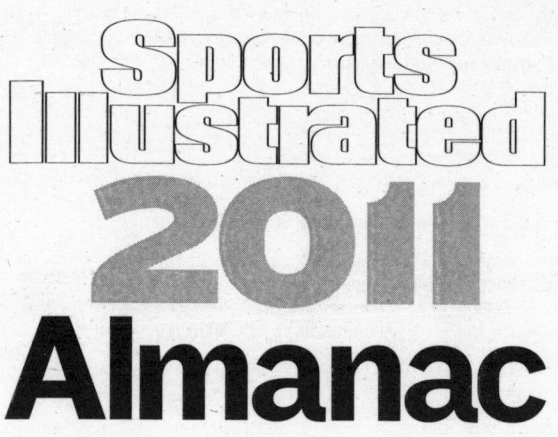

Almanac

By the Editors of Sports Illustrated

First Edition
ISBN10: 1-60320-863-1
ISBN 13: 978-1-60320-863+5

SPORTS ILLUSTRATED is a registered trademark of Time Inc.

SPORTS ILLUSTRATED 2011 Almanac was prepared by Touchpoint Sports Publishing, of White Plains, N.Y.

Editorial Director: Morin Bishop	Managing Editor: Reed Richardson
Art Director: Barbara Chilenskas	Photo Editor: John Blackmar
Proofreader: Wade Martin	

Cover photography credits:
DREW BREES: Chris Gray/Getty Images
PHIL MICKELSON: Fred Vuich
ALBERT PUJOLS : John Biever
SERENA WILLIAMS: Bob Martin

Back cover photography credits:
MARK INGRAM (22): John Biever
BODE MILLER : Carl Yarbrough
JOHN WALL (11): John Biever

Spine photography credit: KOBE BRYANT: Bob Rosato

TIME INC. HOME ENTERTAINMENT

Publisher	Richard Fraiman
General Manager	Steven Sandonato
Executive Director, Marketing Services	Carol Pittard
Director, Retail & Special Sales	Tom Mifsud
Director, New Product Development	Peter Harper
Assistant Director, Bookazine Development & Marketing	Laura Adam
Assistant Director, Brand Marketing	Joy Butts
Assisstant General Counsel	Helen Wan
Brand & Licensing Manager	Alexandra Bliss
Design & Prepress Manager	Anne-Michelle Gallero
Book Production Manager	Susan Chodakiewicz
Associate Brand Manager	Allison Parker
Associate Prepress Manager	Alex Voznesenskiy

Special thanks: Christine Austin, Jeremy Biloon, Glenn Buonocore, Jim Childs, Rose Cirrincione, Jacqueline Fitzgerald, Carrie Frazier, Lauren Hall, Suzanne Janso, Malena Jones, Brynn Joyce, Mona Li, Robert Marasco, Kimberly Marshall, Any Migliaccio, Brooke Reger, Dave Rozzelle, Ilene Schreider, Adriana Tierno, Vanessa Wu

We welcome your comments and suggestions about Sports Illustrated Books. Please write to us at: Sports Illustrated Books, Attention: Book Editors, P.O. Box 11016, Des Moines, IA 50336-1016 If you would like to order any of our hardcover Collector's Edition books, please call us at 1-800-327-6388. (Monday through Friday, 7:00 a.m.- 8:00 p.m. or Saturday, 7:00 a.m.- 6:00 p.m. Central Time)

CONTENTS

In compiling the *Sports Illustrated 2011 Almanac*, the editors would like to extend their gratitude to Robert Yalen as well as to the following organizations for their help in providing information and materials relating to their sports: Major League Baseball; Elias Sports Bureau, the Canadian Football League; the National Football League, Arena Football League; the National Collegiate Athletic Association; the National Basketball Association; the National Hockey League; the Association of Tennis Professionals; the Women's Tennis Association; the U.S. Tennis Association; the U.S. Golf Association; the Ladies Professional Golf Association; the Professional Golfers Association; National Thoroughbred Racing Association; the Breeders' Cup; Churchill Downs; the New York Racing Association, Inc.; the Jockey's Guild, Inc.; the Champ Car Auto Racing circuit; the National Hot Rod Association; the International Motor Sports Association; the National Association for Stock Car Auto Racing; the Professional Bowlers Association; the United Soccer Leagues; Major League Soccer; the Fédération Internationale de Futbol Association; the U.S. Soccer Federation; the U.S. Olympic Committee; USA Track & Field; U.S. Swimming; U.S. Diving; U.S. Skiing; U.S. Figure Skating Association; U.S. Curling; the Iditarod Trail Committee; USA Gymnastics; U.S. Handball Association; the Lacrosse Foundation; the American Power Boat Association; the Unlimited Hydroplane Racing Association; the Professional Rodeo Cowboys Association; U.S. Rowing; the Amateur Softball Association of America; U.S. Speed Skating; U.S. Rugby Football Union; USA Triathlon; the National Archery Association; USA Wrestling; the U.S. Squash Racquets Association; the U.S. Polo Association; NBC Sports; and the U.S. Volleyball Association.

The following sources were consulted in gathering information:

Baseball mlb.com, worldseries.com, baseballhalloffame.org, baseball-almanac.com, *Associated Press* (LCS, WS game recaps)

Pro Football nfl.com, superbowl.com, profootballhof.com, cfl.ca, greycup.cfl.ca

College Football ncaasports.com, heisman.com, *Official 2010 NCAA Division I-A and I-AA Football Records Book, Official 2010 Division II and III Football Records Book*

Pro Basketball nba.com, hoophall.com

College Basketball ncaasports.com, *Official 2011 NCAA Division I Men's Basketball Records Book, Official 2011 NCAA Division I Women's Basketball Records Book, Official 2011 NCAA Division II and III Men's Basketball Records Book*

Hockey nhl.com, hhof.com, ushockeyhall.com

Tennis atptennis.com, sonyericssonwtatour.com, usopen.org, australianopen.com, wimbledon.org, rolandgarros.com, masters-cup.com, daviscup.com, fedcup.com, tennisfame.com

Golf pgatour.com, masters.org, usopen.org, usga.org, opengolf.com, pga.com, randa.org, lpga.com, knc.com, ussenioropen.com, usamateur.org, rydercup.com, walkercup.org, curtiscup.org, pinggolf.com

Boxing wbaonline.com, wbcboxing.com, ibf-usba-boxing.com, ibhof.com, thering-online.com, usaboxing.org, olympic.org

Horse Racing ntra.com, equibase.com, bloodhorse.com, kentuckyderby.com, preakness.com, belmontstakes.nyra.com

Motor Sports nascar.com, formula1.com, indycar.com, americanlemans.com, lemans.org, champcarworldseries.com, indy500.com, daytona24hr.com

Soccer fifa.com, fifaworldcup.yahoo.com, mlsnet.com, ussoccer.com, uefa.com, soccernet.com, premierleague.com, uslsoccer.com,

NCAA Sports ncaasports.com

Olympics olympic.org, usoc.org

Track and Field iaaf.org, usatf.org, usoc.org

Swimming fina.org, usaswimming.org, ishof.org, usoc.org

Miscellaneous Sports letour.fr, usarchery.org, pba.com, fide.com, worldcurling.org, usacurl.org, usacycling.org, iditarod.com, usfigureskating.org, isu.org, fig-gymnastics.com, usa-gymnastics.org, ushandball.org, uscla.com, nll.com, littleleague.org, us-polo.org, prorodeo.org, usrowing.org, usarugby.org, rugbyworldcup.com, amnrl.com, fis-ski.com, asasoftball.com, us-squash.org, ironmanlive.com, usatriathlon.org, fivb.org, usavolleyball.org, themat.com

Obituaries *Associated Press*

AL TIELEMANS

San Francisco ace Tim Lincecum pitched brilliantly to lead the Giants to their first World Series title since 1954

The Year In Sports

Changing of the Guard

The winds of change whipped through the world of sport in 2010 as suprising winners in pro football, baseball, hockey, and even golf, made for an entertaining year

BY HANK HERSCH

SOME SUPER BOWL VICTORIES are more than that—they're harbingers of change (think Joe Namath in Supe III) or crowning achievements (the undefeated Dolphins of 1972) or pillars of a dynasty (the Steelers, the 49ers, the Patriots). But no win has been fraught with more emotional significance than the Saints' in Super Bowl XLIV, when quarterback Drew Brees outdueled Peyton Manning and the Colts 31–17, providing the long-luckless franchise and its fans—swamped by Hurricane Katrina, battered by the recession—a moment of anodyne bliss. Or maybe more than a moment. "I don't know that people in New Orleans are going to go to work for a month," said Brees, the game's MVP, with a grin. "Not that I condone that." As multicolored confetti rained on Brees at Sun Life Stadium in Miami, he held his one-year-old son, Baylen, who wore headphones to mute the ear-splitting revelry.

They would have served Baylen well three weeks later, when a prideful roar went up from British Columbia to Newfoundland. At the Winter Olympics in Vancouver, the host nation took gold in the sport it invented, only because 22-year-old Sidney Crosby slipped a wrist shot past American goaltender Ryan Miller at 7:40 in overtime for a 3–2 win. "It's pretty obvious it's the world's game," Canada coach Mike Babcock said, "but we still think it's ours, and I'm a bit of a redneck."

Not that the U.S. didn't do itself proud too at the Games, taking home a Winter Olympics record 37 medals. Short track skater Apolo Anton Ohno won three, bringing his career total to eight, a record for a U.S. winter Olympian, and Evan Lysacek became the first U.S. male figure skater to win gold in 22 years. The controversial Bode Miller led a record American medal haul in Alpine while confirming his standing as the nation's finest ski racer ever. Miller won three medals, swooshing to his first gold with a dramatic super-combined victory. "My career will be judged however it's judged," he said with a shrug that indicated definitively, *and I don't care* (though it's always possible that he does).

And the other memorable sounds of 2010? How about ole, ole, ole? It was a year of Spanish conquests, most notably that of La Furia Roja in South Africa, where soccer's chronic underachievers became only the third nation to hold the World Cup and European Championship trophies at the same time. In a frequently brutal World Cup final, Spain defeated the Netherlands 1–0 on a goal by midfielder Andrés Iniesta in the 116th minute, the culmination of a 25-second, 100-yard buildup that featured five

SIMON BRUTY

Rafael Nadal became the first man in 41 years to win the French Open, Wimbledon and the U.S. Open in the same year, firmly establishing himself as the No. 1 player in men's tennis.

Spanish players, 10 dribbles and six passes (including one gorgeous backheel). The score was emblematic of tiki-taka—tippy-tap—or what Spaniards call their possession-oriented, short-passing attack. No matter that the team produced only eight goals, the fewest ever by a champion; the players' precision, timing and technical skill were unmatched. "I can't quite believe it yet," said Iniesta. "I simply made a small contribution in a game that was very tough, very rough."

Against the tough, rough Celtics in the NBA Finals, Iniesta's countryman Pau Gasol forever shed his reputation for softness, exhibiting a steely resolve to complement his consummate skill in helping the Lakers repeat as champions. As Kobe Bryant struggled through a 6-for-24 shooting night in Game 7, the 29-year-old Gasol contributed 19 points and 18 rebounds in L.A.'s 83–79 win, establishing himself as the game's most complete 7-footer. And fellow Spaniard Rafael Nadal used the crucible of

the U.S. Open to join the ranks of the all-time greats in tennis. In defeating Novak Djokavic in four sets he not only achieved the career Grand Slam but also became the first man in 41 years to win the French Open, Wimbledon and the U.S. Open in the same year. At 24, Nadal already has nine major singles titles, as well as a 14–7 record against his archrival, Roger Federer, who holds the Grand Slam record with 16.

"When Roger started to be Number 1, he always improves," said Nadal in Flushing, N.Y. "After two years being Number 1 he was a better player than before. That's something I need to do, too, no? If not, well, you always lose something. Maybe lose a little bit more inspiration."

Not all the sights and sounds of '10 were suitable for Baylen's tender eyes and ears. Dogged by reports of serial philandering, Tiger Woods not only failed to win a major—for the first time in his 14-year career he failed to win a tournament. Phil Mickelson claimed the Masters for the third time, but the other majors went to foreign players: Graeme McDowell of Northern Ireland (U.S. Open), Louis Oosthuizen of South Africa (British Open)

Blackhawks captain Jonathan Toews won the Conn Smythe Trophy as the most valuable player in the playoffs as he led Chicago to its first Stanley Cup since 1961.

and Martin Kaymer of Germany (PGA).

Ooohs and aaahs followed the Connecticut women's basketball team, which stretched its winning streak to 78 games, including unprecedented back-to-back unbeaten seasons. The lone team to lose by only single digits over the two undefeated seasons was Stanford, which fell 53–47 in the NCAA final, when UConn rallied behind forward Maya Moore's 23 points and 11 boards. The men's championship game was even closer: Only after a 46-foot heave by Butler forward Gordon Hayward clanged off the rim could Duke celebrate a 61–59 victory and its fourth national championship. "Son of a gun looked good to me," said a relieved Blue Devils forward Kyle Singler, who scored a game-high 19 points.

Behind Heisman Trophy-winning running back Mark Ingram, Alabama rolled to its first title in 17 years, downing Texas 37–21 in the BCS championship game. The victory by the young, deep and well-coached Tide gave rise to talk of a dynasty.

In Chicago, dynasty was the farthest thing from the minds of Blackhawks fans: They were too busy celebrating the franchise's first Stanley Cup in 49 years after a six-game conquest of the Flyers.

An even longer drought ended in San Francisco, where the Giants brought home their first World Series since 1954. With a lineup of castoffs—two of their middle-order hitters, outfielder Scott Burell and Cody Ross, had been released by other teams during the season—and a rotation of brilliant young arms, San Francisco took the championship from the Rangers in five games. The trio of 26-year-old righthander Tim Lincecum (who won the opener and the clincher, fanning 10 in a 3–1 Game 5 victory), 26-year-old righty Matt Cain (21⅓ shutout innings in the postseason) and 21-year-old lefthander Madison Bumgarner (eight shutout innings in Game 4) proved superior to staffs with older and more celebrated starters. Said San Francisco closer Brian Wilson, who had six postseason saves, "It's a hugely difficult task to face pitching like ours if you've never seen us before."

And as Baylen Brees can attest, seeing was believing in 2010.

THE YEAR IN SPORTS CALENDAR

November 2009—December 2009

NOVEMBER 2009

11/1: Meb Keflezighi wins the New York Marathon in 2:09:15, ending a 27-year U.S.-men's drought.

11/1: San Antonio Spurs guard Manu Ginobli knocks a bat out of the air with his bare hand, killing the animal, during a break in the on-court action in a game against the Sacramento Kings.

11/5: Miami Dolphins LB Joey Porter is fined $5,000 by the NFL for wearing his socks incorrectly at an Oct. 25 game against the New Orleans Saints.

11/9: In his just released autobiography, "Open," former tennis great Andre Agassi admits to having taken crystal meth during his playing career.

11/14: Filipino fighting legend Manny Pacquiao wins his seventh different boxing title by scoring a TKO of Miguel Cotto 55 seconds into the final round of their bout at the MGM Grand Hotel in Las Vegas.

11/15: At 20 years old, golfer Michelle Wie wins the LPGA's Lorena Ochoa Invitational, her first career victory after 10 years of playing in pro events.

11/17: Despite playing for a team that finished 32 games under .500, Kansas City Royals pitcher Zack Greinke wins the AL Cy Young Award thanks to his 242 strikeouts and league-leading 2.16 ERA.

11/17: Eight-time NHL All-Star Brendan Shanahan, whose career totals include 656 goals and 1,354 points, announces his retirement after 21 seasons.

11/18: After an obvious but unpenalized hand ball by French striker Thierry Henry sets up a match-tying goal, France defeats Ireland 2–1 in a two-leg playoff and advances to the 2010 FIFA World Cup.

11/22: Jimmie Johnson finishes fourth at the Ford 400, winning an unprecedented fourth-straight NASCAR Sprint Cup season title.

11/22: Real Salt Lake scores a stunning upset over a Los Angeles Galaxy team powered by Landon Donovan and David Beckham in the MLB Cup, winning 5–4 in the penalty kick tiebreaker.

11/23: Minnesota Twins catcher Joe Mauer is named the 2009 AL MVP.

11/24: Roger Federer defeats Andy Murray at the ATP World Tour Finals, cementing his fifth-straight season as the year-end World No. 1 tennis player.

11/27: Tiger Woods crashes his SUV into a tree and fire hydrant while backing out of the driveway of his Florida home at 2:55 a.m. The accident occurs after a reported domestic dispute with his wife, Elin Nordegren, about the golfer's reported infidelities with several different women.

11/30: After posting a disappointing 6–6 record in 2009 and a 35–27 record over the past five seasons, Notre Dame fires coach Charlie Weis.

DECEMBER 2009

12/1: Bobby Bowden, who posted 375 career victories and two national championships while at Florida State, announces his retirement after 44 years of coaching college football.

12/2: The New Jersey Nets lose to the Dallas Mavericks 117–101 and set a new NBA record for most consecutive losses (18) to start a season.

12/5: Alabama rolls over top-ranked Florida in the SEC Championship 32–13, while Texas squeaks by Nebraska on a last-second field goal 13–12, finalizing the BCS National Championship matchup.

12/7: Just nine days after retiring from the Memphis Grizzlies, guard Allen Iverson returns to the NBA after signing a one-year deal with the Philadelphia 76ers, where he played his first 11 seasons.

12/10: Brian Kelly leaves his head football coaching job at the University of Cincinnati to take the same position at Notre Dame, leaving his Bearcats team to be coached by offensive coordinator Jeff Quinn at the team's upcoming Sugar Bowl appearance.

12/11: Citing a policy that prohibits any posthumous pardons, the Justice Department refuses to pardon black heavyweight champion Jack Johnson, who was jailed in the early 20th century for having romantic ties to a white woman.

12/12: Alabama running back Mark Ingram edges out Stanford's Toby Gerhart to win the 2009 Heisman Trophy in the closest vote in the award's 75-year history.

12/13: Denver Broncos wide receiver Brandon Marshall sets a single-game NFL record with 21 receptions against the Indianapolis Colts. The Colts still win, however, 28–16.

12/16: As part of a blockbuster three-team deal, Toronto Blue Jays pitcher Roy Halladay is traded to Philadelphia and Phillies ace Cliff Lee is sent to the Seattle Mariners.

12/17: Cincinnati Bengals receiver Chris Henry dies of injuries sustained from falling out of a pick-up truck driven by his fiancée after a domestic dispute.

12/23: Mercedes announces that, after a four-year retirement, seven-time world champion Michael Schumacher will return to the Formula One circuit in 2010 to race for the carmaker.

12/24: George Michael, longtime Washington D.C.-area sports journalist and host of the late-night TV sports highlight show "The George Michael Sports Machine" dies at age 70.

12/25: Upset at their home team's poor performance against the Cleveland Cavaliers in a game on Christmas Day, L.A. Lakers fans rain promotional foam souvenirs onto the court as the game ends.

12/25: After negotiations involving pre-fight drug testing break down, the blockbuster Floyd Mayweather Jr.–Manny Pacquiao bout scheduled for March 13, 2010 is cancelled.

12/26: Sarah Thomas becomes the first female referee to officiate a college football bowl game, working as line judge for the Little Caesars Pizza Bowl in Detroit.

12/30: Three days before its game in the Alamo Bowl, Texas Tech fires head football coach Mike Leach after allegations arise about his mistreatment of a player who had sustained a concussion.

JANUARY 2010

1/1: In the NHL's Winter Classic, played outdoors in Boston's Fenway Park, a sellout crowd of 38,112 watches the hometown Bruins take a thrilling 2–1 overtime victory over the Philadelphia Flyers.

1/3: Tennessee Titans running back Chris Johnson becomes just the sixth NFL player to rush for more than 2,000 yards in a single season and sets the single-season mark for most yards from scrimmage, breaking Marshall Faulk's previous record.

1/6: Andre "The Hawk" Dawson becomes the sole inductee in the 2010 class of the Baseball Hall of Fame. Pitcher Bert Blyleven falls five votes short.

1/7: Washington Wizards guard Gilbert Arenas is suspended for the remainder of the regular season by the NBA for a Dec. 24 incident where he and teammate Javaris Crittenton brandished pistols at one another in the team's locker room.

1/8: Six months after landing a 22 lb., 4 oz. largemouth bass at a Japanese lake, angler Manabu Kurita is officially rewarded with a share of the world record after passing a polygraph test that questioned the circumstances of his catch.

1/8: On the way to the Africa Cup of Nations soccer tournament, the Togo national team bus is targeted by gunmen as it crosses into Angola. One player, two staff members, and the driver are killed.

1/11: Former MLB slugger Mark McGwire admits to having taken steroids during his career, including his single-season home-run record year of 1998.

1/11: Cuban baseball pitching phenom Aroldis Chapman signs a six-year, $30-million contract with the Cincinnati Reds.

1/12: University of Tennessee head football coach Lane Kiffin is named by USC to replace Pete Carroll just hours after the NFL's Seattle Seahawks introduce Carroll as their new head coach.

1/12: NHL hockey legend Curtis Joseph announces his retirement after 19 seasons, finishing his goalie career with 454 victories, fourth-best all time.

1/13: After injuring his knee in the Los Angeles Clippers' final preseason game in October, the team announces that overall-No. 1 draft pick Blake Griffin will miss the entire 2009–10 regular season.

1/17: Jeremy Abbott wins the men's singles U.S. Figure Skating Championships in Spokane, Wash.

1/18: Filly Rachel Alexandra, undefeated in eight races in 2009, including the Preakness Stakes, beats out Zenyatta for Horse of the Year.

1/19: San Francisco Giants ace Tim Lincecum files a record $13 million salary arbitration case on the same day that he accepts a $513 fine for marijuana possession in a Washington courtroom.

1/20: Defending national champion North Carolina loses its third straight basketball game and falls out of the Associated Press Top 25 rankings for the first time since 2006.

1/21: At 31 years and 151 days-old, Los Angeles Lakers guard Kobe Bryant becomes the youngest-ever NBA player to score 25,000 career points, breaking Wilt Chamberlain's record by 35 days.

1/22: San Antonio Spurs forward Tim Duncan becomes the 35th NBA player to reach 20,000 career points.

1/24: The two No. 1 seeds in the NFL playoffs—the New Orleans Saints and the Indianapolis Colts—win their respective Conference Championships and advance to Super Bowl XLIV in Miami.

1/26: Undefeated and newly No. 1-ranked Kentucky is upset on the road by unranked South Carolina 68–62 after Gamecocks guard Devan Downey pours in 30 points.

1/29: U.S. middle-distance runner Bernard Legat surpasses Irishman Eamonn Coghlan's career record by winning an eighth Wanamaker Mile race at the Millrose Games in New York City.

1/30: Serena Williams defeats Justine Henin in three sets to win her fifth career Australian Open singles title and 12th career Grand Slam title.

1/31: Pakistani national cricket team captain Shahid Afridi is caught on camera trying to doctor the ball by biting it during a match against Australia. After apologizing, he is suspended for two games.

FEBRUARY

2/1: The Minnesota Twins re-sign their catcher, three-time All-Star and 2009 AL MVP Joe Mauer, to a 10-year contract extension.

2/4: David Sills, a 13-year-old quarterback from Bear, Delaware, verbally commits to play for USC after new Trojans head coach Lane Kiffin offers the young phenom the promise of a scholarship.

2/5: In a scandal that roils the soccer world, John Terry is stripped of his captaincy of the English national team after it's reported that the married Terry had an affair with a teammate's girlfriend.

2/7: In the most-watched TV event in U.S. history, the underdog New Orleans Saints defeat the Indianapolis Colts 31–17 in Super Bowl XLIV, thanks to Saints QB and game MVP Drew Brees' 32-of-39 passing performance.

2/8: Newly-reinstated wide receiver Donté Stallworth is cut by the Cleveland Browns after having served a year-long NFL suspension for killing a pedestrian in Miami while driving drunk.

2/12: Hours before the 2010 Winter Olympics opening ceremonies in Vancouver, 21-year-old Georgian luger Nodar Kumaritashvili dies after careening out of control on a training run and striking a nearby exposed support pillar.

2/14: Holding off a late charge by Dale Earnhardt Jr., Jamie McMurray wins the 52nd Daytona 500, a race marred by several wrecks and two extended cautions due to a large pothole on the track.

2/17: Setting a new single-day Winter Olympics record, the U.S. wins six medals—three gold, one silver, and two bronze—on Day 6 of the Vancouver Games.

2/17: Just hours before the NBA trade deadline, Cleveland, Washington, and the Los Angeles Clippers complete a complex three-team deal that, among the more notable moves, sends Cavs center Zydrunas Ilgauskas to Washington and Wizards forward Antawn Jamison to Cleveland.

2/19: Sitting in front of friends and family, including his mother, Tiger Woods reads a prepared statement publicly apologizing for numerous affairs and "irresponsible and foolish behavior," but does not take questions from the press or announce a date for his return to the PGA Tour.

2/22: On a day that included notable Winter Olympic hockey games between Sweden and Finland as well as Russia and the Czech Republic, the U.S. scores a stunning qualifying round upset over Canada 5–3.

2/28: On the last night of the Winter Olympics, Canada wins the rematch, defeating the U.S. 3–2 in the gold-medal hockey game when Sidney Crosby slides the puck past U.S. goalie and Olympics tournament MVP Ryan Miller in overtime.

MARCH

3/2: A full-page ad from a Vikings fan begging QB Brett Favre to return for another season appears in his hometown newspaper, the *Hattiesburg American*.

3/3: Maryland snaps a six-game losing streak to Duke in a 79–72 victory, which prompts Terrapins fans to storm the court and then begin rioting in celebration outside the arena.

3/5: The Miami Dolphins announce they will now charge $5 extra for tickets that are located in the shade on SunLife Stadium's south side.

3/5: To bolster their offense and aging wide receiver corps, the Baltimore Ravens acquire star wideout Anquan Boldin from the Arizona Cardinals for a third- and fourth-round draft pick.

3/6: Duke records its most lopsided defeat of basketball archrival North Carolina, beating the Tar Heels by a score of 82–50.

3/6: In a battle of hapless NBA teams, the New York Knicks lose to the New Jersey Nets 113–93 and break an NBA record while doing so, going 0–18 from beyond the three-point line.

3/8: Golf manufacturer Ping and the PGA Tour come to an agreement eliminating a 20-year-old 'grandfather' loophole that had allowed players to use a Ping Eye 2 wedge with square grooves.

3/9: NASCAR suspends Sprint Cup driver Carl Edwards for three races after Edward intentionally wrecked Brad Keselowski's car in a race at Atlanta Motor Speedway two days earlier.

3/11: Skier Lindsey Vonn clinches her third-straight overall World Cup skiing title and her 33 career victories makes her the most accomplished U.S. skier—male or female—in history.

3/11: Ohio State's Evan Turner drains a 40-foot three-point shot at the buzzer to knock off rival Michigan in the Big Ten conference basketball tournament championship game.

3/15: Coming back after a four-year retirement, legendary racecar driver Michael Schumacher returns to Formula One racing at the circuit's 2010 debut event, the Bahrain Grand Prix.

3/17: *Sports Illustrated* reports that Texas Rangers manager Ron Washington tested positive for cocaine during the 2009 season.

3/19: Less than two months removed from their Super Bowl XLIV victory, the New Orleans Saints announce they will displace 1,200 seats to build a new press box since the old press box is being converted into 16 luxury suites.

3/19: The hot-shooting, No. 14-seed Ohio Bobcats upset Big East powerhouse and No. 3-seed Georgetown Hoyas 97–83 in the first round of March Madness.

3/20: In a successful defense of his IBF heavyweight title, Wladimir Klitschko knocks out Eddie Chambers with five seconds left in the bout.

3/23: A traffic accident in northern New Jersey results in the arrest of former New York Mets pitcher Dwight Gooden for driving under the influence of alchohol.

3/27: After falling just short of gold at the Winter Olympics in Vancouver, Japan's Mao Asada takes home the crown at the World Figure Skating Championships in Turin, Italy.

3/31: In a spring training game, Minnesota Twins outfielder Denard Span hits a foul ball that flies into the stands and plunks his own mother.

APRIL

4/5: On Major League Baseball's Opening Day, Chicago White Sox pitcher Mark Buehrle makes an incredible, no-look, between-the-legs fielding play to get an out at first and Atlanta Braves rookie Jason Heyward hits a home run in his first at-bat.

4/5: In a thrilling, back-and-forth battle, No. 1-seed Duke defeats unheralded but unbowed No. 5-seed Butler 61–59 to win the men's NCAA hoops title.

4/11: With a 5-under 67 in the final round at Augusta National, Phil Mickelson beats out Lee Westwood by three strokes, winning his third Masters.

4/11: The 39-year-old former home of the Dallas Cowboys—Texas Stadium in Irving—is reduced to rubble after being imploded by explosives.

4/13: Boston College defeats Wisconsin 5–0 to take home the men's NCAA hockey crown.

4/16: NBA Commissioner David Stern announces the 2010–11 season salary cap will be $56.1 million, roughly $4 million higher than expected.

4/17: Former Nebraska defensive tackle Ndamukong Suh announces he will donate $2.6 million to his alma mater after he is drafted.

4/21: The NFL confirms that it will suspend Pittsburgh Steelers QB Ben Roethlisberger six games—later reduced to four—for violating the league's personal conduct policy when he engaged in a drunken liaison at a Georgia bar during the off-season.

4/22: March Madness, the annual college basketball tournament, will expand from 65 to 68 teams in 2011, the NCAA announces.

4/22: The WNBA's Seattle Storm unveil their new jerseys, which replace the team's nickname with an ad for Microsoft's new search engine Bing.

4/22: A sharply hit, sixth-inning grounder by Oakland A's catcher Kurt Suzuki is turned into a 5-4-3 triple play by the New York Yankees.

4/22: Oklahoma QB Sam Bradford is the first overall pick by the St. Louis Rams at the NFL Draft in New York City.

4/22: Hudsonville (Mich.) High's Shane Trevino hits his first career home run against opponent West Ottawa only to find out later that the ball crashed through the rear window of his own father's car, which had been parked adjacent to the field.

4/24: Having acquired Donovan McNabb earlier in April, the Washington Redskins trade their 2009 starting QB, Jason Campbell, to the Oakland Raiders for a fourth-round pick in the 2012 draft.

4/25: Jamaican sprinter Usain Bolt is clocked running an incredibly fast 8.79-second split in the final leg of a 4x100-meter race at the Penn Relays.

MAY

5/1: Jockey Calvin Borel wins his second straight Kentucky Derby, this year guiding Super Saver to victory in the Run for the Roses.

5/1: In the fight of the year, a sellout crowd at Las Vegas' MGM Grand Garden Arena watches Floyd Mayweather Jr. retain his unbeaten boxing record by outlasting "Sugar" Shane Mosley to win a unanimous decision.

5/3: During the eighth inning of a Philadelphia Phillies game, a 17-year-old fan runs onto the field and eludes security in the outfield until he is finally brought down by being tasered.

5/4: Ernie Harwell, the legendary broadcast voice of the Detroit Tigers who was the only announcer in baseball history ever traded for a player, passes away at age 92.

5/9: Oakland A's pitcher Dallas Braden throws the 19th perfect game in major league history, a 4–0 blanking of the Tampa Bay Rays.

5/12: After Houston Texans linebacker Brian Cushing tests positive for performance-enhancing drugs, a panel of sportswriters organized by the Associated Press revote on whether to award Cushing the 2009 NFL Defensive Rookie of the Year award. Cushing's 18 votes the second time around is still good enough to win.

5/12: For the second NHL playoff series in a row, the No. 8 seed Montreal Canadiens knock off a heavily favored team in seven games, this time defeating Sidney Crosby and the defending champion Pittsburgh Penguins on the road.

5/12: Lookin at Lucky wins the Preakness Stakes as Kentucky Derby winner Super Saver comes in eighth, making it 32 years since the last horse racing Triple Crown winner, Affirmed.

5/18: Canadian doctor Anthony Galea is arrested and charged in Buffalo, N.Y. with smuggling human growth hormone into the United States and three of the primary witnesses against him are unnamed NFL players.

5/18: Despite having just over a one-in-ten chance, the Washington Wizards win the NBA's Draft Lottery. They will choose Kentucky point guard John Wall as their first pick at the Draft in June.

5/23: Former Houston Astros All-Star pitcher Jose Lima dies of a heart attack at his home in Los Angeles, Calif. at the age of 37.

5/24: In a landmark ruling, the U.S. Supreme Court unanimously overturns a lower court's decision and effectively ends the NFL's antitrust exemption.

5/26: The unexpected appearance of a squirrel on the playing field at Target Field briefly delays a game between the Minnesota Twins and the New York Yankees.

5/30: Scotsman Dario Franchitti wins his second Indianapolis 500, a race marred by a spectacular collision between Ryan Hunter-Reay and Mike Conway that sent the latter's car up into the catch fence.

JUNE

6/1: Robin Soderling defeats Roger Federer in four sets at Wimbledon, ending Federer's streak of appearing in 23 consecutive Grand Slam semifinals.

6/2: Detroit Tigers pitcher Armando Galarraga's bid for a perfect game runs aground on what would be the 27th and final out, when umpire Jim Joyce mistakenly calls Cleveland Indians shortstop Jason Donald safe at first after a ground ball. Joyce later apologizes for the error.

6/3: Nearly three years after the picture is taken, federal prosecutors finally release Barry Bonds' mug shot from his 2007 arrest.

6/5: Drosselmeyer wins the Belmont Stakes, in a race notable for the absence of both Kentucky Derby winner Super Saver and Preakness champ Lookin at Lucky.

6/6: Boston Celtics shooting guard Ray Allen sets a new NBA Finals record when he hits eight three-pointers during Game 2.

6/9: Patrick Kane slides a puck past Philadelphia Flyers goalie Michael Leighton 4:06 into overtime of Game 6 of the Stanely Cup Final, winning the Chicago Blackhawks their first NHL title since 1961.

6/11: Nebraska bolts the Big 12 and applies for membership in the Big Ten as of 2011–12, setting off a college football free-for-all that sees several schools switch conferences before it's over.

6/17: The Los Angeles Lakers defeat the Boston Celtics in Game 7 of the NBA Finals, winning back-to-back titles for the first time since 2002. Finals MVP Kobe Bryant earns his fifth career title and head coach Phil Jackson walks away with his eleventh ring.

6/19: Graeme McDowell struggles with a closing round of 74, but he still wins the U.S. Open at Pebble Beach by one stroke over Gregory Havret.

6/21: After catching a 883-pound marlin in a North Carolina fishing tournament, for which the reward would be $912,000, Andy Thomossan is disqualified when officials discover that one of the other men aboard Thomossan's boat did not have a $5 fishing license.

6/27: In its first game in the Round of 16, the United States is knocked out of the World Cup by Ghana after a disappointing 2–1 defeat.

6/30: After hitting a seventh-inning, tie-breaking solo homer, Baltimore Orioles slugger Luke Scott pulls a hamstring during his trot around the bases and is placed on the disabled list after the game.

JULY

7/8: In a bizarre, hour-long TV special on ESPN entitled "The Decision," NBA free agent LeBron James announces he will leave Cleveland to join Chris Bosh and Dwyane Wade on the Miami Heat.

7/11: After the penalty-filled final match goes into a second extra-time period, Spain's Andres Iniesta finally scores the World Cup-winning goal against the Netherlands in the 116th minute, giving the Spaniards a 1–0 victory.

7/13: George Steinbrenner, the fiery and often controversial longtime owner of the New York Yankees, dies at his home in Tampa, Fla., at age 80.

7/13: The New Jersey Devils announce they have re-signed Ilya Kovalchuk to an eyebrow-raising $100-million, 17-year contract. The deal is rejected by the NHL a week later.

7/13: For the first time since 1996, the National League wins the All-Star Game, thanks to a three-run double by Atlanta Braves catcher Brian McCann.

7/15: Cyclist Mark Renshaw, lead-out man for the HTC-Columbia team, is kicked off the Tour de France for headbutting another rider three times to help his teammate win the Tour's 11th stage.

7/19: Louis Oosthuizen, a 27-year-old South African, easily takes home the British Open's Claret Jug after trouncing the rest of the field by seven strokes at St. Andrews.

7/26: New USC head coach Lane Kiffin is sued by the Tennessee Titans for hiring away the Titans' running backs coach Kennedy Pola.

7/27: The NFL unveils a new locker room poster aimed at improving athlete awareness of the dangers of concussions.

7/28: Memphis Grizzlies forward Lorenzen Wright is found shot to death in a wooded area southeast of the city, a crime that remains unsolved.

7/30: Houston Astros ace Roy Oswalt waives his no-trade clause and is shipped to the Philadelphia Phillies on the last day of MLB's trade deadline.

AUGUST

8/4: At age 35, Alex Rodriguez becomes the youngest player in MLB history to hit 600 home runs.

8/5: At a bankruptcy auction, the Texas Rangers franchise is purchaed by an investment group that includes former Rangers pitcher Nolan Ryan.

8/6: Federal prosecutors interview cycling legend Lance Armstrong over allegations made by a former teammate that Armstrong used performance enhancing drugs during his career.

8/7: On his third try, Washington Redskins defensive lineman Albert Haynesworth finally passes his team's fitness test, ten days after initially reporting to training camp.

8/11: New team owner and Russian billionaire Mikhail Prokhorov officially applies to the NBA to change his team's name to the Brooklyn Nets.

8/11: New York Mets closer Francisco Rodriguez physically assaults his father-in-law in the Mets locker room after a loss. He tears a ligament in his thumb during the fracas and is out for the season.

8/15: German golfer Martin Kaymer wins the PGA Championship after a three-hole playoff, but Dustin Johnson's penalty on himself for grounding his club in a bunker on the 72nd hole—which kept him out of that playoff—is the talk of the tournament.

8/17: A new medical study reports that the numerous concussions suffered by Lou Gehrig during his career may have led to his contracting amyotrophic lateral sclerosis (ALS) and contributed to his subsequent death.

8/27: After a scintillating debut where he struck out a major-league record 32 batters in his first three starts, Washington Nationals ace Stephen Strasburg is shut down after it's reported he needs Tommy John surgery to repair an injured elbow.

8/27: Cuban pitching phenom Aroldis Chapman strikes out the side for the AAA Louisville Bats while being clocked at throwing 105 mph.

8/30: *Washington Post* sports reporter Mike Wise intentionally posts a made-up news report on Twitter concerning the lengths of a suspension of Pittsburgh Steelers QB Ben Roethlisberger. Wise is subsequently suspended from his job for a month.

SEPTEMBER

9/1: Victoria Azarenka passes out in the 90-plus degree heat at an early match of the U.S. Open and is forced to withdraw from the tournament.

9/6: After holding out through the entire New York Jets preseason, cornerback Darrelle Revis returns to the team after signing a new four-year deal.

9/12: Sixteen years removed from its last title, the U.S. team wins the FIBA World Baskeball Championship in Istanbul, Turkey.

9/13: Rafael Nadal completes his career Grand Slam at Flushing Meadows by defeating Novak Djokovic in four sets to win his first U.S. Open title.

9/14: In a pre-emptive move, Reggie Bush decides to forfeit his 2005 Heisman Trophy after USC is punished, in part, for his involvement in several NCAA rules violations from that season.

9/18: Down three points to Notre Dame in overtime and facing a fourth-and-14, Michigan State head football coach Mark Dantonio calls for a fake field goal. It not only works, it scores the Spartans a TD and gives them a thrilling 34–31 victory.

9/23: A pristine one-of-a-kind TV recording of Game 7 of the 1960 World Series is found in the wine cellar of deceased crooner Bing Crosby.

9/23: After Kevin Kolb's injury in Week Two, backup Philadelphia Eagles QB Michael Vick makes his first start in a NFL game since his felony conviction for running a dogfighting ring less than two years ago.

9/25: MLB Commissioner Bud Selig openly discusses changes to his sport's playoff system to allow more teams to qualify for the postseason.

9/29: To protect Commonwealth Games competitors from snakes and mischievous rhesus monkeys, tournament officials in India recruit 40 grey langur monkeys and a squad of snake charmers to guard against future attacks.

OCTOBER

10/6: The New England Patriots trade WR Randy Moss to Minnesota for a third-round pick.

10/6: Philadelphia Phillies pitcher Roy Halladay throws just the second no-hitter in MLB postseason history in Game 1 of the NLDS against the Cincinnati Reds.

10/7: Website Deadspin.com ignites a media firestorm when it posts sexually suggestive pictures and audio allegedly sent by QB Brett Favre to a female New York Jets employee when he played with the team in 2008.

10/13: The diminutive Papua New Guinea steeplechase runner Sapolai Yao is disqualified from a Commonwealth Games race after he uses a potted plant as a stepstool to clear one hurdle.

10/17: Rutgers defensive tackle Eric LeGrand suffers a severe spinal-cord injury after making a tackle on special teams in a game against Army, leaving him paralyzed from the neck down.

10/19: Prompted by a newfound concern for player concussions and a number of violent, helmet-to-helmet hits in the early part of the 2010–11 regular season, the NFL levies heavy fines on three defensive players guilty of the illegal contact.

10/20: Yankees outfielder Brett Gardner loses his grip on his bat during Game 4 of the ALCS and it flies into a TV camera, shattering the lens.

10/24: Jonathan Byrd wins a one-hole playoff at the PGA's Shriner Hospitals for Children Open by carding a hole-in-one on the 204-yard, par-3 17th.

10/26: Paul the Octopus, the World Cup-predicting cephalopod, dies of natural causes in Berlin, Germany, at age two and a half.

10/26: The Boston Celtics defeat the new-look Miami Heat in the NBA season opener 88–80, spoiling the debut of LeBron James.

10/27: A gust of wind toppled a scissor lift during a Notre Dame football practice, killing Declan Sullivan, the team's student manager who was filming practice from atop it.

10/29: After a five-hour, 12-overtime high school football game, the Nacogdoches (Tex.) Dragons finally defeat the Jacksonville Indians 84–81.

10/31: Halfway through the 2010–11 NFL season, the San Diego Chargers have the No. 1-ranked offense and defense, yet only have a 3–5 record.

NOVEMBER

11/1: Edgar Renteria's three-run homer off Texas Rangers' ace Cliff Lee in Game 5 is all the run support Tim Lincecum and the San Francisco Giants need as they cruise to a 3–1 victory and World Series title.

11/1: Less than four weeks after acquiring him from New England, the Minnesota Vikings place WR Randy Moss on waivers.

Baseball

World Series MVP Edgar Renteria hit a three-run home run in Game 5 to clinch the San Francisco Giants' first title since 1954

Mighty Giants They Be

In a year notable for its sparkling pitching performances, a ragged San Francisco team backed into the postseason but then out-pitched everyone on their way to the title

BY MERRELL NODEN

THEY WERE A TEAM OF "CASTOFFS and misfits," words that might have stung had they not been uttered by their own manager, Bruce Bochy, who meant them as a badge of honor. The ragtag San Francisco Giants didn't clinch a playoff berth until the last day of the regular season, and their roster had just one certified star, two-time Cy Young Award winner Tim Lincecum. Many of Lincecum's World Series teammates were not even Giants at the start of the season. Cody Ross, who hit four home runs against the Phillies in the NLCS, was picked up off waivers in late August. Buster Posey, at 23 an astonishingly poised catcher and strong candidate for Rookie of the Year honors, didn't come up to the majors until May 29. Pat Burrell was picked up in June after being released by the Rays.

Yet somehow, in what looked like a run of genius decision-making, Bochy molded this band of castoffs into a superb playoff team that rolled right over the Texas Rangers in the World Series, four games to one. The Giants simply possessed the best pitching in baseball. They had the lowest ERA and the most strikeouts, while black-bearded closer Brian Wilson racked up more saves (48) than anyone else.

Still, their World Series opponents had the highest batting average in baseball and scored the most runs. In the ALCS the Rangers had walked all over the Yankees, making them look their age. AL batting champion Josh Hamilton had four homers to claim MVP honors. But against the Giants' pitching, Hamilton was 2 for 20, which sounds bad, but not as bad as Vladimir Guerrero, who had led the team in RBIs with 115, but was 1 for 14 when it counted most. When Wilson struck out Nelson Cruz for the final out, Bochy was looking very much like a genius.

This was a team that Bay area baseball fans embraced with a loony fervor. They came in droves dressed in orange and black, as if they'd wandered off from a Halloween parade. They wore white panda headdresses in honor of paunchy third baseman Pablo Sandoval, nicknamed "Kung Fu Panda"; they donned fake black beards to celebrate Wilson's preternaturally dark whiskers and held signs warning Fear the Beard; others wore t-shirts urging "Let Timmy Smoke!", a reference to Lincecum's offseason citation for misdemeanor marijuana charges. Heck, the Giants front office recruited members of the Grateful Dead to sing the national anthem before Game 5 of the NLCS. Indeed, what a long, strange, earthquake-plagued trip it has been for the Giants since 1954,

CHUCK SOLOMON

when the team won its last World Series title, back in New York, and Willie Mays made his miracle catch.

Thanks to the Giants superb pitchers the year ended the way it had begun, as the year of the pitcher. From Opening Day to the playoffs, pitchers made headlines. Prior to 2010, there had been only 18 perfect games in major league history. On May 9, Dallas Braden of the Oakland A's used a perfect game to beat Tampa Bay, 4–0, and just 20 days later, Roy Halladay, whom the Phillies had acquired from Toronto in an offseason trade, allowed no one to reach first base in beating the Florida Marlins, 1–0.

And that perfect pair really should have been joined, on June 2, by Armando Galarraga of the Detroit Tigers. Galarraga was one out away from perfection against Cleveland when first base umpire Jim Joyce ruled Indians shortstop Jason Donald safe at first. When replays confirmed that Joyce had indeed blown the call—badly—there were pleas for Commissioner Bud Selig to award Galarraga a perfect game, which Selig refused. In the end, both parties handled the difficult situation as gracefully as was possible, with Joyce expressing his mortification and Galarraga accepting the gesture.

Phillies ace Roy Halladay contributed mightily to the "year of the pitcher," throwing a perfect game during the regular season and a no-hitter in the opening game of the NLDS playoffs.

By the All Star Game, held at Angel Stadium and won by the National League—for the first time since 1996—it even looked as if we might see the first 30-game winner since Denny McLain in 1968. Despite pitching roughly half his games in notoriously batter-friendly Coors Field, Ubaldo Jimenez of the Colorado Rockies was on a tear. He was 15–1 including a no-hitter against Atlanta on April 17. But Jimenez struggled in the second half and won "only" 19 games. Reaching the 20-game plateau were Halladay (21–10), Adam Wainwright of the Cardinals (20–11), and, in the American League, C. C. Sabathia of the Yankees (21–7).

And as if the season needed more incredible pitching, up from the minors came ballyhooed Washington National Stephen Strasburg and his 100 mile-an-hour fastball. Strasburg, who drew 70 credentialed media to his first Double-A start in April, struck out 14 against the Pirates in his debut and seemed to justify all the excitement before injuring his elbow on

JOHN BIEVER

It took Texas five games to beat the pesky Tampa Bay Rays and the Phillies rolled over the Reds in three straight, finding inspiration in Halladay's opening game no hitter—only the second in major league playoff history, after Don Larsen's perfect game in 1956. The Yankees whipped the Twins, and Lincecum gave a hint of things to come when he struck out 14 Braves batters in the NLCS series opener.

Both league series went six games and set up a World Series in which Texas was considered the slight favorite, in large part because of the astonishing roll Cliff Lee was on. Lee was 7–0 in playoff starts, with an ERA of 1.26. His Game 1 start against Lincecum was expected to be a pitcher's duel. It wasn't, as the Giants drove Lee from the game in the fifth inning. Lee would also pitch well but lose Game Five. For the Giants, Matt Cain and Madison Bumgarner pitched shutouts in Games 2 and 4, respectively, and Lincecum struck out 10 and gave up just one earned run in eight innings in the final game.

It was the Giants' hitting that surprised fans. They got the hits they needed at precisely the right times. Freddy Sanchez had three doubles in Game 1. Edgar Renteria, the journeyman infielder who got the game-winning hit for the Florida Marlins in the 1997 World Series, didn't even make the lineup for Game 1. Playing with a painful torn tendon in his left bicep, the 34-year-old Renteria hit a home run in Game 2, had three singles in Game 4, and hit the winning three-run homer in the seventh inning of Game 5 to give the Giants a lead they would not relinquish. Renteria won MVP honors.

When the last out was made and a pile of his delirious teammates were leaping about behind him on the pitcher's mound, Posey sounded like an old San Franciscan at this wonderful ending to his first year in the big leagues. Said Posey, speaking no doubt for the other outcasts and misfits in orange and black, "It's the ultimate high in baseball."

August 21. He underwent season-ending Tommy John surgery on Sept. 3.

Not that the pitchers bamboozled all of the hitters, all of the time. Baseball's last triple crown winner was Carl Yastrzemski in 1967. This year hitters in both leagues seemed to stand a real chance of achieving it. In the National League, St. Louis veteran Albert Pujols—who else?—and Joey Votto of the Reds spent most of August near the top of all three triple crown categories. At season's end, Pujols won the home run (42) and RBI (118) titles, while Carlos Gonzalez of the Rockies took the batting crown (.336), one spot ahead of Votto who wound up with 37 homers and 113 RBIs.

Bobby Cox, in his 29th and final season, became just the fourth manager to win more than 2500 games. And though his Atlanta Braves got off to a slow start, they had a big enough cushion to survive a mid-September collapse during which the team lost 17 of 23 games over one stretch. Not so the Padres. After leading the NL West by as many as six and a half games on August 25, the Padres fell apart, losing ten straight.

FOR THE RECORD•2010

2010 Final Regular Season Standings

National League

EASTERN DIVISION

Team	Won	Lost	Pct	GB	Home	Away
Philadelphia	97	65	.599	--	54–30	43–35
†Atlanta	91	71	.562	6.0	56–25	35–46
Florida	80	82	.494	17.0	41–40	39–42
NY Mets	79	83	.488	18.0	47–34	32–49
Washington	69	93	.426	28.0	41–40	28–53

CENTRAL DIVISION

Team	Won	Lost	Pct	GB	Home	Away
Cincinnati	91	71	.562	--	49–32	42–39
St. Louis	86	76	.531	5.0	52–29	34–47
Milwaukee	77	85	.475	14.0	40–41	37–44
Houston	76	86	.469	15.0	42–39	34–47
Chicago	75	87	.463	16.0	35–46	40–41
Pittsburgh	57	105	.352	34.0	40–41	17–64

WESTERN DIVISION

Team	Won	Lost	Pct	GB	Home	Away
San Francisco	92	70	.568	--	49–32	43–38
San Diego	90	72	.556	2.0	45–36	45–36
Colorado	83	79	.512	9.0	52–29	31–50
LA Dodgers	80	82	.494	12.0	45–36	35–46
Arizona	65	97	.401	27.0	40–41	25–56

†Wild-card teams.

American League

EASTERN DIVISION

Team	Won	Lost	Pct	GB	Home	Away
Tampa Bay	96	66	.593	--	49–32	47–34
†NY Yankees	95	67	.586	1.0	52–29	43–38
Boston	89	73	.549	7.0	46–35	43–38
Toronto	85	77	.525	11.0	45–33	40–44
Baltimore	66	96	.407	30.0	37–44	29–52

CENTRAL DIVISION

Team	Won	Lost	Pct	GB	Home	Away
*Minnesota	94	68	.580	--	53–28	41–40
Chicago	88	74	.543	6.0	45–36	43–38
Detroit	81	81	.500	13.0	52–29	29–52
Cleveland	69	93	.426	25.0	38–43	31–50
Kansas City	67	95	.414	27.0	38–43	29–52

WESTERN DIVISION

Team	Won	Lost	Pct	GB	Home	Away
LA Angels	90	72	.556	--	51–30	39–42
Texas	81	81	.500	9.0	47–34	34–47
Oakland	80	82	.494	10.0	43–38	37–44
Seattle	61	101	.377	29.0	35–46	26–55

2010 Playoffs

National League Division Playoffs

Oct 6 ....Cincinnati 0 at Philadelphia 4
Oct 8 ....Cincinnati 4 at Philadelphia 7
Oct 10 ....Philadelphia 2 at Cincinnati 0

(Philadelphia won series 3–0)

Oct 7 ....Atlanta 0 at San Francisco 1
Oct 8 ....Atlanta 5 at San Francisco 4
Oct 10 ....San Francisco 3 at Atlanta 2
Oct 11 ....San Francisco 3 at Atlanta 2

(San Francisco won series 3–1)

National League Championship Series

Oct 16 ....San Francisco 4 at Philadelphia 3
Oct 17 ....San Francisco 1 at Philadelphia 6
Oct 19 ....Philadelphia 0 at San Francisco 3
Oct 20 ....Philadelphia 5 at San Francisco 6
Oct 21 ....Philadelphia 4 at San Francisco 2
Oct 23 ....San Francisco 3 at Philadelphia 2

(San Francisco won series 4–2)

GAME 1

											R	H	E
San Francisco	0	0	1	0	1	2	0	0	0	**4**	**9**	**0**
Philadelphia	0	0	1	0	0	2	0	0	0	**3**	**7**	**0**

W—SF: Lincecum. **L**—Phi: Halladay. **SV**—SF: Wilson. **LOB**—SF: 7; Phi: 7. **2B**—SF: Burrell, Phi: Howard, Polanco. **HR**—SF: Ross (2); Phi: Ruiz, Werth. **RBI**—SF: Ross (2), Burrell, Uribe; Phi: Ruiz, Werth (2). **GIDP**—Phi: Victorino. **PB**—SF: Posey. **T**—2:59. **A**—45,929.

Recap: The highly anticipated pitching matchup of the Phillies' Roy Halladay versus the Giants' Tim Lincecum was overshadowed by the heroics of Giants' outfielder Cody Ross, whose two home runs off Halladay helped to power San Francisco to a 4–3 win in Game 1 of the NLCS. A two-run shot by Jayson Werth off Linececum in the sixth inning brought the Phillies within one run, but Javier Lopez and Giants' closer Brian Wilson shut the Phillies down in the final two innings to secure the victory.

GAME 2

											R	H	E
San Francisco	0	0	0	0	1	0	0	0	0	**1**	**4**	**1**
Philadelphia	1	0	0	0	1	0	4	0	x	**6**	**8**	**0**

W—Phi: Oswalt. **L**—SF: J Sanchez. **LOB**—SF: 7; Phi: 8. **2B**—Phi: Howard, Victorino, Rollins. **HR**—SF: Ross. **RBI**—SF: Ross; Phi: Rollins (4), Polanco (2). **SB**—Phi: Utley (2), Polanco. **SAC**—Phi: Victorino. **SF**—Phi: Polanco; **E**—SF: Fontenot. **T**—3:01. **A**—46,099.

Recap: Late-season pickup Roy Oswalt made the Phillies' investment pay off with eight dominant innings, nine strikeouts, and only three hits allowed in Philadelphia's 6–1 series-evening victory over San Francisco in Game 2 of the NLCS. The only blemish on his performance was a solo home run by the suddenly potent Giants outfielder Cody Ross that tied the score in the fifth inning. The Phillies broke the game open with a four-run seventh, capped by Jimmy Rollins' bases-clearing three-run double.

National League Championship Series *(Cont.)*

GAME 3

Philadelphia	0	0	0	0	0	0	0	0	0	**0**	**3**	**1**
San Francisco	0	0	0	2	1	0	0	0	x	**3**	**5**	**0**

W—SF: Cain. **L**—Phi: Hamels. **SV**—SF: Wilson.
LOB—Phi 7; SF: 3. **2B**—SF: Rowand. **RBI**—SF: Ross, Huff. **SB**—Phi: Victorino. **SAC**—SF: F Sanchez.
GIDP—Phi: Ibanez. **E**—Phi: Utley.
T—2:39. **A**—43,320.

Recap: Brilliant pitching continued to dominate, but this time it was San Francisco's Matt Cain in command, allowing just a pair of harmless singles in seven shutout innings against the Phillies, before giving way to Javier Lopez and closer Brian Wilson who completed the 3–0 victory for the Giants in a pivotal Game 3. Cody Ross was pivotal for San Francsico yet again, driving in Edgar Renteria with the first run and advancing Pat Burrell to third where he scored on Aubrey Huff's single.

GAME 4

Philadelphia	0	0	0	0	4	0	0	1	0	**5**	**9**	**1**
San Francisco	1	0	1	0	1	2	0	0	1	**6**	**11**	**0**

W—SF: Wilson. **L**—Phi: Oswalt. **LOB**—Phi: 6; SF: 9.
2B—Phi: Polanco, Howard, Werth; SF: Posey (2), Ross, Sandoval. **RBI**—Phi: Victorino, Polanco (2), Werth; SF: Posey (2), Huff, Sandoval (2), Uribe. **CS**—Phi: Rollins; SF: Torres. **SAC**—Phi: Blanton. **SF**—SF: Uribe. **GIDP**—Phi: Polanco; SF: Sandoval. **E**—Phi: Rollins. **T**—3:40. **A**—43,515.

Recap: A see-saw battle featuring two doubles and two RBIs for Giants rookie catcher Buster Posey and another two RBIs from third baseman Pablo Sandoval ended with a walk-off sacrifice fly from banged-up defensive replacement Juan Uribe that scored Aubrey Huff with the game-winning run in Game 4. Uribe, who had just entered the game in the ninth, robbed Philadelphia's Russ Gload of a hit on a hard shot to shortstop in the top of the inning. Second-guessers had a field day with Philadelphia manager Charlie Manuel's decision to bring in starter Roy Oswalt in a relief role in the ninth inning.

GAME 5

Philadelphia	0	0	3	0	0	0	0	0	1	**4**	**6**	**1**
San Francisco	1	0	0	1	0	0	0	0	0	**2**	**7**	**2**

W—Phi: Halladay. **L**—SF: Lincecum. **SV**—Lidge.
LOB—Phi: 6; SF: 7. **2B**—Burrell, Ross. **HR**—Phi: Werth **RBI**—Phi: Victorino, Polanco, Werth; SF: Posey, Ross. **SB**—Phi: Utley, Rollins (2). **SAC**—Phi: Halladay. **E**—Phi: Howard; SF: Huff, Sandoval. **T**—3:15. **A**—43,713.

Recap: In a reprise of the opening-game marquee matchup between Roy Halladay and Tim Lincecum, the winner this time was Halladay, who pitched six strong innings before giving way to the Phillies' bullpen which shut out the Giants the rest of the way as Philadelphia staved off series elimination in Game 5. Lincecum was victimized by first baseman Aubrey Huff's error in the third inning, which allowed two runs to score. Placido Polanco followed with a run-scoring single that would give the Phillies all the runs they would need.

GAME 6

San Francisco	0	0	2	0	0	0	0	1	0	**3**	**13**	**0**
Philadelphia	2	0	0	0	0	0	0	0	0	**2**	**8**	**1**

W—SF: Lopez. **L**—Phi: Madson. **SV**—SF: Wilson.
LOB—SF: 11; Phi: 11. **2B**—SF: Ross, F Sanchez; Phi: Utley, Sandoval. **HR**—SF: Huff, Uribe; Phi: Utley, Werth. **SAC**—SF: F Sanchez; Phi: Ruiz. **SF**—Phi: Werth. **GIDP**—SF: Ross, Renteria. **E**—Phi: Polanco. **T**—3:41. **A**—46,062.

Recap: The real star in the Game 6 series-clinching win for San Francisco was the Giants' bullpen, which took over for a struggling Jonathan Sanchez—who gave up two runs in the first inning and only lasted two innings overall—and proceeded to shut out the Phillies over the remaining seven innings, pitching out of mutiple jams and getting critical outs just when they needed them. That stalwart work was enough to allow the Giants to get back in the game, scoring two runs in the third to tie and getting the go-ahead run in the eighth on a solo home run by Juan Uribe. Brian Wilson notched his third save to go with his victory in Game 4.

American League Division Playoffs

Oct 6 .... Texas 5 at Tampa Bay 1	Oct 10 .... Tampa Bay 5 at Texas 2
Oct 7 .... Texas 6 at Tampa Bay 0	Oct 12 .... Texas 5 at Tampa Bay 1
Oct 9 .... Tampa Bay 6 at Texas 3	*(Texas won series 3–2)*

Oct 6 .... New York 6 at Minnesota 4	Oct 9 .... Minnesota 1 at New York 6
Oct 7 .... New York 5 at Minnesota 2	*(New York won series 3–0)*

American League Championship Series

Oct 15 .... New York 6 at Texas 5	Oct 19 .... Texas 10 at New York 3
Oct 16 .... New York 2 at Texas 7	Oct 20 .... Texas 2 at New York 7
Oct 18 .... Texas 8 at New York 0	Oct 22 .... New York 1 at Texas 6
	(Texas won series 4–2)

GAME 1

New York	0	0	0	0	0	0	1	5	0	**6**	**10**	**1**
Texas	3	0	0	2	0	0	0	0	0	**5**	**7**	**1**

W—NY: Moseley. **L**—Tex: O'Day. **SV**—NY: Rivera.
LOB—NY: 7; Tex: 7. **2B**—NY: Jeter; Tex: Young. **HR**—NY: Cano; Tex: Hamilton. **RBI**—NY: Cano (2), Jeter, Rodriguez (2), Thames; Tex: Hamilton (3), Young (2). **SB**—Tex: Hamilton. **CS**—Tex: Kinsler. **SAC**—Tex: Andrus. **GIDP**—NY: Jeter. **E**—NY: Rodriguez; Tex: Hamilton. **T**—3:50. **A**—50,930.

GAME 1 *(CONT.)*

Recap: It was a tale of two halves in Game 1 of the ALCS: the first half in which the Rangers roughed up usually reliable NY starter CC Sabathia for five runs on a three-run homer by Josh Hamilton in the first inning and a two-run double by Michael Young in the fourth, and the second half, in which the Texas bullpen imploded and the Yankee bats exploded for one run on a solo shot by Robinson Cano in the seventh inning and a stunning five more in the eighth

American League Championship Series *(Cont.)*

GAME 1 *(CONT.)*

with Alex Rodriguez driving in a pair and Cano delivering two more. Kerry Wood and Mariano Rivera shut Texas down in the eighth and ninth to complete the dramatic come-from-behind victory for the Yankees.

GAME 2

New York	0 0 0	1 0 1	0 0 0	**2**	**7**	**0**
Texas	1 2 2	0 2 0	0 0 x	**7**	**12**	**0**

W—Tex: Lewis. **L**—NY: Hughes. **LOB**—NY: 12; Tex: 9. **2B**—NY: Swisher, Cano; Tex: Young, Cruz (2), Murphy, Molina. **3B**—Tex: Kinsler. **HR**—NY: Cano; Tex: Murphy, Molina. **RBI**—NY: Berkman, Cano; Tex: Murphy (2), Young, Molina, Kinsler, Moreland. **SB**—Tex: Andrus (2), Hamilton (2). **SAC**—Tex: Kinsler. **GIDP**—Tex: Young. **IBB**—Tex: Hamilton. **HBP**—NY: Granderson. **WP**—NY: Hughes; Tex: Lewis. **T**—3:52. **A**—50,362.

Recap: Showing no apparent ill effects from their stunning Game 1 loss, the Rangers came flying out of the gate in Game 2, tagging Yankees starter Phil Huges for five runs in the first three innings, the biggest blows being a home run and a double by Texas outfielder David Murphy that drove in one run in the second and another in the third. Texas tacked on two runs in the fifth inning on an Ian Kinsler triple and a Mitch Moreland single to put the game out of reach en route to the 7–2 victory.

GAME 3

Texas	2 0 0	0 0 0	0 0 6	**8**	**11**	**0**
New York	0 0 0	0 0 0	0 0 0	**0**	**2**	**0**

W—Tex: Lee. **L**—NY: Pettitte. **LOB**—Tex: 4; NY: 3. **2B**—Tex: Hamilton. **HR**—Tex: Hamilton. **RBI**—Tex: Hamilton (2), Cruz, Molina, Moreland (2), Andrus. **SB**—NY: Gardner. **IBB**—Tex: Murphy. **WP**—NY: Robertson, Mitre. **T**—3:18. **A**—49,480.

Recap: A simply brilliant performance by Texas starter Cliff Lee sent the Yankee faithful home despondent as the mighty New York offensive machine was held to two hits, one walk, and no runs in the Rangers' 8–0 Game 3 victory. Lee was masterful throughout, striking out 13 Yankees over eight innings and giving way to closer Neftali Feliz in the ninth inning only after Texas had ripped the New York bullpen for six runs in the top of the ninth to put the game out of reach. Josh Hamilton had another productive night for the Rangers with a double, a home run and two RBIs.

GAME 4

Texas	0 0 2	0 0 3	2 0 3	**10**	**13**	**0**
New York	0 1 1	1 0 0	0 0 0	**3**	**7**	**0**

W—Tex: Holland. **L**—NY: Burnett. **SV**—Tex: Oliver. **LOB**—Tex: 7; NY: 8. **2B**—Tex: Guerrero; NY: Jeter. **3B**—NY: Jeter. **HR**—Tex: Molina, Hamilton (2), Cruz; NY: Cano. **RBI**—Tex: Andrus, Young, Molina (3), Hamilton (2), Kinsler, Cruz (2); NY: Cano, Granderson, Gardner. **SB**—Tex: Andrus, Kinsler. **SAC**—Tex: Moreland. **GIDP**—Tex: Moreland, Molina; NY: Rodriguez. **IBB**—Tex: Murphy. **HBP**—Tex: Molina; NY: Rodriguez. **WP**—NY: Burnett. **BK**—Tex: Hunter **T**—4:05. **A**—49,977.

Recap: Struggling Texas starter Tommy Hunter gave

GAME 4 *(CONT.)*

up three runs to the Yankees in just 3⅓ innings of work but Derek Holland and the Rangers bullpen rode to the rescue, shutting New York down the rest of the way as the Texas bats—most notably those of Josh Hamilton (two RBIs), Bengie Molina (three RBIs) and Nelson Cruz (two RBIs)—came to life, producing 10 runs against Yankees starter A.J. Burnett and the New York bullpen to give Texas a commanding three games to one series lead.

GAME 5

Texas	0 0 0	0 1 1	0 0 0	**2**	**13**	**1**
New York	0 3 2	0 1 0	1 0 x	**7**	**9**	**0**

W—NY: Sabathia. **L**—Tex: Wilson. **LOB**—Tex: 7. **2B**—Tex: Cruz; NY: Posada, Rodriguez, Granderson. **HR**—Tex: Treanor; NY: Swisher, Cano, Granderson. **RBI**—Tex: Treanor (2); NY: Posada, Granderson (2), Swisher, Cano, Berkman. **SB**—Tex: Kinsler, Andrus; NY: Rodriguez. **SAC**—NY: Gardner. **SF**—NY: Berkman. **GIDP**—Tex: Young, Hamilton; NY: Swisher. **IBB**—NY: Thames. **WP**—NY: Wood. **E**—Tex: Francoeur; **T**—3:48. **A**—49,832.

Recap: With their season on the line, the Yankees turned to their oversized ace, CC Sabathia, and the big man delivered, limiting the Rangers to two runs over six innings before turning the game over to Kerry Wood and Mariano Rivera, who shut Texas out over the final three innings. Big blows for New York included solo shots for Nick Swisher, Curtis Granderson, and Robinson Cano, whose home run in the third inning was his fourth of the series.

GAME 6

New York	0 0 0	0 1 0	0 0 0	**1**	**3**	**0**
Texas	1 0 0	0 4 0	1 0 x	**6**	**7**	**0**

W—Tex: Lewis. **L**—NY: Hughes. **LOB**—NY: 3; Tex: 7. **2B**—NY: Rodriguez, Posada; Tex: Andrus, Guerrero, Kinsler, Young. **3B**—NY: Berkman. **HR**—Tex: Cruz. **RBI**—Tex: Guerrero (3), Cruz (2), Kinsler. **CS**—NY: Granderson. **SF**—Tex: Kinsler. **GIDP**—NY: Cano. **IBB**—Tex: Hamilton (3), Cruz. **WP**—NY: Hughes; Tex: Lewis. **T**—2:57. **A**—51,404.

Recap: The score was tied 1–1 when Vladimir Guerrero came to the plate in the fifth inning with runners on first and second base. With Guerrero hobbled by injury and seemingly mired in a slump, the Yankees had chosen to intentionally walk Josh Hamilton for the second time in Game 6—they would walk him intentionally again in the seventh inning—but this time Vlad the Destroyer looked like his old self, ripping a double off Yankees starter Phil Hughes into the alley in left-center field to put the Rangers up by two runs. Nelson Cruz followed with a home run off Yankee reliever Dave Robertson to put Texas up 5–1. That was more than enough for the Rangers as Texas starter C.J. Lewis pitched eight superb innings, allowing the Yankees only one run on three hits before giving way to closer Neftali Feliz, who ended the game by striking out Alex Rodriguez to send Texas to its first ever World Series appearance.

Oct 27 ....Texas 7 at San Francisco 11
Oct 28 ....Texas 0 at San Francisco 9
Oct 30 ....San Francisco 2 at Texas 4

Oct 31 ....San Francisco 4 at Texas 0
Nov 1 ....San Francisco 3 at Texas 1

(San Francisco won series 4–1)

GAME 1

Texas	1	1	0	0	0	2	0	0	3	**7**	**11**	**4**
San Francisco	0	0	2	0	6	0	0	3	x	**11**	**14**	**2**

W—SF: Lincecum. **L**—Tex: Lee. **LOB**—Tex: 8; SF: 6. **2B**—Tex: Lee, Moreland, Molina, Cruz; SF: F Sanchez (3), Huff, Torres, Ishikawa. **HR**—SF: Uribe. **RBI**—Tex: Guerrero (2), Andrus, Molina, Murphy, Cruz (2); SF: F Sanchez (3), Posey, Ross, Huff, Uribe (3), Ishikawa, Schierholtz. **CS**—SF: Huff. **GIDP**—Tex: Kinsler. **WP**—SF: Affeldt. **HBP**—SF: Torres, Renteria. **E**—Tex: Young, Andrus, Guerrero (2); SF: Huff, Ishikawa. **T**—3:36. **A**—43,601.

Recap: This was not the World Series Game 1 everyone expected. San Francisco ace Tim Lincecum gave up four runs and eight hits in 5⅔ innings. Texas ace Cliff Lee perfomed even more poorly, allowing seven runs (six earned) on eight hits in just 4⅔ innings of work. The pitcher's duel turned into a slugfest. In the end, the Giants won the battle 11–7, with a six-run fifth inning, capped by a three-run homer from Juan Uribe, proving to be the decisive frame. Giants' second baseman Freddy Sanchez had an especially auspicious start in his first Fall Classic, going 4 for 5, with three doubles, 2 runs scored, and 3 RBIs. Texas, on the other hand, looked a bit overwhelmed by their first visit to the big stage, committing four errors and several base-running mistakes.

GAME 2

Texas	0	0	0	0	0	0	0	0	0	**0**	**4**	**0**
San Francisco	0	0	0	0	1	0	1	7	x	**9**	**8**	**0**

W—SF: Cain. **L**—Tex: C Wilson. **LOB**—Tex: 7, SF: 5. **2B**—Tex: Kinsler; SF: Ross, Torres. **3B**—SF: Rowand. **HR**—SF: Renteria. **RBI**—SF: Renteria (3), Uribe (2), Huff, Rowand (2), Torres. **SB**—SF: Andrus. **SAC**—Tex: C Wilson. **IBB**—Tex: Moreland. **WP**—SF: Cain. **T**—3:17. **A**—43,622.

Recap: Matt Cain pitched his third consecutive brilliant game for the Giants in the postseason, throwing 7⅔ shutout innings—he has yet to allow an earned run in 21⅓ postseason innings—as the Giants defeated the Rangers 9–0 to take a 2–0 lead in the Series. Edgar Renteria's solo shot in the fifth inning was the extent of the offense for either team—C.J. Wilson pitched effectively for the Rangers as well—until Juan Uribe singled in a run for San Francisco in the seventh and the Giant hitters battered the Texas bullpen for seven runs in the eighth to put the game out of reach. Everyone got into the act in the big inning, with Renteria driving in two additional runs with a single, and Aaron Rowand driving in a pair of runs with a bases-clearing triple. The victory represented the Giants third shutout in its nine postseason wins.

GAME 3

San Francisco	0	0	0	0	0	0	1	1	0	**2**	**5**	**1**
Texas	0	3	0	0	1	0	0	0	x	**4**	**8**	**0**

W—Tex: Lewis. **L**—SF: J Sanchez. **SV**—Tex: Feliz. **LOB**—SF: 5; Tex: 5. **2B**—SF: Huff; Tex: Cruz. **HR**—SF: Ross, Torres; Tex: Moreland, Hamilton. **RBI**—SF: Ross, Torres; Tex: Moreland (3), Hamilton. **SB**—Tex: Kinsler. **CS**—Tex: Guerrero. **HBP**—SF: Huff. **E**—SF: Renteria. **T**—2:51. **A**—52,419.

Recap: The brilliant pitching swung to the Rangers side of the diamond in Game 3 as Colby Lewis, just 12–13 in the regular season, gave Texas just the performance it needed to get back in the Series, allowing the Giants just two earned runs in 7⅔ innings in a 4–2 Rangers victory. Rookie Mitch Moreland, batting out of the ninth spot in the batting order, provided all the offense his team would need, smacking a three-run homer off struggling San Francisco starter Jonathan Sanchez in the second inning. Josh Hamilton's fifth home run in the fifth extended the lead to 4–0 before solo shots by Cody Ross and Andres Torres in the seventh and eighth innings, respectively, cut the Rangers lead in half. The Giants managed to get the tying run to the plate in the eighth, but reliever Darren O'Day induced Buster Posey to ground out to end the threat and closer Neftali Feliz retired the Giants 1-2-3 in the ninth.

GAME 4

San Francisco	0	0	2	0	0	0	1	1	0	**4**	**8**	**1**
Texas	0	0	0	0	0	0	0	0	0	**0**	**3**	**0**

W—SF: Bumgarner. **L**—Tex: Hunter. **LOB**—SF: 6; Tex: 3. **2B**—SF: Torres (2). **HR**—SF: Huff, Posey. **RBI**—SF: Huff (2), Torres, Posey. **SB**—SF: Torres. **CS**—Tex: Hamilton. **E**—SF: Uribe. **T**—3:09. **A**—51,920.

Recap: Madison Bumgarner, the Giants' 21-year-old rookie starter, baffled the Rangers over eight innings, closer Brian Wilson shut them down in the ninth, and San Francisco emerged with a 4–0 victory and a commanding 3–1 Series lead. The Giants became the first team since the Baltimore Orioles in 1966 to record at least two shutouts in a World Series. (The Orioles shut out the Dodgers three times.) The Rangers, who were shut out at home only once in the entire regular season, managed just three hits off Bumgarner, who became the youngest lefthander in history to throw at least eight scoreless innings in a World Series. Another bit of history: Bumgarner and catcher Buster Posey, who hit a solo home run in the eighth inning, became the first rookie battery in a World Series game since Yogi Berra and Spec Shea started for the Yankees in 1947. The key blow in the game was a two-run homer by Aubrey Huff in the third inning off Texas starter Tommy Hunter. Andres Torres (two doubles and an RBI) and Edgar Renteria contributed three hits apiece and the Giants got sparkling plays in the field from Cody Ross, Freddy Sanchez, and Posey, who gunned down Josh Hamilton on an attemped steal.

GAME 5

San Francisco	0 0 0	0 0 0	3 0 0	**3**	**7**	**0**
Texas	0 0 0	0 0 0	1 0 1	**I**	**3**	**I**

W—SF: Lincecum. **L**—Tex: Lee. **SV**—SF: B Wilson.
LOB—SF: 4. Tex: 4. **HR**—SF: Renteria; Tex: Cruz.
RBI—SF: Renteria (3); Tex: Cruz. **SAC**—SF: Huff.
GIDP—SF: Renteria. **T**—2:32. **A**—52,045.

Recap: In the biggest game of his life, San Francisco ace and two-time Cy Young award winner Tim Lincecum pitched eight brilliant innings, outdueling Texas starter Cliff Lee in a tense 3–1 victory that delivered the Giants their first championship since 1954 and their only title since the team moved to San Francisco in 1958. Lincecum was nearly unhittable all night, allowing just three hits and one run—on a solo shot by Nelson Cruz in the seventh inning—while striking out 10. It was a fitting finale for San Francisco, which held Texas to a total of just five runs in the final four games of the Series and only one run overall in their final three victories. The hitting star of the game was veteran shortstop and Series MVP Edgar Renteria, whose three-run home run in the seventh inning—delivered after singles by Cody Ross and Juan Uribe—constituted the entire Giants' offense for the evening. Renteria hit .412 for the Series overall, with two home runs and 6 RBIs in the five games. The ancient baseball wisdom about good pitching beating good hitting was confirmed yet again as the Giants, who only made the playoffs on the last day of the regular season but who led the majors in ERA, completely shut down baseball's best hitting team.

2010 World Series Composite Box Score

SAN FRANCISCO

BATTING	AB	R	H	HR	RBI	Avg
Torres	22	4	7	1	3	.318
Sanchez	22	2	6	0	3	.273
Posey	20	2	6	1	2	.300
Uribe	19	3	3	1	5	.158
Ross	17	5	4	1	2	.235
Renteria	17	6	7	2	6	.412
Huff	17	3	5	1	4	.294
Burrell	13	1	0	0	0	.000
Schierholtz	5	1	1	0	1	.200
Rowand	4	1	1	0	2	.250
Ishikawa	4	1	1	0	1	.250
Sandoval	3	0	0	0	0	.000
Fontenot	1	0	0	0	0	.000
Pitchers	6	0	1	0	0	.167
Totals	**170**	**29**	**42**	**7**	**29**	**.247**

PITCHING	G	IP	H	BB	SO	ERA
Lincecum	2	13.2	11	4	13	3.29
Bumgarner	1	8.0	3	2	6	0.00
Cain	1	7.2	4	2	2	0.00
Sanchez	1	4.2	6	3	3	7.71
Wilson	3	2.2	1	0	4	0.00
Mota	2	2.1	1	2	0	0.00
Casilla	1	1.1	0	0	1	0.00
Affeldt	2	1.1	1	1	0	6.75
Ramirez	2	1.0	1	1	1	18.00
Lopez	2	0.2	0	0	0	0.00
Romo	1	0.2	1	0	1	0.00
Totals	**5**	**44.0**	**29**	**15**	**31**	**2.45**

TEXAS

BATTING	AB	R	H	HR	RBI	Avg
Young	20	0	5	0	0	.250
Cruz	20	2	4	1	3	.200
Hamilton	20	2	2	1	1	.100
Andrus	17	2	3	0	1	.176
Kinsler	16	1	3	0	0	.188
Guerrero	14	0	1	0	2	.071
Moreland	13	1	6	1	3	.462
Molina	11	3	2	0	1	.182
Murphy	7	0	1	0	1	.143
Francoeur	6	0	0	0	0	.000
Treanor	3	0	0	0	0	.000
Borbon	2	1	1	0	0	.500
Cantu	1	0	0	0	0	.000
Pitchers	3	0	1	0	0	.333
Totals	**153**	**12**	**29**	**3**	**12**	**.190**

PITCHING	G	IP	H	BB	SO	ERA
Lee	2	11.2	14	1	13	6.94
Lewis	1	7.2	5	2	6	2.35
Wilson	1	6.0	3	2	4	3.00
Hunter	1	4.0	5	1	1	4.50
Ogando	2	3.2	1	0	6	0.00
Feliz	2	3.0	1	0	4	0.00
Oliver	2	2.2	3	0	4	3.38
O'Day	4	2.0	3	0	3	13.50
Holland	2	1.0	0	4	1	27.00
Lowe	2	0.2	4	1	0	67.50
Kirkman	2	0.2	3	0	1	13.50
Totals	**5**	**43.0**	**42**	**11**	**43**	**5.86**

National League Batting

BATTING AVERAGE

Carlos Gonzalez, Col	.336
Joey Votto, Cin	.324
Omar Infante, Atl	.321
Troy Tulowitzki, Col	.315
Matt Holliday, StL	.312
Albert Pujols, StL	.312
Martin Prado, Atl	.307
Ryan Zimmerman, Was	.307
Ryan Braun, Mil	.304
Starlin Castro, CHC	.300
Hanley Ramirez, Fla	.300

HITS

Carlos Gonzalez, Col	197
Ryan Braun, Mil	188
Matt Holliday, StL	186
Martin Prado, Atl	184
Albert Pujols, StL	183
Joey Votto, Cin	177
Adrian Gonzalez, SD	176
Rickie Weeks, Mil	175
Casey McGehee, Mil	174
Hunter Pence, Hou	173

DOUBLES

Jayson Werth, Phi	46
Ryan Braun, Mil	45
Matt Holliday, StL	45
Andres Torres, SF	43
James Loney, LA	41
Martin Prado, Atl	40
Alfonso Soriano, Was	40

TRIPLES

Dexter Fowler, Col	14
Stephen Drew, Ari	12
Alcides Escobar, Mil	10
Jose Reyes, NYM	10
Shane Victorino, Phi	10

STOLEN BASES

Michael Bourn, Hou	52
Angel Pagan, NYM	37
Nyjer Morgan, Was	34
Shane Victorino, Phi	34
Andrew McCutchen, Pit	33
Hanley Ramirez, Fla	32
Jose Reyes, NYM	30
Drew Stubbs, Cin	30

HOME RUNS

Albert Pujols, StL	42
Adam Dunn, Was	38
Joey Votto, Cin	37
Carlos Gonzalez, Col	34
Dan Uggla, Fla	33
Prince Fielder, Mil	32
Mark Reynolds, Ari	32
Adrian Gonzalez, SD	31
Corey Hart, Mil	31
Ryan Howard, Phi	31
Rickie Weeks, Mil	29
David Wright, NYM	29
Matt Holliday, StL	28
Matt Kemp, LAD	28

RUNS SCORED

Albert Pujols, StL	115
Rickie Weeks, Mil	112
Carlos Gonzalez, Col	111
Joey Votto, Cin	106
Jayson Werth, Phi	106
Ryan Braun, Mil	101
Aubrey Huff, SF	100
Brandon Phillips, Cin	100
Martin Prado, Atl	100
Dan Uggla, Fla	100
Matt Holliday, StL	95

RUNS BATTED IN

Albert Pujols, StL	118
Carlos Gonzalez, Col	117
Joey Votto, Cin	113
Ryan Howard, Phi	108
Dan Uggla, Fla	105
Casey McGehee, Mil	104
Ryan Braun, Mil	103
Adam Dunn, Was	103
Matt Holliday, StL	103
David Wright, NYM	103
Corey Hart, Mil	102
Adrian Gonzalez, SD	101
Adam LaRoche, Ari	100
Troy Tulowitzki, Col	95
Hunter Pence, Hous	91
Chris Young, Ari	91

SLUGGING PERCENTAGE

Joey Votto, Cin	.600
Carlos Gonzalez, Col	.598
Albert Pujols, StL	.596
Troy Tulowitzki, Col	.568
Adam Dunn, Was	.536

ON-BASE PERCENTAGE

Joey Votto, Cin	.424
Albert Pujols, StL	.414
Prince Fielder, Mil	.401
Adrian Gonzalez, SD	.393
Jason Heyward, Atl.	.393
Matt Holliday, StL	.390

BASES ON BALLS

Prince Fielder, Mil	114
Albert Pujols, StL	103
Adrian Gonzalez, SD	93
Jason Heyward, Atl	91
Joey Votto, Cin	91

National League Pitching

EARNED RUN AVERAGE

Josh Johnson, Fla	2.30
Adam Wainwright, StL	2.42
Roy Halladay, Phi	2.44
Jaime Garcia, StL	2.70
Roy Oswalt, Hou/Phi	2.76
Tim Hudson, Atl	2.83
R.A. Dickey, NYM	2.84
Ubaldo Jimenez, Col	2.88
Clayton Kershaw, LAD	2.91
Mat Lantos, SD	2.92
Johan Santana, NYM	2.98

SAVES

Brian Wilson, SF	48
Heath Bell, SD	47
Francisco Cordero, Cin	40
Carlos Marmol, CHC	38
Billy Wagner, Atl	37
Leo Nunez, Fla	30
Ryan Franklin, StL	27
Brad Lidge, Phi	27
Matt Capps, Was	26
Francisco Rodriguez, NYM	25

WINS

Roy Halladay, Phi	21
Adam Wainwright, StL	20
Ubaldo Jimenez, Col	19
Bronson Arroyo, Cin	17
Tim Hudson, Atl	17

GAMES PITCHED

Pedro Feliciano, NYM	92
Peter Moylan, Atl	85
Nick Masset, Cin	82
Luke Gregerson, SD	80
Sean Marshall, Cin	80
Brandon Lyon, Hou	79
Jonny Venters, Atl	79

INNINGS PITCHED

Roy Halladay, Phi	250.2
Chris Carpenter, StL	235.0
Adam Wainwright, StL	230.1
Tim Hudson, Atl	228.2
Brett Myers, Hou	223.2
Matt Cain, SF	223.1

STRIKEOUTS

Tim Lincecum, SF	231
Roy Halladay, PHi	219
Ubaldo Jimenez, Col	214
Adam Wainwright, StL	213
Clayton Kershaw, LAD	212
Cole Hamels, Phi	211
Ryan Dempster, CHC	208
Jonathan Sanchez, SF	205
Yovani Gallardo, Mil	200

COMPLETE GAMES

Roy Halladay, Phi	9
Adam Wainwright, StL	5
Three tied with 4.	

SHUTOUTS

Roy Halladay, Phi	4
Matt Cain, SF	2
Yovani Gallardo, Mil	2
Ubaldo Jimenez, Col	2
Roy Oswalt, Hou/Phi	2
Johan Santana, NYM	2
Adam Wainwright, StL	2

American League Batting

BATTING AVERAGE

Josh Hamilton, Tex .... .359
Miguel Cabrera, Det .... .328
Joe Mauer, Min .... .327
Adrian Beltre, Bos .... .321
Robinson Cano, NYY .... .319
Billy Butler, KC .... .318
Ichiro Suzuki, Sea .... .315
Paul Konerko, CWS .... .312
Carl Crawford, TB .... .307
Victor Martinez, Bos .... .302
Shin-Soo Choo, Cle .... .300
Vladimir Guerrero, Tex .... .300

HITS

Ichiro Suzuki, Sea 214
Robinson Cano, NYY 200
Adrian Beltre, Bos 189
Billy Butler, KC 189
Nick Markakis, Bal 187
Josh Hamilton, Tex 186
Michael Young, Tex. 186
Carl Crawford, TB 184
Austin Jackson, Det 181
Miguel Cabrera, Det 180

DOUBLES

Adrian Beltre, Bos. 49
Evan Longoria, TB 46
Delmon Young, Min 46
Billy Butler, KC 45
Miguel Cabrera, Det 45
Nick Markakis, Bal 45
Vernon Wells, Tor 44

TRIPLES

Carl Crawford, TB 13
Austin Jackson, Det 10
Denard Span, Min 10
Cliff Pennington, Oak 8

Two tied with 7.

EARNED RUN AVERAGE

Felix Hernandez, Sea 2.27
Clay Buchholz, Bos 2.33
David Price, TB......................2.72
Trevor Cahill, Oak 2.97
Jered Weaver, LAA 3.01
Cliff Lee, Sea/Tex 3.18
CC Sabathia, NYY 3.18
Gio Gonzalez, Oak 3.23
Jon Lester, Bos 3.25
C.J. Wilson, Tex 3.35
Justin Verlander, Det.............3.37

SAVES

Rafael Soriano, TB 45
Joakim Soria, KC 43
Neftali Feliz, Tex.....................40
Kevin Gregg, Tor 37
Jonathan Papelbon, Bos 37
Mariano Rivera, NYY 33
David Aardsma, Sea................31
Bobby Jenks, CWS...................27
Jose Valverde, Det...................26
Andrew Bailey, Oak 25

STOLEN BASES

Juan Pierre, CWS....................68
Rajai Davis, Oak 50
Carl Crawford, TB....................47
Brett Gardner, NYY 47
Chone Figgins, Sea 42
Ichiro Suzuki, Sea 42
B.J. Upton, TB 42
Alex Rios, CWS........................34
Elvis Andrus, Tex 32
Coco Crisp, Oak 32

HOME RUNS

Jose Bautista, Tor 54
Paul Konerko, CWS 39
Miguel Cabrera, Det 38
Mark Teixeira, NYY 33
Josh Hamilton, Tex 32
David Ortiz, Bos 32
Vernon Wells, Tor 31
Alex Rodriguez, NYY 30
Robinson Cano, NYY 29
Vladimir Guerrero, Tex 29
Nick Swisher, NYY 29
Adrian Beltre, Bos. 28
Carlos Pena, TB........................28
Luke Scott, Bal 27

RUNS SCORED

Mark Teixeira, NYY 113
Miguel Cabrera, Det 111
Derek Jeter, NYY 111
Carl Crawford, TB 110
Jose Bautista, Tor 109
Robinson Cano, NYY 103
Austin Jackson, Det 103
Michael Young, Tex...................99
Brett Gardner, NYY 97
Evan Longoria, TB 96
Juan Pierre, CWS......................96
Josh Hamilton, Tex 95
Michael Cuddyer, Min................93

American League Pitching

WINS

CC Sabathia, NYY 21
Jon Lester, Bos 19
David Price, TB.........................19
Trevor Cahill, Oak 18
Phil Hughes, NYY 18
Justin Verlander, Det.................18

GAMES PITCHED

Randy Choate, TB 85
Craig Breslow, Oak....................75
Phil Coke, Det...........................74
Matt Guerrier, Min 74
Daniel Bard, Bos........................73
Joba Chamberlain, NYY 73

INNINGS PITCHED

Felix Hernandez, Sea 249.2
CC Sabathia, NYY 237.2
Justin Verlander, Det............224.1
Jered Weaver, LAA...............224.1
Ervin Santana, LAA...............222.2
Carl Pavano, Min 221.0
Zack Greinke, KC 220.0

RUNS BATTED IN

Miguel Cabrera, Det 126
Alex Rodriguez, NYY 125
Jose Bautista, Tor 124
Vladimir Guerrero, Tex 115
Delmon Young, Min 112
Paul Konerko, CWS 111
Robinson Cano, NYY 109
Mark Teixeira, NYY 108
Evan Longoria, TB 104
Adrian Beltre, Bos. 102
David Ortiz, Bos 102
Josh Hamilton, Tex 100
Jason Kubel, Min 92
Michael Young, Tex....................91
Shin-Soo Choo, Cle 90
Carl Crawford, TB. 90
Torii Hunter, LAA 90

SLUGGING PERCENTAGE

Josh Hamilton, Tex .... .633
Miguel Cabrera, Det .... .622
Jose Bautista, Tor .... .617
Paul Konerko, CWS .... .584
Adrian Beltre, Bos .... .553
Luke Scott, Bal .... .535
Robinson Cano, NYY .... .534

ON-BASE PERCENTAGE

Miguel Cabrera, Det .... .420
Josh Hamilton, Tex .... .411
Joe Mauer, Min .... .402
Shin-Soo Choo, Cle .... .401
Daric Barton, Oak. .... .393
Paul Konerko, CWS .... .393

BASES ON BALLS

Daric Barton, Oak....................110
Jose Bautista, Tor 100
Mark Teixeira, NYY 93
Ben Zobrist, TB........................92
Miguel Cabrera, Det 89

COMPLETE GAMES

Cliff Lee, Sea/Tex......................7
Carl Pavano, Min 7
Felix Hernandez, Sea 6
Dallas Braden, Oak 5

Three tied with 4.

SHUTOUTS

Dallas Braden, Oak 2
Carl Pavano, Min 2

STRIKEOUTS

Jered Weaver, LAA................ 233
Felix Hernandez, Sea 232
Jon Lester, Bos 225
Justin Verlander, Det 219
Francisco Liriano, Min 201
CC Sabathia, NYY 197
Colby Lewis, Tex. 196
David Price, TB 188
James Shields, TB 187
Cliff Lee, Sea/Tex....................185
Max Scherzer, Det 184
Zack Greinke, KC 181

National League

TEAM BATTING	G	AB	R	H	2B	3B	HR	TB	RBI	OBP	SLG	OPS	BAVG
Cincinnati Reds	162	5579	790	1515	293	30	188	2432	761	.338	.436	.774	.272
St. Louis Cardinals	162	5542	736	1456	285	18	150	2227	689	.332	.402	.733	.263
Colorado Rockies	162	5530	770	1452	270	54	173	2349	741	.336	.425	.760	.263
Milwaukee Brewers	162	5606	750	1471	293	33	182	2376	710	.335	.424	.759	.262
Philadelphia Phillies	162	5581	772	1451	290	34	166	2307	736	.332	.413	.745	.260
Atlanta Braves	162	5463	738	1411	312	25	139	2190	699	.339	.401	.740	.258
San Francisco Giants	162	5488	697	1411	284	30	162	2241	660	.321	.408	.729	.257
Chicago Cubs	162	5512	685	1414	298	27	149	2213	658	.320	.401	.721	.257
Florida Marlins	162	5531	719	1403	294	37	152	2227	686	.321	.403	.724	.254
Los Angeles Dodgers	162	5426	667	1368	270	29	120	2056	621	.322	.379	.700	.252
Arizona Diamondbacks	162	5473	713	1366	301	34	180	2275	691	.325	.416	.740	.250
Washington Nationals	162	5418	655	1355	250	31	149	2114	634	.318	.390	.708	.250
New York Mets	162	5465	656	1361	266	40	128	2091	625	.314	.383	.697	.249
Houston Astros	162	5452	611	1348	252	25	108	1974	577	.303	.362	.665	.247
San Diego Padres	162	5434	665	1338	236	24	132	2018	630	.317	.371	.689	.246
Pittsburgh Pirates	162	5386	587	1303	276	27	126	2011	570	.304	.373	.678	.242

TEAM PITCHING	GP	W	L	SV	SVO	CG	SHO	R	IP	Ks	BB	ERA
San Francisco Giants	162	92	70	57	73	6	17	583	1461.0	1331	578	3.36
San Diego Padres	162	90	72	49	64	2	20	581	1456.1	1295	517	3.39
Atlanta Braves	162	91	71	41	58	2	9	629	1439.1	1241	505	3.56
St. Louis Cardinals	162	86	76	32	42	7	16	641	1453.2	1094	477	3.57
Philadelphia Phillies	162	97	65	40	59	14	21	640	1456.1	1183	416	3.67
New York Mets	162	79	83	36	52	8	19	652	1453.0	1106	545	3.70
Los Angeles Dodgers	162	80	82	41	59	4	16	692	1441.2	1274	539	4.01
Cincinnati Reds	162	91	71	43	63	4	9	685	1453.0	1130	524	4.01
Florida Marlins	162	80	82	39	64	5	17	717	1438.1	1168	549	4.08
Houston Astros	162	76	86	45	60	4	11	729	1439.1	1210	548	4.09
Washington Nationals	162	69	93	37	57	2	5	742	1435.0	1068	512	4.13
Colorado Rockies	162	83	79	35	56	6	12	717	1442.0	1234	525	4.14
Chicago Cubs	162	75	87	40	54	1	14	767	1436.2	1268	605	4.18
Milwaukee Brewers	162	77	85	35	56	3	7	804	1439.0	1258	582	4.58
Arizona Diamondbacks	162	65	97	35	59	3	3	836	1432.0	1070	548	4.81
Pittsburgh Pirates	162	57	105	31	48	1	6	866	1411.2	1026	538	5.00

American League

TEAM BATTING	G	AB	R	H	2B	3B	HR	TB	RBI	OBP	SLG	OPS	BAVG
Texas Rangers	162	5635	787	1556	268	25	162	2360	740	.338	.419	.757	.276
Kansas City Royals	162	5604	676	1534	279	31	121	2238	640	.331	.399	.730	.274
Minnesota Twins	163	5568	781	1521	318	41	142	2347	749	.341	.422	.762	.273
Detroit Tigers	163	5643	751	1515	308	32	152	2343	717	.335	.415	.750	.268
Boston Red Sox	162	5646	818	1511	358	22	211	2546	782	.339	.451	.790	.268
Chicago White Sox	163	5484	752	1467	263	21	177	2303	710	.332	.420	.752	.268
New York Yankees	162	5567	859	1485	275	32	201	2427	823	.350	.436	.786	.267
Baltimore Orioles	162	5554	613	1440	264	21	133	2145	577	.316	.386	.702	.259
Oakland Athletics	162	5448	663	1396	276	30	109	2059	619	.324	.378	.702	.256
Cleveland Indians	162	5487	646	1362	290	20	128	2076	601	.322	.378	.700	.248
Toronto Blue Jays	162	5495	755	1364	319	21	257	2496	732	.312	.454	.766	.248
Los Angeles Angels	162	5488	681	1363	276	19	155	2142	656	.311	.390	.702	.248
Tampa Bay Rays	162	5439	802	1343	295	37	160	2192	769	.333	.403	.736	.247
Seattle Mariners	162	5409	513	1274	227	16	101	1836	485	.298	.339	.637	.236

TEAM PITCHING	GP	W	L	SV	SVO	CG	SHO	R	IP	Ks	BB	ERA
Oakland Athletics	162	81	81	38	51	7	17	626	1431.2	1070	512	3.56
Tampa Bay Rays	162	96	66	51	67	6	12	611	1453.2	1189	478	3.78
Texas Rangers	162	90	72	46	66	7	8	636	1455.1	1181	551	3.93
Seattle Mariners	162	61	101	38	55	11	10	628	1438.0	973	452	3.93
Minnesota Twins	163	94	68	40	58	9	13	638	1452.2	1048	383	3.95
Los Angeles Angels	162	80	82	39	56	10	9	651	1449.1	1130	565	4.04
New York Yankees	162	195	67	39	57	3	8	651	1442.1	1154	540	4.06
Chicago White Sox	162	88	74	43	66	6	11	658	1446.1	1149	490	4.09
Boston Red Sox	162	89	73	44	61	3	9	679	1456.2	1207	580	4.20
Toronto Blue Jays	162	85	77	45	45	5	11	676	1440.2	1184	539	4.22
Detroit Tigers	163	81	81	32	50	6	5	690	1444.1	1056	537	4.30
Cleveland Indians	162	69	93	34	62	10	4	684	1433.0	967	572	4.30
Baltimore Orioles	162	66	96	35	65	3	7	733	1436.1	1007	520	4.59
Kansas City Royals	162	67	95	44	56	7	3	845	1436.2	1.35	551	4.97

Arizona Diamondbacks

BATTING	G	AB	R	H	2B	3B	HR	RBI	TB	BB	SO	SB	OBP	SLG	BAVG
Kelly Johnson	154	585	93	166	36	5	26	71	290	79	148	13	.370	.496	.284
Chris Young	156	584	94	150	33	0	27	91	264	74	145	28	.341	.452	.257
Stephen Drew	151	565	83	157	33	12	15	61	259	62	108	10	.352	.458	.278
Adam LaRoche	151	560	75	146	37	2	25	100	262	48	172	0	.320	.468	.261
Mark Reynolds	145	499	79	99	17	2	32	85	216	83	211	7	.320	.433	.198
Justin Upton	133	495	73	135	27	3	17	69	219	64	152	18	.356	.442	.273
Gerardo Parra	133	364	31	95	19	6	3	30	135	23	76	1	.308	.371	.261
Miguel Montero	85	297	36	79	20	2	9	43	130	29	71	0	.332	.438	.266
Rusty Ryal	104	207	19	54	7	1	3	11	72	8	67	0	.308	.348	.261
*Chris Snyder	65	195	22	45	8	0	10	32	83	36	61	0	.352	.426	.231
Tony Abreu	81	193	16	45	11	1	1	13	61	4	47	2	.244	.316	.233
Conor Jackson	42	151	19	36	11	0	1	11	50	20	18	4	.326	.331	.238
Cole Gillespie	45	104	11	24	8	0	2	12	38	7	29	1	.283	.365	.231
John Hester	38	95	9	20	7	0	2	7	33	11	32	1	.292	.347	.211

PITCHING	GP	GS	W-L	SV	SHO	R	ERA	IP	Ks	BB
Rodrigo Lopez	33	33	7–16	0	0	126	5.00	200.0	116	56
Ian Kennedy	32	32	9–10	0	0	87	3.80	194.0	168	70
*Dan Haren	21	21	7–8	0	0	79	4.60	141.0	141	29
*Edwin Jackson	21	21	6–10	0	1	80	5.16	134.1	104	60
Barry Enright	17	17	6–7	0	0	43	3.91	99.0	49	29
*Joe Saunders	13	13	3–7	0	0	50	4.25	82.2	50	19
*Daniel Hudson	11	11	7–1	0	0	15	1.69	79.2	70	16
Aaron Heilman	70	0	5–8	6	0	37	4.50	72.0	55	26
Blaine Boyer	54	0	3–2	0	0	32	4.26	57.0	29	29
Juan Gutierrez	58	0	0–6	15	0	33	5.08	56.2	47	23
Esmerling Vasquez	57	0	1–6	0	0	32	5.20	53.2	55	38
*Chad Qualls	43	0	1–4	12	0	41	8.29	38.0	34	15

Atlanta Braves

BATTING	G	AB	R	H	2B	3B	HR	RBI	TB	BB	SO	SB	OBP	SLG	BAVG
Martin Prado	140	599	100	184	40	3	15	66	275	40	86	5	.350	.459	.307
Jason Heyward	142	520	83	144	29	5	18	72	237	91	128	11	.393	.456	.277
Brian McCann	143	479	63	129	25	0	21	77	217	74	98	5	.375	.453	.269
Orlando Infante	134	471	65	151	15	3	8	47	196	29	62	7	.359	.416	.321
Melky Cabrera	147	458	50	117	27	3	4	42	162	42	64	7	.317	.354	.255
Troy Glaus	128	412	52	99	18	0	16	71	165	63	100	0	.344	.400	.240
Chipper Jones	95	317	47	84	21	0	10	46	135	61	47	5	.381	.426	.265
Eric Hinske	131	281	38	72	21	1	11	51	128	33	75	0	.338	.456	.256
*Alex Gonzalez	72	267	27	64	17	2	6	38	103	14	53	0	.291	.386	.240
*Yunel Escobar	75	261	28	62	12	0	0	19	74	37	31	5	.334	.284	.238
Nate McLouth	85	242	30	46	12	1	6	24	78	33	57	7	.298	.322	.190
Matt Diaz	84	224	27	56	17	2	7	31	98	13	44	3	.302	.438	.250
Brooks Conrad	103	156	31	39	11	1	8	33	76	16	45	5	.324	.487	.250
*Derrek Lee	39	129	17	37	14	0	3	24	60	31	33	0	.384	.465	.287
David Ross	59	121	15	35	13	2	2	28	58	20	28	0	.392	.479	.289
*Rick Ankiel	47	119	17	25	6	1	2	9	39	19	42	2	.324	.328	.210

PITCHING	GP	GS	W-L	SV	SHO	R	ERA	IP	Ks	BB
Tim Hudson	34	34	17–9	0	0	74	2.83	228.2	139	74
Tommy Hanson	34	34	10–11	0	0	86	3.33	202.2	173	56
Derek Lowe	33	33	16–12	0	0	88	4.00	193.2	136	61
Jair Jurrjens	20	20	7–6	0	0	63	4.64	116.1	86	42
Kris Medlen	31	14	6–2	0	0	48	3.68	107.2	83	21
Kenshin Kawakami	18	16	1–10	0	0	57	5.15	87.1	59	32
Jonny Venters	79	0	4–4	1	0	30	1.95	83.0	93	39
Billy Wagner	71	0	7–2	37	0	14	1.43	69.1	104	22
Peter Moylan	85	0	6–2	1	0	24	2.97	63.2	52	37
Takashi Saito	56	0	2–3	1	0	20	2.83	54.0	69	17
Eric O'Flaherty	56	0	3–2	0	0	14	2.45	44.0	36	18
Mike Minor	9	8	3–2	0	0	28	5.98	40.2	43	11
*Jesse Chavez	28	0	3–2	0	0	24	5.89	36.2	29	12
Cristhian Martinez	18	0	0–0	0	0	14	4.85	26.0	22	6
Craig Kimbrel	21	0	4–0	1	0	2	0.44	20.2	40	16

*Mid-season trade.

Chicago Cubs

BATTING	G	AB	R	H	2B	3B	HR	RBI	TB	BB	SO	SB	OBP	SLG	BAVG
Marlon Byrd	152	580	84	170	39	2	12	66	249	31	98	5	.346	.429	.293
Alfonso Soriano	147	496	67	128	40	3	24	79	246	45	123	5	.322	.496	.258
Aramis Ramirez	124	465	61	112	21	1	25	83	210	34	90	0	.294	.452	.241
Starlin Castro	125	463	53	139	31	5	3	41	189	29	71	10	.347	.408	.300
*Ryan Theriot	96	388	45	110	10	2	1	21	127	19	46	16	.320	.327	.284
Tyler Colvin	135	358	60	91	18	5	20	56	179	30	100	6	.316	.500	.254
Kosuke Fukudome	130	358	45	94	20	2	13	44	157	64	67	7	.371	.439	.263
Geovany Soto	105	322	47	90	19	0	17	53	160	62	83	0	.393	.497	.280
Xavier Nady	119	317	33	81	13	0	6	33	112	17	85	0	.306	.353	.256
Koyie Hill	77	215	18	46	13	1	1	17	64	12	61	1	.254	.298	.214
Jeff Baker	79	206	29	56	13	2	4	21	85	16	50	1	.326	.413	.272
*Blake DeWitt	53	184	18	46	9	1	4	22	69	17	37	1	.314	.375	.250
Darwin Barney	30	79	12	19	4	0	0	2	23	6	12	0	.294	.291	.241

PITCHING	GP	GS	W–L	SV	SHO	R	ERA	IP	Ks	BB
Ryan Dempster	34	34	15–12	0	0	110	3.85	215.1	208	86
Randy Wells	32	32	8–14	0	0	97	4.26	194.1	144	63
Tom Gorzelanny	29	23	7–9	1	0	70	4.09	136.1	119	68
Carlos Zambrano	36	20	11–6	0	0	55	3.33	129.2	117	69
*Ted Lilly	18	18	3–8	0	0	53	3.69	117.0	89	29
Carlos Silva	21	21	10–6	0	0	55	4.22	113.0	80	24
Carlos Marmol	77	0	2–3	38	0	23	2.55	77.2	138	52
Sean Marshall	80	0	7–5	1	0	25	2.65	74.2	90	25
Casey Coleman	12	8	4–2	0	0	27	4.11	57.0	27	25
Andrew Cashner	53	0	2–6	0	0	31	4.80	54.1	50	30
James Russell	57	0	1–1	0	0	37	4.96	49.0	42	11
Justin Berg	41	0	0–1	0	0	27	5.18	40.0	14	20
Thomas Diamond	16	3	1–3	0	0	23	6.83	29.0	36	18
Josh Grabow	28	0	1–3	0	0	24	7.36	25.2	20	13
Marcos Mateo	21	0	0–1	0	0	15	5.82	21.2	26	9

Cincinnati Reds

BATTING	G	AB	R	H	2B	3B	HR	RBI	TB	BB	SO	SB	OBP	SLG	BAVG
Brandon Phillips	155	626	100	172	33	5	18	59	269	46	83	16	.332	.430	.275
Joey Votto	150	547	106	177	36	2	37	113	328	91	125	16	.424	.600	.324
Drew Stubbs	150	514	91	131	19	6	22	77	228	55	168	30	.329	.444	.255
Jonny Gomes	148	511	77	136	24	3	18	86	220	39	123	5	.327	.431	.266
Jay Bruce	148	509	80	143	23	5	25	70	251	58	136	5	.353	.493	.281
Orlando Cabrera	123	494	64	130	33	0	4	42	175	28	53	11	.303	.354	.263
Scott Rolen	133	471	66	134	34	3	20	83	234	50	82	1	.358	.497	.285
Ramon Hernandez	97	313	30	93	18	1	7	48	134	29	49	0	.364	.428	.297
Ryan Hanigan	70	203	25	61	11	0	5	40	87	33	21	0	.405	.429	.300
Chris Heisey	97	201	33	51	10	1	8	21	87	16	57	1	.324	.433	.254
Miguel Cairo	91	200	30	58	12	0	4	28	82	17	30	4	.353	.410	.290
Paul Janish	82	200	23	52	10	0	5	25	77	22	30	1	.338	.385	.260
Lance Nix	97	165	16	48	11	2	4	18	75	15	39	0	.350	.455	.291
Corky Miller	32	74	5	18	5	0	2	9	29	2	16	0	.282	.392	.243

PITCHING	GP	GS	W–L	SV	SHO	R	ERA	IP	Ks	BB
Bronson Arroyo	33	33	17–10	0	0	95	3.88	215.2	121	59
Johnny Cueto	31	31	12–7	0	1	79	3.64	185.2	138	56
Mike Leake	24	22	8–4	0	0	77	4.23	138.1	91	49
Aaron Harang	22	20	6–7	0	0	71	5.32	111.2	82	38
Homer Bailey	19	19	4–3	0	1	55	4.46	109.0	100	40
Travis Wood	17	17	5–4	0	0	45	3.51	102.2	86	26
Nick Masset	82	0	4–4	2	0	31	3.40	76.2	85	33
Francisco Cordero	75	0	6–5	40	0	32	3.84	72.2	59	36
Edinson Volquez	12	12	4–3	0	0	30	4.31	62.2	67	35
Logan Ondrusek	60	0	5–0	0	0	25	3.68	58.2	39	20
Arthur Rhodes	69	0	4–4	0	0	14	2.29	55.0	50	18
Sam LeCure	15	6	2–5	0	0	24	4.50	48.0	37	25
Jordan Smith	37	0	3–2	1	0	18	3.86	42.0	26	11
Micah Owings	22	0	3–2	0	0	20	5.40	33.1	35	25
Bill Bray	35	0	0–2	0	0	13	4.13	28.1	30	10
Danny Herrera	36	0	1–3	0	0	10	3.91	23.0	14	6

*Mid-season trade.

Colorado Rockies

BATTING	G	AB	R	H	2B	3B	HR	RBI	TB	BB	SO	SB	OBP	SLG	BAVG
Carlos Gonzalez	145	587	111	197	34	9	34	117	351	40	135	26	.376	.598	.336
Troy Tulowitzki	122	470	89	148	32	3	27	95	267	48	78	11	.381	.568	.315
Dexter Fowler	132	439	73	114	20	14	6	36	180	57	104	13	.347	.410	.260
Todd Helton	118	398	48	102	18	1	8	37	146	67	90	0	.362	.367	.256
Miguel Olivo	112	394	55	106	17	6	14	58	177	27	117	7	.315	.449	.269
Clint Barmes	133	387	43	91	21	0	8	50	136	35	66	3	.305	.351	.235
Ian Stewart	121	386	54	99	14	2	18	61	171	45	110	5	.338	.443	.256
Seth Smith	133	358	55	88	19	5	17	52	168	35	67	2	.314	.469	.246
Ryan Spilborghs	134	341	41	95	20	2	10	39	149	39	83	4	.360	.437	.279
Melvin Mora	113	316	39	90	12	5	7	45	133	31	53	2	.358	.421	.285
*Brad Hawpe	88	259	24	66	21	2	7	37	112	36	68	2	.343	.432	.255
Jonathan Herrera	76	222	34	63	6	2	1	21	76	25	36	2	.352	.342	.284
Chris Iannetta	61	188	20	37	6	1	9	27	72	30	48	1	.318	.383	.197
Jason Giambi	87	176	17	43	9	0	6	35	70	35	47	2	.378	.398	.244
Eric Young Jr.	51	172	26	42	5	1	0	8	49	17	32	17	.312	.285	.244

PITCHING	GP	GS	W–L	SV	SHO	R	ERA	IP	Ks	BB
Ubaldo Jimenez	33	33	19–8	0	2	73	2.88	221.2	214	92
Jason Hammel	30	30	10–9	0	0	97	4.81	177.2	141	47
Justin Chacin	28	21	9–11	0	0	64	3.28	137.1	138	61
Aaron Cook	23	23	6–8	0	0	77	5.08	127.2	62	52
Jorge De La Rosa	20	20	8–7	0	0	62	4.22	121.2	113	55
Jeff Francis	20	19	4–6	0	0	61	5.00	104.1	67	23
Matt Belisle	76	0	7–5	1	0	34	2.93	92.0	91	16
Esmil Rogers	28	8	2–3	0	0	59	6.13	72.0	66	26
*Octavio Dotel	68	0	3–4	22	0	32	4.08	64.0	75	32
Rafael Betancourt	72	0	5–1	1	0	25	3.61	62.1	89	8
Manny Corpas	56	0	3–5	10	0	33	4.62	62.1	47	22
Huston Street	44	0	4–4	20	0	21	3.61	47.1	45	11
Justin Beimel	71	0	1–2	0	0	18	3.40	45.0	21	15
Greg Smith	8	8	1–2	0	0	28	6.23	39.0	31	24
Franklin Morales	35	0	0–4	3	0	22	6.28	28.2	27	24

Florida Marlins

BATTING	G	AB	R	H	2B	3B	HR	RBI	TB	BB	SO	SB	OBP	SLG	BAVG
Dan Uggla	159	589	100	169	31	0	33	105	299	78	149	4	.369	.508	.287
Gaby Sanchez	151	572	72	156	37	3	19	85	256	57	101	5	.341	.448	.273
Hanley Ramirez	142	543	92	163	28	2	21	76	258	64	93	32	.378	.475	.300
Jorge Cantu	97	374	41	98	25	0	10	54	153	23	76	0	.310	.409	.262
Mike Stanton	100	359	45	93	21	1	22	59	182	34	123	5	.326	.507	.259
Chris Coghlan	91	358	60	96	20	3	5	28	137	33	84	10	.335	.383	.268
Ronny Paulino	91	316	31	82	18	0	4	37	112	25	51	1	.311	.354	.259
Cameron Maybin	82	291	46	68	7	3	8	28	105	24	92	9	.302	.361	.234
Wes Helms	127	254	25	56	12	4	4	39	88	26	76	0	.300	.346	.220
Logan Morrison	62	244	43	69	20	7	2	18	109	41	51	0	.390	.447	.283
Emilio Bonifacio	73	180	30	47	6	3	0	10	59	17	42	12	.320	.328	.261
Brad Davis	33	109	8	23	7	1	3	16	41	9	37	2	.270	.376	.211
*Chad Tracy	41	102	6	25	6	0	1	10	34	6	21	0	.297	.333	.245
John Baker	23	78	7	17	3	1	0	6	22	9	18	0	.307	.282	.218

PITCHING	GP	GS	W–L	SV	SHO	R	ERA	IP	Ks	BB
Anibal Sanchez	32	32	13–12	0	1	89	3.55	195.0	157	70
Josh Johnson	28	28	11–6	0	0	51	2.30	183.2	186	48
Chris Volstad	30	30	12–9	0	1	94	4.58	175.0	102	60
Ricky Nolasco	26	26	14–9	0	0	82	4.51	157.2	147	33
*Nate Robertson	19	18	6–8	0	0	70	5.47	100.1	61	40
Chad Hensley	68	0	3–4	7	0	20	2.16	75.0	77	29
Alex Sanabia	15	12	5–3	0	0	32	3.73	72.1	47	16
Burke Badenhop	53	0	2–5	1	0	33	3.99	67.2	47	21
Leo Nunez	68	0	4–3	30	0	27	3.46	65.0	71	21
Brian Sanches	61	0	2–2	0	0	20	2.26	63.2	54	27
Jose Veras	48	0	3–3	0	0	20	3.75	48.0	54	29
Jorge Sosa	22	2	2–3	0	0	22	4.66	36.2	19	18
Andrew Miller	9	7	1–5	0	0	34	8.54	32.2	28	26
Tim Wood	26	0	0–1	1	0	19	5.53	27.2	10	15
Adalberto Mendez	5	5	1–3	0	0	14	5.11	24.2	11	12
*Chris Leroux	17	0	0–0	0	0	15	7.00	18.0	18	11
Renyel Pinto	20	0	0–0	0	0	5	2.70	16.2	16	9

*Mid-season trade.

Houston Astros

BATTING	G	AB	R	H	2B	3B	HR	RBI	TB	BB	SO	SB	OBP	SLG	BAVG
Hunter Pence	156	614	93	173	29	3	25	91	283	41	105	18	.325	.461	.282
Carlos Lee	157	605	67	149	29	1	24	89	252	37	59	3	.291	.417	.246
Michael Bourn	141	535	84	142	25	6	2	38	185	59	109	52	.341	.346	.265
Jeff Keppinger	137	514	62	148	34	1	6	59	202	51	36	4	.351	.393	.288
Chris Johnson	94	341	40	105	22	2	11	52	164	15	91	3	.337	.481	.308
*Lance Berkman	85	298	39	73	16	1	13	49	130	60	70	7	.372	.436	.245
*Pedro Feliz	97	289	22	64	12	1	4	31	90	9	31	1	.243	.311	.221
Humberto Quintero	88	265	13	62	10	0	4	20	84	8	59	0	.262	.317	.234
Tommy Manzella	83	258	17	58	7	0	1	21	68	13	71	0	.267	.264	.225
*Angel Sanchez	65	250	30	70	9	4	0	25	87	11	45	0	.316	.348	.280
Geoff Blum	93	202	22	54	10	1	2	22	72	15	33	0	.321	.356	.267
Jason Castro	67	195	26	40	8	1	2	8	56	22	41	0	.286	.287	.205
Jason Michaels	106	186	23	47	14	1	8	26	87	12	29	0	.310	.468	.253
Brett Wallace	51	144	14	32	6	1	2	13	46	8	50	0	.296	.319	.222
Jason Bourgeois	69	123	16	27	4	1	0	3	33	13	16	12	.294	.268	.220
Matt Downs	40	97	8	21	7	0	1	7	31	9	20	0	.294	.320	.216

PITCHING	GP	GS	W–L	SV	SHO	R	ERA	IP	Ks	BB
Brett Myers	33	33	14–8	0	0	88	3.14	223.2	180	66
Wandy Rodriguez	32	32	11–12	0	0	95	3.60	195.0	178	68
Bud Norris	27	27	9–10	0	0	94	4.92	153.2	158	77
*Roy Oswalt	20	20	6–12	0	1	52	3.42	129.0	120	34
Nelson Figueroa	31	11	7–4	1	0	38	3.29	93.0	73	34
Felipe Paulino	19	14	1–9	0	0	63	5.11	91.2	83	46
Brandon Lyon	79	0	6–6	20	0	28	3.12	78.0	54	31
*J.A. Happ	13	13	5–4	0	1	33	3.75	72.0	61	35
Wilton Lopez	68	0	5–2	1	0	23	2.96	67.0	50	5
Brian Moehler	20	8	1–4	0	0	32	4.92	56.2	28	26
Matt Lindstrom	58	0	2–5	23	0	26	4.39	53.1	43	20
Jeff Fulchino	50	0	2–1	0	0	30	5.51	47.1	46	22
Tim Byrdak	64	0	2–2	0	0	15	3.49	38.2	29	20

Los Angeles Dodgers

BATTING	G	AB	R	H	2B	3B	HR	RBI	TB	BB	SO	SB	OBP	SLG	BAVG
Matt Kemp	162	602	82	150	25	6	28	89	271	53	170	19	.310	.450	.249
James Loney	161	588	67	157	41	2	10	88	232	52	95	10	.329	.395	.267
*Ryan Theriot	150	586	72	158	15	2	2	29	183	41	74	20	.321	.312	.270
Andre Ethier	139	517	71	151	33	1	23	82	255	59	102	2	.364	.493	.292
Casey Blake	146	509	56	126	28	1	17	64	207	48	138	0	.320	.407	.248
Rafael Furcal	97	383	66	115	23	7	8	43	176	40	60	22	.366	.460	.300
Jamey Carroll	133	351	48	102	15	1	0	23	119	51	64	12	.379	.339	.291
Russell Martin	97	331	45	82	13	0	5	26	110	48	61	6	.347	.332	.248
*Blake DeWitt	82	256	29	69	15	4	1	30	95	30	49	2	.352	.371	.270
Reed Johnson	102	202	24	53	11	2	2	15	74	5	50	2	.291	.366	.262
*Ryan Theriot	54	198	27	48	5	0	1	8	56	22	28	4	.323	.283	.242
*Manny Ramirez	66	196	32	61	15	0	8	40	100	32	38	1	.405	.510	.311
Rafael Belliard	82	162	24	35	10	1	2	19	53	18	35	2	.295	.327	.216
Garret Anderson	80	155	8	28	6	1	2	12	42	5	34	1	.204	.271	.181
*Scott Podsednik	39	149	17	39	6	1	1	7	50	11	26	5	.313	.336	.262
*Juan Castro	55	129	7	25	5	0	0	13	30	8	25	0	.237	.233	.194

PITCHING	GP	GS	W–L	SV	SHO	R	ERA	IP	Ks	BB
Clayton Kershaw	32	32	13–10	0	1	73	2.91	204.1	212	81
Hiroki Kuroda	31	31	11–13	0	0	87	3.39	196.1	159	48
Chad Billingsley	31	31	12–11	0	1	82	3.57	191.2	171	69
John Ely	18	18	4–10	0	0	63	5.49	100.0	76	40
Vincente Padilla	16	16	6–5	0	1	46	4.07	95.0	84	24
Carlos Monasterios	32	13	3–5	0	0	48	4.38	88.1	52	29
*Ted Lilly	12	12	7–4	0	1	30	3.52	76.2	77	15
Jonathan Broxton	64	0	5–6	22	0	30	4.04	62.1	73	28
Hong-Chih Kuo	56	0	3–2	12	0	8	1.20	60.0	73	18
Ronald Belisario	59	0	3–1	2	0	31	5.04	55.1	38	19
Ramon Troncoso	52	0	2–3	0	0	28	4.33	54.0	34	18
Jeff Weaver	43	0	5–1	0	0	30	6.09	44.1	26	20
George Sherrill	65	0	2–2	0	0	28	6.69	36.1	25	24
Charlie Haeger	9	6	0–4	0	0	32	8.40	30.0	30	26
Kenley Jansen	25	0	1–0	4	0	2	0.67	27.0	41	15

*Mid-season trade.

Milwaukee Brewers

BATTING	G	AB	R	H	2B	3B	HR	RBI	TB	BB	SO	SB	OBP	SLG	BAVG
Rickie Weeks	160	651	112	175	32	4	29	83	302	76	184	11	.366	.464	.269
Ryan Braun	157	619	101	188	45	1	25	103	310	56	105	14	.365	.501	.304
Casey McGehee	157	610	70	174	38	1	23	104	283	50	102	1	.337	.464	.285
Prince Fielder	161	578	94	151	25	0	32	83	272	114	138	1	.401	.471	.261
Corey Hart	145	558	91	158	34	4	31	102	293	45	140	7	.340	.525	.283
Alcides Escobar	145	506	57	119	14	10	4	41	165	36	70	10	.288	.326	.235
Carlos Gomez	97	291	38	72	11	3	5	24	104	17	72	18	.298	.357	.247
Jonathan Lucroy	75	277	24	70	9	0	4	26	91	18	44	4	.300	.329	.253
*Jim Edmonds	73	217	38	62	21	0	8	20	107	21	53	2	.350	.493	.286
George Kottaras	67	212	24	43	12	1	9	26	84	33	44	2	.305	.396	.203
Chris Counsell	102	204	16	51	8	0	2	21	65	21	29	1	.322	.319	.250
Lorenzo Cain	43	147	17	45	11	1	1	13	61	9	28	7	.348	.415	.306
Joe Inglett	102	142	15	36	8	5	1	8	57	15	34	1	.331	.401	.254
Gregg Zaun	28	102	11	27	7	0	2	14	40	11	12	0	.350	.392	.265

PITCHING	GP	GS	W-L	SV	SHO	R	ERA	IP	Ks	BB
Randy Wolf	34	34	13–12	0	1	107	4.17	215.2	142	87
Yovani Gallardo	31	31	14–7	0	2	89	3.84	185.0	200	75
Dave Bush	32	31	8–13	0	0	108	4.54	174.1	107	65
Chris Narveson	37	28	12–9	0	0	96	4.99	167.2	137	59
Manny Parra	42	16	3–10	0	0	76	5.02	122.0	129	63
Chris Capuano	24	9	4–4	0	0	29	3.95	66.0	54	21
Todd Coffey	69	0	2–4	0	0	40	4.76	62.1	56	23
Kameron Loe	53	0	3–5	0	0	23	2.78	58.1	46	15
John Axford	50	0	8–2	24	0	17	2.48	58.0	76	27
Carlos Villanueva	50	0	2–0	1	0	27	4.61	52.2	67	22
Trevor Hoffman	50	0	2–7	10	0	31	5.89	47.1	30	19
Doug Davis	8	8	1–4	0	0	36	7.51	38.1	34	21
Zach Braddock	46	0	1–2	0	0	11	2.94	33.2	41	19
*Jeff Suppan	15	0	0–2	0	0	29	7.84	31.0	18	12

New York Mets

BATTING	G	AB	R	H	2B	3B	HR	RBI	TB	BB	SO	SB	OBP	SLG	BAVG
David Wright	157	587	87	166	36	3	29	103	295	69	161	19	.354	.503	.283
Angel Pagan	151	579	80	168	31	7	11	69	246	44	97	37	.340	.425	.290
Jose Reyes	133	563	83	159	29	10	11	54	241	31	63	30	.321	.428	.282
Ike Davis	147	523	73	138	33	1	19	71	230	72	138	3	.351	.440	.264
*Jeff Francoeur	124	401	43	95	16	2	11	54	148	29	76	8	.293	.369	.237
Jason Bay	95	348	48	90	20	6	6	47	140	44	91	10	.347	.402	.259
*Rod Barajas	74	249	30	56	11	0	12	34	103	8	39	0	.263	.414	.225
Luis Castillo	86	247	28	58	4	2	0	17	66	39	25	8	.337	.267	.235
Carlos Beltran	64	220	21	56	11	3	7	27	94	30	39	3	.341	.427	.255
Ruben Tejada	78	216	28	46	12	0	1	15	61	22	38	2	.305	.282	.213
Josh Thole	73	202	17	56	7	1	3	17	74	24	25	1	.357	.366	.277
*Alex Cora	62	169	14	35	6	3	0	20	47	10	16	4	.265	.278	.207
Chris Carter	100	167	15	44	9	0	4	24	65	12	17	1	.317	.389	.263
Henry Blanco	50	130	10	28	5	0	2	8	39	11	26	1	.271	.300	.215
Jesus Feliciano	54	108	12	25	4	1	0	3	31	6	12	1	.276	.287	.231
Lucas Duda	29	84	11	17	6	0	4	13	35	6	22	0	.261	.417	.202

PITCHING	GP	GS	W-L	SV	SHO	R	ERA	IP	Ks	BB
Mike Pelfrey	34	33	15–9	1	0	88	3.66	204.0	113	68
Johan Santana	29	29	11–9	0	2	67	2.98	199.0	144	55
R.A. Dickey	27	26	11–9	0	1	62	2.84	174.1	104	42
Jonathon Niese	30	30	9–10	0	1	97	4.20	173.2	148	62
Hisanori Takahashi	53	12	10–6	8	0	51	3.61	122.0	114	43
Pedro Feliciano	92	0	3–6	0	0	24	3.30	62.2	56	30
Raul Valdes	38	1	3–3	1	0	33	4.91	58.2	56	27
Francisco Rodriguez	53	0	4–2	25	0	14	2.20	57.1	67	21
Elmer Dessens	53	0	4–2	0	0	14	2.30	47.0	16	16
Oliver Perez	17	7	0–5	0	0	37	6.80	46.1	37	42
Fernando Nieve	40	1	2–4	0	0	28	6.00	42.0	38	22
Manny Acosta	41	0	3–2	1	0	13	2.95	39.2	42	18
John Maine	9	9	1–3	0	0	29	6.13	39.2	39	25
Jenrry Mejia	33	3	0–4	0	0	21	4.62	39.0	22	20
Pat Misch	12	6	0–4	0	0	20	3.82	37.2	23	4
Bobby Parnell	41	0	0–1	0	0	13	2.83	35.0	33	8
Dillon Gee	5	5	2–2	0	0	10	2.18	33.0	17	15

*Mid-season trade.

Philadelphia Phillies

BATTING	G	AB	R	H	2B	3B	HR	RBI	TB	BB	SO	SB	OBP	SLG	BAVG
Shane Victorino	147	587	84	152	26	10	18	69	252	53	79	34	.327	.429	.259
Raul Ibanez	155	561	75	154	37	5	16	83	249	68	108	4	.349	.444	.275
Placido Polanco	132	554	76	165	27	2	6	52	214	32	47	5	.339	.386	.298
Jayson Werth	156	554	106	164	46	2	27	85	295	82	147	13	.388	.532	.296
Ryan Howard	143	550	87	152	23	5	31	108	278	59	157	1	.353	.505	.276
Chase Utley	115	425	75	117	20	2	16	65	189	63	63	13	.387	.445	.275
Carlos Ruiz	121	371	43	112	28	1	8	53	166	55	54	0	.400	.447	.302
Jimmy Rollins	88	350	48	85	16	3	8	41	131	40	32	17	.320	.374	.243
Wilson Valdez	111	333	37	86	16	3	4	35	120	21	43	7	.306	.360	.258
Ben Francisco	88	179	24	48	13	0	6	28	79	14	35	8	.327	.441	.268
Greg Dobbs	88	163	13	32	7	0	5	15	54	12	39	1	.251	.331	.196
*Juan Castro	54	126	7	25	5	0	0	13	30	7	23	0	.237	.238	.198
Ross Gload	94	128	16	36	8	0	6	22	62	8	15	1	.328	.484	.281
Brian Schneider	47	125	17	30	4	1	4	15	48	19	25	0	.345	.384	.240

PITCHING	GP	GS	W–L	SV	SHO	R	ERA	IP	Ks	BB
Roy Halladay	33	33	21–10	0	4	74	2.44	250.2	219	30
Cole Hamels	33	33	12–11	0	0	74	3.06	208.2	211	61
Kyle Kendrick	33	31	11–10	0	0	103	4.73	180.2	84	49
Joe Blanton	29	28	9–6	0	0	104	4.82	175.2	134	43
Jamie Moyer	19	19	9–9	0	1	64	4.84	111.2	63	20
*Roy Oswalt	13	12	7–1	0	1	18	1.74	82.2	73	21
Chad Durbin	64	0	4–1	0	0	29	3.80	68.2	63	27
Jose Contreras	67	0	6–4	4	0	22	3.34	56.2	57	16
Ryan Madson	55	0	6–2	5	0	16	2.55	53.0	64	13
David Herndon	47	0	1–3	0	0	27	4.30	52.1	29	17
Danys Baez	51	0	3–4	0	0	31	5.48	47.2	28	23
Brad Lidge	50	0	1–1	27	0	16	2.96	45.2	52	24
J.C. Romero	60	0	1–0	3	0	17	3.68	36.2	28	29
Antonio Bastardo	25	0	2–0	0	0	9	4.34	18.2	26	9
*J.A. Happ	3	3	1–0	0	0	4	1.76	15.1	9	12
Vance Worley	5	2	1–1	0	0	2	1.38	13.0	12	4

Pittsburgh Pirates

BATTING	G	AB	R	H	2B	3B	HR	RBI	TB	BB	SO	SB	OBP	SLG	BAVG
Garrett Jones	158	592	64	146	34	1	21	86	245	53	123	7	.306	.414	.247
Andrew McCutchen	154	570	94	163	35	5	16	56	256	70	89	33	.365	.449	.286
Ronny Cedeno	139	468	42	120	29	3	8	38	179	23	106	12	.293	.382	.256
Neil Walker	110	426	57	126	29	3	12	66	197	34	83	2	.349	.462	.296
Ryan Doumit	124	406	42	102	22	1	13	45	165	41	87	1	.331	.406	.251
Jose Tabata	102	405	61	121	21	4	4	35	162	28	57	19	.346	.400	.299
Lastings Milledge	113	379	38	105	21	3	4	34	144	28	62	5	.332	.380	.277
Pedro Alvarez	95	347	42	89	21	1	16	64	160	37	119	0	.326	.461	.256
Andy LaRoche	102	247	26	51	8	0	4	16	71	19	43	1	.268	.287	.206
Delwyn Young	110	191	22	45	11	1	7	28	79	13	52	1	.286	.414	.236
*Ryan Church	69	170	16	31	11	1	3	18	53	12	46	1	.240	.312	.182
*Akinori Iwamura	54	165	18	30	6	1	2	9	44	26	31	3	.292	.267	.182
*Bobby Crosby	61	156	9	35	8	0	1	11	46	16	33	0	.301	.295	.224
*Chris Snyder	40	124	12	21	1	0	5	16	37	16	33	0	.268	.298	.169

PITCHING	GP	GS	W–L	SV	SHO	R	ERA	IP	Ks	BB
Pat Maholm	32	32	9–15	0	1	119	5.10	185.1	102	62
Zach Duke	29	29	8–15	0	0	115	5.72	159.0	96	51
Jeff Karstens	26	19	3–10	0	0	72	4.92	122.2	72	27
Ross Ohlendorf	21	21	1–11	0	0	54	4.07	108.1	79	44
Evan Meek	70	0	5–4	4	0	25	2.14	80.0	70	31
Charlie Morton	17	17	2–12	0	0	79	7.57	79.2	59	26
Brian Burres	20	13	4–5	0	0	48	4.99	79.1	45	34
Joel Hanrahan	72	0	4–1	6	0	28	3.62	69.2	100	26
Daniel McCutchen	28	9	2–5	0	0	48	6.12	67.2	38	28
*James McDonald	11	11	4–5	0	0	25	3.52	64.0	61	24
*D.J. Carrasco	45	0	2–2	0	0	42	3.88	55.2	45	22
Brad Lincoln	11	9	1–4	0	0	42	6.66	52.2	25	15
*Octavio Dotel	41	0	2–2	21	0	21	4.28	40.0	48	17
*Javier Lopez	50	0	2–2	0	0	14	2.79	38.2	22	18

*Mid-season trade.

St. Louis Cardinals

BATTING	G	AB	R	H	2B	3B	HR	RBI	TB	BB	SO	SB	OBP	SLG	BAVG
Matt Holliday	158	596	95	186	45	1	28	103	317	69	93	9	.390	.532	.312
Albert Pujols	159	587	115	183	39	1	42	118	350	103	76	14	.414	.596	.312
Skip Schumaker	137	476	66	126	18	1	5	42	161	43	64	5	.328	.338	.265
Yadier Molina	136	465	34	122	19	0	6	62	159	42	51	8	.329	.342	.262
Colby Rasmus	144	464	85	128	28	3	23	66	231	63	148	12	.361	.498	.276
Brendan Ryan	139	439	50	98	19	3	2	36	129	33	60	11	.279	.294	.223
*Felipe Lopez	109	376	50	87	18	1	7	36	128	43	77	8	.310	.340	.231
Jon Jay	105	287	47	86	19	2	4	27	121	24	50	2	.359	.422	.300
David Freese	70	240	28	71	12	1	4	36	97	21	59	1	.361	.404	.296
*Randy Winn	87	144	16	36	8	1	3	17	55	13	22	5	.311	.382	.250
Aaron Miles	79	139	14	39	5	0	0	9	44	6	14	0	.311	.317	.281
Nick Stavinoha	79	121	11	31	4	0	2	9	41	4	28	0	.286	.339	.256
*Pedro Feliz	40	120	14	25	0	1	1	9	30	4	10	0	.232	.250	.208
Allen Craig	44	114	12	28	7	0	4	18	47	9	26	0	.298	.412	.246
Tyler Greene	44	104	14	23	3	1	2	10	34	13	24	2	.328	.327	.221

PITCHING	GP	GS	W–L	SV	SHO	R	ERA	IP	Ks	BB
Chris Carpenter	35	35	16–9	0	0	99	3.22	235.0	179	63
Adam Wainwright	33	33	20–11	0	2	68	2.42	230.1	213	56
Jaime Garcia	28	28	13–8	0	1	64	2.70	163.1	132	64
Kyle Lohse	18	18	4–8	0	0	75	6.55	92.0	54	35
Blake Hawksworth	45	8	4–8	0	0	56	4.98	90.1	61	35
Kyle McClellan	68	0	1–4	2	0	20	2.27	75.1	60	23
*Jake Westbrook	12	12	4–4	0	0	31	3.48	75.0	55	24
*Jeff Suppan	15	13	3–6	0	0	32	3.84	70.1	33	25
Mitchell Boggs	61	0	2–3	0	0	29	3.61	67.1	52	27
Ryan Franklin	59	0	6–2	27	0	25	3.46	65.0	42	10
Brad Penny	9	9	3–4	0	0	25	3.23	55.2	35	9
Jason Motte	56	0	4–2	2	0	13	2.24	52.1	54	18
Dennys Reyes	59	0	3–1	1	0	15	3.55	38.0	25	21
Trever Miller	57	0	0–1	0	0	17	4.00	36.0	22	16
Fernando Salas	27	0	0–0	0	0	13	3.52	30.2	29	15

San Diego Padres

BATTING	G	AB	R	H	2B	3B	HR	RBI	TB	BB	SO	SB	OBP	SLG	BAVG
Chase Headley	161	610	77	161	29	3	11	58	229	56	139	17	.327	.375	.264
Adrian Gonzalez	160	591	87	176	33	0	31	101	302	93	114	0	.393	.511	.298
*Ryan Ludwick	136	490	63	123	27	2	17	69	205	48	121	0	.325	.418	.251
David Eckstein	116	442	49	118	23	0	1	29	144	27	35	8	.321	.326	.267
Jerry Hairston Jr.	119	430	53	105	13	2	10	50	152	31	54	9	.299	.353	.244
Will Venable	131	392	60	96	11	7	13	51	160	45	128	29	.324	.408	.245
Yorvit Torrealba	95	325	31	88	14	0	7	37	123	33	67	7	.343	.378	.271
Scott Hairston	104	295	34	62	10	0	10	36	102	31	69	6	.295	.346	.210
Tony Gwynn	117	289	30	59	9	3	3	20	83	41	50	17	.304	.287	.204
Chris Denorfia	99	284	41	77	15	2	9	36	123	27	51	8	.335	.433	.271
Nick Hundley	85	273	33	68	18	2	8	43	114	25	66	0	.308	.418	.249
*Miguel Tejada	59	235	31	63	10	0	8	32	97	15	28	2	.317	.413	.268
Everth Cabrera	76	212	22	44	6	3	1	22	59	19	54	10	.279	.278	.208
Aaron Cunningham	53	132	17	38	12	1	1	15	55	7	28	1	.331	.417	.288
Oscar Salazar	85	131	19	31	4	0	3	19	44	16	23	1	.318	.336	.237
Kyle Blanks	33	102	14	16	6	1	3	15	33	15	46	1	.283	.324	.157
Matt Stairs	78	99	14	23	6	0	6	16	47	11	32	2	.306	.475	.232

PITCHING	GP	GS	W–L	SV	SHO	R	ERA	IP	Ks	BB
Clayton Richard	33	33	14–9	0	1	89	3.75	201.2	153	78
Jon Garland	33	33	14–12	0	0	86	3.47	200.0	136	87
Mat Latos	31	31	14–10	0	1	63	2.92	184.2	189	50
Wade LeBlanc	26	25	8–12	0	0	69	4.25	146.0	110	51
Kevin Correia	28	26	10–10	0	0	89	5.40	145.0	115	64
Tim Stauffer	32	7	6–5	0	0	18	1.85	82.2	61	24
Luke Gregerson	80	0	4–7	2	0	30	3.22	78.1	89	18
Heath Bell	67	0	6–1	47	0	17	1.93	70.0	86	28
Edward Mujica	59	0	2–1	0	0	29	3.62	69.2	72	6
Mike Adams	70	0	4–1	0	0	14	1.76	66.2	73	23
Ryan Webb	54	0	3–1	0	0	21	2.90	59.0	44	19
Joe Thatcher	65	0	1–0	0	0	5	1.29	35.0	45	7
Ernesto Frieri	33	0	1–1	0	0	7	1.71	31.2	41	17

*Mid-season trade.

San Francisco Giants

BATTING	G	AB	R	H	2B	3B	HR	RBI	TB	BB	SO	SB	OBP	SLG	BAVG
Aubrey Huff	157	569	100	165	35	5	26	86	288	83	91	7	.385	.506	.290
Pablo Sandoval	152	563	61	151	34	3	13	63	230	47	81	3	.323	.409	.268
*Cody Ross	153	525	71	141	28	3	14	65	217	37	121	9	.322	.413	.269
Juan Uribe	148	521	64	129	24	2	24	85	229	45	92	1	.310	.440	.248
Andres Torres	139	507	84	136	43	8	16	63	243	56	128	26	.343	.479	.268
Freddy Sanchez	111	431	55	126	22	1	7	47	171	32	68	3	.342	.397	.292
Buster Posey	108	406	58	124	23	2	18	67	205	30	55	0	.357	.505	.305
Aaron Rowand	105	331	42	76	12	2	11	34	125	16	74	5	.281	.378	.230
*Pat Burrell	96	289	41	77	16	0	18	51	147	47	77	0	.364	.509	.266
Edgar Renteria	72	243	26	67	11	2	3	22	91	21	43	3	.332	.374	.276
Mike Fontenot	103	240	24	68	13	3	1	25	90	15	41	1	.331	.375	.283
Nate Schierholtz	137	227	34	55	13	3	3	17	83	20	38	4	.311	.366	.242
*Bengie Molina	61	202	17	52	6	0	3	17	67	14	19	0	.312	.332	.257
Travis Ishikawa	116	158	18	42	11	0	3	22	62	13	29	0	.320	.392	.266
*Jose Guillen	42	128	9	34	5	0	3	15	48	5	29	0	.317	.375	.266
Eli Whiteside	56	126	19	30	6	1	4	10	50	8	35	1	.299	.397	.238
Mark DeRosa	26	93	9	18	3	0	1	10	24	9	16	0	.279	.258	.194

PITCHING	GP	GS	W–L	SV	SHO	R	ERA	IP	Ks	BB
Matt Cain	33	33	13–11	0	2	84	3.14	223.1	177	61
Tim Lincecum	33	33	16–10	0	1	84	3.43	212.1	231	76
Barry Zito	34	33	9–14	0	0	97	4.15	199.1	150	84
Jonathan Sanchez	34	33	13–9	0	0	74	3.07	193.1	205	96
Madison Bumgarner	18	18	7–6	0	0	40	3.00	111.0	86	26
Brian Wilson	70	0	3–3	48	0	16	1.81	74.2	93	26
Sergio Romo	68	0	5–3	0	0	16	2.18	62.0	70	14
Todd Wellemeyer	13	11	3–5	0	0	37	5.68	58.2	41	35
*Javier Lopez	77	0	4–2	0	0	17	2.34	57.2	38	20
Santiago Casilla	52	0	7–2	2	0	14	1.95	55.1	56	26
Guillermo Mota	56	0	1–3	1	0	29	4.33	54.0	38	22
Jeremy Affeldt	53	0	4–3	4	0	25	4.14	50.0	44	24
Denny Bautista	31	0	2–0	0	0	14	3.74	33.2	44	27
Dan Runzler	41	0	3–0	0	0	12	3.03	32.2	37	20

Washington Nationals

BATTING	G	AB	R	H	2B	3B	HR	RBI	TB	BB	SO	SB	OBP	SLG	BAVG
Adam Dunn	158	558	85	145	36	2	38	103	299	77	199	0	.356	.536	.260
Ian Desmond	154	525	59	141	27	4	10	65	206	28	109	17	.308	.392	.269
Ryan Zimmerman	142	525	85	161	32	0	25	85	268	69	98	4	.388	.510	.307
Nyjer Morgan	136	509	60	129	17	7	0	24	160	40	88	34	.319	.314	.253
Roger Bernadina	134	414	52	102	18	3	11	47	159	35	93	16	.307	.384	.246
Ivan Rodriguez	111	398	32	106	18	1	4	49	138	16	66	2	.294	.347	.266
Josh Willingham	114	370	54	99	19	2	16	56	170	67	85	8	.389	.459	.268
Adam Kennedy	135	342	43	85	16	1	3	31	112	37	44	14	.327	.327	.249
*Cristian Guzman	89	319	44	90	11	4	2	25	115	17	53	4	.327	.361	.282
Michael Morse	98	266	36	77	12	2	15	41	138	22	64	0	.352	.519	.289
Willie Harris	132	224	25	41	6	2	10	32	81	33	60	5	.291	.362	.183
Alberto Gonzalez	114	186	19	46	8	1	0	5	56	7	30	0	.277	.301	.247
Wil Nieves	59	158	10	32	8	0	3	16	49	8	29	0	.244	.310	.203
Justin Maxwell	67	104	16	15	6	0	3	12	30	25	43	5	.305	.288	.144
Danny Espinosa	28	103	16	22	4	1	6	15	46	9	30	0	.277	.447	.214

PITCHING	GP	GS	W–L	SV	SHO	R	ERA	IP	Ks	BB
Livan Hernandez	33	33	10–12	0	1	93	3.66	211.2	114	64
John Lannan	25	25	8–8	0	0	82	4.65	143.1	71	49
Craig Stammen	35	19	4–4	0	0	78	5.13	128.0	85	41
Tyler Clippard	78	0	11–8	1	0	33	3.07	91.0	112	41
Luis Atilano	16	16	6–7	0	0	56	5.15	85.2	40	32
Miguel Batista	58	1	1–2	2	0	36	3.70	82.2	55	39
Scott Olsen	17	15	4–8	0	0	54	5.56	81.0	53	27
Stephen Strasburg	12	12	5–3	0	0	25	2.91	68.0	92	17
Sean Burnett	73	0	1–7	3	0	17	2.14	63.0	62	20
Jason Marquis	13	13	2–9	0	0	47	6.60	58.2	31	24
Drew Storen	54	0	4–4	5	0	24	3.58	55.1	52	22
Joel Peralta	39	0	1–0	0	0	12	2.02	49.0	49	9
J.D. Martin	9	9	1–5	0	0	30	4.13	48.0	31	11
*Matt Capps	47	0	3–3	26	0	20	2.74	46.0	38	9
Doug Slaten	49	0	4–1	0	0	18	3.10	40.2	36	19

*Mid-season trade.

American League Team-by-Team Statistical Leaders

Baltimore Orioles

BATTING	G	AB	R	H	2B	3B	HR	RBI	TB	BB	SO	SB	OBP	SLG	BAVG
Nick Markakis	160	629	79	187	45	3	12	60	274	73	93	7	.370	.436	.297
Adam Jones	149	581	76	165	25	5	19	69	257	23	119	7	.325	.442	.284
Ty Wigginton	154	581	63	144	29	1	22	76	241	50	116	0	.312	.415	.248
Cesar Izturis	150	473	42	109	13	1	1	28	127	25	53	11	.277	.268	.230
Luke Scott	131	447	70	127	29	1	27	72	239	59	98	2	.368	.535	.284
Matt Wieters	130	446	37	111	22	1	11	55	168	47	94	0	.319	.377	.249
*Miguel Tejada	97	401	40	108	16	0	7	39	145	15	39	0	.308	.362	.269
Corey Patterson	90	308	43	83	16	1	8	32	125	20	75	21	.315	.406	.269
Felix Pie	82	288	39	79	15	5	5	31	119	13	52	5	.305	.413	.274
Julio Lugo	93	241	26	60	4	2	0	20	68	15	50	5	.298	.282	.249
Brian Roberts	59	230	28	64	14	0	4	15	90	26	40	12	.354	.391	.278
Josh Bell	53	159	15	34	5	0	3	12	48	2	53	0	.224	.302	.214
Garrett Atkins	44	140	5	30	7	0	1	9	40	12	30	0	.276	.286	.214
Nolan Reimold	39	116	9	24	5	0	3	14	38	12	26	0	.282	.328	.207
Craig Tatum	43	114	11	32	4	0	0	9	36	12	21	1	.349	.316	.281
*Jake Fox	38	100	10	22	5	1	5	10	44	8	23	0	.257	.440	.220

PITCHING	GP	GS	W–L	SV	SHO	R	ERA	IP	Ks	BB
Jeremy Guthrie	32	32	11–14	0	0	93	3.83	209.1	119	50
Kevin Millwood	31	31	4–16	0	0	116	5.10	190.2	132	65
Brian Matusz	32	32	10–12	0	0	88	4.30	175.2	143	63
Brad Bergesen	30	28	8–12	0	0	104	4.98	170.0	81	51
Jake Arrieta	18	18	6–6	0	0	57	4.66	100.1	52	48
Daniel Hernandez	41	8	8–8	2	0	40	4.31	79.1	72	42
Matt Albers	62	0	5–3	0	0	41	4.52	75.2	49	34
Mark Hendrickson	52	1	1–6	0	0	47	5.26	75.1	55	20
Jason Berken	41	0	3–3	0	0	24	3.03	62.1	45	19
Chris Tillman	11	11	2–5	0	0	37	5.87	53.2	31	31
Alfredo Simon	49	0	4–2	17	0	30	4.93	49.1	37	22
Koji Uehara	43	0	1–2	13	0	15	2.86	44.0	55	5
*Will Ohman	51	0	0–0	0	0	12	3.30	30.0	29	18
Jim Johnson	26	0	1–1	1	0	11	3.42	26.1	22	5
Mike Gonzalez	29	0	1–3	1	0	11	4.01	24.2	31	14

Boston Red Sox

BATTING	G	AB	R	H	2B	3B	HR	RBI	TB	BB	SO	SB	OBP	SLG	BAVG
Marco Scutaro	150	632	92	174	38	0	11	56	245	53	71	5	.333	.388	.275
Adrian Beltre	154	589	84	189	49	2	28	102	326	40	82	2	.365	.553	.321
David Ortiz	145	518	86	140	36	1	32	102	274	82	145	0	.370	.529	.270
Victor Martinez	127	493	64	149	32	1	20	79	243	40	52	1	.351	.493	.302
J.D. Drew	139	478	69	122	24	2	22	68	216	60	105	3	.341	.452	.255
Kevin Youkilis	102	362	77	111	26	5	19	62	204	58	67	4	.411	.564	.307
Bill Hall	119	344	44	85	16	1	18	46	157	34	104	9	.316	.456	.247
Darnell McDonald	117	319	40	86	18	3	9	34	137	30	85	9	.336	.429	.270
Dustin Pedroia	75	302	53	87	24	1	12	41	149	37	38	9	.367	.493	.288
Mike Lowell	73	218	23	52	13	0	5	26	80	23	34	0	.307	.367	.239
Jed Lowrie	55	171	31	49	14	0	9	24	90	25	25	1	.381	.526	.287
Ryan Kalish	53	163	26	41	11	1	4	24	66	12	38	10	.305	.405	.252
Mike Cameron	48	162	24	42	11	0	4	15	65	14	44	0	.328	.401	.259
Daniel Nava	60	161	23	39	14	1	1	26	58	18	46	1	.351	.360	.242
*Jeremy Hermida	52	158	14	32	8	0	5	27	55	12	45	1	.257	.348	.203
Jason Varitek	39	112	18	26	6	0	7	16	53	10	35	0	.293	.473	.232
*Eric Patterson	45	84	13	19	3	3	2	7	34	7	31	5	.293	.405	.226
Jacoby Ellsbury	18	78	10	15	4	0	0	5	19	4	9	7	.241	.244	.192

PITCHING	GP	GS	W–L	SV	SHO	R	ERA	IP	Ks	BB
John Lackey	33	33	14–11	0	0	114	4.40	215.0	156	72
Jon Lester	32	32	19–9	0	0	81	3.25	208.0	225	83
Clay Buchholz	28	28	17–7	0	1	55	2.33	173.2	120	67
Daisuke Matsuzaka	25	25	9–6	0	0	84	4.69	153.2	133	74
Tim Wakefield	32	19	4–10	0	0	92	5.34	140.0	84	36
Josh Beckett	21	21	6–6	0	0	89	5.78	127.2	116	45
Daniel Bard	73	0	1–2	3	0	18	1.93	74.2	76	30
Jonathan Papelbon	65	0	5–7	37	0	34	3.90	67.0	76	28
Scott Atchison	43	1	2–3	0	0	37	4.50	60.0	41	19
Hideki Okajima	56	0	4–4	0	0	24	4.50	46.0	33	20
*Manny Delcarmen	48	0	3–2	0	0	24	4.70	44.0	32	28
*Ramon Ramirez	44	0	0–3	2	0	21	4.46	42.1	31	16
Felix Doubront	12	3	2–2	2	0	16	4.32	25.0	23	10

*Mid-season trade.

Chicago White Sox

BATTING	G	AB	R	H	2B	3B	HR	RBI	TB	BB	SO	SB	OBP	SLG	BAVG
Juan Pierre	160	651	96	179	18	3	1	47	206	45	47	68	.341	.316	.275
Alexei Ramirez	156	585	83	165	29	2	18	70	252	27	82	13	.313	.431	.282
Alex Rios	147	567	89	161	29	3	21	88	259	38	93	34	.334	.457	.284
Paul Konerko	149	548	89	171	30	1	39	111	320	72	110	0	.393	.584	.312
A.J. Pierzynski	128	474	43	128	29	0	9	56	184	15	39	3	.300	.388	.270
Carlos Quentin	131	453	73	110	25	2	26	87	217	50	83	2	.342	.479	.243
Gordon Beckham	131	444	58	112	25	2	9	49	168	37	92	4	.317	.378	.252
Omar Vizquel	108	344	36	95	11	1	2	30	114	34	45	11	.341	.331	.276
Mark Kotsay	107	327	30	78	17	2	8	31	123	32	36	1	.306	.376	.239
Andruw Jones	107	278	41	64	12	1	19	48	135	45	73	9	.341	.486	.230
Mark Teahen	77	233	31	60	13	2	4	25	89	25	61	3	.327	.382	.258
Raul Castro	37	115	18	32	2	0	8	21	58	9	26	1	.328	.504	.278
Dayan Viciedo	38	104	17	32	7	0	5	13	54	2	25	1	.321	.519	.308
Brent Lillibridge	64	98	19	22	5	2	2	16	37	3	36	5	.248	.378	.224

PITCHING	GP	GS	W–L	SV	SHO	R	ERA	IP	Ks	BB
John Danks	32	32	15–11	0	1	93	3.72	213.0	162	70
Mark Buehrle	33	33	13–13	0	0	105	4.28	210.1	99	49
Gavin Floyd	31	31	10–13	0	0	92	4.08	187.1	151	58
Freddy Garcia	28	28	12–6	0	0	85	4.64	157.0	89	45
Jake Peavy	17	17	7–6	0	1	55	4.63	107.0	93	34
Tony Pena	52	3	5–3	0	0	63	5.10	100.2	56	45
*Edwin Jackson	11	11	4–2	0	0	31	3.24	75.0	77	18
Matt Thornton	61	0	5–4	8	0	18	2.67	60.2	81	20
Scott Linebrink	52	0	3–2	0	0	31	4.40	57.1	52	17
J.J. Putz	60	0	7–5	3	0	18	2.83	54.0	65	15
Bobby Jenks	55	0	1–3	27	0	28	4.44	52.2	61	18
Sergio Santos	56	0	2–2	1	0	18	2.96	51.2	56	26
Randy Williams	27	0	0–1	0	0	17	5.40	25.0	22	21
Lucas Harrell	8	3	1–0	0	0	18	4.88	24.0	15	17
Chris Sale	21	0	2–1	4	0	5	1.93	23.1	32	10

Cleveland Indians

BATTING	G	AB	R	H	2B	3B	HR	RBI	TB	BB	SO	SB	OBP	SLG	BAVG
Shin-Soo Choo	144	550	81	165	31	2	22	90	266	83	118	22	.401	.484	.300
Trevor Crowe	122	442	48	111	24	3	2	36	.147	29	73	20	.302	.333	.251
Travis Hafner	118	396	46	110	29	0	13	50	178	51	94	2	.374	.449	.278
Asdrubal Cabrera	97	381	39	105	16	1	3	29	132	25	60	6	.326	.346	.276
Matt LaPorta	110	376	41	83	15	1	12	41	136	46	82	0	.306	.362	.221
*Jhonny Peralta	91	334	37	82	23	2	7	43	.130	32	69	1	.308	.389	.246
*Austin Kearns	84	301	42	82	18	1	8	42	126	34	78	4	.354	.419	.272
Michael Brantley	72	297	38	73	9	3	3	22	97	22	38	10	.296	.327	.246
Jason Donald	88	296	39	75	19	3	4	24	112	22	70	5	.312	.378	.253
*Jayson Nix	78	282	29	66	14	0	13	29	119	13	75	1	.283	.422	.234
Luis Valbuena	91	275	22	53	12	0	2	24	71	28	61	1	.273	.258	.193
Lou Marson	87	262	29	51	15	0	3	22	75	26	55	4	.274	.286	.195
Shelley Duncan	85	229	29	53	10	0	11	36	96	26	76	1	.317	.419	.231
*Russell Branyan	52	171	24	45	9	0	10	24	84	16	49	0	.328	.491	.263
Andy Marte	80	170	18	39	7	2	5	19	65	17	35	0	.298	.382	.229
Carlos Santana	46	150	23	39	13	0	6	22	70	37	29	3	.401	.467	.260
Grady Sizemore	33	128	15	27	6	2	0	13	37	9	35	4	.271	.289	.211

PITCHING	GP	GS	W–L	SV	SHO	R	ERA	IP	Ks	BB
Fausto Carmona	33	33	13–14	0	1	98	3.77	210.1	124	72
Justin Masterson	34	29	6–13	0	1	107	4.70	180.0	140	73
Mitch Talbot	28	28	10–13	0	0	88	4.41	159.1	88	69
*Jake Westbrook	21	21	6–7	0	0	68	4.65	127.2	73	44
Daniel Huff	15	15	2–11	0	0	61	6.21	79.2	37	34
Josh Tomlin	12	12	6–4	0	0	38	4.56	73.0	43	19
Chris Perez	63	0	2–2	23	0	15	1.71	63.0	61	28
Tony Sipp	70	0	2–2	1	0	30	4.14	63.0	69	39
Rafael Perez	70	0	6–1	0	0	23	3.25	61.0	36	25
Jeanmar Gomez	11	11	4–5	0	0	36	4.68	57.2	34	22
Aaron Laffey	29	5	2–3	0	0	30	4.53	55.2	28	28
Hector Ambriz	34	0	0–2	0	0	36	5.59	48.1	37	17
Carlos Carrasco	7	7	2–2	0	0	20	3.83	44.2	38	14
Frank Herrmann	40	0	0–1	1	0	22	4.03	44.2	24	9

*Mid-season trade.

Detroit Tigers

BATTING	G	AB	R	H	2B	3B	HR	RBI	TB	BB	SO	SB	OBP	SLG	BAVG
Austin Jackson	151	618	103	181	34	10	4	41	247	47	170	27	.345	.400	.293
Miguel Cabrera	150	548	111	180	45	1	38	126	341	89	95	3	.420	.622	.328
Johnny Damon	145	539	81	146	36	5	8	51	216	69	90	11	.355	.401	.271
Brandon Inge	144	514	47	127	28	5	13	70	204	54	134	4	.321	.397	.247
Brennan Boesch	133	464	49	119	26	3	14	67	193	40	99	7	.320	.416	.256
Ryan Raburn	113	371	54	104	25	1	15	62	176	27	92	2	.340	.474	.280
Magglio Ordonez	84	323	56	98	17	1	12	59	153	40	38	1	.378	.474	.303
Ramon Santiago	112	320	38	84	9	1	3	22	104	30	56	2	.337	.325	.263
Alex Avila	104	294	28	67	12	0	7	31	100	36	71	2	.316	.340	.228
Gerald Laird	89	270	22	56	11	0	5	25	82	18	57	3	.263	.304	.207
Carlos Guillen	68	253	26	69	17	1	6	34	106	21	41	1	.327	.419	.273
Don Kelly	119	238	30	58	4	0	9	27	89	8	42	3	.272	.374	.244
*Jhonny Peralta	57	217	23	55	7	0	8	38	86	21	34	0	.314	.396	.253
Will Rhymes	54	191	30	58	12	3	1	19	79	14	16	0	.350	.414	.304
Scott Sizemore	48	143	19	32	7	0	3	14	48	15	40	0	.296	.336	.224
Danny Worth	39	106	10	27	5	0	2	8	38	6	13	1	.295	.358	.255

PITCHING	GP	GS	W-L	SV	SHO	R	ERA	IP	Ks	BB
Justin Verlander	33	33	18-9	0	0	89	3.37	224.1	219	71
Max Scherzer	31	31	12-11	0	0	84	3.50	195.2	184	70
Jeremy Bonderman	30	29	8-10	0	0	113	5.53	171.0	112	60
Ryan Porcello	27	27	10-12	0	0	96	4.92	162.2	84	38
Armando Galarraga	25	24	4-9	0	1	75	4.49	144.1	74	51
Brad Thomas	49	2	6-2	0	0	31	3.89	69.1	30	29
Eddie Bonine	47	1	4-1	0	0	37	4.63	68.0	26	22
Phil Coke	74	1	7-5	2	0	29	3.76	64.2	53	26
Jose Valverde	60	0	2-4	26	0	24	3.00	63.0	63	32
Ryan Perry	60	0	3-5	2	0	26	3.59	62.2	45	23
*Dontrelle Willis	9	8	1-2	0	0	24	4.98	43.1	33	29
Joel Zumaya	31	0	2-1	1	0	13	2.58	38.1	34	11
Robbie Weinhardt	28	0	2-2	0	0	23	6.14	29.1	21	8
Enrique Gonzalez	18	0	0-1	0	0	11	3.81	26.0	13	17

Kansas City Royals

BATTING	G	AB	R	H	2B	3B	HR	RBI	TB	BB	SO	SB	OBP	SLG	BAVG
Billy Butler	158	595	77	189	45	0	15	78	279	69	78	0	.388	.469	.318
Yuniesky Betancourt	151	556	60	144	29	2	16	78	225	23	64	2	.288	.405	.259
Jason Kendall	118	434	39	111	18	0	0	37	129	37	45	12	.318	.297	.256
Mike Aviles	110	424	63	129	16	3	8	32	175	20	49	14	.335	.413	.304
*Jose Guillen	106	396	46	101	17	2	16	62	170	27	84	1	.314	.429	.255
*Scott Podsednik	95	390	46	121	8	6	5	44	156	29	57	30	.353	.400	.310
Mitch Maier	117	373	41	98	15	6	5	39	140	41	68	3	.333	.375	.263
David DeJesus	91	352	46	112	23	3	5	37	156	34	47	3	.384	.443	.318
*Alberto Callaspo	88	349	40	96	19	2	8	43	143	19	29	3	.308	.410	.275
Wilson Betemit	84	276	36	82	20	0	13	43	141	36	74	0	.378	.511	.297
Alex Gordon	74	242	34	52	10	0	8	20	86	34	62	1	.315	.355	.215
Chris Getz	72	224	23	53	9	0	0	18	62	19	28	15	.302	.277	.237
Kila Ka'aihue	52	180	22	39	6	1	8	25	71	24	39	0	.307	.394	.217
*Gregor Blanco	49	179	22	49	8	3	1	16	66	21	35	10	.348	.369	.274
*Willie Bloomquist	72	170	31	45	10	1	3	17	66	8	25	8	.296	.388	.265
Brayan Pena	60	158	11	40	10	0	1	19	53	12	27	2	.306	.335	.253
*Rick Ankiel	27	92	14	24	7	0	4	15	43	7	29	1	.317	.467	.261

PITCHING	GP	GS	W-L	SV	SHO	R	ERA	IP	Ks	BB
Zack Greinke	33	33	10-14	0	0	114	4.17	220.0	181	55
Kyle Davies	32	32	8-12	0	0	114	5.34	183.2	126	80
Bruce Chen	33	23	12-7	1	1	68	4.17	140.1	98	57
Brian Bannister	24	23	7-12	0	0	92	6.34	127.2	77	50
Luke Hochevar	18	17	6-6	0	0	61	4.81	103.0	76	37
*Sean O'Sullivan	14	13	3-6	0	0	50	6.11	70.2	37	27
Joakim Soria	66	0	1-2	43	0	13	1.78	65.2	71	16
Gil Meche	20	9	0-5	0	0	42	5.69	61.2	41	38
Robinson Tejeda	54	0	3-5	0	0	28	3.54	61.0	56	26
Dusty Hughes	57	0	1-3	0	0	28	3.83	56.1	34	24
Brandon Wood	51	0	1-3	0	0	29	5.07	49.2	31	22
*Kyle Farnsworth	37	0	3-0	0	0	13	2.42	44.2	36	12
Bryan Bullington	13	5	1-4	0	0	29	6.12	42.2	29	17
*Kanekoa Texeira	27	0	1-0	0	0	24	4.64	42.2	19	15

*Mid-season trade.

Los Angeles Angels of Anaheim

BATTING	G	AB	R	H	2B	3B	HR	RBI	TB	BB	SO	SB	OBP	SLG	BAVG
Howie Kendrick	158	616	67	172	41	4	10	75	251	28	94	14	.313	.407	.279
Bobby Abreu	154	573	88	146	41	1	20	78	249	87	132	24	.352	.435	.255
Torii Hunter	152	573	76	161	36	0	23	90	266	61	106	9	.354	.464	.281
Erick Aybar	138	534	69	135	18	4	5	29	176	35	81	22	.306	.330	.253
Hideki Matsui	145	482	55	132	24	1	21	84	221	67	98	0	.361	.459	.274
Mike Napoli	140	453	60	108	24	1	26	68	212	42	137	4	.316	.468	.238
Juan Rivera	124	416	53	105	20	0	15	52	170	33	58	2	.312	.409	.252
Brandon Wood	81	226	20	33	2	0	4	14	47	6	71	1	.174	.208	.146
*Alberto Callaspo	58	213	21	53	8	0	2	13	67	12	13	2	.291	.315	.249
Macier Izturis	61	212	27	53	13	1	3	27	77	21	27	7	.321	.363	.250
Jeff Mathis	68	205	19	40	6	1	3	18	57	6	59	3	.219	.278	.195
Kelvin Morales	51	193	29	56	5	0	11	39	94	12	31	0	.346	.487	.290
Peter Bourjos	51	181	19	37	6	4	6	15	69	6	40	10	.237	.381	.204
Kevin Frandsen	54	160	24	40	11	0	0	14	51	9	10	2	.294	.319	.250
Reggie Willits	97	159	23	41	7	0	0	8	48	19	26	2	.341	.302	.258
Bobby Wilson	40	96	12	22	6	0	4	15	40	8	23	0	.288	.417	.229

PITCHING	GP	GS	W–L	SV	SHO	R	ERA	IP	Ks	BB
Jered Weaver	34	34	13–12	0	0	83	3.01	224.1	233	54
Ervin Santana	33	33	17–10	0	1	104	3.92	222.2	169	73
Joel Pineiro	23	23	10–7	0	1	66	3.84	152.1	92	34
Scott Kazmir	28	28	9–15	0	0	103	5.94	150.0	93	79
*Joe Saunders	20	20	6–10	0	1	70	4.62	120.2	64	45
*Dan Haren	14	14	5–4	0	0	31	2.87	94.0	75	25
Fernando Rodney	72	0	4–3	14	0	33	4.24	68.0	53	35
Trevor Bell	25	7	2–5	0	0	35	4.72	61.0	45	21
Kyle Jepsen	68	0	2–4	0	0	26	3.97	59.0	61	29
Francisco Rodriguez	43	0	1–3	0	0	23	4.37	47.1	36	26
Scot Shields	43	1	0–3	0	0	31	5.28	46.0	39	34
*Brian Fuentes	39	0	4–1	23	0	17	3.52	38.1	39	18
Matt Palmer	14	1	1–2	0	0	20	4.54	33.2	17	20

Minnesota Twins

BATTING	G	AB	R	H	2B	3B	HR	RBI	TB	BB	SO	SB	OBP	SLG	BAVG
Denard Span	153	629	85	166	24	10	3	58	219	60	74	26	.331	.348	.264
Michael Cuddyer	157	609	93	165	37	5	14	81	254	58	93	7	.336	.417	.271
Delmon Young	153	570	77	170	46	1	21	112	281	28	81	5	.333	.493	.298
Jason Kubel	143	518	68	129	23	3	21	92	221	56	116	0	.323	.427	.249
Joe Mauer	137	510	88	167	43	1	9	75	239	65	53	1	.402	.469	.327
Orlando Hudson	126	497	80	133	24	5	6	37	185	50	87	10	.338	.372	.268
J.J. Hardy	101	340	44	91	19	3	6	38	134	28	54	1	.320	.394	.268
Danny Valencia	85	299	30	93	18	1	7	40	134	20	46	2	.351	.448	.311
Justin Morneau	81	296	53	102	25	1	18	56	183	50	62	0	.437	.618	.345
Jim Thome	108	276	48	78	16	2	25	59	173	60	82	0	.412	.627	.283
Nick Punto	88	252	24	60	11	1	1	20	76	28	50	6	.313	.302	.238
Alex Casilla	69	152	26	42	7	4	1	20	60	13	17	6	.331	.395	.276
Drew Butera	49	142	12	28	6	1	2	13	42	4	25	0	.237	.296	.197
Jason Repko	58	127	19	29	6	0	3	9	44	13	38	3	.324	.346	.228
Brendan Harris	43	108	11	17	3	0	1	4	23	9	23	0	.233	.213	.157
Matt Tolbert	48	87	8	20	4	3	1	18	33	9	18	1	.293	.379	.230

PITCHING	GP	GS	W–L	SV	SHO	R	ERA	IP	Ks	BB
Carl Pavano	32	32	17–11	0	2	95	3.75	221.0	117	37
Francisco Liriano	31	31	14–10	0	0	77	3.62	191.2	201	58
Scott Baker	29	29	12–9	0	0	87	4.49	170.1	148	43
Nick Blackburn	28	26	10–12	0	0	101	5.42	161.0	68	40
Kevin Slowey	30	28	13–6	0	0	80	4.45	155.2	116	29
Brian Duensing	53	13	10–3	0	1	42	2.62	130.2	78	35
Matt Guerrier	74	0	5–7	1	0	28	3.17	71.0	42	22
Jesse Crain	71	0	1–1	1	0	27	3.04	68.0	62	27
Jon Rauch	59	0	3–1	21	0	20	3.12	57.2	46	14
Aalex Burnett	41	0	2–2	0	0	28	5.29	47.2	37	23
Ron Mahay	41	0	1–1	0	0	15	3.44	34.0	25	8
Jose Mijares	47	0	1–1	0	0	14	3.31	32.2	28	9
Jeff Manship	13	1	2–1	0	0	20	5.28	29.0	21	6
*Matt Capps	27	0	2–0	16	0	7	2.00	27.0	21	4
*Brian Fuentes	9	0	0–0	1	0	0	0.00	9.2	8	2

*Mid-season trade.

New York Yankees

BATTING	G	AB	R	H	2B	3B	HR	RBI	TB	BB	SO	SB	OBP	SLG	BAVG
Derek Jeter	157	663	111	179	30	3	10	67	245	63	106	18	.340	.370	.270
Robinson Cano	160	626	103	200	41	3	29	109	334	57	77	3	.381	.534	.319
Mark Teixeira	158	601	113	154	36	0	33	108	289	93	122	0	.365	.481	.256
Nick Swisher	150	566	91	163	33	3	29	89	289	58	139	1	.359	.511	.288
Alex Rodriguez	137	522	74	141	29	2	30	125	264	59	98	4	.341	.506	.270
Brett Gardner	150	477	97	132	20	7	5	47	181	79	101	47	.383	.379	.277
Curtis Granderson	136	466	76	115	17	7	24	67	218	53	116	12	.324	.468	.247
Jorge Posada	120	383	49	95	23	1	18	57	174	59	99	3	.357	.454	.248
Francisco Cervelli	93	266	27	72	11	3	0	38	89	33	42	1	.359	.335	.271
Marcus Thames	82	212	22	61	7	0	12	33	104	19	61	0	.350	.491	.288
Ramiro Pena	85	154	18	35	1	1	0	18	38	6	27	7	.258	.247	.227
*Lance Berkman	37	106	9	27	7	0	1	9	37	17	15	0	.358	.349	.255
*Austin Kearns	36	102	13	24	3	0	2	7	33	12	38	0	.345	.324	.235
Nick Johnson	24	72	12	12	4	0	2	8	22	24	23	0	.388	.306	.167

PITCHING	GP	GS	W–L	SV	SHO	R	ERA	IP	Ks	BB
CC Sabathia	34	34	21–7	0	0	92	3.18	237.2	197	74
A.J. Burnett	33	33	10–15	0	0	118	5.26	186.2	145	78
Phil Hughes	31	29	18–8	0	0	83	4.19	176.1	146	58
Javier Vazquez	31	26	10–10	0	0	96	5.32	157.1	121	65
Andy Pettitte	21	21	11–3	0	0	52	3.28	129.0	101	41
Joba Chamberlain	73	0	3–4	3	0	37	4.40	71.2	77	22
Dustin Moseley	16	9	4–4	0	0	36	4.96	65.1	33	27
Dave Robertson	64	0	4–5	1	0	26	3.82	61.1	71	33
Mariano Rivera	61	0	3–3	33	0	14	1.80	60.0	45	11
Sergio Mitre	27	3	0–3	1	0	23	3.33	54.0	29	16
*Chad Gaudin	30	0	1–2	0	0	27	4.50	48.0	33	20
Ivan Nova	10	7	1–2	0	0	22	4.50	42.0	26	17
Boone Logan	51	0	2–0	0	0	13	2.93	40.0	38	20
*Chan Ho Park	27	0	2–1	0	0	25	5.60	35.1	29	12
*Kerry Wood	24	0	2–0	0	0	2	0.69	26.0	31	18
Damaso Marte	30	0	0–0	0	0	8	4.08	17.2	12	11
Alfredo Aceves	10	0	3–0	1	0	5	3.00	12.0	2	4
Jonathan Albaladejo	10	0	0–0	0	0	5	3.97	11.1	8	8

Oakland Athletics

BATTING	G	AB	R	H	2B	3B	HR	RBI	TB	BB	SO	SB	OBP	SLG	BAVG
Daric Barton	159	556	79	152	33	5	10	57	225	110	102	7	.393	.405	.273
Kevin Kouzmanoff	143	551	59	136	32	1	16	71	218	24	96	2	.283	.396	.247
Rajai Davis	143	525	66	149	28	3	5	52	198	26	78	50	.320	.377	.284
Cliff Pennington	156	508	64	127	26	8	6	46	187	50	96	29	.319	.368	.250
Kurt Suzuki	131	495	55	120	18	2	13	71	181	33	49	3	.303	.366	.242
Mark Ellis	124	436	45	127	24	0	5	49	166	40	56	7	.358	.381	.291
Jack Cust	112	349	50	95	19	0	13	52	153	68	127	2	.395	.438	.272
Ryan Sweeney	82	303	41	89	20	2	1	36	116	24	41	1	.342	.383	.294
Coco Crisp	75	290	51	81	14	4	8	38	127	30	49	32	.342	.438	.279
Adam Rosales	80	255	31	69	8	2	7	31	102	19	65	2	.321	.400	.271
Gabe Gross	105	222	27	53	11	1	1	25	69	17	39	5	.290	.311	.239
Landon Powell	41	112	13	24	4	0	2	11	34	15	29	1	.305	.304	.214
Endy Chavez	33	111	10	26	8	0	1	10	37	8	31	0	.276	.333	.234
*Eric Patterson	45	103	13	21	5	2	4	9	42	7	31	6	.255	.408	.204
*Jake Fox	39	98	11	21	5	0	2	12	32	3	26	0	.264	.327	.214

PITCHING	GP	GS	W–L	SV	SHO	R	ERA	IP	Ks	BB
Gio Gonzalez	33	33	15–9	0	0	75	3.23	200.2	171	92
Trevor Cahill	30	30	18–8	0	1	73	2.97	196.2	118	63
Dallas Braden	30	30	11–14	0	2	83	3.50	192.2	113	43
Vin Mazzaro	24	18	6–8	0	0	70	4.27	122.1	79	50
Ben Sheets	20	20	4–9	0	0	65	4.53	119.1	84	43
Brett Anderson	19	19	7–6	0	0	41	2.80	112.1	75	22
Craig Breslow	75	0	4–4	5	0	26	3.01	74.2	71	29
Brad Ziegler	64	0	3–7	0	0	24	3.26	60.2	41	28
Andrew Bailey	47	0	1–3	25	0	8	1.47	49.0	42	13
Jerry Blevins	63	0	2–1	1	0	20	3.70	48.2	46	18
Michael Wuertz	48	0	2–3	6	0	21	4.31	39.2	40	21
Tyson Ross	26	2	1–4	1	0	24	5.49	39.1	32	20
Justin Duchscherer	5	5	2–1	0	0	11	2.89	28.0	18	12
Henry Rodriguez	29	0	1–0	0	0	16	4.55	27.2	33	13

*Mid-season trade.

Seattle Mariners

BATTING	G	AB	R	H	2B	3B	HR	RBI	TB	BB	SO	SB	OBP	SLG	BAVG
Ichiro Suzuki	162	680	74	214	30	3	6	43	268	45	86	42	.359	.394	.315
Chone Figgins	161	602	62	156	21	2	1	35	184	74	114	42	.340	.306	.259
Javy Lopez	150	593	49	142	29	0	10	58	201	23	66	3	.270	.339	.239
Franklin Gutierrez	152	568	61	139	25	3	12	64	206	50	137	25	.303	.363	.245
Casey Kotchman	125	414	37	90	20	1	9	51	139	35	57	0	.280	.336	.217
Josh Wilson	108	361	22	82	14	2	2	25	106	14	74	5	.278	.294	.227
Michael Saunders	100	289	29	61	11	2	10	33	106	35	84	6	.295	.367	.211
Milton Bradley	73	244	28	50	9	1	8	29	85	28	75	8	.292	.348	.205
Adam Moore	60	205	12	40	6	0	4	15	58	8	63	0	.230	.283	.195
*Russell Branyan	57	205	23	44	10	0	15	33	99	30	82	1	.319	.483	.215
Jack Wilson	61	193	17	48	11	1	0	14	61	7	35	1	.282	.316	.249
Rob Johnson	61	178	24	34	10	0	2	13	50	25	46	1	.293	.281	.191
Matt Tuiasosopo	50	127	12	22	5	0	4	11	39	9	49	0	.234	.307	.173
*Justin Smoak	30	113	11	27	4	0	5	14	46	8	34	0	.287	.407	.239
Josh Bard	39	112	9	24	7	0	3	10	40	10	27	0	.276	.357	.214
Ryan Langerhans	60	107	16	21	2	1	3	4	34	24	51	4	.344	.318	.196
*Mike Sweeney	30	99	11	26	3	0	6	18	47	9	14	2	.327	.475	.263
Ken Griffey Jr.	33	98	6	18	2	0	0	7	20	9	17	0	.250	.204	.184

PITCHING	GP	GS	W–L	SV	SHO	R	ERA	IP	Ks	BB
Felix Hernandez	34	34	13–12	0	1	80	2.27	249.2	232	70
Jason Vargas	31	31	9–12	0	0	86	3.78	192.2	116	54
Doug Fister	28	28	6–14	0	0	85	4.11	171.0	93	32
Ryan Rowland–Smith	27	20	1–10	0	0	94	6.75	109.1	49	44
*Cliff Lee	13	13	8–3	0	1	31	2.34	103.2	89	6
David Pauley	19	15	4–9	0	0	44	4.07	90.2	51	30
Luke French	16	13	5–7	0	0	47	4.83	87.2	37	29
Brandon League	70	0	9–7	6	0	38	3.42	79.0	56	27
David Aardsma	53	0	0–6	31	0	19	3.44	49.2	49	25
Ian Snell	12	8	0–5	0	0	36	6.41	46.1	26	25
Garrett Olson	35	0	0–3	1	0	20	4.54	37.2	31	15
*Jamey Wright	28	0	0–1	0	0	15	3.41	37.0	19	16

Tampa Bay Rays

BATTING	G	AB	R	H	2B	3B	HR	RBI	TB	BB	SO	SB	OBP	SLG	BAVG
Carl Crawford	154	600	110	184	30	13	19	90	297	46	104	47	.356	.495	.307
Evan Longoria	151	574	96	169	46	5	22	104	291	72	124	15	.372	.507	.294
Ben Zobrist	151	541	77	129	28	2	10	75	191	92	107	24	.346	.353	.238
B.J. Upton	154	536	89	127	38	4	18	62	227	67	164	42	.322	.424	.237
Carlos Pena	144	484	64	95	18	0	28	84	197	87	158	5	.325	.407	.196
Jason Bartlett	135	468	71	119	27	3	4	47	164	45	83	11	.324	.350	.254
Sean Rodriguez	118	343	53	86	19	2	9	40	136	21	97	13	.308	.397	.251
John Jaso	109	339	57	89	18	3	5	44	128	59	39	4	.372	.378	.263
Reid Brignac	113	301	39	77	13	1	8	45	116	20	77	3	.307	.385	.256
Willy Aybar	100	270	22	62	13	0	6	43	93	30	61	0	.309	.344	.230
Matt Joyce	77	216	30	52	15	3	10	40	103	40	55	2	.360	.477	.241
Kelly Shoppach	63	158	17	31	8	0	5	17	54	20	71	0	.308	.342	.196
Gabe Kapler	59	124	19	26	4	0	2	14	36	11	24	1	.288	.290	.210
Dioner Navarro	48	124	11	24	5	0	1	7	32	12	20	0	.270	.258	.194
Dan Johnson	40	111	15	22	3	0	7	23	46	25	27	1	.343	.414	.198
*Pat Burrell	24	84	9	17	5	0	2	13	28	10	28	0	.292	.333	.202

PITCHING	GP	GS	W–L	SV	SHO	R	ERA	IP	Ks	BB
David Price	32	31	19–6	0	1	71	2.72	208.2	188	79
Matt Garza	33	32	15–10	1	1	94	3.91	204.2	150	63
James Shields	34	33	13–15	0	0	128	5.18	203.1	187	51
Jeff Niemann	30	29	12–8	0	1	86	4.39	174.1	131	61
Wade Davis	29	29	12–10	0	0	77	4.07	168.0	113	62
Andy Sonnanstine	41	4	3–1	1	0	40	4.44	81.0	50	27
Rafael Soriano	64	0	3–2	45	0	14	1.73	62.1	57	14
Lance Cormier	60	0	4–3	0	0	28	3.92	62.0	30	34
Joaquin Benoit	63	0	1–2	1	0	10	1.34	60.1	75	11
Grant Balfour	57	0	2–1	0	0	16	2.28	55.1	56	17
Dustin Wheeler	64	0	2–4	3	0	20	3.35	48.1	46	16
Russ Choate	85	0	4–3	0	0	23	4.23	44.2	40	17
Jeremy Hellickson	10	4	4–0	0	0	14	3.47	36.1	33	8
*Chad Qualls	27	0	2–0	0	0	15	5.57	21.0	15	6

*Mid-season trade.

Texas Rangers

BATTING

	G	AB	R	H	2B	3B	HR	RBI	TB	BB	SO	SB	OBP	SLG	BAVG
Michael Young	157	656	99	186	36	3	21	91	291	50	115	4	.330	.444	.284
Vladimir Guerrero	152	593	83	178	27	1	29	115	294	35	60	4	.345	.496	.300
Elvis Andrus	148	588	88	156	15	3	0	35	177	64	96	32	.342	.301	.265
Josh Hamilton	133	518	95	186	40	3	32	100	328	43	95	8	.411	.633	.359
Julio Borbon	137	438	60	121	11	4	3	42	149	19	59	15	.309	.340	.276
David Murphy	138	419	54	122	26	2	12	65	188	45	71	14	.358	.449	.291
Nelson Cruz	108	399	60	127	31	3	22	78	230	38	81	17	.374	.576	.318
Ian Kinsler	103	391	73	112	20	1	9	45	161	56	57	15	.382	.412	.286
Matt Treanor	82	237	22	50	6	1	5	27	73	22	43	1	.287	.308	.211
*Justin Smoak	70	235	29	49	10	0	8	34	83	38	57	1	.316	.407	.239
*Bengie Molina	57	175	10	42	6	1	2	19	56	10	15	0	.279	.320	.240
Andres Blanco	68	166	17	46	10	1	0	13	58	11	24	0	.330	.349	.277
Mitch Moreland	47	145	20	37	4	0	9	25	68	25	36	3	.364	.469	.255
Chris Davis	45	120	7	23	9	0	1	4	35	15	40	3	.279	.292	.192
*Joaquin Arias	50	98	18	27	5	1	0	9	34	2	17	1	.290	.347	.276

PITCHING

	GP	GS	W–L	SV	SHO	R	ERA	IP	Ks	BB
C.J. Wilson	33	33	15–8	0	0	83	3.35	204.0	170	93
Colby Lewis	32	32	12–13	0	0	90	3.72	201.0	196	65
Scott Feldman	29	22	7–11	0	0	98	5.48	141.1	75	45
Tommy Hunter	23	22	13–4	0	0	55	3.73	128.0	68	33
*Cliff Lee	15	15	4–6	0	0	53	3.98	108.2	96	12
Rich Harden	20	18	5–5	0	0	61	5.58	92.0	75	62
Matt Harrison	37	6	3–2	2	0	45	4.71	78.1	46	39
Neftali Feliz	70	0	4–3	40	0	21	2.73	69.1	71	18
Darren O'Day	72	0	6–2	0	0	15	2.03	62.0	45	12
Darren Oliver	64	0	1–2	1	0	20	2.48	61.2	65	15
Dave Holland	14	10	3–4	0	0	30	4.08	57.1	54	24
Dustin Nippert	38	2	4–5	0	0	28	4.29	56.2	47	34
Frank Francisco	56	0	6–4	2	0	23	3.76	52.2	60	18
Alexi Ogando	44	0	4–1	0	0	6	1.30	41.2	39	16
*Chris Ray	35	0	2–0	1	0	12	3.41	31.2	16	16
Doug Mathis	13	0	1–1	0	0	15	6.04	22.1	10	11

Toronto Blue Jays

BATTING

	G	AB	R	H	2B	3B	HR	RBI	TB	BB	SO	SB	OBP	SLG	BAVG
Vernon Wells	157	590	79	161	44	3	31	88	304	50	84	6	.331	.515	.273
Jose Bautista	161	569	109	148	35	3	54	124	351	100	116	9	.378	.617	.260
Adam Lind	150	569	57	135	32	3	23	72	242	38	144	0	.287	.425	.237
Lyle Overbay	154	534	75	130	37	2	20	67	231	67	131	1	.329	.433	.243
Aaron Hill	138	528	70	108	22	0	26	68	208	41	85	2	.271	.394	.205
Fred Lewis	110	428	70	112	31	5	8	36	177	38	104	17	.332	.414	.262
John Buck	118	409	53	115	25	0	20	66	200	16	111	0	.314	.489	.281
Edwin Encarnacion	96	332	47	81	16	0	21	51	160	29	60	1	.305	.482	.244
*Alex Gonzalez	85	328	47	85	25	1	17	50	163	17	65	1	.296	.497	.259
Travis Snider	82	298	36	76	20	0	14	32	138	21	79	6	.304	.463	.255
*Yunel Escobar	60	236	32	65	7	0	4	16	84	19	26	1	.340	.356	.275
Jose Molina	57	167	13	41	4	0	6	12	63	9	36	1	.304	.377	.246
John McDonald	63	152	27	38	9	2	6	23	69	6	26	2	.273	.454	.250
DeWayne Wise	52	112	20	28	3	2	3	14	44	4	29	4	.282	.393	.250
Mike McCoy	46	82	9	16	4	0	0	3	20	8	20	5	.267	.244	.195

PITCHING

	GP	GS	W–L	SV	SHO	R	ERA	IP	Ks	BB
Ricky Romero	32	32	14–9	0	1	98	3.73	210.0	174	82
Shawn Marcum	31	31	13–8	0	0	84	3.64	195.1	165	43
Brett Cecil	28	28	15–7	0	0	87	4.22	172.2	117	54
Brandon Morrow	26	26	10–7	0	1	76	4.49	146.1	178	66
Brian Tallet	34	5	2–6	0	0	60	6.40	77.1	53	38
Shawn Camp	70	0	4–3	2	0	26	2.99	72.1	46	18
Casey Janssen	56	0	5–2	0	0	29	3.67	68.2	63	21
Jason Frasor	69	0	3–4	4	0	30	3.68	63.2	65	27
Marc Rzepczynski	14	12	4–4	0	0	37	4.95	63.2	57	30
Scott Downs	67	0	5–5	0	0	19	2.64	61.1	48	14
Kevin Gregg	63	0	2–6	37	0	24	3.51	59.0	58	30
Jesse Litsch	9	9	1–5	0	0	30	5.79	46.2	16	15
*Dana Eveland	9	9	3–4	0	0	35	6.45	44.2	21	27
David Purcey	33	0	1–1	1	0	16	3.71	34.0	32	15

*Mid-season trade.

FOR THE RECORD • Year by Year

Results

1903	Boston (A) 5, Pittsburgh (N) 3
1904	No series
1905	New York (N) 4, Philadelphia (A) 1
1906	Chicago (A) 4, Chicago (N) 2
1907	Chicago (N) 4, Detroit (A) 0; 1 tie
1908	Chicago (N) 4, Detroit (A) 1
1909	Pittsburgh (N) 4, Detroit (A) 3
1910	Philadelphia (A) 4, Chicago (N) 1
1911	Philadelphia (A) 4, New York (N) 2
1912	Boston (A) 4, New York (N) 3; 1 tie
1913	Philadelphia (A) 4, New York (N) 1
1914	Boston (N) 4, Philadelphia (A) 0
1915	Boston (A) 4, Philadelphia (N) 1
1916	Boston (A) 4, Brooklyn (N) 1
1917	Chicago (A) 4, New York (N) 2
1918	Boston (A) 4, Chicago (N) 2
1919	Cincinnati (N) 5, Chicago (A) 3
1920	Cleveland (A) 5, Brooklyn (N) 2
1921	New York (N) 5, New York (A) 3
1922	New York (N) 4, New York (A) 0; 1 tie
1923	New York (A) 4, New York (N) 2
1924	Washington (A) 4, New York (N) 3
1925	Pittsburgh (N) 4, Washington (A) 3
1926	St. Louis (N) 4, New York (A) 3
1927	New York (A) 4, Pittsburgh (N) 0
1928	New York (A) 4, St. Louis (N) 0
1929	Philadelphia (A) 4, Chicago (N) 1
1930	Philadelphia (A) 4, St. Louis (N) 2
1931	St. Louis (N) 4, Philadelphia (A) 3
1932	New York (A) 4, Chicago (N) 0
1933	New York (N) 4, Washington (A) 1
1934	St. Louis (N) 4, Detroit (A) 3
1935	Detroit (A) 4, Chicago (N) 2
1936	New York (A) 4, New York (N) 2
1937	New York (A) 4, New York (N) 1
1938	New York (A) 4, Chicago (N) 0
1939	New York (A) 4, Cincinnati (N) 0
1940	Cincinnati (N) 4, Detroit (A) 3
1941	New York (A) 4, Brooklyn (N) 1
1942	St. Louis (N) 4, New York (A) 1
1943	New York (A) 4, St. Louis (N) 1
1944	St. Louis (N) 4, St. Louis (A) 2
1945	Detroit (A) 4, Chicago (N) 3
1946	St. Louis (N) 4, Boston (A) 3
1947	New York (A) 4, Brooklyn (N) 3
1948	Cleveland (A) 4, Boston (N) 2
1949	New York (A) 4, Brooklyn (N) 1
1950	New York (A) 4, Philadelphia (N) 0
1951	New York (A) 4, New York (N) 2
1952	New York (A) 4, Brooklyn (N) 3
1953	New York (A) 4, Brooklyn (N) 2
1954	New York (N) 4, Cleveland (A) 0
1955	Brooklyn (N) 4, New York (A) 3
1956	New York (A) 4, Brooklyn (N) 3
1957	Milwaukee (N) 4, New York (A) 3
1958	New York (A) 4, Milwaukee (N) 3
1959	Los Angeles (N) 4, Chicago (A) 2
1960	Pittsburgh (N) 4, New York (A) 3
1961	New York (A) 4, Cincinnati (N) 1
1962	New York (A) 4, San Francisco (N) 3
1963	Los Angeles (N) 4, New York (A) 0
1964	St. Louis (N) 4, New York (A) 3
1965	Los Angeles (N) 4, Minnesota (A) 3
1966	Baltimore (A) 4, Los Angeles (N) 0
1967	St. Louis (N) 4, Boston (A) 3
1968	Detroit (A) 4, St. Louis (N) 3
1969	New York (N) 4, Baltimore (A) 1
1970	Baltimore (A) 4, Cincinnati (N) 1
1971	Pittsburgh (N) 4, Baltimore (A) 3
1972	Oakland (A) 4, Cincinnati (N) 3
1973	Oakland (A) 4, New York (N) 3
1974	Oakland (A) 4, Los Angeles (N) 1
1975	Cincinnati (N) 4, Boston (A) 3
1976	Cincinnati (N) 4, New York (A) 0
1977	New York (A) 4, Los Angeles (N) 2
1978	New York (A) 4, Los Angeles (N) 2
1979	Pittsburgh (N) 4, Baltimore (A) 3
1980	Philadelphia (N) 4, Kansas City (A) 2
1981	Los Angeles (N) 4, New York (A) 2
1982	St. Louis (N) 4, Milwaukee (A) 3
1983	Baltimore (A) 4, Philadelphia (N) 1
1984	Detroit (A) 4, San Diego (N) 1
1985	Kansas City (A) 4, St. Louis (N) 3
1986	New York (N) 4, Boston (A) 3
1987	Minnesota (A) 4, St. Louis (N) 3
1988	Los Angeles (N) 4, Oakland (A) 1
1989	Oakland (A) 4, San Francisco (N) 0
1990	Cincinnati (N) 4, Oakland (A) 0
1991	Minnesota (A) 4, Atlanta (N) 3
1992	Toronto (A) 4, Atlanta (N) 2
1993	Toronto (A) 4, Philadelphia (N) 2
1994	Series canceled due to players' strike.
1995	Atlanta (N) 4, Cleveland (A) 2
1996	New York (A) 4, Atlanta (N) 2
1997	Florida (N) 4, Cleveland (A) 3
1998	New York (A) 4, San Diego (N) 0
1999	New York (A) 4, Atlanta (N) 0
2000	New York (A) 4 , New York (N) 1
2001	Arizona (N) 4, New York (A) 3
2002	Anaheim (A) 4, San Francisco (N) 3
2003	Florida (N) 4, New York (A) 2
2004	Boston (A) 4, St. Louis (N) 0
2005	Chicago (A) 4, Houston (N) 0
2006	St. Louis (N) 4, Detroit (A) 1
2007	Boston (A) 4, Colorado (N) 0
2008	Philadelphia (N) 4, Tampa Bay (A) 1
2009	New York (A) 4, Philadelphia (N) 2
2010	San Francisco (N) 4, Texas (A) 1

Most Valuable Players

1955	Johnny Podres, Bklyn		1983	Rick Dempsey, Balt
1956	Don Larsen, NY (A)		1984	Alan Trammell, Det
1957	Lew Burdette, Mil		1985	Bret Saberhagen, KC
1958	Bob Turley, NY (A)		1986	Ray Knight, NY (N)
1959	Larry Sherry, LA		1987	Frank Viola, Minn
1960	Bobby Richardson, NY (A)		1988	Orel Hershiser, LA
1961	Whitey Ford, NY (A)		1989	Dave Stewart, Oak
1962	Ralph Terry, NY (A)		1990	Jose Rijo, Cin
1963	Sandy Koufax, LA		1991	Jack Morris, Minn
1964	Bob Gibson, StL		1992	Pat Borders, Tor
1965	Sandy Koufax, LA		1993	Paul Molitor, Tor
1966	Frank Robinson, Balt		1994	Series canceled due to strike.
1967	Bob Gibson, StL		1995	Tom Glavine, Atl
1968	Mickey Lolich, Det		1996	John Wetteland, NY (A)
1969	Donn Clendenon, NY (N)		1997	Livan Hernandez, Fla
1970	Brooks Robinson, Balt		1998	Scott Brosius, NY (A)
1971	Roberto Clemente, Pitt		1999	Mariano Rivera, NY (A)
1972	Gene Tenace, Oak		2000	Derek Jeter, NY (A)
1973	Reggie Jackson, Oak		2001	Randy Johnson, Ariz
1974	Rollie Fingers, Oak			Curt Schilling, Ariz
1975	Pete Rose, Cin		2002	Troy Glaus, Ana
1976	Johnny Bench, Cin		2003	Josh Beckett, Fla
1977	Reggie Jackson, NY (A)		2004	Manny Ramirez, Bos
1978	Bucky Dent, NY (A)		2005	Jermaine Dye, Chi (A)
1979	Willie Stargell, Pitt		2006	David Eckstein, StL
1980	Mike Schmidt, Phil		2007	Mike Lowell, Bos
1981	Ron Cey, LA; Steve Yeager, LA;		2008	Cole Hamels, Phi
	Pedro Guerrero, LA		2009	Hideki Matsui, NY (A)
1982	Darrell Porter, StL		2010	Edgar Renteria, SF

Career Batting Leaders (Minimum 40 at bats)

GAMES

Yogi Berra	75
Mickey Mantle	65
Elston Howard	54
Hank Bauer	53
Gil McDougald	53
Phil Rizzuto	52
Joe DiMaggio	51
Frankie Frisch	50
Pee Wee Reese	44
Roger Maris	41
Babe Ruth	41

AT BATS

Yogi Berra	259
Mickey Mantle	230
Joe DiMaggio	199
Frankie Frisch	197
Gil McDougald	190
Hank Bauer	188
Phil Rizzuto	183
Elston Howard	171
Pee Wee Reese	169
Derek Jeter	156
Roger Maris	152

BATTING AVERAGE

Bobby Brown	.439
Paul Molitor	.418
Pepper Martin	.418
Hal McRae	.400
Lou Brock	.391
Marquis Grissom	.390
Thurman Munson	.373
George Brett	.373
Pat Borders	.372
Hank Aaron	.364

RUNS

Mickey Mantle	42
Yogi Berra	41
Babe Ruth	37
Derek Jeter	32
Lou Gehrig	30
Joe DiMaggio	27
Derek Jeter	27
Roger Maris	26
Elston Howard	25
Gil McDougald	23
Jackie Robinson	22

RUNS BATTED IN

Mickey Mantle	40
Yogi Berra	39
Lou Gehrig	35
Babe Ruth	33
Joe DiMaggio	30
Bill Skowron	29
Duke Snider	26
Reggie Jackson	24
Bill Dickey	24
Hank Bauer	24
Gil McDougald	24

TOTAL BASES

Mickey Mantle	123
Yogi Berra	117
Babe Ruth	96
Lou Gehrig	87
Joe DiMaggio	84
Duke Snider	79
Hank Bauer	75
Reggie Jackson	74
Frankie Frisch	74
Gil McDougald	72
Derek Jeter	70

HOME RUNS

Mickey Mantle	18
Babe Ruth	15
Yogi Berra	12
Duke Snider	11
Reggie Jackson	10
Lou Gehrig	10
Frank Robinson	8
Bill Skowron	8
Joe DiMaggio	8
Goose Goslin	7
Hank Bauer	7
Gil McDougald	7
Chase Utley	7

HITS

Yogi Berra	71
Mickey Mantle	59
Frankie Frisch	58
Joe DiMaggio	54
Derek Jeter	50
Pee Wee Reese	46
Hank Bauer	46
Phil Rizzuto	45
Gil McDougald	45
Lou Gehrig	43
Eddie Collins	42
Babe Ruth	42
Elston Howard	42

STOLEN BASES

Lou Brock	14
Eddie Collins	14
Frank Chance	10
Davey Lopes	10
Phil Rizzuto	10
Honus Wagner	9
Frankie Frisch	9
Kenny Lofton	9

Career Batting Leaders *(Cont.)*

STOLEN BASES (CONT.)

Johnny Evers	8
Roberto Alomar	7
Joe Tinker	7
Pepper Martin	7
Joe Morgan	7
Rickey Henderson	7

SLUGGING AVERAGE

Reggie Jackson	.755
Babe Ruth	.744
Lou Gehrig	.731
Bobby Brown	.707
Lenny Dykstra	.700
Al Simmons	.658
Lou Brock	.655
Pepper Martin	.636
Paul Molitor	.636
Joe Harris	.625

STRIKEOUTS

Mickey Mantle	54
Derek Jeter	39
Elston Howard	37
Duke Snider	33
Jorge Posada	31
Babe Ruth	30
David Justice	30
Gil McDougald	29
Bill Skowron	26
Bernie Williams	26
Hank Bauer	25

Career Pitching Leaders

GAMES

Mariano Rivera	24
Whitey Ford	22
Mike Stanton	19
Jeff Nelson	16
Rollie Fingers	16
Allie Reynolds	15
Bob Turley	15
Clay Carroll	14
Clem Labine	13
Mark Wohlers	13
Andy Pettitte	13

INNINGS PITCHED

Whitey Ford	146
Christy Mathewson	101.2
Red Ruffing	85.2
Chief Bender	85
Waite Hoyt	83.2
Bob Gibson	81
Art Nehf	79
Andy Pettitte	77.2
Allie Reynolds	77

WINS

Whitey Ford	10
Bob Gibson	7
Red Ruffing	7
Allie Reynolds	7
Lefty Gomez	6
Chief Bender	6
Waite Hoyt	6
Jack Coombs	5
Three Finger Brown	5
Herb Pennock	5
Christy Mathewson	5
Vic Raschi	5
Catfish Hunter	5
Andy Pettitte	5

*Minimum 25 innings pitched.

LOSSES

Whitey Ford	8
Eddie Plank	5
Schoolboy Rowe	5
Joe Bush	5
Rube Marquard	5
Christy Mathewson	5

SAVES

Mariano Rivera	11
Rollie Fingers	6
Allie Reynolds	4
Johnny Murphy	4
John Wetteland	4
Robb Nen	4

*EARNED RUN AVERAGE

Jack Billingham	0.36
Harry Brecheen	0.83
Babe Ruth	0.87
Sherry Smith	0.89
Sandy Koufax	0.95
Mariano Rivera	0.99
Hippo Vaughn	1.00
Monte Pearson	1.01
Christy Mathewson	1.06
Babe Adams	1.29

SHUTOUTS

Christy Mathewson	4
Three Finger Brown	3
Whitey Ford	3
Bill Hallahan	2
Lew Burdette	2
Bill Dinneen	2
Sandy Koufax	2
Allie Reynolds	2
Art Nehf	2
Bob Gibson	2

COMPLETE GAMES

Christy Mathewson	10
Chief Bender	9
Bob Gibson	8
Red Ruffing	7
Whitey Ford	7
George Mullin	6
Eddie Plank	6
Art Nehf	6
Waite Hoyt	6

STRIKEOUTS

Whitey Ford	94
Bob Gibson	92
Allie Reynolds	62
Sandy Koufax	61
Red Ruffing	61
Chief Bender	59
Andy Pettitte	56
George Earnshaw	56
John Smoltz	52
Waite Hoyt	49
Roger Clemens	49
Christy Mathewson	48

BASES ON BALLS

Whitey Ford	34
Allie Reynolds	32
Art Nehf	32
Jim Palmer	31
Bob Turley	29
Paul Derringer	27
Red Ruffing	27
Don Gullett	26
Burleigh Grimes	26
Andy Pettitte	26
Vic Raschi	25

Alltime Team Rankings, by Championships

Team	W	L	Appearances	Pct.	Most Recent App.	Last Championship
New York Yankees	27	13	40	.675	2009	2009
St. Louis Cardinals	10	7	17	.588	2006	2006
Phila./K.C./Oakland Athletics	9	5	14	.643	1990	1989
Boston Red Sox	7	5	12	.583	2007	2007
New York/San Francisco Giants	6	12	18	.333	2010	2010
Brooklyn/Los Angeles Dodgers	6	12	18	.333	1988	1988
Pittsburgh Pirates	5	2	7	.714	1979	1979
Cincinnati Reds	5	4	9	.556	1990	1990
Detroit Tigers	4	6	10	.400	2006	1984
Chicago White Sox	3	2	5	.600	2005	2005
Wash. Senators/Minnesota Twins	3	3	6	.500	1991	1991
St. Louis Browns/Baltimore Orioles	3	4	7	.429	1983	1983
Boston/Milwaukee/Atlanta Braves	3	6	9	.333	1999	1995
Florida Marlins	2	0	2	1.000	2003	2003

Alltime Team Rankings, by Championships *(Cont.)*

Team	W	L	Appearances	Pct.	Most Recent App.	Last Championship
Toronto Blue Jays	2	0	2	1.000	1993	1993
New York Mets	2	2	4	.500	2000	1986
Cleveland Indians	2	3	5	.400	1997	1948
Philadelphia Phillies	2	5	7	.286	2009	2008
Chicago Cubs	2	8	10	.200	1945	1908
California/Anaheim/L.A. Angels	1	0	1	1.000	2002	2002
Arizona Diamondbacks	1	0	1	1.000	2001	2001
Kansas City Royals	1	1	2	.500	1985	1985
Texas Rangers	0	1	1	.000	2010	—
Tampa Bay Rays	0	1	1	.000	2008	—
Colorado Rockies	0	1	1	.000	2007	—
Houston Astros	0	1	1	.000	2005	—
Seattle Pilots/Milwaukee Brewers	0	1	1	.000	1982	—
San Diego Padres	0	2	2	.000	1998	—

League Pennant Winners

National League

Year	Team	Manager	W	L	Pct	GA
1900	Brooklyn	Ned Hanlon	82	54	.603	4½
1901	Pittsburgh	Fred Clarke	90	49	.647	7½
1902	Pittsburgh	Fred Clarke	103	36	.741	27½
1903	Pittsburgh	Fred Clarke	91	49	.650	6½
1904	New York	John McGraw	106	47	.693	13
1905	New York	John McGraw	105	48	.686	9
1906	Chicago	Frank Chance	116	36	.763	20
1907	Chicago	Frank Chance	107	45	.704	17
1908	Chicago	Frank Chance	99	55	.643	1
1909	Pittsburgh	Fred Clarke	110	42	.724	6½
1910	Chicago	Frank Chance	104	50	.675	13
1911	New York	John McGraw	99	54	.647	7½
1912	New York	John McGraw	103	48	.682	10
1913	New York	John McGraw	101	51	.664	12½
1914	Boston	George Stallings	94	59	.614	10½
1915	Philadelphia	Pat Moran	90	62	.592	7
1916	Brooklyn	Wilbert Robinson	94	60	.610	2½
1917	New York	John McGraw	98	56	.636	10
1918	Chicago	Fred Mitchell	84	45	.651	10½
1919	Cincinnati	Pat Moran	96	44	.686	9
1920	Brooklyn	Wilbert Robinson	93	61	.604	7
1921	New York	John McGraw	94	59	.614	4
1922	New York	John McGraw	93	61	.604	7
1923	New York	John McGraw	95	58	.621	4½
1924	New York	John McGraw	93	60	.608	1½
1925	Pittsburgh	Bill McKechnie	95	58	.621	8½
1926	St. Louis	Rogers Hornsby	89	65	.578	2
1927	Pittsburgh	Donie Bush	94	60	.610	1½
1928	St. Louis	Bill McKechnie	95	59	.617	2
1929	Chicago	Joe McCarthy	98	54	.645	10½
1930	St. Louis	Gabby Street	92	62	.597	2
1931	St. Louis	Gabby Street	101	53	.656	13
1932	Chicago	Charlie Grimm	90	64	.584	4
1933	New York	Bill Terry	91	61	.599	5
1934	St. Louis	Frankie Frisch	95	58	.621	2
1935	Chicago	Charlie Grimm	100	54	.649	4
1936	New York	Bill Terry	92	62	.597	5
1937	New York	Bill Terry	95	57	.625	3
1938	Chicago	Gabby Hartnett	89	63	.586	2
1939	Cincinnati	Bill McKechnie	97	57	.630	4½
1940	Cincinnati	Bill McKechnie	100	53	.654	12
1941	Brooklyn	Leo Durocher	100	54	.649	2½
1942	St. Louis	Billy Southworth	106	48	.688	2
1943	St. Louis	Billy Southworth	105	49	.682	18
1944	St. Louis	Billy Southworth	105	49	.682	14½
1945	Chicago	Charlie Grimm	98	56	.636	3
1946	St. Louis*	Eddie Dyer	98	58	.628	2
1947	Brooklyn	Burt Shotton	94	60	.610	5

National League (Cont.)

Year	Team	Manager	W	L	Pct	GA
1948	Boston	Billy Southworth	91	62	.595	6½
1949	Brooklyn	Burt Shotton	97	57	.630	1
1950	Philadelphia	Eddie Sawyer	91	63	.591	2
1951	New York†	Leo Durocher	98	59	.624	1
1952	Brooklyn	Chuck Dressen	96	57	.627	4½
1953	Brooklyn	Chuck Dressen	105	49	.682	13
1954	New York	Leo Durocher	97	57	.630	5
1955	Brooklyn	Walter Alston	98	55	.641	13½
1956	Brooklyn	Walter Alston	93	61	.604	1
1957	Milwaukee	Fred Haney	95	59	.617	8
1958	Milwaukee	Fred Haney	92	62	.597	8
1959	Los Angeles‡	Walter Alston	88	68	.564	2
1960	Pittsburgh	Danny Murtaugh	95	59	.617	7
1961	Cincinnati	Fred Hutchinson	93	61	.604	4
1962	San Francisco#	Al Dark	103	62	.624	1
1963	Los Angeles	Walter Alston	99	63	.611	6
1964	St. Louis	Johnny Keane	93	69	.574	1
1965	Los Angeles	Walter Alston	97	65	.599	2
1966	Los Angeles	Walter Alston	95	67	.586	1½
1967	St. Louis	Red Schoendienst	101	60	.627	10½
1968	St. Louis	Red Schoendienst	97	65	.599	9
1969	New York (E)††	Gil Hodges	100	62	.617	8
1970	Cincinnati (W)††	Sparky Anderson	102	60	.630	14½
1971	Pittsburgh (E)††	Danny Murtaugh	97	65	.599	7
1972	Cincinnati (W)††	Sparky Anderson	95	59	.617	10½
1973	New York (E)††	Yogi Berra	82	79	.509	1½
1974	Los Angeles (W)††	Walter Alston	102	60	.630	4
1975	Cincinnati (W)††	Sparky Anderson	108	54	.667	20
1976	Cincinnati (W)††	Sparky Anderson	102	60	.630	10
1977	Los Angeles (W)††	Tommy Lasorda	98	64	.605	10
1978	Los Angeles (W)††	Tommy Lasorda	95	67	.586	2½
1979	Pittsburgh (E)††	Chuck Tanner	98	64	.605	2
1980	Philadelphia (E)††	Dallas Green	91	71	.562	1
1981	Los Angeles (W)††	Tommy Lasorda	63	47	.573	**
1982	St. Louis (E)††	Whitey Herzog	92	70	.568	3
1983	Philadelphia (E)††	Pat Corrales/ Paul Owens	90	72	.556	6
1984	San Diego (W)††	Dick Williams	92	70	.568	12
1985	St. Louis (E)††	Whitey Herzog	101	61	.623	3
1986	New York (E)††	Davey Johnson	108	54	.667	21½
1987	St. Louis (E)††	Whitey Herzog	95	67	.586	3
1988	Los Angeles (W)††	Tommy Lasorda	94	67	.584	7
1989	San Francisco (W)††	Roger Craig	92	70	.568	3
1990	Cincinnati (W)††	Lou Piniella	91	71	.562	5
1991	Atlanta (W)††	Bobby Cox	94	68	.580	1
1992	Atlanta (W)††	Bobby Cox	98	64	.605	8
1993	Philadelphia (E)††	Jim Fregosi	97	65	.599	3
1994	Season ended Aug. 11 due to players' strike.					
1995	Atlanta (E)††	Bobby Cox	90	54	.625	21
1996	Atlanta (E)††	Bobby Cox	96	66	.593	8
1997	Florida (wc)††	Jim Leyland	92	70	.568	-9
1998	San Diego (W)††	Bruce Bochy	98	64	.605	9½
1999	Atlanta (E)††	Bobby Cox	103	59	.636	6½
2000	New York (wc)††	Bobby Valentine	94	68	.580	-6½
2001	Arizona (W)††	Bob Brenly	92	70	.568	2
2002	San Francisco (wc)††	Dusty Baker	95	66	.590	-2½
2003	Florida (wc)††	Jack McKeon	91	71	.562	-10
2004	St. Louis (C)††	Tony LaRussa	105	57	.648	13
2005	Houston (wc)††	Phil Garner	89	73	.549	-11
2006	St. Louis (C)††	Tony LaRussa	83	78	.516	1½
2007	Colorado (wc)††§	Clint Hurdle	89	73	.549	-1
2008	Philadelphia (E)††	Charlie Manuel	92	70	.568	3
2009	Philadelphia (E)††	Charlie Manuel	93	69	.574	6
2010	San Francisco (W)††	Bruce Bochy	92	70	.568	2

*Defeated Brooklyn, two games to none, in playoff for pennant. †Defeated Brooklyn, two games to one, in playoff for pennant. ‡Defeated Milwaukee, two games to none, in playoff for pennant. #Defeated Los Angeles, two games to one, in playoff for pennant. § Defeated San Diego in one-game playoff for wild card. ††Won Championship Series. **First half 36–21; second half 27–26, in season split by strike; defeated Houston in playoff for Western Division title.

American League

Year	Team	Manager	W	L	Pct	GA
1901	Chicago	Clark Griffith	83	53	.610	4
1902	Philadelphia	Connie Mack	83	53	.610	5
1903	Boston	Jimmy Collins	91	47	.659	14½
1904	Boston	Jimmy Collins	95	59	.617	1½
1905	Philadelphia	Connie Mack	92	56	.622	2
1906	Chicago	Fielder Jones	93	58	.616	3
1907	Detroit	Hughie Jennings	92	58	.613	1½
1908	Detroit	Hughie Jennings	90	63	.588	½
1909	Detroit	Hughie Jennings	98	54	.645	3½
1910	Philadelphia	Connie Mack	102	48	.680	14½
1911	Philadelphia	Connie Mack	101	50	.669	13½
1912	Boston	Jake Stahl	105	47	.691	14
1913	Philadelphia	Connie Mack	96	57	.627	6½
1914	Philadelphia	Connie Mack	99	53	.651	8½
1915	Boston	Bill Carrigan	101	50	.669	2½
1916	Boston	Bill Carrigan	91	63	.591	2
1917	Chicago	Pants Rowland	100	54	.649	9
1918	Boston	Ed Barrow	75	51	.595	2½
1919	Chicago	Kid Gleason	88	52	.629	3½
1920	Cleveland	Tris Speaker	98	56	.636	2
1921	New York	Miller Huggins	98	55	.641	4½
1922	New York	Miller Huggins	94	60	.610	1
1923	New York	Miller Huggins	98	54	.645	16
1924	Washington	Bucky Harris	92	62	.597	2
1925	Washington	Bucky Harris	96	55	.636	8½
1926	New York	Miller Huggins	91	63	.591	3
1927	New York	Miller Huggins	110	44	.714	19
1928	New York	Miller Huggins	101	53	.656	2½
1929	Philadelphia	Connie Mack	104	46	.693	18
1930	Philadelphia	Connie Mack	102	52	.662	8
1931	Philadelphia	Connie Mack	107	45	.704	13½
1932	New York	Joe McCarthy	107	47	.695	13
1933	Washington	Joe Cronin	99	53	.651	7
1934	Detroit	Mickey Cochrane	101	53	.656	7
1935	Detroit	Mickey Cochrane	93	58	.616	3
1936	New York	Joe McCarthy	102	51	.667	19½
1937	New York	Joe McCarthy	102	52	.662	13
1938	New York	Joe McCarthy	99	53	.651	9½
1939	New York	Joe McCarthy	106	45	.702	17
1940	Detroit	Del Baker	90	64	.584	1
1941	New York	Joe McCarthy	101	53	.656	17
1942	New York	Joe McCarthy	103	51	.669	9
1943	New York	Joe McCarthy	98	56	.636	13½
1944	St. Louis	Luke Sewell	89	65	.578	1
1945	Detroit	Steve O'Neill	88	65	.575	1½
1946	Boston	Joe Cronin	104	50	.675	12
1947	New York	Bucky Harris	97	57	.630	12
1948	Cleveland†	Lou Boudreau	97	58	.626	1
1949	New York	Casey Stengel	97	57	.630	1
1950	New York	Casey Stengel	98	56	.636	3
1951	New York	Casey Stengel	98	56	.636	5
1952	New York	Casey Stengel	95	59	.617	2
1953	New York	Casey Stengel	99	52	.656	8½
1954	Cleveland	Al Lopez	111	43	.721	8
1955	New York	Casey Stengel	96	58	.623	3
1956	New York	Casey Stengel	97	57	.630	9
1957	New York	Casey Stengel	98	56	.636	8
1958	New York	Casey Stengel	92	62	.597	10
1959	Chicago	Al Lopez	94	60	.610	5
1960	New York	Casey Stengel	97	57	.630	8
1961	New York	Ralph Houk	109	53	.673	8
1962	New York	Ralph Houk	96	66	.593	5
1963	New York	Ralph Houk	104	57	.646	10½
1964	New York	Yogi Berra	99	63	.611	1
1965	Minnesota	Sam Mele	102	60	.630	7
1966	Baltimore	Hank Bauer	97	63	.606	9
1967	Boston	Dick Williams	92	70	.568	1
1968	Detroit	Mayo Smith	103	59	.636	12

American League *(Cont.)*

Year	Team	Manager	W	L	Pct	GA
1969	Baltimore (E)‡	Earl Weaver	109	53	.673	19
1970	Baltimore (E)‡	Earl Weaver	108	54	.667	15
1971	Baltimore (E)‡	Earl Weaver	101	57	.639	12
1972	Oakland (W)‡	Dick Williams	93	62	.600	5½
1973	Oakland (W)‡	Dick Williams	94	68	.580	6
1974	Oakland (W)‡	Al Dark	90	72	.556	5
1975	Boston (E)‡	Darrell Johnson	95	65	.594	4½
1976	New York (E)‡	Billy Martin	97	62	.610	10½
1977	New York (E)‡	Billy Martin	100	62	.617	2½
1978	New York (E)†‡	Billy Martin, Bob Lemon	100	63	.613	1
1979	Baltimore (E)‡	Earl Weaver	102	57	.642	8
1980	Kansas City (W)‡	Jim Frey	97	65	.599	14
1981	New York (E)‡	Gene Michael/Bob Lemon	59	48	.551	#
1982	Milwaukee (E)‡	Buck Rodgers, Harvey Kuenn	95	67	.586	1
1983	Baltimore (E)‡	Joe Altobelli	98	64	.605	6
1984	Detroit (E)‡	Sparky Anderson	104	58	.642	15
1985	Kansas City (W)‡	Dick Howser	91	71	.562	1
1986	Boston (E)‡	John McNamara	95	66	.590	5½
1987	Minnesota (W)‡	Tom Kelly	85	77	.525	2
1988	Oakland (W)‡	Tony LaRussa	104	58	.642	13
1989	Oakland (W)‡	Tony LaRussa	99	63	.611	7
1990	Oakland (W)‡	Tony LaRussa	103	59	.636	9
1991	Minnesota (W)‡	Tom Kelly	95	67	.586	8
1992	Toronto‡	Cito Gaston	96	66	.593	4
1993	Toronto‡	Cito Gaston	95	67	.586	7
1994	Season ended Aug. 11 due to players' strike.					
1995	Cleveland (C)‡	Mike Hargrove	100	44	.694	30
1996	New York (E)‡	Joe Torre	92	70	.568	4
1997	Cleveland (C)‡	Mike Hargrove	86	75	.534	6
1998	New York (E)‡	Joe Torre	114	48	.704	22
1999	New York (E)‡	Joe Torre	98	64	.605	4
2000	New York (E)‡	Joe Torre	87	74	.540	2½
2001	New York (E)‡	Joe Torre	95	65	.594	13½
2002	Anaheim (wc)‡	Mike Scioscia	99	63	.611	-4
2003	New York (E)‡	Joe Torre	101	61	.623	6
2004	Boston (wc)‡	Terry Francona	98	64	.605	-3
2005	Chicago (C)‡	Ozzie Guillen	99	63	.611	6
2006	Detroit (wc)‡	Jim Leyland	95	67	.586	-1
2007	Boston (E)‡	Terry Francona	96	66	.593	2
2008	Tampa Bay (E)‡	Joe Maddon	97	65	.599	2
2009	New York (E)‡	Joe Girardi	103	59	.636	8
2010	Texas (W)‡	Ron Washington	90	72	.556	9

†Defeated Boston in one-game playoff. ‡Won championship series.
#First half 34–22; second half 25–26, in season split by strike; defeated Milwaukee in playoff for Eastern Divison title.

National League

1969 ....New York (E) 3, Atlanta (W) 0
1970 ....Cincinnati (W) 3, Pittsburgh (E) 0
1971 ....Pittsburgh (E) 3, San Francisco (W) 1
1972 ....Cincinnati (W) 3, Pittsburgh (E) 2
1973 ....New York (E) 3, Cincinnati (W) 2
1974 ....Los Angeles (W) 3, Pittsburgh (E) 1
1975 ....Cincinnati (W) 3, Pittsburgh (E) 0
1976 ....Cincinnati (W) 3, Philadelphia (E) 0
1977 ....Los Angeles (W) 3, Philadelphia (E) 1
1978 ....Los Angeles (W) 3, Philadelphia (E) 1
1979 ....Pittsburgh (E) 3, Cincinnati (W) 0
1980 ....Philadelphia (E) 3, Houston (W) 2
1981 ....Los Angeles (W) 3, Montreal (E) 2
1982 ....St. Louis (E) 3, Atlanta (W) 0
1983 ....Philadelphia (E) 3, Los Angeles (W) 1
1984 ....San Diego (W) 3, Chicago (E) 2
1985 ....St. Louis (E) 4, Los Angeles (W) 2
1986 ....New York (E) 4, Houston (W) 2
1987 ....St. Louis (E) 4, San Francisco (W) 3
1988 ....Los Angeles (W) 4, New York (E) 3
1989 ....San Francisco (W) 4, Chicago (E) 1
1990 ....Cincinnati (W) 4, Pittsburgh (E) 2
1991 ....Atlanta (W) 4, Pittsburgh (E) 3
1992 ....Atlanta (W) 4, Pitsburgh (E) 3
1993 ....Philadelphia (E) 4, Atlanta (W) 2
1994 ....Playoffs canceled due to players' strike.
1995 ....Atlanta (E) 4, Cincinnati (C) 0
1996 ....Atlanta (E) 4, St. Louis (C) 3
1997 ....Florida (wc) 4, Atlanta (E) 2
1998 ....San Diego (W) 4, Atlanta (E) 2
1999 ....Atlanta (E) 4, New York (wc) 2
2000 ....New York (wc) 4, St. Louis (C) 1
2001 ....Arizona (W) 4, Atlanta (E) 1
2002 ....San Francisco (wc) 4, St. Louis (C) 1
2003 ....Florida (wc) 4, Chicago (C) 3
2004 ....St. Louis (C) 4, Houston (wc) 3
2005 ....Houston (wc) 4, St. Louis (C) 2
2006 ....St. Louis (C) 4, New York (E) 3
2007 ....Colorado (wc) 4, Arizona (W) 0
2008 ....Philadelphia (E) 4, Los Angeles (W) 1
2009 ....Philadelphia (E) 4, Los Angeles (W) 1
2010 ....San Francisco (W) 4, Philadelphia (E) 2

American League

1969 ....Baltimore (E) 3, Minnesota (W) 0
1970 ....Baltimore (E) 3, Minnesota (W) 0
1971 ....Baltimore (E) 3, Oakland (W) 0
1972 ....Oakland (W) 3, Detroit (E) 2
1973 ....Oakland (W) 3, Baltimore (E) 2
1974 ....Oakland (W) 3, Baltimore (E) 1
1975 ....Boston (E) 3, Oakland (W) 0
1976 ....New York (E) 3, Kansas City (W) 2
1977 ....New York (E) 3, Kansas City (W) 2
1978 ....New York (E) 3, Kansas City (W) 1
1979 ....Baltimore (E) 3, California (W) 1
1980 ....Kansas City (W) 3, New York (E) 0
1981 ....New York (E) 3, Oakland (W) 0
1982 ....Milwaukee (E) 3, California (W) 2
1983 ....Baltimore (E) 3, Chicago (W) 1
1984 ....Detroit (E) 3, Kansas City (W) 0
1985 ....Kansas City (W) 4, Toronto (E) 3
1986 ....Boston (E) 4, California (W) 3
1987 ....Minnesota (W) 4, Detroit (E) 1
1988 ....Oakland (W) 4, Boston (E) 0
1989 ....Oakland (W) 4, Toronto (E) 1
1990 ....Oakland (W) 4, Boston (E) 0
1991 ....Minnesota (W) 4, Toronto (E) 1
1992 ....Toronto (E) 4, Oakland (W) 2
1993 ....Toronto (E) 4, Chicago (W) 2
1994 ....Playoffs canceled due to players' strike.
1995 ....Cleveland (C) 4, Seattle (W) 2
1996 ....New York (E) 4, Baltimore (wc) 1
1997 ....Cleveland (C) 4, Baltimore (E) 2
1998 ....New York (E) 4, Cleveland (C) 2
1999 ....New York (E) 4, Boston (wc) 1
2000 ....New York (E) 4, Seattle (wc) 2
2001 ....New York (E) 4, Seattle (W) 1
2002 ....Anaheim (wc) 4, Minnesota (C) 1
2003 ....New York (E) 4, Boston (wc) 3
2004 ....Boston (wc) 4, New York (E) 3
2005 ....Chicago (C) 4, Los Angeles (W) 1
2006 ....Detroit (wc) 4, Oakland (W) 0
2007 ....Boston (E) 4, Cleveland (C) 3
2008 ....Tampa Bay (E) 4, Boston (wc) 3
2009 ....New York (E) 4, Los Angeles (W) 2
2010 ....Texas (W) 4, New York (E) 2

NLCS Most Valuable Player

1977 ....Dusty Baker, LA
1978 ....Steve Garvey, LA
1979 ....Willie Stargell, Pitt
1980 ....Manny Trillo, Phi
1981 ....Burt Hooton, LA
1982 ....Darrell Porter, StL
1983 ....Gary Matthews, Phi
1984 ....Steve Garvey, SD
1985 ....Ozzie Smith, StL
1986 ....Mike Scott, Hou
1987 ....Jeffrey Leonard, SF
1988 ....Orel Hershiser, LA

1989 ....Will Clark, SF
1990 ....R. Myers/R. Dibble, Cin
1991 ....Steve Avery, Atl
1992 ....John Smoltz, Atl
1993 ....Curt Schilling, Phi
1994 ....Playoffs canceled
1995 ....Mike Devereaux, Atl
1996 ....Javier Lopez, Atl
1997 ....Livan Hernandez, Fla
1998 ....Sterling Hitchcock, SD
1999 ....Eddie Perez, Atl
2000 ....Mike Hampton, NY

2001 ....Craig Counsell, Ariz
2002 ....Benito Santiago, SF
2003 ....Ivan Rodriguez, Fla
2004 ....Albert Pujols, StL
2005 ....Roy Oswalt, Hou
2006 ....Jeff Suppan, StL
2007 ....Matt Holliday, Col
2008 ....Cole Hamels, Phi
2009 ....Ryan Howard, Phi
2010 ....Cody Ross, SF

ALCS Most Valuable Player

1980 ....Frank White, KC
1981 ....Graig Nettles, NY
1982 ....Fred Lynn, Calif
1983 ....Mike Boddicker, Balt
1984 ....Kirk Gibson, Det
1985 ....George Brett, KC
1986 ....Marty Barrett, Bos
1987 ....Gary Gaetti, Minn
1988 ....Dennis Eckersley, Oak
1989 ....Rickey Henderson, Oak
1990 ....Dave Stewart, Oak

1991 ....Kirby Puckett, Minn
1992 ....Roberto Alomar, Tor
1993 ....Dave Stewart, Tor
1994 ....Playoffs canceled
1995 ....Orel Hershiser, Clev
1996 ....Bernie Williams, NY
1997 ....Marquis Grissom, Clev
1998 ....David Wells, NY
1999 ....Orlando Hernandez, NY
2000 ....David Justice, NY
2001 ....Andy Pettitte, NY

2002 ....Adam Kennedy, Ana
2003 ....Mariano Rivera, NY
2004 ....David Ortiz, Bos
2005 ....Paul Konerko, Chi
2006 ....Placido Polanco, Det
2007 ....Josh Beckett, Bos
2008 ....Matt Garza, TB
2009 ........C.C. Sabathia, NY
2010 ....Josh Hamilton, Tex

Divisional Playoffs

National League

1995	Atlanta (E) 3, Colorado (wc) 1
	Cincinnati (C) 3, Los Angeles (W) 0
1996	St. Louis (C) 3, San Diego (W) 0
	Atlanta (E) 3, Los Angeles (wc) 0
1997	Atlanta (E) 3, Houston (C) 0
	Florida (wc) 3, San Francisco (W) 0
1998	San Diego (W) 3, Houston (C) 1
	Atlanta (E) 3, Chicago (wc) 0
1999	Atlanta (E) 3, Houston (C) 1
	New York (wc) 3, Arizona (W) 1
2000	St. Louis (C) 3, Atlanta (E) 0
	New York (wc) 3, San Francisco (W) 1
2001	Atlanta (E) 3, Houston (C) 0
	Arizona (W) 3, St. Louis (wc) 2
2002	St. Louis (C) 3, Arizona (W) 0
	San Francisco (wc) 3, Atlanta (E) 2
2003	Chicago (C) 3, Atlanta (E) 2
	Florida (wc) 3, San Francisco (W) 1
2004	St. Louis (C) 3, Los Angeles (W) 1
	Houston (wc) 3, Atlanta (E) 2
2005	Houston (wc) 3, Atlanta (E) 1
	St. Louis (C) 3, San Diego (W) 1
2006	St. Louis (C) 3, San Diego (W) 1
	New York (E) 3, Los Angeles (wc) 0
2007	Colorado (wc) 3, Philadelphia (E) 0
	Arizona (W) 3, Chicago (C) 0
2008	Los Angeles (W) 3, Chicago (C) 0
	Philadelphia (E) 3, Milwaukee (wc) 1
2009	Los Angeles (W) 3, St. Louis, (C) 0
	Philadelphia (E) 3, Colorado (wc) 1
2010	San Francisco (W) 3, Atlanta, (wc) 1
	Philadelphia (E) 3, Cincinnati (C) 0

American League

1995	Cleveland (C) 3, Boston (E) 0
	Seattle (W) 3, New York (wc) 2
1996	Baltimore (wc) 3, Cleveland (C) 1
	New York (E) 3, Texas (W) 1
1997	Baltimore (E) 3, Seattle (W) 1
	Cleveland (C) 3, New York (wc) 2
1998	New York (E) 3, Texas (W) 0
	Cleveland (C) 3, Boston (wc) 1
1999	New York (E) 3, Texas (W) 0
	Boston (wc) 3, Cleveland (C) 2
2000	New York (E) 3, Oakland (W) 2
	Seattle (W) 3, Chicago (C) 0
2001	Seattle (W) 3, Cleveland (wc) 2
	New York (E) 3, Oakland (wc) 2
2002	Minnesota (C) 3, Oakland (W) 2
	Anaheim (W) 3, New York (E) 1
2003	New York (E) 3, Minnesota (C) 1
	Boston (wc) 3, Oakland (W) 2
2004	New York (E) 3, Minnesota (C) 1
	Boston (wc) 3 Anaheim (W) 0
2005	Los Angeles (W) 3, New York (E) 2
	Chicago (C) 3, Boston (wc) 0
2006	Oakland (W) 3, Minnesota (C) 0
	Detroit (wc) 3, New York (E) 1
2007	Boston (E) 3, Los Angeles (W) 0
	Cleveland (C) 3, New York (wc) 1
2008	Boston (wc) 3, Los Angeles (W) 1
	Tampa Bay (E) 3, Chicago (C) 1
2009	Los Angeles (W) 3, Boston (wc) 0
	New York (E) 3, Minnesota (C) 0
2010	Texas (W) 3, Tampa Bay (E) 2
	New York (wc) 3, Minnesota (C) 0

The All-Star Game

Results

Date	Winner	Score	Site
7-6-33	American	4–2	Comiskey Park, Chi
7-10-34	American	9-7	Polo Grounds, NY
7-8-35	American	4–1	Municipal Stadium, Clev
7-7-36	National	4–3	Braves Field, Bos
7-7-37	American	8–3	Griffith Stadium, Wash
7-6-38	National	4–1	Crosley Field, Cin
7-11-39	American	3–1	Yankee Stadium, NY
7-10-40	National	4–0	Sportsman's Park, StL
7-8-41	American	7–5	Briggs Stadium, Det
7-6-42	American	3–1	Polo Grounds, NY
7-13-43	American	5–3	Shibe Park, Phi
7-11-44	National	7–1	Forbes Field, Pitt
1945	No game due to wartime travel restrictions.		
7-9-46	American	12–0	Fenway Park, Bos
7-8-47	American	2–1	Wrigley Field, Chi
7-13-48	American	5–2	Sportsman's Park, StL
7-12-49	American	11–7	Ebbets Field, Bklyn
7-11-50	National	4–3	Comiskey Park, Chi
7-10-51	National	8–3	Briggs Stadium, Det
7-8-52	National	3–2	Shibe Park, Phi
7-14-53	National	5–1	Crosley Field, Cin
7-13-54	American	11–9	Municipal Stadium, Clev
7-12-55	National	6–5	County Stadium, Mil
7-10-56	National	7–3	Griffith Stadium, Wash
7-9-57	American	6–5	Busch Stadium, StL
7-8-58	American	4–3	Memorial Stadium, Balt
7-7-59	National	5–4	Forbes Field, Pitt
8-3-59	American	5–3	Memorial Coliseum, LA
7-11-60	National	5–3	Municipal Stadium, KC
7-13-60	National	6–0	Yankee Stadium, NY
7-11-61	National	5–4	Candlestick Park, SF
7-31-61	Tie*	1–1	Fenway Park, Bos
7-10-62	National	3–1	D.C. Stadium, Wash
7-30-62	American	9–4	Wrigley Field, Chi
7-9-63	National	5–3	Municipal Stadium, Clev
7-7-64	National	7–4	Shea Stadium, NY
7-13-65	National	6–5	Metro. Stadium, Minn
7-12-66	National	2–1	Busch Stadium, StL
7-11-67	National	2–1	Anaheim Stadium, Cal
7-9-68	National	1–0	Astrodome, Hou
7-23-69	National	9–3	R.F.K. Stadium, Wash.
7-14-70	National	5–4	Riverfront Stadium, Cin
7-13-71	American	6–4	Tiger Stadium, Det
7-25-72	National	4–3	Atlanta Stadium, Atl
7-24-73	National	7–1	Royals Stadium, KC
7-23-74	National	7–2	Three Rivers Stadium, Pitt
7-15-75	National	6–3	County Stadium, Mil
7-13-76	National	7–1	Veterans Stadium, Phi
7-19-77	National	7–5	Yankee Stadium, NY
7-11-78	National	7–3	Jack Murphy Stadium, SD
7-17-79	National	7–6	Kingdome, Sea
7-8-80	National	4–2	Dodger Stadium, LA
8-9-81	National	5–4	Municipal Stadium, Clev
7-13-82	National	4–1	Olympic Stadium, Mtl
7-6-83	American	13–3	Comiskey Park, Chi
7-10-84	National	3–1	Candlestick Park, SF
7-16-85	National	6–1	Metrodome, Minn
7-15-86	American	3–2	Astrodome, Hou
7-14-87	National	2–0	Oakland Coliseum, Oak
7-12-88	American	2–1	Riverfront Stadium, Cin
7-11-89	American	5–3	Anaheim Stadium, Cal
7-10-90	American	2–0	Wrigley Field, Chi
7-9-91	American	4–2	SkyDome, Tor
7-14-92	American	13–6	Jack Murphy Stadium, SD

*Game called because of rain after nine innings.

Results (Cont.)

Date	Winner	Score	Site	Date	Winner	Score	Site
7-13-93	American	9–3	Camden Yards, Balt	7-9-02	Tie (11 inn)	7–7	Miller Park, Mil
7-12-94	National	8–7	Three Rivers Stadium, Pitt	7-15-03	American	7–6	Comiskey Park, Chi
7-11-95	National	3–2	Ballpark in Arlington, Tex	7-13-04	American	9–4	Minute Maid Park, Hou
7-9-96	National	6–0	Veterans Stadium, Phi	7-12-05	American	7–5	Comerica Park, Det
7-8-97	American	3–1	Jacobs Field, Cle	7-11-06	American	3–2	PNC Park, Pitt
7-7-98	American	13–8	Coors Field, Col	7-10-07	American	5–4	AT&T Park, SF
7-13-99	American	4–1	Fenway Park, Bos	7-15-08	American	4–3	Yankee Stadium, NY
7-11-00	American	6–3	Turner Field, Atl	7-14-09	American	4–3	Busch Stadium, StL
7-10-01	American	4–1	Safeco Field, Sea	7-13-10	National	3–1	Angel Stadium, LA

Most Valuable Players

1962	Maury Wills, LA	NL	1977	Don Sutton, LA	NL	1994	Fred McGriff, Atl	NL
	Leon Wagner, LA	AL	1978	Steve Garvey, LA	NL	1995	Jeff Conine, Fla	NL
1963	Willie Mays, SF	NL	1979	Dave Parker, Pitt	NL	1996	Mike Piazza, LA	NL
1964	Johnny Callison, Phi	NL	1980	Ken Griffey, Cin	NL	1997	Sandy Alomar, Clev	AL
1965	Juan Marichal, SF	NL	1981	Gary Carter, Mtl	NL	1998	Roberto Alomar, Balt	AL
1966	Brooks Robinson, Balt	AL	1982	Dave Concepcion, Cin	NL	1999	Pedro Martinez, Bos	AL
1967	Tony Perez, Cin	NL	1983	Fred Lynn, Calif	AL	2000	Derek Jeter, NY	AL
1968	Willie Mays, SF	NL	1984	Gary Carter, Mtl	NL	2001	Cal Ripken Jr., Balt	AL
1969	Willie McCovey, SF	NL	1985	LaMarr Hoyt, SD	NL	2002	None selected	
1970	Carl Yastrzemski, Bos	AL	1986	Roger Clemens, Bos	AL	2003	Garret Anderson, Ana	AL
1971	Frank Robinson, Balt	AL	1987	Tim Raines, Mtl	NL	2004	Alfonso Soriano, Tex	AL
1972	Joe Morgan, Cin	NL	1988	Terry Steinbach, Oak	AL	2005	Miguel Tejada, Balt	AL
1973	Bobby Bonds, SF	NL	1989	Bo Jackson, KC	AL	2006	Michael Young, Tex	AL
1974	Steve Garvey, LA	NL	1990	Julio Franco, Tex	AL	2007	Ichiro Suzuki, Sea	AL
1975	Bill Madlock, Chi	NL	1991	Cal Ripken Jr., Balt	AL	2008	J.D. Drew, Bos	AL
	Jon Matlack, NY	NL	1992	Ken Griffey Jr., Sea	AL	2009	Carl Crawford, TB	AL
1976	George Foster, Cin	NL	1993	Kirby Puckett, Minn	AL	2010	Brian McCann, Atl	NL

The Regular Season

Most Valuable Players

NATIONAL LEAGUE

Year	Name and Team	Position	Noteworthy
1911	Wildfire Schulte, Chi	Outfield	21 HR†, 121 RBI†, .300
1912	*Larry Doyle, NY	Second base	10 HR, 90 RBI, .330
1913	Jake Daubert, Bklyn	First base	52 RBI, .350†
1914	*Johnny Evers, Bos	Second base	FA .976†, .279
1915–23	No selection		
1924	Dazzy Vance, Bklyn	Pitcher	28†–6, 2.16 ERA†, 262 K†
1925	Rogers Hornsby, StL	Second base, Manager	39 HR†, 143 RBI†, .403†
1926	*Bob O'Farrell, StL	Catcher	7 HR, 68 RBI, .293
1927	*Paul Waner, Pitt	Outfield	237 hits†, 131 RBI†, .380†
1928	*Jim Bottomley, StL	First base	31 HR†, 136 RBI†, .325
1929	*Rogers Hornsby, Chi	Second base	39 HR, 149 RBI, 156 runs†, .380
1930	No selection		
1931	*Frankie Frisch, StL	Second base	4 HR, 82 RBI, 28 SB†, .311
1932	Chuck Klein, Phi	Outfield	38 HR†, 137 RBI, 226 hits†, .348
1933	*Carl Hubbell, NY	Pitcher	23†–12, 1.66 ERA†, 10 SO†
1934	*Dizzy Dean, StL	Pitcher	30†–7, 2.66 ERA, 195 K†
1935	*Gabby Hartnett, Chi	Catcher	13 HR, 91 RBI, .344
1936	*Carl Hubbell, NY	Pitcher	26†–6, 2.31 ERA†
1937	Joe Medwick, StL	Outfield	31 HR‡, 154 RBI†, 111 runs†, .374†
1938	Ernie Lombardi, Cin	Catcher	19 HR, 95 RBI, .342†
1939	*Bucky Walters, Cin	Pitcher	27†–11, 2.29 ERA†, 137 K‡
1940	*Frank McCormick, Cin	First base	19 HR, 127 RBI, 191 hits†, .309
1941	*Dolph Camilli, Bklyn	First base	34 HR†, 120 RBI†, .285
1942	*Mort Cooper, StL	Pitcher	22†–7, 1.78 ERA†, 10 SO†
1943	*Stan Musial, StL	Outfield	13 HR, 81 RBI, 220 hits†, .357†
1944	*Marty Marion, StL	Shortstop	FA .972†, 63 RBI
1945	*Phil Cavarretta, Chi	First base	6 HR, 97 RBI, .355†
1946	*Stan Musial, StL	First base, Outfield	103 RBI, 124 runs†, 228 hits†, .365†
1947	Bob Elliott, Bos	Third base	22 HR, 113 RBI, .317
1948	Stan Musial, StL	Outfield	39 HR, 131 RBI†, .376†
1949	*Jackie Robinson, Bklyn	Second base	16 HR, 124 RBI, 37 SB†, .342†

*Played for pennant or, after 1968, division winner. †Led league. ‡Tied for league lead.

Most Valuable Players *(Cont.)*
NATIONAL LEAGUE *(Cont.)*

Year	Name and Team	Position	Noteworthy
1950	*Jim Konstanty, Phi	Pitcher	16–7, 22 saves†, 2.66 ERA
1951	Roy Campanella, Bklyn	Catcher	33 HR, 108 RBI, .325
1952	Hank Sauer, Chi	Outfield	37 HR‡, 121 RBI†, .270
1953	*Roy Campanella, Bklyn	Catcher	41 HR, 142 RBI†, .312
1954	*Willie Mays, NY	Outfield	41 HR, 110 RBI, 13 3B†, .345†
1955	*Roy Campanella, Bklyn	Catcher	32 HR, 107 RBI, .318
1956	*Don Newcombe, Bklyn	Pitcher	27†–7, 3.06 ERA
1957	*Hank Aaron, Mil	Outfield	44 HR†, 132 RBI†, .322
1958	Ernie Banks, Chi	Shortstop	47 HR†, 129 RBI†, .313
1959	Ernie Banks, Chi	Shortstop	45 HR, 143 RBI†, .304
1960	*Dick Groat, Pitt	Shortstop	2 HR, 50 RBI, .325†
1961	*Frank Robinson, Cin	Outfield	37 HR, 124 RBI, .323
1962	Maury Wills, LA	Shortstop	104 SB†, 208 hits, .299, GG
1963	*Sandy Koufax, LA	Pitcher	25‡–5, 1.88 ERA†, 306 K†
1964	*Ken Boyer, StL	Third Base	24 HR, 119 RBI†, .295
1965	Willie Mays, SF	Outfield	52 HR†, 112 RBI, .317, GG
1966	Roberto Clemente, Pitt	Outfield	29 HR, 119 RBI, 202 hits, .317, GG
1967	*Orlando Cepeda, StL	First base	25 HR, 111 RBI†, .325
1968	*Bob Gibson, StL	Pitcher	22–9, 1.12 ERA†, 268 K†, 13 SO†, GG
1969	Willie McCovey, SF	First base	45 HR†, 126 RBI†, .320
1970	*Johnny Bench, Cin	Catcher	45 HR†, 148 RBI†, .293, GG
1971	Joe Torre, StL	Third base	24 HR, 137 RBI†, .363†
1972	*Johnny Bench, Cin	Catcher	40 HR†, 125 RBI†, .270, GG
1973	*Pete Rose, Cin	Outfield	5 HR, 64 RBI, .338†, 230 hits†
1974	*Steve Garvey, LA	First base	21 HR, 111 RBI, 200 hits, .312, GG
1975	*Joe Morgan, Cin	Second base	17 HR, 94 RBI, 67 SB, .327, GG
1976	*Joe Morgan, Cin	Second base	27 HR, 111 RBI, 60 SB, .320, GG
1977	George Foster, Cin	Outfield	52 HR†, 149 RBI†, .320
1978	Dave Parker, Pitt	Outfield	30 HR, 117 RBI, .334†, GG
1979	Keith Hernandez, StL	First base	11 HR, 105 RBI, 210 hits, .344†, GG
	*Willie Stargell, Pitt	First base	32 HR, 82 RBI, .281
1980	*Mike Schmidt, Phi	Third base	48 HR†, 121 RBI†, .286, GG
1981	Mike Schmidt, Phi	Third base	31 HR†, 91 RBI†, 78 runs†, .316, GG
1982	*Dale Murphy, Atl	Outfield	36 HR, 109 RBI‡, .281, GG
1983	Dale Murphy, Atl	Outfield	36 HR, 121 RBI†, .302, GG
1984	*Ryne Sandberg, Chi	Second base	19 HR, 84 RBI, 114 runs†, .314, GG
1985	*Willie McGee, StL	Outfield	10 HR, 82 RBI, 18 3B†, .353†, GG
1986	Mike Schmidt, Phi	Third base	37 HR†, 119 RBI†, .290, GG
1987	Andre Dawson, Chi	Outfield	49 HR†, 137 RBI†, .287, GG
1988	*Kirk Gibson, LA	Outfield	25 HR, 76 RBI, 106 runs, .290
1989	*Kevin Mitchell, SF	Outfield	47 HR†, 125 RBI†, .291
1990	*Barry Bonds, Pitt	Outfield	33 HR, 114 RBI, .301
1991	*Terry Pendleton, Atl	Third base	23 HR, 86 RBI, .319†
1992	Barry Bonds, Pitt	Outfield	34 HR, 103 RBI, .311
1993	Barry Bonds, SF	Outfield	46 HR†, 123 RBI†, .336
1994	Jeff Bagwell, Hou	First base	39 HR, 116 RBI†, .368
1995	*Barry Larkin, Cin	Shortstop	15 HR, 66 RBI, 51 SB, .319
1996	*Ken Caminiti, SD	Third base	40 HR, 130 RBI, .326
1997	Larry Walker, Col	Outfield	49 HR†, 130 RBI, .452 OBA†, .366, GG
1998	Sammy Sosa, Chi	Outfield	66 HR, 158 RBI†, 134 runs†, 416 TB†, .308
1999	*Chipper Jones, Atl	Third Base	45 HR, 110 RBI, 116 runs, .319
2000	*Jeff Kent, SF	Second Base	33 HR, 125 RBI, 114 runs, .334
2001	Barry Bonds, SF	Outfield	73 HR†, 137 RBI. 177 BB†, .328, .863 SLG†
2002	*Barry Bonds, SF	Outfield	46 HR, 110 RBI, .582 OBP, 198 BB†, .370
2003	*Barry Bonds, SF	Outfield	45 HR, .341, .529 OBP†, .749 SLG†
2004	Barry Bonds, SF	Outfield	45HR, 101 RBI, .609 OBP, .812 SLG
2005	*Albert Pujols, StL	First Base	41 HR, 117 RBI, .330, .430 OBP†, .609 SLG†
2006	Ryan Howard, Phi	First Base	58 HR†, 149 RBI†, .313, .425 OBP, .659 SLG
2007	*Jimmy Rollins, Phi	Shortstop	30 HR, 94 RBI, .296, 139 runs, 41 SB, GG
2008	Albert Pujols, StL	First Base	37HR, 116RBI, 100 runs, .357, .653 SLG
2009	*Albert Pujols, StL	First Base	47HR, 135RBI, 124 runs, .327, .658 SLG

*Played for pennant or, after 1968, division winner. †Led league. ‡Tied for league lead.

Most Valuable Players (Cont.)

AMERICAN LEAGUE

Year	Name and Team	Position	Noteworthy
1911	Ty Cobb, Det	Outfield	8 HR, 144 RBI†, 24 3B†, .420†
1912	*Tris Speaker, Bos	Outfield	10 HR‡, 98 RBI, 53 2B†, .383
1913	Walter Johnson, Wash	Pitcher	36†–7, 1.09 ERA†, 11 SO†, 243 K†
1914	*Eddie Collins, Phi	Second base	2 HR, 85 RBI, 122 runs†, .344
1915–21	No selection		
1922	George Sisler, StL	First base	8 HR, 105 RBI, 246 hits†, .420†
1923	*Babe Ruth, NY	Outfield	41 HR†, 131 RBI†, .393
1924	*Walter Johnson, Wash	Pitcher	23†–7, 2.72 ERA†, 158 K†
1925	*Roger Peckinpaugh, Wash	Shortstop	4 HR, 64 RBI, .294
1926	George Burns, Clev	First base	114 RBI, 216 hits‡, 64 2B†, .358
1927	*Lou Gehrig, NY	First base	47 HR, 175 RBI†, 52 2B†, .373
1928	Mickey Cochrane, Phi	Catcher	10 HR, 57 RBI, .293
1929	No selection		
1930	No selection		
1931	*Lefty Grove, Phi	Pitcher	31†–4, 2.06 ERA†, 175 K†
1932	Jimmie Foxx, Phi	First base	58 HR†, 169 RBI†, 151 runs†, .364
1933	Jimmie Foxx, Phi	First base	48 HR†, 163 RBI†, .356†
1934	*Mickey Cochrane, Det	Catcher	2 HR, 76 RBI, .320
1935	*Hank Greenberg, Det	First base	36 HR‡, 170 RBI†, 203 hits, .328
1936	*Lou Gehrig, NY	First base	49 HR†, 152 RBI, 167 runs†, .354
1937	Charlie Gehringer, Det	Second base	14 HR, 96 RBI, 133 runs, .371†
1938	Jimmie Foxx, Bos	First base	50 HR, 175 RBI†, .349†
1939	*Joe DiMaggio, NY	Outfield	30 HR, 126 RBI, .381†
1940	*Hank Greenberg, Det	Outfield	41 HR†, 150 RBI†, 50 2B†, .340
1941	*Joe DiMaggio, NY	Outfield	30 HR, 125 RBI†, .357
1942	*Joe Gordon, NY	Second base	18 HR, 103 RBI, .322
1943	*Spud Chandler, NY	Pitcher	20†–4, 1.64 ERA†, 5 SO‡
1944	Hal Newhouser, Det	Pitcher	29†–9, 2.22 ERA†, 187 K†
1945	*Hal Newhouser, Det	Pitcher	25†–9, 1.81 ERA†, 8 SO†, 212 K†
1946	*Ted Williams, Bos	Outfield	38 HR, 123 RBI, 142 runs†, .342
1947	*Joe DiMaggio, NY	Outfield	20 HR, 97 RBI, .315
1948	*Lou Boudreau, Clev	Shortstop	18 HR, 106 RBI, .355
1949	Ted Williams, Bos	Outfield	43 HR†, 159 RBI‡, 150 runs†, .343
1950	*Phil Rizzuto, NY	Shortstop	125 runs, 200 hits, .324
1951	*Yogi Berra, NY	Catcher	27 HR, 88 RBI, .294
1952	Bobby Shantz, Phi	Pitcher	24†–7, 2.48 ERA
1953	Al Rosen, Clev	Third base	43 HR†, 145 RBI†, 115 runs†, .336
1954	Yogi Berra, NY	Catcher	22 HR, 125 RBI, .307
1955	*Yogi Berra, NY	Catcher	27 HR, 108 RBI, .272
1956	*Mickey Mantle, NY	Outfield	52 HR†, 130 RBI†, 132 runs†, .353†
1957	*Mickey Mantle, NY	Outfield	34 HR, 94 RBI, 121 runs†, .365
1958	Jackie Jensen, Bos	Outfield	35 HR, 122 RBI†, .286
1959	*Nellie Fox, Chi	Second base	2 HR, 70 RBI, .306, GG
1960	*Roger Maris, NY	Outfield	39 HR, 112 RBI†, .283, GG
1961	*Roger Maris, NY	Outfield	61 HR†, 142 RBI†, .269
1962	*Mickey Mantle, NY	Outfield	30 HR, 89 RBI, .321, GG
1963	*Elston Howard, NY	Catcher	28 HR, 85 RBI, .287, GG
1964	Brooks Robinson, Balt	Third base	28 HR, 118 RBI†, .317, GG
1965	*Zoilo Versalles, Minn	Shortstop	126 runs†, 45 2B†, 12 3B‡, GG
1966	*Frank Robinson, Balt	Outfield	49 HR†, 122 RBI†, 122 runs†, .316†
1967	*Carl Yastrzemski, Bos	Outfield	44 HR‡, 121 RBI†, 112 runs†, .326†, GG
1968	*Denny McLain, Det	Pitcher	31†–6, 1.96 ERA, 280 K
1969	*Harmon Killebrew, Minn	Third base, First base	49 HR†, 140 RBI†, .276
1970	*Boog Powell, Balt	First base	35 HR, 114 RBI, .297
1971	*Vida Blue, Oak	Pitcher	24–8, 1.82 ERA†, 8 SO†, 301 K
1972	Dick Allen, Chi	First base	37 HR†, 113 RBI†, .308
1973	*Reggie Jackson, Oak	Outfield	32 HR†, 117 RBI†, 99 runs†, .293
1974	Jeff Burroughs, Tex	Outfield	25 HR, 118 RBI†, .301
1975	*Fred Lynn, Bos	Outfield	21 HR, 105 RBI, 103 runs†, .331, GG
1976	*Thurman Munson, NY	Catcher	17 HR, 105 RBI, .302
1977	Rod Carew, Minn	First base	100 RBI, 128 runs†, 239 hits†, .388†
1978	Jim Rice, Bos	Outfield, DH	46 HR†, 139 RBI†, 213 hits†, .315
1979	*Don Baylor, Calif	Outfield, DH	36 HR, 139 RBI†, 120 runs†, .296
1980	*George Brett, KC	Third base	24 HR, 118 RBI, .390†
1981	*Rollie Fingers, Mil	Pitcher	6–3, 28 saves†, 1.04 ERA
1982	*Robin Yount, Mil	Shortstop	29 HR, 114 RBI, 210 hits†, .331, GG

Most Valuable Players *(Cont.)*

AMERICAN LEAGUE *(Cont.)*

Year	Name and Team	Position	Noteworthy
1983	*Cal Ripken Jr., Balt	Shortstop	27 HR, 102 RBI, 121 runs†, 211 hits†, .318
1984	*Willie Hernandez, Det	Pitcher	9–3, 32 saves, 1.92 ERA
1985	Don Mattingly, NY	First base	35 HR, 145 RBI†, 48 2B†, .324, GG
1986	*Roger Clemens, Bos	Pitcher	24†–4, 2.48 ERA†, 238 K
1987	George Bell, Tor	Outfield	47 HR, 134 RBI†, .308
1988	*Jose Canseco, Oak	Outfield	42 HR†, 124 RBI†, 40 SB, .307
1989	Robin Yount, Mil	Outfield	21 HR, 103 RBI, 101 runs, .318
1990	*Rickey Henderson, Oak	Outfield	28 HR, 119 runs†, 65 SB†, .325
1991	Cal Ripken Jr., Balt	Shortstop	34 HR, 114 RBI, .323
1992	Dennis Eckersley, Oak	Pitcher	7–1, 1.91 ERA, 51 saves
1993	Frank Thomas, Chi	First base	41 HR, 128 RBI, .317
1994	Frank Thomas, Chi	First base	38 HR, 101 RBI, .353
1995	*Mo Vaughn, Bos	First base	39 HR, 126 RBI, .300
1996	*Juan Gonzalez, Tex	Outfield	47 HR, 144 RBI, .314
1997	*Ken Griffey Jr., Sea	Outfield	56 HR†, 125 runs†, 393 TB†, 147 RBI†, .304
1998	*Juan Gonzalez, Tex	Outfield	45 HR, 157 RBI†, 50 2B†, .318
1999	*Ivan Rodriguez, Tex	Catcher	35 HR, 113 RBI, 116 runs, .332, GG
2000	*Jason Giambi, Oak	First Base	43 HR, 137 RBI, .333
2001	*Ichiro Suzuki, Sea	Outfield	.350†, 242 H†, 127 runs, 56 SB†, GG
2002	*Miguel Tejada, Oak	Shortstop	34 HR, 131 RBI, .308
2003	Alex Rodriguez, Tex	Shortstop	47 HR†, 118 RBI, .600 SLG†, GG
2004	*Vladimir Guerrero, Ana	Outfield	39 HR, 126 RBI, .598 SLG
2005	*Alex Rodriguez, NYY	Third Base	48 HR†, 130 RBI, .610 SLG†
2006	*Justin Morneau, Min	First Base	30HR, 130 RBI, .321, 190 hits
2007	Alex Rodriguez, NYY	Third Base	54 HR, 156 RBI, .314, 183 hits, 24 SB
2008	Dustin Pedroia, Bos	Second Base	17 HR, 118 runs, 213 hits, .326, 20 SB, GG
2009	*Joe Mauer, Min	Catcher	28 HR, 94 runs, 96 RBIs, 191 hits, .365, GG

*Played for pennant or, after 1968, division winner. †Led league. ‡Tied for league lead.
Notes: 2B=doubles; 3B=triples; FA=fielding average; GG=won Gold Glove, award begun in 1957;
K=strikeouts; O=shutouts; SB=stolen bases; TB=total bases.

Rookies of the Year

NATIONAL LEAGUE		AMERICAN LEAGUE	
1947*	Jackie Robinson, Bklyn (1B)	1949	Roy Sievers, StL (OF)
1948*	Alvin Dark, Bos (SS)	1950	Walt Dropo, Bos (1B)
1949	Don Newcombe, Bklyn (P)	1951	Gil McDougald, NY (3B)
1950	Sam Jethroe, Bos (OF)	1952	Harry Byrd, Phi (P)
1951	Willie Mays, NY (OF)	1953	Harvey Kuenn, Det (SS)
1952	Joe Black, Bklyn (P)	1954	Bob Grim, NY (P)
1953	Junior Gilliam, Bklyn (2B)	1955	Herb Score, Clev (P)
1954	Wally Moon, StL (OF)	1956	Luis Aparicio, Chi (SS)
1955	Bill Virdon, StL (OF)	1957	Tony Kubek, NY (OF, SS)
1956	Frank Robinson, Cin (OF)	1958	Albie Pearson, Wash (OF)
1957	Jack Sanford, Phi (P)	1959	Bob Allison, Wash (OF)
1958	Orlando Cepeda, SF (1B)	1960	Ron Hansen, Balt (SS)
1959	Willie McCovey, SF (1B)	1961	Don Schwall, Bos (P)
1960	Frank Howard, LA (OF)	1962	Tom Tresh, NY (SS)
1961	Billy Williams, Chi (OF)	1963	Gary Peters, Chi (P)
1962	Ken Hubbs, Chi (2B)	1964	Tony Oliva, Minn (OF)
1963	Pete Rose, Cin (2B)	1965	Curt Blefary, Balt (OF)
1964	Dick Allen, Phi (3B)	1966	Tommie Agee, Chi (OF)
1965	Jim Lefebvre, LA (2B)	1967	Rod Carew, Minn (2B)
1966	Tommy Helms, Cin (2B)	1968	Stan Bahnsen, NY (P)
1967	Tom Seaver, NY (P)	1969	Lou Piniella, KC (OF)
1968	Johnny Bench, Cin (C)	1970	Thurman Munson, NY (C)
1969	Ted Sizemore, LA (2B)	1971	Chris Chambliss, Clev (1B)
1970	Carl Morton, Mtl (P)	1972	Carlton Fisk, Bos (C)
1971	Earl Williams, Atl (C)	1973	Al Bumbry, Balt (OF)
1972	Jon Matlack, NY (P)	1974	Mike Hargrove, Tex (1B)
1973	Gary Matthews, SF (OF)	1975	Fred Lynn, Bos (OF)
1974	Bake McBride, StL (OF)	1976	Mark Fidrych, Det (P)
1975	John Montefusco, SF (P)	1977	Eddie Murray, Balt (DH)
1976	Pat Zachry, Cin (P)	1978	Lou Whitaker, Det (2B)
	Butch Metzger, SD (P)	1979	Alfredo Griffin, Tor (SS)
			John Castino, Minn (3B)

*Just one selection for both leagues.

Rookies of the Year *(Cont.)*

NATIONAL LEAGUE *(Cont.)*	AMERICAN LEAGUE *(Cont.)*
1977 ....Andre Dawson, Mtl (OF)	1980 ....Joe Charboneau, Clev (OF)
1978 ....Bob Horner, Atl (3B)	1981 ....Dave Righetti, NY (P)
1979 ....Rick Sutcliffe, LA (P)	1982 ....Cal Ripken Jr., Balt (SS)
1980 ....Steve Howe, LA (P)	1983 ....Ron Kittle, Chi (OF)
1981 ....Fernando Valenzuela, LA (P)	1984 ....Alvin Davis, Sea (1B)
1982 ....Steve Sax, LA (2B)	1985 ....Ozzie Guillen, Chi (SS)
1983 ....Darryl Strawberry, NY (OF)	1986 ....Jose Canseco, Oak (OF)
1984 ....Dwight Gooden, NY (P)	1987 ....Mark McGwire, Oak (1B)
1985 ....Vince Coleman, StL (OF)	1988 ....Walt Weiss, Oak (SS)
1986 ....Todd Worrell, StL (P)	1989 ....Gregg Olson, Balt (P)
1987 ....Benito Santiago, SD (C)	1990 ....Sandy Alomar Jr, Clev (C)
1988 ....Chris Sabo, Cin (3B)	1991 ....Chuck Knoblauch, Minn (2B)
1989 ....Jerome Walton, Chi (OF)	1992 ....Pat Listach, Mil (SS)
1990 ....Dave Justice, Atl (OF)	1993 ....Tim Salmon, Calif (OF)
1991 ....Jeff Bagwell, Hou (3B)	1994 ....Bob Hamelin, KC (DH)
1992 ....Eric Karros, LA (1B)	1995 ....Marty Cordova, Minn (OF)
1993 ....Mike Piazza, LA (C)	1996 ....Derek Jeter, NY (SS)
1994 ....Raul Mondesi, LA (OF)	1997 ....Nomar Garciaparra, Bos (SS)
1995 ....Hideo Nomo, LA (P)	1998 ....Ben Grieve, Oak (OF)
1996 ....Todd Hollandsworth, LA (OF)	1999 ....Carlos Beltran, KC (OF)
1997 ....Scott Rolen, Phi (3B)	2000 ....Kazuhiro Sasaki, Sea (P)
1998 ....Kerry Wood, Chi (P)	2001 ....Ichiro Suzuki, Sea (OF)
1999 ....Scott Williamson, Cin (P)	2002 ....Eric Hinske, Tor (3B)
2000 ....Rafael Furcal, Atl (SS)	2003 ....Angel Berroa, KC (SS)
2001 ....Albert Pujols, StL (OF)	2004 ....Bobby Crosby, Oak (SS)
2002 ....Jason Jennings, Col (P)	2005 ....Huston Street, Oak (P)
2003 ....Dontrelle Willis, Fla (P)	2006 ....Justin Verlander, Det (P)
2004 ....Jason Bay, Pit (OF)	2007 ....Dustin Pedroia, Bos (2B)
2005 ....Ryan Howard, Phi (1B)	2008 ....Evan Longoria, TB (3B)
2006 ....Hanley Ramirez, Fla (SS)	2009 ....Andrew Bailey, Oak (P)
2007 ....Ryan Braun, Mil (OF)	
2008 ....Geovany Soto, Chi (C)	
2009 ....Chris Coghlan, Fla (OF)	

2009 Gold Glove winners

NATIONAL LEAGUE	AMERICAN LEAGUE
C............................Yadier Molina, StL (2)	C............................Joe Mauer, Min (2)
P............................Adam Wainwright, StL	P............................Mark Buerhle, Chi
1B............................Adrian Gonzalez, SD (2)	1B............................Mark Teixeira, NY (3)
2B............................Orlando Hudson, LA (4)	2B............................Placido Polanco, Det (2)
SS............................Jimmy Rollins, Phi (3)	SS............................Derek Jeter, NY (4)
3B............................Ryan Zimmerman, Was	3B............................Evan Longoria, TB
OF ....Matt Kemp, LA	OF ....Ichiro Suzuki, Sea (9)
OF ....Michael Bourn, Hou	OF ....Adam Jones, Balt
OF ....Shane Victorino, Phi (2)	OF ....Torii Hunter, LA (9)

Note: Number in parentheses indicates career totals.

2009 Silver Slugger winners

NATIONAL LEAGUE	AMERICAN LEAGUE
C............................Brian McCann, Atl (3)	C............................Joe Mauer, Min (2)
P............................Carlos Zambrano, Chi (3)	DH............................Adam Lind, Tor
1B............................Albert Pujols, StL (3)	1B............................Mark Teixeira, NY (3)
2B............................Chase Utley, Phi (4)	2B............................Aaron Hill, Tor
SS............................Hanley Ramirez, Fla	SS............................Derek Jeter, NY (4)
3B............................Ryan Zimmerman, Was	3B............................Evan Longoria, TB
OF ....Matt Kemp, LA	OF ....Ichiro Suzuki, Sea (2)
OF ....Ryan Braun, Mil (2)	OF ....Jason Bay, Bos
OF ....Andre Ethier, LA	OF ....Torii Hunter, LA

Note: Number in parentheses indicates career totals.

Cy Young Award

Year	W–L	Sv	ERA	Year	W–L	Sv	ERA
1956....*Don Newcombe, Bklyn (NL)	27–7	0	3.06	1962....Don Drysdale, LA (NL)	25–9	1	2.83
1957....Warren Spahn, Mil (NL)	21–11	3	2.69	1963....*Sandy Koufax, LA (NL)	25–5	0	1.88
1958....Bob Turley, NY (AL)	21–7	1	2.97	1964....Dean Chance, LA (AL)	20–9	4	1.65
1959....Early Wynn, Chi (AL)	22–10	0	3.17	1965....Sandy Koufax, LA (NL)	26–8	2	2.04
1960....Vernon Law, Pitt (NL)	20–9	0	3.08	1966....Sandy Koufax, LA (NL)	27–9	0	1.73
1961....Whitey Ford, NY (AL)	25–4	0	3.21				

NATIONAL LEAGUE

Year	W–L	Sv	ERA
1967.....Mike McCormick, SF	22–10	0	2.85
1968.....*Bob Gibson, StL	22–9	0	1.12
1969.....Tom Seaver, NY	25–7	0	2.21
1970.....Bob Gibson, StL	23–7	0	3.12
1971.....Ferguson Jenkins, Chi	24–13	0	2.77
1972.....Steve Carlton, Phi	27–10	0	1.97
1973.....Tom Seaver, NY	19–10	0	2.08
1974.....Mike Marshall, LA	15–12	21	2.42
1975.....Tom Seaver, NY	22–9	0	2.38
1976.....Randy Jones, SD	22–14	0	2.74
1977.....Steve Carlton, Phi	23–10	0	2.64
1978.....Gaylord Perry, SD	21–6	0	2.72
1979.....Bruce Sutter, Chi	6–6	37	2.23
1980.....Steve Carlton, Phi	24–9	0	2.34
1981.....Fernando Valenzuela, LA	13–7	0	2.48
1982.....Steve Carlton, Phi	23–11	0	3.10
1983.....John Denny, Phi	19–6	0	2.37
1984.....†Rick Sutcliffe, Chi	16–1	0	2.69
1985.....Dwight Gooden, NY	24–4	0	1.53
1986.....Mike Scott, Hou	18–10	0	2.22
1987.....Steve Bedrosian, Phi	5–3	40	2.83
1988.....Orel Hershiser, LA	23–8	1	2.26
1989.....Mark Davis, SD	4–3	44	1.85
1990.....Doug Drabek, Pitt	22–6	0	2.76
1991.....Tom Glavine, Atl	20–11	0	2.55
1992.....Greg Maddux, Chi	20–11	0	2.18
1993.....Greg Maddux, Atl	20–10	0	2.36
1994.....Greg Maddux, Atl	16–6	0	1.56
1995.....Greg Maddux, Atl	19–2	0	1.63
1996.....John Smoltz, Atl	24–8	0	2.94
1997.....Pedro Martinez, Mtl	17–8	0	1.90
1998.....Tom Glavine, Atl	20–6	0	2.47
1999.....Randy Johnson, Ari	17–9	0	2.48
2000.....Randy Johnson, Ari	19–7	0	2.64
2001.....Randy Johnson, Ari	21–6	0	2.49
2002.....Randy Johnson, Ari	24–5	0	2.32
2003.....Eric Gagne, LA	2–3	55	1.20
2004.....Roger Clemens, Hou	18–4	0	2.98
2005.....Chris Carpenter, StL	21-5	0	2.83
2006.....Brandon Webb, Ari	16–8	0	3.10
2007.....Jake Peavy, SD	19–6	0	2.54
2008.....Tim Lincecum, SF	18–5	0	2.62
2009.....Tim Lincecum, SF	15–7	0	2.48

AMERICAN LEAGUE

Year	W–L	Sv	ERA
1967.....Jim Lonborg, Bos	22–9	0	3.16
1968.....*Denny McLain, Det	31–6	0	1.96
1969.....Denny McLain, Det	24–9	0	2.80
Mike Cuellar, Balt	23–11	0	2.38
1970.....Jim Perry, Minn	24–12	0	3.03
1971.....*Vida Blue, Oak	24–8	0	1.82
1972.....Gaylord Perry, Clev	24–16	1	1.92
1973.....Jim Palmer, Balt	22–9	1	2.40
1974.....Catfish Hunter, Oak	25–12	0	2.49
1975.....Jim Palmer, Balt	23–11	1	2.09
1976.....Jim Palmer, Balt	22–13	0	2.51
1977.....Sparky Lyle, NY	13–5	26	2.17
1978.....Ron Guidry, NY	25–3	0	1.74
1979.....Mike Flanagan, Balt	23–9	0	3.08
1980.....Steve Stone, Balt	25–7	0	3.23
1981.....*Rollie Fingers, Mil	6–3	28	1.04
1982.....Pete Vuckovich, Mil	18–6	0	3.34
1983.....LaMarr Hoyt, Chi	24–10	0	3.66
1984.....*Willie Hernandez, Det	9–3	32	1.92
1985.....Bret Saberhagen, KC	20–6	0	2.87
1986.....*Roger Clemens, Bos	24–4	0	2.48
1987.....Roger Clemens, Bos	20–9	0	2.97
1988.....Frank Viola, Minn	24–7	0	2.64
1989.....Bret Saberhagen, KC	23–6	0	2.16
1990.....Bob Welch, Oak	27–6	0	2.95
1991.....Roger Clemens, Bos	18–10	0	2.62
1992.....*Dennis Eckersley, Oak	7–1	51	1.91
1993.....Jack McDowell, Chi	22–10	0	3.37
1994.....David Cone, KC	16–4	0	2.94
1995.....Randy Johnson, Sea	18–2	0	2.48
1996.....Pat Hentgen, Tor	20–10	0	3.22
1997.....Roger Clemens, Tor	21–7	0	2.05
1998.....Roger Clemens, Tor	20–6	0	2.65
1999.....Pedro Martinez, Bos	23–4	0	1.55
2000.....Pedro Martinez, Bos	18–6	0	1.74
2001.....Roger Clemens, NY	20–3	0	3.51
2002.....Barry Zito, Oak	23–5	0	2.75
2003.....Roy Halladay, Tor	22–7	0	3.25
2004.....Johan Santana, Min	20–6	0	2.61
2005.....Bartolo Colon, LA	21-8	0	3.48
2006.....Johan Santana, Min	19–6	0	2.77
2007.....C.C. Sabathia, Cle	19–7	0	3.21
2008.....Cliff Lee, Cle	22–3	0	2.54
2009.....Zack Greinke, KC	16–8	0	2.16

*Won the MVP and Cy Young awards in the same season.
†NL games only. Sutcliffe pitched 15 games with Cleveland before being traded to the Cubs.

Career Individual Batting

GAMES

Pete Rose	3562
Carl Yastrzemski	3308
Hank Aaron	3298
Rickey Henderson	3081
Ty Cobb	3034
Eddie Murray	3026
Stan Musial	3026
Cal Ripken Jr.	3001
Willie Mays	2992
Barry Bonds	2986
Dave Winfield	2973
Rusty Staub	2951
Brooks Robinson	2896
Robin Yount	2856
Craig Biggio	2850
*Omar Vizquel	2850
Al Kaline	2834
Rafael Palmeiro	2831
Harold Baines	2830
Eddie Collins	2826
Reggie Jackson	2820
Frank Robinson	2808
Honus Wagner	2792

AT BATS

Pete Rose	14053
Hank Aaron	12364
Carl Yastrzemski	11988
Cal Ripken Jr.	11551
Ty Cobb	11434
Eddie Murray	11336
Robin Yount	11008
Dave Winfield	11003
Stan Musial	10972
Rickey Henderson	10961
Willie Mays	10881
Craig Biggio	10876
Paul Molitor	10835
Brooks Robinson	10654
Rafael Palmeiro	10472
Honus Wagner	10430
George Brett	10349
Lou Brock	10332

RUNS

Rickey Henderson	2295
Ty Cobb	2246
Barry Bonds	2227
Hank Aaron	2174
Babe Ruth	2174
Pete Rose	2165
Willie Mays	2062
Cap Anson	1996
Stan Musial	1949
Lou Gehrig	1888
Tris Speaker	1882
Mel Ott	1859
Craig Biggio	1834
Frank Robinson	1829
Eddie Collins	1821
Carl Yastrzemski	1816
Ted Williams	1798
Paul Molitor	1782
Charlie Gehringer	1774
*Alex Rodriguez	1757
Jimmie Foxx	1751

BATTING AVERAGE (5,000 AB)

Ty Cobb	.367
Rogers Hornsby	.358
Ed Delahanty	.346
Tris Speaker	.345
Billy Hamilton	.344
Ted Williams	.344
Dan Brouthers	.342
Harry Heilmann	.342
Babe Ruth	.342
Willie Keeler	.341
Bill Terry	.341
Lou Gehrig	.340
George Sisler	.340
Jesse Burkett	.338
Tony Gwynn	.338
Nap Lajoie	.338
Al Simmons	.334
Cap Anson	.333
Eddie Collins	.333
Paul Waner	.333
*Albert Pujols	.331
*Ichiro Suzuki	.331
Sam Thompson	.331
Heinie Manush	.330

HOME RUNS

Barry Bonds	762
Hank Aaron	755
Babe Ruth	714
Willie Mays	660
*Ken Griffey Jr.	630
*Alex Rodriguez	613
Sammy Sosa	609
*Jim Thome	589
Frank Robinson	586
Mark McGwire	583
Harmon Killebrew	573
Rafael Palmeiro	569
Reggie Jackson	563
*Manny Ramirez	555
Mike Schmidt	548
Mickey Mantle	536
Jimmie Foxx	534
Willie McCovey	521
Ted Williams	521
Frank Thomas	521
Ernie Banks	512
Eddie Mathews	512
Mel Ott	511
Gary Sheffield	509
Eddie Murray	504

RUNS BATTED IN

Hank Aaron	2297
Babe Ruth	2213
Cap Anson	2076
Barry Bonds	1996
Lou Gehrig	1995
Stan Musial	1951
Ty Cobb	1937
Jimmie Foxx	1922
Eddie Murray	1917
Willie Mays	1903
Mel Ott	1860
Carl Yastrzemski	1844
Ted Williams	1839
*Ken Griffey Jr.	1836
Rafael Palmeiro	1835
Dave Winfield	1833
*Alex Rodriguez	1831
*Manny Ramirez	1830
Al Simmons	1827
Frank Robinson	1812
Honus Wagner	1732

HITS

Pete Rose	4256
Ty Cobb	4191
Hank Aaron	3771
Stan Musial	3630
Tris Speaker	3515
Carl Yastrzemski	3419
Cap Anson	3418
Honus Wagner	3415
Paul Molitor	3319
Eddie Collins	3313
Willie Mays	3283
Eddie Murray	3255
Nap Lajoie	3251
Cal Ripken Jr.	3184
George Brett	3154
Paul Waner	3152
Robin Yount	3142
Tony Gwynn	3141
Dave Winfield	3110
Craig Biggio	3060
Rickey Henderson	3055
Rod Carew	3053
Lou Brock	3023
Rafael Palmeiro	3020
Wade Boggs	3010
Al Kaline	3007
Roberto Clemente	3000

Career Individual Batting *(Cont.)*

DOUBLES

Tris Speaker	792
Pete Rose	746
Stan Musial	725
Ty Cobb	724
Craig Biggio	668
George Brett	665
Nap Lajoie	657
Carl Yastrzemski	646
Honus Wagner	640
Hank Aaron	624
Paul Molitor	605
Paul Waner	605
Cal Ripken Jr.	603
Barry Bonds	601
Luis Gonzalez	596
Rafael Palmeiro	585
Robin Yount	583
Cap Anson	581
Wade Boggs	578
Charlie Gehringer	574

TRIPLES

Sam Crawford	309
Ty Cobb	295
Honus Wagner	252
Jake Beckley	243
Roger Connor	233
Tris Speaker	222
Fred Clarke	220
Dan Brouthers	205
Joe Kelley	194
Paul Waner	191
Bid McPhee	188
Eddie Collins	187
Ed Delahanty	185
Sam Rice	184
Jesse Burkett	182
Ed Konetchy	182
Edd Roush	182
Buck Ewing	178
Rabbit Maranville	177
Stan Musial	177

BASES ON BALLS

Barry Bonds	2558
Rickey Henderson	2190
Babe Ruth	2062
Ted Williams	2021
Joe Morgan	1865
Carl Yastrzemski	1845
Mickey Mantle	1733
Mel Ott	1708
*Jim Thome	1679
Frank Thomas	1667
Eddie Yost	1614
Darrell Evans	1605
Stan Musial	1599
Pete Rose	1566
Harmon Killebrew	1559
Lou Gehrig	1508
Mike Schmidt	1507
Eddie Collins	1499
Gary Sheffield	1475
Willie Mays	1464
Jimmie Foxx	1452
Eddie Mathews	1444

SLUGGING AVERAGE (5,000 AB)

Babe Ruth	.690
Ted Williams	.634
Lou Gehrig	.632
*Albert Pujols	.624
Jimmie Foxx	.609
Barry Bonds	.607
Hank Greenberg	.605
Mark McGwire	.588
*Manny Ramirez	.586
Joe Dimaggio	.579
Rogers Hornsby	.577
*Alex Rodriguez	.571
Larry Walker	.565
Albert Belle	.564
*Vladimir Guerrero	.563
Johnny Mize	.562
Juan Gonzalez	.561
Stan Musial	.559
*Jim Thome	.559
Mickey Mantle	.557
Willie Mays	.557

STOLEN BASES

Rickey Henderson	1406
Lou Brock	938
Billy Hamilton	912
Ty Cobb	892
Tim Raines	808
Vince Coleman	752
Eddie Collins	745
Max Carey	738
Honus Wagner	722
Joe Morgan	689
Willie Wilson	668
Bert Campaneris	649
Kenny Lofton	622
Otis Nixon	620
George Davis	616
Tom Brown	615
Dummy Hoy	594
Maury Wills	586
George Van Haltren	583
Ozzie Smith	580

ON-BASE PERCENTAGE (5,000 AB)

Ted Williams	.482
Babe Ruth	.469
Barry Bonds	.444
Lou Gehrig	.442
*Albert Pujols	.426
Jimmie Foxx	.425
Ty Cobb	.424
*Todd Helton	.424
Rogers Hornsby	.424
Mickey Mantle	.422
Frank Thomas	.419
Edgar Martinez	.418
Stan Musial	.417
Tris Speaker	.417
Wade Boggs	.415
*Manny Ramirez	.411
Mel Ott	.410
*Lance Berkman	.409
Mickey Cochrane	.409
Hank Greenberg	.409
Jeff Bagwell	.408

TOTAL BASES

Hank Aaron	6856
Stan Musial	6134
Willie Mays	6066
Barry Bonds	5976
Ty Cobb	5859
Babe Ruth	5793
Pete Rose	5752
Carl Yastrzemski	5539
Eddie Murray	5397
Rafael Palmeiro	5388
Frank Robinson	5373
*Ken Griffey Jr.	5271
Dave Winfield	5221
Cal Ripken Jr.	5168
Tris Speaker	5101
Lou Gehrig	5060
George Brett	5044
*Alex Rodriguez	5043
Mel Ott	5041
Jimmie Foxx	4956
Ted Williams	4884

STRIKEOUTS

Reggie Jackson	2597
*Jim Thome	2395
Sammy Sosa	2306
Andres Galarraga	2003
Jose Canseco	1942
Willie Stargell	1936
Mike Schmidt	1883
Fred McGriff	1882
Tony Perez	1867
*Mike Cameron	1842
*Alex Rodriguez	1836
Dave Kingman	1816
*Manny Ramirez	1809
*Ken Griffey Jr.	1779
Bobby Bonds	1757
Craig Biggio	1753
Dale Murphy	1748
Carlos Delgado	1745
Lou Brock	1730
*Jim Edmonds	1729
Mickey Mantle	1710

* Active in 2010.

The 30–30 Club (minimum of 30 HR and 30 SB in single season)

Year		HR	SB	Year		HR	SB
1922	Kenny Williams, StL	39	37	1996	Dante Bichette, Col	31	31
1956	Willie Mays, NYG	36	40	1997	Larry Walker, Col	49	33
1957	Willie Mays, NYG	35	38	1997	Jeff Bagwell, Hou	43	31
1963	Hank Aaron, Mil	44	31	1997	Raul Mondesi, LA	30	32
1969	Bobby Bonds, SF	32	45	1997	Barry Bonds, SF	40	37
1970	Tommy Harper, Mil	31	38	1998	Alex Rodriguez, Sea	42	46
1973	Bobby Bonds, SF	39	43	1998	Shawn Green, Tor	35	35
1975	Bobby Bonds, NYY	32	30	1999	Jeff Bagwell, Hou	42	30
1977	Bobby Bonds, Cal	37	41	1999	Raul Mondesi, LA	33	36
1978	Bobby Bonds, Chi/Tex	31	43	2000	Preston Wilson, Fla	31	36
1983	Dale Murphy, Atl	36	30	2001	Vladimir Guerrero, Mtl	34	37
1987	Joe Carter, Clev	32	31	2001	Jose Cruz Jr., Tor	34	32
1987	Eric Davis, Cin	37	50	2001	Bobby Abreu, Phi	31	36
1987	Darryl Strawberry, NYM	39	36	2002	Alfonso Soriano, NYY	39	41
1987	Howard Johnson, NYM	36	32	2002	Vladimir Guerrero, Mtl	39	40
1988	Jose Canseco, Oak	42	40	2003	Alfonso Soriano, NYY	38	35
1989	Howard Johnson, NYM	36	41	2004	Carlos Beltran, KC/Hou	38	42
1990	Ron Gant, Atl	32	33	2004	Bobby Abreu, Phi	30	40
1990	Barry Bonds, Pitt	33	52	2005	Alfonso Soriano, Tex	36	30
1991	Ron Gant, Atl	32	34	2006	Alfonso Soriano, Wash	46	41
1991	Howard Johnson, NYM	38	30	2007	Brandon Phillips, Cin	30	32
1992	Barry Bonds, Pitt	34	39	2007	Jimmy Rollins, Phi	30	41
1993	Sammy Sosa, ChiC	33	36	2007	David Wright, NYM	30	34
1995	Barry Bonds, SF	33	31	2008	Grady Sizemore, Cle	33	38
1995	Sammy Sosa, ChiC	36	34	2008	Hanley Ramirez, Fla	33	35
1996	Barry Bonds, SF	42	40	2009	Ian Kinsler, Tex	31	31
1996	Ellis Burks, Col	40	32				
1996	Barry Larkin, Cin	33	36				

Career Individual Pitching

GAMES

Jesse Orosco	1251
Mike Stanton	1178
John Franco	1119
Dennis Eckersley	1071
Hoyt Wilhelm	1070
Dan Plesac	1064
Mike Timlin	1058
Kent Tekulve	1050
*Trevor Hoffman	1034
Jose Mesa	1022
Lee Smith	1022
Roberto Hernandez	1010
Mike Jackson	1005
Goose Gossage	1002
Lindy McDaniel	987
Todd Jones	982
*Mariano Rivera	978
David Weathers	964
Rollie Fingers	944
Gene Garber	931
Eddie Guardado	908
Cy Young	906
Sparky Lyle	899
Jim Kaat	898
Tom Gordon	890

INNINGS PITCHED

Cy Young	7356.0
Pud Galvin	6003.1
Walter Johnson	5914.1
Phil Niekro	5404.1
Nolan Ryan	5386.0
Gaylord Perry	5350.1
Don Sutton	5282.1
Warren Spahn	5243.1
Steve Carlton	5217.1
Grover Alexander	5190.0
Kid Nichols	5056.1
Tim Keefe	5049.2
Greg Maddux	5008.1
Bert Blyleven	4970.0
Bobby Mathews	4956.0
Roger Clemens	4916.2
Mickey Welch	4802.0
Tom Seaver	4782.2
Christy Mathewson	4780.2
Tommy John	4710.1
Robin Roberts	4688.2
Early Wynn	4564.0
John Clarkson	4536.1
Charley Radbourn	4535.1
Tony Mullane	4531.1

WINS

Cy Young	511
Walter Johnson	417
Grover Alexander	373
Christy Mathewson	373
Pud Galvin	365
Warren Spahn	363
Kid Nichols	361
Greg Maddux	355
Roger Clemens	354
Tim Keefe	342
Steve Carlton	329
John Clarkson	328
Eddie Plank	326
Nolan Ryan	324
Don Sutton	324
Phil Niekro	318
Gaylord Perry	314
Tom Seaver	311
Charley Radbourn	309
Mickey Welch	307
Tom Glavine	305
Randy Johnson	303
Lefty Grove	300
Early Wynn	300
Bobby Matthews	297

LOSSES

Cy Young	316
Pud Galvin	310
Nolan Ryan	292
Walter Johnson	279
Phil Niekro	274
Gaylord Perry	265
Don Sutton	256
Jack Powell	254
Eppa Rixey	251
Bert Blyleven	250
Bobby Mathews	248
Robin Roberts	245
Warren Spahn	245
Steve Carlton	244
Early Wynn	244
Jim Kaat	237
Frank Tanana	236
Gus Weyhing	232
Tommy John	231
Bob Friend	230
Ted Lyons	230

WINNING PERCENTAGE**

Al Spalding	.795
Spud Chandler	.717
Whitey Ford	.690
Dave Foutz	.690
Bob Caruthers	.688
Pedro Martinez	.687
Don Gullett	.686
Lefty Grove	.680
Joe Wood	.672
Vic Raschi	.667
Roger Clemens	.667
Larry Corcoran	.665
Christy Mathewson	.665
*Roy Halladay	.663
Sam Leever	.660
*Johan Santana	.658
Sal Maglie	.657
Dick McBride	.656
Sandy Koufax	.655
*Tim Hudson	.655

SAVES

*Trevor Hoffman	601
*Mariano Rivera	559
Lee Smith	478
John Franco	424
*Billy Wagner	422
Dennis Eckersley	390
Jeff Reardon	367
Troy Percival	358
Randy Myers	347
Rollie Fingers	341
John Wetteland	330
Roberto Hernandez	326
Jose Mesa	321
Todd Jones	319
Rick Aguilera	318
Robb Nen	314
Tom Henke	311
Goose Gossage	310
Jeff Montgomery	304
Doug Jones	303
Bruce Sutter	300

* Active in 2010. ** Minumum 100 victories.

Career Individual Pitching (Cont.)

EARNED RUN AVERAGE (2,000 IP)

Ed Walsh	1.82
Addie Joss	1.89
Al Spalding	2.04
Three Finger Brown	2.06
John Ward	2.10
Christy Mathewson	2.13
Tommy Bond	2.14
Rube Waddell	2.16
Walter Johnson	2.17
Ed Reulbach	2.28
Will White	2.28
Eddie Plank	2.35
Larry Corcoran	2.36
Eddie Cicotte	2.38
Candy Cummings	2.39
Doc White	2.39
Nap Rucker	2.42
George Bradley	2.43
Jim McCormick	2.43
Chief Bender	2.46

SHUTOUTS

Walter Johnson	110
Grover Alexander	90
Christy Mathewson	79
Cy Young	76
Eddie Plank	69
Warren Spahn	63
Nolan Ryan	61
Tom Seaver	61
Bert Blyleven	60
Don Sutton	58
Pud Galvin	57
Ed Walsh	57
Bob Gibson	56
Three Finger Brown	55
Steve Carlton	55
Jim Palmer	53
Gaylord Perry	53
Juan Marichal	52
Rube Waddell	50
Vic Willis	50

COMPLETE GAMES

Cy Young	749
Pud Galvin	639
Tim Keefe	554
Walter Johnson	531
Kid Nichols	531
Mickey Welch	525
Bobby Mathews	525
Charley Radbourn	489
John Clarkson	485
Tony Mullane	468
Jim McCormick	466
Gus Weyhing	448
Grover Alexander	437
Christy Mathewson	434
Jack Powell	422
Eddie Plank	410
Will White	394
Amos Rusie	392
Vic Willis	388
Tommy Bond	386

STRIKEOUTS

Nolan Ryan	5714
Randy Johnson	4875
Roger Clemens	4672
Steve Carlton	4136
Bert Blyleven	3701
Tom Seaver	3640
Don Sutton	3574
Gaylord Perry	3534
Walter Johnson	3509
Greg Maddux	3371
Phil Niekro	3342
Ferguson Jenkins	3192
Pedro Martinez	3154
Bob Gibson	3117
Curt Schilling	3116
John Smoltz	3084
Jim Bunning	2855
Mickey Lolich	2832
Mike Mussina	2813
Cy Young	2803

BASES ON BALLS

Nolan Ryan	2795
Steve Carlton	1833
Phil Niekro	1809
Early Wynn	1775
Bob Feller	1764
Bobo Newsom	1732
Amos Rusie	1707
Charlie Hough	1665
Roger Clemens	1580
Gus Weyhing	1566
Red Ruffing	1541
Tom Glavine	1500
Randy Johnson	1497
Bump Hadley	1442
Warren Spahn	1434
Earl Whitehill	1431
Tony Mullane	1408
Sad Sam Jones	1396
Jack Morris	1390
Tom Seaver	1390

Alltime Winningest Managers

CAREER

	W	L	Pct	Yrs		W	L	Pct	Yrs
Connie Mack	3755	3967	.486	53	Casey Stengel	1942	1868	.510	25
John McGraw	2810	1987	.586	33	Gene Mauch	1907	2044	.483	26
*Tony LaRussa	2695	2340	.535	32	Bill McKechnie	1904	1737	.523	25
*Bobby Cox	2571	2068	.554	29	*Lou Piniella	1858	1737	.517	23
*Joe Torre	2406	2051	.540	29	Ralph Houk	1627	1539	.514	20
Sparky Anderson	2238	1855	.547	26	Fred Clarke	1609	1189	.575	19
Bucky Harris	2168	2228	.493	29	Dick Williams	1592	1474	.519	21
Joe McCarthy	2155	1346	.616	24	Tommy Lasorda	1589	1434	.526	20
Walter Alston	2063	1634	.558	23	Earl Weaver	1506	1080	.582	17
Leo Durocher	2015	1717	.540	24	Clark Griffith	1491	1367	.522	20

REGULAR SEASON

	W	L	Pct	Yrs		W	L	Pct	Yrs
Connie Mack	3731	3948	.486	53	Casey Stengel	1905	1842	.508	25
John McGraw	2784	1959	.587	33	Gene Mauch	1902	2037	.483	26
*Tony LaRussa	2638	2293	.535	32	Bill McKechnie	1896	1723	.524	25
*Bobby Cox	2504	2001	.556	29	*Lou Piniella	1835	1713	.517	23
*Joe Torre	2326	1997	.538	29	Ralph Houk	1619	1531	.514	20
Sparky Anderson	2194	1834	.545	26	Fred Clarke	1602	1181	.576	19
Bucky Harris	2157	2218	.493	29	Dick Williams	1571	1451	.520	21
Joe McCarthy	2125	1333	.615	24	Tommy Lasorda	1558	1404	.526	20
Walter Alston	2040	1613	.558	23	Lou Piniella	1519	1420	.523	19
Leo Durocher	2008	1709	.540	24	Clark Griffith	1491	1367	.522	20

WORLD SERIES

	W	L	T	Pct	App	WS		W	L	T	Pct	App	WS
Casey Stengel	37	26	0	.587	10	7	Billy Southworth	11	11	0	.500	4	2
Joe McCarthy	30	13	0	.698	9	7	Earl Weaver	11	13	0	.458	4	1
John McGraw	26	28	2	.482	9	2	*Bobby Cox	11	18	0	.379	5	1
Connie Mack	24	19	0	.558	8	5	Whitey Herzog	10	11	0	.476	3	1
*Joe Torre	21	11	0	.657	6	4	*Tony LaRussa	9	13	0	.409	5	2
Walter Alston	20	20	0	.500	7	4	*Terry Francona	8	0	0	1.000	2	2
Miller Huggins	18	15	1	.544	6	3	Bill Carrigan	8	2	0	.800	2	2
Sparky Anderson	16	12	0	.571	5	3	Cito Gaston	8	4	0	.667	2	2
Tommy Lasorda	12	11	0	.522	4	2	Danny Murtaugh	8	6	0	.571	2	2
Dick Williams	12	14	0	.462	4	2	Tom Kelly	8	6	0	.571	2	2
Frank Chance	11	9	1	.548	4	2	Ralph Houk	8	8	0	.500	3	2
Bucky Harris	11	10	0	.524	3	2	Bill McKechnie	8	14	0	.364	4	2

* Active in 2010.

Individual Batting Records (Single Season)

HITS

Ichiro Suzuki, 2004	262
George Sisler, 1920	257
Lefty O'Doul, 1929	254
Bill Terry, 1930	254
Al Simmons, 1925	253
Rogers Hornsby, 1922	250
Chuck Klein, 1930	250
Ty Cobb, 1911	248
George Sisler, 1922	246
Ichiro Suzuki, 2001	242

BATTING AVERAGE

Levi Meyerle, 1871	.492
Hugh Duffy, 1894	.440
Tip O'Neill, 1887	.435
Ross Barnes, 1872	.432
Cal McVey, 1871	.431
Ross Barnes, 1876	.429
Nap Lajoie, 1901	.426
Ross Barnes, 1873	.425
Willie Keeler, 1897	.424
Rogers Hornsby, 1924	.424

DOUBLES

Earl Webb, 1931	67
George Burns, 1926	64
Joe Medwick, 1936	64
Hank Greenberg, 1934	63
Paul Waner, 1932	62
Charlie Gehringer, 1936	60
Tris Speaker, 1923	59
Chuck Klein, 1930	59
Todd Helton, 2000	59
Billy Herman, 1936	57
Billy Herman, 1935	57
Carlos Delgado, 2000	57

TOTAL BASES

Babe Ruth, 1921	457
Rogers Hornsby, 1922	450
Lou Gehrig, 1927	447
Chuck Klein, 1930	445
Jimmie Foxx, 1932	438
Stan Musial, 1948	429
Sammy Sosa, 2001	425
Hack Wilson, 1930	423
Chuck Klein, 1932	420
Luis Gonzalez, 2001	419
Lou Gehrig, 1930	419

TRIPLES

Chief Wilson, 1912	36
Dave Orr, 1886	31
Heinie Reitz, 1894	31
Perry Werden, 1893	29
Harry Davis, 1897	28
George Davis, 1893	27
Sam Thompson, 1894	27
Jimmy Williams, 1899	27
Sam Crawford, 1914	26
Kiki Cuyler, 1925	26
Joe Jackson, 1912	26
John Reilly, 1890	26
George Treadway	26

HOME RUNS

Barry Bonds, 2001	73
Mark McGwire, 1998	70
Sammy Sosa, 1998	66
Mark McGwire, 1999	65
Sammy Sosa, 2001	64
Sammy Sosa, 1999	63
Roger Maris, 1961	61
Babe Ruth, 1927	60
Babe Ruth, 1921	59
Jimmie Foxx, 1932	58
Hank Greenberg, 1938	58
Mark McGwire, 1997	58
Ryan Howard, 2006	58

RUNS BATTED IN

Hack Wilson, 1930	191
Lou Gehrig, 1931	184
Hank Greenberg, 1937	183
Lou Gehrig, 1927	175
Jimmie Foxx, 1938	175
Lou Gehrig, 1930	174
Babe Ruth, 1921	171
Chuck Klein, 1930	170
Hank Greenberg, 1935	170
Jimmie Foxx, 1932	169

STRIKEOUTS

Mark Reynolds, 2009	223
Mark Reynolds, 2010	211
Mark Reynolds, 2008	204
Adam Dunn, 2010	199
Ryan Howard, 2008	199
Ryan Howard, 2007	199
Jack Cust, 2008	197
Adam Dunn, 2004	195
Bobby Bonds, 1970	189
Jose Hernandez, 2002	188
Bobby Bonds, 1969	187
Preston Wilson, 2000	187
Ryan Howard, 2009	186
Rob Deer, 1987	186
Jack Cust, Oakland	185
Jose Hernandez, 2001	185
Pete Incaviglia, 1986	185
Jim Thome, 2001	185

RUNS

Billy Hamilton, 1894	192
Tom Brown, 1891	177
Babe Ruth, 1921	177
Lou Gehrig, 1936	167
Tip O'Neill, 1887	167
Billy Hamilton, 1895	166
Willie Keeler, 1894	165
Joe Kelley, 1894	165
Lou Gehrig, 1931	163
Arlie Latham, 1887	163
Babe Ruth, 1928	163

STOLEN BASES

Hugh Nicol, 1887	138
Rickey Henderson, 1982	130
Arlie Latham, 1887	129
Lou Brock, 1974	118
Charlie Comiskey, 1887	117
Billy Hamilton, 1891	111
Billy Hamilton, 1889	111
John Ward, 1887	111
Vince Coleman, 1985	110
Vince Coleman, 1987	109
Arlie Latham, 1888	109

BASES ON BALLS

Barry Bonds, 2004	232
Barry Bonds, 2002	198
Barry Bonds, 2001	177
Babe Ruth, 1923	170
Ted Williams, 1947	162
Ted Williams, 1949	162
Mark McGwire, 1998	162
Ted Williams, 1946	156
Barry Bonds, 1996	151
Eddie Yost, 1956	151
Babe Ruth, 1920	150

SLUGGING AVERAGE

Barry Bonds, 2001	.863
Babe Ruth, 1920	.847
Babe Ruth, 1921	.846
Barry Bonds, 2004	.812
Barry Bonds, 2002	.799
Babe Ruth, 1927	.772
Lou Gehrig, 1927	.765
Babe Ruth, 1923	.764
Rogers Hornsby, 1925	.756
Mark McGwire, 1998	.752

Individual Pitching Records (Single Season)

GAME APPEARANCES

Mike Marshall, 1974 106
Kent Tekulve, 1979 94
Salomon Torres, 2006............94
*Pedro Feliciano, 2010 92
Mike Marshall, 1973 92
Kent Tekulve, 1978 91
Wayne Granger, 1969............90
Mike Marshall, 1979 90
Kent Tekulve, 1987 90
Steve Kline, 2001..................89
Jim Brower, 2004..................89
Mark Eichhorn, 1987 89
Steve Kline, 2001..................89

GAMES STARTED

Will White, 1879......................75
Pud Galvin, 1883..................75
Jim McCormick, 1880 74
Charley Radbourn, 1884 73
Guy Hecker, 1884..................73
Jim Galvin, 1884..................72
John Clarkson, 1889..............72
Bill Hutchison, 1892..............71
John Clarkson, 1885..............70
Bobby Mathews, 1875..........70

INNINGS PITCHED

Will White, 1878................680.0
Charley Radbourn, 1884 ...678.2
Guy Hecker, 1884..............670.2
Jim McCormick, 1880 ......657.2
Jim Galvin, 1883..............656.1
Jim Galvin, 1884..............636.1
Charley Radbourn, 1883 ..632.1
Bill Hutchison, 1892............627.0
Bobby Mathews, 1875......626.2
John Clarkson, 1885........623.0

WINS

Charley Radbourn, 1884 59
Al Spalding, 1875..................55
John Clarkson, 1885..............53
Guy Hecker, 1884..................52
Al Spalding, 1874..................52
John Clarkson, 1889..............49
Charlie Buffinton, 1884........48
Charley Radbourn, 1883.......48
Al Spalding, 1876..................47
John Ward, 1879 47

LOSSES

John Coleman, 1883 48
Will White, 1880....................42
Larry McKeon, 1884..............41
George Bradley, 1879 40
Jim McCormick, 1879 40
Bobby Mathews, 1875..........38
Kid Carsey, 1891 37
George Cobb, 1892 37
Henry Porter, 1888................37

WINNING PERCENTAGE

Roy Face, 1959 .... .947
Johnny Allen, 1937............ .938
Greg Maddux, 1995............ .905
Randy Johnson, 1995.......... .900
Ron Guidry, 1978 .... .893
Freddie Fitzsimmons, 1940... .889
Lefty Grove, 1931................ .886
Bob Stanley, 1978 .... .882
Preacher Roe, 1951 .... .880
Cliff Lee, 2008 .... .880
Fred Goldsmith, 1880.......... .875
Tom Seaver, 1981................ .875

SAVES

Francisco Rodriguez, 2008 ...62
Bobby Thigpen, 1990............57
Eric Gagne, 2003 55
John Smoltz, 2002..................55
Mariano Rivera, 2004 53
Randy Myers, 1993................53
Trevor Hoffman, 1998 53
Eric Gagne, 2002 52
Rod Beck, 1998......................51
Dennis Eckersley, 1992..........51
Mariano Rivera, 2001............50

EARNED RUN AVERAGE

Tim Keefe, 1880 ....0.86
Dutch Leonard, 1914............0.96
Three Finger Brown, 1906 ...1.04
Bob Gibson, 1968 ....1.12
Christy Mathewson, 1909...1.14
Walter Johnson, 1913..........1.15
Jack Pfiester, 1907 ....1.15
Addie Joss, 1908................1.16
Carl Lundgren, 1907 ....1.17
Denny Driscoll, 1882 ....1.21

SHUTOUTS

Grover Alexander, 1916........16
George Bradley, 1876 16
Jack Coombs, 1910 13
Bob Gibson, 1968..................13
Grover Alexander, 1915........12
Jim Galvin, 1884....................12
Ed Morris, 1886 12
Tommy Bond, 1879................11
Dean Chance, 1964 11
Dave Foutz, 1886 11
Walter Johnson, 1913............11
Sandy Koufax, 1963..............11
Christy Mathewson, 1908......11
Charles Radbourn, 1884 11
Ed Walsh, 1908 11

COMPLETE GAMES

Will White, 1879......................75
Charley Radbourn, 1884 73
Pud Galvin, 1883..................72
Guy Hecker, 1884..................72
Jim McCormick, 1880............72
Pud Galvin, 1884..................71
Bobby Mathews, 1875..........69
John Clarkson, 1885..............68
John Clarkson, 1889..............68

STRIKEOUTS

Matt Kilroy, 1886..................513
Toad Ramsey, 1886..............499
Hugh Daily, 1884..................483
Dupee Shaw, 1884 451
Charley Radbourn, 1884......441
Charlie Buffinton, 1884........417
Guy Hecker, 1884................385
Nolan Ryan, 1973................383
Sandy Koufax, 1965............382

BASES ON BALLS

Amos Rusie, 1890 289
Mark Baldwin, 1889............274
Amos Rusie, 1892 267
Amos Rusie, 1891 262
Mark Baldwin, 1890............249
Jack Stivetts, 1891 232
Mark Baldwin, 1891............227
Phil Knell, 1891....................226
Bob Barr, 1890 219

Manager of the Year

NATIONAL LEAGUE

1983 ....Tommy Lasorda, LA
1984 ....Jim Frey, Chi
1985 ....Whitey Herzog, StL
1986 ....Hal Lanier, Hou
1987 ....Buck Rodgers, Mtl
1988 ....Tommy Lasorda, LA
1989 ....Don Zimmer, Chi
1990 ....Jim Leyland, Pitt
1991 ....Bobby Cox, Atl
1992 ....Jim Leyland, Pitt
1993 ....Dusty Baker, SF
1994 ....Felipe Alou, Mtl
1995 ....Don Baylor, Col
1996 ....Bruce Bochy, SD
1997 ....Dusty Baker, SF
1998 ....Larry Dierker, Hou

AMERICAN LEAGUE

1983 ....Tony LaRussa, Chi
1984 ....Sparky Anderson, Det
1985 ....Bobby Cox, Tor
1986 ....John McNamara, Bos
1987 ....Sparky Anderson, Det
1988 ....Tony LaRussa, Oak
1989 ....Frank Robinson, Balt
1990 ....Jeff Torborg, Chi
1991 ....Tom Kelly, Minn
1992 ....Tony LaRussa, Oak
1993 ....Gene Lamont, Chi
1994 ....Buck Showalter, NY
1995 ....Lou Piniella, Sea
1996 ....Joe Torre, NY/Johnny Oates, Tex
1997 ....Davey Johnson, Balt
1998 ....Joe Torre, NY

Manager of the Year *(Cont.)*

NATIONAL LEAGUE

1999	Jack McKeon, Cin
2000	Dusty Baker, SF
2001	Larry Bowa, Phi
2002	Tony LaRussa, StL
2003	Jack McKeon, Fla
2004	Bobby Cox, Atl
2005	Bobby Cox, Atl
2006	Joe Girardi, Fla
2007	Bob Melvin, Ari
2008	Lou Piniella, Chi
2009	Jim Tracy, Col

AMERICAN LEAGUE

1999	Jimy Williams, Bos
2000	Jerry Manuel, Chi
2001	Lou Piniella, Sea
2002	Mike Scioscia, Ana
2003	Tony Pena, KC
2004	Buck Showalter, Tex
2005	Ozzie Guillen, Chi
2006	Jim Leyland, Det
2007	Eric Wedge, Cle
2008	Joe Maddon, TB
2009	Mike Scioscia, LA

Individual Batting Records (Single Game)

MOST HITS

7	Wilbert Robinson, Balt	June 10, 1892
	Rennie Stennett, Pitt	Sept 16, 1975

MOST HOME RUNS

4	Bobby Lowe, Bos (N)	May 30, 1894
	Ed Delahanty, Phi	July 13, 1896
	Lou Gehrig, NY (A)	June 3, 1932
	Gil Hodges, Bklyn	Aug 31, 1950
	Joe Adcock, Mil (N)	July 31, 1954
	Rocky Colavito, Clev	June 10, 1959
	Willie Mays, SF	April 30, 1961
	Mike Schmidt, Phi	April 17, 1976
	Bob Horner, Atl	July 6, 1986
	Mark Whiten, StL	Sept 7, 1993
	Mike Cameron, Sea	May 2, 2002
	Shawn Green, LA	May 23, 2002
	Carlos Delgado, Tor	Sept 25, 2003

Note: All single-game hitting records for a nine-inning game.

MOST GRAND SLAMS

2	Tony Lazzeri, NY (A)	May 24, 1936
	Jim Tabor, Bos (A)	July 4, 1939
	Rudy York, Bos (A)	July 27, 1946
	Jim Gentile, Balt	May 9, 1961
	Tony Cloninger, Atl	July 3, 1966
	Jim Northrup, Det	June 24, 1968
	Frank Robinson, Balt	June 26, 1970
	Robin Ventura, Chi (A)	Sept 4, 1995
	Chris Hoiles, Balt	Aug 14, 1998
	Fernando Tatis, StL	Apr 23, 1999
	N. Garciaparra, Bos	May 10, 1999
	Bill Mueller, Bos	July 29, 2003

MOST RUNS

7	Guy Hecker, Lou	Aug 15, 1886

MOST RBIs

12	Jim Bottomley, StL	Sept 16, 1924
	Mark Whiten, StL	Sept 7, 1993

Individual Batting Records (Single Inning)

MOST RUNS

3	Tommy Burns, Chi (N)	Sept 6, 1883, 7th inning
	Ned Williamson, Chi (N)	Sept 6, 1883, 7th inning
	Sammy White, Bos (A)	June 18, 1953, 7th inning

MOST HITS

3	Tommy Burns, Chi (N)	Sept 6, 1883, 7th inning
	Fred Pfeiffer, Chi (N)	Sept 6, 1883, 7th inning
	Ned Williamson, Chi (N)	Sept 6, 1883, 7th inning
	Gene Stephens, Bos (A)	June 18, 1953, 7th inning
	Johnny Damon, Bos (A)	June 27, 2003, 1st inning

MOST RBIs

8	Fernando Tatis, StL	Apr 23, 1999, 3rd inning

Individual Pitching Records (Single Game)

MOST INNINGS PITCHED

26	Leon Cadore, Bklyn	May 1, 1920, tie 1–1
	Joe Oeschger, Bos (N)	May 1, 1920, tie 1–1

MOST RUNS ALLOWED

24	Al Travers, Det	May 18, 1912

MOST HITS ALLOWED

36	Jack Wadsworth, Lou	Aug 17, 1894

MOST STRIKEOUTS

20	Roger Clemens, Bos	April 29, 1986
20	Roger Clemens, Bos	Sept 18, 1996
20	Kerry Wood, Chi (N)	May 6, 1998
20	Randy Johnson, Ariz	May 8, 2001

MOST WALKS ALLOWED

16	Bill George, NY (N)	May 30, 1887
	George Van Haltren, Chi (N)	June 27, 1887
	Henry Gruber, Clev	Apr 19, 1890
	Bruno Haas, Phi (A)	June 2, 1915

MOST WILD PITCHES

6	J.R. Richard, Hou	April 10, 1979
	Phil Niekro, Atl	Aug 14, 1979
	Bill Gullickson, Mtl	April 10, 1982

Individual Pitching Records (Single Inning)

MOST RUNS ALLOWED

13 .....Lefty O'Doul, Bos (A)   July 7, 1923

MOST WALKS ALLOWED

8 ....Dolly Gray, Wash   Aug 28, 1909

MOST WILD PITCHES

4	Walter Johnson, Wash	Sept 21, 1914
	Phil Niekro, Atl	Aug 14, 1979
	Kevin Gregg, Ana	July 25, 2004
	Ryan Madson, Phi	July 25, 2006

Miscellaneous Records

LONGEST GAME, BY INNINGS

26 .....Brooklyn 1, Boston 1   May 1, 1920

LONGEST NINE-INNING GAME, BY TIME

4:45...New York (A) 14, Boston 11   Aug 18, 2006

Baseball Hall of Fame

Players

	Position	Career	Selected
Hank Aaron	OF	1954–76	1982
Grover Alexander	P	1911–30	1938
Cap Anson	1B	1876–97	1939
Luis Aparicio	SS	1956–73	1984
Luke Appling	SS	1930–50	1964
Richie Ashburn	OF	1948–62	1995
Earl Averill	OF	1929–41	1975
Jose Mendez Baez*	P	1908–26	2006
Frank Baker	3B	1908–22	1955
Dave Bancroft	SS	1915–30	1971
Ernie Banks	SS-1B	1953–71	1977
Jake Beckley	1B	1888–1907	1971
Cool Papa Bell*	OF		1974
Johnny Bench	C	1967–83	1989
Chief Bender	P	1903–25	1953
Yogi Berra	C	1946–65	1972
Wade Boggs	3B	1982-99	2005
Jim Bottomley	1B	1922–37	1974
Lou Boudreau	SS	1938–52	1970
Roger Bresnahan	C	1897–1915	1945
George Brett	3B	1973–93	1999
Lou Brock	OF	1961–79	1985
Dan Brouthers	1B	1879–1904	1945
Ray Brown*	P	1930–48	2006
Three Finger Brown	P	1903–16	1949
Willard Jesse Brown*	OF	1935–58	2006
Jim Bunning	P	1955–71	1996
Jesse Burkett	OF	1890–1905	1946
Roy Campanella	C	1948–57	1969
Rod Carew	1B-2B	1967–85	1991
Max Carey	OF	1910–29	1961
Steve Carlton	P	1965–88	1994
Gary Carter	C	1974–92	2003
Orlando Cepeda	1B	1958–74	1999
Frank Chance	1B	1898–1914	1946
Oscar Charleston*	OF		1976
Jack Chesbro	P	1899–1909	1946
Fred Clarke	OF	1894–1915	1945
John Clarkson	P	1882–94	1963
Roberto Clemente	OF	1955–72	1973
Ty Cobb	OF	1905–28	1936
Mickey Cochrane	C	1925–37	1947
Eddie Collins	2B	1906–30	1939
Jimmy Collins	3B	1895–1908	1945
Earle Combs	OF	1924–35	1970
Roger Connor	1B	1880–97	1976
Andrew Cooper*	P	1920–41	2006
Stan Coveleski	P	1912–28	1969
Sam Crawford	OF	1899–1917	1957
Joe Cronin	SS	1926–45	1956

	Position	Career	Selected
Candy Cummings	P	1872–77	1939
Kiki Cuyler	OF	1921–38	1968
Ray Dandridge*	3B		1987
George Davis	SS	1890–1909	1998
Andre Dawson	OF	1976–96	2010
Leon Day*	P		1995
Dizzy Dean	P	1930–47	1953
Ed Delahanty	OF	1888–1903	1945
Bill Dickey	C	1928–46	1954
Martin Dihigo*	P-OF		1977
Joe DiMaggio	OF	1936–51	1955
Larry Doby	OF	1947–59	1998
Bobby Doerr	2B	1937–51	1986
Don Drysdale	P	1956–69	1984
Hugh Duffy	OF	1888–1906	1945
Dennis Eckersley	P	1975–98	2004
Johnny Evers	2B	1902–29	1939
Buck Ewing	C	1880–97	1946
Red Faber	P	1914–33	1964
Bob Feller	P	1936–56	1962
Rick Ferrell	C	1929–47	1984
Rollie Fingers	P	1968–85	1992
Carlton Fisk	C	1969–93	2000
Elmer Flick	OF	1898–1910	1963
Whitey Ford	P	1950–67	1974
Bill Foster*	P		1996
Nellie Fox	2B	1947–65	1997
Jimmie Foxx	1B	1925–45	1951
Frankie Frisch	2B	1919–37	1947
Pud Galvin	P	1879–92	1965
Lou Gehrig	1B	1923–39	1939
Charlie Gehringer	2B	1924–42	1949
Bob Gibson	P	1959–75	1981
Josh Gibson*	C		1972
Lefty Gomez	P	1930–43	1972
Joe Gordon	2B	1938-43/46-50	2009
Goose Goslin	OF	1921–38	1968
Rich "Goose" Gossage	P	1972-94	2008
Ulysses F. Grant*	2B	1886–1903	2006
Hank Greenberg	1B	1930–47	1956
Burleigh Grimes	P	1916–34	1964
Lefty Grove	P	1925–41	1947
Tony Gwynn	OF	1982–2001	2007
Chick Hafey	OF	1924–37	1971
Jesse Haines	P	1918–37	1970
Billy Hamilton	OF	1888–1901	1961
Gabby Hartnett	C	1922–41	1955
Harry Heilmann	OF	1914–32	1952
Rickey Henderson	OF	1979–2003	2009
Billy Herman	2B	1931–47	1975

Note: Career dates indicate first and last appearances in the majors.
*Elected on the basis of their career in the Negro leagues.

Players (Cont.)

Name	Position	Career	Selected
Joseph Hill*	OF	1899–1925	2006
Harry Hooper	OF	1909–25	1971
Rogers Hornsby	2B	1915–37	1942
Waite Hoyt	P	1918–38	1969
Carl Hubbell	P	1928–43	1947
Catfish Hunter	P	1965–79	1987
Monte Irvin*	OF	1949–56	1973
Reggie Jackson	OF	1967–87	1993
Travis Jackson	SS	1922–36	1982
Ferguson Jenkins	P	1965–83	1991
Hugh Jennings	SS	1891–1918	1945
Judy Johnson*	3B		1975
Walter Johnson	P	1907–27	1936
Addie Joss	P	1902–10	1978
Al Kaline	OF	1953–74	1980
Tim Keefe	P	1880–93	1964
Willie Keeler	OF	1892–1910	1939
George Kell	3B	1943–57	1983
Joe Kelley	OF	1891–1908	1971
George Kelly	1B	1915–32	1973
King Kelly	C	1878–93	1945
Harmon Killebrew	1B-3B	1954–75	1984
Ralph Kiner	OF	1946–55	1975
Chuck Klein	OF	1928–44	1980
Sandy Koufax	P	1955–66	1972
Nap Lajoie	2B	1896–1916	1937
Tony Lazzeri	2B	1926–39	1991
Bob Lemon	P	1941–58	1976
Buck Leonard*	1B		1977
Fred Lindstrom	3B	1924–36	1976
Pop Lloyd*	SS-1B		1977
Ernie Lombardi	C	1931–47	1986
Ted Lyons	P	1923–46	1955
James Mackey*	C	1920–47	2006
Mickey Mantle	OF	1951–68	1974
Heinie Manush	OF	1923–39	1964
Rabbit Maranville	SS-2B	1912–35	1954
Juan Marichal	P	1960–75	1983
Rube Marquard	P	1908–25	1971
Eddie Mathews	3B	1952–68	1978
Christy Mathewson	P	1900–16	1936
Willie Mays	OF	1951–73	1979
Bill Mazeroski	2B	1956–72	2001
Tommy McCarthy	OF	1884–96	1946
Willie McCovey	1B	1959–80	1986
Joe McGinnity	P	1899–1908	1946
Bid McPhee	2B	1882–99	2000
Joe Medwick	OF	1932–48	1968
Johnny Mize	1B	1936–53	1981
Paul Molitor	3B	1978–98	2004
Joe Morgan	2B	1963–84	1990
Eddie Murray	1B	1977–97	2003
Stan Musial	OF-1B	1941–63	1969
Hal Newhouser	P	1939–55	1992
Kid Nichols	P	1890–1906	1949
Phil Niekro	P	1964–87	1997
Jim O'Rourke	OF	1876–1904	1945
Mel Ott	OF	1926–47	1951
Satchel Paige*	P	1948–65	1971
Jim Palmer	P	1965–84	1990
Herb Pennock	P	1912–34	1948
Tony Perez	1B	1964–86	2000
Gaylord Perry	P	1962–83	1991
Eddie Plank	P	1901–17	1946
Kirby Puckett	OF	1984–95	2001
Charley Radbourn	P	1880–91	1939
Pee Wee Reese	SS	1940–58	1984
Jim Rice	OF	1974–89	2009
Sam Rice	OF	1915–35	1963
Cal Ripken Jr.	SS	1981–2001	2007
Eppa Rixey	P	1912–33	1963
Phil Rizzuto	SS	1941–56	1994
Robin Roberts	P	1948–66	1976
Brooks Robinson	3B	1955–77	1983
Frank Robinson	OF	1956–76	1982
Jackie Robinson	2B	1947–56	1962
Joe (Bullet) Rogan*	P		1998
Edd Roush	OF	1913–31	1962
Red Ruffing	P	1924–47	1967
Amos Rusie	P	1889–1901	1977
Babe Ruth	OF	1914–35	1936
Nolan Ryan	P	1966–93	1999
Ryne Sandberg	2B	1981-97	2005
Louis Santop*	C	1909–26	2006
Ray Schalk	C	1912–29	1955
Mike Schmidt	3B	1972–89	1995
Red Schoendienst	2B	1945–63	1989
Tom Seaver	P	1967–86	1992
Joe Sewell	SS	1920–33	1977
Al Simmons	OF	1924–44	1953
George Sisler	1B	1915–30	1939
Enos Slaughter	OF	1938–59	1985
Hilton Smith*	P		2001
Ozzie Smith	SS	1978–96	2002
Duke Snider	OF	1947–64	1980
Warren Spahn	P	1942–65	1973
Al Spalding	P	1871–78	1939
Tris Speaker	OF	1907–28	1937
Willie Stargell	OF-1B	1962–82	1988
Turkey Stearns*	CF		2000
Don Sutton	P	1966–88	1998
Bruce Sutter	P	1976–88	2006
George Suttles*	C	1923–44	2006
Benjamin Harrison Taylor*	P-1B	1908–29	2006
Bill Terry	1B	1923–36	1954
Sam Thompson	OF	1885–1906	1974
Joe Tinker	SS	1902–16	1946
Cristóbal Torriente*	OF	1913–32	2006
Pie Traynor	3B	1920–37	1948
Dazzy Vance	P	1915–35	1955
Arky Vaughan	SS	1932–48	1985
Rube Waddell	P	1897–1910	1946
Honus Wagner	SS	1897–1917	1936
Bobby Wallace	SS	1894–1918	1953
Ed Walsh	P	1904–17	1946
Lloyd Waner	OF	1927–45	1967
Paul Waner	OF	1926–45	1952
John Ward	2B-P	1878–94	1964
Mickey Welch	P	1880–92	1973
Willie Wells*	SS	1924–49	1997
Zach Wheat	OF	1909–27	1959
Hoyt Wilhelm	P	1952–72	1985
Billy Williams	OF	1959–76	1987
Ted Williams	OF	1939–60	1966
Vic Willis	P	1898–1910	1995
Ernest Judson Wilson*	3B	1922–45	2006
Hack Wilson	OF	1923–34	1979
Dave Winfield	OF	1973–95	2001
Early Wynn	P	1939–63	1972
Carl Yastrzemski	OF	1961–83	1989
Cy Young	P	1890–1911	1937
Ross Youngs	OF	1917–26	1972
Robin Yount	SS	1974–93	1999

*Elected on the basis of their career in the Negro leagues.

Pioneers/Executives

	Selected
Ed Barrow (manager-executive)	1953
Morgan Bulkeley (executive)	1937
Alexander Cartwright (executive)	1938
Henry Chadwick (writer-executive)	1938
Happy Chandler (commissioner)	1982
Charles Comiskey (manager-executive)	1939
Barney Dreyfuss (executive)	2008
Ford Frick (commissioner-executive)	1970
Warren Giles (executive)	1979
Clark Griffith (executive)	1946
Will Harridge (executive)	1972
William Hulbert (executive)	1995
Ban Johnson (executive)	1937
Bowie Kuhn (commissioner)	2008
Kenesaw M. Landis (commissioner)	1944
Larry MacPhail Sr. (executive)	1978
Lee MacPhail Jr. (executive)	1998
Effa Manley (executive)	2006
Walter O'Malley (executive)	2008
Alex Pompez (executive)	2006
Cum Posey (player-manager-owner)	2006
Branch Rickey (manager-executive)	1967
Al Spalding (player-executive)	1939
Bill Veeck Jr. (owner)	1991
George Weiss (executive)	1971
Sol White (player-manager)	2006
J.L. Wilkinson (executive)	2006
George Wright (player-manager)	1937
Harry Wright (player-manager-executive)	1953
Tom Yawkey (executive)	1980

Managers

	Managed	Selected
Walter Alston	1954–76	1983
Sparky Anderson	1970–94	2000
Leo Durocher	1939–73	1994
Rube Foster	1907–26	1981
Ned Hanlon	1899–1907	1996
Bucky Harris	1924–56	1975
Miller Huggins	1913–29	1964
Tommy Lasorda	1977–96	1997
Al Lopez	1951–69	1977
Connie Mack	1894–1950	1937
Joe McCarthy	1926–50	1957
John McGraw	1899–1932	1937
Bill McKechnie	1915–46	1962
Wilbert Robinson	1902–31	1945
Frank Selee	1890–1905	1999
Billy Southworth	1929, 1940–51	2008
Casey Stengel	1934–65	1966
Earl Weaver	1968–82, 85–86	1996
Dick Williams	1967–69, 1971–88	2008

Umpires

	Selected
Al Barlick	1989
Nestor Chylak	1999
Jocko Conlan	1974
Tom Connolly	1953
Billy Evans	1973
Cal Hubbard	1976
Bill Klem	1953
Bill McGowan	1992

Notable Achievements

No-Hit Games, Nine Innings or More

NATIONAL LEAGUE

Date	Pitcher and Game
1876......July 15	George Bradley, StL vs Hart 2–0
1880......June 12	John Richmond, Wor vs Clev 1–0 (perfect game)
June 17	Monte Ward, Prov vs Buff 5–0 (perfect game)
Aug 19	Larry Corcoran, Chi vs Bos 6–0
Aug 20	Pud Galvin, Buff vs Wor 1–0
1882......Sept 20	Larry Corcoran, Chi vs Wor 5–0
Sept 22	Tim Keefe, Bkln vs NY 4–0
1883......July 25	Hoss Radbourn, Prov vs Clev 8–0
Sept 13	Hugh Daily, Clev vs Phi 1–0
1884......June 27	Larry Corcoran, Chi vs Prov 6–0
Aug 4	Pud Galvin, Buff vs Det 18–0
1885......July 27	John Clarkson, Chi vs Prov 4–0
Aug 29	Charles Ferguson, Phi vs Prov 1–0
1891......July 31	Amos Rusie, NY vs Bkln 6–0
June 22	Tom Lovett, Bkln vs NY 4–0
1892......Aug 6	Jack Stivetts, Bos vs Bkln 11–0
Aug 22	Alex Sanders, Lou vs Balt 6–2
Oct 15	Bumpus Jones, Cin vs Pitt 7–1 (first major league game)
1893......Aug 16	Bill Hawke, Balt vs Wash 5–0
1897......Sept 18	Cy Young, Clev vs Cin 6–0
1898......Apr 22	Ted Breitenstein, Cin vs Pitt 11–0
Apr 22	Jim Hughes, Balt vs Bos 8–0
July 8	Frank Donahue, Phi vs Bos 5–0
Aug 21	Walter Thornton, Chi vs Bkln 2–0

Date	Pitcher and Game
1899......May 25	Deacon Phillippe, Lou vs NY 7–0
Aug 7	Vic Willis, Bos vs Wash 7–1
1900......July 12	Noodles Hahn, Cin vs Phi 4–0
1901......July 15	Christy Mathewson, NY vs StL 5–0
1903......Sept 18	Chick Fraser, Phi vs Chi 10–0
1904......June 11	Bob Wicker, Chi at NY 1–0 (hit in 10th; won in 12th)
1905......June 13	Christy Mathewson, NY vs Chi 1–0
1906......May 1	John Lush, Phi vs Bkln 6–0
July 20	Mal Eason, Bkln vs StL 2–0
Aug 1	Harry McIntire, Bkln vs Pitt 0–1 (hit in 11th; lost in 13th)
1907......May 8	Frank Pfeffer, Bos vs Cin 6–0
Sept 20	Nick Maddox, Pitt vs Bkln 2–1
1908......July 4	George Wiltse, NY vs Phi 1–0 (10 innings)
Sept 5	Nap Rucker, Bkln vs Bos 6–0
1909......Apr 15	Leon Ames, NY vs Bkln 0–3 (hit in 10th; lost in 13th)
1912......Sept 6	Jeff Tesreau, NY vs Phi 3–0
1914......Sept 9	George Davis, Bos vs Phi 7–0
1915......Apr 15	Rube Marquard, NY vs Bkln 2–0
Aug 31	Jimmy Lavender, Chi vs NY 2–0
1916......June 16	Tom Hughes, Bos vs Pitt 2–0
1917......May 2	Jim Vaughn, Chi vs Cin 0–1 (hit in 10th; lost in 10th)
May 2	Fred Toney, Cin vs Chi 1–0 (10 innings)

No-Hit Games, Nine Innings or More *(Cont.)*
NATIONAL LEAGUE *(Cont.)*

Date	Pitcher and Game	Date	Pitcher and Game
1919......May 11	Hod Eller, Cin vs StL 6–0	1973......Aug 5	Phil Niekro, Atl vs SD 9–0
1922......May 7	Jesse Barnes, NY vs Phi 6–0	1975......Aug 24	Ed Halicki, SF vs NY 6–0
1924......July 17	Jesse Haines, StL vs Bos 5–0	1976......July 9	Larry Dierker, Hou vs Mtl 6–0
1925......Sept 13	Dazzy Vance, Bklyn vs Phi 10–1	Aug 9	John Candelaria, Pitt vs LA 2–0
1929......May 8	Carl Hubbell, NY vs Phi 11–0	Sept 29	John Montefusco, SF vs Atl 9–0
1934......Sept 21	Paul Dean, StL vs Bklyn 3–0	1978......Apr 16	Bob Forsch, StL vs Phi 5–0
1938......June 11	Johnny Vander Meer, Cin vs Bos 3–0	June 16	Tom Seaver, Cin vs StL 4–0
June 15	Johnny Vander Meer, Cin vs Bklyn 6–0	1979......Apr 7	Ken Forsch, Hou vs Atl 6–0
1940......Apr 30	Tex Carleton, Bklyn vs Cin, 3–0	1980......June 27	Jerry Reuss, LA vs SF 8–0
1941......Aug 30	Lon Warneke, StL vs Cin 2–0	1981......May 10	Charlie Lea, Mtl vs SF 4–0
1944......Apr 27	Jim Tobin, Bos vs Bklyn 2–0	Sept 26	Nolan Ryan, Hou vs LA 5–0
May 15	Clyde Shoun, Cin vs Bos 1–0	1983......Sept 26	Bob Forsch, StL vs Mtl 3–0
1946......Apr 23	Ed Head, Bklyn vs Bos 5–0	1986......Sept 25	Mike Scott, Hou vs SF 2–0
1947......June 18	Ewell Blackwell, Cin vs Bos 6–0	1988......Sept 16	Tom Browning, Cin vs LA 1–0
1948......Sept 9	Rex Barney, Bklyn vs NY 2–0		(perfect game)
1950......Aug 11	Vern Bickford, Bos vs Bklyn 7–0	1990......June 29	Fernando Valenzuela, LA vs StL 6–0
1951......May 6	Cliff Chambers, Pitt vs Bos 3–0	Aug 15	Terry Mulholland, Phi vs SF 6–0
1952......June 19	Carl Erskine, Bklyn vs Chi 5–0	1991......May 23	Tommy Greene, Phi vs Mtl 2–0
1954......June 12	Jim Wilson, Mil vs Phi 2–0	July 26	Mark Gardner, Mtl vs LA 0–1
1955......May 12	Sam Jones, Chi vs Pitt 4–0		(hit in 10th, lost in 10th)
1956......May 12	Carl Erskine, Bklyn vs NY 3–0	July 28	Dennis Martinez, Mtl vs LA 2–0
Sept 25	Sal Maglie, Bklyn vs Phi 5–0		(perfect game)
1959......May 26	Harvey Haddix, Pitt vs Mil 0–1	Sept 11	Kent Mercker (6), Mark Wohlers (2),
	(hit in 13th; lost in 13th)		and Alejandro Pena (1), Atl vs SD 1–0
1960......May 15	Don Cardwell, Chi vs StL 4–0	1992......Aug 17	Kevin Gross, LA vs SF 2–0
Aug 18	Lew Burdette, Mil vs Phi 1–0	1993......Sept 8	Darryl Kile, Hou vs NY 7–1
Sept 16	Warren Spahn, Mil vs Phi 4–0	1994......Apr 8	Kent Mercker, Atl vs LA 6–0
1961......Apr 28	Warren Spahn, Mil vs SF 1–0	1995......June 3	Pedro Martinez, Mtl vs SD 1–0
1962......June 30	Sandy Koufax, LA vs NY 5–0		(perfect through nine, hit in 10th)
1963......May 11	Sandy Koufax, LA vs SF 8–0	July 14	Ramon Martinez, LA vs Fla 7–0
May 17	Don Nottebart, Hou vs Phi 4–1	1996......May 11	Al Leiter, Fla vs Col 11–0
June 15	Juan Marichal, SF vs Hou 1–0	Sept 17	Hideo Nomo, LA vs Col 9–0
1964......Apr 23	Ken Johnson, Hou vs Cin 0–1	1997......June 10	Kevin Brown, Fla vs SF 9–0
June 4	Sandy Koufax, LA vs Phi 3–0	July 12	Francisco Cordova (9) and
June 21	Jim Bunning, Phi vs NY 6–0		Ricardo Rincon (1), Pitt vs Col 3–0
	(perfect game)	1999......June 25	Jose Jimenez, StL vs Ariz 1–0
1965......June 14	Jim Maloney, Cin vs NY 0–1	2001......May 12	A.J. Burnett, Fla vs SD 3–0
	(hit in 11th; lost in 11th)	Sept 3	Bud Smith, StL vs SD 4–0
Aug 19	Jim Maloney, Cin vs Chi 1–0	2003......April 27	Kevin Millwood, Phi vs SF 1–0
	(10 innings)	June 11	R. Oswalt (1), P. Munro (2.2), K.
Sept 9	Sandy Koufax, LA vs Chi 1–0		Saarloos (1.1), B. Lidge (2), O. Dotel
	(perfect game)		(1), B. Wagner (1), Hou vs NYY 8–0
1967......June 18	Don Wilson, Hou vs Atl 2–0	April 27	Kevin Millwood, Phi vs SF 1–0
1968......July 29	George Culver, Cin vs Phi 6–1	2004......May 18	Randy Johnson, Ariz vs Atl 2–0
Sept 17	Gaylord Perry, SF vs StL 1–0		(perfect game)
Sept 18	Ray Washburn, StL vs SF 2–0	2006......Sept 6	Anibal Sanchez, Fla vs Ariz 2–0
1969......Apr 17	Bill Stoneman, Mtl vs Phi 7–0	2008......Sept 14	†Carlos Zambrano, Chi vs Hou 5–0
Apr 30	Jim Maloney, Cin vs Hou 10–0	2009......July 10	Jonathan Sanchez, SF vs SD 8–0
May 1	Don Wilson, Hou vs Cin 4–0	2010......Apr 17	Ubaldo Jimenez, Col vs Atl 4–0
Aug 19	Ken Holtzman, Chi vs Atl 3–0	May 29	Roy Halladay, Phi vs Fla 1–0
Sept 20	Bob Moose, Pitt vs NY 4–0		(perfect game)
1970......June 12	Dock Ellis, Pitt vs SD 2–0	June 26	‡Edwin Jackson, Ariz vs TB 1–0
July 20	Bill Singer, LA vs Phi 5–0	Oct 6	Roy Halladay, Phi vs Cin 4–0
1971......June 3	Ken Holtzman, Chi vs Cin 1–0		(NLDS)
June 23	Rick Wise, Phi vs Cin 4–0		
Aug 14	Bob Gibson, StL vs Pitt 11–0		
1972......Apr 16	Burt Hooton, Chi vs Phi 4–0		
Sept 2	Milt Pappas, Chi vs SD 8–0		
Oct 2	Bill Stoneman, Mtl vs NY 7–0		

Note: Includes the games struck from the official record book on Sept. 4, 1991, when baseball's committee on statistical accuracy voted to define no-hitters as games of nine innings or more that end with a team getting no hits.

†Game played in Milwaukee due to weather-related closure of Houston's home field.

‡Interleague game.

No-Hit Games, Nine Innings or More (Cont.)

AMERICAN LEAGUE

Date	Pitcher and Game	Date	Pitcher and Game
1901......May 9	Earl Moore, Clev vs Chi 2–4 (hit in 10th; lost in 10th)	1957......Aug 20	Bob Keegan, Chi vs Wash 6–0
1902......Sept 20	Jimmy Callahan, Chi vs Det 3–0	1958......July 20	Jim Bunning, Det vs Bos 3–0
1904......May 5	Cy Young, Bos vs Phi 3–0 (perfect game)	Sept 20	Hoyt Wilhelm, Balt vs NY 1–0
Aug 17	Jesse Tannehill, Bos vs Chi 6–0	1962......May 5	Bo Belinsky, LA vs Balt 2–0
1905......July 22	Weldon Henley, Phi vs StL 6–0	June 26	Earl Wilson, Bos vs LA 2–0
Sept 6	Frank Smith, Chi vs Det 15–0	Aug 1	Bill Monbouquette, Bos vs Chi 1–0
Sept 27	Bill Dinneen, Bos vs Chi 2–0	Aug 26	Jack Kralick, Minn vs KC 1–0
1908......June 30	Cy Young, Bos vs NY 8–0	1965......Sept 16	Dave Morehead, Bos vs Clev 2–0
Sept 18	Bob Rhoades, Clev vs Bos 2–1	1966......June 10	Sonny Siebert, Clev vs Wash 2–0
Sept 20	Frank Smith, Chi vs Phi 1–0	1967......Apr 30	Steve Barber (8⅔) and Stu Miller (⅓), Balt vs Det 1–2
Oct 2	Addie Joss, Clev vs Chi 1–0 (perfect game)	Aug 25	Dean Chance, Minn vs Clev 2–1
1910......Apr 20	Addie Joss, Clev vs Chi 1–0	Sept 10	Joel Horlen, Chi vs Det 6–0
May 12	Chief Bender, Phi vs Clev 4–0	1968......Apr 27	Tom Phoebus, Balt vs Bos 6–0
Aug 30	Tom Hughes, NY vs Clev 0–5 (hit in 10th; lost in 11th)	May 8	Catfish Hunter, Oak vs Minn 4–0 (perfect game)
1911......July 29	Joe Wood, Bos vs StL 5–0	1969......Aug 13	Jim Palmer, Balt vs Oak 8–0
Aug 27	Ed Walsh, Chi vs Bos 5–0	1970......July 3	Clyde Wright, Cal vs Oak 4–0
1912......July 4	George Mullin, Det vs StL 7–0	Sept 21	Vida Blue, Oak vs Minn 6–0
Aug 30	Earl Hamilton, StL vs Det 5–1	1973......Apr 27	Steve Busby, KC vs Det 3–0
1914......May 14	Jim Scott, Chi vs Wash 0–1 (hit in 10th; lost in 10th)	May 15	Nolan Ryan, Cal vs KC 3–0
May 31	Joe Benz, Chi vs Clev 6–1	July 15	Nolan Ryan, Cal vs Det 6–0
1916......June 21	George Foster, Bos vs NY 2–0	July 30	Jim Bibby, Tex vs Oak 6–0
Aug 26	Joe Bush, Phi vs Clev 5–0	1974......June 19	Steve Busby, KC vs Mil 2–0
Aug 30	Dutch Leonard, Bos vs StL 4–0	July 19	Dick Bosman, Clev vs Oak 4–0
1917......Apr 14	Ed Cicotte, Chi vs StL 11–0	Sept 28	Nolan Ryan, Cal vs Minn 4–0
Apr 24	George Mogridge, NY vs Bos 2–1	1975......June 1	Nolan Ryan, Cal vs Balt 1–0
May 5	Ernie Koob, StL vs Chi 1–0	Sept 28	Vida Blue (5), Glenn Abbott and Paul Lindblad (1), Rollie Fingers (2), Oak vs Cal 5–0
May 6	Bob Groom, StL vs Chi 3–0		
June 23	Ernie Shore, Bos vs Wash 4–0 (perfect game)	1976......July 28	John Odom (5) and Francisco Barrios (4), Chi vs Oak 2–1
1918......June 3	Dutch Leonard, Bos vs Det 5–0	1977......May 14	Jim Colborn, KC vs Tex 6–0
1919......Sept 10	Ray Caldwell, Clev vs NY 3–0	May 30	Dennis Eckersley, Clev vs Cal 1–0
1920......July 1	Walter Johnson, Wash vs Bos 1–0		
1922......Apr 30	Charlie Robertson, Chi vs Det 2–0 (perfect game)	Sept 22	Bert Blyleven, Tex vs Cal 6–0
1923......Sept 4	Sam Jones, NY vs Phi 2–0	1981......May 15	Len Barker, Clev vs Tor 3–0 (perfect game)
Sept 7	Howard Ehmke, Bos vs Phi 4–0	1983......July 4	Dave Righetti, NY vs Bos 4–0
1926......Aug 21	Ted Lyons, Chi vs Bos 6–0	Sept 29	Mike Warren, Oak vs Chi 3–0
1931......Apr 29	Wes Ferrell, Clev vs StL 9–0	1984......Apr 7	Jack Morris, Det vs Chi 4–0
Aug 8	Bob Burke, Wash vs Bos 5–0	Sept 30	Mike Witt, Cal vs Tex 1–0 (perfect game)
1934......Sept 18	Bobo Newsom, StL vs Bos 1–2 (hit in 10th; lost in 10th)	1986......Sept 19	Joe Cowley, Chi vs Cal 7–1
1935......Aug 31	Vern Kennedy, Chi vs Clev 5–0	1987......Apr 15	Juan Nieves, Mil vs Balt 7–0
1937......June 1	Bill Dietrich, Chi vs StL 8–0	1990......Apr 11	Mark Langston (7), Mike Witt (2), Cal vs Sea 1–0
1938......Aug 27	Mtle Pearson, NY vs Clev 13–0	June 2	Randy Johnson, Sea vs Det 2–0
1940......Apr 16	Bob Feller, Clev vs Chi 1–0 (opening day)	June 11	Nolan Ryan, Tex vs Oak 5–0
1945......Sept 9	Dick Fowler, Phi vs StL 1–0	June 29	Dave Stewart, Oak vs Tor 5–0
1946......Apr 30	Bob Feller, Clev vs NY 1–0	July 1	Andy Hawkins, NY vs Chi 0–4 (pitched eight of nine–inning game)
1947......July 10	Don Black, Clev vs Phi 3–0	Sept 2	Dave Stieb, Tor vs Clev 3–0
Sep 3	Bill McCahan, Phi vs Wash 3–0	1991......May 1	Nolan Ryan, Tex vs Tor 3–0
1948......June 30	Bob Lemon, Clev vs Det 2–0	July 13	Bob Milacki (6), Mike Flanagan (1), Mark Williamson (1), and Gregg Olson (1), Balt vs Oak 2–0
1951......July 1	Bob Feller, Clev vs Det 2–1		
July 12	Allie Reynolds, NY vs Clev 1–0	Aug 11	Wilson Alvarez, Chi vs Balt 7–0
Sept 28	Allie Reynolds, NY vs Bos 8–0	Aug 26	Bret Saberhagen, KC vs Chi 7–0
1952......May 15	Virgil Trucks, Det vs Wash 1–0	1993......Apr 22	Chris Bosio, Sea vs Bos 7–0
Aug 25	Virgil Trucks, Det vs NY 1–0	Sept 4	Jim Abbott, NY vs Clev 4–0
1953......May 6	Bobo Holloman, StL vs Phi 6–0 (first major league start)	1994......Apr 27	Scott Erickson, Minn vs Mil 6–0
1956......July 14	Mel Parnell, Bos vs Chi 4–0	July 28	Kenny Rogers, Texas vs Cal 4–0 (perfect game)
Oct 8	Don Larsen, NY (A) vs Bklyn (N) 2–0 (World Series) (perfect game)	1996......May 14	Dwight Gooden, NY vs Sea 2–0

No-Hit Games, Nine Innings or More *(Cont.)*
AMERICAN LEAGUE *(Cont.)*

Date	Pitcher and Game
1998......May 17	David Wells, NY vs Minn 4–0 (perfect game)
1999......July 18	David Cone, NY vs Mtl 6–0 (perfect game)
Sept 11	Eric Milton, Minn vs Ana 7–0
2001......Apr 4	Hideo Nomo, Bos vs Balt 3–0
2002......Apr 27	Derek Lowe, Bos vs TB 10–0
2007......Apr 19	Mark Buehrle, Chi vs Tex, 6–0
June 12	Justin Verlander, Det vs Mil 4–0
Sep 1	Clay Buchholz, Bos vs Balt 10–0
2008......May 19	Jon Lester, Bos vs KC 7–0
2009......July 23	Mark Buehrle, Chi vs TB 5–0 (perfect game)
2010......May 9	Dallas Braden, Oak vs TB 4–0 (perfect game)
July 26	Matt Garza, TB vs Det 5–0

Longest Hitting Streaks

NATIONAL LEAGUE

Player and Team	Year	G
Willie Keeler, Balt	1897	44
Pete Rose, Cin	1978	44
Bill Dahlen, Chi	1894	42
Tommy Holmes, Bos	1945	37
Billy Hamilton, Phi	1894	36
Jimmy Rollins, Phi	2005–06	36
Fred Clarke, Lou	1895	35
Luis Castillo, Fla	2002	35
Chase Utley, Phi	2006	35
Benito Santiago, SD	1987	34
George Davis, NY	1893	33
Rogers Hornsby, StL	1922	33

AMERICAN LEAGUE

Player and Team	Year	G
Joe DiMaggio, NY	1941	56
George Sisler, StL	1922	41
Ty Cobb, Det	1911	40
Paul Molitor, Mil	1987	39
Ty Cobb, Det	1917	35
George Sisler, StL	1925	34
George McQuinn, StL	1938	34
Dom DiMaggio, Bos	1949	34
Hal Chase, NY	1907	33
Heinie Manush, Wash	1933	33

Triple Crown Hitters

NATIONAL LEAGUE

Player and Team	Year	HR	RBI	BA
Paul Hines, Prov	1878	4	50	.358
Hugh Duffy, Bos	1894	18	145	.438
Heinie Zimmerman*, Chi	1912	14	103	.372
Rogers Hornsby, StL	1922	42	152	.401
	1925	39	143	.403
Chuck Klein, Phi	1933	28	120	.368
Joe Medwick, StL	1937	31	154	.374

*Zimmerman ranked first in RBIs as calculated by Ernie Lanigan, but only third as calculated by Information Concepts Inc.

AMERICAN LEAGUE

Player and Team	Year	HR	RBI	BA
Nap Lajoie, Phi	1901	14	125	.422
Ty Cobb, Det	1909	9	115	.377
Jimmie Foxx, Phi	1933	48	163	.356
Lou Gehrig, NY	1934	49	165	.363
Ted Williams, Bos	1942	36	137	.356
	1947	32	114	.343
Mickey Mantle, NY	1956	52	130	.353
Frank Robinson, Balt	1966	49	122	.316
Carl Yastrzemski, Bos	1967	44	121	.326

Triple Crown Pitchers

NATIONAL LEAGUE				
Player and Team	Year	W	L	SO	ERA
Tommy Bond, Bos	1877	40	17	170	2.11
Hoss Radbourn, Prov	1884	60	12	441	1.38
Tim Keefe, NY	1888	35	12	333	1.74
John Clarkson, Bos	1889	49	19	284	2.73
Amos Rusie, NY	1894	36	13	195	2.78
Christy Mathewson, NY	1905	31	9	206	1.27
	1908	37	11	259	1.43
Grover Alexander, Phi	1915	31	10	241	1.22
	1916	33	12	167	1.55
	1917	30	13	201	1.86
Hippo Vaughn, Chi	1918	22	10	148	1.74
Dazzy Vance, Bklyn	1924	28	6	262	2.16
Bucky Walters, Cin	1939	27	11	137	2.29
Sandy Koufax, LA	1963	25	5	306	1.88
	1965	26	8	382	2.04
	1966	27	9	317	1.73
Steve Carlton, Phi	1972	27	10	310	1.97
Dwight Gooden, NY	1985	24	4	268	1.53
Randy Johnson, Ariz	2002	24	5	334	2.32

AMERICAN LEAGUE				
Player and Team	Year	W	L	SO	ERA
Cy Young, Bos	1901	33	10	158	1.62
Rube Waddell, Phi	1905	26	11	287	1.48
Walter Johnson, Wash	1913	36	7	303	1.09
	1918	23	13	162	1.27
	1924	23	7	158	2.72
Lefty Grove, Phi	1930	28	5	209	2.54
	1931	31	4	175	2.06
Lefty Gomez, NY	1934	26	5	158	2.33
	1937	21	11	194	2.33
Hal Newhouser, Det	1945	25	9	212	1.81
Roger Clemens, Tor	1997	21	7	292	2.05
	1998	20	6	271	2.64
Pedro Martinez, Bos	1999	23	4	313	2.07
*Johan Santana, Minn	2006	19	6	245	2.77

*Tied with another pitcher for most wins

Consecutive Games Played, 500 or More Games

Cal Ripken Jr.	2,632	Frank McCormick	652
Lou Gehrig	2,130	Sandy Alomar Sr.	648
Everett Scott	1,307	Eddie Brown	618
Steve Garvey	1,207	Roy McMillan	585
Miguel Tejada	1,152	George Pinckney	577
Billy Williams	1,117	Steve Brodie	574
Joe Sewell	1,103	Aaron Ward	565
Stan Musial	895	Alex Rodriguez	546
Eddie Yost	829	Candy LaChance	540
Gus Suhr	822	Buck Freeman	535
Nellie Fox	798	Fred Luderus	533
Pete Rose	745	Hideki Matsui	518
Dale Murphy	740	Clyde Milan	511
Richie Ashburn	730	Charlie Gehringer	511
Ernie Banks	717	Vada Pinson	508
Pete Rose	678	Tony Cuccinello	504
Earl Averill	673	Charlie Gehringer	504

Unassisted Triple Plays

Player and Team	Date	Pos	Opp	Opp Batter
Neal Ball, Clev	7-19-09	SS	Bos	Amby McConnell
Bill Wambsganss, Clev	10-10-20	2B	Bklyn	Clarence Mitchell
George Burns, Bos	9-14-23	1B	Clev	Frank Brower
Ernie Padgett, Bos	10-6-23	SS	Phi	Walter Holke
Glenn Wright, Pitt	5-7-25	SS	StL	Jim Bottomley
Jimmy Cooney, Chi	5-30-27	SS	Pitt	Paul Waner
Johnny Neun, Det	5-31-27	1B	Clev	Homer Summa
Ron Hansen, Wash	7-30-68	SS	Clev	Joe Azcue
Mickey Morandini, Phi	9-20-92	2B	Pitt	Jeff King
John Valentin, Bos	7-15-94	SS	Minn	Marc Newfield
Randy Velarde, Oak	5-29-00	2B	NYY	Shane Spencer
Rafael Furcal, Atl	8-10-03	SS	StL	Woody Williams
Troy Tulowitzki, Col	4-29-07	SS	Atl	Chipper Jones
Asdrubal Cabrera, Cle	5-12-08	2B	Tor	Lyle Overbay
Eric Bruntlett, Phi	8-23-09	2B	NYM	Jeff Francoeur

Leading Batsmen

Year	Player and Team	BA	Year	Player and Team	BA
1900	Honus Wagner, Pitt	.381	1956	Hank Aaron, Mil	.328
1901	Jesse Burkett, StL	.382	1957	Stan Musial, StL	.351
1902	Ginger Beaumtl, Pitt	.357	1958	Richie Ashburn, Phi	.350
1903	Honus Wagner, Pitt	.355	1959	Hank Aaron, Mil	.355
1904	Honus Wagner, Pitt	.349	1960	Dick Groat, Pitt	.325
1905	Cy Seymour, Cin	.377	1961	Roberto Clemente, Pitt	.351
1906	Honus Wagner, Pitt	.339	1962	Tommy Davis, LA	.346
1907	Honus Wagner, Pitt	.350	1963	Tommy Davis, LA	.326
1908	Honus Wagner, Pitt	.354	1964	Roberto Clemente, Pitt	.339
1909	Honus Wagner, Pitt	.339	1965	Roberto Clemente, Pitt	.329
1910	Sherry Magee, Phi	.331	1966	Matty Alou, Pitt	.342
1911	Honus Wagner, Pitt	.334	1967	Roberto Clemente, Pitt	.357
1912	Heinie Zimmerman, Chi	.372	1968	Pete Rose, Cin	.335
1913	Jake Daubert, Bklyn	.350	1969	Pete Rose, Cin	.348
1914	Jake Daubert, Bklyn	.329	1970	Rico Carty, Atl	.366
1915	Larry Doyle, NY	.320	1971	Joe Torre, StL	.363
1916	Hal Chase, Cin	.339	1972	Billy Williams, Chi	.333
1917	Edd Roush, Cin	.341	1973	Pete Rose, Cin	.338
1918	Zach Wheat, Bklyn	.335	1974	Ralph Garr, Atl	.353
1919	Edd Roush, Cin	.321	1975	Bill Madlock, Chi	.354
1920	Rogers Hornsby, StL	.370	1976	Bill Madlock, Chi	.339
1921	Rogers Hornsby, StL	.397	1977	Dave Parker, Pitt	.338
1922	Rogers Hornsby, StL	.401	1978	Dave Parker, Pitt	.334
1923	Rogers Hornsby, StL	.384	1979	Keith Hernandez, StL	.344
1924	Rogers Hornsby, StL	.424	1980	Bill Buckner, Chi	.324
1925	Rogers Hornsby, StL	.403	1981	Bill Madlock, Pitt	.341
1926	Bubbles Hargrave, Cin	.353	1982	Al Oliver, Mtl	.331
1927	Paul Waner, Pitt	.380	1983	Bill Madlock, Pitt	.323
1928	Rogers Hornsby, Bos	.387	1984	Tony Gwynn, SD	.351
1929	Lefty O'Doul, Phi	.398	1985	Willie McGee, StL	.353
1930	Bill Terry, NY	.401	1986	Tim Raines, Mtl	.334
1931	Chick Hafey, StL	.349	1987	Tony Gwynn, SD	.370
1932	Lefty O'Doul, Bklyn	.368	1988	Tony Gwynn, SD	.313
1933	Chuck Klein, Phi	.368	1989	Tony Gwynn, SD	.336
1934	Paul Waner, Pitt	.362	1990	Willie McGee, StL	.335
1935	Arky Vaughan, Pitt	.385	1991	Terry Pendleton, Atl	.319
1936	Paul Waner, Pitt	.373	1992	Gary Sheffield, SD	.330
1937	Joe Medwick, StL	.374	1993	Andres Galarraga, Col	.370
1938	Ernie Lombardi, Cin	.342	1994	Tony Gwynn, SD	.394
1939	Johnny Mize, StL	.349	1995	Tony Gwynn, SD	.368
1940	Debs Garms, Pitt	.355	1996	Tony Gwynn, SD	.353
1941	Pete Reiser, Bklyn	.343	1997	Tony Gwynn, SD	.372
1942	Ernie Lombardi, Bos	.330	1998	Larry Walker, Col	.363
1943	Stan Musial, StL	.357	1999	Larry Walker, Col	.379
1944	Dixie Walker, Bklyn	.357	2000	Todd Helton, Col	.372
1945	Phil Cavarretta, Chi	.355	2001	Larry Walker, Col	.350
1946	Stan Musial, StL	.365	2002	Barry Bonds, SF	.370
1947	Harry Walker, StL-Phi	.363	2003	Albert Pujols, StL	.359
1948	Stan Musial, StL	.376	2004	Barry Bonds, SF	.362
1949	Jackie Robinson, Bklyn	.342	2005	Derrek Lee, Chi	.335
1950	Stan Musial, StL	.346	2006	Freddy Sanchez, Pitt	.334
1951	Stan Musial, StL	.355	2007	Matt Holliday, Col	.340*
1952	Stan Musial, StL	.336	2008	Chipper Jones, Atl	.364
1953	Carl Furillo, Bklyn	.344	2009	Hanley Ramirez, Fla	.342
1954	Willie Mays, NY	.345	2010	Carlos Gonzalez, Col	.336
1955	Richie Ashburn, Phi	.338			

*Includes one-game NL Wild Card tiebreaker.

Leaders in Runs Scored

Year	Player and Team	Runs	Year	Player and Team	Runs
1900	Roy Thomas, Phi	131	1955	Duke Snider, Bklyn	126
1901	Jesse Burkett, StL	139	1956	Frank Robinson, Cin	122
1902	Honus Wagner, Pitt	105	1957	Hank Aaron, Mil	118
1903	Ginger Beaumont, Pitt	137	1958	Willie Mays, SF	121
1904	George Browne, NY	99	1959	Vada Pinson, Cin	131
1905	Mike Donlin, NY	124	1960	Bill Bruton, Mil	112
1906	Honus Wagner, Pitt	103	1961	Willie Mays, SF	129
	Frank Chance, Chi	103	1962	Frank Robinson, Cin	134
1907	Spike Shannon, NY	104	1963	Hank Aaron, Mil	121
1908	Fred Tenney, NY	101	1964	Dick Allen, Phi	125
1909	Tommy Leach, Pitt	126	1965	Tommy Harper, Cin	126
1910	Sherry Magee, Phi	110	1966	Felipe Alou, Atl	122
1911	Jimmy Sheckard, Chi	121	1967	Hank Aaron, Atl	113
1912	Bob Bescher, Cin	120		Lou Brock, StL	113
1913	Tommy Leach, Chi	99	1968	Glenn Beckert, Chi	98
	Max Carey, Pitt	99	1969	Bobby Bonds, SF	120
1914	George Burns, NY	100		Pete Rose, Cin	120
1915	Gavvy Cravath, Phi	89	1970	Billy Williams, Chi	137
1916	George Burns, NY	105	1971	Lou Brock, StL	126
1917	George Burns, NY	103	1972	Joe Morgan, Cin	122
1918	Heinie Groh, Cin	88	1973	Bobby Bonds, SF	131
1919	George Burns, NY	86	1974	Pete Rose, Cin	110
1920	George Burns, NY	115	1975	Pete Rose, Cin	112
1921	Rogers Hornsby, StL	131	1976	Pete Rose, Cin	130
1922	Rogers Hornsby, StL	141	1977	George Foster, Cin	124
1923	Ross Youngs, NY	121	1978	Ivan DeJesus, Chi	104
1924	Frankie Frisch, NY	121	1979	Keith Hernandez, StL	116
	Rogers Hornsby, StL	121	1980	Keith Hernandez, StL	111
1925	Kiki Cuyler, Pitt	144	1981	Mike Schmidt, Phi	78
1926	Kiki Cuyler, Pitt	113	1982	Lonnie Smith, StL	120
1927	Lloyd Waner, Pitt	133	1983	Tim Raines, Mtl	133
	Rogers Hornsby, NY	133	1984	Ryne Sandberg, Chi	114
1928	Paul Waner, Pitt	142	1985	Dale Murphy, Atl	118
1929	Rogers Hornsby, Chi	156	1986	Von Hayes, Phi	107
1930	Chuck Klein, Phi	158		Tony Gwynn, SD	107
1931	Bill Terry, NY	121	1987	Tim Raines, Mtl	123
	Chuck Klein, Phi	121	1988	Brett Butler, SF	109
1932	Chuck Klein, Phi	152	1989	Howard Johnson, NY	104
1933	Pepper Martin, StL	122		Will Clark, SF	104
1934	Paul Waner, Pitt	122		Ryne Sandberg, Chi	104
1935	Augie Galan, Chi	133	1990	Ryne Sandberg, Chi	116
1936	Arky Vaughan, Pitt	122	1991	Brett Butler, LA	112
1937	Joe Medwick, StL	111	1992	Barry Bonds, Pitt	109
1938	Mel Ott, NY	116	1993	Lenny Dykstra, Phi	143
1939	Billy Werber, Cin	115	1994	Jeff Bagwell, Hou	104
1940	Arky Vaughan, Pitt	113	1995	Craig Biggio, Hou	123
1941	Pete Reiser, Bklyn	117	1996	Ellis Burks, Col	142
1942	Mel Ott, NY	118	1997	Craig Biggio, Hou	146
1943	Arky Vaughan, Bklyn	112	1998	Sammy Sosa, Chi	134
1944	Bill Nicholson, Chi	116	1999	Jeff Bagwell, Hou	143
1945	Eddie Stanky, Bklyn	128	2000	Jeff Bagwell, Hou	152
1946	Stan Musial, StL	124	2001	Sammy Sosa, Chi	146
1947	Johnny Mize, NY	137	2002	Sammy Sosa, Chi	122
1948	Stan Musial, StL	135	2003	Albert Pujols, StL	137
1949	Pee Wee Reese, Bklyn	132	2004	Albert Pujols, StL	133
1950	Earl Torgeson, Bos	120	2005	Albert Pujols, StL	129
1951	Stan Musial, StL	124	2006	Chase Utley, Phi	131
	Ralph Kiner, Pitt	124	2007	Jimmy Rollins, Phi	139
1952	Stan Musial, StL	105	2008	Hanley Ramirez, Fla	125
	Solly Hemus, StL	105	2009	Albert Pujols, StL	124
1953	Duke Snider, Bklyn	132	2010	Albert Pujols, StL	115
1954	Stan Musial, StL	120			
	Duke Snider, Bklyn	120			

Leaders in Hits

Year	Player and Team	Hits	Year	Player and Team	Hits
1900	Willie Keeler, Bklyn	208	1958	Richie Ashburn, Phi	215
1901	Jesse Burkett, StL	228	1959	Hank Aaron, Mil	223
1902	Ginger Beaumont, Pitt	194	1960	Willie Mays, SF	190
1903	Ginger Beaumont, Pitt	209	1961	Vada Pinson, Cin	208
1904	Ginger Beaumont, Pitt	185	1962	Tommy Davis, LA	230
1905	Cy Seymour, Cin	219	1963	Vada Pinson, Cin	204
1906	Harry Steinfeldt, Chi	176	1964	Roberto Clemente, Pitt	211
1907	Ginger Beaumont, Bos	187		Curt Flood, StL	211
1908	Honus Wagner, Pitt	201	1965	Pete Rose, Cin	209
1909	Larry Doyle, NY	172	1966	Felipe Alou, Atl	218
1910	Bobby Byrne, Pitt	178	1967	Roberto Clemente, Pitt	209
	Honus Wagner, Pitt	178	1968	Felipe Alou, Atl	210
1911	Doc Miller, Bos	192		Pete Rose, Cin	210
1912	Heinie Zimmerman, Chi	207	1969	Matty Alou, Pitt	231
1913	Gavvy Cravath, Phi	179	1970	Pete Rose, Cin	205
1914	Sherry Magee, Phi	171		Billy Williams, Chi	205
1915	Larry Doyle, NY	189	1971	Joe Torre, StL	230
1916	Hal Chase, Cin	184	1972	Pete Rose, Cin	198
1917	Heinie Groh, Cin	182	1973	Pete Rose, Cin	230
1918	Charlie Hollocher, Chi	161	1974	Ralph Garr, Atl	214
1919	Ivy Olson, Bklyn	164	1975	Dave Cash, Phi	213
1920	Rogers Hornsby, StL	218	1976	Pete Rose, Cin	215
1921	Rogers Hornsby, StL	235	1977	Dave Parker, Pitt	215
1922	Rogers Hornsby, StL	250	1978	Steve Garvey, LA	202
1923	Frankie Frisch, NY	223	1979	Garry Templeton, StL	211
1924	Rogers Hornsby, StL	227	1980	Steve Garvey, LA	200
1925	Jim Bottomley, StL	227	1981	Pete Rose, Phi	140
1926	Eddie Brown, Bos	201	1982	Al Oliver, Mtl	204
1927	Paul Waner, Pitt	237	1983	Jose Cruz, Hou	189
1928	Freddy Lindstrom, NY	231		Andre Dawson, Mtl	189
1929	Lefty O'Doul, Phi	254	1984	Tony Gwynn, SD	213
1930	Bill Terry, NY	254	1985	Willie McGee, StL	216
1931	Lloyd Waner, Pitt	214	1986	Tony Gwynn, SD	211
1932	Chuck Klein, Phi	226	1987	Tony Gwynn, SD	218
1933	Chuck Klein, Phi	223	1988	Andres Galarraga, Mtl	184
1934	Paul Waner, Pitt	217	1989	Tony Gwynn, SD	203
1935	Billy Herman, Chi	227	1990	Brett Butler, SF	192
1936	Joe Medwick, StL	223		Lenny Dykstra, Phi	192
1937	Joe Medwick, StL	237	1991	Terry Pendleton, Atl	187
1938	Frank McCormick, Cin	209	1992	Terry Pendleton, Atl	199
1939	Frank McCormick, Cin	209		Andy Van Slyke, Pitt	199
1940	Stan Hack, Chi	191	1993	Lenny Dykstra, Phi	194
	Frank McCormick, Cin	191	1994	Tony Gwynn, SD	165
1941	Stan Hack, Chi	186	1995	Dante Bichette, Col	197
1942	Enos Slaughter, StL	188		Tony Gwynn, SD	197
1943	Stan Musial, StL	220	1996	Lance Johnson, NY	227
1944	Phil Cavarretta, Chi	197	1997	Tony Gwynn, SD	220
	Stan Musial, StL	197	1998	Dante Bichette, Col	219
1945	Tommy Holmes, Bos	224	1999	Luis Gonzalez, Ariz	206
1946	Stan Musial, StL	228	2000	Todd Helton, Col	216
1947	Tommy Holmes, Bos	191	2001	Rich Aurilia, SF	206
1948	Stan Musial, StL	230	2002	Vladimir Guerrero	206
1949	Stan Musial, StL	207	2003	Albert Pujols, StL	212
1950	Duke Snider, Bklyn	199	2004	Juan Pierre, Fla	221
1951	Richie Ashburn, Phi	221	2005	Derrek Lee, Chi	199
1952	Stan Musial, StL	194	2006	Juan Pierre, Chi	204
1953	Richie Ashburn, Phi	205	2007	Matt Holliday, Col	216*
1954	Don Mueller, NY	212	2008	Jose Reyes, NYM	204
1955	Ted Kluszewski, Cin	192	2009	Ryan Braun, Mil	203
1956	Hank Aaron, Mil	200	2010	Carlos Gonzalez, Col	197
1957	Red Schoendienst, NY-Mil	200			

*Includes one-game NL Wild Card tiebreaker.

Home Run Leaders

Year	Player and Team	HR	Year	Player and Team	HR
1900	Herman Long, Bos	12	1952	Ralph Kiner, Pitt	37
1901	Sam Crawford, Cin	16		Hank Sauer, Chi	37
1902	Tommy Leach, Pitt	6	1953	Eddie Mathews, Mil	47
1903	Jimmy Sheckard, Bklyn	9	1954	Ted Kluszewski, Cin	49
1904	Harry Lumley, Bklyn	9	1955	Willie Mays, NY	51
1905	Fred Odwell, Cin	9	1956	Duke Snider, Bklyn	43
1906	Tim Jordan, Bklyn	12	1957	Hank Aaron, Mil	44
1907	Dave Brain, Bos	10	1958	Ernie Banks, Chi	47
1908	Tim Jordan, Bklyn	12	1959	Eddie Mathews, Mil	46
1909	Red Murray, NY	7	1960	Ernie Banks, Chi	41
1910	Fred Beck, Bos	10	1961	Orlando Cepeda, SF	46
	Wildfire Schulte, Chi	10	1962	Willie Mays, SF	49
1911	Wildfire Schulte, Chi	21	1963	Hank Aaron, Mil	44
1912	Heinie Zimmerman, Chi	14		Willie McCovey, SF	44
1913	Gavvy Cravath, Phi	19	1964	Willie Mays, SF	47
1914	Gavvy Cravath, Phi	19	1965	Willie Mays, SF	52
1915	Gavvy Cravath, Phi	24	1966	Hank Aaron, Atl	44
1916	Dave Robertson, NY	12	1967	Hank Aaron, Atl	39
	Cy Williams, Chi	12	1968	Willie McCovey, SF	36
1917	Gavvy Cravath, Phi	12	1969	Willie McCovey, SF	45
	Dave Robertson, NY	12	1970	Johnny Bench, Cin	45
1918	Gavvy Cravath, Phi	8	1971	Willie Stargell, Pitt	48
1919	Gavvy Cravath, Phi	12	1972	Johnny Bench, Cin	40
1920	Cy Williams, Phi	15	1973	Willie Stargell, Pitt	44
1921	George Kelly, NY	23	1974	Mike Schmidt, Phi	36
1922	Rogers Hornsby, StL	42	1975	Mike Schmidt, Phi	38
1923	Cy Williams, Phi	41	1976	Mike Schmidt, Phi	38
1924	Jack Fournier, Bklyn	27	1977	George Foster, Cin	52
1925	Rogers Hornsby, StL	39	1978	George Foster, Cin	40
1926	Hack Wilson, Chi	21	1979	Dave Kingman, Chi	48
1927	Hack Wilson, Chi	30	1980	Mike Schmidt, Phi	48
	Cy Williams, Phi	30	1981	Mike Schmidt, Phi	31
1928	Jim Bottomley, StL	31	1982	Dave Kingman, NY	37
	Hack Wilson, Chi	31	1983	Mike Schmidt, Phi	40
1929	Chuck Klein, Phi	43	1984	Dale Murphy, Atl	36
1930	Hack Wilson, Chi	56		Mike Schmidt, Phi	36
1931	Chuck Klein, Phi	31	1985	Dale Murphy, Atl	37
1932	Chuck Klein, Phi	38	1986	Mike Schmidt, Phi	37
	Mel Ott, NY	38	1987	Andre Dawson, Chi	49
1933	Chuck Klein, Phi	28	1988	Darryl Strawberry, NY	39
1934	Ripper Collins, StL	35	1989	Kevin Mitchell, SF	47
	Mel Ott, NY	35	1990	Ryne Sandberg, Chi	40
1935	Wally Berger, Bos	34	1991	Howard Johnson, NY	38
1936	Mel Ott, NY	33	1992	Fred McGriff, SD	35
1937	Joe Medwick, StL	31	1993	Barry Bonds, SF	46
	Mel Ott, NY	31	1994	Matt Williams, SF	43
1938	Mel Ott, NY	36	1995	Dante Bichette, Col	40
1939	Johnny Mize, StL	28	1996	Andres Galarraga, Col	47
1940	Johnny Mize, StL	43	1997	Larry Walker, Col	49
1941	Dolph Camilli, Bklyn	34	1998	Mark McGwire, StL	70
1942	Mel Ott, NY	30	1999	Mark McGwire, StL	65
1943	Bill Nicholson, Chi	29	2000	Sammy Sosa, Chi	50
1944	Bill Nicholson, Chi	33	2001	Barry Bonds, SF	73
1945	Tommy Holmes, Bos	28	2002	Sammy Sosa, Chi	49
1946	Ralph Kiner, Pitt	23	2003	Jim Thome, Phi	47
1947	Ralph Kiner, Pitt	51	2004	Adrian Beltre, LA	48
	Johnny Mize, NY	51	2005	Andruw Jones, Atl	51
1948	Ralph Kiner, Pitt	40	2006	Ryan Howard, Phi	58
	Johnny Mize, NY	40	2007	Prince Fielder, Mil	50
1949	Ralph Kiner, Pitt	54	2008	Ryan Howard, Phi	48
1950	Ralph Kiner, Pitt	47	2009	Albert Pujols, StL	47
1951	Ralph Kiner, Pitt	42	2010	Albert Pujols, StL	42

Runs Batted In Leaders

Year	Player and Team	RBI	Year	Player and Team	RBI
1900	Elmer Flick, Phi	110	1957	Hank Aaron, Mil	132
1901	Honus Wagner, Pitt	126	1958	Ernie Banks, Chi	129
1902	Honus Wagner, Pitt	91	1959	Ernie Banks, Chi	143
1903	Sam Mertes, NY	104	1960	Hank Aaron, Mil	126
1904	Bill Dahlen, NY	80	1961	Orlando Cepeda, SF	142
1905	Cy Seymour, Cin	121	1962	Tommy Davis, LA	153
1906	Jim Nealon, Pitt	83	1963	Hank Aaron, Mil	130
	Harry Steinfeldt, Chi	83	1964	Ken Boyer, StL	119
1907	Sherry Magee, Phi	85	1965	Deron Johnson, Cin	130
1908	Honus Wagner, Pitt	109	1966	Hank Aaron, Atl	127
1909	Honus Wagner, Pitt	100	1967	Orlando Cepeda, StL	111
1910	Sherry Magee, Phi	123	1968	Willie McCovey, SF	105
1911	Wildfire Schulte, Chi	121	1969	Willie McCovey, SF	126
1912	Heinie Zimmerman, Chi	103	1970	Johnny Bench, Cin	148
1913	Gavvy Cravath, Phi	128	1971	Joe Torre, StL	137
1914	Sherry Magee, Phi	103	1972	Johnny Bench, Cin	125
1915	Gavvy Cravath, Phi	115	1973	Willie Stargell, Pitt	119
1916	Heinie Zimmerman, Chi-NY	83	1974	Johnny Bench, Cin	129
1917	Heinie Zimmerman, NY	102	1975	Greg Luzinski, Phi	120
1918	Sherry Magee, Phi	76	1976	George Foster, Cin	121
1919	Hi Myers, Bklyn	73	1977	George Foster, Cin	149
1920	Rogers Hornsby, StL	94	1978	George Foster, Cin	120
	George Kelly, NY	94	1979	Dave Winfield, SD	118
1921	Rogers Hornsby, StL	126	1980	Mike Schmidt, Phi	121
1922	Rogers Hornsby, StL	152	1981	Mike Schmidt, Phi	91
1923	Irish Meusel, NY	125	1982	Dale Murphy, Atl	109
1924	George Kelly, NY	136		Al Oliver, Mtl	109
1925	Rogers Hornsby, StL	143	1983	Dale Murphy, Atl	121
1926	Jim Bottomley, StL	120	1984	Gary Carter, Mtl	106
1927	Paul Waner, Pitt	131		Mike Schmidt, Phi	106
1928	Jim Bottomley, StL	136	1985	Dave Parker, Cin	125
1929	Hack Wilson, Chi	159	1986	Mike Schmidt, Phi	119
1930	Hack Wilson, Chi	190	1987	Andre Dawson, Chi	137
1931	Chuck Klein, Phi	121	1988	Will Clark, SF	109
1932	Don Hurst, Phi	143	1989	Kevin Mitchell, SF	125
1933	Chuck Klein, Phi	120	1990	Matt Williams, SF	122
1934	Mel Ott, NY	135	1991	Howard Johnson, NY	117
1935	Wally Berger, Bos	130	1992	Darren Daulton, Phi	109
1936	Joe Medwick, StL	138	1993	Barry Bonds, SF	123
1937	Joe Medwick, StL	154	1994	Jeff Bagwell, Hou	116
1938	Joe Medwick, StL	122	1995	Dante Bichette, Col	128
1939	Frank McCormick, Cin	128	1996	Andres Galarraga, Col	150
1940	Johnny Mize, StL	137	1997	Andres Galarraga, Col	140
1941	Dolph Camilli, Bklyn	120	1998	Sammy Sosa, Chi	158
1942	Johnny Mize, NY	110	1999	Mark McGwire, StL	147
1943	Bill Nicholson, Chi	128	2000	Todd Helton, Col	147
1944	Bill Nicholson, Chi	122	2001	Sammy Sosa, Chi	160
1945	Dixie Walker, Bklyn	124	2002	Lance Berkman, Hou	128
1946	Enos Slaughter, StL	130	2003	Preston Wilson, Col	141
1947	Johnny Mize, NY	138	2004	Vinny Castilla, Col	131
1948	Stan Musial, StL	131	2005	Andruw Jones, Atl	128
1949	Ralph Kiner, Pitt	127	2006	Ryan Howard, Phi	149
1950	Del Ennis, Phi	126	2007	Matt Holliday, Col	137*
1951	Monte Irvin, NY	121	2008	Ryan Howard, Phi	146
1952	Hank Sauer, Chi	121	2009	Prince Fielder, Mil	141
1953	Roy Campanella, Bklyn	142		Ryan Howard, Phi	141
1954	Ted Kluszewski, Cin	141	2010	Albert Pujols, StL	118
1955	Duke Snider, Bklyn	136			
1956	Stan Musial, StL	109			

*Includes one-game NL Wild Card tiebreaker.

Leading Base Stealers

Year	Player and Team	SB	Year	Player and Team	SB
1900	George Van Haltren, NY	45	1954	Bill Bruton, Mil	34
	Patsy Donovan, StL	45	1955	Bill Bruton, Mil	35
1901	Honus Wagner, Pitt	48	1956	Willie Mays, NY	40
1902	Honus Wagner, Pitt	43	1957	Willie Mays, NY	38
1903	Jimmy Sheckard, Bklyn	67	1958	Willie Mays, SF	31
	Frank Chance, Chi	67	1959	Willie Mays, SF	27
1904	Honus Wagner, Pitt	53	1960	Maury Wills, LA	50
1905	Billy Maloney, Chi	59	1961	Maury Wills, LA	35
	Art Devlin, NY	59	1962	Maury Wills, LA	104
1906	Frank Chance, Chi	57	1963	Maury Wills, LA	40
1907	Honus Wagner, Pitt	61	1964	Maury Wills, LA	53
1908	Honus Wagner, Pitt	53	1965	Maury Wills, LA	94
1909	Bob Bescher, Cin	54	1966	Lou Brock, StL	74
1910	Bob Bescher, Cin	70	1967	Lou Brock, StL	52
1911	Bob Bescher, Cin	80	1968	Lou Brock, StL	62
1912	Bob Bescher, Cin	67	1969	Lou Brock, StL	53
1913	Max Carey, Pitt	61	1970	Bobby Tolan, Cin	57
1914	George Burns, NY	62	1971	Lou Brock, StL	64
1915	Max Carey, Pitt	36	1972	Lou Brock, StL	63
1916	Max Carey, Pitt	63	1973	Lou Brock, StL	70
1917	Max Carey, Pitt	46	1974	Lou Brock, StL	118
1918	Max Carey, Pitt	58	1975	Davey Lopes, LA	77
1919	George Burns, NY	40	1976	Davey Lopes, LA	63
1920	Max Carey, Pitt	52	1977	Frank Taveras, Pitt	70
1921	Frankie Frisch, NY	49	1978	Omar Moreno, Pitt	71
1922	Max Carey, Pitt	51	1979	Omar Moreno, Pitt	77
1923	Max Carey, Pitt	51	1980	Ron LeFlore, Mtl	97
1924	Max Carey, Pitt	49	1981	Tim Raines, Mtl	71
1925	Max Carey, Pitt	46	1982	Tim Raines, Mtl	78
1926	Kiki Cuyler, Pitt	35	1983	Tim Raines, Mtl	90
1927	Frankie Frisch, StL	48	1984	Tim Raines, Mtl	75
1928	Kiki Cuyler, Chi	37	1985	Vince Coleman, StL	110
1929	Kiki Cuyler, Chi	43	1986	Vince Coleman, StL	107
1930	Kiki Cuyler, Chi	37	1987	Vince Coleman, StL	109
1931	Frankie Frisch, StL	28	1988	Vince Coleman, StL	81
1932	Chuck Klein, Phi	20	1989	Vince Coleman, StL	65
1933	Pepper Martin, StL	26	1990	Vince Coleman, StL	77
1934	Pepper Martin, StL	23	1991	Marquis Grissom, Mtl	76
1935	Augie Galan, Chi	22	1992	Marquis Grissom, Mtl	78
1936	Pepper Martin, StL	23	1993	Chuck Carr, Fla	58
1937	Augie Galan, Chi	23	1994	Craig Biggio, Hou	39
1938	Stan Hack, Chi	16	1995	Quilvio Veras, Fla	56
1939	Stan Hack, Chi	17	1996	Eric Young, Col	53
	Lee Handley, Pitt	17	1997	Tony Womack, Pitt	60
1940	Lonny Frey, Cin	22	1998	Tony Womack, Pitt	58
1941	Danny Murtaugh, Phi	18	1999	Tony Womack, Ariz	72
1942	Pete Reiser, Bklyn	20	2000	Luis Castillo, Fla	62
1943	Arky Vaughan, Bklyn	20	2001	Juan Pierre, Col	46
1944	Johnny Barrett, Pitt	28	2002	Luis Castillo, Fla	48
1945	Red Schoendienst, StL	26	2003	Juan Pierre, Fla	65
1946	Pete Reiser, Bklyn	34	2004	Scott Podsednik, Mil	70
1947	Jackie Robinson, Bklyn	29	2005	Jose Reyes, NY	60
1948	Richie Ashburn, Phi	32	2006	Jose Reyes, NY	64
1949	Jackie Robinson, Bklyn	37	2007	Jose Reyes, NY	78
1950	Sam Jethroe, Bos	35	2008	Willy Taveras, Hou	68
1951	Sam Jethroe, Bos	35	2009	Michael Bourn, Hou	61
1952	Pee Wee Reese, Bklyn	30	2010	Michael Bourn, Hou	52
1953	Bill Bruton, Mil	26			

Leading Pitchers—Winning Percentage

Year	Pitcher and Team	W	L	Pct	Year	Pitcher and Team	W	L	Pct
1900	Jesse Tannehill, Pitt	20	6	.769	1956	Don Newcombe, Bklyn	27	7	.794
1901	Jack Chesbro, Pitt	21	10	.677	1957	Bob Buhl, Mil	18	7	.720
1902	Jack Chesbro, Pitt	28	6	.824	1958	Warren Spahn, Mil	22	11	.667
1903	Sam Leever, Pitt	25	7	.781		Lew Burdette, Mil	20	10	.667
1904	Joe McGinnity, NY	35	8	.814	1959	Roy Face, Pitt	18	1	.947
1905	Sam Leever, Pitt	20	5	.800	1960	Ernie Broglio, StL	21	9	.700
1906	Ed Reulbach, Chi	19	4	.826	1961	Johnny Podres, LA	18	5	.783
1907	Ed Reulbach, Chi	17	4	.810	1962	Bob Purkey, Cin	23	5	.821
1908	Ed Reulbach, Chi	24	7	.774	1963	Ron Perranoski, LA	16	3	.842
1909	Howie Camnitz, Pitt	25	6	.806	1964	Sandy Koufax, LA	19	5	.792
	Christy Mathewson, NY	25	6	.806	1965	Sandy Koufax, LA	26	8	.765
1910	King Cole, Chi	20	4	.833	1966	Juan Marichal, SF	25	6	.806
1911	Rube Marquard, NY	24	7	.774	1967	Dick Hughes, StL	16	6	.727
1912	Claude Hendrix, Pitt	24	9	.727	1968	Steve Blass, Pitt	18	6	.750
1913	Bert Humphries, Chi	16	4	.800	1969	Tom Seaver, NY	25	7	.781
1914	Bill James, Bos	26	7	.788	1970	Bob Gibson, StL	23	7	.767
1915	Grover Alexander, Phi	31	10	.756	1971	Don Gullett, Cin	16	6	.727
1916	Tom Hughes, Bos	16	3	.842	1972	Gary Nolan, Cin	15	5	.750
1917	Ferdie Schupp, NY	21	7	.750	1973	Tommy John, LA	16	7	.696
1918	Claude Hendrix, Chi	19	7	.731	1974	Andy Messersmith, LA	20	6	.769
1919	Dutch Ruether, Cin	19	6	.760	1975	Don Gullett, Cin	15	4	.789
1920	Burleigh Grimes, Bklyn	23	11	.676	1976	Steve Carlton, Phi	20	7	.741
1921	Bill Doak, StL	15	6	.714	1977	John Candelaria, Pitt	20	5	.800
1922	Pete Donohue, Cin	18	9	.667	1978	Gaylord Perry, SD	21	6	.778
1923	Dolf Luque, Cin	27	8	.771	1979	Tom Seaver, Cin	16	6	.727
1924	Emil Yde, Pitt	16	3	.842	1980	Jim Bibby, Pitt	19	6	.760
1925	Bill Sherdel, StL	15	6	.714	1981*	Tom Seaver, Cin	14	2	.875
1926	Ray Kremer, Pitt	20	6	.769	1982	Phil Niekro, Atl	17	4	.810
1927	Larry Benton, Bos-NY	17	7	.708	1983	John Denny, Phi	19	6	.760
1928	Larry Benton, NY	25	9	.735	1984	Rick Sutcliffe, Chi	16	1	.941
1929	Charlie Root, Chi	19	6	.760	1985	Orel Hershiser, LA	19	3	.864
1930	Freddie Fitzsimmons, NY	19	7	.731	1986	Bob Ojeda, NY	18	5	.783
1931	Paul Derringer, StL	18	8	.692	1987	Dwight Gooden, NY	15	7	.682
1932	Lon Warneke, Chi	22	6	.786	1988	David Cone, NY	20	3	.870
1933	Ben Cantwell, Bos	20	10	.667	1989	Mike Bielecki, Chi	18	7	.720
1934	Dizzy Dean, StL	30	7	.811	1990	Doug Drabeck, Pitt	22	6	.786
1935	Bill Lee, Chi	20	6	.769	1991	John Smiley, Pitt	20	8	.714
1936	Carl Hubbell, NY	26	6	.813		Jose Rijo, Cin	15	6	.714
1937	Carl Hubbell, NY	22	8	.733	1992	Bob Tewksbury, StL	16	5	.762
1938	Bill Lee, Chi	22	9	.710	1993	Tom Glavine, Atl	22	6	.786
1939	Paul Derringer, Cin	25	7	.781	1994	Ken Hill, Mtl	16	5	.762
1940	Freddie Fitzsimmons, Bklyn	16	2	.889	1995	Greg Maddux, Atl	19	2	.905
1941	Elmer Riddle, Cin	19	4	.826	1996	John Smoltz, Atl	24	8	.750
1942	Larry French, Bklyn	15	4	.789	1997	Denny Neagle, Atl	20	5	.800
1943	Mort Cooper, StL	21	8	.724	1998	John Smoltz, Atl	17	3	.850
1944	Ted Wilks, StL	17	4	.810	1999	Mike Hampton, Hou	22	4	.846
1945	Harry Brecheen, StL	15	4	.789	2000	Randy Johnson, Ariz	19	7	.730
1946	Murray Dickson, StL	15	6	.714	2001	Curt Schilling, Ariz	22	6	.786
1947	Larry Jansen, NY	21	5	.808	2002	Randy Johnson, Ariz	24	5	.828
1948	Harry Brecheen, StL	20	7	.741	2003	Jason Schmidt, SF	17	5	.773
1949	Preacher Roe, Bklyn	15	6	.714	2004	Roger Clemens, Hou	18	4	.818
1950	Sal Maglie, NY	18	4	.818	2005	Chris Carpenter, StL	21	5	.808
1951	Preacher Roe, Bklyn	22	3	.880	2006	Carlos Zambrano, Chi	16	7	.695
1952	Hoyt Wilhelm, NY	15	3	.833	2007	Brad Penny, LA	16	4	.800
1953	Carl Erskine, Bklyn	20	6	.769	2008	Tim Lincecum, SF	18	5	.783
1954	Johnny Antonelli, NY	21	7	.750	2009	Chris Carpenter, StL	17	4	.810
1955	Don Newcombe, Bklyn	20	5	.800	2010	Ubaldo Jimenez, Col	19	8	.704

*1981 percentages based on 10 or more victories. Note: Percentages based on 15 or more victories in all other years.

Leading Pitchers—Earned Run Average

Year	Player and Team	ERA	Year	Player and Team	ERA
1900	Rube Waddell, Pitt	2.37	1956	Lew Burdette, Mil	2.71
1901	Jesse Tannehill, Pitt	2.18	1957	Johnny Podres, Bklyn	2.66
1902	Jack Taylor, Chi	1.33	1958	Stu Miller, SF	2.47
1903	Sam Leever, Pitt	2.06	1959	Sam Jones, SF	2.82
1904	Joe McGinnity, NY	1.61	1960	Mike McCormick, SF	2.70
1905	Christy Mathewson, NY	1.27	1961	Warren Spahn, Mil	3.01
1906	Three Finger Brown, Chi	1.04	1962	Sandy Koufax, LA	2.54
1907	Jack Pfiester, Chi	1.15	1963	Sandy Koufax, LA	1.88
1908	Christy Mathewson, NY	1.43	1964	Sandy Koufax, LA	1.74
1909	Christy Mathewson, NY	1.14	1965	Sandy Koufax, LA	2.04
1910	George McQuillan, Phi	1.60	1966	Sandy Koufax, LA	1.73
1911	Christy Mathewson, NY	1.99	1967	Phil Niekro, Atl	1.87
1912	Jeff Tesreau, NY	1.96	1968	Bob Gibson, StL	1.12
1913	Christy Mathewson, NY	2.06	1969	Juan Marichal, SF	2.10
1914	Bill Doak, StL	1.72	1970	Tom Seaver, NY	2.81
1915	Grover Alexander, Phi	1.22	1971	Tom Seaver, NY	1.76
1916	Grover Alexander, Phi	1.55	1972	Steve Carlton, Phi	1.98
1917	Grover Alexander, Phi	1.83	1973	Tom Seaver, NY	2.08
1918	Hippo Vaughn, Chi	1.74	1974	Buzz Capra, Atl	2.28
1919	Grover Alexander, Chi	1.72	1975	Randy Jones, SD	2.24
1920	Grover Alexander, Chi	1.91	1976	John Denny, StL	2.52
1921	Bill Doak, StL	2.58	1977	John Candelaria, Pitt	2.34
1922	Rosy Ryan, NY	3.00	1978	Craig Swan, NY	2.43
1923	Dolf Luque, Cin	1.93	1979	J.R. Richard, Hou	2.71
1924	Dazzy Vance, Bklyn	2.16	1980	Don Sutton, LA	2.21
1925	Dolf Luque, Cin	2.63	1981	Nolan Ryan, Hou	1.69
1926	Ray Kremer, Pitt	2.61	1982	Steve Rogers, Mtl	2.40
1927	Ray Kremer, Pitt	2.47	1983	Atlee Hammaker, SF	2.25
1928	Dazzy Vance, Bklyn	2.09	1984	Alejandro Pena, LA	2.48
1929	Bill Walker, NY	3.08	1985	Dwight Gooden, NY	1.53
1930	Dazzy Vance, Bklyn	2.61	1986	Mike Scott, Hou	2.22
1931	Bill Walker, NY	2.26	1987	Nolan Ryan, Hou	2.76
1932	Lon Warneke, Chi	2.37	1988	Joe Magrane, StL	2.18
1933	Carl Hubbell, NY	1.66	1989	Scott Garrelts, SF	2.28
1934	Carl Hubbell, NY	2.30	1990	Danny Darwin, Hou	2.21
1935	Cy Blanton, Pitt	2.59	1991	Dennis Martinez, Mtl	2.39
1936	Carl Hubbell, NY	2.31	1992	Bill Swift, SF	2.08
1937	Jim Turner, Bos	2.38	1993	Greg Maddux, Atl	2.36
1938	Bill Lee, Chi	2.66	1994	Greg Maddux, Atl	1.56
1939	Bucky Walters, Cin	2.29	1995	Greg Maddux, Atl	1.63
1940	Bucky Walters, Cin	2.48	1996	Kevin Brown, Fla	1.89
1941	Elmer Riddle, Cin	2.24	1997	Pedro Martinez, Mtl	1.90
1942	Mort Cooper, StL	1.77	1998	Greg Maddux, Atl	1.98
1943	Howie Pollet, StL	1.75	1999	Randy Johnson, Ariz	2.48
1944	Ed Heusser, Cin	2.38	2000	Kevin Brown, LA	2.58
1945	Hank Borowy, Chi	2.14	2001	Randy Johnson, Ariz	2.49
1946	Howie Pollet, StL	2.10	2002	Randy Johnson, Ariz	2.32
1947	Warren Spahn, Bos	2.33	2003	Jason Schmidt, SF	2.34
1948	Harry Brecheen, StL	2.24	2004	Jake Peavy, SD	2.27
1949	Dave Koslo, NY	2.50	2005	Roger Clemens, Hou	1.87
1950	Jim Hearn, StL-NY	2.49	2006	Roy Oswalt, Hou	2.98
1951	Chet Nichols, Bos	2.88	2007	Jake Peavy, SD	2.54*
1952	Hoyt Wilhelm, NY	2.43	2008	Johan Santana, NYM	2.53
1953	Warren Spahn, Mil	2.10	2009	Chris Carpenter, StL	2.24
1954	Johnny Antonelli, NY	2.29	2010	Josh Johnson, Fla	2.30
1955	Bob Friend, Pitt	2.84			

*Includes one-game NL Wild Card tiebreaker.

Note: Based on 10 complete games through 1950, then 154 innings until National League expanded in 1962, when it became 162 innings. In strike-shortened 1981, one inning per game required.

Leading Pitchers—Strikeouts

Year	Player and Team	SO	Year	Player and Team	SO
1900	Rube Waddell, Pitt	133	1955	Sam Jones, Chi	198
1901	Noodles Hahn, Cin	233	1956	Sam Jones, Chi	176
1902	Vic Willis, Bos	226	1957	Jack Sanford, Phi	188
1903	Christy Mathewson, NY	267	1958	Sam Jones, StL	225
1904	Christy Mathewson, NY	212	1959	Don Drysdale, LA	242
1905	Christy Mathewson, NY	206	1960	Don Drysdale, LA	246
1906	Fred Beebe, Chi-StL	171	1961	Sandy Koufax, LA	269
1907	Christy Mathewson, NY	178	1962	Don Drysdale, LA	232
1908	Christy Mathewson, NY	259	1963	Sandy Koufax, LA	306
1909	Orval Overall, Chi	205	1964	Bob Veale, Pitt	250
1910	Christy Mathewson, NY	190	1965	Sandy Koufax, LA	382
1911	Rube Marquard, NY	237	1966	Sandy Koufax, LA	317
1912	Grover Alexander, Phi	195	1967	Jim Bunning, Phi	253
1913	Tom Seaton, Phi	168	1968	Bob Gibson, StL	268
1914	Grover Alexander, Phi	214	1969	Ferguson Jenkins, Chi	273
1915	Grover Alexander, Phi	241	1970	Tom Seaver, NY	283
1916	Grover Alexander, Phi	167	1971	Tom Seaver, NY	289
1917	Grover Alexander, Phi	200	1972	Steve Carlton, Phi	310
1918	Hippo Vaughn, Chi	148	1973	Tom Seaver, NY	251
1919	Hippo Vaughn, Chi	141	1974	Steve Carlton, Phi	240
1920	Grover Alexander, Chi	173	1975	Tom Seaver, NY	243
1921	Burleigh Grimes, Bklyn	136	1976	Tom Seaver, NY	235
1922	Dazzy Vance, Bklyn	134	1977	Phil Niekro, Atl	262
1923	Dazzy Vance, Bklyn	197	1978	J.R. Richard, Hou	303
1924	Dazzy Vance, Bklyn	262	1979	J.R. Richard, Hou	313
1925	Dazzy Vance, Bklyn	221	1980	Steve Carlton, Phi	286
1926	Dazzy Vance, Bklyn	140	1981	Fernando Valenzuela, LA	180
1927	Dazzy Vance, Bklyn	184	1982	Steve Carlton, Phi	286
1928	Dazzy Vance, Bklyn	200	1983	Steve Carlton, Phi	275
1929	Pat Malone, Chi	166	1984	Dwight Gooden, NY	276
1930	Bill Hallahan, StL	177	1985	Dwight Gooden, NY	268
1931	Bill Hallahan, StL	159	1986	Mike Scott, Hou	306
1932	Dizzy Dean, StL	191	1987	Nolan Ryan, Hou	270
1933	Dizzy Dean, StL	199	1988	Nolan Ryan, Hou	228
1934	Dizzy Dean, StL	195	1989	Jose DeLeon, StL	201
1935	Dizzy Dean, StL	182	1990	David Cone, NY	233
1936	Van Lingle Mungo, Bklyn	238	1991	David Cone, NY	241
1937	Carl Hubbell, NY	159	1992	John Smoltz, Atl	215
1938	Clay Bryant, Chi	135	1993	Jose Rijo, Cin	227
1939	Claude Passeau, Phi-Chi	137	1994	Andy Benes, SD	189
	Bucky Walters, Cin	137	1995	Hideo Nomo, LA	236
1940	Kirby Higbe, Phi	137	1996	John Smoltz, Atl	276
1941	Johnny Vander Meer, Cin	202	1997	Curt Schilling, Phi	319
1942	Johnny Vander Meer, Cin	186	1998	Curt Schilling, Phi	300
1943	Johnny Vander Meer, Cin	174	1999	Randy Johnson, Ariz	364
1944	Bill Voiselle, NY	161	2000	Randy Johnson, Ariz	347
1945	Preacher Roe, Pitt	148	2001	Randy Johnson, Ariz	372
1946	Johnny Schmitz, Chi	135	2002	Randy Johnson, Ariz	334
1947	Ewell Blackwell, Cin	193	2003	Kerry Wood, Chi	266
1948	Harry Brecheen, StL	149	2004	Randy Johnson, Ariz	290
1949	Warren Spahn, Bos	151	2005	Jake Peavy, SD	216
1950	Warren Spahn, Bos	191	2006	Aaron Harang, Cin	216
1951	Warren Spahn, Bos	164	2007	Jake Peavy, SD	240*
	Don Newcombe, Bklyn	164	2008	Tim Lincecum, SF	265
1952	Warren Spahn, Bos	183	2009	Tim Lincecum, SF	261
1953	Robin Roberts, Phi	198	2010	Tim Lincecum, SF	231
1954	Robin Roberts, Phi	185			

*Includes one-game NL Wild Card tiebreaker.

Leading Pitchers—Saves

Year	Player and Team	SV	Year	Player and Team	SV
1947	Hugh Casey, Bklyn	18	1979	Bruce Sutter, Chi	37
1948	Harry Gumpert, Cin	17	1980	Bruce Sutter, Chi	28
1949	Ted Wilks, StL	9	1981	Bruce Sutter, StL	25
1950	Jim Konstanty, Phi	22	1982	Bruce Sutter, StL	36
1951	Ted Wilks, StL, Pitt	13	1983	Lee Smith, Chi	29
1952	Al Brazle, StL	16	1984	Bruce Sutter, StL	45
1953	Al Brazle, StL	18	1985	Jeff Reardon, Mtl	41
1954	Jim Hughes, Bklyn	24	1986	Todd Worrell, StL	36
1955	Jack Meyer, Phi	16	1987	Steve Bedrosian, Phi	40
1956	Clem Labine, Bklyn	19	1988	John Franco, Cin	39
1957	Clem Labine, Bklyn	17	1989	Mark Davis, SD	44
1958	Roy Face, Pitt	20	1990	John Franco, NY	33
1959	Lindy McDaniel, StL	15	1991	Lee Smith, StL	47
	Don McMahon, Mil	15	1992	Lee Smith, StL	42
1960	Lindy McDaniel, StL	26	1993	Randy Myers, Chi	53
1961	Roy Face, Pitt	17	1994	John Franco, NY	30
	Stu Miller, SF	17	1995	Randy Myers, Chi	38
1962	Roy Face, Pitt	28	1996	Jeff Brantley, Cin	44
1963	Lindy McDaniel, Chi	22		Todd Worrell, LA	44
1964	Hal Woodeshick, Hou	23	1997	Jeff Shaw, Cin	42
1965	Ted Abernathy, Chi	31	1998	Trevor Hoffman, SD	53
1966	Phil Regan, LA	21	1999	Ugueth Urbina, Mtl	41
1967	Ted Abernathy, Cin	28	2000	Antonio Alfonseca, Fla	45
1968	Phil Regan, Chi, LA	25	2001	Robb Nen, SF	45
1969	Fred Gladding, Hou	29	2002	John Smoltz, Atl	55
1970	Wayne Granger, Cin	35	2003	Eric Gagne, LA	55
1971	Dave Giusti, Pitt	30	2004	Armando Benitez, Fla	47
1972	Clay Carroll, Cin	37		Jason Isringhausen, StL	47
1973	Mike Marshall, Mtl	13	2005	Chad Cordero, Wash	47
1974	Mike Marshall, LA	21	2006	Trevor Hoffman, SD	46
1975	Rawly Eastwick, Cin	22	2007	Jose Valverde, Ariz	47
	Al Hrabosky, StL	22	2008	Jose Valverde, Hou	44
1976	Rawly Eastwick, Cin	26	2009	Heath Bell, SD	42
1977	Rollie Fingers, SD	35	2010	Brian Wilson, SF	48
1978	Rollie Fingers, SD	37			

Leading Batsmen

Year	Player and Team	BA	Year	Player and Team	BA
1901	Nap Lajoie, Phi	.422	1956	Mickey Mantle, NY	.353
1902	Ed Delahanty, Wash	.376	1957	Ted Williams, Bos	.388
1903	Nap Lajoie, Clev	.355	1958	Ted Williams, Bos	.328
1904	Nap Lajoie, Clev	.381	1959	Harvey Kuenn, Det	.353
1905	Elmer Flick, Clev	.306	1960	Pete Runnels, Bos	.320
1906	George Stone, StL	.358	1961	Norm Cash, Det	.361
1907	Ty Cobb, Det	.350	1962	Pete Runnels, Bos	.326
1908	Ty Cobb, Det	.324	1963	Carl Yastrzemski, Bos	.321
1909	Ty Cobb, Det	.377	1964	Tony Oliva, Minn	.323
1910	Nap Lajoie, Clev†	.383	1965	Tony Oliva, Minn	.321
1911	Ty Cobb, Det	.420	1966	Frank Robinson, Balt	.316
1912	Ty Cobb, Det	.410	1967	Carl Yastrzemski, Bos	.326
1913	Ty Cobb, Det	.390	1968	Carl Yastrzemski, Bos	.301
1914	Ty Cobb, Det	.368	1969	Rod Carew, Minn	.332
1915	Ty Cobb, Det	.369	1970	Alex Johnson, Cal	.329
1916	Tris Speaker, Clev	.386	1971	Tony Oliva, Minn	.337
1917	Ty Cobb, Det	.383	1972	Rod Carew, Minn	.318
1918	Ty Cobb, Det	.382	1973	Rod Carew, Minn	.350
1919	Ty Cobb, Det	.384	1974	Rod Carew, Minn	.364
1920	George Sisler, StL	.407	1975	Rod Carew, Minn	.359
1921	Harry Heilmann, Det	.394	1976	George Brett, KC	.333
1922	George Sisler, StL	.420	1977	Rod Carew, Minn	.388
1923	Harry Heilmann, Det	.403	1978	Rod Carew, Minn	.333
1924	Babe Ruth, NY	.378	1979	Fred Lynn, Bos	.333
1925	Harry Heilmann, Det	.393	1980	George Brett, KC	.390
1926	Heinie Manush, Det	.378	1981	Carney Lansford, Bos	.336
1927	Harry Heilmann, Det	.398	1982	Willie Wilson, KC	.332
1928	Goose Goslin, Wash	.379	1983	Wade Boggs, Bos	.361
1929	Lew Fonseca, Clev	.369	1984	Don Mattingly, NY	.343
1930	Al Simmons, Phi	.381	1985	Wade Boggs, Bos	.368
1931	Al Simmons, Phi	.390	1986	Wade Boggs, Bos	.357
1932	Dale Alexander, Det-Bos	.367	1987	Wade Boggs, Bos	.363
1933	Jimmie Foxx, Phi	.356	1988	Wade Boggs, Bos	.366
1934	Lou Gehrig, NY	.363	1989	Kirby Puckett, Minn	.339
1935	Buddy Myer, Wash	.349	1990	George Brett, KC	.329
1936	Luke Appling, Chi	.388	1991	Julio Franco, Tex	.341
1937	Charlie Gehringer, Det	.371	1992	Edgar Martinez, Sea	.343
1938	Jimmie Foxx, Bos	.349	1993	John Olerud, Tor	.363
1939	Joe DiMaggio, NY	.381	1994	Paul O'Neill, NY	.359
1940	Joe DiMaggio, NY	.352	1995	Edgar Martinez, Sea	.356
1941	Ted Williams, Bos	.406	1996	Alex Rodriguez, Sea	.358
1942	Ted Williams, Bos	.356	1997	Frank Thomas, Chi	.347
1943	Luke Appling, Chi	.328	1998	Bernie Williams, NY	.339
1944	Lou Boudreau, Clev	.327	1999	Nomar Garciaparra, Bos	.357
1945	Snuffy Stirnweiss, NY	.309	2000	Nomar Garciaparra, Bos	.372
1946	Mickey Vernon, Wash	.353	2001	Ichiro Suzuki, Sea	.350
1947	Ted Williams, Bos	.343	2002	Manny Ramirez, Bos	.349
1948	Ted Williams, Bos	.369	2003	Bill Mueller, Bos	.326
1949	George Kell, Det	.343	2004	Ichiro Suzuki, Sea	.372
1950	Billy Goodman, Bos	.354	2005	Michael Young, Tex	.331
1951	Ferris Fain, Phi	.344	2006	Joe Mauer, Minn	.347
1952	Ferris Fain, Phi	.327	2007	Magglio Ordonez, Det	.363
1953	Mickey Vernon, Wash	.337	2008	Joe Mauer, Minn	.330
1954	Bobby Avila, Clev	.341	2009	Joe Mauer, Minn*	.365
1955	Al Kaline, Det	.340	2010	Josh Hamilton, Tex	.359

†League president Ban Johnson declared Ty Cobb batting champion with a .385 average, beating Lajoie's .384. However, subsequent research has led to the revision of Lajoie's average to .383 and Cobb's to .382.
*Includes one-game AL Central playoff tiebreaker.

Leaders in Runs Scored

Year	Player and Team	Runs	Year	Player and Team	Runs
1901	Nap Lajoie, Phi	145	1958	Mickey Mantle, NY	127
1902	Dave Fultz, Phi	110	1959	Eddie Yost, Det	115
1903	Patsy Dougherty, Bos	108	1960	Mickey Mantle, NY	119
1904	Patsy Dougherty, Bos-NY	113	1961	Mickey Mantle, NY	132
1905	Harry Davis, Phi	92		Roger Maris, NY	132
1906	Elmer Flick, Clev	98	1962	Albie Pearson, LA	115
1907	Sam Crawford, Det	102	1963	Bob Allison, Minn	99
1908	Matty McIntyre, Det	105	1964	Tony Oliva, Minn	109
1909	Ty Cobb, Det	116	1965	Zoilo Versalles, Minn	126
1910	Ty Cobb, Det	106	1966	Frank Robinson, Balt	122
1911	Ty Cobb, Det	147	1967	Carl Yastrzemski, Bos	112
1912	Eddie Collins, Phi	137	1968	Dick McAuliffe, Det	95
1913	Eddie Collins, Phi	125	1969	Reggie Jackson, Oak	123
1914	Eddie Collins, Phi	122	1970	Carl Yastrzemski, Bos	125
1915	Ty Cobb, Det	144	1971	Don Buford, Balt	99
1916	Ty Cobb, Det	113	1972	Bobby Murcer, NY	102
1917	Donie Bush, Det	112	1973	Reggie Jackson, Oak	99
1918	Ray Chapman, Clev	84	1974	Carl Yastrzemski, Bos	93
1919	Babe Ruth, Bos	103	1975	Fred Lynn, Bos	103
1920	Babe Ruth, NY	158	1976	Roy White, NY	104
1921	Babe Ruth, NY	177	1977	Rod Carew, Minn	128
1922	George Sisler, StL	134	1978	Ron LeFlore, Det	126
1923	Babe Ruth, NY	151	1979	Don Baylor, Cal	120
1924	Babe Ruth, NY	143	1980	Willie Wilson, KC	133
1925	Johnny Mostil, Chi	135	1981	Rickey Henderson, Oak	89
1926	Babe Ruth, NY	139	1982	Paul Molitor, Mil	136
1927	Babe Ruth, NY	158	1983	Cal Ripken, Balt	121
1928	Babe Ruth, NY	163	1984	Dwight Evans, Bos	121
1929	Charlie Gehringer, Det	131	1985	Rickey Henderson, NY	146
1930	Al Simmons, Phi	152	1986	Rickey Henderson, NY	130
1931	Lou Gehrig, NY	163	1987	Paul Molitor, Mil	114
1932	Jimmie Foxx, Phi	151	1988	Wade Boggs, Bos	128
1933	Lou Gehrig, NY	138	1989	Wade Boggs, Bos	113
1934	Charlie Gehringer, Det	134		Rickey Henderson, NY-Oak	113
1935	Lou Gehrig, NY	125	1990	Rickey Henderson, Oak	119
1936	Lou Gehrig, NY	167	1991	Paul Molitor, Mil	133
1937	Joe DiMaggio, NY	151	1992	Tony Philips, Det	114
1938	Hank Greenberg, Det	144	1993	Rafael Palmeiro, Tex	124
1939	Red Rolfe, NY	139	1994	Frank Thomas, Chi	106
1940	Ted Williams, Bos	134	1995	Albert Belle, Clev	121
1941	Ted Williams, Bos	135		Edgar Martinez, Sea	121
1942	Ted Williams, Bos	141	1996	Alex Rodriguez, Sea	141
1943	George Case, Wash	102	1997	Ken Griffey Jr., Sea	125
1944	Snuffy Stirnweiss, NY	125	1998	Derek Jeter, NY	127
1945	Snuffy Stirnweiss, NY	107	1999	Roberto Alomar, Clev	138
1946	Ted Williams, Bos	142	2000	Johnny Damon, KC	136
1947	Ted Williams, Bos	125	2001	Alex Rodriguez, Tex	133
1948	Tommy Henrich, NY	138	2002	Alfonso Soriano, NY	128
1949	Ted Williams, Bos	150	2003	Alex Rodriguez, Tex	124
1950	Dom DiMaggio, Bos	131	2004	Vladimir Guerrero, Ana	124
1951	Dom DiMaggio, Bos	113	2005	Alex Rodriguez, NY	124
1952	Larry Doby, Clev	104	2006	Grady Sizemore, Clev	134
1953	Al Rosen, Clev	115	2007	Alex Rodriguez, Tex	143
1954	Mickey Mantle, NY	129	2008	Dustin Pedroia, Bos	118
1955	Al Smith, Clev	123	2009	Dustin Pedroia, Bos	115
1956	Mickey Mantle, NY	132	2010	Mark Teixeira, NY	113
1957	Mickey Mantle, NY	121			

Leaders in Hits

Year	Player and Team	Hits	Year	Player and Team	Hits
1901	Nap Lajoie, Phi	229	1955	Al Kaline, Det	200
1902	Piano Legs Hickman, Bos-Clev	194	1956	Harvey Kuenn, Det	196
1903	Patsy Dougherty, Bos	195	1957	Nellie Fox, Chi	196
1904	Nap Lajoie, Clev	211	1958	Nellie Fox, Chi	187
1905	George Stone, StL	187	1959	Harvey Kuenn, Det	198
1906	Nap Lajoie, Clev	214	1960	Minnie Minoso, Chi	184
1907	Ty Cobb, Det	212	1961	Norm Cash, Det	193
1908	Ty Cobb, Det	188	1962	Bobby Richardson, NY	209
1909	Ty Cobb, Det	216	1963	Carl Yastrzemski, Bos	183
1910	Nap Lajoie, Clev	227	1964	Tony Oliva, Minn	217
1911	Ty Cobb, Det	248	1965	Tony Oliva, Minn	185
1912	Ty Cobb, Det	227	1966	Tony Oliva, Minn	191
1913	Joe Jackson, Clev	197	1967	Carl Yastrzemski, Bos	189
1914	Tris Speaker, Bos	193	1968	Bert Campaneris, Oak	177
1915	Ty Cobb, Det	208	1969	Tony Oliva, Minn	197
1916	Tris Speaker, Clev	211	1970	Tony Oliva, Minn	204
1917	Ty Cobb, Det	225	1971	Cesar Tovar, Minn	204
1918	George Burns, Phi	178	1972	Joe Rudi, Oak	181
1919	Ty Cobb, Det	191	1973	Rod Carew, Minn	203
	Bobby Veach, Det	191	1974	Rod Carew, Minn	218
1920	George Sisler, StL	257	1975	George Brett, KC	195
1921	Harry Heilmann, Det	237	1976	George Brett, KC	215
1922	George Sisler, StL	246	1977	Rod Carew, Minn	239
1923	Charlie Jamieson, Clev	222	1978	Jim Rice, Bos	213
1924	Sam Rice, Wash	216	1979	George Brett, KC	212
1925	Al Simmons, Phi	253	1980	Willie Wilson, KC	230
1926	George Burns, Clev	216	1981	Rickey Henderson, Oak	135
	Sam Rice, Wash	216	1982	Robin Yount, Mil	210
1927	Earle Combs, NY	231	1983	Cal Ripken Jr., Balt	211
1928	Heinie Manush, StL	241	1984	Don Mattingly, NY	207
1929	Dale Alexander, Det	215	1985	Wade Boggs, Bos	240
	Charlie Gehringer, Det	215	1986	Don Mattingly, NY	238
1930	Johnny Hodapp, Clev	225	1987	Kirby Puckett, Minn	207
1931	Lou Gehrig, NY	211		Kevin Seitzer, KC	207
1932	Al Simmons, Phi	216	1988	Kirby Puckett, Minn	234
1933	Heinie Manush, Wash	221	1989	Kirby Puckett, Minn	215
1934	Charlie Gehringer, Det	214	1990	Rafael Palmeiro, Tex	191
1935	Joe Vosmik, Clev	216	1991	Paul Molitor, Mil	216
1936	Earl Averill, Clev	232	1992	Kirby Puckett, Minn	210
1937	Beau Bell, StL	218	1993	Paul Molitor, Tor	211
1938	Joe Vosmik, Bos	201	1994	Kenny Lofton, Clev	160
1939	Red Rolfe, NY	213	1995	Lance Johnson, Chi	186
1940	Doc Cramer, Bos	200	1996	Paul Molitor, Minn	225
	Barney McCosky, Det	200	1997	Nomar Garciaparra, Bos	209
	Rip Radcliff, StL	200	1998	Alex Rodriguez, Sea	213
1941	Cecil Travis, Wash	218	1999	Derek Jeter, NY	219
1942	Johnny Pesky, Bos	205	2000	Darin Erstad, Ana	240
1943	Dick Wakefield, Det	200	2001	Ichiro Suzuki, Sea	242
1944	Snuffy Stirnweiss, NY	205	2002	Alfonso Soriano, NY	209
1945	Snuffy Stirnweiss, NY	195	2003	Vernon Wells, Tor	215
1946	Johnny Pesky, Bos	208	2004	Ichiro Suzuki, Sea	262
1947	Johnny Pesky, Bos	207	2005	Michael Young, Tex	221
1948	Bob Dillinger, StL	207	2006	Ichiro Suzuki, Sea	224
1949	Dale Mitchell, Clev	203	2007	Ichiro Suzuki, Sea	238
1950	George Kell, Det	218	2008	Dustin Pedroia, Bos	213
1951	George Kell, Det	191		Ichiro Suzuki, Sea	213
1952	Nellie Fox, Chi	192	2009	Ichiro Suzuki, Sea	225
1953	Harvey Kuenn, Det	209	2010	Ichiro Suzuki, Sea	214
1954	Nellie Fox, Chi	201			
	Harvey Kuenn, Det	201			

Home Run Leaders

Year	Player and Team	HR	Year	Player and Team	HR
1901	Nap Lajoie, Phi	13	1960	Mickey Mantle, NY	40
1902	Socks Seybold, Phi	16	1961	Roger Maris, NY	61
1903	Buck Freeman, Bos	13	1962	Harmon Killebrew, Minn	48
1904	Harry Davis, Phi	10	1963	Harmon Killebrew, Minn	45
1905	Harry Davis, Phi	8	1964	Harmon Killebrew, Minn	49
1906	Harry Davis, Phi	12	1965	Tony Conigliaro, Bos	32
1907	Harry Davis, Phi	8	1966	Frank Robinson, Balt	49
1908	Sam Crawford, Det	7	1967	Harmon Killebrew, Minn	44
1909	Ty Cobb, Det	9		Carl Yastrzemski, Bos	44
1910	Jake Stahl, Bos	10	1968	Frank Howard, Wash	44
1911	Frank Baker, Phi	9	1969	Harmon Killebrew, Minn	49
1912	Frank Baker, Phi	10	1970	Frank Howard, Wash	44
	Tris Speaker, Bos	10	1971	Bill Melton, Chi	33
1913	Frank Baker, Phi	13	1972	Dick Allen, Chi	37
1914	Frank Baker, Phi	9	1973	Reggie Jackson, Oak	32
1915	Braggo Roth, Chi-Clev	7	1974	Dick Allen, Chi	32
1916	Wally Pipp, NY	12	1975	Reggie Jackson, Oak	36
1917	Wally Pipp, NY	9		George Scott, Mil	36
1918	Babe Ruth, Bos	11	1976	Graig Nettles, NY	32
	Tilly Walker, Phi	11	1977	Jim Rice, Bos	39
1919	Babe Ruth, Bos	29	1978	Jim Rice, Bos	46
1920	Babe Ruth, NY	54	1979	Gorman Thomas, Mil	45
1921	Babe Ruth, NY	59	1980	Reggie Jackson, NY	41
1922	Ken Williams, StL	39		Ben Oglivie, Mil	41
1923	Babe Ruth, NY	41	1981	Tony Armas, Oak	22
1924	Babe Ruth, NY	46	1981	Dwight Evans, Bos	22
1925	Bob Meusel, NY	33		Bobby Grich, Cal	22
1926	Babe Ruth, NY	47		Eddie Murray, Balt	22
1927	Babe Ruth, NY	60	1982	Reggie Jackson, Cal	39
1928	Babe Ruth, NY	54		Gorman Thomas, Mil	39
1929	Babe Ruth, NY	46	1983	Jim Rice, Bos	39
1930	Babe Ruth, NY	49	1984	Tony Armas, Bos	43
1931	Babe Ruth/ Lou Gehrig NY	46	1985	Darrell Evans, Det	40
1932	Jimmie Foxx, Phi	58	1986	Jesse Barfield, Tor	40
1933	Jimmie Foxx, Phi	48	1987	Mark McGwire, Oak	49
1934	Lou Gehrig, NY	49	1988	Jose Canseco, Oak	42
1935	Jimmie Foxx, Phi	36	1989	Fred McGriff, Tor	36
	Hank Greenberg, Det	36	1990	Cecil Fielder, Det	51
1936	Lou Gehrig, NY	49	1991	Jose Canseco, Oak	44
1937	Joe DiMaggio, NY	46		Cecil Fielder, Det	44
1938	Hank Greenberg, Det	58	1992	Juan Gonzalez, Tex	43
1939	Jimmie Foxx, Bos	35	1993	Juan Gonzalez, Tex	46
1940	Hank Greenberg, Det	41	1994	Ken Griffey Jr., Sea	40
1941	Ted Williams, Bos	37	1995	Albert Belle, Clev	50
1942	Ted Williams, Bos	36	1996	Mark McGwire, Oak	52
1943	Rudy York, Det	34	1997	Ken Griffey Jr., Sea	56
1944	Nick Etten, NY	22	1998	Ken Griffey Jr., Sea	56
1945	Vern Stephens, StL	24	1999	Ken Griffey Jr., Sea	48
1946	Hank Greenberg, Det	44	2000	Troy Glaus, Ana	47
1947	Ted Williams, Bos	32	2001	Alex Rodriguez, Tex	52
1948	Joe DiMaggio, NY	39	2002	Alex Rodriguez, Tex	57
1949	Ted Williams, Bos	43	2003	Alex Rodriguez, Tex	47
1950	Al Rosen, Clev	37	2004	Manny Ramirez, Bos	43
1951	Gus Zernial, Chi-Phi	33	2005	Alex Rodriguez, NY	48
1952	Larry Doby, Clev	32	2006	David Ortiz, Bos	54
1953	Al Rosen, Clev	43	2007	Alex Rodriguez, NY	54
1954	Larry Doby, Clev	32	2008	Miguel Cabrera, Det	37
1955	Mickey Mantle, NY	37	2009	Carlos Pena, TB	39
1956	Mickey Mantle, NY	52		Mark Teixeira, NY	39
1957	Roy Sievers, Wash	42	2010	Jose Bautista, Tor	54
1958	Mickey Mantle, NY	42			
1959	Rocky Colavito, Clev	42			
	Harmon Killebrew, Wash	42			

Runs Batted In Leaders

Year	Player and Team	RBI	Year	Player and Team	RBI
1907	Ty Cobb, Det	116	1958	Jackie Jensen, Bos	122
1908	Ty Cobb, Det	108	1959	Jackie Jensen, Bos	112
1909	Ty Cobb, Det	107	1960	Roger Maris, NY	112
1910	Sam Crawford, Det	120	1961	Roger Maris, NY	142
1911	Ty Cobb, Det	144	1962	Harmon Killebrew, Minn	126
1912	Frank Baker, Phi	133	1963	Dick Stuart, Bos	118
1913	Frank Baker, Phi	126	1964	Brooks Robinson, Balt	118
1914	Sam Crawford, Det	104	1965	Rocky Colavito, Clev	108
1915	Sam Crawford, Det	112	1966	Frank Robinson, Balt	122
	Bobby Veach, Det	112	1967	Carl Yastrzemski, Bos	121
1916	Del Pratt, StL	103	1968	Ken Harrelson, Bos	109
1917	Bobby Veach, Det	103	1969	Harmon Killebrew, Minn	140
1918	Bobby Veach, Det	78	1970	Frank Howard, Wash	126
1919	Babe Ruth, Bos	114	1971	Harmon Killebrew, Minn	119
1920	Babe Ruth, NY	137	1972	Dick Allen, Chi	113
1921	Babe Ruth, NY	171	1973	Reggie Jackson, Oak	117
1922	Ken Williams, StL	155	1974	Jeff Burroughs, Tex	118
1923	Babe Ruth, NY	131	1975	George Scott, Mil	109
1924	Goose Goslin, Wash	129	1976	Lee May, Balt	109
1925	Bob Meusel, NY	138	1977	Larry Hisle, Minn	119
1926	Babe Ruth, NY	145	1978	Jim Rice, Bos	139
1927	Lou Gehrig, NY	175	1979	Don Baylor, Cal	139
1928	Babe Ruth/ Lou Gehrig, NY	142	1980	Cecil Cooper, Mil	122
1929	Al Simmons, Phi	157	1981	Eddie Murray, Balt	78
1930	Lou Gehrig, NY	174	1982	Hal McRae, KC	133
1931	Lou Gehrig, NY	184	1983	Cecil Cooper, Mil	126
1932	Jimmie Foxx, Phi	169		Jim Rice, Bos	126
1933	Jimmie Foxx, Phi	163	1984	Tony Armas, Bos	123
1934	Lou Gehrig, NY	165	1985	Don Mattingly, NY	145
1935	Hank Greenberg, Det	170	1986	Joe Carter, Clev	121
1936	Hal Trosky, Clev	162	1987	George Bell, Tor	134
1937	Hank Greenberg, Det	183	1988	Jose Canseco, Oak	124
1938	Jimmie Foxx, Bos	175	1989	Ruben Sierra, Tex	119
1939	Ted Williams, Bos	145	1990	Cecil Fielder, Det	132
1940	Hank Greenberg, Det	150	1991	Cecil Fielder, Det	133
1941	Joe DiMaggio, NY	125	1992	Cecil Fielder, Det	124
1942	Ted Williams, Bos	137	1993	Albert Belle, Clev	129
1943	Rudy York, Det	118	1994	Kirby Puckett, Minn	112
1944	Vern Stephens, StL	109	1995	Albert Belle, Clev	126
1945	Nick Etten, NY	111		Mo Vaughn, Bos	126
1946	Hank Greenberg, Det	127	1996	Albert Belle, Clev	148
1947	Ted Williams, Bos	114	1997	Ken Griffey Jr., Sea	147
1948	Joe DiMaggio, NY	155	1998	Juan Gonzales, Tex	157
1949	Vern Stephens, Bos	159	1999	Manny Ramirez, Clev	165
	Ted Williams, Bos	159	2000	Edgar Martinez, Sea	145
1950	Walt Dropo, Bos	144	2001	Bret Boone, Sea	141
	Vern Stephens, Bos	144	2002	Alex Rodriguez, Tex	142
1951	Gus Zernial, Chi-Phi	129	2003	Carlos Delgado, Tor	145
1952	Al Rosen, Clev	105	2004	Miguel Tejada, Balt	150
1953	Al Rosen, Clev	145	2005	David Ortiz, Bos	148
1954	Larry Doby, Clev	126	2006	David Ortiz, Bos	137
1955	Ray Boone, Det	116	2007	Alex Rodriguez, NY	156
	Jackie Jensen, Bos	116	2008	Josh Hamilton, Tex	130
1956	Mickey Mantle, NY	130	2009	Mark Teixeira, NY	122
1957	Roy Sievers, Wash	114	2010	Miguel Cabrera, Det	126

Leading Base Stealers

Year	Player and Team	SB	Year	Player and Team	SB
1901	Frank Isbell, Chi	48	1910	Eddie Collins, Phi	81
1902	Topsy Hartsel, Phi	54	1911	Ty Cobb, Det	83
1903	Harry Bay, Clev	46	1912	Clyde Milan, Wash	88
1904	Harry Bay, Clev	42	1913	Clyde Milan, Wash	75
	Elmer Flick, Clev	42	1914	Fritz Maisel, NY	74
1905	Danny Hoffman, Phi	46	1915	Ty Cobb, Det	96
1906	John Anderson, Wash	39	1916	Ty Cobb, Det	68
	Elmer Flick, Clev	39	1917	Ty Cobb, Det	55
1907	Ty Cobb, Det	49	1918	George Sisler, StL	45
1908	Patsy Dougherty, Chi	47	1919	Eddie Collins, Chi	33
1909	Ty Cobb, Det	76	1920	Sam Rice, Wash	63

Note: Runs Batted In not compiled before 1907; officially adopted in 1920.

Leading Base Stealers *(Cont.)*

Year	Player and Team	SB	Year	Player and Team	SB
1921	George Sisler, StL	35	1966	Bert Campaneris, KC	52
1922	George Sisler, StL	51	1967	Bert Campaneris, KC	55
1923	Eddie Collins, Chi	49	1968	Bert Campaneris, Oak	62
1924	Eddie Collins, Chi	42	1969	Tommy Harper, Sea	73
1925	John Mostil, Chi	43	1970	Bert Campaneris, Oak	42
1926	John Mostil, Chi	35	1971	Amos Otis, KC	52
1927	George Sisler, StL	27	1972	Bert Campaneris, Oak	52
1928	Buddy Myer, Bos	30	1973	Tommy Harper, Bos	54
1929	Charlie Gehringer, Det	27	1974	Bill North, Oak	54
1930	Marty McManus, Det	23	1975	Mickey Rivers, Cal	70
1931	Ben Chapman, NY	61	1976	Bill North, Oak	75
1932	Ben Chapman, NY	38	1977	Freddie Patek, KC	53
1933	Ben Chapman, NY	27	1978	Ron LeFlore, Det	68
1934	Bill Werber, Bos	40	1979	Willie Wilson, KC	83
1935	Bill Werber, Bos	29	1980	Rickey Henderson, Oak	100
1936	Lyn Lary, StL	37	1981	Rickey Henderson, Oak	56
1937	Ben Chapman, Wash-Bos	35	1982	Rickey Henderson, Oak	130
	Bill Werber, Phi	35	1983	Rickey Henderson, Oak	108
1938	Frank Crosetti, NY	27	1984	Rickey Henderson, Oak	66
1939	George Case, Wash	51	1985	Rickey Henderson, NY	80
1940	George Case, Wash	35	1986	Rickey Henderson, NY	87
1941	George Case, Wash	33	1987	Harold Reynolds, Sea	60
1942	George Case, Wash	44	1988	Rickey Henderson, NY	93
1943	George Case, Wash	61	1989	Rickey Henderson, NY-Oak	77
1944	Snuffy Stirnweiss, NY	55	1990	Rickey Henderson, Oak	65
1945	Snuffy Stirnweiss, NY	33	1991	Rickey Henderson, Oak	58
1946	George Case, Clev	28	1992	Kenny Lofton, Clev	66
1947	Bob Dillinger, StL	34	1993	Kenny Lofton, Clev	70
1948	Bob Dillinger, StL	28	1994	Kenny Lofton, Clev	60
1949	Bob Dillinger, StL	20	1995	Kenny Lofton, Clev	54
1950	Dom DiMaggio, Bos	15	1996	Kenny Lofton, Clev	75
1951	Minnie Minoso, Clev-Chi	31	1997	Brian Hunter, Det	74
1952	Minnie Minoso, Chi	22	1998	Rickey Henderson, Oak	66
1953	Minnie Minoso, Chi	25	1999	Brian Hunter, Sea	44
1954	Jackie Jensen, Bos	22	2000	Johnny Damon, KC	46
1955	Jim Rivera, Chi	25	2001	Ichiro Suzuki, Sea	56
1956	Luis Aparicio, Chi	21	2002	Alfonso Soriano, NY	41
1957	Luis Aparicio, Chi	28	2003	Carl Crawford, TB	55
1958	Luis Aparicio, Chi	29	2004	Carl Crawford, TB	59
1959	Luis Aparicio, Chi	56	2005	Chone Figgins, LA	62
1960	Luis Aparicio, Chi	51	2006	Carl Crawford, TB	58
1961	Luis Aparicio, Chi	53	2007	Carl Crawford, TB	50
1962	Luis Aparicio, Chi	31		Brian Roberts, Balt	50
1963	Luis Aparicio, Balt	40	2008	Jacoby Ellsbury, Bos	50
1964	Luis Aparicio, Balt	57	2009	Jacoby Ellsbury, Bos	70
1965	Bert Campaneris, KC	51	2010	Juan Pierre, Chi	68

Leading Pitchers—Winning Percentage

Year	Pitcher and Team	W	L	Pct	Year	Pitcher and Team	W	L	Pct
1901	Clark Griffith, Chi	24	7	.774	1920	Jim Bagby, Clev	31	12	.721
1902	Bill Bernhard, Phi-Clev	18	5	.783	1921	Carl Mays, NY	27	9	.750
1903	Earl Moore, Clev	22	7	.759	1922	Joe Bush, NY	26	7	.788
1904	Jack Chesbro, NY	41	12	.774	1923	Herb Pennock, NY	19	6	.760
1905	Jess Tannehill, Bos	22	9	.710	1924	Walter Johnson, Wash	23	7	.767
1906	Eddie Plank, Phi	19	6	.760	1925	Stan Coveleski, Wash	20	5	.800
1907	Wild Bill Donovan, Det	25	4	.862	1926	George Uhle, Clev	27	11	.711
1908	Ed Walsh, Chi	40	15	.727	1927	Waite Hoyt, NY	22	7	.759
1909	George Mullin, Det	29	8	.784	1928	General Crowder, StL	21	5	.808
1910	Chief Bender, Phi	23	5	.821	1929	Lefty Grove, Phi	20	6	.769
1911	Chief Bender, Phi	17	5	.773	1930	Lefty Grove, Phi	28	5	.848
1912	Smoky Joe Wood, Bos	34	5	.872	1931	Lefty Grove, Phi	31	4	.886
1913	Walter Johnson, Wash	36	7	.837	1932	Johnny Allen, NY	17	4	.810
1914	Chief Bender, Phi	17	3	.850	1933	Lefty Grove, Phi	24	8	.750
1915	Smoky Joe Wood, Bos	15	5	.750	1934	Lefty Gomez, NY	26	5	.839
1916	Eddie Cicotte, Chi	15	7	.682	1935	Eldon Auker, Det	18	7	.720
1917	Reb Russell, Chi	15	5	.750	1936	Monte Pearson, NY	19	7	.731
1918	Sad Sam Jones, Bos	16	5	.762	1937	Johnny Allen, Clev	15	1	.938
1919	Eddie Cicotte, Chi	29	7	.806	1938	Red Ruffing, NY	21	7	.750

Leading Pitchers—Winning Percentage *(Cont.)*

Year	Pitcher and Team	W	L	Pct	Year	Pitcher and Team	W	L	Pct
1939	Lefty Grove, Bos	15	4	.789	1975	Mike Torrez, Balt	20	9	.690
1940	Schoolboy Rowe, Det	16	3	.842	1976	Bill Campbell, Minn	17	5	.773
1941	Lefty Gomez, NY	15	5	.750	1977	Paul Splittorff, KC	16	6	.727
1942	Ernie Bonham, NY	21	5	.808	1978	Ron Guidry, NY	25	3	.893
1943	Spud Chandler, NY	20	4	.833	1979	Mike Caldwell, Mil	16	6	.727
1944	Tex Hughson, Bos	18	5	.783	1980	Steve Stone, Balt	25	7	.781
1945	Hal Newhouser, Det	25	9	.735	1981*	Pete Vuckovich, Mil	14	4	.778
1946	Boo Ferriss, Bos	25	6	.806	1982	Pete Vuckovich, Mil	18	6	.750
1947	Allie Reynolds, NY	19	8	.704		Jim Palmer, Balt	15	5	.750
1948	Jack Kramer, Bos	18	5	.783	1983	Richard Dotson, Chi	22	7	.759
1949	Ellis Kinder, Bos	23	6	.793	1984	Doyle Alexander, Tor	17	6	.739
1950	Vic Raschi, NY	21	8	.724	1985	Ron Guidry, NY	22	6	.786
1951	Bob Feller, Clev	22	8	.733	1986	Roger Clemens, Bos	24	4	.857
1952	Bobby Shantz, Phi	24	7	.774	1987	Roger Clemens, Bos	20	9	.690
1953	Ed Lopat, NY	16	4	.800	1988	Frank Viola, Minn	24	7	.774
1954	Sandy Consuegra, Chi	16	3	.842	1989	Bret Saberhagen, KC	23	6	.793
1955	Tommy Byrne, NY	16	5	.762	1990	Bob Welch, Oak	27	6	.818
1956	Whitey Ford, NY	19	6	.760	1991	Scott Erickson, Minn	20	8	.714
1957	Dick Donovan, Chi	16	6	.727	1992	Mike Mussina, Balt	18	5	.783
	Tom Sturdivant, NY	16	6	.727	1993	Jimmy Key, NY	18	6	.750
1958	Bob Turley, NY	21	7	.750	1994	Jimmy Key, NY	17	4	.810
1959	Bob Shaw, Chi	18	6	.750	1995	Randy Johnson, Sea	18	2	.900
1960	Jim Perry, Clev	18	10	.643	1996	Charles Nagy, Clev	17	5	.773
1961	Whitey Ford, NY	25	4	.862	1997	Randy Johnson, Sea	20	4	.833
1962	Ray Herbert, Chi	20	9	.690	1998	David Wells, NY	18	4	.818
1963	Whitey Ford, NY	24	7	.774	1999	Pedro Martinez, Bos	23	4	.852
1964	Wally Bunker, Balt	19	5	.792	2000	Tim Hudson, Oak	20	6	.769
1965	Mudcat Grant, Minn	21	7	.750	2001	Roger Clemens, NY	20	3	.870
1966	Sonny Siebert, Clev	16	8	.667	2002	Pedro Martinez, Bos	20	4	.833
1967	Joel Horlen, Chi	19	7	.731	2003	Roy Halladay, Tor	22	7	.759
1968	Denny McLain, Det	31	6	.838	2004	Curt Schilling, Bos	21	6	.778
1969	Jim Palmer, Balt	16	4	.800	2005	Cliff Lee, Cle	18	5	.783
1970	Mike Cuellar, Balt	24	8	.750	2006	Roy Halladay, Tor	16	5	.762
1971	Dave McNally, Balt	21	5	.808	2007	Justin Verlander, Det	18	6	.750
1972	Catfish Hunter, Oak	21	7	.750	2008	Cliff Lee, Cle	22	3	.880
1973	Catfish Hunter, Oak	21	5	.808	2009	Felix Hernandez	19	5	.792
1974	Mike Cuellar, Balt	22	10	.688	2010	David Price, TB	19	6	.760

*1981 percentages based on 10 or more victories. Note: Percentages based on 15 or more victories in all other years.

Leading Pitchers—Earned Run Average

Year	Player and Team	ERA	Year	Player and Team	ERA
1913	Walter Johnson, Wash	1.14	1940	Bob Feller, Clev†	2.62
1914	Dutch Leonard, Bos	1.01	1941	Thornton Lee, Chi	2.37
1915	Smoky Joe Wood, Bos	1.49	1942	Ted Lyons, Chi	2.10
1916	Babe Ruth, Bos	1.75	1943	Spud Chandler, NY	1.64
1917	Eddie Cicotte, Chi	1.53	1944	Dizzy Trout, Det	2.12
1918	Walter Johnson, Wash	1.27	1945	Hal Newhouser, Det	1.81
1919	Walter Johnson, Wash	1.49	1946	Hal Newhouser, Det	1.94
1920	Bob Shawkey, NY	2.46	1947	Spud Chandler, NY	2.46
1921	Red Faber, Chi	2.47	1948	Gene Bearden, Clev	2.43
1922	Red Faber, Chi	2.80	1949	Mel Parnell, Bos	2.78
1923	Stan Coveleski, Clev	2.76	1950	Early Wynn, Clev	3.20
1924	Walter Johnson, Wash	2.72	1951	Saul Rogovin, Det-Chi	2.78
1925	Stan Coveleski, Wash	2.84	1952	Allie Reynolds, NY	2.07
1926	Lefty Grove, Phi	2.51	1953	Ed Lopat, NY	2.43
1927	Wilcy Moore, NY#	2.28	1954	Mike Garcia, Clev	2.64
1928	Garland Braxton, Wash	2.52	1955	Billy Pierce, Chi	1.97
1929	Lefty Grove, Phi	2.81	1956	Whitey Ford, NY	2.47
1930	Lefty Grove, Phi	2.54	1957	Bobby Shantz, NY	2.45
1931	Lefty Grove, Phi	2.06	1958	Whitey Ford, NY	2.01
1932	Lefty Grove, Phi	2.84	1959	Hoyt Wilhelm, Balt	2.19
1933	Monte Pearson, Clev	2.33	1960	Frank Baumann, Chi	2.68
1934	Lefty Gomez, NY	2.33	1961	Dick Donovan, Wash	2.40
1935	Lefty Grove, Bos	2.70	1962	Hank Aguirre, Det	2.21
1936	Lefty Grove, Bos	2.81	1963	Gary Peters, Chi	2.33
1937	Lefty Gomez, NY	2.33	1964	Dean Chance, LA	1.65
1938	Lefty Grove, Bos	3.07	1965	Sam McDowell, Clev	2.18
1939	Lefty Grove, Bos	2.54	1966	Gary Peters, Chi	1.98

Leading Pitchers—Earned Run Average *(Cont.)*

Year	Player and Team	ERA	Year	Player and Team	ERA
1967	Joe Horlen, Chi	2.06	1989	Bret Saberhagen, KC	2.16
1968	Luis Tiant, Clev	1.60	1990	Roger Clemens, Bos	1.93
1969	Dick Bosman, Wash	2.19	1991	Roger Clemens, Bos	2.62
1970	Diego Segui, Oak	2.56	1992	Roger Clemens, Bos	2.41
1971	Vida Blue, Oak	1.82	1993	Kevin Appier, KC	2.56
1972	Luis Tiant, Bos	1.91	1994	Steve Ontiveros, Oak	2.65
1973	Jim Palmer, Balt	2.40	1995	Randy Johnson, Sea	2.48
1974	Catfish Hunter, Oak	2.49	1996	Juan Guzman, Tor	2.93
1975	Jim Palmer, Balt	2.09	1997	Roger Clemens, Tor	2.05
1976	Mark Fidrych, Det	2.34	1998	Roger Clemens, Tor	2.64
1977	Frank Tanana, Cal	2.54	1999	Pedro Martinez, Bos	2.07
1978	Ron Guidry, NY	1.74	2000	Pedro Martinez, Bos	1.74
1979	Ron Guidry, NY	2.78	2001	Freddy Garcia, Sea	3.05
1980	Rudy May, NY	2.47	2002	Pedro Martinez, Bos	2.26
1981	Steve McCatty, Oak	2.32	2003	Pedro Martinez, Bos	2.22
1982	Rick Sutcliffe, Clev	2.96	2004	Johan Santana, Minn	2.61
1983	Rick Honeycutt, Tex	2.42	2005	Kevin Millwood, Cle	2.86
1984	Mike Boddicker, Balt	2.79	2006	Johan Santana, Minn	2.77
1985	Dave Stieb, Tor	2.48	2007	John Lackey, LA	3.01
1986	Roger Clemens, Bos	2.48	2008	Cliff Lee, Cle	2.54
1987	Jimmy Key, Tor	2.76	2009	Zack Greinke, KC	2.16
1988	Allan Anderson, Minn	2.45	2010	Felix Hernandez, Sea	2.27

Note: Based on 10 complete games through 1950, then 154 innings until the American League expanded in 1961, when it became 162 innings. In strike-shortened 1981, one inning per game required. Earned runs not tabulated in American League prior to 1913. #Wilcy Moore pitched only six complete games—he started 12—in 1927 but was recognized as leader because of 213 innings pitched. †Ernie Bonham, New York, had 1.91 ERA and 10 complete games in 1940 but appeared in only 12 games and 99 innings, and Bob Feller was recognized as the leader.

Leading Pitchers—Strikeouts

Year	Player and Team	SO	Year	Player and Team	SO
1901	Cy Young, Bos	159	1940	Bob Feller, Clev	261
1902	Rube Waddell, Phi	210	1941	Bob Feller, Clev	260
1903	Rube Waddell, Phi	301	1942	Bobo Newsom, Wash	
1904	Rube Waddell, Phi	349		Tex Hughson, Bos	113
1905	Rube Waddell, Phi	286	1943	Allie Reynolds, Clev	151
1906	Rube Waddell, Phi	203	1944	Hal Newhouser, Det	187
1907	Rube Waddell, Phi	226	1945	Hal Newhouser, Det	212
1908	Ed Walsh, Chi	269	1946	Bob Feller, Clev	348
1909	Frank Smith, Chi	177	1947	Bob Feller, Clev	196
1910	Walter Johnson, Wash	313	1948	Bob Feller, Clev	164
1911	Ed Walsh, Chi	255	1949	Virgil Trucks, Det	153
1912	Walter Johnson, Wash	303	1950	Bob Lemon, Clev	170
1913	Walter Johnson, Wash	243	1951	Vic Raschi, NY	164
1914	Walter Johnson, Wash	225	1952	Allie Reynolds, NY	160
1915	Walter Johnson, Wash	203	1953	Billy Pierce, Chi	186
1916	Walter Johnson, Wash	228	1954	Bob Turley, Balt	185
1917	Walter Johnson, Wash	188	1955	Herb Score, Clev	245
1918	Walter Johnson, Wash	162	1956	Herb Score, Clev	263
1919	Walter Johnson, Wash	147	1957	Early Wynn, Clev	184
1920	Stan Coveleski, Clev	133	1958	Early Wynn, Chi	179
1921	Walter Johnson, Wash	143	1959	Jim Bunning, Det	201
1922	Urban Shocker, StL	149	1960	Jim Bunning, Det	201
1923	Walter Johnson, Wash	130	1961	Camilo Pascual, Minn	221
1924	Walter Johnson, Wash	158	1962	Camilo Pascual, Minn	206
1925	Lefty Grove, Phi	116	1963	Camilo Pascual, Minn	202
1926	Lefty Grove, Phi	194	1964	Al Downing, NY	217
1927	Lefty Grove, Phi	174	1965	Sam McDowell, Clev	325
1928	Lefty Grove, Phi	183	1966	Sam McDowell, Clev	225
1929	Lefty Grove, Phi	170	1967	Jim Lonborg, Bos	246
1930	Lefty Grove, Phi	209	1968	Sam McDowell, Clev	283
1931	Lefty Grove, Phi	175	1969	Sam McDowell, Clev	279
1932	Red Ruffing, NY	190	1970	Sam McDowell, Clev	304
1933	Lefty Gomez, NY	163	1971	Mickey Lolich, Det	308
1934	Lefty Gomez, NY	158	1972	Nolan Ryan, Cal	329
1935	Tommy Bridges, Det	163	1973	Nolan Ryan, Cal	383
1936	Tommy Bridges, Det	175	1974	Nolan Ryan, Cal	367
1937	Lefty Gomez, NY	194	1975	Frank Tanana, Cal	269
1938	Bob Feller, Clev	240	1976	Nolan Ryan, Cal	327
1939	Bob Feller, Clev	246	1977	Nolan Ryan, Cal	341

Leading Pitchers—Strikeouts *(Cont.)*

Year	Player and Team	SO	Year	Player and Team	SO
1978	Nolan Ryan, Cal	260	1995	Randy Johnson, Sea	294
1979	Nolan Ryan, Cal	223	1996	Roger Clemens, Bos	257
1980	Len Barker, Clev	187	1997	Roger Clemens, Tor	292
1981	Len Barker, Clev	127	1998	Roger Clemens, Tor	271
1982	Floyd Bannister, Sea	209	1999	Pedro Martinez, Bos	313
1983	Jack Morris, Det	232	2000	Pedro Martinez, Bos	284
1984	Mark Langston, Sea	204	2001	Hideo Nomo, Bos	220
1985	Bert Blyleven, Clev-Minn	206	2002	Pedro Martinez, Bos	239
1986	Mark Langston, Sea	245	2003	Esteban Loaiza, Chi	207
1987	Mark Langston, Sea	262	2004	Johan Santana, Minn	265
1988	Roger Clemens, Bos	291	2005	Johan Santana, Minn	238
1989	Nolan Ryan, Tex	301	2006	Johan Santana, Minn	245
1990	Nolan Ryan, Tex	232	2007	Scott Kazmir, TB	239
1991	Roger Clemens, Bos	241	2008	A.J. Burnett, Tor	231
1992	Randy Johnson, Sea	241	2009	Justin Verlander, Det	269
1993	Randy Johnson, Sea	308	2010	Jered Weaver, LA	233
1994	Randy Johnson, Sea	204			

Leading Pitchers—Saves

FYear	Player and Team	SV	Year	Player and Team	SV
1947	Joe Page, NY	17	1980	Dan Quisenberry, KC	33
1948	Russ Christopher, Clev	17	1981	Rollie Fingers, Mil	28
1949	Joe Page, NY	29	1982	Dan Quisenberry, KC	35
1950	Mickey Harris, Wash	15	1983	Dan Quisenberry, KC	35
1951	Ellis Kinder, Bos	14	1984	Dan Quisenberry, KC	44
1952	Harry Dorish, Chi	11	1985	Dan Quisenberry, KC	37
1953	Ellis Kinder, Bos	27	1986	Dave Righetti, NY	46
1954	Johnny Sain, NY	22	1987	Tom Henke, Tor	34
1955	Ray Narleski, Clev	19	1988	Dennis Eckersley, Oak	45
1956	George Zuverink, Bal	16	1989	Jeff Russell, Tex	38
1957	Bob Grim, NY	19	1990	Bobby Thigpen, Chi	57
1958	Ryne Duren, NY	20	1991	Bryan Harvey, Cal	46
1959	Turk Lown, Chi	15	1992	Dennis Eckersley, Oak	51
1960	Mike Fornieles, Bos	14	1993	Jeff Montgomery, KC	45
	Johnny Klippstein, Clev	14		Duane Ward, Tor	45
1961	Luis Arroyo, NY	29	1994	Lee Smith, Bal	33
1962	Dick Radatz, Bos	24	1995	Jose Mesa, Clev	46
1963	Stu Miller, Bal	27	1996	John Wetteland, NY	43
1964	Dick Radatz, Bos	29	1997	Randy Myers, Balt	45
1965	Ron Kline, Wash	29	1998	Tom Gordon, Bos	46
1966	Jack Aker, KC	32	1999	Mariano Rivera, NY	45
1967	Minnie Rojas, Cal	27	2000	Todd Jones, Det	42
1968	Al Worthington, Minn	18	2001	Mariano Rivera, NY	50
1969	Ron Perranoski, Minn	31	2002	Eddie Guardado, Minn	45
1970	Ron Perranoski, Minn	34	2003	Keith Foulke, Oak	43
1971	Ken Sanders, Mil	31	2004	Mariano Rivera, NY	53
1972	Sparky Lyle, NY	35	2005	Francisco Rodriguez, LA	45
1973	John Hiller, Det	38		Bob Wickman, Cle	45
1974	Terry Forster, Chi	24	2006	Francisco Rodriguez, LA	47
1975	Goose Gossage, Chi	26	2007	Joe Borowski, Cle	45
1976	Sparky Lyle, NY	23	2008	Francisco Rodriguez, LA	62
1977	Bill Campbell, Bos	31	2009	Brian Fuentes, LA	48
1978	Goose Gossage, NY	27	2010	Rafael Soriano, TB	45
1979	Mike Marshall, Minn	32			

The Commissioners of Baseball

Kenesaw Mountain Landis.....Elected Nov. 12, 1920. Served until his death on Nov. 25, 1944.

Happy Chandler....................Elected April 24, 1945. Served until July 15, 1951.

Ford Frick ....Elected Sept. 20, 1951. Served until Nov. 16, 1965.

William Eckert.......................Elected Nov. 17, 1965. Served until Dec. 20, 1968.

Bowie Kuhn ....Elected Feb. 8, 1969. Served until Sept. 30, 1984.

Peter Ueberroth....................Elected March 3, 1984. Took office Oct. 1, 1984. Served through March 31, 1989.

A. Bartlett Giamatti ....Elected Sept. 8, 1988. Took office April 1, 1989. Served until his death on Sept. 1, 1989.

Francis Vincent Jr. ....Appointed Acting Commissioner Sept. 2, 1989. Elected Commissioner Sept. 13, 1989. Served until Sept. 7, 1992.

Allan H. (Bud) Selig..............Elected chairman of the executive council and given the powers of interim commissioner on Sept. 9, 1992. Unanimously elected Commissioner July 9, 1998.

Super Bowl XLIV MVP Drew Brees orchestrated an aerial attack that led the New Orleans Saints to their first NFL title

AL TIELEMANS

Pro Football

Things Just Ain't the Same

Paced by a potent offense and a suddenly stout defense, the New Orleans Saints marched to their first NFL title, rejuvenating a wounded city's spirits along the way

BY HANK HERSCH

LIKE PLATES OF NACHOS AND barbecue wings, it's a ritual dish enjoyed by every player on a mediocre NFL team at a Super Bowl party: hope. Because as recent years have showed—see the 2007 Giants, the '08 Cardinals—outfits seemingly going nowhere can suddenly, with an off-season pickup here and a lucky bounce there, find themselves playing for the Lombardi Trophy before 100 million viewers a year later. Saints quarterback Drew Brees was among those engaged in such wishful thinking as he watched the Steelers beat Arizona in Super Bowl XLIII. "You say to yourself: Three, four, five games all came down to one or two plays for us, and if we make those plays, that's us in the Super Bowl," he said before the 2009 season kicked off. "Absolutely you do that."

With Brees throwing for a combined total of 9,492 yards in 2007 and 2008, New Orleans had still only gone 8–8 and 7–9 those two seasons. Enter its new defensive coordinator, the former Bills head coach Gregg Williams, to revamp a unit that tied for 26th in the league in points allowed in 2008. The team also signed veteran safety Darren Sharper, who prompltly went out

and picked off nine passes in 2009, setting an NFL record for interception return yardage, with 376, along the way. With game breakers on both sides of the ball—the Brees-led offense set the NFL pace in points (31.9) and yards (403.8) per game—the Saints raced to a 13–0 start before dropping a 24–17 decision to the Cowboys.

New Orleans wasn't the only previously so-so team whose Super Bowl hopes solidified as the season wore on. In the AFC, the Bengals (4–11–1 in '08) used a rugged running game and some last-minute magic to take the daunting NFC North, going 6–0 in the division. But their playoff run ended abruptly against the New York Jets, who were led by a pair of rookies: coach Rex Ryan, who molded the top-ranked D in the league, and quarterback Mark Sanchez, the No. 6 pick out of USC who outplayed the Lions' No. 1 choice, Georgia's Matt Stafford.

And as for the Jets' QB from last season? Well, all he did was come out of retirement (again) after undergoing surgery on his biceps; sign a one-year, $13 million free-agent deal with his former archrival, Minnesota; complete a career-high 68.4% of his passes for 4,202 yards and 33 touchdowns;

Titans RB Chris Johnson had a monster season in 2009, amassing 2,000-plus rushing yards and setting the single-season record for yards from scrimmage.

start his record 285th game; finish fourth in the MVP voting; and, at 40, guide the Vikings to a 12–4 finish, their best since 1998. "The guy's incredible," said Vikings center John Sullivan of Brett Favre. "We know that with this team we're going to fight till the end, and if there's time on the clock, we have a chance because we score points. Brett gives us a swagger."

Of course, for every team whose outlook improved in '09 there was one whose sank. The fortunes of the defending-champion Steelers seemed to fade with a knee injury to All-Pro safety Troy Polamalu, who was sidelined for the last seven games, in which Pittsburgh went 3–4. And the team with the best record in 2008, the 13–3 Titans, tumbled to 8–8 despite the brilliance of Chris Johnson. The second-year running back with 4.24 speed surpassed Marshall Faulk's single-season NFL mark for yards from scrimmage (2,509) and, rolling up 5.6 yards per carry, became only the sixth player to rush for more than 2,000 yards in one season. At one time, Minnesota's Adrian Peterson was the consensus choice as the league's top back; now, it's a footrace. "[Peterson] is going to do something crazy,

run people over or put a disgusting move on them," says Rams defensive end Chris Long. "But people don't touch CJ."

Amid all the ups and downs there was the league's model of consistency: the Colts, who had double digit wins for the eighth straight year. Led by quarterback Peyton Manning, who earned his record fourth MVP award, Indianapolis was unbeaten in its first 14 games and set a record with 23 consecutive regular-season victories. But with his team leading the Jets 15–10 in the third quarter, rookie coach Jim Caldwell pulled Manning and many of his starters. New York rallied for a 29–15 upset, ending the Colts' quest to become the league's first undefeated team since the 1972 Miami Dolphins. "The most important thing for us is to make certain that we're operating on all cylinders come the playoffs," Caldwell said. "That's key, that's important, and that's our focus."

Caldwell's decision to throttle back—

AL TIELEMANS

Metairie, La., served as FEMA headquarters; the battered Superdome had a morgue in the basement. Long a touchstone for the Big Easy, the team became not only an escape but also an inspiration. Over a four-month span in 2006 general manager Mickey Loomis turned last-place New Orleans into what would be a division champ, hiring coach Sean Payton, signing Brees and drafting running back Reggie Bush, safety Roman Harper, guard Jahri Evans and receiver Marques Colston.

It was Payton who sparked New Orleans against the favored Colts; down 10–6 at halftime, he asked his defensive players how they would feel if he chose to come out with an onside kick and the play backfired. "Coach, we've got your back," one piped up, and others nodded. Backup safety Chris Reis recovered the kick, and Brees engineered a six-play, 59-yard scoring drive to give the Saints their first lead.

Indy had regained a 17–16 advantage when, with 10:39 left in the game, Brees gathered the Saints in a huddle and said, "Let's be special." He proceeded to throw seven passes to seven receivers, completing every one of them, the last a two-yard TD to tight end Jeremy Shockey. Then Porter once again made the key defensive play, picking off a Manning pass and going 74 yards for the clinching score in a 31–17 Saints victory.

After the first quarter, Brees connected on an unfathomable 29 of 32 passes and was named MVP. But the origins of the Saints' first-ever Super Bowl victory reached back much further, to those outstanding performances, lucky bounces and key off-season acquisitions. "It was all meant to be," Brees said after the game. "It was destiny."

which infuriated fans in Indy—appeared to pay off: The Colts looked dominant in postseason defeats of the Ravens (20–3) and Jets (30–17). To take Super Bowl XLIV in Miami, though, Manning would have to defeat the team his father, Archie, quarterbacked for a decade: the Saints, who, after defeating Arizona 45–14, toppled the Vikings in the NFC title game 31–28. After New Orleans cornerback Tracy Porter thwarted a late Favre drive in regulation with an interception, Saints kicker Garrett Hartley nailed a 40-yard field goal in overtime to give the 43-year-old franchise its first shot at a championship.

Only 4½ years earlier the Saints were practicing on a high school field in San Antonio and lifting weights in a parking lot, their home city in ruins in the wake of Hurricane Katrina. Their practice facility in

FOR THE RECORD•2009–2010

American Football Conference

EAST DIVISION

	W	L	T	Pct	Pts	OP
New England	10	6	0	.625	427	285
*NY Jets	9	7	0	.563	348	236
Miami	7	9	0	.438	360	390
Buffalo	6	10	0	.375	258	326

NORTH DIVISION

	W	L	T	Pct	Pts	OP
Cincinnati	10	6	0	.625	305	291
*Baltimore	9	7	0	.563	391	261
Pittsburgh	9	7	0	.563	368	324
Cleveland	5	11	0	.313	245	375

SOUTH DIVISION

	W	L	T	Pct	Pts	OP
Indianapolis	14	2	0	.875	416	307
Houston	9	7	0	.563	388	333
Tennessee	8	8	0	.500	354	402
Jacksonville	7	9	0	.438	290	380

WEST DIVISION

	W	L	T	Pct	Pts	OP
San Diego	13	3	0	.813	454	320
Denver	8	8	0	.500	326	324
Oakland	5	11	0	.313	379	379
Kansas City	4	12	0	.250	424	424

National Football Conference

EAST DIVISION

	W	L	T	Pct	Pts	OP
Dallas	11	5	0	.688	361	250
*Philadelphia	11	5	0	.688	429	337
NY Giants	8	8	0	.500	402	427
Washington	4	12	0	.250	266	336

NORTH DIVISION

	W	L	T	Pct	Pts	OP
Minnesota	12	4	0	.750	470	312
*Green Bay	11	5	0	.688	461	297
Chicago	7	9	0	.438	327	375
Detroit	2	14	0	.125	262	494

SOUTH DIVISION

	W	L	T	Pct	Pts	OP
New Orleans	13	3	0	.813	510	341
Atlanta	9	7	0	.563	363	325
Carolina	8	8	0	.500	315	308
Tampa Bay	3	13	0	.188	244	400

WEST DIVISION

	W	L	T	Pct	Pts	OP
Arizona	10	6	0	.625	375	325
San Francisco	8	8	0	.500	330	281
Seattle	5	11	0	.313	280	390
St. Louis	1	15	0	.063	175	436

* Wild-card team.

2009–10 NFL Playoffs

AFC FIRST ROUND	AFC DIVISIONAL PLAYOFF	AFC CHAMPIONSHIP	NFC CHAMPIONSHIP	NFC DIVISIONAL PLAYOFF	NFC FIRST ROUND

SUPER BOWL XLIV
February 7, 2010
Miami, Florida

Baltimore 33
New England 14

Baltimore 3

Indianapolis 30

Indianapolis 20

NY Jets 24
Cincinnati 14

NY Jets 17

NY Jets 17

San Diego 14

**NEW ORLEANS 31
Indianapolis 17**

Minnesota 28

(OT)

Minnesota 34

New Orleans 31

New Orleans 45

Dallas 34
Philadelphia 14

Dallas 3

Arizona 14

Arizona 51 (OT)
Green Bay 45

NFL Playoff Recaps

AFC Wild-card Games

NY Jets	0	14	7	3—24
Cincinnati	7	0	0	7—14

FIRST QUARTER: Cincinnati: TD Coles 11 pass from Palmer (Graham kick), 7:07.

SECOND QUARTER: NY Jets: TD Greene 39 run (Feely kick), 11:52.

NY Jets: TD Keller 45 pass from Sanchez (Feely kick), 6:19.

THIRD QUARTER: NY Jets: TD Jones 9 run (Feely kick), 2:18.

FOURTH QUARTER: Cincinnati: TD Benson 47 run, 11:04.

NY Jets: FG Feely 20, 5:47.

A: 63,686.

Baltimore	24	0	3	6—33
New England	0	7	7	0—14

FIRST QUARTER: Baltimore: TD Rice 83 run (Cundiff kick), 14:43.

Baltimore: TD McClain 1 run (Cundiff kick), 10:29.

Baltimore: TD Rice 1 run (Cundiff kick), 3:55.

Baltimore: FG Cundiff 27, 1:19.

SECOND QUARTER: New England: TD Edelman 6 pass from Brady (Gostkowski kick), 11:23.

THIRD QUARTER: Baltimore: FG Cundiff 23, 6:18.

New England: TD Edelman 1 pass from Brady (Gostkowski kick), 1:47.

FOURTH QUARTER: Baltimore: TD McGahee 3 run (2-pt. conversion failed), 10:32.

A: 68,756.

NFC Wild-card Games

Philadelphia	0	7	0	7—14
Dallas	0	27	7	0—34

SECOND QUARTER: Dallas: TD Phillips 1 pass from Romo (Suisham kick), 14:09.

Philadelphia: TD Maclin 76 pass from Vick (Akers kick), 13:19.

Dallas: TD Choice 1 run (Suisham kick), 9:14.

Dallas: FG Suisham 26, 3:39.

Dallas: TD Austin 6 pass from Romo (Suisham kick), 1:55.

Dallas: FG Suisham 48, 0:02.

THIRD QUARTER: Dallas: TD Jones 73 run, (Suisham kick), 5:33.

FOURTH QUARTER: Philadelphia: Jackson 4 pass from McNabb (Akers kick), 13:30.

A: 92,951.

Green Bay	0	10	14	21	0—45
Arizona	17	7	14	7	6—51

FIRST QUARTER: Arizona: TD Hightower 1 run (Rackers kick), 11:04.

Arizona: TD Doucet 15 pass from Warner (Rackers kick), 9:16.

Arizona: FG Rackers 23, 0:34.

SECOND QUARTER: Green Bay: TD Rodgers 1 run (Crosby kick), 6:52.

Arizona: TD Doucet 15 pass from Warner (Rackers kick), 2:16.

Green Bay: FG Crosby 20, 0:00.

THIRD QUARTER: Arizona: TD Fitzgerald 33 pass from Warner (Rackers kick), 11:15.

Green Bay: TD Jennings 6 pass from Rodgers (Crosby kick), 7:20.

Green Bay: TD Nelson 10 pass from Rodgers (Crosby kick), 4:07.

Arizona: TD Fitzgerald 11 pass from Warner (Rackers kick), 2:34.

FOURTH QUARTER: Green Bay: TD Jones 30 pass from Rodgers (Crosby kick), 14:08.

Green Bay: TD Kuhn 1 run (Crosby kick), 10:57.

Arizona: Breaston TD 17 pass from Warner (Rackers kick), 4:55.

Green Bay: TD Havner 11 pass from Rodgers (Crosby kick), 1:52.

OVERTIME: Arizona: TD Dansby 17 fumble recovery return, 13:42.

A: 61,926.

AFC Divisional Games

Baltimore	3	0	0	0—3
Indianapolis	3	14	0	3—20

FIRST QUARTER: Indianapolis: FG Stover 44, 10:44.

Baltimore: FG Cundiff 25, 2:57.

SECOND QUARTER: Indianapolis: TD Collie 10 pass from Manning (Stover kick), 2:00.

Indianapolis: TD Wayne 3 pass from Manning (Stover kick), 0:03.

FOURTH QUARTER: Indianapolis: FG Stover 33, 13:26.

A: 67,535

NY Jets	0	0	3	14—17
San Diego	0	7	0	7—14

SECOND QUARTER: San Diego: TD Wilson 13 pass from Rivers (Kaeding kick), 12:17.

THIRD QUARTER: NY Jets: FG Feely 46, 10:45.

FOURTH QUARTER: NY Jets: TD Keller 2 pass from Sanchez (Feely kick), 13:35.

NY Jets: TD Greene 53 run (Feely kick), 7:17.

San Diego: TD Rivers 1 run (Kaeding kick), 2:14.

A: 69,498.

NFC Divisional Games

Arizona	7	7	0	0—14
New Orleans	21	14	10	0—45

FIRST QUARTER: Arizona: TD Hightower 70 run (Rackers kick), 14:41.

New Orleans: TD Hamilton 1 run (Hartley kick), 9:17.

New Orleans: TD Shockey 17 pass from Brees (Hartley kick), 7:02.

New Orleans: TD Bush 46 run (Hartley kick), 2:31.

SECOND QUARTER: Arizona: TD Wells 4 run (Rackers kick), 9:40.

New Orleans: TD Henderson 44 pass from Brees (Hartley kick), 6:48.

New Orleans: TD Colston 2 pass from Brees (Hartley kick), 1:10.

THIRD QUARTER: New Orleans: FG Hartley 43, 8:26.

New Orleans: TD Bush 83 punt return (Hartley kick), 6:42.

A: 70,149.

Dallas	0	3	0	0—3
Minnesota	7	10	0	17—34

FIRST QUARTER: Minnesota: TD Rice 47 pass from Favre (Longwell kick), 4:04.

SECOND QUARTER: Dallas: FG Suisham 33, 12:11.

Minnesota: TD Rice 16 pass from Favre (Longwell kick), 7:23.

Minnesota: FG Longwell 23, 3:26.

FOURTH QUARTER: Minnesota: FG Longwell 28, 14:23.

Minnesota: TD Rice 45 pass from Favre (Longwell kick), 7:32.

Minnesota: TD Shiancoe 11 pass from Favre (Longwell kick), 1:55.

A: 63,547.

AFC Championship

NY Jets	0	17	0	0—17
Indianapolis	0	13	7	10—30

SECOND QUARTER: Indianapolis: FG Stover 25, 14:56.

NY Jets: TD Edwards 50 pass from Sanchez (Feely kick), 14:45.

Indianapolis: FG Stover 19, 8:44.

NY Jets: TD Keller 9 pass from Sanchez (Feely kick), 4:53.

NY Jets: FG Feely 48, 2:11.

Indianapolis: TD Collie 16 pass from Manning (Stover kick), 1:13.

THIRD QUARTER: Indianapolis: TD Garcon 4 pass from Manning (Stover kick), 8:03.

FOURTH QUARTER: Indianapolis: TD Clark 15 pass from Manning (Stover kick), 8:52.

Indianapolis: FG Stover 21, 2:29.

A: 67,650.

NFC Championship

Minnesota	14	0	7	7	0—28
New Orleans	7	7	7	7	3—31

FIRST QUARTER: Minnesota: TD Peterson 19 run (Longwell kick), 9:35.

New Orleans: TD Thomas 38 pass from Brees (Hartley kick), 6:30.

Minnesota: TD Rice 5 pass from Favre (Longwell kick), 2:11.

SECOND QUARTER: New Orleans: TD Henderson 9 pass from Brees (Hartley kick), 10:30..

THIRD QUARTER: New Orleans: TD Thomas 9 run (Hartley kick), 12:56.

Minnesota: TD Peterson 1 run (Longwell kick), 7:35.

FOURTH QUARTER: New Orleans: TD Bush 5 pass from Brees (Hartley kick), 12:39.

Minnesota: TD Peterson 2 run (Longwell kick), 4:58.

OVERTIME: New Orleans: FG Hartley 40, 10:15.

A: 71,276.

Super Bowl XLIV Recap

New Orleans	0	6	10	15—31
Indianapolis	10	0	7	0—17

FIRST QUARTER: Indianapolis: FG Stover 38, 7:29.
Indianapolis 3–0.

Indianapolis: TD Garcon 19 pass from Manning (Stover kick), 0:36.
Indianapolis 10–0.

SECOND QUARTER: New Orleans: FG Hartley 46, 9:34.
Indianapolis 10–3.

New Orleans: FG Hartley 44, 0:00.
Indianapolis 10–6.

THIRD QUARTER: New Orleans: TD Thomas 16 pass from Brees (Hartley kick), 11:41.
New Orleans 13–10.

Indianapolis: TD Addai 4 run (Stover kick), 6:15.
Indianapolis 17–13.

New Orleans: FG Hartley 47, 2:01.
Indianapolis 17–16.

FOURTH QUARTER: New Orleans: TD Shockey 2 pass from Brees (Moore 2 pass from Brees for 2-pt. conversion), 5:42.
New Orleans 24–17.

New Orleans: TD Porter 74 interception return (Hartley kick), 3:12.
New Orleans 31–17.

A: 74,059.

Super Bowl XLIV Box Score

Team Statistics

	New Orleans	Indianapolis
FIRST DOWNS	20	23
Rushing	3	6
Passing	16	16
Penalty	1	1
THIRD DOWN EFF	3–9	6–13
FOURTH DOWN EFF	0–1	1–2
TOTAL NET YARDS	332	432
Total plays	58	64
Avg gain	5.7	6.8
NET YARDS RUSHING	51	99
Rushes	18	19
Avg per rush	2.8	5.2
NET YARDS PASSING	281	333
Completed–Att–Int	32–39–0	31–45–1
Yards per pass	7.2	7.4
Sacked–yards lost	1–7	0–0
Had intercepted	0	1
PUNTS–Avg	2–44.0	2–45.0
PENALTIES–Yds	3–19	5–145
FUMBLES–Lost	0–0	0–0

Passing

NEW ORLEANS

	Comp	Att	Yds	Int	TD
Brees	32	39	288	0	2

INDIANAPOLIS

	Comp	Att	Yds	Int	TD
Manning	31	45	333	1	1

Rushing

NEW ORLEANS

	No.	Yds	Lg	TD
P. Thomas	9	30	7	0
Bush	5	25	12	0
Bell	2	4	4	0
Brees	1	-1	-1	0
Henderson	1	-7	-7	0

INDIANAPOLIS

	No.	Yds	Lg	TD
Addai	13	77	26	1
Brown	4	18	5	0
Hart	2	4	3	0

Receiving

NEW ORLEANS

	No.	Yds	Lg	TD
Colston	7	83	27	0
Henderson	7	63	19	0
P. Thomas	6	55	16	1
Bush	4	38	16	0
Moore	2	21	21	0
Shockey	3	13	7	1
D. Thomas	1	9	9	0
Meachem	2	6	6	0

INDIANAPOLIS

	No.	Yds	Lg	TD
Clark	7	86	27	0
Collie	6	66	40	0
Garcon	5	66	19	1
Addai	7	58	17	0
Wayne	5	46	14	0
Brown	1	11	11	0

Defense

NEW ORLEANS

	Tck	Ast	Int	Sack
Harper	8	1	0	0
Vilma	7	0	0	0
Shanie	6	1	0	0
Jenkins	5	0	0	0
Porter	4	0	1	0
Fujita	4	1	0	0
Greer	4	1	0	0
Ellis	3	0	0	0
Sharper	3	1	0	0
Hargrove	3	1	0	0
Gay	2	0	0	0
McCray	2	0	0	0
Reis	1	0	0	0
Young	1	0	0	0
Roby	1	0	0	0
Smith	1	0	0	0
Charleston	1	0	0	0
Prioleau	1	0	0	0

INDIANAPOLIS

	Tck	Ast	Int	Sack
Brackett	13	1	0	0
Lacey	6	0	0	0
Hayden	6	1	0	0
Jennings	5	0	0	0
Bullitt	5	0	0	0
Session	5	2	0	0
Bethea	4	0	0	0
Francisco	2	0	0	0
Foster	2	0	0	0
Johnson	2	1	0	0
Powers	2	1	0	0
Freeney	1	0	0	1
Muir	1	0	0	0
Tamme	1	0	0	0
Brock	1	0	0	0
Dawson	1	1	0	0

2009 *Associated Press* All-Pro Team

First Team

OFFENSE

Peyton Manning, Indianapolis	Quarterback
Adrian Peterson, Minnesota	Running Back
Chris Johnson, Tennessee	Running Back
Leonard Weaver, Philadelphia	Fullback
Dallas Clark, Indianapolis	Tight End
Andre Johnson, Houston	Wide Receiver
Wes Welker, New England	Wide Receiver
Ryan Clady, Denver	Tackle
Joe Thomas, Cleveland	Tackle
Jahri Evans, New Orleans	Guard
Steve Hutchinson, Minnesota	Guard
Nick Mangold, NY Jets	Center

DEFENSE

Jared Allen, Minnesota	Defensive End
Dwight Freeney, Indianapolis	Defensive End
Kevin Williams, Minnesota	Defensive Tackle
Jay Ratliff, Dallas	Defensive Tackle
DeMarcus Ware, Dallas	Linebacker
Elvis Dumervil, Denver	Linebacker
Ray Lewis, Baltimore	Linebacker
Patrick Willis, San Francisco	Linebacker
Charles Woodson, Green Bay	Cornerback
Darelle Revis, NY Jets	Cornerback
Darren Sharper, New Orleans	Safety
Adrian Wilson, Arizona	Safety

SPECIALISTS

Nate Kaeding, San Diego	Kicker
Joshua Cribbs, Cleveland	Kick Returner
Shane Lechler, Oakland	Punter

Second Team

OFFENSE

Drew Brees, New Orleans	Quarterback
Ray Rice, Baltimore	Running Back
Steven Jackson, St. Louis	Running Back
Le'Ron McClain, Baltimore	Fullback
Antonio Gates, San Diego	Tight End
Reggie Wayne, Indianapolis	Wide Receiver
Larry Fitzgerald, Arizona	Wide Receiver
Michael Roos, Tennessee	Tackle
Jake Long, Miami	Tackle
Logan Mankins, New England	Guard
Kris Dielman, San Diego	Guard
Andre Gurode, Dallas	Center

DEFENSE

Trent Cole, Philadelphia	Defensive End
Julius Peppers, Carolina	Defensive End
Darnell Dockett, Arizona	Defensive Tackle
Haloti Ngata, Baltimore	Defensive Tackle
Brian Cushing, Houston	Linebacker
LaMarr Woodley, Pittsburgh	Linebacker
David Harris, NY Jets	Linebacker
Jon Beason, Carolina	Linebacker
Nnamdi Asomugha, Oakland	Cornerback
Leon Hall, Cincinnati	Cornerback (tie)
Asante Samuel, Philadelphia	Cornerback (tie)
Ed Reed, Baltimore	Safety
Brian Dawkins, Philadelphia	Safety

SPECIALISTS

David Akers, Philadelphia	Kicker
DeSean Jackson, Philadelphia	Kick Returner
Donnie Jones, St. Louis	Punter (tie)
Andy Lee, San Francisco	Punter (tie)

BALTIMORE RAVENS (9-7)

38	KANSAS CITY	24
31	at San Diego	26
34	CLEVELAND	3
21	at New England	27
14	CINCINNATI	17
31	at Minnesota	33
30	DENVER	7
7	at Cincinnati	17
16	at Cleveland	0
15	INDIANAPOLIS	17
*20	PITTSBURGH	17
14	at Green Bay	27
48	DETROIT	3
31	CHICAGO	7
20	at Pittsburgh	23
21	at Oakland	13
391		261

CLEVELAND BROWNS (5-11)

20	MINNESOTA	34
6	at Denver	27
3	at Baltimore	34
*20	CINCINNATI	23
6	at Buffalo	3
14	at Pittsburgh	27
3	GREEN BAY	31
6	at Chicago	30
0	BALTIMORE	16
37	at Detroit	38
7	at Cincinnati	16
23	SAN DIEGO	30
13	PITTSBURGH	6
41	at Kansas City	34
23	OAKLAND	9
23	JACKSONVILLE	17
245		375

INDIANAPOLIS COLTS (14-2)

14	JACKSONVILLE	12
27	at Miami	23
31	at Arizona	10
34	SEATTLE	17
31	at Tennessee	9
42	at St. Louis	6
18	SAN FRANCISCO	14
20	HOUSTON	17
35	NEW ENGLAND	34
17	at Baltimore	15
35	at Houston	27
27	TENNESSEE	17
28	DENVER	16
35	at Jacksonville	31
15	NY JETS	29
7	at Buffalo	30
416		307

BUFFALO BILLS (6-10)

24	at New England	25
33	TAMPA BAY	20
7	NEW ORLEANS	27
10	at Miami	38
3	CLEVELAND	6
*16	NY Jets	13
20	at Carolina	9
10	HOUSTON	31
17	at Tennessee	41
15	at Jacksonville	18
31	MIAMI	14
13	NY JETS	19
16	at Kansas City	10
10	NEW ENGLAND	17
3	at Atlanta	31
30	INDIANAPOLIS	7
258		326

DENVER BRONCOS (8-8)

12	at Cincinnati	7
27	CLEVELAND	6
23	at Oakland	3
17	DALLAS	10
*20	NEW ENGLAND	17
34	at San Diego	23
7	at Baltimore	30
10	PITTSBURGH	28
17	at Washington	27
3	SAN DIEGO	32
26	NY GIANTS	6
44	at Kansas City	13
16	at Indianapolis	28
19	OAKLAND	20
27	at Philadelphia	30
24	KANSAS CITY	44
326		324

JACKSONVILLE JAGUARS (7-9)

12	at Indianapolis	14
17	ARIZONA	31
31	at Houston	24
37	TENNESSEE	17
0	at Seattle	41
*23	ST. LOUIS	20
13	at Tennessee	30
24	KANSAS CITY	21
24	at NY Jets	22
18	BUFFALO	15
3	at San Francisco	20
23	HOUSTON	18
10	MIAMI	14
31	INDIANAPOLIS	35
7	at New England	35
17	at Cleveland	23
290		380

CINCINNATI BENGALS (10-6)

7	DENVER	12
31	at Green Bay	24
26	PITTSBURGH	20
*23	at Cleveland	20
17	at Baltimore	14
17	HOUSTON	28
45	CHICAGO	10
17	BALTIMORE	7
18	at Pittsburgh	12
17	at Oakland	20
16	CLEVELAND	7
23	DETROIT	13
10	at Minnesota	30
24	at San Diego	27
17	KANSAS CITY	10
0	at NY Jets	37
305		291

HOUSTON TEXANS (9-7)

7	NY JETS	24
34	at Tennessee	31
24	JACKSONVILLE	31
29	OAKLAND	6
21	at Arizona	28
28	at Cincinnati	17
24	SAN FRANCISCO	21
31	at Buffalo	10
17	at Indianapolis	20
17	TENNESSEE	20
27	INDIANAPOLIS	35
18	at Jacksonville	23
34	SEATTLE	7
16	at St. Louis	13
27	at Miami	20
34	NEW ENGLAND	27
388		333

KANSAS CITY CHIEFS (4-12)

24	at Baltimore	38
10	OAKLAND	13
14	at Philadelphia	34
16	NY GIANTS	27
*20	DALLAS	26
14	at Washington	6
7	SAN DIEGO	37
21	at Jacksonville	24
16	at Oakland	10
*27	PITTSBURGH	24
14	at San Diego	43
13	DENVER	44
10	BUFFALO	16
34	CLEVELAND	41
10	at Cincinnati	17
44	at Denver	24
294		424

MIAMI DOLPHINS (7-9)

7	at Atlanta	19	25	TAMPA BAY		23
23	INDIANAPOLIS	27	24	at Carolina		17
13	at San Diego	23	14	at Buffalo		31
38	BUFFALO	10	22	NEW ENGLAND		21
31	NY JETS	27	14	at Jacksonville		10
34	NEW ORLEANS	46	*24	at Tennessee		27
30	at NY Jets	25	20	HOUSTON		27
17	at New England	27	24	PITTSBURGH		30
			360			390

* overtime

NEW ENGLAND PATRIOTS (10-6)

25	BUFFALO	24
9	at NY Jets	16
26	ATLANTA	10
27	BALTIMORE	21
*17	at Denver	20
59	TENNESSEE	0
35	at Tampa Bay	7
27	MIAMI	17
24	at Indianapolis	35
31	NY JETS	14
17	at New Orleans	38
21	at Miami	22
20	CAROLINA	10
17	at Buffalo	10
35	JACKSONVILLE	7
27	at Houston	34
427		285

NEW YORK JETS (9-7)

24	at Houston	7
16	NEW ENGLAND	9
24	TENNESSEE	17
10	at New Orleans	24
27	at Miami	31
*13	BUFFALO	16
38	at Oakland	0
25	MIAMI	30
22	JACKSONVILLE	24
14	at New England	31
17	CAROLINA	6
19	at Buffalo	13
26	at Tampa Bay	3
7	ATLANTA	10
29	at Indianapolis	15
37	CINCINNATI	0
348		236

OAKLAND RAIDERS (5-11)

20	SAN DIEGO	24
13	at Kansas City	10
3	DENVER	23
6	at Houston	29
7	at NY Giants	44
13	PHILADELPHIA	9
0	NY JETS	38
16	at San Diego	24
10	KANSAS CITY	16
20	CINCINNATI	17
7	at Dallas	24
27	at Pittsburgh	24
13	WASHINGTON	34
20	at Denver	19
9	at Cleveland	23
13	BALTIMORE	21
197		379

PITTSBURGH STEELERS (9-7)

*13	TENNESSEE	10
14	at Chicago	17
20	at Cincinnati	23
38	SAN DIEGO	28
28	at Detroit	20
27	CLEVELAND	14
27	MINNESOTA	17
28	at Denver	10
12	CINCINNATI	18
*24	at Kansas City	27
*17	at Baltimore	20
24	OAKLAND	27
6	at Cleveland	13
37	GREEN BAY	36
23	BALTIMORE	20
30	at Miami	24
368		324

SAN DIEGO CHARGERS (13-3)

24	at Oakland	20
26	BALTIMORE	31
23	MIAMI	13
28	at Pittsburgh	38
23	DENVER	34
37	at Kansas City	7
24	OAKLAND	16
21	at NY Giants	20
31	PHILADELPHIA	23
32	at Denver	3
43	KANSAS CITY	14
30	at Cleveland	23
20	at Dallas	17
27	CINCINNATI	24
42	at Tennessee	17
23	WASHINGTON	20
454		320

TENNESSEE TITANS (8-8)

*10	at Pittsburgh	13
31	HOUSTON	34
17	at NY Jets	24
17	at Jacksonville	37
9	INDIANAPOLIS	31
0	at New England	59
30	JACKSONVILLE	13
34	at San Francisco	27
41	BUFFALO	17
20	at Houston	17
20	ARIZONA	17
17	at Indianapolis	27
47	ST. LOUIS	7
*27	MIAMI	24
17	SAN DIEGO	42
17	at Seattle	13
354		402

2009 NFC Team-by-Team Results

ARIZONA CARDINALS (10-6)

16	SAN FRANCISCO	20
31	at Jacksonville	17
10	INDIANAPOLIS	31
28	HOUSTON	21
27	at Seattle	3
24	at NY Giants	17
21	CAROLINA	34
41	at Chicago	21
31	SEATTLE	20
21	at St. Louis	13
17	at Tennessee	20
30	MINNESOTA	17
9	at San Francisco	24
31	at Detroit	24
31	ST. LOUIS	10
7	GREEN BAY	33
375		325

ATLANTA FALCONS (9-7)

19	MIAMI	7
28	CAROLINA	20
10	at New England	26
45	at San Francisco	10
21	CHICAGO	14
21	at Dallas	37
27	at New Orleans	35
31	WASHINGTON	17
19	at Carolina	28
*31	at NY Giants	34
20	TAMPA BAY	17
7	PHILADELPHIA	34
23	NEW ORLEANS	26
10	at NY Jets	7
31	BUFFALO	3
20	at Tampa Bay	10
363		325

CAROLINA PANTHERS (8-8)

10	PHILADELPHIA	38
20	at Atlanta	28
7	at Dallas	21
20	WASHINGTON	17
28	at Tampa Bay	21
9	BUFFALO	20
34	at Arizona	21
20	at New Orleans	30
28	ATLANTA	19
17	MIAMI	24
6	at NY Jets	17
16	TAMPA BAY	6
10	at New England	20
26	MINNESOTA	7
41	at NY Giants	9
23	NEW ORLEANS	10
315		329

* overtime

CHICAGO BEARS (7-9)

15	at Green Bay	21
17	PITTSBURGH	14
25	at Seattle	19
48	DETROIT	24
14	at Atlanta	21
10	at Cincinnati	45
30	CLEVELAND	6
21	ARIZONA	41
6	at San Francisco	10
20	PHILADELPHIA	24
10	at Minnesota	36
17	ST. LOUIS	9
14	GREEN BAY	21
7	at Baltimore	31
*36	MINNESOTA	30
37	at Detroit	23
327		375

DALLAS COWBOYS (11-5)

34	at Tampa Bay	21
31	NY Giants	33
21	CAROLINA	7
10	at Denver	17
*26	at Kansas City	20
37	ATLANTA	21
38	SEATTLE	17
20	at Philadelphia	16
7	at Green Bay	17
7	WASHINGTON	6
24	OAKLAND	7
24	at NY Giants	31
17	SAN DIEGO	20
24	at New Orleans	17
17	at Washington	0
24	PHILADELPHIA	0
361		250

DETROIT LIONS (2-14)

27	at New Orleans	45
13	MINNESOTA	27
19	WASHINGTON	14
24	at Chicago	48
20	PITTSBURGH	28
0	at Green Bay	26
10	ST. LOUIS	17
20	at Seattle	32
10	at Minnesota	27
38	CLEVELAND	37
12	GREEN BAY	34
13	at Cincinnati	23
3	at Baltimore	48
24	ARIZONA	31
6	at San Francisco	20
23	CHICAGO	37
262		494

GREEN BAY PACKERS (11-5)

21	CHICAGO	15
24	CINCINNATI	31
36	at St. Louis	17
23	at Minnesota	30
26	DETROIT	0
31	at Cleveland	3
26	MINNESOTA	38
28	at Tampa Bay	38
17	DALLAS	7
30	SAN FRANCISCO	24
34	at Detroit	12
27	BALTIMORE	14
21	at Chicago	17
36	at Pittsburgh	37
48	SEATTLE	10
33	at Arizona	7
461		297

MINNESOTA VIKINGS (12-4)

34	at Cleveland	20
27	at Detroit	13
27	SAN FRANCISCO	24
30	GREEN BAY	23
38	at St. Louis	10
33	BALTIMORE	31
17	at Pittsburgh	27
38	at Green Bay	26
27	DETROIT	10
35	SEATTLE	9
36	CHICAGO	10
17	at Arizona	30
30	CINCINNATI	10
7	at Carolina	26
*30	at Chicago	36
44	NY GIANTS	7
470		312

NEW ORLEANS SAINTS (13-3)

45	DETROIT	27
48	at Philadephia	22
27	at Buffalo	7
24	NY JETS	10
48	NY GIANTS	27
46	at Miami	34
35	ATLANTA	27
30	CAROLINA	20
28	at St. Louis	23
38	at Tampa Bay	7
38	NEW ENGLAND	17
*33	at Washington	30
26	at Atlanta	23
17	DALLAS	24
*17	TAMPA BAY	20
10	at Carolina	23
510		341

NEW YORK GIANTS (8-8)

23	WASHINGTON	17
33	at Dallas	31
24	at Tampa Bay	0
27	at Kansas City	16
44	OAKLAND	7
27	at New Orleans	48
17	ARIZONA	24
17	at Philadelphia	40
20	SAN DIEGO	21
*34	ATLANTA	31
6	at Denver	26
31	DALLAS	24
38	PHILADELPHIA	45
45	at Washington	12
9	CAROLINA	41
7	at Minnesota	44
402		427

PHILADELPHIA EAGLES (11-5)

38	at Carolina	10
22	NEW ORLEANS	48
34	KANSAS CITY	14
33	TAMPA BAY	14
9	at Oakland	13
27	at Washington	17
40	NY GIANTS	17
16	DALLAS	20
23	at San Diego	31
24	at Chicago	20
27	WASHINGTON	24
34	at Atlanta	7
45	at NY Giants	38
27	SAN FRANCISCO	13
30	DENVER	27
0	at Dallas	24
449		337

SAN FRANCISCO 49ERS (8-8)

20	at Arizona	16
23	SEATTLE	10
24	at Minnesota	27
35	ST. LOUIS	0
10	ATLANTA	45
21	at Houston	24
14	at Indianapolis	18
27	TENNESSEE	34
10	CHICAGO	6
24	at Green Bay	30
20	JACKSONVILLE	3
17	at Seattle	20
24	ARIZONA	9
13	at Philadelphia	27
20	DETROIT	6
28	at St. Louis	6
330		281

* overtime

SEATTLE SEAHAWKS (5-11)

28	ST. LOUIS	0
10	at San Francisco	23
19	CHICAGO	25
17	at Indianapolis	34
41	JACKSONVILLE	0
3	ARIZONA	27
17	at Dallas	38
32	DETROIT	20
20	at Arizona	31
9	at Minnesota	35
27	at St. Louis	17
20	SAN FRANCISCO	17
7	at Houston	34
7	TAMPA BAY	24
10	at Green Bay	48
13	TENNESSEE	17
280		**390**

ST. LOUIS RAMS (1-15)

0	at Seattle	28
7	at Washington	9
17	GREEN BAY	36
0	at San Francisco	35
10	MINNESOTA	38
*20	at Jacksonville	23
6	INDIANAPOLIS	42
17	at Detroit	10
23	NEW ORLEANS	28
13	ARIZONA	21
17	SEATTLE	27
9	at Chicago	17
7	at Tennessee	47
13	HOUSTON	16
10	at Arizona	31
6	SAN FRANCISCO	28
175		**436**

TAMPA BAY BUCCANEERS (3-13)

21	DALLAS	34
20	at Buffalo	33
0	NY GIANTS	24
13	at Washington	16
14	at Philadelphia	33
21	CAROLINA	28
7	NEW ENGLAND	35
38	GREEN BAY	28
23	at Miami	25
7	NEW ORLEANS	38
17	at Atlanta	20
6	at Carolina	16
3	NY JETS	26
24	at Seattle	7
*20	at New Orleans	17
10	ATLANTA	20
244		**400**

WASHINGTON REDSKINS (4-12)

17	at NY Giants	23	27	DENVER	17
9	ST. LOUIS	7	6	at Dallas	7
14	at Detroit	19	24	at Philadelphia	27
16	TAMPA BAY	13	*30	NEW ORLEANS	33
17	at Carolina	20	34	at Oakland	13
6	KANSAS CITY	14	12	NY GIANTS	45
17	PHILADELPHIA	27	0	DALLAS	17
17	at Atlanta	31	20	at San Diego	23
			266		**336**

* overtime

American Football Conference

Scoring

TOUCHDOWNS	TD	Rush	Rec	Ret	2PT	Pts
C. Johnson, Ten	16	14	2	0	1	98
Jones-Drew, Jax	16	15	1	0	0	96
T. Jones, NYJ	14	14	0	0	0	84
McGahee, Balt	14	12	2	0	0	84
Moss, NE	13	0	13	0	1	80
R. Williams, Mia	13	11	2	0	1	80
Addai, Ind	13	10	3	0	0	78
Tomlinson, SD	12	12	0	0	0	72
Wayne, Ind	10	0	10	0	0	60
D. Clark, Ind	10	0	10	0	0	60
Marshall, Den	0	0	10	0	0	60

KICKING	PAT	FG	Pts
Kaeding, SD	50	32	146
Gostkowski, NE	47	26	125
Feely, NYJ	32	30	122
Prater, Den	32	30	122
Reed, Pit	41	27	122
Bironas, Ten	37	27	118
Carpenter, Mia	37	25	112
Lindell, Buf	24	28	108
K. Brown, Hou	43	21	106
Succop, KC	29	25	104
Graham, Cin	28	23	98

Passing

	Att	Comp	Yds	TD	Int	Lg	Rating Pts
Rivers, SD	486	317	4254	28	9	81	104.4
Roethlisberger, Pit	506	337	4328	26	12	60	100.5
P. Manning, Ind	571	393	4500	33	16	80	99.9
Schaub, Hou	583	396	4770	29	15	72	98.6
Brady, NE	565	371	4398	28	13	81	96.2
Flacco, Balt	499	315	3613	21	12	72	88.9
Orton, Den	541	336	3802	21	12	87	86.8
Palmer, Cin	466	282	3094	21	13	73	83.6
Garrard, Jax	516	314	3597	15	10	63	83.5
Young, Ten	259	152	1879	10	7	66	82.8

American Football Conference (Cont.)

Pass Receiving

RECEPTIONS	No.	Yds	Avg	Lg	TD	YARDS	Yds	No.	Avg	Lg	TD
Welker, NE	123	1348	11.0	58	4	A. Johnson, Hou	1569	101	15.5	72	9
A. Johnson, Hou	101	1569	15.5	72	9	Welker, NE	1348	123	11.0	58	4
Marshall, Den	101	1120	11.1	75	10	Moss, NE	1264	83	15.2	71	13
Wayne, Ind	100	1264	12.6	65	10	Wayne, Ind	1264	100	12.6	65	10
D. Clark, Ind	100	1106	11.1	80	10	Holmes, Pit	1248	79	15.8	57	5
Ward, Pit	95	1167	12.3	54	6	Ward, Pit	1167	68	17.2	55	9
Moss, NE	83	1264	15.2	71	13	V. Jackson, SD	1167	95	12.3	54	6
Holmes, Cin	79	1248	15.8	57	5	Gates, SD	1157	79	14.6	56	8
Gates, Den	79	1157	14.6	56	8	Marshall, Den	1120	101	11.1	75	10
Rice, Bal	78	702	9.0	63	1	D. Clark, Ind	1106	100	11.1	80	10

Rushing

	Att	Yds	Avg	Lg	TD	Interceptions	No.	Yds	Lg	TD
C. Johnson, Ten	358	2006	5.6	91	14	Byrd, Buf	9	118	37	0
T. Jones, NYJ	331	1402	4.2	71	14	Joseph, Cin	6	92	32	1
Jones-Drew, Jax	312	1391	4.5	80	15	Revis, NYJ	6	121	67	1
Rice, Bal	254	1339	5.3	59	7	Hall, Cin	6	47	26	0
Benson, Cin	301	1251	4.2	42	6	Goodman, Den	5	65	30	0
R. Williams, Mia	241	1121	4.7	68	11	Bodden, NE	5	60	53	1
J. Charles, KC	190	1120	5.9	76	7	Finnegan, Ten	5	194	80	1
Mendenhall, Pit	242	1108	4.6	60	7	Meriweather, NE	5	149	56	1
F. Jackson, Buf	237	1062	4.5	43	2	Flowers, KC	5	38	33	0
Moreno, Den	247	947	3.8	36	7					

Sacks

	Att	Yds	Avg	Lg	TD		
J. Harrison, Clev	194	862	4.4	71	5	Dumervil, Den	17.0
Addai, Ind	219	828	3.8	21	10	Freeney, Ind	13.5
Maroney, NE	194	757	3.9	45	9	Woodley, Pit	13.5
Tomlinson, SD	223	730	3.3	36	12	Schobel, Buf	10.0
R. Brown, Mia	147	648	4.4	45	8	J. Harrison, Pit	10.0

Punting

	No.	Yds	Avg	Net Avg	TB	In 20	Lg	Blk	Ret	Ret Avg
Lechler, Oak	96	4909	51.1	43.9	12	30	70	0	63	7.3
Moorman, Buf	90	4192	46.7	40.2	10	25	73	0	49	7.7
Fields, Mia	75	3472	46.3	39.8	6	25	66	0	43	8.6
Kern, Den/Ten	64	2910	45.5	38.5	10	27	67	0	27	9.2
Colquitt, KC	96	4361	45.4	41.2	6	41	70	1	40	7.1

Punt Returns

	No.	Yds	Avg	Lg	TD	Kickoff Returns	No.	Yds	Avg	Lg	TD
Welker, NE	27	338	12.5	69	0	J. Cribbs, Cle	56	1542	27.5	103	3
Cribbs, Cle	38	452	11.9	67	1	S. Logan, Pit	55	1466	26.7	83	0
Cosby, Cin	40	474	11.9	67	1	J. Jones, Hou	24	638	26.6	95	1
Royal, Den	30	335	11.2	71	1	L. Webb, Bal	35	918	26.2	95	1
J. Jones, Hou	39	426	10.9	62	0	J. Charles, KC	36	925	25.7	97	1

National Football Conference

Scoring

TOUCHDOWNS	TD	Rush	Rec	Ret	2PT	Pts	KICKING	PAT	FG	Pts
Peterson, Min	18	18	0	0	0	108	Akers, Phi	43	32	139
Fitzgerald, Ari	13	0	13	0	0	78	Longwell, Min	54	26	132
Gore, SF	13	10	3	0	0	78	Crosby, GB	48	27	129
V. Davis, SF	13	0	13	0	0	78	Tynes, NYG	45	27	126
D. Jackson, Phi	12	1	9	2	0	72	Gould, Chi	33	24	105
Shiancoe, Min	11	0	11	0	0	66	Mare, Sea	28	24	100
R. White, Atl	11	0	11	0	0	66	Kasay, Car	31	22	97
Grant, GB	11	11	0	0	0	66	Folk, Dal	36	18	90
Austin, Dal	11	0	11	0	0	66	Carney, NO	50	13	89
J. Stewart, Car	11	10	1	0	0	66	Hanson, Det	25	21	88
Turner, Atl	10	10	0	0	0	60	Rackers, Ari	37	16	85
Meachem, NO	10	0	9	1	0	60	Suisham, Dal/Was	25	20	85
Colston, NO	9	0	9	0	0	54	Nedney, SF	33	17	84

National Football Conference (Cont.)

Passing

	Att	Comp	Yds	TD	Int	Lg	Rating Pts
Brees, NO	514	363	4388	34	11	75	109.6
Favre, Min	531	363	4202	33	7	63	107.2
Rodgers, GB	541	350	4434	30	7	83	103.2
Romo, Dal	550	347	4483	26	9	80	97.6
Warner, Ari	513	339	3753	26	14	45	93.2
E. Manning, NYG	509	317	4021	27	14	74	93.1
McNabb, Phi	443	267	3553	22	10	60	92.9
Campbell, Wash	507	327	3618	20	15	84	86.4
Smith, SF	372	225	2350	18	12	73	81.5
Ryan, Atl	451	263	2913	22	14	90	80.9

Pass Receiving

RECEPTIONS	No.	Yds	Avg	Lg	TD	YARDS	Yds	No.	Avg	Lg	TD
S. Smith, NYG	107	1220	11.4	51	7	Austin, Dal	1320	81	16.3	60	11
Fitzgerald, Ari	97	1092	11.3	34	13	Rice, Min	1312	83	15.8	63	8
Witten, Dal	94	1030	11.0	69	2	S. Smith, NYG	1220	107	11.4	51	7
R. White, Atl	85	1153	13.6	90	11	D. Jackson, Phi	1167	63	18.5	71	9
Boldin, Ari	84	1024	12.2	44	4	R. White, Atl	1153	85	13.6	90	11
Rice, Min	83	1312	15.8	63	8	Jennings, GB	1113	68	16.4	83	4
Gonzalez, Atl	83	867	10.4	27	6	Fitzgerald, Ari	1092	97	11.3	34	13
Austin, Dal	81	1320	16.3	60	11	Colston, NO	1074	70	15.3	68	9
Houshmandzadeh, Sea	79	911	11.5	53	3	Driver, GB	1061	70	15.2	71	6
V. Davis, SF	78	965	12.4	73	13	Witten, Dal	1030	94	11.0	69	2
Winslow, TB	77	165	11.5	42	5	Boldin, Ari	1024	84	12.2	44	4

Rushing

	Att	Yds	Avg	Lg	TD
Jackson, StL	324	1416	4.4	58	4
Peterson, Min	314	1383	4.4	64	18
Grant, GB	282	1253	4.4	62	11
J. Stewart, Car	221	1133	5.1	67	10
Gore, SF	229	1120	4.9	80	10
D. Williams, Car	216	1117	5.2	77	17
Barber, Dal	214	932	4.4	35	7
Forte, Chi	258	929	3.6	61	4
Turner, Atl	178	871	4.9	58	10
Jacobs, NYG	224	835	3.7	31	5
C. Williams, TB	210	821	3.9	35	4
P. Thomas, NO	147	793	5.4	34	6
Wells, Ari	176	793	4.5	33	7
Bradshaw, NYG	163	778	4.8	38	7
K. Smith, Det	217	747	3.4	31	4

Interceptions

	No.	Yds	Lg	TD
Sharper, NO	9	376	99	3
Woodson, GB	9	179	45	3
Samuel, Phi	9	117	37	0
Collins, GB	6	110	31	0
Grimes, Atl	6	17	11	0
Rodgers-Cromartie, Ari	6	77	49	1
Bowman, Chi	6	67	39	0

Sacks

J. Allen, Min	14.5
W. Smith, NO	13.0
Cole, Phi	12.5
Carter, Wash	11.0
Ware, Dal	11.0
Orakpo, Was	10.5
Peppers, Car	10.0
Matthews, GB	8.5

Punting

	No.	Yds	Avg	Net Avg	TB	In 20	Lg	Blk	Ret	Ret Avg
A. Lee, SF	99	4711	47.6	41.0	8	30	64	0	57	8.7
B. Graham, Ari	86	4045	47.0	40.6	3	42	64	0	47	10.5
D. Jones, StL	90	4212	46.8	41.7	10	34	63	0	41	6.3
J. Ryan, Sea	88	4068	46.2	38.7	9	28	70	0	43	11.1
McBriar, Dal	72	3249	45.1	39.9	3	38	63	0	38	8.3

Punt Returns

	No.	Yds	Avg	Lg	TD
D. Jackson, Phi	29	441	15.2	85	2
Crayton, Dal	36	437	12.1	82	2
Amendola, StL	31	360	11.6	56	0
Reynaud, Min	30	308	10.3	36	0
C. Smith, TB	23	232	10.1	21	0
Weems, Atl	27	270	10.0	28	0
Munnerlyn, Car	31	278	9.0	37	0

Kickoff Returns

	No.	Yds	Avg	Lg	TD
C. Smith, TB	31	902	29.1	83	0
Knox, Chi	32	927	29.0	102	1
Harvin, Min	42	1156	27.5	101	2
Roby, NO	42	1154	27.5	97	1
Manning, Chi	28	744	26.6	59	0
J. Nelson, GB	25	635	25.4	54	0
Weems, Atl	48	1214	25.3	62	0

AFC Total Offense

	Total Plays	Yds/ Game	Pts/ Game	1st Dwns/ Game	Time of Poss
New England	1076	397.3	26.7	23.3	33:05
Houston	1043	383.1	24.3	21.2	31:54
Pittsburgh	1014	371.3	23.0	20.7	32:52
Indianapolis	980	363.1	26.0	21.2	27:40
San Diego	972	360.1	28.4	20.6	29:58
Tennessee	990	351.4	22.1	18.0	28:42
Baltimore	1014	351.2	24.4	20.0	29:33
Denver	1032	341.4	20.4	19.1	30:12
Miami	1088	337.6	22.5	20.8	32:01
Jacksonville	1010	336.6	18.1	18.8	30:21
NY Jets	1030	321.0	21.8	17.5	32:07
Cincinnati	1011	309.1	19.1	18.4	32:29
Kansas City	1019	303.2	18.4	16.0	27:59
Buffalo	911	273.9	16.1	14.6	28:12
Oakland	944	266.1	12.3	14.6	28:18
Cleveland	971	260.2	15.3	14.8	28:54

AFC Total Defense

	Opp Total Plays	Opp Yds/ Game	Opp Yds/ Play	Opp Pts/ Game
NY Jets	953	252.3	4.2	14.8
Baltimore	991	300.5	4.9	16.3
Cincinnati	980	301.4	4.9	18.2
Pittsburgh	967	305.3	5.1	20.3
Denver	1007	315.0	5.0	20.3
New England	941	320.2	5.4	17.8
Houston	974	324.9	5.3	20.8
San Diego	991	326.9	5.3	20.0
Indianapolis	1084	339.2	5.0	19.2
Buffalo	1086	340.6	5.0	20.4
Miami	968	349.3	5.8	24.4
Jacksonville	982	352.3	5.7	23.8
Oakland	1023	361.9	5.7	23.7
Tennessee	1038	365.6	5.6	25.1
Kansas City	1062	388.2	5.8	26.5
Cleveland	1072	389.3	5.8	23.4

NFC Total Offense

	Total Plays	Yds/ Game	Pts/ Game	1st Dwns/ Game	Time of Poss
New Orleans	1032	403.8	31.9	21.8	31:36
Dallas	1020	399.4	22.6	20.9	32:17
Minnesota	1054	379.6	29.4	21.4	32:51
Green Bay	1042	379.1	28.8	20.9	33:03
NY Giants	1017	366.0	25.1	20.2	31:41
Philadelphia	975	357.9	26.8	18.1	28:14
Arizona	985	344.4	23.4	19.8	29:52
Atlanta	1048	340.4	22.7	20.6	29:54
Carolina	1023	331.1	19.7	18.1	30:13
Seattle	1045	316.8	17.5	18.6	27:31
Washington	970	312.4	16.6	17.5	29:01
Chicago	971	310.3	20.4	16.4	28:37
Detroit	1037	299.0	16.4	17.6	28:57
San Francisco	939	290.8	20.6	14.9	29:46
Tampa Bay	961	287.5	15.3	15.4	28:44
St. Louis	998	279.4	10.9	16.2	29:10

NFC Total Defense

	Opp Total Plays	Opp Yds/ Game	Opp Yds/ Play	Opp Pts/ Game
Green Bay	948	284.4	4.8	18.6
Minnesota	940	305.5	5.2	19.5
Carolina	976	315.8	5.2	19.3
Dallas	979	315.9	5.2	15.6
Washington	1000	319.7	5.1	21.0
Philadelphia	1037	321.1	5.0	21.1
NY Giants	953	324.9	5.5	26.7
San Francisco	1050	326.4	5.0	17.6
Chicago	1033	337.8	5.2	23.4
Arizona	1038	346.4	5.3	20.3
Atlanta	997	348.9	5.6	20.3
Seattle	1024	356.4	5.6	24.4
New Orleans	1044	357.8	5.5	21.3
Tampa Bay	1039	365.6	5.6	25.0
St. Louis	1016	372.8	5.9	27.3
Detroit	1029	392.1	6.1	30.9

Takeaways/Giveaways

American Football Conference

	Takeaways			Giveaways			Net Diff
	Int	Fum	Total	Int	Fum	Total	
Baltimore	22	10	32	13	9	22	10
San Diego	14	11	25	10	7	17	8
Denver	17	13	30	13	10	23	7
New England	18	10	28	13	9	22	6
Buffalo	28	5	33	19	11	30	3
Indianapolis	16	10	26	19	5	24	2
Jacksonville	15	10	25	10	13	23	2
Kansas City	15	13	28	17	10	27	1
NY Jets	17	14	31	21	9	30	1
Cincinnati	19	6	25	13	12	25	0
Houston	14	13	27	17	11	28	-1
Pittsburgh	12	10	22	14	11	25	-3
Tennessee	20	7	27	15	16	31	-4
Miami	15	6	21	19	10	29	-8
Cleveland	10	9	19	18	13	31	-12
Oakland	8	12	20	18	15	33	-13

National Football Conference

	Takeaways			Giveaways			Net Diff
	Int	Fum	Total	Int	Fum	Total	
Green Bay	30	10	40	8	8	16	24
Philadelphia	25	13	38	13	10	23	15
New Orleans	26	13	39	12	16	28	11
San Francisco	18	15	33	14	10	24	9
Minnesota	11	13	24	7	11	18	6
Carolina	22	15	37	20	11	31	6
Atlanta	15	13	28	17	8	25	3
Dallas	11	10	21	9	10	19	2
Tampa Bay	19	10	29	29	5	34	-5
Chicago	13	15	28	27	7	34	-6
Arizona	21	8	29	18	18	36	-7
NY Giants	13	11	24	14	17	31	-7
Seattle	13	10	23	19	12	31	-8
Washington	11	6	17	16	12	28	-11
St. Louis	8	12	20	21	12	33	-13
Detroit	9	14	23	32	9	41	-18

Baltimore Ravens

SCORING

	Rush	Rec	Ret	PAT	FG	2PT	Pts
McGahee	12	2	0	0	0	0	84
Cundiff	0	0	0	19	12	0	55
Hauschka	0	0	0	27	9	0	54
Rice	7	1	0	0	0	0	48
Mason	0	7	0	0	0	0	42
Heap	0	6	0	0	0	0	36
K. Washington	0	2	0	0	0	0	12
Clayton	0	2	0	0	0	0	12
McClain	2	0	0	0	0	0	12

RUSHING

	No.	Yds	Avg	Lg	TD
Rice	254	1339	5.3	59	7
McGahee	109	544	5.0	77	12

PASSING

	Att	Comp	Pct Comp	Yds	Avg Gain	TD	Int	Rating Pts
Flacco	499	315	63.1	3613	7.2	21	12	88.9

RECEIVING

	No.	Yds	Avg	Lg	TD
Mason	73	1028	14.1	72	7
Rice	78	702	9.0	63	1
Heap	53	593	11.2	31	6
Clayton	34	480	14.1	54	2
K. Washington	34	431	12.7	28	2
D. Williams	8	142	17.8	34	1

INTERCEPTIONS: Foxworth, Landry, 4

PUNTING

	No.	Yds	Avg	Net Avg	TB	In 20	Lg	Blk
Koch	73	3188	43.7	37.9	5	26	60	1

SACKS: Pryce, 6.5

Cincinnati Bengals

SCORING

	Rush	Rec	Ret	PAT	FG	2PT	Pts
Graham	0	0	0	28	23	0	97
Ochocinco	0	9	0	0	0	0	64
Benson	6	0	0	0	0	0	36
Coles	0	5	0	0	0	0	30
Palmer	3	0	0	0	0	1	20
Caldwell	0	3	0	0	0	0	18
Henry	0	2	0	0	0	0	12
Foschi	0	2	0	0	0	0	12

RUSHING

	No.	Yds	Avg	Lg	TD
Benson	301	1251	4.2	42	6
Scott	74	321	4.3	61	0

PASSING

	Att	Comp	Pct Comp	Yds	Avg Gain	TD	Int	Rating Pts
Palmer	466	282	60.5	3094	6.6	21	13	83.6

RECEIVING

	No.	Yds	Avg	Lg	TD
Ochocinco	72	1047	14.5	50	9
Coles	43	514	12.0	40	5
Caldwell	51	432	8.5	24	3
Foschi	27	260	9.6	27	2
Henry	12	236	19.7	73	2
Leonard	30	217	7.2	18	0

INTERCEPTIONS: Hall, Joseph 6

PUNTING

	No.	Yds	Avg	Net Avg	TB	In 20	Lg	Blk
Huber	86	3713	43.2	36.3	10	24	61	1

SACKS: Odom, 8

Buffalo Bills

SCORING

	Rush	Rec	Ret	PAT	FG	2PT	Pts
Lindell	0	0	0	24	28	0	108
Evans	0	7	0	0	0	0	42
Owens	1	5	0	0	0	0	36
F. Jackson	2	2	0	0	0	0	24
Lynch	2	0	0	0	0	0	12

RUSHING

	No.	Yds	Avg	Lg	TD
F. Jackson	237	1062	4.5	43	2
Lynch	120	450	3.8	47	2

PASSING

	Att	Comp	Pct Comp	Yds	Avg Gain	TD	Int	Rating Pts
Fitzpatrick	227	127	55.9	1422	6.3	9	10	69.7
Edwards	183	110	60.1	1169	6.4	6	7	73.8

RECEIVING

	No.	Yds	Avg	Lg	TD
Owens	55	829	15.1	98	5
Evans	44	612	13.9	50	7
F. Jackson	46	371	8.1	21	2
Reed	27	291	10.8	29	1
Lynch	28	179	6.4	35	0
Nelson	18	157	8.7	25	1

INTERCEPTIONS: Byrd, 9

PUNTING

	No.	Yds	Avg	Net Avg	TB	In 20	Lg	Blk
Moorman	90	4192	46.6	40.2	10	25	73	0

SACKS: Schobel, 10

Cleveland Browns

SCORING

	Rush	Rec	Ret	PAT	FG	2PT	Pts
Dawson	0	0	0	18	17	0	69
Harrison	5	2	0	0	0	0	42
Cribbs	1	1	4	0	0	0	36
Cundiff	0	0	0	4	6	0	22
Massaquoi	0	3	0	0	0	0	18
Anderson	2	0	0	0	0	0	12

RUSHING

	No.	Yds	Avg	Lg	TD
Harrison	194	862	4.4	71	5
J. Lewis	143	500	3.5	18	0
Cribbs	55	381	6.9	37	1

PASSING

	Att	Comp	Pct Comp	Yds	Avg Gain	TD	Int	Rating Pts
Quinn	256	136	53.1	1339	5.2	8	7	67.2
Anderson	182	81	44.5	888	4.9	3	10	42.1

RECEIVING

	No.	Yds	Avg	Lg	TD
Massaquoi	34	624	18.4	59	3
Harrison	34	220	6.5	18	2
Stuckey	19	198	10.4	40	1
Furrey	23	170	7.4	22	0
Moore	12	158	13.2	24	0

INTERCEPTIONS: Pool, Wright, 4

PUNTING

	No.	Yds	Avg	Net Avg	TB	In 20	Lg	Blk
Zastudil	49	2188	44.7	39.1	5	25	60	0
Hodges	45	1789	39.8	36.4	3	15	54	0

SACKS: Wimbley, 6.5

Denver Broncos

SCORING

	TD			PAT	FG	2PT	Pts
	Rush	Rec	Ret				
Prater	0	0	0	32	30	0	122
Marshall	0	10	0	0	0	0	60
Moreno	7	2	0	0	0	0	54
Stokley	0	4	0	0	0	0	24
Gaffney	0	2	0	0	0	0	12
Scheffler	0	2	0	0	0	0	12
Royal	0	0	2	0	0	0	12

RUSHING

	No.	Yds	Avg	Lg	TD
Moreno	247	947	3.8	36	7
Buckhalter	120	642	5.4	45	1

PASSING

	Att	Comp	Pct Comp	Yds	Avg Gain	TD	Int	Rating Pts
Orton	541	336	62.1	3802	7.0	21	12	86.8

RECEIVING

	No.	Yds	Avg	Lg	TD
Marshall	101	1120	11.1	75	10
Gaffney	54	732	13.6	49	2
Scheffler	31	416	13.4	52	2
Royal	37	345	9.3	20	0
Stokley	19	327	17.2	87	4

INTERCEPTIONS: Goodman, 5

PUNTING

	No.	Yds	Avg	Net Avg	TB	In 20	Lg	Blk
Berger	51	2142	42.0	37.9	2	13	65	0
Kern	27	1245	46.1	34.5	6	9	64	0

SACKS: Dumervil, 17.0

Houston Texans

SCORING

	TD			PAT	FG	2PT	Pts
	Rush	Rec	Ret				
Brown	0	0	0	43	21	0	106
A. Johnson	0	9	0	0	0	1	56
J. Jones	0	6	1	0	0	0	42
Slaton	3	4	0	0	0	0	42
Moats	4	1	0	0	0	0	30
Daniels	0	5	0	0	0	0	30
Brown	3	0	0	0	0	0	18
Foster	3	0	0	0	0	0	18

RUSHING

	No.	Yds	Avg	Lg	TD
Slaton	131	437	3.3	32	3
Moats	101	390	3.9	17	4

PASSING

	Att	Comp	Pct Comp	Yds	Avg Gain	TD	Int	Rating Pts
Schaub	583	396	67.9	4770	8.2	29	15	98.6

RECEIVING

	No.	Yds	Avg	Lg	TD
A. Johnson	101	1569	15.5	72	9
Walter	53	611	11.5	44	2
Daniels	40	519	13.0	44	5
J. Jones	27	437	16.2	45	6
Slaton	44	417	9.5	38	4
Anderson	38	370	9.7	27	0

INTERCEPTIONS: Cushing, Pollard, 4

PUNTING

	No.	Yds	Avg	Net Avg	TB	In 20	Lg	Blk
Turk	67	2866	42.8	35.8	6	24	62	0

SACKS: Williams, 9

Indianapolis Colts

SCORING

	TD			PAT	FG	2PT	Pts
	Rush	Rec	Ret				
Addai	10	3	0	0	0	0	78
Stover	0	0	0	33	9	0	60
Wayne	0	10	0	0	0	0	60
Clark	0	10	0	0	0	0	60
Collie	0	7	0	0	0	0	42
Vinatieri	0	0	0	17	7	0	38
Garcon	0	4	0	0	0	0	24
Simpson	2	0	1	0	0	0	18
D. Brown	3	0	0	0	0	0	18

RUSHING

	No.	Yds	Avg	Lg	TD
Addai	219	828	3.8	21	10
D. Brown	78	281	3.6	45	3

PASSING

	Att	Comp	Pct Comp	Yds	Avg Gain	TD	Int	Rating Pts
Manning	571	393	68.8	4500	7.9	33	16	99.9

RECEIVING

	No.	Yds	Avg	Lg	TD
Wayne	100	1264	12.6	65	10
Clark	100	1106	11.1	80	10
Garcon	47	765	16.3	66	4
Collie	60	676	11.3	39	7
Addai	51	336	6.6	25	3

INTERCEPTIONS: Bethea, 4

PUNTING

	No.	Yds	Avg	Net Avg	TB	In 20	Lg	Blk
McAfee	64	2837	44.3	37.8	6	21	60	0

SACKS: Freeney, 13.5

Jacksonville Jaguars

SCORING

	TD			PAT	FG	2PT	Pts
	Rush	Rec	Ret				
Jones-Drew	15	1	0	0	0	0	96
Scobee	0	0	0	30	18	0	84
Sims-Walker	0	7	0	0	0	0	42
Garrard	3	0	0	0	0	1	20
M. Lewis	0	2	0	0	0	0	12
Z. Miller	0	2	0	0	0	0	12

RUSHING

	No.	Yds	Avg	Lg	TD
Jones-Drew	312	1391	4.5	80	15
Garrard	77	323	4.2	30	3
R. Jennings	39	202	5.2	28	1

PASSING

	Att	Comp	Pct Comp	Yds	Avg Gain	TD	Int	Rating Pts
Garrard	516	314	60.9	3597	7.0	15	10	83.5

RECEIVING

	No.	Yds	Avg	Lg	TD
Sims-Walker	63	869	13.8	61	7
Holt	51	722	14.2	63	0
M. Lewis	32	518	16.2	47	2
M. Thomas	48	453	9.4	28	1
Jones-Drew	53	374	7.1	19	1
Z. Miller	21	212	10.1	62	2
Wilford	11	123	11.2	30	1

INTERCEPTIONS: Cox, 4

PUNTING

	No.	Yds	Avg	Net Avg	TB	In 20	Lg	Blk
Podlesh	72	3017	41.9	38.3	5	23	64	0

SACKS: Henderson, 3

Kansas City Chiefs

SCORING

	TD						
	Rush	Rec	Ret	PAT	FG	2PT	Pts
Succop	0	0	0	29	25	0	104
J. Charles	7	1	0	0	0	1	56
Chambers	0	4	0	0	0	0	24
Bowe	0	4	0	0	0	0	24
Wade	0	2	0	7	6	0	12
Ryan	0	2	0	0	0	0	12
D. Johnson	0	0	2	0	0	0	12
Bradley	0	2	0	0	0	0	12

RUSHING

	No.	Yds	Avg	Lg	TD
J. Charles	190	1120	5.9	76	7
L. Johnson	132	377	2.9	19	0

PASSING

	Att	Comp	Pct Comp	Yds	Avg Gain	TD	Int	Rating Pts
Cassel	493	271	55.0	2924	5.9	16	16	69.9
Croyle	40	23	57.5	230	5.8	2	0	90.6

RECEIVING

	No.	Yds	Avg	Lg	TD
Chambers	36	608	16.9	61	4
Bowe	47	589	12.5	41	4
Wade	36	367	10.2	25	2
Bradley	24	320	13.3	50	2
J. Charles	40	297	7.4	49	1

INTERCEPTIONS: Flowers, 5

PUNTING

	No.	Yds	Avg	Net Avg	TB	In 20	Lg	Blk
Colquitt	96	4361	45.4	41.2	6	41	70	1

SACKS: Hali, 8.5

New England Patriots

SCORING

	TD						
	Rush	Rec	Ret	PAT	FG	2PT	Pts
Gostkowski	0	0	0	47	26	0	125
Moss	0	13	0	0	0	1	80
Maroney	9	0	0	0	0	0	54
Watson	0	5	0	0	0	0	30
F. Taylor	4	0	0	0	0	0	24
Welker	0	4	0	0	0	0	24
Faulk	2	1	0	0	0	0	18

RUSHING

	No.	Yds	Avg	Lg	TD
Maroney	194	757	3.9	45	9
Faulk	62	335	5.4	29	2
Morris	73	319	4.4	55	2
F. Taylor	63	269	4.3	19	4

PASSING

	Att	Comp	Pct Comp	Yds	Avg Gain	TD	Int	Rating Pts
Brady	565	371	65.7	4398	7.8	28	13	96.2

RECEIVING

	No.	Yds	Avg	Lg	TD
Welker	123	1348	11.0	58	4
Moss	83	1264	15.2	71	13
Watson	29	404	13.9	36	5
Edelman	37	359	9.7	29	1
Aiken	20	326	16.3	81	2
Faulk	37	301	8.1	38	1

INTERCEPTIONS: Meriweather, Bodden, 5

PUNTING

	No.	Yds	Avg	Net Avg	TB	In 20	Lg	Blk
Hanson	56	2221	39.7	34.7	5	18	56	1

SACKS: Banta-Cain, 9.5

Miami Dolphins

SCORING

	TD						
	Rush	Rec	Ret	PAT	FG	2PT	Pts
Carpenter	0	0	0	37	25	0	112
R. Williams	11	2	0	0	0	1	80
Brown	8	0	0	0	0	0	48
Hartline	1	3	0	0	0	0	24
Ginn Jr.	0	1	2	0	0	0	18
Hilliard	1	2	0	0	0	0	18

RUSHING

	No.	Yds	Avg	Lg	TD
R. Williams	241	1121	4.7	68	11
Brown	147	648	4.4	45	8

PASSING

	Att	Comp	Pct Comp	Yds	Avg Gain	TD	Int	Rating Pts
Henne	451	274	60.8	2878	6.4	12	14	75.2
Pennington	74	51	68.9	413	5.6	1	2	76.0

RECEIVING

	No.	Yds	Avg	Lg	TD
Bess	76	758	10.0	34	2
Camarillo	50	552	11.0	29	0
Hartline	31	506	16.3	67	3
Ginn Jr.	38	454	11.9	53	1
Fasano	31	339	10.9	27	2
R. Williams	35	264	7.5	59	2
Haynos	19	162	8.5	21	2

INTERCEPTIONS: Davis, 4

PUNTING

	No.	Yds	Avg	Net Avg	TB	In 20	Lg	Blk
Fields	75	3472	46.3	39.8	6	25	66	0

SACKS: Porter, 9

New York Jets

SCORING

	TD						
	Rush	Rec	Ret	PAT	FG	2PT	Pts
Feely	0	0	0	32	30	0	122
Jones	14	0	0	0	0	0	84
Edwards	0	4	0	0	0	1	26
Cotchery	1	3	0	0	0	0	24
B. Smith	1	0	2	0	0	0	18
Sanchez	3	0	0	0	0	0	18
Keller	0	2	0	0	0	1	14
Greene	2	0	0	0	0	0	12

RUSHING

	No.	Yds	Avg	Lg	TD
Jones	331	1402	4.2	71	14
Greene	108	540	5.0	33	2
L. Washington	72	331	4.6	33	0

PASSING

	Att	Comp	Pct Comp	Yds	Avg Gain	TD	Int	Rating Pts
Sanchez	364	196	53.8	2444	6.7	12	20	63.0

RECEIVING

	No.	Yds	Avg	Lg	TD
Cotchery	57	821	14.4	53	3
Edwards	35	541	15.5	65	4
Keller	45	522	11.6	40	2
Clowney	14	191	13.6	53	1
L. Washington	15	131	8.7	33	0
Stuckey	11	120	10.9	30	1

INTERCEPTIONS: Revis, 6

PUNTING

	No.	Yds	Avg	Net Avg	TB	In 20	Lg	Blk
Weatherford	80	3357	42.0	36.7	9	25	66	0

SACKS: Pace, 8

Oakland Raiders

SCORING

SCORING	Rush	Rec	Ret	PAT	FG	2PT	Pts
Janikowski	0	0	0	17	26	0	95
Murphy	0	4	0	0	0	0	24
Fargas	3	0	0	0	0	0	18
Z. Miller	0	3	0	0	0	0	18
M. Bush	3	0	0	0	0	0	18
Schilens	0	2	0	0	0	0	12

RUSHING

RUSHING	No.	Yds	Avg	Lg	TD
M. Bush	123	589	4.8	60	3
Fargas	129	491	3.8	35	3
McFadden	104	357	3.4	28	1

PASSING

PASSING	Att	Comp	Pct Comp	Yds	Avg Gain	TD	Int	Rating Pts
Russell	246	120	48.8	1287	5.2	3	11	50.0
Gradkowski	150	82	54.7	1007	6.7	6	3	80.6
Frye	87	53	60.9	581	6.7	1	4	65.3

RECEIVING

RECEIVING	No.	Yds	Avg	Lg	TD
Z. Miller	66	805	12.2	86	3
Murphy	34	521	15.3	75	4
Schilens	29	365	12.6	25	2
Higgins	19	263	13.8	33	0
McFadden	21	245	11.7	48	0
Heyward-Bey	9	124	13.8	24	1

INTERCEPTIONS: C. Johnson, Huff, 3

PUNTING	No.	Yds	Avg	Net Avg	TB	In 20	Lg	Blk
Lechler	90	4391	48.8	41.	13	33	70	0

SACKS: Ellis Scott, 7

San Diego Chargers

SCORING

SCORING	Rush	Rec	Ret	PAT	FG	2PT	Pts
Kaeding	0	0	0	50	32	0	146
Tomlinson	12	0	0	0	0	0	72
V. Jackson	0	9	0	0	0	0	54
Gates	0	8	0	0	0	0	48
Sproles	3	4	1	0	0	0	48
Tolbert	1	3	0	0	0	0	24
Naanee	0	2	0	0	0	0	12
J. Hester	0	0	2	0	0	0	12

RUSHING

RUSHING	No.	Yds	Avg	Lg	TD
Tomlinson	223	730	3.3	36	12
Sproles	93	343	3.7	21	3

PASSING

PASSING	Att	Comp	Pct Comp	Yds	Avg Gain	TD	Int	Rating Pts
Rivers	486	317	65.2	4254	8.8	28	9	104.4

RECEIVING

RECEIVING	No.	Yds	Avg	Lg	TD
V. Jackson	68	1167	17.2	55	9
Gates	79	1157	14.6	56	8
Floyd	45	776	17.2	53	1
Sproles	45	497	11.0	81	4
Naanee	24	242	10.1	23	2
Tolbert	17	192	11.3	66	3
Tomlinson	20	154	7.7	36	0
Chambers	9	122	13.6	20	1

INTERCEPTIONS: Cromarie, Jammer, 3

PUNTING	No.	Yds	Avg	Net Avg	TB	In 20	Lg	Blk
Scifres	52	2342	45.0	39.2	2	23	65	0

SACKS: Phillips, 7

Pittsburgh Steelers

SCORING

SCORING	Rush	Rec	Ret	PAT	FG	2PT	Pts
Reed	0	0	0	41	27	0	122
Mendenhall	7	1	0	0	0	0	48
Ward	0	6	0	0	0	0	36
H. Miller	0	6	0	0	0	0	36
Wallace	0	6	0	0	0	0	36
Holmes	0	5	0	0	0	0	30
Roethlisberger	2	0	0	0	0	0	12
Moore	0	2	0	0	0	0	12

RUSHING

RUSHING	No.	Yds	Avg	Lg	TD
Mendenhall	242	1108	4.6	60	7
Parker	98	389	4.0	34	0

PASSING

PASSING	Att	Comp	Pct Comp	Yds	Avg Gain	TD	Int	Rating Pts
Roethlisberger	506	337	66.6	4328	8.6	26	12	100.5

RECEIVING

RECEIVING	No.	Yds	Avg	Lg	TD
Holmes	79	1248	15.8	57	5
Ward	95	1167	12.3	54	6
H. Miller	76	789	10.4	41	6
Wallace	39	756	19.4	60	6
Mendenhall	25	261	10.4	26	1
Moore	21	153	7.3	19	2

INTERCEPTIONS: Polamalu, Clark, 3

PUNTING	No.	Yds	Avg	Net Avg	TB	In 20	Lg	Blk
Sepulveda	72	3074	42.7	37.1	4	29	60	0

SACKS: Woodley, 13.5

Tennessee Titans

SCORING

SCORING	Rush	Rec	Ret	PAT	FG	2PT	Pts
Bironas	0	0	0	37	27	0	118
C. Johnson	14	2	0	0	0	1	98
N. Washington	0	6	0	0	0	0	36
Gage	0	3	0	0	0	0	18
Britt	0	3	0	0	0	0	18
Fuller	0	2	0	0	0	0	12
Young	2	0	0	0	0	0	12
White	2	0	0	0	0	0	12

RUSHING

RUSHING	No.	Yds	Avg	Lg	TD
C. Johnson	358	2006	5.6	91	14
Young	55	281	5.1	44	2
White	64	222	3.5	11	2

PASSING

PASSING	Att	Comp	Pct Comp	Yds	Avg Gain	TD	Int	Rating Pts
Young	259	152	58.7	1879	7.3	10	9	82.8
Collins	216	119	55.1	1225	5.7	6	8	65.5

RECEIVING

RECEIVING	No.	Yds	Avg	Lg	TD
Britt	42	701	16.7	57	3
N. Washington	47	569	12.1	35	6
C. Johnson	50	503	10.1	69	2
Scaife	45	440	9.8	27	1
Gage	28	383	13.7	49	3
Crumpler	27	222	8.2	27	1

INTERCEPTIONS: Finnegan, 5

PUNTING	No.	Yds	Avg	Net Avg	TB	In 20	Lg	Blk
Kern	37	1665	46.9	44.1	4	18	67	0
Hodges	22	868	39.5	31.8	2	1	50	0

SACKS: Ford, 5.5

Arizona Cardinals

SCORING

| | TD | | | | | | |
	Rush	Rec	Ret	PAT	FG	2PT	Pts
Rackers	0	0	0	37	16	0	85
Fitzgerald	0	13	0	0	0	0	78
Hightower	8	0	0	0	0	0	48
Wells	7	0	0	0	0	0	42
Boldin	1	4	0	0	0	0	30
Breaston	0	3	0	0	0	0	18
Nugent	0	0	0	8	2	0	14

RUSHING

	No.	Yds	Avg	Lg	TD
Wells	176	793	4.5	33	7
Hightower	133	598	4.2	50	8

PASSING

	Att	Comp	Pct Comp	Yds	Avg Gain	TD	Int	Rating Pts
Warner	513	339	66.1	3753	7.3	26	14	93.2

RECEIVING

	No.	Yds	Avg	Lg	TD
Fitzgerald	97	1092	11.3	34	13
Boldin	84	1024	12.2	45	4
Breaston	55	712	12.9	45	3
Hightower	63	428	6.8	23	0
Doucet	17	214	12.6	29	1
Urban	18	186	10.3	40	0

INTERCEPTIONS: Rodgers-Cromartie, 6

PUNTING

	No.	Yds	Avg	Net Avg	TB	In 20	Lg	Blk
Graham	86	4045	47.0	40.6	3	42	64	0

SACKS: Dockett, Campbell, 7

Carolina Panthers

SCORING

| | TD | | | | | | |
	Rush	Rec	Ret	PAT	FG	2PT	Pts
Kasay	0	0	0	31	22	0	97
Stewart	10	1	0	0	0	0	66
S. Smith	0	7	0	0	0	1	44
D. Williams	7	0	0	0	0	1	44
King	0	3	0	0	0	0	18
Hoover	1	1	0	0	0	0	12
Rosario	0	2	0	0	0	0	12

RUSHING

	No.	Yds	Avg	Lg	TD
Stewart	221	1133	5.1	67	10
D. Williams	216	1117	5.2	77	7

PASSING

	Att	Comp	Pct Comp	Yds	Avg Gain	TD	Int	Rating Pts
Delhomme	321	178	55.5	2015	6.3	8	18	59.4
Moore	138	85	61.6	1053	7.6	8	2	98.5

RECEIVING

	No.	Yds	Avg	Lg	TD
S. Smith	65	982	15.1	66	7
Muhammad	53	581	11.0	27	1
Rosario	26	313	12.0	26	2
D. Williams	29	252	8.7	30	2
Barnidge	12	242	20.2	55	3
King	25	200	8.0	32	1
Jarrett	17	196	11.5	30	1

INTERCEPTIONS: Marshall, Gamble, 4

PUNTING

	No.	Yds	Avg	Net Avg	TB	In 20	Lg	Blk
Baker	76	3352	44.1	37.1	4	22	61	1

SACKS: Peppers, 10.5

Atlanta Falcons

SCORING

| | TD | | | | | | |
	Rush	Rec	Ret	PAT	FG	2PT	Pts
Elam	0	0	0	32	12	0	68
White	0	11	0	0	0	0	66
Turner	10	0	0	0	0	0	60
Gonzalez	0	6	0	0	0	0	36
Bryant	0	0	0	10	7	0	31
Snelling	4	1	0	0	0	0	30

RUSHING

	No.	Yds	Avg	Lg	TD
Turner	178	871	4.9	58	10
Snelling	142	613	4.3	31	4
Norwood	76	252	3.3	21	0

PASSING

	Att	Comp	Pct Comp	Yds	Avg Gain	TD	Int	Rating Pts
Ryan	451	263	58.3	2916	6.5	22	14	80.9
Redman	119	69	58.0	781	6.6	4	3	78.4

RECEIVING

	No.	Yds	Avg	Lg	TD
White	85	1153	13.6	90	11
Gonzalez	83	867	10.4	27	6
Jenkins	50	635	12.7	50	1
Snelling	30	259	8.6	38	1
Norwood	19	186	9.8	38	1
Booker	16	181	11.3	27	1
Peelle	12	115	9.6	32	2

INTERCEPTIONS: Grimes, 6

PUNTING

	No.	Yds	Avg	Net Avg	TB	In 20	Lg	Blk
Koenen	61	2598	42.6	36.9	3	18	70	1

SACKS: Abraham, 16.5

Chicago Bears

SCORING

| | TD | | | | | | |
	Rush	Rec	Ret	PAT	FG	2PT	Pts
Gould	0	0	0	33	24	0	105
Olsen	0	8	0	0	0	0	48
Knox	0	5	1	0	0	0	36
Forte	4	0	0	0	0	1	26
Aromashodu	0	4	0	0	0	0	24
Bennett	0	2	1	0	0	1	20
Hester	0	2	1	0	0	0	18
K. Davis	0	3	0	0	0	0	18

RUSHING

	No.	Yds	Avg	Lg	TD
Forte	258	929	3.6	61	4
K. Bell	40	220	5.5	72	0

PASSING

	Att	Comp	Pct Comp	Yds	Avg Gain	TD	Int	Rating Pts
Cutler	555	336	60.5	3666	6.6	27	26	76.8

RECEIVING

	No.	Yds	Avg	Lg	TD
Hester	57	757	13.3	48	3
Bennett	54	717	13.3	71	2
Olsen	60	612	10.2	41	8
Knox	45	527	11.7	68	5
Forte	57	471	8.3	37	0
Aromashodu	24	298	12.4	39	4
Clark	19	145	7.6	26	2

INTERCEPTIONS: Bowman, 6

PUNTING

	No.	Yds	Avg	Net Avg	TB	In 20	Lg	Blk
Maynard	77	3191	41.4	37.4	2	26	66	0

SACKS: Ogunleye 6.5

Dallas Cowboys

SCORING	Rush	TD Rec	Ret	PAT	FG	2PT	Pts
Folk	0	0	0	36	18	0	90
Austin	0	11	0	0	0	0	66
Roy E. Williams	0	7	0	0	0	0	42
Crayton	0	5	2	0	0	0	42
Barber	7	0	0	0	0	0	42
Choice	3	0	0	0	0	1	20
F. Jones	3	0	0	0	0	0	18
Witten	0	2	0	0	0	0	12

RUSHING	No.	Yds	Avg	Lg	TD
Barber	214	932	4.4	35	7
F. Jones	116	685	5.9	56	3
Choice	64	349	5.5	66	3

PASSING	Att	Comp	Pct Comp	Yds	Avg Gain	TD	Int	Rating Pts
Romo	550	347	63.1	4483	8.2	26	9	97.6

RECEIVING	No.	Yds	Avg	Lg	TD
Austin	81	1320	16.3	60	11
Witten	94	1030	11.0	69	2
Crayton	37	622	16.8	80	5
Roy E. Williams	38	596	15.7	66	7
Barber	26	221	8.5	42	0

INTERCEPTIONS: Jenkins, 5

PUNTING	No.	Yds	Avg	Net Avg	TB	In 20	Lg	Blk
McBriar	72	3249	45.1	39.9	3	38	63	0

SACKS: Ware, 11

Green Bay Packers

SCORING	Rush	TD Rec	Ret	PAT	FG	2PT	Pts
Crosby	0	0	0	48	27	0	129
Grant	11	0	0	0	0	0	66
Driver	0	6	0	0	0	0	36
Rodgers	5	0	0	0	0	0	30
J. Jones	0	5	0	0	0	0	30
Finley	0	5	0	0	0	0	30
Jennings	0	4	0	0	0	2	28

RUSHING	No.	Yds	Avg	Lg	TD
Grant	282	1253	4.4	62	11
Rodgers	58	316	5.4	35	5

PASSING	Att	Comp	Pct Comp	Yds	Avg Gain	TD	Int	Rating Pts
Rodgers	541	350	64.7	4434	8.2	30	7	103.2

RECEIVING	No.	Yds	Avg	Lg	TD
Jennings	68	1113	16.4	83	4
Driver	70	1061	15.2	71	6
Finley	55	676	12.3	62	5
J. Jones	32	440	13.8	74	5
Nelson	22	320	14.5	51	2
Lee	37	260	7.0	19	1
Grant	25	197	7.9	27	0

INTERCEPTIONS: Woodson, 9

PUNTING	No.	Yds	Avg	Net Avg	TB	In 20	Lg	Blk
Kapinos	66	2891	43.8	34.7	10	15	58	1

SACKS: Matthews, 10

Detroit Lions

SCORING	Rush	TD Rec	Ret	PAT	FG	2PT	Pts
Hanson	0	0	0	25	21	0	88
K. Smith	4	1	0	0	0	0	32
C. Johnson	0	5	0	0	0	0	30
B. Johnson	0	3	0	0	0	0	18
Heller	0	3	0	0	0	0	18
Morris	2	0	0	0	0	1	14
Delmas	0	0	2	0	0	0	14

RUSHING	No.	Yds	Avg	Lg	TD
K. Smith	217	747	3.4	31	4
Morris	93	384	4.1	64	2

PASSING	Att	Comp	Pct Comp	Yds	Avg Gain	TD	Int	Rating Pts
Stafford	377	201	53.3	2267	6.0	13	20	61.0
Culpepper	157	89	56.7	945	6.0	3	6	64.8

RECEIVING	No.	Yds	Avg	Lg	TD
C. Johnson	67	984	14.7	75	5
B. Johnson	35	417	11.9	36	3
K. Smith	41	415	10.1	63	1
Northcutt	35	357	10.2	47	1
Pettigrew	30	346	11.5	30	2
Heller	29	296	10.2	24	3

INTERCEPTIONS: Delmas, James, Henry, 2

PUNTING	No.	Yds	Avg	Net Avg	TB	In 20	Lg	Blk
Harris	74	3174	42.9	36.8	5	20	56	0

SACKS: Avril, 5.5

Minnesota Vikings

SCORING	Rush	TD Rec	Ret	PAT	FG	2PT	Pts
Longwell	0	0	0	54	26	0	132
Peterson	18	0	0	0	0	0	108
Shiancoe	0	11	0	0	0	0	66
Rice	0	8	0	0	0	0	48
Harvin	0	6	2	0	0	0	48
Berrian	0	4	0	0	0	0	24
Taylor	1	1	0	0	0	0	12
Dugan	0	2	0	0	0	0	12

RUSHING	No.	Yds	Avg	Lg	TD
Peterson	314	1383	4.4	64	18
Taylor	94	338	3.6	25	1

PASSING	Att	Comp	Pct Comp	Yds	Avg Gain	TD	Int	Rating Pts
Favre	531	363	68.4	4202	7.9	33	7	107.2

RECEIVING	No.	Yds	Avg	Lg	TD
Rice	83	1312	15.8	63	8
Harvin	60	790	13.2	51	6
Berrian	55	618	11.2	40	4
Shiancoe	56	566	10.1	27	11
Peterson	43	436	10.1	63	0
Taylor	44	389	8.8	33	1

INTERCEPTIONS: Griffin, 4

PUNTING	No.	Yds	Avg	Net Avg	TB	In 20	Lg	Blk
Kluwe	73	3202	43.9	37.8	9	24	60	0

SACKS: J. Allen, 14.5

New Orleans Saints

SCORING	Rush	Rec	Ret	PAT	FG	2PT	Pts
		TD					
Carney	0	0	0	50	13	0	89
Meachem	0	9	1	0	0	0	60
Colston	0	9	0	0	0	0	54
Bush	5	3	0	0	0	0	48
P. Thomas	6	2	0	0	0	0	48
Hartley	0	0	0	10	9	0	37
Bell	5	0	0	0	0	0	30

RUSHING	No.	Yds	Avg	Lg	TD
P. Thomas	147	793	5.4	34	6
Bell	172	654	3.8	35	5
Bush	70	390	5.6	55	5

PASSING	Att	Comp	Pct Comp	Yds	Avg Gain	TD	Int	Rating Pts
Brees	514	363	70.6	4388	8.5	34	11	109.6

RECEIVING	No.	Yds	Avg	Lg	TD
Colston	70	1074	15.3	68	9
Henderson	51	804	15.8	75	2
Meachem	45	722	16.0	54	9
Shockey	48	569	11.9	66	3
D. Thomas	35	356	10.2	37	1
Bush	47	335	7.1	29	3
P. Thomas	39	302	7.7	36	2
Moore	14	153	10.9	22	2

INTERCEPTIONS: Sharper, 9

PUNTING	No.	Yds	Avg	Net Avg	TB	In 20	Lg	Blk
Morstead	58	2528	43.6	36.0	4	18	60	0

SACKS: W. Smith, 13

New York Giants

SCORING	Rush	Rec	Ret	PAT	FG	2PT	Pts
		TD					
Tynes	0	0	0	45	27	0	126
S. Smith	0	7	0	0	0	0	42
Bradshaw	7	0	0	0	0	0	42
Jacobs	5	1	0	0	0	0	36
Nicks	0	6	0	0	0	0	36
Boss	0	5	0	0	0	0	30
Manningham	0	5	0	0	0	0	30
Hixon	0	1	1	0	0	0	12

RUSHING	No.	Yds	Avg	Lg	TD
Jacobs	224	835	3.7	31	5
Bradshaw	163	778	4.8	38	7

PASSING	Att	Comp	Pct Comp	Yds	Avg Gain	TD	Int	Rating Pts
Manning	509	317	62.3	4021	7.9	27	14	93.1

RECEIVING	No.	Yds	Avg	Lg	TD
S. Smith	107	1220	11.4	51	7
Manningham	57	822	14.4	49	5
Nicks	47	790	16.8	68	6
Boss	42	567	13.5	35	5
Bradshaw	21	207	9.9	55	0
Hixon	15	187	12.5	61	1
Jacobs	18	184	10.2	74	1

INTERCEPTIONS: Thomas, 5

PUNTING	No.	Yds	Avg	Net Avg	TB	In 20	Lg	Blk
Feagles	64	2604	40.7	36.0	2	23	59	0

SACKS: Umenyiora, 7

Philadelphia Eagles

SCORING	Rush	Rec	Ret	PAT	FG	2PT	Pts
		TD					
Akers	0	0	0	43	32	0	139
D. Jackson	1	9	2	0	0	0	72
Celek	0	8	0	0	0	0	48
McCoy	4	0	0	0	0	1	26
Weaver	2	2	0	0	0	0	24
Maclin	0	4	0	0	0	0	24
Avant	0	3	0	0	0	1	20

RUSHING	No.	Yds	Avg	Lg	TD
McCoy	155	637	4.1	66	4
Weaver	70	323	4.6	41	2
Westbrook	61	274	4.5	25	1

PASSING	Att	Comp	Pct Comp	Yds	Avg Gain	TD	Int	Rating Pts
McNabb	443	267	60.3	3553	8.0	22	10	92.9
Kolb	96	62	64.6	741	7.7	4	3	88.9

RECEIVING	No.	Yds	Avg	Lg	TD
D. Jackson	63	1167	18.5	71	9
Celek	76	971	12.8	47	8
Maclin	55	762	13.9	56	4
Avant	41	587	14.3	58	3
McCoy	40	308	7.7	45	0

INTERCEPTIONS: Samuel, 9

PUNTING	No.	Yds	Avg	Net Avg	TB	In 20	Lg	Blk
Rocca	76	3222	42.4	38.3	4	26	61	0

SACKS: Cole, 12.5

St. Louis Rams

SCORING	Rush	Rec	Ret	PAT	FG	2PT	Pts
		TD					
Brown	0	0	0	16	19	0	73
Avery	0	5	0	0	0	0	30
S. Jackson	4	0	0	0	0	0	24
Fells	0	3	0	0	0	0	18

RUSHING	No.	Yds	Avg	Lg	TD
S. Jackson	324	1416	4.4	58	4
Darby	27	152	5.6	51	0

PASSING	Att	Comp	Pct Comp	Yds	Avg Gain	TD	Int	Rating Pts
Bulger	247	140	56.7	1469	6.0	5	6	70.7
Boller	176	98	55.7	899	5.1	3	6	61.2
Null	119	73	61.3	566	4.7	3	9	49.9

RECEIVING	No.	Yds	Avg	Lg	TD
Avery	47	589	12.5	50	5
Gibson	34	348	10.2	23	1
McMichael	34	332	9.7	35	1
Amendola	43	326	7.6	25	1
S. Jackson	51	322	6.3	38	0
Fells	21	273	13.0	36	3
Burton	25	253	10.1	25	0
Robinson	13	167	12.8	45	1

INTERCEPTIONS: Butler, 3

PUNTING	No.	Yds	Avg	Net Avg	TB	In 20	Lg	Blk
Jones	90	4212	46.8	41.7	10	34	63	0

SACKS: Little, 6.5

San Francisco 49ers

SCORING	Rush	Rec	Ret	PAT	FG	2PT	Pts
Nedney	0	0	0	33	17	0	84
Gore	10	3	0	0	0	0	78
V. Davis	0	13	0	0	0	0	78
Morgan	0	3	0	0	0	0	18
Hill	0	2	0	0	0	0	12
Crabtree	0	2	0	0	0	0	12

RUSHING	No.	Yds	Avg	Lg	TD
Gore	229	1120	4.9	80	10
Coffee	83	226	2.7	17	1

PASSING	Att	Comp	Pct Comp	Yds	Avg Gain	TD	Int	Rating Pts
A. Smith	372	225	60.5	2350	6.3	18	12	81.5
Hill	155	87	56.1	943	6.1	5	2	79.6

RECEIVING	No.	Yds	Avg	Lg	TD
V. Davis	78	965	12.4	73	13
Crabtree	48	625	13.0	50	2
Morgan	52	527	10.1	61	3
Gore	52	406	7.8	48	3
Bruce	21	264	12.6	50	0
Walker	21	233	11.1	39	0

INTERCEPTIONS: Goldson, 4

PUNTING	No.	Yds	Avg	Net Avg	TB	In 20	Lg	Blk
Lee	99	4711	47.6	41.0	8	30	64	0

SACKS: Lawson, 6.5

Tampa Bay Buccaneers

SCORING	Rush	Rec	Ret	PAT	FG	2PT	Pts
Barth	0	0	0	12	14	0	54
Williams	4	3	0	0	0	0	42
Winslow	0	5	0	0	0	0	30
A. Bryant	0	4	0	0	0	0	24
Ward	1	2	0	0	0	0	18
Nugent	0	0	0	6	2	0	12
T. Jackson	0	2	0	0	0	0	12
Stroughter	0	1	1	0	0	0	12

RUSHING	No.	Yds	Avg	Lg	TD
Williams	210	821	3.9	35	4
Ward	114	409	3.9	28	1

PASSING	Att	Comp	Pct Comp	Yds	Avg Gain	TD	Int	Rating Pts
Freeman	291	159	54.6	1857	6.4	10	18	59.9
J. Johnson	125	63	50.4	685	5.5	4	8	50.9
Leftwich	107	58	54.2	594	5.6	4	3	71.2

RECEIVING	No.	Yds	Avg	Lg	TD
Winslow	77	884	11.5	42	5
A. Bryant	39	600	15.4	42	4
Stovall	24	366	15.3	38	1
Stroughter	31	334	10.8	35	1
Clayton	16	230	14.4	47	1
Williams	29	219	7.6	22	3

INTERCEPTIONS: Jackson, Talib, 5

PUNTING	No.	Yds	Avg	Net Avg	TB	In 20	Lg	Blk
D. Johnson	62	2558	41.3	36.7	3	16	63	0
Paulescu	24	1022	42.6	35.5	5	8	61	0

SACKS: S. Whtie, 6.5

Seattle Seahawks

SCORING	Rush	Rec	Ret	PAT	FG	2PT	Pts
Mare	0	0	0	28	24	0	100
Carlson	0	7	0	0	0	0	42
Forsett	4	1	0	0	0	0	30
Ju. Jones	2	2	0	0	0	0	24
Houshmandzadeh	0	3	0	0	0	0	18
Burleson	0	3	0	0	0	0	18

RUSHING	No.	Yds	Avg	Lg	TD
Ju. Jones	177	663	3.7	62	2
Forsett	114	619	5.4	35	4

PASSING	Att	Comp	Pct Comp	Yds	Avg Gain	TD	Int	Rating Pts
Hasselbeck	488	293	60.0	3029	6.2	17	17	75.1
Wallace	120	78	65.0	700	5.8	3	2	81.9

RECEIVING	No.	Yds	Avg	Lg	TD
Houshmandzadeh	79	911	11.5	53	3
Burleson	63	812	12.9	44	3
Carlson	51	574	11.3	42	7
Branch	45	437	9.7	35	2
Forsett	41	350	8.5	47	1
Ju. Jones	35	232	6.6	49	2

INTERCEPTIONS: Hawthorne, Grant, 3

PUNTING	No.	Yds	Avg	Net Avg	TB	In 20	Lg	Blk
Ryan	88	4068	46.2	38.7	9	28	70	0

SACKS: Kerney, 5

Washington Redskins

SCORING	Rush	Rec	Ret	PAT	FG	2PT	Pts
Suisham	0	0	0	20	18	0	74
Davis	0	6	0	0	0	0	36
Yoder	0	3	0	0	0	0	18
Moss	0	3	0	0	0	0	18
Ganther	3	0	0	0	0	0	18
D. Thomas	0	3	0	0	0	0	18
Gano	0	0	0	6	4	0	18

RUSHING	No.	Yds	Avg	Lg	TD
Portis	124	494	4.0	78	1
Campbell	46	236	5.1	21	1
Cartwright	64	228	3.6	34	0

PASSING	Att	Comp	Pct Comp	Yds	Avg Gain	TD	Int	Rating Pts
Campbell	507	327	64.5	3618	7.1	20	15	86.4

RECEIVING	No.	Yds	Avg	Lg	TD
Moss	70	902	12.9	59	3
Randle El	50	530	10.6	44	0
Davis	48	509	10.6	29	6
Kelly	25	347	13.9	84	0
Cooley	29	332	11.4	25	2
D. Thomas	25	325	13.0	40	3
Cartwright	27	242	9.0	51	1

INTERCEPTIONS: Hall, 4

PUNTING	No.	Yds	Avg	Net Avg	TB	In 20	Lg	Blk
H. Smith	57	2356	41.3	36.8	5	23	59	0
Pakulak	13	498	38.3	33.2	1	4	57	0

SACKS: Carter, Orakpo, 11

2010 NFL Draft

First two rounds of the 74th annual NFL Draft, held April 22–23, 2010 in New York City.

First Round

	Team	Selection	Position
1.	St. Louis	Sam Bradford, Oklahoma	QB
2.	Detroit	Ndamukong Suh, Nebraska	DT
3.	Tampa Bay	Gerald McCoy, Oklahoma	DT
4.	Washington	Trent Williams, Oklahoma	OT
5.	Kansas City	Eric Berry, Tennessee	DB
6.	Seattle	Russell Okung, Oklahoma	OT
7.	Cleveland	Joe Haden, Florida	DB
8.	Oakland	Rolando McClain, Alabama	LB
9.	Buffalo	C.J. Spiller, Clemson	RB
10.	Jacksonville	Tyson Alualu, California	DE
11.	San Francisco (from Chicago through Denver)	Anthony Davis, Rutgers	OT
12.	San Diego (from Miami)	Ryan Mathews, Fresno St	RB
13.	Philadelphia (from San Francisco through Denver)	Brandon Graham, Michigan	DE
14.	Seattle (from Denver)	Earl Thomas, Texas	DB
15.	NY Giants	Jason Pierre-Paul, South Florida	DE
16.	Tennessee	Derrick Morgan, Georgia Tech	DE
17.	San Francisco (from Carolina)	Mike Iupati, Idaho	OG
18.	Pittsburgh	Maurkice Pouncey, Florida	C
19.	Atlanta	Sean Weatherspoon, Missouri	LB
20.	Houston	Kareem Jackson, Alabama	DB
21.	Cincinnati	Jermaine Gresham, Oklahoma	TE
22.	Denver (from New England)	Demaryius Thomas, Georgia Tech	WR
23.	Green Bay	Bryan Bulaga, Iowa	OT
24.	Dallas (from Philadelphia through Denver and New England)	Dez Bryant, Oklahoma St	WR
25.	Denver (from Baltimore)	Tim Tebow, Florida	QB
26.	Arizona	Dan Williams, Tennessee	DT
27.	New England (from Dallas)	Devin McCourty, Rutgers	DB
28.	Miami (from San Diego)	Jared Odrick, Penn St	DT
29.	NY Jets	Kyle Wilson, Boise St	DB
30.	Detroit (from Minnesota)	Jahvid Best, California	RB
31.	Indianapolis	Jerry Hughes, TCU	DE
32.	New Orleans	Patrick Robinson, Florida St	DB

Second Round

	Team	Selection	Position
33.	St. Louis	Rodger Saffold, Indiana	DT
34.	Minnesota (from Detroit)	Chris Cook, Virginia	DB
35.	Tampa Bay	Brian Price, UCLA	DT
36.	Kansas City	Dexter McCluster, Mississippi	RB
37.	Philadelphia (from Washington)	Nathaniel Allen, South Florida	DB
38.	Cleveland	T.J.Ward, Oregon	DB
39.	Tampa Bay (from Oakland)	Arrelious Benn, Illinois	WR
40.	Miami (from Seattle through San Diego)	Koa Misi, Utah	DE
41.	Buffalo	Torell Troup, Central Florida	DT
42.	New England	Rob Gronkowski, Arizona	TE
	(from Chicago through Tampa Bay and Oakland)		
43.	Baltimore (from Miami through Denver)	Sergio Kindle, Texas	DE
44.	Oakland	Lamarr Houston, Texas	DT
	(from Jacksonville through New England)		
45.	Denver	Zane Beadles, Utah	OT
46.	NY Giants	Linval Joseph, East Carolina	DT
47.	Arizona	Daryl Washington, TCU	LB
	(from Tennessee through New England)		
48.	Carolina	Jimmy Clausen, Notre Dame	QB
49.	San Francisco	Taylor Mays, USC	DB
50.	Kansas City (from Atlanta)	Javier Arenas, Alabama	DB
51.	Minnesota (from Houston)	Toby Gerhart, Stanford	RB
52.	Pittsburgh	Jason Worilds, Virginia Tech	DE
53.	New England	Jermaine Cunningham, Florida	DE
54.	Cincinnati	Carlos Dunlap, Florida	DE
55.	Dallas (from Philadephia)	Sean Lee, Penn St	LB
56.	Green Bay	Mike Neal, Purdue	DT
57.	Baltimore	Terrence Cody, Alabama	DT
58.	Houston	Ben Tate, Auburn	RB
	(from Arizona through New England)		
59.	Cleveland	Montario Hardesty, Tennessee	RB
	(from Dallas through Philadelphia)		
60.	Seattle	Golden Tate, Notre Dame	WR
61.	NY Jets	Vlad Ducasse, Massachusetts	OT
62.	New England	Brandon Spikes, Florida	LB
	(from Minnesota through Houston)		
63.	Indianapolis	Pat Angerer, Iowa	LB
64.	New Orleans	Charles Brown, USC	OT

Regular Season Results

WEST DIVISION						
	W	L	T	Pts	PF	PA
†Saskatchewan	10	7	1	21	514	484
*Edmonton	10	7	1	21	514	443
*Calgary	9	9	0	18	469	502
*British Columbia	8	10	0	16	431	502

EAST DIVISION						
	W	L	T	Pts	PF	PA
†Montreal	15	3	0	30	600	324
*Hamilton	9	9	0	18	449	428
Winnipeg	7	11	0	14	386	506
Toronto	3	15	0	6	328	502

†Clinched division title.

*Clinched playoff berth.

Playoff Results

DIVISION SEMI-FINALS

Nov. 15, 2009

British Columbia 34, HAMILTON 27
CALGARY 24, Edmonton 21

DIVISION FINALS

Nov. 22, 2009

MONTREAL 56, British Columbia 18
SASKATCHEWAN 27, Calgary 17

Home team in caps.

2009 Grey Cup Championship

Nov. 29, 2009, Calgary, Saskatchewan

Montreal Alouettes	0	3	7	18	28
Sask. Roughriders	10	7	3	7	27

FIRST QUARTER: Saskatchewan: FG Congi 40, 7:30 **Saskatchewan 3–0.**

Saskatchewan: TD Fantuz 8 pass from Durant (Congi kick), 1:44. **Saskatchewan 10–0.**

SECOND QUARTER: Montreal: FG Duval 28, 12:56. **Saskatchewan 10–3.**

Saskatchewan: FG Congi 44, 1:36. **Saskatchewan 13–3.**

Saskatchewean: Kickoff single Sakoda 85, 1:32. **Saskatchewan 14–3.**

Saskatchewan: FG Congi 9, 0:02. **Saskatchewan 17–3.**

THIRD QUARTER: Montreal: TD Richardson 8 pass from Calvillo (Duval kick), 8:38. **Saskatchewan 17–10.**

Saskatchewan: FG Congi 23, 1:20. **Saskatchewan 20–10.**

FOURTH QUARTER: Montreal: Punt single Duval 52, 13:32. **Saskatchewan 20–11.**

Saskatchewan: TD Durant 16 run (Congi kick), 11:35. **Saskatchewan 27–11.**

Montreal: TD Cobourne 3 run (2-pt. conversion Carter pass from Calvillo), 7:42. **Saskatchewan 27–19.**

Montreal: TD Cahoon 11 pass from Calvillo (2-pt. conversion failed), 1:45. **Saskatchewan 27–25.**

Montreal: FG Duval 33, 0:00. **Montreal 28–27.**

A: 46,020.

FOR THE RECORD • Year by Year

Season-by-Season NFL Final Standings

1920*

	W	L	T	Pct	Pts	OP
Akron Pros	8	0	3	1.000	151	7
Decatur Staleys	10	1	2	.909	164	21
Buffalo All-Americans	9	1	1	.900	258	32
Chicago Cardinals	6	2	1	.750	101	29
Rock Island Independents	6	2	2	.750	201	49
Dayton Triangles	5	2	2	.714	150	54
Rochester Jeffersons	6	3	2	.667	156	57
Canton Bulldogs	7	4	2	.636	208	57
Detroit Heralds	2	3	3	.400	53	82
Cleveland Tigers	2	4	2	.333	28	46
Chicago Tigers	2	5	1	.286	49	63
Hammond Pros	2	5	0	.286	41	154
Columbus Panhandles	2	6	2	.250	41	121
Muncie Flyers	0	1	0	.000	0	45

*no official standings kept

1921

	W	L	T	Pct	Pts	OP
Buffalo All-Americans	9	1	2	.900	211	29
Chicago Staleys	9	1	1	.900	128	53
Akron Pros	8	3	1	.727	148	31
Canton Bulldogs	5	2	3	.714	106	55
Rock Island Independents	4	2	1	.667	65	30
Evansville Crimson Giants	3	2	0	.600	89	46
Green Bay Packers	3	2	1	.600	70	55
Chicago Cardinals	3	3	2	.500	54	53
Dayton Triangles	4	4	1	.500	96	67
Rochester Jeffersons	2	3	0	.400	85	76
Cleveland Tigers	3	5	0	.375	95	58
Washington Senators	1	2	0	.333	21	43
Cincinnati Celts	1	3	0	.250	14	117
Hammond Pros	1	3	1	.250	17	45
Minneapolis Marines	1	3	0	.250	37	41
Detroit Tigers	1	5	1	.167	19	109
Columbus Panhandles	1	8	0	.111	47	222
Muncie Flyers	0	2	0	.000	0	28
Louisville Brecks	0	2	0	.000	0	27
New York Giants	0	2	0	.000	0	72
Tonawanda Kardex	0	1	0	.000	0	45

1922

	W	L	T	Pct	Pts	OP
Canton Bulldogs	10	0	2	1.000	184	15
Chicago Bears	9	3	0	.750	123	44
Chicago Cardinals	8	3	0	.727	96	50
Toledo Maroons	5	2	2	.714	94	59
Rock Island Independents	4	2	1	.667	154	27
Racine Legion	6	4	1	.600	122	56
Dayton Triangles	4	3	1	.571	80	62
Green Bay Packers	4	3	3	.571	70	54
Buffalo All-Americans	5	4	1	.556	87	41
Akron Pros	3	5	2	.375	146	95
Milwaukee Badgers	2	4	3	.333	51	71
Oorang Indians	3	6	0	.333	69	190
Minneapolis Marines	1	3	0	.250	19	40
Louisville Brecks	1	3	0	.250	13	140
Evansville Crimson Giants	0	3	0	.000	6	88
Rochester Jeffersons	0	4	1	.000	13	76
Hammond Pros	0	5	1	.000	0	69
Columbus Panhandles	0	8	0	.000	24	174

1923

	W	L	T	Pct	Pts	OP
Canton Bulldogs	11	0	1	1.000	246	19
Chicago Bears	9	2	1	.818	123	35
Green Bay Packers	7	2	1	.778	85	34
Milwaukee Badgers	7	2	3	.778	100	49
Cleveland Indians	3	1	3	.750	52	49
Chicago Cardinals	8	4	0	.667	139	37
Duluth Kelleys	4	3	0	.571	35	33
Buffalo All-Americans	5	4	3	.556	94	43
Columbus Tigers	5	4	1	.556	119	35
Racine Legion	4	4	2	.500	86	76
Toledo Maroons	3	3	2	.500	35	66
Rock Island Independents	2	3	2	.400	83	62
Minneapolis Marines	2	5	1	.286	48	80
St. Louis All-Stars	1	4	2	.200	14	32
Hammond Pros	1	5	1	.167	14	59
Dayton Triangles	1	6	1	.143	16	95
Akron Pros	1	6	0	.143	25	74
Oorang Indians	1	10	0	.091	24	235
Louisville Brecks	0	3	0	.000	0	90
Rochester Jeffersons	0	4	0	.000	6	141

1924

	W	L	T	Pct	Pts	OP
Cleveland Bulldogs	7	1	1	.875	229	60
Chicago Bears	6	1	4	.857	136	55
Frankfort Yellow Jackets	11	2	1	.846	326	109
Duluth Kelleys	5	1	0	.833	56	16
Rock Island Independents	5	2	2	.714	81	15
Green Bay Packers	7	4	0	.636	108	38
Racine Legion	4	3	3	.571	69	47
Chicago Cardinals	5	4	1	.556	90	67
Buffalo Bisons	6	5	0	.545	120	140
Columbus Tigers	4	4	0	.500	91	68
Hammond Pros	2	2	1	.500	18	45
Milwaukee Badgers	5	8	0	.385	142	188
Akron Pros	2	6	0	.250	59	132
Dayton Triangles	2	6	0	.250	45	148
Kansas City Blues	2	7	0	.222	46	124
Kenosha Maroons	0	4	1	.000	12	117
Minneapolis Marines	0	6	0	.000	14	108
Rochester Jeffersons	0	7	0	.000	14	179

1925

	W	L	T	Pct	Pts	OP
Chicago Cardinals	11	2	1	.846	230	65
Pottsville Maroons	10	2	0	.833	280	45
Detroit Panthers	8	2	2	.800	118	42
New York Giants	8	4	0	.667	122	67
Akron Pros	4	2	2	.650	65	51
Frankfort Yellow Jackets	13	7	0	.643	196	189
Chicago Bears	9	5	3	.625	158	96
Rock Island Independents	5	3	3	.615	99	58
Green Bay Packers	8	5	0	.545	151	120
Providence Steam Roller	6	5	1	.500	131	108
Canton Bulldogs	4	4	0	.385	50	73
Cleveland Bulldogs	5	8	1	.286	75	134
Kansas City Cowboys	2	5	1	.200	68	106
Hammond Pros	1	4	0	.143	23	87

1925 *(Cont.)*

	W	L	T	Pct	Pts	OP
Buffalo Bisons	1	6	2	.143	33	113
Duluth Kelleys	0	3	0	.000	6	25
Rochester Jeffersons	0	6	1	.000	26	91
Milwaukee Badgers	0	6	0	.000	7	191
Dayton Triangles	0	7	1	.000	3	84
Columbus Tigers	0	9	0	.000	28	124

1926

	W	L	T	Pct	Pts	OP
Frankfort Yellow Jackets	14	1	2	.765	223	43
Chicago Bears	12	1	3	.844	216	63
Pottsville Maroons	10	2	2	.714	155	29
Kansas City Cowboys	8	3	0	.727	76	54
Green Bay Packers	7	3	3	.462	144	68
Los Angeles Buccaneers	6	3	1	.600	67	57
NY Giants	8	4	1	.583	140	45
Duluth Eskimos	6	5	3	.429	114	81
Buffalo Rangers	4	4	2	.400	53	62
Chicago Cardinals	5	6	1	.417	67	86
Providence Steam Roller	5	7	1	.417	94	96
Detroit Panthers	4	6	2	.500	115	52
Hartford Blues	3	7	0	.300	57	99
Brooklyn Lions	3	8	0	.273	60	150
Milwaukee Badgers	2	7	0	.222	41	66
Akron Indians	1	4	3	.125	23	89
Dayton Triangles	1	4	1	.167	15	82
Racine Tornadoes	1	4	0	.200	8	92
Columbus Tigers	1	6	0	.143	26	93
Canton Bulldogs	1	9	3	.077	46	172
Hammond Pros	0	4	0	.000	3	56
Louisville Colonels	0	4	0	.000	0	108

1927

	W	L	T	Pct	Pts	OP
NY Giants	11	1	1	.917	197	20
Green Bay Packers	7	2	1	.778	113	43
Chicago Bears	9	3	2	.750	149	98
Cleveland Bulldogs	8	4	1	.667	209	107
Providence Steam Roller	8	5	1	.615	105	88
New York Yankees	7	8	1	.467	142	174
Frankfort Yellow Jackets	6	9	3	.400	152	166
Pottsville Maroons	5	8	0	.385	80	163
Chicago Cardinals	3	7	1	.300	69	134
Dayton Triangles	1	6	1	.143	15	57
Duluth Eskimos	1	8	0	.111	68	134
Buffalo Bisons	0	5	0	.000	8	123

1928

	W	L	T	Pct	Pts	OP
Providence Steam Roller	8	1	1	.889	128	36
Frankfort Yellow Jackets	11	3	1	.786	169	84
Detroit Wolverines	7	2	1	.778	189	76
Green Bay Packers	6	4	3	.600	120	92
Chicago Bears	7	5	1	.583	182	85
NY Giants	4	7	2	.364	79	137
NY Yankees	4	8	1	.333	104	179
Pottsville Maroons	2	8	0	.200	74	134
Chicago Cardinals	1	5	0	.167	7	107
Dayton Triangles	0	7	0	.000	9	131

1929

	W	L	T	Pct	Pts	OP
Green Bay Packers	12	0	1	1.000	198	22
NY Giants	13	1	1	.929	312	86
Frankfort Yellow Jackets	10	4	5	.714	139	128
Chicago Cardinals	6	6	1	.500	154	83
Boston Bulldogs	4	4	0	.500	98	73
Staten Island Stapletons	3	6	3	.429	89	62
Providence Steam Roller	4	5	2	.400	107	117
Orange Tornadoes	3	6	4	.375	32	90
Chicago Bears	4	9	2	.308	119	227
Buffalo Bisons	1	7	1	.125	48	142
Minneapolis Red Jackets	1	9	0	.100	48	185
Dayton Triangles	0	6	0	.000	7	136

1930

	W	L	T	Pct	Pts	OP
Green Bay Packers	10	3	1	.769	234	111
NY Giants	13	4	0	.765	308	98
Chicago Bears	9	4	1	.692	169	71
Brooklyn Dodgers	7	4	1	.636	154	59
Providence Steam Roller	6	4	1	.600	90	125
Staten Island Stapletons	5	5	2	.500	95	112
Chicago Cardinals	5	6	2	.455	128	132
Portsmouth Spartans	5	6	3	.455	176	161
Frankfort Yellow Jackets	4	13	1	.222	113	321
Minneapolis Red Jackets	1	7	1	.125	27	165
Newark Tornadoes	1	10	1	.091	51	190

1931

	W	L	T	Pct	Pts	OP
Green Bay Packers	12	2	0	.857	318	94
Portsmouth Spartans	11	3	0	.786	161	77
Chicago Bears	8	5	0	.615	145	92
Chicago Cardinals	5	4	0	.556	120	128
NY Giants	7	6	1	.538	161	127
Providence Steam Roller	4	4	3	.500	78	127
Staten Island Stapletons	4	6	1	.400	79	118
Cleveland Indians	2	8	0	.200	45	137
Brooklyn Dodgers	2	12	0	.143	64	199
Frankfort Yellow Jackets	1	6	1	.143	13	85

1932

	W	L	T	Pct	Pts	OP
Chicago Bears	7	1	6	.875	160	44
Green Bay Packers	10	3	1	.769	152	63
Portsmouth Spartans	6	2	4	.750	116	71
Boston Braves	4	4	2	.500	55	79
NY Giants	4	6	2	.400	93	113
Brooklyn Dodgers	3	9	0	.250	63	131
Chiago Cardinals	2	6	2	.250	72	114
Staten Island Stapletons	2	7	3	.222	77	173

1933

EAST	W	L	T	Pct	Pts	OP
NY Giants	11	3	0	.786	244	101
Brooklyn Dodgers	5	4	1	.556	93	54
Boston Redskins	5	5	2	.500	103	97
Philadelphia Eagles	3	5	1	.375	77	158
Pittsburgh Pirates	3	6	2	.333	67	208

1933 *(Cont.)*

WEST	W	L	T	Pct	Pts	OP
Chicago Bears	10	2	1	.833	133	82
Portsmouth Spartans	6	5	0	.545	128	87
Green Bay Packers	5	7	1	.417	170	107
Cincinnati Reds	3	6	1	.333	38	110
Chicago Cardinals	1	9	1	.100	52	101

1934

EAST	W	L	T	Pct	Pts	OP
NY Giants	8	5	0	.615	147	107
Boston Redskins	6	6	0	.500	107	93
Brooklyn Dodgers	4	7	0	.364	60	153
Philadelphia Eagles	4	7	0	.364	127	85
Pittsburgh Pirates	2	10	0	.167	51	206

WEST	W	L	T	Pct	Pts	OP
Chicago Bears	13	0	0	1.000	286	86
Detroit Lions	10	3	0	.769	238	59
Green Bay Packers	7	6	0	.538	156	112
Chicago Cardinals	5	6	0	.455	80	84
St. Louis Gunners	1	2	0	.333	27	61
Cincinnati Reds	0	8	0	.000	10	243

1935

EAST	W	L	T	Pct	Pts	OP
NY Giants	9	3	0	.750	180	96
Brooklyn Dodgers	5	6	1	.455	90	141
Pittsburgh Pirates	4	8	0	.333	99	209
Boston Redskins	2	8	1	.200	65	122
Philadelphia Eagles	2	9	0	.182	60	179

WEST	W	L	T	Pct	Pts	OP
Detroit Lions	7	3	2	.700	191	111
Green Bay Packers	8	4	0	.667	181	96
Chicago Bears	6	4	2	.600	192	106
Chicago Cardinals	6	4	2	.600	99	97

1936

EAST	W	L	T	Pct	Pts	OP
Boston Redskins	7	5	0	.583	149	110
Pittsburgh Pirates	6	6	0	.500	98	187
NY Giants	5	6	1	.455	115	163
Brooklyn Dodgers	3	8	1	.273	92	161
Philadelphia Eagles	1	11	0	.083	51	206

WEST	W	L	T	Pct	Pts	OP
Green Bay	10	1	1	.909	248	118
Chicago Bears	9	3	0	.750	222	94
Detroit Lions	8	4	0	.667	235	102
Chicago Cardinals	3	8	1	.273	74	143

1937

EAST	W	L	T	Pct	Pts	OP
Washington Redskins	8	3	0	.727	195	120
NY Giants	6	3	2	.667	128	109
Pittsburgh Pirates	4	7	0	.364	122	145
Brooklyn Dodgers	3	7	1	.300	82	174
Philadelphia Eagles	2	8	1	.200	86	177

WEST	W	L	T	Pct	Pts	OP
Chicago Bears	9	1	1	.900	201	100
Green Bay Packers	7	4	0	.636	220	122
Detroit Lions	7	4	0	.636	180	105
Chicago Cardinals	5	5	1	.500	135	165
Cleveland Rams	1	10	0	.091	75	207

1938

EAST	W	L	T	Pct	Pts	OP
NY Giants	8	2	1	.800	194	79
Washington Redskins	6	3	2	.667	148	154
Brooklyn Dodgers	4	4	3	.500	131	161
Philadelphia Eagles	5	6	0	.455	154	164
Pittsburgh Pirates	2	9	0	.182	79	169

WEST	W	L	T	Pct	Pts	OP
Green Bay Packers	8	3	0	.727	223	118
Detroit Lions	7	4	0	.636	119	108
Chicago Bears	6	5	0	.545	194	148
Cleveland Rams	4	7	0	.364	131	215
Chicago Cardinals	2	9	0	.182	111	168

1939

EAST	W	L	T	Pct	Pts	OP
NY Giants	9	1	1	.168	168	85
Washington Redskins	8	2	1	.242	242	94
Brooklyn Dodgers	4	6	1	.108	108	219
Philadelphia Eagles	1	9	1	.105	105	200
Pittsburgh Pirates	1	9	1	.114	114	216

WEST	W	L	T	Pct	Pts	OP
Green Bay Packers	9	2	0	.818	233	153
Chicago Bears	8	3	0	.727	298	157
Detroit Lions	6	5	0	.545	145	150
Cleveland Rams	5	5	1	.195	195	164
Chicago Cardinals	1	10	0	.091	84	254

1940

EAST	W	L	T	Pct	Pts	OP
Washington Redskins	9	2	0	.818	245	142
Brooklyn Dodgers	8	2	0	.800	179	110
NY Giants	6	4	1	.545	131	133
Pittsburgh Pirates	2	7	2	.182	67	174
Philadelphia Eagles	1	10	0	.091	121	200

WEST	W	L	T	Pct	Pts	OP
Chicago Bears	8	3	0	.727	238	152
Green Bay Packers	6	4	1	.600	238	155
Detroit Lions	5	5	1	.500	120	177
Cleveland Rams	4	6	1	.400	181	191
Chicago Cardinals	2	7	2	.222	139	222

1941

EAST

	W	L	T	Pct	Pts	OP
NY Giants	8	3	0	.727	238	114
Brooklyn Dodgers	7	4	0	.636	158	127
Washington	6	5	0	.545	176	174
Philadelphia	2	8	1	.200	119	218
Pittsburgh Steelers	1	9	1	.100	103	276

WEST

	W	L	T	Pct	Pts	OP
Green Bay	10	1	0	.909	258	120
Chicago Bears	10	1	0	.909	396	147
Detroit	4	6	1	.400	121	195
Chicago Cardinals	3	7	1	.300	127	197
Cleveland Rams	2	9	0	.182	116	244

1942

EAST

	W	L	T	Pct	Pts	OP
Washington	10	1	0	.909	227	102
Pittsburgh Steelers	7	4	0	.636	167	119
NY Giants	5	5	1	.500	155	139
Brooklyn Dodgers	3	8	0	.273	100	168
Philadelphia	2	9	0	.182	134	239

WEST

	W	L	T	Pct	Pts	OP
Chicago Bears	11	0	0	1.000	376	84
Green Bay	8	2	1	.800	300	215
Cleveland Rams	5	6	0	.455	150	207
Chicago Cardinals	3	8	0	.273	98	209
Detroit	0	11	0	.000	38	263

1943

EAST

	W	L	T	Pct	Pts	OP
Washington	6	3	1	.667	229	137
NY Giants	6	3	1	.667	197	170
Phi/Pitt Eagles/Steelers	5	4	1	.556	225	230
Brooklyn Dodgers	2	8	0	.200	65	234

WEST

	W	L	T	Pct	Pts	OP
Chicago Bears	8	1	1	.889	303	157
Green Bay	7	2	1	.778	264	172
Detroit	3	6	1	.333	178	218
Chicago Cardinals	0	10	0	.000	95	238

1944

EAST

	W	L	T	Pct	Pts	OP
NY Giants	8	1	1	.889	206	75
Philadelphia	7	1	2	.875	267	131
Washington	6	3	1	.667	169	180
Boston Yanks	2	8	0	.200	82	233
Brooklyn Tigers	0	10	0	.000	69	166

WEST

	W	L	T	Pct	Pts	OP
Green Bay	8	2	0	.800	238	141
Chicago Bears	6	3	1	.667	258	172
Detroit	6	3	1	.667	216	151
Cleveland Rams	4	6	0	.400	188	224
Chi/Pitt Cards/Steelers	0	10	0	.000	116	336

1945

EAST

	W	L	T	Pct	Pts	OP
Washington	8	2	0	.800	209	121
Philadelphia	7	3	0	.700	272	133
NY Giants	3	6	1	.333	179	198
Bos/Bkn Yanks/Tigers	3	6	1	.333	123	211
Pittsburgh	2	8	0	.200	79	220

WEST

	W	L	T	Pct	Pts	OP
Cleveland Rams	9	1	0	.900	244	136
Detroit	7	3	0	.700	195	194
Green Bay	6	4	0	.600	258	173
Chicago Bears	3	7	0	.300	192	235
Chicago Cardinals	1	9	0	.100	98	228

1946

EAST

	W	L	T	Pct	Pts	OP
NY Giants	7	3	1	.700	236	162
Philadelphia	6	5	0	.545	231	220
Washington	5	5	1	.500	171	191
Pittsburgh	5	5	1	.500	136	117
Boston Yanks	2	8	1	.200	189	273

WEST

	W	L	T	Pct	Pts	OP
Chicago Bears	8	2	1	.800	289	193
LA Rams	6	4	1	.600	277	257
Chicago Cardinals	6	5	0	.545	260	198
Green Bay	6	5	0	.545	148	158
Detroit	1	10	0	.091	142	310

1947

EAST

	W	L	T	Pct	Pts	OP
Pittsburgh	8	4	0	.667	240	259
Philadelphia	8	4	0	.667	308	242
Boston Yanks	4	7	1	.364	168	256
Washington	4	8	0	.333	295	367
NY Giants	2	8	2	.200	190	309

WEST

	W	L	T	Pct	Pts	OP
Chicago Cardinals	9	3	0	.750	306	231
Chicago Bears	8	4	0	.667	363	241
Green Bay	6	5	1	.542	274	210
LA Rams	6	6	0	.500	259	214
Detroit-Lions	3	9	0	.250	231	305

1948

EAST

	W	L	T	Pct	Pts	OP
Philadelphia	9	2	1	.818	376	156
Washington	7	5	0	.583	291	287
Pittsburgh	4	8	0	.333	200	243
NY Giants	4	8	0	.333	297	388
Boston Yanks	3	9	0	.250	174	372

WEST

	W	L	T	Pct	Pts	OP
Chicago Cardinals	11	1	0	.917	395	226
Chicago Bears	10	2	0	.833	375	151
LA Rams	6	5	1	.545	327	269
Green Bay	3	9	0	.250	154	290
Detroit Lions	2	10	0	.167	200	407

1949

EAST

	W	L	T	Pct	Pts	OP
Philadelphia	11	1	0	.917	364	134
Pittsburgh	6	5	1	.545	224	214
NY Giants	6	6	0	.500	287	298
Washington	4	7	1	.364	268	339
NY Bulldogs	1	10	1	.091	153	368

WEST

	W	L	T	Pct	Pts	OP
LA Rams	8	2	2	.800	360	239
Chicago Bears	9	3	0	.750	332	218
Chicago Cardinals	6	5	1	.545	360	301
Detroit Lions	4	8	0	.333	237	259
Green Bay	2	10	0	.167	114	329

1950

EAST

	W	L	T	Pct	Pts	OP
Cleveland Browns	10	2	0	.833	310	144
NY Giants	10	2	0	.833	268	150
Philadelphia	6	6	0	.500	254	141
Pittsburgh	6	6	0	.500	180	195
Chicago Cardinals	5	7	0	.417	233	287
Washington	3	9	0	.250	232	326

WEST

	W	L	T	Pct	Pts	OP
Chicago Bears	9	3	0	.750	279	207
LA Rams	9	3	0	.750	466	309
New York Yanks	7	5	0	.583	366	367
Detroit	6	6	0	.500	321	285
San Francisco 49ers	3	9	0	.250	213	300
Green Bay	3	9	0	.250	244	406
Baltimore Colts	1	11	0	.067	213	462

1951

AMERICAN

	W	L	T	Pct	Pts	OP
Cleveland	11	1	0	.917	331	152
NY Giants	9	2	1	.818	254	161
Washington	5	7	0	.417	183	296
Pittsburgh	4	7	1	.364	183	235
Philadelphia	4	8	0	.333	234	264
Chicago Cardinals	3	9	0	.250	210	287

NATIONAL

	W	L	T	Pct	Pts	OP
LA Rams	8	4	0	.667	392	261
Detroit Lions	7	4	1	.636	336	259
San Francisco 49ers	7	4	1	.636	255	205
Chicago Bears	7	5	0	.583	286	282
Green Bay	3	9	0	.250	254	375
New York Yanks	1	9	2	.100	241	382

1952

AMERICAN

	W	L	T	Pct	Pts	OP
Cleveland	8	4	0	.667	310	213
Philadelphia	7	5	0	.583	252	271
NY Giants	7	5	0	.583	234	231
Pittsburgh	5	7	0	.417	300	273
Washington	4	8	0	.333	240	287
Chicago Cardinals	4	8	0	.333	172	221

NATIONAL

	W	L	T	Pct	Pts	OP
Detroit	9	3	0	.750	344	192
LA Rams	9	3	0	.750	349	234
San Francisco	7	5	0	.583	285	221
Green Bay	6	6	0	.500	295	312
Chicago Bears	5	7	0	.417	245	326
Dallas Texans	1	11	0	.083	182	427

1953

EAST

	W	L	T	Pct	Pts	OP
Cleveland	11	1	0	.917	348	162
Philadelphia	7	4	1	.636	352	215
Washington	6	5	1	.545	208	215
Pittsburgh	5	7	0	.417	211	272
NY Giants	4	8	0	.333	188	277
Chicago Cardinals	1	10	1	.091	190	337

WEST

	W	L	T	Pct	Pts	OP
Detroit	10	2	0	.833	271	205
San Francisco	9	3	0	.750	372	237
LA Rams	8	3	1	.727	366	236
Chicago Bears	3	8	1	.273	218	262
Baltimore Colts	3	9	0	.250	182	350
Green Bay	2	9	1	.182	200	338

1954

EAST

	W	L	T	Pct	Pts	OP
Cleveland	9	3	0	.750	336	162
Philadelphia	7	4	1	.636	284	230
NY Giants	7	5	0	.583	293	184
Pittsburgh	5	7	0	.417	219	263
Washington	3	9	0	.250	207	432
Chicago Cardinals	2	10	0	.167	183	347

WEST

	W	L	T	Pct	Pts	OP
Detroit	9	2	1	.818	337	189
Chicago Bears	8	4	0	.667	301	279
San Francisco	7	4	1	.636	313	251
LA Rams	6	5	1	.545	314	285
Green Bay	4	8	0	.333	234	251
Baltimore	3	9	0	.250	131	279

1955

EAST

	W	L	T	Pct	Pts	OP
Cleveland	9	2	1	.818	349	218
Washington	8	4	0	.667	246	222
NY Giants	6	5	1	.545	267	223
Philadelphia	4	7	1	.364	248	231
Chicago Cardinals	4	7	1	.364	224	252
Pittsburgh	4	8	0	.333	195	285

WEST

	W	L	T	Pct	Pts	OP
LA Rams	8	3	1	.727	260	231
Chicago Bears	8	4	0	.667	294	251
Green Bay	6	6	0	.500	258	276
Baltimore	5	6	1	.455	214	239
San Francisco	4	8	0	.333	216	298
Detroit	3	9	0	.250	230	275

1956

EAST

	W	L	T	Pct	Pts	OP
NY Giants	8	3	1	.727	264	197
Chicago Cardinals	7	5	0	.583	240	182
Washington	6	6	0	.500	183	225
Pittsburgh	5	7	0	.417	217	250
Cleveland	5	7	0	.417	167	177
Philadelphia	3	8	1	.273	143	215

WEST

	W	L	T	Pct	Pts	OP
Chicago Bears	9	2	1	.818	269	169
Detroit	9	3	0	.750	300	188
San Francisco	5	6	1	.455	233	284
Baltimore	5	7	0	.417	270	322
Green Bay	4	8	0	.333	264	342
LA Rams	4	8	0	.333	291	307

1957

EAST

	W	L	T	Pct	Pts	OP
Cleveland	9	2	1	.818	269	169
NY Giants	7	5	0	.583	251	211
Pittsburgh	6	6	0	.500	155	178
Washington	5	6	1	.455	251	230
Philadelphia	4	8	0	.333	173	224
Chicago Cardinals	3	9	0	.250	200	299

WEST

	W	L	T	Pct	Pts	OP
San Francisco	8	4	0	.667	260	264
Detroit	8	4	0	.667	251	231
Baltimore	7	5	0	.583	303	235
LA Rams	6	6	0	.500	307	278
Chicago Bears	5	7	0	.417	203	211
Green Bay	3	9	0	.250	218	311

1958

EAST

	W	L	T	Pct	Pts	OP
Cleveland	9	3	0	.750	302	217
NY Giants	9	3	0	.750	246	183
Pittsburgh	7	4	1	.636	261	230
Washington	4	7	1	.364	214	268
Chicago Cardinals	2	9	1	.182	261	356
Philadelphia	2	9	1	.182	235	306

WEST

	W	L	T	Pct	Pts	OP
Baltimore	9	3	0	.750	381	203
LA Rams	8	4	0	.667	344	278
Chicago Bears	8	4	0	.667	298	230
San Francisco	6	6	0	.500	257	324
Detroit	4	7	1	.364	261	276
Green Bay	1	10	1	.091	193	382

1959

EAST

	W	L	T	Pct	Pts	OP
NY Giants	10	2	0	.833	284	167
Philadelphia	7	5	0	.583	268	278
Cleveland	7	5	0	.583	270	214
Pittsburgh	6	5	1	.545	257	216
Washington	3	9	0	.250	185	350
Chicago Cardinals	2	10	0	.167	231	324

WEST

	W	L	T	Pct	Pts	OP
Baltimore	9	3	0	.750	374	251
Chicago Bears	8	4	0	.667	246	196
Green Bay	7	5	0	.583	248	240
San Francisco	7	5	0	.583	255	237
Detroit	3	8	1	.273	203	275
LA Rams	2	10	0	.167	242	315

1960

NFL EAST

	W	L	T	Pct	Pts	OP
Philadelphia	10	2	0	.833	321	246
Cleveland	8	3	1	.727	362	217
NY Giants	6	4	2	.600	271	261
St. Louis Cardinals	6	5	1	.545	288	230
Pittsburgh	5	6	1	.455	240	275
Washington	1	9	2	.100	178	309

NFL WEST

	W	L	T	Pct	Pts	OP
Green Bay	8	4	0	.667	332	209
Detroit	7	5	0	.583	239	212
San Francisco	7	5	0	.583	208	205
Baltimore	6	6	0	.500	288	234
Chicago Bears	5	6	1	.455	194	299
LA Rams	4	7	1	.364	265	297
Dallas Cowboys	0	11	1	.000	177	369

AFL EAST

	W	L	T	Pct	Pts	OP
Houston Oilers	10	4	0	.714	379	285
NY Titans	7	7	0	.500	382	399
Buffalo Bills	5	8	1	.385	296	303
Boston Patriots	5	9	0	.357	286	349

AFL WEST

	W	L	T	Pct	Pts	OP
Los Angeles Chargers	10	4	0	.714	373	336
Dallas Texans	8	6	0	.571	361	253
Oakland Raiders	6	8	0	.429	319	388
Denver Broncos	4	9	1	.308	309	393

1961

NFL EAST

	W	L	T	Pct	Pts	OP
NY Giants	10	3	1	.769	368	220
Philadelphia	10	4	0	.714	361	297
Cleveland	8	5	1	.615	319	270
St. Louis Cardinals	7	7	0	.500	279	267
Pittsburgh	6	8	0	.429	295	287
Dallas Cowboys	4	9	1	.308	236	380
Washington	1	12	1	.077	174	392

NFL WEST

	W	L	T	Pct	Pts	OP
Green Bay	11	3	0	.786	391	223
Detroit	8	5	1	.615	270	258
Baltimore	8	6	0	.571	302	307
Chicago	8	6	0	.571	326	302
San Francisco	7	6	1	.538	346	272
LA Rams	4	10	0	.286	263	407
Minnesota Vikings	3	11	0	.214	285	407

AFL EAST

	W	L	T	Pct	Pts	OP
Houston Oilers	10	3	1	.769	513	242
Boston Patriots	9	4	1	.692	413	313
New York Titans	7	7	0	.500	301	390
Buffalo Bills	6	8	0	.429	294	342

AFL WEST

	W	L	T	Pct	Pts	OP
San Diego Chargers	12	2	0	.857	396	219
Dallas Texans	6	8	0	.429	334	343
Denver	3	11	0	.214	251	432
Oakland	2	12	0	.143	237	458

1962

NFL EAST

	W	L	T	Pct	Pts	OP
NY Giants	12	2	0	.857	398	283
Pittsburgh	9	5	0	.642	312	363
Cleveland	7	6	1	.538	291	257
Washington	5	7	2	.417	305	376
Dallas Cowboys	5	8	1	.385	398	402
St. Louis Cardinals	4	9	1	.308	287	361
Philadelphia	3	10	1	.231	282	356

NFL WEST

	W	L	T	Pct	Pts	OP
Green Bay	13	1	0	.929	415	148
Detroit	11	3	0	.786	315	177
Chicago	9	5	0	.643	321	287
Baltimore	7	7	0	.500	293	288
San Francisco	6	8	0	.429	282	331
Minnesota	2	11	1	.154	254	410
LA Rams	1	12	1	.077	220	334

AFL EAST

	W	L	T	Pct	Pts	OP
Houston	11	3	0	.786	387	270
Boston	9	4	1	.692	346	295
Buffalo	7	6	1	.538	309	272
NY Titans	5	9	0	.357	278	423

AFL WEST

	W	L	T	Pct	Pts	OP
Dallas Texans	11	3	0	.786	389	233
Denver	6	7	0	.462	322	313
San Diego	4	9	0	.308	293	362
Oakland	1	13	0	.071	213	370

1963

NFL EAST

	W	L	T	Pct	Pts	OP
NY Giants	11	3	0	.786	448	280
Cleveland	10	4	0	.714	343	262
St. Louis	9	5	0	.643	341	283
Pittsburgh	7	4	3	.636	321	295
Dallas Cowboys	4	10	0	.286	305	378
Washington	3	11	0	.214	279	398
Philadelphia	2	10	2	.214	242	381

NFL WEST

	W	L	T	Pct	Pts	OP
Chicago	11	1	2	.917	301	144
Green Bay	11	2	1	.846	369	206
Baltimore	8	6	0	.571	316	285
Minnesota	5	8	1	.385	309	390
Detroit	5	8	1	.385	326	265
LA Rams	5	9	0	.357	210	350
San Francisco	2	12	0	.143	198	391

AFL EAST

	W	L	T	Pct	Pts	OP
Boston	7	6	1	.538	327	257
Buffalo	7	6	1	.538	304	291
Houston	6	8	0	.429	302	372
NY Jets	5	8	1	.385	249	399

AFL WEST

	W	L	T	Pct	Pts	OP
San Diego	11	3	0	.786	399	255
Oakland	10	4	0	.714	363	282
Kansas City Chiefs	5	7	2	.417	347	263
Denver	2	11	1	.154	301	473

1964

NFL EAST

	W	L	T	Pct	Pts	OP
Cleveland	10	3	1	.769	415	293
St. Louis	9	3	2	.750	357	331
Philadelphia	6	8	0	.429	312	313
Washington	6	8	0	.429	307	305
Dallas	5	8	1	.385	250	289
Pittsburgh	5	9	0	.357	253	315
NY Giants	2	10	2	.167	241	399

NFL WEST

	W	L	T	Pct	Pts	OP
Baltimore	12	2	0	.857	428	225
Green Bay	8	5	1	.615	342	245
Minnesota	8	5	1	.615	355	296
Detroit	7	5	2	.583	280	260
LA Rams	5	7	2	.417	283	339
Chicago	5	9	0	.357	260	379
San Francisco	4	10	0	.286	236	330

AFL EAST

	W	L	T	Pct	Pts	OP
Buffalo	12	2	0	.857	400	242
Boston	10	3	1	.769	365	297
NY Jets	5	8	1	.385	278	315
Houston	4	10	0	.286	310	355

AFL WEST

	W	L	T	Pct	Pts	OP
San Diego	8	5	1	.615	341	300
Kansas City Chiefs	7	7	0	.500	366	306
Oakland	5	7	2	.417	303	350
Denver	2	11	1	.154	240	438

1965

NFL EAST

	W	L	T	Pct	Pts	OP
Cleveland	11	3	0	.786	363	325
NY Giants	7	7	0	.500	270	338
Dallas	7	7	0	.500	325	280
Washington	6	8	0	.429	257	301
St. Louis	5	9	0	.357	296	309
Philadelphia	5	9	0	.357	363	359
Pittsburgh	2	12	0	.143	202	397

NFL WEST

	W	L	T	Pct	Pts	OP
Green Bay	10	3	1	.769	316	224
Baltimore	9	3	1	.769	389	263
Chicago	9	5	0	.643	409	275
San Francisco	7	6	1	.538	421	402
Minnesota	7	6	0	.500	383	362
Detroit	6	7	1	.462	257	295
LA Rams	4	10	0	.286	269	328

AFL EAST

	W	L	T	Pct	Pts	OP
Buffalo	10	3	1	.769	313	226
NY Jets	5	8	1	.385	285	303
Boston	4	8	2	.333	244	302
Houston	4	10	0	.286	298	429

AFL WEST

	W	L	T	Pct	Pts	OP
San Diego	9	2	3	.818	340	227
Oakland	8	5	1	.615	298	239
Kansas City	7	5	2	.583	322	285
Denver	4	10	0	.286	303	392

1966

NFL EAST

	W	L	T	Pct	Pts	OP
Dallas	10	3	1	.769	445	239
Cleveland	9	5	0	.643	403	259
Philadelphia	9	5	0	.643	326	340
St. Louis	8	5	1	.625	264	265
Washington	7	7	0	.500	351	355
Pittsburgh	5	8	1	.385	316	347
Atlanta Falcons	3	11	0	.214	204	437
NY Giants	1	12	1	.077	263	501

NFL WEST

	W	L	T	Pct	Pts	OP
Green Bay	12	2	0	.857	335	163
Baltimore	9	5	0	.643	314	226
LA Rams	8	6	0	.571	289	212
San Francisco	6	6	2	.500	320	325
Chicago	5	7	2	.417	234	272
Detroit	4	9	1	.308	206	317
Minnesota	4	9	1	.308	292	304

AFL EAST

	W	L	T	Pct	Pts	OP
Buffalo	9	4	1	.692	358	255
Boston	8	4	2	.677	315	283
NY Jets	6	6	2	.500	322	312
Houston	3	11	0	.214	335	396
Miami Dolphins	3	11	0	.214	213	362

AFL WEST

	W	L	T	Pct	Pts	OP
Kansas City	11	2	1	.846	448	276
Oakland	8	5	1	.615	315	288
San Diego	7	6	1	.538	335	284
Denver	4	10	0	.286	196	381

1967

NFL CAPITOL

	W	L	T	Pct	Pts	OP
Dallas	9	5	0	.643	342	268
Philadelphia	6	7	1	.462	351	409
Washington	5	6	3	.455	347	353
New Orleans Saints	3	11	0	.214	233	379

NFL CENTURY

	W	L	T	Pct	Pts	OP
Cleveland	9	5	0	.643	334	297
NY Giants	7	7	0	.500	369	379
St. Louis	6	7	1	.462	333	356
Pittsburgh	4	9	1	.308	281	320

NFL COASTAL

	W	L	T	Pct	Pts	OP
LA Rams	11	1	2	.917	398	196
Baltimore	11	1	2	.917	394	198
San Francisco	7	7	0	.500	273	337
Atlanta	1	12	1	.077	175	422

NFL CENTRAL

	W	L	T	Pct	Pts	OP
Green Bay	9	4	1	.692	332	209
Chicago	7	6	1	.538	239	218
Detroit	5	7	2	.417	260	259
Minnesota	3	8	3	.273	233	294

AFL EAST

	W	L	T	Pct	Pts	OP
Houston	9	4	1	.692	258	199
NY Jets	8	5	1	.615	371	329
Buffalo	4	10	0	.286	237	285
Miami	4	10	0	.286	219	407
Boston	3	10	1	.231	280	389

1967 *(Cont.)*

AFL WEST

	W	L	T	Pct	Pts	OP
Oakland	13	1	0	.929	468	233
Kansas City	9	5	0	.643	408	254
San Diego	8	5	1	.615	360	352
Denver	3	11	0	.214	256	409

1968

NFL CAPITOL

	W	L	T	Pct	Pts	OP
Dallas	12	2	0	.857	431	186
NY Giants	7	7	0	.500	294	325
Washington	5	9	0	.357	249	358
Philadelphia	2	12	0	.143	202	351

NFL CENTURY

	W	L	T	Pct	Pts	OP
Cleveland	10	4	0	.714	394	273
St. Louis	9	4	1	.692	325	289
New Orleans	4	9	1	.308	246	327
Pittsburgh	2	11	1	.154	244	397

NFL COASTAL

	W	L	T	Pct	Pts	OP
Baltimore	13	1	0	.929	402	144
LA Rams	10	3	1	.769	312	200
San Francisco	7	6	1	.538	303	310
Atlanta	2	12	0	.143	202	351

NFL CENTRAL

	W	L	T	Pct	Pts	OP
Minnesota	8	6	0	.571	282	242
Chicago	7	7	0	.500	250	333
Green Bay	6	7	1	.462	281	227
Detroit	4	8	2	.333	207	241

AFL EAST

	W	L	T	Pct	Pts	OP
NY Jets	11	3	0	.786	419	280
Houston	7	7	0	.500	303	248
Miami	5	8	1	.385	276	355
Boston	4	10	0	.286	229	406
Buffalo	1	12	1	.077	199	367

AFL WEST

	W	L	T	Pct	Pts	OP
Oakland	12	2	0	.857	453	233
Kansas City	12	2	0	.857	371	170
San Diego	9	5	0	.643	382	310
Denver	5	9	0	.357	255	404
Cincinnati Bengals	3	11	0	.214	215	329

1969

NFL CAPITOL

	W	L	T	Pct	Pts	OP
Dallas	11	2	1	.846	369	223
Washington	7	5	2	.583	307	319
New Orleans	5	9	0	.357	311	393
Philadelphia	4	9	1	.308	279	377

NFL CENTURY

	W	L	T	Pct	Pts	OP
Cleveland	10	3	1	.769	351	300
NY Giants	6	8	0	.429	264	298
St. Louis	4	9	1	.308	314	389
Pittsburgh	1	13	0	.071	218	404

NFL COASTAL

	W	L	T	Pct	Pts	OP
LA Rams	11	3	0	.786	320	243
Baltimore	7	5	2	.615	307	319
Atlanta	6	8	0	.429	276	268
San Francisco	4	8	2	.333	277	319

1969 *(Cont.)*

NFL CENTRAL

	W	L	T	Pct	Pts	OP
Minnesota	12	2	0	.857	379	133
Detroit	9	4	1	.692	259	188
Green Bay	8	6	0	.571	269	221
Chicago	1	13	0	.071	210	339

AFL EAST

	W	L	T	Pct	Pts	OP
NY Jets	10	4	0	.714	353	269
Houston	6	6	2	.500	278	279
Buffalo	4	10	0	.286	230	359
Boston	4	10	0	.286	266	316
Miami	3	10	1	.231	233	332

AFL WEST

	W	L	T	Pct	Pts	OP
Oakland	12	1	1	.923	377	242
Kansas City	11	3	0	.786	359	177
San Diego	8	6	0	.571	288	276
Denver	5	8	1	.385	297	344
Cincinnati	4	9	1	.308	280	367

1970

AFC EAST

	W	L	T	Pct	Pts	OP
Baltimore	11	2	1	.846	321	234
Miami	10	4	0	.714	297	228
NY Jets	4	10	0	.286	255	286
Buffalo	3	10	1	.231	204	337
Boston	2	12	0	.143	149	361

AFC CENTRAL

	W	L	T	Pct	Pts	OP
Cincinnati	8	6	0	.571	312	255
Cleveland	7	7	0	.500	286	265
Pittsburgh	5	9	0	.357	210	272
Houston	3	10	1	.231	217	352

AFC WEST

	W	L	T	Pct	Pts	OP
Oakland	8	4	2	.667	300	293
Kansas City	7	5	2	.583	272	244
San Diego	5	6	3	.455	282	278
Denver	5	8	1	.385	253	264

NFC EAST

	W	L	T	Pct	Pts	OP
Dallas	10	4	0	.714	299	221
NY Giants	9	5	0	.643	301	270
St. Louis	8	5	1	.615	325	228
Washington	6	8	0	.429	297	314
Philadelphia	3	10	1	.231	241	332

NFC CENTRAL

	W	L	T	Pct	Pts	OP
Minnesota	12	2	0	.857	335	143
Detroit	10	4	0	.714	347	202
Green Bay	6	8	0	.429	196	293
Chicago	6	8	0	.429	256	261

NFC WEST

	W	L	T	Pct	Pts	OP
San Francisco	10	3	1	.769	352	267
LA Rams	9	4	1	.692	325	202
Atlanta	4	8	2	.333	206	261
New Orleans	2	11	1	.154	172	347

1971

AFC EAST

	W	L	T	Pct	Pts	OP
Miami	10	3	1	.769	315	174
Baltimore	10	4	0	.714	313	140
New England Patriots	6	8	0	.429	238	325
NY Jets	6	8	0	.429	212	299
Buffalo	1	13	0	.071	184	394

AFC CENTRAL

	W	L	T	Pct	Pts	OP
Cleveland	9	5	0	.643	285	273
Pittsburgh	6	8	0	.429	246	292
Houston	4	9	1	.308	251	330
Cincinnati	4	10	0	.286	284	265

AFC WEST

	W	L	T	Pct	Pts	OP
Kansas City	10	3	1	.769	302	208
Oakland	8	4	2	.667	344	278
San Diego	6	8	0	.429	311	341
Denver	4	9	1	.308	203	275

NFC EAST

	W	L	T	Pct	Pts	OP
Dallas	11	3	0	.786	406	222
Washington	9	4	1	.692	276	190
Philadelphia	6	7	1	.462	221	302
St. Louis	4	9	1	.308	231	279
NY Giants	4	10	0	.286	228	362

NFC CENTRAL

	W	L	T	Pct	Pts	OP
Minnesota	11	3	0	.786	245	139
Detroit	7	6	1	.538	341	286
Chicago	6	8	0	.429	185	276
Green Bay	4	8	2	.333	274	298

NFC WEST

	W	L	T	Pct	Pts	OP
San Francisco	9	5	0	.643	300	216
LA Rams	8	5	1	.615	313	260
Atlanta	7	6	1	.538	274	277
New Orleans	4	8	2	.333	266	347

1972

AFC EAST

	W	L	T	Pct	Pts	OP
Miami	14	0	0	1.000	385	171
NY Jets	7	7	0	.500	367	324
Baltimore	5	9	0	.357	235	252
Buffalo	4	9	1	.321	257	377
New England	3	11	0	.214	192	446

AFC CENTRAL

	W	L	T	Pct	Pts	OP
Pittsburgh	11	3	0	.786	343	175
Cleveland	10	4	0	.714	268	249
Cincinnati	8	6	0	.571	299	229
Houston	1	13	0	.071	164	380

AFC WEST

	W	L	T	Pct	Pts	OP
Oakland	10	3	1	.750	365	248
Kansas City	8	6	0	.571	287	254
Denver	5	9	0	.357	325	350
San Diego	4	9	1	.321	264	344

NFC EAST

	W	L	T	Pct	Pts	OP
Washington	11	3	0	.786	336	218
Dallas	10	4	0	.286	319	240
NY Giants	8	6	0	.571	331	247
St. Louis	4	9	1	.321	193	303
Philadelphia	2	11	1	.179	145	352

1972 *(Cont.)*

NFC CENTRAL

	W	L	T	Pct	Pts	OP
Green Bay	10	4	0	.714	304	226
Detroit	8	5	1	.607	339	290
Minnesota	7	7	0	.500	301	252
Chicago	4	9	1	.321	225	275

NFC WEST

	W	L	T	Pct	Pts	OP
San Francisco	8	5	1	.607	353	249
Atlanta	7	7	0	.500	269	274
LA Rams	6	7	1	.464	291	286
New Orleans	2	11	1	.179	215	361

1973

AFC EAST

	W	L	T	Pct	Pts	OP
Miami	12	2	0	.857	343	150
Buffalo	9	5	0	.643	259	230
New England	5	9	0	.357	258	300
Baltimore	4	10	0	.286	226	341
NY Jets	4	10	0	.286	240	306

AFC CENTRAL

	W	L	T	Pct	Pts	OP
Pittsburgh	10	4	0	.714	347	210
Cincinnati	10	4	0	.714	286	231
Cleveland	7	5	2	.571	234	255
Houston	1	13	0	.071	199	447

AFC WEST

	W	L	T	Pct	Pts	OP
Oakland	9	4	1	.679	292	175
Kansas City	7	5	2	.571	231	192
Denver	7	5	2	.571	354	296
San Diego	2	11	1	.179	188	386

NFC EAST

	W	L	T	Pct	Pts	OP
Washington	10	4	0	.714	325	198
Dallas	10	4	0	.714	325	198
Philadelphia	5	8	1	.393	310	393
St. Louis	4	9	1	.321	286	365
NY Giants	2	11	1	.179	226	362

NFC CENTRAL

	W	L	T	Pct	Pts	OP
Minnesota	12	2	0	.857	296	168
Detroit	6	7	1	.464	271	247
Green Bay	5	7	2	.429	202	259
Chicago	3	11	0	.214	195	334

NFC WEST

	W	L	T	Pct	Pts	OP
LA Rams	12	2	0	.857	388	178
Atlanta	9	5	0	.643	318	224
New Orleans	5	9	0	.357	163	312
San Francisco	5	9	0	.357	262	319

1974

AFC EAST

	W	L	T	Pct	Pts	OP
Miami	11	3	0	.786	327	216
Buffalo	9	5	0	.643	264	244
NY Jets	7	7	0	.500	279	300
New England	7	7	0	.500	348	289
Baltimore	2	12	0	.143	190	329

AFC CENTRAL

	W	L	T	Pct	Pts	OP
Pittsburgh	10	3	1	.750	305	189
Houston	7	7	0	.500	236	282
Cincinnati	7	7	0	.500	283	259
Cleveland	4	10	0	.283	251	344

1974 *(Cont.)*

AFC WEST

	W	L	T	Pct	Pts	OP
Oakland	12	2	0	.857	355	228
Denver	7	6	1	.536	302	294
Kansas City	5	9	0	.357	233	293
San Diego	5	9	0	.357	212	285

NFC EAST

	W	L	T	Pct	Pts	OP
Washington	10	4	0	.714	320	196
St. Louis	10	4	0	.714	285	218
Dallas	8	6	0	.571	297	235
Philadelphia	7	7	0	.500	242	217
NY Giants	2	12	0	.143	195	299

NFC CENTRAL

	W	L	T	Pct	Pts	OP
Minnesota	10	4	0	.714	310	195
Detroit	7	7	0	.500	256	270
Green Bay	6	8	0	.429	210	206
Chicago	4	10	0	.286	152	279

NFC WEST

	W	L	T	Pct	Pts	OP
LA Rams	10	4	0	.714	263	181
San Francisco	6	8	0	.429	226	236
New Orleans	5	9	0	.357	166	263
Atlanta	3	11	0	.214	111	271

1975

AFC EAST

	W	L	T	Pct	Pts	OP
Miami	10	4	0	.714	357	222
Baltimore	10	4	0	.714	395	269
Buffalo	8	6	0	.571	420	355
NY Jets	3	11	0	.214	258	433
New England	3	11	0	.214	258	358

AFC CENTRAL

	W	L	T	Pct	Pts	OP
Pittsburgh	12	2	0	.857	373	162
Cincinnati	11	3	0	.786	340	246
Houston	10	4	0	.714	293	226
Cleveland	3	11	0	.214	218	372

AFC WEST

	W	L	T	Pct	Pts	OP
Oakland	11	3	0	.786	375	255
Denver	6	8	0	.429	254	307
Kansas City	5	9	0	.357	282	341
San Diego	2	12	0	.143	189	345

NFC EAST

	W	L	T	Pct	Pts	OP
St. Louis	11	3	0	.786	356	276
Dallas	10	4	0	.714	350	268
Washington	8	6	0	.571	325	276
NY Giants	5	9	0	.357	216	306
Philadelphia	4	10	0	.286	225	302

NFC CENTRAL

	W	L	T	Pct	Pts	OP
Minnesota	12	2	0	.857	377	180
Detroit	7	7	0	.500	245	262
Green Bay	4	10	0	.286	226	285
Chicago	4	10	0	.286	191	379

NFC WEST

	W	L	T	Pct	Pts	OP
LA Rams	12	2	0	.857	312	135
San Francisco	5	9	0	.357	255	286
Atlanta	4	10	0	.286	240	289
New Orleans	2	12	0	.143	165	360

1976

AFC EAST
	W	L	T	Pct	Pts	OP
Baltimore	11	3	0	.786	417	246
New England	11	3	0	.786	376	236
Miami	6	8	0	.429	263	264
NY Jets	3	11	0	.214	169	383
Buffalo	2	12	0	.143	246	363

AFC CENTRAL
	W	L	T	Pct	Pts	OP
Cincinnati	10	4	0	.714	335	210
Pittsburgh	10	4	0	.714	342	138
Cleveland	9	5	0	.643	267	287
Houston	5	9	0	.357	222	273

AFC WEST
	W	L	T	Pct	Pts	OP
Oakland	13	1	0	.929	350	237
Denver	9	5	0	.643	315	206
San Diego	6	8	0	.429	248	285
Kansas City	5	9	0	.357	290	376
Tampa Bay Buccaneers	0	14	0	.000	125	412

NFC EAST
	W	L	T	Pct	Pts	OP
Dallas	11	3	0	.786	296	194
Washington	10	4	0	.714	291	217
St. Louis	10	4	0	.714	309	267
Philadelphia	4	10	0	.286	165	286
NY Giants	3	11	0	.214	170	250

NFC CENTRAL
	W	L	T	Pct	Pts	OP
Minnesota	11	2	1	.821	305	176
Chicago	7	7	0	.500	253	216
Detroit	6	8	0	.429	218	299
Green Bay	5	9	0	.357	218	299

NFC WEST
	W	L	T	Pct	Pts	OP
LA Rams	10	3	1	.750	351	190
San Francisco	8	6	0	.571	270	190
Atlanta	4	10	0	.286	172	312
New Orleans	4	10	0	.286	253	346
Seattle Seahawks	2	12	0	.143	229	429

1977

AFC EAST
	W	L	T	Pct	Pts	OP
Miami	10	4	0	.714	313	197
Baltimore	10	4	0	.714	295	221
New England	9	5	0	.643	279	217
Buffalo	3	11	0	.214	160	313
NY Jets	3	11	0	.214	191	313

AFC CENTRAL
	W	L	T	Pct	Pts	OP
Pittsburgh	9	5	0	.643	283	243
Houston	8	6	0	.571	299	230
Cincinnati	8	6	0	.571	238	235
Cleveland	6	8	0	.429	269	267

AFC WEST
	W	L	T	Pct	Pts	OP
Denver	12	2	0	.857	274	148
Oakland	11	3	0	.786	351	230
San Diego	7	7	0	.500	222	205
Seattle	5	9	0	.357	282	373
Kansas City	2	12	0	.143	225	349

1977 (Cont.)

NFC EAST
	W	L	T	Pct	Pts	OP
Dallas	12	2	0	.857	345	212
Washington	9	5	0	.643	196	189
St. Louis	7	7	0	.500	272	287
NY Giants	5	9	0	.357	181	265
Philadelphia	5	9	0	.357	220	207

NFC CENTRAL
	W	L	T	Pct	Pts	OP
Chicago	9	5	0	.643	255	253
Minnesota	9	5	0	.643	231	227
Detroit	6	8	0	.429	183	252
Green Bay	4	10	0	.286	134	219
Tampa Bay	2	12	0	.143	103	223

NFC WEST
	W	L	T	Pct	Pts	OP
LA Rams	10	4	0	.714	302	146
Atlanta	7	7	0	.500	179	129
San Francisco	5	9	0	.357	220	260
New Orleans	3	11	0	.214	232	336

1978

AFC EAST
	W	L	T	Pct	Pts	OP
New England	11	5	0	.688	358	286
Miami	11	5	0	.688	372	254
NY Jets	8	8	0	.500	359	364
Buffalo	5	11	0	.313	302	354
Baltimore	5	11	0	.313	239	421

AFC CENTRAL
	W	L	T	Pct	Pts	OP
Pittsburgh	14	2	0	.875	356	195
Houston	10	6	0	.625	283	298
Cleveland	8	8	0	.500	334	356
Cincinnati	4	12	0	.250	252	284

AFC WEST
	W	L	T	Pct	Pts	OP
Denver	10	6	0	.625	282	198
Seattle	9	7	0	.563	345	358
Oakland	9	7	0	.563	311	283
San Diego	9	7	0	.563	355	309
Kansas City	4	12	0	.250	243	327

NFC EAST
	W	L	T	Pct	Pts	OP
Dallas	12	4	0	.750	384	208
Philadelphia	9	7	0	.563	270	250
Washington	8	8	0	.500	273	283
St. Louis	6	10	0	.375	248	296
NY Giants	6	10	0	.375	264	298

NFC CENTRAL
	W	L	T	Pct	Pts	OP
Green Bay	8	7	1	.531	249	269
Minnesota	8	7	1	.531	294	306
Detroit	7	9	0	.438	290	300
Chicago	7	9	0	.438	253	274
Tampa Bay	5	11	0	.313	241	259

NFC WEST
	W	L	T	Pct	Pts	OP
LA Rams	12	4	0	.750	316	245
Atlanta	9	7	0	.563	240	290
New Orleans	7	9	0	.438	281	298
San Francisco	2	14	0	.125	219	350

1979

AFC EAST

	W	L	T	Pct	Pts	OP
Miami	10	6	0	.625	341	257
New England	9	7	0	.563	411	326
NY Jets	8	8	0	.500	337	383
Buffalo	7	9	0	.438	268	279
Baltimore	5	11	0	.313	271	351

AFC CENTRAL

	W	L	T	Pct	Pts	OP
Pittsburgh	12	4	0	.750	416	262
Houston	11	5	0	.688	362	331
Cleveland	9	7	0	.563	359	352
Cincinnati	4	12	0	.250	337	421

AFC WEST

	W	L	T	Pct	Pts	OP
San Diego	12	4	0	.750	411	246
Denver	10	6	0	.625	289	262
Seattle	9	7	0	.563	378	372
Oakland	9	7	0	.563	365	337
Kansas City	7	9	0	.438	238	262

NFC EAST

	W	L	T	Pct	Pts	OP
Dallas	11	5	0	.688	371	313
Philadelphia	11	5	0	.688	339	282
Washington	10	6	0	.625	348	295
NY Giants	6	10	0	.375	237	323
St. Louis	5	11	0	.313	307	358

NFC CENTRAL

	W	L	T	Pct	Pts	OP
Chicago	10	6	0	.625	306	249
Tampa Bay	10	6	0	.625	273	237
Minnesota	7	9	0	.438	259	337
Green Bay	5	11	0	.313	246	316
Detroit	2	14	0	.125	219	365

NFC WEST

	W	L	T	Pct	Pts	OP
LA Rams	9	7	0	.563	323	309
New Orleans	8	8	0	.500	370	360
Atlanta	6	10	0	.375	300	388
San Francisco	2	14	0	.125	308	416

1980

AFC EAST

	W	L	T	Pct	Pts	OP
Buffalo	11	5	0	.688	320	260
New England	10	6	0	.625	441	325
Miami	8	8	0	.500	266	305
Baltimore	7	9	0	.438	355	387
NY Jets	4	12	0	.250	302	395

AFC CENTRAL

	W	L	T	Pct	Pts	OP
Cleveland	11	5	0	.688	357	310
Houston	11	5	0	.688	295	251
Pittsburgh	9	7	0	.563	352	313
Cincinnati	6	10	0	.375	244	312

AFC WEST

	W	L	T	Pct	Pts	OP
San Diego	11	5	0	.688	418	327
Oakland	11	5	0	.688	364	306
Denver	8	8	0	.500	310	323
Kansas City	8	8	0	.500	319	336
Seattle	4	12	0	.250	291	408

NFC EAST

	W	L	T	Pct	Pts	OP
Dallas	12	4	0	.750	454	311
Philadelphia	12	4	0	.750	384	222
Washington	6	10	0	.375	261	293
St. Louis	5	11	0	.313	299	350
NY Giants	4	12	0	.250	249	425

1980 *(Cont.)*

NFC CENTRAL

	W	L	T	Pct	Pts	OP
Detroit	9	7	0	.563	334	272
Minnesota	9	7	0	.563	317	308
Chicago	7	9	0	.438	304	264
Tampa Bay	5	10	1	.344	271	341
Green Bay	5	10	1	.344	231	371

NFC WEST

	W	L	T	Pct	Pts	OP
Atlanta	12	4	0	.750	405	272
LA Rams	11	5	0	.688	424	289
San Francisco	6	10	0	.375	320	415
New Orleans	1	15	0	.063	291	487

1981

AFC EAST

	W	L	T	Pct	Pts	OP
Miami	11	4	1	.719	345	275
NY Jets	10	5	1	.656	355	287
Buffalo	10	6	0	.625	311	276
Baltimore	2	14	0	.125	259	533
New England	2	14	0	.125	322	370

AFC CENTRAL

	W	L	T	Pct	Pts	OP
Cincinnati	12	4	0	.750	421	304
Pittsburgh	8	8	0	.500	356	297
Houston	7	9	0	.438	281	355
Cleveland	5	11	0	.313	276	375

AFC WEST

	W	L	T	Pct	Pts	OP
Denver	10	6	0	.625	321	289
San Diego	10	6	0	.625	478	390
Kansas City	9	7	0	.563	343	290
Oakland	7	9	0	.438	273	343
Seattle	6	10	0	.375	322	388

NFC EAST

	W	L	T	Pct	Pts	OP
Dallas	12	4	0	.750	367	277
Philadelphia	10	6	0	.625	368	221
NY Giants	9	7	0	.563	295	257
Washington	8	8	0	.500	347	349
St. Louis	7	9	0	.438	315	407

NFC CENTRAL

	W	L	T	Pct	Pts	OP
Tampa Bay	9	7	0	.563	315	268
Detroit	8	8	0	.500	397	322
Green Bay	8	8	0	.500	324	361
Minnesota	7	9	0	.438	325	369
Chicago	6	10	0	.375	253	324

NFC WEST

	W	L	T	Pct	Pts	OP
San Francisco	13	3	0	.813	357	250
Atlanta	7	9	0	.438	426	355
LA Rams	6	10	0	.375	303	351
New Orleans	4	12	0	.250	207	378

1982

AFC EAST

	W	L	T	Pct	Pts	OP
Miami	7	2	0	.778	198	131
NY Jets	6	3	0	.667	245	166
New England	5	4	0	.556	143	157
Buffalo	4	5	0	.444	150	154
Baltimore	0	8	1	.056	113	236

AFC CENTRAL

	W	L	T	Pct	Pts	OP
Cincinnati	7	2	0	.778	232	177
Pittsburgh	6	3	0	.667	204	146
Cleveland	4	5	0	.444	140	182
Houston	1	8	0	.111	136	245

AFC WEST

	W	L	T	Pct	Pts	OP
Los Angeles Raiders	8	1	0	.889	260	200
San Diego	6	3	0	.667	288	221
Seattle	4	5	0	.444	127	147
Kansas City	3	6	0	.333	176	184
Denver	2	7	0	.222	148	226

NFC EAST

	W	L	T	Pct	Pts	OP
Washington	8	1	0	.889	190	128
Dallas	6	3	0	.667	226	145
St. Louis	5	4	0	.556	135	170
NY Giants	4	5	0	.444	164	160
Philadelphia	3	6	0	.333	191	195

NFC CENTRAL

	W	L	T	Pct	Pts	OP
Green Bay	5	3	1	.611	226	169
Tampa Bay	5	4	0	.556	158	178
Minnesota	5	4	0	.556	187	198
Detroit	4	5	0	.444	181	176
Chicago	3	6	0	.333	141	174

NFC WEST

	W	L	T	Pct	Pts	OP
Atlanta	5	4	0	.556	183	199
New Orleans	4	5	0	.444	129	160
San Francisco	3	6	0	.333	209	206
Los Angeles Rams	2	7	0	.222	200	250

1983

AFC EAST

	W	L	T	Pct	Pts	OP
Miami	12	4	0	.750	389	250
Buffalo	8	8	0	.500	283	351
New England	8	8	0	.500	274	289
Baltimore	7	9	0	.438	264	354
NY Jets	7	9	0	.438	313	331

AFC CENTRAL

	W	L	T	Pct	Pts	OP
Pittsburgh	10	6	0	.625	355	303
Cleveland	9	7	0	.563	356	342
Cincinnati	7	9	0	.438	346	302
Houston	2	14	0	.125	288	460

AFC WEST

	W	L	T	Pct	Pts	OP
LA Raiders	12	4	0	.750	442	338
Seattle	9	7	0	.563	403	397
Denver	9	7	0	.563	302	327
San Diego	6	10	0	.375	358	462
Kansas City	6	10	0	.375	386	367

NFC EAST

	W	L	T	Pct	Pts	OP
Washington	14	2	0	.875	541	332
Dallas	12	4	0	.750	479	360
St. Louis	8	7	1	.531	374	428
Philadelphia	5	11	0	.313	233	322
NY Giants	3	12	1	.219	267	347

1983 *(Cont.)*

NFC CENTRAL

	W	L	T	Pct	Pts	OP
Detroit	9	7	0	.563	47	286
Minnesota	8	8	0	.500	316	348
Chicago	8	8	0	.500	311	301
Green Bay	8	8	0	.500	429	439
Tampa Bay	2	14	0	.125	241	380

NFC WEST

	W	L	T	Pct	Pts	OP
San Francisco	10	6	0	.625	432	293
LA Rams	9	7	0	.563	361	344
New Orleans	8	8	0	.500	319	337
Atlanta	7	9	0	.438	370	389

1984

AFC EAST

	W	L	T	Pct	Pts	OP
Miami	14	2	0	.875	513	298
New England	9	7	0	.563	362	352
NY Jets	7	9	0	.438	332	364
Indianapolis Colts	4	12	0	.250	239	414
Buffalo	2	14	0	.125	250	454

AFC CENTRAL

	W	L	T	Pct	Pts	OP
Pittsburgh	9	7	0	.563	387	310
Cincinnati	8	8	0	.500	339	339
Cleveland	5	11	0	.313	250	297
Houston	3	13	0	.188	240	437

AFC WEST

	W	L	T	Pct	Pts	OP
Denver	13	3	0	.813	353	241
Seattle	12	4	0	.750	418	282
LA Raiders	11	5	0	.313	368	278
Kansas City	8	8	0	.500	314	324
San Diego	7	9	0	.438	394	413

NFC EAST

	W	L	T	Pct	Pts	OP
Washington	11	5	0	.688	426	310
NY Giants	9	7	0	.563	299	301
Dallas	9	7	0	.563	308	308
St. Louis	9	7	0	.563	423	345
Philadelphia	6	9	1	.406	278	320

NFC CENTRAL

	W	L	T	Pct	Pts	OP
Chicago	10	6	0	.625	325	248
Green Bay	8	8	0	.500	390	309
Tampa Bay	6	10	0	.375	335	380
Detroit	4	11	1	.281	283	408
Minnesota	3	13	0	.188	276	484

NFC WEST

	W	L	T	Pct	Pts	OP
San Francisco	15	1	0	.938	475	227
LA Rams	10	6	0	.625	346	316
New Orleans	7	9	0	.438	298	361
Atlanta	4	12	0	.250	281	382

1985

AFC EAST

	W	L	T	Pct	Pts	OP
Miami	12	4	0	.750	428	320
New England	11	5	0	.688	362	290
NY Jets	11	5	0	.688	393	264
Indianapolis	5	11	0	.313	320	386
Buffalo	2	14	0	.125	200	381

AFC CENTRAL

	W	L	T	Pct	Pts	OP
Cleveland	8	8	0	.500	287	294
Cincinnati	7	9	0	.438	441	437
Pittsburgh	7	9	0	.438	379	355
Houston	5	11	0	.313	284	412

AFC WEST

	W	L	T	Pct	Pts	OP
LA Raiders	12	4	0	.750	354	308
Denver	11	5	0	.688	380	329
Seattle	8	8	0	.500	349	303
San Diego	8	8	0	.500	467	435
Kansas City	6	10	0	.375	317	360

NFC EAST

	W	L	T	Pct	Pts	OP
Washington	10	6	0	.625	297	312
NY Giants	10	6	0	.625	399	283
Dallas	10	6	0	.625	357	333
Philadelphia	7	9	0	.438	286	310
St. Louis	5	11	0	.313	278	414

NFC CENTRAL

	W	L	T	Pct	Pts	OP
Chicago	15	1	0	.938	456	198
Green Bay	8	8	0	.500	337	355
Detroit	7	9	0	.438	307	366
Minnesota	7	9	0	.438	346	359
Tampa Bay	2	14	0	.125	294	448

NFC WEST

	W	L	T	Pct	Pts	OP
LA Rams	11	5	0	.688	340	277
San Francisco	10	6	0	.625	411	263
New Orleans	5	11	0	.313	294	401
Atlanta	4	12	0	.250	282	452

1986

AFC EAST

	W	L	T	Pct	Pts	OP
New England	11	5	0	.688	412	307
NY Jets	10	6	0	.625	364	386
Miami	8	8	0	.500	430	405
Buffalo	4	12	0	.250	287	348
Indianapolis	3	13	0	.188	299	400

AFC CENTRAL

	W	L	T	Pct	Pts	OP
Cleveland	12	4	0	.750	391	310
Cincinnati	10	6	0	.625	409	394
Pittsburgh	6	10	0	.375	307	336
Houston	5	11	0	.313	274	329

AFC WEST

	W	L	T	Pct	Pts	OP
Denver	11	5	0	.688	378	327
Kansas City	10	6	0	.625	358	326
Seattle	10	6	0	.625	366	293
LA Raiders	8	8	0	.500	323	346
San Diego	4	12	0	.250	335	396

NFC EAST

	W	L	T	Pct	Pts	OP
NY Giants	14	2	0	.875	371	236
Washington	12	4	0	.750	368	296
Dallas	7	9	0	.438	346	337
Philadelphia	5	10	1	.344	256	312
St. Louis	4	11	1	.281	518	351

1986 *(Cont.)*

NFC CENTRAL

	W	L	T	Pct	Pts	OP
Chicago	14	2	0	.875	352	187
Minnesota	9	7	0	.563	398	271
Detroit	5	11	0	.313	277	326
Green Bay	4	12	0	.250	254	418
Tampa Bay	2	14	0	.125	239	473

NFC WEST

	W	L	T	Pct	Pts	OP
San Francisco	10	5	1	.656	374	247
LA Rams	10	6	0	.625	309	267
Atlanta	7	8	1	.469	280	280
New Orleans	7	9	0	.438	288	287

1987

AFC EAST

	W	L	T	Pct	Pts	OP
Indianapolis	9	6	0	.643	300	238
Miami	8	7	0	.533	362	335
New England	8	7	0	.533	320	293
Buffalo	7	8	0	.467	320	293
NY Jets	6	9	0	.400	334	360

AFC CENTRAL

	W	L	T	Pct	Pts	OP
Cleveland	10	5	0	.700	390	239
Houston	9	6	0	.600	345	349
Pittsburgh	8	7	0	.533	285	299
Cincinnati	4	11	0	.267	285	370

AFC WEST

	W	L	T	Pct	Pts	OP
Denver	10	4	1	.667	379	288
Seattle	9	6	0	.600	371	314
San Diego	8	7	0	.563	253	317
LA Raiders	5	10	0	.333	301	289
Kansas City	4	11	0	.267	276	388

NFC EAST

	W	L	T	Pct	Pts	OP
Washington	11	4	0	.733	379	285
Dallas	7	8	0	.467	340	348
St. Louis	7	8	0	.467	362	368
Philadelphia	7	8	0	.467	337	380
NY Giants	6	9	0	.400	280	312

NFC CENTRAL

	W	L	T	Pct	Pts	OP
Chicago	11	4	0	.733	356	282
Minnesota	8	7	0	.533	336	335
Green Bay	5	9	1	.367	255	300
Tampa Bay	4	11	0	.267	286	360
Detroit	4	11	0	.267	269	384

NFC WEST

	W	L	T	Pct	Pts	OP
San Francisco	13	2	0	.867	459	253
New Orleans	12	3	0	.800	422	283
LA Rams	6	9	0	.400	317	361
Atlanta	3	12	0	.200	205	436

1988

AFC EAST

	W	L	T	Pct	Pts	OP
Buffalo	12	4	0	.750	329	237
New England	9	7	0	.563	250	284
Indianapolis	9	7	0	.563	354	315
NY Jets	8	7	1	.531	372	354
Miami	6	10	0	.375	319	380

AFC CENTRAL

	W	L	T	Pct	Pts	OP
Cincinnati	12	4	0	.750	448	329
Cleveland	10	6	0	.625	304	288
Houston	10	6	0	.625	424	365
Pittsburgh	5	1	0	.313	336	421

AFC WEST

	W	L	T	Pct	Pts	OP
Seattle	9	7	0	.563	339	329
Denver	8	8	0	.500	327	352
LA Raiders	7	9	0	.438	325	369
San Diego	6	10	0	.375	231	332
Kansas City	4	11	1	.281	254	320

NFC EAST

	W	L	T	Pct	Pts	OP
NY Giants	10	6	0	.625	359	304
Philadelphia	10	6	0	.625	379	319
Phoenix Cardinals	7	9	0	.438	344	398
Washington	7	9	0	.438	345	387
Dallas	3	13	0	.188	265	381

NFC CENTRAL

	W	L	T	Pct	Pts	OP
Chicago	12	4	0	.750	312	215
Minnesota	11	5	0	.688	406	233
Tampa Bay	5	11	0	.313	261	350
Detroit	4	12	0	.250	220	313
Green Bay	4	12	0	.250	240	315

NFC WEST

	W	L	T	Pct	Pts	OP
New Orleans	10	6	0	.625	312	283
San Francisco	10	6	0	.625	369	294
LA Rams	10	6	0	.625	407	293
Atlanta	5	11	0	.313	244	315

1989

AFC EAST

	W	L	T	Pct	Pts	OP
Buffalo	9	7	0	.563	407	317
Miami	8	8	0	.500	331	379
Indianapolis	8	8	0	.500	298	301
New England	5	11	0	.313	297	391
NY Jets	4	12	0	.250	253	411

AFC CENTRAL

	W	L	T	Pct	Pts	OP
Cleveland	9	6	1	.594	334	254
Houston	9	7	0	.563	365	412
Pittsburgh	9	7	0	.563	265	326
Cincinnati	8	8	0	.500	404	285

AFC WEST

	W	L	T	Pct	Pts	OP
Denver	11	5	0	.688	362	226
Kansas City	8	7	1	.531	318	286
LA Raiders	8	8	0	.500	315	297
Seattle	7	9	0	.438	241	327
San Diego	6	10	0	.375	266	290

1989 *(Cont.)*

NFC EAST

	W	L	T	Pct	Pts	OP
NY Giants	12	4	0	.750	348	252
Philadelphia	11	5	0	.688	342	274
Washington	10	6	0	.625	386	308
Phoenix	5	11	0	.313	258	377
Dallas	1	15	0	.063	204	393

NFC CENTRAL

	W	L	T	Pct	Pts	OP
Green Bay	10	6	0	.625	362	356
Minnesota	10	6	0	.625	351	275
Detroit	7	9	0	.438	312	364
Chicago	6	10	0	.375	358	377
Tampa Bay	5	11	0	.313	320	419

NFC WEST

	W	L	T	Pct	Pts	OP
San Francisco	14	2	0	.875	442	253
LA Rams	11	5	0	.688	426	344
New Orleans	9	7	0	.563	386	301
Atlanta	3	13	0	.188	279	437

1990

AFC EAST

	W	L	T	Pct	Pts	OP
Buffalo	13	3	0	.813	428	263
Miami	12	4	0	.750	336	242
Indianapolis	7	9	0	.438	281	353
NY Jets	6	10	0	.375	295	345
New England	1	15	0	.063	181	446

AFC CENTRAL

	W	L	T	Pct	Pts	OP
Pittsburgh	9	7	0	.563	292	240
Cincinnati	9	7	0	.563	360	352
Houston	9	7	0	.563	405	307
Cleveland	3	13	0	.188	228	462

AFC WEST

	W	L	T	Pct	Pts	OP
LA Raiders	12	4	0	.750	337	268
Kansas City	11	5	0	.688	369	257
Seattle	9	7	0	.563	306	286
San Diego	6	10	0	.375	315	281
Denver	5	11	0	.313	331	374

NFC EAST

	W	L	T	Pct	Pts	OP
NY Giants	13	3	0	.813	335	211
Washington	10	6	0	.625	381	301
Philadelphia	10	6	0	.625	396	299
Dallas	7	9	0	.438	244	308
Phoenix	5	11	0	.313	268	396

NFC CENTRAL

	W	L	T	Pct	Pts	OP
Chicago	11	5	0	.688	348	280
Green Bay	6	10	0	.375	271	347
Minnesota	6	10	0	.375	351	326
Detroit	6	10	0	.375	373	413
Tampa Bay	6	10	0	.375	264	367

NFC WEST

	W	L	T	Pct	Pts	OP
San Francisco	14	2	0	.875	353	239
New Orleans	8	8	0	.500	274	275
LA Rams	5	11	0	.313	345	412
Atlanta	5	11	0	.313	348	365

1991

AFC EAST

	W	L	T	Pct	Pts	OP
Buffalo	13	3	0	.813	458	318
Miami	8	8	0	.500	343	349
NY Jets	8	8	0	.500	314	293
New England	6	10	0	.375	211	305
Indianapolis	1	15	0	.063	143	381

AFC CENTRAL

	W	L	T	Pct	Pts	OP
Houston	11	5	0	.688	386	251
Pittsburgh	7	9	0	.438	292	344
Cleveland	6	10	0	.375	293	298
Cincinnati	3	13	0	.188	263	435

AFC WEST

	W	L	T	Pct	Pts	OP
Denver	12	4	0	.750	304	235
Kansas City	10	6	0	.625	322	252
LA Raiders	9	7	0	.563	298	297
Seattle	7	9	0	.438	276	261
San Diego	4	12	0	.250	274	342

NFC EAST

	W	L	T	Pct	Pts	OP
Washington	14	2	0	.875	485	224
Dallas	11	5	0	.688	342	310
Philadelphia	10	6	0	.625	285	244
NY Giants	8	8	0	.500	281	297
Phoenix	4	12	0	.250	196	344

NFC CENTRAL

	W	L	T	Pct	Pts	OP
Detroit	12	4	0	.750	339	295
Chicago	11	5	0	.688	299	269
Minnesota	8	8	0	.500	301	306
Green Bay	4	12	0	.250	273	313
Tampa Bay	3	13	0	.188	199	365

NFC WEST

	W	L	T	Pct	Pts	OP
New Orleans	11	5	0	.688	341	211
Atlanta	10	6	0	.625	361	338
San Francisco	10	6	0	.625	393	239
LA Rams	3	13	0	.188	234	390

1992

AFC EAST

	W	L	T	Pct	Pts	OP
Buffalo	11	5	0	.688	381	283
Miami	11	5	0	.688	340	281
Indianapolis	9	7	0	.563	216	302
NY Jets	4	12	0	.250	220	315
New England	2	14	0	.125	205	363

AFC CENTRAL

	W	L	T	Pct	Pts	OP
Pittsburgh	11	5	0	.688	299	225
Houston	10	6	0	.625	352	258
Cleveland	7	9	0	.438	272	275
Cincinnati	5	11	0	.313	274	364

AFC WEST

	W	L	T	Pct	Pts	OP
San Diego	11	5	0	.688	335	241
Kansas City	10	6	0	.625	348	282
Denver	8	8	0	.500	262	329
LA Raiders	7	9	0	.438	249	281
Seattle	2	14	0	.125	140	312

1992 *(Cont.)*

NFC EAST

	W	L	T	Pct	Pts	OP
Dallas	13	3	0	.813	409	243
Philadelphia	11	5	0	.688	354	245
Washington	9	7	0	.563	300	255
NY Giants	6	10	0	.375	306	367
Phoenix	4	12	0	.250	243	332

NFC CENTRAL

	W	L	T	Pct	Pts	OP
Minnesota	11	5	0	.688	374	249
Green Bay	9	7	0	.563	276	296
Tampa Bay	5	11	0	.313	267	365
Detroit	5	11	0	.313	273	332
Chicago	5	11	0	.313	295	361

NFC WEST

	W	L	T	Pct	Pts	OP
San Francisco	14	2	0	.875	431	236
New Orleans	12	4	0	.750	330	202
Atlanta	6	10	0	.375	327	414
LA Rams	6	10	0	.375	313	383

1993

AFC EAST

	W	L	T	Pct	Pts	OP
Buffalo	12	4	0	.750	329	242
Miami	9	7	0	.563	349	351
NY Jets	8	8	0	.500	270	247
New England	5	11	0	.313	238	286
Indianapolis	4	12	0	.250	189	378

AFC CENTRAL

	W	L	T	Pct	Pts	OP
Houston	12	4	0	.750	368	238
Pittsburgh	9	7	0	.563	308	281
Cleveland	7	9	0	.438	304	307
Cincinnati	3	13	0	.188	187	319

AFC WEST

	W	L	T	Pct	Pts	OP
Kansas City	11	5	0	.688	328	291
LA Raiders	10	6	0	.625	306	326
Denver	9	7	0	.563	373	284
San Diego	8	8	0	.500	322	290
Seattle	6	10	0	.375	280	314

NFC EAST

	W	L	T	Pct	Pts	OP
Dallas	12	4	0	.750	376	229
NY Giants	11	5	0	.688	288	205
Philadelphia	8	8	0	.500	293	315
Phoenix	7	9	0	.438	326	269
Washington	4	12	0	.250	230	345

NFC CENTRAL

	W	L	T	Pct	Pts	OP
Detroit	10	6	0	.625	298	292
Green Bay	9	7	0	.563	340	282
Minnesota	9	7	0	.563	277	290
Chicago	7	9	0	.438	234	230
Tampa Bay	5	11	0	.313	237	375

NFC WEST

	W	L	T	Pct	Pts	OP
San Francisco	10	6	0	.625	473	295
New Orleans	8	8	0	.500	317	343
Atlanta	6	10	0	.375	316	385
LA Rams	5	11	0	.313	221	367

1994

AFC EAST
	W	L	T	Pct	Pts	OP
Miami	10	6	0	.625	389	327
New England	10	6	0	.625	351	312
Indianapolis	8	8	0	.500	307	320
Buffalo	7	9	0	.438	340	356
NY Jets	6	10	0	.375	264	320

AFC CENTRAL
	W	L	T	Pct	Pts	OP
Pittsburgh	12	4	0	.750	316	234
Cleveland	11	5	0	.688	340	204
Cincinnati	3	13	0	.188	276	406
Houston	2	14	0	.125	226	352

AFC WEST
	W	L	T	Pct	Pts	OP
San Diego	11	5	0	.688	384	306
LA Raiders	9	7	0	.563	303	327
Kansas City	9	7	0	.563	319	298
Denver	7	9	0	.438	347	396
Seattle	6	10	0	.375	287	323

NFC EAST
	W	L	T	Pct	Pts	OP
Dallas	12	4	0	.750	414	248
NY Giants	9	7	0	.563	279	305
Arizona Cardinals	8	8	0	.500	235	267
Philadelphia	7	9	0	.438	308	308
Washington	3	13	0	.188	320	412

NFC CENTRAL
	W	L	T	Pct	Pts	OP
Minnesota	10	6	0	.625	356	314
Green Bay	9	7	0	.563	382	287
Detroit	9	7	0	.563	357	342
Chicago	9	7	0	.563	271	307
Tampa Bay	6	10	0	.375	251	351

NFC WEST
	W	L	T	Pct	Pts	OP
San Francisco	13	3	0	.813	505	296
New Orleans	7	9	0	.438	348	407
Atlanta	7	9	0	.438	317	385
LA Rams	4	12	0	.250	286	365

1995

AFC EAST
	W	L	T	Pct	Pts	OP
Buffalo	10	6	0	.625	350	335
Miami	9	7	0	.563	398	332
Indianapolis	9	7	0	.563	331	316
New England	6	10	0	.375	294	377
NY Jets	3	13	0	.188	233	384

AFC CENTRAL
	W	L	T	Pct	Pts	OP
Pittsburgh	11	5	0	.688	407	327
Houston	7	9	0	.438	348	324
Cincinnati	7	9	0	.438	349	374
Cleveland	5	11	0	.313	289	356
Jacksonville Jaguars	4	12	0	.250	275	404

AFC WEST
	W	L	T	Pct	Pts	OP
Kansas City	13	3	0	.813	358	241
San Diego	9	7	0	.563	321	323
Oakland Raiders	8	8	0	.500	348	332
Denver	8	8	0	.500	388	345
Seattle	8	8	0	.500	363	366

1995 (Cont.)

NFC EAST
	W	L	T	Pct	Pts	OP
Dallas	12	4	0	.750	435	291
Philadelphia	10	6	0	.625	318	338
Washington	6	10	0	.375	326	359
NY Giants	5	11	0	.313	290	340
Arizona	4	12	0	.250	275	422

NFC CENTRAL
	W	L	T	Pct	Pts	OP
Green Bay	11	5	0	.688	404	314
Detroit	10	6	0	.625	436	336
Chicago	9	7	0	.563	392	360
Minnesota	8	8	0	.500	412	385
Tampa Bay	7	9	0	.438	238	335

NFC WEST
	W	L	T	Pct	Pts	OP
San Francisco	11	5	0	.688	457	258
Atlanta	9	7	0	.563	362	349
St. Louis Rams	7	9	0	.438	309	418
Carolina Panthers	7	9	0	.438	289	325
New Orleans	7	9	0	.438	319	348

1996

AFC EAST
	W	L	T	Pct	Pts	OP
New England	11	5	0	.688	418	313
Buffalo	10	6	0	.625	319	266
Indianapolis	9	7	0	.563	317	334
Miami	8	8	0	.500	339	325
NY Jets	1	15	0	.063	279	454

AFC CENTRAL
	W	L	T	Pct	Pts	OP
Pittsburgh	10	6	0	.625	344	257
Jacksonville	9	7	0	.563	325	334
Houston	8	8	0	.500	345	319
Cincinnati	8	8	0	.500	372	369
Baltimore Ravens	4	12	0	.250	371	441

AFC WEST
	W	L	T	Pct	Pts	OP
Denver	13	3	0	.813	391	275
Kansas City	9	7	0	.563	297	300
San Diego	8	8	0	.500	310	376
Seattle	7	9	0	.438	317	375
Oakland	7	9	0	.438	340	293

NFC EAST
	W	L	T	Pct	Pts	OP
Dallas	10	6	0	.625	286	250
Philadelphia	10	6	0	.625	363	341
Washington	9	7	0	.563	364	312
Arizona	7	9	0	.438	300	397
NY Giants	6	10	0	.375	242	297

NFC CENTRAL
	W	L	T	Pct	Pts	OP
Green Bay	13	3	0	.813	456	210
Minnesota	9	7	0	.563	298	315
Chicago	7	9	0	.438	283	305
Tampa Bay	6	10	0	.375	221	293
Detroit	5	11	0	.313	302	368

NFC WEST
	W	L	T	Pct	Pts	OP
San Francisco	12	4	0	.750	398	257
Carolina	12	4	0	.750	367	218
St. Louis	6	10	0	.375	303	409
New Orleans	3	13	0	.188	229	339
Atlanta	3	13	0	.188	309	461

1997

AFC EAST

	W	L	T	Pct	Pts	OP
New England	10	6	0	.625	369	289
Miami	9	7	0	.563	339	327
NY Jets	9	7	0	.563	348	287
Buffalo	6	10	0	.375	255	367
Indianapolis	3	13	0	.188	313	401

AFC CENTRAL

	W	L	T	Pct	Pts	OP
Jacksonville	11	5	0	.688	394	318
Pittsburgh	11	5	0	.688	372	307
Tennessee Oilers	8	8	0	.500	333	310
Cincinnati	7	9	0	.438	355	405
Baltimore	6	9	1	.375	326	345

AFC WEST

	W	L	T	Pct	Pts	OP
Kansas City	13	3	0	.813	375	232
Denver	12	4	0	.750	472	287
Seattle	8	8	0	.500	365	362
Oakland	4	12	0	.250	324	419
San Diego	4	12	0	.250	266	425

NFC EAST

	W	L	T	Pct	Pts	OP
NY Giants	10	5	1	.656	307	265
Washington	8	7	1	.531	327	289
Philadelphia	6	9	1	.406	317	372
Dallas	6	10	0	.375	304	314
Arizona	4	12	0	.250	283	379

NFC CENTRAL

	W	L	T	Pct	Pts	OP
Green Bay	13	3	0	.813	422	282
Tampa Bay	10	6	0	.625	299	263
Detroit	9	7	0	.563	379	306
Minnesota	9	7	0	.563	354	359
Chicago	4	12	0	.250	263	421

NFC WEST

	W	L	T	Pct	Pts	OP
San Francisco	13	3	0	.813	375	265
Carolina	7	9	0	.438	265	314
Atlanta	7	9	0	.438	320	361
New Orleans	6	10	0	.375	237	327
St. Louis	5	11	0	.313	299	359

1998

AFC EAST

	W	L	T	Pct	Pts	OP
NY Jets	12	4	0	.750	416	266
Miami	10	6	0	.625	321	265
Buffalo	10	6	0	.625	400	333
New England	9	7	0	.563	337	329
Indianapolis	3	13	0	.188	310	444

AFC CENTRAL

	W	L	T	Pct	Pts	OP
Jacksonville	11	5	0	.688	392	338
Tennessee	8	8	0	.500	330	320
Pittsburgh	7	9	0	.438	263	303
Baltimore	6	10	0	.375	269	335
Cincinnati	3	13	0	.188	268	452

AFC WEST

	W	L	T	Pct	Pts	OP
Denver	14	2	0	.875	501	309
Oakland	8	8	0	.500	288	356
Seattle	8	8	0	.500	372	310
Kansas City	7	9	0	.438	327	363
San Diego	5	11	0	.313	241	342

1998 *(Cont.)*

NFC EAST

	W	L	T	Pct	Pts	OP
Dallas	10	6	0	.625	381	275
Arizona	9	7	0	.563	325	378
NY Giants	8	8	0	.500	287	309
Washington	6	10	0	.375	319	421
Philadelphia	3	13	0	.188	161	344

NFC CENTRAL

	W	L	T	Pct	Pts	OP
Minnesota	15	1	0	.938	556	296
Green Bay	11	5	0	.688	408	319
Tampa Bay	8	8	0	.500	314	295
Detroit	5	11	0	.313	306	378
Chicago	4	12	0	.250	276	368

NFC WEST

	W	L	T	Pct	Pts	OP
Atlanta	14	2	0	.875	442	289
San Francisco	12	4	0	.750	479	328
New Orleans	6	10	0	.375	305	359
Carolina	4	12	0	.250	336	413
St. Louis	4	12	0	.250	285	378

1999

AFC EAST

	W	L	T	Pct	Pts	OP
Indianapolis	13	3	0	.813	423	333
Buffalo	11	5	0	.688	320	229
Miami	9	7	0	.563	326	336
NY Jets	8	8	0	.500	309	309
New England	8	8	0	.500	299	284

AFC CENTRAL

	W	L	T	Pct	Pts	OP
Jacksonville	14	2	0	.875	396	217
Tennessee Titans	13	3	0	.813	392	324
Baltimore	8	8	0	.500	324	277
Pittsburgh	6	10	0	.375	317	320
Cincinnati	4	12	0	.250	283	460
Cleveland Browns	2	14	0	.125	217	437

AFC WEST

	W	L	T	Pct	Pts	OP
Seattle	9	7	0	.563	338	298
Kansas City	9	7	0	.563	390	322
Oakland	8	8	0	.500	390	329
San Diego	8	8	0	.500	269	316
Denver	6	10	0	.375	314	318

NFC EAST

	W	L	T	Pct	Pts	OP
Washington	10	6	0	.625	443	377
Dallas	8	8	0	.500	352	276
NY Giants	7	9	0	.438	299	358
Arizona	6	10	0	.375	245	329
Philadelphia	5	11	0	.313	272	357

NFC CENTRAL

	W	L	T	Pct	Pts	OP
Tampa Bay	11	5	0	.688	270	235
Minnesota	10	6	0	.625	399	335
Green Bay	8	8	0	.500	357	341
Detroit	8	8	0	.500	322	323
Chicago	6	10	0	.375	272	341

NFC WEST

	W	L	T	Pct	Pts	OP
St. Louis	13	3	0	.813	526	242
Carolina	8	8	0	.500	421	381
Atlanta	5	11	0	.313	285	380
San Francisco	4	12	0	.250	295	453
New Orleans	3	13	0	.188	260	434

2000

AFC EAST

	W	L	T	Pct	Pts	OP
Miami	11	5	0	.688	323	226
Indianapolis	10	6	0	.625	429	326
NY Jets	9	7	0	.563	321	321
Buffalo	8	8	0	.500	315	350
New England	5	11	0	.313	276	338

AFC CENTRAL

	W	L	T	Pct	Pts	OP
Tennessee	13	3	0	.813	346	191
Baltimore	12	4	0	.750	333	165
Pittsburgh	9	7	0	.563	321	255
Jacksonville	7	9	0	.438	367	327
Cincinnati	4	12	0	.250	185	359
Cleveland	3	13	0	.188	161	419

AFC WEST

	W	L	T	Pct	Pts	OP
Oakland	12	4	0	.750	479	299
Denver	11	5	0	.688	485	369
Kansas City	7	9	0	.438	355	354
Seattle	6	10	0	.375	320	405
San Diego	1	15	0	.063	269	440

NFC EAST

	W	L	T	Pct	Pts	OP
NY Giants	12	4	0	.750	328	246
Philadelphia	11	5	0	.688	351	245
Washington	8	8	0	.500	281	269
Dallas	5	11	0	.313	294	361
Arizona	3	13	0	.188	210	443

NFC CENTRAL

	W	L	T	Pct	Pts	OP
Minnesota	11	5	0	.688	397	371
Tampa Bay	10	6	0	.625	388	269
Green Bay	9	7	0	.563	353	323
Detroit	9	7	0	.563	307	307
Chicago	5	11	0	.313	216	355

NFC WEST

	W	L	T	Pct	Pts	OP
New Orleans	10	6	0	.625	354	306
St. Louis	10	6	0	.625	540	471
Carolina	7	9	0	.438	310	310
San Francisco	6	10	0	.375	388	422
Atlanta	4	12	0	.250	252	413

2001

AFC EAST

	W	L	T	Pct	Pts	OP
New England	11	5	0	.688	371	272
Miami	11	5	0	.688	344	290
NY Jets	10	6	0	.625	413	486
Indianapolis	6	10	0	.375	413	486
Buffalo	3	13	0	.188	265	420

AFC CENTRAL

	W	L	T	Pct	Pts	OP
Pittsburgh	13	3	0	.813	352	212
Baltimore	10	6	0	.625	303	265
Cleveland	7	9	0	.438	285	319
Tennessee	7	9	0	.438	336	388
Jacksonville	6	10	0	.375	294	286
Cincinnati	6	10	0	.375	226	309

AFC WEST

	W	L	T	Pct	Pts	OP
Oakland	10	6	0	.625	399	327
Seattle	9	7	0	.563	301	324
Denver	8	8	0	.500	340	339
Kansas City	6	10	0	.375	320	344
San Diego	5	11	0	.313	332	321

2001 *(Cont.)*

NFC EAST

	W	L	T	Pct	Pts	OP
Philadelphia	11	5	0	.688	343	208
Washington	8	8	0	.500	256	303
NY Giants	7	9	0	.438	294	321
Arizona	7	9	0	.438	295	343
Dallas	5	11	0	.313	246	338

NFC CENTRAL

	W	L	T	Pct	Pts	OP
Chicago	13	3	0	.813	338	203
Green Bay	12	4	0	.750	390	266
Tampa Bay	9	7	0	.563	324	280
Minnesota	5	11	0	.313	290	390
Detroit	2	14	0	.125	270	424

NFC WEST

	W	L	T	Pct	Pts	OP
St. Louis	14	2	0	.875	503	273
San Francisco	12	4	0	.750	409	282
Atlanta	7	9	0	.438	291	377
New Orleans	7	9	0	.438	333	409
Carolina	1	15	0	.938	253	410

2002

AFC EAST

	W	L	T	Pct	Pts	OP
New England	9	7	0	.563	384	346
Miami	9	7	0	.563	378	301
NY Jets	9	7	0	.563	359	336
Buffalo	8	8	0	.500	379	397

AFC NORTH

	W	L	T	Pct	Pts	OP
Pittsburgh	10	5	1	.656	390	345
Cleveland	9	7	0	.563	344	320
Baltimore	7	9	0	.438	316	354
Cincinnati	2	14	0	.125	279	456

AFC SOUTH

	W	L	T	Pct	Pts	OP
Tennessee	11	5	0	.688	367	324
Indianapolis	10	6	0	.625	349	313
Jacksonville	6	10	0	.375	328	315
Houston Texans	4	12	0	.250	213	356

AFC WEST

	W	L	T	Pct	Pts	OP
Oakland	11	5	0	.688	450	304
Denver	9	7	0	.563	392	344
Kansas City	8	8	0	.500	467	399
San Diego	8	8	0	.500	333	367

NFC EAST

	W	L	T	Pct	Pts	OP
Philadelphia	12	4	0	.750	415	241
NY Giants	10	6	0	.625	320	279
Washington	7	9	0	.438	307	365
Dallas	5	11	0	.313	217	329

NFC NORTH

	W	L	T	Pct	Pts	OP
Green Bay	12	4	0	.750	398	328
Minnesota	6	10	0	.375	390	442
Chicago	4	12	0	.250	281	379
Detroit	3	13	0	.188	306	451

2002 *(Cont.)*

NFC SOUTH

	W	L	T	Pct	Pts	OP
Tampa Bay	12	4	0	.750	346	196
Atlanta	9	6	1	.594	402	314
New Orleans	9	7	0	.563	432	388
Carolina	7	9	0	.438	258	302

NFC WEST

	W	L	T	Pct	Pts	OP
San Francisco	10	6	0	.625	367	351
St. Louis	7	9	0	.438	316	367
Seattle	7	9	0	.438	355	369
Arizona	5	11	0	.313	262	417

2003

AFC EAST

	W	L	T	Pct	Pts	OP
New England	14	2	0	.875	348	238
Miami	10	6	0	.625	311	261
Buffalo	6	10	0	.375	243	279
NY Jets	6	10	0	.375	283	299

AFC NORTH

	W	L	T	Pct	Pts	OP
Baltimore	10	6	0	.625	391	281
Cincinnati	8	8	0	.500	346	384
Pittsburgh	6	10	0	.375	300	327
Cleveland	5	11	0	.313	254	322

AFC SOUTH

	W	L	T	Pct	Pts	OP
Indianapolis	12	4	0	.750	447	336
Tennessee	12	4	0	.750	435	324
Houston	5	11	0	.313	255	380
Jacksonville	5	11	0	.313	276	331

AFC WEST

	W	L	T	Pct	Pts	OP
Kansas City	13	3	0	.813	484	332
Denver	10	6	0	.625	381	301
Oakland	4	12	0	.250	270	379
San Diego	4	12	0	.250	313	441

NFC EAST

	W	L	T	Pct	Pts	OP
Philadelphia	12	4	0	.750	374	287
Dallas	10	6	0	.625	289	260
Washington	5	11	0	.313	287	372
NY Giants	4	12	0	.250	243	387

NFC NORTH

	W	L	T	Pct	Pts	OP
Green Bay	10	6	0	.625	442	307
Minnesota	9	7	0	.563	416	353
Chicago	7	9	0	.438	283	346
Detroit	5	11	0	.313	270	379

NFC SOUTH

	W	L	T	Pct	Pts	OP
Carolina	11	5	0	.688	325	304
New Orleans	8	8	0	.500	340	326
Tampa Bay	7	9	0	.438	301	264
Atlanta	5	11	0	.313	299	422

NFC WEST

	W	L	T	Pct	Pts	OP
St. Louis	12	4	0	.750	447	328
Seattle	10	6	0	.625	404	327
San Francisco	7	9	0	.438	384	337
Arizona	4	12	0	.250	225	452

2004

AFC EAST

	W	L	T	Pct	Pts	OP
New England	14	2	0	.875	437	260
NY Jets	10	6	0	.625	333	261
Buffalo	9	7	0	.562	395	284
Miami	4	12	0	.250	275	354

AFC NORTH

	W	L	T	Pct	Pts	OP
Pittsburgh	15	1	0	.938	372	251
Baltimore	9	7	0	.562	317	268
Cincinnati	8	8	0	.500	374	372
Cleveland	4	12	0	.250	275	354

AFC SOUTH

	W	L	T	Pct	Pts	OP
Indianapolis	12	4	0	.750	522	351
Jacksonville	9	7	0	.562	261	280
Houston	7	9	0	.438	309	339
Tennessee	5	11	0	.312	344	439

AFC WEST

	W	L	T	Pct	Pts	OP
San Diego	12	4	0	.750	446	313
Denver	10	6	0	.625	381	304
Kansas City	7	9	0	.438	483	435
Oakland	5	11	0	.312	320	442

NFC EAST

	W	L	T	Pct	Pts	OP
Philadelphia	13	3	0	.812	386	260
NY Giants	6	10	0	.375	303	347
Dallas	6	10	0	.375	293	405
Washington	6	10	0	.375	240	265

NFC NORTH

	W	L	T	Pct	Pts	OP
Green Bay	10	6	0	.625	424	380
Minnesota	8	8	0	.500	405	395
Detroit	6	10	0	.375	296	350
Chicago	5	11	0	.312	231	331

NFC SOUTH

	W	L	T	Pct	Pts	OP
Atlanta	11	5	0	.688	340	337
New Orleans	8	8	0	.500	348	405
Carolina	7	9	0	.438	355	339
Tampa Bay	5	11	0	.312	301	304

NFC WEST

	W	L	T	Pct	Pts	OP
Seattle	9	7	0	.562	371	373
St. Louis	8	8	0	.500	319	392
Arizona	6	10	0	.375	284	322
San Francisco	2	14	0	.125	259	452

2005

AFC EAST

	W	L	T	Pct	Pts	OP
New England	10	6	0	.625	379	338
Miami	9	7	0	.562	318	317
Buffalo	5	11	0	.312	271	367
NY Jets	4	12	0	.250	240	355

AFC NORTH

	W	L	T	Pct	Pts	OP
Cincinnati	11	5	0	.688	421	350
Pittsburgh	11	5	0	.688	389	258
Cleveland	6	10	0	.375	232	301
Baltimore	6	10	0	.375	265	299

AFC SOUTH

	W	L	T	Pct	Pts	OP
Indianapolis	14	2	0	.875	439	247
Jacksonville	12	4	0	.750	361	269
Tennessee	4	12	0	.250	299	421
Houston	2	14	0	.125	260	431

2005 (Cont.)

AFC WEST

	W	L	T	Pct	Pts	OP
Denver	13	3	0	.812	395	258
Kansas City	10	6	0	.625	403	325
San Diego	9	7	0	.562	418	312
Oakland	4	12	0	.250	290	383

NFC EAST

	W	L	T	Pct	Pts	OP
NY Giants	11	5	0	.688	422	314
Washington	10	6	0	.625	359	293
Dallas	9	7	0	.562	325	308
Philadelphia	6	10	0	.375	310	388

NFC NORTH

	W	L	T	Pct	Pts	OP
Chicago	11	5	0	.688	260	202
Minnesota	9	7	0	.562	306	344
Detroit	5	11	0	.312	254	345
Green Bay	4	12	0	.250	298	344

NFC SOUTH

	W	L	T	Pct	Pts	OP
Carolina	11	5	0	.688	391	259
Tampa Bay	11	5	0	.688	300	274
Atlanta	8	8	0	.500	351	341
New Orleans	3	13	0	.188	235	398

NFC WEST

	W	L	T	Pct	Pts	OP
Seattle	13	3	0	.812	452	271
St. Louis	6	10	0	.375	363	429
Arizona	5	11	0	.312	311	387
San Francisco	4	12	0	.250	239	428

2006

AFC EAST

	W	L	T	Pct	Pts	OP
New England	12	4	0	.750	385	237
NY Jets	10	6	0	.625	316	295
Buffalo	7	9	0	.438	300	311
Miami	6	10	0	.375	260	283

AFC NORTH

	W	L	T	Pct	Pts	OP
Baltimore	13	3	0	.812	353	201
Cincinnati	8	8	0	.500	373	331
Pittsburgh	8	8	0	.500	353	315
Cleveland	4	12	0	.250	238	356

AFC SOUTH

	W	L	T	Pct	Pts	OP
Indianapolis	12	4	0	.750	427	360
Tennessee	8	8	0	.500	324	400
Jacksonville	8	8	0	.500	371	274
Houston	6	10	0	.375	267	366

AFC WEST

	W	L	T	Pct	Pts	OP
San Diego	14	2	0	.875	492	303
Kansas City	9	7	0	.562	331	315
Denver	9	7	0	.562	319	305
Oakland	2	14	0	.125	168	332

NFC EAST

	W	L	T	Pct	Pts	OP
Philadelphia	10	6	0	.625	398	328
Dallas	9	7	0	.562	425	350
NY Giants	8	8	0	.500	355	362
Washington	5	11	0	.312	307	376

NFC NORTH

	W	L	T	Pct	Pts	OP
Chicago	13	3	0	.812	427	255
Green Bay	8	8	0	.500	301	366
Minnesota	6	10	0	.375	282	327
Detroit	3	13	0	.188	305	398

2006 (Cont.)

NFC SOUTH

	W	L	T	Pct	Pts	OP
New Orleans	10	6	0	.625	413	322
Carolina	8	8	0	.500	270	305
Atlanta	7	9	0	.438	292	328
Tampa Bay	4	12	0	.250	211	353

NFC WEST

	W	L	T	Pct	Pts	OP
Seattle	9	7	0	.562	335	341
St. Louis	8	8	0	.500	367	381
San Francisco	7	9	0	.438	298	412
Arizona	5	11	0	.312	314	389

2007

AFC EAST

	W	L	T	Pct	Pts	OP
New England	16	0	0	1.000	589	274
Buffalo	7	9	0	.438	252	354
NY Jets	4	12	0	.250	268	355
Miami	1	15	0	.063	267	437

AFC NORTH

	W	L	T	Pct	Pts	OP
Pittsburgh	10	6	0	.625	393	269
Cleveland	10	6	0	.625	402	382
Cincinnati	7	9	0	.438	380	385
Baltimore	5	11	0	.313	275	384

AFC SOUTH

	W	L	T	Pct	Pts	OP
Indianapolis	13	3	0	.813	450	262
Jacksonville	11	5	0	.688	411	304
Tennessee	10	6	0	.625	301	297
Houston	8	8	0	.500	379	384

AFC WEST

	W	L	T	Pct	Pts	OP
San Diego	11	5	0	.688	412	284
Denver	7	9	0	.438	320	409
Kansas City	4	12	0	.250	226	335
Oakland	4	12	0	.250	286	398

NFC EAST

	W	L	T	Pct	Pts	OP
Dallas	13	3	0	.813	455	325
NY Giants	10	6	0	.625	373	351
Washington	9	7	0	.563	334	310
Philadelphia	8	8	0	.500	336	300

NFC NORTH

	W	L	T	Pct	Pts	OP
Green Bay	13	3	0	.813	435	291
Minnesota	8	8	0	.500	365	311
Detroit	7	9	0	.438	346	444
Chicago	7	9	0	.438	334	348

NFC SOUTH

	W	L	T	Pct	Pts	OP
Tampa Bay	9	7	0	.563	334	270
Carolina	7	9	0	.438	267	347
New Orleans	7	9	0	.438	379	388
Atlanta	4	12	0	.250	259	414

NFC WEST

	W	L	T	Pct	Pts	OP
Seattle	10	6	0	.625	393	291
Arizona	8	8	0	.500	404	399
San Francisco	5	11	0	.313	219	364
St. Louis	3	13	0	.188	263	438

2008

AFC EAST
	W	L	T	Pct	Pts	OP
Miami	11	5	0	.688	345	317
New England	11	5	0	.688	410	309
NY Jets	9	7	0	.563	405	356
Buffalo	7	9	0	.438	336	342

AFC NORTH
	W	L	T	Pct	Pts	OP
Pittsburgh	12	4	0	.750	347	223
*Baltimore	11	5	0	.688	385	244
Cincinnati	4	11	1	.281	204	364
Cleveland	4	12	0	.250	232	350

AFC SOUTH
	W	L	T	Pct	Pts	OP
Tennessee	13	3	0	.813	375	234
*Indianapolis	12	4	0	.750	377	298
Houston	8	8	0	.500	366	394
Jacksonville	5	11	0	.313	302	367

AFC WEST
	W	L	T	Pct	Pts	OP
San Diego	8	8	0	.500	439	347
Denver	8	8	0	.500	370	448
Oakland	5	11	0	.313	263	388
Kansas City	2	14	0	.125	291	440

NFC EAST
	W	L	T	Pct	Pts	OP
NY Giants	12	4	0	.750	427	294
*Philadelphia	9	6	1	.594	416	289
Dallas	9	7	0	.563	362	365
Washington	8	8	0	.500	265	296

NFC NORTH
	W	L	T	Pct	Pts	OP
Minnesota	10	6	0	.625	379	333
Chicago	9	7	0	.563	375	350
Green Bay	6	10	0	.375	419	380
Detroit	0	16	0	.000	268	517

NFC SOUTH
	W	L	T	Pct	Pts	OP
Carolina	12	4	0	.750	414	329
*Atlanta	11	5	0	.688	391	325
Tampa Bay	9	7	0	.563	361	323
New Orleans	8	8	0	.500	463	393

NFC WEST
	W	L	T	Pct	Pts	OP
Arizona	9	7	0	.563	427	426
San Francisco	7	9	0	.438	339	381
Seattle	4	12	0	.250	294	392
St. Louis	2	14	0	.125	232	465

2009

AFC EAST
	W	L	T	Pct	Pts	OP
New England	10	6	0	.625	427	285
*NY Jets	9	7	0	.563	348	236
Miami	7	9	0	.438	360	390
Buffalo	6	10	0	.375	258	326

AFC NORTH
	W	L	T	Pct	Pts	OP
Cincinnati	10	6	0	.625	305	291
*Baltimore	9	7	0	.563	391	261
Pittsburgh	9	7	0	.563	368	324
Cleveland	5	11	0	.313	245	375

AFC SOUTH
	W	L	T	Pct	Pts	OP
Indianapolis	14	2	0	.875	416	307
Houston	9	7	0	.563	388	333
Tennessee	8	8	0	.500	354	402
Jacksonville	7	9	0	.438	290	380

AFC WEST
	W	L	T	Pct	Pts	OP
San Diego	13	3	0	.813	454	320
Denver	8	8	0	.500	326	324
Oakland	5	11	0	.313	379	379
Kansas City	4	12	0	.250	424	424

NFC EAST
	W	L	T	Pct	Pts	OP
Dallas	11	5	0	.688	361	250
*Philadelphia	11	5	0	.688	429	337
NY Giants	8	8	0	.500	402	427
Washington	4	12	0	.250	266	336

NFC NORTH
	W	L	T	Pct	Pts	OP
Minnesota	12	4	0	.750	470	312
*Green Bay	11	5	0	.688	461	297
Chicago	7	9	0	.438	327	375
Detroit	2	14	0	.125	262	494

NFC SOUTH
	W	L	T	Pct	Pts	OP
New Orleans	13	3	0	.813	510	341
Atlanta	9	7	0	.563	363	325
Carolina	8	8	0	.500	315	308
Tampa Bay	3	13	0	.188	244	400

NFC WEST
	W	L	T	Pct	Pts	OP
Arizona	10	6	0	.625	375	325
San Francisco	8	8	0	.500	330	281
Seattle	5	11	0	.313	280	390
St. Louis	1	15	0	.063	175	436

Results

	Date	Winner (Share)	Loser (Share)	Score	Site (Attendance)
I	1-15-67	Green Bay ($15,000)	Kansas City ($7,500)	35–10	Los Angeles (61,946)
II	1-14-68	Green Bay ($15,000)	Oakland ($7,500)	33–14	Miami (75,546)
III	1-12-69	NY Jets ($15,000)	Baltimore ($7,500)	16–7	Miami (75,389)
IV	1-11-70	Kansas City ($15,000)	Minnesota ($7,500)	23–7	New Orleans (80,562)
V	1-17-71	Baltimore ($15,000)	Dallas ($7,500)	16–13	Miami (79,204)
VI	1-16-72	Dallas ($15,000)	Miami ($7,500)	24–3	New Orleans (81,023)
VII	1-14-73	Miami ($15,000)	Washington ($7,500)	14–7	Los Angeles (90,182)
VIII	1-13-74	Miami ($15,000)	Minnesota ($7,500)	24–7	Houston (71,882)
IX	1-12-75	Pittsburgh ($15,000)	Minnesota ($7,500)	16–6	New Orleans (80,997)
X	1-18-76	Pittsburgh ($15,000)	Dallas ($7,500)	21–17	Miami (80,187)
XI	1-9-77	Oakland ($15,000)	Minnesota ($7,500)	32–14	Pasadena (103,438)
XII	1-15-78	Dallas ($18,000)	Denver ($9,000)	27–10	New Orleans (76,400)
XIII	1-21-79	Pittsburgh ($18,000)	Dallas ($9,000)	35–31	Miami (79,484)
XIV	1-20-80	Pittsburgh ($18,000)	Los Angeles ($9,000)	31–19	Pasadena (103,985)
XV	1-25-81	Oakland ($18,000)	Philadelphia ($9,000)	27–10	New Orleans (76,135)
XVI	1-24-82	San Francisco ($18,000)	Cincinnati ($9,000)	26–21	Pontiac, Mich. (81,270)
XVII	1-30-83	Washington ($36,000)	Miami ($18,000)	27–17	Pasadena (103,667)
XVIII	1-22-84	LA Raiders ($36,000)	Washington ($18,000)	38–9	Tampa (72,920)
XIX	1-20-85	San Francisco ($36,000)	Miami ($18,000)	38–16	Stanford, Calif. (84,059)
XX	1-26-86	Chicago ($36,000)	New England ($18,000)	46–10	New Orleans (73,818)
XXI	1-25-87	NY Giants ($36,000)	Denver ($18,000)	39–20	Pasadena (101,063)
XXII	1-31-88	Washington ($36,000)	Denver ($18,000)	42–10	San Diego (73,302)
XXIII	1-22-89	San Francisco ($36,000)	Cincinnati ($18,000)	20–16	Miami (75,129)
XXIV	1-28-90	San Francisco ($36,000)	Denver ($18,000)	55–10	New Orleans (72,919)
XXV	1-27-91	NY Giants ($36,000)	Buffalo ($18,000)	20–19	Tampa (73,813)
XXVI	1-26-92	Washington ($36,000)	Buffalo ($18,000)	37–24	Minneapolis (63,130)
XXVII	1-31-93	Dallas ($36,000)	Buffalo ($18,000)	52–17	Pasadena (98,374)
XXVIII	1-30-94	Dallas ($38,000)	Buffalo ($23,500)	30–13	Atlanta (72,817)
XXIX	1-29-95	San Francisco ($42,000)	San Diego ($26,000)	49–26	Miami (74,107)
XXX	1-28-96	Dallas ($42,000)	Pittsburgh ($27,000)	27–17	Tempe, Ariz. (76,347)
XXXI	1-26-97	Green Bay ($48,000)	New England ($29,000)	35–21	New Orleans (72,301)
XXXII	1-25-98	Denver ($48,000)	Green Bay ($27,500)	31–24	San Diego (68,912)
XXXIII	1-31-99	Denver ($53,000)	Atlanta ($32,500)	34–19	Miami (74,803)
XXXIV	1-30-00	St. Louis ($58,000)	Tennessee ($33,000)	23–16	Atlanta (72,625)
XXXV	1-28-01	Baltimore ($58,000)	NY Giants ($34,500)	34–7	Tampa (71,921)
XXXVI	2-3-02	New England ($63,000)	St. Louis ($34,500)	20–17	New Orleans (72,922)
XXXVII	1-26-03	Tampa Bay ($64,000)	Oakland ($35,000)	48–21	San Diego (67,603)
XXXVIII	2-1-04	New England ($64,000)	Carolina ($35,000)	32–29	Houston (71,525)
XXXIX	2-6-05	New England ($68,000)	Philadelphia ($36,500)	24–21	Jacksonville (78,125)
XL	2-5-06	Pittsburgh ($73,000)	Seattle ($38,000)	21–10	Detroit (68,206)
XLI	2-4-07	Indianapolis ($78,000)	Chicago ($40,000)	29–17	Miami (74,512)
XLII	2-3-08	NY Giants ($78,000)	New England ($40,000)	17–14	Glendale, Ariz. (71,101)
XLIII	2-1-09	Pittsburgh ($78,000)	Arizona ($40,000)	27–23	Tampa (70,774)
XLIV	2-7-10	New Orleans ($83,000)	Indianapolis ($42,000)	31–17	Miami (74,059)

Most Valuable Players

Super Bowl	Player/ Team	Position	Super Bowl	Player/ Team	Position
I	Bart Starr, GB	QB	XXIII	Jerry Rice, SF	WR
II	Bart Starr, GB	QB	XXIV	Joe Montana, SF	QB
III	Joe Namath, NYJ	QB	XXV	Ottis Anderson, NYG	RB
IV	Len Dawson, KC	QB	XXVI	Mark Rypien, Wash	QB
V	Chuck Howley, Dal	LB	XXVII	Troy Aikman, Dal	QB
VI	Roger Staubach, Dal	QB	XXVIII	Emmitt Smith, Dal	RB
VII	Jake Scott, Mia	S	XXIX	Steve Young, SF	QB
VIII	Larry Csonka, Mia	RB	XXX	Larry Brown, Dal	CB
IX	Franco Harris, Pit	RB	XXXI	Desmond Howard, GB	KR
X	Lynn Swann, Pit	WR	XXXII	Terrell Davis, Den	RB
XI	Fred Biletnikoff, Oak	WR	XXXIII	John Elway, Den	QB
XII	Randy White/Harvey Martin, Dal	DT/DE	XXXIV	Kurt Warner, StL	QB
XIII	Terry Bradshaw, Pit	QB	XXXV	Ray Lewis, Balt	LB
XIV	Terry Bradshaw, Pit	QB	XXXVI	Tom Brady, NE	QB
XV	Jim Plunkett, Oak	QB	XXXVII	Dexter Jackson, TB	S
XVI	Joe Montana, SF	QB	XXXVIII	Tom Brady, NE	QB
XVII	John Riggins, Wash	RB	XXXIX	Deion Branch, NE	WR
XVIII	Marcus Allen, LA Rai	RB	XL	Hines Ward, Pit	WR
XIX	Joe Montana, SF	QB	XLI	Peyton Manning, Ind	QB
XX	Richard Dent, Chi	DE	XLII	Eli Manning, NYG	QB
XXI	Phil Simms, NYG	QB	XLIII	Santonio Holmes, Pit	WR
XXII	Doug Williams, Wash	QB	XLIV	Drew Brees, NO	QB

Composite Standings, by Win Percentage

	W	L	Pct	Pts	Opp Pts
San Francisco 49ers	5	0	1.000	188	89
Tampa Bay Buccaneers	1	0	1.000	48	21
Baltimore Ravens	1	0	1.000	34	7
New Orleans Saints	1	0	1.000	34	17
New York Jets	1	0	1.000	16	7
Pittsburgh Steelers	6	1	.857	168	133
Green Bay Packers	3	1	.750	127	76
New York Giants	3	1	.750	83	87
Dallas Cowboys	5	3	.625	221	132
Oakland/LA Raiders	3	2	.600	132	114
Washington Redskins	3	2	.600	122	103
New England Patriots	3	3	.500	121	165
Baltimore/Indianapolis Colts	2	2	.500	69	77
Chicago Bears	1	1	.500	63	39
Kansas City Chiefs	1	1	.500	33	42
Miami Dolphins	2	3	.400	74	103
Denver Broncos	2	4	.333	115	206
Los Angeles/St. Louis Rams	1	2	.333	59	67
Carolina Panthers	0	1	.000	29	32
San Diego Chargers	0	1	.000	26	49
Arizona Cardinals	0	1	.000	23	27
Atlanta Falcons	0	1	.000	19	34
Tennessee Titans	0	1	.000	16	23
Seattle Seahawks	0	1	.000	10	21
Cincinnati Bengals	0	2	.000	37	46
Philadelphia Eagles	0	2	.000	31	51
Buffalo Bills	0	4	.000	73	139
Minnesota Vikings	0	4	.000	34	95

Career Leaders

Passing

	GP	Att	Comp	Pct Comp	Yds	Avg Gain/ Att	TD	Pct TD	Int	Pct Int	Lg	Rating Pts
Joe Montana, SF	4	122	83	68.0	1142	9.36	11	9.0	0	0.0	44	127.8
Jim Plunkett, Oak/LA Rai.	2	46	29	63.0	433	9.41	4	8.7	0	0.0	t80	122.8
Terry Bradshaw, Pit	4	84	49	58.3	932	11.10	9	10.7	4	4.8	t75	112.8
Troy Aikman, Dal	3	80	56	70.0	689	8.61	5	6.3	1	1.3	t56	111.9
Bart Starr, GB	2	47	29	61.7	452	9.62	3	6.4	1	2.1	t62	106.0
Brett Favre, GB	2	69	39	56.5	502	7.28	5	7.2	1	1.4	t81	97.7
Kurt Warner, StL, Ari	3	132	83	62.9	1156	8.76	6	4.5	3	2.3	t73	96.7
Roger Staubach, Dal	4	98	61	62.2	734	7.49	8	8.2	4	4.1	t45	95.4
Tom Brady, NE	4	156	100	64.1	1001	6.42	7	4.5	1	0.1	52	94.5
Peyton Manning, Ind	2	83	58	67.5	580	6.99	2	2.4	2	2.4	t53	85.4
Len Dawson, KC	2	44	28	63.6	353	8.02	2	4.5	2	4.5	t46	84.8

Note: Minimum 40 attempts.

Rushing Yards

	GP	Yds	Att	Avg	Lg	TD
Franco Harris, Pit	4	354	101	3.5	25	4
Larry Csonka, Mia	3	297	57	5.2	49	2
Emmitt Smith, Dal	3	289	70	4.1	38	5
Terrell Davis, Den	2	259	55	4.7	27	3
John Riggins, Was	2	230	64	3.6	43	2
Timmy Smith, Was	1	204	22	9.3	58	2
Thurman Thomas, Buf	4	204	52	3.9	31	4
Roger Craig, SF	3	217	44	4.9	20	3
Marcus Allen, LA Rai	1	191	20	9.6	t74	2
Antowain Smith, NE	2	175	44	4.0	17	1

t-scored touchdown

Receptions

	GP	No.	Yds	Avg	Lg	TD
Jerry Rice, SF	4	33	589	17.9	t48	8
Andre Reed, Buf	4	27	323	12.0	40	0
Roger Craig, SF	3	20	212	10.6	40	2
Deion Branch, NE	2	21	276	13.1	52	1
Thurman Thomas, Buf	4	20	144	7.2	24	0
Jay Novacek, Dal	3	17	148	8.7	23	2
Joseph Addai, Ind	2	17	124	7.3	17	0
Lynn Swann, Pit	4	16	364	22.8	t74	3
Michael Irvin, Dal	3	16	256	16.0	25	2
Troy Brown, NE	3	16	182	11.4	23	0

Single-Game Leaders

Scoring

	Pts
Roger Craig: XIX, San Francisco vs Miami (1 rush, 2 rec)	18
Jerry Rice: XXIV, San Francisco vs Denver (3 rec); XXIX, SF vs San Diego (3 rec)	18
Ricky Watters: XXIX, San Francisco vs San Diego (1 rush, 2 rec)	18
Terrell Davis: XXXII, Denver vs Green Bay (3 rec)	18

Rushing Yards

	Yds
Timmy Smith: XXII, Washington vs Denver	204
Marcus Allen: XVIII, LA Raiders vs Washington	191
John Riggins: XVII, Washington vs Miami	166
Franco Harris: IX, Pittsburgh vs Minnesota	158
Terrell Davis: XXXII, Denver vs Green Bay	157
Larry Csonka: VIII, Miami vs Minnesota	145
Clarence Davis: XI, Oakland vs Minnesota	137
Thurman Thomas: XXV, Buffalo vs NY Giants	135
Emmitt Smith: XXVIII, Dallas vs Buffalo	132
Michael Pittman: XXXVII, Tampa Bay vs Oakland	124

Receptions

	No.
Deion Branch: XXXIX, New England vs Phila.	11
Jerry Rice: XXIII, San Francisco vs Cincinnati	11
Dan Ross: XVI, Cincinnati vs San Francisco	11
Wes Welker: XLII, New England vs NY Giants	11
Joseph Addai: XLI, Indianapolis vs Chicago	10
Deion Branch: XXXVIII, New England vs Carolina	10
Andre Hastings: XXX, Pittsburgh vs Dallas	10
Tony Nathan: XIX, Miami vs San Francisco	10
Jerry Rice: XXIX, San Francisco vs San Diego	10
Antonio Freeman: XXXII, Green Bay vs Denver	9
Santonio Holmes: XLIII, Pittsburgh vs Arizona	9
Terrell Owens: XXXIX, Philadelphia vs New England	9
Ricky Sanders: XXII, Washington vs Denver	9
Eight tied with eight.	

Touchdown Passes

	No.
Steve Young: XXIX, San Francisco vs San Diego	6
Joe Montana: XXIV, San Francisco vs Denver	5
Terry Bradshaw: XIII, Pittsburgh vs Dallas	4
Doug Williams: XXII, Washington vs Denver	4
Troy Aikman: XXVII, Dallas vs Buffalo	4
Eight tied with three.	

Passing Yards

	Yds
Kurt Warner: XXXIV, St. Louis vs Tennessee	414
Kurt Warner: XLIII, Arizona vs Pittsburgh	377
Kurt Warner: XXXVI, St. Louis vs New England	365
Joe Montana: XXIII, San Francisco vs Cincinnati	357
Donovan McNabb: XXXIX, Phila. vs. New England	357
Tom Brady: XXXVIII, New England vs Carolina	354
Doug Williams: XXII, Washington vs Denver	340
John Elway: XXXIII, Denver vs Atlanta	336
Peyton Manning: XLIV, Indianapolis vs New Orl'ns	333
Joe Montana: XIX, San Francisco vs Miami	331
Steve Young: XXIX, San Francisco vs San Diego	325
Jake Delhomme: XXXVIII Carolina vs New England	323
Terry Bradshaw: XIII, Pittsburgh vs Dallas	318
Dan Marino: XIX, Miami vs San Francisco	318

Receiving Yards

	Yds
Jerry Rice: XXIII, San Francisco vs Cincinnati	215
Ricky Sanders: XXII, Washington vs Denver	193
Isaac Bruce: XXXIV, St. Louis vs Tennessee	162
Lynn Swann: X, Pittsburgh vs Dallas	161
Andre Reed: XXVII, Buffalo vs Dallas	152
Rod Smith: XXXIII, Denver vs Atlanta	152
Jerry Rice: XXIX, San Francisco vs San Diego	149
Jerry Rice: XXIV, San Francisco vs Denver	148
Deion Branch: XXXVIII, New England vs Carolina	143

Super Bowl History Recaps*

I - 1967

Green Bay	7	7	14	7—35
Kansas City	0	10	0	0—10

FIRST QUARTER: GB: McGee 37 pass from Starr (Chandler kick), 8:56. **Green Bay 7-0.**

SECOND QUARTER: KC: McClinton 7 pass from Dawson (Mercer kick), 4:20. **7-7.**
GB: Taylor 14 run (Chandler kick), 10:23. **Green Bay 14-7.**
KC: FG Mercer 31, 14:06. **Green Bay 14-10.**

THIRD QUARTER: GB: Pitts 5 run (Chandler kick), 2:27. **Green Bay 21-10.**
GB: McGee 13 pass from Starr (Chandler kick), 14:09. **Green Bay 28-10.**

FOURTH QUARTER: GB: Pitts 1 run (Chandler kick), 8:25. **Green Bay 35-10.**

A: 61,946.

II - 1968

Green Bay	3	13	10	7—33
Oakland	0	7	0	7—14

FIRST QUARTER: GB: FG Chandler 39 5:07. **Green Bay 3-0.**

SECOND QUARTER: GB: FG Chandler, 20, 3:08. **Green Bay 6-0.**
GB: Dowler 62 pass from Starr (Chandler kick), 4:10. **Green Bay 13-0.**

SECOND QUARTER (CONT.): Oak: Miller 23 pass from Lamonica (Blanda kick), 8:45. **Green Bay 13-7.**
GB: FG Chandler 43, 14:59. **Green Bay 16-7.**

THIRD QUARTER: GB: Anderson 2 run (Chandler kick), 9:06. **Green Bay 23-7.**
GB: FG Chandler 31, 14:58. **Green Bay 26-7.**

FOURTH QUARTER:
GB: Adderley 60 int return (Chandler kick), 3:57. **Green Bay 33-7.**
Oak: Miller 23 pass from Lamonica (Blanda kick), 5:47. **Green Bay 33-14.**

A: 75,546.

*From 1967 to 1999, Super Bowl scoring times indicate the time elapsed in each quarter. Starting in 2000, times listed give the time remaining in each quarter.

III - 1969

NY Jets	0	7	6	3—16
Baltimore	0	0	0	7—7

SECOND QUARTER: Jets: Snell 4 run (Turner kick), 5:57. **Jets: 7-0.**

THIRD QUARTER: Jets: FG Turner 32, 4:52. **Jets: 10-0.** Jets: FG Turner 30, 11:02. **Jets: 13-0.**

FOURTH QUARTER: Jets: FG Turner 9, 1:34. **Jets: 16-0.** Balt: Hill 1 run (Michaels kick), 11:41. **Jets: 16-7.** A: 75,389.

IV - 1970

Kansas City	3	13	7	0—23
Minnesota	0	0	7	0—7

FIRST QUARTER: KC: FG Stenerud 48, 8:08. **Kansas City 3-0.**

SECOND QUARTER: KC: FG Stenerud 32, 1:40. **Kansas City 6-0.** KC: FG Stenerud 25, 7:08. **Kansas City 9-0.** KC: Garrett 5 run (Stenerud kick), 9:26. **Kansas City 16-0.**

THIRD QUARTER: Minn: Osborn 4 run (Cox kick), 10:28. **Kansas City 16-7.** KC: Taylor 46 pass from Dawson (Stenerud kick), 13:38. **Kansas City 23-7.** A: 80,562.

V - 1971

Baltimore	0	6	0	10—16
Dallas	3	10	0	0—13

FIRST QUARTER: Dal (9:28): FG Clark 14, 9:28. **Dallas 3-0.**

SECOND QUARTER: Dal: FG Clark 30, 0:08. **Dallas 6-0.** Balt: Mackey 75 pass from Unitas (kick blocked). 0:50. **6-6.** Dal: Thomas 7 pass from Morton (Clark kick), 7:07. **Dallas 13-6.**

FOURTH QUARTER: Balt: Nowatzke 2 run (O'Brien kick), 7:25. **13-13.** Balt: FG O'Brien 32, 14:55. **Baltimore 16-13.** A: 79,204.

VI - 1972

Dallas	3	7	7	7—24
Miami	0	3	0	0—3

FIRST QUARTER: Dal: FG Clark 9, 13:37. **Dallas 3-0.**

SECOND QUARTER: Dal: Alworth 7 pass from Staubach (Clark kick), 13:45. **Dallas 10-0.** Mia: FG Yepremian, 31, 14:56. **Dallas 10-3.**

THIRD QUARTER: Dal: D. Thomas 3 run (Clark kick), 5:17. **Dallas 17-3.**

FOURTH QUARTER: Dal: Ditka 7 pass from Staubach (Clark kick), 3:18. **Dallas 24-3.** A: 81,023.

VII - 1973

Miami	7	7	0	0—14
Washington	0	0	0	7—7

FIRST QUARTER: Mia: Twilley 28 pass from Griese (Yepremian kick), 14:59. **Miami 7-0.**

SECOND QUARTER: Mia: Kiick 1 run (Yepremian kick), 14:42. **Miami 14-0.**

FOURTH QUARTER: Wash: Bass 49 fumble recovery return (Knight kick), 12:53. **Miami 14-7.** A: 90,182.

VIII - 1974

Miami	14	3	7	0—24
Minnesota	0	0	0	7—7

FIRST QUARTER: Mia: Csonka 5 run (Yepremian kick), 5:27. **Miami 7-0.** Mia: Kiick 1 run (Yepremian kick), 13:38. **Miami 14-0.**

SECOND QUARTER: Mia: FG Yepremian 28, 8:58. **Miami 17-0.**

THIRD QUARTER: Mia: Csonka 2 run (Yepremian kick), 6:16. **Miami 24-0.**

FOURTH QUARTER: Minn: Tarkenton 4 run (Cox kick), 1:35. **Miami 24-7.** A: 71,882.

IX - 1975

Pittsburgh	0	2	7	7—16
Minnesota	0	0	0	6—6

SECOND QUARTER: Pit: White tackled Tarkenton for safety, 7:49. **Pittsburgh 2-0.**

THIRD QUARTER: Pit: Harris 9 run (Gerela kick), 1:35. **Pittsburgh 9-0.**

FOURTH QUARTER: Minn: T. Brown recovered blocked punt in end zone (kick failed), 4:27. **Pittsburgh 9-6.** Pit: L. Brown 4 pass from Bradshaw (Gerela kick), 11:29. **Pittsburgh 16-6.** A: 80,997.

X - 1976

Pittsburgh	7	0	0	14—21
Dallas	7	3	0	7—17

FIRST QUARTER: Dal: D. Pearson 29 pass from Staubach (Fritsch kick), 4:36. **Dallas 7-0.** Pit: Grossman 7 pass from Bradshaw (Gerela kick), 9:03. **7-7.**

SECOND QUARTER: Dal: FG Fritsch 36, 0:15. **Dallas 10-7.**

FOURTH QUARTER: Pit: Harrison blocked Hoopes's punt for safety, 3:32. **Dallas 10-9.** Pit: FG Gerela 36, 6:19. **Pittsburgh 12-10.** Pit: FG Gerela 18, 8:32. **Pittsburgh 15-10.** Pit: Swann 64 pass from Bradshaw (kick failed), 11:58. **Pittsburgh 21-10.** Dal: P. Howard 34 pass from Staubach (Fritsch kick), 13:12. **Pittsburgh 21-17.** A: 80,187.

XI - 1977

Oakland	0	16	3	13—32
Minnesota	0	0	7	7—14

SECOND QUARTER: Oak: FG Mann, 24, 0:48. **Oakland 3-0.** Oak: Casper 1 pass from Stabler (Mann kick), 7:50. **Oakland 10-0.** Oak: Banaszak 1 run (kick failed), 11:27. **Oakland 16-0.**

THIRD QUARTER: Oak: FG Mann, 40, 9:44. **Oakland 19-0.** Min: S. White 8 pass from Tarkenton (Cox kick), 14:13. **Oakland 19-7.**

FOURTH QUARTER: Oak: Banaszak 2 run (Mann kick), 7:21. **Oakland 26-7.** Oak: Brown 75 int return (kick failed), 9:17. **Oakland 32-7.** Min: Voigt 13 pass from Lee (Cox kick), 14:35. **Oakland 32-14.** A: 103,438.

XII - 1978

Dallas	10	3	7	7—27
Denver	0	0	10	0—10

FIRST QUARTER: FIRST QUARTER: Dal: Dorsett 3 run (Herrera kick), 10:31. **Dallas 7-0.**
Dal: FG Herrera 35, 13:29. **Dallas 10-0.**

SECOND QUARTER: Dal: FG Herrera 43, 3:44. **Dallas 13-0.**

THIRD QUARTER: Den: FG Turner 47, 2:28. **Dallas 13-3.**
Dal: Johnson 45 pass from Staubach (Herrera kick), 8:01. **Dallas 20-3.**
Den: Lytle 1 run (Turner kick), 9:21. **Dallas 20-10.**

FOURTH QUARTER: Dal: Richards 29 pass from Newhouse (Herrera kick), 7:56. **Dallas 27-10.**

A: 76,400.

XIII - 1979

Pittsburgh	7	14	0	14—35
Dallas	7	7	3	14—31

FIRST QUARTER: Pit: Stallworth 28 pass from Bradshaw (Gerela kick), 5:13. **Pittsburgh 7-0.**
Dal: Hill 39 pass from Staubach (Septien kick), 15:00. **7-7.**

SECOND QUARTER: Dal: Hegman 37 fumble recovery return (Septien kick), 2:52. **Dallas 14-7.**
Pit: Stallworth 75 pass from Bradshaw (Gerela kick), 4:35. **14-14.**
Pit: Bleier 7 pass from Bradshaw (Gerela kick), 14:34. **Pittsburgh 21-14.**

THIRD QUARTER: Dal: FG Septien 27, 12:24. **Pittsburgh 21-17.**

FOURTH QUARTER: Pit: Harris 22 run (Gerela kick), 7:50. **Pittsburgh 28-17.**
Pit: Swann 18 pass from Bradshaw (Gerela kick), 8:09. **Pittsburgh 35-17.**
Dal: DuPree 7 pass from Staubach (Septien kick), 12:33. **Pittsburgh 35-24.**
Dal: B. Johnson 4 pass from Staubach (Septien kick), 14:38. **Pittsburgh 35-31.**

A: 79,484.

XIV - 1980

Pittsburgh	3	7	7	14—31
LA Rams	7	6	6	0—19

FIRST QUARTER: Pit: FG Bahr, 41, 7:29. **Pittsburgh 3-0.**
LA: Bryant 1 run (Corral kick), 12:16. **LA Rams 7-3.**

SECOND QUARTER: Pit: Harris 1 run (Bahr kick), 2:08. **Pittsburgh 10-7.**
LA: FG Corral 31, 7:39. **10-10.**
LA: FG Corral 45, 14:46. **LA Rams 13-10.**

THIRD QUARTER: Pit: Swann 47 pass from Bradshaw (Bahr kick), 2:48. **Pittsburgh 17-13.**
LA: Smith 24 pass from McCutcheon (kick failed), 4:45. **LA Rams 19-17.**

FOURTH QUARTER: Pit: Stallworth 73 pass from Bradshaw (Bahr kick), 2:56. **Pittsburgh 24-19.**
Pit: Harris 1 run (Bahr kick), 13:11. **Pittsburgh 31-19.**

A: 103,985.

XV - 1981

Oakland	14	0	10	3—27
Philadelphia	0	3	0	7—10

FIRST QUARTER: Oak: Branch 2 pass from Plunkett (Bahr kick), 6:04. **Oakland 7-0.**
Oak: King 80 pass from Plunkett (Bahr kick), 14:51. **Oakland 14-0.**

SECOND QUARTER: Phi: FG Franklin 30, 4:32. **Oakland 14-3.**

THIRD QUARTER: Oak: Branch 29 pass from Plunkett (Bahr kick), 2:36. **Oakland 21-3.**
Oak: FG Bahr 46, 10:25. **Oakland 24-3.**

FOURTH QUARTER: Phi: Krepfle 8 pass from Jaworski (Franklin kick), 1:01. **Oakland 24-10.**
Oak: FG Bahr, 35, 6:31. **Oakland 27-10.**

A: 76,135.

XVI - 1982

San Francisco	7	13	0	6—26
Cincinnati	0	0	7	14—21

FIRST QUARTER: SF: Montana 1 run (Wersching kick), 9:08. **San Francisco 7-0.**

SECOND QUARTER: SF: E. Cooper 11 pass from Montana (Wersching kick), 8:07. **San Francisco 14-0.**
SF: FG Wersching 22, 14:45. **San Francisco 17-0.**
SF: FG Wersching 26, 14:58. **San Francisco 20-0.**

THIRD QUARTER: Cin: Anderson 5 run (Breech kick), 3:35. **San Francisco 20-7.**

FOURTH QUARTER: Cin: Ross 4 pass from Anderson (Breech kick), 4:54. **San Francisco 20-14.**
SF: FG Wersching 40, 9:35. **San Francisco 23-14.**
SF: FG Wersching 23, 13:03. **San Francisco 26-14.**
Cin: Ross 3 pass from Anderson (Breech kick), 14:44. **San Francisco 26-21.**

A: 81,270.

XVII - 1983

Washington	0	10	3	14—27
Miami	7	10	0	0—17

FIRST QUARTER: Mia: Cefalo 76 pass from Woodley (Von Schamann kick), 6:49. **Miami 7-0.**

SECOND QUARTER: Wash: FG Moseley 31, 0:21. **Miami 7-3.**
Mia: FG Von Schamann 20, 9:00. **Miami 10-3.**
Wash: Garrett 4 pass from Theismann (Moseley kick), 13:09. **10-10.**
Mia: Walker 98 kick return (Von Schamann kick), 13:22. **Miami 17-10.**

THIRD QUARTER: Wash: FG Moseley 20, 6:51. **Miami 17-13.**

FOURTH QUARTER: Wash: Riggins 43 run (Moseley kick), 4:59. **Washington 20-17.**
Wash: Brown 6 pass from Theismann (Moseley kick), 13:05. **Washington 27-17.**

A: 103,667.

XVIII - 1984

LA Raiders	7	14	14	3—38
Washington	0	3	6	0—9

FIRST QUARTER: LA: Jensen 0 blocked punt return (Bahr kick), 4:52. **LA Raiders 7-0.**

SECOND QUARTER: LA: Branch 12 pass from Plunkett (Bahr kick), 5:46. **LA Raiders 14-0.**
Wash: FG Moseley 24, 11:55. **LA Raiders 14-3.**
LA: Squirek 5 int return (Bahr kick), 14:53. **LA Raiders 21-3.**

THIRD QUARTER: Wash: Riggins 1 run (kick blocked), 4:08. **LA Raiders 21-9.**
LA: Allen 5 run (Bahr kick), 7:54. **LA Raiders 28-9.**
LA: Allen 74 run (Bahr kick), 15:00. **LA Raiders 35-9.**

FOURTH QUARTER: LA: FG Bahr 21, 12:36. **LA Raiders 38-9.**
A: 72,920.

XIX - 1985

San Francisco	7	21	10	0—38
Miami	10	6	0	0—16

FIRST QUARTER: Mia: FG Von Schamann 37, 7:36. **Miami 3-0.**
SF: Monroe 33 pass from Montana (Wersching kick), 11:48. **San Francisco 7-3.**
Mia: D. Johnson 2 pass from Marino (Von Schamann kick), 14:15. **Miami 10-7.**

SECOND QUARTER: SF: Craig 8 pass from Montana (Wersching kick), 3:26. **San Francisco 14-10.**
SF: Montana 6 run (Wersching kick), 8:02. **San Francisco 21-10.**
SF: Craig 2 run (Wersching kick), 12:55. **San Francisco 28-10.**
Mia: FG Von Schamann 31, 14:48. **San Francisco 28-13.**
Mia: FG Von Schamann 30, 15:00. **San Francisco 28-16.**

THIRD QUARTER: SF: FG Wersching 27, 4:48. **San Francisco 31-16.**
SF: Craig 16 pass from Montana (Wershing kick), 8:42. **San Francisco 38-16.**
A: 84,059.

XX - 1986

Chicago	13	10	21	2—46
New England	3	0	0	7—10

FIRST QUARTER: NE: FG Franklin 36, 1:19. **New England 3-0.**
Chi: FG Butler 28, 5:40. **3-3.**
Chi: FG Butler 24, 13:34. **Chicago 6-3.**
Chi: Suhey 11 run (Butler kick), 14:37. **Chicago 13-3.**

SECOND QUARTER: Chi: McMahon 2 run (Butler kick), 7:36. **Chicago 20-3.**
Chi: FG Butler 24, 15:00. **Chicago 23-3.**

THIRD QUARTER: Chi: McMahon 1 run (Butler kick), 7:38. **Chicago 30-3.**
Chi: Phillips 28 int return (Butler kick), 8:44. **Chicago 37-3.**
Chi: Perry 1 run (Butler kick), 11:38. **Chicago 44-3.**

FOURTH QUARTER: NE: Fryar 8 pass from Grogan (Franklin kick), 1:46. **Chicago 44-10.**
Chi: Waechter safety, 9:24. **Chicago 46-10.**

A: 73,818.

XXI - 1987

NY Giants	7	2	17	13—39
Denver	10	0	0	10—20

FIRST QUARTER: Den: FG Karlis 48, 4:09. **Denver 3-0.**
NYG: Mowatt 6 pass from Simms (Allegre kick), 9:33. **NY Giants 7-3.**
Den: Elway 4 run (Karlis kick), 12:54. **Denver 10-7.**

SECOND QUARTER: NYG: Martin safety, 12:14. **Denver 10-9.**

THIRD QUARTER: NYG: Bavaro 13 pass from Simms (Allegre kick), 4:52. **NY Giants 16-10.**
NYG: FG Allegre 21, 11:06. **NY Giants 19-10.**
NYG: Morris 1 run (Allegre kick), 14:36. **NY Giants 26-10.**

FOURTH QUARTER: NYG: McConkey 6 pass from Simms (Allegre kick), 4:04. **NY Giants 33-10.**
Den: FG Karlis 28, 8:59. **NY Giants 33-13.**
NYG: Anderson 2 run (kick failed), 11:42. **NY Giants 39-13.**
Den: Johnson 47 pass from Elway (Karlis kick), 12:54. **NY Giants 39-20.**

A: 101,063.

XXII - 1988

Washington	0	35	0	7—42
Denver	10	0	0	0—10

FIRST QUARTER: Den: Nattiel 56 pass from Elway (Karlis kick), 1:57. **Denver 7-0.**
Den: FG Karlis 24, 5:51. **Denver 10-0.**

SECOND QUARTER: Wash: Sanders 80 pass from D. Williams (Haji-Sheikh kick), 0:53. **Denver 10-7.**
Wash: Clark 27 pass from D. Williams (Haji-Sheikh kick), 4:45. **Washington 14-10.**
Wash: Smith 58 run (Haji-Sheikh kick), 8:33. **Washington 21-10.**
Wash: Sanders 50 pass from D. Williams (Haji-Sheikh kick), 11:18. **Washington 28-10.**
Wash: Didier 8 pass from D. Williams (Haji-Sheikh kick), 13:56. **Washington 35-10.**

FOURTH QUARTER: Wash: Smith 4 run (Haji-Sheikh kick), 1:51. **Washington 42-10.**

A: 73,302.

XXIII - 1989

San Francisco	3	0	3	14—20
Cincinnati	0	3	10	3—16

FIRST QUARTER: SF: FG Cofer 41, 11:46. **San Francisco 3-0.**

SECOND QUARTER: Cin: FG Breech 34, 13:41. **3-3.**

THIRD QUARTER: Cin: FG Breech 43, 9:15. **Cincinnati 6-3.**
SF: FG Cofer 32, 14:10. **6-6.**
Cin: Jennings 93 kick return (Breech kick), 14:26. **Cincinnati 13-6.**

FOURTH QUARTER: SF: Rice 14 pass from Montana (Cofer kick), 0:57. **13-13.**
Cin: FG Breech 40, 11:40. **Cincinnati 16-13.**
SF: Taylor 10 pass from Montana (Cofer kick), 14:26. **San Francisco 20-16.**

A: 75,129.

XXIV - 1990

San Francisco	13	14	14	14—55
Denver	3	0	7	0—10

FIRST QUARTER: SF: Rice 20 pass from Montana (Cofer kick), 4:54. **San Francisco 7-0.**
Den: FG Treadwell 42, 8:13. **San Francisco 7-3.**
SF: Jones 7 pass from Montana (kick failed), 14:57. **San Francisco 13-3.**

SECOND QUARTER: SF: Rathman 1 run (Cofer kick), 7:45. **San Francisco 20-3.**
SF: Rice 38 pass from Montana (Cofer kick), 14:26. **San Francisco 27-3.**

THIRD QUARTER: SF: Rice 28 pass from Montana (Cofer kick), 2:12. **San Francisco 34-3.**
SF: Taylor 35 pass from Montana (Cofer kick), 5:16. **San Francisco 41-3.**
Den: Elway 3 run (Treadwell kick), 8:07. **San Francisco 41-10.**

FOURTH QUARTER: SF: Rathman 3 run (Cofer kick), 0:03. **San Francisco 48-10.**
SF: Craig 1 run (Cofer kick), 1:13. **San Francisco 55-10.**
A: 72,919.

XXV - 1991

NY Giants	3	7	7	3—20
Buffalo	3	9	0	7—19

FIRST QUARTER: NYG: FG Bahr 28, 7:46. **NY Giants 3-0.**
Buff: FG Norwood 23, 9:09. **3-3.**

SECOND QUARTER: Buff: D. Smith 1 run (Norwood kick), 2:30. **Buffalo 10-3.**
Buff: B. Smith safety 0, 6:33. **Buffalo 12-3.**
NYG: Baker 14 pass from Hostetler (Bahr kick), 14:35. **Buffalo 12-10.**

THIRD QUARTER: NYG: Anderson 1 run (Bahr kick), 9:29. **NY Giants 17-12.**

FOURTH QUARTER: Buff: Thomas 31 run (Norwood kick), 0:08. **Buffalo 19-17.**
NYG: FG Bahr 21, 7:40. **NY Giants 20-19.**
A: 73,813.

XXVI - 1992

Washington	0	17	14	6—37
Buffalo	0	0	10	14—24

SECOND QUARTER: Wash: FG Lohmiller 34, 1:58. **Washington 3-0.**
Wash: Byner 10 pass from Rypien (Lohmiller kick), 5:06. **Washington 10-0.**
Wash: Riggs 1 run (Lohmiller kick), 7:43. **Washington 17-0.**

THIRD QUARTER: Wash: Riggs 2 run (Lohmiller kick), 0:16. **Washington 24-0.**
Buff: FG Norwood 21, 3:01. **Washington 24-3.**
Buff: Thomas 1 run (Norwood kick), 9:02. **Washington 24-10.**
Wash: Clark 30 pass from Rypien (Lohmiller kick), 13:36. **Washington 31-10.**

FOURTH QUARTER: Wash: FG Lohmiller 25, 0:06. **Washington 34-10.**
Wash: FG Lohmiller 39, 3:24. **Washington 37-10.**
Buff: Metzelaars 2 pass from Kelly (Norwood kick), 9:01. **Washington 37-17.**
Buff: Beebe 4 pass from Kelly (Norwood kick), 11:05. **Washington 37-24.**
A: 63,130.

XXVII - 1993

Dallas	14	14	3	21—52
Buffalo	7	3	7	0—17

FIRST QUARTER: Buff: Thomas 2 run (Christie kick), 5:00. **Buffalo 7-0.**
Dal: Novacek 23 pass from Aikman (Elliott kick), 13:24. **7-7.**
Dal: J.Jones 2 fumble return (Elliott kick), 13:39. **Dallas 14-7.**

SECOND QUARTER: Buff: FG Christie 21, 11:36. **Dallas 14-10.**
Dal: Irvin 19 pass from Aikman (Elliott kick) 13:06. **Dallas 21-10.**
Dal: Irvin 18 pass from Aikman (Elliott kick), 13:24. **Dallas 28-10.**

THIRD QUARTER: Dal: FG Elliott 20, 6:39. **Dallas 31-10.**
Buff: Beebe 40 pass from Reich (Christie kick), 15:00. **Dallas 31-17.**

FOURTH QUARTER: Dal: Harper 45 pass from Aikman (Elliott kick), 4:56. **Dallas 38-17.**
Dal: E. Smith 10 run (Elliott kick), 6:48. **Dallas 45-17.**
Dal: Norton 9 fumble return (Elliott kick), 7:29. **Dallas 52-17.**
A: 98,374.

XXVIII - 1994

Dallas	6	0	14	10—30
Buffalo	3	10	0	0—13

FIRST QUARTER: Dal: FG Murray 41, 2:19. **Dallas 3-0.**
Buff: FG Christie 54: 4:41. **3-3.**
Dal: FG Murray 24, 11:05. **Dallas 6-3.**

SECOND QUARTER: Buff: Thomas 4 run (Christie kick), 2:34. **Buffalo 10-6.**
Buff: FG Christie 28, 15:00. **Buffalo 13-6.**

THIRD QUARTER: Dal: Washington fumble return (Murray kick), 0:55. **13-13.**
Dal: Smith 15 run (Murray kick), 0:55. **Dallas 20-13.**

FOURTH QUARTER: Dal: Smith 1 run (Murray kick), 5:10. **Dallas 27-13.**
Dal: FG Murray 20, 12:10. **Dallas 30-13.**
A: 72,817.

XXIX - 1995

San Francisco	14	14	14	7—49
San Diego	7	3	8	8—26

FIRST QUARTER: SF: Rice 44 pass from Young (Brien kick), 1:24. **San Francisco 7-0.**
SF: Watters 51 pass from Young (Brien kick, 4:55. **San Francisco 14-0.**
SD: Means 1 run (Carney kick), 12:16. **San Francisco 14-7.**

SECOND QUARTER: SF: Floyd 5 pass from Young (Brien kick), 1:58. **San Francisco 21-7.**
SF: Watters 8 pass from Young (Brien kick), 10:16. **San Francisco 28-7.**
SD: FG Carney 31, 13:16. **San Francisco 28-10.**

THIRD QUARTER: SF: Watters 9 run (Brien kick), 5:25. **San Francisco 35-10.**
SF: Rice 15 pass from Young (Brien kick), 11:42. **San Francisco 42-10.**

XXIX - 1995 *(Cont.)*

THIRD QUARTER *(CONT.):*SD: Coleman 98 kickoff return (Humphries 2-pt conv pass to Seay), 11:59. **San Francisco 42-18.**

FOURTH QUARTER: SF: Rice 7 pass from Young (Brien kick), 1:11. **San Francisco 49-18.**
SD: Martin 30 pass from Humphries (Humphries 2 pt-conv pass to Pupunu), 12:35. **San Francisco 49-26.**
A: 74,107.

XXX - 1996

Dallas	10	3	7	7—27
Pittsburgh	0	7	0	10—17

FIRST QUARTER: Dal: FG Boniol 42, 2:55. **Dallas 3-0.**
Dal: Novacek 3 pass from Aikman (Boniol kick), 9:37. **Dallas 10-0.**

SECOND QUARTER: Dal: FG Boniol 35, 8:57. **Dallas 13-0.**
Pitt: Thigpen 6 pass from O'Donnell (N. Johnson kick), 14:47. **Dallas 13-7.**

THIRD QUARTER: Dal: E. Smith 1 run (Boniol kick), 8:18. **Dallas 20-7.**

FOURTH QUARTER: Pitt: FG N. Johnson 46, 3:40. **Dallas 20-10.**
Pitt: Morris 1 run (N. Johnson kick), 8:24. **Dallas 20-17.**
Dal: E. Smith 4 run (Boniol kick), 11:17. **Dallas 27-17.**

A: 76,347.

XXXI - 1997

Green Bay	10	17	8	0—35
New England	14	0	7	0—21

FIRST QUARTER: GB: Rison 54 pass from Favre (Jacke kick), 3:32. **Green Bay 7-0.**
GB: FG Jacke 37, 6:18. **Green Bay 10-0.**
NE: Byars 1 pass from Bledsoe (Vinatieri kick), 8:25. **Green Bay 10-7.**
NE: Coates 4 pass from Bledsoe (Vinatieri kick), 12:27. **New England 14-10.**

SECOND QUARTER: GB: Freeman 81 pass from Favre (Jacke kick), 0:56. **Green Bay 17-14.**
GB: FG Jacke 31, 6:45. **Green Bay 20-14.**
GB: Favre 2 run (Jacke kick), 13:49. **Green Bay 27-14.**

THIRD QUARTER: NE: Martin 18 run (Vinatieri kick), 11:33. **Green Bay 27-21.**
GB: Howard 99 kickoff return (Favre 2 pt conv pass to Chmura), 11:50. **Green Bay 35-21.**

A: 72,301.

XXXII - 1998

Denver	7	10	7	7—31
Green Bay	7	7	3	7—24

FIRST QUARTER: GB: Freeman 22 pass from Favre (Longwell kick), 4:02. **Green Bay 7-0.**
Den: Davis 1 run (Elam kick), 9:21. **7-7.**

SECOND QUARTER: Den: Elway 1 run (Elam kick), 0:05. **Denver 14-7.**
Den: FG Elam 51, 2:39. **Denver 17-7.**
GB: Chmura 6 pass from Favre (Longwell kick), 14:48. **Denver 17-14.**

THIRD QUARTER: GB: FG Longwell 27, 3:01. **17-17.**
Den: Davis 1 run (Elam kick), 14:26. **Denver 24-17.**

FOURTH QUARTER: GB: Freeman 13 pass from Favre (Longwell kick), 1:28. **24-24.**
Den: Davis 1 run (Elam kick), 13:15. **Denver 31-24.**

A: 68,912.

XXXIII - 1999

Denver	7	10	0	17—34
Atlanta	3	3	0	13—19

FIRST QUARTER: Atl: FG Andersen 32, 5:25. **Atlanta 3-0.**
Den: Griffith 1 run (Elam kick), 11:05. **Denver 7-3.**

SECOND QUARTER: Den: FG Elam 26, 5:43. **Denver 10-3.**
Den: Smith 80 pass from Elway (Elam kick), 10:06. **Denver 17-3.**
Atl: FG Andersen 28, 12:35. **Denver 17-6.**

FOURTH QUARTER: Den: Griffith 1 run (Elam kick), 0:04. **Denver 24-6.**
Den: Elway 3 run (Elam kick), 3:40. **Denver 31-6.**
Atl: Dwight 94 kickoff return (Andersen kick), 3:59. **Denver 31-13.**
Den: FG Elam 37, 7:52. **Denver 34-13.**
Atl: Mathis 3 pass from Chandler (2-pt conv failed), 12:56. **Denver 34-19.**

A: 74,803.

XXXIV - 2000

St. Louis	3	6	7	7—23
Tennessee	0	0	6	10—16

FIRST QUARTER: StL: FG Wilkins 27, 3:00. **St. Louis 3-0.**

SECOND QUARTER: StL: FG Wilkins 29, 4:16. **St. Louis 6-0.**
StL: FG Wilkins 28, 0:15. **St. Louis 9-0.**

THIRD QUARTER: StL: Holt 9 pass from Warner (Wilkins kick), 7:20. **St. Louis 16-0.**
Tenn: George 1 run (2-pt conv failed), 0:14. **St. Louis 16-6.**

FOURTH QUARTER: Tenn: George 2 run (Del Greco kick), 7:21. **St. Louis 16-13.**
Tenn: FG Del Greco 43, 2:15. **16-16.**
StL: Bruce 73 pass from Warner, 1:54. **St. Louis 23-16.**

A: 72,265.

XXXV - 2001

Baltimore	7	3	14	10—34
NY Giants	0	0	7	0—7

FIRST QUARTER: Balt: Stokely 38 pass from Dilfer (Stover kick), 6:50. **Baltimore 7-0.**

SECOND QUARTER: Balt: FG Stover 47, 1:41. **Baltimore 10-0.**

THIRD QUARTER: Balt: Starks 49 int return (Stover kick), 3:49. **Baltimore 17-0.**
NYG: Dixon 97 kickoff return (Daluiso kick), 3:31. **Baltimore 17-7.**
Balt: Je. Lewis 84 kickoff return (Stover kick), 3:13. **Baltimore 24-7.**

FOURTH QUARTER: Balt: Ja. Lewis 3 run (Stover kick), 8:45. **Baltimore 31-7.**
Balt: FG Stover 34, 5:28. **Baltimore 34-7.**
A: 71,921.

XXXVI - 2002

New England	0	14	3	3—20
St. Louis	3	0	0	14—17

FIRST QUARTER: StL: FG Wilkins 50, 3:50. **St. Louis 3-0.**

SECOND QUARTER: NE: Law 47 int return (Vinatieri kick), 8:49. **New England 7-3.**
NE: Patten 8 pass from Brady (Vinatieri kick), 0:31. **New England 14-3.**

THIRD QUARTER: NE: FG Vinatieri 37, 1:18. **New Eng. 17-3.**

FOURTH QUARTER: StL: Warner 2 run (Wilkins kick), 9:31. **New England 17-10.**
StL: Proehl 26 pass from Warner (Wilkins kick), 1:30. **17-17.**
NE: FG Vinatieri 48, 0:00. **New England 20-17.**
A: 72,922.

XXXVII - 2003

Tampa Bay	3	17	14	14—48
Oakland	3	0	6	12—21

FIRST QUARTER: Oak: FG Janikowski 40, 10:20. **Oakland 3-0.**
TB: FG Gramatica 31, 7:51. **3-3.**

SECOND QUARTER: TB: FG Gramatica 43, 11:16. **Tampa Bay 6-3.**
TB: Alstott 2 run (Gramatica kick), 6:24. **Tampa Bay 13-3.**
TB: McCardell 5 pass from B. Johnson (Gramatica kick), 0:30. **Tampa Bay 20-3.**

THIRD QUARTER: TB: McCardell 8 pass from B. Johnson (Gramatica kick), 5:30. **Tampa Bay 27-3.**
TB: Smith 44 int. return (Gramatica kick), 4:47. **Tampa Bay 34-3.**
Oak: Porter 39 pass from Gannon (2-pt conv failed), 2:14. **Tampa Bay 34-9.**

FOURTH QUARTER: Oak: Johnson 13 return of blocked punt (two-pt. conversion failed), 14:14. **Tampa Bay 34-15.**
Oak: Rice 48 pass from Gannon (2-pt conv failed), 6:06. **Tampa Bay 34-21.**
TB: Brooks 44 int. return (Gramatica kick), 1:18. **Tampa Bay 41-21.**
TB: Smith 50 int. return (Gramatica kick), 0:02. **Tampa Bay 48-21.**
A: 67,603.

XXXVIII - 2004

New England	0	14	0	18—32
Carolina	0	10	0	19—29

SECOND QUARTER: NE: Branch 5 pass from Brady (Vinatieri kick), 3:11. **New England 7-0.**
Car: Smith 39 pass from Delhomme (Kasay kick), 1:17. **7-7.**
NE: Givens 5 pass from Brady (Vinatieri kick), 0:28. **New England 14-7.**
Car: FG Kasay 50, 0:00. **New England 14-10.**

FOURTH QUARTER: NE: Smith 2 run (Vinatieri kick), 14:49. **New England 21-10.**
Car: Foster 33 run (2-pt conv failed), 12:49. **New England 21-16.**
Car: Muhammad 85 pass from Delhomme (2-pt conv failed), 7:13. **Carolina 22-21.**
NE: Vrabel 1 pass from Brady (Faulk ran for 2-pt conv), 2:51. **New England 29-22.**
Car: Proehl 12 pass from Delhomme (Kasay kick), 1:18. **29-29.**
NE: FG Vinatieri 41, 0:04. **New England 32-29.**

A: 71,525.

XXXIX - 2005

New England	0	7	7	10—24
Philadelphia	0	7	7	7—21

SECOND QUARTER: Phil: Smith 6 pass from McNabb (Akers kick), 10:05. **Philadelphia 7-0.**
NE: Givens 4 pass from Brady (Vinatieri kick), 1:10. **7-7.**

THIRD QUARTER: NE: Vrabel 2 pass from Brady (Vinatieri kick), 11:04. **New England 14-7.**
Phil: Westbrook 10 pass from McNabb (Akers kick), 3:45. **14-14.**

FOURTH QUARTER: NE: Dillon 2 run (Vinatieri kick), 1:16. **New England 21-14.**
NE: FG Vinatieri 22, 6:20. **New England 24-14.**
Phil: Lewis 30 pass from McNabb (Akers kick), 13:12. **New England 24-21.**

A: 78,125.

XL - 2006

Pittsburgh	0	7	7	7—21
Seattle	3	0	7	0—10

FIRST QUARTER: Sea: FG Brown 47, 0:22. **Seattle 3-0.**

SECOND QUARTER: Pit: Roethlisberger 1 run (Reed kick), 1:55. **Pittsburgh 7-3.**

THIRD QUARTER: Pit: Parker 75 run (Reed kick), 14:38. **Pittsburgh 14-3.**
Sea: Stevens 16 pass from Hasselbeck (Brown kick), 6:45. **Pittsburgh 14-10.**

FOURTH QUARTER: Pit: Ward 43 pass from Randle El (Reed kick), 8:56. **Pittsburgh 21-10.**

A: 68,206.

XLI - 2007

Indianapolis	6	10	6	7—29
Chicago	14	0	3	0—17

FIRST QUARTER: Chicago: TD Hester 92 kick return (Gould kick)14:46. **Chicago 7-0.**
Indianapolis: TD Wayne 53 pass from Manning, 6:50 (Vinatieri kick failed). **Chicago 7-6.**
Chicago: TD Muhammad 4 pass from Grossman (Gould kick), 4:34. **Chicago 14-6.**

SECOND QUARTER: Indianapolis: FG Vinatieri 29, 11:17. **Chicago 14-9.**
Indianapolis: TD Rhodes 1 run (Vinatieri kick), 6:09. **Indianapolis 16-14.**

THIRD QUARTER: Indianapolis: FG Vinatieri 24, 7:26. **Indianapolis 19-14.**
Indianapolis: FG Vinatieri 20, 3:16. **Indianapolis 22-14.**
Chicago: FG Gould 44, 1:14. **Indianapolis 22-17.**

FOURTH QUARTER: Indianapolis: TD Hayden 56 interception return (Vinatieri kick) 11:44. **Indianapolis 29-17.**

A: 74,512.

XLII - 2008

NY Giants	3	0	0	14—17
New England	0	7	0	7—14

FIRST QUARTER: NY Giants: FG Tynes 32, 5:01. **NY Giants 3-0.**
SECOND QUARTER: New England: TD Maroney 1 run (Gostkowski kick), 14:57. **New England 7-3.**
FOURTH QUARTER: NY Giants: TD Tyree 5 pass from Manning (Tynes kick), 11:05. **NY Giants 10-7.**

XLII - 2008 *(Cont.)*

FOURTH QUARTER *(CONT.)***:**New England: TD Moss 6 pass from Brady (Gostkowski kick), 02:42. **New England 14-10.**
NY Giants: TD Burress 13 pass from Manning (Tynes kick), 00:35. **NY Giants 17-14.**

A: 71,101.

XLIII - 2009

Pittsburgh	3	14	3	7—27
Arizona	0	7	0	16—23

FIRST QUARTER: Pit: FG Reed 18, 9:45. **Pittsburgh 3-0.**

SECOND QUARTER: Pit: Russell 1 run (Reed kick), 14:01. **Pittsburgh 10-0.**
Ari: Patrick 1 pass from Warner (Rackers kick), 8:34. **Pittsburgh 10-7.**
Pit: Harrison 100 Int return (Rackers kick), 0:00. **Pittsburgh 17-7.**

THIRD QUARTER: Pit: FG Reed 21, 2:11. **Pittsburgh 20-7.**

FOURTH QUARTER: Ari: Fitzgerald 1 pass from Warner (Rackers kick), 7:33. **Pittsburgh 20-14.**
Ari: Safety (Hartwig offensive holding penalty in end zone), 2:58. **Pittsburgh 20-16.**
Ari: Fitzgerald 64 pass from Warner (Rackers kick), 2:37. **Arizona 23-20.**
Pit: Holmes 6 pass from Roethlisberger (Reed kick), 0:35. **Pittsburgh 27-23.**

A: 70,774.

NFL Playoff History

	1933
NFL championship	Chicago Bears 23, NY Giants 21
	1934
NFL championship	NY Giants 30, Chicago Bears 13
	1935
NFL championship	Detroit 26, NY Giants 7
	1936
NFL championship	Green Bay 21, Boston 6
	1937
NFL championship	Washington 28, Chicago Bears 21
	1938
NFL championship	NY Giants 23, Green Bay 17
	1939
NFL championship	Green Bay 27, NY Giants 0
	1940
NFL championship	Chicago Bears 73, Washington 0
	1941
W. div. playoff	Chicago Bears 33, Green Bay 14
NFL championship	Chicago Bears 37, NY Giants 9
	1942
NFL championship	Washington 14, Chicago Bears 6

	1943
E. div. playoff	Washington 28, NY Giants 0
NFL championship	Chicago Bears 41, Washington 21
	1944
NFL championship	Green Bay 14, NY Giants 7
	1945
NFL championship	Cleveland 15, Washington 14
	1946
NFL championship	Chicago Bears 24, NY Giants 14
	1947
E. div. playoff	Philadelphia 21, Pittsburgh 0
NFL championship	Chi Cardinals 28, Philadelphia 21
	1948
NFL championship	Philadelphia 7, Chi Cardinals 0
	1949
NFL championship	Philadelphia 14, Los Angeles 0
	1950
Am. Conf. playoff	Cleveland 8, NY Giants 3
Nat. Conf. playoff	Los Angeles 24, Chicago Bears 14
NFL championship	Cleveland 30, Los Angeles 28
	1951
NFL championship	Los Angeles 24, Cleveland 17

1952

Nat. Conf. playoff	Detroit 31, Los Angeles 21
NFL championship	Detroit 17, Cleveland 7

1953

NFL championship	Detroit 17, Cleveland 16

1954

NFL championship	Cleveland 56, Detroit 10

1955

NFL championship	Cleveland 38, Los Angeles 14

1956

NFL championship	NY Giants 47, Chicago Bears 7

1957

W. Conf. playoff	Detroit 31, San Francisco 27
NFL championship	Detroit 59, Cleveland 14

1958

E. Conf. playoff	NY Giants 10, Cleveland 0
NFL championship	Baltimore 23, NY Giants 17

1959

NFL championship	Baltimore 31, NY Giants 16

1960

NFL championship	Philadelphia 17, Green Bay 13
AFL championship	Houston 24, LA Chargers 16

1961

NFL championship	Green Bay 37, NY Giants 0
AFL championship	Houston 10, San Diego 3

1962

NFL championship	Green Bay 16, NY Giants 7
AFL championship	Dallas Texans 20, Houston 17

1963

NFL championship	Chicago 14, NY Giants 10
AFL E. div. playoff	Boston 26, Buffalo 8
AFL championship	San Diego 51, Boston 10

1964

NFL championship	Cleveland 27, Baltimore 0
AFL championship	Buffalo 20, San Diego 7

1965

NFL W. Conf. playoff	Green Bay 13, Baltimore 10
NFL championship	Green Bay 23, Cleveland 12
AFL championship	Buffalo 23, San Diego 0

1966

NFL championship	Green Bay 34, Dallas 27
AFL championship	Kansas City 31, Buffalo 7

1967

NFL E. Conf. championship	Dallas 52, Cleveland 14
NFL W. Conf. championship	Green Bay 28, Los Angeles 7
NFL championship	Green Bay 21, Dallas 17
AFL championship	Oakland 40, Houston 7

1968

NFL E. Conf. championship	Cleveland 31, Dallas 20
NFL W. Conf. championship	Baltimore 24, Minnesota 14
NFL championship	Baltimore 34, Cleveland 0
AFL W. div. playoff	Oakland 41, Kansas City 6
AFL championship	NY Jets 27, Oakland 23

1969

NFL E. Conf. championship	Cleveland 38, Dallas 14
NFL W. Conf. championship	Minnesota 23, Los Angeles 20
NFL championship	Minnesota 27, Cleveland 7
AFL div. playoffs	Kansas City 13, NY Jets 6
	Oakland 56, Houston 7
AFL championship	Kansas City 17, Oakland 7

1970

AFC div. playoffs	Baltimore 17, Cincinnati 0
	Oakland 21, Miami 14
AFC championship	Baltimore 27, Oakland 17
NFC div. playoffs	Dallas 5, Detroit 0
	San Francisco 17, Minnesota 14
NFC championship	Dallas 17, San Francisco 10

1971

AFC div. playoffs	Miami 27, Kansas City 24
	Baltimore 20, Cleveland 3
AFC championship	Miami 21, Baltimore 0
NFC div. playoffs	Dallas 20, Minnesota 12
	San Francisco 24, Washington 20
NFC championship	Dallas 14, San Francisco 3

1972

AFC div. playoffs	Pittsburgh 13, Oakland 7
	Miami 20, Cleveland 14
AFC championship	Miami 21, Pittsburgh 17
NFC div. playoffs	Dallas 30, San Francisco 28
	Washington 16, Green Bay 3
NFC championship	Washington 26, Dallas 3

1973

AFC div. playoffs	Oakland 33, Pittsburgh 14
	Miami 34, Cincinnati 16
AFC championship	Miami 27, Oakland 10
NFC div. playoffs	Minnesota 27, Washington 20
	Dallas 27, Los Angeles 16
NFC championship	Minnesota 27, Dallas 10

1974

AFC div. playoffs	Oakland 28, Miami 26
	Pittsburgh 32, Buffalo 14
AFC championship	Pittsburgh 24, Oakland 13
NFC div. playoffs	Minnesota 30, St Louis 14
	Los Angeles 19, Washington 10
NFC championship	Minnesota 14, Los Angeles 10

1975

AFC div. playoffs	Pittsburgh 28, Baltimore 10
	Oakland 31, Cincinnati 28
AFC championship	Pittsburgh 16, Oakland 10
NFC div. playoffs	Los Angeles 35, St Louis 23
	Dallas 17, Minnesota 14
NFC championship	Dallas 37, Los Angeles 7

1976

AFC div. playoffs	Oakland 24, New England 21
	Pittsburgh 40, Baltimore 14
AFC championship	Oakland 24, Pittsburgh 7
NFC div. playoffs	Minnesota 35, Washington 20
	Los Angeles 14, Dallas 12
NFC championship	Minnesota 24, Los Angeles 13

1977

AFC div. playoffs	Denver 34, Pittsburgh 21
	Oakland 37, Baltimore 31
AFC championship	Denver 20, Oakland 17
NFC div. playoffs	Dallas 37, Chicago 7
	Minnesota 14, Los Angeles 7
NFC championship	Dallas 23, Minnesota 6

1978

AFC 1st-rd. playoff	Houston 17, Miami 9
AFC div. playoffs	Houston 31, New England 14
	Pittsburgh 33, Denver 10
AFC championship	Pittsburgh 34, Houston 5
NFC 1st-rd. playoff	Atlanta 14, Philadelphia 13
NFC div. playoffs	Dallas 27, Atlanta 20
	Los Angeles 34, Minnesota 10
NFC championship	Dallas 28, Los Angeles 0

1979

AFC 1st-rd. playoff	Houston 13, Denver 7
AFC div. playoffs	Houston 17, San Diego 14
	Pittsburgh 34, Miami 14
AFC championship	Pittsburgh 27, Houston 13
NFC 1st-rd. playoff	Philadelphia 27, Chicago 17
NFC div. playoffs	Tampa Bay 24, Philadelphia 17
	Los Angeles 21, Dallas 19
NFC championship	Los Angeles 9, Tampa Bay 0

1980

AFC 1st-rd. playoff	Oakland 27, Houston 7
AFC div. playoffs	San Diego 20, Buffalo 14
	Oakland 14, Cleveland 12
AFC championship	Oakland 34, San Diego 27
NFC 1st-rd. playoff	Dallas 34, Los Angeles 13
NFC div. playoffs	Philadelphia 31, Minnesota 16
	Dallas 30, Atlanta 27
NFC championship	Philadelphia 20, Dallas 7

1981

AFC 1st-rd. playoff	Buffalo 31, NY Jets 27
AFC div. playoffs	San Diego 41, Miami 38
	Cincinnati 28, Buffalo 21
AFC championship	Cincinnati 27, San Diego 7
NFC 1st-rd. playoff	NY Giants 27, Philadelphia 21
NFC div. playoffs	Dallas 38, Tampa Bay 0
	San Francisco 38, NY Giants 24
NFC championship	San Francisco 28, Dallas 27

1982

AFC 1st-rd. playoffs	Miami 28, New England 13
	LA Raiders 27, Cleveland 10
	NY Jets 44, Cincinnati 17
	San Diego 31, Pittsburgh 28
AFC div. playoffs	NY Jets 17, LA Raiders 14
	Miami 34, San Diego 13
AFC championship	Miami 14, NY Jets 0
NFC 1st-rd. playoffs	Washington 31, Detroit 7
	Green Bay 41, St Louis 16
	Minnesota 30, Atlanta 24
	Dallas 30, Tampa Bay 17
NFC div. playoffs	Washington 21, Minnesota 7
	Dallas 37, Green Bay 26
NFC championship	Washington 31, Dallas 17

1983

AFC 1st-rd. playoff	Seattle 31, Denver 7
AFC div. playoffs	Seattle 27, Miami 20
	LA Raiders 38, Pittsburgh 10
AFC championship	LA Raiders 30, Seattle 14
NFC 1st-rd. playoff	LA Rams 24, Dallas 17
NFC div. playoffs	San Francisco 24, Detroit 23
	Washington 51, LA Rams 7
NFC championship	Washington 24, San Francisco 21

1984

AFC 1st-rd. playoff	Seattle 13, LA Raiders 7
AFC div. playoffs	Miami 31, Seattle 10
	Pittsburgh 24, Denver 17
AFC championship	Miami 45, Pittsburgh 28
NFC 1st-rd. playoff	NY Giants 16, LA Rams 13
NFC div. playoffs	San Francisco 21, NY Giants 10
	Chicago 23, Washington 19
NFC championship	San Francisco 23, Chicago 0

1985

AFC 1st-rd. playoff	New England 26, NY Jets 14
AFC div. playoffs	Miami 24, Cleveland 21
	New England 27, LA Raiders 20
AFC championship	New England 31, Miami 14
NFC 1st-rd. playoff	NY Giants 17, San Francisco 3
NFC div. playoffs	LA Rams 20, Dallas 0
	Chicago 21, NY Giants 0
NFC championship	Chicago 24, LA Rams 0

1986

AFC 1st-rd. playoff	NY Jets 35, Kansas City 15
AFC div. playoffs	Cleveland 23, NY Jets 20
	Denver 22, New England 17
AFC championship	Denver 23, Cleveland 20
NFC 1st-rd. playoff	Washington 19, LA Rams 7
NFC div playoffs	Washington 27, Chicago 13
	NY Giants 49, San Francisco 3
NFC championship	NY Giants 17, Washington 0

1987

AFC 1st-rd. playoff	Houston 23, Seattle 20
AFC div. playoffs	Cleveland 38, Indianapolis 21
	Denver 34, Houston 10
AFC championship	Denver 38, Cleveland 33
NFC 1st-rd. playoff	Minnesota 44, New Orleans 10
NFC div playoffs	Minnesota 36, San Francisco 24
	Washington 21, Chicago 17
NFC championship	Washington 17, Minnesota 10

1988

AFC 1st-rd. playoff	Houston 24, Cleveland 23
AFC div. playoffs	Cincinnati 21, Seattle 13
	Buffalo 17, Houston 10
AFC championship	Cincinnati 21, Buffalo 10
NFC 1st-rd. playoff	Minnesota 28, LA Rams 17
NFC div. playoffs	Chicago 20, Philadelphia 12
	San Francisco 34, Minnesota 9
NFC championship	San Francisco 28, Chicago 3

1989

AFC 1st-rd. playoff	Pittsburgh 26, Houston 23
AFC div. playoffs	Cleveland 34, Buffalo 30
	Denver 24, Pittsburgh 23
AFC championship	Denver 37, Cleveland 21
NFC 1st-rd. playoff	LA Rams 21, Philadelphia 7
NFC div. playoffs	LA Rams 19, NY Giants 13
	San Francisco 41, Minnesota 13
NFC championship	San Francisco 30, LA Rams 3

1990

AFC 1st-rd. playoffs	Miami 17, Kansas City 16
	Cincinnati 41, Houston 14
AFC div. playoffs	Buffalo 44, Miami 34
	LA Raiders 20, Cincinnati 10
AFC championship	Buffalo 51, LA Raiders 3
NFC 1st-rd. playoffs	Chicago 16, New Orleans 6
	Washington 20, Philadelphia 6
NFC div. playoffs	NY Giants 31, Chicago 3
	San Francisco 28, Washington 10
NFC championship	NY Giants 15, San Francisco 13

1991

AFC 1st-rd. playoffs	Houston 17, NY Jets 10
	Kansas City 10, LA Raiders 6
AFC div. playoffs	Denver 26, Houston 24
	Buffalo 37, Kansas City 14
AFC championship	Buffalo 10, Denver 7
NFC 1st-rd. playoffs	Atlanta 27, New Orleans 20
	Dallas 17, Chicago 13
NFC div. playoffs	Washington 24, Atlanta 7
	Detroit 38, Dallas 6
NFC championship	Washington 41, Detroit 10

1992

AFC 1st-rd. playoffs	San Diego 17, Kansas City 0
	Buffalo 41, Houston 38 (OT)
AFC div. playoffs	Buffalo 24, Pittsburgh 3
	Miami 31, San Diego 0
AFC championship	Buffalo 29, Miami 10
NFC 1st-rd. playoffs	Washington 24, Minnesota 7
	Philadelphia 36, New Orleans 20
NFC div. playoffs	San Francisco 20, Washington 13
	Dallas 34, Philadelphia 10
NFC championship	Dallas 30, San Francisco 20

1993

AFC 1st-rd. playoffs	LA Raiders 42, Denver 24
	Kansas City 27, Pittsburgh 24 (OT)
AFC div. playoffs	Buffalo 29, LA Raiders 23
	Kansas City 28, Houston 20
AFC championship	Buffalo 30, Kansas City 13
NFC 1st-rd. playoffs	NY Giants 17, Minnesota 10
	Green Bay 28, Detroit 24
NFC div. playoffs	San Francisco 44, NY Giants 3
	Dallas 27, Green Bay 17
NFC championship	Dallas 38, San Francisco 21

1994

AFC 1st-rd. playoffs	Miami 27, Kansas City 17
	Cleveland 20, New England 13
AFC div. playoffs	San Diego 22, Miami 21
	Pittsburgh 29, Cleveland 9
AFC championship	San Diego 17, Pittsburgh 13
NFC 1st-rd. playoffs	Green Bay 16, Detroit 12
	Chicago 35, Minnesota 18
NFC div. playoffs	Dallas 35, Green Bay 9
	San Francisco 44, Chicago 15
NFC championship	San Francisco 38, Dallas 28

1995

AFC 1st-rd. playoffs	Buffalo 37, Miami 22
	Indianapolis 35, San Diego 20
AFC div. playoffs	Pittsburgh 40, Buffalo 21
	Indianapolis 10, Kansas City 7
AFC championship	Pittsburgh 20, Indianapolis 16
NFC 1st-rd. playoffs	Philadelphia 58, Detroit 37
	Green Bay 37, Atlanta 20
NFC div. playoffs	Dallas 30, Philadelphia 11
	Green Bay 27, San Francisco 17
NFC championship	Dallas 38, Green Bay 27

1996

AFC 1st-rd. playoffs	Jacksonville 30, Buffalo 27
	Pittsburgh 42, Indianapolis 14
AFC div. playoffs	Jacksonville 30, Denver 27
	New England 28, Pittsburgh 3
AFC championship	New England 20, Jacksonville 6
NFC 1st-rd. playoffs	Dallas 40, Minnesota 15
	San Francisco 14, Philadelphia 0
NFC div. playoffs	Green Bay 35, San Francisco 14
	Carolina 26, Dallas 17
NFC championship	Green Bay 30, Carolina 13

1997

AFC 1st-rd. playoffs	Denver 42, Jacksonville 17
	New England 17, Miami 3
AFC div. playoffs	Denver 14, Kansas City 10
	Pittsburgh 7, New England 6
AFC championship	Denver 24, Pittsburgh 21
NFC 1st-rd. playoffs	Minnesota 23, NY Giants 22
	Tampa Bay 20, Detroit 10
NFC div. playoffs	Green Bay 21, Tampa Bay 7
	San Francisco 38, Minnesota 22
NFC championship	Green Bay 23, San Francisco 10

1998

AFC 1st-rd. playoffs	Miami 24, Buffalo 17
	Jacksonville 25, New England 10
AFC div. playoffs	Denver 38, Miami 3
	NY Jets 34, Jacksonville 24
AFC championship	Denver 23, NY Jets 10
NFC 1st-rd. playoffs	Arizona 20, Dallas 7
	San Francisco 30, Green Bay 27
NFC div. playoffs	Atlanta 20, San Francisco 18
	Minnesota 41, Arizona 21
NFC championship	Atlanta 30, Minnesota 27 (OT)

1999

AFC 1st-rd. playoffs	Tennessee 22, Buffalo 16
	Miami 20, Seattle 17
AFC div. playoffs	Jacksonville 62, Miami 7
	Tennessee 19, Indianapolis 16
AFC championship	Tennessee 33, Jacksonville 14
NFC 1st-rd. playoffs	Washington 27, Detroit 13
	Minnesota 27, Dallas 10
NFC div. playoffs	Tampa Bay 14, Washington 13
	St Louis 49, Minnesota 37
NFC championship	St Louis 11, Tampa Bay 6

2000

AFC 1st-rd. playoffs	Baltimore 21, Denver 3
	Miami 23, Indianapolis 17 (OT)
AFC div. playoffs	Baltimore 24, Tennessee 10
	Oakland 27, Miami 0
AFC championship	Baltimore 16, Oakland 3
NFC 1st-rd. playoffs	New Orleans 31, St. Louis 28
	Philadelphia 21, Tampa Bay 3
NFC div. playoffs	NY Giants 20, Philadelphia 10
	Minnesota 34, New Orleans 16
NFC championship	NY Giants 41, Minnesota 0

2001

AFC 1st-rd. playoffs	Oakland 38, NY Jets 24
	Baltimore 20, Miami 3
AFC div. playoffs	New England 16, Oakland 13(OT)
	Pittsburgh 27, Baltimore 10
AFC championship	New England 24, Pittsburgh 17
NFC 1st-rd. playoffs	Philadelphia 31, Tampa Bay 9
	Green Bay 25, San Francisco 15
NFC div. playoffs	Philadelphia 33, Chicago 19
	St. Louis 45, Green Bay 17
NFC championship	St. Louis 29, Philadelphia 24

2002

AFC 1st-rd. playoffs	NY Jets 41, Indianapolis 0
	Pittsburgh 36, Cleveland 33
AFC div. playoffs	Tennessee 34, Pittsburgh 31 (OT)
	Oakland 30, NY Jets 10
AFC championship	Oakland 41, Tennessee 24
NFC 1st-rd. playoffs	Atlanta 27, Green Bay 7
	San Francisco 39, NY Giants 38
NFC div. playoffs	Philadelphia 20, Atlanta 6
	Tampa Bay 31, San Francisco 6
NFC championship	Tampa Bay 27, Philadelphia 10

2003

AFC 1st-rd. playoffs	Tennessee 20, Baltimore 17
	Indianapolis 41, Denver 10
AFC div. playoffs	New England 17, Tennessee 14
	Indianapolis 38, Kansas City 31
AFC championship	New England 24, Indianapolis 14
NFC 1st-rd. playoffs	Carolina 29, Dallas 10
	Green Bay 37, Seattle 31 (OT)
NFC div. playoffs	Carolina 29, St. Louis 23
	Philadelphia 20, Green Bay 17 (OT)
NFC championship	Carolina 14, Philadelphia 3

2004

AFC 1st-rd. playoffs	Indianapolis 49, Denver 24
	NY Jets 20, San Diego 17
AFC div. playoffs	New England 20, Indianapolis 3
	Pittsburgh 20, NY Jets 17
AFC championship	New England 41, Pittsburgh 27
NFC 1st-rd. playoffs	Minnesota 31, Green Bay 17
	St. Louis 27, Seattle 20
NFC div. playoffs	Atlanta 47, St. Louis 17
	Philadelphia 27, Minnesota 14
NFC championship	Philadelphia 27, Atlanta 10

2005

AFC 1st-rd. playoffs	Pittsburgh 31, Cincinnati 17
	New England 28, Jacksonville 3
AFC div. playoffs	Pittsburgh 21, Indianapolis 18
	Denver 27, New England 13
AFC championship	Pittsburgh 34, Denver 17
NFC 1st-rd. playoffs	Washington 17, Tampa Bay 10
	Carolina 23, NY Giants 0
NFC div. playoffs	Seattle 20, Washington 10
	Carolina 29, Chicago 21
NFC championship	Seattle 34, Carolina 14

2006

AFC 1st-rd. playoffs	Indianapolis 23, Kansas City 8
	New England 37, NY Jets 16
AFC div. playoffs	Indianapolis 15, Baltimore 6
	New England 24, San Diego 21
AFC championship	Indianapolis 38, New England 34
NFC 1st-rd. playoffs	Seattle 21, Dallas 20
	Philadelphia 23, NY Giants 20
NFC div. playoffs	Chicago 27, Seattle 24
	New Orleans 27, Philadelphia 24
NFC championship	Chicago 39, New Orleans 14

2007

AFC 1st-rd. playoffs	Jacksonville 31, Pittsburgh 29
	San Diego 17, Tennessee 6
AFC Div. Playoffs	New England 31, Jacksonville 20
	San Diego 28, Indianapolis 24
AFC Championship	New England 21, San Diego 12
NFC 1st-rd. playoffs	Seattle 35, Washington 14
	NY Giants 24, Tampa Bay 14
NFC Div. Playoffs	NY Giants 21, Dallas 17
	Green Bay 42, Seattle 20
NFC Championship	NY Giants 23, Green Bay 20 (OT)

2008

AFC 1st-rd. playoffs	Baltimore 27, Miami 9
	San Diego 23, Indianapolis 17 (OT)
AFC Div. Playoffs	Baltimore 13, Tennessee 10
	Pittsburgh 35, San Diego 24
AFC Championship	Pittsburgh 23, Baltimore 14
NFC 1st-rd. playoffs	Philadelphia 26, Minnesota 14
	Arizona 30, Atlanta 24
NFC Div. Playoffs	Philadelphia 23, NY Giants 11
	Arizona 33, Carolina 13
NFC Championship	Arizona 32, Philadelphia 25

2009

AFC 1st-rd. playoffs	NY Jets 24, Cincinnati 14
	Baltimore 33, New England 14
AFC Div. Playoffs	NY Jets 17, San Diego 14
	Indianapolis 20, Baltimore 3
AFC Championship	Indianapolis 30, NY Jets 17
NFC 1st-rd. playoffs	Dallas 34, Philadelphia 14
	Arizona 51, Green Bay 45 (OT)
NFC Div. Playoffs	Minnesota 34, Dallas 3
	New Orleans 45, Arizona 14
NFC Championship	New Orleans 31, Minnesota 28 (OT)

Career Leaders

Scoring

	Yrs	TD	FG	PAT	Pts
Morten Andersen	25	0	565	849	2,544
Gary Anderson	23	0	538	820	2,434
†John Carney	21	0	473	625	2,044
†Matt Stover	20	0	471	591	2,004
George Blanda	26	9	335	943	2,002
†Jason Elam	17	0	436	675	1,983
†Jason Hanson	18	0	427	554	1,835
Norm Johnson	18	0	366	638	1,736
†John Kasay	19	0	408	507	1,731
Nick Lowery	18	0	383	562	1,711
Jan Stenerud	19	0	373	580	1,699
Lou Groza	21	1	264	810	1,608
Eddie Murray	19	0	352	538	1,594
Al Del Greco	17	0	347	543	1,584
†Adam Vinatieri	14	0	338	514	1,528
Steve Christie	15	0	336	468	1,476

Rushing

	Yrs	Att	Yds	Avg	Lg	TD
Emmitt Smith	15	4,409	18,355	4.2	75	164
Walter Payton	13	3,838	16,726	4.4	76	110
Barry Sanders	10	3,062	15,269	5.0	85	99
Curtis Martin	11	3,518	14,101	4.0	70	90
Jerome Bettis	13	3,479	13,662	3.9	71	91
Eric Dickerson	11	2,996	13,259	4.4	85	90
Tony Dorsett	12	2,936	12,739	4.3	99	77
†LaD. Tomlinson	9	2,880	12,490	4.3	85	138
Jim Brown	9	2,359	12,312	5.2	80	106
Marshall Faulk	12	2,836	12,279	4.3	71	100
†Edgerrin James	11	3,028	12,246	4.0	72	80
Marcus Allen	16	3,022	12,243	4.1	61	123
Franco Harris	13	2,949	12,120	4.1	75	91
Thurman Thomas	13	2,877	12,074	4.2	80	66
†Fred Taylor	12	2,491	11,540	4.6	80	66
John Riggins	14	2,916	11,352	3.9	66	104

Touchdowns

	Yrs	Rush	Rec	Ret	Total TD
Jerry Rice	20	10	197	0	207
Emmitt Smith	15	164	11	0	175
†LaDainian Tomlinson	9	138	15	0	153
†Randy Moss	12	0	148	1	149
†Terrell Owens	14	3	144	0	147
Marcus Allen	16	123	21	0	144
Marshall Faulk	12	100	36	0	136
Cris Carter	16	0	130	0	130
Marvin Harrison	13	0	128	0	128
Jim Brown	9	106	20	0	126

	Yrs	Rush	Rec	Ret	Total TD
Walter Payton	13	110	15	0	125
John Riggins	14	104	12	0	116
Lenny Moore	12	63	48	1	112
Shaun Alexander	9	100	12	0	112
Barry Sanders	10	99	10	0	109
Tim Brown	17	1	100	4	105
Don Hutson	11	3	99	0	102
Steve Largent	14	1	100	0	101
Curtis Martin	12	90	10	0	100
Franco Harris	13	91	9	0	100

Combined Yards Gained

	Yrs	Total	Rush	Rec	Int Ret	Punt Ret	Kickoff Ret	Fum Ret
Jerry Rice	20	23,546	645	22,895	0	0	6	0
Brian Mitchell	14	23,330	1,967	2,336	0	4,999	14,014	14
Walter Payton	13	21,803	16,726	4,538	0	0	539	0
Emmitt Smith	15	21,583	18,355	3,224	0	0	0	4
Tim Brown	17	19,682	190	14,934	0	3,320	1,235	3
Marshall Faulk	12	19,154	12,279	6,875	0	0	18	18
Barry Sanders	10	18,308	15,269	2,921	0	0	118	0
Herschel Walker	12	18,168	8,225	4,859	0	0	5,084	0
Marcus Allen	16	17,654	12,243	5,411	0	0	0	0
Curtis Martin	11	17,430	14,101	3,329	0	0	0	0
Tiki Barber	10	17,359	10,449	5,183	0	1,181	544	2
Eric Metcalf	13	17,230	2,392	5,572	0	3,453	5,813	0
Thurman Thomas	13	16,532	12,074	4,458	0	0	0	0
†LaDainian Tomlinson	9	16,445	12,490	3,955	0	0	0	0
Tony Dorsett	12	16,293	12,739	3,554	0	0	0	0
Henry Ellard	16	15,718	50	13,777	0	1,527	364	0
†Edgerrin James	11	15,610	12,246	3,364	0	0	0	0
†Isaac Bruce	16	15,347	139	15,208	0	0	0	0
†Terrell Owens	14	15,202	251	14,951	0	0	0	0

†-Active in 2009.

Career Leaders *(Cont.)*

Passing
PASSER RATING*

	Yrs	Att	Comp	Pct Comp	Yds	Avg Gain	TD	Pct TD	Int	Pct Int	Rating Pts
Steve Young	15	4,149	2,667	64.3	33,124	8.0	232	5.6	107	2.6	96.8
†Philip Rivers	6	1,914	1,207	63.1	14,951	7.8	106	5.5	45	2.4	95.8
†Tony Romo	7	1,857	1,178	63.4	15,045	8.1	107	5.8	55	3.0	95.6
†Peyton Manning	12	6,531	4,232	64.8	50,128	7.7	366	5.6	181	2.8	95.2
†Kurt Warner	12	4,070	2,666	65.5	32,344	7.9	208	5.1	128	3.1	93.7
†Tom Brady	10	4,218	2,672	63.3	30,844	7.3	225	5.3	99	2.3	93.3
Joe Montana	15	5,391	3,409	63.2	40,551	7.5	273	5.2	139	2.6	92.3
†Drew Brees	9	4,164	2,697	64.8	30,646	7.4	202	4.9	110	2.6	91.9
†Ben Roethlisberger	6	2,411	1,526	63.3	19,302	8.0	127	5.3	81	3.4	91.7
†Chad Pennington	10	2,469	1,631	66.1	17,804	7.2	102	4.1	64	2.6	90.1
†Carson Palmer	7	2,631	1,662	63.2	18,724	7.1	128	4.9	80	3.0	87.9
†Daunte Culpepper	11	3,199	2,016	63.0	24,123	7.6	149	4.7	106	3.3	87.8
†Jeff Garcia	11	3,676	2,264	61.6	25,537	6.9	161	4.4	83	2.3	87.5
†Brett Favre	19	9,811	6,083	62.0	69,329	7.1	497	5.1	317	3.2	86.6
†Donovan McNabb	11	4,746	2,801	59.0	32,873	6.9	216	4.6	100	2.1	86.5
Dan Marino	17	8,358	4,967	59.4	61,361	7.3	420	5.0	252	3.0	86.4
Trent Green	15	3,740	2,266	60.6	28,475	7.6	162	4.3	114	3.0	86.0
†David Garrard	8	1,915	1,170	61.1	13,269	6.9	66	3.4	69	2.0	84.9
Rich Gannon	18	4,206	2,533	60.2	28,743	6.8	180	4.3	104	2.3	84.7
Jim Kelly	11	4,779	2,874	60.1	35,467	7.4	237	5.0	175	3.7	84.4
†Marc Bulger	9	3,171	1,969	62.1	22,814	7.2	122	3.8	93	2.9	84.4
†Mark Brunell	17	4,624	2,753	59.5	31,928	6.9	182	3.9	107	2.3	83.9
†Jay Cutler	4	1,775	1,098	61.9	12,690	7.1	81	4.6	63	3.5	83.8

*1,500 or more attempts. The passer ratings are based on performance standards established for completion percentage, interception percentage, touchdown percentage and average gain. Passers are allocated points according to how their marks compare with those standards.

PASSING YARDS

	Yrs	Att	Comp	Pct Comp	Yds		Yrs	Att	Comp	Pct Comp	Yds
†Brett Favre	19	9,811	6,083	62.0	69,329	Dave Krieg	19	5,311	3,105	58.5	38,147
Dan Marino	17	8,358	4,967	59.4	61,361	Boomer Esiason	14	5,205	2,969	57.0	37,920
John Elway	16	7,250	4,123	56.9	51,475	Jim Kelly	11	4,779	2,874	60.1	35,467
†Peyton Manning	12	6,531	4,232	64.8	50,128	Jim Everett	12	4,923	2,841	57.7	34,837
Warren Moon	17	6,823	3,988	58.5	49,325	Jim Hart	19	5,076	2,593	51.1	34,665
Fran Tarkenton	18	6,467	3,686	57.0	47,003	Steve DeBerg	17	4,746	2,924	61.6	34,241
Vinny Testaverde	21	6,701	3,787	56.5	46,233	John Hadl	16	4,687	2,363	50.4	33,503
Drew Bledsoe	14	6,717	3,839	57.2	44,611	Phil Simms	14	4,647	2,576	55.4	33,462
Dan Fouts	15	5,604	3,297	58.8	43,040	Steve Young	15	5,149	2,667	64.3	33,124
Joe Montana	15	5,391	3,409	63.2	40,551	*Y.A. Tittle	17	4,395	2,427	55.2	33,070
Johnny Unitas	18	5,186	2,830	54.6	40,239	Troy Aikman	12	4,715	2,898	61.5	32,942
†Kerry Collins	15	5,885	3,279	55.7	38,618	†Donovan McNabb	11	4,746	2,801	59.0	32,873

PASSING TOUCHDOWNS

	No.		No.		No.
†Brett Favre	497	Dan Fouts	254	John Brodie	214
Dan Marino	420	Drew Bledsoe	251	Terry Bradshaw	212
†Peyton Manning	366	Boomer Esiason	247	Jim Hart	209
Fran Tarkenton	342	John Hadl	244	†Kurt Warner	208
John Elway	300	*Y.A. Tittle	242	Randall Cunningham	207
Warren Moon	291	Len Dawson	239	Jim Everett	203
Johnny Unitas	290	Jim Kelly	237	†Drew Brees	202
Vinny Testaverde	275	George Blanda	236	Roman Gabriel	201
Joe Montana	273	Steve Young	232	Phil Simms	199
Dave Krieg	261	†Tom Brady	225	Ken Anderson	197
Sonny Jurgensen	255	†Donovan McNabb	216		

* Includes 4,731 passing yards and 30 TDs with Baltimore Colts (1948–49) in All-American Football Conference.

† Active in 2009.

Career Leaders *(Cont.)*

Receiving

RECEPTIONS

	Yrs	No.	Yds	Avg	Lg	TD		Yrs	No.	Yds	Avg	Lg	TD
Jerry Rice	20	1,549	22,895	14.8	96	197	Jimmy Smith	13	862	12,287	14.3	75	67
Marvin Harrison	12	1,102	14,580	13.2	80	128	†Muhsin Muhammad	14	860	11,438	13.3	72	62
Cris Carter	16	1,101	13,899	12.6	80	130	Irving Fryar	17	851	12,785	15.0	80	84
Tim Brown	17	1,094	14,934	13.7	80	100	Rod Smith	12	849	11,389	13.4	85	68
†Isaac Bruce	16	1,024	15,208	14.9	80	91	Larry Centers	14	827	6,797	8.2	54	28
†Terrell Owens	14	1,006	14,951	14.9	98	144	Steve Largent	14	819	13,089	16.0	74	100
†Tony Gonzalez	13	999	11,807	11.8	73	82	Shannon Sharpe	15	815	10,060	12.3	82	62
Andre Reed	16	951	13,198	13.9	83	87	Henry Ellard	16	814	13,777	16.9	81	65
Art Monk	16	940	12,721	13.5	79	68	Keyshawn Johnson	11	814	10,571	13.0	76	64
†Randy Moss	12	926	14,465	15.6	82	148	Marshall Faulk	11	767	6,875	9.0	85	36
†Torry Holt	11	920	13,382	14.5	85	74	James Lofton	16	764	14,004	18.3	80	75
†Hines Ward	12	895	10,947	12.2	85	78	Eric Moulds	12	764	9,995	13.1	84	49
Keenan McCardell	17	883	11,373	12.9	76	63	Michael Irvin	12	750	11,904	15.9	87	65
†Derrick Mason	13	863	11,089	12.8	79	59	Charlie Joiner	18	750	12,146	16.2	87	65

YARDS

Jerry Rice	22,895	Henry Ellard	13,777	Michael Irvin	11,904
†Isaac Bruce	15,208	†Torry Holt	13,382	Don Maynard	11,834
†Terrell Owens	14,951	Andre Reed	13,198	†Tony Gonzalez	11,807
Tim Brown	14,934	Steve Largent	13,089	†Muhsin Muhammad	11,438
Marvin Harrison	14,580	Irving Fryar	12,785	Rod Smith	11,389
†Randy Moss	14,465	Art Monk	12,721	Keenan McCardell	11,373
James Lofton	14,004	Jimmy Smith	12,287	†Derrick Mason	11,089
Cris Carter	13,899	Charlie Joiner	12,146	†Hines Ward	10,947

SACKS

Bruce Smith	200.0	Michael Strahan	141.5
Reggie White	198.0	John Randle	137.5
Kevin Greene	160.0	Richard Dent	137.5
Chris Doleman	150.5		

Note: Stat officially compiled since 1982.

Interceptions

	Yrs	No.	Yds	Avg	Lg	TD
Paul Krause	16	81	1,185	14.6	81	3
Emlen Tunnell	14	79	1,282	16.2	55	4
Rod Woodson	17	71	1,483	20.9	98	17
Dick (Night Train) Lane	14	68	1,207	17.8	80	5
Ken Riley	15	65	596	9.2	66	5
†Darren Sharper	13	63	1,412	22.4	99	11

Punting

	Yrs	No.	Yds	Avg	Lg	Blk
†Shane Lechler	10	778	36,811	47.3	73	3
†Donnie Jones	6	449	20,451	45.5	80	2
†Jon Ryan	4	310	14,028	45.3	72	3
Sammy Baugh	16	338	15,245	45.1	85	9
†Mat McBriar	6	371	16,712	45.0	75	0
†Andy Lee	6	554	24,896	44.9	82	2
Tommy Davis	11	511	22,833	44.7	82	2
†Chris Kluwe	5	391	17,360	44.4	70	0
†Ben Graham	5	335	14,886	44.4	69	2

Note: 250 or more punts.

Punt Returns

	Yrs	No.	Yds	Avg	Lg	TD
George McAfee	8	112	1,431	12.8	74	2
Jack Christiansen	8	85	1,084	12.8	89	8
Claude Gibson	5	110	1,381	12.6	85	3
Bill Dudley	9	124	1,515	12.2	96	3
†Roscoe Parrish	5	118	1,445	12.2	82	3

Note: 75 or more returns.

Kickoff Returns

	Yrs	No.	Yds	Avg	Lg	TD
Gale Sayers	7	91	2,781	30.6	103	6
Lynn Chandnois	7	92	2,720	29.6	93	3
Abe Woodson	9	193	5,538	28.7	105	5
Claude (Buddy) Young	6	90	2,514	27.9	104	2
Travis Williams	5	102	2,801	27.5	105	6
†Ellis Hobbs	5	125	3,394	27.2	108	3

Note: 75 or more returns.

† Active in 2009.

Single-Season Leaders
Scoring

POINTS

	Year	TD	PAT	FG	Pts
†LaDainian Tomlinson,SD	2006	31	0	0	186
Paul Hornung, GB	1960	15	41	15	176
Shaun Alexander, Sea	2005	28	0	0	168
Gary Anderson, Min	1998	0	59	35	164
Jeff Wilkins, StL	2003	0	46	39	163
Priest Holmes, KC	2003	27	0	0	162
Mark Moseley, Was	1983	0	62	33	161
Marshall Faulk, StL	2000	26	2	0	160
Mike Vanderjagt, Ind	2003	0	46	37	157
Gino Cappelletti, Bos	1964	7	37	25	155
Emmitt Smith, Dal	1995	25	0	0	150
Chip Lohmiller, Was	1991	0	56	31	149
†Jay Feely, NYG	2005	0	43	35	148
†Stephen Gostkowski, NE	2008	0	40	36	148
Gino Cappelletti, Bos	1961	8	48	17	147

Note: Faulk's (2) and Cappelletti's (1) totals include two-point conversions.

TOUCHDOWNS

	Year	Rush	Rec	Ret	Total
†LaDainian Tomlinson, SD	2006	28	3	0	31
Shaun Alexander, Sea	2005	27	1	0	28
Priest Holmes, KC	2003	27	0	0	27
Marshall Faulk, StL	2000	18	8	0	26
Emmitt Smith, Dal	1995	25	0	0	25
John Riggins, Was	1983	24	0	0	24
Priest Holmes, KC	2002	21	3	0	24
O.J. Simpson, Buf	1975	16	7	0	23
Jerry Rice, SF	1987	1	22	0	23
Terrell Davis, Den	1998	21	2	0	23
†Randy Moss, NE	2007	0	0	23	23

FIELD GOALS

	Year	FGA	FGM
†Neil Rackers, Ari	2005	42	40
Jeff Wilkins, StL	2003	42	39
†Olindo Mare, Mia	1999	46	39
Mike Vanderjagt, Ind	2003	37	37
†John Kasay, Car	1996	45	37
Al Del Greco, Ten	1998	39	36
Cary Blanchard, Ind	1996	40	36
†Stephen Gostkowski, NE	2008	40	36

Rushing

YARDS GAINED

	Year	Att	Yds	Avg
Eric Dickerson, LA Rams	1984	379	2,105	5.6
†Jamal Lewis, Bal	2003	387	2,066	5.3
Barry Sanders, Det	1997	335	2,053	6.1
Terrell Davis, Den	1998	392	2,008	5.1
†Chris Johnson, Ten	2009	358	2,006	5.6
O.J. Simpson, Buf	1973	332	2,003	6.0
Earl Campbell, Hou	1980	373	1,934	5.2
†Ahman Green, GB	2003	355	1,883	5.3
Barry Sanders, Det	1994	331	1,883	5.7
Shaun Alexander, Sea	2005	370	1,880	5.1
Jim Brown, Cle	1963	291	1,863	6.4
Tiki Barber, NYG	2005	357	1,860	5.2
†Ricky Williams, Mia	2002	383	1,853	4.8

AVERAGE GAIN

	Year	Avg
Beattie Feathers, Chi	1934	8.44
Randall Cunningham, Phi	1990	7.98
†Michael Vick, Atl	2004	7.50
†Michael Vick, Atl	2002	6.88
Bobby Douglass, Chi	1972	6.87

Minimum 100 attempts.

TOUCHDOWNS

	Year	No.
†LaDainian Tomlinson, SD	2006	28
Shaun Alexander, Sea	2005	27
Priest Holmes, KC	2003	27
Emmitt Smith, Dal	1995	25
John Riggins, Was	1983	24
Priest Holmes, KC	2002	21
Emmitt Smith, Dal	1994	21
Joe Morris, NYG	1985	21
Terry Allen, Wash	1996	21
Terrell Davis, Den	1998	21

Passing

YARDS GAINED

	Year	Att	Comp	Pct	Yds
Dan Marino, Mia	1984	564	362	64.2	5,084
†Drew Brees, NO	2008	635	413	65.0	5,069
†Kurt Warner, StL Rams	2001	546	375	68.7	4,830
†Tom Brady, NE	2007	578	398	68.9	4,806
Dan Fouts, SD	1981	609	360	59.1	4,802
†Matt Schaub, Hou	2009	583	396	67.9	4,770
Dan Marino, Mia	1986	623	378	60.7	4,746
†D. Culpepper, Min	2004	548	379	69.2	4,717
Dan Fouts, SD	1980	589	348	59.1	4,715
Warren Moon, Hou	1991	655	404	61.7	4,690
Warren Moon, Hou	1990	584	362	62.0	4,689
Rich Gannon, Oak	2002	618	418	67.6	4,689
Neil Lomax, StL Cards	1984	560	345	61.6	4,614
Trent Green, StL Rams	2004	556	369	66.4	4,591
†Kurt Warner, Ari	2008	598	401	67.1	4,583
†Peyton Manning, Ind	2004	497	336	67.6	4,557
Drew Bledsoe, NE	1994	691	400	57.9	4,555

PASSER RATING

	Year	Rat.
†Peyton Manning, Ind	2004	121.1
†Tom Brady, NE	2007	117.2
Steve Young, SF	1994	112.8
Joe Montana, SF	1989	112.4
†Daunte Culpepper, Min	2004	110.9
Milt Plum, Clev	1960	110.4

TOUCHDOWNS

	Year	No.
†Tom Brady, NE	2007	50
†Peyton Manning, Ind	2004	49
Dan Marino, Mia	1984	48
Dan Marino, Mia	1986	44
†Kurt Warner, StL Rams	1999	41
†Daunte Culpepper, Min	2004	39
†Brett Favre, GB	1996	39
†Brett Favre, GB	1995	38

Six tied with 36.

† Active in 2009.

Single-Season Leaders (Cont.)

Receiving

RECEPTIONS

	Year	No.	Yds
Marvin Harrison, Ind	2002	143	1,722
Herman Moore, Det	1995	123	1,686
†Wes Welker, NE	2009	123	1,348
Cris Carter, Min	1994	122	1,256
Jerry Rice, SF	1995	122	1,848
Cris Carter, Min	1995	122	1,371
†Isaac Bruce, StL	1995	119	1,781
†Torry Holt, StL	2003	117	1,696
Jimmy Smith, Jac	1999	116	1,636
Marvin Harrison, Ind	1999	115	1,663
†Andre Johnson, Hou	2008	115	1,575
Rod Smith, Den	2001	113	1,343

Six tied at 112.

YARDS GAINED

	Year	Yds
Jerry Rice, SF	1995	1,848
†Isaac Bruce, StL	1995	1,781
Charley Hennigan, Hou	1961	1,746
Marvin Harrison, Ind	2002	1,722
†Torry Holt, StL	2003	1,696

TOUCHDOWNS

	Year	No.
†Randy Moss, NE	2007	23
Jerry Rice, SF	1987	22
Mark Clayton, Mia	1984	18
Sterling Sharpe, GB	1994	18

Seven tied with 17.

All-Purpose Yards

	Year	Run	Rec	Ret	Total
†Derrick Mason, Ten	2000	1	895	1794	2690
Michael Lewis, NO	2002	15	200	2432	2647
†Chris Johnson, Ten	2009	2006	503	0	2509
Lionel James, SD	1985	516	1027	992	2535
Brian Mitchell, Was	1994	311	236	1930	2477
Dante Hall, KC	2003	73	423	1950	2446
Mack Herron, NE	1974	824	474	1146	2444
Gale Sayers, Chi	1966	1231	447	762	2440
Terry Metcalf, StL Cards	1975	816	378	1245	2439
Marshall Faulk, StL Rams	1999	1381	1048	0	2429
Timmy Brown, Phi	1963	841	487	1097	2425
MarTay Jenkins, Ari	2000	-4	219	2187	2402
Tiki Barber, NYG	2005	1860	530	0	2390
†LaD. Tomlinson, SD	2003	1645	725	0	2370
Barry Sanders, Det	1997	2053	305	0	2358
Brian Mitchell, Was	1998	208	306	1843	2357

Punting

	Year	No.	Yds	Avg
Sammy Baugh, Was	1940	35	1,799	51.4
†Shane Lechler, Oak	2009	96	4,909	51.1
†Donnie Jones, StL	2008	82	4,100	50.0
†Shane Lechler, Oak	2007	73	3,585	49.1
†Mat McBriar, Dal	2008	24	1,175	49.0
Yale Lary, Det	1963	35	1,713	48.9
†Shane Lechler, Oak	2008	90	4,391	48.8
Sammy Baugh, Was	1941	30	1,462	48.7

Interceptions

	Year	No.
Dick (Night Train) Lane, LA Rams	1952	14
Dan Sandifer, Was	1948	13
Spec Sanders, NY Yanks	1950	13
Lester Hayes, Oak	1980	13

Nine tied with 12.

Sacks

	Year	No.
Michael Strahan, NYG	2001	22.5
Mark Gastineau, NYJ	1984	22
Reggie White, Phi	1987	21
Chris Doleman, Min	1989	21
Lawrence Taylor, NYG	1986	20.5
Derrick Thomas, KC	1990	20
†DeMarcus Ware, Dal	2008	20

Three tied with 19.0.

Punt Returns

	Year	Avg
Jack Christiansen, Det	1952	21.5
Dick Christy, NY Titans	1961	21.3
Bob Hayes, Dal	1968	20.8

Two tied at 19.1.

Kickoff Returns

	Year	Avg
Travis Williams, GB	1967	41.1
Gale Sayers, Chi	1967	37.7
Ollie Matson, Chi Cards	1958	35.5
Jim Duncan, Balt Colts	1970	35.4
Lynn Chandnois, Pit	1952	35.2

Single-Game Leaders

Scoring

POINTS

	Date	Pts
Ernie Nevers, Chi Cards vs Chi	11-28-29	40
Dub Jones, Clev vs Chi	11-25-51	36
Gale Sayers, Chi vs SF	12-12-65	36
Paul Hornung, GB vs Balt Colts	10-8-61	33

On Thanksgiving Day, 1929, Nevers scored all the Cardinals' points on six rushing TDs and four PATs. The Cards defeated Red Grange and the Bears, 40–6. Jones and Sayers each rushed for four touchdowns and scored two more on returns in their teams' victories. Hornung scored four touchdowns and kicked 6 PATs and a field goal in a 45-7 win over the Colts.

FIELD GOALS

	Date	No.
†Rob Bironas, Ten vs Hou	10-21-07	8
Jim Bakken, StL Cards vs Pit	9-24-67	7
Rich Karlis, Min vs LA Rams	11-5-89	7
Chris Boniol, Dal vs GB	11-18-96	7
Billy Cundiff, Dal vs NYG	9-15-03	7

Bironas was 8 for 8.

Bakken was 7 for 9; Cundiff was 7 for 8; and Karlis and Boniol went 7 for 7.

† Active in 2009.

Single-Game Leaders (Cont.)

Scoring (Cont.)

TOUCHDOWNS

	Date	No.
Ernie Nevers, Chi Cards vs Chi	11-28-29	6
Dub Jones, Clev vs Chi	11-25-51	6
Gale Sayers, Chi vs SF	12-12-65	6
Bob Shaw, Chi Cards vs Balt Colts	10-2-50	5
Jim Brown, Clev vs Balt Colts	11-1-59	5
Abner Haynes, Dal Texans vs Oak	11-26-61	5
Billy Cannon, Hou vs NY Titans	12-10-61	5
Cookie Gilchrist, Buf vs NYJ	12-8-63	5
Paul Hornung, GB vs Balt Colts	12-12-65	5
Kellen Winslow, SD vs Oak	11-22-81	5
Jerry Rice, SF vs Atl	10-14-90	5
James Stewart, Jac vs Phil	10-12-97	5
Shaun Alexander, Sea vs Min	9-29-02	5
†Clinton Portis, Den vs KC	12-07-03	5

Rushing

YARDS GAINED

	Date	Yds
†Adrian Peterson, Min vs SD	11-4-07	296
†Jamal Lewis, Balt vs Clev	9-14-03	295
Corey Dillon, Cin vs Den	10-22-00	278
Walter Payton, Chi vs Min	11-20-77	275
O.J. Simpson, Buf vs Det	11-25-76	273

CARRIES

	Date	No.
Jamie Morris, Wash vs Cin	12-17-88	45
Butch Woolfolk, NYG vs Phil	11-20-83	43
James Wilder, TB vs GB	9-30-84	43
Rudi Johnson, Cin vs Hou	11-9-03	43
James Wilder, TB vs Pit	10-30-83	42
Terrell Davis, Den vs Buf (OT)	10-26-97	42
†Ricky Williams, Mia vs Buf	9-21-03	42

TOUCHDOWNS

	Date	No.
Ernie Nevers, Chi Cards vs Chi	11-28-29	6
Jim Brown, Clev vs Balt Colts	11-1-59	5
Cookie Gilchrist, Buf vs NYJ	12-8-63	5
James Stewart, Jac vs Phil	10-12-97	5
†Clinton Portis, Den vs KC	12-7-03	5

Passing

YARDS GAINED

	Date	Yds
N. Van Brocklin, Rams vs NY Yanks	9-28-51	554
Warren Moon, Hou vs KC	12-16-90	527
Boomer Esiason, Ariz vs Wash	11-10-96	522
Dan Marino, Mia vs NYJ	10-23-88	521
Phil Simms, NYG vs Cin	10-13-85	513

COMPLETIONS

	Date	No.
Drew Bledsoe, NE vs Min	11-13-94	45
Rich Gannon, Oak vs Pit	9-15-02	43
Richard Todd, NYJ vs SF	9-21-80	42
Vinny Testaverde, NYJ vs Sea	12-6-98	42
Warren Moon, Hou vs Dal	11-10-91	41
†Tony Romo, Dal vs NYG	12-06-09	41
Ken Anderson, Cin vs SD	12-20-82	40
Phil Simms, NYG vs Cin	10-13-85	40
Brad Johnson, TB vs Chi	11-18-01	40
†Marc Bulger, StL Rams vs NYG	10-02-05	40
†Kurt Warner, Ari vs NYJ	9-28-08	40

TOUCHDOWNS

	Date	No.
Sid Luckman, Chi vs NYG	11-14-43	7
Adrian Burk, Phil vs Wash	10-17-54	7
George Blanda, Hou vs NY Titans	11-19-61	7
Y. A. Tittle, NYG vs Wash	10-28-62	7
Joe Kapp, Min vs Balt Colts	9-28-69	7

Receiving

YARDS GAINED

	Date	Yds
Flipper Anderson, LA Rams vs NO	11-26-89	336
Stephone Paige, KC vs SD	12-22-85	309
Jim Benton, Clev vs Det	11-22-45	303
Cloyce Box, Det vs Balt Colts	12-3-50	302
Jimmy Smith, Jax vs Balt Ravens	9-10-00	291

RECEPTIONS

	Date	No.
†Brandon Marshall, Den vs Ind	12-13-09	21
†Terrell Owens, SF vs Chi	12-17-00	20
Tom Fears, Rams vs GB	12-3-50	18
†Brandon Marshall, Den vs SD	9-14-08	18
Clark Gaines, NYJ vs SF	9-21-80	17
Sonny Randle, StL Cards vs NYG	11-4-62	16
Jerry Rice, SF vs Rams	11-20-94	16
Keenan McCardell, Jax vs Rams	10-20-96	16
Troy Brown, NE vs KC	9-22-02	16

† Active in 2009.

Six tied with 15.

Single-Game Leaders *(Cont.)*

Receiving *(Cont.)*

TOUCHDOWNS

	Date	No.
Bob Shaw, Chi Cards vs Balt Colts	10-2-50	5
Kellen Winslow, SD vs Oak	11-22-81	5
Jerry Rice, SF vs Atl	10-14-90	5

All-Purpose Yards

	Date	Yds
Glyn Milburn, Den vs Sea	12-10-95	404
Billy Cannon, Hou vs NY Titans	12-10-61	373
Tyrone Hughes, NO vs LA Rams	10-23-94	347
Lionel James, SD vs LA Rai	11-10-85	345
Timmy Brown, Phi vs StL Cards	12-16-62	341

Longest Plays

RUSHING

	Opponent	Year	Yds
Tony Dorsett, Dal	Min	1983	99
†Ahman Green, GB	Den	2003	98
Andy Uram, GB	Chi Cards	1939	97
Bob Gage, Pit	Chi	1949	97
Jim Spavital, Balt Colts	GB	1950	96
Bob Hoernschemeyer, Det	NY Yanks	1950	96
Garrison Hearst, SF	NYJ	1998	96
Corey Dillon, Cin	Det	2001	96

PASSING

	Opponent	Year	Yds
Frank Filchock to Andy Farkas, Wash	Pit	1939	99
George Izo to Bobby Mitchell, Wash	Clev	1963	99
Karl Sweetan to Pat Studstill, Det	Balt Colts	1966	99
Sonny Jurgensen to Gerry Allen, Wash	Chi	1968	99
Jim Plunkett to Cliff Branch, LA Rai	Wash	1983	99
Ron Jaworski to Mike Quick, Phil	Atl	1985	99
Stan Humphries to Tony Martin, SD	Sea	1994	99
†Brett Favre to Robert Brooks, GB	Chi	1995	99
Trent Green to Marc Boerigter, KC	SD	2002	99
†Jeff Garcia to Andre Davis, Clev	Cin	2004	99
Gus Frerotte to Bernard Berrian, Min	Chi	2008	99

FIELD GOALS

	Opponent	Year	Yds
Tom Dempsey, NO	Det	1970	63
†Jason Elam, Den	Jac	1998	63
†Matt Bryant, TB	Phi	2006	62
†Rob Bironas, Ten	Ind	2006	62

PUNTS

	Opponent	Year	Yds
Steve O'Neal, NYJ	Den	1969	98
Joe Lintzenich, Chi	NYG	1931	94
Shawn McCarthy, NE	Buf	1991	93
Randall Cunningham, Phil	NYG	1989	91

INTERCEPTION RETURNS

	Opponent	Year	Yds
†Ed Reed, Balt	Phi	2008	107
†Ed Reed, Balt	Clev	2004	106
Vencie Glenn, SD	Den	1987	103
Louis Oliver, Mia	Buf	1992	103
Nine players tied at 102.			

KICKOFF RETURNS

	Opponent	Year	Yds
†Ellis Hobbs, NE	NYJ	2007	108
Al Carmichael, GB	Chi	1956	106
Noland Smith, KC	Den	1967	106
Roy Green, StL Cards	Dal	1979	106
†Brad Smith, NYJ	Ind	2009	106

PUNT RETURNS

	Opponent	Year	Yds
Robert Bailey, LA Rams	NO	1994	103
Gil LeFebvre, Cin	Brooklyn	1933	98
Charlie West, Min	Wash	1968	98
Dennis Morgan, Dal	StL Cards	1974	98
Terance Mathis, NYJ	Dal	1990	98

MISSED FIELD GOAL RETURNS

	Opponent	Year	Yds
†Antonio Cromartie, SD	Min	2007	109
†Devin Hester, Chi	NYG	2006	108
†Nathan Vasher, Chi	SF	2005	108
†Chris McAlister, Balt	Den	2002	107
Aaron Glenn, NYJ	Ind	1998	104

† Active in 2009.

Rushing

Year	Player, Team	Att	Yards	Avg	TD
1932	Cliff Battles, Bos	148	576	3.9	3
1933	Jim Musick, Bos	173	809	4.7	5
1934	Beattie Feathers, Chi	119	1,004	8.4	8
1935	Doug Russell, Chi Cards	140	499	3.6	0
1936	Alphonse Leemans, NY	206	830	4.0	2
1937	Cliff Battles, Wash	216	874	4.0	5
1938	Byron White, Pit	152	567	3.7	4
1939	Bill Osmanski, Chi	121	699	5.8	7
1940	Byron White, Det	146	514	3.5	5
1941	Clarence Manders, Bklyn	111	486	4.4	5
1942	Bill Dudley, Pit	162	696	4.3	5
1943	Bill Paschal, NY	147	572	3.9	10
1944	Bill Paschal, NY	196	737	3.8	9
1945	Steve Van Buren, Phil	143	832	5.8	15
1946	Bill Dudley, Pit	146	604	4.1	3
1947	Steve Van Buren, Phil	217	1,008	4.6	13
1948	Steve Van Buren, Phil	201	945	4.7	10
1949	Steve Van Buren, Phil	263	1,146	4.4	11
1950	Marion Motley, Clev	140	810	5.8	3
1951	Eddie Price, NY	271	971	3.6	7
1952	Dan Towler, LA	156	894	5.7	10
1953	Joe Perry, SF	192	1,018	5.3	10
1954	Joe Perry, SF	173	1,049	6.1	8
1955	Alan Ameche, Balt	213	961	4.5	9
1956	Rick Casares, Chi	234	1,126	4.8	12
1957	Jim Brown, Clev	202	942	4.7	9
1958	Jim Brown, Clev	257	1,527	5.9	17
1959	Jim Brown, Clev	290	1,329	4.6	14
1960	Jim Brown, Clev, NFL	215	1,257	5.8	9
	Abner Haynes, Dallas Texans, AFL	156	875	5.6	9
1961	Jim Brown, Clev, NFL	305	1,408	4.6	8
	Billy Cannon, Hou, AFL	200	948	4.7	6
1962	Jim Taylor, GB, NFL	272	1,474	5.4	19
	Cookie Gilchrist, Buf, AFL	214	1,096	5.1	13
1963	Jim Brown, Clev, NFL	291	1,863	6.4	12
	Clem Daniels, Oak, AFL	215	1,099	5.1	3
1964	Jim Brown, Clev, NFL	280	1,446	5.2	7
	Cookie Gilchrist, Buf, AFL	230	981	4.3	6
1965	Jim Brown, Clev, NFL	289	1,544	5.3	17
	Paul Lowe, SD, AFL	222	1,121	5.0	7
1966	Jim Nance, Bos, AFL	299	1,458	4.9	11
	Gale Sayers, Chi, NFL	229	1,231	5.4	8
1967	Jim Nance, Bos, AFL	269	1,216	4.5	7
	Leroy Kelly, Clev, NFL	235	1,205	5.1	11
1968	Leroy Kelly, Clev, NFL	248	1,239	5.0	16
	Paul Robinson, Cin, AFL	238	1,023	4.3	8
1969	Gale Sayers, Chi, NFL	236	1,032	4.4	8
	Dickie Post, SD, AFL	182	873	4.8	6
1970	Larry Brown, Wash, NFC	237	1,125	4.7	5
	Floyd Little, Den, AFC	209	901	4.3	3
1971	Floyd Little, Den, AFC	284	1,133	4.0	6
	John Brockington, GB, NFC	216	1,105	5.1	4
1972	O.J. Simpson, Buf, AFC	292	1,251	4.3	6
	Larry Brown, Wash, NFC	285	1,216	4.3	8
1973	O.J. Simpson, Buf, AFC	332	2,003	6.0	12
	John Brockington, GB, NFC	265	1,144	4.3	3
1974	Otis Armstrong, Den, AFC	263	1,407	5.3	9
	Lawrence McCutcheon, LA, NFC	236	1,109	4.7	3
1975	O.J. Simpson, Buf, AFC	329	1,817	5.5	16
	Jim Otis, StL, NFC	269	1,076	4.0	5
1976	O.J. Simpson, Buf, AFC	290	1,503	5.2	8
	Walter Payton, Chi, NFC	311	1,390	4.5	13
1977	Walter Payton, Chi, NFC	339	1,852	5.5	14
	Mark van Eeghen, Oak, AFC	324	1,273	3.9	7
1978	Earl Campbell, Hou, AFC	302	1,450	4.8	13
	Walter Payton, Chi, NFC	333	1,395	4.2	11
1979	Earl Campbell, Hou, AFC	368	1,697	4.6	19
	Walter Payton, Chi, NFC	369	1,610	4.4	14
1980	Earl Campbell, Hou, AFC	373	1,934	5.2	13
	Walter Payton, Chi, NFC	317	1,460	4.6	6
1981	George Rogers, NO, NFC	378	1,674	4.4	13
	Earl Campbell, Hou, AFC	361	1,376	3.8	10
1982	Freeman McNeil, NYJ, AFC	151	786	5.2	6
	Tony Dorsett, Dal, NFC	177	745	4.2	5
1983	Eric Dickerson, LA, NFC	390	1,808	4.6	18
	Curt Warner, Sea, AFC	335	1,449	4.3	13
1984	Eric Dickerson, LA, NFC	379	2,105	5.6	14
	Earnest Jackson, SD, AFC	296	1,179	4.0	8
1985	Marcus Allen, LA, AFC	380	1,759	4.6	11
	Gerald Riggs, Atl, NFC	397	1,719	4.3	10
1986	Eric Dickerson, LA, NFC	404	1,821	4.5	11
	Curt Warner, Sea, AFC	319	1,481	4.6	13
1987	Charles White, LA, NFC	324	1,374	4.2	11
	Eric Dickerson, Ind, AFC	223	1,011	4.5	5
1988	Eric Dickerson, Ind, AFC	388	1,659	4.3	14
	Herschel Walker, Dal, NFC	361	1,514	4.2	5
1989	Christian Okoye, KC, AFC	370	1,480	4.0	12
	Barry Sanders, Det, NFC	280	1,470	5.3	14
1990	Barry Sanders, Det, NFC	255	1,304	5.1	13
	Thurman Thomas, Buf, AFC	271	1,297	4.8	11
1991	Emmitt Smith, Dal, NFC	365	1,563	4.3	12
	Thurman Thomas, Buf, AFC	288	1,407	4.9	7
1992	Emmitt Smith, Dal, NFC	373	1,713	4.6	18
	Barry Foster, Pit, AFC	390	1,690	4.3	11
1993	Emmitt Smith, Dal, NFC	283	1,486	5.3	9
	Thurman Thomas, Buf, AFC	355	1,315	3.7	6

Rushing *(Cont.)*

Year	Player, Team	Att	Yards	Avg	TD
1994	Barry Sanders, Det, NFC	331	1,883	5.7	7
	Chris Warren, Sea, AFC	333	1,545	4.6	9
1995	Emmitt Smith, Dal, NFC	377	1,773	4.7	25
	Curtis Martin, NE, AFC	368	1,487	4.0	14
1996	Barry Sanders, Det, NFC	307	1,553	5.1	11
	Terrell Davis, Den, AFC	345	1,538	4.5	13
1997	Barry Sanders, Det, NFC	335	2,053	6.1	11
	Terrell Davis, Den, AFC	369	1,750	4.7	15
1998	Terrell Davis, Den, AFC	392	2,008	5.1	21
	Jamal Anderson, Atl, NFC	410	1,846	4.5	14
1999	Edgerrin James, Ind, AFC	369	1,553	4.2	13
	Stephen Davis, Wash, NFC	290	1,405	4.8	17
2000	Edgerrin James, Ind, AFC	387	1,709	4.4	13
	Robert Smith, Min, NFC	295	1,521	5.2	7
2001	Priest Holmes, Kan, AFC	327	1,555	4.8	8
	Stephen Davis, Wash, NFC	356	1,432	4.0	5
2002	Ricky Williams, Mia, AFC	383	1,853	4.8	16
	Deuce McAllister, NO, NFC	325	1,388	4.3	13
2003	Jamal Lewis, Balt, AFC	387	2,066	5.3	14
	Ahman Green, GB, NFC	355	1,883	5.3	15

Year	Player, Team	Att	Yards	Avg	TD
2004	Curtis Martin, NY Jets, AFC	371	1,697	4.6	12
	Shaun Alexander, Sea, NFC	353	1,696	4.8	16
2005	Shaun Alexander, Sea, NFC	370	1,880	5.1	27
	Larry Johnson, KC, AFC	336	1,750	5.2	20
2006	LaDainian Tomlinson, SD, AFC	348	1,815	5.2	28
	Frank Gore, SF, NFC	312	1,695	5.4	8
2007	LaDainian Tomlinson, SD, AFC	315	1,474	4.7	15
	Adrian Peterson, Min, NFC	238	1,341	5.6	12
2008	Adrian Peterson, Min, NFC	363	1,760	4.8	10
	Thomas Jones, NYJ, AFC	290	1,312	4.5	13
2009	Chris Johnson, Ten, AFC	358	2,006	5.6	14
	Steven Jackson, StL, NFC	324	1,416	4.4	4

Passing

Year	Player, Team	Att	Comp	Yards	TD	Int
1932	Arnie Herber, GB	101	37	639	9	9
1933	Harry Newman, NYG	136	53	973	11	17
1934	Arnie Herber, GB	115	42	799	8	12
1935	Ed Danowski, NYG	113	57	794	10	9
1936	Arnie Herber, GB	173	77	1,239	11	13
1937	Sammy Baugh, Wash	171	81	1,127	8	14
1938	Ed Danowski, NYG	129	70	848	7	8
1939	Parker Hall, Clev	208	106	1,227	9	13
1940	Sammy Baugh, Wash	177	111	1,367	12	10
1941	Cecil Isbell, GB	206	117	1,479	15	11
1942	Cecil Isbell, GB	268	146	2,021	24	14
1943	Sammy Baugh, Wash	239	133	1,754	23	19
1944	Frank Filchock, Wash	147	84	1,139	13	9
1945	Sid Luckman, Chi	217	117	1,725	14	10
1946	Bob Waterfield, LA	251	127	1,747	18	17
1947	Sammy Baugh, Wash	354	210	2,938	25	15
1948	Tommy Thompson, Phil	246	141	1,965	25	11
1949	Sammy Baugh, Wash	255	145	1,903	18	14
1950	Norm Van Brocklin, LA	233	127	2,061	18	14
1951	Bob Waterfield, LA	176	88	1,566	13	10
1952	Norm Van Brocklin, LA	205	113	1,736	14	17
1953	Otto Graham, Clev	258	167	2,722	11	9
1954	Norm Van Brocklin, LA	260	139	2,637	13	21
1955	Otto Graham, Clev	185	98	1,721	15	8
1956	Ed Brown, Chi	168	96	1,667	11	12
1957	Tommy O'Connell, Clev	110	63	1,229	9	8
1958	Eddie LeBaron, Wash	145	79	1,365	11	10

Year	Player, Team	Att	Comp	Yards	TD	Int
1959	Charlie Conerly, NYG	194	113	1,706	14	4
1960	Milt Plum, Clev, NFL	250	151	2,297	21	5
	Jack Kemp, LA, AFL	406	211	3,018	20	25
1961	George Blanda, Hou, AFL	362	187	3,330	36	22
	Milt Plum, Clev, NFL	302	177	2,416	18	10
1962	Len Dawson, Dal, AFL	310	189	2,759	29	17
	Bart Starr, GB, NFL	285	178	2,438	12	9
1963	Y.A. Tittle, NY, NFL	367	221	3,145	36	14
	Tobin Rote, SD, AFL	286	170	2,510	20	17
1964	Len Dawson, KC, AFL	354	199	2,879	30	18
	Bart Starr, GB, NFL	272	163	2,144	15	4
1965	Rudy Bukich, Chi, NFL	312	176	2,641	20	9
	John Hadl, SD, AFL	348	174	2,798	20	21
1966	Bart Starr, GB, NFL	251	156	2,257	14	3
	Len Dawson, KC, AFL	284	159	2,527	26	10
1967	Sonny Jurgensen, Wash, NFL	508	288	3,747	31	16
	Daryle Lamonica, Oak, AFL	425	220	3,228	30	20
1968	Len Dawson, KC, AFL	224	131	2,109	17	9
	Earl Morrall, Balt, NFL	317	182	2,909	26	17
1969	S. Jurgensen, Wash, NFL	442	274	3,102	22	15
	Greg Cook, Cin, AFL	197	106	1,854	15	11
1970	John Brodie, SF, NFC	378	223	2,941	24	10
	Daryle Lamonica, Oak, AFC	356	179	2,516	22	15
1971	Roger Staubach, Dal, NFC	211	126	1,882	15	4
	Bob Griese, Mia, AFC	263	145	2,089	19	9
1972	Norm Snead, NY, NFC	325	196	2,307	17	12
	Earl Morrall, Mia, AFC	150	83	1,360	11	7

Passing* *(Cont.)*

*Since 1973, the annual passing NFL leaders have been determined by a passer rating system that compares individual performances to a fixed performance standard. Before 1973, total passing yards gained was used.

Year	Player, Team	Comp%	Yds	TD	Int	Rating	Year	Player, Team	Comp%	Yds	TD	Int	Rating
1973	Roger Staubach, Dal, NFC	62.6	2,428	23	15	94.6	1988	Boomer Esiason, Cin, AFC	57.5	3,572	28	14	97.4
	Ken Stabler, Oak, AFC	62.7	1,997	14	10	88.3		Wade Wilson, Min, NFC	61.4	2,746	15	9	91.5
1974	Ken Anderson, Cin, AFC	64.9	2,667	18	10	95.7	1989	Joe Montana, SF, NFC	70.2	3,521	26	8	112.4
	Sonny Jurgensen, Wash, NFC	64.1	1,185	11	5	94.5		Boomer Esiason, Cin, AFC	56.7	3,525	28	11	92.1
1975	Ken Anderson, Cin, AFC	60.5	3,169	21	11	93.9	1990	Jim Kelly, Buf, AFC	63.3	2,829	24	9	101.2
	Fran Tarkenton, Min, NFC	64.2	2,994	25	13	91.8		Phil Simms, NY, NFC	59.2	2,284	15	4	92.7
1976	Ken Stabler, Oak, AFC	66.7	2,737	27	17	103.4	1991	Steve Young, SF, NFC	64.5	2,517	17	8	101.8
	James Harris, LA, NFC	57.6	1,460	8	6	89.6		Jim Kelly, Buf, AFC	64.1	3,844	33	17	97.6
1977	Bob Griese, Mia, AFC	58.6	2,252	22	13	87.8	1992	Steve Young, SF, NFC	66.7	3,465	25	7	107.0
	Roger Staubach, Dal, NFC	58.2	2,620	18	9	87.0		Warren Moon, Hou, AFC	64.7	2,521	18	12	89.3
1978	Roger Staubach, Dal, NFC	55.9	3,190	25	16	84.9	1993	Steve Young, SF, NFC	68.0	4,023	29	16	101.5
	Terry Bradshaw, Pit, AFC	56.3	2,915	28	20	84.7		John Elway, Den, AFC	63.2	4,030	25	10	92.8
1979	Roger Staubach, Dal, NFC	57.9	3,586	27	11	92.3	1994	Steve Young, SF, NFC	70.3	3,969	35	10	112.8
	Dan Fouts, SD, AFC	62.6	4,082	24	24	82.6		Dan Marino, Mia, AFC	62.0	4,453	30	17	89.2
1980	Brian Sipe, Clev, AFC	60.8	4,132	30	14	91.4	1995	Brett Favre, GB, NFC	62.9	4,413	38	13	99.5
	Ron Jaworski, Phi, NFC	57.0	3,529	27	12	91.0		Jim Harbaugh, Ind, AFC	61.2	2,575	17	5	100.7
1981	Ken Anderson, Cin, AFC	62.6	3,754	29	10	98.4	1996	John Elway, Den, AFC	61.6	3,328	26	14	89.2
	Joe Montana, SF, NFC	63.7	3,565	19	12	88.4		Steve Young, SF, NFC	67.7	2,410	14	6	97.2
1982	Ken Anderson, Cin, AFC	70.6	2,495	12	9	95.3	1997	Steve Young, SF, NFC	67.7	3,029	19	6	104.7
	Joe Theismann, Wash, NFC	63.9	2,033	13	9	91.3		Mark Brunell, Jax, AFC	60.7	3,281	18	7	91.2
1983	Steve Bartkowski, Atl, NFC	63.4	3,167	22	5	97.6	1998	Randall Cunningham, Min, NFC	60.9	3,704	34	10	106.0
	Dan Marino, Mia AFC	58.4	2,210	20	6	96.0		Vinny Testaverde, NYJ, AFC	61.5	3,256	29	7	101.6
1984	Dan Marino, Mia, AFC	64.2	5,084	48	17	108.9	1999	Kurt Warner, StL, NFC	65.1	4,353	41	13	109.2
	Joe Montana, SF, NFC	64.6	3,630	28	10	102.9		Peyton Manning, Ind, AFC	62.1	4,135	26	15	90.7
1985	Ken O'Brien, NY, AFC	60.9	3,888	25	8	96.2	2000	Trent Green, StL, NFC	60.4	2,063	16	5	101.8
	Joe Montana, SF, NFC	61.3	3,653	27	13	91.3		Brian Griese, Den, AFC	64.3	2,688	19	4	102.9
1986	Tommy Kramer, Min, NFC	55.9	3,000	24	10	92.6	2001	Kurt Warner, StL, NFC	68.7	4,830	36	22	101.4
	Dan Marino, Mia, AFC	60.7	4,746	44	23	92.5		Rich Gannon, Oak, AFC	65.8	3,828	27	9	95.5
1987	Joe Montana, SF, NFC	66.8	3,054	31	13	102.1	2002	Brad Johnson, TB, NFC	62.3	3,049	22	6	92.9
	Bernie Kosar, Clev, AFC	61.9	3,033	22	9	95.4		Chad Pennington, NY, AFC	68.9	3,120	22	6	104.2

Passing *(Cont.)*

Year	Player, Team	Comp%	Yds	TD	Int	Rating
2003	Steve McNair, Ten, AFC	62.5	3,215	24	7	100.4
	Daunte Culpepper, Min, NFC	65.0	3,479	25	11	96.4
2004	Peyton Manning, Ind, AFC	67.6	4,557	49	10	121.1
	Daunte Culpepper, Min, NFC	69.2	4,717	39	11	110.9
2005	Peyton Manning, Ind, AFC	67.3	3,747	28	10	104.1
	Matt Hasselbeck, GB, NFC	65.5	3,459	24	9	98.2
2006	Peyton Manning, Ind, AFC	65.0	4,397	31	9	101.0
	Drew Brees, NO, NFC	64.3	4,418	26	11	96.2
2007	Tom Brady, NE, AFC	68.9	4,806	50	8	117.2
	Tony Romo, Dal, NFC	64.4	4,211	36	19	97.4
2008	Philip Rivers, SD, AFC	65.3	4,009	34	11	105.5
	Kurt Warner, Ari, NFC	67.1	4,583	30	14	96.9
2009	Drew Brees, NO, NFC	70.6	4,388	34	11	109.6
	Philip Rivers, SD, AFC	65.2	4,254	28	9	104.4

Pass Receiving†

Year	Player, Team	No.	Yds	Avg	TD
1932	Ray Flaherty, NY	21	350	16.7	3
1933	John Kelly, Brooklyn	22	246	11.2	3
1934	Joe Carter, Phil	16	238	14.9	4
	Morris Badgro, NY	16	206	12.9	1
1935	Tod Goodwin, NY	26	432	16.6	4
1936	Don Hutson, GB	34	536	15.8	8
1937	Don Hutson, GB	41	552	13.5	7
1938	Gaynell Tinsley, Chi Cards	41	516	12.6	1
1939	Don Hutson, GB	34	846	24.9	6
1940	Don Looney, Phil	58	707	12.2	4
1941	Don Hutson, GB	58	738	12.7	10
1942	Don Hutson, GB	74	1,211	16.4	17
1943	Don Hutson, GB	47	776	16.5	11
1944	Don Hutson, GB	58	866	14.9	9
1945	Don Hutson, GB	47	834	17.7	9
1946	Jim Benton, LA	63	981	15.6	6
1947	Jim Keane, Chi	64	910	14.2	10
1948	Tom Fears, LA	51	698	13.7	4
1949	Tom Fears, LA	77	1,013	13.2	9
1950	Tom Fears, LA	84	1,116	13.3	7
1951	Elroy Hirsch, LA	66	1,495	22.7	17
1952	Mac Speedie, Clev	62	911	14.7	5
1953	Pete Pihos, Phil	63	1,049	16.7	10
1954	Pete Pihos, Phil	60	872	14.5	10
	Billy Wilson, SF	60	830	13.8	5
1955	Pete Pihos, Phil	62	864	13.9	7
1956	Billy Wilson, SF	60	889	14.8	5
1957	Billy Wilson, SF	52	757	14.6	6
1958	Raymond Berry, Balt	56	794	14.2	9
	Pete Retzlaff, Phil	56	766	13.7	2
1959	Raymond Berry, Balt	66	959	14.5	14
1960	Lionel Taylor, Den, AFL	92	1,235	13.4	12
	Raymond Berry, Balt, NFL	74	1,298	17.5	10
1961	Lionel Taylor, Den, AFL	100	1,176	11.8	4
	Jim Phillips, LA, NFL	78	1,092	14.0	5
1962	Lionel Taylor, Den, AFL	77	908	11.8	4
	Bobby Mitchell, Wash, NFL	72	1,384	19.2	11
1963	Lionel Taylor, Den, AFL	78	1,101	14.1	10
	Bobby Joe Conrad, St. Louis, NFL	73	967	13.2	10
1964	Charley Hennigan, Houston, AFL	101	1,546	15.3	8
	Johnny Morris, Chi, NFL	93	1,200	12.9	10
1965	Lionel Taylor, Den, AFL	85	1,131	13.3	6
	Dave Parks, SF, NFL	80	1,344	16.8	12
1966	Lance Alworth, SD, AFL	73	1,383	18.9	13
	Charley Taylor, Wash, NFL	72	1,119	15.5	12
1967	George Sauer, NY, AFL	75	1,189	15.9	6
	Charley Taylor, Wash, NFL	70	990	14.1	9
1968	Clifton McNeil, SF, NFL	71	994	14.0	7
	Lance Alworth, SD, AFL	68	1,312	19.3	10
1969	Dan Abramowicz, NO, NFL	73	1,015	13.9	7
	Lance Alworth, SD, AFL	64	1,003	15.7	4
1970	Dick Gordon, Chi, NFC	71	1,026	14.5	13
	Marlin Briscoe, Buf, AFC	57	1,036	18.2	8
1971	Fred Biletnikoff, Oak, AFC	61	929	15.2	9
	Bob Tucker, NY, NFC	59	791	13.4	4
1972	Harold Jackson, Phil, NFC	62	1,048	16.9	4
	Fred Biletnikoff, Oak, AFC	58	802	13.8	7
1973	Harold Carmichael, Phil, NFC	67	1,116	16.7	9
	Fred Willis, Hou, AFC	57	371	6.5	1
1974	Lydell Mitchell, Balt, AFC	72	544	7.6	2
	Charles Young, Phil, NFC	63	696	11.0	3
1975	Chuck Foreman, Min, NFC	73	691	9.5	9
	Reggie Rucker, Clev, AFC	60	770	12.8	3
	Lydell Mitchell, Balt, AFC	60	544	9.1	4
1976	MacArthur Lane, KC, AFC	66	686	10.4	1
	Drew Pearson, Dal, NFC	58	806	13.9	6
1977	Lydell Mitchell, Balt, AFC	71	620	8.7	4
	Ahmad Rashad, Min, NFC	51	681	13.4	2
1978	Rickey Young, Min, NFC	88	704	8.0	5
	Steve Largent, Sea, AFC	71	1,168	16.5	8

†Most catches.

Pass Receiving† *(Cont.)*

Year	Player, Team	No.	Yds	Avg	TD
1979	Joe Washington, Balt, AFC	82	750	9.1	3
	Ahmad Rashad, Min, NFC	80	1,156	14.5	9
1980	Kellen Winslow, SD, AFC	89	1,290	14.5	9
	Earl Cooper, SF, NFC	83	567	6.8	4
1981	Kellen Winslow, SD, AFC	88	1,075	12.2	10
	Dwight Clark, SF, NFC	85	1,105	13.0	4
1982	Dwight Clark, SF, NFC	60	913	15.2	5
	Kellen Winslow, SD, AFC	54	721	13.4	6
1983	Todd Christensen, LA, AFC	92	1,247	13.6	12
	Roy Green, StL, NFC	78	1,227	15.7	14
	Charlie Brown, Wash, NFC	78	1,225	15.7	8
	Earnest Gray, NY, NFC	78	1,139	14.6	5
1984	Art Monk, Wash, NFC	106	1,372	12.9	7
	Ozzie Newsome, Clev, AFC	89	1,001	11.2	5
1985	Roger Craig, SF, NFC	92	1,016	11.0	6
	Lionel James, SD, AFC	86	1,027	11.9	6
1986	Todd Christensen, LA, AFC	95	1,153	12.1	8
	Jerry Rice, SF, NFC	86	1,570	18.3	15
1987	J.T. Smith, StL Card, NFC	91	1,117	12.3	8
	Al Toon, NY, AFC	68	976	14.4	5
1988	Al Toon, NY, AFC	93	1,067	11.5	5
	Henry Ellard, LA, NFC	86	1,414	16.4	10
1989	Sterling Sharpe, GB, NFC	90	1,423	15.8	12
	Andre Reed, Buf, AFC	88	1,312	14.9	9
1990	Jerry Rice, SF, NFC	100	1,502	15.0	13
	Haywood Jeffires, Hou, AFC	74	1,048	14.2	8
	Drew Hill, Hou, AFC	74	1,019	13.8	5
1991	Haywood Jeffires, Hou, AFC	100	1,181	11.8	7
	Michael Irvin, Dal, NFC	93	1,523	16.4	8
1992	Sterling Sharpe, GB, NFC	108	1,461	13.5	13
	Haywood Jeffires, Hou, AFC	90	913	10.1	9
1993	Sterling Sharpe, GB, NFC	112	1,274	11.4	11
	Reggie Langhorne, Ind, AFC	85	1,038	12.2	3
1994	Cris Carter, Min, NFC	122	1,256	10.3	7
	Ben Coates, NE, AFC	96	1,174	12.2	7
1995	Herman Moore, Det, NFC	123	1,686	13.7	14
	Carl Pickens, Cin, AFC	99	1,234	12.5	17
1996	Jerry Rice, SF, NFC	108	1,254	11.6	8
	Carl Pickens, Cin, AFC	100	1,180	11.8	12
1997	Herman Moore, Det, NFC	104	1,293	12.4	8
	Tim Brown, Oak, AFC	104	1,408	13.5	5
1998	Frank Sanders, Ariz, NFC	89	1,145	12.9	3
	O.J. McDuffie, Mia, AFC	90	1,050	11.7	5
1999	Muhsin Muhammad, Car, NFC	96	1,253	13.1	8
	Jimmy Smith, Jax, AFC	116	1,636	14.1	6
2000	Muhsin Muhammad, Car, NFC	102	1,183	11.6	6
	Marvin Harrison, Ind, AFC	102	1,413	13.9	14
2001	Rod Smith, Den, AFC	113	1,343	11.9	11
	Keyshawn Johnson, TB, NFC	106	1,266	11.9	1
2002	Marvin Harrison, Ind, AFC	143	1,722	12.0	11
	Randy Moss, Min, NFC	106	1,347	12.7	7
2003	LaDainian Tomlinson, SD, AFC	100	725	7.3	4
	Torry Holt, StL, NFC	117	1,696	14.5	12
2004	Tony Gonzalez, KC, AFC	102	1,258	12.3	7
	Joe Horn, NO, NFC	94	1,399	14.9	11
2005	Chad Johnson, Cin, AFC	97	1,432	14.8	9
	Steve Smith, Car, NFC	103	1,563	15.2	12
2006	Chad Johnson, Cin, AFC	87	1,369	15.7	7
	Roy Williams, Det, NFC	82	1,310	16.0	7
2007	Reggie Wayne, Ind, AFC	104	1,510	14.5	10
	Larry Fitzgerald, Ari, NFC	100	1,409	14.1	10
2008	Andre Johnson, Hou, AFC	115	1,575	13.7	8
	Larry Fitzgerald, Ari, NFC	96	1,431	14.9	12
2009	Wes Welker, NE, AFC	123	1,348	11.0	4
	Steve Smith, NYG, NFC	107	1,220	11.4	7

†Most catches.

Scoring

Year	Player, Team	TD	FG	PAT	TP
1932	Earl Clark, Portsmouth	6	3	10	55
1933	Ken Strong, NY	6	5	13	64
	Glenn Presnell, Ports	6	6	10	64
1934	Jack Manders, Chi	3	10	31	79
1935	Earl Clark, Det	6	1	16	55
1936	Earl Clark, Det	7	4	19	73
1937	Jack Manders, Chi	5	18	15	69
1938	Clarke Hinkle, GB	7	3	7	58
1939	Andy Farkas, Wash	11	0	2	68
1940	Don Hutson, GB	7	0	15	57
1941	Don Hutson, GB	12	1	20	95
1942	Don Hutson, GB	17	1	33	138
1943	Don Hutson, GB	12	3	36	117
1944	Don Hutson, GB	9	0	31	85
1945	Steve Van Buren, Phil	18	0	2	110
1946	Ted Fritsch, GB	10	9	13	100
1947	Pat Harder, Chicago Cards	7	7	39	102
1948	Pat Harder, Chicago Cards	6	7	53	110
1949	Pat Harder, Chicago Cards	8	3	45	102
	Gene Roberts, NY	17	0	0	102
1950	Doak Walker, Det	11	8	38	128
1951	Elroy Hirsch, LA	17	0	0	102

Scoring *(Cont.)*

Year	Player, Team	TD	FG	PAT	TP
1952	Gordy Soltau, SF	7	6	34	94
1953	Gordy Soltau, SF	6	10	48	114
1954	Bobby Walston, Phi	11	4	36	114
1955	Doak Walker, Det	7	9	27	96
1956	Bobby Layne, Det	5	12	33	99
1957	Sam Baker, Was	1	14	29	77
	Lou Groza, Cle	0	15	32	77
1958	Jim Brown, Cle	18	0	0	108
1959	Paul Hornung, GB	7	7	31	94
1960	Paul Hornung, GB, NFL	15	15	41	176
	Gene Mingo, Den, AFL	6	18	33	123
1961	Gino Cappelletti, Bos, AFL	8	17	48	147
	Paul Hornung, GB, NFL	10	15	41	146
1962	Gene Mingo, Den, AFL	4	27	32	137
	Jim Taylor, GB, NFL	19	0	0	114
1963	Gino Cappelletti, Bos, AFL	2	22	35	113
	Don Chandler, NY, NFL	0	18	52	106
1964	Gino Cappelletti, Bos, AFL	7	25	36	155
	Lenny Moore, Balt, NFL	20	0	0	120
1965	Gale Sayers, Chi, NFL	22	0	0	132
	Gino Cappelletti, Bos, AFL	9	17	27	132
1966	Gino Cappelletti, Bos, AFL	6	16	35	119
	Bruce Gossett, LA, NFL	0	28	29	113
1967	Jim Bakken, StL, NFL	0	27	36	117
	George Blanda, Oak, AFL	0	20	56	116
1968	Jim Turner, NY, AFL	0	34	43	145
	Leroy Kelly, Clev, NFL	20	0	0	120
1969	Jim Turner, NY, AFL	0	32	33	129
	Fred Cox, Min, NFL	0	26	43	121
1970	Fred Cox, Min, NFC	0	30	35	125
	Jan Stenerud, KC, AFC	0	30	26	116
1971	Garo Yepremian, Mia, AFC	0	28	33	117
	Curt Knight, Was, NFC	0	29	27	114
1972	Chester Marcol, GB, NFC	0	33	29	128
	Bobby Howfield, NY AFC	0	27	40	121
1973	David Ray, LA, NFC	0	30	40	130
	Roy Gerela, Pit, AFC	0	29	36	123
1974	Chester Marcol, GB, NFC	0	25	19	94
	Roy Gerela, Pit, AFC	0	20	33	93
1975	O.J. Simpson, Buf, AFC	23	0	0	138
	Chuck Foreman, Min, NFC	22	0	0	132
1976	Toni Linhart, Balt, AFC	0	20	49	109
	Mark Moseley, Wash, NFC	0	22	31	97
1977	Errol Mann, Oak, AFC	0	20	39	99
	Walter Payton, Chi, NFC	16	0	0	96
1978	Frank Corral, LA, NFC	0	29	31	118
	Pat Leahy, NY, AFC	0	22	41	107
1979	John Smith, NE, AFC	0	23	46	115
	Mark Moseley, Was, NFC	0	25	39	114
1980	John Smith, NE, AFC	0	26	51	129
	Ed Murray, Det, NFC	0	27	35	116
1981	Ed Murray, Det, NFC	0	25	46	121
	Rafael Septien, Dal, NFC	0	27	40	121
	Jim Breech, Cin, AFC	0	22	49	115
	Nick Lowery, KC, AFC	0	26	37	115
1982	Marcus Allen, LA, AFC	14	0	0	84
	Wendell Tyler, LA, NFC	13	0	0	78
1983	Mark Moseley, Was, NFC	0	33	62	161
	Gary Anderson, Pit, AFC	0	27	38	119
1984	Ray Wersching, SF, NFC	0	25	56	131
	Gary Anderson, Pit, AFC	0	24	45	117
1985	Kevin Butler, Chi, NFC	0	31	51	144
	Gary Anderson, Pit, AFC	0	33	40	139
1986	Tony Franklin, NE, AFC	0	32	44	140
	Kevin Butler, Chi, NFC	0	28	36	120
1987	Jerry Rice, SF, NFC	23	0	0	138
	Jim Breech, Cin, AFC	0	24	25	97
1988	Scott Norwood, Buf, AFC	0	32	33	129
	Mike Cofer, SF, NFC	0	27	40	121
1989	Mike Cofer, SF, NFC	0	29	49	136
	David Treadwell, Den, AFC	0	27	39	120
1990	Nick Lowery, KC, AFC	0	34	37	139
	Chip Lohmiller, Was, NFC	0	30	41	131
1991	Chip Lohmiller, Was, NFC	0	31	56	149
	Pete Stoyanovich, Mia, AFC	0	31	28	121
1992	Pete Stoyanovich, Mia, AFC	0	30	34	124
	Morten Anderson, NO, NFC	0	29	33	120
	Chip Lohmiller, Was, NFC	0	30	30	120
1993	Jeff Jaeger, Rai, AFC	0	35	27	132
	Jason Hanson, Det, NFC	0	34	28	130
1994	John Carney, SD, AFC	0	34	33	135
	Fuad Reveiz, Min, NFC	0	34	30	132
	Emmitt Smith, Dal, NFC	22	0	0	132
1995	Emmitt Smith, Dal, NFC	25	0	0	150
	Norm Johnson, Pit, AFC	0	34	39	141
1996	John Kasay, Car, NFC	0	37	34	145
	Cary Blanchard, Ind, AFC	0	36	27	135
1997	Richie Cunningham, Dal, NFC	0	34	24	126
	Mike Hollis, Jax, AFC	0	41	31	134
1998	Gary Anderson, Min, NFC	0	35	59	164
	Steve Christie, Buf, AFC	0	33	41	140
1999	Jeff Wilkins, StL, NFC	0	20	64	124
	Mike Vanderjagt, Ind, AFC	0	34	43	145
2000	Marshall Faulk, StL, NFC	26	0	0	160
	Matt Stover, Balt, AFC	0	35	30	135
2001	Marshall Faulk, StL, NFC	21	0	0	128
	Mike Vanderjagt, Ind, AFC	0	28	41	125
2002	Jay Feely, Atl, NFC	0	32	42	138
	Priest Holmes, KC, AFC	24	0	0	144
2003	Jeff Wilkins StL, NFC	0	39	46	163
	Priest Holmes, KC, AFC	27	0	0	162
2004	Adam Vinatieri, NE, AFC	0	31	48	141
	David Akers, Phi, NFC	0	27	41	122
2005	Shayne Graham, Cin, AFC	0	28	47	131
	Shaun Alexander, Sea, NFC	28	0	0	168
2006	LaDainian Tomlinson, SD, AFC	31	0	0	186
	Robbie Gould, Chi, NFC	0	32	47	143
2007	Randy Moss, NE, AFC	23	0	0	138
	Mason Crosby, GB, NFC	0	31	48	141
2008	Stephen Gostkowski, NE, AFC	0	36	40	148
	David Akers, Phi, NFC	0	33	45	144
2009	Nate Kaeding, SD, AFC	0	32	50	146
	David Akers, Phi, NFC	0	32	43	139

Interceptions

Year	Player, Team	Int	Yds
1940	Clarence Parker, Brooklyn	6	146
	Kent Ryan, Det	6	65
	Don Hutson, GB	6	24
1941	Marshall Goldberg, Chicago Card	7	54
	Art Jones, Pit	7	35
1942	Clyde Turner, Chicago Bears	8	96
1943	Sammy Baugh, Wash	11	112
1944	Howard Livingston, NYG	9	172
1945	Ray Zimmerman, Phil	7	90
1946	Bill Dudley, Pittsburgh	10	242
1947	Frank Reagan, NYG	10	203
	Frank Seno, Bos	10	100
1948	Dan Sandifer, Wash	13	258
1949	Bob Nussbaumer, Chicago Car	12	157
1950	Orban Sanders, NY Yanks	13	199
1951	Otto Schnellbacher, NYG	11	194
1952	Dick Lane, LA	14	298
1953	Jack Christiansen, Det	12	238
1954	Dick Lane, Chicago Card	10	181
1955	Will Sherman, LA	11	101
1956	Lindon Crow, Chicago Card	11	170
1957	Milt Davis, Balt	10	219
	Jack Christiansen, Det	10	137
	Jack Butler, Pit	10	85
1958	Jim Patton, NYG	11	183
1959	Dean Derby, Pit	7	127
	Milt Davis, Balt	7	119
	Don Shinnick, Balt	7	70
1960	Goose Gonsoulin, Den, AFL	11	98
	Dave Baker, SF, NFL	10	96
	Jerry Norton, StL, NFL	10	96
1961	Billy Atkins, Buf, AFL	10	158
	Dick Lynch, NYG, NFL	9	60
1962	Lee Riley, NY Titans, AFL	11	122
	Willie Wood, GB, NFL	9	132
1963	Fred Glick, Hous, AFL	12	180
	Dick Lynch, NYG, NFL	9	251
	Roosevelt Taylor, Chi, NFL	9	172
1964	Dainard Paulson, NYJ, AFL	12	157
	Paul Krause, Wash, NFL	12	140
1965	W. K. Hicks, Hous, AFL	9	156
	Bobby Boyd, Balt, NFL	9	78
1966	Larry Wilson, StL, NFL	10	180
	Johnny Robinson, KC, AFL	10	136
	Bobby Hunt, KC, AFL	10	113
1967	Lem Barney, Det, NFL	10	232
	Dave Whitsell, NO, NFL	10	178
	Miller Farr, Hous, AFL	10	264
	Tom Janik, Buf, AFL	10	222
	Dick Westmoreland, Mia, AFL	10	127
1968	Dave Grayson, Oak, AFL	10	195
	Willie Williams, NYG, NFL	10	103
1969	Mel Renfro, Dal, NFL	10	118
	Emmitt Thomas, KC, AFL	9	146
1970	Johnny Robinson, KC, AFC	10	155
	Dick LeBeau, Det, NFC	9	96
1971	Bill Bradley, Phil, NFC	11	248
	Ken Houston, Hou, AFC	9	220

Year	Player, Team	Int	Yds
1972	Bill Bradley, Phil, NFC	9	73
	Mike Sensibaugh, KC, AFC	8	65
1973	Dick Anderson, Mia, AFC	8	163
	Mike Wagner, Pit, AFC	8	134
	Bobby Bryant, Min, NFC	7	105
1974	Emmitt Thomas, KC, AFC	12	214
	Ray Brown, Atl, NFC	8	164
1975	Mel Blount, Pit, AFC	11	121
	Paul Krause, Min, NFC	10	201
1976	Monte Jackson, LA, NFC	10	173
	Ken Riley, Cin, AFC	9	141
1977	Lyle Blackwood, Balt, AFC	10	163
	Rolland Lawrence, Atl, NFC	7	138
1978	Thom Darden, Clev, AFC	10	200
	Ken Stone, StL, NFC	9	139
	Willie Buchanon, GB, NFC	9	93
1979	Mike Reinfeldt, Hou, AFC	12	205
	Lemar Parrish, Wash, NFC	9	65
1980	Lester Hayes, Oak, AFC	13	273
	Nolan Cromwell, LA, NFC	8	140
1981	Everson Walls, Dal, NFC	11	133
	John Harris, Sea, AFC	10	155
1982	Everson Walls, Dal, NFC	7	61
	Ken Riley, Cin, AFC	5	88
	Bobby Jackson, NYJ, AFC	5	84
	Dwayne Woodruff, Pit, AFC	5	53
	Donnie Shell, Pit, AFC	5	27
1983	Mark Murphy, Wash, NFC	9	127
	Ken Riley, Cin, AFC	8	89
	Vann McElroy, LA, AFC	8	68
1984	Ken Easley, Sea, AFC	10	126
	Tom Flynn, GB, NFC	9	106
1985	Everson Walls, Dal, NFC	9	31
	Albert Lewis, KC, AFC	8	59
	Eugene Daniel, Ind, AFC	8	53
1986	Ronnie Lott, SF, NFC	10	134
	Deron Cherry, KC, AFC	9	150
1987	Barry Wilburn, Wash, NFC	9	135
	Mike Prior, Ind, AFC	6	57
	Mark Kelso, Buf, AFC	6	25
	Keith Bostic, Hou, AFC	6	-14
1988	Scott Case, Atl, NFC	10	47
	Erik McMillan, NYJ, AFC	8	168
1989	Felix Wright, Clev, AFC	9	91
	Eric Allen, Phil, NFC	8	38
1990	Mark Carrier, Chi, NFC	10	39
	Richard Johnson, Hou, AFC	8	100
1991	Ronnie Lott, LA, AFC	8	52
	Ray Crockett, Det, NFC	6	141
	Deion Sanders, Atl, NFC	6	119
	Aeneas Williams, Phoenix, NFC	6	60
	Tim McKyer, Atl, NFC	6	24
1992	Henry Jones, Buf, AFC	8	263
	Audray McMillian, Min, NFC	8	157
1993	Eugene Robinson, Sea, AFC	9	80
	Nate Odomes, Buf, AFC	9	65
	Deion Sanders, Atl, NFC	7	91
1994	Eric Turner, Clev, AFC	9	199
	Aeneas Williams, Ariz, NFC	9	89

Interceptions (Cont.)

Year	Player, Team	Int	Yds	Year	Player, Team	Int	Yds
1995	Orlando Thomas, Min, NFC	9	108	2004	Ed Reed, Balt, AFC	9	358
	Willie Williams, Pit, NFC	7	122		Chris Gamble, Car, NFC	6	15
1996	Tyrone Braxton, Den, AFC	9	128		Ken Lucas, Sea, NFC	6	46
	Keith Lyle, StL, NFC	9	152	2005	Ty Law, NYJ, AFC	10	195
1997	Ryan McNeil, StL, NFC	9	127		Deltha O'Neal, Cin, AFC	10	103
	Mark McMillian, KC, AFC	8	274		Darren Sharper, Min, NFC	9	276
	Darryl Williams, Sea, AFC	8	172	2006	Champ Bailey, Den, AFC	10	162
1998	Ty Law, NE, AFC	9	133		Asante Samuel, NE, AFC	10	120
	Kwamie Lassiter, Ariz, NFC	8	80		Walt Harris, SF, NFC	8	84
1999	Rod Woodson, Balt, AFC	7	195		Charles Woodson, GB, NFC	8	61
	Sam Madison, Mia, AFC	7	164	2007	Antonio Cromartie, SD, AFC	10	144
	James Hasty, KC, AFC	7	98		O. J. Atogwe, StL, NFC	8	125
	Donnie Abraham, TB, NFC	7	115	2008	Ed Reed, Balt, AFC	9	264
	Troy Vincent, Phil, NFC	7	91		Nick Collins, GB, NFC	7	295
2000	Darren Sharper, GB, NFC	9	109		Charles Woodson, GB, NFC	7	169
	Samari Rolle, Ten, AFC	7	140	2009	Darren Sharper, NO, NFC	9	376
	Brian Walker, Mia, AFC	7	80		Charles Woodson, GB, NFC	9	179
2001	Ronde Barber, TB, NFC	10	86		Asante Samuel, Phi, NFC	9	117
	Anthony Henry, Clev, AFC	10	177		Jairus Byrd, Buf, AFC	9	118
2002	Rod Woodson, Oak, AFC	8	225				
	Brian Kelly, TB, NFC	8	68				
2003	Brian Russell, Min, NFC	9	185				
	Tony Parrish, SFo, NFC	9	202				
	Patrick Surtain, Mia, AFC	7	59				
	Ed Reed, Balt, AFC	7	132				
	Marcus Coleman, Hou, AFC	7	95				

Sacks*

Year	Player, Team	Sacks	Year	Player, Team	Int	Yds
1982	Doug Martin, Min, NFC	11.5	1996	Kevin Greene, Car, NFC		14.5
	Jesse Baker, Hou, AFC	7.5		Michael McCrary, Sea, AFC		13.5
1983	Mark Gastineau, NYJ, AFC	19.0		Bruce Smith, Buf, AFC		13.5
	Fred Dean, SF, NFC	17.5	1997	John Randle, Min, NFC		15.5
1984	Mark Gastineau, NYJ, AFC	22.0		Bruce Smith, Buf, AFC		14.0
	Richard Dent, Chi, NFC	17.5	1998	Michael Sinclair, Sea, AFC		16.5
1985	Richard Dent, Chi, NFC	17.0		Reggie White, GB, NFC		16.0
	Andre Tippett, NE, AFC	16.5	1999	Kevin Carter, StL, NFC		17.0
1986	Lawrence Taylor, NYG, NFC	20.5		Jevon Kearse, Ten, AFC		14.5
	Sean Jones, LA, AFC	15.5	2000	La'Roi Glover, NO, NFC		17.0
1987	Reggie White, Phil, NFC	21.0		Trace Armstrong, Mia, AFC		16.5
	Andre Tippett, NE, AFC	12.5	2001	Michael Strahan, NYG, NFC		22.5
1988	Reggie White, Phil, NFC	18.0		Peter Boulware, Balt, AFC		15.0
	G. Townsend, LA, AFC	11.5	2002	Jason Taylor, Mia, AFC		18.5
1989	Chris Doleman, Min, NFC	21.0		Simeon Rice, TB, NFC		15.5
	Lee Williams, SD, AFC	14.0	2003	Michael Strahan, NYG, NFC		18.5
1990	Derrick Thomas, KC, AFC	20.0		Adewale Ogunleye, Mia, AFC		15.0
	Charles Haley, SF, NFC	16.0	2004	Dwight Freeney, Ind, AFC		16.0
1991	Pat Swilling, NO, NFC	17.0		Bertrand Berry, Ariz, NFC		14.5
	William Fuller, Hou, AFC	15.0	2005	Derrick Burgess, Oak, AFC		16.0
1992	Clyde Simmons, Phil, NFC	19.0		Osi Umenyiora, NYG, NFC		14.5
	Leslie O'Neal, SD, AFC	17.0	2006	Shawne Merriman, SD, AFC		17.0
1993	Neil Smith, KC, AFC	15.0		Aaron Kampman, GB, NFC		15.5
	Renaldo Turnbull, NO, NFC	13.0	2007	Jared Allen, KC, AFC		15.5
	Reggie White, GB, NFC	13.0		Patrick Kerney, Sea, NFC		14.5
1994	Kevin Greene, Pit, AFC	14.0	2008	DeMarcus Ware, Dal, NFC		20.0
	Ken Harvey, Wash, NFC	13.5		Joey Porter, Mia, AFC		17.5
	John Randle, Min, NFC	13.5	2009	Elvis Dumervil, Den, AFC		17.0
1995	Bryce Paup, Buf, AFC	17.5		Jared Allen, Min, NFC		14.5
	William Fuller, Phil, NFC	13.0				
	Wayne Martin, NO, NFC	13.0				

*Sacks were not kept as an official NFL statistic until 1982.

Pro Bowl Alltime Results

Date	Result
1-15-39	NY Giants 13, Pro All-Stars 10
1-14-40	Green Bay 16, NFL All-Stars 7
12-29-40	Chi Bears 28, NFL All-Stars 14
1-4-42	Chi Bears 35, NFL All-Stars 24
12-27-42	NFL All-Stars 17, Washington 14
1-14-51	A. Conf. 28, N. Conf. 27
1-12-52	N. Conf. 30, A. Conf. 13
1-10-53	N. Conf. 27, A. Conf. 7
1-17-54	East 20, West 9
1-16-55	West 26, East 19
1-15-56	East 31, West 30
1-13-57	West 19, East 10
1-12-58	West 26, East 7
1-11-59	East 28, West 21
1-17-60	West 38, East 21
1-15-61	West 35, East 31
1-7-62	AFL West 47, East 27
1-14-62	NFL West 31, East 30
1-13-63	AFL West 21, East 14
1-13-63	NFL East 30, West 20
1-12-64	NFL West 31, East 17
1-19-64	AFL West 27, East 24

Date	Result
1-10-65	NFL West 34, East 14
1-16-65	AFL West 38, East 14
1-15-66	AFL All-Stars 30, Buffalo 19
1-15-66	NFL East 36, West 7
1-21-67	AFL East 30, West 23
1-22-67	NFL East 20, West 10
1-21-68	AFL East 25, West 24
1-21-68	NFL West 38, East 20
1-19-69	AFL West 38, East 25
1-19-69	NFL West 10, East 7
1-17-70	AFL West 26, East 3
1-18-70	NFL West 16, East 13
1-24-71	NFC 27, AFC 6
1-23-72	AFC 26, NFC 13
1-21-73	AFC 33, NFC 28
1-20-74	AFC 15, NFC 13
1-20-75	NFC 17, AFC 10
1-26-76	NFC 23, AFC 20
1-17-77	AFC 24, NFC 14
1-23-78	NFC 14, AFC 13
1-29-79	NFC 13, AFC 7
1-27-80	NFC 37, AFC 27
2-1-81	NFC 21, AFC 7
1-31-82	AFC 16, NFC 13
2-6-83	NFC 20, AFC 19
1-29-84	NFC 45, AFC 3

Date	Result
1-27-85	AFC 22, NFC 14
2-2-86	NFC 28, AFC 24
2-1-87	AFC 10, NFC 6
2-7-88	AFC 15, NFC 6
1-29-89	NFC 34, AFC 3
2-4-90	NFC 27, AFC 21
2-3-91	AFC 23, NFC 21
2-2-92	NFC 21, AFC 15
2-7-93	AFC 23, NFC 20
2-6-94	NFC 17, AFC 3
2-5-95	AFC 41, NFC 13
2-4-96	NFC 20, AFC 13
2-2-97	AFC 26, NFC 23
2-1-98	AFC 29, NFC 24
2-7-99	AFC 23, NFC 10
2-6-00	NFC 51, AFC 31
2-4-01	AFC 38, NFC 17
2-10-02	AFC 38, NFC 30
2-2-03	AFC 45, NFC 20
2-8-04	NFC 55, AFC 52
2-13-05	AFC 38, NFC 27
2-12-06	NFC 23, AFC 17
2-10-07	AFC 31, NFC 28
2-10-08	NFC 42, AFC 30
2-8-09	NFC 30, AFC 21

Chicago All-Star Game* Results

Date	Result (Attendance)
8-31-34	Chi Bears 0, All-Stars 0 (79,432)
8-29-35	Chi Bears 5, All-Stars 0 (77,450)
9-2-36	All-Stars 7, Detroit 7 (76,000)
9-1-37	All-Stars 6, Green Bay 0 (84,560)
8-31-38	All-Stars 28, Washington 16 (74,250)
8-30-39	NY Giants 9, All-Stars 0 (81,456)
8-29-40	Green Bay 45, All-Stars 28 (84,567)
8-28-41	Chi Bears 37, All-Stars 13 (98,203)
8-28-42	Chi Bears 21, All-Stars 0 (101,100)
8-25-43	All-Stars 27, Washington 7 (48,471)
8-30-44	Chi Bears 24, All-Stars 21 (48,769)
8-30-45	Green Bay 19, All-Stars 7 (92,753)
8-23-46	All-Stars 16, Los Angeles 0 (97,380)
8-22-47	All-Stars 16, Chi Bears 0 (105,840)
8-20-48	Chi Cardinals 28, All-Stars 0 (101,220)
8-12-49	Philadelphia 38, All-Stars 0 (93,780)
8-11-50	All-Stars 17, Philadelphia 7 (88,885)
8-17-51	Cleveland 33, All-Stars 0 (92,180)
8-15-52	Los Angeles 10, All-Stars 7 (88,316)
8-14-53	Detroit 24, All-Stars 10 (93,818)
8-13-54	Detroit 31, All-Stars 6 (93,470)
8-12-55	All-Stars 30, Cleveland 27 (75,000)

Date	Result (Attendance)
8-10-56	Cleveland 26, All-Stars 0 (75,000)
8-9-57	NY Giants 22, All-Stars 12 (75,000)
8-15-58	All-Stars 35, Detroit 19 (70,000)
8-14-59	Baltimore 29, All-Stars 0 (70,000)
8-12-60	Baltimore 32, All-Stars 7 (70,000)
8-4-61	Philadelphia 28, All-Stars 14 (66,000)
8-3-62	Green Bay 42, All-Stars 20 (65,000)
8-2-63	All-Stars 20, Green Bay 17 (65,000)
8-7-64	Chicago 28, All-Stars 17 (65,000)
8-6-65	Cleveland 24, All-Stars 16 (68,000)
8-5-66	Green Bay 38, All-Stars 0 (72,000)
8-4-67	Green Bay 27, All-Stars 0 (70,934)
8-2-68	Green Bay 34, All-Stars 17 (69,917)
8-1-69	NY Jets 26, All-Stars 24 (74,208)
7-31-70	Kansas City 24, All-Stars 3 (69,940)
7-30-71	Baltimore 24, All-Stars 17 (52,289)
7-28-72	Dallas 20, All-Stars 7 (54,162)
7-27-73	Miami 14, All-Stars 3 (54,103)
1974	No game
8-1-75	Pittsburgh 21, All-Stars 14 (54,562)
7-23-76	Pittsburgh 24, All-Stars 0 (52,895)

*Discontinued.

Alltime Winningest NFL Head Coaches

Most Career Wins

Coach	Yrs	Teams	Regular Season				Career			
			W	L	T	Pct	W	L	T	Pct
Don Shula	33	Colts, Dolphins	328	156	6	.676	347	173	6	.665
George Halas	40	Bears	318	148	31	.671	324	151	31	.671
Tom Landry	29	Cowboys	250	162	6	.605	270	178	6	.601
Curly Lambeau	33	Packers, Cardinals, Redskins	226	132	22	.624	229	134	22	.623
*Paul Brown	25	Browns, Bengals	213	104	9	.672	222	116	9	.668
Chuck Noll	23	Steelers	193	148	1	.566	209	156	1	.572
M. Schottenheimer	20	Browns, Chiefs, Redskins, Chargers	200	126	1	.613	205	139	1	.596
Dan Reeves	23	Broncos, Giants, Falcons	190	165	2	.535	201	174	2	.536
Chuck Knox	22	Rams, Bills, Seahawks	186	147	1	.558	193	158	1	.550
Bill Parcells	18	Giants, Patriots, Jets, Cowboys	172	130	1	.569	183	138	1	.570
Mike Holmgren	17	Packers, Seahawks	161	111	0	.592	174	122	0	.588
Joe Gibbs	15	Redskins	154	94	0	.621	171	101	0	.629
Bud Grant	18	Vikings	158	96	5	.620	168	108	5	.607
Bill Cowher	14	Steelers	149	90	1	.623	161	99	1	.619
†Mike Shanahan	16	Raiders, Broncos	146	98	0	.598	154	103	0	.599
Marv Levy	17	Chiefs, Bills	143	112	0	.561	154	120	0	.562
†Bill Belichick	14	Browns, Patriots	138	86	0	.616	153	90	0	.630
Steve Owen	23	Giants	151	100	17	.595	153	108	17	.581
Tony Dungy	13	Buccaneers, Colts	139	69	0	.668	148	79	0	.652
Hank Stram	17	Chiefs, Saints	131	97	10	.571	136	100	10	.573
Weeb Ewbank	20	Colts, Jets	130	129	7	.502	134	130	7	.507
†Jeff Fisher	15	Oilers, Titans	128	102	0	.557	133	108	0	.552

Top Winning Percentages

	W	L	T	Pct		W	L	T	Pct
Vince Lombardi	105	35	6	.740	Don Shula	347	173	6	.665
John Madden	112	39	7	.731	Tony Dungy	148	79	0	.652
George Allen	118	54	5	.681	George Seifert	124	67	0	.650
George Halas	324	151	31	.671	†Bill Belichick	153	90	0	.630
*Paul Brown	222	116	9	.668	Joe Gibbs	162	93	0	.629

Note: Minimum 100 victories.

†Active in 2009. *Includes a 52–4–3 (5–0 playoff) record with Browns in AAFC and a 7–20–1 record with Bengals in AFL.

Pro Football Most Valuable Players

Year	Player/ Team	Position
1938	Mel Hein, NYG (NFL)	C
1939	Parker Hall, Clev (NFL)	HB
1940	Ace Parker, Brooklyn (NFL)	QB
1941	Don Hutson, GB (NFL)	E
1942	Don Hutson, GB (NFL)	E
1943	Sid Luckman, Chi Bears (NFL)	QB
1944	Frank Sinkwich, Det (NFL)	HB
1945	Bob Waterfield, Clev (NFL)	QB
1946	Bill Dudley, Pit (NFL)	HB
	Glenn Dobbs, Brooklyn (AAFC)	HB
1947	No Selection (NFL)	
	Otto Graham, Clev (AAFC)	QB
1948	No Selection (NFL)	
	Otto Graham, Clev (AAFC-tie)	QB
	Frankie Albert, SF (AAFC-tie)	QB
1949	No Selection (NFL)	
1950	No Selection (NFL)	
1951	Otto Graham, Clev (UP)	QB
1952	No Selection (NFL)	
1953	Otto Graham, Clev (UP)	QB
1954	Joe Perry, SF (UP)	FB
	Lou Groza, Clev (TSN)	OT/K

Year	Player/ Team	Position
1955	Otto Graham, Clev (UP, TSN)	QB
	Harlon Hill, Chi Bears (NEA)	E
1956	Frank Gifford, NYG (UP, NEA, TSN)	HB
1957	Y.A. Tittle, SF (UP)	QB
	Jim Brown, Clev (AP, TSN)	FB
	John Unitas, Balt (NEA)	QB
1958	Jim Brown, Clev (UP, AP, NEA, TSN)	FB
1959	John Unitas, Balt (UP, MCP, TSN)	QB
	Charley Conerly, NYG (AP, NEA)	QB
1960	Norm Van Brocklin, Phil, NFL (UP, AP, NEA, TSN, MCP)	QB
	Joe Schmidt, Det, NFL (UP- tie)	LB
	Abner Haynes, Dal Texans, AFL (UP, TSN)	HB
1961	Paul Hornung, GB, NFL (UP, AP, TSN, MCP)	HB
	Y.A. Tittle, NYG, NFL (NEA)	QB
	George Blanda, Hous, AFL (UP, TSN)	QB
1962	Y.A. Tittle, NYG, NFL (UP, TSN)	QB
	Jim Taylor, GB, NFL (AP, NEA)	FB
	Andy Robustelli, NYG, NFL (MCP)	DE
	Cookie Gilchrist, Buf, AFL (UP)	FB
	Len Dawson, Dal Texans, AFL (TSN)	QB
1963	Jim Brown, Clev, NFL (UP, NEA tie, MCP)	FB
	Y.A. Tittle, NYG, NFL (AP, NEA tie, TSN)	QB
	Lance Alworth, SD, AFL (UP)	WR
	Clem Daniels, Oak, AFL (TSN)	HB

Year	Player/ Team	Position
1964	Johnny Unitas, Balt, NFL (UP, AP, TSN, MCP)	QB
	Lenny Moore, Balt, NFL (NEA)	HB
	Gino Cappelletti, Boston, AFL (UP, TSN)	WR
1965	Jim Brown, Clev, NFL (UP, AP, TSN, NEA)	FB
	Pete Retzlaff, Phil, NFL (MCP)	TE
	Jack Kemp, Buf, AFL (UP)	QB
	Paul Lowe, SD, AFL (TSN)	RB
1966	Bart Starr, GB, NFL (UP, AP, NEA, TSN)	QB
	Don Meredith, Dal, NFL (MCP)	QB
	Jim Nance, Boston, AFL (UP, AP, TSN)	FB
1967	Johnny Unitas, Balt, NFL (UP, AP, NEA, TSN, MCP)	QB
	Daryl Lamonica, Oak, AFL (UP, AP, TSN)	QB
1968	Earl Morrall, Balt, NFL (UP, AP, NEA, TSN, PFW)	QB
	Leroy Kelly, Clev, AFL (MCP)	HB
	Joe Namath, NY Jets, AFL (UP, TSN, PFW)	QB
1969	Roman Gabriel, LA Rams, NFL (UP, AP, NEA, MCP, TSN, PFW)	QB
	Daryle Lamonica, Oak, AFL (UP, TSN, PFW)	QB
	Joe Namath, NY Jets, AFL (AP)	QB
1970	John Brodie, SF (AP, NEA)	QB
	George Blanda, Oak (MCP)	QB/K
1971	Alan Page, Min (AP)	DT
	Bob Griese, Miami (NEA)	QB
	Roger Staubach, Dal (MCP)	QB
1972	Larry Brown, Washington (AP, NEA, MCP)	RB
1973	O.J. Simpson, Buf (AP, NEA, MCP)	RB
1974	Ken Stabler, Oak (AP, NEA)	QB
	Merlin Olsen, LA Rams (MCP)	DT
1975	Fran Tarkenton, Min (PFWA, AP, NEA, MCP)	QB
1976	Bert Jones, Balt (PFWA, AP, NEA)	QB
	Ken Stabler, Oak (MCP)	QB
1977	Walter Payton, Chi (PFWA, AP, NEA)	RB
	Bob Griese, Miami (MCP)	QB
1978	Earl Campbell, Hous (PFWA, NEA)	RB
	Terry Bradshaw, Pit (AP, MCP)	QB
1979	Earl Campbell, Hous (PFWA, AP, NEA, MCP)	RB
1980	Brian Sipe, Clev (PFWA, AP, TSN)	QB
	Earl Campbell, Hous (NEA)	RB
	Ron Jaworski, Phil (MCP)	QB
1981	Ken Anderson, Cin (PFWA, AP, NEA, TSN, MCP)	QB
1982	Dan Fouts, SD (PFWA, NEA)	QB
	Mark Moseley, Washington (AP, TSN)	K
	Joe Theismann, Washington (MCP)	QB
1983	Joe Theismann, Washington (PFWAA, AP, NEA)	QB

Year	Player/ Team	Position
	Eric Dickerson, LA Rams (TSN)	RB
	John Riggins, Washington (MCP)	RB
1984	Dan Marino, Miami (PFWAA, AP, NEA, MCP, TSN)	QB
1985	Marcus Allen, LA Raiders (PFWAA, AP, TSN)	RB
	Walter Payton, Chi Bears (NEA, MCP)	RB
1986	Lawrence Taylor, NYG (PFWAA, AP, MCP, TSN)	LB
	Phil Simms, NYG (NEA)	QB
1987	Jerry Rice, SF (PFWAA, NEA, MCP, TSN)	WR
	John Elway, Den (AP)	QB
1988	Boomer Esiason, Cin (PFWAA, AP, TSN)	QB
	Roger Craig, SF (NEA)	RB
	Randall Cunningham, Phil (MCP)	QB
1989	Joe Montana, SF (PFWAA, AP, NEA, MCP, TSN)	QB
1990	Randall Cunningham, Phil (PFWAA)	QB
	Joe Montana, SF (AP)	QB
	Jerry Rice, SF (TSN)	WR
1991	Thurman Thomas, Buf (PFWAA, AP, TSN)	RB
	Barry Sanders, Det (MCP)	RB
1992	Steve Young, SF (PFWAA, AP, MCP, TSN)	QB
1993	Emmitt Smith, Dal (PFWAA, AP, MCP, TSN)	RB
1994	Steve Young, SF (PFWAA, AP, MCP, TSN)	QB
1995	Brett Favre, GB (PFWAA, AP, MCP, TSN)	QB
1996	Brett Favre, GB (PFWAA, AP, MCP, TSN)	QB
1997	Brett Favre, GB (AP – tie)	QB
	Barry Sanders, Det (PFWAA, AP (tie), MCP, TSN)	RB
1998	Terrell Davis, Den (PFWAA, AP, TSN)	RB
	Randall Cunningham, Min (MCP)	QB
1999	Kurt Warner, StL (AP, PFWAA, MCP)	QB
2000	Marshall Faulk, StL (AP, PFWAA)	RB
	Rich Gannon, Oak (MCP)	QB
2001	Kurt Warner, StL (AP)	QB
	Marshall Faulk, StL (PFWAA, MCP, TSN)	RB
2002	Rich Gannon, Oak (AP)	QB
2003	Peyton Manning, Ind (AP - tie)	QB
	Steve McNair, Ten (AP - tie)	QB
2004	Peyton Manning, Ind (AP)	QB
2005	Shaun Alexander, Sea (AP)	RB
2006	LaDainian Tomlinson, SD (AP)	RB
2007	Tom Brady, NE (AP)	QB
2008	Peyton Manning, Ind (AP)	QB
2009	Peyton Manning, Ind (AP)	QB

NOTE: AP-Associated Press, UP-United Press, PFW-*Pro Football Weekly*, TSN-*The Sporting News*, PFWAA-Pro Football Writers Association of America, PFWA-Pro Football Writers of America, MCP-Maxwell Club of Philadelphia, NEA-Newspaper Enterprise Association.

The NFL began awarding its MVP award, the Joe F. Carr Trophy (Carr was league president from 1921-39), in 1938, and continued to do so until 1946. Since that time, the NFL's Most Valuable Players and Players of the Year have been named by a variety of sources, among them, the United Press, the Associated Press, the Maxwell Club of Philadelphia, and the Pro Football Writers Association of America as well as magazines such as *Pro Football Weekly* and *The Sporting News*.

Year	Player/ Team	Position
1955	Alan Ameche, Balt (UP, TSN)	FB
1956	Lenny Moore, Balt (UP)	HB
	J.C. Caroline, Chi Bears (TSN)	DB
1957	Jim Brown, Clev (UP, AP, TSN)	FB
1958	Jimmy Orr, Pit (UP, AP)	OE
	Bobby Mitchell, Cleveland (TSN)	HB
1959	Nick Pietrosante, Det (AP, TSN)	FB
	Boyd Dowler, GB (UP)	OE
1960	Gail Cogdill, Det, NFL (AP, UP, TSN)	OE
	Abner Haynes, Dal Texans, AFL (UP, TSN)	HB
1961	Mike Ditka, Chi Bears, NFL (AP, UP, TSN)	OE
	Earl Faison, SD, AFL (UP, TSN)	DE
1962	Ronnie Bull, Chi Bears, NFL (AP, UP, TSN)	HB
	Curtis McClinton, Dal, AFL (UP, TSN)	FB
1963	Paul Flatley, Min, NFL (AP, UP, TSN)	OE
	Billy Joe, Den, AFL (UP, TSN)	FB
1964	Charley Taylor, Wash, NFL (AP, UP, TSN, NEA)	HB
	Matt Snell, NYJ, AFL (UP, TSN)	FB
1965	Gale Sayers, Chi, NFL (AP, UP, TSN, NEA)	HB
	Joe Namath, NYJ, AFL (UP, TSN)	QB
1966	Johnny Roland, StL, NFL (UP)	HB
	Tommy Nobis, Atl, NFL (AP, TSN, NEA)	LB
	Bobby Burnett, Buf, AFL (UP, TSN)	HB
1967	Mel Farr, Det, NFL (AP-Off, UP, TSN, NEA)	HB
	Lem Barney, Det NFL (AP-Def)	CB
	George Webster, Hous, AFL (UP)	LB
	Dickie Post, SD, AFL (TSN)	HB
1968	Earl McCullouch, Det, NFL (AP-Off, UP, TSN, NEA)	OE
	Claude Humphrey NFL (AP-Def)	DE
	Paul Robinson, Cin, AFL (UP, TSN)	HB
1969	Calvin Hill, Dal, NFL (AP-Off, UP, TSN, NEA)	HB
	Joe Greene NFL (AP-Def)	DT
	Greg Cook, Cin, AFL (UP)	QB
	Carl Garrett, Boston, AFL (TSN)	HB
1970	Raymond Chester, Oak (NEA)	TE
	Dennis Shaw Buf (AP-Off, UP-AFC)	QB
	Bruce Taylor, DB SF (AP-Def, UP-NFC)	DB
1971	Jim Plunkett NE (UP-AFC)	QB
	John Brockington GB (AP-Off, UP-NFC)	RB
	Isiah Robertson, SF (AP-Def)	LB
1972	Franco Harris, Pit (AP-Off, PFW, UP-AFC)	RB
	Chester Marcol, GB (UP-NFC)	PK
	Willie Buchanan, GB (AP-Def)	CB
1973	Chuck Foreman, Min (AP-Off, PFW)	RB
	Wally Chambers, Chi (AP-Def)	DT
	Bobbie Clark, Cin (UP-AFC)	RB
	Charle Young Phil (UP-NFC)	TE
1974	Don Woods, SD (AP-Off, PFW, UP-AFC)	RB
	John Hicks, NYG (UP-NFC)	G
	Jack Lambert, Pit (AP-Def)	LB
1975	Steve Bartkowski, Atl (PFW)	QB
	Robert Brazile, Hous (AP-Def, UP-AFC)	LB
	Mike Thomas, Wash (AP-Off, UP-NFC)	RB
1976	Mike Haynes, DB NE (AP-Def, UP-AFC)	DB
	Sammy White, Min (AP-Off, UP-NFC)	WR
1977	Tony Dorsett, Dal (NEA, AP-Off, UP-NFC)	RB
	A.J. Duhe, Mia (AP-Def, UP-AFC)	DE
1978	Earl Campbell, Hous Oilers (NEA, PFWA, AP-Off, UP-AFC)	RB
	Al "Bubba" Baker, Det (AP-Def, UP-NFC)	DE

Year	Player/ Team	Position
1979	Ottis Anderson, StL Card (NEA, PFWA, AP-Off, UP-NFC)	RB
	Jerry Butler, Buf (UP-AFC)	WR
	Jim Haslett, Buf (AP-Def)	LB
1980	Billy Sims, Det (NEA, TSN, PFWA, AP-Off, UP-NFC)	RB
	Joe Cribbs Buf (UP-AFC)	RB
	Buddy Curry, Atl (AP-Def tie)	LB
	Al Richardson, Atl (AP-Def tie)	LB
1981	Lawrence Taylor, NYG (NEA, AP-Def)	LB
	George Rogers, NO (TSN, PFWA, AP-Off, UP-NFC)	RB
	Joe Delaney, KC (UP-AFC)	RB
1982	Marcus Allen, LA Raiders (NEA, TSN, PFWA, AP-Off, UP-AFC)	RB
	Jim McMahon, Chi (UP-NFC)	QB
	Chip Banks, Cle (AP-Def)	LB
1983	Eric Dickerson, LA Rams (NEA, PFWA, AP-Off, UP-NFC)	RB
	Dan Marino, Mia (TSN)	QB
	Curt Warner, Sea (UP-AFC)	RB
	Vernon Maxwell, Balt (AP-Def)	LB
1984	Louis Lipps, Pit (NEA, TSN, PFWA, AP-Off, UP-AFC)	WR
	Paul McFadden, Phil (UP-NFC)	PK
	Bill Maas, KC (AP-Def)	DT
1985	Eddie Brown, Cin (NEA, TSN, AP-Off, PFWA)	WR
	Kevin Mack, Clev (UP-AFC)	RB
	Jerry Rice, SF (UP-NFC)	WR
	Duane Bickett, Ind (AP-Def)	LB
1986	Reuben Mayes, NO (NEA, TSN, PFWA, AP-Off, UP-NFC)	RB
	Leslie O'Neal, SD (AP-Def, UP-AFC)	DE
1987	Shane Conlan, Buf (PFWA, AP-Def, UP-AFC)	LB
	Bo Jackson, LA Raiders (NEA)	RB
	Robert Awalt, StL Card (TSN, UP-NFC)	TE
	Troy Stradford, Mia (AP-Off)	RB
1988	John Stephens, NE (NEA, AP-Off, PFWA)	RB
	Keith Jackson, Phil (TSN, UP-NFC)	TE
	Eric McMillan, NYJ (AP-Def)	S
1989	Barry Sanders, Det (NEA, TSN, PFWA, AP-Off, UP-NFC)	RB
	Derrick Thomas KC (AP-Def, UP-AFC)	LB
1990	Mark Carrier, Chi (PFWA, UP-NFC, AP-Def)	S
	Emmitt Smith, Dal (AP-Off)	RB
	Richmond Webb, Mia (TSN, UP-AFC)	OT
1991	Mike Croel, Den (PFWA, TSN, AP-Def, UP-AFC)	LB
	Lawrence Dawsey TB (UP-NFC)	WR
	Leonard Russell, NE (AP-Off)	RB
1992	Dale Carter, KC (PFWA, AP-Def, UP-AFC)	CB
	Carl Pickens, Cin (AP-Off)	WR
	Santana Dotson, TB (TSN)	DE
	Robert Jones, Dal (UP-NFC)	LB
1993	Jerome Bettis, LA Rams (PFWA, TSN, AP-Off, UP-NFC)	RB
	Rick Mirer, Sea (UP-AFC)	QB
	Dana Stubblefield, SF (AP-Def)	DT
1994	Marshall Faulk, Ind (PFWA, TSN, AP-Off, UP-AFC)	RB
	Bryant Young, SF (UP-NFC)	DT
	Tim Bowens, Mia (AP-Def)	DT
1995	Curtis Martin, NE (PFWA, TSN, AP-Off, UP-AFC)	RB
	Rashaan Salaam Chi (UP-NFC)	RB
	Hugh Douglas, NYJ (AP-Def)	DE

Year	Player/ Team	Position	Year	Player/ Team	Position
1996	Eddie George, Ten (AP, PFWA, AP-Off, TSN)	RB	2003	Anquan Boldin, Ariz (AP-Off)	WR
	Terry Glenn, NE (UP-AFC)	WR		Terrell Suggs, Bal (AP-Def)	LB
	Simeon Rice, Ariz (AP-Def, UP-NFC)	DE	2004	Ben Roethlisberger, Pit (AP-Off)	QB
1997	Warrick Dunn, TB (PFWA, AP-Off, TSN)	RB		Jonathan Vilma, NYJ (AP-Def)	LB
	Peter Boulware, Balt (AP-Def)	LB	2005	Carnell Williams, TB (AP-Off)	RB
1998	Randy Moss, Min (PFWA, AP-Off, TSN)	WR		Shawne Merriman, SD (AP-Def)	LB
	Charles Woodson LA Raiders (AP-Def)	CB	2006	Vince Young, Ten (AP-Off)	QB
1999	Edgerrin James, Ind (AP-Off, TSN)	RB		DeMeco Ryans, Hou (AP-Def)	LB
	Jevon Kearse, Ten (AP-Def)	DE	2007	Adrian Peterson, Min (AP-Off)	RB
2000	Mike Anderson, Den (AP-Off, TSN)	RB		Patrick Willis, SF (AP-Def)	LB
	Brian Urlacher, Chi (AP-Def)	LB	2008	Matt Ryan, Atl (AP-Off)	QB
2001	Anthony Thomas, Chi (AP-Off)	RB		Jerod Mayo, NE (AP-Def)	LB
	Kendrell Bell, Pit (AP-Def)	LB	2009	Percy Harvin, Min (AP-Off)	WR
2002	Clinton Ports, Den (AP-Off)	RB		Brian Cushing, Hou (AP-Def)	LB
	Julius Peppers, Car (AP-Def)	DE			

NOTE: AP-Associated Press, UP-United Press, PFW-*Pro Football Weekly*, TSN-*The Sporting News*, PFWAA-Pro Football Writers Association of America, PFWA-Pro Football Writers of America, MCP-Maxwell Club of Philadelphia, NEA-Newspaper Enterprise Association
Starting in 1960, the United Press annually awarded two Rookie of the Year awards, one to an AFL player and one to a NFL player. After the AFL-NFL merger, the UP kept the two-award format for the AFC and NFC. The UP stopped awarding RoY awards after the 1996 season.
Starting in 1967, the Associated Press began announcing two annual Rookie of the Year awards, as well. One went to the best offensive rookie in the NFL, the other to the best defensive rookie.

Alltime Number-One Draft Choices

Year	Team	Selection	Position
1936	Philadelphia	Jay Berwanger, Chicago	HB
1937	Philadelphia	Sam Francis, Nebraska	FB
1938	Cleveland	Corbett Davis, Indiana	FB
1939	Chicago Cardinals	Ki Aldrich, Texas Christian	C
1940	Chicago Cardinals	George Cafego, Tennessee	HB
1941	Chicago Bears	Tom Harmon, Michigan	HB
1942	Pittsburgh	Bill Dudley, Virginia	HB
1943	Detroit	Frank Sinkwich, Georgia	HB
1944	Boston	Angelo Bertelli, Notre Dame	QB
1945	Chicago Cardinals	Charley Trippi, Georgia	HB
1946	Boston	Frank Dancewicz, Notre Dame	QB
1947	Chicago Bears	Bob Fenimore, Oklahoma A&M	HB
1948	Washington	Harry Gilmer, Alabama	QB
1949	Philadelphia	Chuck Bednarik, Pennsylvania	C
1950	Detroit	Leon Hart, Notre Dame	E
1951	New York Giants	Kyle Rote, SMU	HB
1952	Los Angeles	Bill Wade, Vanderbilt	QB
1953	San Francisco	Harry Babcock, Georgia	E
1954	Cleveland	Bobby Garrett, Stanford	QB
1955	Baltimore	George Shaw, Oregon	QB
1956	Pittsburgh	Gary Glick, Colorado A&M	DB
1957	Green Bay	Paul Hornung, Notre Dame	HB
1958	Chicago Cardinals	King Hill, Rice	QB
1959	Green Bay	Randy Duncan, Iowa	QB
1960	Los Angeles	Billy Cannon, LSU	RB
1961	Minnesota	Tommy Mason, Tulane	RB
	Buffalo (AFL)	Ken Rice, Auburn	G
1962	Washington	Ernie Davis, Syracuse	RB
	Oakland (AFL)	Roman Gabriel, North Carolina St	QB
1963	LA Rams	Terry Baker, Oregon St	QB
	Kansas City (AFL)	Buck Buchanan, Grambling	DT
1964	San Francisco	Dave Parks, Texas Tech	E
	Boston (AFL)	Jack Concannon, Boston College	QB
1965	NY Giants	Tucker Frederickson, Auburn	RB
	Houston (AFL)	Lawrence Elkins, Baylor	E
1966	Atlanta	Tommy Nobis, Texas	LB
	Miami (AFL)	Jim Grabowski, Illinois	RB

Year	Team	Selection	Position
1967	Baltimore	Bubba Smith, Michigan St	DT
1968	Minnesota	Ron Yary, USC	T
1969	Buffalo (AFL)	O.J. Simpson, USC	RB
1970	Pittsburgh	Terry Bradshaw, Louisiana Tech	QB
1971	New England	Jim Plunkett, Stanford	QB
1972	Buffalo	Walt Patulski, Notre Dame	DE
1973	Houston	John Matuszak, Tampa	DE
1974	Dallas	Ed Jones, Tennessee St	DE
1975	Atlanta	Steve Bartkowski, California	QB
1976	Tampa Bay	Lee Roy Selmon, Oklahoma	DE
1977	Tampa Bay	Ricky Bell, USC	RB
1978	Houston	Earl Campbell, Texas	RB
1979	Buffalo	Tom Cousineau, Ohio St	LB
1980	Detroit	Billy Sims, Oklahoma	RB
1981	New Orleans	George Rogers, South Carolina	RB
1982	New England	Kenneth Sims, Texas	DT
1983	Baltimore	John Elway, Stanford	QB
1984	New England	Irving Fryar, Nebraska	WR
1985	Buffalo	Bruce Smith, Virginia Tech	DE
1986	Tampa Bay	Bo Jackson, Auburn	RB
1987	Tampa Bay	Vinny Testaverde, Miami (Fla.)	QB
1988	Atlanta	Aundray Bruce, Auburn	LB
1989	Dallas	Troy Aikman, UCLA	QB
1990	Indianapolis	Jeff George, Illinois	QB
1991	Dallas	Russell Maryland, Miami (Fla.)	DT
1992	Indianapolis	Steve Emtman, Washington	DT
1993	New England	Drew Bledsoe, Washington St	QB
1994	Cincinnati	Dan Wilkinson, Ohio St	DT
1995	Cincinnati	Ki-Jana Carter, Penn St	RB
1996	New York Jets	Keyshawn Johnson, USC	WR
1997	St Louis	Orlando Pace, Ohio St	OT
1998	Indianapolis	Peyton Manning, Tennessee	QB
1999	Cleveland	Tim Couch, Kentucky	QB
2000	Cleveland	Courtney Brown, Penn St	DE
2001	Atlanta	Michael Vick, Virginia Tech	QB
2002	Houston	David Carr, Fresno St	QB
2003	Cincinnati	Carson Palmer, USC	QB
2004	San Diego	Eli Manning, Mississippi	QB
2005	San Francisco	Alex Smith, Utah	QB
2006	Houston	Mario Williams, North Carolina St	DE
2007	Oakland	JaMarcus Russell, LSU	QB
2008	Miami	Jake Long, Michigan	OT
2009	Detroit	Matthew Stafford, Georgia	QB
2009	St. Louis	Sam Bradford, Oklahoma	QB

From 1947 through 1958, the first selection in the draft was a bonus pick, awarded to the winner of a random draw. That club, in turn, forfeited its last-round draft choice. The winner of the bonus choice was eliminated from future draws. The system was abolished after 1958, by which time all clubs had received a bonus choice.

Members of the Pro Football Hall of Fame

Herb Adderley
Troy Aikman
George Allen
Marcus Allen
Lance Alworth
Doug Atkins
Morris (Red) Badgro
Lem Barney
Cliff Battles
Sammy Baugh
Chuck Bednarik
Bert Bell
Bobby Bell
Raymond Berry
Elvin Bethea
Charles W. Bidwill Sr.
Fred Biletnikoff
George Blanda
Mel Blount
Terry Bradshaw
Bob (the Boomer) Brown
Jim Brown
Paul Brown
Roosevelt Brown
Willie Brown
Junios (Buck) Buchanan
Nick Buoniconti
Dick Butkus
Earl Campbell
Tony Canadeo
Joe Carr
Harry Carson
Dave Casper
Guy Chamberlin
Jack Christiansen
Earl (Dutch) Clark
George Connor
Jimmy Conzelman
Lou Creekmur
Larry Csonka
Al Davis
Willie Davis
Len Dawson
Fred Dean
Joe DeLamielleure
Eric Dickerson
Dan Dierdorf
Mike Ditka
Art Donovan
Tony Dorsett
John (Paddy) Driscoll
Bill Dudley
Albert Glen (Turk) Edwards
Carl Eller
John Elway
Weeb Ewbank
Tom Fears
Jim Finks
Ray Flaherty
Len Ford
Dan Fortmann
Dan Fouts
Benny Friedman
Frank Gatski
Bill George

Joe Gibbs
Frank Gifford
Sid Gillman
Otto Graham
Harold (Red) Grange
Bud Grant
Darrell Green
Joe Greene
Forrest Gregg
Bob Griese
Russ Grimm
Lou Groza
Joe Guyon
George Halas
Jack Ham
Dan Hampton
John Hannah
Franco Harris
Bob Hayes
Mike Haynes
Ed Healey
Mel Hein
Ted Hendricks
Wilbur (Pete) Henry
Arnie Herber
Bill Hewitt
Gene Hickerson
Clarke Hinkle
Elroy (Crazylegs) Hirsch
Paul Hornung
Ken Houston
Robert (Cal) Hubbard
Sam Huff
Lamar Hunt
Don Hutson
Michael Irvin
Rickey Jackson
Jimmy Johnson
John Henry Johnson
Charlie Joiner
David (Deacon) Jones
Stan Jones
Henry Jordan
Sonny Jurgensen
Jim Kelly
Leroy Kelly
Walt Kiesling
Frank (Bruiser) Kinard
Paul Krause
Earl (Curly) Lambeau
Jack Lambert
Tom Landry
Dick (Night Train) Lane
Jim Langer
Willie Lanier
Steve Largent
Yale Lary
Dante Lavelli
Bobby Layne
Dick LeBeau
Alphonse (Tuffy) Leemans
Marv Levy
Bob Lilly
Floyd Little
Larry Little

James Lofton
Vince Lombardi
Howie Long
Ronnie Lott
Sid Luckman
William Roy (Link) Lyman
Tom Mack
John Mackey
John Madden
Tim Mara
Wellington Mara
Gino Marchetti
Dan Marino
George Preston Marshall
Ollie Matson
Bruce Matthews
Don Maynard
George McAfee
Mike McCormack
Randall McDaniel
Tommy McDonald
Hugh McElhenny
John (Blood) McNally
Mike Michalske
Wayne Millner
Bobby Mitchell
Ron Mix
Art Monk
Joe Montana
Warren Moon
Lenny Moore
Marion Motley
Mike Munchak
Anthony Munoz
George Musso
Bronko Nagurski
Joe Namath
Earle (Greasy) Neale
Ernie Nevers
Ozzie Newsome
Ray Nitschke
Chuck Noll
Leo Nomellini
Merlin Olsen
Jim Otto
Steve Owen
Alan Page
Clarence (Ace) Parker
Jim Parker
Walter Payton
Joe Perry
Pete Pihos
Fritz Pollard
John Randle
Hugh (Shorty) Ray
Dan Reeves
Mel Renfro
Jerry Rice
John Riggins
Jim Ringo
Andy Robustelli
Art Rooney
Dan Rooney
Pete Rozelle
Bob St. Clair

Barry Sanders
Charlie Sanders
Gale Sayers
Joe Schmidt
Tex Schramm
Lee Roy Selmon
Billy Shaw
Art Shell
Don Shula
O.J. Simpson
Mike Singletary
Jackie Slater
Bruce Smith
Emmitt Smith
Jackie Smith
John Stallworth
Bart Starr
Roger Staubach
Ernie Stautner
Jan Stenerud
Dwight Stephenson
Hank Stram
Ken Strong
Joe Stydahar
Lynn Swann
Fran Tarkenton
Charley Taylor
Jim Taylor
Lawrence Taylor
Derrick Thomas
Emmitt Thomas
Thurman Thomas
Jim Thorpe
Andre Tippett
Y.A. Tittle
George Trafton
Charley Trippi
Emlen Tunnell
Clyde (Bulldog) Turner
Johnny Unitas
Gene Upshaw
Norm Van Brocklin
Steve Van Buren
Doak Walker
Bill Walsh
Paul Warfield
Bob Waterfield
Mike Webster
Roger Wehrli
Arnie Weinmeister
Randy White
Reggie White
Dave Wilcox
Bill Willis
Larry Wilson
Ralph Wilson
Kellen Winslow
Alex Wojciechowicz
Willie Wood
Rod Woodson
Rayfield Wright
Ron Yary
Steve Young
Jack Youngblood
Gary Zimmerman

Canadian Football League Grey Cup

Year	Results	Site	Attendance
1909	U of Toronto 26, Parkdale 6	Toronto	3,807
1910	U of Toronto 16, Hamilton Tigers 7	Hamilton	12,000
1911	U of Toronto 14, Toronto 7	Toronto	13,687
1912	Hamilton Alerts 11, Toronto 4	Hamilton	5,337
1913	Hamilton Tigers 44, Parkdale 2	Hamilton	2,100
1914	Toronto 14, U of Toronto 2	Toronto	10,500
1915	Hamilton Tigers 13, Toronto RAA 7	Toronto	2,808
1916–19	No game	—	—
1920	U of Toronto 16, Toronto 3	Toronto	10,088
1921	Toronto 23, Edmonton 0	Toronto	9,558
1922	Queen's U 13, Edmonton 1	Kingston	4,700
1923	Queen's U 54, Regina 0	Toronto	8,629
1924	Queen's U 11, Balmy Beach 3	Toronto	5,978
1925	Ottawa Senators 24, Winnipeg 1	Ottawa	6,900
1926	Ottawa Senators 10, Toronto U 7	Toronto	8,276
1927	Balmy Beach 9, Hamilton Tigers 6	Toronto	13,676
1928	Hamilton Tigers 30, Regina 0	Hamilton	4,767
1929	Hamilton Tigers 14, Regina 3	Hamilton	1,906
1930	Balmy Beach 11, Regina 6	Toronto	3,914
1931	Montreal AAA 22, Regina 0	Montreal	5,112
1932	Hamilton Tigers 25, Regina 6	Hamilton	4,806
1933	Toronto 4, Sarnia 3	Sarnia	2,751
1934	Sarnia 20, Regina 12	Toronto	8,900
1935	Winnipeg 18, Hamilton Tigers 12	Hamilton	6,405
1936	Sarnia 26, Ottawa RR 20	Toronto	5,883
1937	Toronto 4, Winnipeg 3	Toronto	11,522
1938	Toronto 30, Winnipeg 7	Toronto	18,778
1939	Winnipeg 8, Ottawa 7	Ottawa	11,738
1940	Ottawa 8, Balmy Beach 2	Toronto	4,998
1940	Ottawa 12, Balmy Beach 5	Ottawa	1,700
1941	Winnipeg 18, Ottawa 16	Toronto	19,065
1942	Toronto RCAF 8, Winnipeg RCAF 5	Toronto	12,455
1943	Hamilton F Wild 23, Winnipeg RCAF 14	Toronto	16,423
1944	Montreal St H-D Navy 7, Hamilton F Wild 6	Hamilton	3,871
1945	Toronto 35, Winnipeg 0	Toronto	18,660
1946	Toronto 28, Winnipeg 6	Toronto	18,960
1947	Toronto 10, Winnipeg 9	Toronto	18,885
1948	Calgary 12, Ottawa 7	Toronto	20,013
1949	Montreal Als 28, Calgary 15	Toronto	20,087
1950	Toronto 13, Winnipeg 0	Toronto	27,101
1951	Ottawa 21, Saskatchewan 14	Toronto	27,341
1952	Toronto 21, Edmonton 11	Toronto	27,391
1953	Hamilton Ticats 12, Winnipeg 6	Toronto	27,313
1954	Edmonton 26, Montreal 25	Toronto	27,321
1955	Edmonton 34, Montreal 19	Vancouver	39,417
1956	Edmonton 50, Montreal 27	Toronto	27,425
1957	Hamilton 32, Winnipeg 7	Toronto	27,051
1958	Winnipeg 35, Hamilton 28	Vancouver	36,567
1959	Winnipeg 21, Hamilton 7	Toronto	33,133
1960	Ottawa 16, Edmonton 6	Vancouver	38,102
1961	Winnipeg 21, Hamilton 14	Toronto	32,651
1962	Winnipeg 28, Hamilton 27	Toronto	32,655
1963	Hamilton 21, British Columbia 10	Vancouver	36,545
1964	British Columbia 34, Hamilton 24	Toronto	32,655
1965	Hamilton 22, Winnipeg 16	Toronto	32,655
1966	Saskatchewan 29, Ottawa 14	Vancouver	36,553
1967	Hamilton 24, Saskatchewan 1	Ottawa	31,358
1968	Ottawa 24, Calgary 21	Toronto	32,655
1969	Ottawa 29, Saskatchewan 11	Montreal	33,172
1970	Montreal 23, Calgary 10	Toronto	32,669
1971	Calgary 14, Toronto 11	Vancouver	34,484
1972	Hamilton 13, Saskatchewan 10	Hamilton	33,993
1973	Ottawa 22, Edmonton 18	Toronto	36,653
1974	Montreal 20, Edmonton 7	Vancouver	34,450
1975	Edmonton 9, Montreal 8	Calgary	32,454
1976	Ottawa 23, Saskatchewan 20	Toronto	53,467
1977	Montreal 41, Edmonton 6	Montreal	68,318

Canadian Football League Grey Cup

Year	Results	Site	Attendance
1978	Edmonton 20, Montreal 13	Toronto	54,695
1979	Edmonton 17, Montreal 9	Montreal	65,113
1980	Edmonton 48, Hamilton 10	Toronto	54,661
1981	Edmonton 26, Ottawa 23	Montreal	52,478
1982	Edmonton 32, Toronto 16	Toronto	54,741
1983	Toronto 18, British Columbia 17	Vancouver	59,345
1984	Winnipeg 47, Hamilton 17	Edmonton	60,081
1985	British Columbia 37, Hamilton 24	Montreal	56,723
1986	Hamilton 39, Edmonton 15	Vancouver	59,621
1987	Edmonton 38, Toronto 36	Vancouver	59,478
1988	Winnipeg 22, British Columbia 21	Ottawa	50,604
1989	Saskatchewan 43, Hamilton 40	Toronto	54,088
1990	Winnipeg 50, Edmonton 11	Vancouver	46,968
1991	Toronto 36, Calgary 21	Winnipeg	51,985
1992	Calgary 24, Winnipeg 10	Toronto	45,863
1993	Edmonton 33, Winnipeg 23	Calgary	50,035
1994	British Columbia 26, Baltimore 23	Vancouver	55,097
1995	Baltimore 37, Calgary 20	Regina, Saskatchewan	52,564
1996	Toronto 43, Edmonton 37	Hamilton, Ontario	38,595
1997	Toronto 47, Saskatchewan 23	Edmonton	60,431
1998	Calgary 26, Hamilton 24	Winnipeg	34,157
1999	Hamilton 32, Calgary 21	Vancouver	45,118
2000	British Columbia 28, Montreal 26	Calgary	43,822
2001	Calgary 27, Winnipeg 19	Montreal	65,255
2002	Montreal 25, Edmonton 16	Edmonton	62,531
2003	Edmonton 34, Montreal 22	Regina, Saskatchewan	50,909
2004	Toronto 27, British Columbia 19	Ottawa	51,242
2005	Edmonton 38, Montreal 35 (OT)	Vancouver	59,157
2006	British Columbia 25, Montreal 14	Winnipeg	44,786
2007	Saskatchewan 23, Winnipeg 19	Toronto	52,230
2008	Calgary 22, Montreal 14	Montreal	66,308
2009	Montreal 28, Saskatchewan 27	Calgary	46,020

In 1909, Earl Grey, the Governor-General of Canada, donated a trophy for the Rugby Football Championship of Canada. The trophy, which subsequently became known as the Grey Cup, was originally open only to teams registered with the Canada Rugby Union. Since 1954, it has been awarded to the winner of the Canadian Football League's championship game.

AMERICAN FOOTBALL LEAGUE I

Year	Champion	Record
1926	Philadelphia Quakers	7-2

AMERICAN FOOTBALL LEAGUE II

Year	Champion	Record
1936	Boston Shamrocks	8-3
1937	LA Bulldogs	8-0

AMERICAN FOOTBALL LEAGUE III

Year	Champion	Record
1940	Columbus Bullies	8-1-1
1941	Columbus Bullies	5-1-2

ALL-AMERICAN FOOTBALL CONFERENCE

Year	Championship Game
1946	Cleveland 14, NY Yankees 9
1947	Cleveland 14, NY Yankees 3
1948	Cleveland 49, Buffalo 7
1949	Cleveland 21, San Francisco 7

WORLD FOOTBALL LEAGUE

Year	World Bowl Championship
1974	Birmingham 22, Florida 21
1975	Disbanded midseason

UNITED STATES FOOTBALL LEAGUE

Year	Championship Game
1983	Michigan 24, Philadelphia 22
1984	Philadelphia 23, Arizona 3
1985	Baltimore 28, Oakland 24

X FOOTBALL LEAGUE

Year	Championship Game
2001	Los Angeles 38, San Francisco 6

NFL EUROPE*

Year	Champion	Record
1991	London	9-1-0
1992	Sacramento	8-2-0
1995	Frankfurt	6-4-0
1996	Scotland	7-3-0
1997	Barcelona	5-5-0
1998	Rhein	7-3-0
1999	Frankfurt	6-4-0
2000	Rhein	7-3-0
2001	Berlin	6-4-0
2002	Berlin	6-4-0
2003	Frankfurt	6-4-0
2004	Berlin	9-1-0
2005	Amsterdam	6-4-0
2006	Frankfurt	7-3-0
2007	Hamburg	7-3-0

*Known as World League of American Football until 1998. League folded after the 2007 season.

UNITED FOOTBALL LEAGUE

Year	Championship Game
2009	Las Vegas 20, Florida 17

College Football

Head coach Nick Saban (l.) and RB Mark Ingram led Alabama to the 2010 National Championship

Time and Tide

Powered by a stout defense and tailback Mark Ingram, the Crimson Tide's first-ever Heisman Trophy winner, Alabama ran the table to claim another national title

B.J. SCHECTER

EVER SINCE PAUL W. "BEAR" Bryant made the University of Alabama one of the nation's most iconic football programs, Crimson Tide fans have worshiped their football coaches. Literally. Outside Bryant-Denny Stadium there are four bronze statues of the coaches who have led the Tide to national championships: Wallace Wade, Frank Thomas, Bryant and Gene Stallings. Now they can add a fifth. From the second Nick Saban left the Miami Dolphins in 2007 to become the coach at Alabama he was treated like a deity, the savior who could bring the Crimson Tide back to the top of the college football world. Saban was the type of driven, maniacal perfectionist that Alabama had lacked as the football program slid into mediocrity, and much to the delight of a rabid and impatient fan base he delivered the Crimson Tide's first national title in 17 years ahead of schedule.

Saban learned from every loss and found a way to use it as motivation. After Alabama finished the 2008 season by losing to Florida in the SEC title game then fell to Utah in the Sugar Bowl, Saban made sure his team didn't forget. Alabama came into the season determined and focused, and though much of the attention was given to Tim Tebow and defending champion Florida, the Tide proved they were a better team. Alabama crushed Florida 32–13 in an SEC championship game rematch and then outclassed Texas 37–21 in the national title game when Longhorns star quarterback Colt McCoy was knocked out of action on Texas' first series.

Afterward, as confetti rained down in the Rose Bowl and Saban was doused with Gatorade (he looked upset afterward), Saban's wife, Terry, knew the celebration would be short-lived. "I guarantee you he's already thinking about next week," she said. Indeed, Saban would give his wife of 38 years all of two days away from football and then it was back to work. "The adage that 'success breeds success' is not necessarily true," he said. "The challenge to our returning players will be: Is this the beginning, or the end?"

Talk about a Debbie Downer. Consider all Alabama accomplished in a remarkable season. The Crimson Tide's massive defensive lineman Terrence Cody, a.k.a. Mt. Cody, blocked not one but two field goals to preserve a 12–10 win over Tennessee; Alabama rallied from a 14-point deficit for a 26–21 victory over archrival Auburn in the Iron Bowl; sophomore running back Mark Ingram became the first player in school history to win the Heisman Trophy; and Alabama managed to throttle Texas in the BCS National Championship despite the fact that 'Bama quarterback Greg McElroy completed just six passes for 58 yards.

Alabama caught a break early in the title game when McCoy was knocked out five

In the closest vote in history, Alabama's Mark Ingram edged out fellow running back Toby Gerhart of Stanford to win the first Heisman Trophy in Crimson Tide history.

snaps into the game with a shoulder injury on a seemingly innocuous hit, but the Crimson Tide quickly took advantage. Ingram and dynamic freshman Trent Richardson combined for 225 yards and four touchdowns against the nation's No. 1 rushing defense. Just when Alabama looked like it was going to make the game ugly, Texas stormed back behind true freshman quarterback Garrett Gilbert. But the Crimson Tide's defense stepped up and Alabama was able to pull away. With McCoy out, it wasn't the showdown many fans had hoped for, but it still counted as a national championship and Alabama players and fans weren't going to let anything taint their long-awaited title.

"I don't write the script. I just play it out," said McElroy. "On my ring it's not going to stay BEAT TEXAS WITHOUT COLT. It's going to say NATIONAL CHAMPIONS."

Coming into the season, Florida was the overwhelming favorite to be wearing national championship rings come January. With Tebow returning for his senior season, the pressure was on the Gators and nobody felt it more than coach Urban Meyer. Like many coaches, Meyer is more relieved than elated when his team wins and is devastated when they lose. And no defeat tore him up more the Alabama one. Hours after the Gators were pounded, Meyer's wife Shelley, called 911 and said her husband was lying on the floor experiencing intense chest pains. Meyer was rushed to the hospital and later he revealed that he had been experiencing chest pains all season.

A few weeks later, as Florida was preparing to face undefeated Cincinnati in the Sugar Bowl, Meyer announced that he would be taking an indefinite leave of absence following the bowl game. But less than 24 hours later he changed his mind and said he would come back after a temporary layoff (he claimed he was inspired after watching his team practice), leaving everyone unsure as to how much time he would spend away from the sidelines. The whole saga was surreal and one had to wonder if Meyer was endangering his life by staying in coaching. He admitted that his health problems (chest pains, dropping considerable weight during the season) were stress-related and self-inflicted.

BOB ROSATO

Tech, Oklahoma and Oklahoma State to the Pac-10. Eulogies were written for the Big 12, but thanks to some last-minute back-room negotiations, conference linchpin Texas decided to stay and only Colorado left for the Pac-10. Utah, from the Mountain West, soon followed the Buffaloes, making a Pac-10 conference championship game all but a certainty come fall 2011.

This step up by Utah comes as little surprise, since teams outside the BCS conferences once again proved that there's some pretty good football played in other parts of the country. Boise State and TCU, for example, marched through the regular season undefeated. And as protests over the BCS grew louder and some politicians threatened congressional intervention (even President Obama chimed in, lobbying for a playoff), Boise State earned a trip to the Fiesta Bowl, where they would face...TCU.

Many wondered whether two non-BCS teams would attract a large TV audience and put on an entertaining bowl game. The Broncos and Horned Frogs more than delivered with Boise State prevailing 17–10 in arguably the best of the major bowl games. In what was expected to be a shootout, Boise State's D overshadowed TCU's highly-touted defense. In the end, however, the Broncos delivered on yet another crunch-time trick play, calling a gutsy fourth-quarter fake punt from their own 33-yard-line to set up the winning touchdown.

Though Boise State finished the season undefeated there was no doubt which team was national champion. Alabama emerged from the nation's toughest conference unscathed, then beat an unbeaten Texas team. The Crimson Tide climbed back to the top of the mountain and with Saban as their sherpa they planned to stay there.

Meyer vowed to do some soul-searching and reevaluate his priorities, but the man is wired a certain way and it's hard to change. As Shelley Meyer pointed out, when Florida loses Urban is "miserable. He can't sleep, and he can't eat. He's in the tank." Meyer eventually led Florida to a Sugar Bowl win, oversaw another top recruiting class and was back for spring practice. For his sake, let's hope he can get his health under control.

The health of the Big 12 was in serious jeopardy this past summer as the Big Ten and Pac-10 attempted to raid the conference and radically alter the landscape of college football. Initial talk of expansion centered around the Big Ten, which has long courted Notre Dame and talked about expanding to 12, 14 or even 16 teams. Notre Dame vowed to stay independent, however, and so five-time national champion Nebraska became the first school to jump ship, leaving the Big 12 for the Big Ten starting in the 2011–12 season. That move triggered a series of events that turned the Big 12 upside down as the Pac-10, under the leadership of new commissioner Larry Scott, appeared to work a deal to bring Colorado, Texas, Texas A&M, Texas

Final Polls

Associated Press

	Record	Pts	Head Coach	SI Preseason Rank
1. ....Alabama (60)	14–0	1500	Nick Saban	8
2. ....Texas	13–1	1399	Mack Brown	2
3. ....Florida	13–1	1370	Urban Meyer	1
4. ....Boise St	14–0	1366	Chris Petersen	9
5. ....Ohio St	11–2	1224	Jim Tressel	10
6. ....TCU	12–1	1163	Gary Patterson	17
7. ....Iowa	11–2	1126	Kirk Ferentz	24
8. ....Cincinnati	12–1	1060	Brian Kelly*	39
9. ....Penn St	11–2	1016	Joe Paterno	14
10. ....Virginia Tech	10–3	953	Frank Beamer	5
11. ....Oregon	10–3	886	Mike Bellotti	11
12. ....BYU	11–2	806	Bronco Mendenhall	22
13. ....Georgia Tech	11–3	768	Paul Johnson	12
14. ....Nebraska	10–4	724	Bo Pelini	34
15. ....Pittsburgh	10–3	697	Dave Wannstedt	25
16. ....Wisconsin	10–3	571	Bret Bielema	48
17. ....LSU	9–4	501	Les Miles	13
18. ....Utah	10–3	491	Kyle Whittingham	19
19. ....Miami (Fla.)	9–4	310	Randy Shannon	36
20. ....Mississippi	9–4	296	Houston Nutt	6
21. ....Texas Tech	9–4	224	Mike Leach*	26
22. ....USC	9–4	216	Pete Carroll	4
23. ....Central Michigan	12–2	166	Dan Enos	47
24. ....Clemson	9–5	125	Dabo Swinney	43
25. ....West Virginia	9–4	91	Bill Stewart	28

Note: As voted by a panel of 60 sportswriters and broadcasters following bowl games (first place votes in parentheses). *Did not coach team's 2009–10 bowl game.

USA Today/ESPN/Coaches

	Pts	SI Preseason Rank		Pts	SI Preseason Rank
1. ....Alabama (58)	1450	8	14. ....Nebraska	671	34
2. ....Texas	1360	2	15. ....Pittsburgh	667	25
3. ....Florida	1323	1	16. ....Wisconsin	587	48
4. ....Boise St	1312	9	17. ....LSU	530	13
5. ....Ohio St	1190	10	18. ....Utah	466	19
6. ....TCU	1104	17	19. ....Miami (Fla.)	336	36
7. ....Iowa	1087	24	20. ....USC	217	4
8. ....Penn St	1071	14	21. ....Mississippi	192	6
9. ....Cincinnati	943	39	22. ....West Virginia	159	28
10. ....Virginia Tech	940	5	23. ....Texas Tech	152	26
11. ....Oregon	846	11	24. ....Central Michigan	123	47
12. ....BYU	814	22	25. ....Oklahoma St	92	7
13. ....Georgia Tech	741	12			

Note: Voted by a panel of 58 FBS (I-A) head coaches; 25 points for 1st, 24 for 2nd, etc. (First place votes in parentheses).

Bowls and Playoffs

NCAA Football Bowl Subdivision (I-A) Bowl Results

Date	Bowl	Result	Payout/Team ($)	Attendance
12-19-09	New Mexico	Wyoming 35, Fresno St 28	750,000	24,989
12-19-09	St. Petersburg	Rutgers 45, Central Florida 24	1 million	29,736
12-20-09	New Orleans	Middle Tennessee St, 42, Southern Miss 32	325,000	30,228
12-22-09	Las Vegas	BYU 44, Oregon St 20	1 million	40,018
12-23-09	Poinsettia	Utah 37, California 27	750,000	32,665
12-24-09	Hawaii	SMU 45, Nevada 10	750,000	32,650
12-26-09	Little Caesars	Marshall 21, Ohio 17	750,000	30,311
12-26-09	Emerald	USC 24, Boston College 13	750,000	40,121
12-26-09	Meineke	Pittsburgh 19, North Carolina 17	1 million	50,389
12-27-09	Music City	Clemson 21, Kentucky 13	1.65 million	57,280

NCAA Football Bowl Subdivision (I-A) Bowl Results *(Cont.)*

Date	Bowl	Result	Payout/Team($)	Attendance
12-28-09	Independence	Georgia 44, Texas A&M 20	1.1 million	49,653
12-29-09	Champs Sports	Wisconsin 20, Miami (Fla.)	2.13 million	56,747
12-29-09	EagleBank	UCLA 30, Temple 21	1 million	23,072
12-30-09	Humanitarian	Idaho 43, Bowling Green 42	750,000	26,726
12-30-09	Holiday	Nebraska 33, Arizona 0	2.2 million	64,607
12-31-09	Texas	Navy 35, Missouri 13	1.25 million	69,441
12-31-09	Armed Forces	Air Force 47, Houston 20	750,000	41,414
12-31-09	Insight	Iowa St 14, Minnesota 13	1.2 million	45,090
12-31-09	Sun	Oklahoma 31, Stanford 27	1.9 million	53,713
12-31-09	Chick-fil-A	Virginia Tech 37, Tennessee 14	5.83 million	73,777
01-01-10	Outback	Auburn 38, Northwestern 35	3.1 million	49,383
01-01-10	Capital One	Penn St 19, LSU 17	4.25 million	63,025
01-01-10	Gator	Florida St 33, West Virginia 21	2.25 million	84,129
01-01-10	Rose	Ohio St 26, Oregon 17	17 million	93,963
01-01-10	Sugar	Florida 51, Cincinnati 24	17 million	65,207
01-02-10	International	South Florida 27, Northern Illinois 3	750,000	22,185
01-02-10	Papajohns.com	Connecticut 20, South Carolina 7	300,000	45,254
01-02-10	Liberty	Arkansas 20, East Carolina 17	1.35 million	62,742
01-02-10	Alamo	Texas Tech 41, Michigan St 31	2.25 million	64,757
01-02-10	Cotton	Mississippi 21, Oklahoma St 7	3 million	77,928
01-04-10	Fiesta	Boise St 17, TCU 10	17 million	73,227
01-05-10	Orange	Iowa 24, Georgia Tech 14	17 million	66,131
01-06-10	GMAC	Central Michigan 44, Troy 41 (OT)	750,000	34,486
01-08-09	BCS Championship	Alabama 37, Texas 21	17 million	94,906

NCAA FCS (I-AA) Championship Box Score

Montana	7	7	0	7—21
Villanova	3	6	7	7—23

FIRST QUARTER

Villanova: FG Yako 23, 5:12.
Montana: TD Mariani 24 pass from Selle (McKnight kick), 3:15.

SECOND QUARTER

\Montana: TD Sambrano 4 pass from Selle (McKnight kick), 6:48.
Villanova: TD Szczur 5 run (kick failed), 3:34.

THIRD QUARTER

Villanova: TD Farmer 3 pass from Whitney (Yako kick), 5:27.

FOURTH QUARTER

Villanova: TD Szczur 3 run (Yako kick), 11:04.
Montana: TD Sambrano 53 pass from Selle (McKnight kick), 1:07.

	MONTANA	VILLANOVA
First downs	18	22
Rushes-net yards	19-60	51-351
Net passing yards	365	142
Comp/Att/Int	28-37-0	10-13-1
Punts/total yards	5-199	3-125
Fumbles-lost	0-0	1-0
Penalties-yards	3-25	6-40
Time of possession	26:33	33:27

12-18-09, Chattanooga, Tennessee; Att: 14,328.

Small College Championship Summaries

NCAA DIVISION II

First round: Neb.-Kearney 35, Saginaw Valley 20; Hillsdale 27, Minn St.-Mankato 24; Arkansas Tech 41, UNC-Pembroke 13; West Alabama 24, Albany St (Ga.) 22; Edinboro 31, East Stroudsburg 16; California (Pa.) 42, Fayetteville St 13; Tarleton St 57, Texas A&M-Kingsville 56 (2OT); Abilene Christian 24, Midwestern St 21.
Second Round: Minn.-Duluth 42, Neb.-Kearney 7; Grand Valley St 44, Hillsdale 27; North Alabama 41, Arkansas Tech 28; Carson-Newman 59, West Alabama 21; West Liberty 84, Edinboro 63; California (Pa.) 26, Shippensburg 21; Central Washington 27, Tarleton St 6; NW Missouri St 35, Abilene Christian 10.
Quarterfinals: Grand Valley St 24, Minn.-Duluth 10; Carson-Newman 24, North Alabama 21; California (Pa.) 57, West Liberty 35; NW Missouri St 21, Central Washington 20.
Semifinals: NW Missouri St 56, California (Pa.) 31; Grand Valley St 41, Carson-Newman 27.

NCAA DIVISION II

Championship: 12-12-09, Florence, Ala., Att: 6,211.				
NW Missouri St	7	14	2	7—30
Grand Valley St	0	0	13	10—23

NCAA DIVISION III

First round: Mount Union 55, Wash. & Jeff. 0; Montclair St 38, Maine Maritime 22; Albright 35, Alfred 25; Delaware Valley 66, Susquehanna 7; Wesley 55, N.C. Wesleyan 23; Mississippi Coll. 56, Huntingdon 25; Johns Hopkins 23, Hampden-Sydney 7; Thomas More 49, DePauw 39; UW-Whitewater 70, Lakeland 7; Illinois Wesleyan 41, Wabash 35; Trine 51, Case 38; Wittenberg 42, Mt. St. Joseph 14; Coe 34, St. John's (Minn.) 27; St. Thomas (Minn.) 43, Monmouth (Ill.) 21; Mary Hardin-Baylor 42, Central (Iowa) 40; Linfield 38, Cal Lutheran 17.

NCAA DIVISION III *(CONT.)*

Second Round: Mount Union 62, Montclair St 14; Albright 27, Delaware Valley 7; Wesley 43, Miss. Coll. 9; Johns Hopkins 31, Thomas More 29; UW-Whitewater 45, Illinois Wesleyan 7; Wittenberg 34, Trine 17; St. Thomas (Minn.) 34, Coe 7; Linfield 53, Mary Hardin-Baylor 21.
Quarterfinals: Mount Union 55, Albright 3; Wesley 12, Johns Hopkins 0; UW-Whitewater 31, Wittenberg 13; Linfield 31, St. Thomas (Minn.) 20.
Semifinals: Mount Union 24, Wesley 7; UW-Whitewater 27, Linfield 17.

NCAA DIVISION III

Championship: 12-19-09, Salem, Virginia, Att: 3,468

Mount Union	0	14	7	7—28
UW-Whitewater	7	21	0	10—38

NAIA CHAMPIONSHIP

12-19-09, Rome, Georgia, Att: 5,000

Lindenwood	0	14	8	0—22
Sioux Falls (S.D.)	5	3	14	3—25

Awards

Heisman Memorial Trophy

Player, School	Class	Pos	1st	2nd	3rd	Total
Mark Ingram, Alabama	So.	RB	227	236	151	1304
Toby Gerhart, Stanford	Sr.	RB	222	225	160	1276
Colt McCoy, Texas	Sr.	QB	203	188	160	1145
Ndamukong Suh, Nebraska	Sr.	DT	161	105	122	815
Tim Tebow, Florida	Sr.	QB	43	70	121	390

Note: Former Heisman winners and the media vote, with ballots allowing for three names (3 points for 1st, 2 for 2nd, 1 for 3rd).

Other Awards

Maxwell Award (Player) .... Colt McCoy, Texas, QB
Sporting News Player of the Year .... Mark Ingram, Alabama, RB
Walter Camp Player of the Year .... Colt McCoy, Texas, QB
Chuck Bednarik Award (Defense) .... Ndamukong Suh, Nebraska, DT
Vince Lombardi/Rotary Award (Lineman/LB) ..... Ndamukong Suh, Nebraska, DT
Outland Trophy (Interior Lineman) .... Ndamukong Suh, Nebraska, OT
Davey O'Brien Award (QB) .... Colt McCoy, Texas, QB
Unitas Golden Arm Award (Senior QB) .... Colt McCoy, Texas, QB
Doak Walker Award (RB) .... Toby Gerhart, Stanford, RB
Biletnikoff Award (WR) .... Golden Tate, Notre Dame, WR
Butkus Award (Linebacker) .... Rolando McClain, Alabama, LB
Jim Thorpe Award (Defensive Back) .... Eric Berry, Tennessee, CB
Associated Press Player of the Year .... Ndamukong Suh, Nebraska, DT
Walter Payton Award (FCS Player) .... Armanti Edwards, Appalachian St, QB
Harlon Hill Trophy (Div. II Player) .... Joique Bell, Wayne St, RB
Gagliardi Trophy (Div. III Player) .... Blaine Westemeyer, Augustana, OT

Coaches' Awards

Walter Camp Award .... Gary Patterson, TCU
Eddie Robinson Award (FCS) ..... Henry Frazier III, Prairie View A&M
Bobby Dodd Award .... Gary Patterson, TCU
Bear Bryant Award .... Chris Petersen, Boise St

AFCA COACHES OF THE YEAR

FBS (Division I-A) .... Gary Patterson, TCU
FCS (Division I-AA) .... Andy Talley, Villanova
Division II .... Mel Tjeerdsma, NW Missouri St
Division III .... Lance Leipold, UW-Whitewater

Football Writers Association of America All-America Team

OFFENSE

QB .... Colt McCoy, Texas, Sr.
RB .... Toby Gerhart, Stanford, Sr.
RB .... Mark Ingram, Alabama, So.
WR ...... Freddie Barnes, Bowling Green, Sr.
WR ...... Golden Tate, Notre Dame, Jr.
TE .... Dorin Dickerson, Pittsburgh, Sr.
OL .... Zane Beadles, Utah, Sr.
OL .... Rodney Hudson, Florida St, Jr.
OL .... Mike Iupati, Idaho, Sr.
OL .... Russell Okung, Oklahoma St, Sr.
C .... Maurice Pouncey, Florida, Jr.
K .... Kai Forbath, UCLA, Jr.
RS .... C.J. Spiller, Clemson, Sr.

DEFENSE

DL .... Terrence Cody, Alabama, Sr.
DL .... Jerry Hughes, TCU, Sr.
DL .... Gerald McCoy, Oklahoma, Jr.
DL .... Ndamukong Suh, Nebraska, Sr.
LB .... Pat Angerer, Iowa, Sr.
LB .... Greg Jones, Michigan St, Jr.
LB .... Rolando McClain, Alabama, Jr.
DB .... Eric Berry, Tennessee, Jr.
DB .... Joe Haden, Florida, Jr.
DB .... DeAndre McDaniel, Clemson, Jr.
DB .... Earl Thomas, Texas, So.
P .... Drew Butler, Georgia, So.

Football Bowl Subdivision (I-A)

ATLANTIC COAST CONFERENCE

ATLANTIC	Conference		Full Season		
	W	L	W	L	Pct
Clemson	6	2	9	5	.642
Boston College	5	3	8	5	.615
Florida St	4	4	7	6	.538
Wake Forest	3	5	5	7	.417
North Carolina St	2	6	5	7	.417
Maryland	1	7	2	10	.167

COASTAL					
Georgia Tech	7	1	11	3	.786
Virginia Tech	6	2	10	3	.769
Miami (Fla.)	5	3	9	4	.692
North Carolina	4	4	8	5	.615
Duke	3	5	5	7	.417
Virginia	2	6	3	9	.250

BIG EAST CONFERENCE

	Conference		Full Season		
	W	L	W	L	Pct
Cincinnati	7	0	12	1	.923
Pittsburgh	5	2	10	3	.769
West Virginia	5	2	9	4	.692
Rutgers	3	4	9	4	.691
Connecticut	3	4	8	5	.615
South Florida	3	4	8	5	.615
Louisville	1	6	4	8	.333
Syracuse	1	6	4	8	.333

BIG TEN CONFERENCE

	Conference		Full Season		
	W	L	W	L	Pct
Ohio St	7	1	11	2	.846
Iowa	6	2	11	2	.846
Penn St	6	2	11	2	.846
Northwestern	5	3	8	5	.615
Wisconsin	5	3	10	3	.769
Michigan St	4	4	6	7	.462
Purdue	4	4	5	7	.417
Minnesota	3	5	6	7	.461
Illinois	2	6	3	9	.250
Michigan	1	7	5	7	.417
Indiana	1	7	4	8	.333

BIG 12 CONFERENCE

NORTH	Conference		Full Season		
	W	L	W	L	Pct
Nebraska	6	2	10	4	.714
Missouri	4	4	8	5	.615
Kansas St	4	4	6	6	.500
Iowa St	3	5	7	6	.538
Colorado	2	6	3	9	.250
Kansas	1	7	5	7	.417

SOUTH					
Texas	8	0	13	1	.929
Oklahoma St	6	6	9	4	.692
Texas Tech	5	3	9	4	.692
Oklahoma	5	3	8	5	.615
Texas A&M	3	5	6	7	.462
Baylor	1	7	4	8	.333

Football Bowl Subdivision (I-A) *(Cont.)*

CONFERENCE USA

EAST	Conference		Full Season		
	W	L	W	L	Pct
East Carolina	7	1	9	5	.642
Central Florida	6	2	8	5	.615
Southern Miss	5	3	7	6	.538
Marshall	4	4	7	6	.538
UAB	4	4	5	7	.417
Memphis	1	7	2	10	.167

WEST					
Houston	6	2	10	4	.714
SMU	6	2	8	5	.615
Tulsa	3	5	5	7	.538
UTEP	3	5	4	8	.333
Rice	2	6	2	10	.167
Tulane	1	7	3	9	.250

MID-AMERICAN ATHLETIC CONFERENCE

EAST	Conference		Full Season		
	W	L	W	L	Pct
Ohio	7	1	9	5	.642
Temple	7	1	9	4	.692
Bowling Green	6	2	7	6	.538
Kent St	4	4	5	7	.417
Buffalo	3	5	5	7	.417
Akron	2	6	3	9	.250
Miami (Ohio)	1	7	1	11	.083

WEST					
Central Michigan	8	0	12	2	.857
Northern Illinois	5	3	7	6	.538
Western Michigan	4	4	5	7	.417
Toledo	3	5	5	7	.417
Ball St	2	6	2	10	.167
Eastern Michigan	0	8	0	12	.000

MOUNTAIN WEST CONFERENCE

	Conference		Full Season		
	W	L	W	L	Pct
TCU	8	0	12	1	.923
BYU	7	1	11	2	.846
Utah	6	2	10	3	769
Air Force	5	3	8	5	.615
Wyoming	4	4	7	6	.538
UNLV	3	5	5	7	.417
San Diego St	2	6	4	8	.333
New Mexico	1	7	1	11	.083
Colorado St	0	8	3	9	.250

PACIFIC 10 CONFERENCE

	Conference		Full Season		
	W	L	W	L	Pct
Oregon	8	1	10	3	.763
Arizona	6	3	8	5	.615
Oregon St	6	3	8	5	.615
Stanford	6	3	8	5	.615
USC	5	4	9	4	.692
California	5	4	8	5	.615
Washington	4	5	5	7	.417
UCLA	3	6	7	6	.538
Arizona St	2	7	4	8	.333
Washington St	0	9	1	11	.083

Football Bowl Subdivision (I-A) *(Cont.)*

SOUTHEASTERN CONFERENCE

	Conference		Full Season		
EAST	**W**	**L**	**W**	**L**	**Pct**
Florida	8	0	13	1	.929
Georgia	4	4	8	5	.615
Tennessee	4	4	7	6	.538
Kentucky	3	5	7	6	.538
South Carolina	3	5	7	6	.538
Vanderbilt	0	8	2	10	.167
WEST					
Alabama	8	0	14	0	1.000
LSU	5	3	9	4	.692
Mississippi	4	4	9	4	.692
Arkansas	3	5	8	5	.615
Auburn	3	5	8	5	.615
Mississippi St	3	5	5	7	.417

SUN BELT CONFERENCE

	Conference		Full Season		
	W	**L**	**W**	**L**	**Pct**
Troy	8	0	9	4	.692
Middle Tennessee St	7	1	10	3	.769
La.-Monroe	5	3	6	6	.500
Florida Atlantic	5	3	5	7	.417
La.-Lafayette	4	4	6	6	.500
Arkansas St	3	5	4	8	.333
Florida International	3	5	3	9	.250
North Texas	1	7	2	10	.167
Western Kentucky	0	8	0	12	.000

WESTERN ATHLETIC CONFERENCE

	Conference		Full Season		
	W	**L**	**W**	**L**	**Pct**
Boise St	8	0	14	0	1.000
Nevada	7	1	8	5	.615
Fresno St	6	2	8	5	.615
Idaho	4	4	8	5	.615
Hawaii	3	5	6	7	.462
Louisiana Tech	3	5	4	8	.333
Utah St	3	5	4	8	.333
New Mexico St	1	7	3	10	.231
San Jose St	1	7	2	10	.167

INDEPENDENTS

	Full Season		
	W	**L**	**Pct**
Navy	10	4	.714
Notre Dame	6	6	.500
Army	5	7	.417

Football Championship Subdivision (I-AA)

BIG SKY CONFERENCE

	Conference		Full Season		
	W	**L**	**W**	**L**	**Pct**
Montana	8	0	14	1	.933
Eastern Washington	6	2	8	4	.667
Weber St	6	2	7	5	.583
Montana St	5	3	7	4	.636
Northern Arizona	4	4	5	6	.455
Sacramento St	4	4	5	6	.455
Northern Colorado	1	7	3	8	.273
Portland St	1	7	2	9	.182
Idaho St	1	7	1	10	.091

BIG SOUTH CONFERENCE

	Conference		Full Season		
	W	**L**	**W**	**L**	**Pct**
Liberty	5	1	8	3	.727
Stony Brook	5	1	6	5	.545
Charleston Southern	4	2	6	5	.545
Gardner-Webb	3	3	6	5	.545
Coastal Carolina	3	3	5	6	.455
Virginia Military Inst.	1	5	2	9	.182

COLONIAL CONFERENCE

	Conference		Full Season		
NORTH	**W**	**L**	**W**	**L**	**Pct**
New Hampshire	6	2	10	3	.769
Maine	4	4	5	6	.455
Hofstra	3	5	5	6	.455
Massachusetts	3	5	5	6	.455
Northeastern	3	5	3	8	.273
Rhode Island	0	8	1	10	.091
SOUTH					
Villanova	7	1	14	1	.933
Richmond	7	1	11	2	.846
William & Mary	6	2	11	3	.786
Delaware	4	4	6	5	.545
James Madison	4	4	6	5	.545
Towson	1	7	2	9	.182

GREAT WEST

	Conference		Full Season		
	W	**L**	**W**	**L**	**Pct**
UC-Davis	3	1	6	5	.545
North Dakota	2	2	6	5	.545
South Dakota	2	2	5	6	.455
Southern Utah	2	2	5	6	.455
Cal Poly	1	3	4	7	.364

IVY LEAGUE

	Conference		Full Season		
	W	**L**	**W**	**L**	**Pct**
Pennsylvania	7	0	8	2	.800
Harvard	6	1	7	3	.700
Brown	4	3	6	4	.600
Columbia	3	4	4	6	.400
Princeton	3	4	4	6	.400
Yale	2	5	4	6	.400
Dartmouth	2	5	2	8	.200
Cornell	1	6	2	8	.200

Football Champ. Subdivision (I-AA) (Cont.)

MID-EASTERN ATHLETIC CONFERENCE

	Conference		Full Season		
	W	L	W	L	Pct
South Carolina St	8	0	10	2	.833
Florida A&M	6	2	8	3	.727
Norfolk St	5	3	7	4	.636
Morgan St	4	4	6	5	.545
Bethune-Cookman	4	4	5	6	.455
Delaware St	3	4	4	6	.400
Hampton	3	5	5	6	.455
North Carolina A&T	2	5	4	6	.400
Howard	0	8	2	9	.182

MISSOURI VALLEY CONFERENCE

	Conference		Full Season		
	W	L	W	L	Pct
Southern Illinois	8	0	11	2	.846
South Dakota St	7	1	8	4	.667
Northern Iowa	5	3	7	4	.636
Illinois St	5	3	6	5	.545
Missouri St	4	4	6	5	.545
Youngstown St	4	4	6	5	.545
North Dakota St	2	6	3	8	.273
Indiana St	1	7	1	10	.091
Western Illinois	0	8	1	10	.091

NORTHEAST CONFERENCE

	Conference		Full Season		
	W	L	W	L	Pct
Central Connecticut St	7	1	9	3	.750
Albany	6	2	7	4	.636
Wagner	5	3	6	5	.545
Robert Morris	5	3	5	6	.455
Bryant	4	4	5	6	.455
Monmouth (N.J.)	4	4	5	6	.455
Duquesne	2	6	3	8	.273
Sacred Heart	2	6	2	8	.200
St. Francis (Pa.)	1	7	2	9	.182

OHIO VALLEY CONFERENCE

	Conference		Full Season		
	W	L	W	L	Pct
Jacksonville St	6	1	8	3	.727
Eastern Illinois	6	2	8	4	.667
Tennessee Tech	5	3	6	5	.545
Eastern Kentucky	5	3	5	6	.455
Tenn.-Martin	4	4	5	6	.455
Tennessee St	3	4	4	7	.364
Austin Peay	3	5	4	7	.364
Murray St	2	6	3	8	.273
SE Missouri St	1	7	2	9	.182

PATRIOT LEAGUE

	Conference		Full Season		
	W	L	W	L	Pct
Holy Cross	5	1	9	3	.750
Colgate	4	2	9	2	.818
Lafayette	4	2	8	3	.727
Lehigh	4	2	4	7	.364
Fordham	2	4	5	6	.455
Bucknell	2	4	4	7	.364
Georgetown	0	6	0	11	.000

Football Champ. Subdivision (I-AA) (Cont.)

PIONEER LEAGUE

	Conference		Full Season		
	W	L	W	L	Pct
Butler	7	1	11	1	.917
Dayton	7	1	9	2	.818
Drake	6	2	8	3	.727
Jacksonville	6	2	7	4	.636
Marist	5	3	7	4	.636
San Diego	3	5	4	7	.364
Davidson	3	5	3	7	.300
Campbell	2	6	3	8	.273
Morehead St	1	7	3	8	.273
Valparaiso	0	8	1	10	.091

SOUTHERN CONFERENCE

	Conference		Full Season		
	W	L	W	L	Pct
Appalachian St	8	0	11	3	.786
Elon	7	1	9	3	.750
Furman	5	3	6	5	.545
Chattanooga	4	4	6	5	.545
Georgia Southern	4	4	5	6	.455
Samford	3	5	5	6	.455
Citadel	2	6	4	7	.364
Wofford	2	6	3	8	.273
Western Carolina	1	7	2	9	.182

SOUTHLAND CONFERENCE

	Conference		Full Season		
	W	L	W	L	Pct
Stephen F. Austin	6	1	10	3	.769
McNeese St	6	1	9	3	.750
Texas St	5	2	7	4	.636
SE Louisiana	4	3	6	5	.545
Sam Houston St	3	4	5	6	.455
Central Arkansas	2	5	5	7	.417
Nicholls St	2	5	3	8	.273
Northwestern St	0	7	0	11	.000

SOUTHWESTERN ATHLETIC CONFERENCE

	Conference		Full Season		
	W	L	W	L	Pct
EAST					
Alabama A&M	4	3	7	5	.583
Alcorn St	3	4	3	6	.333
Jackson St	3	5	3	7	.300
Alabama St	1	6	4	7	.364
Mississippi Valley St	1	7	3	8	.273
WEST					
Prairie View A&M	8	0	9	1	.900
Grambling St	6	2	6	5	.545
Texas Southern	5	2	6	5	.545
Southern Univ.	3	4	6	6	.500
Ark.-Pine Bluff	3	4	5	5	.500

INDEPENDENTS

	Full Season		
	W	L	Pct
Old Dominion	9	2	.818
North Carolina Central	4	7	.364
Savannah St	2	8	.200
Winston-Salem	1	10	.091

Football Bowl Subdivision (I-A)

SCORING

	Class	GP	TD	XP	FG	Pts	Pts/Game
Toby Gerhart, Stanford	Sr.	13	28	0	0	172	13.23
Ricky Dobbs, Navy	Jr.	13	27	0	0	162	12.46
Donald Buckram, UTEP	Jr.	12	21	0	0	126	10.50
Jacquizz Rodgers, Oregon St	So.	13	22	0	0	132	10.15
Ryan Williams, Virginia Tech	Fr.	13	22	0	0	132	10.15
Freddie Barnes, Bowling Green	Sr.	13	21	0	0	126	9.69
Curtis Steele, Memphis	Sr.	10	16	0	0	96	9.60
Hunter Lawrence, Texas	Sr.	14	0	61	24	133	9.50
Lance Dunbar, North Texas	So.	12	19	0	0	114	9.50
Ryan Mathews, Fresno St	Jr.	12	19	0	0	114	9.50
Leigh Tiffin, Alabama	Sr.	14	0	42	30	132	9.43
Chad Spann, Northern Illinois	Jr.	13	20	0	0	120	9.23
Robert Turpin, Utah St	So.	12	18	0	0	110	9.17
C.J. Spiller, Clemson	Sr.	14	21	0	0	128	9.14
Grant Ressel, Missouri	So.	13	0	39	26	117	9.00
Golden Tate, Notre Dame	Jr.	12	18	0	0	108	9.00

FIELD GOALS

	Class	GP	FGA	FG	Pct	FG/Game
Kai Forbath, UCLA	Jr.	13	31	28	.903	2.15
Leigh Tiffin, Alabama	Sr.	14	35	30	.857	2.14
Grant Ressel, Missouri	So.	13	27	26	.963	2.00
Dan Hutchins, Pittsburgh	Jr.	13	29	23	.763	1.77
Hunter Lawrence, Texas	Sr.	14	27	24	.889	1.71
Alex Henery, Nebraska	Jr.	14	28	24	.857	1.71

TOTAL OFFENSE

	Class	GP	Rushing		Passing			Total Offense	
			Car	Net	Att	Yds	Yds	Yds/Play	Yds/Game
Case Keenum, Houston	Jr.	14	60	158	700	5671	5829	7.67	416.4
Levi Brown, Troy	Sr.	13	54	7	504	4254	4261	7.64	327.8
Jerrod Johnson, Texas A&M	Jr.	13	145	506	497	3579	4085	6.36	314.2
Todd Reesing, Kansas	Sr.	12	104	119	496	3616	3735	6.23	311.3
Tyler Sheehan, Bowling Green	Sr.	13	73	-8	575	4051	4043	6.24	311.0
Joe Webb, UAB	Sr.	12	227	1427	271	2299	3726	7.48	310.5
Dwight Dasher, Middle Tenn. St	Jr.	13	224	1154	399	2789	3943	6.33	303.3
Jimmy Clausen, Notre Dame	Jr.	12	59	-95	425	3722	3627	7.49	302.3
Taylor Potts, Texas Tech	Jr.	11	24	-166	470	3440	3274	6.63	297.6
Dan LeFevour, Central Michigan	Sr.	14	183	713	456	3438	4151	6.50	296.5

RUSHING

	Class	GP	Car	Yds	TD	Avg	Yds/Game
Ryan Mathews, Fresno St	Jr.	12	276	1808	19	6.55	150.67
Toby Gerhart, Stanford	Sr.	13	343	1871	28	5.45	143.92
Dion Lewis, Pittsburgh	Fr.	13	325	1799	17	5.54	138.38
Donald Buckram, UTEP	Jr.	12	259	1594	18	6.15	132.83
Ryan Williams, Virginia Tech	Fr.	13	293	1655	21	5.65	127.31
Anthony Dixon, Mississippi St	Sr.	11	257	1391	12	5.41	126.45
Curtis Steele, Memphis	Sr.	10	198	1239	15	6.26	123.90
Vai Taua, Nevada	Jr.	11	172	1345	10	7.82	122.27
LaMichael James, Oregon	Fr.	13	230	1546	14	6.72	118.92
Joe Webb, UAB	Sr.	12	227	1427	11	6.29	118.92

PASSING EFFICIENCY

	Class	GP	Att	Comp	Pct Comp	Yds	Yds/Att	TD	Int	Rating Pts
Tim Tebow, Florida	Sr.	14	314	213	67.8	2895	9.2	21	5	164.17
Kellen Moore, Boise St	So.	14	431	277	64.3	3536	8.2	39	3	161.65
Jimmy Clausen, Notre Dame	Jr.	12	425	289	68.0	3722	8.8	28	4	161.42
Max Hall, BYU	Sr.	13	409	275	67.2	3560	8.7	33	14	160.13
Nathan Enderle, Idaho	Jr.	11	312	192	61.5	2906	9.3	22	9	157.28
Case Keenum, Houston	Jr.	14	700	492	70.3	5671	8.1	44	15	154.79
Ryan Mallett, Arkansas	So.	13	403	225	55.8	3624	9.0	30	7	152.46
Andy Dalton, TCU	Jr.	13	323	199	61.6	2756	8.5	23	8	151.83
Joe Webb, UAB	Sr.	12	271	162	59.8	2299	8.5	21	8	150.71
Bill Stull, Pittsburgh	Sr.	13	321	209	65.1	2633	8.2	21	8	150.61

Note: Minimum 15 attempts per game.

Football Bowl Subdivision (I-A) *(Cont.)*

RECEPTIONS PER GAME

	Class	GP	No.	Yds	TD	R/Game
Freddie Barnes, Bowling Green	Sr.	13	155	1770	19	11.92
Danario Alexander, Missouri	Sr.	13	113	1781	14	8.69
James Cleveland, Houston	Jr.	12	104	1214	14	8.67
Kerry Meier, Kansas	Sr.	12	102	985	8	8.50
Jordan Shipley, Texas	Sr.	14	116	1485	13	8.29

RECEIVING YARDS PER GAME

	Class	GP	No.	Yds	TD	Yds/Game
Danario Alexander, Missouri	Sr.	13	113	1781	14	137.0
Freddie Barnes, Bowling Green	Sr.	13	155	1770	19	136.2
Golden Tate, Notre Dame	Jr.	12	93	1496	15	124.7
Greg Salas, Hawaii	Jr.	13	106	1590	8	122.3
Dezmon Briscoe, Kansas	Jr.	11	84	1337	9	121.6

ALL-PURPOSE RUNNING

	Class	GP	Rush	Rec	PR	KOR	Total Yds	Yds/Game
Damaris Johnson, Tulsa	So.	12	175	1131	256	1131	2693	224.4
Mardy Gilyard, Cincinnati	Sr.	13	16	1191	202	1281	2690	206.9
Brandon West, Western Michigan	Sr.	12	1164	217	17	960	2358	196.5
C.J. Spiller, Clemson	Sr.	14	1212	503	210	755	2680	191.4
Antonio Brown, Central Michigan	Jr.	14	341	1198	270	773	2582	184.4

INTERCEPTIONS

	Class	GP	No.	Int/Game
Rahim Moore, UCLA	So.	13	10	.77
Brian Lainhart, Kent St.	Jr.	12	7	.58
DeAndre McDaniel, Clemson	Jr.	14	8	.57
Earl Thomas, Texas	So.	14	8	.57
Chris May, Eastern Mich.	Sr.	11	6	.55
Anthony Wright, Air Force	So.	13	7	.54
Marcus Udell, Mid. Tenn. St	Sr.	13	7	.54

PUNTING

	Class	No.	Avg
Drew Butler, Georgia	So.	56	48.1
Matt Dodge, East Carolina	Sr.	67	45.8
Tress Way, Oklahoma.	Fr.	61	45.7
Matt Reagan, Memphis	Sr.	63	45.5
Quinn Sharp, Oklahoma St	Fr.	67	45.1

Note: Minimum of 3.6 punts per game.

PUNT RETURNS

	Class	No.	Yds	TD	Avg
Greg Reid, Florida St	Fr.	21	387	1	18.4
Trindon Holliday, LSU	Sr.	20	362	1	18.1
Ryan Broyles, Oklahoma	So.	31	492	1	15.9
Javier Arenas, Alabama	Sr.	32	493	1	15.4
Da'Norris Searcy, N. Carolina	Jr.	23	335	1	14.6

Note: Minimum 1.2 punt returns per game.

KICKOFF RETURNS

	Class	No.	Yds	TD	Avg
Ray Fisher, Indiana	Sr.	17	635	2	37.4
D.J. Monroe, Texas	Fr.	16	537	2	33.6
C.J. Spiller, Clemson	Sr.	23	755	4	32.8
Dyrell Roberts, Virginia Tech	So.	18	574	1	31.9
Chris Owusu, Stanford	So.	37	1167	3	31.5

Note: Minimum of 1.2 kickoff returns per game.

Football Bowl Subdivision (I-A) Single-Game Highs

RUSHING AND PASSING

Rushing and passing yards: 569—Case Keenum, Houston, QB, Oct. 31, 2009 (vs Southern Miss)
Rushing and passing plays: 98—Mike Kafka, Northwestern, QB, Jan. 1, 2010 (vs Auburn)
Rushing plays: 47—Dion Lewis, Pittsburgh, RB, Dec. 5, 2009 (vs Cincinnati)
Net rushing yards: 308—MiQuale Lewis, Ball St, RB, Oct. 24, 2009 (vs Eastern Michigan)
Passes attempted: 78—Mike Kafka, Northwestern, QB, Jan. 1, 2010 (vs Auburn)
Passes completed: 56—Case Keenum, Houston, QB, Dec. 5, 2009 (vs East Carolina)
Net passing yards: 559—Case Keenum, Houston, QB, Oct. 31, 2009 (vs Southern Miss)

RECEIVING AND RETURNS

Passes caught: 22—Freddie Barnes, Bowling Green, WR, Oct. 10, 2009 (vs Kent St)
Receiving yards: 278—Freddie Barnes, Bowling Green, WR, Oct. 10, 2009 (vs Kent St)
Punt return Yards: 209—Ryan Broyles, Oklahoma, WR, Nov. 28, 2009 (vs Oklahoma St)
Kickoff return yards: 256—Mardy Gilyard, Cincinnati, WR, Dec. 5, 2009 (vs Pittsburgh)

Football Championship Subdivision (I-AA)

SCORING

	Class	GP	TD	XP	FG	Pts	Pts/Game
Toddrick Pendland, McNeese St	Sr.	11	19	0	0	118	10.73
Tysson Poots, Southern Utah	Jr.	9	15	0	0	90	10.00
Matt Bevins, Liberty	So.	11	0	41	22	107	9.73
Chase Reynolds, Montana	Jr.	15	24	0	0	144	9.60
Pat Paschall, North Dakota St	Sr.	10	16	0	0	96	9.60

FIELD GOALS

	Class	GP	FGA	FG	Pct	FG/Game
Matt Bevins, Liberty	So.	11	26	22	.846	2.00
Zach Kutch, Illinois St	Sr.	11	29	22	.759	2.00
Armando Cuko, Massachusetts	Sr.	10	24	19	.792	1.90
Brian Pate, William & Mary	Fr.	14	35	23	.657	1.64
Ari Johnson, Grambling St	So.	11	23	18	.783	1.64
Zach Brown, Portland St	So.	11	25	18	.720	1.64

TOTAL OFFENSE

			Rushing		Passing			Total Offense	
	Class	GP	Car	Net	Att	Yds	Total Yds	Yds/Play	Yds/Game
Dominic Randolph, Holy Cross	Sr.	12	113	480	485	3776	4256	7.1	354.7
John Skelton, Fordham	Sr.	11	86	122	441	3708	3830	7.3	348.2
Armanti Edwards, Appalachian St	Sr.	12	137	679	378	3291	3970	7.7	330.8
Matt Nichols, Eastern Washington	Sr.	12	69	102	458	3830	3932	7.5	327.7
Jeremy Moses, Stephen F. Austin	Jr.	13	48	43	566	4124	4167	6.8	320.5

RUSHING

	Class	GP	Car	Yds	Avg	TD	Yds/Game
Pat Paschall, North Dakota St	Sr.	10	207	1397	6.8	16	139.7
David Sinisi, Monmouth	Sr.	11	300	1437	4.8	13	130.6
Deji Karim, Southern Illinois	Sr.	13	240	1694	7.1	18	130.3
James Mallory, Central Connecticut St.	Sr.	12	278	1352	4.9	16	112.7
Kyle Minett, South Dakota St	Jr.	12	270	1304	4.8	16	108.7

PASSING EFFICIENCY

	Class	GP	Att	Comp	Pct Comp	Yds	Yds/Att	TD	Int	Rating Pts
KJ Black, Prairie View A&M	Jr.	9	230	162	70.4	2033	9.6	22	4	172.77
Ryan Perrilloux, Jacksonville St	Sr.	10	236	138	58.5	2350	9.8	23	2	172.58
Robert Curley, Lafayette	Sr.	11	336	231	68.8	3044	8.3	28	12	165.21
Andrew Selle, Montana	Jr.	15	356	224	62.9	3043	7.9	28	6	157.31
Pat Grace, Northern Iowa	Sr.	11	253	155	61.3	1180	7.9	20	8	156.73

Note: Minimum 15 attempts per game.

RECEPTIONS PER GAME

	Class	GP	No.	Yds	TD	R/G
Terrell Hudgens, Elon	Sr.	12	123	1633	16	10.3
Tysson Poots, Southern Utah	Jr.	9	85	1081	15	9.4
Duane Brooks, Stephen F. Austin	Sr.	13	118	1076	6	9.1
Eyad Salem, Illinois St	Sr.	11	92	943	6	8.4
Chris Carter, UC-Davis	Sr.	11	85	889	4	7.7

RECEIVING YARDS PER GAME

	Class	GP	No.	Yds	TD	Yds/G
Terrell Hudgens, Elon	Sr.	12	123	1633	16	136.1
Tysson Poots, Southern Utah	Jr.	9	85	1081	15	120.1
Jason Caldwell, Fordham	Sr.	11	79	1252	9	113.8
Buddy Farnham, Brown	Sr.	10	74	1003	11	100.3
Marc Mariani, Montana	Sr.	15	80	1479	13	98.6

INTERCEPTIONS

	Class	GP	No.	Yds	TD	Int/G
Jason House, Southern U.	Jr.	11	10	230	1	.91
Kerry Hoskins, Jackson St	Sr	9	7	68	0	.78
Josh Norman, Coastal Caro.	So.	11	8	72	0	.73
Jeremy Caldwell, East. Ky.	So.	10	7	84	1	.70
Three tied at .60.						

PUNTING

	Class	No.	Avg
Jonathan Plisco, Old Dominion	Fr.	62	44.8
Jon Vandewielen, Idaho St	Sr.	74	44.7
Jahmal Blanchard, Hampton	Sr.	59	43.9
Pedro Ventura, Prairie View A&M	Jr.	44	43.8
Patrick Dolan, Nicholls St	Jr.	59	42.7

Football Championship Subdivision (I-AA) *(Cont.)*

ALL-PURPOSE RUNNING

	Class	GP	Rush	Rec	PR	KOR	Total Yds	Yds/Game
Terrence Holt, Austin Peay	Jr.	11	793	187	199	1194	2373	215.7
Taiwan Joens, Eastern Washington	So.	12	1213	561	0	571	2345	195.4
Deji Karim, Southern Illinois	Sr.	13	1694	212	0	433	2339	179.9
Aaron Woods, Portland St	Sr.	11	-2	535	82	1314	1929	175.4
Bryan Walters, Cornell	Sr.	10	1	764	174	777	1716	171.6

Division II

SCORING

	Class	GP	TD	XP	FG	Pts	Pts/Game
Joique Bell, Wayne St (Mich.)	Sr.	11	33	0	0	192	17.5
Isaac Odim, Minn.-Duluth	Jr.	13	33	0	0	198	15.2
Buck Wakefield, Carson-Newman	Sr.	11	24	0	0	144	13.1
DaRante Hunter, Charleston (W.V.)	Jr.	11	23	0	0	140	12.7
Kevon Calhoun, West Liberty St	Jr.	13	26	0	0	156	12.0

FIELD GOALS

	Class	GP	FGA	FG	Pct	FG/Game
David Van Voris, Adams St	Fr.	9	21	17	.810	1.89
Steve Ivanisevic, Washburn	Sr.	11	21	19	.905	1.73
Travis Atter, Chadron St	Sr.	11	24	18	.750	1.64
Matt Dineen, Kutztown	Jr.	11	20	17	.850	1.55
Garrett Rolsma, Central Washington	Sr.	13	25	20	.800	1.54

TOTAL OFFENSE

			Rushing		Passing		Total Offense		
	Class	GP	Car	Net	Att	Yds	Total Yds	Yds/Play	Yds/Game
J.J. Harp, Eastern New Mexico	So.	10	87	-6	547	4373	4367	6.0	436.7
Nick Graziano, Arkansas Tech	Sr.	12	76	455	538	4313	4768	7.8	397.3
Zach Amedro, West Liberty St	Jr.	13	44	-24	526	4945	4921	8.6	378.5
Steven Gachette, SW Baptist	Jr.	11	140	975	396	3013	3988	7.4	362.6
Silas Fluellen, Wayne St (Neb.)	Sr.	11	135	458	390	3253	3711	7.1	337.4

RUSHING

	Class	GP	Car	Yds	TD	Yds/Game
Joique Bell, Wayne St (Mich.)	Sr.	11	326	2084	29	189.5
Jonas Randolph, Mars Hill	So.	10	312	1804	19	180.4
Anthony Smalls, Merrimack	So.	8	157	1161	6	145.1
Isaac Odim, Minn.-Duluth	Jr.	13	259	1808	29	139.1
Quinn Porter, Stillman	Sr.	9	193	1243	8	138.1

PASSING EFFICIENCY

	Class	GP	Att	Comp	Pct Comp	Yds	TD	Int	Rating Pts
Zack Eskridge, Midwestern St	Jr.	12	330	236	71.5	3295	29	6	180.75
Blake Bolles, NW Missouri St	Jr.	15	449	312	69.5	4145	42	13	172.11
Zach Amedro, West Liberty St	Jr.	13	526	343	65.2	4945	49	14	169.60
Brad Iciek, Grand Valley St	Sr.	15	368	226	61.4	3194	35	3	164.07
Billy Cundiff, Ashland	Sr.	11	305	199	65.3	2653	24	1	163.62

Note: Minimum 15 attempts per game.

RECEPTIONS PER GAME

	Class	GP	No.	Yds	TD	R/G
Justin Johnson, Fort Lewis	Jr.	11	124	1136	5	11.3
Robert Holland, Chowan	Fr.	10	86	1078	7	8.6
Marc Wilson, St. Anselm	So.	10	82	860	7	8.2
Ryan Travis, West Liberty St	Jr.	13	104	1250	14	8.0
Landon Turner, Arkansas Tech	Sr.	11	86	1164	9	7.8

RECEIVING YARDS PER GAME

	Class	GP	No.	Yds	TD	Yds/G
Thomas Mayo, Concord	So.	11	72	1368	11	124.4
Frantz Simeon, Arkansas Tech	Sr.	12	90	1359	14	113.3
Adam Saur, Colorado Mines	Sr.	11	84	1219	15	110.8
Kashif Walls, West Liberty St	Jr.	12	61	1321	21	110.1
Robert Holland, Chowan	Fr.	10	86	1078	7	107.8

Division II (Cont.)

INTERCEPTIONS

	Class	GP	No.	Yds	Int/ Game
Quintez Smith, Shaw	Sr.	10	9	302	.90
Justin Hamilton, Elizabeth City St.	Sr.	11	9	123	.82
Chris Carroll, Bentley	Sr.	10	8	63	.80
Derek Evans, West Liberty St.	Sr.	13	10	23	.77
Josh Jones, Harding	Sr.	11	8	116	.73
Giorgilo Durham, Central Okla.	So.	11	8	90	.73

PUNTING

	Class	No.	Avg
Justin Hinson, N.C.-Pembroke	Sr.	40	43.05
Joe Kok, Northeastern St	Sr.	71	42.31
Kyle Witman, Slippery Rock	Sr.	54	41.76
Will Batson, North Alabama	Sr.	56	41.71
Kevin Berg, Chadron St	Jr.	44	41.66

Note: Minimum 3.6 per game.

Division III

SCORING

	Class	GP	TD	XP	FG	Pts	Pts/Game
Levell Coppage, UW-Whitewater	So.	15	35	0	0	210	14.0
Jim Bower, Maine Maritime	Sr.	10	22	0	0	138	13.8
Cory McCain, Kalamazoo	Jr.	9	19	0	0	114	12.7
Cory Sartorelli, UW-Eau Claire	Sr.	10	17	0	0	117	11.7
James Spanopolous, Maritime (N.Y.)	So.	10	19	0	0	114	11.4
Justin Fuller, Bridgewater St	Jr.	10	19	0	0	114	11.4

FIELD GOALS

	Class	GP	FGA	FG	Pct	FG/Game
Garrett Biel, Trinity (Tex.)	Fr.	10	19	17	.895	1.70
Tony Smidl, UW-Platteville	Sr.	10	19	15	.789	1.50
Zach Egger, Nebraska Wesleyan	Jr.	10	22	14	.636	1.40
Dan Winsey, Concordia (Wisc.)	Jr.	10	15	13	.867	1.30
Carl Hauser, Concorida (Minn.)	Sr.	10	18	13	.722	1.30

TOTAL OFFENSE

	Class	GP	Rushing Car	Net	Passing Att	Yds	Total Offense Total Yds	Yds/Play	Yds/Game
Brandon Luczak, Kalamazoo	Sr.	10	80	155	516	3663	3818	6.4	381.8
Donald McKillop, Middlebury	Jr.	8	59	94	405	2873	2967	6.4	370.9
Evan Jones, Carthage	Jr.	10	60	101	464	3554	3655	7.0	365.5
Alex Tanney, Monmouth (Ill.)	Jr.	11	27	-20	484	3856	3836	7.5	348.7
Justin Ridgeway, Huntingdon	Sr.	10	87	249	339	3165	3414	8.0	341.4

RUSHING

	Class	GP	Car	Yds	TD	Yds/Game
Jim Bower, Maine Maritime	Sr.	10	256	1605	22	160.5
DeRon Brown, MIT	Sr.	9	269	1363	10	151.4
Johrone Bunch, Mount Ida	So.	11	304	1613	14	146.6
Levell Coppage, UW-Whitewater	So.	15	310	2107	35	140.5
Ben Wartman, St. Thomas (Minn.)	Jr.	13	295	1819	21	139.9

PASSING EFFICIENCY

	Class	GP	Att	Comp	Pct Comp	Yds	TD	Int	Rating Pts
Kurt Rocco, Mount Union	Sr.	15	341	236	69.2	3926	42	8	201.87
Aaron Fanthrope, North Central (Ill.)	Sr.	10	208	142	68.3	2096	28	7	190.61
Jeff Donovan, UW-Whitewater	Sr.	15	374	269	71.9	3682	29	6	177.00
Dan Whalen, Chase	Sr.	11	361	247	68.4	3340	34	8	172.97
Matt Hudson, Wabash	Sr.	9	273	185	67.8	2516	25	8	169.54

Note: Minimum 15 attempts per game.

RECEPTIONS PER GAME

	Class	GP	No.	Yds	TD	Rec/Game
Daniel Passaflume, Hanover	So.	10	113	1055	14	11.3
Michael Zweifel, Dubuque	Jr.	10	111	1522	15	11.1
R.J. Maki, Pomona-Pitzer	Jr.	9	91	1219	8	10.1
Jimmy Semeslberger, Kalamazoo	Sr.	10	96	1116	10	9.6
Patrick Noone, Bowdoin	So.	8	76	997	7	9.5

RECEIVING YARDS PER GAME

	Class	GP	No.	Yds	TD	Yds/Game
Michael Zweifel, Dubuque	Jr.	10	111	1522	15	152.2
R.J. Maki, Pomona-Pitzer	Jr.	9	91	1219	8	135.4
Alex Koors, DePauw	Jr.	10	73	1266	13	126.6
Wes Schimndgall, Eureka	So.	10	63	1247	16	124.7
Patrick Noone, Bowdoin	So.	8	76	997	7	124.6

Division III (Cont.)

INTERCEPTIONS

	Class	GP	No.	Yds	Int/G
Corry Stewart, Hanover	Sr.	10	9	138	.90
Scott Driscoll, Curry	Sr.	11	9	257	.82
Bill Doody, Hampden-Sydney	Jr.	11	9	135	.82
Brandon Hudson, Salisbury	Sr.	11	9	130	.82
Keith Anthony, Huntingdon	So.	10	8	140	.80
Jordan Nelson, Guilford	Jr.	10	8	92	.80

PUNTING

	Class	No.	Avg
Tyler Funk, Carthage	So.	36	44.4
Kyle Trella, Trinty (Tex.)	Fr.	45	44.0
Jared Jenkins, UW-Stevens Point	Jr.	37	42.8
Marc Zucconi, Coll. of New Jersey	Sr.	41	41.9
Ethan Hunke, Nebraska Wesleyan	Jr.	49	41.7

Note: Minimum 3.6 per game.

2009 NCAA FBS (I-A) Team Leaders

Offense

SCORING

	GP	Pts	Avg
Boise St.	14	591	42.21
Houston	14	591	42.21
Texas	14	550	39.29
Cincinnati	13	502	38.62
TCU	13	498	38.31
Nevada	13	497	38.23
Texas Tech	13	481	37.00
Oregon	13	469	36.08
Arkansas	13	468	36.00
Florida	14	502	35.86

RUSHING

	GP	Car	Yds	Avg	TD	Yds/Game
Nevada	13	607	4484	7.39	48	344.92
Georgia Tech	14	792	4136	5.22	47	295.43
Air Force	13	815	3685	4.52	31	283.46
Navy	14	820	3927	4.79	44	280.50
TCU	13	595	3114	5.23	35	239.54
Oregon	13	547	3012	5.51	38	231.69
UAB	12	463	2759	5.96	17	229.92
Fresno St.	13	555	3976	5.36	30	228.92
Mississippi St	12	555	2731	4.92	21	227.58
Florida	14	555	3105	5.59	30	221.79

TOTAL OFFENSE

	GP	Plays	Yds	Avg	TD	Yds/Game
Houston	14	1150	7887	6.86	77	563.36
Nevada	13	900	6573	7.30	69	505.62
Troy	13	973	6314	6.49	55	485.69
Texas Tech	13	988	6120	6.19	64	470.77
Texas A&M	13	1053	6055	5.75	56	465.77
Florida	14	919	6410	6.97	63	457.86
TCU	13	921	5937	6.45	65	456.69
Notre Dame	12	848	5421	6.39	44	451.75
Idaho	13	849	5868	6.91	55	451.38
Boise St	14	966	6303	6.52	76	450.21

PASSING

	GP	Att	Comp	Int	Pct Comp	Yds	Yds/Gm	TD
Houston	14	747	525	15	70.3	6072	433.7	47
Texas Tech	13	669	448	17	67.0	5028	486.8	38
Hawaii	13	569	339	17	59.6	4381	337.0	25
Troy	13	529	333	10	63.0	4375	336.5	24
Notre Dame	12	447	301	5	67.3	3882	323.5	30
Bowling Green	13	596	381	7	63.9	4110	316.2	27
Kansas	12	506	320	10	63.2	3724	310.3	22
Cincinnati	13	472	311	8	65.9	4014	308.8	39
Duke	12	501	308	10	61.5	3660	305.0	24
Arkansas	13	439	247	9	56.3	3842	295.5	32

Single-Game Highs

Points Scored: 73—Houston, Nov. 28, 2009 (vs Rice)
Net Rushing Yards: 574—Nevada, Nov. 21, 2009 (vs New Mexico St)
Net Passing Yards: 578—Houston, Nov. 21, 2009 (vs Memphis)
Rushing and Passing Yards: 773—Nevada, Oct. 3, 2009 (vs UNLV)
Fewest Rushing and Passing Yards Allowed: 36—North Carolina St, Sept. 12, 2009
(vs Murray St)

Defense

OPPONENTS' SCORING

	GP	Pts	Avg
Nebraska	14	146	10.4
Alabama	14	164	11.7
Penn St	13	159	12.2
Florida	14	174	12.4
Ohio St	13	163	12.5
TCU	13	166	12.8
Oklahoma	13	189	14.5
Iowa	13	200	15.4
Virginia Tech	13	203	15.6
Air Force	13	204	15.7

TOTAL DEFENSE

	GP	Plays	Yds	Avg Y/Play	Avg Y/G
TCU	13	801	3116	3.89	239.69
Alabama	14	844	3418	4.05	244.14
Texas	14	918	3527	4.18	251.93
Florida	14	845	3536	4.18	252.57
Ohio St	13	827	3410	4.12	262.31
North Carolina	13	835	3505	4.20	269.62
Nebraska	14	955	3808	3.99	272.00
Oklahoma	13	866	3544	4.09	272.62
Penn St	13	811	3568	4.40	274.46
Iowa	13	844	3595	4.26	276.54

OPPONENTS' RUSHING

	GP	Car	Yds	Avg	TD	Yds/Game
Texas	14	458	1013	2.21	9	72.4
Alabama	14	395	1094	2.77	5	78.1
TCU	13	402	1043	2.59	8	80.2
Central Florida	13	416	1076	2.59	12	82.8
Wisconsin	13	397	1147	2.89	8	88.2
Penn St	13	410	1168	2.85	6	89.9
Ohio St	13	410	1180	2.88	6	90.8
Oklahoma	13	432	1208	2.80	10	92.9
Nebraska	14	465	1304	2.80	7	93.1
North Carolina	13	439	1243	2.83	12	95.6

TURNOVER MARGIN

		Turnovers Gained			Turnovers Lost			
	GP	Fum	Int	Total	Fum	Int	Total	Mar/Gm
Air Force	13	14	20	34	9	3	12	1.69
Rutgers	13	19	15	34	4	10	14	1.54
Boise St	14	11	24	35	11	3	14	1.50
Alabama	14	7	24	31	7	5	12	1.36
Ohio St	13	11	24	35	7	11	18	1.31
Arkansas	13	17	13	30	6	9	15	1.15
Ohio	14	17	20	37	11	13	24	0.93
Middle Tenn.St.	13	14	19	33	6	15	21	0.92
East Carolina	14	17	17	34	11	12	23	0.79
Pittsburgh	13	9	15	24	6	8	14	0.77
Southern Miss	13	15	12	27	11	6	17	0.77

OPPONENTS' PASSING EFFICIENCY

	GP	Att	Comp	Pct Comp	Int	Pct Int	Yds	Yds/Att	TD	Pct TD	Rating Pts
Nebraska	14	490	234	47.8	20	4.08	2504	5.11	7	1.43	87.28
Alabama	14	449	210	46.8	24	5.35	2324	5.18	11	2.45	87.67
Iowa	13	383	190	49.6	21	5.48	1988	5.19	9	2.35	89.99
TCU	13	399	189	47.4	14	3.51	2073	5.20	10	2.51	92.30
Ohio St	13	417	226	54.2	24	5.76	2230	5.35	10	2.40	95.52
Florida	14	396	208	52.5	20	5.05	2139	5.40	10	2.53	96.11
Oklahoma	13	434	233	53.7	18	4.15	2336	5.38	11	2.53	98.98
Virginia Tech	13	367	174	47.4	11	3.00	2172	5.92	9	2.45	99.21
Utah	13	397	201	50.6	17	4.28	2288	5.76	12	3.02	100.42
Texas	14	460	255	55.4	25	5.43	2514	5.47	14	3.04	100.48

FOR THE RECORD•Year by Year

NCAA Football Bowl Subdivision* National Champions

Year	Champion	Record	Bowl Game	Head Coach
1883	Yale	8-0-0	No bowl	Ray Tompkins (Captain)
1884	Yale	9-0-0	No bowl	Eugene L. Richards (Captain)
1885	Princeton	9-0-0	No bowl	Charles DeCamp (Captain)
1886	Yale	9-0-1	No bowl	Robert N. Corwin (Captain)
1887	Yale	9-0-0	No bowl	Harry W. Beecher (Captain)
1888	Yale	13-0-0	No bowl	Walter Camp
1889	Princeton	10-0-0	No bowl	Edgar Poe (Captain)
1890	Harvard	11-0-0	No bowl	George A. Stewart/George C. Adams
1891	Yale	13-0-0	No bowl	Walter Camp
1892	Yale	13-0-0	No bowl	Walter Camp
1893	Princeton	11-0-0	No bowl	Tom Trenchard (Captain)
1894	Yale	16-0-0	No bowl	William C. Rhodes
1895	Pennsylvania	14-0-0	No bowl	George Woodruff
1896	Princeton	10-0-1	No bowl	Garrett Cochran
1897	Pennsylvania	15-0-0	No bowl	George Woodruff
1898	Harvard	11-0-0	No bowl	W. Cameron Forbes
1899	Harvard	10-0-1	No bowl	Benjamin H. Dibblee
1900	Yale	12-0-0	No bowl	Malcolm McBride
1901	Michigan	11-0-0	Won Rose	Fielding Yost
1902	Michigan	11-0-0	No bowl	Fielding Yost
1903	Princeton	11-0-0	No bowl	Art Hillebrand
1904	Pennsylvania	12-0-0	No bowl	Carl Williams
1905	Chicago	11-0-0	No bowl	Amos Alonzo Stagg
1906	Princeton	9-0-1	No bowl	Bill Roper
1907	Yale	9-0-1	No bowl	Bill Knox
1908	Pennsylvania	11-0-1	No bowl	Sol Metzger
1909	Yale	10-0-0	No bowl	Howard Jones
1910	Harvard	8-0-1	No bowl	Percy Houghton
1911	Princeton	8-0-2	No bowl	Bill Roper
1912	Harvard	9-0-0	No bowl	Percy Houghton
1913	Harvard	9-0-0	No bowl	Percy Houghton
1914	Army	9-0-0	No bowl	Charley Daly
1915	Cornell	9-0-0	No bowl	Al Sharpe
1916	Pittsburgh	8-0-0	No bowl	Pop Warner
1917	Georgia Tech	9-0-0	No bowl	John Heisman
1918	Pittsburgh	4-1-0	No bowl	Pop Warner
1919	Harvard	9-0-1	Won Rose	Bob Fisher
1920	California	9-0-0	Won Rose	Andy Smith
1921	Cornell	8-0-0	No bowl	Gil Dobie
1922	Cornell	8-0-0	No bowl	Gil Dobie
1923	Illinois	8-0-0	No bowl	Bob Zuppke
1924	Notre Dame	10-0-0	Won Rose	Knute Rockne
1925	Alabama (H)	10-0-0	Won Rose	Wallace Wade
	Dartmouth (D)	8-0-0	No bowl	Jesse Hawley
1926	Alabama (H)	9-0-1	Tied Rose	Wallace Wade
	Stanford (D)(H)	10-0-1	Tied Rose	Pop Warner
1927	Illinois	7-0-1	No bowl	Bob Zuppke
1928	Georgia Tech (H)	10-0-0	Won Rose	Bill Alexander
	USC (D)	9-0-1	No bowl	Howard Jones
1929	Notre Dame	9-0-0	No bowl	Knute Rockne
1930	Notre Dame	10-0-0	No bowl	Knute Rockne
1931	USC	10-1-0	Won Rose	Howard Jones
1932	USC (H)	10-0-0	Won Rose	Howard Jones
	Michigan (D)	8-0-0	No bowl	Harry Kipke
1933	Michigan	7-0-1	No bowl	Harry Kipke
1934	Minnesota	8-0-0	No bowl	Bernie Bierman
1935	Minnesota (H)	8-0-0	No bowl	Bernie Bierman
	SMU (D)	12-1-0	Lost Rose	Matty Bell
1936	Minnesota	7-1-0	No bowl	Bernie Bierman
1937	Pittsburgh	9-0-1	No bowl	Jock Sutherland
1938	TCU (AP)	11-0-0	Won Sugar	Dutch Meyer
	Notre Dame (D)	8-1-0	No bowl	Elmer Layden
1939	USC (D)	8-0-2	Won Rose	Howard Jones
	Texas A&M (AP)	11-0-0	Won Sugar	Homer Norton

*In 2007, the NCAA renamed Division I-A as the "Football Bowl Subdivision" and Division I-AA as the "Football Championship Subdivision."

Year	Champion	Record	Bowl Game	Head Coach
1940	Minnesota	8-0-0	No bowl	Bernie Bierman
1941	Minnesota	8-0-0	No bowl	Bernie Bierman
1942	Ohio St	9-1-0	No bowl	Paul Brown
1943	Notre Dame	9-1-0	No bowl	Frank Leahy
1944	Army	9-0-0	No bowl	Red Blaik
1945	Army	9-0-0	No bowl	Red Blaik
1946	Notre Dame	8-0-1	No bowl	Frank Leahy
1947	Notre Dame	9-0-0	No bowl	Frank Leahy
	Michigan*	10-0-0	Won Rose	Fritz Crisler
1948	Michigan	9-0-0	No bowl	Bennie Oosterbaan
1949	Notre Dame	10-0-0	No bowl	Frank Leahy
1950	Oklahoma	10-1-0	Lost Sugar	Bud Wilkinson
1951	Tennessee	10-1-0	Lost Sugar	Bob Neyland
1952	Michigan St	9-0-0	No bowl	Biggie Munn
1953	Maryland	10-1-0	Lost Orange	Jim Tatum
1954	Ohio St	10-0-0	Won Rose	Woody Hayes
	UCLA (UPI)	9-0-0	No bowl	Red Sanders
1955	Oklahoma	11-0-0	Won Orange	Bud Wilkinson
1956	Oklahoma	10-0-0	No bowl	Bud Wilkinson
1957	Auburn	10-0-0	No bowl	Shug Jordan
	Ohio St (UPI)	9-1-0	Won Rose	Woody Hayes
1958	LSU	11-0-0	Won Sugar	Paul Dietzel
1959	Syracuse	11-0-0	Won Cotton	Ben Schwartzwalder
1960	Minnesota	8-2-0	Lost Rose	Murray Warmath
1961	Alabama	11-0-0	Won Sugar	Bear Bryant
1962	USC	11-0-0	Won Rose	John McKay
1963	Texas	11-0-0	Won Cotton	Darrell Royal
1964	Alabama	10-1-0	Lost Orange	Bear Bryant
1965	Alabama	9-1-1	Won Orange	Bear Bryant
	Michigan St (UPI)	10-1-0	Lost Rose	Duffy Daugherty
1966	Notre Dame	9-0-1	No bowl	Ara Parseghian
1967	USC	10-1-0	Won Rose	John McKay
1968	Ohio St	10-0-0	Won Rose	Woody Hayes
1969	Texas	11-0-0	Won Cotton	Darrell Royal
1970	Nebraska	11-0-1	Won Orange	Bob Devaney
	Texas (UPI)	10-1-0	Lost Cotton	Darrell Royal
1971	Nebraska	13-0-0	Won Orange	Bob Devaney
1972	USC	12-0-0	Won Rose	John McKay
1973	Notre Dame	11-0-0	Won Sugar	Ara Parseghian
	Alabama (UPI)	11-1-0	Lost Sugar	Bear Bryant
1974	Oklahoma	11-0-0	No bowl	Barry Switzer
	USC (UPI)	10-1-1	Won Rose	John McKay
1975	Oklahoma	11-1-0	Won Orange	Barry Switzer
1976	Pittsburgh	12-0-0	Won Sugar	Johnny Majors
1977	Notre Dame	11-1-0	Won Cotton	Dan Devine
1978	Alabama	11-1-0	Won Sugar	Bear Bryant
	USC (UPI)	12-1-0	Won Rose	John Robinson
1979	Alabama	12-0-0	Won Sugar	Bear Bryant
1980	Georgia	12-0-0	Won Sugar	Vince Dooley
1981	Clemson	12-0-0	Won Orange	Danny Ford
1982	Penn St	11-1-0	Won Sugar	Joe Paterno
1983	Miami (Fla.)	11-1-0	Won Orange	Howard Schnellenberger
1984	BYU	13-0-0	Won Holiday	LaVell Edwards
1985	Oklahoma	11-1-0	Won Orange	Barry Switzer
1986	Penn St	12-0-0	Won Fiesta	Joe Paterno
1987	Miami (Fla.)	12-0-0	Won Orange	Jimmy Johnson
1988	Notre Dame	12-0-0	Won Fiesta	Lou Holtz
1989	Miami (Fla.)	11-1-0	Won Sugar	Dennis Erickson
1990	Colorado	11-1-1	Won Orange	Bill McCartney
	Georgia Tech (UPI)	11-0-1	Won Citrus	Bobby Ross
1991	Miami (Fla.)	12-0-0	Won Orange	Dennis Erickson
	Washington (CNN)	12-0-0	Won Rose	Don James
1992	Alabama	13-0-0	Won Sugar	Gene Stallings
1993	Florida St	12-1-0	Won Orange	Bobby Bowden
1994	Nebraska	13-0-0	Won Orange	Tom Osborne
1995	Nebraska	12-0-0	Won Fiesta	Tom Osborne
†1996	Florida	12-1	Won Sugar	Steve Spurrier
1997	Michigan	12-0	Won Rose	Lloyd Carr
	Nebraska (ESPN)	13-0	Won Orange	Tom Osborne

Year	Champion	Record	Bowl Game	Head Coach
1998	Tennessee	13–0	Won Fiesta	Phillip Fulmer
1999	Florida St	12–0	Won Sugar	Bobby Bowden
2000	Oklahoma	13–0	Won Orange	Bob Stoops
2001	Miami (Fla.)	12–0	Won Rose	Larry Coker
2002	Ohio St	14–0	Won Fiesta	Jim Tressel
2003	LSU	13–1	Won Sugar	Nick Saban
	USC	12–1	Won Rose	Pete Carroll
§2004	Vacated			
2005	Texas	13–0	Won Rose	Mack Brown
‡2006	Florida	13–1	Won BCS Nat'l Championship	Urban Meyer
2007	LSU	12–2	Won BCS Nat'l Championship	Les Miles
2008	Florida	13–1	Won BCS Nat'l Championship	Urban Meyer
2009	Alabama	14–0	Won BCS Nat'l Championship	Nick Saban

*The AP, which had voted Notre Dame No. 1, took a second vote, giving the national title to Michigan after its 49–0 win over USC in the Rose Bowl. Note: Selectors: Helms Athletic Foundation (H) 1883–1935, The Dickinson System (D) 1924–40, The Associated Press (AP) 1936–present, United Press International (UPI) 1958–90, *USA Today*/CNN (CNN) 1991–96, and *USA Today*/ESPN (ESPN) 1997–present. †In 1996 the NCAA introduced overtime to break ties.
‡In 2006, the BCS established a separate national championship game in addition to its existing four-bowl structure.
§USC's 2005 Orange Bowl victory and 2004 national championship were vacated in 2010 due to rules violations.

Results of Major Bowl Games

Rose Bowl

1-1-02	Michigan 49, Stanford 0	1-1-53	USC 7, Wisconsin 0
1-1-16	Washington St 14, Brown 0	1-1-54	Michigan St 28, UCLA 20
1-1-17	Oregon 14, Pennsylvania 0	1-1-55	Ohio St 20, USC 7
1-1-18	Mare Island 19, Camp Lewis 7	1-2-56	Michigan St 17, UCLA 14
1-1-19	Great Lakes 17, Mare Island 0	1-1-57	Iowa 35, Oregon St 19
1-1-20	Harvard 7, Oregon 6	1-1-58	Ohio St 10, Oregon 7
1-1-21	California 28, Ohio St 0	1-1-59	Iowa 38, California 12
1-2-22	Washington & Jefferson 0, California 0	1-1-60	Washington 44, Wisconsin 8
1-1-23	USC 14, Penn St 3	1-2-61	Washington 17, Minnesota 7
1-1-24	Navy 14, Washington 14	1-1-62	Minnesota 21, UCLA 3
1-1-25	Notre Dame 27, Stanford 10	1-1-63	USC 42, Wisconsin 37
1-1-26	Alabama 20, Washington 19	1-1-64	Illinois 17, Washington 7
1-1-27	Alabama 7, Stanford 7	1-1-65	Michigan 34, Oregon St 7
1-2-28	Stanford 7, Pittsburgh 6	1-1-66	UCLA 14, Michigan St 12
1-1-29	Georgia Tech 8, California 7	1-2-67	Purdue 14, USC 13
1-1-30	USC 47, Pittsburgh 14	1-1-68	USC 14, Indiana 3
1-1-31	Alabama 24, Washington St 0	1-1-69	Ohio St 27, USC 16
1-1-32	USC 21, Tulane 12	1-1-70	USC 10, Michigan 3
1-2-33	USC 35, Pittsburgh 0	1-1-71	Stanford 27, Ohio St 17
1-1-34	Columbia 7, Stanford 0	1-1-72	Stanford 13, Michigan 12
1-1-35	Alabama 29, Stanford 13	1-1-73	USC 42, Ohio St 17
1-1-36	Stanford 7, Southern Methodist 0	1-1-74	Ohio St 42, USC 21
1-1-37	Pittsburgh 21, Washington 0	1-1-75	USC 18, Ohio St 17
1-1-38	California 13, Alabama 0	1-1-76	UCLA 23, Ohio St 10
1-2-39	USC 7, Duke 3	1-1-77	USC 14, Michigan 6
1-1-40	USC 14, Tennessee 0	1-2-78	Washington 27, Michigan 20
1-1-41	Stanford 21, Nebraska 13	1-1-79	USC 17, Michigan 10
1-1-42	Oregon St 20, Duke 16	1-1-80	USC 17, Ohio St 16
1-1-43	Georgia 9, UCLA 0	1-1-81	Michigan 23, Washington 6
1-1-44	USC 29, Washington 0	1-1-82	Washington 28, Iowa 0
1-1-45	USC 25, Tennessee 0	1-1-83	UCLA 24, Michigan 14
1-1-46	Alabama 34, USC 14	1-2-84	UCLA 45, Illinois 9
1-1-47	Illinois 45, UCLA 14	1-1-85	USC 20, Ohio St 17
1-1-48	Michigan 49, USC 0	1-1-86	UCLA 45, Iowa 28
1-1-49	Northwestern 20, California 14	1-1-87	Arizona St 22, Michigan 15
1-2-50	Ohio St 17, California 14	1-1-88	Michigan St 20, USC 17
1-1-51	Michigan 14, California 6	1-2-89	Michigan 22, USC 14
1-1-52	Illinois 40, Stanford 7	1-1-90	USC 17, Michigan 10

Note: The Fiesta, Orange, Rose and Sugar Bowls constitute the Bowl Alliance, formed in 1995 and running through the 2009 regular season and 2010 bowl season. Starting in January 2007, it has included a separate BCS National Championship game as well. The four other BCS Bowls will host the following conference champions with consideration for the following conference tie-ins: the ACC or Big East champion in the FedEx Orange Bowl, the SEC champion in the Allstate Sugar Bowl, the Big Ten and the Pac-10 champions in the Rose Bowl and the Big 12 champion in the Tostitos Fiesta Bowl. There are also four at-large positions in the BCS that are open to any Division I-A team. This allows any Division I-A school in the nation the opportunity to play in a BCS bowl game.

Rose Bowl *(Cont.)*

1-1-91 ....Washington 46, Iowa 34
1-1-92 ....Washington 34, Michigan 14
1-1-93 ....Michigan 38, Washington 31
1-1-94 ....Wisconsin 21, UCLA 16
1-2-95 ....Penn St 38, Oregon 20
1-1-96 ....USC 41, Northwestern 32
1-1-97 ....Ohio St 20, Arizona St 17
1-1-98 ....Michigan 21, Washington St 16
1-1-99 ....Wisconsin 38, UCLA 31
1-1-00 ....Wisconsin 17, Stanford 9
1-1-01 ....Washington 34, Purdue 24
1-3-02 ....Miami 37, Nebraska 14
1-1-03 ....Oklahoma 34, Washington St 14
1-1-04 ....USC 28, Michigan 14
1-1-05 ....Texas 38, Michigan 37
1-4-06 ....Texas 41, USC 38
1-1-07 ....USC 32, Michigan 18
1-1-08 ....USC 49, Illinois 17
1-1-09 ....USC 38, Penn St 24
1-1-10 ....Ohio St 26, Oregon 17

City: Pasadena. Stadium: Rose Bowl, capacity 96,576.
Playing Sites: Tournament Park (1902, 1916–22), Rose Bowl (1923–41, since 1943), Duke Stadium, Durham, NC (1942).

Orange Bowl

1-1-35 ....Bucknell 26, Miami (Fla.) 0
1-1-36 ....Catholic 20, Mississippi 19
1-1-37 ....Duquesne 13, Mississippi St 12
1-1-38 ....Auburn 6, Michigan St 0
1-2-39 ....Tennessee 17, Oklahoma 0
1-1-40 ....Georgia Tech 21, Missouri 7
1-1-41 ....Mississippi St 14, Georgetown 7
1-1-42 ....Georgia 40, TCU 26
1-1-43 ....Alabama 37, Boston College 21
1-1-44 ....LSU 19, Texas A&M 14
1-1-45 ....Tulsa 26, Georgia Tech 12
1-1-46 ....Miami (Fla.) 13, Holy Cross 6
1-1-47 ....Rice 8, Tennessee 0
1-1-48 ....Georgia Tech 20, Kansas 14
1-1-49 ....Texas 41, Georgia 28
1-2-50 ....Santa Clara 21, Kentucky 13
1-1-51 ....Clemson 15, Miami (Fla.) 14
1-1-52 ....Georgia Tech 17, Baylor 14
1-1-53 ....Alabama 61, Syracuse 6
1-1-54 ....Oklahoma 7, Maryland 0
1-1-55 ....Duke 34, Nebraska 7
1-2-56 ....Oklahoma 20, Maryland 6
1-1-57 ....Colorado 27, Clemson 21
1-1-58 ....Oklahoma 48, Duke 21
1-1-59 ....Oklahoma 21, Syracuse 6
1-1-60 ....Georgia 14, Missouri 0
1-2-61 ....Missouri 21, Navy 14
1-1-62 ....LSU 25, Colorado 7
1-1-63 ....Alabama 17, Oklahoma 0
1-1-64 ....Nebraska 13, Auburn 7
1-1-65 ....Texas 21, Alabama 17
1-1-66 ....Alabama 39, Nebraska 28
1-2-67 ....Florida 27, Georgia Tech 12
1-1-68 ....Oklahoma 26, Tennessee 24
1-1-69 ....Penn St 15, Kansas 14
1-1-70 ....Penn St 10, Missouri 3
1-1-71 ....Nebraska 17, LSU 12
1-1-72 ....Nebraska 38, Alabama 6
1-1-73 ....Nebraska 40, Notre Dame 6
1-1-74 ....Penn St 16, LSU 9
1-1-75 ....Notre Dame 13, Alabama 11
1-1-76 ....Oklahoma 14, Michigan 6

Orange Bowl *(Cont.)*

1-1-77 ....Ohio St 27, Colorado 10
1-2-78 ....Arkansas 31, Oklahoma 6
1-1-79 ....Oklahoma 31, Nebraska 24
1-1-80 ....Oklahoma 24, Florida St 7
1-1-81 ....Oklahoma 18, Florida St 17
1-1-82 ....Clemson 22, Nebraska 15
1-1-83 ....Nebraska 21, LSU 20
1-2-84 ....Miami (Fla.) 31, Nebraska 30
1-1-85 ....Washington 28, Oklahoma 17
1-1-86 ....Oklahoma 25, Penn St 10
1-1-87 ....Oklahoma 42, Arkansas 8
1-1-88 ....Miami (Fla.) 20, Oklahoma 14
1-2-89 ....Miami (Fla.) 23, Nebraska 3
1-1-90 ....Notre Dame 21, Colorado 6
1-1-91 ....Colorado 10, Notre Dame 9
1-1-92 ....Miami (Fla.) 22, Nebraska 0
1-1-93 ....Florida St 27, Nebraska 14
1-1-94 ....Florida St 18, Nebraska 16
1-1-95 ....Nebraska 24, Miami (Fla.) 17
1-1-96 ....Florida St 31, Notre Dame 26
12-31-96 ....Nebraska 41, Virginia Tech 21
1-2-98 ....Nebraska 42, Tennessee 17
1-2-99 ....Florida 31, Syracuse 10
1-1-00 ....Michigan 35, Alabama 34 (ot)
1-3-01 ....Oklahoma 13, Florida St 2
1-2-02 ....Florida 56, Maryland 23
1-2-03 ....USC 38, Iowa 17
1-1-04 ....Miami (Fla.) 16, Florida St 15
1-4-05 ....*Vacated
1-3-06 ....Penn State 26, Florida State 23 (3OT)
1-2-07 ....Louisville 24, Wake Forest 13
1-3-08 ....Kansas 24, Virginia Tech 21
1-1-09 ....Virginia Tech 20, Cincinnati 7
1-5-10 ....Iowa 24, Georgia Tech 14

City: Miami. Stadium: Pro Player Stadium, capacity 75,192.
Playing Sites: Orange Bowl (1935–96), Pro Player Stadium (1996–2005), Dolphin(s) Stadium (2005–09), Land Shark Stadium (2010). *USC's 2005 Orange Bowl victory was vacated in 2010 due to rules violations.

Sugar Bowl

1-1-35 ....Tulane 20, Temple 14
1-1-36 ....TCU 3, LSU 2
1-1-37 ....Santa Clara 21, LSU 14
1-1-38 ....Santa Clara 6, LSU 0
1-2-39 ....TCU 15, Carnegie Tech 7
1-1-40 ....Texas A&M 14, Tulane 13
1-1-41 ....Boston Col 19, Tennessee 13
1-1-42 ....Fordham 2, Missouri 0
1-1-43 ....Tennessee 14, Tulsa 7
1-1-44 ....Georgia Tech 20, Tulsa 18
1-1-45 ....Duke 29, Alabama 26
1-1-46 ....Oklahoma St 33, St. Mary's (Ca.) 13
1-1-47 ....Georgia 20, North Carolina 10
1-1-48 ....Texas 27, Alabama 7
1-1-49 ....Oklahoma 14, North Carolina 6
1-2-50 ....Oklahoma 35, LSU 0
1-1-51 ....Kentucky 13, Oklahoma 7
1-1-52 ....Maryland 28, Tennessee 13
1-1-53 ....Georgia Tech 24, Mississippi 7
1-1-54 ....Georgia Tech 42, W Virginia 19
1-1-55 ....Navy 21, Mississippi 0
1-2-56 ....Georgia Tech 7, Pittsburgh 0
1-1-57 ....Baylor 13, Tennessee 7
1-1-58 ....Mississippi 39, Texas 7
1-1-59 ....LSU 7, Clemson 0
1-1-60 ....Mississippi 21, LSU 0

Sugar Bowl *(Cont.)*

1-2-61.............Mississippi 14, Rice 6
1-1-62.............Alabama 10, Arkansas 3
1-1-63.............Mississippi 17, Arkansas 13
1-1-64.............Alabama 12, Mississippi 7
1-1-65.............LSU 13, Syracuse 10
1-1-66.............Missouri 20, Florida 18
1-2-67.............Alabama 34, Nebraska 7
1-1-68.............LSU 20, Wyoming 13
1-1-69.............Arkansas 16, Georgia 2
1-1-70.............Mississippi 27, Arkansas 22
1-1-71.............Tennessee 34, Air Force 13
1-1-72.............Oklahoma 40, Auburn 22
12-31-72.........Oklahoma 14, Penn St 0
12-31-73.........Notre Dame 24, Alabama 23
12-31-74.........Nebraska 13, Florida 10
12-31-75.........Alabama 13, Penn St 6
1-1-77.............Pittsburgh 27, Georgia 3
1-2-78.............Alabama 35, Ohio St 6
1-1-79.............Alabama 14, Penn St 7
1-1-80.............Alabama 24, Arkansas 9
1-1-81.............Georgia 17, Notre Dame 10
1-1-82.............Pittsburgh 24, Georgia 20
1-1-83.............Penn St 27, Georgia 23
1-2-84.............Auburn 9, Michigan 7
1-1-85.............Nebraska 28, LSU 10
1-1-86.............Tennessee 35, Miami (Fla.) 7
1-1-87.............Nebraska 30, LSU 15
1-1-88.............Syracuse 16, Auburn 16
1-2-89.............Florida St 13, Auburn 7
1-1-90.............Miami (Fla.) 33, Alabama 25
1-1-91.............Tennessee 23, Virginia 22
1-1-92.............Notre Dame 39, Florida 28
1-1-93.............Alabama 34, Miami (Fla.) 13
1-1-94.............Florida 41, West Virginia 7
1-2-95.............Florida St 23, Florida 17
12-31-95.........Virginia Tech 28, Texas 10
1-2-97.............Florida St 52, Florida 20
1-1-98.............Florida St 31, Ohio St 14
1-1-99.............Ohio St 24, Texas A&M 14
1-4-00.............Florida St 46, Virginia Tech 29
1-2-01.............Miami (Fla.) 37, Florida 20
1-1-02.............LSU 47, Illinois 34
1-1-03.............Georgia 26, Florida St 13
1-4-04.............LSU 21, Oklahoma 14
1-3-05.............Auburn 16, Virginia Tech 13
1-2-06.............West Virginia 38, Georgia 35
1-3-07.............LSU 41, Notre Dame 14
1-1-08.............Georgia 41, Hawaii 10
1-2-09.............Utah 31, Alabama 17
1-1-10.............Florida 51, Cincinnati 24

City: New Orleans. Stadium: Louisiana Superdome, capacity 76,791. Playing Sites: Tulane Stadium (1935–74), Louisiana Superdome (since 1975). Due to Hurricane Katrina, 2006 Sugar Bowl played at Atlanta's Georgia Dome.

Cotton Bowl

1-1-37.............TCU 16, Marquette 6
1-1-38.............Rice 28, Colorado 14
1-2-39.............St. Mary's (Ca.) 20, Texas Tech 13
1-1-40.............Clemson 6, Boston Col 3
1-1-41.............Texas A&M 13, Fordham 12
1-1-42.............Alabama 29, Texas A&M 21
1-1-43.............Texas 14, Georgia Tech 7
1-1-44.............Texas 7, Randolph Field 7
1-1-45.............Oklahoma St 34, TCU 0
1-1-46.............Texas 40, Missouri 27
1-1-47.............Arkansas 0, LSU 0

Cotton Bowl *(Cont.)*

1-1-48.............Southern Methodist 13, Penn St 13
1-1-49.............Southern Methodist 21, Oregon 13
1-2-50.............Rice 27, North Carolina 13
1-1-51.............Tennessee 20, Texas 14
1-1-52.............Kentucky 20, TCU 7
1-1-53.............Texas 16, Tennessee 0
1-1-54.............Rice 28, Alabama 6
1-1-55.............Georgia Tech 14, Arkansas 6
1-2-56.............Mississippi 14, TCU 13
1-1-57.............TCU 28, Syracuse 27
1-1-58.............Navy 20, Rice 7
1-1-59.............TCU 0, Air Force 0
1-1-60.............Syracuse 23, Texas 14
1-2-61.............Duke 7, Arkansas 6
1-1-62.............Texas 12, Mississippi 7
1-1-63.............LSU 13, Texas 0
1-1-64.............Texas 28, Navy 6
1-1-65.............Arkansas 10, Nebraska 7
1-1-66.............LSU 14, Arkansas 7
12-31-66.........Georgia 24, Southern Methodist 9
1-1-68.............Texas A&M 20, Alabama 16
1-1-69.............Texas 36, Tennessee 13
1-1-70.............Texas 21, Notre Dame 17
1-1-71.............Notre Dame 24, Texas 11
1-1-72.............Penn St 30, Texas 6
1-1-73.............Texas 17, Alabama 13
1-1-74.............Nebraska 19, Texas 3
1-1-75.............Penn St 41, Baylor 20
1-1-76.............Arkansas 31, Georgia 10
1-1-77.............Houston 30, Maryland 21
1-2-78.............Notre Dame 38, Texas 10
1-1-79.............Notre Dame 35, Houston 34
1-1-80.............Houston 17, Nebraska 14
1-1-81.............Alabama 30, Baylor 2
1-1-82.............Texas 14, Alabama 12
1-1-83.............SMU 7, Pittsburgh 3
1-2-84.............Georgia 10, Texas 9
1-1-85.............Boston Col 45, Houston 28
1-1-86.............Texas A&M 36, Auburn 16
1-1-87.............Ohio St 28, Texas A&M 12
1-1-88.............Texas A&M 35, Notre Dame 10
1-2-89.............UCLA 17, Arkansas 3
1-1-90.............Tennessee 31, Arkansas 27
1-1-91.............Miami (Fla.) 46, Texas 3
1-1-92.............Florida St 10, Texas A&M 2
1-1-93.............Notre Dame 28, Texas A&M 3
1-1-94.............Notre Dame 24, Texas A&M 21
1-2-95.............USC 55, Texas Tech 14
1-1-96.............Colorado 38, Oregon 6
1-1-97.............BYU 19, Kansas St 15
1-1-98.............UCLA 29, Texas A&M 23
1-1-99.............Texas 38, Mississippi St 11
1-1-00.............Arkansas 27, Texas 6
1-1-01.............Kansas St 35, Tennessee 21
1-1-02.............Oklahoma 10, Arkansas 3
1-1-03.............Texas 35, LSU 20
1-2-04.............Mississippi 31, Oklahoma St 28
1-1-05.............Tennessee 38, Texas A&M 7
1-2-06.............Alabama 13, Texas Tech 10
1-1-07.............Auburn 17, Nebraska 14
1-1-08.............Missouri 38, Arkansas 7
1-2-09.............Mississippi 47, Texas Tech 34
1-2-10.............Mississippi 21, Oklahoma St 7

City: Dallas. Stadium: Cotton Bowl (1937–2009), capacity 88,175. Cowboys Stadium (2010–), capacity 71,167.

Results of Major Bowl Games *(Cont.)*

Sun Bowl

1-1-36............Hardin-Simmons 14, New Mexico St 14
1-1-37............Hardin-Simmons 34, UTEP 6
1-1-38............W Virginia 7, Texas Tech 6
1-2-39............Utah 26, New Mexico 0
1-1-40............Catholic 0, Arizona St 0
1-1-41............Case Reserve 26, Arizona St 13
1-1-42............Tulsa 6, Texas Tech 0
1-1-43............2nd Air Force 13, Hardin-Simmons 7
1-1-44............Southwestern (Tex.) 7, New Mexico 0
1-1-45............Southwestern (Tex.) 35, New Mexico 0
1-1-46............New Mexico 34, Denver 24
1-1-47............Cincinnati 18, Virginia Tech 6
1-1-48............Miami (OH) 13, Texas Tech 12
1-1-49............W Virginia 21, UTEP 12
1-2-50............UTEP 33, Georgetown 20
1-1-51............W Texas 14, Cincinnati 13
1-1-52............Texas Tech 25, Pacific 14
1-1-53............Pacific 26, Southern Miss 7
1-1-54............UTEP 37, Southern Miss 14
1-1-55............UTEP 47, Florida St 20
1-2-56............Wyoming 21, Texas Tech 14
1-1-57............George Washington 13, UTEP 0
1-1-58............Louisville 34, Drake 20
12-31-58............Wyoming 14, Hardin-Simmons 6
12-31-59............New Mexico St 28, N Texas 8
12-31-60............New Mexico 20, Utah St 13
12-30-61............Villanova 17, Wichita St 9
12-31-62............W Texas 15, Ohio 14
12-31-63............Oregon 21, Southern Methodist 14
12-26-64............Georgia 7, Texas Tech 0
12-31-65............UTEP 13, TCU 12
12-24-66............Wyoming 28, Florida St 20
12-30-67............UTEP 14, Mississippi 7
12-28-68............Auburn 34, Arizona 10
12-20-69............Nebraska 45, Georgia 6
12-19-70............Georgia Tech 17, Texas Tech 9
12-18-71............LSU 33, Iowa 15
12-30-72............North Carolina 32, Texas Tech 28
12-29-73............Missouri 34, Auburn 17
12-28-74............Mississippi St 26, North Carolina 24
12-26-75............Pittsburgh 33, Kansas 19
1-2-77............Texas A&M 37, Florida 14
12-31-77............Stanford 24, LSU 14
12-23-78............Texas 42, Maryland 0
12-22-79............Washington 14, Texas 7
12-27-80............Nebraska 31, Mississippi St 17
12-26-81............Oklahoma 40, Houston 14
12-25-82............North Carolina 26, Texas 10
12-24-83............Alabama 28, Southern Methodist 7
12-22-84............Maryland 28, Tennessee 27
12-28-85............Georgia 13, Arizona 13
12-25-86............Alabama 28, Washington 6
12-25-87............Oklahoma St 35, W Virginia 33
12-24-88............Alabama 29, Army 28
12-30-89............Pittsburgh 31, Texas A&M 28
12-31-90............Michigan St 17, USC 16
12-31-91............UCLA 6, Illinois 3
12-31-92............Baylor 20, Arizona 15
12-24-93............Oklahoma 41, Texas Tech 10
12-30-94............Texas 35, North Carolina 31
12-29-95............Iowa 38, Washington 18
12-31-96............Stanford 38, Michigan St 0
12-31-97............Arizona St 17, Iowa 7
12-31-98............TCU 28, USC 19
12-31-99............Oregon 24, Minnesota 20
12-29-00............Wisconsin 21, UCLA 20
12-31-01............Washington St 33, Purdue 27
12-31-02............Purdue 34, Washington 24

Sun Bowl

12-31-03............Minnesota 31, Oregon 30
12-31-04............Arizona State 27, Purdue 23
12-30-05............UCLA 50, Northwestern 39
12-29-06............Oregon State 39, Missouri 38
12-31-07............Oregon 56, South Florida 21
12-31-08............Oregon St 3, Pittsburgh 0
12-31-09............Oklahoma 31, Stanford 27

City: El Paso. Stadium: Sun Bowl, capacity 51,270.
Name Changes: Sun Bowl (1936–86; 94–), John Hancock
Sun Bowl (1987–88), John Hancock Bowl (1989–93).
Playing Sites: Kidd Field (1936–62), Sun Bowl (since
1963).

Gator Bowl

1-1-46............Wake Forest 26, South Carolina 14
1-1-47............Oklahoma 34, North Carolina St 13
1-1-48............Maryland 20, Georgia 20
1-1-49............Clemson 24, Missouri 23
1-2-50............Maryland 20, Missouri 7
1-1-51............Wyoming 20, Washington & Lee 7
1-1-52............Miami (Fla.) 14, Clemson 0
1-1-53............Florida 14, Tulsa 13
1-1-54............Texas Tech 35, Auburn 13
12-31-54............Auburn 33, Baylor 13
12-31-55............Vanderbilt 25, Auburn 13
12-29-56............Georgia Tech 21, Pittsburgh 14
12-28-57............Tennessee 3, Texas A&M 0
12-27-58............Mississippi 7, Florida 3
1-2-60............Arkansas 14, Georgia Tech 7
12-31-60............Florida 13, Baylor 12
12-30-61............Penn St 30, Georgia Tech 15
12-29-62............Florida 17, Penn St 7
12-28-63............North Carolina 35, Air Force 0
1-2-65............Florida 36, Oklahoma 19
12-31-65............Georgia Tech 31, Texas Tech 21
12-31-66............Tennessee 18, Syracuse 12
12-30-67............Penn St 17, Florida St 17
12-28-68............Missouri 35, Alabama 10
12-27-69............Florida 14, Tennessee 13
1-2-71............Auburn 35, Mississippi 28
12-31-71............Georgia 7, North Carolina 3
12-30-72............Auburn 24, Colorado 3
12-29-73............Texas Tech 28, Tennessee 19
12-30-74............Auburn 27, Texas 3
12-29-75............Maryland 13, Florida 0
12-27-76............Notre Dame 20, Penn St 9
12-30-77............Pittsburgh 34, Clemson 3
12-29-78............Clemson 17, Ohio St 15
12-28-79............North Carolina 17, Michigan 15
12-29-80............Pittsburgh 37, South Carolina 9
12-28-81............North Carolina 31, Arkansas 27
12-30-82............Florida St 31, W Virginia 12
12-30-83............Florida 14, Iowa 6
12-28-84............Oklahoma St 21, South Carolina 14
12-30-85............Florida St 34, Oklahoma St 23
12-27-86............Clemson 27, Stanford 21
12-31-87............LSU 30, South Carolina 13
1-1-89............Georgia 34, Michigan St 27
12-30-89............Clemson 27, W Virginia 7
1-1-91............Michigan 35, Mississippi 3
12-29-91............Oklahoma 48, Virginia 14
12-31-92............Florida 27, North Carolina St 10
12-31-93............Alabama 24, North Carolina 10
12-30-94............Tennessee 45, Virginia Tech 23
1-1-96............Syracuse 41, Clemson 0
1-1-97............North Carolina 20, W Virginia 13
1-1-98............North Carolina 42, Viginia Tech 13

Gator Bowl *(Cont.)*

1-1-99 ....Georgia Tech 35, Notre Dame 28
1-1-00 ....Miami 27, Georgia Tech 13
1-1-01 ....Virginia Tech 41, Clemson 20
1-1-02 ....Florida St 30, Virginia Tech 17
1-1-03 ....North Carolina St 28, Notre Dame 6
1-1-04 ....Maryland 41, W Virginia 7
1-1-05 ....Florida State 30, West Virginia 18
1-2-06 ....Virginia Tech 35, Louisville 24
1-1-07 ....West Virginia 38, Georgia Tech 35
1-1-08 ....Texas Tech 31, Virginia 28
1-1-09 ....Nebraska 26, Clemson 21
1-1-10 ....Florida St 33, West Virginia 21

City: Jacksonville, FL. Stadium: Gator Bowl Stadium (1946-1993); Ben Hill Griffin Stadium (1994); Alltel Stadium (1997–2007, capacity 76,976. Jacksonville Municipal Stadium (1995–95, 2007–)

Florida Citrus Bowl

1-1-47 ....Catawba 31, Maryville (Tenn.) 6
1-1-48 ....Catawba 7, Marshall 0
1-1-49 ....Murray St 21, Sul Ross St 21
1-2-50 ....St. Vincent 7, Emory & Henry 6
1-1-51 ....Morris Harvey 35, Emory & Henry 14
1-1-52 ....Stetson 35, Arkansas St 20
1-1-53 ....E Texas St 33, Tennessee Tech 0
1-1-54 ....E Texas St 7, Arkansas St 7
1-1-55 ....NE-Omaha 7, Eastern Kentucky 6
1-2-56 ....Juniata 6, Missouri Valley 1
1-1-57 ....W Texas St 20, Southern Miss 13
1-1-58 ....E Texas St 10, Southern Miss 9
12-27-58 ....E Texas St 26, Missouri Valley 7
1-1-60 ....Middle Tennessee St 21, Presbyterian 12
12-30-60 ....Citadel 27, Tennessee Tech 0
12-29-61 ....Lamar 21, Middle Tennessee St 14
12-22-62 ....Houston 49, Miami (Ohio) 21
12-28-63 ....Western Kentucky 27, Coast Guard 0
12-12-64 ....E Carolina 14, Massachusetts 13
12-11-65 ....E Carolina 31, Maine 0
12-10-66 ....Morgan St 14, W Chester 6
12-16-67 ....TN-Martin 25, W Chester 8
12-27-68 ....Richmond 49, Ohio 42
12-26-69 ....Toledo 56, Davidson 33
12-28-70 ....Toledo 40, William & Mary 12
12-28-71 ....Toledo 28, Richmond 3
12-29-72 ....Tampa 21, Kent St 18
12-22-73 ....Miami (Ohio) 16, Florida 7
12-21-74 ....Miami (Ohio) 21, Georgia 10
12-20-75 ....Miami (Ohio) 20, South Carolina 7
12-18-76 ....Oklahoma St 49, BYU 21
12-23-77 ....Florida St 40, Texas Tech 17
12-23-78 ....North Carolina St 30, Pittsburgh 17
12-22-79 ....LSU 34, Wake Forest 10
12-20-80 ....Florida 35, Maryland 20
12-19-81 ....Missouri 19, Southern Miss 17
12-18-82 ....Auburn 33, Boston Col 26
12-17-83 ....Tennessee 30, Maryland 23
12-22-84 ....Georgia 17, Florida St 17
12-28-85 ....Ohio St 10, BYU 7
1-1-87 ....Auburn 16, USC 7
1-1-88 ....Clemson 35, Penn St 10
1-2-89 ....Clemson 13, Oklahoma 6
1-1-90 ....Illinois 31, Virginia 21
1-1-91 ....Georgia Tech 45, Nebraska 21
1-1-92 ....California 37, Clemson 13
1-1-93 ....Georgia 21, Ohio State 14
1-1-94 ....Penn State 31, Tennessee 13
1-2-95 ....Alabama 24, Ohio St 17
1-1-96 ....Tennessee 20, Ohio St 14

Florida Citrus Bowl *(Cont.)*

1-1-97 ....Tennessee 48, Northwestern 28
1-1-98 ....Florida 21, Penn St 6
1-1-99 ....Michigan 45, Arkansas 31
1-1-00 ....Michigan St 37, Florida 34
1-1-01 ....Michigan 31, Auburn 28
1-1-02 ....Tennessee 45, Michigan 17
1-1-03 ....Auburn 13, Penn St 9
1-1-04 ....Georgia 34, Purdue 27 (OT)
1-1-05 ....Iowa 30, LSU 25
1-2-06 ....Wisconsin 24, Auburn 10
1-1-07 ....Wisconsin 17, Arkansas 14
1-1-08 ....Michigan 41, Florida 35
1-1-09 ....Georgia 24, Michigan St 12
1-1-10 ....Penn St 19, LSU 17

City: Orlando, FL. Stadium: Florida Citrus Bowl, capacity 70,000. Name Change: Tangerine Bowl (1947–82). Capital One Bowl (since 2008). Playing Sites: Tangerine Bowl (1947–72, 1974–82); Florida Field, Gainesville (1973); Orlando Stadium/Florida Citrus Bowl-Orlando (1983–2007).

Liberty Bowl

12-19-59 ....Penn St 7, Alabama 0
12-17-60 ....Penn St 41, Oregon 12
12-16-61 ....Syracuse 15, Miami (Fla.) 14
12-15-62 ....Oregon St 6, Villanova 0
12-21-63 ....Mississippi St 16, North Carolina St 12
12-19-64 ....Utah 32, W Virginia 6
12-18-65 ....Mississippi 13, Auburn 7
12-10-66 ....Miami (Fla.) 14, Virginia Tech 7
12-16-67 ....North Carolina St 14, Georgia 7
12-14-68 ....Mississippi 34, Virginia Tech 17
12-13-69 ....Colorado 47, Alabama 33
12-12-70 ....Tulane 17, Colorado 3
12-20-71 ....Tennessee 14, Arkansas 13
12-18-72 ....Georgia Tech 31, Iowa St 30
12-17-73 ....North Carolina St 31, Kansas 18
12-16-74 ....Tennessee 7, Maryland 3
12-22-75 ....USC 20, Texas A&M 0
12-20-76 ....Alabama 36, UCLA 6
12-19-77 ....Nebraska 21, North Carolina 17
12-23-78 ....Missouri 20, LSU 15
12-22-79 ....Penn St 9, Tulane 6
12-27-80 ....Purdue 28, Missouri 25
12-30-81 ....Ohio St 31, Navy 28
12-29-82 ....Alabama 21, Illinois 15
12-29-83 ....Notre Dame 19, Boston Col 18
12-27-84 ....Auburn 21, Arkansas 15
12-27-85 ....Baylor 21, LSU 7
12-29-86 ....Tennessee 21, Minnesota 14
12-29-87 ....Georgia 20, Arkansas 17
12-28-88 ....Indiana 34, South Carolina 10
12-28-89 ....Mississippi 42, Air Force 29
12-27-90 ....Air Force 23, Ohio St 11
12-29-91 ....Air Force 38, Mississippi St 15
12-31-92 ....Mississippi 13, Air Force 0
12-28-93 ....Louisville 18, Michigan St 7
12-31-94 ....Illinois 30, E Carolina 0
12-30-95 ....East Carolina 19, Stanford 13
12-27-96 ....Syracuse 30, Houston 17
12-31-97 ....Southern Miss 41, Pittsburgh 7
12-31-98 ....Tulane 41, BYU 27
12-31-99 ....Southern Miss 23, Colorado St 17
12-29-01 ....Colorado St 22, Louisville 17
12-31-01 ....Louisville 28, BYU 10
12-31-02 ....TCU 17, Colorado St 3
12-31-03 ....Utah 17, Southern Mississippi 0
12-31-04 ....Louisville 44, Boise State 40

Results of Major Bowl Games (Cont.)

Liberty Bowl (Cont.)

12-31-05..........Tulsa 31, Fresno State 24
12-29-06..........South Carolina 44, Houston 36
12-29-07..........Mississippi St 10, Central Florida 3
1-2-09..............Kentucky 25, East Carolina 19
1-2-10..............Arkansas 20, East Carolina 17

City: Memphis (since 1965). Stadium: Liberty Bowl Memorial Stadium, capacity 62,921.
Playing Sites: Philadelphia (Municipal Stadium, 1959–63), Atlantic City (Convention Center, 1964).

Bluebonnet Bowl

12-19-59..........Clemson 23, TCU 7
12-17-60..........Texas 3, Alabama 3
12-16-61..........Kansas 33, Rice 7
12-22-62..........Missouri 14, Georgia Tech 10
12-21-63..........Baylor 14, LSU 7
12-19-64..........Tulsa 14, Mississippi 7
12-18-65..........Tennessee 27, Tulsa 6
12-17-66..........Texas 19, Mississippi 0
12-23-67..........Colorado 31, Miami (Fla.) 21
12-31-68..........Southern Methodist 28, Oklahoma 27
12-31-69..........Houston 36, Auburn 7
12-31-70..........Alabama 24, Oklahoma 24
12-31-71..........Colorado 29, Houston 17
12-30-72..........Tennessee 24, LSU 17
12-29-73..........Houston 47, Tulane 7
12-23-74..........North Carolina St 31, Houston 31
12-27-75..........Texas 38, Colorado 21
12-31-76..........Nebraska 27, Texas Tech 24
12-31-77..........USC 47, Texas A&M 28
12-31-78..........Stanford 25, Georgia 22
12-31-79..........Purdue 27, Tennessee 22
12-31-80..........North Carolina 16, Texas 7
12-31-81..........Michigan 33, UCLA 14
12-31-82..........Arkansas 28, Florida 24
12-31-83..........Oklahoma St 24, Baylor 14
12-31-84..........W Virginia 31, TCU 14
12-31-85..........Air Force 24, Texas 16
12-31-86..........Baylor 21, Colorado 9
12-31-87..........Texas 32, Pittsburgh 27

City: Houston. Playing sites: Rice Stadium (1959–67; 1985–86), Astrodome (1968–84, 1987).
Name change: Astro-Bluebonnet Bowl (1968–76). Bowl was discontinued after 1987.

Peach Bowl

12-3-68............LSU 31, Florida St 27
12-30-69..........W Virginia 14, South Carolina 3
12-30-70..........Arizona St 48, North Carolina 26
12-30-71..........Mississippi 41, Georgia Tech 18
12-29-72..........North Carolina St 49, W Virginia 13
12-28-73..........Georgia 17, Maryland 16
12-28-74..........Vanderbilt 6, Texas Tech 6
12-31-75..........W Virginia 13, North Carolina St 10
12-31-76..........Kentucky 21, North Carolina 0
12-31-77..........North Carolina St 24, Iowa St 14
12-25-78..........Purdue 41, Georgia Tech 21
12-31-79..........Baylor 24, Clemson 18
1-2-81..............Miami (Fla.) 20, Virginia Tech 10
12-31-81..........W Virginia 26, Florida 6
12-31-82..........Iowa 28, Tennessee 22
12-30-83..........Florida St 28, North Carolina 3
12-31-84..........Virginia 27, Purdue 24
12-31-85..........Army 31, Illinois 29
12-31-86..........Virginia Tech 25, North Carolina St 24
1-2-88..............Tennessee 27, Indiana 22
12-31-88..........North Carolina St 28, Iowa 23

Peach Bowl (Cont.)

12-30-89..........Syracuse 19, Georgia 18
12-29-90..........Auburn 27, Indiana 23
1-1-92..............E Carolina 37, North Carolina St 34
1-2-93..............North Carolina 21, Mississippi St 17
12-31-93..........Clemson 14, Kentucky 13
1-1-95..............North Carolina St 28, Mississippi St 24
12-30-95..........Virginia 34, Georgia 27
12-28-96..........LSU 10, Clemson 7
1-2-98..............Auburn 21, Clemson 17
12-31-98..........Georgia 35, Virginia 33
12-30-99..........Mississippi St 17, Clemson 7
12-29-00..........LSU 28, Georgia Tech 14
12-31-01..........North Carolina 16, Auburn 10
12-31-02..........Maryland 30, Tennessee 3
1-2-04..............Clemson 27, Tennessee 14
12-31-04..........Miami (Fla.) 27, Florida 10
12-30-05..........LSU 40, Miami (Fla.) 3
12-30-06..........Georgia 31, Virginia Tech 24
12-31-07..........Auburn 23, Clemson 20 (OT)
12-31-08..........LSU 38, Georgia Tech 3
12-31-09..........Virginia Tech 37, Tennessee 14

City: Atlanta. Stadium: Georgia Dome, capacity 71,500.
Name change: Chick-fil-A Bowl (2006–). Playing Sites: Grant Field (1968–70), Atlanta–Fulton County Stadium (1971–92), Georgia Dome (since 1993).

Fiesta Bowl

12-27-71..........Arizona St 45, Florida St 38
12-23-72..........Arizona St 49, Missouri 35
12-21-73..........Arizona St 28, Pittsburgh 7
12-28-74..........Oklahoma St 16, BYU 6
12-26-75..........Arizona St 17, Nebraska 14
12-25-76..........Oklahoma 41, Wyoming 7
12-25-77..........Penn St 42, Arizona St 30
12-25-78..........Arkansas 10, UCLA 10
12-25-79..........Pittsburgh 16, Arizona 10
12-26-80..........Penn St 31, Ohio St 19
1-1-82..............Penn St 26, USC 10
1-1-83..............Arizona St 32, Oklahoma 21
1-2-84..............Ohio St 28, Pittsburgh 23
1-1-85..............UCLA 39, Miami (Fla.) 37
1-1-86..............Michigan 27, Nebraska 23
1-2-87..............Penn St 14, Miami (Fla.) 10
1-1-88..............Florida St 31, Nebraska 28
1-2-89..............Notre Dame 34, W Virginia 21
1-1-90..............Florida St 41, Nebraska 17
1-1-91..............Louisville 34, Alabama 7
1-1-92..............Penn St 42, Tennessee 17
1-1-93..............Syracuse 26, Colorado 22
1-1-94..............Arizona 29, Miami (Fla.) 0
1-2-95..............Colorado 41, Notre Dame 24
1-2-96..............Nebraska 62, Florida 24
1-1-97..............Penn St 38, Texas 15
12-31-97..........Kansas St 35, Syracuse 18
1-4-99..............Tennessee 23, Florida St 16
1-2-00..............Nebraska 31, Tennessee 21
1-1-01..............Oregon St 41, Notre Dame 9
1-1-02..............Oregon 38, Colorado 16
1-3-03..............Ohio St 31, Miami (Fla.) 24 [2 OT]
1-2-04..............Ohio St 35, Kansas St 28
1-1-05..............Utah 35, Pittsburgh 7
1-2-06..............Ohio State 34, Notre Dame 20
1-1-07..............Boise State 43, Oklahoma 42
1-2-08..............West Virginia 48, Oklahoma 28
1-5-09..............Texas 24, Ohio St 21

Stadium: Sun Devil Stadium, Tempe, Ariz. (1971–2006), capacity 73,471. University of Phoenix Stadium, Glendale, Ariz. (2006–), capacity 72,200.

Independence Bowl

12-13-76	McNeese St 20, Tulsa 16
12-17-77	Louisiana Tech 24, Louisville 14
12-16-78	E Carolina 35, Louisiana Tech 13
12-15-79	Syracuse 31, McNeese St 7
12-13-80	Southern Miss 16, McNeese St 14
12-12-81	Texas A&M 33, Oklahoma St 16
12-11-82	Wisconsin 14, Kansas St 3
12-10-83	Air Force 9, Mississippi 3
12-15-84	Air Force 23, Virginia Tech 7
12-21-85	Minnesota 20, Clemson 13
12-20-86	Mississippi 20, Texas Tech 17
12-19-87	Washington 24, Tulane 12
12-23-88	Southern Miss 38, UTEP 18
12-16-89	Oregon 27, Tulsa 24
12-15-90	Louisiana Tech 34, Maryland 34
12-29-91	Georgia 24, Arkansas 15
12-31-92	Wake Forest 39, Oregon 35
12-31-93	Virginia Tech 45, Indiana 20
12-28-94	Virginia 20, TCU 10
12-29-95	LSU 45, Michigan St 26
12-31-96	Auburn 32, Army 29
12-28-97	LSU 27, Notre Dame 9
12-31-98	Mississippi 35, Texas Tech 18
12-31-99	Mississippi 27, Oklahoma 25
12-31-00	Mississippi St 43, Texas A&M 41
12-27-01	Alabama 14, Iowa St 13
12-27-02	Mississippi 27, Nebraska 23
12-31-03	Arkansas 27, Missouri 14
12-28-04	Iowa State 17, Miami (Ohio) 13
12-30-05	Missouri 38, South Carolina 31
12-28-06	Oklahoma State 34, Alabama 31
12-30-07	Alabama 30, Colorado 24
12-28-08	Louisiana Tech 17, Northern Ill. 10
12-28-09	Georgia 44, Texas A&M 20

City: Shreveport, LA. Stadium: Independence Stadium, capacity 50,459.

All-American Bowl

12-22-77	Maryland 17, Minnesota 7
12-20-78	Texas A&M 28, Iowa St 12
12-29-79	Missouri 24, South Carolina 14
12-27-80	Arkansas 34, Tulane 15
12-31-81	Mississippi St 10, Kansas 0
12-31-82	Air Force 36, Vanderbilt 28
12-22-83	W Virginia 24, Kentucky 16
12-29-84	Kentucky 20, Wisconsin 19
12-31-85	Georgia Tech 17, Michigan St 14
12-31-86	Florida St 27, Indiana 13
12-22-87	Virginia 22, BYU 16
12-29-88	Florida 14, Illinois 10
12-28-89	Texas Tech 49, Duke 21
12-28-90	North Carolina St 31, Southern Miss 27

City: Birmingham, AL. Stadium: Legion Field.
Name Change: Hall of Fame Classic (1977–84). Bowl was discontinued after 1990.

Holiday Bowl

12-22-78	Navy 23, BYU 16
12-21-79	Indiana 38, BYU 37
12-19-80	BYU 46, SMU 45
12-18-81	BYU 38, Washington St 36
12-17-82	Ohio St 47, BYU 17
12-23-83	BYU 21, Missouri 17
12-21-84	BYU 24, Michigan 17
12-22-85	Arkansas 18, Arizona St 17
12-30-86	Iowa 39, San Diego St 38
12-30-87	Iowa 20, Wyoming 19

Holiday Bowl *(Cont.)*

12-30-88	Oklahoma St 62, Wyoming 14
12-29-89	Penn St 50, BYU 39
12-29-90	Texas A&M 65, BYU 14
12-30-91	Iowa 13, BYU 13
12-30-92	Hawaii 27, Illinois 17
12-30-93	Ohio St 28, BYU 21
12-30-94	Michigan 24, Colorado St 14
12-29-95	Kansas St 54, Colorado St 21
12-30-96	Colorado 33, Washington 21
12-29-97	Colorado St 35, Missouri 24
12-30-98	Arizona 23, Nebraska 20
12-29-99	Kansas St 24, Washington 20
12-29-00	Oregon 35, Texas 30
12-28-01	Texas 47, Washington 43
12-27-02	Kansas St 34, Arizona St 27
12-30-03	Washington St 28, Texas 20
12-30-04	Texas Tech 45, California 31
12-29-05	Oklahoma 17, Oregon 14
12-28-06	California 45, Texas A&M 10
12-27-07	Texas 52, Arizona St 34
12-30-08	Oregon 42, Oklahoma St 31
12-30-09	Nebraska 33, Arizona 0

City: San Diego. Stadium: Qualcomm Stadium, capacity 70,000.

Las Vegas Bowl

12-19-81	Toledo 27, San Jose St 25
12-18-82	Fresno St 29, Bowling Green 28
12-17-83	Northern Illinois 20, Cal St–Fullerton 13
12-15-84	UNLV 30, Toledo 13*
12-14-85	Fresno St 51, Bowling Green 7
12-13-86	San Jose St 37, Miami (Ohio) 7
12-12-87	Eastern Michigan 30, San Jose St 27
12-10-88	Fresno St 35, Western Michigan 30
12-9-89	Fresno St 27, Ball St 6
12-8-90	San Jose St 48, Central Michigan 24
12-14-91	Bowling Green 28, Fresno St 21
12-18-92	Bowling Green 35, Nevada 34
12-17-93	Utah St 42, Ball St 33
12-15-94	UNLV 52, Central Michigan 24
12-14-95	Toledo 40, Nevada 37
12-19-96	Nevada 18, Ball St 15
12-19-97	Oregon 41, Air Force 13
12-19-98	North Carolina 20, San Diego St 13
12-18-99	Utah 17, Fresno St 16
12-21-00	UNLV 31, Arkansas 14
12-25-01	Utah 10, USC 6
12-25-02	UCLA 27, New Mexico 13
12-24-03	Oregon St 55, New Mexico 14
12-23-04	Wyoming 24, UCLA, 21
12-22-05	California 35, BYU 28
12-21-06	BYU 38, Oregon 8
12-22-07	BYU 17, UCLA 16
12-20-08	Arizona 31, BYU 21
12-22-09	BYU 44, Oregon St 20

* Toledo won later by forfeit. City: Las Vegas (since 1992). Stadium: Sam Boyd Silver Bowl Stadium, capacity 40,000. Name change: California Bowl (1981–91). Playing sites: Fresno, CA (Bulldog Stadium, 1981–91), Las Vegas.

Aloha Bowl

12-25-82	Washington 21, Maryland 20
12-26-83	Penn St 13, Washington 10
12-29-84	Southern Methodist 27, Notre Dame 20
12-28-85	Alabama 24, USC 3

Aloha Bowl *(Cont.)*

12-27-86 ....Arizona 30, North Carolina 21
12-25-87 ....UCLA 20, Florida 16
12-25-88 ....Washington St 24, Houston 22
12-25-89 ....Michigan St 33, Hawaii 13
12-25-90 ....Syracuse 28, Arizona 0
12-25-91 ....Georgia Tech 18, Stanford 17
12-25-92 ....Kansas 23, BYU 20
12-25-93 ....Colorado 41, Fresno St 30
12-25-94 ....Boston College 12, Kansas St 7
12-25-95 ....Kansas 51, UCLA 30
12-25-96 ....Navy 42, California 38
12-25-97 ....Washington 51, Michigan St 23
12-25-98 ....Colorado 51, Oregon 43
12-25-99 ....Wake Forest 23, Arizona St 3
12-25-00 ....Boston College 31, Arizona St 17

City: Honolulu. Stadium: Aloha Stadium. Bowl was discontinued after 2000.

Freedom Bowl

12-16-84 ....Iowa 55, Texas 17
12-30-85 ....Washington 20, Colorado 17
12-30-86 ....UCLA 31, BYU 10
12-30-87 ....Arizona St 33, Air Force 28
12-29-88 ....BYU 20, Colorado 17
12-30-89 ....Washington 34, Florida 7
12-29-90 ....Colorado St 32, Oregon 31
12-30-91 ....Tulsa 28, San Diego St 17
12-29-92 ....Fresno St 24, USC 7
12-30-93 ....USC 28, Utah 21
12-29-94 ....Utah 16, Arizona 13

City: Anaheim. Stadium: Anaheim Stadium. Bowl was discontinued after 1994.

Outback Bowl

12-23-86 ....Boston College 27, Georgia 24
1-2-88 ....Michigan 28, Alabama 24
1-2-89 ....Syracuse 23, LSU 10
1-1-90 ....Auburn 31, Ohio St 14
1-1-91 ....Clemson 30, Illinois 0
1-1-92 ....Syracuse 24, Ohio St 17
1-1-93 ....Tennessee 38, Boston College 23
1-1-94 ....Michigan 42, North Carolina St 7
1-2-95 ....Wisconsin 34, Duke 20
1-1-96 ....Penn St 43, Auburn 14
1-1-97 ....Alabama 17, Michigan 14
1-1-98 ....Georgia 33, Wisconsin 6
1-1-99 ....Penn St 26, Kentucky 14
1-1-00 ....Georgia 28, Purdue 25
1-1-01 ....South Carolina 24, Ohio St 7
1-1-02 ....South Carolina 31, Ohio St 28
1-1-03 ....Michigan 38, Florida 30
1-1-04 ....Iowa 37, Florida 17
1-1-05 ....Georgia 24, Wisconsin 21
1-2-06 ....Florida 31, Iowa 24
1-1-07 ....Penn State 20, Tennessee 10
1-1-08 ....Tennessee 21, Wisconsin 17
1-1-09 ....Iowa 31, South Carolina 10
1-1-10 ....Auburn 38, Northwestern 35

City: Tampa. Stadium: Raymond James Stadium, capacity 75,000. Name change: Hall of Fame Bowl (1986–95).

Insight Bowl

12-31-89 ....Arizona 17, North Carolina St 10
12-31-90 ....California 17, Wyoming 15
12-31-91 ....Indiana 24, Baylor 0

Insight Bowl *(Cont.)*

12-29-92 ....Washington St 31, Utah 28
12-29-93 ....Kansas St 52, Wyoming 17
12-29-94 ....BYU 31, Oklahoma 6
12-27-95 ....Texas Tech 55, Air Force 41
12-27-96 ....Wisconsin 38, Utah 10
12-27-97 ....Arizona 20, New Mexico 14
12-26-98 ....Missouri 34, W Virginia 31
12-31-99 ....Colorado 62, Boston College 28
12-28-00 ....Iowa St 37, Pittsburgh 29
12-29-01 ....Syracuse 26, Kansas St 3
12-26-02 ....Pittsburgh 38, Oregon St 13
12-26-03 ....California 52, Virginia Tech 49
12-28-04 ....Oregon State 38, Notre Dame 21
12-27-05 ....Arizona State 45, Rutgers 40
12-29-06 ....Texas Tech 44, Minnesota 41
12-31-07 ....Oklahoma St 49, Indiana 33
12-31-08 ....Kansas 42, Minnesota 21
12-31-09 ....Iowa St 14, Minnesota 13

City: Tucson. Stadium: Arizona Stadium, capacity 55,883. Name change: Copper Bowl (1989–97), Insight.com Bowl (1998–2000).

Tangerine Bowl

12-28-90 ....Florida St 24, Penn St 17
12-28-91 ....Alabama 30, Colorado 25
1-1-93 ....Stanford 24, Penn St 3
1-1-94 ....Boston College 31, Virginia 13
1-2-95 ....South Carolina 24, W Virginia 21
12-30-95 ....North Carolina 20, Arkansas 10
12-27-96 ....Miami (Fla.) 31, Virginia 21
12-29-97 ....Georgia Tech 35, W Virginia 30
12-29-98 ....Miami (Fla.) 46, North Carolina St 23
12-30-99 ....Illinois 62, Virginia 21
12-28-00 ....North Carolina St 38, Minnesota 30
12-20-01 ....Pittsburgh 34, North Carolina St 19
12-23-02 ....Texas Tech 55, Clemson 15
12-22-03 ....North Carolina 56, Kansas 26

City: Miami. Stadium: Pro Player Stadium, capacity 75,192. Name change: Blockbuster Bowl (1990–93), Carquest Bowl (1994–97), Micron PC Bowl (1998–01). Discontinued after 2003.

Alamo Bowl

12-31-93 ....California 37, Iowa 3
12-31-94 ....Washington St 10, Baylor 3
12-28-95 ....Texas A&M 22, Michigan 20
12-29-96 ....Iowa 27, Texas Tech 0
12-30-97 ....Purdue 33, Oklahoma St 20
12-29-98 ....Purdue 37, Kansas St 34
12-28-99 ....Penn St 24, Texas A&M 0
12-30-00 ....Nebraska 66, Northwestern 17
12-29-01 ....Iowa 16, Texas Tech 13
12-28-02 ....Wisconsin 31, Colorado 28 (OT)
12-29-03 ....Nebraska 17, Michigan St 3
12-29-04 ....Ohio State 33, Oklahoma State 7
12-28-05 ....Nebraska 32, Michigan 28
12-30-06 ....Texas 26, Iowa 24
12-29-07 ....Penn St 24, Texas A&M 17
12-29-08 ....Missouri 30, Northwestern 23
1-2-10 ....Texas Tech 41, Michigan St 31

City: San Antonio, TX. Stadium: Alamodome, capaciity 67,000.

1936

		Record	Coach
1.	Minnesota	7-1-0	Bernie Bierman
2.	LSU	9-0-1	Bernie Moore
3.	Pittsburgh	7-1-1	Jock Sutherland
4.	Alabama	8-0-1	Frank Thomas
5.	Washington	7-1-1	Jimmy Phelan
6.	Santa Clara	7-1-0	Buck Shaw
7.	Northwestern	7-1-0	Pappy Waldorf
8.	Notre Dame	6-2-1	Elmer Layden
9.	Nebraska	7-2-0	Dana X. Bible
10.	Pennsylvania	7-1-0	Harvey Harman
11.	Duke	9-1-0	Wallace Wade
12.	Yale	7-1-0	Ducky Pond
13.	Dartmouth	7-1-1	Red Blaik
14.	Duquesne	7-2-0	John Smith
15.	Fordham	5-1-2	Jim Crowley
16.	TCU	8-2-2	Dutch Meyer
17.	Tennessee	6-2-2	Bob Neyland
18.	Arkansas	7-3-0	Fred Thomsen
19.	Navy	6-3-0	Tom Hamilton
20.	Marquette	7-1-0	Frank Murray

1937

		Record	Coach
1.	Pittsburgh	9-0-1	Jock Sutherland
2.	California	9-0-1	Stub Allison
3.	Fordham	7-0-1	Jim Crowley
4.	Alabama	9-0-0	Frank Thomas
5.	Minnesota	6-2-0	Bernie Bierman
6.	Villanova	8-0-1	Clipper Smith
7.	Dartmouth	7-0-2	Red Blaik
8.	LSU	9-1-0	Bernie Moore
9.	Notre Dame	6-2-1	Elmer Layden
	Santa Clara	8-0-0	Buck Shaw
11.	Nebraska	6-1-2	Biff Jones
12.	Yale	6-1-1	Ducky Pond
13.	Ohio St	6-2-0	Francis Schmidt
14.	Holy Cross	8-0-2	Eddie Anderson
	Arkansas	6-2-2	Fred Thomsen
16.	TCU	4-2-2	Dutch Meyer
17.	Colorado	8-0-0	Bunnie Oakes
18.	Rice	5-3-2	Jimmy Kitts
19.	North Carolina	7-1-1	Ray Wolf
20.	Duke	7-2-1	Wallace Wade

1938

		Record	Coach
1.	TCU	10-0-0	Dutch Meyer
2.	Tennessee	10-0-0	Bob Neyland
3.	Duke	9-0-0	Wallace Wade
4.	Oklahoma	10-0-0	Tom Stidham
5.	#Notre Dame	8-1-0	Elmer Layden
6.	Carnegie Tech	7-1-0	Bill Kern
7.	USC	8-2-0	Howard Jones
8.	Pittsburgh	8-2-0	Jock Sutherland
9.	Holy Cross	8-1-0	Eddie Anderson
10.	Minnesota	6-2-0	Bernie Bierman
11.	Texas Tech	10-0-0	Pete Cawthon
12.	Cornell	5-1-1	Carl Snavely
13.	Alabama	7-1-1	Frank Thomas
14.	California	10-1-0	Stub Allison
15.	Fordham	6-1-2	Jim Crowley
16.	Michigan	6-1-1	Fritz Crisler
17.	Northwestern	4-2-2	Pappy Waldorf

1938 (Cont.)

		Record	Coach
18.	Villanova	8-0-1	Clipper Smith
19.	Tulane	7-2-1	Red Dawson
20.	Dartmouth	7-2-0	Red Blaik

#Selected No. 1 by the Dickinson System.

1939

		Record	Coach
1.	Texas A&M	10-0-0	Homer Norton
2.	Tennessee	10-0-0	Bob Neyland
3.	#USC	7-0-2	Howard Jones
4.	Cornell	8-0-0	Carl Snavely
5.	Tulane	8-0-1	Red Dawson
6.	Missouri	8-1-0	Don Faurot
7.	UCLA	6-0-4	Babe Horrell
8.	Duke	8-1-0	Wallace Wade
9.	Iowa	6-1-1	Eddie Anderson
10.	Duquesne	8-0-1	Buff Donelli
11.	Boston College	9-1-0	Frank Leahy
12.	Clemson	8-1-0	Jess Neely
13.	Notre Dame	7-2-0	Elmer Layden
14.	Santa Clara	5-1-3	Buck Shaw
15.	Ohio St	6-2-0	Francis Schmidt
16.	Georgia Tech	7-2-0	Bill Alexander
17.	Fordham	6-2-0	Jim Crowley
18.	Nebraska	7-1-1	Biff Jones
19.	Oklahoma	6-2-1	Tom Stidham
20.	Michigan	6-2-0	Fritz Crisler

#Selected No. 1 by the Dickinson System.

1940

		Record	Coach
1.	Minnesota	8-0-0	Bernie Bierman
2.	Stanford	9-0-0	C. Shaughnessy
3.	Michigan	7-1-0	Fritz Crisler
4.	Tennessee	10-0-0	Bob Neyland
5.	Boston College	10-0-0	Frank Leahy
6.	Texas A&M	8-1-0	Homer Norton
7.	Nebraska	8-1-0	Biff Jones
8.	Northwestern	6-2-0	Pappy Waldorf
9.	Mississippi St	9-0-1	Allyn McKeen
10.	Washington	7-2-0	Jimmy Phelan
11.	Santa Clara	6-1-1	Buck Shaw
12.	Fordham	7-1-0	Jim Crowley
13.	Georgetown	8-1-0	Jack Hagerty
14.	Pennsylvania	6-1-1	George Munger
15.	Cornell	6-2-0	Carl Snavely
16.	SMU	8-1-1	Matty Bell
17.	Hard.-Simmons	9-0-0	Abe Woodson
18.	Duke	7-2-0	Wallace Wade
19.	Lafayette	9-0-0	Hooks Mylin
20.	—		

Only 19 teams selected.

1941

		Record	Coach
1.	Minnesota	8-0-0	Bernie Bierman
2.	Duke	9-0-0	Wallace Wade
3.	Notre Dame	8-0-1	Frank Leahy
4.	Texas	8-1-1	Dana X. Bible
5.	Michigan	6-1-1	Fritz Crisler

Note: Except where indicated with an asterisk, the polls from 1936 through 1964 were taken before the bowl games and those from 1965 through the present were taken after the bowl games.

1941 *(Cont.)*

		Record	Coach
6.	Fordham	7-1-0	Jim Crowley
7.	Missouri	8-1-0	Don Faurot
8.	Duquesne	8-0-0	Buff Donelli
9.	Texas A&M	9-1-0	Homer Norton
10.	Navy	7-1-1	Swede Larson
11.	Northwestern	5-3-0	Pappy Waldorf
12.	Oregon St	7-2-0	Lon Stiner
13.	Ohio St	6-1-1	Paul Brown
14.	Georgia	8-1-1	Wally Butts
15.	Pennsylvania	7-1-1	George Munger
16.	Mississippi St	8-1-1	Allyn McKeen
17.	Mississippi	6-2-1	Harry Mehre
18.	Tennessee	8-2-0	John Barnhill
19.	Washington St	6-4-0	Babe Hollingbery
20.	Alabama	8-2-0	Frank Thomas

1942

		Record	Coach
1.	Ohio St	9-1-0	Paul Brown
2.	Georgia	10-1-0	Wally Butts
3.	Wisconsin	8-1-1	H. Stuhldreher
4.	Tulsa	10-0-0	Henry Frnka
5.	Georgia Tech	9-1-0	Bill Alexander
6.	Notre Dame	7-2-2	Frank Leahy
7.	Tennessee	8-1-1	John Barnhill
8.	Boston College	8-1-0	Denny Myers
9.	Michigan	7-3-0	Fritz Crisler
10.	Alabama	7-3-0	Frank Thomas
11.	Texas	8-2-0	Dana X. Bible
12.	Stanford	6-4-0	Marchie Schwartz
13.	UCLA	7-3-0	Babe Horrell
14.	William & Mary	9-1-1	Carl Voyles
15.	Santa Clara	7-2-0	Buck Shaw
16.	Auburn	6-4-1	Jack Meagher
17.	Washington St	6-2-2	Babe Hollingbery
18.	Mississippi St	8-2-0	Allyn McKeen
19.	Minnesota	5-4-0	George Hauser
	Holy Cross	5-4-1	Ank Scanlon
	Penn St	6-1-1	Bob Higgins

1943

		Record	Coach
1.	Notre Dame	9-1-0	Frank Leahy
2.	Iowa Pre-Flight	9-1-0	Don Faurot
3.	Michigan	8-1-0	Fritz Crisler
4.	Navy	8-1-0	Billick Whelchel
5.	Purdue	9-0-0	Elmer Burnham
6.	Great Lakes	10-2-0	Tony Hinkle
7.	Duke	8-1-0	Eddie Cameron
8.	Del Monte P-F	7-1-0	Bill Kern
9.	Northwestern	6-2-0	Pappy Waldorf
10.	March Field	9-1-0	Paul Schissler
11.	Army	7-2-1	Red Blaik
12.	Washington	4-0-0	Ralph Welch
13.	Georgia Tech	7-3-0	Bill Alexander
14.	Texas	7-1-0	Dana X. Bible
15.	Tulsa	6-0-1	Henry Frnka
16.	Dartmouth	6-1-0	Earl Brown
17.	Bainbridge NTS	7-0-0	Joe Maniaci
18.	Colorado College	7-0-0	Hal White
19.	Pacific	7-2-0	Amos A. Stagg
20.	Pennsylvania	6-2-1	George Munger

1944

		Record	Coach
1.	Army	9-0-0	Red Blaik
2.	Ohio St	9-0-0	Carroll Widdoes
3.	Randolph Field	11-0-0	Frank Tritico
4.	Navy	6-3-0	Oscar Hagberg
5.	Bainbridge NTS	9-0-0	Joe Maniaci
6.	Iowa Pre-Flight	10-1-0	Jack Meagher
7.	USC	7-0-2	Jeff Cravath
8.	Michigan	8-2-0	Fritz Crisler
9.	Notre Dame	8-2-0	Ed McKeever
10.	March Field	7-1-2	Paul Schissler
11.	Duke	5-4-0	Eddie Cameron
12.	Tennessee	8-0-1	John Barnhill
13.	Georgia Tech	8-2-0	Bill Alexander
	Norman P-F	6-0-0	John Gregg
15.	Illinois	5-4-1	Ray Eliot
16.	El Toro Marines	8-1-0	Dick Hanley
17.	Great Lakes	9-2-1	Paul Brown
18.	Fort Pierce	9-0-0	Hamp Pool
19.	St. Mary's P-F	4-4-0	Jules Sikes
20.	2nd Air Force	7-2-1	Bill Reese

1945

		Record	Coach
1.	Army	9-0-0	Red Blaik
2.	Alabama	9-0-0	Frank Thomas
3.	Navy	7-1-1	Oscar Hagberg
4.	Indiana	9-0-1	Bo McMillan
5.	Oklahoma A&M	8-0-0	Jim Lookabaugh
6.	Michigan	7-3-0	Fritz Crisler
7.	St. Mary's (CA)	7-1-0	Jimmy Phelan
8.	Pennsylvania	6-2-0	George Munger
9.	Notre Dame	7-2-1	Hugh Devore
10.	Texas	9-1-0	Dana X. Bible
11.	USC	7-3-0	Jeff Cravath
12.	Ohio St	7-2-0	Carroll Widdoes
13.	Duke	6-2-0	Eddie Cameron
14.	Tennessee	8-1-0	John Barnhill
15.	LSU	7-2-0	Bernie Moore
16.	Holy Cross	8-1-0	John DeGrosa
17.	Tulsa	8-2-0	Henry Frnka
18.	Georgia	8-2-0	Wally Butts
19.	Wake Forest	4-3-1	Peahead Walker
20.	Columbia	8-1-0	Lou Little

1946

		Record	Coach
1.	Notre Dame	8-0-1	Frank Leahy
2.	Army	9-0-1	Red Blaik
3.	Georgia	10-0-0	Wally Butts
4.	UCLA	10-0-0	B. LaBrucherie
5.	Illinois	7-2-0	Ray Eliot
6.	Michigan	6-2-1	Fritz Crisler
7.	Tennessee	9-1-0	Bob Neyland
8.	LSU	9-1-0	Bernie Moore
9.	North Carolina	8-1-1	Carl Snavely
10.	Rice	8-2-0	Jess Neely
11.	Georgia Tech	8-2-0	Bobby Dodd
12.	Yale	7-1-1	Howard Odell
13.	Pennsylvania	6-2-0	George Munger
14.	Oklahoma	7-3-0	Jim Tatum
15.	Texas	8-2-0	Dana X. Bible
16.	Arkansas	6-3-1	John Barnhill
17.	Tulsa	9-1-0	J.O. Brothers
18.	North Carolina St	8-2-0	Beattie Feathers
19.	Delaware	9-0-0	Bill Murray
20.	Indiana	6-3-0	Bo McMillan

1947

		Record	Coach
1.	Notre Dame	9-0-0	Frank Leahy
2.	#Michigan	9-0-0	Fritz Crisler
3.	SMU	9-0-1	Matty Bell
4.	Penn St	9-0-0	Bob Higgins
5.	Texas	9-1-0	Blair Cherry
6.	Alabama	8-2-0	Red Drew
7.	Pennsylvania	7-0-1	George Munger
8.	USC	7-1-1	Jeff Cravath
9.	North Carolina	8-2-0	Carl Snavely
10.	Georgia Tech	9-1-0	Bobby Dodd
11.	Army	5-2-2	Red Blaik
12.	Kansas	8-0-2	George Sauer
13.	Mississippi	8-2-0	Johnny Vaught
14.	William & Mary	9-1-0	Rube McCray
15.	California	9-1-0	Pappy Waldorf
16.	Oklahoma	7-2-1	Bud Wilkinson
17.	North Carolina St	5-3-1	Beattie Feathers
18.	Rice	6-3-1	Jess Neely
19.	Duke	4-3-2	Wallace Wade
20.	Columbia	7-2-0	Lou Little

#The AP, which had voted Notre Dame No. 1 before the bowl games, took a second vote, giving the title to Michigan after its 49–0 win over USC in the Rose Bowl.

1948

		Record	Coach
1.	Michigan	9-0-0	Bennie Oosterbaan
2.	Notre Dame	9-0-1	Frank Leahy
3.	North Carolina	9-0-1	Carl Snavely
4.	California	10-0-0	Pappy Waldorf
5.	Oklahoma	9-1-0	Bud Wilkinson
6.	Army	8-0-1	Red Blaik
7.	Northwestern	7-2-0	Bob Voigts
8.	Georgia	9-1-0	Wally Butts
9.	Oregon	9-1-0	Jim Aiken
10.	SMU	8-1-1	Matty Bell
11.	Clemson	10-0-0	Frank Howard
12.	Vanderbilt	8-2-1	Red Sanders
13.	Tulane	9-1-0	Henry Frnka
14.	Michigan St	6-2-2	Biggie Munn
15.	Mississippi	8-1-0	Johnny Vaught
16.	Minnesota	7-2-0	Bernie Bierman
17.	William & Mary	6-2-2	Rube McCray
18.	Penn St	7-1-1	Bob Higgins
19.	Cornell	8-1-0	Lefty James
20.	Wake Forest	6-3-0	Peahead Walker

1949

		Record	Coach
1.	Notre Dame	10-0-0	Frank Leahy
2.	Oklahoma	10-0-0	Bud Wilkinson
3.	California	10-0-0	Pappy Waldorf
4.	Army	9-0-0	Red Blaik
5.	Rice	9-1-0	Jess Neely
6.	Ohio St	6-1-2	Wes Fesler
7.	Michigan	6-2-1	Bennie Oosterbaan
8.	Minnesota	7-2-0	Bernie Bierman
9.	LSU	8-2-0	Gaynell Tinsley
10.	Pacific	11-0-0	Larry Siemering
11.	Kentucky	9-2-0	Bear Bryant
12.	Cornell	8-1-0	Lefty James
13.	Villanova	8-1-0	Jim Leonard
14.	Maryland	8-1-0	Jim Tatum

1949 *(Cont.)*

		Record	Coach
15.	Santa Clara	7-2-1	Len Casanova
16.	North Carolina	7-3-0	Carl Snavely
17.	Tennessee	7-2-1	Bob Neyland
18.	Princeton	6-3-0	Charlie Caldwell
19.	Michigan St	6-3-0	Biggie Munn
20.	Missouri	7-3-0	Don Faurot
	Baylor	8-2-0	Bob Woodruff

1950

		Record	Coach
1.	Oklahoma	10-0-0	Bud Wilkinson
2.	Army	8-1-0	Red Blaik
3.	Texas	9-1-0	Blair Cherry
4.	Tennessee	10-1-0	Bob Neyland
5.	California	9-0-1	Pappy Waldorf
6.	Princeton	9-0-0	Charlie Caldwell
7.	Kentucky	10-1-0	Bear Bryant
8.	Michigan St	8-1-0	Biggie Munn
9.	Michigan	5-3-1	Bennie Oosterhaan
10.	Clemson	8-0-1	Frank Howard
11.	Washington	8-2-0	Howard Odell
12.	Wyoming	9-0-0	Bowden Wyatt
13.	Illinois	7-2-0	Ray Eliot
14.	Ohio St	6-3-0	Wes Fesler
15.	Miami (FL)	9-0-1	Andy Gustafson
16.	Alabama	9-2-0	Red Drew
17.	Nebraska	6-2-1	Bill Glassford
18.	Washington & Lee	8-2-0	George Barclay
19.	Tulsa	9-1-1	J.O. Brothers
20.	Tulane	6-2-1	Henry Frnka

1951

		Record	Coach
1.	Tennessee	10-0-0	Bob Neyland
2.	Michigan St	9-0-0	Biggie Munn
3.	Maryland	9-0-0	Jim Tatum
4.	Illinois	8-0-1	Ray Eliot
5.	Georgia Tech	10-0-1	Bobby Dodd
6.	Princeton	9-0-0	Charlie Caldwell
7.	Stanford	9-1-0	Chuck Taylor
8.	Wisconsin	7-1-1	Ivy Williamson
9.	Baylor	8-1-1	George Sauer
10.	Oklahoma	8-2-0	Bud Wilkinson
11.	TCU	6-4-0	Dutch Meyer
12.	California	8-2-0	Pappy Waldorf
13.	Virginia	8-1-0	Art Guepe
14.	San Francisco	9-0-0	Joe Kuharich
15.	Kentucky	7-4-0	Bear Bryant
16.	Boston University	6-4-0	Buff Donelli
17.	UCLA	5-3-1	Red Sanders
18.	Washington St	7-3-0	Forest Evashevski
19.	Holy Cross	8-2-0	Eddie Anderson
20.	Clemson	7-2-0	Frank Howard

1952

		Record	Coach
1.	Michigan St	9-0-0	Biggie Munn
2.	Georgia Tech	11-0-0	Bobby Dodd
3.	Notre Dame	7-2-1	Frank Leahy
4.	Oklahoma	8-1-1	Bud Wilkinson
5.	USC	9-1-0	Jess Hill
6.	UCLA	8-1-0	Red Sanders
7.	Mississippi	8-0-2	Johnny Vaught

1952 *(Cont.)*

		Record	Coach
8.	Tennessee	8-1-1	Bob Neyland
9.	Alabama	9-2-0	Red Drew
10.	Texas	8-2-0	Ed Price
11.	Wisconsin	6-2-1	Ivy Williamson
12.	Tulsa	8-1-1	J.O. Brothers
13.	Maryland	7-2-0	Jim Tatum
14.	Syracuse	7-2-0	Ben Schwartzwalder
15.	Florida	7-3-0	Bob Woodruff
16.	Duke	8-2-0	Bill Murray
17.	Ohio St	6-3-0	Woody Hayes
18.	Purdue	4-3-2	Stu Holcomb
19.	Princeton	8-1-0	Charlie Caldwell
20.	Kentucky	5-4-2	Bear Bryant

1953

		Record	Coach
1.	Maryland	10-0-0	Jim Tatum
2.	Notre Dame	9-0-1	Frank Leahy
3.	Michigan St	8-1-0	Biggie Munn
4.	Oklahoma	8-1-1	Bud Wilkinson
5.	UCLA	8-1-0	Red Sanders
6.	Rice	8-2-0	Jess Neely
7.	Illinois	7-1-1	Ray Eliot
8.	Georgia Tech	8-2-1	Bobby Dodd
9.	Iowa	5-3-1	Forest Evashevski
10.	W Virginia	8-1-0	Art Lewis
11.	Texas	7-3-0	Ed Price
12.	Texas Tech	10-1-0	DeWitt Weaver
13.	Alabama	6-2-3	Red Drew
14.	Army	7-1-1	Red Blaik
15.	Wisconsin	6-2-1	Ivy Williamson
16.	Kentucky	7-2-1	Bear Bryant
17.	Auburn	7-2-1	Shug Jordan
18.	Duke	7-2-1	Bill Murray
19.	Stanford	6-3-1	Chuck Taylor
20.	Michigan	6-3-0	Bennie Oosterbaan

1954

		Record	Coach
1.	Ohio St	9-0-0	Woody Hayes
2.	#UCLA	9-0-0	Red Sanders
3.	Oklahoma	10-0-0	Bud Wilkinson
4.	Notre Dame	9-1-0	Terry Brennan
5.	Navy	7-2-0	Eddie Erdelatz
6.	Mississippi	9-1-0	Johnny Vaught
7.	Army	7-2-0	Red Blaik
8.	Maryland	7-2-1	Jim Tatum
9.	Wisconsin	7-2-0	Ivy Williamson
10.	Arkansas	8-2-0	Bowden Wyatt
11.	Miami (FL)	8-1-0	Andy Gustafson
12.	W Virginia	8-1-0	Art Lewis
13.	Auburn	7-3-0	Shug Jordan
14.	Duke	7-2-1	Bill Murray
15.	Michigan	6-3-0	Bennie Oosterbaan
16.	Virginia Tech	8-0-1	Frank Moseley
17.	USC	8-3-0	Jess Hill
18.	Baylor	7-3-0	George Sauer
19.	Rice	7-3-0	Jess Neely
20.	Penn St	7-2-0	Rip Engle

#Selected No. 1 by UP.

1955

		Record	Coach
1.	Oklahoma	10-0-0	Bud Wilkinson
2.	Michigan St	8-1-0	Duffy Daugherty
3.	Maryland	10-0-0	Jim Tatum
4.	UCLA	9-1-0	Red Sanders
5.	Ohio St	7-2-0	Woody Hayes
6.	TCU	9-1-0	Abe Martin
7.	Georgia Tech	8-1-1	Bobby Dodd
8.	Auburn	8-1-1	Shug Jordan
9.	Notre Dame	8-2-0	Terry Brennan
10.	Mississippi	9-1-0	Johnny Vaught
11.	Pittsburgh	7-3-0	John Michelosen
12.	Michigan	7-2-0	Bennie Oosterbaan
13.	USC	6-4-0	Jess Hill
14.	Miami (FL)	6-3-0	Andy Gustafson
15.	Miami (OH)	9-0-0	Ara Parseghian
16.	Stanford	6-3-1	Chuck Taylor
17.	Texas A&M	7-2-1	Bear Bryant
18.	Navy	6-2-1	Eddie Erdelatz
19.	W Virginia	8-2-0	Art Lewis
20.	Army	6-3-0	Red Blaik

1956

		Record	Coach
1.	Oklahoma	10-0-0	Bud Wilkinson
2.	Tennessee	10-0-0	Bowden Wyatt
3.	Iowa	8-1-0	Forest Evashevski
4.	Georgia Tech.	9-1-0	Bobby Dodd
5.	Texas A&M	9-0-1	Bear Bryant
6.	Miami (FL)	8-1-0	Andy Gustafson
7.	Michigan	7-2-0	Bennie Oosterbaan
8.	Syracuse	7-1-0	Ben Schwartzwalder
9.	Michigan St	7-2-0	Duffy Daugherty
10.	Oregon St	7-2-1	Tommy Prothro
11.	Baylor	8-2-0	Sam Boyd
12.	Minnesota	6-1-2	Murray Warmath
13.	Pittsburgh	7-2-1	John Michelosen
14.	TCU	7-3-0	Abe Martin
15.	Ohio St	6-3-0	Woody Hayes
16.	Navy	6-1-2	Eddie Erdelatz
17.	Geo Washington	7-1-1	Gene Sherman
18.	USC	8-2-0	Jess Hill
19.	Clemson	7-1-2	Frank Howard
20.	Colorado	7-2-1	Dallas Ward
	Penn St	6-2-1	Rip Engle

1957

		Record	Coach
1.	Auburn	10-0-0	Shug Jordan
2.	#Ohio St	8-1-0	Woody Hayes
3.	Michigan St	8-1-0	Duffy Daugherty
4.	Oklahoma	9-1-0	Bud Wilkinson
5.	Navy	8-1-1	Eddie Erdelatz
6.	Iowa	7-1-1	Forest Evashevski
7.	Mississippi	8-1-1	Johnny Vaught
8.	Rice	7-3-0	Jess Neely
9.	Texas A&M	8-2-0	Bear Bryant
10.	Notre Dame	7-3-0	Terry Brennan
11.	Texas	6-3-1	Darrell Royal
12.	Arizona St	10-0-0	Dan Devine
13.	Tennessee	7-3-0	Bowden Wyatt
14.	Mississippi St	6-2-1	Wade Walker
15.	North Carolina St	7-1-2	Earle Edwards
16.	Duke	6-2-2	Bill Murray

1957 *(Cont.)*

		Record	Coach
17.	Florida	6-2-1	Bob Woodruff
18.	Army	7-2-0	Red Blaik
19.	Wisconsin	6-3-0	Milt Brunt
20.	VMI	9-0-1	John McKenna

#Selected No. 1 by UP.

1958

		Record	Coach
1.	LSU	10-0-0	Paul Dietzel
2.	Iowa	7-1-1	Forest Evashevski
3.	Army	8-0-1	Red Blaik
4.	Auburn	9-0-1	Shug Jordan
5.	Oklahoma	9-1-0	Bud Wilkinson
6.	Air Force	9-0-1	Ben Martin
7.	Wisconsin	7-1-1	Milt Bruhn
8.	Ohio St	6-1-2	Woody Hayes
9.	Syracuse	8-1-0	Ben Schwartzwalder
10.	TCU	8-2-0	Abe Martin
11.	Mississippi	8-2-0	Johnny Vaught
12.	Clemson	8-2-0	Frank Howard
13.	Purdue	6-1-2	Jack Mollenkopf
14.	Florida	6-3-1	Bob Woodruff
15.	South Carolina	7-3-0	Warren Giese
16.	California	7-3-0	Pete Elliott
17.	Notre Dame	6-4-0	Terry Brennan
18.	SMU	6-4-0	Bill Meek
19.	Oklahoma St	7-3-0	Cliff Speegle
20.	Rutgers	8-1-0	John Stiegman

1959

		Record	Coach
1.	Syracuse	10-0-0	Ben Schwartzwalder
2.	Mississippi	9-1-0	Johnny Vaught
3.	LSU	9-1-0	Paul Dietzel
4.	Texas	9-1-0	Darrell Royal
5.	Georgia	9-1-0	Wally Butts
6.	Wisconsin	7-2-0	Milt Bruhn
7.	TCU	8-2-0	Abe Martin
8.	Washington	9-1-0	Jim Owens
9.	Arkansas	8-2-0	Frank Broyles
10.	Alabama	7-1-2	Bear Bryant
11.	Clemson	8-2-0	Frank Howard
12.	Penn St	8-2-0	Rip Engle
13.	Illinois	5-3-1	Ray Eliot
14.	USC	8-2-0	Don Clark
15.	Oklahoma	7-3-0	Bud Wilkinson
16.	Wyoming	9-1-0	Bob Devaney
17.	Notre Dame	5-5-0	Joe Kuharich
18.	Missouri	6-4-0	Dan Devine
19.	Florida	5-4-1	Bob Woodruff
20.	Pittsburgh	6-4-0	John Michelosen

1960

		Record	Coach
1.	Minnesota	8-1-0	Murray Warmath
2.	Mississippi	9-0-1	Johnny Vaught
3.	Iowa	8-1-0	Forest Evashevski
4.	Navy	9-1-0	Wayne Hardin
5.	Missouri	9-1-0	Dan Devine
6.	Washington	9-1-0	Jim Owens
7.	Arkansas	8-2-0	Frank Broyles
8.	Ohio St	7-2-0	Woody Hayes
9.	Alabama	8-1-1	Bear Bryant

1960 *(Cont.)*

		Record	Coach
10.	Duke	7-3-0	Bill Murray
11.	Kansas	7-2-1	Jack Mitchell
12.	Baylor	8-2-0	John Bridgers
13.	Auburn	8-2-0	Shug Jordan
14.	Yale	9-0-0	Jordan Oliver
15.	Michigan St	6-2-1	Duffy Daugherty
16.	Penn St	6-3-0	Rip Engle
17.	New Mexico St	10-0-0	Warren Woodson
18.	Florida	8-2-0	Ray Graves
19.	Syracuse	7-2-0	Ben Schwartzwalder
	Purdue	4-4-1	Jack Mollenkopf

1961

		Record	Coach
1.	Alabama	10-0-0	Bear Bryant
2.	Ohio St	8-0-1	Woody Hayes
3.	Texas	9-1-0	Darrell Royal
4.	LSU	9-1-0	Paul Dietzel
5.	Mississippi	9-1-0	Johnny Vaught
6.	Minnesota	7-2-0	Murray Warmath
7.	Colorado	9-1-0	Sonny Grandelius
8.	Michigan St	7-2-0	Duffy Daugherty
9.	Arkansas	8-2-0	Frank Broyles
10.	Utah St	9-0-1	John Ralston
11.	Missouri	7-2-1	Dan Devine
12.	Purdue	6-3-0	Jack Mollenkopf
13.	Georgia Tech	7-3-0	Bobby Dodd
14.	Syracuse	7-3-0	Ben Schwartzwalder
15.	Rutgers	9-0-0	John Bateman
16.	UCLA	7-3-0	Bill Barnes
17.	Rice	7-3-0	Jess Neely
	Penn St	7-3-0	Rip Engle
	Arizona	8-1-1	Jim LaRue
20.	Duke	7-3-0	Bill Murray

1962

		Record	Coach
1.	USC	10-0-0	John McKay
2.	Wisconsin	8-1-0	Milt Bruhn
3.	Mississippi	9-0-0	Johnny Vaught
4.	Texas	9-0-1	Darrell Royal
5.	Alabama	9-1-0	Bear Bryant
6.	Arkansas	9-1-0	Frank Broyles
7.	LSU	8-1-1	Charlie McClendon
8.	Oklahoma	8-2-0	Bud Wilkinson
9.	Penn St	9-1-0	Rip Engle
10.	Minnesota	6-2-1	Murray Warmath
11–20: UPI			
11.	Georgia Tech	7-2-1	Bobby Dodd
12.	Missouri	7-1-2	Dan Devine
13.	Ohio St	6-3-0	Woody Hayes
14.	Duke	8-2-0	Bill Murray
	Washington	7-1-2	Jim Owens
16.	Northwestern	7-2-0	Ara Parseghian
	Oregon St	8-2-0	Tommy Prothro
18.	Arizona St	7-2-1	Frank Kush
	Miami (FL)	7-3-0	Andy Gustafson
	Illinois	2-7-0	Pete Elliott

1963

		Record	Coach
1.	Texas	10-0-0	Darrell Royal
2.	Navy	9-1-0	Wayne Hardin
3.	Illinois	7-1-1	Pete Elliott
4.	Pittsburgh	9-1-0	John Michelosen
5.	Auburn	9-1-0	Shug Jordan
6.	Nebraska	9-1-0	Bob Devaney
7.	Mississippi	7-0-2	Johnny Vaught
8.	Alabama	8-2-0	Bear Bryant
9.	Oklahoma	8-2-0	Bud Wilkinson
10.	Michigan St	6-2-1	Duffy Daugherty

11–20: UPI

11.	Mississippi St	6-2-2	Paul Davis
12.	Syracuse	8-2-0	Ben Schwartzwalder
13.	Arizona St	8-1-0	Frank Kush
14.	Memphis St	9-0-1	Billy J. Murphy
15.	Washington	6-4-0	Jim Owens
16.	Penn St	7-3-0	Rip Engle
	USC	7-3-0	John McKay
	Missouri	7-3-0	Dan Devine
19.	North Carolina	8-2-0	Jim Hickey
20.	Baylor	7-3-0	John Bridgers

1964

		Record	Coach
1.	Alabama	10-0-0	Bear Bryant
2.	Arkansas	10-0-0	Frank Broyles
3.	Notre Dame	9-1-0	Ara Parseghian
4.	Michigan	8-1-0	Bump Elliott
5.	Texas	9-1-0	Darrell Royal
6.	Nebraska	9-1-0	Bob Devaney
7.	LSU	7-2-1	Charlie McClendon
8.	Oregon St	8-2-0	Tommy Prothro
9.	Ohio St	7-2-0	Woody Hayes
10.	USC	7-3-0	John McKay

11–20: UPI

11.	Florida St	8-1-1	Bill Peterson
12.	Syracuse	7-3-0	Ben Schwartzwalder
13.	Princeton	9-0-0	Dick Colman
14.	Penn St	6-4-0	Rip Engle
	Utah	8-2-0	Ray Nagel
16.	Illinois	6-3-0	Pete Elliott
	New Mexico	9-2-0	Bill Weeks
18.	Tulsa	8-2-0	Glenn Dobbs
19.	Missouri	6-3-1	Dan Devine
20.	Mississippi	5-4-1	Johnny Vaught
	Michigan St	4-5-1	Duffy Daugherty

1965

		Record	Coach
1.	Alabama	9-1-1	Bear Bryant
2.	#Michigan St	10-1-0	Duffy Daugherty
3.	Arkansas	10-1-0	Frank Broyles
4.	UCLA	8-2-1	Tommy Prothro
5.	Nebraska	10-1-0	Bob Devaney
6.	Missouri	8-2-1	Dan Devine
7.	Tennessee	8-1-2	Doug Dickey
8.	LSU	8-3-0	Charlie McClendon
9.	Notre Dame	7-2-1	Ara Parseghian
10.	USC	7-2-1	John McKay

11–20: UPI

11.	Texas Tech	8-2-0	J.T. King
12.	Ohio St	7-2-0	Woody Hayes

1965 *(Cont.)*

		Record	Coach
13.	Florida	7-3-0	Ray Graves
14.	Purdue	7-2-1	Jack Mollenkopf
15.	Georgia	6-4-0	Vince Dooley
16.	Tulsa	8-2-0	Glenn Dobbs
17.	Mississippi	6-4-0	Johnny Vaught
18.	Kentucky	6-4-0	Charlie Bradshaw
19	Syracuse	7-3-0	Ben Schwartzwalder
20.	Colorado	6-2-2	Eddie Crowder

#Selected No. 1 by UPI.

1966

		Record	Coach
1.	Notre Dame	9-0-1	Ara Parseghian
2.	Michigan St	9-0-1	Duffy Daugherty
3.	Alabama	10-0-0	Bear Bryant
4.	Georgia	9-1-0	Vince Dooley
5.	UCLA	9-1-0	Tommy Prothro
6.	Nebraska	9-1-0	Bob Devaney
7.	Purdue	8-2-0	Jack Mollenkopf
8.	Georgia Tech	9-1-0	Bobby Dodd
9.	Miami (FL)	7-2-1	Charlie Tate
10.	SMU	8-2-0	Hayden Fry

11–20: UPI

11.	Florida	8-2-0	Ray Graves
12.	Mississippi	8-2-0	Johnny Vaught
13.	Arkansas	8-2-0	Frank Broyles
14.	Tennessee	7-3-0	Doug Dickey
15.	Wyoming	9-1-0	Lloyd Eaton
16.	Syracuse	8-2-0	Ben Schwartzwalder
17.	Houston	8-2-0	Bill Yeoman
18.	USC	7-3-0	John McKay
19.	Oregon St	7-3-0	Dee Andros
20.	Virginia Tech	8-1-1	Jerry Claiborne

1967

		Record	Coach
1.	USC	9-1-0	John McKay
2.	Tennessee	9-1-0	Doug Dickey
3.	Oklahoma	9-1-0	Chuck Fairbanks
4.	Indiana	9-1-0	John Pont
5.	Notre Dame	8-2-0	Ara Parseghian
6.	Wyoming	10-0-0	Lloyd Eaton
7.	Oregon St	7-2-1	Dee Andros
8.	Alabama	8-1-1	Bear Bryant
9.	Purdue	8-2-0	Jack Mollenkopf
10.	Penn St	8-2-0	Joe Paterno

11–20: UPI†

11.	UCLA	7-2-1	Tommy Prothro
12.	Syracuse	8-2-0	Ben Schwartzwalder
13.	Colorado	8-2-0	Eddie Crowder
14.	Minnesota	8-2-0	Murray Warmath
15.	Florida St	7-2-1	Bill Peterson
16.	Miami (FL)	7-3-0	Charlie Tate
17.	North Carolina St	8-2-0	Earle Edwards
18.	Georgia	7-3-0	Vince Dooley
19.	Houston	9-2-0	Bill Yeoman
20.	Arizona St	8-2-0	Frank Kush

†UPI ranked Penn St 11th and did not rank Alabama, which was on probation.

1968

		Record	Coach
1.	Ohio St	10-0-0	Woody Hayes
2.	Penn St	11-0-0	Joe Paterno
3.	Texas	9-1-1	Darrell Royal
4.	USC	9-1-1	John McKay
5.	Notre Dame	7-2-1	Ara Parseghian
6.	Arkansas	10-1-0	Frank Broyles
7.	Kansas	9-2-0	Pepper Rodgers
8.	Georgia	8-1-2	Vince Dooley
9.	Missouri	8-3-0	Dan Devine
10.	Purdue	8-2-0	Jack Mollenkopf
11.	Oklahoma	7-4-0	Chuck Fairbanks
12.	Michigan	8-2-0	Bump Elliott
13.	Tennessee	8-2-1	Doug Dickey
14.	SMU	8-3-0	Hayden Fry
15.	Oregon St	7-3-0	Dee Andros
16.	Auburn	7-4-0	Shug Jordan
17.	Alabama	8-3-0	Bear Bryant
18.	Houston	6-2-2	Bill Yeoman
19.	LSU	8-3-0	Charlie McClendon
20.	Ohio	10-1-0	Bill Hess

1969

		Record	Coach
1.	Texas	11-0-0	Darrell Royal
2.	Penn St	11-0-0	Joe Paterno
3.	USC	10-0-1	John McKay
4.	Ohio St	8-1-0	Woody Hayes
5.	Notre Dame	8-2-1	Ara Parseghian
6.	Missouri	9-2-0	Dan Devine
7.	Arkansas	9-2-0	Frank Broyles
8.	Mississippi	8-3-0	Johnny Vaught
9.	Michigan	8-3-0	Bo Schembechler
10.	LSU	9-1-0	Charlie McClendon
11.	Nebraska	9-2-0	Bob Devaney
12.	Houston	9-2-0	Bill Yeoman
13.	UCLA	8-1-1	Tommy Prothro
14.	Florida	9-1-1	Ray Graves
15.	Tennessee	9-2-0	Doug Dickey
16.	Colorado	8-3-0	Eddie Crowder
17.	W Virginia	10-0-1	Jim Carlen
18.	Purdue	8-2-0	Jack Mollenkopf
19.	Stanford	7-2-1	John Ralston
20.	Auburn	8-3-0	Shug Jordan

1970

		Record	Coach
1.	Nebraska	11-0-1	Bob Devaney
2.	Notre Dame	10-1-0	Ara Parseghian
3.	#Texas	10-1-0	Darrell Royal
4.	Tennessee	11-0-1	Bill Battle
5.	Ohio St	9-1-0	Woody Hayes
6.	Arizona St	11-0-0	Frank Kush
7.	LSU	9-3-0	Charlie McClendon
8.	Stanford	9-3-0	John Ralston
9.	Michigan	9-1-0	Bo Schembechler
10.	Auburn	9-2-0	Shug Jordan
11.	Arkansas	9-2-0	Frank Broyles
12.	Toledo	12-0-0	Frank Lauterbur
13.	Georgia Tech	9-3-0	Bud Carson
14.	Dartmouth	9-0-0	Bob Blackman
15.	USC	6-4-1	John McKay

1970 *(Cont.)*

		Record	Coach
16.	Air Force	9-3-0	Ben Martin
17.	Tulane	8-4-0	Jim Pittman
18.	Penn St	7-3-0	Joe Paterno
19.	Houston	8-3-0	Bill Yeoman
20.	Oklahoma	7-4-1	Chuck Fairbanks
	Mississippi	7-4-0	Johnny Vaught

#Selected No. 1 by UPI.

1971

		Record	Coach
1.	Nebraska	13-0-0	Bob Devaney
2.	Oklahoma	11-1-0	Chuck Fairbanks
3.	Colorado	10-2-0	Eddie Crowder
4.	Alabama	11-1-0	Bear Bryant
5.	Penn St	11-1-0	Joe Paterno
6.	Michigan	11-1-0	Bo Schembechler
7.	Georgia	11-1-0	Vince Dooley
8.	Arizona St	11-1-0	Frank Kush
9.	Tennessee	10-2-0	Bill Battle
10.	Stanford	9-3-0	John Ralston
11.	LSU	9-3-0	Charlie McClendon
12.	Auburn	9-2-0	Shug Jordan
13.	Notre Dame	8-2-0	Ara Parseghian
14.	Toledo	12-0-0	John Murphy
15.	Mississippi	10-2-0	Billy Kinard
16.	Arkansas	8-3-1	Frank Broyles
17.	Houston	9-3-0	Bill Yeoman
18.	Texas	8-3-0	Darrell Royal
19.	Washington	8-3-0	Jim Owens
20.	USC	6-4-1	John McKay

1972

		Record	Coach
1.	USC	12-0-0	John McKay
2.	Oklahoma	11-1-0	Chuck Fairbanks
3.	Texas	10-1-0	Darrell Royal
4.	Nebraska	9-2-1	Bob Devaney
5.	Auburn	10-1-0	Shug Jordan
6.	Michigan	10-1-0	Bo Schembechler
7.	Alabama	10-2-0	Bear Bryant
8.	Tennessee	10-2-0	Bill Battle
9.	Ohio St	9-2-0	Woody Hayes
10.	Penn St	10-2-0	Joe Paterno
11.	LSU	9-2-1	Charlie McClendon
12.	North Carolina	11-1-0	Bill Dooley
13.	Arizona St	10-2-0	Frank Kush
14.	Notre Dame	8-3-0	Ara Parseghian
15.	UCLA	8-3-0	Pepper Rodgers
16.	Colorado	8-4-0	Eddie Crowder
17.	North Carolina St	8-3-1	Lou Holtz
18.	Louisville	9-1-0	Lee Corso
19.	Washington St	7-4-0	Jim Sweeney
20.	Georgia Tech	7-4-1	Bill Fulch

1973

		Record	Coach
1.	Notre Dame	11-0-0	Ara Parseghian
2.	Ohio St	10-0-1	Woody Hayes
3.	Oklahoma	10-0-1	Barry Switzer
4.	#Alabama	11-1-0	Bear Bryant
5.	Penn St	12-0-0	Joe Paterno
6.	Michigan	10-0-1	Bo Schembechler

1973 *(Cont.)*

		Record	Coach
7.	Nebraska	9-2-1	Tom Osborne
8.	USC	9-2-1	John McKay
9.	Arizona St	11-1-0	Frank Kush
	Houston	11-1-0	Bill Yeoman
11.	Texas Tech	11-1-0	Jim Carlen
12.	UCLA	9-2-0	Pepper Rodgers
13.	LSU	9-3-0	Charlie McClendon
14.	Texas	8-3-0	Darrell Royal
15.	Miami (OH)	11-0-0	Bill Mallory
16.	North Carolina St	9-3-0	Lou Holtz
17.	Missouri	8-4-0	Al Onofrio
18.	Kansas	7-4-1	Don Fambrough
19.	Tennessee	8-4-0	Bill Battle
20.	Maryland	8-4-0	Jerry Claiborne
	Tulane	9-3-0	Bennie Ellender

#Selected No. 1 by UPI.

1974

		Record	Coach
1.	Oklahoma	11-0-0	Barry Switzer
2.	#USC	10-1-1	John McKay
3.	Michigan	10-1-0	Bo Schembechler
4.	Ohio St	10-2-0	Woody Hayes
5.	Alabama	11-1-0	Bear Bryant
6.	Notre Dame	10-2-0	Ara Parseghian
7.	Penn St	10-2-0	Joe Paterno
8.	Auburn	10-2-0	Shug Jordan
9.	Nebraska	9-3-0	Tom Osborne
10.	Miami (Ohio)	10-0-1	Dick Crum
11.	North Carolina St	9-2-1	Lou Holtz
12.	Michigan St	7-3-1	Denny Stolz
13.	Maryland	8-4-0	Jerry Claiborne
14.	Baylor	8-4-0	Grant Teaff
15.	Florida	8-4-0	Doug Dickey
16.	Texas A&M	8-3-0	Emory Ballard
17.	Mississippi St	9-3-0	Bob Tyler
	Texas	8-4-0	Darrell Royal
19.	Houston	8-3-1	Bill Yeoman
20.	Tennessee	7-3-2	Bill Battle

#Selected No. 1 by UPI

1975

		Record	Coach
1.	Oklahoma	11-1-0	Barry Switzer
2.	Arizona St	12-0-0	Frank Kush
3.	Alabama	11-1-0	Bear Bryant
4.	Ohio St	11-1-0	Woody Hayes
5.	UCLA	9-2-1	Dick Vermeil
6.	Texas	10-2-0	Darrell Royal
7.	Arkansas	10-2-0	Frank Broyles
8.	Michigan	8-2-2	Bo Schembechler
9.	Nebraska	10-2-0	Tom Osborne
10.	Penn St	9-3-0	Joe Paterno
11.	Texas A&M	10-2-0	Emory Bellard
12.	Miami (OH)	11-1-0	Dick Crum
13.	Maryland	9-2-1	Jerry Claiborne
14.	California	8-3-0	Mike White
15.	Pittsburgh	8-4-0	Johnny Majors
16.	Colorado	9-3-0	Bill Mallory
17.	USC	8-4-0	John McKay
18.	Arizona	9-2-0	Jim Young
19.	Georgia	9-3-0	Vince Dooley
20.	W Virginia	9-3-0	Bobby Bowden

1976

		Record	Coach
1.	Pittsburgh	12-0-0	Johnny Majors
2.	USC	11-1-0	John Robinson
3.	Michigan	10-2-0	Bo Schembechler
4.	Houston	10-2-0	Bill Yeoman
5.	Oklahoma	9-2-1	Barry Switzer
6.	Ohio St	9-2-1	Woody Hayes
7.	Texas A&M	10-2-0	Emory Bellard
8.	Maryland	11-1-0	Jerry Claiborne
9.	Nebraska	9-3-1	Tom Osborne
10.	Georgia	10-2-0	Vince Dooley
11.	Alabama	9-3-0	Bear Bryant
12.	Notre Dame	9-3-0	Dan Devine
13.	Texas Tech	10-2-0	Steve Sloan
14.	Oklahoma St	9-3-0	Jim Stanley
15.	UCLA	9-2-1	Terry Donahue
16.	Colorado	8-4-0	Bill Mallory
17.	Rutgers	11-0-0	Frank Burns
18.	Kentucky	9-3-0	Fran Curci
19.	Iowa St	8-3-0	Earle Bruce
20.	Mississippi St	9-2-0	Bob Tyler

1977

		Record	Coach
1.	Notre Dame	11-1-0	Dan Devine
2.	Alabama	11-1-0	Bear Bryant
3.	Arkansas	11-1-0	Lou Holtz
4.	Texas	11-1-0	Fred Akers
5.	Penn St	11-1-0	Joe Paterno
6.	Kentucky	10-1-0	Fran Curci
7.	Oklahoma	10-2-0	Barry Switzer
8.	Pittsburgh	9-2-1	Jackie Sherrill
9.	Michigan	10-2-0	Bo Schembechler
10.	Washington	10-2-0	Don James
11.	Ohio St	9-3-0	Woody Hayes
12.	Nebraska	9-3-0	Tom Osborne
13.	USC	8-4-0	John Robinson
14.	Florida St	10-2-0	Bobby Bowden
15.	Stanford	9-3-0	Bill Walsh
16.	San Diego St	10-1-0	Claude Gilbert
17.	North Carolina	8-3-1	Bill Dooley
18.	Arizona St	9-3-0	Frank Kush
19.	Clemson	8-3-1	Charley Pell
20.	BYU	9-2-0	LaVell Edwards

1978

		Record	Coach
1.	Alabama	11-1-0	Bear Bryant
2.	#USC	12-1-0	John Robinson
3.	Oklahoma	11-1-0	Barry Switzer
4.	Penn St	11-1-0	Joe Paterno
5.	Michigan	10-2-0	Bo Schembechler
6.	Clemson	11-1-0	Charley Pell
7.	Notre Dame	9-3-0	Dan Devine
8.	Nebraska	9-3-0	Tom Osborne
9.	Texas	9-3-0	Fred Akers
10.	Houston	9-3-0	Bill Yeoman
11.	Arkansas	9-2-1	Lou Holtz
12.	Michigan St	8-3-0	Darryl Rogers
13.	Purdue	9-2-1	Jim Young
14.	UCLA	8-3-1	Terry Donahue
15.	Missouri	8-4-0	Warren Powers
16.	Georgia	9-2-1	Vince Dooley
17.	Stanford	8-4-0	Bill Walsh
18.	North Carolina St	9-3-0	Bo Rein
19.	Texas A&M	8-4-0	Emory Bellard (4–2)
			Tom Wilson (4–2)
20.	Maryland	9-3-0	Jerry Claiborne

#Selected No. 1 by UPI.

1979

		Record	Coach
1.	Alabama	12-0-0	Bear Bryant
2.	USC	11-0-1	John Robinson
3.	Oklahoma	11-1-0	Barry Switzer
4.	Ohio St	11-1-0	Earle Bruce
5.	Houston	11-1-0	Bill Yeoman
6.	Florida St	11-1-0	Bobby Bowden
7.	Pittsburgh	11-1-0	Jackie Sherrill
8.	Arkansas	10-2-0	Lou Holtz
9.	Nebraska	10-2-0	Tom Osborne
10.	Purdue	10-2-0	Jim Young
11.	Washington	10-1-0	Don James
12.	Texas	9-3-0	Fred Akers
13.	BYU	11-1-0	LaVell Edwards
14.	Baylor	8-4-0	Grant Teaff
15.	North Carolina	8-3-1	Dick Crum
16.	Auburn	8-3-0	Doug Barfield
17.	Temple	10-2-0	Wayne Hardin
18.	Michigan	8-4-0	Bo Schembechler
19.	Indiana	8-4-0	Lee Corso
20.	Penn St	8-4-0	Joe Paterno

1980

		Record	Coach
1.	Georgia	12-0-0	Vince Dooley
2.	Pittsburgh	11-1-0	Jackie Sherrill
3.	Oklahoma	10-2-0	Barry Switzer
4.	Michigan	10-2-0	Bo Schembechler
5.	Florida St	10-2-0	Bobby Bowden
6.	Alabama	10-2-0	Bear Bryant
7.	Nebraska	10-2-0	Tom Osborne
8.	Penn St	10-2-0	Joe Paterno
9.	Notre Dame	9-2-1	Dan Devine
10.	North Carolina	11-1-0	Dick Crum
11.	USC	8-2-1	John Robinson
12.	BYU	12-1-0	LaVell Edwards
13.	UCLA	9-2-0	Terry Donahue
14.	Baylor	10-2-0	Grant Teaff
15.	Ohio St	9-3-0	Earle Bruce
16.	Washington	9-3-0	Don James
17.	Purdue	9-3-0	Jim Young
18.	Miami (FL)	9-3-0	H. Schnellenberger
19.	Mississippi St	9-3-0	Emory Bellard
20.	SMU	8-4-0	Ron Meyer

1981

		Record	Coach
1.	Clemson	12-0-0	Danny Ford
2.	Texas	10-1-1	Fred Akers
3.	Penn St	10-2-0	Joe Paterno
4.	Pittsburgh	11-1-0	Jackie Sherrill
5.	SMU	10-1-0	Ron Meyer
6.	Georgia	10-2-0	Vince Dooley
7.	Alabama	9-2-1	Bear Bryant
8.	Miami (FL)	9-2-0	H. Schnellenberger
9.	North Carolina	10-2-0	Dick Crum
10.	Washington	10-2-0	Don James
11.	Nebraska	9-3-0	Tom Osborne
12.	Michigan	9-3-0	Bo Schembechler
13.	BYU	11-2-0	LaVell Edwards
14.	USC	9-3-0	John Robinson

1981 *(Cont.)*

		Record	Coach
15.	Ohio St	9-3-0	Earle Bruce
16.	Arizona St	9-2-0	Darryl Rogers
17.	W Virginia	9-3-0	Don Nehlen
18.	Iowa	8-4-0	Hayden Fry
19.	Missouri	8-4-0	Warren Powers
20.	Oklahoma	7-4-1	Barry Switzer

1982

		Record	Coach
1.	Penn St	11-1-0	Joe Paterno
2.	SMU	11-0-1	Bobby Collins
3.	Nebraska	12-1-0	Tom Osborne
4.	Georgia	11-1-0	Vince Dooley
5.	UCLA	10-1-1	Terry Donahue
6.	Arizona St	10-2-0	Darryl Rogers
7.	Washington	10-2-0	Don James
8.	Clemson	9-1-1	Danny Ford
9.	Arkansas	9-2-1	Lou Holtz
10.	Pittsburgh	9-3-0	Foge Fazio
11.	LSU	8-3-1	Jerry Stovall
12.	Ohio St	9-3-0	Earle Bruce
13.	Florida St	9-3-0	Bobby Bowden
14.	Auburn	9-3-0	Pat Dye
15.	USC	8-3-0	John Robinson
16.	Oklahoma	8-4-0	Barry Switzer
17.	Texas	9-3-0	Fred Akers
18.	North Carolina	8-4-0	Dick Crum
19.	W Virginia	9-3-0	Don Nehlen
20.	Maryland	8-4-0	Bobby Ross

1983

		Record	Coach
1.	Miami (Fla.)	11-1-0	H. Schnellenberger
2.	Nebraska	12-1-0	Tom Osborne
3.	Auburn	11-1-0	Pat Dye
4.	Georgia	10-1-1	Vince Dooley
5.	Texas	11-1-0	Fred Akers
6.	Florida	9-2-1	Charlie Pell
7.	BYU	11-1-0	LaVell Edwards
8.	Michigan	9-3-0	Bo Schembechler
9.	Ohio St	9-3-0	Earle Bruce
10.	Illinois	10-2-0	Mike White
11.	Clemson	9-1-1	Danny Ford
12.	SMU	10-2-0	Bobby Collins
13.	Air Force	10-2-0	Ken Hatfield
14.	Iowa	9-3-0	Hayden Fry
15.	Alabama	8-4-0	Ray Perkins
16.	W Virginia	9-3-0	Don Nehlen
17.	UCLA	7-4-1	Terry Donahue
18.	Pittsburgh	8-3-1	Foge Fazio
19.	Boston College	9-3-0	Jack Bicknell
20.	E Carolina	8-3-0	Ed Emory

1984

		Record	Coach
1.	BYU	13-0-0	LaVell Edwards
2.	Washington	11-1-0	Don James
3.	Florida	9-1-1	Chas Pell (0-1-1)
			Galen Hall (9-0)

1984 (Cont.)

		Record	Coach
4.	Nebraska	10-2-0	Tom Osborne
5.	Boston College	10-2-0	Jack Bicknell
6.	Oklahoma	9-2-1	Barry Switzer
7.	Oklahoma St	10-2-0	Pat Jones
8.	SMU	10-2-0	Bobby Collins
9.	UCLA	9-3-0	Terry Donahue
10.	USC	10-3-0	Ted Tollner
11.	South Carolina	10-2-0	Joe Morrison
12.	Maryland	9-3-0	Bobby Ross
13.	Ohio St	9-3-0	Earle Bruce
14.	Auburn	9-4-0	Pat Dye
15.	LSU	8-3-1	Bill Arnsparger
16.	Iowa	8-4-1	Hayden Fry
17.	Florida St	7-3-2	Bobby Bowden
18.	Miami (Fla.)	8-5-0	Jimmy Johnson
19.	Kentucky	9-3-0	Jerry Claiborne
20.	Virginia	8-2-2	George Welsh

1985

		Record	Coach
1.	Oklahoma	11-1-0	Barry Switzer
2.	Michigan	10-1-1	Bo Schembechler
3.	Penn St	11-1-0	Joe Paterno
4.	Tennessee	9-1-2	Johnny Majors
5.	Florida	9-1-1	Galen Hall
6.	Texas A&M	10-2-0	Jackie Sherrill
7.	UCLA	9-2-1	Terry Donahue
8.	Air Force	12-1-0	Fisher DeBerry
9.	Miami (Fla.)	10-2-0	Jimmy Johnson
10.	Iowa	10-2-0	Hayden Fry
11.	Nebraska	9-3-0	Tom Osborne
12.	Arkansas	10-2-0	Ken Hatfield
13.	Alabama	9-2-1	Ray Perkins
14.	Ohio St	9-3-0	Earle Bruce
15.	Florida St	9-3-0	Bobby Bowden
16.	BYU	11-3-0	LaVell Edwards
17.	Baylor	9-3-0	Grant Teaff
18.	Maryland	9-3-0	Bobby Ross
19.	Georgia Tech.	9-2-1	Bill Curry
20.	LSU	9-2-1	Bill Arnsparger

1986

		Record	Coach
1.	Penn St	12-0-0	Joe Paterno
2.	Miami (Fla.)	11-1-0	Jimmy Johnson
3.	Oklahoma	11-1-0	Barry Switzer
4.	Arizona St	10-1-1	John Cooper
5.	Nebraska	10-2-0	Tom Osborne
6.	Auburn	10-2-0	Pat Dye
7.	Ohio St	10-3-0	Earle Bruce
8.	Michigan	11-2-0	Bo Schembechler
9.	Alabama	10-3-0	Ray Perkins
10.	LSU	9-3-0	Bill Arnsparger
11.	Arizona	9-3-0	Larry Smith
12.	Baylor	9-3-0	Grant Teaff
13.	Texas A&M	9-3-0	Jackie Sherrill
14.	UCLA	8-3-1	Terry Donahue
15.	Arkansas	9-3-0	Ken Hatfield
16.	Iowa	9-3-0	Hayden Fry
17.	Clemson	8-2-2	Danny Ford

1986 (Cont.)

		Record	Coach
18.	Washington	8-3-1	Don James
19.	Boston College	9-3-0	Jack Bicknell
20.	Virginia Tech.	9-2-1	Bill Dooley

1987

		Record	Coach
1.	Miami (Fla.)	12-0-0	Jimmy Johnson
2.	Florida St	11-1-0	Bobby Bowden
3.	Oklahoma	11-1-0	Barry Switzer
4.	Syracuse	11-0-1	Dick MacPherson
5.	LSU	10-1-1	Mike Archer
6.	Nebraska	10-2-0	Tom Osborne
7.	Auburn	9-1-2	Pat Dye
8.	Michigan St	9-2-1	George Perles
9.	UCLA	10-2-0	Terry Donahue
10.	Texas A&M	10-2-0	Jackie Sherrill
11.	Oklahoma St	10-2-0	Pat Jones
12.	Clemson	10-2-0	Danny Ford
13.	Georgia	9-3-0	Vince Dooley
14.	Tennessee	10-2-1	Johnny Majors
15.	South Carolina	8-4-0	Joe Morrison
16.	Iowa	10-3-0	Hayden Fry
17.	Notre Dame	8-4-0	Lou Holtz
18.	USC	8-4-0	Larry Smith
19.	Michigan	8-4-0	Bo Schembechler
20.	Arizona St	7-4-1	John Cooper

1988

		Record	Coach
1.	Notre Dame	12-0-0	Lou Holtz
2.	Miami (Fla.)	11-1-0	Jimmy Johnson
3.	Florida St	11-1-0	Bobby Bowden
4.	Michigan	9-2-1	Bo Schembechler
5.	West Virginia	11-1-0	Don Nehlen
6.	UCLA	10-2-0	Terry Donahue
7.	USC	10-2-0	Larry Smith
8.	Auburn	10-2-0	Pat Dye
9.	Clemson	10-2-0	Danny Ford
10.	Nebraska	11-2-0	Tom Osborne
11.	Oklahoma St	10-2-0	Pat Jones
12.	Arkansas	10-2-0	Ken Hatfield
13.	Syracuse	10-2-0	Dick MacPherson
14.	Oklahoma	9-3-0	Barry Switzer
15.	Georgia	9-3-0	Vince Dooley
16.	Washington St	9-3-0	Dennis Erickson
17.	Alabama	9-3-0	Bill Curry
18.	Houston	9-3-0	Jack Pardee
19.	LSU	8-4-0	Mike Archer
20.	Indiana	8-3-1	Bill Mallor

†1989

		Record	Coach
1.	Miami (Fla.)	11-1-0	Dennis Erickson
2.	Notre Dame	12-1-0	Lou Holtz
3.	Florida St	10-2-0	Bobby Bowden
4.	Colorado	11-1-0	Bill McCartney
5.	Tennessee	11-1-0	Johnny Majors
6.	Auburn	10-2-0	Pat Dye
7.	Michigan	10-2-0	Bo Schembechler
8.	USC	9-2-1	Larry Smith
9.	Alabama	10-2-0	Bill Curry

†In 1989 the AP expanded its final poll to 25 teams.

†1989 *(Cont.)*

		Record	Coach
10.	Illinois	10-2-0	John Mackovic
11.	Nebraska	10-2-0	Tom Osborne
12.	Clemson	10-2-0	Danny Ford
13.	Arkansas	10-2-0	Ken Hatfield
14.	Houston	9-2-0	Jack Pardee
15.	Penn St	8-3-1	Joe Paterno
16.	Michigan St	8-4-0	George Perles
17.	Pittsburgh	8-3-1	Mike Gottfried
18.	Virginia	10-3-0	George Welsh
19.	Texas Tech	9-3-0	Spike Dykes
20.	Texas A&M	8-4-0	R.C. Slocum
21.	W Virginia	8-3-1	Don Nehlen
22.	BYU	10-3-0	LaVell Edwards
23.	Washington	8-4-0	Don James
24.	Ohio St	8-4-0	John Cooper
25.	Arizona	8-4-0	Dick Tomey

1990

		Record	Coach
1.	Colorado	11-1-1	Bill McCartney
2.	#Ga. Tech (UPI)	11-0-1	Bobby Ross
3.	Miami (Fla.)	10-2-0	Dennis Erickson
4.	Florida St	10-2-0	Bobby Bowden
5.	Washington	10-2-0	Don James
6.	Notre Dame	9-3-0	Lou Holtz
7.	Michigan	9-3-0	Gary Moeller
8.	Tennessee	9-2-2	Johnny Majors
9.	Clemson	10-2-0	Ken Hatfield
10.	Houston	10-1-0	John Jenkins
11.	Penn St	9-3-0	Joe Paterno
12.	Texas	10-2-0	David McWilliams
13.	Florida	9-2-0	Steve Spurrier
14.	Louisville	10-1-1	H. Schnellenberger
15.	Texas A&M	9-3-1	R.C. Slocum
16.	Michigan St	8-3-1	George Perles
17.	Oklahoma	8-3-0	Gary Gibbs
18.	Iowa	8-4-0	Hayden Fry
19.	Auburn	8-3-1	Pat Dye
20.	USC I	8-4-1	Larry Smith
21.	Mississippi	9-3-0	Billy Brewer
22.	BYU	10-3-0	LaVell Edwards
23.	Virginia	8-4-0	George Wells
24.	Nebraska	9-3-0	Tom Osborne
25.	Illinois	8-4-0	John Mackovic

1991

		Record	Coach
1.	Miami (Fla.)	12-0-0	Dennis Erickson
2.	#Washington	12-0-0	Don James
3.	Penn St	11-2-0	Joe Paterno
4.	Florida St	11-2-0	Bobby Bowden
5.	Alabama	11-1-0	Gene Stallings
6.	Michigan	10-2-0	Gary Moeller
7.	Florida	10-2-0	Steve Spurrier
8.	California	10-2-0	Bruce Snyder
9.	E Carolina	11-1-0	Bill Lewis
10.	Iowa	10-1-1	Hayden Fry
11.	Syracuse	10-2-0	Paul Pasqualoni
12.	Texas A&M	10-2-0	R.C. Slocum
13.	Notre Dame	10-3-0	Lou Holtz

1991 *(Cont.)*

		Record	Coach
14.	Tennessee	9-3-0	Johnny Majors
15.	Nebraska	9-2-1	Tom Osborne
16.	Oklahoma	9-3-0	Gary Gibbs
17.	Georgia	9-3-0	Ray Goff
18.	Clemson	9-2-1	Ken Hatfield
19.	UCLA	9-3-0	Terry Donahue
20.	Colorado	8-3-1	Bill McCartney
21.	Tulsa	10-2-0	David Rader
22.	Stanford	8-4-0	Dennis Green
23.	BYU	8-3-2	LaVell Edwards
24.	North Carolina St	9-3-0	Dick Sheridan
25.	Air Force	10-3-0	Fisher DeBerry

#Selected No. 1 by *USA Today*/CNN.

1992

		Record	Coach
1.	Alabama	13-0-0	Gene Stallings
2.	Florida St	11-1-0	Bobby Bowden
3.	Miami	11-1-0	Dennis Erickson
4.	Notre Dame	10-1-1	Lou Holtz
5.	Michigan	9-0-3	Gary Moeller
6.	Syracuse	10-2-0	Paul Pasqualoni
7.	Texas A&M	12-1-0	R.C. Slocum
8.	Georgia	10-2-0	Ray Goff
9.	Stanford	10-3-0	Bill Walsh
10.	Florida	9-4-0	Steve Spurrier
11.	Washington	9-3-0	Don James
12.	Tennessee	9-3-0	Johnny Majors
13.	Colorado	9-2-1	Bill McCartney
14.	Nebraska	9-3-0	Tom Osborne
15.	Washington St	9-3-0	Mike Price
16.	Mississippi	9-3-0	Billy Brewer
17.	North Carolina St	9-3-1	Dick Sheridan
18.	Ohio St	8-3-1	John Cooper
19.	North Carolina	9-3-0	Mack Brown
20.	Hawaii	11-2-0	Bob Wagner
21.	Boston College	8-3-1	Tom Coughlin
22.	Kansas	8-4-0	Glen Mason
23.	Mississippi St	7-5-0	Jackie Sherrill
24.	Fresno St	9-4-0	Jim Sweeney
25.	Wake Forest	8-4-0	Bill Dooley

1993

		Record	Coach
1.	Florida St	12-1-0	Bobby Bowden
2.	Notre Dame	11-1-0	Lou Holtz
3.	Nebraska	11-1-0	Tom Osborne
4.	Auburn	11-0-0	Terry Bowden
5.	Florida	11-2-0	Steve Spurrier
6.	Wisconsin	10-1-1	Barry Alvarez
7.	W Virginia	11-1-0	Don Nehlen
8.	Penn St	10-2-0	Joe Paterno
9.	Texas A&M	10-2-0	R.C. Slocum
10.	Arizona	10-2-0	Dick Tomey
11.	Ohio St	10-1-1	John Cooper
12.	Tennessee	9-2-1	Phil Fulmer
13.	Boston College	9-3-0	Tom Coughlin
14.	Alabama	9-3-1	Gene Stallings
15.	Miami	9-3-0	Dennis Erickson
16.	Colorado	8-3-1	Bill McCartney

†In 1989 the AP expanded its final poll to 25 teams.

1993 *(Cont.)*

		Record	Coach
17.	Oklahoma	9-3-0	Gary Gibbs
18.	UCLA	8-4-0	Terry Donahue
19.	North Carolina	10-3-0	Mack Brown
20.	Kansas St.	9-2-1	Bill Snyder
21.	Michigan	8-4-0	Gary Moeller
22.	Virginia Tech	9-3-0	Frank Beamer
23.	Clemson	9-3-0	Ken Hatfield
24.	Louisville	9-3-0	H. Schnellenberger
25.	California	9-4-0	Keith Gilbertson

1994

		Record	Coach
1.	Nebraska	13-0-0	Tom Osborne
2.	Penn St	12-0-0	Joe Paterno
3.	Colorado	11-1-0	Bill McCartney
4.	Florida St.	10-1-1	Bobby Bowden
5.	Alabama	12-1-0	Gene Stallings
6.	Miami (Fla.)	10-2-0	Dennis Erickson
7.	Florida	10-2-1	Steve Spurrier
8.	Texas A&M	10-0-1	R.C. Slocum
9.	Auburn	9-1-1	Terry Bowden
10.	Utah	10-2-0	Ron McBride
11.	Oregon	9-4-0	Rich Brooks
12.	Michigan	8-4-0	Gary Moeller
13.	USC	8-3-1	John Robinson
14.	Ohio St	9-4-0	John Cooper
15.	Virginia	9-3-0	George Welsh
16.	Colorado St.	10-2-0	Sonny Lubick
17.	North Carolina St	9-3-0	Mike O'Cain
18.	BYU	10-3-0	LaVell Edwards
19.	Kansas St.	9-3-0	Bill Snyder
20.	Arizona	8-4-0	Dick Tomey
21.	Washington St.	8-4-0	Mike Price
22.	Tennessee	8-4-0	Phillip Fulmer
23.	Boston College	7-4-1	Dan Henning
24.	Mississippi St.	8-4-0	Jackie Sherrill
25.	Texas	8-4-0	John Mackovic

1995

		Record	Coach
1.	Nebraska	12-0-0	Tom Osborne
2.	Florida	12-1-0	Steve Spurrier
3.	Tennessee	11-1-0	Phillip Fulmer
4.	Florida St.	10-2-0	Bobby Bowden
5.	Colorado	10-2-0	Rick Neuheisel
6.	Ohio St	11-2-0	John Cooper
7.	Kansas St.	10-2-0	Bill Snyder
8.	Northwestern	10-2-0	Gary Barnett
9.	Kansas	10-2-0	Glen Mason
10.	Virginia Tech	10-2-0	Frank Beamer
11.	Notre Dame	9-3-0	Lou Holtz
12.	USC	9-2-1	John Robinson
13.	Penn St	9-3-0	Joe Paterno
14.	Texas	10-2-1	John Mackovic
15.	Texas A&M	9-3-0	S.C. Slocum
16.	Virginia	9-4-0	George Welsh
17.	Michigan	9-4-0	Lloyd Carr
18.	Oregon	9-3-0	Mike Bellotti
19.	Syracuse	9-3-0	Paul Pasqualoni
20.	Miami (Fla.)	8-3-0	Butch Davis
21.	Alabama	8-3-0	Gene Stallings

*In 1996 the NCAA introduced overtime to break ties.

1995 *(Cont.)*

		Record	Coach
22.	Auburn	8-4-0	Terry Bowden
23.	Texas Tech	9-3-0	Spike Dykes
24.	Toledo	11-0-1	Gary Pinkel
25.	Iowa	8-4-0	Hayden Fry

1996

		Record*	Coach
1.	Florida	12–1	Steve Spurrier
2.	Ohio St	11–1	John Cooper
3.	Florida St	11–1	Bobby Bowden
4.	Arizona St	11–1	Bruce Snyder
5.	BYU	14–1	LaVell Edwards
6.	Nebraska	11–2	Tom Osborne
7.	Penn St	11–2	Joe Paterno
8.	Colorado	10–2	Rick Neuheisel
9.	Tennessee	10–2	Phillip Fulmer
10.	North Carolina	10–2	Mack Brown
11.	Alabama	10–3	Gene Stallings
12.	LSU	10–2	Gerry DiNardo
13.	Virginia Tech	10–2	Frank Beamer
14.	Miami (Fla.)	9–3	Butch Davis
15.	Northwestern	9–3	Gary Barnett
16.	Washington	9–3	Jim Lambright
17.	Kansas St	9–3	Bill Snyder
18.	Iowa	9–3	Hayden Fry
19.	Notre Dame	8–3	Lou Holtz
20.	Michigan	8–4	Lloyd Carr
21.	Syracuse	9–3	Paul Pasqualoni
22.	Wyoming	10–2	Joe Tiller
23.	Texas	8–5	John Mackovic
24.	Auburn	8–4	Terry Bowden
25.	Army	10–2	Bob Sutton

1997

		Record	Coach
1.	Michigan	12–0	Lloyd Carr
#2.	Nebraska	13–0	Tom Osborne
3.	Florida St	11–1	Bobby Bowden
4.	Florida	10–2	Steve Spurrier
5.	UCLA	10–2	Bob Toledo
6.	North Carolina	11–1	Mack Brown
7.	Tennessee	11–2	Phillip Fulmer
8.	Kansas St	11–1	Bill Snyder
9.	Washington St	10–2	Mike Price
10.	Georgia	10–2	Jim Donnan
11.	Auburn	10–3	Terry Bowden
12.	Ohio St	10–3	John Cooper
13.	LSU	9–3	Gerry DiNardo
14.	Arizona St	8–3	Bruce Snyder
15.	Purdue	9–3	Joe Tiller
16.	Penn St	9–3	Joe Paterno
17.	Colorado St	11–2	Sonny Lubick
18.	Washington	8–4	Jim Lambright
19.	Southern Mississippi	9–3	Jeff Bower
20.	Texas A&M	9–4	R. C. Slocum
21.	Syracuse	9–4	Paul Pasqualoni
22.	Mississippi	8–4	Tommy Tuberville
23.	Missouri	7–5	Larry Smith
24.	Oklahoma St	8–4	Bob Simmons
25.	Georgia Tech	7–5	George O'Leary

#Selected No. 1 by *USA Today*/CNN.

Annual Associated Press Top 25 *(Cont.)*

1998

		Record	Coach
1.	Tennessee	13–0	Phillip Fulmer
2.	Ohio St.	11–1	John Cooper
3.	Florida St	11–2	Bobby Bowden
4.	Arizona	12–1	Dick Tomey
5.	Florida	10–2	Steve Spurrier
6.	Wisconsin	11–1	Barry Alvarez
7.	Tulane	12–0	Tommy Bowden
8.	UCLA	10–2	Bob Toledo
9.	Georgia Tech	10–2	George O'Leary
10.	Kansas St	11–2	Bill Snyder
11.	Texas A&M	11–3	R.C. Slocum
12.	Michigan	10–3	Lloyd Carr
13.	Air Force	12–1	Fisher DeBerry
14.	Georgia	9–3	Jim Donnan
15.	Texas	9–3	Mack Brown
16.	Arkansas	9–3	Houston Nutt
17.	Penn St	9–3	Joe Paterno
18.	Virginia	9–3	George Welsh
19.	Nebraska	9–4	Frank Solich
20.	Miami (Fla.)	9–3	Butch Davis
21.	Missouri	8–4	Larry Smith
22.	Notre Dame	9–3	Bob Davie
23.	Virginia Tech	9–3	Frank Beamer
24.	Purdue	9–4	Joe Tiller
25.	Syracuse	8–4	Paul Pasqualoni

1999

		Record	Coach
1.	Florida St	12–0	Bobby Bowden
2.	Virginia Tech	11–1	Frank Beamer
3.	Nebraska	12–1	Frank Solich
4.	Wisconsin	10–2	Barry Alvarez
5.	Michigan	10–2	Lloyd Carr
6.	Kansas St	11–1	Bill Snyder
7.	Michigan St	10–2	Nick Saban
8.	Alabama	10–3	Mike DuBose
9.	Tennessee	9–3	Phillip Fulmer
10.	Marshall	13–0	Bob Pruett
11.	Penn St	10–3	Joe Paterno
12.	Florida	9–4	Steve Spurrier
13.	Mississippi St	10–2	Jackie Sherrill
14.	Southern Miss	9–3	Jeff Bower
15.	Miami (Fla.)	9–4	Butch Davis
16.	Georgia	8–4	Jim Donnan
17.	Arkansas	8–4	Houston Nutt
18.	Minnesota	8–4	Glen Mason
19.	Oregon	9–3	Mike Bellotti
20.	Georgia Tech	8–4	Goerge O'Leary
21.	Texas	9–5	Mack Brown
22.	Mississippi	8–4	David Cutcliffe
23.	Texas A&M	8–4	R.C. Slocum
24.	Illinois	8–4	Ron Turner
25.	Purdue	7–5	Joe Tiller

2000

		Record	Coach
1.	Oklahoma	13–0	Bob Stoops
2.	Miami (Fla.)	11–1	Butch Davis
3.	Washington	11–1	Rick Neuheisel
4.	Oregon St	11–1	Dennis Erickson
5.	Florida St	11–2	Bobby Bowden
6.	Virginia Tech	11–1	Frank Beamer
7.	Oregon	10–2	Mike Belotti

2000 *(Cont.)*

		Record	Coach
8.	Nebraska	10–2	Frank Solich
9.	Kansas St	11–3	Bill Snyder
10.	Florida	10–3	Steve Spurrier
11.	Michigan	9–3	Lloyd Carr
12.	Texas	9–3	Mack Brown
13.	Purdue	8–4	Joe Tiller
14.	Colorado St	10–2	Sonny Lubeck
15.	Notre Dame	9–3	Bob Davie
16.	Clemson	9–3	Tommy Bowden
17.	Georgia Tech	9–3	George O'Leary
18.	Auburn	9–4	Tommy Tuberville
19.	South Carolina	8–4	Lou Holtz
20.	Georgia	8–4	Jim Donnan
21.	TCU	10–2	Dennis Franchione
22.	LSU	8–4	Nick Saban
23.	Wisconsin	9–4	Barry Alvarez
24.	Mississippi St	8–4	Jackie Sherrill
25.	Iowa St	9–3	Dan McCarney

2001

		Record	Coach
1.	Miami (Fla.)	12–0	Larry Coker
2.	Oregon	11–1	Mike Belotti
3.	Florida	10–2	Steve Spurrier
4.	Tennessee	11–2	Phillip Fulmer
5.	Texas	11–2	Mack Brown
6.	Oklahoma	11–2	Bob Stoops
7.	LSU	10–3	Nick Saban
8.	Nebraska	11–2	Frank Solich
9.	Colorado	10–3	Gary Barnett
10.	Washington St	10–2	Mike Price
11.	Maryland	10–2	Ralph Friedgen
12.	Illinois	10–2	Ron Turner
13.	South Carolina	9–3	Lou Holtz
14.	Syracuse	10–3	Paul Pasqualoni
15.	Florida St	8–4	Bobby Bowden
16.	Stanford	9–3	Tyrone Willingham
17.	Louisville	11–2	John Smith
18.	Virginia Tech	8–4	Frank Beamer
19.	Washington	8–4	Rick Neuheisel
20.	Michigan	8–4	Lloyd Carr
21.	Boston College	8–4	Tom O'Brien
22.	Georgia	8–4	Mark Richt
23.	Toledo	10–2	Tom Amstutz
24.	Georgia Tech	8–5	George O'Leary
25.	BYU	12–2	Gary Crowton

2002

		Record	Coach
1.	Ohio St	14–0	Jim Tressel
2.	Miami (Fla.)	12–1	Larry Coker
3.	Georgia	13–1	Mark Richt
4.	USC	11–2	Pete Carroll
5.	Oklahoma	12–2	Bob Stoops
6.	Texas	11–2	Mack Brown
7.	Kansas St	11–2	Bill Snyder
8.	Iowa	11–2	Kirk Ferentz
9.	Michigan	10–3	Lloyd Carr
10.	Washington St	10–3	Mike Price
11.	Alabama	10–3	Dennis Franchione
12.	North Carolina St	11–3	Chuck Amato
13.	Maryland	11–3	Ralph Friedgen

2002 *(Cont.)*

		Record	Coach
14.	Auburn	9-4	Tommy Tuberville
15.	Boise St	12-1	Dan Hawkins
16.	Penn St	9-4	Joe Paterno
17.	Notre Dame	10-3	Tyrone Willingham
18.	Virginia Tech	10-4	Frank Beamer
19.	Pittsburgh	9-4	Walt Harris
20.	Colorado	9-5	Gary Barnett
21.	Florida St	9-5	Bobby Bowden
22.	Virginia	9-5	Al Groh
23.	TCU	10-2	Gary Patterson
24.	Marshall	11-2	Bob Pruett
25.	W Virginia	9-4	Rich Rodriguez

2003

		Record	Coach
1.	USC	12-1	Pete Carroll
#2.	LSU	13-1	Nick Saban
3.	Oklahoma	12-2	Bob Stoops
4.	Ohio St	11-2	Jim Tressel
5.	Miami (Fla.)	11-2	Larry Coker
6.	Michigan	10-3	Lloyd Carr
7.	Georgia	11-3	Mark Richt
8.	Iowa	10-3	Kirk Ferentz
9.	Washington St	10-3	Bill Doba
10.	Miami (Ohio)	13-1	Terry Hoeppner
11.	Florida St	10-3	Bobby Bowden
12.	Texas	10-3	Mack Brown
13.	Kansas St	11-4	Bill Snyder
	Mississippi	10-3	David Cutcliffe
15.	Tennessee	10-3	Phillip Fulmer
16.	Boise St	13-1	Dan Hawkins
17.	Maryland	10-3	Ralph Friedgen
18.	Nebraska	10-3	Frank Solich/Bo Pelini
	Purdue	9-4	Joe Tiller
20.	Minnesota	10-3	Glen Mason
21.	Utah	10-2	Urban Meyer
22.	Clemson	9-4	Tommy Bowden
23.	Bowling Green	11-3	Gregg Brandon
24.	Florida	8-5	Ron Zook
25.	TCU	11-2	Gary Patterson

#Selected No. 1 by *USA Today*/CNN.

2004

		Record	Coach
1.	*Vacated		
2.	Auburn	13-0	Tommy Tuberville
3.	Oklahoma	12-1	Bob Stoops
4.	Utah	12-0	Kyle Whittingham
5.	Texas	11-1	Mack Brown
6.	Louisville	11-1	Bobby Petrino
7.	Georgia	10-2	Mark Richt
8.	Iowa	10-2	Kirk Ferentz
9.	California	10-2	Jeff Tedford
10.	Virginia Tech	10-3	Frank Beamer
11.	Miami (Fla.)	9-3	Larry Coker
12.	Boise St	11-1	Dan Hawkins
13.	Tennessee	10-3	Phillip Fulmer
14.	Michigan	9-3	Lloyd Carr
15.	Florida St	8-5	Bobby Bowden
16.	LSU	9-3	Les Miles
17.	Wisconsin	9-3	Barry Alvarez
18.	Texas Tech	8-4	Mike Leach
19.	Arizona St	9-3	Dirk Koetter

2004 *(Cont.)*

		Record	Coach
20.	Ohio St	8-4	Jim Tressel
21.	Boston College	9-3	Tom O'Brien
22.	Fresno St	9-3	Pat Hill
23.	Virginia	8-4	Al Groh
24.	Navy	10-2	Paul Johnson
25.	Pittsburgh	8-4	Walt Harris

*USC was stripped of its 2004 BCS victory in 2010.

2005

		Record	Coach
1.	Texas	13-0	Mack Brown
2.	*Vacated		
3.	Penn St	11-1	Joe Paterno
4.	Ohio St	10-2	Jim Tressel
5.	Texas	11-1	Mack Brown
6.	LSU	11-2	Les Miles
7.	Virginia Tech	10-3	Frank Beamer
8.	Alabama	10-2	Mike Shula
9.	Notre Dame	9-3	Charlie Weis
10.	Georgia	10-3	Mark Richt
11.	TCU	11-1	Gary Patterson
12.	Florida	9-3	Urban Meyer
12.	Oregon	10-2	Mike Bellotti
14.	Auburn	9-3	Tommy Tuberville
15.	Wisconsin	9-3	Barry Alvarez
15.	Michigan	9-3	Lloyd Carr
16.	UCLA	10-2	Karl Dorrell
17.	Miami (Fla.)	9-3	Larry Coker
18.	Boston College	9-3	Tom O'Brien
19.	Louisville	9-3	Bobby Petrino
20.	Texas Tech	9-3	Mike Leach
21.	Clemson	8-4	Tommy Bowden
22.	Oklahoma	8-4	Bob Stoops
23.	Florida St	8-5	Bobby Bowden
24.	Nebraska	8-4	Bill Callahan
25.	California	8-4	Jeff Tedford

*USC was stripped of its 2005 season victories in 2010.

2006

		Record	Coach
1.	Florida	13-1	Urban Meyer
2.	Ohio St	12-1	Jim Tressel
3.	LSU	11-2	Les Miles
4.	USC	11-2	Pete Carroll
5.	Boise St	13-0	Chris Petersen
6.	Louisville	12-1	Steve Kragthorpe
7.	Wisconsin	12-1	Bret Bielema
8.	Michigan	11-2	Lloyd Carr
9.	Auburn	11-2	Tommy Tuberville
10.	West Virginia	11-2	Rich Rodriguez
11.	Oklahoma	11-3	Bob Stoops
12.	Rutgers	11-2	Greg Schiano
13.	Texas	10-3	Mack Brown
14.	California	10-3	Jeff Tedford
15.	Arkansas	10-4	Houston Nutt
16.	BYU	11-2	Bronco Mendenhall
17.	Notre Dame	10-3	Charlie Weis
18.	Wake Forest	11-3	Jim Grobe
19.	Virginia Tech	10-3	Frank Beamer
20.	Boston College	10-3	Jeff Jagodzinski
21.	Oregon St	10-4	Mike Riley
22.	TCU	11-2	Gary Patterson
23.	Georgia	9-4	Mark Richt
24.	Penn St	9-4	Joe Paterno
25.	Tennessee	9-4	Phillip Fulmer

2007

		Record	Coach
1.	LSU	12-2	Les Miles
2.	Georgia	11-2	Mark Richt
3.	USC	11-2	Pete Carroll
4.	Missouri	12-2	Gary Pinkell
5.	Ohio St	11-2	Jim Tressel
6.	West Virginia	11-2	Rich Rodriguez
7.	Kansas	12-1	Mark Mangino
8.	Oklahoma	11-3	Bob Stoops
9.	Virginia Tech	11-3	Frank Beamer
10.	Texas	10-3	Mack Brown
10.	Boston College	11-3	Jeff Jagodzinski
12.	Tennessee	10-4	Philip Fulmer
13.	Florida	9-4	Urban Meyer
14.	BYU	11-2	Bronco Mendenhall
15.	Auburn	9-4	Tommy Tuberville
16.	Arizona St	10-3	Dennis Erickson
17.	Cincinnati	10-3	Brian Kelly
18.	Michigan	9-4	Lloyd Carr
19.	Hawaii	12-1	June Jones
20.	Illinois	9-4	Ron Zook
21.	Clemson	9-4	Tommy Bowden
22.	Texas Tech	9-4	Mike Leach
23.	Oregon	9-4	Mike Bellotti
24.	Wisconsin	9-4	Bret Bielema
25.	Oregon St	9-4	Mike Riley

2009

		Record	Coach
1.	LSU	12-2	Les Miles
2.	Georgia	11-2	Mark Richt
3.	USC	11-2	Pete Carroll
4.	Missouri	12-2	Gary Pinkell
5.	Ohio St	11-2	Jim Tressel
6.	West Virginia	11-2	Rich Rodriguez
7.	Kansas	12-1	Mark Mangino
8.	Oklahoma	11-3	Bob Stoops
9.	Virginia Tech	11-3	Frank Beamer
10.	Texas	10-3	Mack Brown
10.	Boston College	11-3	Jeff Jagodzinski
12.	Tennessee	10-4	Philip Fulmer
13.	Florida	9-4	Urban Meyer
14.	BYU	11-2	Bronco Mendenhall
15.	Auburn	9-4	Tommy Tuberville
16.	Arizona St	10-3	Dennis Erickson
17.	Cincinnati	10-3	Brian Kelly
18.	Michigan	9-4	Lloyd Carr
19.	Hawaii	12-1	June Jones
20.	Illinois	9-4	Ron Zook
21.	Clemson	9-4	Tommy Bowden
22.	Texas Tech	9-4	Mike Leach
23.	Oregon	9-4	Mike Bellotti
24.	Wisconsin	9-4	Bret Bielema
25.	Oregon St	9-4	Mike Riley

2008

		Record	Coach
1.	Florida	13-1	Urban Meyer
2.	Ohio St	12-1	Jim Tressel
3.	LSU	11-2	Les Miles
4.	USC	11-2	Pete Carroll
5.	Boise St	13-0	Chris Petersen
6.	Louisville	12-1	Steve Kragthorpe
7.	Wisconsin	12-1	Bret Bielema
8.	Michigan	11-2	Lloyd Carr
9.	Auburn	11-2	Tommy Tuberville
10.	West Virginia	11-2	Rich Rodriguez
11.	Oklahoma	11-3	Bob Stoops
12.	Rutgers	11-2	Greg Schiano
13.	Texas	10-3	Mack Brown
14.	California	10-3	Jeff Tedford
15.	Arkansas	10-4	Houston Nutt
16.	BYU	11-2	Bronco Mendenhall
17.	Notre Dame	10-3	Charlie Weis
18.	Wake Forest	11-3	Jim Grobe
19.	Virginia Tech	10-3	Frank Beamer
20.	Boston College	10-3	Jeff Jagodzinski
21.	Oregon St	10-4	Mike Riley
22.	TCU	11-2	Gary Patterson
23.	Georgia	9-4	Mark Richt
24.	Penn St	9-4	Joe Paterno
25.	Tennessee	9-4	Phillip Fulmer

Football Championship Subdivision (Div. I-AA)

Year	Winner	Runner-Up	Score
1978	Florida A&M	Massachusetts	35–28
1979	Eastern Kentucky	Lehigh	30–7
1980	Boise St	Eastern Kentucky	31–29
1981	Idaho St	Eastern Kentucky	34–23
1982	Eastern Kentucky	Delaware	17–14
1983	Southern Illinois	Western Carolina	43–7
1984	Montana St	Louisiana Tech	19–6
1985	Georgia Southern	Furman	44–42
1986	Georgia Southern	Arkansas St	48–21
1987	NE Louisiana	Marshall	43–42
1988	Furman	Georgia Southern	17–12
1989	Georgia Southern	Stephen F. Austin St	37–34
1990	Georgia Southern	Nevada-Reno	36–13
1991	Youngstown St	Marshall	25–17
1992	Marshall	Youngstown St	31–28
1993	Youngstown St	Marshall	17–5
1994	Youngstown St	Boise St	28–14
1995	Montana	Marshall	22–20
1996	Marshall	Montana	49–29
1997	Youngstown St	McNesse St	10–9
1998	Massachusetts	Georgia Southern	55–43
1999	Georgia Southern	Youngstown St	59–24
2000	Georgia Southern	Montana	27–25
2001	Montana	Furman	13–6
2002	Western Kentucky	McNeese St	34–14
2003	Delaware	Colgate	40–0
2004	James Madison	Montana	31–21
2005	Appalachian St	Northern Iowa	21–16
2006	Appalachian St	Massachusetts	28–17
2007	Appalachian St	Delaware	49–21
2008	Richmond	Montana	24–7
2009	Villanova	Montana	23–21

Division II

Year	Winner	Runner-Up	Score
1973	Louisiana Tech	Western Kentucky	34–0
1974	Central Michigan	Delaware	54–14
1975	Northern Michigan	Western Kentucky	16–14
1976	Montana St	Akron	24–13
1977	Lehigh	Jacksonville St	33–0
1978	Eastern Illinois	Delaware	10–9
1979	Delaware	Youngstown St	38–21
1980	Cal Poly SLO	Eastern Illinois	21–13
1981	SW Texas St	North Dakota St	42–13
1982	SW Texas St	UC–Davis	34–9
1983	North Dakota St	Central St (Ohio)	41–21
1984	Troy St	North Dakota St	18–17
1985	North Dakota St	North Alabama	35–7
1986	North Dakota St	South Dakota	27–7
1987	Troy St	Portland St	31–17
1988	North Dakota St	Portland St	35–21
1989	Mississippi College	Jacksonville St	3–0
1990	N Dakota St	Indiana (Pa.)	51–11
1991	Pittsburg St	Jacksonville St	23–6
1992	Jacksonville St	Pittsburg St	17–13
1993	North Alabama	Indiana (Pa.)	41–34
1994	North Alabama	Texas A&M–Kingsville	16–10
1995	North Alabama	Pittsburg St	27–7
1996	Northern Colorado	Carson-Newman	23–14
1997	Northern Colorado	New Haven	51–0
1998	NW Missouri St	Carson-Newman	24–6
1999	NW Missouri St	Carson-Newman	58–52 (OT)
2000	Delta St	Bloomsburg	63–34
2001	Grand Valley St	North Dakota	17–14

Division II (Cont.)

Year	Winner	Runner-Up	Score
2002	Grand Valley St	Valdosta St	31–24
2003	Grand Valley St	North Dakota	10–3
2004	Valdosta State	Pittsburg State	36–31
2005	Grand Valley St	NW Missouri St	21–17
2006	Grand Valley St	NW Missouri St	17–14
2007	Valdosta St	NW Missouri St	25-20
2008	Minnesota-Duluth	NW Missouri St	21–14
2009	NW Missouri St	Grand Valley St	30–23

Division III

Year	Winner	Runner-Up	Score
1973	Wittenberg	Juniata	41–0
1974	Central (Iowa)	Ithaca	10–8
1975	Wittenberg	Ithaca	28–0
1976	St. John's (Minn.)	Towson St	31–28
1977	Widener	Wabash	39–36
1978	Baldwin-Wallace	Wittenberg	24–10
1979	Ithaca	Wittenberg	14–10
1980	Dayton	Ithaca	63–0
1981	Widener	Dayton	17–10
1982	West Georgia	Augustana (Ill.)	14–0
1983	Augustana (Ill.)	Union (N.Y.)	21–17
1984	Augustana (Ill.)	Central (Iowa)	21–12
1985	Augustana (Ill.)	Ithaca	20–7
1986	Augustana (Ill.)	Salisbury St	31–3
1987	Wagner	Dayton	19–3
1988	Ithaca	Central (Iowa)	39–24
1989	Dayton	Union (N.Y.)	17–7
1990	Allegheny	Lycoming	21–14 (OT)
1991	Ithaca	Dayton	34–20
1992	UW-LaCrosse	Washington & Jefferson	16–12
1993	Mount Union	Rowan	34–24
1994	Albion	Washington & Jefferson	38–15
1995	UW-LaCrosse	Rowan	36–7
1996	Mount Union	Rowan	56–24
1997	Mount Union	Lycoming	61–12
1998	Mount Union	Rowan	44–24
1999	Pacific Lutheran	Rowan	42–13
2000	Mount Union	St. John's (Minn.)	10–7
2001	Mount Union	Bridgewater	30–27
2002	Mount Union	Trinity (Tex.)	48–7
2003	St. John's (Minn.)	Mount Union	24–6
2004	Linfield	Mary Hardin-Baylor	28–21
2005	Mount Union	UW-Whitewater	35–28
2006	Mount Union	UW-Whitewater	35–16
2007	UW-Whitewater	Mount Union	31–21
2008	Mount Union	UW-Whitewater	31–26
2009	UW-Whitewater	Mount Union	38–28

Division I

Year	Winner	Runner-Up	Score
1956	St. Joseph's (Ind.)/Montana St		0–0
1957	Pittsburg St (Kan.)	Hillsdale	27–26
1958	NE Oklahoma	Northern Arizona	19–13
1959	Texas A&I	Lenoir-Rhyne	20–7
1960	Lenoir-Rhyne	Humboldt St	15–14
1961	Pittsburg St (Kan.)	Linfield	12–7
1962	Central St (Okla.)	Lenoir-Rhyne	28–13
1963	St. John's (Minn.)	Prairie View	33–27
1964	Concordia-Moorhead/ Sam Houston St		7–7
1965	St. John's (Minn.)	Linfield	33–0
1966	Waynesburg	UW-Whitewater	42–21
1967	Fairmont St	Eastern Washington	28–21
1968	Troy St (Mich.)	Texas A&I	43–35
1969	Texas A&I	Concordia-Moorhead (Minn.)	32–7
1970	Texas A&I	Wofford	48–7
1971	Livingston (Ala.)	Arkansas Tech	14–12
1972	E Texas St	Carson-Newman	21–18
1973	Abilene Christian	Elon	42–14
1974	Texas A&I	Henderson St	34–23
1975	Texas A&I	Salem (W.V.)	37–0
1976	Texas A&I	Central Arkansas	26–0
1977	Abilene Christian	SW Oklahoma	24–7
1978	Angelo St	Elon	34–14
1979	Texas A&I	Central St (Okla.)	20–14
1980	Elon	NE Oklahoma	17–10
1981	Elon	Pittsburg St	3–0
1982	Central St (Okla.)	Mesa	14–11
1983	Carson-Newman	Mesa	36–28
1984	Carson-Newman/Central Arkansas		19–19
1985	Central Arkansas/Hillsdale		10–10
1986	Carson-Newman	Cameron	17–0
1987	Cameron	Carson-Newman	30–2
1988	Carson-Newman	Adams St (Col.)	56–21
1989	Carson-Newman	Emporia St	34–20
1990	Central St (Ohio)	Mesa St	38–16
1991	Central Arkansas	Central St (Ohio)	19–16
1992	Central St (Ohio)	Gardner-Webb	19–16
1993	East Central (Okla.)	Glenville St	49–35
1994	Northeastern St (Okla.)	Arkansas–Pine Bluff	13–12
1995	Central St (Ohio)	Northeastern St (Okla.)	37–7
1996	SW Oklahoma St	Montana Tech	33–31
1997	Findlay	Willamette	14–7
1998	Azusa Pacific	Olivet Nazarene	17–14
1999	Northwestern Oklahoma St	Georgetown (Ky.)	34–26
2000	Georgetown (Ky.)	Northwestern Oklahoma St	20–0
2001	Georgetown (Ky.)	Sioux Falls	49–27
2002	Carroll (Mont.)	Georgetown (Ky.)	28–7
2003	Carroll (Mont.)	Northwestern Oklahoma St	41–28
2004	Carroll (Mont.)	St. Francis (Ind.)	15–13
2005	Carroll (Mont.)	St. Francis (Ind.)	27–10
2006	Sioux Falls (S.D.)	St. Francis (Ind.)	23–19
2007	Carroll (Mont.)	Sioux Falls (S.D.)	17–9
2008	Sioux Falls (S.D.)	Carroll (Mont.)	23–7
2009	Sioux Falls (S.D.)	Lindenwood	25–22

Division II†

Year	Winner	Runner-Up	Score
1970	Westminster (Pa.)	Anderson	21–16
1971	California Lutheran	Westminster (Pa.)	30–14
1972	Missouri Southern	Northwestern (Iowa)	21–14
1973	Northwestern (Iowa)	Glenville St	10–3
1974	Texas Lutheran	Missouri Valley	42–0
1975	Texas Lutheran	California Lutheran	34–8
1976	Westminster (Pa.)	Redlands	20–13
1977	Westminster (Pa.)	California Lutheran	17–9

†In 1997 the NAIA consolidated its two divisions into one.

†Division II (Cont.)

Year	Winner	Runner-Up	Score
1978	Concordia-Moorhead (Minn.)	Findlay	7–0
1979	Findlay	Northwestern (Iowa)	51–6
1980	Pacific Lutheran	Wilmington (Ohio)	38–10
1981	Austin Coll./Conc.-Moorhead (Minn.)		24–24
1982	Linfield	William Jewell	33–15
1983	Northwestern (Iowa)	Pacific Lutheran	25–21
1984	Linfield	Northwestern (Iowa)	33–22
1985	UW-La Crosse	Pacific Lutheran	24–7
1986	Linfield	Baker	17–0
1987	Pacific Lutheran	UW-Stevens Point*	16–16
1988	Westminster (Pa.)	UW-La Crosse	21–14
1989	Westminster (Pa.)	UW-La Crosse	51–30
1990	Peru St	Westminster (Pa.)	17–7
1991	Georgetown (Ky.)	Pacific Lutheran	28–20
1992	Findlay	Linfield	26–13
1993	Pacific Lutheran	Westminster (Pa.)	50–20
1994	Westminster (Pa.)	Pacific Lutheran	27–7
1995	Findlay	Central Washington	21–21
1996	Sioux Falls (S.D.)	Western Washington	47–25

*Forfeited 1987 season due to use of an ineligible player.   †In 1997 the NAIA consolidated its two divisions into one.

Awards

Heisman Memorial Trophy

Awarded to the best college player by the Downtown Athletic Club of New York City. The trophy is named after John W. Heisman, who coached Georgia Tech to the national championship in 1917 and later served as DAC athletic director.

Year	Winner, College, Position	Winner's Season Statistics	Runner-Up, College
1935	Jay Berwanger, Chicago, HB	Rush: 119 Yds: 577 TD: 6	Monk Meyer, Army
1936	Larry Kelley, Yale, E	Rec: 17 Yds: 372 TD: 6	Sam Francis, Nebraska
1937	Clint Frank, Yale, HB	Rush: 157 Yds: 667 TD: 11	Byron White, Colorado
1938	†Davey O'Brien, TCU, QB	Att/Comp: 194/110 Yds: 1733 TD: 19	Marshall Goldberg, Pittsburgh
1939	Nile Kinnick, Iowa, HB	Rush: 106 Yds: 374 TD: 5	Tom Harmon, Michigan
1940	Tom Harmon, Michigan, HB	Rush: 191 Yds: 852 TD: 16	John Kimbrough, Texas A&M
1941	†Bruce Smith, Minnesota, HB	Rush: 98 Yds: 480 TD: 6	Angelo Bertelli, Notre Dame
1942	Frank Sinkwich, Georgia, HB	Att/Comp: 166/84 Yds: 1392 TD: 10	Paul Governali, Columbia
1943	Angelo Bertelli, Notre Dame, QB	Att/Comp: 36/25 Yds: 511 TD: 10	Bob Odell, Pennsylvania
1944	Les Horvath, Ohio State, QB	Rush: 163 Yds: 924 TD: 12	Glenn Davis, Army
1945	*†Doc Blanchard, Army, FB	Rush: 101 Yds: 718 TD: 13	Glenn Davis, Army
1946	Glenn Davis, Army, HB	Rush: 123 Yds: 712 TD: 7	Charley Trippi, Georgia
1947	†John Lujack, Notre Dame, QB	Att/Comp: 109/61 Yds: 777 TD: 9	Bob Chappius, Michigan
1948	*Doak Walker, SMU, HB	Rush: 108 Yds: 532 TD: 8	Charlie Justice, North Carolina
1949	†Leon Hart, Notre Dame, E	Rec: 19 Yds: 257 TD: 5	Charlie Justice, North Carolina
1950	*Vic Janowicz, Ohio St, HB	Att/Comp: 77/32 Yds: 561 TD: 12	Kyle Rote, SMU
1951	Dick Kazmaier, Princeton, HB	Rush: 149 Yds: 861 TD: 9	Hank Lauricella, Tennessee
1952	Billy Vessels, Oklahoma, HB	Rush: 167 Yds: 1072 TD: 17	Jack Scarbath, Maryland
1953	John Lattner, Notre Dame, HB	Rush: 134 Yds: 651 TD: 6	Paul Giel, Minnesota
1954	Alan Ameche, Wisconsin, FB	Rush: 146 Yds: 641 TD: 9	Kurt Burris, Oklahoma
1955	Howard Cassady, Ohio St, HB	Rush: 161 Yds: 958 TD: 15	Jim Swink, TCU
1956	Paul Hornung, Notre Dame, QB	Att/Comp: 111/59 Yds: 917 TD: 3	Johnny Majors, Tennessee
1957	John David Crow, Texas A&M, HB	Rush: 129 Yds: 562 TD: 10	Alex Karras, Iowa
1958	Pete Dawkins, Army, HB	Rush: 78 Yds: 428 TD: 6	Randy Duncan, Iowa
1959	Billy Cannon, LSU, HB	Rush: 139 Yds: 598 TD: 6	Rich Lucas, Penn St
1960	Joe Bellino, Navy, HB	Rush: 168 Yds: 834 TD: 18	Tom Brown, Minnesota
1961	Ernie Davis, Syracuse, HB	Rush: 150 Yds: 823 TD: 15	Bob Ferguson, Ohio St
1962	Terry Baker, Oregon St, QB	Att/Comp: 203/112 Yds: 1738 TD: 15	Jerry Stovall, LSU
1963	*Roger Staubach, Navy, QB	Att/Comp: 161/107 Yds: 1474 TD: 7	Billy Lothridge, Georgia Tech
1964	John Huarte, Notre Dame, QB	Att/Comp: 205/114 Yds: 2062 TD: 16	Jerry Rhome, Tulsa

Heisman Memorial Trophy *(Cont.)*

1965 ...Mike Garrett, USC, HB — Rush: 267 Yds: 1440 TD: 16 — Howard Twilley, Tulsa
1966 ...Steve Spurrier, Florida, QB — Att/Comp: 291/179 Yds: 2012 TD: 16 — Bob Griese, Purdue

1967 ...Gary Beban, UCLA, QB — Att/Comp: 156/87 Yds: 1359 TD: 8 — O.J. Simpson, USC

1968 ...O.J. Simpson, USC, HB — Rush: 383 Yds: 1880 TD: 23 — Leroy Keyes, Purdue
1969 ...Steve Owens, Oklahoma, FB — Rush: 358 Yds: 1523 TD: 23 — Mike Phipps, Purdue
1970 ...Jim Plunkett, Stanford, QB — Att/Comp: 358/191 Yds: 2715 TD: 18 — Joe Theismann, Notre Dame

1971 ...Pat Sullivan, Auburn, QB — Att/Comp: 281/162 Yds: 2012; 20 TD — Ed Marinaro, Cornell
1972 ...Johnny Rodgers, Nebraska, FL — Rec: 55 Yds: 942 TD: 17 — Greg Pruitt, Oklahoma
1973 ...John Cappelletti, Penn St, HB — Rush: 286 Yds: 1522 TD: 17 — John Hicks, Ohio St
1974 ...*Archie Griffin, Ohio St, HB — Rush: 256 Yds: 1695 TD: 12 — Anthony Davis, USC
1975 ...Archie Griffin, Ohio St, HB — Rush: 262 Yds: 1450 TD: 4 — Chuck Muncie, California
1976 ...†Tony Dorsett, Pittsburgh, HB — Rush: 370 Yds: 2150 TD: 23 — Ricky Bell, USC
1977 ...Earl Campbell, Texas, FB — Rush: 267 Yds: 1744 TD: 19 — Terry Miller, Oklahoma St
1978 ...*Billy Sims, Oklahoma, HB — Rush: 231 Yds: 1762 TD: 20 — Chuck Fusina, Penn St
1979 ...Charles White, USC, HB — Rush: 332 Yds: 1803 TD: 19 — Billy Sims, Oklahoma
1980 ...George Rogers, South Carolina, HB — Rush: 324 Yds: 1894 TD: 14 — Hugh Green, Pittsburgh
1981 ...Marcus Allen, USC, HB — Rush: 433 Yds: 2427 TD: 23 — Herschel Walker, Georgia
1982 ...*Herschel Walker, Georgia, HB — Rush: 335 Yds: 1752 TD: 17 — John Elway, Stanford
1983 ...Mike Rozier, Nebraska, HB — Rush: 275 Yds: 2148 TD: 29 — Steve Young, BYU
1984 ...Doug Flutie, Boston College, QB — Att/Comp: 396/233 Yds: 3454 TD: 27 — Keith Byars, Ohio St

1985 ...Bo Jackson, Auburn, HB — Rush: 278 Yds: 1786 TD: 17 — Chuck Long, Iowa
1986 ...Vinny Testaverde, Miami (Fla.), QB — Att/Comp: 276/175 Yds: 2557 TD: 26 — Paul Palmer, Temple

1987 ...Tim Brown, Notre Dame, WR — Rec: 39 Yds: 846 TD: 7 — Don McPherson, Syracuse
1988 ...*Barry Sanders, Oklahoma St, RB — Rush: 344 Yds: 2628 TD: 39 — Rodney Peete, USC
1989 ...*Andre Ware, Houston, QB — Att/Comp: 578/365 Yds: 4699 TD: 46 — Anthony Thompson, Indiana

1990 ...*Ty Detmer, BYU, QB — Att/Comp: 562/361 Yds: 5188 TD: 41 — Raghib Ismail, Notre Dame

1991 ...*Desmond Howard, Michigan, WR — Rec: 61 Yds: 950 TD: 23 — Casey Weldon, Florida St
1992 ...Gino Torretta, Miami (FL), QB — Att/Comp: 402/228 Yds: 3060 TD: 19 — Marshall Faulk, San Diego St

1993 ...†Charlie Ward, Florida St, QB — Att/Comp: 380/264 Yds: 3032 TD: 27 — Heath Shuler, Tennessee

1994 ...Rashaan Salaam, Colorado, RB — Rush: 298 Yds: 2055 TD: 24 — Ki-Jana Carter, Penn St
1995 ...Eddie George, Ohio State, RB — Rush: 303 Yds: 1826 TD: 23 — Tommie Frazier, Nebraska
1996 ...†Danny Wuerffel, Florida, QB — Att/Comp: 360/207 Yds: 3625 TD: 39 — Troy Davis, Iowa St

1997 ...†Charles Woodson, Michigan, CB/WR — 7 interceptions; Rec: 11 Yds: 231 TD: 4 — Peyton Manning, Tennessee

1998 ...Ricky Williams, Texas, RB — Rush: 361 Yds: 2124 TD: 28 — Michael Bishop, Kansas St
1999 ...Ron Dayne, Wisconsin, RB — Rush: 303 Yds: 1834 TD: 19 — Joe Hamilton, Georgia Tech
2000 ...Chris Weinke, Florida St, QB — Att/Comp: 431/266 Yds: 4167 TD: 33 — Josh Heupel, Oklahoma

2001 ...Eric Crouch, Nebraska, QB — Att/Comp: 189/105 Yds: 1510 TD: 7; Rush: 1115 Yds, 18 TD — Rex Grossman, Florida

2002 ...Carson Palmer, USC, QB — Att/Comp: 450/228 Yds: 3639 TD: 32 — Brad Banks, Iowa

2003 ... Jason White, Oklahoma, QB — Pct. Comp: 64; 3744 Yds; TD: 40 — Larry Fitzgerald, Pittsburgh

2004 ... *†Matt Leinart, USC, QB — Att/Comp: 269/412 Yds: 2990 TD: 28 — Adrian Peterson, Oklahoma

2005 ... **Vacated — — Vince Young, Texas
2006 ... Troy Smith, Ohio State, QB — Att/Comp: 311/203 Yds: 2542 TD: 30 — Darren McFadden, Arkansas

2007 ... ^Tim Tebow, Florida, QB — Att/Comp: 350/234 Yds: 3286 TD: 32 — Darren McFadden, Arkansas
2008 ... ^Sam Bradford, Oklahoma, QB — Att/Comp: 483/328 Yds: 4720 TD: 50 — Colt McCoy, Texas

2009 ... ^†Mark Ingram, Alabama, RB — Rush: 249 Yds: 1,542 TD: 15 — Toby Gerhart, Stanford

*Juniors; ^Sophomore; (all others seniors). †Winners who played for national championship teams the same year. Note: Former Heisman winners and national media cast votes, with ballots allowing for three names (3 points for first, 2 for second and 1 for third). **In September 2010, Reggie Bush forfeited the 2005 Heisman Trophy he won while at USC.

Maxwell Award

Given to the outstanding college player of the year by the Maxwell Club of Philadelphia.

Year	Player, College, Position	Year	Player, College, Position
1937	Clint Frank, Yale, HB	1974	Steve Joachim, Temple, QB
1938	Davey O'Brien, TCU, QB	1975	Archie Griffin, Ohio St, RB
1939	Nile Kinnick, Iowa, HB	1976	Tony Dorsett, Pittsburgh, RB
1940	Tom Harmon, Michigan, HB	1977	Ross Browner, Notre Dame, DE
1941	Bill Dudley, Virginia, HB	1978	Chuck Fusina, Penn St, QB
1942	Paul Governali, Columbia, QB	1979	Charles White, USC, RB
1943	Bob Odell, Pennsylvania, HB	1980	Hugh Green, Pittsburgh, DE
1944	Glenn Davis, Army, HB	1981	Marcus Allen, USC, RB
1945	Doc Blanchard, Army, FB	1982	Herschel Walker, Georgia, RB
1946	Charley Trippi, Georgia, HB	1983	Mike Rozier, Nebraska, RB
1947	Doak Walker, SMU, HB	1984	Doug Flutie, Boston College, QB
1948	Chuck Bednarik, Pennsylvania, C	1985	Chuck Long, Iowa, QB
1949	Leon Hart, Notre Dame, E	1986	Vinny Testaverde, Miami (Fla.), QB
1950	Reds Bagnell, Pennsylvania, HB	1987	Don McPherson, Syracuse, QB
1951	Dick Kazmaier, Princeton, HB	1988	Barry Sanders, Oklahoma St, RB
1952	John Lattner, Notre Dame, HB	1989	Anthony Thompson, Indiana, RB
1953	John Lattner, Notre Dame, HB	1990	Ty Detmer, BYU, QB
1954	Ron Beagle, Navy, E	1991	Desmond Howard, Michigan, WR
1955	Howard Cassady, Ohio St, HB	1992	Gino Torretta, Miami (Fla.), QB
1956	Tommy McDonald, Oklahoma, HB	1993	Charlie Ward, Florida St, QB
1957	Bob Reifsnyder, Navy, T	1994	Kerry Collins, Penn St, QB
1958	Pete Dawkins, Army, HB	1995	Eddie George, Ohio St, RB
1959	Rich Lucas, Penn St, QB	1996	Danny Wuerffel, Florida, QB
1960	Joe Bellino, Navy, HB	1997	Peyton Manning, Tennessee, QB
1961	Bob Ferguson, Ohio St, FB	1998	Ricky Williams, Texas, RB
1962	Terry Baker, Oregon St, QB	1999	Ron Dayne, Wisconsin, RB
1963	Roger Staubach, Navy, QB	2000	Drew Brees, Purdue, QB
1964	Glenn Ressler, Penn St, C	2001	Ken Dorsey, Miami (Fla.), QB
1965	Tommy Nobis, Texas, LB	2002	Larry Johnson, Penn St, RB
1966	Jim Lynch, Notre Dame, LB	2003	Eli Manning, Mississippi, QB
1967	Gary Beban, UCLA, QB	2004	Jason White, Oklahoma, QB
1968	O.J. Simpson, USC, RB	2005	Vince Young, Texas, QB
1969	Mike Reid, Penn St, DT	2006	Brady Quinn, Notre Dame, QB
1970	Jim Plunkett, Stanford, QB	2007	Tim Tebow, Florida, QB
1971	Ed Marinaro, Cornell, RB	2008	Tim Tebow, Florida, QB
1972	Brad Van Pelt, Michigan St, DB	2009	Colt McCoy, Texas, QB
1973	John Cappelletti, Penn St, RB		

Davey O'Brien National Quarterback Award

Given to the top quarterback in the nation by the Davey O'Brien Educational and Charitable Trust of Fort Worth. Named for TCU Hall of Fame quarterback Davey O'Brien (1936–38).

Year	Player, College	Year	Player, College
1981	Jim McMahon, BYU	1996	Danny Wuerffel, Florida
1982	Todd Blackledge, Penn St	1997	Peyton Manning, Tennessee
1983	Steve Young, BYU	1998	Michael Bishop, Kansas St
1984	Doug Flutie, Boston College	1999	Joe Hamilton, Georgia Tech
1985	Chuck Long, Iowa	2000	Chris Weinke, Florida St
1986	Vinny Testaverde, Miami (Fla.)	2001	Eric Crouch, Nebraska
1987	Don McPherson, Syracuse	2002	Brad Banks, Iowa
1988	Troy Aikman, UCLA	2003	Jason White, Oklahoma
1989	Andre Ware, Houston	2004	Jason White, Oklahoma
1990	Ty Detmer, BYU	2005	Vince Young, Texas
1991	Ty Detmer, BYU	2006	Troy Smith, Ohio St
1992	Gino Torretta, Miami (Fla.)	2007	Tim Tebow, Florida
1993	Charlie Ward, Florida St	2008	Sam Bradford, Oklahoma
1994	Kerry Collins, Penn St	2009	Colt McCoy, Texas
1995	Danny Wuerffel, Florida		

Note: Originally honored the outstanding football player in the Southwest as follows: 1977—Earl Campbell, Texas, RB; 1978—Billy Sims, Oklahoma, RB; 1979—Mike Singletary, Baylor, LB; 1980—Mike Singletary, Baylor, LB.

Vince Lombardi/Rotary Award

Given to the outstanding college lineman of the year, the award is sponsored by the Rotary Club of Houston.

Year	Player, College, Position	Year	Player, College, Position
1970	Jim Stillwagon, Ohio St, MG	1990	Chris Zorich, Notre Dame, NG
1971	Walt Patulski, Notre Dame, DE	1991	Steve Emtman, Washington, DT
1972	Rich Glover, Nebraska, MG	1992	Marvin Jones, Florida St, LB
1973	John Hicks, Ohio St, OT	1993	Aaron Taylor, Notre Dame, OT
1974	Randy White, Maryland, DT	1994	Warren Sapp, Miami (Fla.), DT
1975	Lee Roy Selmon, Oklahoma, DT	1995	Orlando Pace, Ohio St, OT
1976	Wilson Whitley, Houston, DT	1996	Orlando Pace, Ohio St, OT
1977	Ross Browner, Notre Dame, DE	1997	Grant Wistrom, Nebraska, DE
1978	Bruce Clark, Penn St, DT	1998	Dat Nguyen, Texas A&M, LB
1979	Brad Budde, USC, G	1999	Corey Moore, Virginia Tech, DE
1980	Hugh Green, Pittsburgh, DE	2000	Jamal Reynolds, Florida St, DE
1981	Kenneth Sims, Texas, DT	2001	Julius Peppers, North Carolina, DE
1982	Dave Rimington, Nebraska, C	2002	Terrell Suggs, Arizona St, DL
1983	Dean Steinkuhler, Nebraska, G	2003	Tommie Harris, Oklahoma, DT
1984	Tony Degrate, Texas, DT	2004	David Pollack, Georgia, DE
1985	Tony Casillas, Oklahoma, NG	2005	A.J. Hawk, Ohio St, LB
1986	Cornelius Bennett, Alabama, LB	2006	LaMarr Woodley, Michigan, DE
1987	Chris Spielman, Ohio St, LB	2007	Glenn Dorsey, LSU, DT
1988	Tracy Rocker, Auburn, DT	2008	Brian Orakpo, Texas, DE
1989	Percy Snow, Michigan St, LB	2009	Ndamukong Suh, Nebraska, DT

Outland Trophy

Given to the outstanding interior lineman, selected by the Football Writers Association of America.

Year	Player, College, Position	Year	Player, College, Position
1946	George Connor, Notre Dame, T	1978	Greg Roberts, Oklahoma, G
1947	Joe Steffy, Army, G	1979	Jim Ritcher, North Carolina St, C
1948	Bill Fischer, Notre Dame, G	1980	Mark May, Pittsburgh, OT
1949	Ed Bagdon, Michigan St, G	1981	Dave Rimington, Nebraska, C
1950	Bob Gain, Kentucky, T	1982	Dave Rimington, Nebraska, C
1951	Jim Weatherall, Oklahoma, T	1983	Dean Steinkuhler, Nebraska, G
1952	Dick Modzelewski, Maryland, T	1984	Bruce Smith, Virginia Tech, DT
1953	J.D. Roberts, Oklahoma, G	1985	Mike Ruth, Boston College, NG
1954	Bill Brooks, Arkansas, G	1986	Jason Buck, BYU, DT
1955	Calvin Jones, Iowa, G	1987	Chad Hennings, Air Force, DT
1956	Jim Parker, Ohio St, G	1988	Tracy Rocker, Auburn, DT
1957	Alex Karras, Iowa, T	1989	Mohammed Elewonibi, BYU, G
1958	Zeke Smith, Auburn, G	1990	Russell Maryland, Miami (Fla.), DT
1959	Mike McGee, Duke, T	1991	Steve Emtman, Washington, DT
1960	Tom Brown, Minnesota, G	1992	Will Shields, Nebraska, G
1961	Merlin Olsen, Utah St, T	1993	Rob Waldrop, Arizona, NG
1962	Bobby Bell, Minnesota, T	1994	Zach Wiegert, Nebraska, G
1963	Scott Appleton, Texas, T	1995	Jonathan Ogden, UCLA, OT
1964	Steve DeLong, Tennessee, T	1996	Orlando Pace, Ohio St, OT
1965	Tommy Nobis, Texas, G	1997	Aaron Taylor, Nebraska, G
1966	Loyd Phillips, Arkansas, T	1998	Kris Farris, UCLA, OL
1967	Ron Yary, USC, T	1999	Chris Samuels, Alabama, OL
1968	Bill Stanfill, Georgia, T	2000	John Henderson, Tennessee, DT
1969	Mike Reid, Penn St, DT	2001	Bryant McKinnie, Miami (Fla.), OT
1970	Jim Stillwagon, Ohio St, MG	2002	Rien Long, Washington St, DL
1971	Larry Jacobson, Nebraska, DT	2003	Robert Gallery, Iowa, OT
1972	Rich Glover, Nebraska, MG	2004	Jammal Brown, Oklahoma, OT
1973	John Hicks, Ohio St, OT	2005	Greg Eslinger, Minnesota, LB
1974	Randy White, Maryland, DE	2006	Joe Thomas, Wisconsin, OT
1975	Lee Roy Selmon, Oklahoma, DT	2007	Glenn Dorsey, LSU, DT
1976	Ross Browner, Notre Dame, DE	2008	Andre Smith, Alabama, OT
1977	Brad Shearer, Texas, DT	2009	Ndamukong Suh, Nebraska, DT

Butkus Award

Given to the top collegiate linebacker, the award was established by the Downtown Athletic Club of Orlando and named for college Hall of Famer Dick Butkus of Illinois.

Year	Player, College	Year	Player, College
1985	Brian Bosworth, Oklahoma	1998	Chris Claiborne, USC
1986	Brian Bosworth, Oklahoma	1999	LaVar Arrington, Penn St
1987	Paul McGowan, Florida St	2000	Dan Morgan, Miami (Fla.)
1988	Derrick Thomas, Alabama	2001	Rocky Calmus, Oklahoma
1989	Percy Snow, Michigan St	2002	E.J. Henderson, Maryland
1990	Alfred Williams, Colorado	2003	Teddy Lehman, Oklahoma
1991	Erick Anderson, Michigan	2004	Derrick Johnson, Texas
1992	Marvin Jones, Florida St	2005	Paul Posluszny, Penn State
1993	Trev Alberts, Nebraska	2006	Patrick Willis, Mississippi
1994	Dana Howard, Illinois	2007	James Laurinaitis, Ohio St
1995	Kevin Hardy, Illinois	2008	Aaron Curry, Wake Forest
1996	Matt Russell, Colorado	2009	Rolando McClain, Alabama
1997	Andy Katzenmoyer, Ohio St		

Jim Thorpe Award

Given to the best defensive back of the year, the award is presented by the Jim Thorpe Athletic Club of Oklahoma City.

Year	Player, College	Year	Player, College
1986	Thomas Everett, Baylor	1998	Antoine Winfield, Ohio St
1987	Bennie Blades, Miami (Fla.)	1999	Tyrone Carter, Minnesota
	Rickey Dixon, Oklahoma	2000	Jamar Fletcher, Wisconsin
1988	Deion Sanders, Florida St	2001	Roy Williams, Oklahoma
1989	Mark Carrier, USC	2002	Terence Newman, Kansas St
1990	Darryl Lewis, Arizona	2003	Derrick Strait, Oklahoma
1991	Terrell Buckley, Florida St	2004	Carlos Rogers, Auburn
1992	Deon Figures, Colorado	2005	Michael Huff, Texas
1993	Antonio Langham, Alabama	2006	Aaron Ross, Texas
1994	Chris Hudson, Colorado	2007	Antoine Cason, Arizona
1995	Greg Myers, Colorado St	2008	Malcolm Jenkins, Ohio St
1996	Lawrence Wright, Florida	2009	Eric Berry, Tennessee
1997	Charles Woodson, Michigan		

Walter Payton Player of the Year Award

Given to the top FCS (I-AA) player, voted by Div. I-AA sports information directors. Sponsored by Sports Network.

Year	Player, College, Position	Year	Player, College, Position
1987	Kenny Gamble, Colgate, RB	1999	Adrian Peterson, Georgia Southern, RB
1988	Dave Meggett, Towson St, RB	2000	Louis Ivory, Furman, RB
1989	John Friesz, Idaho, QB	2001	Brian Westbrook, Villanova, RB
1990	Walter Dean, Grambling, RB	2002	Tony Romo, Eastern Ilinois, QB
1991	Jamie Martin, Weber St, QB	2003	Jamaal Branch, Colgate, RB
1992	Michael Payton, Marshall, QB	2004	Lang Campbell, William & Mary, QB
1993	Doug Nussmeier, Idaho, QB	2005	Erik Meyer, Eastern Washington, QB
1994	Steve McNair, Alcorn St, QB	2006	Ricky Santos, New Hampshire, QB
1995	Dave Dickenson, Montana, QB	2007	Jayson Foster, Georgia Southern, QB
1996	Archie Amerson, Northern Arizona, RB	2008	Armanti Edwards, Appalachian St, QB
1997	Brian Finneran, Villanova, WR	2009	Armanti Edwards, Appalachian St, QB
1998	Jerry Azumah, New Hampshire, RB		

Career

SCORING

Most Points Scored: 468—Travis Prentice, Miami (Ohio), 1996–99
Most Points Scored per Game: 12.1—Marshall Faulk, San Diego St, 1991–93
Most Touchdowns Scored: 78—Travis Prentice, Miami (Ohio), 1996–99 (73 rushing, 5 receiving)
Most Touchdowns Scored per Game: 2.0—Marshall Faulk, San Diego St, 1991–93
Most Touchdowns Scored, Rushing: 73—Travis Prentice, Miami (Ohio), 1996–99
Most Touchdowns Scored, Passing: 134—Graham Harrell, Texas Tech, 2005–08
Most Touchdowns Scored, Receiving: 60—Jarrett Dillard, Rice, 2005–08
Most Touchdowns Scored, Interception Returns: 5—Ken Thomas, San Jose St, 1979–82; Jackie Walker, Tennessee, 1969–71; Deltha O'Neal, California, 1996–99; Darrent Williams, Okla St, 2001–04
Most Touchdowns Scored, Punt Returns: 8—Wes Welker, Texas Tech, 2000–03; Antonio Perkins, Oklahoma, 2001–04
Most Touchdowns Scored, Kickoff Returns: 6—Anthony Davis, USC, 1972–74; Ashlan Davis, Tulsa, 2004–05

TOTAL OFFENSE

Most Plays: 2,587—Timmy Chang, Hawaii, 2000–04
Most Plays per Game: 50.1—Kliff Kingsbury, Texas Tech, 1999–2002
Most Yards Gained: 16,910—Timmy Chang, Hawaii, 2000–04 (17,072 rushing)
Most Yards Gained per Game: 387.9—Colt Brennan, Hawaii, 2005–07
Most 300+ Yard Games: 33 —Ty Detmer, BYU, 1988–91

RUSHING

Most Rushes: 1,215—Steve Bartalo, Colorado St, 1983–86 (4813 yds)
Most Rushes per Game: 34.0—Ed Marinaro, Cornell, 1969–71
Most Yards Gained: 6,397—Ron Dayne, Wisconsin, 1996–99
Most Yards Gained per Game: 174.6—Ed Marinaro, Cornell, 1969–71
Most 100+ Yard Games: 34—DeAngelo Williams, Memphis, 2002–05
Most 200+ Yard Games: 11—Marcus Allen, USC, 1978–81; Ricky Williams, Texas, 1995–98; Ron Dayne, Wisconsin, 1996–99

SPECIAL TEAMS

Highest Punt Return Average: 23.6—Jack Mitchell, Oklahoma, 1946–48
Highest Kickoff Return Average: 36.2—Forrest Hall, San Francisco, 1946–47
Highest Average Yards per Punt: 46.3—Todd Sauerbrun, West Virginia, 1991–93 (150–199 punts). 45.3—Ryan Plackemeier, Wake Forest, 2002–05 (200–250 punts). 45.2—Daniel Sepulveda, Baylor, 2003–06 (250+ punts).

PASSING

Highest Passing Efficiency Rating: 168.9—Ryan Dinwiddie, Boise St, 2000–03
Most Passes Attempted: 2,436—Timmy Chang, Hawaii, 2000–04
Most Passes Attempted per Game: 47.0—Tim Rattay, Louisiana Tech, 1997–99
Most Passes Completed: 1,403—Graham Harrell, Texas Tech, 2005–08
Most Passes Completed per Game: 31.2—Graham Harrell, Texas Tech, 2005–08
*Highest Completion Percentage: 70.4—Colt Brennan, Hawaii, 2005–07
Most Yards Gained: 17,072—Timmy Chang, Hawaii, 2000–04
Most Yards Gained per Game: 386.2—Tim Rattay, Louisiana Tech, 1997–99 (3 years); 351.0—Graham Harrell, Texas Tech, 2005–08 (4 years)

RECEIVING

Most Passes Caught: 316—Taylor Stubblefield, Purdue, 2001–04
Most Passes Caught per Game: 10.5—Emmanuel Hazard, Houston, 1989–90
Most Yards Gained: 5,005—Trevor Insley, Nevada, 1996–99
Most Yards Gained per Game: 140.9—Alex Van Dyke, Nevada, 1994–95
†Highest Average Gain per Reception: 22.0—Herman Moore, Virginia, 1988–90

ALL-PURPOSE RUNNING

Most Plays: 1,347—Steve Bartalo, Colorado St, 1983–86 (1,215 rushes, 132 receptions)
Most Yards Gained: 7,573—DeAngelo Williams, Memphis, 2002–05 (6,026 rushing, 723 receiving, 824 KO retrurns)
Most Yards Gained per Game: 237.8—Ryan Benjamin, Pacific, 1990–92
Highest Average Gain per Play: 17.4—Anthony Carter, Michigan, 1979–82

INTERCEPTIONS

Most Passes Intercepted: 29—Al Brosky, Illinois, 1950–52
Most Passes Intercepted per Game: 1.1—Al Brosky, Illinois, 1950–52
Most Yards on Interception Returns: 501—Terrell Buckley, Florida St, 1989–91
Highest Average Gain per Interception: 26.5—Tom Pridemore, West Virginia, 1975–77

*Minimum 1,000 attempts.
†Minimum 105 receptions.

Single Season

SCORING

Most Points Scored: 234—Barry Sanders, Oklahoma St, 1988
Most Points Scored per Game: 21.3—Barry Sanders, Oklahoma St, 1988
Most Touchdowns Scored: 39—Barry Sanders, Oklahoma St, 1988
Most Touchdowns Scored, Rushing: 37—Barry Sanders, Oklahoma St, 1988
Most Touchdowns Scored, Passing: 58—Colt Brennan, Hawaii, 2006
Most Touchdowns Scored, Receiving: 27—Troy Edwards, Louisiana Tech, 1998
Most Touchdowns Scored, Interception Returns: 4—Deltha O'Neal, California, 1999
Most Touchdowns Scored, Punt Returns: 5—Chad Owens, Hawaii, 2004
Most Touchdowns Scored, Kickoff Returns: 5—Ashlan Davis, Tulsa, 2004

TOTAL OFFENSE

Most Plays: 814—Kliff Kingsbury, Texas Tech, 2002
Most Yards Gained: 5,976—B.J. Symons, Texas Tech, 2003
Most Yards Gained per Game: 474.6—David Klingler, Houston, 1990
Most 300+ Yard Games: 14—Colt Brennan, Hawaii, 2006; Paul Smith, Tulsa, 2007

RUSHING

Most Rushes: 450—Kevin Smith, Central Florida, 2007
Most Rushes per Game: 39.6—Ed Marinaro, Cornell, 1971
Most Yards Gained: 2,628—Barry Sanders, Oklahoma St, 1988
Most Yards Gained per Game: 238.9—Barry Sanders, Oklahoma St, 1988
Most 100+ Yard Games: 13—Shonn Green, Iowa, 2008

PASSING

Highest Passing Efficiency Rating: 186.0—Colt Brennan, Hawaii, 2006
Most Passes Attempted: 719—B.J. Symons, Texas Tech, 2003
Most Passes Attempted per Game: 58.5—David Klingler, Houston, 1990
Most Passes Completed: 512—Graham Harrell, Texas Tech, 2007

PASSING *(Cont.)*

Most Passes Completed per Game: 39.4—Graham Harrell, Texas Tech, 2007
Highest Completion Percentage: 76.7—Colt McCoy, Texas, 2008
Most Yards Gained: 5,140—David Klingler, Houston, 1990 (11 games); 5,336—B.J. Symons, Texas Tech, 2003 (12 games); 5,833—B.J. Symons, Texas Tech, 2003 (13 games; 5,829—Case Keenum, Houston, 2009 (14 games)
Most Yards Gained per Game: 467.3—David Klingler, Houston, 1990

RECEIVING

Most Passes Caught: 155—Freddie Barnes, Bowling Green, 2009
Most Passes Caught per Game: 13.4—Howard Twilley, Tulsa, 1965
Most Yards Gained: 2,060—Trevor Insley, Nevada, 1999
Most Yards Gained per Game: 187.3—Trevor Insley, Nevada, 1999
Highest Average Gain per Reception: 31.9—Brennan Marion, Tulsa, 2007 (min. 30 receptions)

ALL-PURPOSE RUNNING

Most Plays: 432—Marcus Allen, USC, 1981
Most Yards Gained: 3,250—Barry Sanders, Oklahoma St, 1988
Most Yards Gained per Game: 295.5—Barry Sanders, Oklahoma St, 1988
Highest Average Gain per Play: 22.3—Chris Owusu, Stanford, 2009

INTERCEPTIONS

Most Passes Intercepted: 14—Al Worley, Washington, 1968
Most Yards on Interception Returns: 302 — Charles Phillips, USC, 1974
Highest Average Gain per Interception: 51.8 — Norm Thompson, Utah, 1969

SPECIAL TEAMS

Highest Punt Return Average: 28.5—Maurice Drew, UCLA, 2005
Highest Kickoff Return Average: 40.1 — Paul Allen, BYU, 1961
Highest Average Yards per Punt: 50.3 — Chad Kessler, LSU, 1997

Single Game

SCORING

Most Points Scored: 48—Howard Griffith, Illinois, 1990 (vs Southern Illinois)
Most Field Goals: 7—Dale Klein, Nebraska, 1985 (vs Missouri); Mike Prindle, Western Michigan, 1984 (vs Marshall)
Most Extra Points (Kick): 13—Derek Mahoney, Fresno St, 1991 (vs New Mexico); Terry Leiweke, Houston, 1968 (vs Tulsa)
Most Extra Points (2-Pts): 6—Jim Pilot, New Mexico St, 1961 (vs Hardin-Simmons), all 6 rush

PASSING

Most Passes Completed: 58—Andy Schmitt, Eastern Michigan, 2008 (vs Central Michigan)
Most Yards Gained: 716—David Klingler, Houston, 1990 (vs Arizona St)
Most Touchdown Passes: 11—David Klingler, Houston, 1990 [vs Eastern Washington (I-AA)]

TOTAL OFFENSE

Most Yards Gained: 732—David Klingler, Houston, 1990 (vs Arizona St); (716 pass, 16 rush)

RUSHING

Most Yards Gained: 406—LaDainian Tomlinson, TCU, 1999 (vs UTEP)
Most Touchdowns Rushed: 8—Howard Griffith, Illinois, 1990 (vs Southern Illinois)

RECEIVING

Most Passes Caught: 23—Randy Gatewood, UNLV, 1994 (vs Idaho); Tyler Jones, Eastern Michigan, 2008 (vs Central Michigan)
Most Yards Gained: 405—Troy Edwards, Louisiana Tech, 1998 (vs Nebraska)
Most Touchdown Catches: 7—Rashaun Woods, Oklahoma St, 2003 (vs SMU)

*Minimum 1,000 attempts.

Career

SCORING

Most Points Scored: 544—Brian Westbrook, Villanova, 1997–98, 2000-01
Most Touchdowns Scored: 89—Brian Westbrook, Villanova, 1997–98, 2000-01
Most Touchdowns Scored, Rushing: 84—Adrian Peterson, Georgia Southern, 1998–2001
Most Touchdowns Scored, Passing: 140—Bruce Eugene, Grambling St, 2001–05
Most Touchdowns Scored, Receiving: 58—David Ball, New Hampshire, 2003–06

RUSHING

Most Rushes: 1,240—Jordan Scott, Colgate, 2005–08
Most Rushes per Game: 38.2—Arnold Mickens, Butler, 1994–95
Most Yards Gained: 6,559—Adrian Peterson, Georgia Southern, 1998–2001
Most Yards Gained per Game: 190.7—Arnold Mickens, Butler, 1994–95 (2 years); 164.5—Adrian Peterson, Georgia Southern, 1998–2000 (3 years); 156.2—Adrian Peterson, Georgia Southern, 1998–2001 (4 years)

PASSING

Highest Passing Efficiency Rating: 170.8—Shawn Knight, William & Mary, 1991–94 (3 years); 176.7—Josh Johnson, San Diego, 2004–07 (4 years)
Most Passes Attempted: 1,680—Marcus Brady, Cal St-Northridge, 1998–2001; Steve McNair, Alcorn St, 1991–94
Most Passes Completed: 1,122—Ricky Santos, New Hampsire, 2004–07
Most Passes Completed per Game: 26.5—Chris Sanders, Chattanooga, 1999–2000
Highest Completion Percentage: 69.6—Eric Sanders, Northern Iowa, 2004–07
Most Yards Gained: 14,496—Steve McNair, Alcorn St, 1991–94
Most Yards Gained per Game: 350.0—Neil Lomax, Portland St, 1978–80

RECEIVING

Most Passes Caught: 317—Jacquay Nunnally, Florida A&M, 1997–2000
Most Yards Gained: 4,693—Jerry Rice, Mississippi Valley St, 1981–84
Most Yards Gained per Game: 114.5—Jerry Rice, Mississippi Valley St, 1981–84 (min. 3,000 yds)
Highest Average Gain per Reception: 22.0—Dedric Ward, Northern Iowa, 1993–96 (min. 125 rec.)

Single Season

SCORING

Most Points Scored: 234—Omar Cuff, Delaware, 2007
Most Touchdowns Scored: 39—Omar Cuff, Delaware, 2007 (15 games)
Most Touchdowns Scored, Rushing: 35—Omar Cuff, Delaware, 2007
Most Touchdowns Scored, Passing: 56—Willie Totten, Mississippi Valley St, 1984; Bruce Eugene, Grambling St, 2005
Most Touchdowns Scored, Receiving: 27—Jerry Rice, Mississippi Valley St, 1984

PASSING

Highest Passing Efficiency Rating: 204.6—Shawn Knight, William & Mary, 1993
Most Passes Attempted: 598—Jeremy Moses, Stephen F. Austin, 2008
Most Passes Completed: 385—Brett Gordon, Villanova, 2002; Jeremy Moses, Stephen F. Austin, 2009
Most Passes Completed per Game: 32.4—Willie Totten, Mississippi Valley St, 1984
Highest Completion Percentage: 75.2—Eric Sanders, Northern Iowa, 2007
Most Yards Gained: 4,863—Steve McNair, Alcorn St, 1994
Most Yards Gained per Game: 455.7—Willie Totten, Mississippi Valley St, 1984

RUSHING

Most Rushes: 450—Jamaal Branch, Colgate, 2003
Most Rushes per Game: 40.9—Arnold Mickens, Butler, 1994
Most Yards Gained: 2,326—Jamaal Branch, Colgate, 2003
Most Yards Gained per Game: 225.5—Arnold Mickens, Butler, 1994

RECEIVING

Most Passes Caught: 123—Terrell Hudgins, Elon, 2009
Most Yards Gained: 1,712—Eddie Conti, Delaware, 1998
Most Yards Gained per Game: 168.2—Jerry Rice, Mississippi Valley St, 1984
Highest Average Gain per Reception: 28.9—Mikhael Ricks, Stephen F. Austin, 1997; (min. 35 receptions); 20.7—Golden Tate, Tennessee St, 1983 (min 60 receptions)

Single Game

SCORING

Most Points Scored: 42—Omar Cuff, Delaware, 2007 (vs William & Mary); Jesse Burton, McNeese St, 1998 (vs Southern Utah); Archie Amerson, Northern Arizona, 1996 (vs Weber St)
Most Field Goals: 8—Goran Lingmerth, Northern Arizona, 1986 (vs Idaho)

RUSHING

Most Yards Gained: 437—Maurice Hicks, North Carolina A&T, 2001 (vs Morgan St)
Most Touchdowns Rushed: 7—Archie Amerson, Northern Arizona, 1996 (vs Weber St)

PASSING

Most Passes Completed: 57—Jeremy Moses, Stephen F. Austin, 2008, (vs. Sam Houston St)
Most Yards Gained: 624—Jamie Martin, Weber St, 1991 (vs Idaho St)
Most Touchdown Passes: 9—Willie Totten, Mississippi Valley St, 1984 (vs Kentucky St); Drew Hubel, Portland St, 2007 (vs Weber St)

RECEIVING

Most Passes Caught: 24—Chas Gessner, Brown, 2002, (vs Rhode Island); Jerry Rice, Mississippi Valley St, 1983 (vs Southern–Birmingham)
Most Yards Gained: 376—Kassim Osgood, Cal Poly, 2000 (vs Northern Iowa)
Most Touchdown Catches: 6—Cos DeMatteo, Chattanooga, 2000 (vs Mississippi Valley St)

NCAA Division II Individual Records

Career

SCORING

Most Points Scored: 656—Germaine Rice, Pittsburg St, 2003–06
Most Touchdowns Scored: 109—Germaine Rice, Pittsburg St, 2003–06
Most Touchdowns Scored, Rushing: 107—Germaine Rice, Pittsburg St, 2003–06
Most Touchdowns Scored, Passing: 148—Jimmy Terwilliger, East Stroudsburg, 2003–06
Most Touchdowns Scored, Receiving: 78—Dallas Mall, Bentley, 2001–04

RUSHING

Most Rushes: 1,271—Xavier Omon, NW Missouri St, 2004–07
Most Rushes per Game: 29.8—Bernie Peeters, Luther, 1968–71
Most Yards Gained: 7,962—Danny Woodhead, Chadron St, 2004–07
Most Yards Gained per Game: 183.4—Anthony Gray, Western New Mexico, 1997–98

PASSING

Highest Passing Efficiency Rating: 170.7—Jimmy Terwilliger, East Stroudsburg, 2003–06 (Min. 750 comp.)
Most Passes Attempted: 1,898—Andrew Webb, Fort Lewis, 2000–03

PASSING *(Cont.)*

Most Passes Completed: 1,055—Ted Schlafke, Wayne St (Neb.), 2005–08
Most Passes Completed per Game: 25.9—Evan Gray, Missouri S&T*, 2003–05
Highest Completion Percentage: 69.0—Chris Hatcher, Valdosta St, 1991–94 (min. 1,000 att.)
Most Yards Gained: 14,350—Jimmy Terwilliger, East Stroudsburg, 2003–06
Most Yards Gained per Game: 323.7—Dusty Bonner, Valdosta St, 2000–01

RECEIVING

Most Passes Caught: 323—Clarence Coleman, Ferris St, 1998–2001
Most Yards Gained: 4,983—Clarence Coleman, Ferris St, 1998–2001
Most Yards Gained per Game: 160.8—Chris George, Glenville St, 1993–94
Highest Average Gain per Reception: 23.2—Romar Crenshaw, SE Oklahoma, 2000–03 (min. 135 receptions)

*Missouri S&T was formerly known as Missouri-Rolla.

Single Season

SCORING

Most Points Scored: 234—Bernard Scott, Abilene Christian, 2007

Most Touchdowns Scored: 39—Bernard Scott, Abilene Christian, 2007

Most Touchdowns Scored, Rushing: 37—Xavier Omon, NW Missouri St, 2007

Most Touchdowns Scored, Passing: 54—Dusty Bonner, Valdosta St, 2000

Most Touchdowns Scored, Receiving: 35—David Kircus, Grand Valley St, 2002

RUSHING

Most Rushes: 385—Joe Gough, Wayne St (Mich.), 1994

Most Rushes per Game: 38.6—Mark Perkins, Hobart, 1968

Most Yards Gained: 2,756—Danny Woodhead, Chadron St, 2006

Most Yards Gained per Game: 222.0—Anthony Gray, Western New Mexico, 1997

PASSING

Highest Passing Efficiency Rating: 221.63—Curt Anes, Grand Valley St, 2001 (min. 100 comp.); 196.5—Dusty Bonner, Valdosta St, 2001 (min. 200 comp.)

PASSING *(Cont.)*

Most Passes Attempted: 583—Dalton Bell, West Texas A&M, 2006

Most Passes Completed: 386—Dalton Bell, West Texas A&M, 2006

Most Passes Completed per Game: 32.4—Lance Funderburk, Valdosta St, 1995

Highest Completion Percentage: 74.7—Chris Hatcher, Valdosta St, 1994 (min. 250 att.)

Most Yards Gained: 5,097—Keith Null, West Texas A&M, 2008

Most Yards Gained per Game: 393.4—Grady Benton, West Texas A&M, 1994

RECEIVING

Most Passes Caught: 143—Nick Smart, Southwest Baptist, 2007

Most Yards Gained: 1,876—Chris George, Glenville St, 1993

Most Yards Gained per Game: 187.6—Chris George, Glenville St, 1993

Highest Average Gain per Reception: 32.5—Tyrone Johnson, Western St, 1991 (min. 30 receptions)

Single Game

SCORING

Most Points Scored: 48—Paul Zaeske, North Park, 1968 (vs North Central [Ill.]); Junior Wolf, Okla. Panhandle St, 1958 (vs St. Mary [Ks.])

Most Field Goals: 6—Steve Huff, Central Missouri St, 1985 (vs SE Missouri St); Austin Wellock, Ashland, 2002 (vs. Wayne St); Taylor Cannon, Eastern New Mexico, 2009 (vs SE Oklahoma)

RUSHING

Most Yards Gained: 418—Jarom Freeman, Southern Connecticut St, 2007 (vs Bryant)

Most Touchdowns Rushed: 8—Junior Wolf, Okla. Panhandle St, 1958 (vs St. Mary [Ks.])

PASSING

Most Passes Completed: 76—Jarrod DeGeorgia, Wayne St (Neb.),1996 (vs Drake)

Most Yards Gained: 695—J.J. Harp, Eastern New Mexico, 2009 (vs SE Oklahoma)

Most Touchdowns Passed: 10—Bruce Swanson, North Park, 1968 (vs North Central [Ill.])

RECEIVING

Most Passes Caught: 23—Chris George, Glenville St, 1994 (vs W.V. Wesleyan); Barry Wagner, Alabama A&M, 1989 (vs Clark Atlanta)

Most Yards Gained: 401—Kevin Ingram, West Chester, 1998 (vs Clarion)

Most Touchdown Catches: 8—Paul Zaeske, North Park, 1968 (vs North Central [Ill.])

NCAA Division III Individual Records

Career

SCORING

Most Points Scored: 780—Nate Kmic, Mount Union, 2005–08

Most Touchdowns Scored: 130—Nate Kmic, Mount Union, 2005–08

Most Touchdowns Scored, Rushing: 125—Nate Kmic, Mount Union, 2005–08

Most Touchdowns Scored, Passing: 148—Justin Peery, Westminster (Mo.), 1996–99

Most Touchdowns Scored, Receiving: 75—Scott Pingel, Westminster (Mo.), 1996–99

RUSHING

Most Rushes: 1,190—Steve Tardif, Maine Maritime, 1996–99

Most Rushes per Game: 32.7—Chris Sizemore, Bridgewater (Va.), 1972–74

RUSHING *(Cont.)*

Most Yards Gained: 8,074—Nate Kmic, Mount Union, 2005–08

Most Yards Gained per Game: 187.1—Tony Sutton, Wooster, 2002–04

PASSING

Highest Passing Efficiency Rating: 194.2—Bill Borchert, Mount Union, 1994–97

Most Passes Attempted: 1,982—Josh Vogelbach, Guilford, 2005–08

Most Passes Completed: 1,189—Josh Vogelbach, Guilford, 2005–08

Most Passes Completed per Game: 49.6—Josh Vogelbach, Guilford, 2005–08

Highest Completion Percentage: 74.1—Greg Micheli, Mount Union, 2005–08 (min. 750 att.)

Career *(Cont.)*

PASSING *(Cont.)*

Most Yards Gained: 13,605—Josh Vogelbach, Guilford, 2005–08
Most Yards Gained per Game: 358.9—Brett Elliott, Linfield, 2004–05

RECEIVING

Most Passes Caught: 436—Scott Pingel, Westminster (Mo.), 1996–99
Most Yards Gained: 6,108—Scott Pingel, Westminster (Mo.), 1996–99
Most Yards Gained per Game: 156.6—Scott Pingel, Westminster (Mo.), 1996–99
Highest Average Gain per Reception: 23.4—Michael Coleman, Widener, 1998–2001

Single Season

SCORING

Most Points Scored: 264—Nate Kmic, Mount Union, 2008
Most Points Scored per Game: 20.8—James Regan, Pomona-Pitzer, 1997
Most Touchdowns Scored: 44—Nate Kmic, Mount Union, 2008
Most Touchdowns Scored, Rushing: 43—Nate Kmic, Mount Union, 2008
Most Touchdowns Scored, Passing: 61—Brett Elliott, Linfield, 2004
Most Touchdowns Scored, Receiving: 26—Scott Pingel, Westminster (Mo.), 1998; Jack Phelan, Hartwick, 2008

RUSHING

Most Rushes: 463—Dante Washington, Carthage, 2004
Most Rushes per Game: 38.0—Mike Birosak, Dickinson, 1989
Most Yards Gained: 2,790—Nate Kmic, Mount Union, 2008

PASSING

Highest Passing Efficiency Rating: 225.0—Mike Simpson, Eureka, 1994
Most Passes Attempted: 575—Brett Dietz, Hanover, 2003
Most Passes Completed: 360—Brett Dietz, Hanover, 2003
Most Passes Completed per Game: 32.9—Justin Peery, Westminster (Mo.), 1999
Highest Completion Percentage: 75.0—Greg Micheli, Mount Union, 2008
Most Yards Gained: 4,595—Brett Elliott, Linfield, 2004
Most Yards Gained per Game: 450.1—Justin Peery, Westminster (Mo.), 1998

RECEIVING

Most Passes Caught: 136—Scott Pingel, Westminster (Mo.), 1999
Most Yards Gained: 2,157—Scott Pingel, Westminster, (Mo.), 1998
Most Yards Gained per Game: 215.7—Scott Pingel, Westminster, (Mo.), 1998
Highest Average Gain per Reception: 26.9—Marty Redlawsk, Concordia (Ill.), 1985 (min. 35 receptions)

Single Game

SCORING

Most Field Goals: 6—Jim Hever, Rhodes, 1984 (vs Millsaps)

PASSING

Most Passes Completed: 56—Brandon Luczak, Kalamazoo, 2009 (vs Hope)
Most Yards Gained: 731—Zamir Amin, Menlo, 2000 (vs California Lutheran)
Most Touchdown Passes: 9—Joe Zarlinga, Ohio Northern, 1998 (vs Capital)

RUSHING

Most Yards Gained: 441—Dante Brown, Marietta, 1996 (vs Baldwin-Wallace)
Most Touchdowns Rushed: 8—Carey Bender, Coe, 1994 (vs Beloit)

RECEIVING

Most Passes Caught: 25—Daniel Passaflume, Hanover, 2009 (vs Franklin)
Most Yards Gained: 418—Lewis Howes, Principia, 2002 (vs Martin Luther)
Most Touchdown Catches: 7—Matt Perceval, Wesleyan (Conn.), 1998 (vs Middlebury)

Career

Scoring

POINTS (KICKERS)

	Years	Pts
Art Carmody, Louisville	2004–07	433
‡Kevin Kelly, Penn St	2005–08	425
Roman Anderson, Houston	1988–91	423
Billy Bennett, Georgia	2000–03	409
Jeremy Ito, Rutgers	2004–07	400

‡includes one TD and one 2-pt. conversion (rush)

POINTS (NON-KICKERS)

	Years	Pts
Travis Prentice, Miami (Ohio)	1996–99	468
Ricky Williams, Texas	1995–98	452
Taurean Henderson, Texas Tech	2002–05	414
Brock Forsey, Boise St	1999–02	408
Cedric Benson, Texas	2001–04	404

POINTS PER GAME (NON-KICKERS)

	Years	Pts/Game
Marshall Faulk, San Diego St	1991–93	12.1
Ed Marinaro, Cornell	1969–71	11.8
Bill Burnett, Arkansas	1968–70	11.3
Steve Owens, Oklahoma	1967–69	11.2
Eddie Talboom, Wyoming	1948–50	10.8

Total Offense

YARDS GAINED

	Years	Yds
Timmy Chang, Hawaii	2000–04	16,910
Graham Harrell, Texas Tech	2005–08	15,599
Colt Brennan, Hawaii	2005–07	14,740
Ty Detmer, BYU	1988–91	14,665
Kevin Kolb, Houston	2003–06	13,715

YARDS PER GAME

	Years	Yds/Game
Colt Brennan, Hawaii	2005–07	387.9
Tim Rattay, Louisiana Tech	1997–99	382.4
Graham Harrell, Texas Tech	2005–08	346.6
Chase Holbrook, New Mexico St	2005–08	321.4
Chris Vargas, Nevada	1992–93	320.9

Rushing

YARDS GAINED

	Years	Yds
Ron Dayne, Wisconsin	1996–99	6,397
Ricky Williams, Texas	1995–98	6,279
Tony Dorsett, Pittsburgh	1973–76	6,082
DeAngelo Williams, Memphis	2002–05	6,026
Charles White, USC	1976–79	5,598
Travis Prentice, Miami (Ohio)	1996–99	5,596

YARDS PER GAME

	Years	Yds/Game
Ed Marinaro, Cornell	1969–71	174.6
O.J. Simpson, USC	1967–68	164.4
Herschel Walker, Georgia	1980–82	159.4
Garrett Wolfe, Northern Illinois	2004-06	156.5
LeShon Johnson, Northern Illinois	1992–93	150.6

TOUCHDOWNS RUSHING

	Years	TD
Travis Prentice, Miami (Ohio)	1996–99	73
Ricky Williams, Texas	1995–98	72
Anthony Thompson, Indiana	1986–89	64
Cedric Benson, Texas	2001–04	64
Ron Dayne, Wisconsin	1996–99	63

Passing

PASSING EFFICIENCY

	Years	Rating
Ryan Dinwiddie, Boise St	2000–03	168.9
Colt Brennan, Hawaii	2005–07	167.7
Danny Wuerffel, Florida	1993–96	163.6
Omar Jacobs, Bowling Green	2003–05	163.5
Ty Detmer, BYU	1988–91	162.7

Note: Minimum 500 completions.

YARDS GAINED

	Years	Yds
Timmy Chang, Hawaii	2000–04	17,072
Graham Harrell, Texas Tech	2005–08	15,793
Ty Detmer, BYU	1988–91	15,031
Colt Brennan, Hawaii	2005–07	14,193
Philip Rivers, North Carolina St	2000–03	13,484

COMPLETIONS

	Years	Comp
Graham Harrell, Texas Tech	2005–08	1,403
Timmy Chang, Hawaii	2000–04	1,388
Kliff Kingsbury, Texas Tech	1999–02	1,231
Philip Rivers, North Carolina St	2000–03	1,147
Colt Brennan, Hawaii	2005–07	1,115

TOUCHDOWNS PASSING

	Years	TD
Graham Harrell, Texas Tech	2005–08	134
Colt Brennan, Hawaii	2005–07	131
Ty Detmer, BYU	1988–91	121
Timmy Chang, Hawaii	2000–04	117
Tim Rattay, Louisiana Tech	1997–99	115

Receiving

CATCHES

	Years	No.
Taylor Stubblefield, Purdue	2001–04	316
Josh Davis, Marshall	2001–04	306
Taurean Henderson, Texas Tech	2002–05	303
Arnold Jackson, Louisville	1997–00	300
Trevor Insley, Nevada	1996–99	298

CATCHES PER GAME

	Years	No./Game
Emmanuel Hazard, Houston	1989–90	10.5
Alex Van Dyke, Nevada	1994–95	10.3
Howard Twilley, Tulsa	1963–65	10.0
Jason Phillips, Houston	1987–88	9.4
Michael Crabtree, Texas Tech	2007–08	8.9

YARDS GAINED

	Years	Yds
Trevor Insley, Nevada	1996–99	5,005
Marcus Harris, Wyoming	1993–96	4,518
Rashaun Woods, Oklahoma St	2000–03	4,412
Ryan Yarborough, Wyoming	1990–93	4,357
Troy Edwards, Louisiana Tech	1996–98	4,352

TOUCHDOWN CATCHES

	Years	TD
Jarrett Dillard, Rice	2005–08	60
Troy Edwards, Louisiana Tech	1996–98	50
Darius Watts, Marshall	2000–03	47
Aaron Turner, Pacific	1989–92	43
Ryan Yarborough, Wyoming	1990–93	42
Rashaun Woods, Oklahoma St	2000–03	42

Career *(Cont.)*

All-Purpose Running

YARDS GAINED	Years	Yds
DeAngelo Williams, Memphis	2002–05	7,573
Ricky Williams, Texas	1996–98	7,206
Napoleon McCallum, Navy	1981–85	7,172
Chris Johnson, East Carolina	2004–07	6,993
Darrin Nelson, Stanford	1977–78, '80–81	6,885

YARDS PER GAME	Years	Yds/Game
Ryan Benjamin, Pacific	1990–92	237.8
Sheldon Canley, San Jose St	1988–90	205.8
Jeremy Maclin, Missouri	2007–08	200.3
Howard Stevens, Louisville	1971–72	193.7
O.J. Simpson, USC	1967–68	192.9

Interceptions

PLAYER/SCHOOL	Years	Int
Al Brosky, Illinois	1950–52	29
John Provost, Holy Cross	1972–74	27
Martin Bayless, Bowling Green	1980–83	27
Tom Curtis, Michigan	1967–69	25
Tony Thurman, Boston College	1981–84	25
Tracy Saul, Texas Tech	1989–92	25

Punting Average

PLAYER/SCHOOL	Years	Avg
Daniel Sepulveda, Baylor	2003–06	45.2
Shane Lechler, Texas A&M	1996–99	44.7
Bill Smith, Mississippi	1983–86	44.3
Jim Arnold, Vanderbilt	1979–82	43.9
Ralf Mojsiejenko, Michigan St	1981–84	43.6

Note: 250+ punts.

Punt Return Average

PLAYER/SCHOOL	Years	Avg
Jack Mitchell, Oklahoma	1946–48	23.6
Gene Gibson, Cincinnati	1949–50	20.5
Eddie Macon, Pacific	1949–51	18.9
Jackie Robinson, UCLA	1939–40	18.8
Dan Shelton, Illinois	2001–04	17.9

Note: Minimum 30 returns.

Kickoff Return Average

PLAYER/SCHOOL	Years	Avg
Anthony Davis, USC	1972–74	35.1
Eric Booth, Southern Miss	1994–97	32.4
Overton Curtis, Utah St	1957–58	31.0
Fred Montgomery, New Mexico St	1991–92	30.5
Bryan Williams, Akron	2005–08	30.5

Note: Minimum 30 returns.

Single Season

Scoring

POINTS	Year	Pts
Barry Sanders, Oklahoma St	1988	234
Brock Forsey, Boise St	2002	192
Troy Edwards, Louisiana Tech	1998	186
Kevin Smith, Central Florida	2007	180
Mike Rozier, Nebraska	1983	174
Lydell Mitchell, Penn St	1971	174

FIELD GOALS	Year	FG
Billy Bennett, Georgia	2003	31
Leigh Tiffin, Alabama	2009	30
John Lee, UCLA	1984	29
John Sullivan, New Mexico	2007	29
Paul Woodside, West Virginia	1982	28
Luis Zendejas, Arizona St	1983	28
Nick Browne, TCU	2003	28
Justin Medlock, UCLA	2006	28
Kai Forbath, UCLA	2009	28

Four tied with 27.

All-Purpose Running

YARDS GAINED	Year	Yds
Barry Sanders, Oklahoma St	1988	3,250
Ryan Benjamin, Pacific	1991	2,995
Chris Johnson, East Carolina	2007	2,960
Reggie Bush, USC	2005	2,890
Jeremy Maclin, Missouri	2008	2,833

YARDS PER GAME	Year	Yds/Game
Barry Sanders, Oklahoma St	1988	295.5
Ryan Benjamin, Pacific	1991	249.6
Byron (Whizzer) White, Colorado	1937	246.3
Mike Pringle, Fullerton St	1989	244.6
Paul Palmer, Temple	1986	239.4

Total Offense

YARDS GAINED	Year	Yds
B.J. Symons, Texas Tech	2003	5,976
Colt Brennan, Hawaii	2006	5,915
Case Keenum, Houston	2009	5,829
Graham Harrell, Texas Tech	2007	5,614
Case Keenum, Houston	2008	5,241

YARDS PER GAME	Year	Yds/Game
David Klingler, Houston	1990	474.6
B.J. Symons, Texas Tech	2003	459.7
Graham Harrell, Texas Tech	2007	431.8
Andre Ware, Houston	1989	423.7
Colt Brennan, Hawaii	2006	422.5

Rushing

YARDS GAINED	Year	Yds
Barry Sanders, Oklahoma St	1988	2,628
Kevin Smith, Central Florida	2007	2,567
Marcus Allen, USC	1981	2,342
Troy Davis, Iowa St	1996	2,185
LaDainian Tomlinson, TCU	2000	2,158

YARDS PER GAME	Year	Yds/Game
Barry Sanders, Oklahoma St	1988	238.9
Marcus Allen, USC	1981	212.9
Ed Marinaro, Cornell	1971	209.0
Troy Davis, Iowa St	1996	198.6
LaDainian Tomlinson, TCU	2000	196.2

TOUCHDOWNS RUSHING	Year	TD
Barry Sanders, Oklahoma St	1988	37
Kevin Smith, Central Florida	2007	29
Mike Rozier, Nebraska	1983	29
Toby Gerhart, Stanford	2009	28
Willis McGahee, Miami (Fla.)	2002	28
Ricky Williams, Texas	1998	27
Lee Suggs, Virginia Tech	2000	27

Single Season *(Cont.)*

Passing

PASSING EFFICIENCY	Year	Rating
Colt Brennan, Hawaii	2006	186.0
Shaun King, Tulane	1998	183.3
Stefan LeFors, Louisville	2004	181.7
Sam Bradford, Oklahoma	2008	180.8
Michael Vick, Virginia Tech	1999	180.4

YARDS GAINED	Year	Yds
B.J. Symons, Texas Tech	2003	5,833
Graham Harrell, Texas Tech	2007	5,705
Case Keenum, Houston	2009	5,671
Colt Brennan, Hawaii	2006	5,549
Ty Detmer, BYU	1990	5,188
David Klingler, Houston	1990	5,140

COMPLETIONS	Year	Att	Comp
Graham Harrell, Texas Tech	2007	713	512
Case Keenum, Houston	2009	700	492
Kliff Kingsbury, Texas Tech	2002	712	479
B.J. Symons, Texas Tech	2003	719	470
Graham Harrell, Texas Tech	2008	626	442

TOUCHDOWNS PASSING	Year	TD
Colt Brennan, Hawaii	2006	58
David Klingler, Houston	1990	54
B.J. Symons, Texas Tech	2003	52
Sam Bradford, Oklahoma	2008	50
Graham Harrell, Texas Tech	2007	48

Receiving

CATCHES	Year	GP	No.
Freddie Barnes, Bowling Green	2009	13	155
Emmanuel Hazard, Houston	1989	11	142
Troy Edwards, Louisiana Tech	1998	12	140
Nate Burleson, Nevada	2002	12	138
Howard Twilley, Tulsa	1965	10	134
Trevor Insley, Nevada	1999	11	134
Michael Crabtree, Texas Tech	2008	13	134

CATCHES PER GAME	Year	No.	No./Game
Howard Twilley, Tulsa	1965	134	13.4
Emmanuel Hazard, Houston	1989	142	12.9
Trevor Insley, Nevada	1999	134	12.2
Freddie Barnes, Bowling Green	2009	155	11.9
Alex Van Dyke, Nevada	1995	129	11.7
Troy Edwards, Louisiana Tech	1998	140	11.7

YARDS GAINED	Year	Yds
Trevor Insley, Nevada	1999	2,060
Troy Edwards, Louisiana Tech	1998	1,996
Michael Crabtree, Texas Tech	2007	1,962
Alex Van Dyke, Nevada	1995	1,854
J.R. Tolver, San Diego St	2002	1,785

TOUCHDOWN CATCHES	Year	TD
Troy Edwards, Louisiana Tech	1998	27
Randy Moss, Marshall	1997	25
Emmanuel Hazard, Houston	1989	22
Larry Fitzgerald, Pittsburgh	2003	22
Michael Crabtree, Texas Tech	2007	22

Single Game

Scoring

POINTS	Opponent	Year	Pts
Howard Griffith, Illinois	Southern Illinois	1990	48
Marshall Faulk, San Diego St	Pacific	1991	44
Jim Brown, Syracuse	Colgate	1956	43
Fred Wendt, UTEP*	New Mexico St	1948	42
Arnold Boykin, Mississippi	Mississippi St	1951	42
Rashaun Woods, Okla. St	SMU	2003	42

*UTEP was Texas Mines in 1948.

FIELD GOALS	Opponent	Year	FG
Dale Klein, Nebraska	Missouri	1985	7
Mike Prindle, Western Michigan	Marshall	1984	7

Note: 15 tied with 6.

Klein's distances were 32-22-43-44-29-43-43.
Prindle's distances were 32-44-42-23-48-41-27.

Total Offense

YARDS GAINED	Opponent	Year	Yds
David Klingler, Houston	Arizona St	1990	732
Matt Vogler, TCU	Houston	1990	696
B.J. Symons, Texas Tech	Mississippi	2003	681
Brian Lindgren, Idaho	Middle Tenn St	2001	657
Graham Harrell, Texas Tech	Oklahoma St	2007	643
David Klingler, Houston	TCU	1990	625
Scott Mitchell, Utah	Air Force	1988	625

Passing

YARDS GAINED	Opponent	Year	Yds
David Klingler, Houston	Arizona St	1990	716
Matt Vogler, TCU	Houston	1990	690
B.J. Symons, Texas Tech	Mississippi	2003	661
Graham Harrell, Texas Tech	Oklahoma St	2007	646
Cody Hodges, Texas Tech	Kansas St	2005	643

Passing *(Cont.)*

COMPLETIONS	Opponent	Year	Comp
Andy Schmitt, E. Michigan	Central Mich.	2008	58
Case Keenum, Houston	East Carolina	2009	56
Drew Brees, Purdue	Wisconsin	1998	55
Rusty LaRue, Wake Forest	Duke	1995	55
Case Keenum, Houston	UTEP	2009	51
Andy Schmitt, E. Michigan	Temple	2008	50
Rusty LaRue, Wake Forest	No.Carolina St	1995	50

Note: 5 tied with 49.

TOUCHDOWNS PASSING	Opponent	Year	TD
David Klingler, Houston	E Wash	1990	11

Note: Klingler's TD passes were for 5-48-29-7-3-7-40-10-7-8-51 yards, respectively.

Rushing

YARDS GAINED	Opponent	Year	Yds
LaDainian Tomlinson, TCU	UTEP	1999	406
Tony Sands, Kansas	Missouri	1991	396
Marshall Faulk, San Diego St.	Pacific	1991	386
Troy Davis, Iowa St	Missouri	1996	378
Anthony Thompson, Indiana	Wisconsin	1989	377
Robbie Mixon, Cent. Mich.	Eastern Mich	2002	377

TOUCHDOWNS RUSHING	Opponent	Year	TD
Howard Griffith, Illinois	Southern Illinois	1990	8

Note: Griffith's TD runs were for 5-51-7-41-5-18-5-3 yards, respectively.

Single Game (Cont.)

Receiving

CATCHES	Opponent	Year	No.
Tyler Jones, E. Michigan.....Central Mich.		2008	23
Randy Gatewood, UNLV .....Idaho		1994	23
Freddie Barnes, Bowl. Green..Kent St		2009	22
Jay Miller, BYU ....New Mexico		1973	22
Troy Edwards, La. Tech .....Nebraska		1998	21
Chris Daniels, Purdue ....Michigan St		1999	21

Note: 3 tied with 20.

Receiving (Cont.)

YARDS GAINED	Opponent	Year	Yds
Troy Edwards, Louisiana Tech...Nebraska		1998	405
Randy Gatewood, UNLV ....Idaho		1994	363
Chuck Hughes, UTEP*...........North Texas		1965	349
Donnie Avery, Houston ....Rice		2007	346
Casey Fitzgerald, North Texas..SMU		2007	327

*UTEP was Texas Western in 1965.

TOUCHDOWN CATCHES	Opponent	Year	TD
Rashaun Woods, Okla. St .....SMU		2003	7
Tim Delaney, San Diego St....New Mex. St		1969	6

Longest Plays (since 1941)

PASSING	Opponent	Year	Yds
Fred Owens to Jack Ford, Portland................................St. Mary's (Ca.)1947			99
Bo Burris to Warren McVea, Houston................................Washington St		1966	99
Colin Clapton to Eddie Jenkins, Holy Cross ....Boston Univ.		1970	99
Terry Peel to Robert Ford, Houston................................Syracuse		1970	99
Terry Peel to Robert Ford, Houston................................San Diego St		1972	99
Cris Collinsworth to Derrick Gaffney, Florida ....Rice		1977	99
Scott Ankrom to James Maness, TCU ....Rice		1984	99
Gino Toretta to Horace Copeland, Miami (Fla.) ....Arkansas		1991	99
John Paci to Thomas Lewis, Indiana ....Penn St		1993	99
Troy DeGar to Wes Caswell Tulsa ....Oklahoma		1996	99
Drew Brees to Vinny Sutherland, Purdue ....Northwestern		1999	99
Dan Urban to Justin McCariens, Northern Illinois....................Ball St		2000	99
Jason Johnson to Brandon Marshall, Arizona..................................Idaho		2001	99
Dondrial Pinkins to Troy Williamson, South Carolina ....Virginia		2003	99
Jim Sorgi to Lee Evans, Wisconsin..............................Akron		2003	99
Giovanni Vizza to Casey Fitzgerald, North Texas...........................La.-Monroe		2007	99
Jeff Tuel to Johnny Forzani, Washington St......................Arizona St		2009	99

RUSHING	Opponent	Year	Yd
Gale Sayers, Kansas ....Nebraska		1963	99
Max Anderson, Arizona St....Wyoming		1967	99
Ralph Thompson, West Texas St ....Wichita St		1970	99
Kelsey Finch, Tennessee ......Florida		1977	99
Eric Vann, Kansas................Oklahoma		1997	99
Terry Caulley, Connecticut....Army		2006	99
Broderick Green, Arkansas ..E. Michigan		2009	-99

FIELD GOALS	Opponent	Year	Yds
Steve Little, Arkansas ....Texas		1977	67
Russell Erxleben, Texas ....Rice		1977	67
Joe Williams, Wichita St ....Southern Ill.		1978	67
Martin Gramatica, Kansas St...Northern Ill.		1998	65
Tony Franklin, Texas A&M ......Baylor		1976	65

PUNTS	Opponent	Year	Yds
Pat Brady, Nevada*................Loyola (Ca.)		1950	99
George O'Brien, Wisconsin ...Iowa		1952	96
John Hadl, Kansas.................Oklahoma		1959	94
Carl Knox, TCU ....Oklahoma St		1947	94
Preston Johnson, SMU...........Pittsburgh		1940	94

*Nevada was Nevada-Reno in 1950.

FOOTBALL BOWL SUBDIVISION (I-A) WINNINGEST TEAMS

Alltime Winning Percentage

	Yrs	W	L	T	Pct	GP	Bowl Record
Michigan	130	877	302	36	.737	1,215	19-20-0
Notre Dame	121	837	290	42	.734	1,169	14-15-0
Texas	117	845	318	33	.720	1,196	25-22-2
Ohio St.	120	819	308	53	.717	1,180	19-22-0
Oklahoma	115	799	302	53	.715	1,154	25-17-1
Boise St	42	353	144	2	.709	499	6-4-0
*Alabama	115	792	316	43	.707	1,151	32-22-3
*USC	117	761	307	54	.702	1,122	30-16-0
Nebraska	120	826	341	41	.701	1,208	24-22-0
Tennessee	113	783	333	53	.692	1,169	25-23-0
Penn St	123	811	351	41	.691	1,203	27-13-2
*Florida St	63	454	227	17	.663	698	20-14-2
Georgia	116	731	389	54	.646	1,174	26-16-3
LSU	116	709	387	47	.641	1,143	21-19-1
Miami (Fla.)	84	561	314	19	.638	894	18-15-0
Florida	103	654	374	40	.631	1,068	18-19-0
Auburn	117	689	400	47	.627	1,136	20-13-2
South Florida	13	95	57	0	.625	152	3-2-0
Miami (Ohio)	121	650	390	44	.620	1,084	6-3-0
Arizona St	97	549	343	24	.612	916	12-11-1
Washington	120	656	406	50	.612	1,112	14-14-1
Central Michigan	109	570	357	36	.611	963	2-4-0
Virginia Tech	116	667	429	46	.604	1,142	9-14-0
Colorado	120	666	435	36	.602	1,137	12-16-0
West Virginia	117	682	450	45	.599	1,177	13-16-0

Note: Includes bowl games. *Indicates record adjustment made by NCAA in 2010 due to past rules infractions.
**Reclassified as FBS (Div. I-A) on November 2, 2006.

Alltime Victories

Michigan	877	Georgia	731	Arkansas	659
Texas	845	LSU	709	Washington	656
Notre Dame	837	Auburn	689	Florida	654
Nebraska	826	West Virginia	682	Miami (Ohio)	650
Ohio St	819	Syracuse	678	North Carolina	647
Penn St.	811	Georgia Tech	673	California	643
Oklahoma	799	Virginia Tech	667	Army	642
Alabama	792	Colorado	666	Navy	642
Tennessee	783	Texas A&M	665	Clemson	641
USC	761	Pittsburgh	663	Minnesota	640

NUMBER ONE VS NUMBER TWO

The No. 1 and No. 2 teams, according to the Associated Press Poll, have met 33 times, including 13 bowl games, since the poll's inception in 1936. The No. 1 teams have a 20-11-2 record in these matchups. Notre Dame (4-3-2) has played in nine of the games.

Date	Results	Stadium
10-9-43	No. 1 Notre Dame 35, No. 2 Michigan 12	Michigan (Ann Arbor)
11-20-43	No. 1 Notre Dame 14, No. 2 Iowa Pre-Flight 13	Notre Dame (South Bend)
12-2-44	No. 1 Army 23, No. 2 Navy 7	Municipal (Baltimore)
11-10-45	No. 1 Army 48, No. 2 Notre Dame 0	Yankee (New York)
12-1-45	No. 1 Army 32, No. 2 Navy 13	Municipal (Philadelphia)
11-9-46	No. 1 Army 0, No. 2 Notre Dame 0	Yankee (New York)
1-1-63	No. 1 USC 42, No. 2 Wisconsin 37 (Rose Bowl)	Rose Bowl (Pasadena)
10-12-63	No. 2 Texas 28, No. 1 Oklahoma 7	Cotton Bowl (Dallas)
1-1-64	No. 1 Texas 28, No. 2 Navy 6 (Cotton Bowl)	Cotton Bowl (Dallas)
11-19-66	No. 1 Notre Dame 10, No. 2 Michigan St 10	Spartan (East Lansing)
9-28-68	No. 1 Purdue 37, No. 2 Notre Dame 22	Notre Dame (South Bend)
1-1-69	No. 1 Ohio St 27, No. 2 USC 16 (Rose Bowl)	Rose Bowl (Pasadena)
12-6-69	No. 1 Texas 15, No. 2 Arkansas 14	Razorback (Fayetteville)
11-25-71	No. 1 Nebraska 35, No. 2 Oklahoma 31	Owen Field (Norman)
1-1-72	No. 1 Nebraska 38, No. 2 Alabama 6 (Orange Bowl)	Orange Bowl (Miami)
1-1-79	No. 2 Alabama 14, No. 1 Penn St 7 (Sugar Bowl)	Sugar Bowl (New Orleans)
9-26-81	No. 1 USC 28, No. 2 Oklahoma 24	Coliseum (Los Angeles)
1-1-83	No. 2 Penn St 27, No. 1 Georgia 23 (Sugar Bowl)	Sugar Bowl (New Orleans)
10-19-85	No. 1 Iowa 12, No. 2 Michigan 10	Kinnick (Iowa City)
9-27-86	No. 2 Miami (Fla.) 28, No. 1 Oklahoma 16	Orange Bowl (Miami)

NUMBER ONE VS NUMBER TWO *(Cont.)*

Date	Results	Stadium
1-2-87	No. 2 Penn St 14, No. 1 Miami (Fla.) 10 (Fiesta Bowl)	Sun Devil (Tempe)
11-21-87	No. 2 Oklahoma 17, No. 1 Nebraska 7	Memorial (Lincoln)
1-1-88	No. 2 Miami (Fla.) 20, No. 1 Oklahoma 14 (Orange Bowl)	Orange Bowl (Miami)
11-26-88	No. 1 Notre Dame 27, No. 2 USC 10	Coliseum (Los Angeles)
9-16-89	No. 1 Notre Dame 24, No. 2 Michigan 19	Michigan (Ann Arbor)
11-16-91	No. 2 Miami (Fla.) 17, No. 1 Florida St 16	Doak Campbell (Tallahassee)
1-1-93	No. 2 Alabama 34, No. 1 Miami (Fla.) 13 (Sugar Bowl)	Superdome (New Orleans)
11-13-93	No. 2 Notre Dame 31, No. 1 Florida St 24	Notre Dame (South Bend)
1-1-94	No. 1 Florida St 18, No. 2 Nebraska 16 (Orange Bowl)	Orange Bowl (Miami)
1-2-96	No. 1 Nebraska 62, No. 2 Florida 24 (Fiesta Bowl)	Sun Devil (Tempe)
11-30-96	No. 2 Florida St 24, No. 1 Florida 21	Doak Campbell (Tallahassee)
1-4-99	No. 1 Tennessee 23, No. 2 Florida St 16 (Fiesta Bowl)	Sun Devil (Tempe)
1-4-00	No. 1 Florida St 46, No. 2 Virginia Tech 29 (Sugar Bowl)	Superdome (New Orleans)
1-3-03	No. 2 Ohio St 31, No. 1 Miami (Fla.) 24 [2OT] (Fiesta Bowl)	Sun Devil (Tempe)
1-5-06	No. 2 Texas 41, No. 1 USC 38 (Rose Bowl)	Rose Bowl (Pasadena)
9-9-06	No. 1 Ohio St 24, No. 2 Texas 7	Texas Memorial (Austin)
11-18-06	No. 1 Ohio St 42, No. 2 Michigan 39	Ohio (Columbus)
1-8-07	No. 2 Florida 41, No. 1 Ohio St 14 (BCS Championship)	Univ. of Phoenix (Glendale)
1-7-08	No. 2 LSU 38, No. 1 Ohio St. 24 (BCS Championship)	Superdome (New Orleans)
12-6-08	No. 2 Florida 31, No. 1 Alabama 20 (SEC Championship)	Georgia Dome (Atlanta)
1-8-09	No. 1 Florida 24, No. 2 Oklahoma 14 (BCS Championship)	Dolphins Stadium (Miami)
12-5-09	No. 1 Florida 13, No. 2 Alabama 32 (SEC Championship)	Georgia Dome (Atlanta)
1-6-10	No. 1 Alabama 37, No. 2 Texas 21 (BCS Championship)	Rose Bowl (Pasadena)

Note: #1 USC's Orange Bowl victory over #2 Oklahoma on Jan. 4, 2005 was vacated in 2010 for rules violations.

LONGEST FBS (I-A) WINNING STREAKS

Wins	Team	Yrs	Ended by	Score
47	Oklahoma	1953–57	Notre Dame	7–0
39	Washington	1908–14	Oregon St	0–0
37	Yale	1890–93	Princeton	6–0
37	Yale	1887–89	Princeton	10–0
35	Toledo	1969–71	Tampa	21–0
34	Miami	2000–03	Ohio St	31–24 (2 OT)
34	Pennsylvania	1894–96	Lafayette	6–4
31	Oklahoma	1948–50	Kentucky	13–7
31	Pittsburgh	1914–18	Cleveland Naval Reserve	10–9
31	Pennsylvania	1896–98	Harvard	10–0
30	Texas	1968–70	Notre Dame	24–11

LONGEST FBS (I-A) UNBEATEN STREAKS

No.	W	T	Team	Yrs	Ended by	Score
63	59	4	Washington	1907–17	California	27–0
56	55	1	Michigan	1901–05	Chicago	2–0
50	46	4	California	1920–25	Olympic Club	15–0
48	47	1	Oklahoma	1953–57	Notre Dame	7–0
48	47	1	Yale	1885–89	Princeton	10–0
47	42	5	Yale	1879–85	Princeton	6–5
44	42	2	Yale	1894–96	Princeton	24–6
42	39	3	Yale	1904–08	Harvard	4–0
39	37	2	Notre Dame	1946–50	Purdue	28–14
37	36	1	Oklahoma	1972–75	Kansas	23–3
37	37	0	Yale	1890–93	Princeton	6–0
35	35	0	Toledo	1969–71	Tampa	21–0
35	34	1	Minnesota	1903–05	Wisconsin	16–12
34	34	0	Miami	2000–03	Ohio St	31–24 (2 OT)
34	33	1	Nebraska	1912–16	Kansas	7–3
34	34	0	Pennsylvania	1894–96	Lafayette	6–4
34	32	2	Princeton	1884–87	Harvard	12–0
34	29	5	Princeton	1877–82	Harvard	1–0
33	30	3	Tennessee	1926–30	Alabama	18–6
33	31	2	Georgia Tech	1914–18	Pittsburgh	32–0
33	30	3	Harvard	1911–15	Cornell	10–0
32	31	1	Nebraska	1969–71	UCLA	20–17
32	30	2	Army	1944–47	Columbia	21–20
32	31	1	Harvard	1898–1900	Yale	28–0

Note: Includes bowl games.

LONGEST FBS (I-A) LOSING STREAKS

Losses		Seasons	Ended Against	Score
34	Northwestern	1979–82	Northern Illinois	31–6
28	Virginia	1958–61	William & Mary	21–6
28	Kansas St	1945–48	Arkansas St	37–6
27	New Mexico St	1988–90	Cal St–Fullerton	43–9
27	Eastern Michigan	1980–82	Kent St	9–7

MOST-PLAYED FBS (I-A) RIVALRIES

GP	Opponents (Series Leader Listed First)	Record	First Game
119	Minnesota–Wisconsin	59-52-8	1890
118	Kansas–Missouri	55-54-9	1891
116	Nebraska–Kansas	90-23-3	1892
116	Texas–Texas A&M	75-36-5	1894
114	Miami (Ohio)–Cincinnati	59-48-7	1888
114	North Carolina–Virginia	†57-53-4	1892
113	Auburn–Georgia	53-52-8	1892
113	Oregon–Oregon St	57-46-10	1894
112	Purdue–Indiana	70-36-6	1891
112	Stanford–California	55-46-11	1892
110	Navy–Army	54-49-7	1890
109	Utah–Utah St	77-28-4	1892
107	Clemson–South Carolina	65-38-4	1896

GP	Opponents (Series Leader Listed First)	Record	First Game
107	Kansas–Kansas St	65-37-5	1902
106	Michigan–Ohio St	57-43-6	1897
106	Mississippi–Mississippi St	60-40-6	1901
105	Baylor–TCU	49-49-7	1899
105	Tennessee–Kentucky	73-23-9	1893
104	Georgia–Georgia Tech	60-39-5	1893
104	Nebraska–Iowa St	85-17-2	1896
104	Texas–Oklahoma	59-40-5	1900
104	Oklahoma–Oklahoma St	81-16-7	1904
103	North Carolina–Wake Forest	67-34-2	1897

†Disputed series record: Virginia claims North Carolina leads series 55-51-4 based on a forfeited game in 1956.

NCAA Coaches' Records

ALLTIME WINNINGEST FBS (I-A) COACHES

By Percentage

Coach (Alma Mater)	Colleges Coached	Yrs	W	L	T	Pct
Knute Rockne (Notre Dame '14)†	Notre Dame 1918–30	13	105	12	5	.881
Frank W. Leahy (Notre Dame '31)†	Boston College 1939–40; Notre Dame 1941–43, 1946–53	13	107	13	9	.864
George W. Woodruff (Yale 1889)†	Pennsylvania 1892–01; Illinois 1903; Carlisle 1905	12	142	25	2	.846
Barry Switzer (Arkansas '60)	Oklahoma 1973–88	16	157	29	4	.837
Tom Osborne (Hastings '59)†	Nebraska 1973–97	25	255	49	3	.836
Percy D. Haughton (Harvard 1899)†	Cornell 1899–1900; Harvard 1908–16; Columbia 1923–24	13	96	17	6	.832
Bob Neyland (Army '16)†	Tennessee 1926–34, 1936–40, 1946–52	21	173	31	12	.829
Fielding Yost (West Virginia 1895)†	Ohio Wesleyan 1897; Nebraska 1898; Kansas 1899; Stanford 1900; Michigan 1901–23, 1925–26	29	196	36	12	.828
Bud Wilkinson (Minnesota '37)†	Oklahoma 1947–63	17	145	29	4	.826
Jock Sutherland (Pittsburgh '18)†	Lafayette 1919–23; Pittsburgh 1924–38	20	144	28	14	.812
Bob Devaney (Alma [Mich] '39)†	Wyoming 1957–61; Nebraska 1962–72	16	136	30	7	.806
*Bob Stoops (Iowa '83)	Oklahoma 1999–	11	117	29	0	.801
Frank W. Thomas (Notre Dame '23)†	Tenn.-Chattanooga 1925–28; Alabama 1931–42, 1944–46	19	141	33	9	.795
Henry L. Williams (Yale 1891)†	Army 1891; Minnesota 1900–21	23	141	34	12	.786
Gil Dobie (Minnesota '02)†	North Dakota St 1906–07; Washington 1908-16; Navy 1917–19; Cornell 1920–35; Boston College 1936–38	33	180	45	15	.781
Fred Folsom (Dartmouth 1895)	Colorado 1895–99, 1901–02; Dartmouth 1903–06; Colorado 1908–15	19	107	28	6	.780
Paul "Bear" Bryant (Alabama '36)†	Maryland 1945; Kentucky 1946–53;	38	323	85	17	.780
Bo Schembechler (Miami [Ohio] '51)	Miami (Ohio) 1963–68; Michigan 1969–89	27	234	65	8	.775
Fritz Crisler (Chicago '22)	Minnesota 1930–31, Princeton 1931–37– Michigan 1938–47	18	116	32	9	.768
Wallace Wade (Brown, '17)	Alabama 1923–30; Duke 1931–41, 46–50	24	171	49	10	.765

*Active in 2009. †Hall of Fame member.

Note: Minimum 10 years as head coach at Division I institutions; record at four-year colleges only; bowl games included; ties computed as half won, half lost.

ALLTIME WINNINGEST FBS (I-A) COACHES *(Cont.)*
By Victories

	Yrs	W	L	T	Pct		Yrs	W	L	T	Pct
*Joe Paterno	44	394	129	3	.752	Hayden Fry	37	232	178	10	.564
*Bobby Bowden	44	377	129	4	.743	*Jim Tressel	24	229	78	2	.744
Paul (Bear) Bryant	38	323	85	17	.780	*Frank Beamer	29	229	115	4	.664
Glenn (Pop) Warner	44	319	106	32	.733	*Mack Brown	26	214	101	1	.679
Amos Alonzo Stagg	57	314	199	35	.605	Jess Neely	40	207	176	19	.539
LaVell Edwards	29	257	100	3	.718	Warren Woodson	31	203	95	14	.673
Tom Osborne	25	255	49	3	.836	Don Nehlen	30	202	128	8	.609
Lou Holtz	33	249	132	7	.651	Vince Dooley	25	201	77	10	.715
Woody Hayes	33	238	72	10	.759	Eddie Anderson	39	201	128	15	.606
Bo Schembechler	27	234	65	8	.775						

*Active in 2009. Record at four-year colleges only.

Most Bowl Victories

	W	L	T		W	L	T
*Joe Paterno	24	11	1	Philip Fulmer	8	7	0
*Bobby Bowden	21	10	1	Darrell Royal	8	7	1
Paul (Bear) Bryant	15	12	2	*Frank Beamer	8	9	0
Lou Holtz	12	8	2	Vince Dooley	8	10	2
Tom Osborne	12	13	0	Mark Richt	7	2	0
*Mack Brown	11	7	0	Pat Dye	7	2	1
Don James	10	5	0	Tommy Tuberville	7	3	0
John Vaught	10	8	0	Bob Devaney	7	3	0
Bobby Dodd	9	4	0	Dan Devine	7	3	0
Johnny Majors	9	7	0	Earle Bruce	7	5	0
John Robinson	8	1	0	Charlie McClendon	7	6	0
Barry Alvarez	8	3	0	*Steve Spurrier	7	8	0
Terry Donahue	8	4	1	Hayden Fry	7	9	1
Barry Switzer	8	5	0	LaVell Edwards	7	14	1
Jackie Sherrill	8	6	0				

WINNINGEST ACTIVE* FBS (I-A) COACHES
By Percentage

Coach, College	Yrs	W	L	T	Pct.	Bowls W	L	T
Urban Meyer, Florida	9	96	18	0	.842	6	1	0
†Pete Carroll, USC	9	83	19	0	.813	6	2	0
Bob Stoops, Oklahoma	11	117	29	0	.801	5	5	0
Mark Richt, Georgia	9	90	27	0	.769	7	2	0
Bronco Mendenhall, Boise St	5	49	15	0	.766	3	2	0
Gary Patterson, TCU	10	85	28	0	.752	5	4	0
Joe Paterno, Penn St	44	394	129	3	.752	24	11	1
Brian Kelly, Cincinnati	20	171	57	2	.748	2	1	0
Jim Tressel, Ohio St	24	229	78	2	.744	5	4	0
**Bobby Bowden, Florida St	44	377	129	4	.743	21	10	1
Kyle Whittingham, Utah	5	47	17	0	.734	5	0	0
Paul Johnson, Georgia Tech	13	127	46	0	.734	2	4	0
Steve Spurrier, South Carolina	20	177	68	2	.721	7	8	0
Bobby Petrino, Arkansas	6	54	21	0	.720	3	2	0
Nick Saban, Alabama	14	119	50	1	.701	5	6	0
Les Miles, LSU	9	79	36	0	.687	5	3	0
Chris Ault, Nevada	25	206	96	1	.682	1	5	0
Mack Brown, Texas	26	214	101	1	.679	11	7	0
Dennis Erickson, Arizona St	21	167	83	1	.667	5	6	0
Frank Beamer, Virginia Tech	29	229	115	4	.664	8	9	0

#Bowl games included. Ties computed as half win, half loss. Note: Min. five years as Div. I-A head coach at four-year collges only. **Fourteen regular season wins and one bowl victory from Bowden's 2006 and 2007 seasons at Florida St were vacated in early 2010. †One bowl win and 14 regular-season victories from Carroll's totals, starting in December 2004 and running through the 2005 season, were vacated in 2010.

By Victories

Joe Paterno, Penn St	394	Steve Spurrier, South Carolina	177
Bobby Bowden, Florida St	377	Brian Kelly, Cincinnati	171
Jim Tressel, Ohio St	229	Dennis Erickson, Arizona St	167
Frank Beamer, Viginia Tech	229	Mike Price, UTEP	163
Mack Brown, Texas	214	Howard Schellenberger, Fla. Atlantic	153
Chris Ault, Nevada	206	Larry Blakeney, Troy	152
Dick Tomey, San Jose St	183	Bill Snyder, Kansas St	142

*Active in 2009.

WINNINGEST ACTIVE* FCS (I-AA) COACHES
By Percentage

Coach, College	Yrs	W	L	T	Pct
Bob Hauck, Montana	7	80	17	0	.825
Al Bagnoli, Pennsylvania	28	213	70	0	.753
Buddy Pough, South Carolina St	8	67	26	0	.720
Joe Taylor, Florida A&M	27	214	82	4	.720
Mark Farley, Northern Iowa	9	82	32	0	.713
K.C. Keeler, Delaware	17	150	60	1	.713
David Bennett, Coastal Carolina	14	113	46	0	.711
Pete Lembo, Elon	9	73	31	0	.702
Pete Richardson, Southern Univ.	22	175	76	1	.696
Dick Biddle, Colgate	14	113	51	0	.689
Bobby Lamb, Furman	8	62	34	0	.646
Walt Hameline, Wagner	29	195	110	2	.638

Ties computed as half win, half loss. Playoff games included.
Note: Minimum five years as a FBS and/or FCS head coach; record at four-year colleges only.

By Victories

Bob Ford, Albany St	241	Rob Ash, Montana St	196
Jerry Moore, Appalachian St	216	Walt Hameline, Wagner	195
Joe Taylor, Florida A&M	214	Pete Richardson, Southern U.	175
Al Bagnoli, Pennsylvania	213	Mike Ayers, Wofford	155
Andy Talley, Villanova	206	K.C. Keeler, Delaware	150
Jimmye Laycock, William & Mary	200	Bob Spoo, Eastern Illinois	140

WINNINGEST ACTIVE* DIVISION II COACHES
By Percentage

Coach, College	Yrs	W	L	T	Pct
Chuck Martin, Grand Valley St	6	74	7	0	.914
Chuck Broyles, Pittsburg St (Kan.)	20	198	47	2	.806
Ken Sparks, Carson-Newman	30	287	70	2	.802
Bill O'Boyle, Chadron St	5	46	14	0	.767
John Luckhardt, California (Pa.)	25	205	65	2	.757
Danny Hale, Bloomsburg	22	184	62	1	.747
Bill Zwaan, West Chester	13	115	39	0	.747
Mel Tjeerdsma, NW Missouri St	26	230	80	4	.739
Tom Sawyer, Winona St	14	116	46	0	.716
Bob Nielson, Minn.-Duluth	17	134	54	1	.712
Bryan Collins, LIU-C.W. Post	12	93	39	0	.705
Roger Waialae, West Liberty	5	39	18	0	.684

Ties computed as half win, half loss. Playoff games included.
Note: Minimum five years as a college head coach; record at four-year colleges only.

By Victories

Ken Sparks, Carson-Newman	287	Chuck Broyles, Pittsburg St	198
Billy Joe, Miles	243	Monte Cater, Shepherd	190
Mel Tjeerdsma, NW Missouri St	230	Danny Hale, Bloomsburg	184
Willard Bailey, St. Paul's	228	Pat Behrns, Neb.-Omaha	154
Dennis Douds, East Stroudsburg	226	Rocky Rees, Shippensburg	154
John Luckhardt, California (Pa.)	205	Richard Cavanagh, Southern Connecticut St	150

*Active in 2009.

WINNINGEST ACTIVE* DIVISION III COACHES
By Percentage

Coach, College	Yrs	W	L	T	Pct
Larry Kehres, Mount Union	24	289	22	3	.925
Mike Sirianni, Washington and Jefferson	7	70	12	0	.854
Joe Fincham, Wittenberg	14	126	230	0	.808
Jeff McMartin, Central (Iowa)	6	53	13	0	.803
Rick Willis, Wartburg	11	95	24	0	.798
Mike Whalen, Williams	6	38	10	0	.792
Jim Purtill, St. Norbert	12	100	26	1	.791
John Gagliardi, St. John's (Minn.)	61	471	126	11	.784
Pete Fredenberg, Mary Hardin-Baylor	12	109	31	0	.779
Mike Swider, Wheaton (Ill.)	14	114	35	0	.765
Jimmie Keeling, Hardin-Simmons	20	164	51	0	.763
Mike Drass, Wesley	17	142	44	1	.762

Ties computed as half won, half lost. Playoff games included.
Note: Minimum five years as a college head coach; record at four-year colleges only.

By Victories

John Gagliardi, St John's (Minn.)	471
Larry Kehres, Mount Union	289
Eric Hamilton, The College of New Jersey	196
Rick Giancola, Montclair St.	191
Dale Widolff, Occidental	169
Rich Lackner, Carnegie Mellon	165
Jimmie Keeling, Hardin-Simmons	164
Michael DeLong, Springfield	162
Steve Mohr, Trinity (Texas)	160
Larry Kindbom, Wash U.-St. Louis	158
Barry Streeter, Gettysburg	155
Joe King, Rensselaer	145
John Miech, UW-Stevens Point	145

NAIA Coaches' Records

WINNINGEST ACTIVE* NAIA COACHES
By Percentage

Coach, College	Yrs	W	L	T	Pct
Mike Van Diest, Carroll, (Mont.)	11	130	20	0	.867
Bill Cronin, Georgetown (Ky.)	13	125	31	0	.801
John Bland, Cumberlands (Ky.)	5	33	11	0	.750
Patrick Ross, Lindenwood (Mo.)	8	71	24	0	.747
Hank Biesiot, Dickinson St (N.D.)	34	242	93	1	.722
Steve Ryan, Morningside (Ia.)	8	66	26	0	.717
Carl Poelker, McKendree (Ill.)	28	191	82	1	.699
Mike Feminis, St. Xavier (Ill.)	11	89	39	0	.695
Monty Lewis, Friends (Ks.)	17	112	50	0	.691
Mike Gardner, Malone (Ohio)	6	45	21	0	.682
Mike Cochran, Southern Nazarene (Okla.)	9	68	32	0	.680
Kevin Donley, St. Francis (Ind.)	31	236	112	1	.678
Paul Troth, Missouri Valley	13	98	47	0	.676
Keith Barefield, Northwestern Oklahoma St.	14	88	44	2	.664
Larry Wilcox, Benedictine (Ks.)	31	213	119	0	.642

Playoff games included.
Note: Minimum five years as a collegiate head coach and includes record against four-year institutions only.

By Victories

Hank Biesiot, Dickinson St (N.D.)	242
Kevin Donley, St. Francis (Ind.)	236
Larry Wilcox, Benedictine (Kan.)	213
Carl Poelker, McKendree (Ill.)	191
Jim Dennison, Walsh (Ohio)	184
Fran Schwenk, William Jewell (Mo.)	136
Bob Green, Montana Tech	135
Mike Van Dienst, Carroll (Mont.)	130
Bill Cronin, Georgetown (Ky.)	125
Monty Lewis, Friends (Ks.)	112

*Active in 2009.

Pro Basketball

The indomnitable
Kobe Bryant led the
L.A. Lakers to the
NBA title in 2009-10

LeBron Who?

Though the off-season free agent moves got the hype, Kobe and the Lakers provided real basketball drama, defeating the Celtics in a classic, seven-game Finals

BY MARK BEECH

IN THE RECORD BOOKS, IT LOOKS LIKE no big deal, really. Another NBA season written into history. Another championship for the Lakers, for Phil Jackson, their decorated coach, and for Kobe Bryant, their incomparable shooting guard. If you're counting, that's 16 titles for the franchise (dating back to 1949, when it was in Minneapolis), 11 for the coach and five for the best player in the game. So, besides the impressive totals, what was so special about any of it?

Well, a whole lot, actually, starting with the fact that L.A.'s triumph over the never-say-die Boston Celtics in the NBA Finals at the Staples Center this past June—the club's second straight championship—took all of seven games to complete. It was the first time that either Jackson or Bryant, who have won five championships together, had needed so many games to close out a finals. *Ever.*

Against a gritty and resilient Boston club that refused to give in, Bryant, a bloodless competitor who is widely regarded as the toughest-minded player in the sport, actually gave out in Game 7. He missed 16 of his first 21 shots. He dropped passes and dribbled the ball off the side of his feet. He even threw up one shot that clanged off the side of the backboard. It was hardly a surprise to look up and see that the Celtics led by 13 points midway through the third quarter. "I was on E," said Bryant, who nevertheless averaged 28.6 points in the finals and won his second straight Finals MVP.

Enter Ron Artest, one of the more unlikely championship closers in recent memory. A talented forward with an incendiary reputation, he was all business in Game 7. While Bryant busied himself by pulling down rebounds (15) and driving the lane with abandon, he turned crunch time over to the 6'7" Artest, who responded with 20 points and a dagger of a three-pointer. With 1:01 remaining in the game and the Lakers leading 76-73, he took a pass from a double-teamed Bryant on the wing and calmy drained a three. As Artest ran back on defense, he blew kisses to the crowd. "He passed me the ball," Artest said of Bryant and the play after the game. "He never passes me the ball! And he passed me the ball! Kobe passed me the ball, and I shot a three."

Oddly, draining high-pressure jump shots wasn't the reason the Lakers signed Artest away from Houston in the offseason. The defensive specialist was brought in specifically to add menace and a deft scoring touch to a less-than-imposing L.A. frontcourt. He was one of a string of off-season deals made by NBA contenders to gird for a championship run. The Magic added explosive Vince Carter to complement power forward Dwight Howard. The Celtics added the mercurial Rasheed Wallace in order to become even more versatile (and more experienced). The Spurs added athleticism in the figure of forward Richard Jefferson.

Rising above all other player moves, however, was the Cavaliers' acquisition of

Ray Allen (r.) and an aging Celtics team beat a Who's Who of NBA Eastern Conference All-Stars to reach the Finals, but couldn't overcome Kobe and the Lakers.

the redoubtable Shaquille O'Neal, who joined Cleveland in an attempt to lead LeBron James to the promised land ("to win a ring for the King," in the words of Shaq). And for a time—pretty much the entire regular season—it seemed to be working. Cleveland won an NBA-best 61 games, and James averaged a career-high 29.7 points and earned his second straight regular season MVP award.

But Cleveland never seemed quite sure what to do with the aging O'Neal, who won three straight titles with Bryant in L.A. from 2000 to '02. He played just 53 games and suffered career-lows in scoring (12.0) and rebounding average (6.7). His mind may have been willing, but his big body, all 7'1" and 350 pounds of it, was no longer able. James, O'Neal and the Cavs flopped in the playoffs, losing in six games to the Celtics in the second round. "They're starting Shaq," said one Eastern Conference G.M. during the postseason as he watched O'Neal lumber up and down the court. "But you know [coach] Mike [Brown] can't wait to get Andy [Varejao] in the game."

As crushing as the playoff defeat was for Cleveland, it was just as uplifting for Boston, which fought off age and injuries to make one last gallant run at a title. The nucleus of the club—forwards Kevin Garnett and Paul Pierce, and guard Ray Allen—were all at least 32 years old, and Garnett, who hasn't played a full season since 2004–05, was struggling with a gimpy knee. But the trio gathered themselves in the postseason, subduing a raft of NBA superstars on their run to the finals. Dwyane Wade and the Heat fell in the first round, then LeBron and the Cavs, and finally, NBA Defensive Player of the Year Dwight Howard and the Magic. The Celtics were lifted not only by veterans like Wallace, but new stars like speedy point guard Rajon Rondo, a capable scorer (13.7 points per game) and wily defender (he led the NBA with 189 steals) who was a revelation in his third season.

"Without his speed," says Boston coach Doc Rivers, "we're a slow-ass basketball team."

Cleveland's loss to Boston on May 13 had

DOUG BENC/GETTY IMAGES

LeBron James announced his move to Miami via an awkward, one-hour special on ESPN that left many fans shaking their heads.

still another 33 minutes left in the show—just enough time for ESPN and everybody associated with the project to shred what remained of their credibility. "His brand is [bleep] now," one high-level NBA official said later that night of James. "He's destroyed everything." By 9:52 fans in Cleveland were already burning his jersey.

James's move was merely the biggest of an eventful summer on the NBA free-agent market. Joining him in Miami was Raptors forward Chris Bosh, who like James signed for six years and $110.1 million. With Bosh and James in the frontcourt, and former NBA MVP Dwyane Wade at guard, the Heat enter the 2010–11 season as prohibitive championship favorites. Challenging them again in the East will be the Celtics, who bolstered their aging lineup by signing both Shaquille and Jermaine O'Neal. At 32 and 38, respectively, Jermaine and Shaq should fit right in. The moribund Knicks also made some noise, landing Amar'e Stoudemire, though it's doubtful New York will morph into a title contender overnight.

The irony of the Summer of LeBron, of course, is that James had supposedly supplanted Kobe Bryant as the best player in the NBA. Bryant's fifth championship, however, stands in stark contrast to James' inability to lift his team in a second-round playoff series.

"LeBron has the pullup jumper and he takes you to the rim," says Suns forward Grant Hill. "He has the two pitches, and, trust me, both of them are great. But Kobe is like the guy with all the pitches. He brings his fastball, his change, gives you something on the corner. LeBron will overpower you but you might know what's coming. With Kobe, you're never comfortable."

There is also that ineffable something known as will. And at the end of the 2009–10 season, Bryant clearly had more of it than James. For one more year, at least, he remains the NBA's main man.

lasting repercussions, as it opened the bidding on James, perhaps the biggest and most coveted free agent in NBA history. Speculation began almost immediately that he was leaving to play for the Knicks. Two weeks later, in a move that was seen as an attempt to win James back, the Cavaliers fired Brown as their coach.

They needn't have bothered. On July 8, one week after he became a free agent, James signed a deal with the Miami Heat. The forum he chose for his announcement was an awkward, one-hour special on ESPN titled "The Decision" that was broadcast live to a bewildered public. It was one of the more cynical media spectacles in recent memory, filled with puffball interviews, stilted panel discussions and a man of the hour who looked like he would have rather been anywhere else in the world—maybe even back in Cleveland. But the train was already moving, and at 9:27 p.m. King James announced to the world, "This fall, I am taking my talents to South Beach." At that point, there were

NBA Final Standings

Western Conference
NORTHWEST DIVISION

Team	W	L	Pct	GB
†Denver	53	29	.646	—
*Utah	53	29	.646	—
*Portland	50	32	.610	3
*Oklahoma City	50	32	.610	3
Minnesota	15	67	.183	38

PACIFIC DIVISION

Team	W	L	Pct	GB
‡LA Lakers	57	25	.695	—
*Phoenix	54	28	.659	3
Golden State	29	53	.354	28
LA Clippers	26	56	.317	31
Sacramento	25	57	.305	32

SOUTHWEST DIVISION

Team	W	L	Pct	GB
†Dallas	55	27	.671	—
*San Antonio	50	32	.610	5
Houston	42	40	.512	13
New Orleans	40	42	.488	15
Memphis	37	45	.451	18

Eastern Conference
ATLANTIC DIVISION

Team	W	L	Pct	GB
†Boston	50	32	.610	—
Toronto	40	42	.488	10
New York	29	53	.354	21
Philadelphia	27	55	.329	23
New Jersey	12	70	.146	38

CENTRAL DIVISION

Team	W	L	Pct	GB
‡Cleveland	61	21	.744	—
*Milwaukee	46	36	.561	15
*Chicago	41	41	.500	20
Indiana	32	50	.390	29
Detroit	27	55	.329	34

SOUTHEAST DIVISION

Team	W	L	Pct	GB
†Orlando	59	23	.720	—
*Atlanta	53	29	.646	6
*Miami	47	35	.573	12
*Charlotte	44	38	.537	15
Washington	26	56	.317	33

†Clinched division title. *Clinched playoff berth. ‡Clinched conference title.

2010 NBA Playoffs

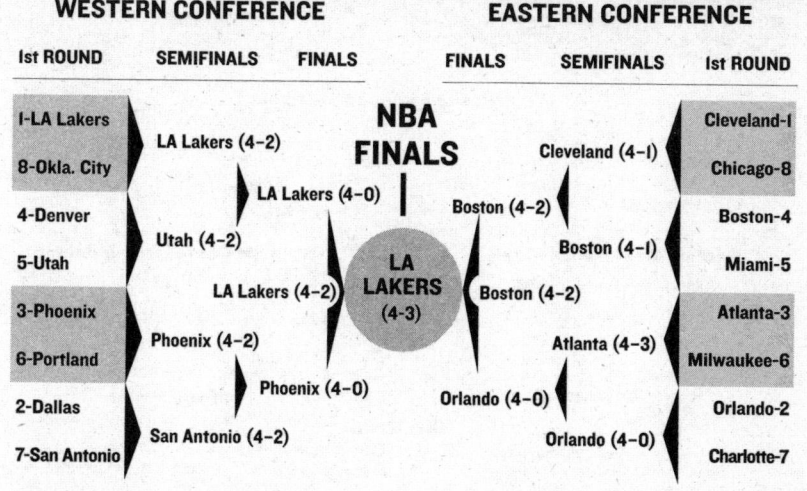

WESTERN CONFERENCE

1st ROUND — SEMIFINALS — FINALS

- 1-LA Lakers
- 8-Okla. City
- LA Lakers (4–2)
- LA Lakers (4–0)
- 4-Denver
- 5-Utah
- Utah (4–2)
- LA Lakers (4–2)
- 3-Phoenix
- 6-Portland
- Phoenix (4–2)
- Phoenix (4–0)
- 2-Dallas
- 7-San Antonio
- San Antonio (4–2)

NBA FINALS

LA LAKERS (4–3)

EASTERN CONFERENCE

FINALS — SEMIFINALS — 1st ROUND

- Cleveland (4–1)
- Boston (4–2)
- Boston (4–1)
- Boston (4–2)
- Atlanta (4–3)
- Orlando (4–0)
- Orlando (4–0)
- Cleveland-1
- Chicago-8
- Boston-4
- Miami-5
- Atlanta-3
- Milwaukee-6
- Orlando-2
- Charlotte-7

2010 NBA Playoff Results

Eastern Conference First Round

Game 1......Chicago	83	at Cleveland	96
Game 2......Chicago	102	at Cleveland	112
Game 3......Cleveland	106	at Chicago	108
Game 4......Cleveland	121	at Chicago	98
Game 5......Chicago	94	at Cleveland	96

Cleveland won series 4–1.

Game 1......Miami	76	at Boston	85
Game 2......Miami	77	at Boston	106
Game 3......Boston	100	at Miami	98
Game 4......Boston	92	at Miami	101
Game 5......Miami	86	at Boston	96

Boston won series 4–1.

Game 1......Charlotte	89	at Orlando	98
Game 2......Charlotte	77	at Orlando	92
Game 3......Orlando	90	at Charlotte	86
Game 4......Orlando	99	at Charlotte	90

Orlando won series 4–0.

Game 1......Milwaukee	92	at Atlanta	102
Game 2......Milwaukee	86	at Atlanta	96
Game 3......Atlanta	89	at Milwaukee	107
Game 4......Atlanta	104	at Milwaukee	111
Game 5......Milwaukee	91	at Atlanta	87
Game 6......Atlanta	83	at Milwaukee	69
Game 7......Milwaukee	74	at Atlanta	95

Atlanta won series 4–3.

Western Conference First Round

Game 1......Okla. City	79	at LA Lakers	87
Game 2......Okla. City	92	at LA Lakers	95
Game 3......LA Lakers	96	at Okla. City	101
Game 4......LA Lakers	89	at Okla. City	110
Game 5......Okla. City	87	at LA Lakers	111
Game 6......LA Lakers	95	at Okla. City	94

LA Lakers won series 4–2.

Game 1......Utah	113	at Denver	126
Game 2......Utah	114	at Denver	111
Game 3......Denver	93	at Utah	105
Game 4......Denver	106	at Utah	117
Game 5......Utah	102	at Denver	116
Game 6......Denver	104	at Utah	112

Utah won series 4–2.

Game 1......San Antonio	94	at Dallas	100
Game 2......San Antonio	102	at Dallas	88
Game 3......Dallas	90	at San Antonio	94
Game 4......Dallas	89	at San Antonio	92
Game 5......San Antonio	81	at Dallas	103
Game 6......Dallas	87	at San Antonio	97

San Antonio won series 4–2.

Game 1......Portland	105	at Phoenix	100
Game 2......Portland	90	at Phoenix	119
Game 3......Phoenix	108	at Portland	89
Game 4......Phoenix	87	at Portland	96
Game 5......Portland	88	at Phoenix	107
Game 6......Phoenix	99	at Portland	90

Phoenix won series 4–2.

Eastern Conference Semifinals

Game 1......Boston	93	at Cleveland	101
Game 2......Boston	104	at Cleveland	86
Game 3......Cleveland	124	at Boston	95
Game 4......Cleveland	87	at Boston	97
Game 5......Boston	120	at Cleveland	88
Game 6......Cleveland	85	at Boston	94

Boston won series 4–2.

Game 1......Atlanta	71	at Orlando	114
Game 2......Atlanta	98	at Orlando	112
Game 3......Orlando	105	at Atlanta	75
Game 4......Orlando	98	at Atlanta	84

Orlando won series 4–0.

Western Conference Semifinals

Game 1......Utah	99	at LA Lakers	104
Game 2......Utah	103	at LA Lakers	111
Game 3......LA Lakers	111	at Utah	110
Game 4......LA Lakers	111	at Utah	96

LA Lakers won series 4–0.

Game 1......San Antonio	102	at Phoenix	111
Game 2......San Antonio	102	at Phoenix	110
Game 3......Phoenix	110	at San Antonio	96
Game 4......Phoenix	107	at San Antonio	101

Phoenix won series 4–0.

Eastern Conference Finals

Game 1......Boston	92	at Orlando	88
Game 2......Boston	95	at Orlando	92
Game 3......Orlando	71	at Boston	94
Game 4......Orlando	96	at Boston	92
Game 5......Boston	92	at Orlando	113
Game 6......Orlando	84	at Boston	96

Boston won series 4–2.

Western Conference Finals

Game 1......Phoenix	107	at LA Lakers	128
Game 2......Phoenix	112	at LA Lakers	124
Game 3......LA Lakers	109	at Phoenix	118
Game 4......LA Lakers	106	at Phoenix	115
Game 5......Phoenix	101	at LA Lakers	103
Game 6......LA Lakers	111	at Phoenix	103

LA Lakers won series 4–2.

NBA Finals

Game 1......Boston	89	at LA Lakers	102
Game 2......Boston	103	at LA Lakers	94
Game 3......LA Lakers	91	at Boston	84
Game 4......LA Lakers	89	at Boston	96
Game 5......LA Lakers	86	at Boston	92
Game 6......Boston	67	at LA Lakers	89
Game 7......Boston	79	at LA Lakers	83

LA Lakers won series 4–3.

NBA Finals Composite Box Score

BOSTON CELTICS

Player	GP	Mpg	FG%	3FG%	FT%	Reb./per game Off.	Reb./per game Total	Apg	Spg	Bpg	TOpg	Ppg
Paul Pierce	7	39.9	.439	.400	.865	0.6	5.3	3.0	0.6	0.9	2.6	18.0
Kevin Garnett	7	33.3	.511	.000	.737	1.1	5.6	3.0	1.4	1.3	1.6	15.3
Ray Allen	7	39.3	.367	.293	.960	0.6	2.7	1.7	0.3	0.1	1.7	14.6
Rajon Rondo	7	38.9	.453	.333	.263	2.3	6.3	7.6	1.4	0.3	2.7	13.6
Glen Davis	7	20.6	.461	.000	.688	2.3	5.6	0.8	0.7	0.4	1.0	6.7
Kendrick Perkins	6	23.5	.571	.000	.647	2.0	5.0	1.0	0.1	0.1	1.1	5.8
Rasheed Wallace	7	20.7	.366	.238	1.000	0.4	4.6	0.9	0.4	0.7	3.3	5.3
Nate Robinson	7	10.4	.400	.333	1.000	0.3	1.1	1.9	0.1	0.0	0.6	4.9
Tony Allen	7	14.6	.333	.000	.858	0.4	1.0	0.4	1.0	0.7	0.7	3.1
Marquis Daniels	2	2.2	.500	1.000	1.000	0.1	0.1	0.0	0.0	0.0	0.5	2.5
Michael Finley	2	2.5	.000	.000	.000	0.0	0.0	0.0	0.0	0.0	0.0	0.0
Brian Scalabrine	1	0.9	.000	.000	.000	0.0	0.0	0.0	0.0	0.0	0.0	0.0
Shelden Williams	2	9.2	.000	.000	.000	0.0	0.6	0.0	0.0	0.0	2.0	0.0
Avg/Total	**7**	**336.0**	**.433**	**.308**	**.772**	**10.1**	**37.9**	**19.7**	**4.6**	**4.3**	**13.7**	**87.1**

LOS ANGELES LAKERS

Player	GP	Mpg	FG%	3FG%	FT%	Reb./per game Off.	Reb./per game Total	Apg	Spg	Bpg	TOpg	Ppg
Kobe Bryant	7	41.3	.405	.319	.883	1.7	8.0	3.9	2.0	0.7	3.9	28.6
Pau Gasol	7	41.9	.478	.000	.721	5.0	11.6	3.7	0.7	2.6	1.9	18.6
Ron Artest	7	35.9	.361	.344	.550	1.7	4.6	1.3	0.7	0.6	1.6	10.6
Derek Fisher	7	30.6	.420	.200	.941	0.4	3.0	2.0	0.7	0.0	1.3	8.6
Lamar Odom	7	27.4	.489	.100	.545	1.4	6.6	1.3	0.4	0.6	1.4	7.6
Andrew Bynum	7	25.0	.452	.000	.700	2.3	5.1	0.0	0.1	1.3	0.9	7.4
Shannon Brown	7	11.9	.450	.000	1.000	0.0	0.9	0.4	0.0	0.1	0.0	3.0
Jordan Farmar	7	12.6	.321	.200	.500	0.1	1.1	0.9	1.1	0.0	1.1	3.0
Sasha Vujacic	7	7.6	.375	.400	.833	0.4	1.0	1.7	0.3	0.0	0.1	3.0
Luke Walton	4	7.8	.333	.000	.000	0.0	0.5	0.8	0.0	0.5	0.5	0.5
D.J. Mbenga	1	2.7	.000	.000	.000	0.0	1.0	0.0	0.0	0.0	0.0	0.0
Josh Powell	2	4.1	.000	.000	.000	0.0	0.5	0.0	0.0	0.0	0.0	0.0
Avg/Total	**7**	**336.0**	**.418**	**.280**	**.765**	**13.1**	**42.4**	**14.6**	**6.1**	**6.1**	**13.3**	**90.6**

NBA Finals Game Box Scores

Game 1

BOSTON 89

Player	Min	FG M–A	FT M–A	Reb O–T	A	PF	S	TO	TP
P. Pierce	46	6–13	12–13	0–9	4	5	0	3	24
K. Garnett	35	7–16	2–2	2–4	1	3	2	1	16
K. Perkins	25	2–2	4–5	1–3	1	3	1	1	8
R. Allen	27	3–8	6–6	0–0	0	5	0	2	12
R. Rondo	40	6–14	1–4	4–6	8	2	0	2	13
T. Allen	17	1–4	2–2	0–0	0	4	1	2	4
R. Wallace	18	3–4	2–2	0–4	0	3	0	1	9
G. Davis	19	4–3	1–2	1–3	1	1	1	1	3
M. Finley	2	0–0	0–0	0–0	0	0	0	0	0
N.Robinson	13	0–3	0–2	0–2	4	2	0	0	0
Totals	240	29–67	30–36	8–31	19	28	5	13	89

Percentages: FG—.433, FT—.833. 3-pt goals: 1–10, .100 (Pierce 0–4, Allen 0–2, Wallace 1–2, Robinson 0–2).
Technical Fouls 2 (Pierce, Wallace). Team rebounds: 7. Blocked shots: 5 (Pierce 2, Garnett 1, Allen 1, Wallace 1).

LOS ANGELES 102

Player	Min	FG M–A	FT M–A	Reb O–T	A	PF	S	TO	TP
R. Artest	33	5–10	2–2	1–4	1	4	2	0	15
P. Gasol	47	8–14	7–10	8–14	3	4	1	3	23
A. Bynum	28	4–6	2–4	0–6	0	3	0	1	10
K. Bryant	39	10–22	9–10	1–7	6	4	1	4	30
D. Fisher	28	3–8	3–3	0–3	3	3	1	0	9
S. Vujacic	8	0–1	0–0	0–1	2	1	0	0	0
L. Odom	21	2–6	1–2	1–4	1	5	0	2	5
J. Farmar	13	2–4	0–0	0–2	1	1	1	1	4
S. Brown	17	3–5	0–0	0–1	0	0	0	0	6
L. Walton	5	0–0	0–0	0–0	1	1	0	1	0
Totals	240	37–76	24–31	12–42	18	26	6	12	102

Percentages: FG—.487, FT—.774. 3-pt goals: 4–10, .400 (Artest 3–5, Bryant 1–2, Vujacic 0–1, Odom 0–2)).
Technical Fouls 1 (Artest). Team rebounds: 10. Blocked shots: 7 (Artest 1, Gasol 3, Bryant 1, Odom 1, Walton 1).

A: 18,997. Officials: J. Crawford, DeRosa, Stafford.–

Game 2

BOSTON 103

Player	Min	FG M-A	FT M-A	Reb O-T	A	PF	S	TO	TP
P. Pierce	40	2-11	6-6	1-4	4	3	1	2	10
K. Garnett	24	2-5	2-2	0-4	6	5	0	0	6
K. Perkins	32	4-7	4-6	1-6	3	4	0	2	12
R. Allen	44	11-20	2-2	1-3	2	3	0	2	32
R. Rondo	42	8-18	2-5	4-12	10	2	2	3	19
G. Davis	18	4-13	0-1	5-7	1	4	1	1	8
R. Wallace	18	3-5	0-0	1-7	1	4	0	1	7
T. Allen	12	0-2	2-2	0-1	1	2	0	0	2
S. Williams	4	0-1	0-0	0-1	0	2	2	0	0
N. Robinson	6	2-2	2-2	0-0	0	0	0	0	7
Totals	240	36-84	20-26	13-44	28	29	6	13	103

Percentages: FG—.408, FT—.769. 3-pt goals: 11-16, .688 (Allen 8-11, Rondo 1-1, Wallace 1-3, Robinson 1-1). Team rebounds: 12. Blocked shots: 3 (Pierce 1, Rondo 1, Davis 1).

LOS ANGELES 94

Player	Min	FG M-A	FT M-A	Reb O-T	A	PF	S	TO	TP
R. Artest	41	1-10	3-0	2-5	1	6	2	3	6
P. Gasol	42	7-10	11-11	3-8	3	3	1	1	25
A. Bynum	39	6-10	9-11	3-6	0	5	0	2	21
K. Bryant	34	8-20	3-10	0-5	6	5	4	5	21
D. Fisher	35	2-8	2-2	1-7	4	3	0	1	6
L. Odom	15	1-3	1-4	0-5	1	5	0	1	3
S. Vujacic	7	1-1	0-0	1-1	1	0	0	2	3
J. Farmar	13	3-7	0-0	0-0	1	1	1	0	7
S. Brown	15	0-2	0-0	0-2	1	1	0	0	2
Totals	240	29-71	31-41	10-39	18	29	8	15	94

Percentages: FG—.408, FT—.756. 3-pt goals: 5-22, .227 (Artest 1-6, Gasol 0-1, Bryant 2-7, Fisher 0-2, Odom 0-1, Vujacic 1-1, Farmar 1-4, Brown 0-2). Team rebounds: 11. Blocked shots: 14 (Gasol 6, Bynum 7, Brown 1).

A: 18,997. Officials: Javie, Washington, McCutchen.

Game 3

LOS ANGELES 91

Player	Min	FG M-A	FT M-A	Reb O-T	A	PF	S	TO	TP
R. Artest	23	1-4	0-0	1-3	1	2	0	1	2
P. Gasol	39	5-11	3-6	2-10	4	2	0	1	13
A. Bynum	29	3-9	3-3	5-10	0	2	0	1	9
K. Bryant	44	10-29	8-8	2-7	4	2	2	1	29
D. Fisher	41	6-12	4-4	0-3	1	5	0	2	16
L. Walton	13	1-1	0-0	0-2	1	2	0	0	2
L. Odom	28	5-5	1-1	1-5	1	4	0	1	12
S. Brown	16	2-3	0-0	0-1	0	1	0	0	4
J. Farmar	7	1-2	0-0	0-2	1	0	0	1	2
S. Vujacic	1	0-0	2-2	0-0	0	0	0	0	2
Totals	240	34-76	21-24	11-43	13	20	2	8	91

Percentages: FG—.447, FT—.875. 3-pt goals: 2-15, .133 (Artest 0-2, Bryant 1-7, Fisher 0-3, Odom 1-1, Brown 0-1, Farmar 0-1). Team rebounds: 5. Blocked shots: 7 (Artest 1, Gasol 2, Bynum 1, Bryant 3).

BOSTON 84

Player	Min	FG M-A	FT M-A	Reb O-T	A	PF	S	TO	TP
P. Pierce	34	5-12	2-3	0-2	2	5	0	0	15
K. Garnett	32	11-16	3-4	2-6	3	5	0	3	25
K. Perkins	22	1-4	3-4	5-11	1	2	0	2	5
R. Allen	42	0-13	2-2	1-4	2	2	0	2	2
R. Rondo	43	5-10	1-4	0-3	8	4	2	0	11
R. Wallace	19	1-5	0-0	0-4	3	4	2	0	2
G. Davis	24	4-5	4-5	0-3	0	3	0	3	12
T. Allen	20	3-4	1-2	0-2	1	1	0	0	7
N. Robinson	6	2-4	0-0	0-0	1	0	0	0	5
Totals	240	32-73	16-24	8-35	20	27	4	10	84

Percentages: FG—.438, FT—.667. 3-pt goals: 4-18, .222 (Pierce 3-4, Allen 0-8, Rondo 0-1, Wallace 0-3, Robinson 1-2). Team rebounds: 11. Blocked shots: 2 (Garnett 1, Wallace 1).

A: 18,624. Officials: D. Crawford, Salvatore, Kennedy.

Game 4

LOS ANGELES 89

Player	Min	FG M-A	FT M-A	Reb O-T	A	PF	S	TO	TP
R. Artest	42	4-10	1-1	4-7	3	2	0	0	9
P. Gasol	44	6-13	9-10	1-6	3	4	0	4	21
A. Bynum	12	1-2	0-0	0-3	0	1	0	1	2
K. Bryant	43	10-22	7-8	0-6	2	5	2	7	33
D. Fisher	31	3-6	0-1	0-1	2	4	1	1	6
L. Odom	39	5-10	0-1	1-7	1	5	1	1	10
S. Vujacic	7	0-1	0-0	2-2	1	0	0	0	0
S. Brown	11	2-5	1-1	0-0	0	1	0	0	5
J. Farmar	11	1-2	0-0	0-2	1	1	1	1	3
Totals	240	32-71	18-22	8-34	13	23	6	15	89

Percentages: FG—.451, FT—.818. 3-pt goals: 7-20, .350 (Artest 0-1, Gasol 0-1, Bryant 6-11, Fisher 0-2, Odom 0-1, Vujacic 0-1, Brown 0-1, Farmar 1-2). Technical Fouls 2 (Robinson 1, Wallace 1). Team rebounds: 8. Blocked shots: 3 (Artest 1, Gasol 2).

BOSTON 96

Player	Min	FG M-A	FT M-A	Reb O-T	A	PF	S	TO	TP
P. Pierce	36	7-12	5-7	1-6	5	3	1	5	19
K. Garnett	27	5-13	3-3	3-6	3	3	2	2	13
K. Perkins	25	3-5	0-0	3-7	0	2	0	2	6
R. Allen	41	4-11	4-4	0-5	1	3	1	0	12
R. Rondo	31	5-15	0-2	2-5	3	0	3	1	10
G. Davis	22	7-10	4-4	4-5	0	2	0	0	18
R. Wallace	22	1-1	0-0	0-2	0	5	1	1	3
T. Allen	18	1-4	1-1	2-3	1	3	1	1	3
N. Robinson	16	4-8	2-2	1-2	2	2	1	0	12
M. Daniels	1	0-0	0-0	0-0	0	0	0	0	0
Totals	240	37-83	19-23	16-41	15	21	12	12	96

Percentages: FG—.446, FT—.826. 3-pt goals: 3-12, .250 (Pierce 0-1, Allen 0-4, Rondo 0-1, Wallace 1-1, Allen 0-1, Robinson 2-4). Team rebounds: 10. Blocked shots: 2 (Garnett 1, Allen 1).

A: 18,624. Officials: Foster, Rush, Willard.

Game 5

LOS ANGELES 86

Player	Min	FG M-A	FT M-A	Reb O-T	A	PF	S	TO	TP
R. Artest	34	2-9	1-4	1-2	2	4	1	1	7
P. Gasol	38	5-12	2-3	7-12	0	4	2	1	12
A. Bynum	32	3-6	0-1	1-1	0	3	0	1	6
K. Bryant	44	13-27	8-9	2-5	4	5	1	4	38
D. Fisher	34	2-9	5-5	2-4	2	3	1	2	9
L. Odom	26	4-6	0-2	3-8	2	2	2	3	8
J. Farmar	14	0-4	1-2	0-1	1	0	1	0	1
S. Brown	1	0-0	0-0	0-0	0	0	0	0	0
S. Vujacic	10	2-5	0-0	0-1	0	1	1	0	5
L. Walton	7	0-0	0-0	0-0	1	0	0	1	0
Totals	240	31-78	17-26	16-34	12	22	9	13	86

Percentages: FG—.397, FT—.654. 3-pt goals: 7-19, .368 (Artest 2-5, Bryant 4-10, Fisher 0-1, Farmar 0-1, Vujacic 1-2). Technical Fouls: 1 (Fisher). Team rebounds: 9. Blocked shots: 1 (Bryant).

BOSTON 92

Player	Min	FG M-A	FT M-A	Reb O-T	A	PF	S	TO	TP
P. Pierce	43	12-21	1-2	0-2	2	4	1	0	18
K. Garnett	36	6-11	6-7	1-10	3	4	5	3	17
K. Perkins	32	2-2	0-2	4-7	1	4	0	2	11
R. Allen	40	5-10	2-2	0-3	2	5	1	2	13
R. Rondo	38	9-12	0-0	1-5	8	1	1	7	14
T. Allen	13	2-6	0-0	0-1	0	2	0	1	0
G. Davis	13	0-1	0-0	1-3	1	2	0	0	6
R. Wallace	15	2-4	0-0	0-4	0	0	0	0	11
N.Robinson	10	2-4	0-0	4-4	0	0	4	0	1
Totals	240	40-71	9-13	8-32	21	23	8	16	92

Percentages: FG—.563, FT—.692. 3-pt goals: 3-12, .250 (Pierce 2-4, Allen 0-4, Wallace 1-2, Robinson 0-2). Technical Fouls 2 (Allen, Rondo). Team rebounds: 13. Blocked shots: 7 (Pierce 2, Garnett 2, Rondo 1, Allen 1, Wallace 1).

A: 18,624. Officials: J. Crawford, Callahan, Stafford.

Game 6

BOSTON 67

Player	Min	FG M-A	FT M-A	Reb O-T	A	PF	S	TO	TP
P. Pierce	34	6-14	0-0	1-4	2	1	1	5	13
K. Garnett	31	6-14	0-0	0-6	3	3	1	0	12
K. Perkins	7	0-1	0-0	0-1	0	1	0	1	0
R. Allen	36	7-14	3-3	2-2	3	2	0	4	19
R. Rondo	33	5-15	0-2	1-5	6	1	2	3	10
R. Wallace	17	0-7	0-0	0-3	0	4	0	0	0
T. Allen	17	1-4	0-0	1-1	0	3	3	0	2
N.Robinson	16	2-8	1-1	1-4	3	0	0	2	6
G. Davis	27	0-3	0-2	4-9	0	3	1	0	0
S. Williams	14	0-1	0-0	0-3	0	2	0	0	0
M. Daniels	4	1-2	2-2	1-1	0	1	0	1	5
M. Finley	3	0-1	0-0	0-0	0	0	0	0	0
Totals	240	28-84	6-10	11-39	17	21	8	14	67

Percentages: FG—.333, FT—.600. 3-pt goals: 5-23, .217 (Pierce 1-4, Garnett 0-1, Allen 2-5, Rondo 0-4, Robinson 1-4, Daniels 1-1, Finley 0-1). Team rebounds: 10. Blocked shots: 4 (Allen 2, Davis 2).

LOS ANGELES 89

Player	Min	FG M-A	FT M-A	Reb O-T	A	PF	S	TO	TP
R. Artest	32	6-11	0-0	0-6	0	3	0	2	15
P. Gasol	41	6-14	5-6	5-13	9	2	1	2	17
A. Bynum	16	1-4	0-0	3-4	0	1	1	0	2
K. Bryant	40	9-19	7-7	3-11	3	2	4	2	26
D. Fisher	15	1-1	2-2	0-2	0	4	2	3	4
S. Brown	19	2-4	0-0	0-2	2	1	0	0	4
L. Odom	28	3-9	2-2	1-10	1	2	1	1	8
S. Vujacic	14	3-6	1-2	0-1	1	1	1	1	9
J. Farmar	17	2-6	0-0	0-1	1	0	3	2	4
J. Powell	7	0-2	0-0	0-0	0	0	0	0	0
L. Walton	6	0-2	0-0	0-0	0	0	0	0	0
D. Mbenga	3	0-1	0-0	0-1	0	1	0	0	0
Totals	240	33-79	17-19	12-52	17	17	12	13	89

Percentages: FG—.418, FT—.895. 3-pt goals: 6-19, .316 (Artest 3-6, Bryant 1-4, Brown 0-2, Vujacic 2-4, Farmar 0-1, Powell 0-1). Technical Fouls 1 (Bryant). Team rebounds: 7. Blocked shots: 8 (Artest 1, Gasol 3, Bynum 1, Odom 2, Walton 1).

A: 18,997. Officials: McCutchen, DeRosa, Mauer.

Game 7

BOSTON 79

Player	Min	FG M-A	FT M-A	Reb O-T	A	PF	S	TO	TP
P. Pierce	46	5-15	6-6	1-10	2	4	0	3	18
K. Garnett	38	8-13	1-1	0-3	2	5	0	2	17
R. Wallace	36	5-11	0-0	2-8	2	6	0	1	11
R. Allen	45	3-14	5-6	0-2	2	3	0	4	13
R. Rondo	45	6-13	1-2	4-8	10	2	0	3	14
G. Davis	21	2-4	2-2	1-9	0	4	0	2	6
N.Robinson	3	0-1	0-0	0-0	0	0	0	0	0
T. Allen	5	0-0	0-0	0-0	0	1	0	0	0
B.Scalabrine	1	0-0	0-0	0-0	0	0	0	0	0
Totals	240	29-71	15-17	8-32	18	25	0	14	79

Percentages: FG—.408, FT—.882. 3-pt goals: 6-16, .375 (Pierce 2-3, Wallace 1-4, Allen 2-7, Rondo 1-2). Team rebounds: 6. Blocked shots: 7 (Pierce 1, Garnett 4, Wallace 2).

LOS ANGELES 83

Player	Min	FG M-A	FT M-A	Reb O-T	A	PF	S	TO	TP
R. Artest	46	7-18	4-5	3-5	1	3	0	4	20
P. Gasol	42	6-16	7-13	9-18	4	2	0	1	19
A. Bynum	19	1-5	0-0	4-6	0	2	0	0	2
K. Bryant	45	6-24	11-15	4-15	2	4	0	2	23
D. Fisher	30	4-6	0-0	0-1	2	3	0	2	10
L. Odom	35	3-8	1-2	3-7	2	0	0	1	7
J. Farmar	13	0-3	0-0	0-0	0	2	0	1	0
S. Vujacic	5	0-2	2-2	0-1	0	2	0	0	2
S. Brown	5	0-1	0-0	0-0	0	1	0	0	0
J. Powell	1	0-0	0-0	0-0	0	0	0	0	0
Totals	240	27-83	25-37	23-53	11	19	0	11	83

Percentages: FG—.325, FT—.676. 3-pt goals: 4-20, .200 (Artest 2-6, Bryant 0-6, Fisher 2-2, Odom 0-3, Farmar 0-1, Vujacic 0-1). Team rebounds: 13. Blocked shots: 3 (Gasol 2, Odom 1).

A: 18,997. Officials: D. Crawford, J. Crawford, Foster

2009–10 All-NBA Teams

FIRST TEAM	SECOND TEAM	THIRD TEAM
F LeBron James, Cle	F Carmelo Anthony, Den	F Tim Duncan, SA
F Kevin Durant, OKC	F Dirk Nowitzki, Dal	F Pau Gasol, LAL
C Dwight Howard, Orl	C Amare Stoudemire, Phx	C Andrew Bogut, Mil
G Kobe Bryant, LAL	G Steve Nash, Phx	G Joe Johnson, Atl
G Dwyane Wade, Mia	G Deron Williams, Utah	G Brandon Roy, Por

All-Rookie Teams

FIRST TEAM	SECOND TEAM
Tyreke Evans, Sac	Marcus Thornton, NO
Brandon Jennings, Mil	DeJuan Blair, SA
Stephen Curry, GS	James Harden, OKC
Darren Collison, NO	Jonny Flynn, Min
Taj Gibson, Chi	Jonas Jerebko, Det

All-Defensive Team

FIRST TEAM	SECOND TEAM
F LeBron James, Cle	F Josh Smith, Atl
F Gerald Wallace, Cha	F Anderson Varejao, Cle
C Dwight Howard, Orl	C Tim Duncan, SA
G Kobe Bryant, LAL	G Dwyane Wade, Mia
G Rajon Rondo, Bos	G Thabo Sefolosha, OKC

2009–10 NBA Regular Season Individual Leaders

Scoring

	GP	Pts	Avg
Kevin Durant, OKC	82	2,472	30.1
LeBron James, Cle	76	2,228	29.7
Carmelo Anthony, Den	69	1,943	28.2
Kobe Bryant, LAL	73	1,970	27.0
Dwyane Wade, Mia	77	2,045	26.5
Monta Ellis, GS	64	1,641	25.5
Dirk Nowitzki, Dal	81	2,027	25.0
Danny Granger, Ind	62	1,497	24.1
Chris Bosh, Tor	72	1,678	24.0
Amare Stoudemire, Phx	82	1,896	23.1

Rebounds

	GP	Reb	Avg
Dwight Howard, Orl	82	1,082	13.2
Marcus Camby, Por/LAC	74	871	11.8
Zach Randolph, Mem	81	950	11.7
David Lee, NY	81	949	11.7
Pau Gasol, LAL	65	734	11.3
Carlos Boozer, Utah	78	874	11.2
Joakim Noah, Chi	64	704	11.0
Kevin Love, Min	60	658	11.0
Chris Bosh, Tor	70	759	10.8
Troy Murphy, Ind	72	737	10.2

Assists

	GP	Ast	Avg
Steve Nash, Phx	81	892	11.0
Chris Paul, NO	45	480	10.7
Deron Williams, Utah	76	798	10.5
Rajon Rondo, Bos	81	794	9.8
Jason Kidd, Dal	80	724	9.0
LeBron James, Cle	76	651	8.6
Baron Davis, LAC	75	598	8.0
Russell Westbrook, OKC	82	652	8.0
Gilbert Arenas, Was	32	230	7.2
Devin Harris, NJ	64	423	6.6

Field-Goal Percentage

	FGA	FGM	Pct
Erick Dampier, Dal	213	133	.624
Dwight Howard, Orl	834	510	.612
DeAndre Jordan, LAC	238	144	.605
Kendrick Perkins, Bos	522	314	.602
Nick Collison, OKC	309	182	.589
Robin Lopez, Phx	291	171	.588
Nene Hilario, Den	717	421	.587
Marc Gasol, Mem	651	378	.581
Anderson Varejao, Cle	467	267	.572
Andrew Bynum, LAL	688	392	.570

Free-Throw Percentage

	FTA	FTM	Pct
Steve Nash, Phx	225	211	.938
Dirk Nowitzki, Dal	586	536	.915
Ray Allen, Bos	253	231	.913
Chauncey Billups, Den	512	466	.910
Kevin Durant, OKC	840	756	.900
Mo Williams, Cle	198	177	.894
Stephen Curry, GS	200	177	.885
Kevin Martin, Hou/Sac	340	298	.876
Manu Ginobli, SA	355	309	.870
Jason Terry, Dal	268	232	.866

Three-Point Field-Goal Percentage

	3FGA	3FGM	Pct
Mike Miller, Was	171	82	.480
Jared Dudley, Phx	262	120	.458
Anthony Morrow, GS	307	140	.456
Channing Frye, Phx	392	172	.439
Stephen Curry, GS	380	166	.437
Arron Afflalo, Den	249	108	.434
Mo Williams, Cle	371	159	.429
Steve Nash, Phx	291	124	.426
Jason Kidd, Dal	414	176	.425
Anthony Parker, Cle	261	108	.414

Steals

	GP	Steals	Avg
Rajon Rondo, Bos	81	189	2.33
Monta Ellis, GS	64	143	2.23
Chris Paul, NO	45	96	2.13
Stephen Curry, GS	80	152	1.90
Dwyane Wade, Mia	77	142	1.84
Jason Kidd, Dal	80	145	1.81
Trevor Ariza, Hou	72	126	1.75
Andre Iguodala, Phi	82	141	1.72
Baron Davis, LAC	75	126	1.68
LeBron James, Cle	76	125	1.64

Blocked Shots

	GP	BS	Avg
Dwight Howard, Orl	82	228	2.78
Andrew Bogut, Mil	69	175	2.54
Josh Smith, Atl	81	172	2.12
Brendan Haywood, Dal/Was	77	158	2.05
Marcus Camby, LAC	74	146	1.97
Chris Andersen, Den	76	143	1.88
Samuel Dalembert, Phi	82	151	1.84
Pau Gasol, LAL	65	113	1.74
Brook Lopez, NJ	82	139	1.70
Kendrick Perkins, Bos	78	132	1.69

Offense

Team	FG Pct	3FG Pct	FT Pct	Rebound Avg Off	Total	A	TO	Stl	Scoring Avg
Phoenix	.49.2	41.2	77.0	11.1	43.0	23.3	14.8	5.8	110.2
Golden State	.46.9	37.5	78.2	9.2	38.4	22.4	14.7	9.3	108.8
Denver	.46.8	35.9	77.2	10.8	41.4	21.0	13.9	8.3	106.5
Utah	.49.1	36.4	74.1	10.6	42.2	26.7	15.2	8.2	104.2
Toronto	.48.2	37.1	76.4	9.8	40.4	22.0	13.4	5.7	104.1
Orlando	.47.0	37.5	72.4	9.9	43.2	19.7	14.1	6.2	102.8
Memphis	.46.9	33.7	73.3	13.0	43.5	18.8	15.2	7.9	102.5
Houston	.44.7	35.1	77.2	11.8	42.0	21.8	14.5	7.1	102.4
Cleveland	.48.5	38.1	72.0	9.6	42.5	22.4	13.9	6.9	102.1
New York	.45.5	34.6	78.2	10.2	40.4	21.6	14.0	7.1	102.1
Dallas	.46.4	37.2	81.6	10.2	41.7	23.4	12.9	7.6	102.0
LA Lakers	.45.7	34.1	76.5	11.9	44.3	21.1	13.4	7.5	101.7
Atlanta	.46.8	36.0	75.9	11.8	41.7	21.8	12.0	7.2	101.7
Oklahoma City	.46.2	34.0	80.5	11.7	43.5	20.0	15.0	8.0	101.5
San Antonio	.47.3	35.8	74.0	10.8	42.8	22.3	13.6	6.3	101.4
Indiana	.44.3	34.8	77.5	9.6	41.5	21.1	15.0	7.1	100.8
New Orleans	.46.4	36.3	77.8	10.4	40.3	22.3	13.5	7.6	100.2
Sacramento	.45.6	34.9	72.6	11.9	42.6	20.5	15.0	6.9	100.0
Boston	.48.3	35.8	74.6	8.7	38.6	23.5	14.9	8.5	99.2
Minnesota	.44.9	34.1	74.6	11.7	42.9	19.8	16.3	7.3	98.2
Portland	.46.1	35.4	79.0	11.1	40.2	20.4	12.3	6.4	98.1
Philadelphia	.46.0	34.3	75.6	11.5	41.0	21.0	14.5	8.1	97.7
Milwaukee	.43.6	35.6	75.5	11.8	43.0	21.2	13.2	7.1	97.7
Chicago	.45.1	33.0	75.4	11.4	44.5	20.8	14.3	6.5	97.5
Miami	.45.8	34.6	75.2	10.7	41.8	18.9	13.2	7.4	96.5
Washington	.44.9	35.3	76.2	11.8	41.8	19.0	14.9	6.0	96.2
Charlotte	.45.5	33.2	73.0	10.5	40.8	22.1	15.7	7.7	95.7
LA Clippers	.45.3	34.6	75.1	11.3	41.8	20.2	15.7	6.5	95.3
Detroit	.44.5	31.4	72.8	12.8	40.2	19.4	13.4	7.3	94.0
New Jersey	.42.9	31.8	78.0	10.9	39.7	18.8	14.4	7.0	92.4

Defense (Opponents' Statistics)

Team	FG Pct	3FG Pct	FT Pct	Rebound Avg. Off	Total	A	TO	Stl	Scoring Avg
Charlotte	.46.9	37.5	78.2	10.6	39.6	22.4	15.3	7.5	93.8
Miami	.44.9	34.1	74.6	10.4	40.7	19.8	14.4	6.3	94.2
Portland	.45.5	34.6	78.2	9.8	38.1	21.6	13.5	5.9	94.8
Orlando	.48.2	37.1	76.4	9.8	40.0	22.0	12.8	6.7	95.3
Boston	.49.2	41.2	77.0	10.6	40.1	23.3	15.6	7.0	95.6
Cleveland	.45.6	34.9	72.6	9.7	38.5	20.5	12.7	6.6	95.6
Milwaukee	.46.9	33.7	73.3	9.6	42.8	18.8	15.3	7.0	96.0
San Antonio	.44.3	34.8	77.5	9.9	39.5	21.1	12.6	6.9	96.3
LA Lakers	.44.7	35.1	77.2	11.1	42.2	21.9	14.1	7.0	97.0
Atlanta	.46.4	36.3	77.8	11.2	41.4	22.3	13.8	6.2	97.0
Oklahoma City	.46.8	35.9	77.2	11.4	40.7	21.0	15.1	7.5	98.0
Utah	.45.5	33.2	73.0	10.2	39.2	22.1	15.1	7.7	98.9
Chicago	.46.0	34.3	75.6	11.2	42.7	21.0	13.3	7.0	99.1
Detroit	.42.9	31.8	78.0	9.9	39.4	18.8	14.3	6.7	99.1
Dallas	.44.9	35.3	76.2	11.2	42.9	19.0	14.6	6.9	99.3
Washington	.46.4	37.2	81.6	11.4	42.3	23.4	13.6	6.9	101.0
New Jersey	.44.5	31.4	72.8	11.3	44.0	19.4	14.0	7.8	101.5
Philadelphia	.45.1	33.0	75.4	10.8	41.0	20.8	14.5	7.6	101.6
LA Clippers	.49.1	36.4	74.1	10.7	41.1	26.7	12.9	8.4	102.1
Denver	.46.2	34.0	80.5	11.6	42.3	20.0	15.1	7.0	102.4
New Orleans	.46.8	36.0	75.9	10.6	42.1	21.8	14.4	7.0	102.7
Houston	.45.7	34.1	76.5	10.7	42.8	21.1	14.7	7.3	102.7
Indiana	.47.3	35.8	74.0	11.8	46.6	22.3	15.0	8.0	103.8
Memphis	.43.6	35.6	75.5	11.1	39.7	21.2	14.2	7.7	104.0
Sacramento	.48.5	38.1	72.0	11.1	42.0	22.4	13.7	7.1	104.4
Phoenix	.48.3	34.8	74.6	13.2	42.3	23.5	13.0	7.9	105.3
Toronto	.47.0	37.5	72.4	11.4	41.3	19.7	12.7	7.1	105.9
New York	.46.1	35.4	79.0	11.7	44.9	20.4	14.4	7.1	105.9
Minnesota	.45.8	34.6	75.2	11.2	43.4	18.9	14.3	8.8	107.8
Golden State	.45.3	34.6	74.3	13.4	48.1	20.2	17.6	7.9	112.4

Atlanta Hawks

Player	GP	MPG	FG%	3Pt%	FT%	OFF	DEF	Total	APG	SPG	BPG	TO	PF	PPG
Joe Johnson	76	38.0	45.8	36.9	81.8	1.0	3.7	4.6	4.9	1.1	0.1	1.9	1.9	21.3
Jamal Crawford	79	31.1	44.9	38.2	85.7	0.4	2.1	2.5	3.0	0.8	0.2	1.7	1.7	18.0
Josh Smith	81	35.4	50.5	0.0	61.8	2.8	6.0	8.7	4.2	1.6	2.1	2.4	3.0	15.7
Al Horford	81	35.1	55.1	100.0	78.9	2.9	7.0	9.9	2.3	0.7	1.1	1.5	2.8	14.2
Marvin Williams	81	30.5	45.5	30.3	81.9	1.3	3.8	5.1	1.1	0.8	0.6	0.9	2.0	10.1
Mike Bibby	80	27.4	41.6	39.9	86.1	0.3	2.1	2.3	3.9	0.8	0.0	1.1	2.0	9.1
Maurice Evans	79	16.7	44.5	33.7	75.4	0.7	1.2	1.9	0.6	0.4	0.2	0.3	1.6	5.7
Zaza Pachulia	78	14.0	48.8	0.0	65.0	1.5	2.3	3.8	0.5	0.5	0.4	0.7	2.4	4.3
Jeff Teague	71	10.1	39.6	21.9	83.7	0.1	0.9	0.9	1.7	0.5	0.2	0.7	1.2	3.2
Joe Smith	64	9.3	39.9	14.3	81.3	1.0	1.4	2.5	0.3	0.1	0.3	0.3	1.5	3.0
Randolph Morris	28	4.4	56.1	0.0	59.3	0.9	0.9	1.7	0.0	0.2	0.1	0.4	1.2	2.2
Mario West	39	3.6	33.3	0.0	60.0	0.2	0.5	0.7	0.2	0.2	0.0	0.2	0.6	0.8
Jason Collins	24	4.8	34.8	0.0	0.0	0.2	0.4	0.6	0.2	0.1	0.1	0.2	0.9	0.7
Hawks	**82**	**242.1**	**46.8**	**36.0**	**75.9**	**11.8**	**29.9**	**41.7**	**21.8**	**7.4**	**5.0**	**12.0**	**19.9**	**101.7**
Opponents	**82**	**242.1**	**46.0**	**34.5**	**74.5**	**11.2**	**30.1**	**41.4**	**21.0**	**6.5**	**4.4**	**13.8**	**19.3**	**97.0**

Boston Celtics

Player	GP	MPG	FG%	3Pt%	FT%	OFF	DEF	Total	APG	SPG	BPG	TO	PF	PPG
Paul Pierce	71	34.0	47.2	41.4	85.2	0.5	3.8	4.4	3.1	1.2	0.4	2.3	2.8	18.3
Ray Allen	80	35.2	47.7	36.3	91.3	0.6	2.6	3.2	2.6	0.8	0.3	1.6	2.3	16.3
Kevin Garnett	69	29.9	52.1	20.0	83.7	1.1	6.2	7.3	2.7	1.0	0.8	1.5	2.5	14.3
Rajon Rondo	81	36.6	50.8	21.3	62.1	1.2	3.2	4.4	9.8	2.3	0.1	3.0	2.4	13.7
Kendrick Perkins	78	27.6	60.2	0.0	58.2	2.0	5.6	7.6	1.0	0.3	1.7	2.1	2.8	10.1
Rasheed Wallace	79	22.5	40.9	28.3	76.8	0.5	3.6	4.1	1.0	1.0	0.9	0.8	2.8	9.0
*Nate Robinson	26	14.7	40.1	41.4	61.5	0.2	1.3	1.5	2.0	0.9	0.0	0.8	1.9	6.5
Glen Davis	54	17.3	43.7	0.0	69.9	1.9	1.9	3.8	0.6	0.4	0.3	1.0	2.4	6.3
Tony Allen	54	16.5	51.0	0.0	60.5	1.0	1.7	2.7	1.3	1.1	0.4	1.2	2.0	6.1
Marquis Daniels	51	18.4	49.8	21.4	60.7	0.5	1.3	1.9	1.3	0.5	0.1	0.8	1.8	5.6
*Michael Finley	21	15.0	50.6	46.3	33.3	0.0	1.5	1.6	1.1	0.2	0.1	0.4	1.0	5.2
Shelden Williams	54	11.1	52.1	0.0	76.5	0.9	1.8	2.7	0.4	0.2	0.4	0.6	1.6	3.7
Brian Scalabrine	52	9.1	34.1	32.7	66.7	0.2	0.8	0.9	0.5	0.0	0.1	0.3	1.1	1.5
Celtics	**82**	**241.2**	**48.3**	**34.8**	**74.6**	**8.7**	**29.9**	**38.6**	**23.5**	**8.6**	**4.9**	**14.9**	**22.1**	**99.2**
Opponents	**82**	**241.2**	**45.1**	**34.2**	**74.6**	**10.6**	**29.5**	**40.1**	**19.3**	**7.0**	**4.7**	**15.6**	**21.7**	**95.6**

Charlotte Bobcats

Player	GP	MPG	FG%	3Pt%	FT%	OFF	DEF	Total	APG	SPG	BPG	TO	PF	PPG
*Stephen Jackson	72	39.3	42.3	33.4	78.6	1.0	4.1	5.1	3.6	1.6	0.5	3.2	2.5	21.1
Gerald Wallace	76	41.0	48.4	37.1	77.6	2.0	8.1	10.0	2.1	1.5	1.1	2.3	2.6	18.2
Raymond Felton	80	33.0	45.9	38.5	76.3	0.7	2.9	3.6	5.6	1.5	0.3	2.1	2.2	12.1
*Raja Bell	5	31.4	43.6	37.5	100.0	1.0	3.2	4.2	2.0	0.8	0.4	1.0	2.6	12.0
Boris Diaw	82	35.4	48.3	32.0	76.9	1.6	3.6	5.2	4.0	0.7	0.7	2.2	2.7	11.3
*Tyrus Thomas	25	21.7	44.2	0.0	72.9	1.6	4.5	6.1	0.9	0.9	1.5	1.6	2.6	10.1
*Ronald Murray	46	21.6	38.9	31.3	71.0	0.3	1.8	2.1	1.8	0.6	0.3	1.4	1.7	9.9
*Larry Hughes	14	21.1	32.7	35.7	85.3	0.5	1.8	2.3	2.0	0.9	0.3	1.4	1.2	8.1
Nazr Mohammed	58	17.0	55.3	0.0	64.8	2.0	3.3	5.2	0.5	0.3	0.7	0.9	1.8	7.9
Tyson Chandler	51	22.8	57.4	0.0	73.2	2.2	4.0	6.3	0.3	0.3	1.1	1.8	2.7	6.5
D.J. Augustin	80	18.4	38.6	39.3	77.9	0.1	1.1	1.2	2.4	0.6	0.1	0.9	1.6	6.4
*Theo Ratliff	28	22.3	46.6	0.0	78.3	1.6	2.6	4.2	0.6	0.3	1.5	0.9	2.1	5.1
*V. Radmanovic	8	16.6	33.3	31.8	66.7	1.0	2.6	3.6	0.9	0.4	0.1	0.6	2.3	4.9
Stephen Graham	70	11.5	49.6	32.0	64.6	0.3	1.6	1.9	0.3	0.3	0.1	0.5	1.3	4.2
Derrick Brown	57	9.4	46.3	28.6	66.7	0.5	0.8	1.4	0.3	0.4	0.2	0.3	0.9	3.3
Gerald Henderson	43	8.3	35.6	21.1	74.5	0.3	0.9	1.3	0.3	0.2	0.2	0.3	0.6	2.6
*Acie Law	9	3.7	31.3	0.0	85.7	0.0	0.1	0.1	0.3	0.1	0.1	0.3	0.3	1.8
Alexis Ajinca	6	5.0	50.0	0.0	0.0	0.2	0.5	0.7	0.0	0.2	0.2	0.3	0.8	1.7
DeSagana Diop	27	9.7	51.7	0.0	22.2	0.9	1.5	2.4	0.0	0.2	0.5	0.4	1.1	1.2
Bobcats	**82**	**241.7**	**45.3**	**34.6**	**75.1**	**10.5**	**30.4**	**40.8**	**20.2**	**7.7**	**5.4**	**15.7**	**19.5**	**95.3**
Opponents	**82**	**241.7**	**44.8**	**33.8**	**74.3**	**10.6**	**29.0**	**39.6**	**20.3**	**7.5**	**6.1**	**15.3**	**22.0**	**93.8**

* mid-season trade

Chicago Bulls

Player	GP	MPG	FG%	3Pt%	FT%	OFF	DEF	Total	APG	SPG	BPG	TO	PF	PPG
Derrick Rose	78	36.8	48.9	26.7	76.6	0.8	2.9	3.8	6.0	0.7	0.4	2.8	1.2	20.8
Luol Deng	70	37.9	46.6	38.6	76.4	1.9	5.4	7.3	2.0	0.9	0.9	1.9	1.8	17.6
Kirk Hinrich	74	33.5	40.9	37.1	75.2	0.3	3.2	3.5	4.5	1.2	0.3	1.5	2.8	10.9
Joakim Noah	64	30.1	50.4	0.0	74.4	3.4	7.6	11.0	2.1	0.5	1.6	1.8	3.1	10.7
*Ronald Murray	29	23.4	39.7	31.1	76.2	0.4	2.5	2.9	1.8	0.6	0.1	0.9	1.7	10.1
Taj Gibson	82	26.9	49.4	0.0	64.6	2.8	4.7	7.5	0.9	0.6	1.3	1.4	3.4	9.0
Brad Miller	82	23.8	43.0	28.0	82.7	1.0	3.9	4.9	1.9	0.5	0.4	1.3	2.3	8.8
*Hakim Warrick	28	19.0	48.3	0.0	75.5	1.4	2.2	3.6	0.6	0.3	0.3	0.8	1.5	8.7
*Acie Law	12	11.3	46.7	33.3	74.1	0.3	0.9	1.2	1.3	0.3	0.0	1.0	0.7	5.5
Jannero Pargo	63	13.2	34.6	27.5	93.3	0.1	1.1	1.21	1.4	0.5	0.0	0.8	1.1	5.5
James Johnson	65	11.6	45.2	32.6	72.9	0.5	1.4	2.0	0.7	0.3	0.7	1.0	1.9	3.9
Chris Richard	18	12.4	51.7	0.0	63.6	1.1	2.2	3.3	0.4	0.4	0.2	0.8	2.8	2.1
*Devin Brown	11	8.5	22.2	23.5	0.0	0.2	1.2	1.4	0.6	0.3	0.1	0.5	0.9	1.8
Lindsey Hunter	13	9.4	16.7	7.7	100.0	0.1	1.0	1.1	0.7	0.1	0.0	0.3	0.9	1.0
Joe Alexander	8	3.6	16.7	0.0	66.7	0.3	0.4	0.6	0.3	0.1	0.1	0.0	1.1	0.5
Bulls	82	242.7	45.1	33.0	75.4	11.4	33.1	44.5	20.8	6.5	5.8	14.3	20.1	97.5
Opponents	82	242.7	44.2	34.8	74.4	11.2	31.6	42.7	20.9	7.0	5.3	13.3	20.0	99.1

Cleveland Cavaliers

Player	GP	MPG	FG%	3Pt%	FT%	OFF	DEF	Total	APG	SPG	BPG	TO	PF	PPG
LeBron James	76	39.0	50.3	33.3	76.7	0.9	6.4	7.3	8.6	1.6	1.0	3.4	1.6	29.7
Mo Williams	69	34.2	44.7	42.9	89.4	0.4	2.6	3.0	5.3	1.0	0.3	2.5	2.5	15.8
*Antawn Jamison	25	32.4	48.5	34.2	50.6	1.5	6.2	7.7	1.3	1.1	0.5	1.2	2.7	15.8
Shaquille O'Neal	53	23.4	56.6	0.0	49.6	1.8	4.9	6.7	1.5	0.3	1.2	2.0	3.2	12.0
*Sebastian Telfair	4	19.3	45.7	22.2	83.3	0.0	1.0	1.0	3.0	0.5	0.0	1.5	1.5	9.8
Delonte West	60	25.0	44.5	32.5	81.0	0.5	2.3	2.8	3.3	0.9	0.5	1.5	1.4	8.8
Anderson Varejao	76	28.5	57.2	20.0	66.3	2.5	5.1	7.6	1.1	0.9	0.9	0.9	2.9	8.6
J.J. Hickson	81	20.9	55.4	0.0	68.1	1.4	3.6	4.9	0.5	0.4	0.5	1.1	1.6	8.5
Zydrunas Ilgauskas	64	20.9	44.3	47.8	74.3	1.8	3.6	5.4	0.8	0.2	0.8	1.0	2.9	7.4
Anthony Parker	81	28.3	43.4	41.4	78.9	0.4	2.5	2.9	1.9	0.8	0.2	0.9	1.9	7.3
Daniel Gibson	56	19.1	46.6	47.7	69.4	0.2	1.1	1.3	1.3	0.5	0.1	0.6	1.4	6.3
Jamario Moon	61	17.2	46.2	32.0	80.0	0.4	2.7	3.1	0.8	0.6	0.5	0.4	1.1	4.9
Jawad Williams	54	13.7	39.3	32.3	71.1	0.3	1.2	1.5	0.6	0.2	0.1	0.3	1.4	4.1
Leon Powe	20	11.8	42.9	0.0	58.7	1.0	2.1	3.1	0.0	0.3	0.1	0.6	1.8	4.0
Daniel Green	20	5.8	38.5	27.3	66.7	0.4	0.5	0.9	0.3	0.3	0.2	0.3	0.5	2.0
Cavaliers	82	241.2	48.5	38.1	72.0	9.6	32.8	42.5	22.4	6.9	5.2	13.9	19.4	102.1
Opponents	82	241.2	44.2	34.7	75.7	9.7	28.9	38.5	20.3	6.6	4.0	12.7	20.8	95.6

Dallas Mavericks

Player	GP	MPG	FG%	3Pt%	FT%	OFF	DEF	Total	APG	SPG	BPG	TO	PF	PPG
Dirk Nowitzki	81	37.5	48.1	42.1	91.5	1.0	6.7	7.7	2.7	0.9	1.0	1.8	2.6	25.0
Jason Terry	77	33.0	43.8	36.5	86.6	0.2	1.6	1.8	3.8	1.2	0.2	1.4	1.8	16.6
*Caron Butler	27	34.4	44.0	34.0	76.0	1.3	4.0	5.4	1.8	1.8	0.3	1.7	2.5	15.2
Shawn Marion	75	31.8	50.8	15.8	75.5	2.1	4.3	6.4	1.4	0.9	0.8	1.3	1.9	12.0
Jason Kidd	80	36.0	42.3	42.5	80.8	0.6	5.0	5.6	9.1	1.8	0.4	2.4	1.8	10.3
*Bren. Haywood	28	26.5	56.4	0.0	57.5	2.8	4.6	7.4	0.9	0.3	2.0	1.1	2.3	8.1
Jose Barea	78	19.8	44.0	35.7	84.4	0.2	1.7	1.9	3.3	0.5	0.1	1.3	1.5	7.6
Tim Thomas	18	15.8	46.2	37.2	87.5	0.7	1.6	2.3	0.8	0.6	0.1	0.8	1.7	7.5
Rodrigue Beaubois	56	12.5	51.8	40.9	80.8	0.2	1.2	1.4	1.3	0.5	0.2	1.0	1.5	7.1
Erick Dampier	55	23.3	62.4	33.3	60.4	2.3	4.9	7.3	0.6	0.3	1.4	1.1	2.8	6.0
*Eduardo Najera	33	14.6	45.2	34.0	66.7	0.7	1.7	2.3	0.4	0.5	0.4	0.4	1.8	3.3
*DeS. Stevenson	24	11.1	28.3	32.0	70.0	0.2	0.9	1.1	0.5	0.2	0.0	0.3	1.0	2.0
*Matt Carroll	25	4.8	36.0	21.1	1.000	0.2	0.3	0.5	0.2	0.2	0.0	0.3	0.5	1.8
Mavericks	82	242.4	46.4	37.2	81.6	10.2	31.5	41.7	23.4	7.6	5.5	12.9	19.1	102.0
Opponents	82	242.4	45.7	34.7	75.8	11.2	31.6	42.9	20.2	6.9	4.1	14.6	20.1	99.3

* mid-season trade

Denver Nuggets

Player	GP	MPG	FG%	3Pt%	FT%	OFF	DEF	Total	APG	SPG	BPG	TO	PF	PPG
Carmelo Anthony	.69	38.2	45.8	31.6	83.0	2.2	4.4	6.6	3.2	1.3	0.4	3.0	3.3	28.2
Chauncey Billups	.73	34.1	41.8	38.6	91.0	0.3	2.8	3.1	5.6	1.1	0.1	2.4	2.1	19.5
J.R. Smith	.75	27.7	41.4	33.8	70.6	0.4	2.7	3.1	2.4	1.3	0.3	1.9	2.3	15.4
Nenê	.82	33.6	58.7	0.0	70.4	2.0	5.6	7.6	2.5	1.4	1.0	1.5	3.4	13.8
Kenyon Martin	.58	34.2	45.6	27.6	55.7	2.4	7.0	9.4	1.9	1.2	1.1	1.6	3.2	11.5
Arron Afflalo	.82	27.2	46.5	43.4	73.5	0.7	2.4	3.1	1.7	0.6	0.4	0.9	2.7	8.8
Ty Lawson	.65	20.2	51.5	41.0	75.7	0.6	1.3	1.9	3.1	0.7	0.0	1.3	1.4	8.3
Chris Andersen	.76	22.3	56.6	0.0	69.5	1.9	4.4	6.4	0.4	0.6	1.9	0.8	2.3	5.9
Joey Graham	.63	12.0	52.0	15.4	74.0	0.6	1.3	2.0	0.3	0.4	0.1	0.7	1.7	4.2
Johan Petro	.36	12.1	53.5	0.0	66.7	0.9	2.7	3.6	0.4	0.3	0.4	0.6	2.2	3.4
Anthony Carter	.54	15.9	42.0	27.0	84.6	0.3	1.3	1.6	3.0	0.7	0.2	1.1	1.3	3.3
Malik Allen	.51	8.9	39.7	16.7	92.3	0.7	0.9	1.6	0.3	0.2	0.1	0.4	1.3	2.1
Renaldo Balkman	.13	7.0	33.3	0.0	33.3	0.3	1.5	1.8	0.5	0.6	0.2	0.5	1.2	1.1
Nuggets	**82**	**241.2**	**46.8**	**35.9**	**77.2**	**10.8**	**30.5**	**41.4**	**21.0**	**8.3**	**5.1**	**13.8**	**22.5**	**106.5**
Opponents	**82**	**241.2**	**45.6**	**34.9**	**76.8**	**11.6**	**30.6**	**42.3**	**21.0**	**7.0**	**5.3**	**15.1**	**23.7**	**102.4**

Detroit Pistons

Player	GP	MPG	FG%	3Pt%	FT%	OFF	DEF	Total	APG	SPG	BPG	TO	PF	PPG
Richard Hamilton	...46	33.7	40.9	29.7	84.6	0.7	2.0	2.7	4.4	0.7	0.1	2.5	2.5	18.1
Rodney Stuckey	.73	34.2	40.5	22.8	83.3	0.9	2.9	3.8	4.8	1.4	0.2	2.2	2.8	16.6
Ben Gordon	...62	27.9	41.6	32.1	86.1	0.4	1.5	1.9	2.7	0.8	0.1	1.9	2.4	13.8
Tayshaun Prince	.49	34.0	48.6	37.0	71.4	1.4	3.6	5.1	3.3	0.7	0.5	1.2	1.6	13.5
Charlie Villanueva	.78	23.7	43.9	35.1	81.5	1.1	3.6	4.7	0.7	0.6	0.7	1.0	2.9	11.9
Will Bynum	...63	26.5	44.4	21.8	79.8	0.4	1.9	2.3	4.5	0.9	0.1	1.8	2.3	10.0
Jonas Jerebko	...80	27.9	48.1	31.3	71.0	2.4	3.6	6.0	0.7	1.0	0.4	1.0	2.9	9.3
Jason Maxiell	76	20.4	51.1	0.0	57.4	2.1	3.2	5.3	0.5	0.5	0.9	0.9	2.3	6.8
Ben Wallace	...69	28.6	54.1	0.0	40.6	3.6	5.1	8.7	1.5	1.3	1.2	0.9	1.9	5.5
Austin Daye	...69	13.3	46.4	30.5	82.1	0.5	2.0	2.5	0.5	0.4	0.4	0.7	1.7	5.1
Chris Wilcox	...34	13.0	52.5	0.0	50.0	1.3	2.1	3.4	0.4	0.4	0.4	1.1	1.9	4.5
Chucky Atkins	...16.1	36.3	30.1	92.6	0.1	0.6	0.7	2.3	0.4	0.0	0.8	1.3	4.0	
Kwame Brown	48	13.8	50.0	0.0	33.7	1.1	2.6	3.7	0.5	0.3	0.3	0.9	1.9	3.3
DaJuan Summers	44	9.2	35.4	35.7	71.1	0.3	0.7	1.0	0.4	0.2	0.2	0.4	1.2	3.0
Pistons	**82**	**241.2**	**44.5**	**31.4**	**72.8**	**12.8**	**27.3**	**40.2**	**19.4**	**7.3**	**3.8**	**13.4**	**22.2**	**94.0**
Opponents	**82**	**241.2**	**48.0**	**37.5**	**76.7**	**9.9**	**29.5**	**39.4**	**23.1**	**6.7**	**4.9**	**14.3**	**20.8**	**99.1**

Golden State Warriors

Player	GP	MPG	FG%	3Pt%	FT%	OFF	DEF	Total	APG	SPG	BPG	TO	PF	PPG
Monta Ellis	...64	41.4	44.9	33.8	75.3	0.7	3.3	4.0	5.3	2.2	0.4	3.8	3.0	25.5
Corey Maggette	...70	29.7	51.6	26.0	83.5	1.3	4.0	5.3	2.5	0.7	0.1	2.4	3.3	19.8
Stephen Curry	80	36.2	46.2	43.7	88.5	0.6	3.9	4.5	5.9	1.9	0.2	3.0	3.2	17.5
Reggie Williams	...24	32.6	49.5	35.9	83.9	0.8	3.8	4.6	2.8	1.0	0.3	1.2	2.0	15.2
Kelenna Azubuike	..9	25.7	54.5	37.0	67.9	1.3	3.2	4.6	1.1	0.6	1.0	0.8	1.8	13.9
Anthony Morrow	...69	29.2	46.8	45.6	88.6	0.9	2.9	3.8	1.5	0.9	0.2	1.2	2.3	13.0
*Anthony Tolliver	..44	32.3	43.1	33.1	76.9	1.9	5.3	7.3	2.0	0.7	0.8	1.1	2.9	12.3
Anthony Randolph	..33	22.7	44.3	20.0	80.1	2.2	4.3	6.5	1.3	0.9	1.6	1.5	2.8	11.6
*Raja Bell	1	23.0	66.7	100.0	0.0	0.0	2.0	2.0	3.0	0.0	0.0	0.0	2.0	11.0
C.J. Watson	...65	27.5	46.8	31.0	77.1	0.4	2.2	2.6	2.8	1.6	0.1	1.1	1.9	10.3
*V. Radmanovic	...33	23.0	38.5	26.7	76.2	1.3	3.2	4.5	1.2	0.8	0.2	1.2	2.4	6.6
Devean George	...45	16.9	43.2	39.0	69.6	0.5	2.1	2.5	0.7	0.9	0.2	0.3	2.0	5.4
Mikki Moore	...23	17.7	60.0	0.0	63.6	1.1	1.9	3.0	1.6	0.2	0.6	0.9	2.4	5.0
Andris Biedrins	33	23.1	59.1	0.0	16.0	1.9	5.9	7.8	1.7	0.6	1.3	1.0	3.5	5.0
Ronny Turiaf	42	20.8	58.2	0.0	47.4	1.3	3.3	4.5	2.1	0.6	1.3	1.2	2.3	4.9
Chris Hunter	60	13.1	50.2	0.0	75.4	0.9	1.9	2.8	0.6	0.2	0.6	0.5	2.2	4.5
Warriors	**82**	**240.6**	**46.9**	**37.5**	**78.2**	**9.2**	**29.2**	**38.4**	**22.4**	**9.3**	**4.2**	**14.7**	**23.0**	**108.8**
Opponents	**82**	**240.6**	**48.5**	**37.5**	**76.7**	**13.4**	**34.7**	**48.1**	**24.1**	**7.9**	**5.0**	**17.6**	**21.4**	**112.4**

* mid-season trade

Houston Rockets

Player	GP	MPG	FG%	3Pt%	FT%	OFF	DEF	Total	APG	SPG	BPG	TO	PF	PPG
*Kevin Martin	24	35.8	43.5	31.0	92.4	0.4	2.5	2.9	2.3	1.0	0.1	2.4	1.9	21.3
Aaron Brooks	82	35.6	43.2	39.8	82.2	0.7	2.0	2.6	5.3	0.8	0.2	2.8	2.4	19.6
Luis Scola	82	32.6	51.4	20.0	77.9	2.1	6.5	8.6	2.1	0.8	0.3	2.0	3.0	16.2
Trevor Ariza	72	36.5	39.4	33.4	64.9	1.1	4.5	5.6	3.8	1.8	0.6	2.2	2.3	14.9
Kyle Lowry	68	24.3	39.7	27.2	82.7	1.3	2.3	3.6	4.5	0.9	0.1	1.7	2.5	9.1
Chase Budinger	74	20.1	44.1	36.9	77.0	0.5	2.5	3.0	1.2	0.5	0.2	0.7	1.1	8.9
Shane Battier	67	32.4	39.8	36.2	72.6	1.1	3.6	4.7	2.4	0.8	1.1	1.0	2.1	8.0
*Jordan Hill	23	16.2	53.2	0.0	66.0	1.9	3.0	5.0	0.6	0.2	0.5	0.8	2.4	6.4
David Andersen	63	14.1	43.2	34.6	68.7	0.9	2.4	3.3	0.7	0.2	0.2	0.6	1.9	5.8
*Jared Jeffries	18	18.4	42.9	11.1	55.6	1.7	1.9	3.6	1.0	0.5	0.7	0.8	2.6	4.9
Chuck Hayes	82	21.6	48.9	0.0	54.5	1.8	3.8	5.7	1.7	0.9	0.5	0.9	2.7	4.4
Jermaine Taylor	31	9.8	37.8	22.7	71.7	0.7	0.8	1.5	0.5	0.3	0.1	0.6	0.5	4.1
*Mike Harris	8	10.3	37.0	0.0	55.6	1.1	1.4	2.5	0.4	0.5	0.1	1.1	1.3	3.1
Brian Cook	15	2.9	30.4	22.2	71.4	0.1	0.5	0.6	0.1	0.0	0.1	0.4	0.3	1.4
Will Conroy	5	7.2	30.0	0.0	0.0	0.0	0.6	0.6	1.4	0.0	0.0	0.8	1.0	1.2
*Hilton Armstrong	9	4.4	29.4	0.0	0.0	0.6	0.1	0.7	0.3	0.6	0.0	0.6	1.1	1.1
Rockets	**82**	**242.7**	**44.7**	**35.1**	**77.2**	**11.8**	**30.1**	**42.0**	**21.8**	**7.1**	**3.9**	**14.5**	**20.9**	**102.4**
Opponents	**82**	**242.7**	**47.5**	**36.4**	**76.4**	**10.7**	**32.1**	**42.8**	**20.9**	**7.3**	**6.5**	**14.7**	**22.4**	**102.7**

Indiana Pacers

Player	GP	MPG	FG%	3Pt%	FT%	OFF	DEF	Total	APG	SPG	BPG	TO	PF	PPG
Danny Granger	62	36.7	42.8	36.1	84.8	1.1	4.4	5.5	2.8	1.5	0.8	2.5	3.0	24.1
Troy Murphy	72	32.6	47.2	38.4	79.8	1.8	8.4	10.2	2.1	1.0	0.5	1.4	2.4	14.6
Roy Hibbert	81	25.1	49.5	50.0	75.4	2.2	3.5	5.7	2.0	0.4	1.6	1.8	3.5	11.7
T.J. Ford	47	25.3	44.5	16.0	77.0	0.9	2.3	3.2	3.8	0.9	0.2	1.9	2.2	10.3
Dahntay Jones	76	24.9	46.1	12.5	77.0	0.6	2.4	3.0	2.0	0.5	0.5	1.7	3.1	10.2
Mike Dunleavy	67	22.2	41.0	31.8	84.2	0.4	3.1	3.5	1.5	0.6	0.2	1.1	1.6	9.9
Brandon Rush	82	24.0	42.3	41.1	62.9	0.5	3.7	4.2	1.4	0.7	0.8	1.1	1.9	9.4
Tyler Hansbrough	29	17.6	36.0	0.0	74.3	2.1	2.7	4.8	1.0	0.6	0.3	0.7	2.4	8.5
Earl Watson	79	29.4	42.6	28.8	71.0	0.7	2.4	3.0	5.1	1.3	0.2	2.2	2.3	7.8
Luther Head	47	17.3	43.7	35.2	82.8	0.1	1.6	1.7	1.5	0.4	0.2	1.2	1.1	7.6
A.J. Price	56	15.4	41.0	34.5	80.0	0.2	1.4	1.6	1.9	0.6	0.1	1.1	0.9	7.3
Josh McRoberts	42	12.5	52.1	34.8	50.0	1.0	2.1	3.0	1.0	0.4	0.4	0.5	1.8	4.3
Solomon Jones	52	13.0	44.3	0.0	71.8	1.0	1.8	2.8	0.6	0.3	0.7	0.8	2.4	4.0
Jeff Foster	16	15.9	47.8	0.0	55.6	2.1	2.9	5.1	1.3	0.2	0.3	0.9	2.8	3.1
Pacers	**82**	**240.3**	**44.3**	**34.8**	**77.5**	**9.6**	**31.9**	**41.5**	**21.1**	**7.1**	**5.4**	**15.0**	**22.5**	**100.8**
Opponents	**82**	**240.3**	**45.3**	**36.3**	**75.6**	**11.8**	**34.8**	**46.6**	**20.7**	**8.0**	**5.0**	**15.0**	**20.8**	**103.8**

Los Angeles Clippers

Player	GP	MPG	FG%	3Pt%	FT%	OFF	DEF	Total	APG	SPG	BPG	TO	PF	PPG
Chris Kaman	76	34.3	49.0	0.0	74.9	2.4	6.8	9.3	1.6	0.5	1.2	2.9	2.8	18.5
Eric Gordon	62	36.0	44.9	37.1	74.2	0.4	2.2	2.6	3.0	1.1	0.2	2.3	1.5	16.9
Baron Davis	75	33.6	40.6	27.7	82.1	0.7	2.9	3.5	8.0	1.7	0.6	2.8	2.8	15.3
*Drew Gooden	24	30.2	49.2	0.0	92.1	3.5	5.9	9.4	0.9	0.6	0.3	2.2	2.7	14.8
Rasual Butler	82	30.4	40.0	33.6	84.1	0.5	2.5	2.9	1.4	0.4	0.8	1.0	1.5	11.9
*Travis Outlaw	23	21.7	40.0	37.8	80.0	0.9	2.7	3.6	1.1	0.5	0.4	0.9	1.3	8.7
Craig Smith	75	16.4	56.9	20.0	63.5	1.3	2.5	3.8	1.1	0.4	0.3	1.2	2.6	7.8
*Steve Blake	29	26.3	44.3	43.7	75.0	0.2	2.2	2.4	6.1	0.7	0.1	2.2	1.3	6.8
DeAndre Jordan	70	16.2	60.5	0.0	37.5	1.7	3.3	5.0	0.3	0.2	0.9	1.1	2.2	4.8
Ricky Davis	36	13.9	43.4	38.1	58.1	0.3	1.3	1.6	1.1	0.4	0.1	0.8	1.1	4.4
*Bobby Brown	23	8.3	32.9	28.1	71.4	0.3	0.5	0.9	1.8	0.3	0.0	1.0	0.6	3.0
Mardy Collins	43	10.9	36.7	23.5	61.9	0.3	0.9	1.2	1.0	0.5	0.0	0.7	1.0	2.6
Steve Novak	54	6.7	38.9	31.0	77.8	0.0	0.6	0.6	0.1	0.1	0.0	0.0	0.4	2.1
Brian Skinner	16	7.7	40.0	0.0	75.0	0.6	1.1	1.7	0.0	0.2	0.3	0.4	1.3	1.6
Kareem Rush	7	8.3	36.4	33.3	0.0	0.1	0.7	0.9	0.6	0.3	0.4	0.4	1.1	1.3
Clippers	**82**	**240.3**	**45.5**	**33.2**	**73.0**	**11.3**	**30.5**	**41.8**	**22.1**	**6.5**	**5.7**	**15.7**	**19.3**	**95.7**
Opponents	**82**	**240.3**	**47.0**	**36.3**	**76.2**	**10.7**	**30.4**	**41.1**	**23.5**	**8.4**	**4.4**	**12.9**	**19.4**	**102.1**

* mid-season trade

Los Angeles Lakers

Player	GP	MPG	FG%	3Pt%	FT%	OFF	DEF	Total	APG	SPG	BPG	TO	PF	PPG
Kobe Bryant	73	38.8	45.6	32.9	81.1	1.1	4.3	5.4	5.0	1.6	0.3	3.2	2.6	27.0
Pau Gasol	65	37.0	53.6	0.0	79.0	3.7	7.6	11.3	3.4	0.6	1.7	2.2	2.3	18.3
Andrew Bynum	65	30.4	57.0	0.0	73.9	2.7	5.6	8.3	1.0	0.5	1.5	1.8	3.0	15.0
Ron Artest	77	33.8	41.4	35.5	68.8	1.3	3.0	4.3	3.0	1.4	0.3	1.6	2.1	11.0
Lamar Odom	82	31.5	46.3	31.9	69.3	2.2	7.5	9.8	3.3	0.9	0.7	1.8	2.8	10.8
Shannon Brown	82	20.7	42.7	32.8	81.8	0.4	1.9	2.2	1.3	0.7	0.4	0.8	1.6	8.1
Derek Fisher	82	27.2	38.0	34.8	85.6	0.3	1.8	2.1	2.5	1.1	0.1	1.0	2.5	7.5
Jordan Farmar	82	18.0	43.5	37.6	67.1	0.2	1.4	1.6	1.5	0.6	0.6	0.9	1.3	7.2
Sasha Vujacic	67	8.6	40.2	30.9	84.8	0.4	0.8	1.2	0.6	0.3	0.1	0.3	1.0	2.8
Josh Powell	63	9.2	36.6	43.8	64.5	0.7	1.1	1.8	0.6	0.1	0.1	0.5	1.1	2.7
Luke Watson	29	9.4	35.7	41.2	50.0	0.4	0.9	1.3	1.4	0.3	0.0	0.4	0.7	2.4
Adam Morrison	31	7.8	37.6	23.8	62.5	0.3	0.7	1.0	0.6	0.1	0.1	0.3	0.5	2.4
D. Ilunga-Mbenga	49	7.2	46.6	0.0	47.4	0.7	1.1	1.8	0.2	0.1	0.6	0.3	1.1	2.1
Lakers	**82**	**241.8**	**45.7**	**34.1**	**76.5**	**11.9**	**32.5**	**44.3**	**21.1**	**7.5**	**4.9**	**13.4**	**19.4**	**101.7**
Opponents	**82**	**241.8**	**44.6**	**32.8**	**75.0**	**11.1**	**31.0**	**42.2**	**21.9**	**7.0**	**4.4**	**14.1**	**21.2**	**97.0**

Memphis Grizzlies

Player	GP	MPG	FG%	3Pt%	FT%	OFF	DEF	Total	APG	SPG	BPG	TO	PF	PPG
Zach Randolph	81	37.7	48.8	28.8	77.8	4.1	7.7	11.7	1.8	1.0	0.4	2.2	2.8	20.8
Rudy Gay	80	39.7	46.6	32.7	75.3	1.4	4.5	5.9	1.9	1.5	0.8	2.1	2.5	19.6
O.J. Mayo	82	38	45.8	38.3	80.9	0.7	3.0	3.8	3.0	1.2	0.2	2.2	2.1	17.5
Marc Gasol	69	35.8	58.1	0.0	67.0	3.0	6.3	9.3	2.4	1.0	1.6	2.0	3.7	14.6
Mike Conley	80	32.1	44.5	38.7	74.3	0.4	2.0	2.4	5.3	1.4	0.2	2.1	2.2	12.0
Sam Young	80	16.5	45.1	19.6	77.7	1.0	1.6	2.5	0.7	0.4	0.3	1.2	1.3	7.4
Darrell Arthur	32	14.3	43.2	0.0	56.7	1.2	2.3	3.4	0.5	0.4	0.4	0.7	1.9	4.5
Marcus Williams	62	14.1	38.4	29.6	67.3	0.2	1.3	1.5	2.6	0.5	0.0	1.2	0.7	4.3
*Lester Hudson	9	6.8	40.0	18.2	85.7	0.4	0.7	1.1	0.6	0.6	0.1	0.6	0.6	4.0
Jamaal Tinsley	38	15.5	37.1	17.9	81.5	0.3	1.4	1.7	2.8	0.9	0.1	1.7	1.8	3.5
Hasheem Thabeet	68	13	58.8	0.0	58.1	1.3	2.3	3.6	0.2	0.2	1.3	0.6	2.4	3.1
DeMarre Carroll	71	11.2	39.6	0.0	62.3	0.7	1.4	2.1	0.5	0.4	0.1	0.3	1.5	2.9
Steven Hunter	21	7.5	39.5	0.0	52.8	0.9	1.1	2.0	0.0	0.1	0.5	0.4	0.5	2.5
*Ronnie Brewer	5	16	23.1	0.0	80.0	0.2	1.2	1.4	0.6	1.2	0.0	0.4	0.0	2.0
Hamed Haddadi	36	6.7	38.7	0.0	73.7	0.7	1.4	2.1	0.3	0.0	0.6	0.6	1.6	1.7
Trey Gilder	2	2.5	100.0	0.0	0.0	0.0	0.5	0.5	0.0	0.5	0.0	0.0	0.0	1.0
Grizzlies	**82**	**242.7**	**46.9**	**33.7**	**73.3**	**13.0**	**30.4**	**43.5**	**18.8**	**7.9**	**4.9**	**15.2**	**20.2**	**102.5**
Opponents	**82**	**242.7**	**47.8**	**35.4**	**75.5**	**11.1**	**28.6**	**39.7**	**22.9**	**7.7**	**6.1**	**14.2**	**22.4**	**104.0**

Miami Heat

Player	GP	MPG	FG%	3Pt%	FT%	OFF	DEF	Total	APG	SPG	BPG	TO	PF	PPG
Dwyane Wade	77	36.3	47.6	30.0	76.1	1.4	3.5	4.8	6.5	1.8	1.1	3.3	2.4	26.6
Michael Beasley	78	29.8	45.0	27.5	80.0	1.6	4.8	6.4	1.3	1.0	0.6	1.7	2.8	14.8
Jermaine O'Neal	70	28.4	52.9	0.0	72.0	1.8	5.2	6.9	1.3	0.4	1.4	1.8	3.0	13.6
Udonis Haslem	78	27.9	49.4	0.0	76.2	2.1	5.9	8.1	0.7	0.4	0.3	1.0	2.2	9.9
Q. Richardson	76	27.4	43.1	39.7	73.2	0.8	4.1	4.9	1.2	0.9	0.2	0.8	2.2	8.9
Dorell Wright	72	20.8	46.3	38.9	88.4	0.7	2.6	3.3	1.3	0.7	0.4	0.7	1.3	7.1
Mario Chalmers	73	24.8	40.1	31.8	74.5	0.3	1.5	1.8	3.4	1.3	0.2	1.7	2.4	7.1
*Rafer Alston	25	26.2	35.5	37.0	55.6	0.2	2.0	2.2	2.9	0.9	0.2	1.4	2.1	6.6
Carlos Arroyo	72	22.0	47.5	28.0	84.4	0.4	1.4	1.8	3.1	0.5	0.1	0.8	1.4	6.1
Daequan Cook	45	15.4	32.0	31.7	84.0	0.2	1.6	1.8	1.0	0.3	0.2	0.5	1.1	5.0
James Jones	36	14.0	36.1	41.1	82.1	0.1	1.1	1.3	0.5	0.5	0.3	0.3	1.3	4.1
*Shavlik Randolph	3	15.7	33.3	0.0	0.0	2.3	2.0	4.3	0.0	0.3	0.3	0.7	3.0	3.3
Joel Anthony	80	16.5	47.8	0.0	71.7	1.5	1.6	3.1	0.2	0.3	1.4	0.6	2.0	2.7
Jamaal Magloire	36	10.0	50.0	0.0	35.6	1.1	2.2	3.4	0.0	0.3	0.3	0.5	1.6	2.1
Yakhouba Diawara	6	7.3	20.0	16.7	0.0	0.2	0.5	0.7	0.5	0.2	0.0	0.5	1.3	0.8
Heat	**82**	**242.4**	**45.8**	**34.6**	**75.2**	**10.7**	**31.1**	**41.8**	**18.9**	**7.4**	**5.6**	**13.2**	**20.9**	**96.5**
Opponents	**82**	**242.4**	**43.9**	**34.2**	**75.4**	**10.4**	**30.3**	**40.7**	**18.8**	**6.3**	**4.3**	**14.4**	**20.0**	**94.2**

* mid-season trade

Milwaukee Bucks

Player	GP	MPG	FG%	3Pt%	FT%	OFF	DEF	Total	APG	SPG	BPG	TO	PF	PPG
*John Salmons	30	37.6	46.7	38.5	86.7	0.6	2.6	3.2	3.3	1.1	0.1	1.8	2.2	19.9
Andrew Bogut	69	32.3	52.0	0.0	62.9	3.0	7.1	10.2	1.8	0.6	2.5	1.9	3.2	15.9
Brandon Jennings	82	32.6	37.1	37.4	81.7	0.6	2.8	3.4	5.7	1.3	0.2	2.4	2.3	15.5
Michael Redd	18	27.3	35.2	30.0	71.2	0.6	2.4	3.0	2.2	1.1	0.1	0.8	1.3	11.9
Carlos Delfino	75	30.4	40.8	36.7	78.2	0.7	4.6	5.3	2.7	1.1	0.3	1.6	1.8	11.0
Luke Ridnour	82	21.5	47.8	38.1	90.7	0.3	1.5	1.7	4.0	0.7	0.1	1.3	2.2	10.4
Ersan Ilyasova	81	23.4	44.3	33.6	71.5	1.9	4.4	6.4	1.0	0.7	0.3	0.9	3.1	10.4
Jerry Stackhouse	42	20.4	40.8	34.6	79.7	0.5	1.9	2.4	1.7	0.5	0.2	1.6	1.3	8.5
Charlie Bell	71	22.7	38.1	36.5	71.6	0.4	1.4	1.9	1.5	0.6	0.2	0.8	1.9	6.5
Luc Mbah a Moute	73	25.6	48.0	35.3	69.9	2.3	3.1	5.5	1.1	0.8	0.5	1.0	2.5	6.2
Roko Ukic	13	7.5	46.7	25.0	81.8	0.0	0.2	0.2	0.9	0.1	0.0	0.5	0.5	3.1
Kurt Thomas	70	15.0	47.6	0.0	80.0	1.2	3.0	4.2	0.7	0.4	0.7	0.7	2.3	3.0
Dan Gadzuric	32	9.8	43.8	0.0	40.0	1.2	1.7	2.9	0.4	0.2	0.4	0.5	2.0	2.8
*Darnell Jackson	1	9.0	20.0	0.0	0.0	1.0	1.0	2.0	0.0	0.0	0.0	0.0	2.0	2.0
*Royal Ivey	18	5.0	32.1	18.2	60.0	0.1	0.4	0.4	0.6	0.5	0.0	0.3	0.8	1.3
*Primoz Brezec	14	4.2	53.8	0.0	0.0	0.4	0.5	0.9	0.1	0.0	0.1	0.1	0.7	1.0
Bucks	**82**	**243.7**	**43.6**	**35.6**	**75.5**	**11.8**	**31.2**	**43.0**	**21.2**	**7.1**	**4.7**	**13.2**	**22.2**	**97.7**
Opponents	**82**	**243.7**	**45.1**	**34.3**	**76.5**	**9.6**	**33.2**	**42.8**	**19.3**	**7.0**	**5.1**	**15.3**	**20.3**	**96.0**

Minnesota Timberwolves

Player	GP	MPG	FG%	3Pt%	FT%	OFF	DEF	Total	APG	SPG	BPG	TO	PF	PPG
Al Jefferson	76	32.4	49.8	0.0	68.0	2.4	6.9	9.3	1.8	0.8	1.3	1.8	2.7	17.1
Kevin Love	60	28.6	45.0	33.0	81.5	3.8	7.2	11.0	2.3	0.7	0.4	2.0	2.3	14.0
Jonny Flynn	81	28.9	41.7	35.8	82.6	0.3	2.1	2.4	4.4	1.0	0.0	2.9	1.2	13.5
Corey Brewer	82	30.3	43.1	34.6	64.8	0.9	2.5	3.4	2.4	1.4	0.4	2.0	2.7	13.0
Ryan Gomes	76	29.1	44.7	37.2	82.5	1.0	3.6	4.6	1.6	0.8	0.2	1.3	2.0	10.9
*Darko Milicic	24	25.6	49.2	0.0	53.6	1.8	3.8	5.5	1.8	0.8	1.4	1.4	3.1	8.3
Ramon Sessions	82	21.1	45.6	6.7	71.7	0.7	1.9	2.6	3.1	0.7	0.1	1.7	1.7	8.2
Wayne Ellington	76	18.2	42.4	39.5	87.1	0.4	1.7	2.1	1.0	0.3	0.1	1.0	0.9	6.6
Ryan Hollins	73	16.8	55.8	0.0	69.0	1.1	1.8	2.8	0.7	0.3	0.5	1.3	2.7	6.1
Damien Wilkins	80	19.8	43.3	29.5	79.8	0.9	2.2	3.1	1.7	0.8	0.3	1.0	1.8	5.6
Oleksiy Pecherov	44	10.2	41.0	26.9	90.6	0.7	2.1	2.8	0.3	0.2	0.3	0.7	1.3	4.5
Aleksandar Pavlovic	71	12.4	36.3	29.7	38.5	0.2	1.5	1.6	0.8	0.3	0.1	0.8	1.2	3.7
Nathan Jawai	39	10.6	44.1	0.0	68.4	1.3	1.4	2.7	0.6	0.3	0.2	0.7	1.5	3.2
*Alando Tucker	4	6.3	44.4	0.0	0.0	0.3	0.5	0.8	0.0	0.0	0.0	0.3	0.3	2.0
*Brian Cardinal	29	9.2	38.9	33.3	94.4	0.2	0.8	1.0	0.8	0.3	0.1	0.2	1.9	1.7
Timberwolves	**82**	**241.2**	**44.9**	**34.1**	**74.6**	**11.7**	**31.2**	**42.9**	**19.8**	**7.3**	**3.7**	**16.3**	**20.7**	**98.2**
Opponents	**82**	**241.2**	**48.0**	**36.6**	**77.4**	**11.2**	**32.2**	**43.4**	**25.6**	**8.8**	**5.4**	**14.3**	**20.6**	**107.8**

New Jersey Nets

Player	GP	MPG	FG%	3Pt%	FT%	OFF	DEF	Total	APG	SPG	BPG	TO	PF	PPG
Brook Lopez	82	36.9	49.9	0.0	81.7	3.3	5.4	8.6	2.3	0.7	1.7	2.5	3.1	18.8
Devin Harris	64	34.7	40.3	27.6	79.8	0.4	2.8	3.2	6.6	1.2	0.3	2.8	2.8	16.9
Courtney Lee	71	33.5	43.6	33.8	86.9	0.8	2.7	3.5	1.7	1.3	0.3	1.1	1.8	12.5
Yi Jianlian	52	28.8	40.3	36.6	79.8	2.2	4.9	7.2	0.9	0.7	1.0	1.5	3.3	12.0
C. Douglas-Roberts	67	25.8	44.5	25.9	84.7	0.7	2.3	3.0	1.4	0.8	0.3	1.5	1.5	9.8
Terrence Williams	78	22.6	40.1	31.0	71.5	0.6	3.9	4.5	2.9	0.6	0.1	1.6	1.6	8.4
*Kris Humphries	44	20.6	43.3	0.0	69.9	1.9	4.6	6.4	0.6	0.7	0.8	1.2	2.3	8.1
Jarvis Hayes	45	23.0	42.1	33.5	77.8	0.2	2.2	2.4	0.9	0.6	0.2	0.6	2.0	7.8
Keyon Dooling	53	18.3	39.8	37.6	77.0	0.2	0.9	1.0	2.5	0.6	0.0	1.1	1.5	6.9
Bobby Simmons	23	17.2	35.9	31.7	90.0	0.5	2.3	2.7	0.7	0.7	0.1	0.8	2.3	5.3
Trenton Hassell	52	21.3	41.1	0.0	75.4	1.1	1.8	2.9	1.0	0.3	0.2	0.9	1.8	4.5
Josh Boone	63	16.6	52.5	0.0	32.8	2.0	3.0	5.0	0.5	0.5	0.8	0.6	1.8	4.0
Sean Williams	20	11.4	42.9	0.0	52.6	1.1	1.3	2.3	0.1	0.4	1.0	1.0	2.1	2.6
Tony Battie	15	8.9	35.0	25.0	70.0	0.3	1.3	1.5	0.2	0.3	0.1	0.2	1.3	2.4
*Chris Quinn	25	8.9	35.7	31.3	100.0	0.0	0.6	0.6	1.2	0.4	0.0	0.4	0.6	2.2
Nets	**82**	**241.2**	**42.9**	**31.8**	**78.0**	**10.9**	**28.8**	**39.7**	**18.8**	**7.0**	**4.8**	**14.4**	**20.0**	**92.4**
Opponents	**82**	**241.2**	**48.1**	**36.6**	**74.8**	**11.3**	**32.7**	**44.0**	**23.9**	**7.8**	**5.1**	**14.0**	**20.1**	**101.5**

* mid-season trade

New Orleans Hornets

Player	GP	MPG	FG%	3Pt%	FT%	OFF	DEF	Total	APG	SPG	BPG	TO	PF	PPG
David West	81	36.4	50.5	25.9	86.5	2.0	5.4	7.5	3.0	0.9	0.7	2.1	2.9	19.0
Chris Paul	45	38	49.3	40.9	84.7	0.4	3.8	4.2	10.7	2.1	0.2	2.5	2.6	18.7
Marcus Thornton	73	25.6	45.1	37.4	81.4	1.0	1.9	2.9	1.6	0.8	0.2	1.0	1.7	14.5
Peja Stojakovic	62	31.4	40.4	37.5	89.7	0.6	3.0	3.7	1.5	0.8	0.1	0.9	1.3	12.6
Darren Collison	76	27.8	47.7	40.0	85.1	0.5	2.0	2.5	5.7	1.0	0.1	2.7	1.2	12.4
Emeka Okafor	82	28.9	53.0	0.0	56.2	3.1	6.0	9.0	0.7	0.7	1.6	1.4	2.7	10.4
Darius Songaila	75	18.8	49.4	16.7	81.1	0.8	2.3	3.1	0.9	0.8	0.2	1.1	2.7	7.2
Morris Peterson	46	21.2	38.5	36.3	61.1	0.4	2.4	2.7	0.9	0.5	0.1	0.6	1.8	7.1
James Posey	72	22.5	36.5	33.5	82.5	0.4	3.9	4.3	1.5	0.6	0.3	0.7	2.6	5.2
Julian Wright	68	12.8	50.0	33.3	61.0	0.9	1.3	2.1	0.6	0.4	0.3	0.7	0.7	3.8
*Aaron Gray	24	10.9	55.7	0.0	85.7	1.7	2.1	3.8	0.8	0.4	0.5	0.7	1.8	3.6
Sean Marks	14	5.4	50.0	0.0	40.0	1.0	0.6	1.6	0.1	0.0	0.2	0.1	1.2	0.7
*Jason Hart	4	4.3	100.0	0.0	0.0	0.0	0.5	0.5	1.3	0.3	0.3	0.8	1.0	0.5
Hornets	82	241.8	46.4	36.3	77.8	10.4	29.9	40.3	22.3	7.6	3.7	13.4	19.6	100.2
Opponents	82	241.8	48.3	35.5	75.1	10.6	31.5	42.1	23.5	7.0	4.5	14.4	19.5	102.7

New York Knicks

Player	GP	MPG	FG%	3Pt%	FT%	OFF	DEF	Total	APG	SPG	BPG	TO	PF	PPG
David Lee	81	37.3	54.5	0.0	81.2	2.8	8.9	11.7	3.6	1.1	0.5	2.3	3.2	20.2
Al Harrington	72	30.5	43.5	34.2	75.7	1.2	4.4	5.6	1.5	0.9	0.4	1.8	2.9	17.7
Wilson Chandler	65	35.7	47.9	26.7	80.6	1.4	3.9	5.4	2.1	0.7	0.8	1.7	2.8	15.3
Danilo Gallinari	81	33.9	42.3	38.1	81.8	0.8	4.1	4.9	1.7	0.9	0.7	1.4	2.4	15.1
*Bill Walker	27	27.4	51.8	43.1	78.7	0.6	2.5	3.1	1.4	0.9	0.1	1.0	2.9	11.9
Earl Barron	7	33.1	44.1	0.0	75.9	4.4	6.6	11.0	1.1	0.6	0.6	1.6	3.4	11.7
*Tracy McGrady	24	26.1	38.9	24.2	75.4	0.9	2.8	3.7	3.9	0.6	0.5	1.8	1.6	9.4
Toney Douglas	56	19.4	45.8	38.9	80.9	0.7	1.2	1.9	2.0	0.8	0.1	1.0	2.1	8.6
Chris Duhon	67	30.9	37.3	34.9	71.6	0.4	2.2	2.7	5.6	0.9	0.0	1.6	1.2	7.4
*Sergio Rodriguez	27	19.7	49.1	34.7	80.6	0.3	1.1	1.4	3.4	0.8	0.1	2.0	1.4	7.4
*Eddie House	18	20.6	33.1	25.0	100.0	0.3	1.9	2.2	2.1	0.7	0.0	1.1	1.1	6.4
Jonathan Bender	25	11.7	40.0	35.9	92.3	0.6	1.5	2.1	0.6	0.1	0.7	1.1	1.3	4.7
*J.R. Giddens	11	12.7	48.7	0.0	63.6	1.1	1.7	2.8	0.6	0.5	0.1	0.9	1.7	4.1
Eddy Curry	7	8.9	38.1	0.0	58.8	0.6	1.3	1.9	0.0	0.0	0.1	1.9	1.9	3.7
Knicks	82	242.4	45.5	34.6	78.2	10.2	30.2	40.4	21.6	7.2	3.7	14.0	20.0	102.1
Opponents	82	242.4	48.6	35.2	75.4	11.7	33.2	44.9	21.0	7.1	4.5	14.4	19.2	105.9

Oklahoma City Thunder

Player	GP	MPG	FG%	3Pt%	FT%	OFF	DEF	Total	APG	SPG	BPG	TO	PF	PPG
Kevin Durant	82	39.5	47.6	36.5	90.0	1.3	6.3	7.6	2.8	1.4	1.0	3.3	2.1	30.1
Russell Westbrook	82	34.3	41.8	22.1	78.0	1.7	3.1	4.9	8.0	1.3	0.4	3.3	2.5	16.1
Jeff Green	82	37.1	45.3	33.3	74.0	1.4	4.6	6.0	1.6	1.3	0.9	1.7	2.7	15.1
James Harden	76	22.9	40.3	37.5	80.8	0.6	2.6	3.2	1.8	1.1	0.3	1.4	2.6	9.9
Nenad Krstic	76	22.9	50.2	20.0	71.7	1.8	3.3	5.0	0.7	0.4	0.6	0.8	2.3	8.4
Serge Ibaka	73	18.1	54.3	50.0	63.0	1.9	3.5	5.4	0.1	0.3	1.3	0.9	2.7	6.3
Thabo Sefolosha	82	28.6	44.0	31.3	67.4	0.9	3.8	4.7	1.8	1.2	0.6	1.1	1.9	6.0
Nick Collison	75	20.8	58.9	25.0	69.2	2.0	3.1	5.1	0.5	0.5	0.6	0.8	3.1	5.9
D.J. White	12	8.5	61.0	0.0	90.0	0.8	1.1	1.9	0.3	0.4	0.3	0.3	1.0	4.9
*Eric Maynor	55	16.5	43.4	36.2	69.2	0.2	1.5	1.7	3.4	0.5	0.2	1.0	1.5	4.5
Ryan Bowen	1	8	100.0	0.0	100.0	1.0	1.0	2.0	0.0	1.0	0.0	0.0	2.0	4.0
Mike Wilks	4	14.8	50.0	66.7	50.0	0.3	0.8	1.0	1.0	0.0	0.0	1.0	1.3	4.0
Etan Thomas	23	14	45.6	0.0	59.1	0.8	2.0	2.8	0.0	0.2	0.7	0.8	1.7	3.3
Kyle Weaver	12	12	36.4	36.8	83.3	0.1	1.4	1.5	0.9	0.5	0.5	0.3	1.1	3.0
Antonio Anderson	1	15	33.3	0.0	0.0	1.0	0.0	1.0	1.0	0.0	0.0	1.0	1.0	2.0
Kevin Ollie	25	10.5	40.0	0.0	100.0	0.1	0.9	1.0	0.8	0.4	0.0	0.2	0.6	1.8
Byron Mullens	13	4.2	36.8	0.0	0.0	0.2	0.5	0.8	0.1	0.2	0.0	0.3	1.0	1.1
Thunder	82	241.5	46.2	34.0	80.5	11.7	31.8	43.5	20.0	8.0	5.9	15.0	21.3	101.5
Opponents	82	241.5	44.8	34.0	76.4	11.4	29.2	40.7	19.7	7.5	4.7	15.1	21.4	98.0

* mid-season trade

Orlando Magic

Player	GP	MPG	FG%	3Pt%	FT%	OFF	DEF	Total	APG	SPG	BPG	TO	PF	PPG
Dwight Howard	82	34.7	61.2	0.0	59.2	3.5	9.7	13.2	1.8	0.9	2.8	3.3	3.5	18.3
Vince Carter	75	30.8	42.8	36.7	84.0	0.4	3.5	3.9	3.1	0.7	0.2	1.4	2.5	16.6
Rashard Lewis	72	32.9	43.5	39.7	80.6	0.9	3.6	4.4	1.5	1.1	0.4	1.5	2.5	14.1
Jameer Nelson	65	28.6	44.9	38.1	84.5	0.4	2.6	3.0	5.4	0.7	0.0	2.1	2.3	12.6
J.J. Redick	82	22.0	43.9	40.5	86.0	0.2	1.7	1.9	1.9	0.3	0.1	0.8	1.4	9.6
Matt Barnes	81	25.9	48.7	31.9	74.0	1.3	4.2	5.5	1.7	0.7	0.4	1.4	2.3	8.8
Mickael Pietrus	75	22.5	43.2	37.9	63.3	0.5	2.3	2.9	0.7	0.7	0.4	0.9	1.8	8.7
Ryan Anderson	63	14.5	43.6	37.0	86.6	1.1	2.1	3.2	0.6	0.4	0.2	0.9	1.3	7.7
Jason Williams	82	20.8	44.4	38.0	75.6	0.1	1.5	1.5	3.6	0.7	0.0	1.1	0.8	6.0
Brandon Bass	50	13.0	51.1	0.0	82.5	1.1	1.5	2.5	0.4	0.2	0.5	0.6	1.4	5.8
Anthony Johnson	31	13.1	44.1	33.3	95.0	0.3	1.3	1.5	2.0	0.4	0.0	0.8	1.0	4.2
Marcin Gortat	81	13.4	53.3	0.0	68.0	1.3	2.9	4.2	0.2	0.2	0.9	0.6	1.7	3.6
Magic	82	240.6	47.0	37.5	72.4	9.9	33.4	43.2	19.7	6.2	5.6	14.1	19.9	102.8
Opponents	82	240.6	43.8	36.3	75.4	9.8	30.3	40.0	18.9	6.7	3.5	12.8	22.2	95.3

Philadelphia 76ers

Player	GP	MPG	FG%	3Pt%	FT%	OFF	DEF	Total	APG	SPG	BPG	TO	PF	PPG
Andre Iguodala	82	38.9	44.3	31.0	73.3	1.0	5.5	6.5	5.8	1.7	0.7	2.7	1.8	17.1
Louis Williams	64	29.9	47.0	34.0	82.4	0.4	2.5	2.9	4.2	1.3	0.2	1.7	1.7	14.0
*Allen Iverson	25	31.9	41.7	33.3	82.4	0.6	2.4	3.0	4.1	0.7	0.1	2.3	1.7	13.9
Thaddeus Young	67	32.0	47.0	34.8	69.1	1.9	3.3	5.2	1.4	1.2	0.2	1.9	2.0	13.8
Elton Brand	76	30.2	48.0	0.0	73.8	2.4	3.7	6.1	1.4	1.1	1.1	1.7	3.1	13.1
Willie Green	73	21.3	45.7	34.6	83.3	0.3	1.5	1.8	2.1	0.4	0.2	0.9	1.8	8.7
Marreese Speights	62	16.4	47.7	0.0	74.5	1.4	2.7	4.1	0.6	0.5	0.6	0.8	2.5	8.6
Samuel Dalembert	82	25.9	54.5	0.0	72.9	2.9	6.6	9.6	0.8	0.5	1.8	1.5	3.1	8.1
Jrue Holiday	73	24.2	44.2	39.0	75.6	0.8	1.8	2.6	3.8	1.1	0.3	2.1	2.1	8.0
*Jodie Meeks	19	12.3	44.0	38.0	72.2	0.2	1.2	1.4	0.9	0.3	0.1	0.3	1.0	5.9
Jason Kapono	57	17.1	41.9	36.8	60.0	0.2	0.9	1.2	0.7	0.4	0.1	0.6	1.4	5.7
Rodney Carney	68	12.6	40.1	30.4	82.5	0.4	1.6	2.0	0.5	0.4	0.3	0.3	1.2	4.7
Jason Smith	56	11.8	43.1	34.5	69.0	1.0	1.4	2.4	0.6	0.4	0.5	0.6	2.0	3.4
*Francisco Elson	1	4.0	50.0	0.0	0.0	1.0	0.0	1.0	0.0	0.0	0.0	0.0	0.0	2.0
76ers	82	241.5	46.0	34.3	75.6	11.5	29.5	41.0	21.0	8.1	5.4	14.5	20.5	97.7
Opponents	82	241.5	47.2	39.3	76.6	10.8	30.1	41.0	22.1	7.6	4.0	14.5	18.7	101.6

Phoenix Suns

Player	GP	MPG	FG%	3Pt%	FT%	OFF	DEF	Total	APG	SPG	BPG	TO	PF	PPG
Amar'e Stoudemire	82	34.6	55.7	16.7	77.1	2.8	6.1	8.9	1.0	0.6	1.0	2.6	3.4	23.1
Steve Nash	81	32.8	50.7	42.6	93.8	0.4	2.9	3.3	11.0	0.5	0.2	3.6	1.3	16.5
Jason Richardson	79	31.5	47.4	39.3	73.9	1.0	4.1	5.1	1.8	0.8	0.4	1.2	2.1	15.7
Grant Hill	81	30.0	47.8	43.8	81.7	0.9	4.6	5.5	2.4	0.7	0.4	1.3	2.0	11.3
Channing Frye	81	27.0	45.1	43.9	81.0	0.8	4.5	5.3	1.4	0.8	0.9	0.9	3.2	11.2
Leandro Barbosa	44	17.9	42.5	32.4	87.7	0.3	1.3	1.6	1.5	0.5	0.3	1.1	1.6	9.5
Robin Lopez	51	19.3	58.8	0.0	70.4	2.0	2.8	4.9	0.1	0.2	1.0	0.8	2.3	8.4
Jared Dudley	82	24.3	45.9	45.8	75.4	1.2	2.2	3.4	1.4	1.0	0.2	0.8	2.0	8.2
Goran Dragic	80	18.0	45.2	39.4	73.6	0.5	1.7	2.1	3.0	0.6	0.1	1.6	1.6	7.9
Louis Amundson	79	14.8	55.1	0.0	54.5	1.6	2.8	4.4	0.4	0.3	0.9	0.7	2.1	4.7
Earl Clark	51	7.5	37.1	40.0	72.2	0.4	0.9	1.2	0.4	0.1	0.3	0.5	0.5	2.7
Taylor Griffin	8	4.0	40.0	0.0	50.0	0.0	0.3	0.3	0.1	0.0	0.3	0.1	0.5	1.3
Jarron Collins	34	7.7	38.7	0.0	40.0	0.6	1.2	1.8	0.2	0.1	0.1	0.3	1.2	1.0
Dwayne Jones	2	3.5	0.0	0.0	0.0	0.0	1.0	1.0	0.0	0.0	0.0	0.0	0.5	0.0
Suns	82	240.6	49.2	41.2	77.0	11.1	31.9	43.0	23.3	5.8	5.1	14.8	20.9	110.2
Opponents	82	240.6	45.2	35.5	76.0	13.2	29.2	42.3	20.8	7.9	4.4	13.0	21.8	105.3

* mid-season trade

Portland Trail Blazers

Player	GP	MPG	FG%	3Pt%	FT%	OFF	DEF	Total	APG	SPG	BPG	TO	PF	PPG
Brandon Roy	65	37.2	47.3	33.0	78.0	1.1	3.3	4.4	4.7	0.9	0.3	2.0	2.1	21.5
LaMarcus Aldridge	78	37.5	49.5	31.3	75.7	2.5	5.6	8.0	2.1	0.9	0.6	1.3	3.0	17.9
Andre Miller	82	30.5	44.5	20.0	82.1	1.0	2.3	3.2	5.4	1.1	0.1	2.1	2.1	14.0
Greg Oden	21	23.9	60.5	0.0	76.6	3.0	5.4	8.5	0.9	0.4	2.3	1.9	4.0	11.1
Nicolas Batum	37	24.8	51.9	40.9	84.3	0.9	2.9	3.8	1.2	0.7	0.7	0.7	2.2	10.1
Martell Webster	82	24.5	40.5	37.3	81.3	0.6	2.7	3.3	0.8	0.6	0.5	0.7	1.9	9.4
Jerryd Bayless	74	17.6	41.4	31.5	83.1	0.2	1.4	1.6	2.3	0.4	0.1	1.3	2.1	8.5
Rudy Fernandez	62	23.2	37.8	36.8	86.7	0.6	2.1	2.6	2.0	1.0	0.2	1.2	1.4	8.1
*Marcus Camby	23	31.2	49.7	0.0	58.1	3.6	7.5	11.1	1.5	1.1	2.0	1.2	2.4	7.0
Juwan Howard	73	22.4	50.9	0.0	78.6	1.5	3.1	4.6	0.8	0.4	0.1	1.0	2.6	6.0
Joel Przybilla	30	22.7	52.3	0.0	64.7	2.4	5.5	7.9	0.3	0.3	1.4	1.3	3.2	4.1
Dante Cunningham	63	11.2	49.5	0.0	64.6	0.9	1.7	2.5	0.2	0.4	0.4	0.2	1.5	3.9
Jeff Pendergraph	39	10.4	66.2	0.0	90.0	0.6	1.9	2.5	0.0	0.2	0.4	0.3	1.9	2.7
Patrick Mills	10	3.8	41.7	50.0	57.1	0.1	0.1	0.2	0.5	0.0	0.0	0.4	0.6	2.6
*Travis Diener	5	5.2	25.0	0.0	50.0	0.0	0.2	0.2	0.8	0.2	0.0	0.0	0.2	0.6
Trail Blazers	82	242.1	46.1	35.4	79.0	11.1	29.1	40.2	20.4	6.4	4.3	12.3	20.9	98.1
Opponents	82	242.1	46.4	34.3	74.5	9.8	28.3	38.1	19.3	5.9	4.1	13.5	21.5	94.8

Sacramento Kings

Player	GP	MPG	FG%	3Pt%	FT%	OFF	DEF	Total	APG	SPG	BPG	TO	PF	PPG
Tyreke Evans	72	37.2	45.8	25.5	74.8	0.9	4.4	5.3	5.8	1.5	0.4	3.0	2.8	20.1
*Carl Landry	28	37.6	52.0	33.3	74.1	2.4	4.1	6.5	0.9	1.0	0.6	1.8	3.1	18.0
Beno Udrih	79	31.4	49.3	37.7	83.7	0.5	2.3	2.8	4.7	1.1	0.1	1.7	2.1	12.9
Jason Thompson	75	31.4	47.2	10.0	71.5	3.0	5.5	8.5	1.7	0.6	1.0	1.9	3.7	12.5
Omri Casspi	77	25.1	44.6	36.9	67.2	1.0	3.6	4.5	1.2	0.7	0.2	1.3	1.6	10.3
Spencer Hawes	72	26.4	46.8	29.9	68.9	2.0	4.0	6.1	2.2	0.4	1.2	1.8	2.8	10.0
Donte Greene	76	21.4	44.1	37.7	64.3	0.7	2.4	3.1	0.9	0.5	0.7	1.2	2.0	8.5
Andres Nocioni	75	19.7	39.9	38.6	71.7	0.4	2.5	3.0	1.0	0.4	0.4	0.9	2.1	8.5
Francisco Garcia	25	23	46.6	39.0	88.2	0.4	2.2	2.6	1.8	0.4	0.8	0.8	2.0	8.1
Ime Udoka	69	13.7	37.8	28.6	73.7	0.7	2.0	2.8	0.8	0.5	0.1	0.6	1.2	3.6
Sean May	37	8.9	45.9	0.0	65.6	0.5	1.4	1.9	0.5	0.3	0.2	0.5	1.2	3.3
Jon Brockman	52	12.6	53.4	0.0	59.7	2.0	2.1	4.1	0.4	0.3	0.1	0.4	2.2	2.8
Desmond Mason	5	13.2	41.7	0.0	75.0	0.8	1.8	2.6	0.4	0.2	0.2	0.8	1.0	2.6
Kenny Thomas	26	12	48.6	0.0	58.3	1.3	2.0	3.3	0.6	0.4	0.4	0.7	1.6	1.6
*Dominic McGuire	10	6.7	33.3	0.0	0.0	0.6	1.2	1.8	0.3	0.1	0.1	0.7	0.3	0.8
Kings	82	242.4	45.6	34.9	72.6	11.9	30.7	42.6	20.5	6.9	4.5	15.0	22.3	100.0
Opponents	82	242.4	46.9	35.7	77.4	11.1	31.0	42.0	20.5	7.2	5.7	13.7	20.1	104.4

San Antonio Spurs

Player	GP	MPG	FG%	3Pt%	FT%	OFF	DEF	Total	APG	SPG	BPG	TO	PF	PPG
Tim Duncan	78	31.3	51.8	18.2	72.5	2.8	7.3	10.1	3.2	0.6	1.5	1.8	1.9	17.9
Manu Ginobili	75	28.7	44.1	37.7	87.0	0.9	2.9	3.8	4.9	1.4	0.3	2.1	2.1	16.5
Tony Parker	56	30.9	48.7	29.4	75.6	0.1	2.3	2.4	5.7	0.5	0.1	2.7	1.7	16.0
George Hill	78	29.2	47.8	39.9	77.2	0.5	2.1	2.6	2.9	0.9	0.3	1.3	2.8	12.3
Richard Jefferson	81	31.1	46.7	31.6	73.5	0.7	3.7	4.4	2.0	0.6	0.5	1.3	2.2	12.3
DeJuan Blair	82	18.2	55.6	0.0	54.7	2.4	4.0	6.4	0.8	0.6	0.5	1.4	2.7	7.8
Matt Bonner	65	17.9	44.6	39.0	72.9	0.8	2.5	3.3	1.0	0.5	0.4	0.6	1.7	7.0
Roger Mason	79	19.2	38.9	33.3	79.4	0.1	1.9	2.1	1.7	0.4	0.2	0.8	1.3	6.3
*Garrett Temple	13	14.8	43.8	43.5	66.7	0.2	0.8	1.1	0.9	0.6	0.2	0.9	1.9	6.2
Antonio McDyess	77	21	47.9	0.0	63.2	1.9	4.0	5.9	1.1	0.6	0.4	1.0	1.9	5.8
Keith Bogans	79	19.7	40.3	35.7	74.0	0.3	1.9	2.2	1.2	0.6	0.2	0.7	2.0	4.4
Ian Mahinmi	26	6.3	63.6	0.0	66.0	0.5	1.5	2.0	0.1	0.1	0.3	0.6	1.2	3.9
Marcus Haislip	10	4.4	47.6	60.0	40.0	0.4	0.6	1.0	0.0	0.0	0.2	0.3	0.5	2.5
Malik Hairston	47	6.7	52.6	18.2	56.7	0.3	0.8	1.0	0.3	0.1	0.2	0.2	0.6	2.1
Spurs	82	241.2	47.3	35.8	74.0	10.8	32.0	42.8	22.3	6.3	4.6	13.6	20.4	101.
Opponents	82	241.2	45.2	34.3	75.6	9.9	29.6	39.5	19.2	6.9	5.1	12.6	20.4	96.

* mid-season trade

Toronto Raptors

Player	GP	MPG	FG%	3Pt%	FT%	OFF	DEF	Total	APG	SPG	BPG	TO	PF	PPG
Chris Bosh 70		36.1	51.8	36.4	79.7	2.9	7.9	10.8	2.4	0.6	1.0	2.4	2.4	24.0
Andrea Bargnani..80		35.0	47.0	37.2	77.4	1.3	4.9	6.2	1.2	0.3	1.4	1.5	2.7	17.2
Jarrett Jack 82		27.4	48.1	41.2	84.2	0.4	2.3	2.7	5.0	0.7	0.1	2.0	1.8	11.4
Hedo Turkoglu......74		30.7	40.9	37.4	77.4	0.6	4.1	4.6	4.1	0.7	0.4	1.7	3.0	11.3
Jose Calderon......68		26.7	48.2	39.8	79.8	0.3	1.8	2.1	5.9	0.7	0.1	1.5	2.0	10.3
DeMar DeRozan ..77		21.6	49.8	25.0	76.3	0.9	2.0	2.9	0.7	0.6	0.2	0.8	2.3	8.6
Sonny Weems 69		19.8	51.5	13.3	68.8	0.6	2.2	2.8	1.5	0.6	0.4	0.9	1.8	7.5
Marco Belinelli...66		17.0	40.6	38.0	83.5	0.2	1.2	1.4	1.3	0.6	0.1	0.9	1.2	7.1
Antoine Wright......67		20.8	40.6	33.5	68.8	0.6	2.3	2.8	1.1	0.5	0.2	0.9	2.0	6.5
Amir Johnson.......82		17.7	62.3	0.0	63.8	1.9	2.9	4.8	0.6	0.5	0.8	0.8	3.1	6.2
Marcus Banks 22		11.1	53.4	29.2	82.8	0.1	0.9	1.0	1.2	0.6	0.1	0.9	1.4	5.0
Rasho Nesterovic.42		9.8	54.4	0.0	20.0	0.9	1.2	2.1	0.6	0.2	0.4	0.4	1.3	3.9
Reggie Evans.......28		11.1	49.3	0.0	45.0	1.1	2.7	3.8	0.3	0.5	0.1	0.8	1.6	3.4
*P. Mensah-Bonsu16		6.7	41.4	0.0	55.6	0.9	1.0	1.9	0.1	0.2	0.5	0.6	1.1	2.1
Patrick O'Bryant ...11		4.6	53.3	0.0	50.0	0.2	0.8	1.0	0.1	0.2	0.4	0.5	1.1	1.7
Raptors.................82		241.2	48.2	37.1	76.4	9.8	30.6	40.4	22.0	5.7	4.7	13.4	22.2	104.1
Opponents.............82		241.2	46.8	36.6	78.4	11.4	29.9	41.3	23.0	7.1	4.4	12.7	21.1	105.9

Utah Jazz

Player	GP	MPG	FG%	3Pt%	FT%	OFF	DEF	Total	APG	SPG	BPG	TO	PF	PPG
Carlos Boozer 78		34.3	56.2	0.0	74.2	2.3	8.9	11.2	3.2	1.1	0.5	2.7	3.5	19.5
Deron Williams 76		36.9	46.9	37.1	80.1	0.7	3.3	4.0	10.5	1.3	0.2	3.3	2.7	18.7
Mehmet Okur 73		29.4	45.8	38.5	82.0	1.8	5.2	7.1	1.6	0.5	1.1	1.7	3.1	13.5
Andrei Kirilenko....58		29.0	50.6	29.2	74.4	1.3	3.2	4.6	2.7	1.4	1.2	1.4	1.8	11.9
Paul Millsap...........82		27.8	53.8	11.1	69.3	2.3	4.5	6.8	1.6	0.8	1.2	1.4	3.5	11.6
C.J. Miles 63		23.8	42.9	34.1	69.5	0.7	2.0	2.7	1.7	0.9	0.3	1.3	3.0	9.9
Wesley Matthews .82		24.7	48.3	38.2	82.9	0.6	1.7	2.3	1.5	0.8	0.2	1.1	1.9	9.4
Kyle Korver...........52		18.3	49.3	53.6	79.6	0.2	1.9	2.1	1.7	0.5	0.2	0.8	1.5	7.2
Ronnie Price.........60		13.4	40.5	28.6	69.5	0.5	0.8	1.2	2.1	0.7	0.2	0.9	1.8	4.3
Sundiata Gaines ..32		6.8	46.3	26.9	50.0	0.2	0.7	0.9	1.2	0.4	0.0	0.4	0.5	3.3
Kyrylo Fesenko 49		8.3	54.7	0.0	42.1	0.7	1.2	1.8	0.3	0.1	0.4	0.5	1.6	2.6
Othyus Jeffers......14		5.2	41.4	0.0	68.4	0.6	0.8	1.4	0.1	0.3	0.0	0.4	0.7	2.6
Kosta Koufos........36		4.8	46.8	0.0	60.0	0.4	0.8	1.3	0.2	0.1	0.1	0.4	0.7	1.5
Jazz.......................82		240.9	49.1	36.4	74.1	10.6	31.6	42.2	26.7	8.2	4.9	15.2	22.7	104.2
Opponents.............82		240.9	44.9	35.4	76.2	10.2	29.0	39.2	19.9	7.7	5.4	15.1	22.2	98.9

Washington Wizards

Player	GP	MPG	FG%	3Pt%	FT%	OFF	DEF	Total	APG	SPG	BPG	TO	PF	PPG
Gilbert Arenas......32		36.5	41.1	34.8	73.9	0.5	3.6	4.2	7.2	1.3	0.3	3.7	3.0	22.6
*Josh Howard.........4		22.8	43.5	27.3	75.0	1.0	2.3	3.3	1.0	0.8	0.5	0.8	3.3	14.5
Andray Blatche 81		27.9	47.8	29.5	74.4	2.0	4.3	6.3	2.1	1.1	0.9	2.3	2.7	14.1
Mike Miller............54		33.4	50.1	48.0	82.4	1.0	5.2	6.2	3.9	0.7	0.2	2.1	2.4	10.9
*Al Thornton 24		28.1	46.3	35.3	69.4	1.3	3.0	4.3	1.2	0.8	0.5	1.5	2.6	10.7
Randy Foye..........70		23.8	41.4	34.6	89.0	0.2	1.6	1.9	3.3	0.5	0.1	1.3	1.8	10.1
*Shaun Livingston 26		25.6	53.5	0.0	87.5	0.5	1.8	2.2	4.4	0.5	0.4	1.9	2.0	9.2
Nick Young...........74		19.2	41.8	40.6	80.0	0.3	1.1	1.4	0.6	0.4	0.1	0.8	2.0	8.6
Earl Boykins 67		16.7	42.7	31.7	86.5	0.3	0.9	1.1	2.6	0.4	0.0	1.0	0.7	6.6
JaVale McGee.......60		16.1	50.8	0.0	63.8	1.5	2.6	4.1	0.2	0.3	1.7	0.9	2.0	6.4
*Cartier Martin.......8		14.3	37.5	38.9	88.9	1.0	1.6	2.6	0.9	0.4	0.1	0.8	1.5	6.4
*James Singleton .32		23.9	38.4	13.3	83.9	2.8	4.1	6.9	0.7	0.5	1.1	1.2	2.6	6.1
Mike James 11		11.5	30.0	33.3	50.0	0.3	0.5	0.8	1.3	0.8	0.0	1.3	0.8	4.5
*Cedric Jackson 4		9.8	36.4	33.3	75.0	0.2	0.5	0.8	1.5	0.0	0.0	2.0	1.3	3.0
Paul Davis.............2		4.0	50.0	0.0	50.0	0.0	0.0	0.0	1.5	0.0	0.5	0.0	0.0	2.5
*Quinton Ross 25		10.4	30.9	12.5	50.0	0.3	0.9	1.1	0.9	0.2	0.1	0.3	1.4	1.5
Fabricio Oberto 57		11.4	62.5	0.0	76.5	0.6	1.2	1.8	0.9	0.2	0.2	0.6	2.1	1.5
Wizards 82		241.8	44.9	35.3	76.2	11.8	30.0	41.8	19.0	6.0	5.1	14.9	21.4	96.2
Opponents.............82		241.8	46.3	36.0	76.1	11.4	30.9	42.3	21.6	6.9	5.1	13.6	20.5	101.0

* mid-season trade

2010 NBA Draft

The 2010 NBA Draft was held on June 24, 2010 in New York City.

First Round

1. WAS—John Wall, Kentucky
2. PHI—Evan Turner, Ohio St
3. NJN—Derrick Favors, Georgia Tech
4. MIN—Wesley Johnson, Syracuse
5. SAC—DeMarcus Cousins, Kent'ky
6. GSW—Ekpe Udoh, Baylor
7. DET—Greg Monroe, Georgetown
8. LAC—Al-Farouq Aminu, Wake F.
9. UTA—Gordon Hayward, Butler
   (from NYK via PHX)
10. IND—Paul George, Fresno St
11. NOH—Cole Aldrich, Kansas
    (traded to OKC)
12. MEM—Xavier Henry, Kansas
13. TOR—Ed Davis, North Carolina
14. HOU—Patrick Patterson, Kent'ky
15. MIL—Larry Sanders, VCU
    (from CHI)
16. MIN—Luke Babbitt, Nevada
    (from DEN via CHA, traded to POR)
17. CHI—Kevin Seraphin, France
    (from MIL)
18. OKC—Eric Bledsoe, Kentucky
    (from MIA, traded to LAC)
19. BOS—Avery Bradley, Texas
20. SAS—James Anderson, Okla St
21. OKC—Craig Brackins, Iowa St
    (traded to NOH)
22. POR—Elliot Williams, Memphis
23. MIN—Trevor Booker, Clemson
    (from PHI via UTA, traded to WAS)
24. ATL—Damion James, Texas
    (traded to NJN)
25. MEM—Dominique Jones, S. Fla
    (from DEN, traded to DAL)
26. OKC—Quincy Pondexter, Wash.
    (from PHX, traded to NOH)
27. NJN—Jordan Crawford, Xavier
    (from DAL, traded to ATL)
28. MEM—Greivis Vasquez, Md.
    (from LAL)
29. ORL—Daniel Orton, Kentucky
30. WAS—Lazar Hayward, Marq'tte
    (from CLE, traded to MIN)

Second Round

31. NJN—Tibor Pleiss, Germany
    (traded to OKC)
32. MIA—Dexter Pittman, Texas
    (from OKC via MIN)
33. SAC—Hassan Whiteside, Marshall
34. POR—Armon Johnson, Nevada
    (from GSW)
35. WAS—Nemanja Bjelica, Serbia
    (traded to MIN)
36. DET—Terrico White, Mississippi
37. MIL—Darington Hobson, N. Mex.
    (from PHI)
38. NYK—Andy Rautins, Syracuse
39. NYK—Landry Fields, Stanford
    (from DEN via LAC)
40. IND—Lance Stephenson, Cincy.
41. MIA—Jarvis Varnado, Miss. St
    (from NOH)
42. MIA—Da'Sean Butler, W. Virg.
    (from TOR)
43. LAL—Devin Ebanks, W. Virg.
    (from MEM)
44. MIL—Jerome Jordan, Tulas
    (from CHI via POR and GSW)
45. MIN—Paulao Prestes, Brazil
    (from HOU)
46. PHX—Gani Lawal, Ga. Tech
    (from CHA)
47. MIL—Keith Gallon, Oklahoma
48. MIA—Latavious Williams, NBDL
49. SAS—Ryan Richards, England
50. DAL—Solomon Alabi, Fla. St
    (from OKC, traded to TOR)
51. OKC—Magnum Rolle, La. Tech
    (from DAL and MIN via POR,
    traded to IND)
52. BOS—Luke Harangody,
    Notre Dame
53. LAC—Pape Sy, Senegal
54. LAC—Willie Warren, Oklahoma
    (from DEN)
55. UTA—Jeremy Evans, W. Ky.
56. MIN—Hamady N'diaye, Rutgers
    (from PHX)
57. IND—Ryan Reid, Florida St
    (from DAL, traded to OKC)
58. LAL—Derrick Caracter, UTEP
59. ORL—Stanley Robinson, Conn.
60. PHX—Dwayne Collins,
    Miami (Fla.)

Women's National Basketball Association

2010 Final Regular Season Standings

WESTERN CONFERENCE

Team	W	L	Pct	GB
†Seattle	28	6	.588	—
*Phoenix	15	19	.441	13.0
*San Antonio	14	20	.412	14.0
*Los Angeles	13	21	.382	15.0
Minnesota	13	21	.382	15.0
Tulsa	6	28	.176	22.0

EASTERN CONFERENCE

Team	W	L	Pct	GB
†Washington	22	12	.647	—
*New York	22	12	.647	—
*Indiana	21	13	.618	1.0
*Atlanta	19	15	.559	3.0
Connecticut	17	17	.500	5.0
Chicago	14	20	.412	8.0

†Clinched conference title. *Clinched playoff berth.

2010 Playoffs

FIRST ROUND

WESTERN CONFERENCE

Game 1......San Antonio 93   at Phoenix 106
Game 2......Phoenix 92   at San Antonio 73
Phoenix won series 2–0.

Game 1......Los Angeles 66   at Seattle 79
Game 2......Seattle 81   at Los Angeles 66
Seattle won series 2–0.

EASTERN CONFERENCE

Game 1......Atlanta 95   at Washington 90
Game 2......Washington 77   at Atlanta 101
Atlanta won series 2–0.

Game 1......Indiana 73   at New York 85
Game 2......New York 67   at Indiana 75
Game 3......Indiana 74   at New York 77
New York won series 2–1.

WESTERN CONFERENCE FINALS

Game 1......Phoenix 72   at Seattle 82
Game 2......Seattle 91   at Phoenix 88
Seattle won series 2–0.

EASTERN CONFERENCE FINALS

Game 1......Atlanta 81   at New York 75
Game 2......New York 93   at Atlanta 105
Atlanta won series 2–0.

WNBA FINALS

Game 1..........Atlanta 77   at Seattle 79
Game 2..........Atlanta 84   at Seattle 87
Game 3..........Seattle 87   at Atlanta 84
Seattle won series 3–0.

*2010 WNBA Regular Season and Finals MVP: Lauren Jackson, Seattle Storm

NBA Champions

Season	Winner	Series	Runner-Up	Winning Coach	Finals MVP
1946–47	Philadelphia	4–1	Chicago	Eddie Gottlieb	—
1947–48	Baltimore	4–2	Philadelphia	Buddy Jeannette	—
1948–49	Minneapolis	4–2	Washington	John Kundla	—
1949–50	Minneapolis	4–2	Syracuse	John Kundla	—
1950–51	Rochester	4–3	New York	Les Harrison	—
1951–52	Minneapolis	4–3	New York	John Kundla	—
1952–53	Minneapolis	4–1	New York	John Kundla	—
1953–54	Minneapolis	4–3	Syracuse	John Kundla	—
1954–55	Syracuse	4–3	Ft Wayne	Al Cervi	—
1955–56	Philadelphia	4–1	Ft Wayne	George Senesky	—
1956–57	Boston	4–3	St Louis	Red Auerbach	—
1957–58	St Louis	4–2	Boston	Alex Hannum	—
1958–59	Boston	4–0	Minneapolis	Red Auerbach	—
1959–60	Boston	4–3	St Louis	Red Auerbach	—
1960–61	Boston	4–1	St Louis	Red Auerbach	—
1961–62	Boston	4–3	LA Lakers	Red Auerbach	—
1962–63	Boston	4–2	LA Lakers	Red Auerbach	—
1963–64	Boston	4–1	San Francisco	Red Auerbach	—
1964–65	Boston	4–1	LA Lakers	Red Auerbach	—
1965–66	Boston	4–3	LA Lakers	Red Auerbach	—
1966–67	Philadelphia	4–2	San Francisco	Alex Hannum	—
1967–68	Boston	4–2	LA Lakers	Bill Russell	—
1968–69	Boston	4–3	LA Lakers	Bill Russell	Jerry West, LA
1969–70	New York	4–3	LA Lakers	Red Holzman	Willis Reed, NY
1970–71	Milwaukee	4–0	Baltimore	Larry Costello	Kareem Abdul-Jabbar, Mil
1971–72	LA Lakers	4–1	New York	Bill Sharman	Wilt Chamberlain, LA
1972–73	New York	4–1	LA Lakers	Red Holzman	Willis Reed, NY
1973–74	Boston	4–3	Milwaukee	Tommy Heinsohn	John Havlicek, Bos
1974–75	Golden State	4–0	Washington	Al Attles	Rick Barry, GS
1975–76	Boston	4–2	Phoenix	Tommy Heinsohn	JoJo White, Bos
1976–77	Portland	4–2	Philadelphia	Jack Ramsay	Bill Walton, Port
1977–78	Washington	4–3	Seattle	Dick Motta	Wes Unseld, Wash
1978–79	Seattle	4–1	Washington	Lenny Wilkens	Dennis Johnson, Sea
1979–80	LA Lakers	4–2	Philadelphia	Paul Westhead	Magic Johnson, LA
1980–81	Boston	4–2	Houston	Bill Fitch	Cedric Maxwell, Bos
1981–82	LA Lakers	4–2	Philadelphia	Pat Riley	Magic Johnson, LA
1982–83	Philadelphia	4–0	LA Lakers	Billy Cunningham	Moses Malone, Phil
1983–84	Boston	4–3	LA Lakers	K.C. Jones	Larry Bird, Bos
1984–85	LA Lakers	4–2	Boston	Pat Riley	Kareem Abdul-Jabbar, LA
1985–86	Boston	4–2	Houston	K.C. Jones	Larry Bird, Bos
1986–87	LA Lakers	4–2	Boston	Pat Riley	Magic Johnson, LA
1987–88	LA Lakers	4–3	Detroit	Pat Riley	James Worthy, LA
1988–89	Detroit	4–0	LA Lakers	Chuck Daly	Joe Dumars, Det
1989–90	Detroit	4–1	Portland	Chuck Daly	Isiah Thomas, Det
1990–91	Chicago	4–1	LA Lakers	Phil Jackson	Michael Jordan, Chi
1991–92	Chicago	4–2	Portland	Phil Jackson	Michael Jordan, Chi
1992–93	Chicago	4–2	Phoenix	Phil Jackson	Michael Jordan, Chi
1993–94	Houston	4–3	New York	Rudy Tomjanovich	Hakeem Olajuwon, Hou
1994–95	Houston	4–0	Orlando	Rudy Tomjanovich	Hakeem Olajuwon, Hou
1995–96	Chicago	4–2	Seattle	Phil Jackson	Michael Jordan, Chi
1996–97	Chicago	4–2	Utah	Phil Jackson	Michael Jordan, Chi
1997–98	Chicago	4–2	Utah	Phil Jackson	Michael Jordan, Chi
1998–99	San Antonio	4–1	New York	Gregg Popovich	Tim Duncan, SA
1999–00	LA Lakers	4–2	Indiana	Phil Jackson	Shaquille O'Neal, LA
2000–01	LA Lakers	4–1	Philadelphia	Phil Jackson	Shaquille O'Neal, LA
2001–02	LA Lakers	4–0	New Jersey	Phil Jackson	Shaquille O'Neal, LA
2002–03	San Antonio	4–2	New Jersey	Gregg Popovich	Tim Duncan, SA
2003–04	Detroit	4–1	LA Lakers	Larry Brown	Chauncey Billups, Det
2004–05	San Antonio	4–3	Detroit	Gregg Popovich	Tim Duncan, SA
2005–06	Miami	4–2	Dallas	Pat Riley	Dwyane Wade, Mia
2006–07	San Antonio	4–0	Cleveland	Gregg Popovich	Tony Parker, SA
2007–08	Boston	4–2	LA Lakers	Doc Rivers	Paul Pierce, Bos
2008–09	LA Lakers	4–2	Orlando	Phil Jackson	Kobe Bryant, LA
2009–10	LA Lakers	4–3	Boston	Phil Jackson	Kobe Bryant, LA

Regular Season Most Valuable Player: Maurice Podoloff Trophy

Season	Player, Team	GP	Field Goals FGM	Pct	3-Pt FG FGM	Pct	Free Throws FTM	Pct	Rebounds Off	Total	A	Stl	BS	Avg
1955–56	Bob Pettit, StL	72	646	42.9	–	–	557	73.6	–	1,164	189	–	–	25.7
1956–57	Bob Cousy, Bos	64	478	37.8	–	–	363	82.1	–	309	478	–	–	20.6
1957–58	Bill Russell, Bos	69	456	44.2	–	–	230	51.9	–	1,564	202	–	–	16.6
1958–59	Bob Pettit, StL	72	719	43.8	–	–	667	75.9	–	1,182	221	–	–	29.2
1959–60	Wilt Chamberlain, Phil	72	1,065	46.1	–	–	577	58.2	–	1,941	168	–	–	37.6
1960–61	Bill Russell, Bos	78	532	42.6	–	–	258	55.0	–	1,868	264	–	–	16.9
1961–62	Bill Russell, Bos	76	575	45.7	–	–	286	59.5	–	1,891	341	–	–	18.9
1962–63	Bill Russell, Bos	78	511	43.2	–	–	287	55.5	–	1,843	348	–	–	16.8
1963–64	Oscar Robertson, Cin	79	840	48.3	–	–	800	85.3	–	783	868	–	–	31.4
1964–65	Bill Russell, Bos	78	429	43.8	–	–	244	57.3	–	1,878	410	–	–	14.1
1965–66	Wilt Chamberlain, Phil	79	1,074	54.0	–	–	501	51.3	–	1,943	414	–	–	33.5
1966–67	Wilt Chamberlain, Phil	81	785	68.3	–	–	386	44.1	–	1,957	630	–	–	24.1
1967–68	Wilt Chamberlain, Phil	82	819	59.5	–	–	354	38.0	–	1,952	702	–	–	24.3
1968–69	Wes Unseld, Balt	82	427	47.6	–	–	277	60.5	–	1,491	213	–	–	13.8
1969–70	Willis Reed, NY	81	702	50.7	–	–	351	75.6	–	1,126	161	–	–	21.7
1970–71	Lew Alcindor*, Mil	82	1,063	57.7	–	–	470	69.0	–	1,311	272	–	–	31.7
1971–72	Kareem Abdul-Jabbar, Mil	81	1,159	57.4	–	–	504	68.9	–	1,346	370	–	–	34.8
1972–73	Dave Cowens, Bos	82	740	45.2	–	–	204	77.9	–	1,329	333	–	–	20.5
1973–74	Kareem Abdul-Jabbar, Mil	81	948	53.9	–	–	295	70.2	287	1,178	386	112	283	27.0
1974–75	Bob McAdoo, Buff	82	1,095	51.2	–	–	641	80.5	307	1,155	179	92	174	34.5
1975–76	Kareem Abdul-Jabbar, LAL	82	914	52.9	–	–	447	70.3	272	1,383	413	119	338	37.7
1976–77	Kareem Abdul-Jabbar, LAL	82	888	57.9	–	–	376	70.1	266	1,090	319	101	261	26.2
1977–78	Bill Walton, Port	58	460	52.2	–	–	177	72.0	118	766	291	60	146	18.9
1978–79	Moses Malone, Hou	82	716	54.0	–	–	599	73.9	587	1,444	147	79	119	24.8
1979–80	Kareem Abdul-Jabbar, LAL	82	835	60.4	0	00.0	364	76.5	190	886	371	81	280	24.8
1980–81	Julius Erving, Phil	82	794	52.1	4	22.2	422	78.7	244	657	364	173	147	24.6
1981–82	Moses Malone, Hou	81	945	51.9	0	00.0	630	76.2	558	1,188	142	76	125	31.1
1982–83	Moses Malone, Phil	78	654	50.1	0	00.0	600	76.1	445	1,194	101	89	157	24.5
1983–84	Larry Bird, Bos	79	758	49.2	18	24.7	374	88.8	181	796	520	144	69	24.2
1984–85	Larry Bird, Bos	80	918	52.2	56	42.7	403	88.2	164	842	531	129	98	28.7
1985–86	Larry Bird, Bos	82	796	49.6	82	42.3	441	89.6	190	805	557	166	51	25.8
1986–87	Magic Johnson, LAL	80	683	52.2	8	20.5	535	84.8	122	504	977	138	36	23.9
1987–88	Michael Jordan, Chi	82	1,069	53.5	7	13.2	723	84.1	139	449	485	259	131	35.0
1988–89	Magic Johnson, LAL	77	579	50.9	59	31.4	513	91.1	111	607	988	138	22	22.5
1989–90	Magic Johnson, LAL	79	546	48.0	106	38.4	567	89.0	128	522	907	132	34	22.3
1990–91	Michael Jordan, Chi	82	990	53.9	29	31.2	571	85.1	118	492	453	223	83	31.5
1991–92	Michael Jordan, Chi	80	943	51.9	27	27.0	491	83.2	91	511	489	182	75	30.1
1992–93	Charles Barkley, Phx	76	716	52.0	67	30.5	445	76.5	237	928	385	119	74	25.6
1993–94	Hakeem Olajuwon, Hou	80	894	52.8	8	42.1	388	71.6	229	955	287	128	297	27.3
1994–95	David Robinson, SA	81	788	53.0	6	30.0	656	77.4	234	877	236	134	262	27.6
1995–96	Michael Jordan, Chi	82	916	49.5	111	42.7	548	83.4	148	543	352	180	42	30.4
1996–97	Karl Malone, Utah	82	864	55.0	0	00.0	521	75.5	193	809	368	113	48	27.4
1997–98	Michael Jordan, Chi	82	881	46.5	30	23.8	565	78.4	130	475	283	141	45	28.7
1998–99	Karl Malone, Utah	49	393	49.3	0	00.0	378	78.8	107	463	201	62	28	23.8
1999–00	Shaquille O'Neal, LAL	79	956	57.4	0	00.0	432	52.4	336	1078	299	36	239	29.7
2000–01	Allen Iverson, Phil	71	762	42.0	98	32.0	585	81.4	50	273	325	78	20	31.1
2001–02	Tim Duncan, SA	82	764	50.8	1	10.0	560	79.9	268	1042	307	61	203	25.5
2002–03	Tim Duncan, SA	81	714	51.3	6	27.3	450	71.0	260	1045	316	55	237	23.3
2003–04	Kevin Garnett, Minn	82	804	49.9	11	25.6	368	79.1	245	1139	409	120	178	24.2
2004–05	Steve Nash, Phx	75	430	50.2	94	43.1	211	88.7	80	330	861	74	6	26.0
2005–06	Steve Nash, Phx	79	541	51.2	150	43.9	257	92.1	47	333	826	61	12	18.8
2006–07	Dirk Nowitzki, Dal	78	673	50.2	72	41.6	498	90.4	122	693	263	52	62	24.6
2007–08	Kobe Bryant, LAL	82	775	45.9	150	36.1	623	84.0	94	517	441	151	40	28.3
2008–09	LeBron James, Cle	81	789	48.9	132	34.4	594	78.0	106	613	587	137	93	28.4
2009–10	LeBron James, Cle	76	768	50.3	129	33.3	756	76.7	71	554	651	125	77	29.7

*Alcindor changed his name to Kareem Abdul-Jabbar after the 1970–71 season.

Coach of the Year: Arnold (Red) Auerbach Trophy

1962–63...Harry Gallatin, StL
1963–64...Alex Hannum, SF
1964–65...Red Auerbach, Bos
1965–66...Dolph Schayes, Phil
1966–67...Johnny Kerr, Chi
1967–68...Richie Guerin, StL
1968–69...Gene Shue, Balt
1969–70...Red Holzman, NY
1970–71...Dick Motta, Chi
1971–72...Bill Sharman, LA
1972–73...Tom Heinsohn, Bos
1973–74...Ray Scott, Det
1974–75...Phil Johnson, KC-Oma
1975–76...Bill Fitch, Clev
1976–77...Tom Nissalke, Hou
1977–78...Hubie Brown, Atl

1978–79...Cotton Fitzsimmons, KC
1979–80...Bill Fitch, Bos
1980–81...Jack McKinney, Ind
1981–82...Gene Shue, Wash
1982–83...Don Nelson, Mil
1983–84...Frank Layden, Utah
1984–85...Don Nelson, Mil
1985–86...Mike Fratello, Atl
1986–87...Mike Schuler, Port
1987–88...Doug Moe, Den
1988–89...Cotton Fitzsimmons, Phx
1989–90...Pat Riley, LAL
1990–91...Don Chaney, Hou
1991–92...Don Nelson, GS
1992–93...Pat Riley, NY
1993–94...Lenny Wilkens, Atl

1994–95...Del Harris, LAL
1995–96...Phil Jackson, Chi
1996–97...Pat Riley, Mia
1997–98...Larry Bird, Ind
1998–99...Mike Dunleavy, Port
1999–00...Glenn (Doc) Rivers, Orl
2000–01...Larry Brown, Phil
2001–02...Rick Carlisle, Det
2002–03...Gregg Popovich, SA
2003–04...Hubie Brown, Mem
2004–05...Mike D'Antoni, Phx
2005–06...Avery Johnson, Dal
2006–07...Sam Mitchell, Tor
2007–08...Byron Scott, NO
2008–09...Mike Brown, Cle
2009–10...Scott Brooks, OKC

Note: Award named after Auerbach in 1986.

Rookie of the Year: Eddie Gottlieb Trophy

1952–53...Don Meineke, FW
1953–54...Ray Felix, Balt
1954–55...Bob Pettit, Mil
1955–56...Maurice Stokes, Roch
1956–57...Tom Heinsohn, Bos
1957–58...Woody Sauldsberry, Phil
1958–59...Elgin Baylor, Minn
1959–60...Wilt Chamberlain, Phil
1960–61...Oscar Robertson, Cin
1961–62...Walt Bellamy, Chi
1962–63...Terry Dischinger, Chi
1963–64...Jerry Lucas, Cin
1964–65...Willis Reed, NY
1965–66...Rick Barry, SF
1966–67...Dave Bing, Det
1967–68...Earl Monroe, Balt
1968–69...Wes Unseld, Balt
1969–70...K. Abdul-Jabbar, Mil
1970–71...Dave Cowens, Bos
        Geoff Petrie, Port
1971–72...Sidney Wicks, Port

1972–73...Bob McAdoo, Buff
1973–74...Ernie DiGregorio, Buf
1974–75...Keith Wilkes, GS
1975–76...Alvan Adams, Phx
1976–77...Adrian Dantley, Buf
1977–78...Walter Davis, Phx
1978–79...Phil Ford, KC
1979–80...Larry Bird, Bos
1980–81...Darrell Griffith, Utah
1981–82...Buck Williams, NJ
1982–83...Terry Cummings, SD
1983–84...Ralph Sampson, Hou
1984–85...Michael Jordan, Chi
1985–86...Patrick Ewing, NY
1986–87...Chuck Person, Ind
1987–88...Mark Jackson, NY
1988–89...Mitch Richmond, GS
1989–90...David Robinson, SA
1990–91...Derrick Coleman, NJ
1991–92...Larry Johnson, Cha
1992–93...Shaquille O'Neal, Orl

1993–94...Chris Webber, GS
1994–95...Grant Hill, Det
        Jason Kidd, Dal
1995–96...Damon Stoudamire, Tor
1996–97...Allen Iverson, Phil
1997–98...Tim Duncan, SA
1998–99...Vince Carter, Tor
1999–00...Elton Brand, Chi
        Steve Francis, Hou
2000–01...Mike Miller, Orl
2001–02...Pau Gasol, Mem
2002–03...Amare Stoudemire, Phx
2003–04...LeBron James, Clev
2004–05...Emeka Okafor, Cha
2005–06...Chris Paul, NO
2006–07...Brandon Roy, Port
2007–08...Kevin Durant, Sea
2008–09...Derrick Rose, Chi
2009–10...Tyreke Evans, Sac

Defensive Player of the Year

1982–83...Sidney Moncrief, Mil
1983–84...Sidney Moncrief, Mil
1984–85...Mark Eaton, Utah
1985–86...Alvin Robertson, SA
1986–87...Michael Cooper, LAL
1987–88...Michael Jordan, Chi
1988–89...Mark Eaton, Utah
1989–90...Dennis Rodman, Det
1990–91...Dennis Rodman, Det
1991–92...David Robinson, SA

1992–93...Hakeem Olajuwon, Hou
1993–94...Hakeem Olajuwon, Hou
1994–95...Dikembe Mutombo, Den
1995–96...Gary Payton, Sea
1996–97...Dikembe Mutombo, Atl
1997–98...Dikembe Mutombo, Atl
1998–99...Alonzo Mourning, Mia
1999–00...Alonzo Mourning, Mia
2000–01...Dikembe Mutombo, Phil/Atl
2001–02...Ben Wallace, Det

2002–03...Ben Wallace, Det
2003–04...Ron Artest, Ind
2004–05...Ben Wallace, Det
2005–06...Ben Wallace, Det
2006–07...Marcus Camby, Den
2007–08...Kevin Garnett, Bos
2008–09...Dwight Howard, Orl
2009–10...Dwight Howard, Orl

Sixth Man Award

1982–83...Bobby Jones, Phil
1983–84...Kevin McHale, Bos
1984–85...Kevin McHale, Bos
1985–86...Bill Walton, Bos
1986–87...Ricky Pierce, Mil
1987–88...Roy Tarpley, Dal
1988–89...Eddie Johnson, Phx
1989–90...Ricky Pierce, Mil
1990–91...Detlef Schrempf, Ind
1991–92...Detlef Schrempf, Ind

1992–93...Cliff Robinson, Port
1993–94...Dell Curry, Cha
1994–95...Anthony Mason, NY
1995–96...Tony Kukoc, Chi
1996–97...John Starks, NY
1997–98...Danny Manning, Phx
1998–99...Darrell Armstrong, Orl
1999–00...Rodney Rogers, Phx
2000–01...Aaron McKie, Phil
2001–02...Corliss Williamson, Det

2002–03...Bobby Jackson, Sac
2003–04...Antawn Jamison, Dal
2004–05...Ben Gordon, Chi
2005–06...Mike Miller, Mem
2006–07...Leandro Barbosa, Phx
2007–08...Manu Ginobli, SA
2008–09...Jason Terry, Dal
2009–10...Jamal Crawford, Atl

J. Walter Kennedy Citizenship Award

1974–75...Wes Unseld, Wash
1975–76...Slick Watts, Sea
1976–77...Dave Bing, Wash
1977–78...Bob Lanier, Det
1978–79...Calvin Murphy, Hou
1979–80...Austin Carr, Cle
1980–81...Mike Glenn, NY
1981–82...Kent Benson, Det
1982–83...Julius Erving, Phi
1983–84...Frank Layden, Utah
1984–85...Dan Issel, Den
1985–86...Michael Cooper, LAL
Rory Sparrow, NY

1986–87...Isiah Thomas, Det
1987–88...Alex English, Den
1988–89...Thurl Bailey, Utah
1989–90...Glenn (Doc) Rivers, Atl
1990–91...Kevin Johnson, Phx
1991–92...Magic Johnson, LAL
1992–93...Terry Porter, Port
1993–94...Joe Dumars, Det
1994–95...Joe O'Toole, Atl
1995–96...Chris Dudley, Port
1996–97...P.J. Brown, Mia
1997–98...Steve Smith, Atl

1998–99...Brian Grant, Port
1999–00...Vlade Divac, Sac
2000–01...Dikembe Mutombo, Phi
2001–02...Alonzo Mourning, Mia
2002–03...David Robinson, SA
2003–04...Reggie Miller, Ind
2004–05...Eric Snow, Clev
2005–06...Kevin Garnett, Min
2006–07...Luol Deng, Chi
2007–08...Grant Hill, Phx
2008–09...Dikembe Mutombo, Hou
2009–10...Samuel Dalembert, Phi

Most Improved Player

1985–86...Alvin Robertson, SA
1986–87...Dale Ellis, Sea
1987–88...Kevin Duckworth, Port
1988–89...Kevin Johnson, Phx
1989–90...Rony Seikaly, Mia
1990–91...Scott Skiles, Orl
1991–92...Pervis Ellison, Wash
1992–93...Mahmoud Abdul-Rauf, Den
1993–94...Don MacLean, Wash

1994–95...Dana Barros, Phil
1995–96....Gheorghe Muresan, Wash
1996–97...Isaac Austin, Mia
1997–98...Alan Henderson, Atl
1998–99...Darrell Armstrong, Orl
1999–00...Jalen Rose, Ind
2000–01...Tracy McGrady, Orl
2001–02....Jermaine O'Neal, Ind
2002–03...Gilbert Arenas, GS

2003–04...Zach Randolph, Port
2004–05...Bobby Simmons, LAC
2005–06...Boris Diaw, Phx
2006–07...Monta Ellis, GS
2007–08...Hedo Turkoglu, Orl
2008–09...Danny Granger, Ind
2009–10...Aaron Brooks, Hou

Executive of the Year

1972–73...Joe Axelson, KC-Oma
1973–74...Eddie Donovan, Buf
1974–75...Dick Vertlieb, GS
1975–76...Jerry Colangelo, Phx
1976–77...Ray Patterson, Hou
1977–78...Angelo Drossos, SA
1978–79...Bob Ferry, Wash
1979–80...Red Auerbach, Bos
1980–81...Jerry Colangelo, Phx
1981–82...Bob Ferry, Wash
1982–83...Zollie Volchok, Sea
1983–84...Frank Layden, Utah
1984–85...Vince Boryla, Den

1985–86...Stan Kasten, Atl
1986–87...Stan Kasten, Atl
1987–88...Jerry Krause, Chi
1988–89...Jerry Colangelo, Phx
1989–90...Bob Bass, SA
1990–91...Bucky Buckwalter, Port
1991–92...Wayne Embry, Clev
1992–93...Jerry Colangelo, Phx
1993–94...Bob Whitsitt, Sea
1994–95...Jerry West, LAL
1995–96...Jerry Krause, Chi
1996–97...Bob Bass, Cha
1997–98...Wayne Embry, Clev

1998–99...Geoff Petrie, Sac
1999–00...John Gabriel, Orl
2000–01...Geoff Petrie, Sac
2001–02...Rod Thorn, NJ
2002–03...Joe Dumars, Det
2003–04...Jerry West, Mem
2004–05...Bryan Colangelo, Phx
2005–06...Elgin Baylor, LAC
2006–07...Bryan Colangelo, Tor
2007–08...Danny Ainge, Bos
2008–09...Mark Warkentien, Den
2009–10...John Hammond, Mil

NBA Alltime Individual Leaders

Scoring

MOST POINTS, CAREER

	Pts	Avg
Kareem Abdul-Jabbar	38,387	24.6
Karl Malone	36,928	25.0
Michael Jordan	32,292	30.1
Wilt Chamberlain	31,419	30.1
*Shaquille O'Neal	28,255	24.1
Moses Malone	27,409	20.6
Elvin Hayes	27,313	21.0
Hakeem Olajuwon	26,946	21.8
Oscar Robertson	26,710	25.7
Dominique Wilkins	26,668	24.8

*Active in 2009–10.

HIGHEST SCORING AVERAGE, CAREER

Michael Jordan	30.1	1,072 games
Wilt Chamberlain	30.1	1,045 games
*LeBron James	27.8	547 games
Elgin Baylor	27.4	846 games
Jerry West	27.0	932 games
*Allen Iverson	26.7	914 games
Bob Pettit	26.4	792 games
George Gervin	26.2	791 games
Oscar Robertson	25.7	1,040 games
*Dwyane Wade	25.4	471 games

*Acitve in 2009–10. Note: Minimum 400 games.

MOST POINTS, SEASON

Wilt Chamberlain, Phil	4,029	1961–62
Wilt Chamberlain, SF	3,586	1962–63
Michael Jordan, Chi	3,041	1986–87
Wilt Chamberlain, Phil	3,033	1960–61
Wilt Chamberlain, SF	2,948	1963–64
Michael Jordan, Chi	2,868	1987–88
Kobe Bryant, LA	2,832	2005–06
Bob McAdoo, Buff	2,831	1974–75
Rick Barry, SF	2,775	1966–67
Michael Jordan, Chi	2,753	1989–90

HIGHEST SCORING AVERAGE, SEASON

Wilt Chamberlain, Phil	50.4	1961–62
Wilt Chamberlain, SF	44.8	1962–63
Wilt Chamberlain, Phil	38.4	1960–61
Wilt Chamberlain, Phil	37.6	1959–60
Michael Jordan, Chi	37.1	1986–87
Wilt Chamberlain, SF	36.9	1963–64
Rick Barry, SF	35.6	1966–67
Kobe Bryant, LA	35.4	2005–06
Michael Jordan, Chi	35.0	1987–88
Elgin Baylor, LA	34.8	1960–61

Note: Minimum 70 games.

Scoring (Cont.)

MOST POINTS, SINGLE GAME

	Player, Team	Opp	Date
100	Wilt Chamberlain, Phil	NY	3/2/62
81	Kobe Bryant, LAL	Tor	1/22/06
78	Wilt Chamberlain, Phil	LAL	12/8/61
73	Wilt Chamberlain, Phil	Chi	1/13/62
73	Wilt Chamberlain, SF	NY	11/16/62
73	David Thompson, Den	Det	4/9/78
72	Wilt Chamberlain, SF	LAL	11/3/62
71	David Robinson, SA	LAC	4/24/94
71	Elgin Baylor, LAL	NY	11/15/60
70	Wilt Chamberlain, SF	Syr	3/10/63

Field-Goal Percentage

Highest FG Percentage, Career: .599—Artis Gilmore

Highest FG Percentage, Season: .727—Wilt Chamberlain, LA Lakers, 1972–73 (426/586)

Free Throws

HIGHEST FREE-THROW PERCENTAGE, CAREER

Mark Price	.904
*Steve Nash	.903
Rick Barry	.900
*Peja Stojakovic	.895
*Ray Allen	.894

Note: Minimum 1200 free throws made. *Active 2009–10.

HIGHEST FREE-THROW PERCENTAGE, SEASON

Jose Calderon, Tor	.981	2008–09
Calvin Murphy, Hou	.958	1980–81
Mahmoud Abdul-Rauf, Den	.956	1993–94
Ray Allen, Bos	.952	2008–09
Jeff Hornacek, Utah	.950	1999–00
Mark Price, Clev	.948	1992–93

MOST FREE THROWS MADE, CAREER

	No.	Yrs	Pct
Karl Malone	9,787	19	.742
Moses Malone	8,531	19	.769
Oscar Robertson	7,694	14	.838
Michael Jordan	7,327	15	.835
Jerry West	7,160	14	.814

Three-Point Field Goals

Most Three-Point Field-Goals, Career: 2,560—Reggie Miller

Highest Three-Point Field-Goal Percentage, Career: .454—Steve Kerr

Most Three-Point Field Goals, Season: 269—Ray Allen, Sea, 2005–06

Highest Three-Point Field-Goal Percentage, Season: .524—Steve Kerr, Chi, 1994–95

Most Three-Point Field Goals, Game: 12—Kobe Bryant, LA Lakers vs Seattle, 1/7/03; Donyell Marshall, Toronto vs. Philadelphia, 3/13/05

Note: First season of three-point field goal: 1979–80. *Active 2009–10.

Steals

Most Steals, Career: 3,265—John Stockton

Most Steals, Season: 301—Alvin Robertson, San Antonio, 1985–86

Most Steals, Game: 11—Kendall Gill, New Jersey vs Miami, 4/3/99; Larry Kenon, San Antonio vs Kansas City, 12/26/76

Rebounds

MOST REBOUNDS, CAREER

	No.	Yrs	Avg
Wilt Chamberlain	23,924	14	22.9
Bill Russell	21,620	13	22.5
Kareem Abdul-Jabbar	17,440	20	11.2
Elvin Hayes	16,279	16	12.5
Moses Malone	16,212	19	12.2
Karl Malone	14,968	19	10.1
Robert Parish	14,715	21	9.1
Nate Thurmond	14,464	14	15.0
Walt Bellamy	14,241	14	13.7
Wes Unseld	13,769	13	14.0

MOST REBOUNDS, SEASON

Wilt Chamberlain, Phil	2,149	1960–61
Wilt Chamberlain, Phil	2,052	1961–62
Wilt Chamberlain, Phil	1,957	1966–67
Wilt Chamberlain, Phil	1,952	1967–68
Wilt Chamberlain, SF	1,946	1962–63
Wilt Chamberlain, Phil	1,943	1965–66
Wilt Chamberlain, Phil	1,941	1959–60
Bill Russell, Bos	1,930	1963–64
Bill Russell, Bos	1,878	1964–65
Bill Russell, Bos	1,868	1960–61

MOST REBOUNDS, GAME

	Player, Team	Opp	Date
55	Wilt Chamberlain, Phil	Bos	11/24/60
51	Bill Russell, Bos	Syr	02/05/60
49	Bill Russell, Bos	Phil	11/16/57
49	Bill Russell, Bos	Det	03/11/65
45	Wilt Chamberlain, Phil	Syr	02/06/60
45	Wilt Chamberlain, Phil	LA	01/21/61

Assists

MOST ASSISTS, CAREER

John Stockton	15,806
*Jason Kidd	10,923
Mark Jackson	10,334
Magic Johnson	10,141
Oscar Robertson	9,887

*Active in 2009–10.

MOST ASSISTS, SEASON

John Stockton, Utah	1,164	1990–91
John Stockton, Utah	1,134	1989–90
John Stockton, Utah	1,128	1987–88
John Stockton, Utah	1,126	1991–92
Isiah Thomas, Det	1,123	1984–85

MOST ASSISTS, GAME: 30—Scott Skiles, Orlando vs Denver, 12/30/90

Blocked Shots

MOST BLOCKED SHOTS, CAREER

Hakeem Olajuwon	3,830
Dikembe Mutombo	3,289
Kareem Abdul-Jabbar	3,189
Mark Eaton	3,064
David Robinson	2,954

MOST BLOCKED SHOTS, SEASON

Mark Eaton, Utah	456	1984–85
Manute Bol, Wash	397	1985–86
Elmore Smith, LAL	393	1973–74

MOST BLOCKED SHOTS, GAME: 17—Elmore Smith, LA Lakers vs Portland, 10/28/73

Scoring

MOST POINTS, CAREER

	Pts	App.	Avg
Michael Jordan	5,987	13	33.4
Kareem Abdul-Jabbar	5,762	18	24.3
*Shaquille O'Neal	5,248	16	24.5
*Kobe Bryant	5,052	13	25.5
Karl Malone	4,761	19	24.7
Jerry West	4,457	13	29.1
*Tim Duncan	3,914	12	23.0
Larry Bird	3,897	12	23.8
John Havlicek	3,776	13	22.0
Hakeem Olajuwon	3,755	15	25.9
Magic Johnson	3,701	13	19.5
Scottie Pippen	3,642	16	17.5

*Active 2009–10.

†HIGHEST SCORING AVERAGE, CAREER

	Avg	Games
Michael Jordan	33.4	179
*Allen Iverson	29.7	71
*LeBron James	29.3	71
Jerry West	29.1	153
*Tracy McGrady	28.5	38
Elgin Baylor	27.0	134
George Gervin	27.0	59
*Dwyane Wade	26.3	66
Hakeem Olajuwon	25.9	145
*Dirk Nowitzki	25.6	103
Bob Pettit	25.5	88
*Kobe Bryant	25.5	198
Dominique Wilkins	25.4	55
Ricky Barry	24.8	74
Karl Malone	24.7	193

†Minimum of 25 games. *Active 2009–10.

MOST POINTS, GAME

	Player, Team	Opp	Date
†63	Michael Jordan, Chi	Bos	4/20/86
61	Elgin Baylor, LAL	Bos	4/14/62
56	Wilt Chamberlain, Phil	Syr	3/22/62
56	Michael Jordan, Chi	Mia	4/29/92
56	Charles Barkley, Phx	GS	5/4/94
55	Rick Barry, SF	Phil	4/18/67
55	Michael Jordan, Chi	Cle	5/1/88
55	Michael Jordan, Chi	Phx	4/16/95
55	Michael Jordan, Chi	Wash	4/27/97

†Double overtime game.

Rebounds

MOST REBOUNDS, CAREER

	No.	App.	Avg
Bill Russell	4,104	13	24.9
Wilt Chamberlain	3,913	13	24.5
*Shaquille O'Neal	2,508	16	11.7
Kareem Abdul-Jabbar	2,481	18	10.5
*Tim Duncan	2,114	12	12.4
Karl Malone	2,062	19	10.7

*Active 2009–10.

MOST REBOUNDS, GAME

	Player, Team	Opp	Date
41	Wilt Chamberlain, Phil	Bos	4/5/67
40	Bill Russell, Bos	Phil	3/23/58
40	Bill Russell, Bos	StL	3/29/60
†40	Bill Russell, Bos	LA	4/18/62

†Overtime game. Three tied at 39.

Assists

MOST ASSISTS, CAREER

	No.	Games
Magic Johnson	2,346	190
John Stockton	1,839	182
*Jason Kidd	1,062	115
Larry Bird	1,062	164
Scottie Pippen	1,048	208
Michael Jordan	1,022	179

*Active 2009–10.

MOST ASSISTS, GAME

	Player, Team	Opp	Date
24	Magic Johnson, LAL	Phx	5/15/84
24	John Stockton, Utah	LAL	5/17/88
23	Magic Johnson, LAL	Port	5/3/85
23	John Stockton, Utah	Port	4/25/96
23	Steve Nash, Phx	LAL	4/24/07

Games played

Robert Horry	244
Kareem Abdul-Jabbar	237
*Shaquille O'Neal	214
Scottie Pippen	208
*Kobe Bryant	198
Danny Ainge	193
Karl Malone	193
Magic Johnson	190
Robert Parish	184
Byron Scott	183

Appearances

John Stockton	19
Karl Malone	19
Kareem Abdul-Jabbar	18
Robert Horry	16
Robert Parish	16
Scottie Pippen	16
Terry Porter	16
*Shaquille O'Neal	16
Dolph Schayes	15
Clyde Drexler	15
Jerome Kersey	15
Hakeem Olajuwon	15
Tree Rollins	15

*Active 2009–10.

Scoring

1946–47	Joe Fulks, Phil	1389
1947–48	Max Zaslofsky, Chi	1007
1948–49	George Mikan, Min	1698
1949–50	George Mikan, Min	1865
1950–51	George Mikan, Min	1932
1951–52	Paul Arizin, Phil	1674
1952–53	Neil Johnston, Phil	1564
1953–54	Neil Johnston, Phil	1759
1954–55	Neil Johnston, Phil	1631
1955–56	Bob Pettit, StL	1849
1956–57	Paul Arizin, Phil	1817
1957–58	George Yardley, Det	2001
1958–59	Bob Pettit, StL	2105
1959–60	Wilt Chamberlain, Phil	2707
1960–61	Wilt Chamberlain, Phil	3033
1961–62	Wilt Chamberlain, Phil	4029
1962–63	Wilt Chamberlain, SF	3586
1963–64	Wilt Chamberlain, SF	2948
1964–65	Wilt Chamberlain, SF-Phil	2534
1965–66	Wilt Chamberlain, Phil	2649
1966–67	Rick Barry, SF	2775
1967–68	Dave Bing, Det	2142
1968–69	Elvin Hayes, SD	2327
1969–70	Jerry West, LAL	*31.2
1970–71	Kareem Abdul-Jabbar, Mil	31.7
1971–72	Kareem Abdul-Jabbar, Mil	34.8
1972–73	Nate Archibald, KC-Oma	34.0
1973–74	Bob McAdoo, Buff	30.6
1974–75	Bob McAdoo, Buff	34.5
1975–76	Bob McAdoo, Buff	31.1
1976–77	Pete Maravich, NO	31.1
1977–78	George Gervin, SA	27.2
1978–79	George Gervin, SA	29.6
1979–80	George Gervin, SA	33.1
1980–81	Adrian Dantley, Utah	30.7
1981–82	George Gervin, SA	32.3
1982–83	Alex English, Den	28.4
1983–84	Adrian Dantley, Utah	30.6
1984–85	Bernard King, NY	32.9
1985–86	Dominique Wilkins, Atl	30.3
1986–87	Michael Jordan, Chi	37.1
1987–88	Michael Jordan, Chi	35.0
1988–89	Michael Jordan, Chi	32.5
1989–90	Michael Jordan, Chi	33.6
1990–91	Michael Jordan, Chi	31.5
1991–92	Michael Jordan, Chi	30.1
1992–93	Michael Jordan, Chi	32.6
1993–94	David Robinson, SA	29.8
1994–95	Shaquille O'Neal, Orl	29.3
1995–96	Michael Jordan, Chi	30.4
1996–97	Michael Jordan, Chi	29.6
1997–98	Michael Jordan, Chi	28.7
1998–99	Allen Iverson, Phil	26.8
1999–00	Shaquille O'Neal, LAL	29.7
2000–01	Allen Iverson, Phil	31.1
2001–02	Allen Iverson, Phil	31.4
2002–03	Tracy McGrady, Orl	32.1
2003–04	Tracy McGrady, Orl	28.0
2004–05	Allen Iverson, Phil	30.7
2005–06	Kobe Bryant, LAL	35.4
2006–07	Kobe Bryant, LAL	31.6
2007–08	LeBron James, Cle	30.0
2008–09	Dwyane Wade, Mia	30.2
2009–10	Kevin Durant, OKC	30.1

*Based on per game average since 1969–70.

Rebounding

1950–51	Dolph Schayes, Syr	1080
1951–52	Larry Foust, FW	880
	Mel Hutchins, Mil	880
1952–53	George Mikan, Min	1007
1953–54	Harry Gallatin, NY	1098
1954–55	Neil Johnston, Phil	1085
1955–56	Bob Pettit, StL	1164
1956–57	Maurice Stokes, Roch	1256
1957–58	Bill Russell, Bos	1564
1958–59	Bill Russell, Bos	1612
1959–60	Wilt Chamberlain, Phil	1941
1960–61	Wilt Chamberlain, Phil	2149
1961–62	Wilt Chamberlain, Phil	2052
1962–63	Wilt Chamberlain, SF	1946
1963–64	Bill Russell, Bos	1930
1964–65	Bill Russell, Bos	1878
1965–66	Wilt Chamberlain, Phil	1943
1966–67	Wilt Chamberlain, Phil	1957
1967–68	Wilt Chamberlain, Phil	1952
1968–69	Wilt Chamberlain, LAL	1712
1969–70	Elvin Hayes, SD	*16.9
1970–71	Wilt Chamberlain, LAL	18.2
1971–72	Wilt Chamberlain, LAL	19.2
1972–73	Wilt Chamberlain, LAL	18.6
1973–74	Elvin Hayes, Capital (Wash.)	18.1
1974–75	Wes Unseld, Wash	14.8
1975–76	Kareem Abdul-Jabbar, LAL	16.9
1976–77	Bill Walton, Port	14.4
1977–78	Len Robinson, NO	15.7
1978–79	Moses Malone, Hou	17.6
1979–80	Swen Nater, SD	15.0
1980–81	Moses Malone, Hou	14.8
1981–82	Moses Malone, Hou	14.7
1982–83	Moses Malone, Phil	15.3
1983–84	Moses Malone, Phil	13.4
1984–85	Moses Malone, Phil	13.1
1985–86	Bill Laimbeer, Det	13.1
1986–87	Charles Barkley, Phil	14.6
1987–88	Michael Cage, LAC	13.0
1988–89	Hakeem Olajuwon, Hou	13.5
1989–90	Hakeem Olajuwon, Hou	14.0
1990–91	David Robinson, SA	13.0
1991–92	Dennis Rodman, Det	18.7
1992–93	Dennis Rodman, Det	18.3
1993–94	Dennis Rodman, SA	17.3
1994–95	Dennis Rodman, SA	16.8
1995–96	Dennis Rodman, Chi	14.9
1996–97	Dennis Rodman, Chi	16.1
1997–98	Dennis Rodman, Chi	15.0
1998–99	Chris Webber, Sac	13.0
1999–00	Dikembe Mutombo, Atl	14.1
2000–01	Dikembe Mutombo, Atl	13.5
2001–02	Ben Wallace, Det	13.0
2002–03	Ben Wallace, Det	15.4
2003–04	Kevin Garnett, Min	13.9
2004–05	Kevin Garnett, Min	13.5
2005–06	Kevin Garnett, Min	12.7
2006–07	Kevin Garnett, Min	12.8
2007–08	Dwight Howard, Orl	14.2
2008–09	Dwight Howard, Orl	13.8
2009–10	Dwight Howard, Orl	12.7

*Based on per game average since 1969–70.

Assists

1946–47	Ernie Calverly, Prov	202	1979–80	Micheal Ray Richardson, NY	10.1
1947–48	Howie Dallmar, Phil	120	1980–81	Kevin Porter, Wash	9.1
1948–49	Bob Davies, Roch	321	1981–82	Johnny Moore, SA	9.6
1949–50	Dick McGuire, NY	386	1982–83	Magic Johnson, LAL	10.5
1950–51	Andy Phillip, Phil	414	1983–84	Magic Johnson, LAL	13.1
1951–52	Andy Phillip, Phil	539	1984–85	Isiah Thomas, Det	13.9
1952–53	Bob Cousy, Bos	547	1985–86	Magic Johnson, LAL	12.6
1953–54	Bob Cousy, Bos	518	1986–87	Magic Johnson, LAL	12.2
1954–55	Bob Cousy, Bos	557	1987–88	John Stockton, Utah	13.8
1955–56	Bob Cousy, Bos	642	1988–89	John Stockton, Utah	13.6
1956–57	Bob Cousy, Bos	478	1989–90	John Stockton, Utah	14.5
1957–58	Bob Cousy, Bos	463	1990–91	John Stockton, Utah	14.2
1958–59	Bob Cousy, Bos	557	1991–92	John Stockton, Utah	13.7
1959–60	Bob Cousy, Bos	715	1992–93	John Stockton, Utah	12.0
1960–61	Oscar Robertson, Cin	690	1993–94	John Stockton, Utah	12.6
1961–62	Oscar Robertson, Cin	899	1994–95	John Stockton, Utah	12.3
1962–63	Guy Rodgers, SF	825	1995–96	John Stockton, Utah	11.2
1963–64	Oscar Robertson, Cin	868	1996–97	Mark Jackson, Ind	11.4
1964–65	Oscar Robertson, Cin	861	1997–98	Rod Strickland, Wash	10.5
1965–66	Oscar Robertson, Cin	847	1998–99	Jason Kidd, Phx	10.8
1966–67	Guy Rodgers, Chi	908	1999–00	Jason Kidd, Phx	10.1
1967–68	Wilt Chamberlain, Phil	702	2000–01	Jason Kidd, Phx	9.8
1968–69	Oscar Robertson, Cin	772	2001–02	Andre Miller, Cle	10.9
1969–70	Lenny Wilkens, Sea	*9.1	2002–03	Jason Kidd, NJ	8.9
1970–71	Norm Van Lier, Cin	10.1	2003–04	Jason Kidd, NJ	9.2
1971–72	Jerry West, LAL	9.7	2004–05	Steve Nash, Phx	11.5
1972–73	Nate Archibald, KC-Oma	11.4	2005–06	Steve Nash, Phx	10.5
1973–74	Ernie DiGregorio, Buf	8.2	2006–07	Steve Nash, Phx	11.6
1974–75	Kevin Porter, Wash	8.0	2007–08	Chris Paul, NO	11.6
1975–76	Don Watts, Sea	8.1	2008–09	Chris Paul, NO	11.0
1976–77	Don Buse, Ind	8.5	2009–10	Steve Nash, Phx	11.0
1977–78	Kevin Porter, NJ-Det	10.2			
1978–79	Kevin Porter, Det	13.4	*Based on per game average since 1969–70.		

Field-Goal Percentage

1946–47	Bob Feerick, Wash	40.1	1978–79	Cedric Maxwell, Bos	58.4
1947–48	Bob Feerick, Wash	34.0	1979–80	Cedric Maxwell, Bos	60.9
1948–49	Arnie Risen, Roch	42.3	1980–81	Artis Gilmore, Chi	67.0
1949–50	Alex Groza, Ind	47.8	1981–82	Artis Gilmore, Chi	65.2
1950–51	Alex Groza, Ind	47.0	1982–83	Artis Gilmore, SA	62.6
1951–52	Paul Arizin, Phil	44.8	1983–84	Artis Gilmore, SA	63.1
1952–53	Neil Johnston, Phil	45.2	1984–85	James Donaldson, LAC	63.7
1953–54	Ed Macauley, Bos	48.6	1985–86	Steve Johnson, SA	63.2
1954–55	Larry Foust, FW	48.7	1986–87	Kevin McHale, Bos	60.4
1955–56	Neil Johnston, Phil	45.7	1987–88	Kevin McHale, Bos	60.4
1956–57	Neil Johnston, Phil	44.7	1988–89	Dennis Rodman, Det	59.5
1957–58	Jack Twyman, Cin	45.2	1989–90	Mark West, Phx	62.5
1958–59	Ken Sears, NY	49.0	1990–91	Buck Williams, Port	60.2
1959–60	Ken Sears, NY	47.7	1991–92	Buck Williams, Port	60.4
1960–61	Wilt Chamberlain, Phil	50.9	1992–93	Cedric Ceballos, Phx	57.6
1961–62	Walt Bellamy, Chi	51.9	1993–94	Shaquille O'Neal, Orl	59.9
1962–63	Wilt Chamberlain, SF	52.8	1994–95	Chris Gatling, GS	63.3
1963–64	Jerry Lucas, Cin	52.7	1995–96	Gheorghe Muresan, Wash	58.4
1964–65	Wilt Chamberlain, SF-Phil	51.0	1996–97	Gheorghe Muresan, Wash	60.4
1965–66	Wilt Chamberlain, Phil	54.0	1997–98	Shaquille O'Neal, LAL	58.4
1966–67	Wilt Chamberlain, Phil	68.3	1998–99	Shaquille O'Neal, LAL	57.6
1967–68	Wilt Chamberlain, Phil	59.5	1999–00	Shaquille O'Neal, LAL	57.4
1968–69	Wilt Chamberlain, LAL	58.3	2000–01	Shaquille O'Neal, LAL	57.2
1969–70	Johnny Green, Cin	55.9	2001–02	Shaquille O'Neal, LAL	57.9
1970–71	Johnny Green, Cin	58.7	2002–03	Eddy Curry, Chi	58.5
1971–72	Wilt Chamberlain, LAL	64.9	2003–04	Shaquille O'Neal, LAL	58.4
1972–73	Wilt Chamberlain, LAL	72.7	2004–05	Shaquille O'Neal, Mia	60.1
1973–74	Bob McAdoo, Buf	54.7	2005–06	Shaquille O'Neal, Mia	60.0
1974–75	Don Nelson, Bos	53.9	2006–07	Mikki Moore, NJ	60.9
1975–76	Wes Unseld, Wash	56.1	2007–08	Andris Biedrins, GS	62.6
1976–77	Kareem Abdul-Jabbar, LAL	57.9	2008–09	Erick Dampier, Dal	65.0
1977–78	Bobby Jones, Den	57.8	2009–10	Erick Dampier, Dal	62.4

Free-Throw Percentage

1946–47	Fred Scolari, Wash	81.1
1947–48	Bob Feerick, Wash	78.8
1948–49	Bob Feerick, Wash	85.9
1949–50	Max Zaslofsky, Chi	84.3
1950–51	Joe Fulks, Phil	85.5
1951–52	Bob Wanzer, Roch	90.4
1952–53	Bill Sharman, Bos	85.0
1953–54	Bill Sharman, Bos	84.4
1954–55	Bill Sharman, Bos	89.7
1955–56	Bill Sharman, Bos	86.7
1956–57	Bill Sharman, Bos	90.5
1957–58	Dolph Schayes, Syr	90.4
1958–59	Bill Sharman, Bos	93.2
1959–60	Dolph Schayes, Syr	89.3
1960–61	Bill Sharman, Bos	92.1
1961–62	Dolph Schayes, Syr	89.7
1962–63	Larry Costello, Syr	88.1
1963–64	Oscar Robertson, Cin	85.3
1964–65	Larry Costello, Phil	87.7
1965–66	Larry Siegfried, Bos	88.1
1966–67	Adrian Smith, Cin	90.3
1967–68	Oscar Robertson, Cin	87.3
1968–69	Larry Siegfried, Bos	86.4
1969–70	Flynn Robinson, Mil	89.8
1970–71	Chet Walker, Chi	85.9
1971–72	Jack Marin, Balt	89.4
1972–73	Rick Barry, GS	90.2
1973–74	Ernie DiGregorio, Buf	90.2
1974–75	Rick Barry, GS	90.4
1975–76	Rick Barry, GS	92.3
1976–77	Ernie DiGregorio, Buf	94.5
1977–78	Rick Barry, GS	92.4
1978–79	Rick Barry, Hou	94.7
1979–80	Rick Barry, Hou	93.5
1980–81	Calvin Murphy, Hou	95.8
1981–82	Kyle Macy, Phx	89.9
1982–83	Calvin Murphy, Hou	92.0
1983–84	Larry Bird, Bos	88.8
1984–85	Kyle Macy, Phx	90.7
1985–86	Larry Bird, Bos	89.6
1986–87	Larry Bird, Bos	91.0
1987–88	Jack Sikma, Mil	92.2
1988–89	Magic Johnson, LAL	91.1
1989–90	Larry Bird, Bos	93.0
1990–91	Reggie Miller, Ind	91.8
1991–92	Mark Price, Clev	94.7
1992–93	Mark Price, Clev	94.8
1993–94	Mahmoud Abdul-Rauf, Den	95.6
1994–95	Spud Webb, Sac	93.4
1995–96	Mahmoud Abdul-Rauf, Den	93.0
1996–97	Mark Price, GS	90.6
1997–98	Chris Mullin, Ind	93.9
1998–99	Reggie Miller, Ind	91.5
1999–00	Jeff Hornacek, Utah	95.0
2000–01	Reggie Miller, Ind	92.8
2001–02	Reggie Miller, Ind	91.1
2002–03	Allan Houston, NY	91.9
2003–04	Peja Stojakovic, Sac	92.7
2004–05	Reggie Miller, Ind	93.3
2005–06	Steve Nash, Phx	92.1
2006–07	Kyle Korver, Phil	91.4
2007–08	Peja Stojakovic, NO	92.9
2008–09	Jose Calderon, Tor	98.1
2009–10	Steve Nash, Phx	93.8

Three-Point Field-Goal Percentage

1979–80	Fred Brown, Sea	44.3
1980–81	Brian Taylor, SD	38.3
1981–82	Campy Russell, NY	43.9
1982–83	Mike Dunleavy, SA	34.5
1983–84	Darrell Griffith, Utah	36.1
1984–85	Byron Scott, LAL	43.3
1985–86	Craig Hodges, Mil	45.1
1986–87	Kiki Vandeweghe, Por	48.1
1987–88	Craig Hodges, Mil-Phx	49.1
1988–89	Jon Sundvold, Mia	52.2
1989–90	Steve Kerr, Clev	50.7
1990–91	Jim Les, Sac	46.1
1991–92	Dana Barros, Sea	44.6
1992–93	Chris Mullin, GS	45.1
1993–94	Tracy Murray, Por	45.9
1994–95	Steve Kerr, Chi	52.4
1995–96	Tim Legler, Wash	52.2
1996–97	Glen Rice, Cha	47.0
1997–98	Dale Ellis, Sea	46.0
1998–99	Dell Curry, Cha	47.6
1999–00	Hubert Davis, Dal	49.1
2000–01	Brent Barry, Sea	47.6
2001–02	Steve Smith, SA	47.2
2002–03	Bruce Bowen, SA	44.1
2003–04	Anthony Peeler, Sac	48.2
2004–05	Fred Hoiberg, Min	48.3
2005–06	Richard Hamilton, Det	45.8
2006–07	Jason Kapono, Mia	51.4
2007–08	Jason Kapono, Tor	48.3
2008–09	Anthony Morrow, GS	46.7
2009–10	Mike Miller, Wash	48.0

Steals

1973–74	Larry Steele, Por	2.68
1974–75	Rick Barry, GS	2.85
1975–76	Don Watts, Sea	3.18
1976–77	Don Buse, Ind	3.47
1977–78	Ron Lee, Phx	2.74
1978–79	M.L. Carr, Det	2.46
1979–80	Micheal Ray Richardson, NY	3.23
1980–81	Magic Johnson, LAL	3.43
1981–82	Magic Johnson, LAL	2.67
1982–83	Micheal Ray Richardson, GS-NJ	2.84
1983–84	Rickey Green, Utah	2.65
1984–85	Micheal Ray Richardson, NJ	2.96
1985–86	Alvin Robertson, SA	3.67
1986–87	Alvin Robertson, SA	3.21
1987–88	Michael Jordan, Chi	3.16
1988–89	John Stockton, Utah	3.21
1989–90	Michael Jordan, Chi	2.77
1990–91	Alvin Robertson, Mil	3.04
1991–92	John Stockton, Utah	2.98
1992–93	Michael Jordan, Chi	2.83
1993–94	Nate McMillan, Sea	2.96
1994–95	Scottie Pippen, Chi	2.94
1995–96	Gary Payton, Sea	2.85
1996–97	Mookie Blaylock, Atl	2.72
1997–98	Mookie Blaylock, Atl	2.61
1998–99	Kendall Gill, NJ	2.68
1999–00	Eddie Jones, Cha	2.67
2000–01	Allen Iverson, Phil	2.51
2001–02	Allen Iverson, Phil	2.80
2002–03	Allen Iverson, Phil	2.74
2003–04	Baron Davis, NO	2.36
2004–05	Larry Hughes, Wash	2.89
2005–06	Gerald Wallace, Cha	2.51
2006–07	Baron Davis, GS	2.14
2007–08	Chris Paul, NO	2.71
2008–09	Chris Paul, NO	2.77
2009–10	Rajon Rondo, Bos	2.33

Blocked Shots

1973–74	Elmore Smith, LAL	4.85	1992–93	Hakeem Olajuwon, Hou	4.17
1974–75	Kareem Abdul-Jabbar, Mil	3.26	1993–94	Dikembe Mutombo, Den	4.10
1975–76	Kareem Abdul-Jabbar, LAL	4.12	1994–95	Dikembe Mutombo, Den	3.91
1976–77	Bill Walton, Port	3.25	1995–96	Dikembe Mutombo, Den	4.49
1977–78	George Johnson, NJ	3.38	1996–97	Shawn Bradley, NJ	3.40
1978–79	Kareem Abdul-Jabbar, LAL	3.95	1997–98	Marcus Camby, Tor	3.65
1979–80	Kareem Abdul-Jabbar, LAL	3.41	1998–99	Alonzo Mourning, Mia	3.91
1980–81	George Johnson, SA	3.39	1999–00	Alonzo Mourning, Mia	3.72
1981–82	George Johnson, SA	3.12	2000–01	Theo Ratliff, Phil/Atl	3.74
1982–83	Wayne Rollins, Atl	4.29	2001–02	Ben Wallace, Det	3.48
1983–84	Mark Eaton, Utah	4.28	2002–03	Theo Ratliff, Atl	3.23
1984–85	Mark Eaton, Utah	5.56	2003–04	Theo Ratliff, Port	3.61
1985–86	Manute Bol, Wash	4.96	2004–05	Andrei Kirilenko, Utah	3.32
1986–87	Mark Eaton, Utah	4.06	2005–06	Marcus Camby, Den	3.29
1987–88	Mark Eaton, Utah	3.71	2006–07	Marcus Camby, Den	3.30
1988–89	Manute Bol, GS	4.31	2007–08	Marcus Camby, Den	3.61
1989–90	Hakeem Olajuwon, Hou	4.59	2008–09	Dwight Howard, Orl	2.92
1990–91	Hakeem Olajuwon, Hou	3.95	2009–10	Dwight Howard, Orl	2.78
1991–92	David Robinson, SA	4.49			

NBA All-Star Game Results

Year	Result	Site	Winning Coach	Most Valuable Player
1951	East 111, West 94	Boston	Joe Lapchick	Ed Macauley, Bos
1952	East 108, West 91	Boston	Al Cervi	Paul Arizin, Phil
1953	West 79, East 75	Ft Wayne	John Kundla	George Mikan, Min
1954	East 98, West 93 (OT)	New York	Joe Lapchick	Bob Cousy, Bos
1955	East 100, West 91	New York	Al Cervi	Bill Sharman, Bos
1956	West 108, East 94	Rochester	Charley Eckman	Bob Pettit, StL
1957	East 109, West 97	Boston	Red Auerbach	Bob Cousy, Bos
1958	East 130, West 118	St Louis	Red Auerbach	Bob Pettit, StL
1959	West 124, East 108	Detroit	Ed Macauley	B. Pettit, StL/ E. Baylor, Min
1960	East 125, West 115	Philadelphia	Red Auerbach	Wilt Chamberlain, Phil
1961	West 153, East 131	Syracuse	Paul Seymour	Oscar Robertson, Cin
1962	West 150, East 130	St Louis	Fred Schaus	Bob Pettit, StL
1963	East 115, West 108	Los Angeles	Red Auerbach	Bill Russell, Bos
1964	East 111, West 107	Boston	Red Auerbach	Oscar Robertson, Cin
1965	East 124, West 123	St Louis	Red Auerbach	Jerry Lucas, Cin
1966	East 137, West 94	Cincinnati	Red Auerbach	Adrian Smith, Cin
1967	West 135, East 120	San Francisco	Fred Schaus	Rick Barry, SF
1968	East 144, West 124	New York	Alex Hannum	Hal Greer, Phil
1969	East 123, West 112	Baltimore	Gene Shue	Oscar Robertson, Cin
1970	East 142, West 135	Philadelphia	Red Holzman	Willis Reed, NY
1971	West 108, East 107	San Diego	Larry Costello	Lenny Wilkens, Sea
1972	West 112, East 110	Los Angeles	Bill Sharman	Jerry West, LA
1973	East 104, West 84	Chicago	Tom Heinsohn	Dave Cowens, Bos
1974	West 134, East 123	Seattle	Larry Costello	Bob Lanier, Det
1975	East 108, West 102	Phxnix	K.C. Jones	Walt Frazier, NY
1976	East 123, West 109	Philadelphia	Tom Heinsohn	Dave Bing, Wash
1977	West 125, East 124	Milwaukee	Larry Brown	Julius Erving, Phil
1978	East 133, West 125	Atlanta	Billy Cunningham	Randy Smith, Buff
1979	West 134, East 129	Detroit	Lenny Wilkens	David Thompson, Den
1980	East 144, West 135 (OT)	Washington	Billy Cunningham	George Gervin, SA
1981	East 123, West 120	Cleveland	Billy Cunningham	Nate Archibald, Bos
1982	East 120, West 118	New Jersey	Bill Fitch	Larry Bird, Bos
1983	East 132, West 123	Los Angeles	Billy Cunningham	Julius Erving, Phil
1984	East 154, West 145 (OT)	Denver	K.C. Jones	Isiah Thomas, Det
1985	West 140, East 129	Indiana	Pat Riley	Ralph Sampson, Hou
1986	East 139, West 132	Dallas	K.C. Jones	Isiah Thomas, Det
1987	West 154, East 149 (OT)	Seattle	Pat Riley	Tom Chambers, Sea
1988	East 138, West 133	Chicago	Mike Fratello	Michael Jordan, Chi
1989	West 143, East 134	Houston	Pat Riley	Karl Malone, Utah
1990	East 130, West 113	Miami	Chuck Daly	Magic Johnson, LAL
1991	East 116, West 114	Charlotte	Chris Ford	Charles Barkley, Phil
1992	West 153, East 113	Orlando	Don Nelson	Magic Johnson, LAL
1993	West 135, East 132	Salt Lake City	Paul Westphal	K. Malone/J. Stockton, Utah
1994	East 127, West 118	Minneapolis	Lenny Wilkens	Scottie Pippen, Chi
1995	West 139, East 112	Phoenix	Paul Westphal	Mitch Richmond, Sac

Year	Result	Site	Winning Coach	Most Valuable Player
1996	East 129, West 118	San Antonio	Phil Jackson	Michael Jordan, Chi
1997	East 132, West 120	Cleveland	Doug Collins	Glen Rice, Cha
1998	East 135, West 114	New York	Larry Bird	Michael Jordan, Chi
1999	Cancelled due to lockout.			
2000	West 137, East 126	Oakland	Phil Jackson	S. O'Neal, LAL/T. Duncan, SA
2001	East 111, West 110	Washington	Larry Brown	Allen Iverson, Phill
2002	West 135, East 120	Philadelphia	Don Nelson	Kobe Bryant, LAL
2003	West 155, East 145 (2OT)	Atlanta	Rick Adelman	Kevin Garnett, Min
2004	West 136, East 132	Los Angeles	Flip Saunders	Shaquille O'Neal, LAL
2005	East 125, West 115	Denver	Stan Van Gundy	Allen Iverson, Phil
2006	East 122, West 120	Houston	Flip Saunders	LeBron James, Cle
2007	West 153, East 132	Las Vegas	Mike D'Antoni	Kobe Bryant, LAL
2008	East 134, West 128	New Orleans	Doc Rivers	LeBron James, Cle
2009	West 146, East 119	Phoenix	Phil Jackson	K. Bryant, LAL/S. O'Neal, Phx
2010	East 141, West 139	Dallas	Stan Van Gundy	Dwyane Wade, Mia

Members of the Basketball Hall of Fame

Contributors

Senda Abbott (1984)
Clair F. Bee (1967)
Danny Biasone (2000)
Hubie Brown (2005)
Walter A. Brown (1965)
John W. Bunn (1964)
Jerry Buss (2010)
Jerry Colangelo (2004)
William Davidson (2008)
Bob Douglas (1971)
Al Duer (1981)
Wayne Embry (1999)
Clifford Fagan (1983)
Harry A. Fisher (1973)
Larry Fleisher (1991)
Dave Gavitt (2006)
Edward Gottlieb (1971)
Luther H. Gulick (1959)
Lester Harrison (1979)

Chick Hearn (2003)
Ferenc Hepp (1980)
Edward J. Hickox (1959)
Paul D. (Tony) Hinkle (1965)
Ned Irish (1964)
R. William Jones (1964)
J. Walter Kennedy (1980)
Meadowlark Lemon (2003)
Emil S. Liston (1974)
Earl Lloyd (2003)
Bill Mokray (1965)
Ralph Morgan (1959)
Frank Morgenweck (1962)
James Naismith (1959)
C.M. Newton (2000)
John J. O'Brien (1961)
Larry O'Brien (1991)
Harold G. Olsen (1959)
Maurice Podoloff (1973)

H. V. Porter (1960)
William A. Reid (1963)
Elmer Ripley (1972)
Lynn W. St. John (1962)
Abe Saperstein (1970)
Arthur A. Schabinger (1961)
Amos Alonzo Stagg (1959)
Boris Stankovic (1991)
Edward Steitz (1983)
Chuck Taylor (1968)
Bertha F. Teague (1984)
Oswald Tower (1959)
Arthur L. Trester (1961)
Dick Vitale (2008)
Clifford Wells (1971)
Lou Wilke (1982)
Fred Zollner (1999)

Players

Kareem Abdul-Jabbar (1995)
Nate (Tiny) Archibald (1991)
Paul J. Arizin (1977)
Charles Barkley (2006)
Thomas B. Barlow (1980)
Rick Barry (1987)
Elgin Baylor (1976)
John Beckman (1972)
Walt Bellamy (1993)
Sergei Belov (1992)
Dave Bing (1990)
Larry Bird (1998)
Carol Blazejowski (1994)
Bennie Borgmann (1961)
Bill Bradley (1982)
Joseph Brennan (1974)
Al Cervi (1984)
Wilt Chamberlain (1978)
Charles (Tarzan) Cooper (1976)
Cynthia Cooper (20100)
Kresimir Cosic (1996)
Bob Cousy (1970)
Dave Cowens (1991)
Joan Crawford (1997)

Billy Cunningham (1986)
Denise Curry (1997)
Drazen Dalipagic (2004)
Adrian Dantley (2008)
Bob Davies (1969)
Forrest S. DeBernardi (1961)
Dave DeBusschere (1982)
H.G. (Dutch) Dehnert (1968)
Anne Donovan (1995)
Clyde Drexler (2004)
Joe Dumars (2006)
Paul Endacott (1971)
Alex English (1997)
Julius Erving (1993)
Patrick Ewing (2008)
Harold (Bud) Foster (1964)
Walter (Clyde) Frazier (1987)
Max (Marty) Friedman (1971)
Joe Fulks (1977)
Lauren (Laddie) Gale (1976)
Harry (the Horse) Gallatin (1991)
William Gates (1989)
George Gervin (1996)
Tom Gola (1975)

Gail Goodrich (1996)
Hal Greer (1981)
Robert (Ace) Gruenig (1963)
Clifford O. Hagan (1977)
Victor Hanson (1960)
Lusia Harris-Stewart (1992)
John Havlicek (1983)
Connie Hawkins (1992)
Elvin Hayes (1990)
Marques Haynes (1998)
Tom Heinsohn (1986)
Nat Holman (1964)
Robert J. Houbregs (1987)
Bailey Howell (1997)
Chuck Hyatt (1959)
Dan Issel (1993)
Harry (Buddy) Jeannette (1994)
Dennis Johnson (2010)
Earvin (Magic) Johnson (2002)
Gus Johnson (2010)
William C. Johnson (1976)
D. Neil Johnston (1990)
K.C. Jones (1989)
Sam Jones (1983)

Players *(Cont.)*

Michael Jordan (2009)
Edward (Moose) Krause (1975)
Bob Kurland (1961)
Bob Lanier (1992)
Joe Lapchick (1966)
Nancy Lieberman-Cline (1996)
Clyde Lovellette (1988)
Jerry Lucas (1979)
Angelo (Hank) Luisetti (1959)
C. Edward Macauley (1960)
Karl Malone (2010)
Moses Malone (2001)
Peter P. Maravich (1987)
Hortencia Marcari (2005)
Slater Martin (1981)
Bob McAdoo (2000)
Branch McCracken (1960)
Jack McCracken (1962)
Bobby McDermott (1988)
Dick McGuire (1993)
Kevin McHale (1999)
Dino Meneghin (2003)
Ann Meyers (1993)
George L. Mikan (1959)
Vern Mikkelsen (1995)

Cheryl Miller (1995)
Earl Monroe (1990)
Calvin Murphy (1993)
Charles (Stretch) Murphy (1960)
Hakeem Olajuwon (2008)
H. O. (Pat) Page (1962)
Robert Parish (2003)
Maciel (Ubiratan) Pereira (2010)
Drazen Petrovic (2002)
Bob Pettit (1970)
Andy Phillip (1961)
Scottie Pippen (2010)
Jim Pollard (1977)
Frank Ramsey (1981)
Willis Reed (1981)
Arnie Risen (1998)
Oscar Robertson (1979)
David Robinson (2009)
John S. Roosma (1961)
Bill Russell (1974)
John (Honey) Russell (1964)
Adolph Schayes (1972)
Ernest J. Schmidt (1973)
John J. Schommer (1959)
Barney Sedran (1962)

Uljana Semjonova (1993)
Bill Sharman (1975)
Christian Steinmetz (1961)
Lusia Harris Stewart (1992)
John Stockton (2009)
Maurice Stokes (2004)
Isiah Thomas (2000)
David Thompson (1996)
John A. (Cat) Thompson (1962)
Nate Thurmond (1984)
Jack Twyman (1982)
Wes Unseld (1988)
Robert (Fuzzy) Vandivier (1974)
Edward A. Wachter (1961)
Bill Walton (1993)
Robert F. Wanzer (1987)
Jerry West (1979)
Nera White (1992)
Lenny Wilkens (1989)
Dominique Wilkins (2006)
Lynette Woodard (2004)
John R. Wooden (1960)
James Worthy (2003)
George (Bird) Yardley (1996)

Coaches

Forest C. (Phog) Allen (1959)
Harold Anderson (1984)
Red Auerbach (1968)
Geno Auriemma (2006)
Leon Barmore (2003)
Sam Barry (1978)
Ernest A. Blood (1960)
Jim Boeheim (2005)
Larry Brown (2002)
Jim Calhoun (2005)
Howard G. Cann (1967)
H. Clifford Carlson (1959)
Lou Carnesecca (1992)
Ben Carnevale (1969)
Pete Carril (1997)
Everett Case (1945)
Van Chancellor (2007)
John Chaney (2001)
Jody Conradt (1998)
Denny Crum (1994)
Chuck Daly (1994)
Everett S. Dean (1966)
Antonio Diaz-Miguel (1997)
Edgar A. Diddle (1971)
Bruce Drake (1972)
Pedro Ferrandiz (2007)
Sandro Gamba (2006)
Clarence Gaines (1981)
Jack Gardner (1983)

Amory T. (Slats) Gill (1967)
Aleksandr Gomelsky (1995)
Sue Gunter (2005)
Alex Hannum (1998)
Marv Harshman (1984)
Don Haskins (1997)
Edgar S. Hickey (1978)
Howard A. Hobson (1965)
Red Holzman (1986)
Bob Hurley Sr. (2010)
Hank Iba (1968)
Phil Jackson (2007)
Alvin F. (Doggie) Julian (1967)
Frank W. Keaney (1960)
George E. Keogan (1961)
Bob Knight (1991)
Mike Krzyzewski (2001)
John Kundla (1995)
Ward L. Lambert (1960)
Harry Litwack (1975)
Kenneth D. Loeffler (1964)
A.C. (Dutch) Lonborg (1972)
John B. McLendon (1978)
Arad A. McCutchan (1980)
Al McGuire (1992)
Frank McGuire (1976)
Walter E. Meanwell (1959)
Raymond J. Meyer (1978)
Ralph Miller (1988)

Billie Moore (1999)
Peter F. Newell (1978)
Aleksandar Nikolic (1998)
Mirko Novosel (2007)
Lute Olson (2002)
Jack Ramsay (1992)
Pat Riley (2008)
Cesare Rubini (1994)
Adolph F. Rupp (1968)
Cathy Rush (2008)
Leonard D. Sachs (1961)
Bill Sharman (2004)
Everett F. Shelton (1979)
Jerry Sloan (2009)
Dean Smith (1982)
C. Vivian Stringer (2009)
Pat Summitt (2000)
Fred R. Taylor (1985)
John Thompson (1999)
Margaret Wade (1984)
Stanley H. Watts (1985)
Lenny Wilkens (1998)
Roy Williams (2007)
John R. Wooden (1972)
Morgan Wooten (2000)
Phil Woolpert (1992)
Kay Yow (2002)

Referees

James E. Enright (1978)
George T. Hepbron (1960)
George Hoyt (1961)
Matthew P. Kennedy (1959)
Lloyd Leith (1982)
Zigmund J. Mihalik (1985)
John P. Nucatola (1977)

Ernest C. Quigley (1961)
Marvin Rudolph (2007)
J. Dallas Shirley (1979)
Earl Strom (1995)
David Tobey (1961)
David H. Walsh (1961)

Teams

Buffalo Germans (1961)
First Team (1959)
Harlem Globetrotters (2002)
Original Celtics (1959)
Renaissance (1963)
1960 USA Olympic Team (2010)
1966 Texas Western (2007)
1992 USA Olympic "Dream" Team
(2010)

Note: Year of election in parentheses.

American Basketball Association

Champions

Year	Champion	Series	Runner-up	Winning Coach
1968	Pittsburgh Pipers	4–3	New Orleans Bucs	Vince Cazetta
1969	Oakland Oaks	4–1	Indiana Pacers	Alex Hannum
1970	Indiana Pacers	4–2	Los Angeles Stars	Bob Leonard
1971	Utah Stars	4–3	Kentucky Colonels	Bill Sharman
1972	Indiana Pacers	4–2	New York Nets	Bob Leonard
1973	Indiana Pacers	4–3	Kentucky Colonels	Bob Leonard
1974	New York Nets	4–1	Utah Stars	Kevin Loughery
1975	Kentucky Colonels	4–1	Indiana Pacers	Hubie Brown
1976	New York Nets	4–2	Denver Nuggets	Kevin Loughery

ABA Postseason Awards

Most Valuable Player

1967–68	Connie Hawkins, Pitt
1968–69	Mel Daniels, Ind
1969–70	Spencer Haywood, Den
1970–71	Mel Daniels, Ind
1971–72	Artis Gilmore, Ken
1972–73	Billy Cunningham, Car
1973–74	Julius Erving, NY
1974–75	Julius Erving, NY
	George McGinnis, Ind
1975–76	Julius Erving, NY

Rookie of the Year

1967–68	Mel Daniels, Minn
1968–69	Warren Armstrong, Oak
1969–70	Spencer Haywood, Den
1970–71	Dan Issel, Ken
	Charlie Scott, Vir
1971–72	Artis Gilmore, Ken
1972–73	Brian Taylor, NY
1973–74	Swen Nater, SA
1974–75	Marvin Barnes, StL
1975–76	David Thompson, Den

Coach of the Year

1967–68	Vince Cazetta, Pitt
1968–69	Alex Hannum, Oak
1969–70	Joe Belmont, Den
	Bill Sharman, LA
1970–71	Al Bianchi, Vir
1971–72	Tom Nissalke, Dal
1972–73	Larry Brown, Car
1973–74	Babe McCarthy, Ken
	Joe Mullaney, Utah
1974–75	Larry Brown, Den
1975–76	Larry Brown, Den

ABA Season Leaders

Scoring

		GP	Pts	Avg
1967–68	Connie Hawkins, Pitt	70	1875	26.8
1968–69	Rick Barry, Oak	35	1190	34.0
1969–70	Spencer Haywood, Den	84	2519	30.0
1970–71	Dan Issel, Ken	83	2480	29.9
1971–72	Charlie Scott, Vir	79	2637	33.4
1972–73	Julius Erving, Vir	71	2268	31.9
1973–74	Julius Erving, NY	84	2299	27.4
1974–75	George McGinnis, Ind	79	2353	29.8
1975–76	Julius Erving, NY	84	2462	29.3

Rebounds

1967–68	Mel Daniels, Minn	15.6
1968–69	Mel Daniels, Ind	16.5
1969–70	Spencer Haywood, Den	19.5
1970–71	Mel Daniels, Ind	18.0
1971–72	Artis Gilmore, Ken	17.8
1972–73	Artis Gilmore, Ken	17.6
1973–74	Artis Gilmore, Ken	18.3
1974–75	Swen Nater, SA	16.4
1975–76	Artis Gilmore, Ken	15.5

Assists

1967–68	Larry Brown, NO	6.5
1968–69	Larry Brown, Oak	7.1
1969–70	Larry Brown, Wash	7.1
1970–71	Bill Melchionni, NY	8.3
1971–72	Bill Melchionni, NY	8.4
1972–73	Bill Melchionni, NY	7.4
1973–74	Al Smith, Den	8.2
1974–75	Mack Calvin, Den	7.7
1975–76	Don Buse, Ind	8.2

Steals

1973–74	Ted McClain, Car	2.98
1974–75	Brian Taylor, NY	2.80
1975–76	Don Buse, Ind	4.12

Blocked Shots

1973–74	Caldwell Jones, SD	4.00
1974–75	Caldwell Jones, SD	3.24
1975–76	Billy Paultz, SA	3.05

World Championship of Basketball

Year	Winner	Runner-Up	Score	Site
1950	Argentina	United States	†	Buenos Aires
1954	United States	Brazil	†	Rio de Janeiro
1959	Brazil	United States	†	Santiago, Chile
1963	Brazil	Yugoslavia	†	Rio de Janeiro
1967	Soviet Union	Yugoslavia	†	Montevideo, Uruguay
1970	Yugoslavia	Brazil	†	Ljubljana, Yugoslavia
1974	Soviet Union	Yugoslavia	†	San Juan
1978	Yugoslavia	Soviet Union	82–81 (OT)	Manila
1982	Soviet Union	United States	95–94	Cali, Colombia
1986	United States	Soviet Union	87–85	Madrid
1990	Yugoslavia	Soviet Union	92–75	Buenos Aires
*1994	United States	Russia	137–91	Toronto
†1998	Yugoslavia	Russia	64–62	Athens
2002	Yugoslavia	Argentina	84–77 (OT)	Indianapolis
2006	Spain	Greece	70–47	Saitama, Japan
2010	United States	Turkey	81–64	Turkey

*U.S. professionals began competing in 1994. †In 1998, a labor dispute resulted in a boycott of the World Championship by NBA stars; the U.S. roster was filled by members of the CBA and European professional leagues and college players.

†Result determined by overall record in final round of competition.

Duke Coach Mike Krzyzewski won his fourth career NCAA title in 2010

College Basketball

A Game & Team for the Ages

While Butler and Duke played an unforgettable title game in the men's tourney, the UConn women steamrolled to the school's seventh title and fourth undefeated season

BY B.J. SCHECTER

A S THE FINAL SHOT HUNG IN the air—a 45-foot heave—history hung in the balance. There was blueblooded Duke, a solid but unspectacular team all season that had underachieved for nearly a decade but made the most of its talent in this season. And then there was Butler, the Cinderella mid-major and a modern-day Hoosiers. The script couldn't have been written any better: small Indianapolis school fights its way to the Final Four in its home city, and now...Butler has a chance to win the game.

This wouldn't be a mere upset. It would be one of the biggest upsets in history in what many would call the greatest championship game ever. The two teams fought so valiantly, scrapping for every loose ball, every rebound; every shot was contested and Butler just wouldn't let Duke pull away.

And now...holy smokes, the ball looks like it's going in. In fact, later several people sitting courtside said they were sure Gordon Hayward's half-court, game-winning three was good. It's right on line as the seconds tick down and 80,000 fans in attendance collectively hold their breath. Hayward would later say that the shot felt like it had a

chance when it left his hands just before the final buzzer, but it hits the backboard, then the front rim and bounces out. Duke players celebrate as they hang on for a 61–59 victory and win another championship under coach Mike Krzyzewski. Meanwhile, Butler is dejected, collapsing on the floor as fans on both sides applaud the incredible effort. Duke may have won the game, but Butler won the Blue Devils'—and the nation's—respect.

This is what the NCAA tournament is about and why the thought of expanding the field to 96 teams is such a horrible idea. Who in their right mind had filled out their bracket predicting Butler would win it all? On paper, it was not such an outrageous pick. The Bulldogs entered the tournament with the nation's longest winning streak— 20 games—and weren't some flash-in-the-pan team. Butler has been on the rise and a Top 25 team for several years, but let's face it: the Butlers of the world don't win national championships in today's game. As prevalent as upsets have been in the NCAA tournament, titles are usually reserved for the Kansases, Dukes and North Carolinas— the establishment.

Butler came into the tournament and

Butler's Gordon Hayward matched Duke forward and Final Four MOP Kyle Singler (l.) shot-for-shot, but his last-second heave to win the title game for the Bulldogs just missed.

said the heck with the establishment. The Bulldogs beat up Michigan State in an ugly-but-impressive national semifinal and then looked at Duke and essentially said, "So, you expect us to be impressed?" As Butler boy-wonder coach Brad Stevens said after the game, "These guys didn't come in here thinking they were just going to roll over."

No, Butler came in expecting to win—and nearly did. This is not to take anything away from Duke, which played extremely hard and capped a fantastic season with a title. Or the quality of the game, which was played at a very high level. But the story was Butler, the small school with the huge heart. In 2006, the nation cheered as George Mason became the first mid-major in the modern era to make it to the Final Four. It was a great story, but Mason was just happy to be there and got drilled in the semifinal by eventual champion Florida. Butler was there to win it.

The Duke-Butler final was the culmination of a terrific tournament. In the first two rounds, 19 of the 48 games were decided in the final minute and eight of the 16 teams left after the first weekend were seeded fourth or lower, including four teams seeded ninth or lower. There were buzzer-beaters and head-scratchers (Ohio U. crushing Georgetown), but the headline of the first week was FAROKHMANESH.

Little little-known Northern Iowa 6-foot guard Ali Farokhmanesh led the Panthers to a stunning upset of No. 1-overall seed Kansas in the second round, and after his unconscious assassin-like three-point shooting, Farokhmanesh became a verb to basketball fans. Northern Iowa had dominated Kansas and led by one point with 42.8 seconds remaining when Farokhmanesh, the son of a former Iranian Olympic volleyball player, received the ball alone outside the three-point line. Conventional wisdom holds that you pull back and wait to be fouled. But Farokhmanesh, seeing daggers, instead launched a three that hit nothing but net. Ballgame.

With Kansas gone, the prohibitive favorite became Kentucky. In the offseason, John Calipari jumped from Memphis to take over the game's most storied program and quickly made his mark, signing four top freshmen, including eventual No. 1 NBA Draft pick John Wall and first-rounders DeMarcus Cousins and Eric Bledsoe. After an overtime win over Mississippi State in the SEC title game, the Wildcats

NCAA Women's Final Four MOP Maya Moore helped UConn coach Geno Auriemma (l.) to his fourth undefeated season and seventh career title with the Huskies.

The stars never seem to leave UConn in women's basketball, however. They stay for four years and then coach Geno Auriemma just reloads with more high school All-America athletes. But as dominant as the Huskies have been, nothing compared to this year's group. After going undefeated and winning the 2009 title, UConn did it again, finishing undefeated for the fourth time and increasing their winning streak to 78 games. Throughout the season there was little doubt that the Huskies would win it all as they toyed with the competition. But in the NCAA final against Stanford, UConn played its worst first half in its history, shooting 5 for 29 (17.2 percent) from the field and trailed 20-12. But UConn being the powerhouse it is finally got things together as Maya Moore and Tina Charles delivered a 53–47 victory. It wasn't pretty but it was still a championship.

"Looking back at what we've done, I'm almost incredulous that it actually happened because I can't imagine having done it," said Auriemma. "It's something that's there and I know we did it, but I'm so astounded that it's happened. Four undefeated teams. It's just too hard to comprehend."

The same could be said for Butler and Duke. While UConn made history, Butler and Duke delivered a game for the ages.

cruised through the first two rounds of the NCAA tournament and faced an intriguing foe in Cornell in the Sweet 16.

It was the ultimate in contrasts—the basketball school vs. the Ivy League scholar-athletes—and making matters more interesting, the game was played in Syracuse, 45 miles from the Cornell campus. Kentucky did its best to stay focused as Cornell was impressive in the first two rounds with decisive victories over Temple and Wisconsin. But a day before, all the media attention surrounding the geeks vs. jocks storyline was wearing on the Wildcats. Finally, Cousins had enough. "I think it's stupid," he said. "I'm not going to let it get to me. We're here to play basketball. It's not a spelling bee."

In the end, Kentucky's athleticism was too much for Cornell as the Wildcats used a blistering 30–6 run to close out the first half en route to a 62–45 victory. But Kentucky was denied a trip to the Final Four by Bob Huggins and West Virginia, and soon the Wildcats' stars left school and decamped to the NBA.

NCAA Men's Championship Game Box Score

Duke 61

	Min	FG M–A	FT M–A	Reb O–T	A	PF	TP
L. Thomas	35	3–5	0–0	1–4	0	4	6
K. Singler	40	7–13	2–2	1–9	2	1	19
B. Zoubek	31	3–4	2–4	6–10	1	4	8
J. Scheyer	37	5–12	4–5	1–6	5	3	15
N. Smith	40	5–15	2–5	1–3	4	0	13
Mi. Plumlee	9	0–2	0–0	1–3	0	2	0
A. Dawkins	5	0–1	0–0	0–0	0	0	0
Ma. Plumlee	3	0–0	0–0	0–1	0	0	0
Totals		**23–52**	**10–16**	**11–36**	**12**	**14**	**61**

Percentages: FG-.442, FT-.625. 3-Point Goals: 5–17, .294 (K. Singler 3–6, J. Scheyer 1–5, N. Smith 1–5, A. Dawkins 0–1). Team Rebounds: 0. Blocked Shots: 7 (Singler 2, Zoubek 2, Scheyer 2, Mi. Plumlee 1). Turnovers: 12 (L. Thomas 3, K. Singler 2, B. Zoubek 1, J. Scheyer 2, N. Smith 3, Mi. Plumlee 1). Steals: 5 (L. Thomas 2, K. Singler 1, J. Scheyer 1, Mi. Plumlee 1). Technical Fouls: None.

Butler 59

	Min	FG M–A	FT M–A	Reb O–T	A	PF	TP
M. Howard	19	3–8	5–8	2–4	0	4	11
G. Hayward	40	2–11	8–8	3–8	1	1	12
W. Veasley	38	1–9	0–0	3–3	3	2	2
S. Mack	31	5–14	0–0	1–5	2	1	12
R. Nored	27	3–8	0–0	1–6	1	3	7
A. Jukes	18	4–6	0–2	2–4	0	4	10
Z. Hahn	11	1–1	0–0	0–1	0	1	3
S. Vanzant	15	1–1	0–0	0–1	0	2	2
A. Smith	1	0–0	0–0	0–0	0	0	0
Totals		**20–58**	**13–18**	**12–32**	**7**	**18**	**59**

Percentages: FG-.345, FT-.722. 3-Point Goals: 6–18, .333 (G. Hayward 0–3, W. Veasley 0–5, S. Mack 2–4, R. Nored 1–2, A. Jukes 2–3, Z. Hahn 1–1). Team Rebounds: 0. Blocked Shots: 0. Turnovers: 8 (M. Howard 1, G. Hayward 1, W. Veasley 2, S. Mack 2, R. Nored 2). Steals: 4 (G. Hayward 1, S. Mack 2, R. Nored 1). Technical Fouls: None.

Halftime: Duke 33, Butler 32.

Officials: John Cahill, Tom Eades, Ted Valentine.
A: 70,930.

Final ESPN/USA Today Top 25 Poll

1. Duke (31)	33–5
2. Butler	32–4
3. West Virginia	31–6
4. Michigan St.	28–8
5. Kentucky	35–3
6. Kansas	33–3
7. Kansas St.	29–8
8. Syracuse	30–5
9. Tennessee	28–9
10. Baylor	28–8
11. Ohio St.	29–8
12. Purdue	29–6
13. Northern Iowa	30–5
14. Xavier	26–9
15. Villanova	25–8
16. New Mexico	30–5
17. Cornell	29–5
18. Maryland	24–9
19. Saint Mary's	28–6
20. Pittsburgh	25–9
21. Washington	26–10
22. BYU	30–6
23. Gonzaga	27–7
24. Wisconsin	24–9
25. Texas A&M	24–10

National Invitation Tournament Scores

First round: Illinois 76, Stony Brook 66; Kent St 75, Tulsa 74; Dayton 3, Illinois St 42; Cincinnati 76, Weber St 62; Jacksonville 67, Arizona St 66; Texas Tech 87, Seton Hall 69; Memphis 73, St. John's 71; Mississippi 84, Troy 65; Vermont 81, Quinnipiac 61; Connecticut 59, Northeastern 57; Nevada 74, Wichita St 70; Rhode Island 76, Northwestern 64; Mississippi St 81, Jackson St 67; North Carolina 80, William & Mary 72; North Carolina St 58, South Florida 57; UAB 65, Coastal Carolina 49.

Second round: Illinois 75, Kent St 58; Dayton 63, Illinois St 42; Texas Tech 69, Jacksonville 64; Mississippi 90, Memphis 81; Vermont 65, Connecticut 63; Rhode Island 85, Nevada 83; North Carolina 76, Mississippi St 74; UAB 75, North Carolina St 52.

Quarterfinals: Dayton 77, Illinois 71; Mississippi 90, Texas Tech 87; Rhode Island 79, Vermont 72; North Carolina 60, UAB 55.

Semifinals: Dayton 68, Mississippi 63; North Carolina 68, Rhode Island 67.

Championship Game: Dayton 79, North Carolina 68.

2010 NCAA Basketball Men's Division I Tournament

1st ROUND	2nd ROUND	REGIONALS	2nd ROUND	1st ROUND

EAST
Syracuse

1 Kansas (32-2)
16 Lehigh (22-10)
Kansas 90-74
8 UNLV (25-8)
9 Northern Iowa (28-4)
Northern Iowa 69-67
Northern Iowa 69-66
5 Michigan St (24-8)
12 New Mexico St (22-11)
Michigan St 70-67
Michigan St 70-67
4 Maryland (23-8)
13 Houston (19-15)
Maryland 89-77
Michigan St 85-53
6 Tennessee (25-8)
11 San Diego St (25-8)
Tennessee 62-59
Tennessee 83-68
3 Georgetown (23-10)
14 Ohio (21-14)
Ohio 97-83
Tennessee 76-73
10 Oklahoma St (22-10)
10 Georgia Tech (22-12)
Georgia Tech 64-59
Ohio 75-66
2 Ohio St (27-7)
15 UC-Santa Barbara (20-9)
Ohio St 68-51

Michigan St 59-52

MIDWEST
St. Louis

Michigan St 70-69

Butler 52-50

NATIONAL CHAMPIONSHIP
Indianapolis

DUKE 61
Butler 59

Butler 63-56

1 Syracuse (28-4)
6 Vermont (25-9)
Syracuse 79-56
Syracuse 87-65
8 Gonzaga (26-6)
9 Florida St (22-9)
Gonzaga 67-60
Butler 63-59
5 Butler (28-4)
12 UTEP (26-6)
Butler 77-59
Butler 64-62
4 Vanderbilt (24-8)
13 Murray St (30-4)
Murray St 66-65
Xavier 71-68
6 Xavier (24-8)
11 Minnesota (21-13)
Xavier 65-54
3 Pittsburgh (24-8)
14 Oakland (26-8)
Pittsburgh 89-66
Kansas St 101-96 (2OT)
7 BYU (29-5)
10 Florida (21-12)
BYU 99-92 (2OT)
Kansas St 84-72
2 Kansas St (26-7)
15 North Texas (24-8)
Kansas St 82-62

WEST
Salt Lake City

1 Kentucky (32-2)
16 East Tennessee St (20-14)
Kentucky 100-71
Kentucky 90-60
8 Texas (24-9)
9 Wake Forest (19-10)
Wake Forest 81-80 (OT)
Kentucky 62-45
5 Temple (29-5)
12 Cornell (27-4)
Cornell 78-65
Cornell 87-69
4 Wisconsin (23-8)
13 Wofford (26-8)
Wisconsin 53-49
6 Marquette (22-11)
11 Washington (24-9)
Washington 80-78
Washington 82-64
14 New Mexico (29-4)
14 Montana (22-9)
New Mexico 62-57
West Virginia 69-56
7 Clemson (21-10)
10 Missouri (22-10)
Missouri 86-78
2 West Virginia (27-6)
15 Morgan St (27-9)
West Virginia 77-50
West Virginia 68-59

West Virginia 73-66

Duke 78-57

Duke 61

Duke 76-71

1 Duke (29-5)
16 Ark.-Pine Bluff* (17-15)
Duke 73-44
Duke 68-53
8 California (23-10)
9 Louisville (20-12)
California 77-62
Duke 70-57
5 Texas A&M (23-90)
12 Utah St (27-7)
Texas A&M 69-53
4 Purdue (27-5)
13 Siena (27-6)
Purdue 72-64
Purdue 63-61 (OT)
11 Old Dominion (26-8)
11 Old Dominion (26-8)
Old Dominion 51-50
Duke 70-57
3 Baylor (25-7)
14 Sam Houston St (25-7)
Baylor 68-59
Baylor 76-68
7 Richmond (26-9)
10 Saint Mary's (26-5)
Saint Mary's 80-71
Baylor 72-49
2 Villanova (24-7)
15 Robert Morris (23-11)
Villanova 73-70 (OT)
Saint Mary's 75-68

SOUTH
Houston

*won 61-44 vs Winthrop (19-13) in opening game at Dayton, Ohio.

America East

	Conference			All Games		
	W	L	Pct	W	L	Pct
SUNY-Stony Brook	13	3	.813	22	10	.688
*Vermont	12	4	.750	25	10	.714
Maine	11	5	.688	19	11	.633
Boston Univ.	11	5	.688	21	14	.600
SUNY-Binghamton	8	8	.500	13	18	.419
New Hampshire	6	10	.375	13	17	.433
Hartford	6	10	.375	8	22	.267
Md.-Baltimore Cty.	3	13	.188	4	26	.133
SUNY-Albany	2	14	.125	7	25	.219

Atlantic Coast

	Conference			All Games		
	W	L	Pct	W	L	Pct
*Duke	13	3	.813	35	5	.875
Maryland	13	3	.813	24	9	.727
Virginia Tech	10	6	.625	25	9	.735
Florida St	10	6	.625	22	10	.688
Clemson	9	7	.563	21	11	.656
Wake Forest	9	7	.563	20	11	.645
Georgia Tech	7	9	.438	23	13	.639
Boston College	6	10	.375	15	16	.484
North Carolina St	5	11	.313	20	16	.556
North Carolina	5	11	.313	20	17	.541
Virginia	5	11	.313	15	16	.484
Miami (Fla.)	4	12	.250	20	13	.606

Atlantic Sun

	Conference			All Games		
	W	L	Pct	W	L	Pct
Campbell	14	6	.700	19	11	.633
Belmont	14	6	.700	19	12	.613
Jacksonville	14	6	.700	20	13	.606
Lipscomb	14	6	.700	17	13	.567
*East Tennnessee St	13	7	.650	20	15	.571
Mercer	10	10	.500	16	17	.485
North Florida	8	12	.400	13	18	.419
Kennesaw St.	7	13	.350	13	20	.394
S.C.-Upstate	6	14	.300	6	23	.207
Florida Gulf Coast	5	15	.250	8	21	.276
Stetson	5	15	.250	7	22	.241

Atlantic 10

	Conference			All Games		
	W	L	Pct	W	L	Pct
*Temple	14	2	.875	29	6	.829
Xavier	14	2	.875	26	9	.743
Richmond	13	3	.813	26	9	.743
St. Louis	11	5	.688	23	13	.639
Rhode Island	9	7	.563	26	10	.722
Charlotte	9	7	.563	19	12	.613
Dayton	8	8	.500	25	12	.676
Duquesne	7	9	.438	16	16	.500
St. Bonaventure	7	9	.438	15	16	.484
George Washington	6	10	.375	16	15	.516
Massachusetts	5	11	.313	12	20	.375
St. Joseph's	5	11	.313	11	20	.355
La Salle	4	12	.250	12	18	.400
Fordham	0	16	.000	2	26	.071

Big East

	Conference			All Games		
	W	L	Pct	W	L	Pct
Syracuse	15	3	.833	30	5	.857
*West Virginia	13	5	.722	31	7	.816
Villanova	13	5	.722	25	8	.758
Pittsburgh	13	5	.722	25	9	.735
Marquette	11	7	.611	22	12	.647
Louisville	11	7	.611	20	13	.606
Georgetown	10	8	.556	23	11	.676
Notre Dame	10	8	.556	23	12	.657
South Florida	9	9	.500	20	13	.606
Seton Hall	9	9	.500	19	13	.594
Cincinnati	7	11	.389	19	16	.543
Connecticut	7	11	.389	18	16	.529
St. John's	6	12	.333	17	16	.515
Rutgers	5	13	.278	15	17	.468
Providence	4	14	.222	12	19	.387
DePaul	1	17	.056	8	23	.258

Big Sky

	Conference			All Games		
	W	L	Pct	W	L	Pct
Weber St	13	3	.813	20	11	.645
Northern Colorado	12	4	.750	25	8	.758
*Montana	10	6	.625	22	10	.688
Montana St	10	6	.625	15	14	.517
Northern Arizona	8	8	.500	14	14	.500
Portland St	7	9	.438	13	19	.406
Eastern Washington	5	11	.313	9	21	.300
Idaho St	4	12	.250	7	22	.241
Sacramento St	3	13	.188	9	21	.300

Big South

	Conference			All Games		
	W	L	Pct	W	L	Pct
Coastal Carolina	15	3	.833	28	7	.800
Radford	13	5	.722	19	12	.613
*Winthrop	12	6	.667	19	14	.576
UNC-Asheville	11	7	.611	15	16	.484
High Point	10	8	.556	15	15	.500
Liberty	10	8	.556	15	16	.484
Charleston Southern	7	11	.389	13	17	.433
Virginia Military Inst.	5	13	.278	10	19	.345
Gardner-Webb	5	13	.278	8	21	.276
Presbyterian	2	16	.111	5	26	.161

Big 10

	Conference			All Games		
	W	L	Pct	W	L	Pct
Purdue	14	4	.777	29	6	.829
Michigan St	14	4	.777	29	8	.784
*Ohio St	14	4	.777	28	9	.757
Wisconsin	13	5	.722	24	9	.727
Illinois	10	8	.556	21	15	.583
Minnesota	9	9	.500	21	14	.600
Northwestern	7	11	.389	20	15	.588
Michigan	7	11	.389	15	17	.469
Indiana	4	14	.222	10	21	.322
Iowa	4	14	.222	10	22	.313
Penn St	3	15	.167	11	20	.355

Note: Standings based on regular-season conference play only; overall records include all tournament play.
*Conference tournament winner.

Big 12

	Conference			All Games		
	W	L	Pct	W	L	Pct
*Kansas	15	1	.938	33	3	.917
Kansas St	11	5	.688	29	8	.784
Baylor	11	5	.688	28	8	.778
Texas A&M	11	5	.688	24	10	.706
*Missouri	10	6	.625	23	11	.676
Texas	9	7	.563	24	10	.706
Oklahoma St	9	7	.563	22	11	.667
Colorado	6	10	.375	15	16	.484
Texas Tech	4	12	.250	19	16	.543
Iowa St	4	12	.250	15	17	.469
Oklahoma	4	12	.250	13	18	.419
Nebraska	2	14	.125	15	18	.455

Big West

	Conference			All Games		
	W	L	Pct	W	L	Pct
*UC-Santa Barbara	12	4	.750	20	10	.667
Pacific	12	4	.750	23	12	.657
CSU-Fullerton	8	8	.500	16	15	.516
Long Beach St	8	8	.500	17	16	.515
UC-Davis	8	8	.500	14	18	.438
Cal Poly	7	9	.438	12	19	.387
UC-Irvine	6	10	.375	14	18	.438
CSU-Northridge	6	10	.375	11	21	.344
UC-Riverside	5	11	.313	12	17	.414

Colonial

	Conference			All Games		
	W	L	Pct	W	L	Pct
*Old Dominion	15	3	.833	27	9	.750
Northeastern	14	4	.778	20	13	.606
William & Mary	12	6	.667	22	11	.667
George Mason	12	6	.667	17	15	.531
VCU	11	7	.611	27	9	.750
Drexel	11	7	.611	16	16	.500
Hofstra	10	8	.556	19	15	.559
Towson	6	12	.333	10	21	.323
Georgia St	5	13	.278	12	20	.375
UNC-Wilmington	5	13	.278	9	22	.290
James Madison	4	14	.222	13	20	.394
Delaware	3	15	.167	7	24	.226

Conference USA

	Conference			All Games		
	W	L	Pct	W	L	Pct
UTEP	15	1	.938	26	7	.788
Memphis	13	3	.813	24	10	.706
UAB	11	5	.688	25	9	.735
Marshall	11	5	.688	24	10	.706
Tulsa	10	6	.625	23	12	.657
Southern Miss	8	8	.500	20	14	.588
*Houston	7	9	.438	19	16	.543
SMU	7	9	.438	14	17	.452
Central Florida	6	10	.375	15	17	.469
East Carolina	4	12	.250	10	21	.323
Tulane	3	13	.188	8	22	.267
Rice	1	15	.063	8	23	.348

Horizon League

	Conference			All Games		
	W	L	Pct	W	L	Pct
*Butler	18	0	1.000	33	5	.868
Wright St	12	6	.667	20	12	.625
UW-Green Bay	11	7	.611	22	13	.629
UW-Milwaukee	10	8	.556	20	14	.588
Cleveland St	10	8	.556	16	17	.485
Valparaiso	10	8	.556	15	17	.469
Detroit	9	9	.500	20	14	.588
Loyola (Ill.)	5	13	.278	14	16	.467
Ill.-Chicago	3	15	.167	8	22	.300
Youngstown St	2	16	.111	8	22	.300

Ivy League†

	Conference			All Games		
	W	L	Pct	W	L	Pct
Cornell	11	3	.786	21	9	.700
Brown	8	6	.571	13	14	.481
Pennsylvania	8	6	.571	13	15	.464
Columbia	7	7	.500	12	16	.429
Yale	7	7	.500	9	19	.321
Dartmouth	6	8	.429	14	14	.500
Harvard	6	8	.429	10	18	.357
Princeton	3	11	.214	9	19	.321

Metro Atlantic

	Conference			All Games		
	W	L	Pct	W	L	Pct
*Siena	17	1	.944	27	7	.794
Fairfield	13	5	.722	23	11	.676
Iona	12	6	.667	21	10	.677
St. Peter's	11	7	.611	16	14	.533
Niagara	9	9	.500	18	15	.545
Rider	9	9	.500	17	16	.515
Canisius	8	10	.444	15	17	.469
Loyola (Md.)	6	12	.333	13	17	.433
Manhattan	4	14	.222	11	20	.355
Marist	1	17	.056	1	29	.033

Mid-American

	Conference			All Games		
EAST	W	L	Pct	W	L	Pct
Kent St	13	3	.813	24	10	.706
Akron	12	4	.750	24	11	.686
Buffalo	9	7	.563	18	12	.600
Miami (Ohio)	9	7	.563	14	18	.438
*Ohio	7	9	.438	22	15	.647
Bowling Green	6	10	.375	14	16	.467
WEST						
Central Michigan	9	7	.563	15	15	.500
Western Michigan	8	8	.500	18	15	.545
Eastern Michigan	8	8	.500	17	15	.531
Ball St	8	8	.500	15	15	.500
Northern Illinois	6	10	.375	10	20	.333
Toledo	1	15	.063	4	28	.125

*Conference tournament winner.
†Does not hold end-of-season conference tournament.

Mid-Eastern Athletic

	Conference			All Games		
	W	L	Pct	W	L	Pct
*Morgan St	15	1	.938	27	10	.730
Delaware St	11	5	.688	17	12	.586
South Carolina St	10	6	.625	18	14	.563
Norfolk St	9	7	.563	11	19	.367
Hampton	8	8	.500	14	18	.438
Md.-Eastern Shore	8	8	.500	11	21	.344
Bethune-Cookman	7	9	.438	17	16	.515
North Carolina A&T	6	10	.375	11	22	.333
Howard	6	10	.375	7	25	.219
Florida A&M	5	11	.313	9	22	.290
Coppin St	3	13	.188	8	22	.267

Missouri Valley

	Conference			All Games		
	W	L	Pct	W	L	Pct
*Northern Iowa	15	3	.833	30	5	.857
Wichita St	12	6	.667	25	10	.714
Illinois St	11	7	.611	22	11	.667
Creighton	10	8	.556	18	16	.514
Indiana St	9	9	.500	17	15	.531
Bradley	9	9	.500	16	15	.516
Missouri St	8	10	.444	24	12	.667
Drake	7	11	.389	14	19	.424
Southern Illinois	6	12	.333	15	15	.500
Evansville	3	15	.167	9	21	.300

Mountain West

	Conference			All Games		
	W	L	Pct	W	L	Pct
New Mexico	14	2	.875	30	5	.857
BYU	13	3	.750	30	6	.833
*San Diego St	11	5	.688	25	9	.735
UNLV	11	5	.688	25	9	.735
Colorado St	7	9	.438	16	16	.500
Utah	7	9	.438	14	17	.452
TCU	5	11	.313	13	19	.406
Wyoming	3	13	.188	10	21	.323
Air Force	1	15	.063	10	21	.323

Northeast

	Conference			All Games		
	W	L	Pct	W	L	Pct
Quinnipiac	15	3	.833	23	10	.767
*Robert Morris	15	3	.833	23	12	.657
Mount St. Mary's	12	6	.667	16	15	.516
Long Island	11	7	.611	14	17	.452
Fairleigh Dickinson	10	8	.556	11	21	.344
Central Conn. St	9	9	.500	12	18	.400
St. Francis (Pa.)	9	9	.500	11	19	.367
Monmouth	8	10	.444	12	19	.387
St. Francis (N.Y.)	8	10	.444	11	18	.379
Sacred Heart	7	11	.389	14	18	.438
Wagner	3	15	.167	5	26	.161
Bryant	1	17	.056	1	29	.033

Ohio Valley

	Conference			All Games		
	W	L	Pct	W	L	Pct
*Murray St	17	1	.944	31	5	.861
Morehead St	15	3	.833	24	11	.686
Eastern Illinois	11	7	.611	19	12	.613
Eastern Kentucky	11	7	.611	20	13	.606
Austin Peay	11	7	.611	17	15	.531
Tennessee Tech	8	10	.444	15	17	.469
Jacksonville St	7	11	.389	11	19	.367
Tennessee St	6	12	.333	9	23	.281
SE Missouri St	3	15	.167	7	23	.233
Tenn.-Martin	1	17	.056	4	25	.138

Pac 10

	Conference			All Games		
	W	L	Pct	W	L	Pct
California	13	5	.722	24	11	.686
Arizona St	12	6	.667	22	11	.667
*Washington	11	7	.611	26	10	.722
Arizona	10	8	.556	16	15	.516
USC	8	10	.444	16	14	.533
UCLA	8	10	.444	14	18	.438
Oregon St	8	10	.444	14	18	.438
Oregon	7	11	.389	16	16	.500
Stanford	7	11	.389	14	18	.438
Washington St	6	12	.333	16	18	.471

Patriot League

	Conference			All Games		
	W	L	Pct	W	L	Pct
*Lehigh	10	4	.714	22	11	.667
Bucknell	9	5	.643	14	17	.452
Lafayette	8	6	.571	19	13	.594
Navy	7	7	.500	13	17	.433
American	7	7	.500	11	20	.355
Colgate	6	8	.429	10	19	.345
Holy Cross	5	9	.357	9	22	.290
Army	4	10	.286	14	15	.483

Southeastern

	Conference			All Games		
	W	L	Pct	W	L	Pct
EAST						
*Kentucky	14	2	.875	35	3	.921
Vanderbilt	12	4	.750	24	9	.727
Tennessee	11	5	.688	28	9	.757
Florida	9	7	.563	21	13	.618
South Carolina	6	10	.375	15	16	.484
Georgia	5	11	.313	14	17	.452
WEST						
Mississippi	9	7	.563	24	11	.686
Mississippi St	9	7	.563	24	12	.667
Arkansas	7	9	.438	14	18	.438
Alabama	6	10	.375	17	15	.531
Auburn	6	10	.375	15	17	.569
LSU	2	14	.125	11	20	.355

*Conference tournament winner.

Southern

	Conference			All Games		
NORTH	**W**	**L**	**Pct**	**W**	**L**	**Pct**
Appalachian St	13	5	.722	24	13	.706
Western Carolina	11	7	.611	22	12	.647
Chattanooga	6	12	.333	15	18	.455
UNC-Greensboro	6	12	.333	8	23	.258
Samford	5	13	.278	11	20	.355
Elon	5	13	.278	9	23	.391
SOUTH						
*Wofford	15	3	.833	26	9	.743
Coll. of Charleston	14	4	.778	22	12	.647
Davidson	11	7	.611	16	15	.516
Citadel	9	9	.500	16	16	.600
Furman	7	11	.389	13	17	.433
Georgia Southern	6	12	.333	9	23	.391

Sun Belt

	Conference			All Games		
EAST	**W**	**L**	**Pct**	**W**	**L**	**Pct**
Troy	13	5	.722	20	13	.606
Middle Tenn. St	13	5	.722	19	14	.576
Western Kentucky	12	6	.667	21	13	.618
Florida Atlantic	10	8	.556	14	16	.467
South Alabama	8	10	.444	17	15	.531
Florida Int'l	4	14	.222	7	25	.219
WEST						
*North Texas	13	5	.722	24	9	.727
Arkansas St	11	7	.611	17	14	.549
Denver	10	8	.556	19	13	.594
La.-Lafayette	10	8	.556	13	17	.433
La.-Monroe	6	12	.333	12	19	.387
Ark.-Little Rock	4	14	.222	8	22	.300
New Orleans	3	15	.167	8	22	.300

Southland

	Conference			All Games		
EAST	**W**	**L**	**Pct**	**W**	**L**	**Pct**
Stephen F. Austin	11	5	.688	23	9	.719
SE Louisiana	10	6	.625	19	12	.613
Nicholls St	7	9	.438	11	19	.367
Northwestern St	5	11	.313	10	19	.345
McNeese St	5	11	.313	10	20	.333
Central Arkansas	3	13	.188	9	21	.300
WEST						
*Sam Houston St	14	2	.875	25	8	.758
Tex. A&M-Corp. Chrs.	10	6	.625	17	15	.531
Tex.-San Antonio	9	7	.563	19	11	.633
Texas St	9	7	.563	15	16	.484
Tex.-Arlington	8	8	.500	16	14	.533
Lamar	5	11	.313	14	18	.438

West Coast

	Conference			All Games		
	W	**L**	**Pct**	**W**	**L**	**Pct**
Gonzaga	12	2	857	27	7	.794
*St. Mary's (Ca.)	11	3	.786	28	6	.824
Portland	10	4	.714	21	11	.656
Loyola Marymount	7	7	.500	18	16	.529
San Francisco	7	7	.500	12	18	.400
San Diego	3	11	.214	11	21	.344
Santa Clara	3	11	.214	11	21	.344
Pepperdine	3	11	.214	7	24	.292

Southwestern Athletic

	Conference			All Games		
	W	**L**	**Pct**	**W**	**L**	**Pct**
Jackson St	17	1	.944	19	13	.594
*Ark.-Pine Bluff	14	4	.778	18	16	.529
Alabama St	12	6	.667	16	15	.516
Prairie View A&M	11	7	.611	16	14	.533
Texas Southern	11	7	.611	17	16	.515
Alabama A&M	8	10	.444	11	16	.407
Mississippi Valley St	8	10	.444	9	23	.281
Grambling St	4	14	.222	7	21	.250
Southern Univ.	3	15	.167	5	25	.167
Alcorn St	2	16	.111	2	29	.065

Western Athletic

	Conference			All Games		
	W	**L**	**Pct**	**W**	**L**	**Pct**
Utah St	14	2	.875	27	8	.771
*New Mexico St	11	5	.688	22	12	.647
Nevada	11	5	.688	21	13	.618
Louisiana Tech	9	7	.563	24	11	.686
Fresno St	7	9	.438	15	18	.455
Idaho	6	10	.375	15	16	.484
San Jose St	6	10	.375	14	17	.452
Boise St	5	11	.313	15	17	.469
Hawaii	3	13	.188	10	20	.333

Summit

	Conference			All Games		
	W	**L**	**Pct**	**W**	**L**	**Pct**
*Oakland	17	1	.944	26	9	.743
IUPUI	15	3	.833	25	11	.694
Oral Roberts	13	5	.722	20	13	.606
South Dakota St	10	8	.556	14	16	.467
IPFW	9	9	.500	16	15	.516
North Dakota St	8	10	.444	11	18	.379
Western Illinois	6	12	.333	13	17	.433
Mo.-Kansas City	6	12	.333	12	18	.400
Centenary	3	15	.167	8	21	.276
Southern Utah	3	15	.167	7	22	.241

Independents

	All Games		
	W	**L**	**Pct**
Seattle	17	14	.548
Savannah St	11	15	.423
Winston-Salem	12	17	.414
Longwood	12	19	.387
North Carolina Central	7	22	.241
CSU-Bakersfield	7	22	.241
SIU-Edwardsville	5	23	.179

*Conference tournament winner.

Scoring

	Class	GP	FG	3FG	FT	Pts	Avg
Aubrey Coleman, Houston	Sr.	35	305	51	235	896	25.6
Adnan Hodzic, Lipscomb	Jr.	30	269	0	144	682	22.7
Marquez Haynes, Texas-Arlington	Sr.	30	215	63	185	678	22.6
Devan Downey, South Carolina	Sr.	31	237	69	156	699	22.5
Adrian Oliver, San Jose St	Jr.	31	230	51	188	699	22.5
James Anderson, Oklahoma St	Jr.	33	226	74	209	735	22.3
Jimmer Fredette, BYU	Jr.	34	225	77	224	751	22.1
Landry Fields, Stanford	Sr.	32	248	29	179	704	22.0
Luke Babbitt, Nevada	So.	34	251	42	199	743	21.9
Luke Harangody, Notre Dame	Sr.	30	244	25	140	653	21.8
Michael Deloach, Norfolk St	Sr.	30	238	36	140	652	21.7
David Kool, Western Michigan	Sr.	33	221	63	209	714	21.6
Reggie Holmes, Morgan St	Sr.	37	226	100	241	793	21.4
Dominique Jones, South Florida	Jr.	33	222	52	209	705	21.4
Artsiom Parakhouski, Radford	Sr.	31	250	3	159	662	21.4
Omar Samhan, St. Mary's (Calif.)	Sr.	34	282	0	160	724	21.3
Anatoly Bose, Nicholls St	Jr.	30	194	86	159	633	21.1
Chris Harris, Navy	Sr.	30	183	88	178	632	21.1
Denzel Bowles, James Madison	Jr.	25	203	0	114	520	20.8
Charles Jenkins, Hofstra	Jr.	34	235	63	169	702	20.6
Jordan Crawford, Xavier	So.	35	260	79	119	718	20.5
Jeremy Hazell, Seton Hall	Jr.	32	220	98	116	654	20.4
Evan Turner, Ohio St	Jr.	31	237	20	138	632	20.4
Donald Sims, Appalachian St	Jr.	37	228	123	175	754	20.4
Jahmar Young, New Mexico St	Jr.	34	228	73	160	689	20.3

FIELD-GOAL PERCENTAGE

	Class	GP	FG	FGA	Pct
Adnan Hodzic, Lipscomb	Jr.	30	269	445	60.4
Jeremy Simmons, Coll. of Charl.	Jr.	29	148	248	59.7
Denzel Bowles, James Madison	So.	25	203	342	59.4
Willie Reed, St. Louis	Sr.	35	176	300	58.7
Jamal Boykin, California	Sr.	35	177	303	58.4
Jamie Jones, Portland St	Sr.	32	180	309	58.3
Jarvis Varnado, Mississippi St	Sr.	36	184	316	58.2
Artsiom Parakhouski, Radford	Sr.	31	250	430	58.1
Robert Glenn, IUPUI	Sr.	36	259	446	58.1
Noah Dahlman, Wofford	Jr.	35	224	387	57.9

Note: Minimum 5 made per game.

REBOUNDS

	Class	GP	Reb	Avg
Artsiom Parakhouski, Radford	Sr.	31	414	13.4
Kenneth Faried, Morehead St	Jr.	35	456	13.0
Daniel Emerson, Mercer	Sr.	32	385	12.0
Kevin Thompson, Morgan St	So.	37	438	11.8
Chris Gaston, Fordham	Fr.	28	319	11.4
Damian Saunders, Duquesne	Jr.	32	360	11.3
Ryan Rossiter, Siena	Jr.	34	379	11.1
Justin Rutty, Quinnipiac	Jr.	33	359	10.9
Omar Samhan, St. Mary's (Calif.)	Sr.	34	369	10.9
Herb Pope, Seton Hall	So.	32	343	10.7
Lavoy Allen, Temple	Jr.	35	375	10.7
Al-Farouq Aminu, Wake Forest	So.	31	332	10.7
George Odufuwa, North Texas	Jr.	33	353	10.7

FREE-THROW PERCENTAGE

	Class	GP	FT	FTA	Pct
Donald Sims, Appalachian St	Jr.	37	175	184	95.1
Jerome Randle, California	Sr.	35	139	149	93.3
Luke Babbitt, Nevada	So.	34	199	217	91.7
Tyler Haws, BYU	Fr.	35	110	120	91.7
Paul George, Fresno St	So.	29	120	132	90.9
Clevin Hannah, Wichita St	Sr.	32	85	94	90.4
Dominic Waters, Portland St	Sr.	32	138	153	90.2
Robbie Hummel, Purdue	Jr.	27	110	122	90.2
Bryan Sherrer, South Alabama	Sr.	28	91	101	90.1
T.J. Campbell, Portland	Sr.	32	116	129	89.9

Note: Minimum 2.5 made per game.

ASSISTS

	Class	GP	Ast	Avg
Ronald Moore, Siena	Sr.	34	261	7.7
Demetri McCamey, Illinois	Jr.	36	254	7.1
John Wall, Kentucky	Fr.	37	241	6.5
Johnathan Jones, Oakland	Sr.	35	224	6.4
Greivis Vasquez, Maryland	Sr.	33	208	6.3
Ishmael Smith, Wake Forest	Sr.	31	185	6.0
Evan Turner, Ohio St	Jr.	31	185	6.0
Larry Drew II, North Carolina	So.	37	220	5.9
Junard Hartley, Campbell	Jr.	30	178	5.9
Ronnie Moss, TCU	So.	32	189	5.9
Raymond Taylor, Florida Atlantic	Fr.	30	177	5.9
D.J. Cooper, Ohio	Fr.	37	218	5.9
Tweety Carter, Baylor	Sr.	32	177	5.9

*Includes games played in tournaments.

THREE-POINT FIELD-GOAL PERCENTAGE

	Class	GP	3FG	3FGA	Avg
Jared Stohl, Portland	Jr.	32	98	205	47.8
Tommy Freeman, Ohio	Jr.	37	93	195	47.7
Jim Mower, Lafayette	So.	32	92	198	46.5
Frank Davis, Tennessee Tech	Sr.	32	88	198	44.4
Devon Beitzel, Northern Colo.	Jr.	26	68	153	44.4
Jordan Burgason, Lipscomb	So.	29	96	219	43.8
Robbie Harman, Central Mich.	Sr.	30	105	245	42.9
Ryan Wittman, Cornell	Sr.	34	109	255	42.7
Rotnei Clarke, Arkansas	So.	31	100	234	42.7
Donald Sims, Appalachian St.	Jr.	37	123	288	42.7

Note: Minimum 2.5 made per game

THREE-POINT FIELD GOALS MADE PER GAME

	Class	GP	3FG	Avg
Robbie Harman, Central Michigan	Sr.	30	105	3.5
Gerald McLemore, Maine	So.	30	102	3.4
Joe Zegliniski, Hartford	Jr.	29	98	3.4
Tay Waller, Auburn	Sr.	26	87	3.3
Donald Sims, Appalachian St.	Jr.	37	123	3.3
Jordan Burgason, Lipscomb.	So.	29	96	3.3
Chris Matthews, St. Bonaventure	Sr.	31	101	3.3
E.J. Kusnyer, Mercer	Sr.	33	107	3.2
Rotnei Clarke, Arkansas	So.	31	100	3.2
LaceDarius Dunn, Baylor	Jr.	36	116	3.2
Tyrone Lewis, Niagara.	Sr.	27	87	3.2
Corey Hassan, Sacred Heart	Sr.	28	90	3.2
Ryan Wittman, Cornell	Sr.	34	109	3.2
Chris Warren, Mississippi	Jr.	35	111	3.2

BLOCKED SHOTS

	Class	GP	BS	Avg
Hassan Whiteside, Marshall	Fr.	34	182	5.4
Jarvis Varnado, Mississippi St	Sr.	36	170	4.7
Hamady Ndiaye, Rutgers	Sr.	32	145	4.5
David Foster, Utah	So.	29	115	4.0
Ekpe Udoh, Baylor	Jr.	36	133	3.7
Cole Aldrich, Kansas	Jr.	36	125	3.5
William Mosley, Northwestern St	So.	29	98	3.4
Keith Benson, Oakland	Jr.	35	117	3.3
Patrick Sullivan, Southeastern La.	Sr.	34	102	3.3
Sam Muldow, South Carolina	Sr.	31	97	3.1
Robert Nwankwo, Towson	Jr.	27	83	3.1

STEALS

	Class	GP	Stl	Avg
Jay Threatt, Delaware St	So.	29	82	2.8
Damian Saunders, Duquesne	Jr.	32	89	2.8
Devan Downey, South Carolina	Sr.	31	85	2.7
Chris Jones, Prairie View A&M	Sr.	24	65	2.7
Ceola Clark, Western Illinois	So.	27	72	2.7
Aubrey Coleman, Houston	Sr.	35	93	2.7
Brigham Waginger, Western Carolina	Sr.	34	90	2.6
Michael Deloach, Norfolk St	Sr.	30	79	2.6
A.J. Rompza, Central Florida	So.	31	81	2.6
Jackson Emery, BYU	Jr.	35	91	2.6
La'Shard Anderson, Boise St.	Jr.	32	83	2.6
Junard Hartley, Campbell	Jr.	30	77	2.6

Single-Game Highs

POINTS

51 .... Rotnei Clarke, Arkansas, November 13, 2009 (vs Alcorn St)
49 .... Jimmer Fredette, BYU, December 28, 2009 (vs Arizona)
46 .... Anatoly Bose, Nicholls St, January 23, 2010 (vs Northwestern St)
46 .... Dominique Jones, South Florida, January 23, 2010 (vs Providence)
45 .... Jimmer Fredette, BYU, March 22, 2010 (vs TCU)
45 .... Randy Culpepper, UTEP, February 13, 2010 (vs East Carolina)

REBOUNDS

25 .... Kevin Thompson, Morgan St, December 22, 2009 (vs Towson)
24 .... Justin Nabors, Lamar, December 9, 2009 (vs Louisiana College)
23 .... George Odufuwa, North Texas, November 13, 2009 (vs Cameron)
23 .... Anthony Johnson, Fairfield, February 28, 2010 (vs Niagara)

ASSISTS

16 .... Demetri McCamey, Illiinois, February 20, 2010 (vs Purdue)
16 .... Alex Tucker, Florida Atlantic, January 30, 2010 (vs Florida International)
16 .... John Wall, Kentucky, December 29, 2009 (vs Hartford)
15 .... Tory Jackson, Notre Dame, January 18, 2010 (vs Syracuse)
Three tied with 14.

THREE-POINT FIELD GOALS

13 .... Rotnei Clarke, Arkanas, November 13, 2009 (vs Alcorn St)
12 .... Jamel Jackson, Seton Hall, December 12, 2009 (vs Virginia Military Institute)
11 .... Corey Almond, Sam Houston St, November 19, 2009 (vs Kentucky)
Six tied with 10.

STEALS

9 .... Jay Threatt, Delaware St, November 16, 2009 (vs Wilmington)
Ten tied with 8.

BLOCKED SHOTS

14 .... Darrius Garrett, Richmond, January 13, 2010 (vs Massachusetts)
13 .... Hassan Whiteside, Marshall, February 27, 2010 (vs Central Florida)
11 .... Hassan Whiteside, Marshall, December 16, 2009 (vs Brescia)
Six tied with 10.

SCORING OFFENSE

	GP	W	L	Pts	Avg
Virginia Military Institute	29	10	19	2569	88.6
BYU	36	30	6	2992	83.1
Providence	31	12	19	2554	82.4
Villanova	33	25	8	2700	81.8
Kansas	36	33	3	2937	81.6
Texas	34	24	10	2761	81.2
Syracuse	35	30	5	2832	80.9
Seton Hall	32	19	13	2563	80.1
Marshall	34	24	10	2717	79.9
Xavier	35	26	9	2793	79.8

SCORING DEFENSE

	GP	W	L	Pts	Avg
Princeton	31	22	9	1652	53.3
Northern Iowa	35	30	5	1929	55.1
Temple	35	29	6	1987	56.8
Wisconsin	33	24	9	1878	56.9
USC	30	16	14	1715	57.2
Old Dominion	36	27	9	2069	57.5
Delaware St	29	17	12	1691	58.3
Arizona St	33	22	11	1938	58.7
Butler	38	33	5	2258	59.4
The Citadel	32	16	16	1914	59.8
Stephen F. Austin	32	23	9	1914	59.8

SCORING MARGIN

	Off	Def	Mar
Kansas	81.6	64.2	17.4
BYU	83.1	66.4	16.7
Murray St	76.5	60.4	16.1
Duke	77.0	61.0	16.0
Syracuse	80.9	66.4	14.5
Kentucky	79.3	64.9	14.3
Coastal Carolina	73.8	60.1	13.7
Utah St	73.1	59.9	13.2
Ohio St	74.1	61.5	12.6
St. Mary's (Calif.)	78.5	66.4	12.1

FIELD-GOAL PERCENTAGE

	FGM	FGA	Pct
Syracuse	1042	2021	51.6
IUPUI	953	1891	50.4
Murray St	978	1961	49.9
Georgetown	905	1815	49.9
Ohio St	983	1999	49.2
Gonzaga	912	1856	49.1
Denver	689	1406	49.0
Kansas	1033	2111	48.9
Utah St	941	1928	48.8
Baylor	993	2040	48.7

FIELD-GOAL PERCENTAGE DEFENSE

	Opp FG	Opp FGA	Opp Pct
Florida St	660	1751	37.7
St. Peter's	606	1607	37.7
Kentucky	875	2314	37.8
Kansas	811	2142	37.9
Coastal Carolina	767	2008	38.2
Baylor	816	2136	38.2
Temple	727	1897	38.3
USC	591	1540	38.4
Georgia Tech	818	2129	38.4
Murray St	761	1967	38.7

FREE-THROW PERCENTAGE

	FT	FTA	Pct
BYU	650	823	79.0
Indiana St	476	619	76.9
Colorado	561	732	76.6
Harvard	514	672	76.5
Lafayette	512	670	76.4
St. Mary's (Calif,)	496	652	76.1
Texas-San Antonio	451	593	76.1
Duke	682	899	75.9
Northern Iowa	489	645	75.8
Utah St	435	574	75.8

THREE-POINT FIELD GOALS MADE PER GAME

	GP	3FG	Avg
Virginia Military Institute	29	335	11.6
Eastern Kentucky	33	327	9.9
College of Charleston	34	326	9.6
Cornell	34	326	9.6
Northwestern	34	317	9.3
Mississippi St	36	329	9.1
Davidson	31	279	9.0
William & Mary	33	295	8.9
Sam Houston St	33	287	8.7
Sacred Heart	29	252	8.7

REBOUNDING MARGIN

	GP	Reb	Opp Reb	Margin Avg
Michigan St	37	1426	1109	8.6
Quinnipiac	33	1333	1052	8.5
Old Dominion	36	1394	1102	8.1
Kentucky	38	1584	1277	8.1
Appalachian St	37	1424	1134	7.8
Morehead St	35	1301	1029	7.8
Radford	31	1340	1112	7.4
Southern Miss	34	1285	1047	7.0
Kansas	36	1457	1211	6.8
San Diego St	34	1257	1035	6.5

2010 NCAA Basketball Women's Division I Tournament

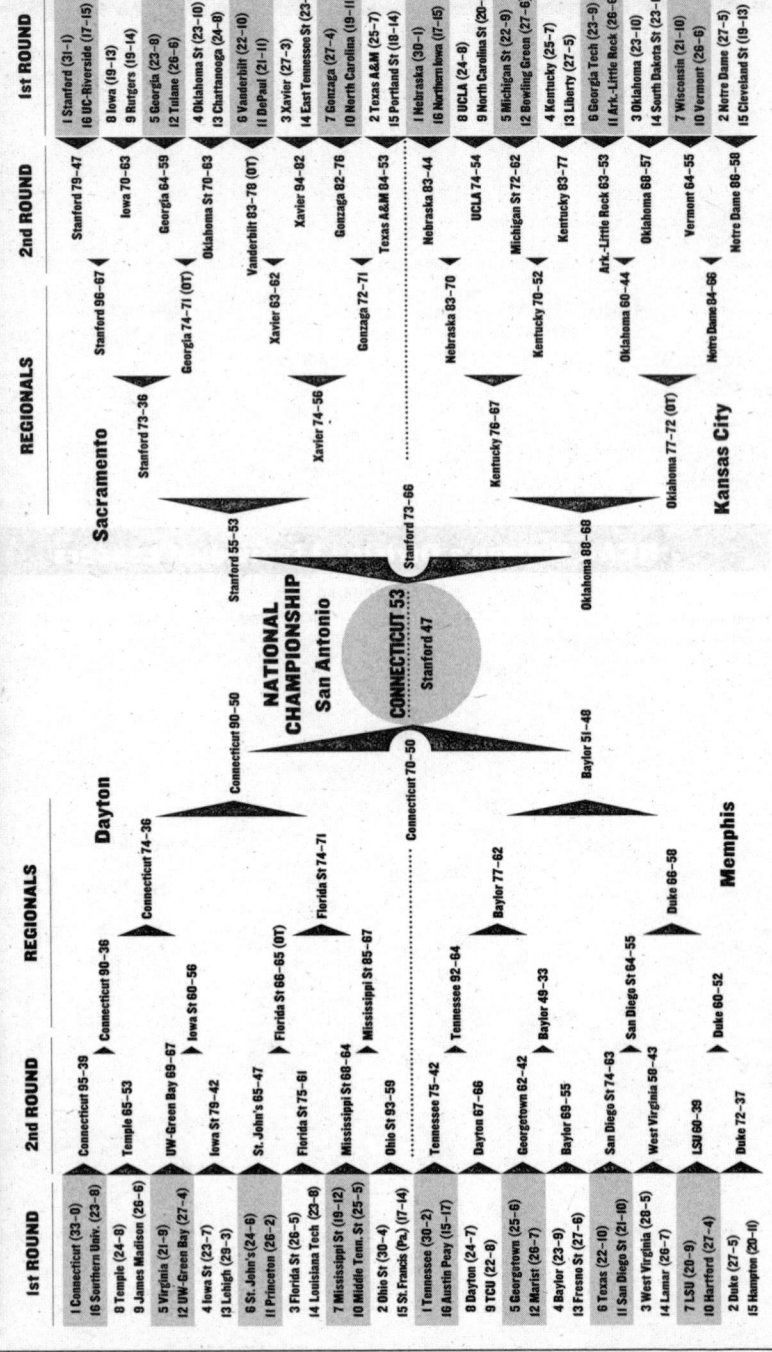

1st ROUND — **2nd ROUND** — **REGIONALS** — Sacramento

1 Stanford (31–1)
16 UC-Riverside (17–15) — Stanford 79–47
8 Rutgers (19–14)
9 Rutgers (19–14) — Iowa 70–63
5 Georgia (23–8)
12 Tulane (26–6) — Georgia 64–59
4 Oklahoma St (23–10)
13 Chattanooga (24–8) — Oklahoma St 70–63
6 Vanderbilt (22–10)
11 DePaul (21–11) — Vanderbilt 83–78 (OT)
3 Xavier (27–3)
14 East Tennessee St (23–8) — Xavier 94–82
7 Gonzaga (27–4)
10 North Carolina (19–11) — Gonzaga 82–76
2 Texas A&M (25–7)
15 Portland St (18–14) — Texas A&M 84–53

Stanford 96–67
Georgia 74–71 (OT)
Xavier 63–62
Gonzaga 72–71

Stanford 73–36
Xavier 74–56

Stanford 55–53

1 Nebraska (30–1)
16 Northern Iowa (17–15) — Nebraska 83–44
8 UCLA (24–8)
9 North Carolina St (20–13) — UCLA 74–54
5 Michigan St (22–9)
12 Bowling Green (27–6) — Michigan St 72–62
4 Kentucky (25–7)
13 Liberty (27–5) — Kentucky 83–77
6 Georgia Tech (23–9)
11 Ark-Little Rock (26–6) — Ark-Little Rock 63–53
3 Oklahoma (23–10)
14 South Dakota St (23–10) — Oklahoma 60–57
7 Wisconsin (26–6)
10 Vermont (26–6) — Vermont 64–55
2 Notre Dame (27–5)
15 Cleveland St (19–13) — Notre Dame 86–58

Nebraska 83–70
Kentucky 70–52
Oklahoma 68–68

Kentucky 76–67
Oklahoma 77–72 (OT)

Notre Dame 84–66

Kansas City

Stanford 73–66

NATIONAL CHAMPIONSHIP
San Antonio

CONNECTICUT 53
Stanford 47

Stanford 70–50

Connecticut 70–50

Baylor 51–48

REGIONALS — Dayton

Connecticut 90–50
Connecticut 74–36
Florida St 74–71
Mississippi St 65–67

Baylor 77–62
Duke 66–58

1 Connecticut (33–0)
16 Southern Univ. (23–8) — Connecticut 95–39
8 Temple (24–8)
9 James Madison (26–6) — Temple 65–53
5 Virginia (21–9)
12 UW-Green Bay (27–4) — UW-Green Bay 69–67
4 Iowa St (23–7)
13 Lehigh (28–3) — Iowa St 79–42
6 St. John's (24–6)
11 Princeton (26–2) — St. John's 65–47
3 Florida St (26–5)
14 Louisiana Tech (23–8) — Florida St 75–61
7 Mississippi St (19–12)
10 Middle Tenn. St (25–5) — Mississippi St 68–64
2 Ohio St (30–4)
15 St. Francis (Pa.) (17–14) — Ohio St 93–59

Connecticut 90–36
Florida St 66–65 (OT)

1 Tennessee (30–2)
16 Austin Peay (15–17) — Tennessee 75–42
8 Dayton (24–7)
9 TCU (22–8) — Dayton 67–66
5 Georgetown (25–6)
12 Marist (26–7) — Georgetown 62–42
4 Baylor (23–9)
13 Fresno St (27–6) — Baylor 69–55
6 Texas (22–10)
11 San Diego St (21–10) — San Diego St 74–63
3 West Virginia (28–5)
14 Lamar (26–7) — West Virginia 59–43
7 LSU (20–9)
10 Hartford (27–4) — LSU 60–39
2 Duke (27–5)
15 Hampton (20–11) — Duke 72–37

Tennessee 92–64
Baylor 49–33
San Diego St 64–55
Duke 60–52

Memphis

NCAA Div. I Women's Championship Game Box Score

Connecticut 53

	Min	FG M-A	FT M-A	Reb O-T	A	PF	TP
M. Moore	37	9-18	2-5	5-11	1	2	23
T. Charles	38	4-13	1-5	2-11	2	1	9
K. Greene	32	1-4	4-6	2-5	1	3	6
T. Hayes	30	2-8	2-6	1-3	1	3	7
C. Doty	36	3-11	0-0	0-5	3	0	8
K. McLaren	2	0-0	0-0	0-0	0	0	0
K. Faris	25	0-4	0-0	0-7	1	0	0
Totals		**19-58**	**9-22**	**10-42**	**9**	**9**	**53**

Percentages: FG-.328, FT-.409, 3-pt goals: 6-20, .300 (M. Moore 3-5, T. Hayes 1-5, C. Doty 2-8, K. Faris 0-4). Blocked shots: 7 (T. Charles 6, K. Greene 1). Turnovers: 120 (M. Moore 3, T. Charles 3, K. Greene 1, T. Hayes 3). Steals: 5 (T. Charles 1, K. Greene 1, T. Hayes 1, K. Faris 2). Technical Fouls: None.

Halftime: Stanford 20, Connecticut 12.
Final Four Most Outstanding Player: Maya Moore.

Stanford 47

	Min	FG M-A	FT M-A	Reb O-T	A	PF	TP
K. Pedersen	40	5-13	2-2	4-17	3	4	15
N. Ogwumike	38	5-14	1-2	1-13	0	4	11
J. Appel	30	0-12	0-0	4-7	2	3	0
R. Gold-Onwude	11	0-3	0-0	0-0	0	0	0
J. Pohlen	33	4-8	0-0	1-2	2	5	11
M. Harrison	1	0-0	0-0	0-0	0	1	0
J. Hones	21	1-9	0-0	1-2	1	1	3
M. Murphy	15	2-5	0-0	0-2	1	0	4
J. Tinkle	11	1-4	0-0	2-2	2	2	3
Totals		**18-68**	**3-4**	**13-45**	**11**	**20**	**47**

Percentages: FG-.265 FT-.750, 3-pt goals: 8-22, .364 (K. Pedersen 3-5, R. Gold Onwude 0-1, J. Pohlen 3-5, J. Hones 1-6, M. Murphy 0-1, J. Tinkle 1-4). Blocked shots: 1 (J. Tinkle). Turnovers: 10 (N. Ogwumike 1, J. Appel 3, R. Gold-Onwude 1, J. Pohlen 1, J. Hones 2, M. Murphy 2). Steals: 2 (K. Pedersen 1, J. Tinkle 1). Technical Fouls: None.

Officials: Eric Brewton, Denise Kantner, Lisa Jones.
A: 22,936.

NCAA Women's Division I Individual Leaders

SCORING

Player and Team	Class	GP	TFG	3FG	FT	Pts	Avg
Alysha Clark, Middle Tennessee St	Sr.	29	306	17	192	821	28.3
Andrea Riley, Oklahoma St	Sr.	34	296	78	239	909	26.7
Elena Delle Donne, Delaware	Fr.	29	257	66	194	774	26.7
Chastity Reed, Arkansas-Little Rock	Jr.	34	346	0	150	842	24.8
Dawn Evans, James Madison	Jr.	31	237	112	177	763	24.6
Kevi Luper, Oral Roberts	Fr.	31	260	43	194	757	24.4
Monica Wright, Virginia	Sr.	31	270	31	163	734	23.7
Gabriela Marginean, Drexel	Sr.	31	255	39	178	727	23.5
Jantel Lavender, Ohio St	Jr.	36	304	2	159	769	21.4
Bianca Thomas, Mississippi	Sr.	32	219	100	132	670	20.9
Tavleyn James, Eastern Michigan	So.	31	220	86	115	641	20.7
Kelsey Griffin, Nebraska	Sr.	34	245	6	189	685	20.1
Casey Garrison, Missouri St	So.	33	234	32	158	658	19.9
Riquna Williams, Miami (Fla.)	So.	36	253	106	95	707	19.6
Chynna Bozeman, Morehead St	Jr.	33	203	121	121	648	19.6
Kristina Santiago, Cal Poly	Jr.	29	226	1	116	569	19.6
Corin Adams, Morgan St	Sr.	30	196	58	131	581	19.4
Tyra Grant, Penn St	Sr.	31	186	49	176	597	19.3
Brittany Carter, Memphis	So.	34	245	26	138	654	19.2
Shenise Johnson, Miami (Fla.)	So.	36	251	50	133	685	19.0
Kailey Klein, Cleveland St	Sr.	33	213	48	152	626	19.0
Maya Moore, Connecticut	Jr.	39	279	80	98	736	18.9
Ricshanda Bickham, Nicholls St	Jr.	27	167	54	123	508	18.8
Charday Hunt, Sacramento St	Sr.	30	169	44	177	559	18.6
Judie Lomax, Columbia	Jr.	28	201	0	119	521	18.6
Amy Patton, Northern Arizona	Fr.	29	207	65	60	539	18.6

FIELD-GOAL PERCENTAGE

Player and Team	Class	GP	FG	FGA	Pct
Carolyn Swords, Boston College	Jr.	32	188	283	66.4
Diana Delva, Hartford	Sr.	32	178	275	64.7
Kaetlyn Murdoch, Denver	So.	31	209	334	62.6
Ta'Shia Phillips, Xavier	Jr.	34	195	314	62.1
Tina Charles, Connecticut	Sr.	39	299	484	61.8
Alysha Clark, Middle Tenn. St.	Sr.	29	306	498	61.4
Nnemkadi Ogwumike, Stanford	So.	38	266	445	59.8
Kelsey Griffin, Nebraska	Sr.	34	245	411	59.6
Maria Boever, South Dakota St	Sr.	33	186	316	58.9
Taryn Wicijowski, Utah	Fr.	35	204	353	57.8

Note: Minimum 5 FG per game.

REBOUNDS

Player and Team	Class	GP	Reb	Avg
Judie Lomax, Connecitcut	Jr.	28	398	14.2
Pauline Love, Southern Miss	Sr.	28	359	12.8
Shanavia Dowdell, Louisiana Tech	Sr.	32	398	12.4
Ta'Shia Phillips, Xavier	Jr.	34	399	11.7
Alysha Clark, Middle Tenn. St	Sr.	29	337	11.6
Kourtney Brown, Buffalo	Jr.	30	346	11.5
Stephanie Geehan, Fairfield	Sr.	34	388	11.4
Jenna Smith, Illinois	Sr.	34	387	11.4
Ify Ibekwe, Arizona	Jr.	31	352	11.4
Chelsea Cole, Pittsburgh	Jr.	30	340	11.3

FREE-THROW PERCENTAGE

Player and Team	Class	GP	FT	FTA	Pct
Kelsey Luna, Indiana St	Sr.	31	125	134	93.3
Laiken Dollente, Portland	Sr.	31	148	161	91.9
Reiko Thomas, Arizona	So.	29	75	83	90.4
Emily London, Samford	Jr.	29	101	112	90.2
Lauren Prochaska, Bowl. Green	Jr.	34	151	168	89.9
Elene Delle Donne, Delaware St	Fr.	29	194	216	89.8
Jacqui Kalin, Northern Iowa	So.	33	96	107	89.7
Chelsea Marandola, Providence	Sr.	34	106	119	89.1
Gabriela Marginean, Drexel	Sr.	31	178	200	89.0
Jenna Smith, Illinois	Sr.	34	137	155	88.4

Note: Minimum 2.5 made per game.

ASSISTS

Player and Team	Class	GP	Ast	Avg
Courtney Vandersloot, Gonzaga	Jr.	34	321	9.4
Samantha Prahalis, Ohio St	So.	36	289	8.0
Naama Shafir, Toledo	So.	34	227	6.7
Claire Faucher, Portland St	Sr.	32	213	6.7
Jenna Plumley, Lamar	Jr.	34	224	6.6
Tonya Schnibbe, Weber St	Sr.	29	191	6.6
Andrea Riley, Oklahoma St	Sr.	34	220	6.5
Kiara Evans, Long Island	So.	32	206	6.4
Alison Lacey, Iowa St	Sr.	30	187	6.2
Kayla Melson, Mississippi	Jr.	30	178	5.9
Sarah Miles, West Virginia	Jr.	34	200	5.9

THREE-POINT FIELD-GOAL PERCENTAGE

Player and Team	Class	GP	3FG	3FGA	Pct
Brigid Mulroy, Detroit	Sr.	31	92	182	50.5
Brittany Johnson, Ohio St	So.	36	77	160	48.1
Kathleen Nash, Texas	Jr.	33	68	144	47.2
Erica Carter, SUNY-Binghamton	Sr.	30	100	214	46.7
Anne Marie Lanning, Md. Ten. St.	Jr.	30	64	137	46.7
Emily London, Samford	Jr.	29	68	147	46.3
Maggie Cosgrove, Sacred Heart	Jr.	30	76	167	45.5
Lauren Prochaska, Bowl. Green	Jr.	34	92	205	44.9
Kelly McManmon, St. John's (N.Y.)	Sr.	32	69	155	44.5
Carmen Reynolds, Michigan	So.	35	85	191	44.5

Note: Minimum 2.0 made per game.

BLOCKED SHOTS

Player and Team	Class	GP	BS	Avg
Brittany Griner, Baylor	Fr.	35	223	6.4
Louella Tomlinson, St. Mary's (Ca.)	Jr.	31	195	6.3
Mekia Valentine, UC-Santa Barbara	Jr.	30	120	4.0
Stephanie Geehan, Fairfield	Sr.	34	118	3.5
Kelley Cain, Tennessee	So.	33	113	3.4
Amy Jaeschke, Northwestern	Jr.	33	106	3.2
Ashley Gayle, Texas	So.	33	103	3.1
Allyssa DeHaan, Michigan St	Sr.	33	101	3.1
Alisha Nelson, Savannah St	So.	30	91	3.0
Jess Fuller, Hofstra	Sr.	34	103	3.0
Kaetlyn Murdoch, Denver	So.	31	93	3.0
Hillary Carlson, Wyoming	Jr.	33	98	3.0

NCAA Men's Division II Individual Leaders

SCORING

Player and Team	Class	GP	TFG	3FG	FT	Pts	Avg
Stephen Dennis, Kutztown	Sr.	31	281	27	228	817	26.4
Gage Daye, Bloomfield	Jr.	29	243	60	207	753	26.0
Kyle Moore, Tusculum	Sr.	28	207	117	162	693	24.8
Justin Swidowski, Holy Family	So.	27	262	11	115	650	24.1
Roman Andrande, New Mexico Highlands	Sr.	31	215	82	234	746	24.1
Kendrick Easley, Mount Olive	Sr.	29	212	106	154	684	23.6
LaMarshall Corbett, Angelo St	Jr.	28	186	81	203	656	23.4
Danny Sanders, Mars Hill	Sr.	28	221	95	108	645	23.0
Matt Rosinski, Regis (Colo.)	Sr.	27	223	50	111	607	22.5
Paul Harrison, North Greenville	So.	28	141	0	141	627	22.4
Chris Woods, Pfeiffer	Jr.	28	220	0	185	625	22.3
Kyle White, Goldey-Beacom	Sr.	29	217	34	172	640	22.1
DeAndre Landsdowne, Fort Lewis	Jr.	28	216	26	150	608	21.7
Sanijay Watts, Central Missouri	Sr.	31	267	0	139	673	21.7
Sharif Bray, Cheyney	Jr.	28	193	67	154	607	21.7

REBOUNDS

Player and Team	Class	GP	Reb	Avg
Nathan Schumacher, Oakland City	Sr.	28	414	14.8
Lance Smith, Henderson St	Jr.	27	360	13.3
Blake Poole, St. Martin's	Jr.	27	329	12.2
William Eason, Concordia (N.Y.)	Jr.	27	328	12.1
Laurence Ekperigin, Le Moyne	Sr.	28	340	12.1
C.J. Jackson, Hawaii Pacific	Sr.	27	316	11.7
Michel Vidal, Lynn	Jr.	28	323	11.5
Matt Schneck, St. Cloud St	Sr.	34	386	11.4
Scott Dennis, Christian Brothers	So.	27	305	11.3
D'Mario Curry, Lincoln Memorial	Jr.	28	312	11.1

ASSISTS

Player and Team	Class	GP	Ast	Avg
D.J. Ferguson, Flagler	Jr.	27	254	9.4
P.J. Turner, Davis & Elkins	Jr.	27	231	8.6
Chad Akins, Delta St	Sr.	21	154	7.3
Ben Fischer, Winona St	Jr.	28	201	7.2
Darren Duncan, Merrimack	Sr.	30	204	6.8
Josh Magette, Alabama-Huntsville	So.	30	200	6.7
Desmond Stephens, Ky. Wesleyan	Sr.	31	204	6.6
Andrew Bridger, Nebraska-Omaha	Sr.	30	193	6.4
Robby Pines, East Stroudsburg	Sr.	30	193	6.4
Michael Mathey, West Liberty	Sr.	32	203	6.3

FIELD-GOAL PERCENTAGE

Player and Team	Class	GP	FG	FGA	Pct
Patrick Grubbs, Pitt.-Johnstown	So.	28	191	288	66.3
Ken Mitchell, West Florida	Jr.	21	112	169	66.3
Terrell Ray, Franklin Pierce	Sr.	27	165	249	66.3
Kevin Kotzur, St. Mary's (Tex.)	Fr.	30	189	288	65.6
Brandon Hopf, Oakland City	Sr.	28	176	271	64.9
Gerard Devaughn, Stillman	Sr.	29	151	233	64.8
Laurence Ekperigin, Le Moyne	Sr.	28	221	344	64.2
Dion Malachi, Mars Hill	Jr.	27	152	239	63.6
Paul Harrison, North Greenville	So.	28	243	384	63.3
Dominique Nhniman, W.V. Wesleyan	So.	23	127	201	63.2

Note: Minimum 5 made per game.

FREE-THROW PERCENTAGE

Player and Team	Class	GP	FT	FTA	Pct
Girod Adams, NW Mo. St	Sr.	27	86	92	93.5
Edward Freeman, Molloy	So.	28	81	89	91.0
LaMarshall Corbett, Angelo St	Jr.	28	203	224	90.6
Bryan Smothers, Wayne St. (Mich.)	Jr.	27	85	94	90.4
Mitch Boeck, Northern St	Sr.	27	103	114	90.4
Kyle Caiola, Mass.-Lowell	So.	32	178	198	89.9
Jake Driscoll, Minn St.-Moorhead	So.	27	113	126	89.7
Gerald Boston, Barton	Fr.	26	104	116	89.7
Zac Tiderman, Humboldt St	Sr.	30	111	124	89.5
Alex Hall, Drury	Fr.	29	84	94	89.4

Note: Minimum 2.5 made per game.

NCAA Women's Division II Individual Leaders

SCORING

Player and Team	Class	GP	TFG	3FG	FT	Pts	Avg
Johannah Leedham, Franklin Pierce	Sr.	34	305	90	215	915	26.9
Donita Adams, Greenville St	Sr.	28	205	69	154	633	22.6
Tori Hansen, West Liberty	Jr.	32	260	19	166	705	22.0
Brittni Young, Mars Hill	Jr.	27	178	64	173	593	22.0
Ashley Vavrek, Fairmont St	Sr.	32	206	87	200	699	21.8
Lauren Beckley, Shippensburg	Sr.	30	214	69	157	654	21.8
Amelia Simmons, Wilmington (Del.)	Sr.	28	211	41	146	609	21.8
Jasmine Gunn, Tusculum	Jr.	33	240	10	223	713	21.6
Brooque Williams, California (Pa.)	Sr.	32	270	5	134	679	21.2
Jamie Meyer, Abilene Christian	Sr.	28	224	20	121	589	21.0
Veronica Walker, Delta St	So.	31	254	0	137	645	20.8
Kmaria Hobbs, Southern Arkansas	So.	26	192	3	151	538	20.7
Jheri Booker, Minnesotia-Duluth	So.	31	265	22	86	638	20.6
Veronica Jackson, Lane	Jr.	25	178	26	122	504	20.2
Kirsty Leedham, Caldwell	Jr.	27	170	60	132	532	19.7

REBOUNDS

Player and Team	Class	GP	Reb	Avg
Lillian McGill, District of Columbia	Jr.	25	306	12.2
Phebe Smith, Columbus St	Sr.	28	339	12.1
Donisha Tate, San Francisco St	Sr.	31	372	12.0
Kayla Smith, California (Pa.)	Jr.	32	381	11.9
Delmara Reece, Mercy	Jr.	25	296	11.8
Anita Bucher, Newberry	Sr.	29	338	11.7
Jennifer Robbins, Queens (N.Y.)	Sr.	28	317	11.3
Katie Wysocky, Michigan Tech	Sr.	34	384	11.3
Dana Hicks, Catawba	So.	27	303	11.2
Jody Meyer, Abilene Christian	Sr.	28	303	10.8
Utivia Barnes, Benedict	Jr.	30	324	10.8

ASSISTS

Player and Team	Class	GP	Ast	Avg
Bug Cooper, Delta St	Jr.	31	265	8.5
Kath. Kundermuellier, Abilene Christian	Sr.	28	213	7.6
Jenni Robbins, West Liberty	Fr.	32	200	6.3
Megan Stadler, SW Missouri St	Sr.	27	167	6.2
Helin Marte, New Haven	Sr.	29	174	6.0
Ja'Nell Jones, Drury	Jr.	28	167	6.0
Brooke Knight, Hillsdale	Sr.	27	159	5.9
Amanda Harris, Alderson-Broaddus	So.	28	164	5.9
Tiffany Crocker, Gannon	Sr.	38	218	5.7
Porsha Morgan, Erskine	So.	28	159	5.7

FIELD-GOAL PERCENTAGE

Player and Team	Class	GP	FG	FGA	Pct
Veronica Walker, Delta St	So.	31	254	399	63.7
JaToya Kemp, N.C.-Pembroke	Jr.	28	181	287	63.1
Stephanie Harper, Kentucky St	Fr.	28	167	277	60.3
Mariesa Greene, Barry	Sr.	31	223	376	59.3
Katie Wysocky, Michigan Tech	Sr.	34	224	380	58.9
Erin Chesnavich, Phila. Sciences	Sr.	23	125	213	58.7
Allison Rosel, Fort Lewis	Sr.	39	230	396	58.1
Danae Danen, Michigan Tech	Sr.	30	171	299	57.2
Courtney Shuman, Quincy	Jr.	29	170	301	56.5
Phebe Smith, Columbus St	Sr.	28	183	325	56.3

Note: Minimum 5 FG per game.

FREE-THROW PERCENTAGE

Player and Team	Class	GP	FT	FTA	Pct
Tricia Principe, Ferris St	So.	27	86	93	92.5
Maurika Hickman, Concordia-St. Paul	Jr.	32	93	102	91.2
Samantha Reimer, Edinboro	Sr.	28	174	192	90.6
Lyndie NeVille, Camerion	Jr.	27	84	93	90.3
Lizzie Suwala, Clarion	Sr.	27	82	92	89.1
Amanda Gibson, UW-Parkside	Sr.	31	120	135	88.9
Traci Keyser, Fort Hays St	Fr.	27	72	81	88.9
Lauren Beckley, Shippensburg	Sr.	30	157	177	88.7
Carolyn Mills, Lincoln Memorial	Jr.	28	76	81	88.4
Amy Drake, West Florida	Sr.	28	86	177	87.8

Note: Minimum 2.5 made per game.

NCAA Men's Division III Individual Leaders

SCORING

Player and Team	Class	GP	TFG	3FG	FT	Pts	Avg
Rui Carmo, Green Mountain	Sr.	26	244	14	147	649	25.0
John Hoch, Carroll (Wisc.)	Sr.	25	211	40	158	620	24.8
Steve Djurickovic, Carthage	Jr.	30	231	41	228	731	24.4
Lamonte Thomas, Johnson & Wales	So.	26	204	63	154	625	24.0
Derek D'Amours, Keene St	So.	26	212	75	119	618	23.8
Jake Schwarz, Lakeland	So.	22	194	26	94	508	23.1
Gabriel Davis, City Tech	Jr.	25	199	14	150	562	22.5
Aris Wurtz, Ripon	So.	24	199	39	98	535	22.3
Tony Mane, UW-LaCrosse	Jr.	25	209	64	75	557	22.3
D.J. Marsh, UW-Oshkosh	Sr.	25	184	17	172	557	22.3
Scott Gillespie, Ripon	Jr.	24	206	5	114	531	22.1
Dominic Trawick, Bridgewater (Pa.)	Sr.	25	180	70	119	549	22.0
Nick Rose, Colorado College	Jr.	25	191	47	119	548	21.9
Tyler Gordon, Finlandia	Sr.	20	161	43	72	437	21.9
Blair Rozenblad, Thiel	Fr.	25	198	17	131	544	21.8

REBOUNDS

Player and Team	Class	GP	Reb	Avg
Juan Paulino, Wells	Sr.	27	445	16.5
Marcel Esonwune, York (N.Y.)	Jr.	31	459	14.8
Tyler Sanborn, Guilford	Sr.	33	465	14.1
Derek Mitchell, Ferrum	Jr.	22	299	13.6
Jon Greenberg, Mass. Liberal Arts	Jr.	25	312	12.5
Jonathan Jones, Kean	Jr.	25	312	12.5
Cameron Mitchell, Willamette	Jr.	25	312	12.5
Raymond Askew, Albertus Magnus	So.	30	365	12.2
Rui Como, Green Mountain	Sr.	26	314	12.1
Matt Pepdjonovic, Suffolk	Fr.	25	290	11.6
Joshua Jones, Husson	So.	28	324	11.6

ASSISTS

Player and Team	Class	GP	Ast	Avg
Sean Rossi, Ithaca	Fr.	28	221	7.9
Sean Wallis, Washington-St. Louis	Sr.	27	207	7.7
Scott Gillespie, Ripon	Jr.	24	176	7.3
Steve Kjurickovic, Carthage	Jr.	30	218	7.3
Lance Robinson, Aurora	Sr.	29	208	7.2
Zach Spitz, Penn St-Altoona	Sr.	26	175	6.7
Robbie Kunke, Willamette	Jr.	22	138	6.3
Shane Denully, SUNY-Old Westbury	Sr.	26	159	6.1
Oppong Agyemang, SUNY-New Paltz	Sr.	25	152	6.1
Austin Claunch, Emory	So.	25	151	6.0

FIELD-GOAL PERCENTAGE

Player and Team	Class	GP	FG	FGA	Pct
Juan Paulino, Wells	Sr.	27	190	271	70.1
Travis Clark, Lake Forest	So.	24	188	274	68.6
Andy O'Keefe, Grove City	Sr.	28	175	263	66.5
Antonio Samedi, SUNY-Buffalo	Sr.	22	120	183	65.6
Paul Reynolds, Wesley	Fr.	28	146	223	65.5
Phil Barera, Ithaca	Jr.	28	198	303	65.3
Kevin Knab, Marietta	So.	26	149	229	65.1
Justin Riley, Chapman	Jr.	27	161	250	64.4
Tyler Sanborn, Guilford	Sr.	33	268	417	64.3
Aaron Burtzel, St. John's (Minn.)	Jr.	26	132	208	63.5

Note: Minimum 5 made per game.

SCORING

Player and Team	Class	GP	TFG	3FG	FT	Pts	Avg
Kimberly Blakney, Farmingdale St.	Sr.	26	224	65	153	666	25.6
Chelsie Schweers, Christopher Newport	Jr.	31	262	122	113	759	24.5
Lyndsie Long, Elmhurst	Sr.	27	241	74	100	656	24.3
Katie Dewitt, Northwestern (Minn.)	So.	29	268	65	88	689	23.8
Jennings Chantelle, La Roche	Jr.	26	224	45	117	610	23.5
Krystina Agard, SUNY-Old Westbury	Fr.	25	172	39	196	579	23.2
Colleen Clarke, Cazenovia	Sr.	25	207	48	104	566	22.6
Margo Muhlbauer, Buena Vista	Sr.	27	218	23	136	595	22.0
Lee Jennings, John Carroll	Jr.	25	196	7	151	550	22.0
Julia Hirssig, UW-Stout	Sr.	27	217	0	145	579	21.4
Jessica Berry, Utica	Sr.	29	243	16	117	619	21.3
Kym Wenz, Wooster	Sr.	26	178	72	113	541	20.8
Nikki Wilborn, Greensboro	Jr.	24	184	60	69	497	20.7
Brittany Whetts, Neumann	Sr.	27	203	1	151	558	20.7
Jessica Laing, SUNY-Cortland	Sr.	29	191	41	168	591	20.4

REBOUNDS

Player and Team	Class	GP	Reb	Avg
Courtney Bailey, Penn St-Berks	Sr.	28	445	15.9
Tiffany Thompson, Medgar Evers	Fr.	26	408	15.7
Catherine O'Connell, Newbury	Fr.	23	346	15.0
Melissa Teel, Western Conn. St	Jr.	29	422	14.6
Emma Buckley, Green Mountain	Sr.	24	346	14.4
Kelsey Wilcox, Pitt-Greensburgh.	Sr.	27	383	14.2
Kathryn Stockbower, Swarthmore	Jr.	25	338	13.5
Katy Williams, Austin	Sr.	24	320	13.5
Juanita Whyms, Hunter	Sr.	28	365	13.3
Sharon Dennis, Roch. Inst. of Tech.	So.	25	325	13.0

FIELD-GOAL PERCENTAGE

Player and Team	Class	GP	FG	FGA	Pct
Julia Hirssig, UW-Stout	Sr.	27	217	318	68.2
Megan Lawler, Rockford	Jr.	24	123	188	65.4
Sam Jewell, Luther	Jr.	25	132	208	63.5
Melissa Teel, Western Conn. St	Jr.	29	170	269	63.2
Rachel Macon, Illinois College	Jr.	24	130	215	60.5
Amanda Jennings, Rowan	Sr.	26	221	366	60.4
Lisa Nassin, Lake Forest	Sr.	24	147	244	60.2
Morgan Korinek, Kenyon	So.	27	161	268	60.1
Alison Harmon, Maryville (Tenn.)	Fr.	28	153	255	60.0
Easter Faafiti, Gallaudet	Jr.	25	190	318	59.7

Note: Minimum 5 made per game.

ASSISTS

Player and Team	Class	GP	Ast	Avg
Monique Salmon, Baruch.	Jr.	26	189	7.3
Andrea Bailey, Wheaton (Mass.)	Sr.	27	168	6.2
Amy Doyle, Texas Lutheran	So.	24	149	6.2
Alicia Brown, Maryville (Tenn.)	Sr.	28	167	6.0
Annie Burns, Bates	So.	26	155	6.0
Jakoya Wilkins, Salem St	Sr.	25	149	6.0
Samantha Allen Cazenovia	Jr.	25	143	5.7
Danielle Barber, Drew	So.	27	154	5.7
Cory Boyd, Wesley	Jr.	23	130	5.7
Allison Anderson, Oberlin	Fr.	26	146	5.6
Lee Jennings, John Carroll	Jr.	27	140	5.6
Jackie Berry, Montclair St	Sr.	26	133	5.6

FREE-THROW PERCENTAGE

Player and Team	Class	GP	FT	FTA	Pct
Jessie Domes, SUNY-Purchase	Sr.	27	85	93	91.4
Julianna Eagles, Simmons	Sr.	26	85	94	90.4
Stephanie Coro, Rhode Island Coll.	So.	25	66	73	90.4
Kelly Dunne, Nazareth	Sr.	25	74	82	90.2
Christina Byler, Hendrix	Sr.	25	129	143	90.2
Lyndsie Long, Elmhurst	Sr.	27	100	112	89.3
Amanda Schroeder, Bald.-Wall.	Jr.	26	115	131	87.8
Brook Van Eck, Calvin	Sr.	29	79	90	87.8
Margo Muhlbauer, Buena Vista	Sr.	27	136	155	87.7
Lyndsey Seewald, Carroll (Wisc.)	Jr.	23	104	119	87.4

Note: Minimum 2.5 made per game.

NCAA Men's Division I Championship Results

NCAA Final Four Results

Year	Winner	Score	Runner-up	Third Place	Fourth Place	Winning Coach
1939	Oregon	46–33	Ohio St	*Oklahoma	*Villanova	Howard Hobson
1940	Indiana	60–42	Kansas	*Duquesne	*USC	Branch McCracken
1941	Wisconsin	39–34	Washington St	*Pittsburgh	*Arkansas	Harold Foster
1942	Stanford	53–38	Dartmouth	*Colorado	*Kentucky	Everett Dean
1943	Wyoming	46–34	Georgetown	*Texas	*DePaul	Everett Shelton
1944	Utah	42–40 (OT)	Dartmouth	*Iowa St	*Ohio St	Vadal Peterson
1945	Oklahoma St	49–45	NYU	*Arkansas	*Ohio St	Hank Iba
1946	Oklahoma St	43–40	North Carolina	Ohio St	California	Hank Iba
1947	Holy Cross	58–47	Oklahoma	Texas	CCNY	Alvin Julian
1948	Kentucky	58–42	Baylor	Holy Cross	Kansas St	Adolph Rupp
1949	Kentucky	46–36	Oklahoma St	Illinois	Oregon St	Adolph Rupp
1950	CCNY	71–68	Bradley	North Carolina St	Baylor	Nat Holman
1951	Kentucky	68–58	Kansas St	Illinois	Oklahoma St	Adolph Rupp
1952	Kansas	80–63	St. John's (N.Y.)	Illinois	Santa Clara	Forrest Allen
1953	Indiana	69–68	Kansas	Washington	LSU	Branch McCracken
1954	La Salle	92–76	Bradley	Penn St	USC	Kenneth Loeffler
1955	San Francisco	77–63	La Salle	Colorado	Iowa	Phil Woolpert
1956	San Francisco	83–71	Iowa	Temple	SMU	Phil Woolpert
1957	North Carolina	54–53 (3OT)	Kansas	San Francisco	Michigan St	Frank McGuire
1958	Kentucky	84–72	Seattle	Temple	Kansas St	Adolph Rupp
1959	California	71–70	West Virginia	Cincinnati	Louisville	Pete Newell
1960	Ohio St	75–55	California	Cincinnati	NYU	Fred Taylor
1961	Cincinnati	70–65 (OT)	Ohio St	Vacated‡	Utah	Edwin Jucker
1962	Cincinnati	71–59	Ohio St	Wake Forest	UCLA	Edwin Jucker
1963	Loyola (Ill.)	60–58 (OT)	Cincinnati	Duke	Oregon St	George Ireland
1964	UCLA	98–83	Duke	Michigan	Kansas St	John Wooden
1965	UCLA	91–80	Michigan	Princeton	Wichita St	John Wooden
1966	UTEP	72–65	Kentucky	Duke	Utah	Don Haskins
1967	UCLA	79–64	Dayton	Houston	North Carolina	John Wooden
1968	UCLA	78–55	North Carolina	Ohio St	Houston	John Wooden
1969	UCLA	92–72	Purdue	Drake	North Carolina	John Wooden
1970	UCLA	80–69	Jacksonville	New Mexico St	St. Bonaventure	John Wooden
1971	UCLA	68–62	Vacated‡	Vacated‡	Kansas	John Wooden
1972	UCLA	81–76	Florida St	North Carolina	Louisville	John Wooden
1973	UCLA	87–66	Memphis St	Indiana	Providence	John Wooden
1974	North Carolina St	76–64	Marquette	UCLA	Kansas	Norm Sloan
1975	UCLA	92–85	Kentucky	Louisville	Syracuse	John Wooden
1976	Indiana	86–68	Michigan	UCLA	Rutgers	Bob Knight
1977	Marquette	67–59	North Carolina	UNLV	UNC-Charlotte	Al McGuire
1978	Kentucky	94–88	Duke	Arkansas	Notre Dame	Joe Hall
1979	Michigan St	75–64	Indiana St	DePaul	Penn	Jud Heathcote
1980	Louisville	59–54	Vacated‡	Purdue	Iowa	Denny Crum
1981	Indiana	63–50	North Carolina	Virginia	LSU	Bob Knight
1982	North Carolina	63–62	Georgetown	*Houston	*Louisville	Dean Smith
1983	North Carolina St	54–52	Houston	*Georgia	*Louisville	Jim Valvano
1984	Georgetown	84–75	Houston	*Kentucky	*Virginia	John Thompson
1985	Villanova	66–64	Georgetown	St. John's (N.Y.)	Vacated‡	Rollie Massimino
1986	Louisville	72–69	Duke	*Kansas	*LSU	Denny Crum
1987	Indiana	74–73	Syracuse	*UNLV	*Providence	Bob Knight
1988	Kansas	83–79	Oklahoma	*Arizona	*Duke	Larry Brown
1989	Michigan	80–79 (OT)	Seton Hall	*Duke	*Illinois	Steve Fisher
1990	UNLV	103–73	Duke	*Arkansas	*Georgia Tech	Jerry Tarkanian
1991	Duke	72–65	Kansas	*UNLV	*North Carolina	Mike Krzyzewski
1992	Duke	71–51	Michigan	*Cincinnati	*Indiana	Mike Krzyzewski
1993	North Carolina	77–71	Michigan	*Kansas	*Kentucky	Dean Smith
1994	Arkansas	76–72	Duke	*Arizona	*Florida	Nolan Richardson
1995	UCLA	89–78	Arkansas	*North Carolina	*Oklahoma St	Jim Harrick
1996	Kentucky	76–67	Syracuse	Vacated‡	Mississippi St	Rick Pitino
1997	Arizona	84–79 (OT)	Kentucky	*Minnesota	*North Carolina	Lute Olson
1998	Kentucky	78–69	Utah	*Stanford	*North Carolina	Tubby Smith
1999	Connecticut	77–74	Duke	*Michigan St	*Ohio St	Jim Calhoun
2000	Michigan St	89–76	Florida	*Wisconsin	*North Carolina	Tom Izzo
2001	Duke	82–72	Arizona	*Maryland	*Michigan St	Mike Krzyzewski

NCAA Final Four Results *(Cont.)*

Year	Winner	Score	Runner-up	Third Place	Fourth Place	Winning Coach
2002	Maryland	64–52	Indiana	*Kansas	*Oklahoma	Gary Williams
2003	Syracuse	81–78	Kansas	*Marquette	*Texas	Jim Boeheim
2004	Connecticut	82–73	Georgia Tech	*Oklahoma St	*Duke	Jim Calhoun
2005	North Carolina	75-70	Illinois	*Louisville	*Michigan St	Roy Williams
2006	Florida	73–57	UCLA	*George Mason	*LSU	Billy Donovan
2007	Florida	84-75	Ohio St	*UCLA	*Georgetown	Billy Donovan
2008	Kansas	75–68 (OT)	Vacated‡	*UCLA	*North Carolina	Bill Self
2009	North Carolina	89–72	Michigan St	*Villanova	*Connecticut	Roy Williams
2010	Duke	61–59	Butler	*West Virginia	*Michigan St	Mike Krzyzewski

*Tied for third place. ‡Student-athletes representing St. Joseph's (Pa.) in 1961, Villanova in 1971, Western Kentucky in 1971, UCLA in 1980, Memphis State in 1985, Massachusetts in 1996, and Memphis in 2008 were declared ineligible subsequent to the tournament. Under NCAA rules, the teams' and ineligible student-athletes' records were deleted, and the teams' places in the standings were vacated.

NCAA Final Four Most Outstanding Players

Year	Winner, School	GP	Field Goals FGM	Pct	3-Pt FG FGA	FGM	Free Throws FTM	Pct	Reb	Asst	Stl	BS	Avg
1939	None selected												
1940	Marv Huffman, Indiana	2	7	—	—	—	4	—	—	—	—	—	9.0
1941	John Kotz, Wisconsin	2	8	—	—	—	6	—	—	—	—	—	11.0
1942	Howard Dallmar, Stanford	2	8	—	—	—	4	66.7	—	—	—	—	10.0
1943	Ken Sailors, Wyoming	2	10	—	—	—	8	72.7	—	—	—	—	14.0
1944	Arnie Ferrin, Utah	2	11	—	—	—	6	—	—	—	—	—	14.0
1945	Bob Kurland, Oklahoma St	2	16	—	—	—	5	—	—	—	—	—	18.5
1946	Bob Kurland, Oklahoma St	2	21	—	—	—	10	66.7	—	—	—	—	26.0
1947	George Kaftan, Holy Cross	2	18	—	—	—	12	70.6	—	—	—	—	24.0
1948	Alex Groza, Kentucky	2	16	—	—	—	5	—	—	—	—	—	18.5
1949	Alex Groza, Kentucky	2	19	—	—	—	14	—	—	—	—	—	26.0
1950	Irwin Dambrot, CCNY	2	12	42.9	—	—	4	50.0	—	—	—	—	14.0
1951	None selected												
1952	Clyde Lovellette, Kansas	2	24	—	—	—	18	—	—	—	—	—	33.0
1953	*B.H. Horn, Kansas	2	17	—	—	—	17	—	—	—	—	—	25.5
1954	Tom Gola, La Salle	2	12	—	—	—	14	—	—	—	—	—	19.0
1955	Bill Russell, San Francisco	2	19	—	—	—	9	—	—	—	—	—	23.5
1956	*Hal Lear, Temple	2	32	—	—	—	16	—	—	—	—	—	40.0
1957	*Wilt Chamberlain, Kansas	2	18	51.4	—	—	19	70.4	25	—	—	—	32.5
1958	*Elgin Baylor, Seattle	2	18	34.0	—	—	12	75.0	41	—	—	—	24.0
1959	*Jerry West, West Virginia	2	22	66.7	—	—	22	68.8	25	—	—	—	33.0
1960	Jerry Lucas, Ohio St	2	16	66.7	—	—	3	100.0	23	—	—	—	17.5
1961	*Jerry Lucas, Ohio St	2	20	71.4	—	—	16	94.1	25	—	—	—	28.0
1962	Paul Hogue, Cincinnati	2	23	63.9	—	—	12	63.2	38	—	—	—	29.0
1963	Art Heyman, Duke	2	18	41.0	—	—	15	68.2	19	—	—	—	25.5
1964	Walt Hazzard, UCLA	2	11	55.0	—	—	8	66.7	10	—	—	—	15.0
1965	*Bill Bradley, Princeton	2	34	63.0	—	—	19	95.0	24	—	—	—	43.5
1966	*Jerry Chambers, Utah	2	25	53.2	—	—	20	83.3	35	—	—	—	35.0
1967	Lew Alcindor, UCLA	2	14	60.9	—	—	11	45.8	38	—	—	—	19.5
1968	Lew Alcindor, UCLA	2	22	62.9	—	—	9	90.0	34	—	—	—	26.5
1969	Lew Alcindor, UCLA	2	23	67.7	—	—	16	64.0	41	—	—	—	31.0
1970	Sidney Wicks, UCLA	2	15	71.4	—	—	9	60.0	34	—	—	—	19.5
1971	*†Howard Porter, Villanova	2	20	48.8	—	—	7	77.8	24	—	—	—	23.5
1972	Bill Walton, UCLA	2	20	69.0	—	—	17	73.9	41	—	—	—	28.5
1973	Bill Walton, UCLA	2	28	82.4	—	—	2	40.0	30	—	—	—	29.0
1974	David Thompson, N.C. St	2	19	51.4	—	—	11	78.6	17	—	—	—	24.5
1975	Richard Washington, UCLA	2	23	54.8	—	—	8	72.7	20	—	—	—	27.0
1976	Kent Benson, Indiana	2	17	50.0	—	—	7	63.6	18	—	—	—	20.5
1977	Butch Lee, Marquette	2	11	34.4	—	—	8	100.0	6	2	1	1	15.0
1978	Jack Givens, Kentucky	2	28	65.1	—	—	8	66.7	17	4	.1	3	32.0
1979	Earvin Johnson, Michigan St	2	17	68.0	—	—	19	86.4	17	3	0	2	26.5
1980	Darrell Griffith, Louisville	2	23	62.2	—	—	11	68.8	7	15	0	2	28.5
1981	Isiah Thomas, Indiana	2	14	56.0	—	—	9	81.8	4	9	3	4	18.5
1982	James Worthy, North Carolina	2	20	74.1	—	—	2	28.6	8	9	0	4	21.0
1983	*Akeem Olajuwon, Houston	2	16	55.2	—	—	9	64.3	40	3	2	5	20.5
1984	Patrick Ewing, Georgetown	2	8	57.1	—	—	2	100.0	18	1	1	15	9.0
1985	Ed Pinckney, Villanova	2	8	57.1	—	—	12	75.0	15	6	3	0	14.0
1986	Pervis Ellison, Louisville	2	15	60.0	—	—	6	75.0	24	2	3	1	18.0

*Not a member of the championship-winning team. †Record later vacated.

NCAA Final Four MOPs *(Cont.)*

Year	Winner, School	GP	Field Goals		3-Pt FG		Free Throws		Reb	Ast	Stl	BS	Avg
			FGM	Pct	FGA	FGM	FTM	Pct					
1987	Keith Smart, Indiana	2	14	63.6	1	0	7	77.8	7	7	0	2	17.5
1988	Danny Manning, Kansas	2	25	55.6	1	0	6	66.7	17	4	8	9	28.0
1989	Glen Rice, Michigan	2	24	49.0	16	7	4	100.0	16	1	0	3	29.5
1990	Anderson Hunt, UNLV	2	19	61.3	16	9	2	50.0	4	9	1	1	24.5
1991	Christian Laettner, Duke	2	12	54.5	1	1	21	91.3	17	2	1	2	23.0
1992	Bobby Hurley, Duke	2	10	41.7	12	7	8	80.0	3	11	0	3	17.5
1993	Donald Williams, North Carolina	2	15	65.2	14	10	10	100.0	4	2	2	0	25.0
1994	Corliss Williamson, Arkansas	2	21	50.0	0	0	10	71.4	21	8	4	3	26.0
1995	Ed O'Bannon, UCLA	2	16	45.7	8	3	10	76.9	25	3	7	1	22.5
1996	Tony Delk, Kentucky	2	15	41.7	16	8	6	54.6	9	2	3	2	22.0
1997	Miles Simon, Arizona	2	17	45.9	10	3	17	77.3	8	6	0	1	27.0
1998	Jeff Sheppard, Kentucky	2	16	55.2	10	4	7	77.8	10	7	4	0	21.5
1999	Richard Hamilton, Connecticut	2	20	51.3	7	3	8	72.7	12	4	2	1	25.5
2000	Mateen Cleaves, Michigan St	2	8	44.4	4	3	10	83.3	6	5	2	0	14.5
2001	Shane Battier, Duke	2	13	50.0	12	5	12	70.6	19	8	2	6	21.5
2002	Juan Dixon, Maryland	2	16	59.3	15	7	12	80.0	8	5	7	0	25.5
2003	Carmelo Anthony, Syracuse	2	19	54.3	6	9	9	81.1	24	8	4	0	26.5
2004	Emeka Okafor, Connecticut	2	17	65.4	0	0	8	53.3	22	2	1	4	21.0
2005	Sean May, North Carolina	2	19	65.5	0	0	10	71.4	17	5	1	2	24.0
2006	Joakim Noah, Florida	2	12	60.0	1	0	4	100.0	17	5	2	10	14.0
2007	Corey Brewer, Florida	2	9	47.3	13	7	7	87.5	10	2	3	5	16.0
2008	Mario Chalmers, Kansas	2	10	43.5	9	3	6	75.0	7	6	7	0	14.5
2009	Wayne Ellington, North Carolina	2	14	53.8	11	8	3	75.0	13	4	0	0	19.5
2010	Kyle Singler, Duke	2	15	34.1	10	6	4	100.0	18	7	3	2	20.0

Best NCAA Tournament Single-Game Scoring Performances

Player and Team	Year	Round	FG	3FG	FT	TP
Austin Carr, Notre Dame vs Ohio	1970	1st	25	—	11	61
Bill Bradley, Princeton vs Wichita St	1965	C*	22	—	14	58
Oscar Robertson, Cincinnati vs Arkansas	1958	C	21	—	14	56
Austin Carr, Notre Dame vs Kentucky	1970	2nd	22	—	8	52
Austin Carr, Notre Dame vs TCU	1971	1st	20	—	12	52
David Robinson, Navy vs Michigan	1987	1st	22	0	6	50
Elvin Hayes, Houston vs Loyola (Ill.)	1968	1st	20	—	9	49
Hal Lear, Temple vs SMU	1956	C*	17	—	14	48
Austin Carr, Notre Dame vs Houston	1971	C	17	—	13	47
Dave Corzine, DePaul vs Louisville	1978	2nd	18	—	10	46

C=regional third place; C*=third-place game.

NIT Championship Results

Year	Winner	Score	Runner-up	Year	Winner	Score	Runner-up
1938	Temple	60–36	Colorado	1958	Xavier (Ohio)	78–74 (OT)	Dayton
1939	Long Island U.	44–32	Loyola (Ill.)	1959	St. John's (N.Y.)	76–71 (OT)	Bradley
1940	Colorado	51–40	Duquesne	1960	Bradley	88–72	Providence
1941	Long Island U.	56–42	Ohio U	1961	Providence	62–59	St. Louis
1942	West Virginia	47–45	W. Kentucky	1962	Dayton	73–67	St. John's (N.Y.)
1943	St. John's (N.Y.)	48–27	Toledo	1963	Providence	81–66	Canisius
1944	St. John's (N.Y.)	47–39	DePaul	1964	Bradley	86–54	New Mexico
1945	DePaul	71–54	Bowling Green	1965	St. John's (N.Y.)	55–51	Villanova
1946	Kentucky	46–45	Rhode Island	1966	BYU	97–84	NYU
1947	Utah	49–45	Kentucky	1967	Southern Illinois	71–56	Marquette
1948	St. Louis	65–52	NYU	1968	Dayton	61–48	Kansas
1949	San Francisco	48–47	Loyola (Ill.)	1969	Temple	89–76	Boston College
1950	CCNY	69–61	Bradley	1970	Marquette	65–53	St. John's (N.Y.)
1951	BYU	62–43	Dayton	1971	North Carolina	84–66	Georgia Tech
1952	La Salle	75–64	Dayton	1972	Maryland	100–69	Niagara
1953	Seton Hall	58–46	St. John's (N.Y.)	1973	Virginia Tech	92–91 (OT)	Notre Dame
1954	Holy Cross	71–62	Duquesne	1974	Purdue	97–81	Utah
1955	Duquesne	70–58	Dayton	1975	Princeton	80–69	Providence
1956	Louisville	93–80	Dayton	1976	Kentucky	71–67	UNC-Charlotte
1957	Bradley	84–83	Memphis St	1977	St. Bonaventure	94–91	Houston

NIT Championship Results *(Cont.)*

Year	Winner	Score	Runner-up	Year	Winner	Score	Runner-up
1978	Texas	101–93	North Carolina St	1995	Virginia Tech	65–64 (OT)	Marquette
1979	Indiana	53–52	Purdue	1996	Nebraska	60–56	St. Joseph's
1980	Virginia	58–55	Minnesota	1997	Michigan	82–73	Florida St
1981	Tulsa	86–84 (OT)	Syracuse	1998	Minnesota	79–72	Penn St
1982	Bradley	67–58	Purdue	1999	California	61–60	Clemson
1983	Fresno St	69–60	DePaul	2000	Wake Forest	71–61	Notre Dame
1984	Michigan	83–63	Notre Dame	2001	Tulsa	79–60	Alabama
1985	UCLA	65–62	Indiana	2002	Memphis	72–62	South Carolina
1986	Ohio St	73–63	Wyoming	2003	St. John's	70–67	Georgetown
1987	Southern Miss	84–80	La Salle	2004	Michigan	62–55	Rutgers
1988	Connecticut	72–67	Ohio St	2005	South Carolina	60–57	Saint Joseph's
1989	St. John's (N.Y.)	73–65	St. Louis	2006	South Carolina	76–64	Michigan
1990	Vanderbilt	74–72	St. Louis	2007	West Virginia	78–73	Clemson
1991	Stanford	78–72	Oklahoma	2008	Ohio St	92–85	Massachusetts
1992	Virginia	81–76	Notre Dame	2009	Penn St	69–63	Baylor
1993	Minnesota	62–61	Georgetown	2010	Dayton	79–68	North Carolina
1994	Villanova	80–73	Vanderbilt				

NCAA Men's Division I Season Leaders

Scoring Average

Year	Player and Team	Ht	Class	GP	FG	3FG	FT	Pts	Avg
1948	Murray Wier, Iowa	5-9	Sr.	19	152	—	95	399	21.0
1949	Tony Lavelli, Yale	6-3	Sr.	30	228	—	215	671	22.4
1950	Paul Arizin, Villanova	6-3	Sr.	29	260	—	215	735	25.3
1951	Bill Mlkvy, Temple	6-4	Sr.	25	303	—	125	731	29.2
1952	Clyde Lovellette, Kansas	6-9	Sr.	28	315	—	165	795	28.4
1953	Frank Selvy, Furman	6-3	Jr.	25	272	—	194	738	29.5
1954	Frank Selvy, Furman	6-3	Sr.	29	427	—	355	1209	41.7
1955	Darrell Floyd, Furman	6-1	Jr.	25	344	—	209	897	35.9
1956	Darrell Floyd, Furman	6-1	Sr.	28	339	—	268	946	33.8
1957	Grady Wallace, South Carolina	6-4	Sr.	29	336	—	234	906	31.2
1958	Oscar Robertson, Cincinnati	6-5	So.	28	352	—	280	984	35.1
1959	Oscar Robertson, Cincinnati	6-5	Jr.	30	331	—	316	978	32.6
1960	Oscar Robertson, Cincinnati	6-5	Sr.	30	369	—	273	1011	33.7
1961	Frank Burgess, Gonzaga	6-1	Sr.	26	304	—	234	842	32.4
1962	Billy McGill, Utah	6-9	Sr.	26	394	—	221	1009	38.8
1963	Nick Werkman, Seton Hall	6-3	Jr.	22	221	—	208	650	29.5
1964	Howard Komives, Bowling Green	6-1	Sr.	23	292	—	260	844	36.7
1965	Rick Barry, Miami (Fla.)	6-7	Sr.	26	340	—	293	973	37.4
1966	Dave Schellhase, Purdue	6-4	Sr.	24	284	—	213	781	32.5
1967	Jim Walker, Providence	6-3	Sr.	28	323	—	205	851	30.4
1968	Pete Maravich, LSU	6-5	So.	26	432	—	274	1138	43.8
1969	Pete Maravich, LSU	6-5	Jr.	26	433	—	282	1148	44.2
1970	Pete Maravich, LSU	6-5	Sr.	31	522	—	337	1381	44.5
1971	Johnny Neumann, Mississippi	6-6	So.	23	366	—	191	923	40.1
1972	Dwight Lamar, SW Louisiana	6-1	Jr.	29	429	—	196	1054	36.3
1973	William Averitt, Pepperdine	6-1	Sr.	25	352	—	144	848	33.9
1974	Larry Fogle, Canisius	6-5	So.	25	326	—	183	835	33.4
1975	Bob McCurdy, Richmond	6-7	Sr.	26	321	—	213	855	32.9
1976	Marshall Rodgers, Tex.-Pan American	6-2	Sr.	25	361	—	197	919	36.8
1977	Freeman Williams, Portland St	6-4	Jr.	26	417	—	176	1010	38.8
1978	Freeman Williams, Portland St	6-4	Sr.	27	410	—	149	969	35.9
1979	Lawrence Butler, Idaho St	6-3	Sr.	27	310	—	192	812	30.1
1980	Tony Murphy, Southern-Birmingham	6-3	Sr.	29	377	—	178	932	32.1
1981	Zam Fredrick, South Carolina	6-2	Sr.	27	300	—	181	781	28.9
1982	Harry Kelly, Texas Southern	6-7	Jr.	29	336	—	190	862	29.7
1983	Harry Kelly, Texas Southern	6-7	Sr.	29	333	—	169	835	28.8
1984	Joe Jakubick, Akron	6-5	Sr.	27	304	—	206	814	30.1
1985	Xavier McDaniel, Wichita St	6-8	Sr.	31	351	—	142	844	27.2
1986	Terrance Bailey, Wagner	6-2	Jr.	29	321	—	212	854	29.4
1987	Kevin Houston, Army	5-11	Sr.	29	311	63	268	953	32.9
1988	Hersey Hawkins, Bradley	6-3	Sr.	31	377	87	284	1125	36.3
1989	Hank Gathers, Loyola Marymount	6-7	Jr.	31	419	0	177	1015	32.7
1990	Bo Kimble, Loyola Marymount	6-5	Sr.	32	404	92	231	1131	35.3

Scoring Average *(Cont.)*

Year	Player and Team	Ht	Class	GP	FG	3FG	FT	Pts	Avg
1991	Kevin Bradshaw, U.S. Int'l	6-6	Sr.	28	358	60	278	1054	37.6
1992	Brett Roberts, Morehead St	6-8	Sr.	29	278	66	193	815	28.1
1993	Greg Guy, Tex.-Pan American	6-1	Jr.	19	189	67	111	556	29.3
1994	Glenn Robinson, Purdue	6-8	Jr.	34	368	79	215	1030	30.3
1995	Kurt Thomas, TCU	6-9	Sr.	27	288	3	202	781	28.9
1996	Kevin Granger, Texas Southern	6-3	Sr.	24	194	30	230	648	27.0
1997	Charles Jones, LIU-Brooklyn	6-3	Jr.	30	338	109	118	903	30.1
1998	Charles Jones, LIU-Brooklyn	6-3	Sr.	30	326	116	101	869	29.0
1999	Alvin Young, Niagara	6-3	Sr.	29	253	65	157	728	25.1
2000	Courtney Alexander, Fresno St	6-6	Sr.	27	252	58	107	669	24.8
2001	Ronnie McCollum, Centenary	6-4	Sr.	27	244	85	214	787	29.1
2002	Jason Conley, Virginia Military	6-5	Fr.	28	285	79	171	820	29.3
2003	Ruben Douglas, New Mexico	6-5	Sr.	28	218	94	253	783	28.0
2004	Keydren Clark, St. Peter's	5-8	So.	29	233	112	197	775	26.7
2005	Keydren Clark, St. Peter's	5-9	Jr.	28	230	109	152	721	25.8
2006	Adam Morrison, Gonzaga	6-8	Jr.	33	306	74	240	926	28.1
2007	Reggie Williams, Virginia Military Institute	6-5	Jr.	33	338	76	176	928	28.1
2008	Stephen Curry, Davidson	6-3	Jr.	34	312	130	220	974	28.6
2009	Aubrey Coleman, Houston	6-4	Sr.	35	305	51	235	896	25.6

Rebounds

Year	Player and Team	Ht	Class	GP	Reb	Avg
1951	Ernie Beck, Pennsylvania	6-4	So.	27	556	20.6
1952	Bill Hannon, Army	6-3	So.	17	355	20.9
1953	Ed Conlin, Fordham	6-5	So.	26	612	23.5
1954	Art Quimby, Connecticut	6-5	Jr.	26	588	22.6
1955	Charlie Slack, Marshall	6-5	Jr.	21	538	25.6
1956	Joe Holup, George Washington	6-6	Sr.	26	604	†.256
1957	Elgin Baylor, Seattle	6-6	Jr.	25	508	†.235
1958	Alex Ellis, Niagara	6-5	Sr.	25	536	†.262
1959	Leroy Wright, Pacific	6-8	Jr.	26	652	†.238
1960	Leroy Wright, Pacific	6-8	Sr.	17	380	†.234
1961	Jerry Lucas, Ohio St	6-8	Jr.	27	470	†.198
1962	Jerry Lucas, Ohio St	6-8	Sr.	28	499	†.211
1963	Paul Silas, Creighton	6-7	Sr.	27	557	20.6
1964	Bob Pelkington, Xavier (Ohio)	6-7	Sr.	26	567	21.8
1965	Toby Kimball, Connecticut	6-8	Sr.	23	483	21.0
1966	Jim Ware, Oklahoma City	6-8	Sr.	29	607	20.9
1967	Dick Cunningham, Murray St	6-10	Jr.	22	479	21.8
1968	Neal Walk, Florida	6-10	Jr.	25	494	19.8
1969	Spencer Haywood, Detroit	6-8	So.	22	472	21.5
1970	Artis Gilmore, Jacksonville	7-2	Jr.	28	621	22.2
1971	Artis Gilmore, Jacksonville	7-2	Sr.	26	603	23.2
1972	Kermit Washington, American	6-8	Jr.	23	455	19.8
1973	Kermit Washington, American	6-8	Sr.	22	439	20.0
1974	Marvin Barnes, Providence	6-9	Sr.	32	597	18.7
1975	John Irving, Hofstra	6-9	So.	21	323	15.4
1976	Sam Pellom, Buffalo	6-8	So.	26	420	16.2
1977	Glenn Mosley, Seton Hall	6-8	Sr.	29	473	16.3
1978	Ken Williams, North Texas St	6-7	Sr.	28	411	14.7
1979	Monti Davis, Tennessee St	6-7	Jr.	26	421	16.2
1980	Larry Smith, Alcorn St	6-8	Sr.	26	392	15.1
1981	Darryl Watson, Miss. Valley St	6-7	Sr.	27	379	14.0
1982	LaSalle Thompson, Texas	6-10	Jr.	27	365	13.5
1983	Xavier McDaniel, Wichita St	6-7	So.	28	403	14.4
1984	Akeem Olajuwon, Houston	7-0	Jr.	37	500	13.5
1985	Xavier McDaniel, Wichita St	6-8	Sr	31	460	14.8
1986	David Robinson, Navy	6-11	Jr.	35	455	13.0
1987	Jerome Lane, Pittsburgh	6-6	So.	33	444	13.5
1988	Kenny Miller, Loyola (Ill.)	6-9	Fr.	29	395	13.6
1989	Hank Gathers, Loyola (Calif.)	6-7	Jr.	31	426	13.7
1990	Anthony Bonner, St. Louis	6-8	Sr.	33	456	13.8
1991	Shaquille O'Neal, LSU	7-1	So.	28	411	14.7
1992	Popeye Jones, Murray St	6-8	Sr.	30	431	14.4

Rebounds (Cont.)

Year	Player and Team	Ht	Class	GP	Reb	Avg
1993	Warren Kidd, Middle Tenn. St	6-9	Sr.	26	386	14.8
1994	Jerome Lambert, Baylor	6-8	Jr.	24	355	14.8
1995	Kurt Thomas, TCU	6-9	Sr.	27	393	14.6
1996	Marcus Mann, Miss. Valley St	6-8	Sr.	29	394	13.6
1997	Tim Duncan, Wake Forest	6-11	Sr.	31	457	14.7
1998	Ryan Perryman, Dayton	6-7	Sr.	33	412	12.5
1999	Ian McGinnis, Dartmouth	6-8	So.	26	317	12.2
2000	Darren Phillips, Fairfield	6-7	Sr.	29	405	14.0
2001	Chris Marcus, Western Kentucky	7-1	Jr.	31	374	12.1
2002	Jeremy Bishop, Quinnipiac	6-6	J..	29	347	12.0
2003	Brandon Hunter, Ohio	6-7	Sr.	30	378	12.6
2004	Paul Millsap, Louisiana Tech	6-7	Fr.	30	374	12.5
2005	Paul Millsap, Louisiana Tech	6-8	So.	29	360	12.4
2006	Paul Millsap, Louisiana Tech	6-8	Jr.	33	438	13.3
2007	Rashad Jones-Jennings, Ark-Little Rock	6-8	Sr.	30	392	13.3
2008	Blake Griffin, Oklahoma	6-10	So.	35	504	14.4
2009	Artsiom Parakhouski, Radford	6-11	Sr.	31	414	13.4

†From 1956–1962, title was based on highest individual recoveries out of total by both teams in all games.

Assists

Year	Player and Team	Class	GP	Ast	Avg
1984	Craig Lathen, Ill.-Chicago	Jr.	29	274	9.45
1985	Rob Weingard, Hofstra	Sr.	24	228	9.50
1986	Mark Jackson, St. John's (N.Y.)	Jr.	36	328	9.11
1987	Avery Johnson, Southern-Birm.	Jr.	31	333	10.74
1988	Avery Johnson, Southern-Birm.	Sr.	30	399	13.30
1989	Glenn Williams, Holy Cross	Sr.	28	278	9.93
1990	Todd Lehmann, Drexel	Sr.	28	260	9.29
1991	Chris Corchiani, North Carolina St	Sr.	31	299	9.65
1992	Van Usher, Tennessee Tech	Sr.	29	254	8.76
1993	Sam Crawford, New Mex. St	Sr.	34	310	9.12
1994	Jason Kidd, California	So.	30	272	9.06
1995	Nelson Haggerty, Baylor	Sr.	28	284	10.10
1996	Raimonds Miglinieks, UC-Irvine	Sr.	27	230	8.52
1997	Kenny Mitchell, Dartmouth	Sr.	26	203	7.81
1998	Ahlon Lewis, Arizona St	Sr.	32	294	9.19
1999	Doug Gottlieb, Oklahoma St	Jr.	34	299	8.79
2000	Mark Dickel, UNLV	Sr.	31	280	9.03
2001	Markus Carr, CSU–Northridge	Jr.	32	286	8.94
2002	T.J. Ford, Texas	Fr.	33	273	8.27
2003	Martell Bailey, Ill.-Chicago	Jr.	30	244	8.13
2004	Greg Davis, Troy St	Sr.	31	256	8.26
2005	Damitrius Coleman, Mercer	Jr.	28	224	8.00
	Will Funn, Portland St	Sr.	28	224	8.00
2006	Jared Jordan, Marist	Jr.	29	247	8.52
2007	Jared Jordan, Marist	Sr.	31	274	8.83
2008	Johnathon Jones, Oakland	Jr.	36	290	8.06
2009	Ronald Moore, Siena	Sr.	34	261	7.68

Blocked Shots

Year	Player and Team	Class	GP	BS	Avg
1986	David Robinson, Navy	Jr.	35	207	5.91
1987	David Robinson, Navy	Sr.	32	144	4.50
1988	Rodney Blake, St. Joseph's (Pa.)	Sr.	29	116	4.00
1989	Alonzo Mourning, Georgetown	Fr.	34	169	4.97
1990	Kenny Green, Rhode Island	Sr.	26	124	4.77
1991	Shawn Bradley, BYU	Fr.	34	177	5.21
1992	Shaquille O'Neal, LSU	Jr.	30	157	5.23
1993	Theo Ratliff, Wyoming	Jr.	28	124	4.43
1994	Grady Livingston, Howard	Jr.	26	115	4.42
1995	Keith Closs, Central Conn. St	Fr.	26	139	5.35
1996	Keith Closs, Central Conn. St	So.	28	178	6.36
1997	Adonal Foyle, Colgate	Jr.	28	180	6.43
1998	Jerome James, Florida A&M	Sr.	27	125	4.63
1999	Tarvis Williams, Hampton	Jr.	27	135	5.00
2000	Ken Johnson, Ohio St	Sr.	30	161	5.37
2001	Tarvis Williams, Hampton	Sr	32	147	4.59
2002	Wojciech Myrda, La.-Monroe	Sr.	32	172	5.38
2003	Emeka Okafor, Connecticut	So.	33	156	4.73
2004	Anwar Ferguson, Houston	Sr.	27	111	4.11
2005	Deng Gai, Fairfield	Sr.	30	165	5.50
2006	Shawn James, Northeastern	So.	30	196	6.53
2007	Mickell Gladness, Ala.-A&M	Jr.	30	188	6.26
2008	Jarvis Varnado, Mississippi St	Jr.	36	170	4.72
2009	Hassan Whiteside, Marshall	Fr.	34	182	5.35

Steals

Year	Player and Team	Class	GP	Stl	Avg
1986	Darron Brittman, Chicago St	Sr.	28	139	4.96
1987	Tony Fairley, Charleston South.	Sr.	28	114	4.07
1988	Aldwin Ware, Florida A&M	Sr.	29	142	4.90
1989	Kenny Robertson, Cleveland St	Jr.	28	111	3.96
1990	Ronn McMahon, E. Washington	Sr.	29	130	4.48
1991	Van Usher, Tennessee Tech	Jr.	28	104	3.71
1992	Victor Snipes, NE Illinois	So.	25	86	3.44
1993	Jason Kidd, California	Fr.	29	110	3.80
1994	Shawn Griggs, SW Louisiana	Sr.	30	120	4.00
1995	Roderick Anderson, Texas	Sr.	30	101	3.37
1996	Pointer Williams, McNeese St	Sr.	27	118	4.37
1997	Joel Hoover, Md.-Eastern Shore	Fr.	28	90	3.21
1998	Bonzi Wells, Ball St	Sr.	29	103	3.55
1999	Shawnta Rogers, George Wash.	Sr.	29	103	3.55
2000	Carl Williams, Liberty	Sr.	28	107	3.82
2001	Greedy Daniels, TCU	Jr.	25	108	4.32
2002	Desmond Cambridge, Ala. A&M	Sr.	29	160	5.52
2003	Alexis McMillan, Stetson	Sr.	22	87	3.95
2004	Marques Green, St. Bonaventure	Sr.	27	107	3.96
2005	Obie Trotter, Alabama A&M	Jr.	32	125	3.91
2006	Tim Smith, East Tennessee St	Sr.	28	95	3.39
2007	Travis Holmes, Virg. Mil. Inst.	So.	33	111	3.36
2008	Chavis Holmes, Virg. Mil. Inst.	Sr.	31	105	3.39
2009	Jay Threatt, Delaware St	So.	29	82	2.83

Single Game Records

SCORING HIGHS VS DIVISION I OPPONENT

Pts	Player and Team vs Opponent	Date
72	Kevin Bradshaw, U.S. Int'l vs Loyola Marymount	1-5-91
69	Pete Maravich, LSU vs Alabama	2-7-70
68	Calvin Murphy, Niagara vs Syracuse	12-7-68
66	Jay Handlan, Washington & Lee vs Furman	2-17-51
66	Pete Maravich, LSU vs Tulane	2-10-69
66	Anthony Roberts, Oral Roberts vs North Carolina A&T	2-19-77
65	Anthony Roberts, Oral Roberts vs Oregon	3-9-77
65	Scott Haffner, Evansville vs Dayton	2-18-89
64	Pete Maravich, LSU vs Kentucky	2-21-70
63	Johnny Neumann, Mississippi vs LSU	1-30-71
63	Hersey Hawkins, Bradley vs Detroit	2-22-88

SCORING HIGHS VS NON-DIVISION I OPPONENT

Pts	Player and Team vs Opponent	Date
100	Frank Selvy, Furman vs Newberry	2-13-54
85	Paul Arizin, Villanova vs Philadelphia NAMC	2-12-49
81	Freeman Williams, Portland St vs Rocky Mountain	2-3-78
73	Bill Mlkvy, Temple vs Wilkes	3-3-51
71	Freeman Williams, Portland St vs S. Oregon	2-9-77

REBOUNDING HIGHS ALL-TIME

Reb	Player and Team vs Opponent	Date
51	Bill Chambers, William & Mary vs Virginia	2-14-53
43	Charlie Slack, Marshall vs Morris Harvey	1-12-54
42	Tom Heinsohn, Holy Cross vs Boston College	3-1-55
40	Art Quimby, Connecticut vs Boston University	1-11-55
39	Maurice Stokes, St. Francis (Pa.) vs John Carroll	1-28-55
39	Dave DeBusschere, Detroit vs C. Michigan	1-30-60
39	Keith Swagerty, Pacific vs UC-Santa Barbara	3-5-65

REBOUNDING HIGHS SINCE 1973*

Reb	Player and Team vs Opponent	Date
35	Larry Abney, Fresno St vs SMU	2-17-00
34	David Vaughn, Oral Roberts vs Brandeis	1-8-73
32	Jervaughn Scales, Southern-Birm. vs Grambling	2-7-94
32	Durand Macklin, LSU vs Tulane	11-26-76
31	Jim Bradley, Northern Illinois vs UW-Milwaukee	2-19-73
31	Calvin Natt, NE Louisiana vs Georgia Southern	12-29-76

ASSISTS

Asst	Player and Team vs Opponent	Date
22	Tony Fairley, Baptist vs Armstrong St	2-9-87
22	Avery Johnson, Southern-Birm. vs Texas Southern	1-25-88
22	Sherman Douglas, Syracuse vs Providence	1-28-89
21	Kelvin Scarborough, New Mexico vs Hawaii	2-13-87
21	Anthony Manuel, Bradley vs UC-Irvine	12-19-87
21	Avery Johnson, Southern-Birm. vs Alabama St	1-16-88

STEALS

Stl	Player and Team vs Opponent	Date
13	Mookie Blaylock, Oklahoma vs Centenary	12-12-87
13	Mookie Blaylock, Oklahoma vs Loyola Marymount	12-17-88
12	Kenny Robertson, Cleveland St vs Wagner	12-3-88
12	Terry Evans, Oklahoma vs Florida A&M	1-27-93
12	Richard Duncan, Middle Tenn. St vs Eastern Kentucky	2-20-99
12	Greedy Daniels, Texas Christian vs Ark.–Pine Bluff	12-30-00
12	Jehiel Lewis, Navy vs Bucknell	1-12-02
12	Carldell Johnson, Ala.-Birmingham vs. South Carolina St	11-27-05

BLOCKED SHOTS

BS	Player and Team vs Opponent	Date
16	Mickell Gladness, Alabama A&M vs Texas Southern	2-24-07
14	David Robinson, Navy vs UNC–Wilmington	1-4-86
14	Shawn Bradley, BYU vs Eastern Kentucky	12-7-90
14	Roy Rogers, Alabama vs Georgia	2-10-96
14	Loren Woods, Arizona vs Oregon	2-3-00
14	Darrius Garrett, Richmond vs Massachusetts	1-13-10

Eleven players tied with 13

Single Season Records

POINTS

Player and Team	Year	GP	FG	3FG	FT	Pts
Pete Maravich, LSU	1970	31	522	—	337	1381
Elvin Hayes, Houston	1968	33	519	—	176	1214
Frank Selvy, Furman	1954	29	427	—	355	1209
Pete Maravich, LSU	1969	26	433	—	282	1148
Pete Maravich, LSU	1968	26	432	—	274	1138
Bo Kimble, Loyola Marymount	1990	32	404	92	231	1131
Hersey Hawkins, Bradley	1988	31	377	87	284	1125
Austin Carr, Notre Dame	1970	29	444	—	218	1106
Austin Carr, Notre Dame	1971	29	430	—	241	1101
Otis Birdsong, Houston	1977	36	452	—	186	1090

SCORING AVERAGE

Player and Team	Year	GP	FG	3FG	FT	Pts
Pete Maravich, LSU	1970	31	522	337	1381	44.5
Pete Maravich, LSU	1969	26	433	282	1148	44.2
Pete Maravich, LSU	1968	26	432	274	1138	43.8
Frank Selvy, Furman	1954	29	427	355	1209	41.7
Johnny Neumann, Mississippi	1971	23	366	191	923	40.1
Freeman Williams, Portland St	1977	26	417	176	1010	38.8
Billy McGill, Utah	1962	26	394	221	1009	38.8
Calvin Murphy, Niagara	1968	24	337	242	916	38.2
Austin Carr, Notre Dame	1970	29	444	218	1106	38.1
Austin Carr, Notre Dame	1971	29	430	241	1101	38.0

REBOUNDS

Player and Team	Year	GP	Reb	Player and Team	Year	GP	Reb
Walt Dukes, Seton Hall	1953	33	734	Artis Gilmore, Jacksonville	1970	28	621
Leroy Wright, Pacific	1959	26	652	Tom Gola, La Salle	1955	31	618
Tom Gola, La Salle	1954	30	652	Ed Conlin, Fordham	1953	26	612
Charlie Tyra, Louisville	1956	29	645	Art Quimby, Connecticut	1955	25	611
Paul Silas, Creighton	1964	29	631	Bill Russell, San Francisco	1956	29	609
Elvin Hayes, Houston	1968	33	624	Jim Ware, Oklahoma City	1966	29	607

REBOUND AVERAGE ALL-TIME

Player and Team	Year	GP	Reb	Avg
Charlie Slack, Marshall	1955	21	538	25.6
Leroy Wright, Pacific	1959	26	652	25.1
Art Quimby, Connecticut	1955	25	611	24.4
Charlie Slack, Marshall	1956	22	520	23.6
Ed Conlin, Fordham	1953	26	612	23.5

REBOUND AVERAGE SINCE 1973*

Player and Team	Year	GP	Reb	Avg
Kermit Washington, American	1973	22	439	20.0
Marvin Barnes, Providence	1973	30	571	19.0
Marvin Barnes, Providence	1974	32	597	18.7
Pete Padgett, Nev.-Reno	1973	26	462	17.8
Jim Bradley, Northern Illinois	1973	24	426	17.8

ASSISTS

Player and Team	Year	GP	Asst	Player and Team	Year	GP	Asst
Mark Wade, UNLV	1987	38	406	Sherman Douglas, Syracuse	1989	38	326
Avery Johnson, Southern-Birm.	1988	30	399	Sam Crawford, New Mex. St	1993	34	310
Anthony Manuel, Bradley	1988	31	373	Greg Anthony, UNLV	1991	35	310
Avery Johnson, Southern-Birm.	1987	31	333	Reid Gettys, Houston	1984	37	309
Mark Jackson, St. John's (N.Y.)	1986	32	328	Carl Golston, Loyola (Ill.)	1985	33	305

ASSIST AVERAGE

Player and Team	Year	GP	Asst	Avg	Player and Team	Year	GP	Asst	Avg
Avery Johnson, Southern-Birm.	1988	30	399	13.3	Chris Corchiani, North Carolina St.	1991	31	299	9.6
Anthony Manuel, Bradley	1988	31	373	12.0	Tony Fairley, Charleston South.†	1987	28	270	9.6
Avery Johnson, Southern-Birm.	1987	31	333	10.7	Tyrone Bogues, Wake Forest	1987	29	276	9.5
Mark Wade, UNLV	1987	38	406	10.7	Ron Weingard, Hofstra	1985	24	228	9.5
Nelson Haggerty, Baylor	1995	28	284	10.1	Craig Neal, Georgia Tech	1988	32	303	9.5
Glenn Williams, Holy Cross	1989	28	278	9.9					

*Freshmen became eligible for varsity play in 1973. †Formerly Baptist College.

Single Season Records *(Cont.)*

FIELD-GOAL PERCENTAGE

Player and Team	Year	GP	FG	FGA	Pct
Steve Johnson, Oregon St	1981	28	235	315	74.6
Dwayne Davis, Florida	1989	33	179	248	72.2
Keith Walker, Utica	1985	27	154	216	71.3
Steve Johnson, Oregon St	1980	30	211	297	71.0
Adam Mark, Belmont	2002	26	150	212	70.8
Oliver Miller, Arkansas	1991	38	254	361	70.4
Alan Williams, Princeton	1987	25	163	232	70.3
Mark McNamara, California	1982	27	231	329	70.2
Warren Kidd, Middle Tennessee St	1991	30	173	247	70.0
Pete Freeman, Akron	1991	28	175	250	70.0

Based on qualifiers for annual championship.

FREE-THROW PERCENTAGE

Player and Team	Year	GP	FT	FTA	Pct
Blake Ahearn, SW Missouri St†	2004	33	117	120	97.5
Ryan Toolson, Utah Valley St	2006	29	96	99	97.0
Derek Raivio, Gonzaga	2006	33	146	152	96.1
Craig Collins, Penn St	1985	27	94	98	95.9
A.J. Graves, Butler	2006	32	137	143	95.8
J.J. Redick, Duke	2004	37	143	150	95.3
Steve Drabyn, Belmont	2003	29	78	82	95.1
Donald Sims, Appalachian St	2009	37	175	184	95.1
Rod Foster, UCLA	1982	27	95	100	95.0
Clay McKnight, Pacific	2000	24	74	78	94.9
Matt Logie, Lehigh	2003	28	91	96	94.8

THREE-POINT FIELD-GOAL PERCENTAGE

Player and Team	Year	GP	3FG	3FGA	Pct
Glenn Tropf, Holy Cross	1988	29	52	82	63.4
Sean Wightman, Western Michigan	1992	30	48	76	63.2
Keith Jennings, East Tennessee St	1991	33	84	142	59.2
Dave Calloway, Monmouth (N.J.)	1989	28	48	82	58.5
Steve Kerr, Arizona	1988	38	114	199	57.3
Reginald Jones, Prairie View	1987	28	64	112	57.1
Jim Cantamessa, Siena	1998	29	66	117	56.4
Joel Tribelhorn, Colorado St	1989	33	76	135	56.3
Mike Joseph, Bucknell	1988	28	65	116	56.0
Brian Jackson, Evansville	1995	27	53	95	55.8

Based on qualifiers for annual championship.

STEALS

Player and Team	Year	GP	Stl
Desmond Cambridge, Alabama A&M	2002	29	160
Mookie Blaylock, Oklahoma	1988	39	150
Aldwin Ware, Florida A&M	1988	29	142
Darron Brittman, Chicago St	1986	28	139
John Linehan, Providence	2002	31	139

STEAL AVERAGE

Player and Team	Year	GP	Stl	Avg
D. Cambridge, Alabama A&M	2002	29	160	5.52
Darron Brittman, Chicago St	1986	28	139	4.96
Aldwin Ware, Florida A&M	1988	29	142	4.90
John Linehan, Providence	2002	31	139	4.48
Ronn McMahon, E. Washington	1990	29	130	4.48

BLOCKED SHOTS

Player and Team	Year	GP	BS
David Robinson, Navy	1986	35	207
Shawn James, Northeastern	2005	30	196
Mickell Gladness, Alabama A&M	2006	30	188
Hassan Whiteside, Marshall	2010	34	182
Adonal Foyle, Colgate	1997	28	180

BLOCKED-SHOT AVERAGE

Player and Team	Year	GP	BS	Avg
Shawn James, Northeastern	2005	30	196	6.53
Adonal Foyle, Colgate	1997	28	180	6.43
Keith Closs, Central Conn. St	1996	28	178	6.36
Mickell Gladness, Alabama A&M	2006	30	188	6.26
David Robinson, Navy	1986	35	207	5.91

†Southwest Missouri State changed name to Missouri State after 2004–05 season
Based on qualifiers for annual championship.

Career Records

POINTS

Player and Team	Ht	Final Year	GP	FG	3FG*	FT	Pts
Pete Maravich, LSU	6-5	1970	83	1387	—	893	3667
Freeman Williams, Portland St.	6-4	1978	106	1369	—	511	3249
Lionel Simmons, La Salle	6-7	1990	131	1244	56	673	3217
Alphonso Ford, Mississippi Valley St.	6-2	1993	109	1121	333	590	3165
Harry Kelly, Texas Southern	6-7	1983	110	1234	—	598	3066
Keydren Clark, St. Peter's	5-9	2006	118	967	435	689	3058
Hersey Hawkins, Bradley	6-3	1988	125	1100	118	690	3008
Oscar Robertson, Cincinnati	6-5	1960	88	1052	—	869	2973
Danny Manning, Kansas	6-10	1988	147	1216	10	509	2951
Alfredrick Hughes, Loyola (Ill.)	6-5	1985	120	1226	—	462	2914
Elvin Hayes, Houston	6-8	1968	93	1215	—	454	2884
Tyler Hansbrough, North Carolina	6-9	2009	142	939	12	982	2872
Larry Bird, Indiana St.	6-9	1979	94	1154	—	542	2850
Otis Birdsong, Houston	6-4	1977	116	1176	—	480	2832
Kevin Bradshaw, Bethune-Cookman, U.S. Int'l	6-6	1991	111	1027	132	618	2804
Allan Houston, Tennessee	6-6	1993	128	902	346	651	2801
J.J. Redick, Duke	6-4	2006	139	825	457	662	2769
Hank Gathers, USC, Loyola Marymount	6-7	1990	117	1127	0	469	2723
Reggie Lewis, Northeastern	6-7	1987	122	1043	30 (1)	592	2708
Daren Queenan, Lehigh	6-5	1988	118	1024	29	626	2703

*Listed is the number of three-pointers scored since it became the national rule in 1987; the number in the parentheses is number scored prior to 1987—these counted as three points in the game but counted as two-pointers in the national rankings. The three-pointers in the parentheses are not included in total points.

SCORING AVERAGE

Player and Team	Final Year	GP	FG	FT	Pts	Avg
Pete Maravich, LSU	1968	83	1387	893	3667	44.2
Austin Carr, Notre Dame	1971	74	1017	526	2560	34.6
Oscar Robertson, Cincinnati	1960	88	1052	869	2973	33.8
Calvin Murphy, Niagara	1970	77	947	654	2548	33.1
Dwight Lamar, SW Louisiana	1973	57	768	326	1862	32.7
Frank Selvy, Furman	1954	78	922	694	2538	32.5
Rick Mount, Purdue	1970	72	910	503	2323	32.3
Darrell Floyd, Furman	1956	71	868	545	2281	32.1
Nick Werkman, Seton Hall	1964	71	812	649	2273	32.0
Willie Humes, Idaho St.	1971	48	565	380	1510	31.5
William Averitt, Pepperdine	1973	49	615	311	1541	31.4
Elgin Baylor, Coll. of Idaho; Seattle	1958	80	956	588	2500	31.3
Elvin Hayes, Houston	1968	93	1215	454	2884	31.0
Freeman Williams, Portland St	1978	106	1369	511	3249	30.7
Larry Bird, Indiana St	1979	94	1154	542	2850	30.3

Career Records *(Cont.)*

REBOUNDS ALL-TIME

Player and Team	Final Year	GP	Reb
Tom Gola, La Salle	1955	118	2201
Joe Holup, George Washington	1956	104	2030
Charlie Slack, Marshall	1956	88	1916
Ed Conlin, Fordham	1955	102	1884
Dickie Hemric, Wake Forest	1955	104	1802

REBOUNDS SINCE 1973*

Player and Team	Final Year	GP	Reb
Tim Duncan, Wake Forest	1997	128	1570
Derrick Coleman, Syracuse	1990	143	1537
Malik Rose, Drexel	1996	120	1514
Ralph Sampson, Virginia	1983	132	1511
Pete Padgett, Nev.-Reno	1976	104	1464

ASSISTS

Player and Team	Final Year	GP	Asst
Bobby Hurley, Duke	1993	140	1076
Chris Corchiani, North Carolina St	1991	124	1038
Ed Cota, North Carolina	2000	138	1030
Keith Jennings, East Tennessee St	1991	127	983
Steve Blake, Maryland	2003	138	972

FIELD-GOAL PERCENTAGE

Player and Team	Final Year	FG	FGA	Pct
Steve Johnson, Oregon St	1981	828	1222	67.8
Michael Bradley, Kentucky/Villanova	2001	441	651	67.7
Murray Brown, Florida St	1980	566	847	66.8
Lee Campbell, SW Missouri St	1990	411	618	66.5
Warren Kidd, Middle Tennessee St	1993	496	747	66.4

Note: Minimum 400 field goals and 4 FG made per game.

FREE-THROW PERCENTAGE

Player and Team	Final Year	FT	FTA	Pct
Blake Ahearn, Missouri St	2007	435	460	94.6
Derek Raivio, Gonzaga	2007	343	370	92.7
Gary Buchanan, Villanova	2003	324	355	91.3
J.J. Redick, Duke	2006	662	726	91.2
Greg Starrick, Kentucky/Southern Illinois	1972	341	375	90.9

Note: Minimum 300 free throws made.

*Freshmen became eligible for varsity play in 1973.

Career Records *(Cont.)*

THREE-POINT FIELD GOALS MADE

Player and Team	Final Year	GP	3FG
J.J. Redick, Duke	2006	139	457
David Holston, Chicago St.	2009	119	450
Keydren Clark, St. Peter's	2006	118	435
Chris Lofton, Tennessee	2008	128	431
Stephen Curry, Davidson	2009	104	414

THREE-POINT FIELD-GOAL PERCENTAGE

Player and Team	Final Year	3FG	3FGA	Pct
Tony Bennett, UW–Green Bay	1992	290	584	49.7
Stephen Sir, San Diego St/Northern Ariz.	2007	323	689	46.9
David Olson, Eastern Illinois	1992	262	562	46.6
Jaycee Carroll, Utah St	2008	369	793	46.5
Ross Land, Northern Arizona	2000	308	664	46.4

Note: Minimum 200 3-point field goals and 2.0 3FG/G.

STEALS

Player and Team	Final Year	GP	Stl
John Linehan, Providence	2002	122	385
Eric Murdock, Providence	1991	117	376
Pepe Sanchez, Temple	2000	116	365
Cookie Belcher, Nebraska	2001	131	353
Kevin Braswell, Georgetown	2002	128	349

BLOCKED SHOTS

Player and Team	Final Year	GP	BS
Jarvis Varnado, Mississipi St	2010	141	564
Wojciech Myrda, La.-Monroe	2002	115	535
Adonal Foyle, Colgate	1997	87	492
Tim Duncan, Wake Forest	1997	128	481
Alonzo Mourning, Georgetown	1992	120	453

NCAA Men's Division I Team Leaders

Division I Team Alltime Wins

Team	First Year	Yrs	W	L	T
Kentucky	1903	107	2023	638	1
North Carolina	1911	100	2004	720	0
Kansas	1899	112	2003	796	0
Duke	1906	105	1912	822	0
Syracuse	1901	109	1783	811	0
Temple	1895	114	1740	966	0
St. John's (N.Y.)	1908	103	1703	884	0
UCLA	1920	91	1686	744	0
Notre Dame	1898	105	1674	920	1
Pennsylvania	1897	110	1664	971	2
Indiana	1901	110	1651	930	0
Utah	1909	102	1651	875	0
Illinois	1906	105	1630	868	0
Western Kentucky	1915	91	1623	793	0
Washington	1896	108	1617	1057	0

Note: Minimum of 25 years in Division I.

Division I Alltime Winning Percentage

Team	First Year	Yrs	W	L	T	Pct
Kentucky	1903	106	2023	638	1	.758
North Carolina	1911	99	2004	720	0	.738
Kansas	1899	111	2003	796	0	.713
UNLV	1959	51	1083	438	0	.711
Duke	1906	104	1912	822	0	.697
UCLA	1920	90	1686	744	0	.697
Syracuse	1901	108	1783	811	0	.685
Western Kentucky	1915	90	1623	793	0	.673
St. John's (N.Y.)	1908	102	1703	884	0	.660
Louisville	1912	95	1607	844	0	.656
Utah	1909	101	1651	875	0	.656
Illinois	1906	104	1630	868	0	.654
Notre Dame	1898	104	1674	920	1	.645
Temple	1895	114	1740	966	0	.643
Missouri St	1909	98	1522	845	0	.643

NCAA Men's Division I Winning Streaks

Longest—Full Season

Team	Games	Years	Ended by
UCLA	88	1971–74	Notre Dame (71–70)
San Francisco	60	1955–57	Illinois (62–33)
UCLA	47	1966–68	Houston (71–69)
UNLV	45	1990–91	Duke (79–77)
Texas	44	1913–17	Rice (24–18)
Seton Hall	43	1939–41	LIU-Brooklyn (49–26)
LIU-Brooklyn	43	1935–37	Stanford (45–31)
UCLA	41	1968–69	USC (46–44)
Marquette	39	1970–71	Ohio St (60–59)
Cincinnati	37	1962–63	Wichita St (65–64)
North Carolina	37	1957–58	West Virginia (75–64)

Longest—Regular Season

Team	Games	Years	Ended by
UCLA	76	1971–74	Notre Dame (71–70)
Indiana	57	1975–77	Toledo (59–57)
Marquette	56	1970–72	Detroit (70–49)
Kentucky	54	1952–55	Georgia Tech (59–58)
San Francisco	51	1955–57	Illinois (62–33)
Pennsylvania	48	1970–72	Temple (57–52)
Ohio State	47	1960–62	Wisconsin (86–67)
Texas	44	1913–17	Rice (24–18)
UCLA	43	1966–68	Houston (71–69)
LIU-Brooklyn	43	1935–37	Stanford (45–31)
Seton Hall	42	1939–41	LIU-Brooklyn (49–26)

Longest—Home Court

Team	Games	Years	Team	Games	Years
Kentucky	129	1943–55	Lamar	80	1978–84
St. Bonaventure	99	1948–61	Long Beach St	75	1968–74
UCLA	98	1970–76	UNLV	72	1974–78
Cincinnati	86	1957–64	Arizona	71	1987–92
Marquette	81	1967–73	Cincinnati	68	1972–78
Arizona	81	1945–51	Western Kentucky	67	1949–55

Active Coaches*

WINS

Coach and Team	W
Mike Krzyzewski, Duke	.868
Jim Boeheim, Syracuse	.829
Jim Calhoun, Connecticut	.823
Bob Huggins, West Virginia	.670
Gary Williams, Maryland	.649
Tom Penders, Houston	.648
Homer Drew, Valparaiso	.617
Roy Williams, North Carolina	.614
Bo Ryan, Wisconsin	.600
Mike Montgomery, California	.593

Note: Minimum 5 years as a Division I head coach; includes record at 4-year colleges only.

WINNING PERCENTAGE

Coach and Team	Yrs	W	L	Pct
Mark Few, Gonzaga	11	291	73	.799
Roy Williams, North Carolina	22	614	155	.798
Jamie Dixon, Pittsburgh	7	188	54	.777
Bruce Pearl, Tennessee	18	443	130	.773
Bo Ryan, Wisconsin	26	600	185	.764
Dave Rose, BYU	5	127	40	.760
Mike Krzyzewski, Duke	35	868	279	.757
John Calipari, Kentucky	18	438	141	.756
Thad Matta, Ohio St	10	258	85	.752
Jim Boeheim, Syracuse	34	829	293	.739

Note: Minimum 5 years as a Division I head coach; includes record at 4-year colleges only.

Alltime Winningest Men's Division I Coaches

	W
Bob Knight (Army, Indiana, Texas Tech)	.902
Dean Smith (North Carolina)	.879
Adolph Rupp (Kentucky)	.876
*Mike Krzyzewski (Army, Duke)	.868
Jim Phelan (Mt. St. Mary's)	.830
*Jim Boeheim (Syracuse)	.829
*Jim Calhoun (Northeastern, Connecticut)	.823
Eddie Sutton (Creighton, Arkansas, Kentucky, Oklahoma St)	.804
Lefty Driesell (Davidson, Maryland, James Madison, Georgia St)	.786
Lute Olson (Long Beach St, Iowa, Arizona)	.780
Lou Henson (Hardin-Simmons, New Mexico St, Illinois, New Mexico St)	.779
Henry Iba (NW Missouri St, Colorado, Oklahoma St)	.764
Ed Diddle (Western Kentucky)	.759
Phog Allen (Baker, Kansas, Haskell, Central Missouri St, Kansas)	.746
John Chaney (Cheyney St, Temple)	.741
Jerry Tarkanian (Long Beach St, UNLV, Fresno St)	.729
Norm Stewart (Northern Iowa, Missouri)	.728
Ray Meyer (DePaul)	.724
Don Haskins (Oklahoma St, UTEP)	.719
Denny Crum (UCLA, Louisville)	.675
*Bob Huggins (Akron, Cincinnati, Kansas St, West Virginia)	.670
John Wooden (Purdue, Indiana St, UCLA)	.664
Ralph Miller (Wichita St, Iowa, Oregon St)	.657
*Gary Williams (American, Boston College, Ohio St, Maryland)	.649
*Tom Penders (Tufts, Columbia, Fordham, URI, Texas, George Wash., Houston)	.648
Gene Bartow (C. Missouri St, Valparaiso, Memphis, Illinois, UCLA, UAB)	.647
Billy Tubbs (Lamar, Southwestern [Tex.], Oklahoma, TCU)	.641
Marv Harshman (Pacific Lutheran, Washington St, Washington)	.637

Note: Minimum 10 head coaching seasons in Division I.

*Active in 2009–10.

Alltime Winningest Men's Division I Coaches *(Cont.)*
WINNING PERCENTAGE

Coach (Team, Years)	Yrs	W	L	Pct
Clair Bee (Rider 1929–31, LIU-Brooklyn 1932–45, 1946–51)	21	412	87	.826
Adolph Rupp (Kentucky 1931–72)	41	876	190	.822
John Wooden (Indiana St 1947–48, UCLA 1949–75)	29	664	162	.804
*Mark Few (Gonzaga 1999–)	11	291	73	.799
*Roy Williams (Kansas 1989–2003, North Carolina 2003–)	22	614	155	.798
John Kresse (College of Charleston 1980–2002)	23	560	143	.797
Jerry Tarkanian (Long Beach St 1969–73, UNLV 1974–92, Fresno St 1995–2002)	31	729	201	.784
Francis Schmidt (Tulsa 1916–17, Arkansas 1924–29, TCU 1930–34)	17	258	72	.782
Dean Smith (North Carolina 1962–97)	36	879	254	.776
Jack Ramsay (St. Joseph's [Pa.] 1956–66)	11	231	71	.765
Frank Keaney (Rhode Island 1921–48)	28	401	124	.764
*Bo Ryan (UW-Milwaukee 1999–2001, Wisconsin 2001–)	26	600	185	.764
George Keogan (St. Louis 1916, Allegheny 1919, Valparaiso 1920–21, Notre Dame 1924–43)	27	414	127	.764
Vic Bubas (Duke 1960–69)	10	213	67	.761
Harry Fisher (Columbia 1907–16, Army 1922–23, 1925)	16	189	60	.759
*Mike Krzyzewski (Army 1976–80, Duke 1981–)	35	868	279	.757
*John Calipari (Massachusetts 1989–96, Memphis 2001–09, Kentucky 2009–)	18	438	141	.756
Fred Bennion (Brigham Young 1909–10, Utah 1911-14, Montana St 1915-19)	11	95	31	.756
*Thad Matta (Butler 2001, Xavier 2002–04, Ohio St 2005–)	10	258	85	.752
Charles (Chick) Davies (Duquesne 1925–43, 1947–48)	21	314	106	.748
Ray Mears (Wittenberg 1957–62, Tennessee 1963–77)	21	399	135	.747
Edward McNichol (Penn 1921-30)	10	186	63	.747
Al McGuire (Belmont Abbey 1958–64, Marquette 1965–77)	20	406	142	.741
*Jim Boeheim (Syracuse 1977–)	34	829	293	.739
Phog Allen (Baker 1906–08, Haskell 1909, C. Mo. St 1913–19, Kansas 1908–09, 1920–56)	50	746	264	.739
Everett Case (North Carolina St 1947–65)	19	377	134	.738
Lute Olson (Long Beach St 1973–74, Iowa 1974–83, Arizona 1983–)	34	780	280	.736
Arthur Schabinger (Ottawa 1917–20, Emporia St 1921–22, Creighton 1924–25)	19	245	88	.736
*Bob Huggins (Akron 1985–89, Cincinnati 1990–2005, Kans. St 2007, W. Va. 2008–10)	19	245	88	.735

*Active in 2009–10. Note: Minimum 10 head coaching seasons in Division I.

NCAA Women's Division I Winningest Coaches

Alltime Winningest Women's Division I Coaches
WINNING PERCENTAGE

Coach (Team, Years)	Yrs	W	L	Pct
Leon Barmore (Louisiana Tech 1983–02)	20	576	87	.869
*Geno Auriemma (Connecticut 1986–)	25	735	122	.858
*Pat Summitt (Tennessee 1975–)	36	1037	196	.841
*Tara VanDerveer (Idaho 1979-80, Ohio St 1981–85, Stanford 1986–95, 97–)	31	793	195	.803
Bill Sheahan (Mt. St. Mary's 1982–98)	17	372	104	.782
*Wes Moore (Maryville 1988–93, Francis Marion 1996–98, Chattanooga 1999–)	21	490	141	.777
*Kim Mulkey (Baylor 2001–)	10	264	76	.776
*Gail Goestenkors (Duke 1993–07, Texas 2007–)	18	461	135	.773
*Robin Selvig (Montana 1979–)	32	740	218	.772
*Carey Green (Liberty 2000–)	11	264	83	.761

Note: Minimum 10 head coaching seasons in Division I.
*Active in 2009–10.

Alltime Winningest Women's Division I Coaches

	W
*Pat Summitt (Tennessee)	1,037
Jody Conradt (Sam Houston St, Tex.-Arlington, Texas)	900
*C. Vivian Stringer (Cheyney St, Iowa, Rutgers)	843
*Sylvia Rhyne Hatchell (Francis Marison, North Carolina)	831
*Tara VanDerveer (Idaho, Ohio St, Stanford)	793
*Andy Landers (Georgia)	750
*Robin Selvig (Montana)	740
Kay Yow (Elon, North Carolina St)	737
*Geno Auriemma (Connecticut)	735
*Debbie Ryan (Virginia)	720

Note: Minimum 10 head coaching seasons in Division I.
*Active in 2009–10.

NCAA Women's Division I Championship Results

Year	Winner	Score	Runner-up	Winning Coach
1982	Louisiana Tech	76–62	Cheyney	Sonja Hogg/Leon Barmore
1983	USC	69–67	Louisiana Tech	Linda Sharp
1984	USC	72–61	Tennessee	Linda Sharp
1985	Old Dominion	70–65	Georgia	Marianne Stanley
1986	Texas	97–81	USC	Jody Conradt
1987	Tennessee	67–44	Louisiana Tech	Pat Summitt
1988	Louisiana Tech	56–54	Auburn	Leon Barmore
1989	Tennessee	76–60	Auburn	Pat Summitt
1990	Stanford	88–81	Auburn	Tara VanDerveer
1991	Tennessee	70–67 (OT)	Virginia	Pat Summitt
1992	Stanford	78–62	Western Kentucky	Tara VanDerveer
1993	Texas Tech	84–82	Ohio State	Marsha Sharp
1994	North Carolina	60–59	Louisiana Tech	Sylvia Hatchell
1995	Connecticut	70–64	Tennessee	Geno Auriemma
1996	Tennessee	83–65	Georgia	Pat Summitt
1997	Tennessee	68–59	Old Dominion	Pat Summitt
1998	Tennessee	93–75	Louisiana Tech	Pat Summitt
1999	Purdue	62–45	Duke	Carolyn Peck
2000	Connecticut	71–52	Tennessee	Geno Auriemma
2001	Notre Dame	68–66	Purdue	Muffet McGraw
2002	Connecticut	82–70	Oklahoma	Geno Auriemma
2003	Connecticut	73–68	Tennessee	Geno Auriemma
2004	Connecticut	70–61	Tennessee	Geno Auriemma
2005	Baylor	84–62	Michigan St	Kim Mulkey-Robinson
2006	Maryland	78–75	Duke	Brenda Frese
2007	Tennessee	59–46	Rutgers	Pat Summitt
2008	Tennessee	64–48	Stanford	Pat Summitt
2009	Connecticut	76–54	Louisville	Geno Auriemma
2010	Connecticut	53–47	Stanford	Geno Auriemma

NCAA Women's Division I Alltime Individual Leaders

Single-Game Records

SCORING HIGHS

Pts	Player and Team vs Opponent	Year
60	Cindy Brown, Long Beach St vs San Jose St	1987
58	Kim Perrot, SW Louisiana vs SE Louisiana	1990
58	Lorri Bauman, Drake vs SW Missouri St*	1984
56	Jackie Stiles, SW Missouri St vs Evansville	2000
55	Patricia Hoskins, Mississippi Valley St vs Southern-Birm.	1989
55	Patricia Hoskins, Mississippi Valley St vs Alabama St	1989
54	Anjinea Hopson, Grambling vs Jackson St	1994
54	Mary Lowry, Baylor vs Texas	1994
54	Wanda Ford, Drake vs SW Missouri St*	1986
54	Elena Delle Donne, Delaware vs James Madison	2010

Three tied with 53.

REBOUNDS

Reb	Player and Team vs Opponent	Year
40	Deborah Temple, Delta St vs UAB	1983
37	Rosina Pearson, Bethune-Cookman vs Florida Memorial	1985
33	Maureen Formico, Pepperdine vs Loyola (Calif.)	1985
32	Lachelle Lyles, Southeast Mo. St. vs Tennessee St.	2006
31	Darlene Beale, Howard vs South Carolina St	1987
30	Cindy Bonforte, Wagner vs Queens (N.Y.)	1983
30	Kayone Hankins, New Orleans vs. Nicholls St	1994
30	Wanda Ford, Drake vs Eastern Illinois	1985
30	Jennifer Butler, Massachusetts vs Florida	2003

Three tied with 29.

*School changed name to Missouri State after 2004–05 season.

Single Game Records *(Cont.)*
ASSISTS

Asst	Player and Team vs Opponent	Year
23	Michelle Burden, Kent St vs Ball St	1991
22	Shawn Monday, Tennessee Tech vs Morehead St	1988
22	Veronica Pettry, Loyola (Ill.) vs Detroit	1989
22	Tine Freil, Pacific vs Wichita St	1991
21	Tine Freil, Pacific vs Fresno St	1992
21	Amy Bauer, Wisconsin vs Detroit	1989
21	Neacole Hall, Alabama St vs Southern-Birm.	1989

Six tied with 20.

Single Season Records
POINTS

Player and Team	Year	GP	FG	3FG	FT	Pts
Jackie Stiles, SW Missouri St*	2001	35	365	65	267	1062
Cindy Brown, Long Beach St	1987	35	362	—	250	974
Genia Miller, CSU-Fullerton	1991	33	376	0	217	969
Sheryl Swoopes, Texas Tech	1993	34	356	32	211	955
Alysha Clark, Middle Tennessee St	2008	34	343	12	237	935
Andrea Congreaves, Mercer	1992	28	353	77	142	925
Wanda Ford, Drake	1986	30	390	—	139	919
Chamique Holdsclaw, Tennessee	1998	39	370	9	166	915
Andrea Riley, Oklahoma St	2010	34	296	78	239	909
Barbara Kennedy, Clemson	1982	31	392	—	124	908
Patricia Hoskins, Mississippi Valley St	1989	27	345	13	205	908

SEASON SCORING AVERAGE

Player and Team	Year	GP	FG	3FG	FT	Pts	Avg
Patricia Hoskins, Mississippi Valley St	1989	27	345	13	205	908	33.6
Andrea Congreaves, Mercer	1992	28	353	77	142	925	33.0
Deborah Temple, Delta St	1984	28	373	—	127	873	31.2
Andrea Congreaves, Mercer	1993	26	302	51	150	805	31.0
Wanda Ford, Drake	1986	30	390	—	139	919	30.6
Anucha Browne, Northwestern	1985	28	341	—	173	855	30.5
LeChandra LeDay, Grambling	1988	28	334	36	146	850	30.4
Jackie Stiles, SW Missouri St*	2001	35	365	65	267	1062	30.3
Kim Perrot, SW Louisiana	1990	28	308	95	128	839	30.0
Tina Hutchinson, San Diego St	1984	30	383	—	132	898	29.9
Jan Jensen, Drake	1991	30	358	6	166	888	29.6
Genia Miller, CSU-Fullerton	1991	33	376	0	217	969	29.4
Barbara Kennedy, Clemson	1982	31	392	—	124	908	29.3
LaTaunya Pollard, Long Beach St	1983	31	376	—	155	907	29.3
Lisa McMullen, Alabama St	1991	28	285	126	119	815	29.1

REBOUNDS

Player and Team	Year	GP	Reb	Player and Team	Year	GP	Reb
Courtney Paris, Oklahoma	2006	36	539	Darlene Jones, Miss Valley St	1983	31	487
Wanda Ford, Drake	1985	30	534	Melanie Simpson, Okla. City	1982	37	481
Lachelle Lyles, SE Missouri St	2006	30	517	R. Pearson, Beth.-Cookman	1985	26	480
Wanda Ford, Drake	1986	30	506	Patricia Hoskins, Miss. Valley St	1987	28	476
Anne Donovan, Old Dominion	1983	35	504	Cheryl Miller, USC	1985	30	474

REBOUND AVERAGE

Player and Team	Year	GP	Reb	Avg
Rosina Pearson, Bethune-Cookman	1985	26	480	18.5
Wanda Ford, Drake	1985	30	534	17.8
Katie Beck, East Tennessee St	1988	25	441	17.6
DeShawne Blocker, East Tennessee St	1994	26	450	17.3
Lachelle Lyles, SE Missouri St	2006	30	517	17.2
Patricia Hoskins, Mississippi Valley St	1987	28	476	17.0
Wanda Ford, Drake	1986	30	506	16.9
Patricia Hoskins, Mississippi Valley St	1989	27	440	16.3
Joy Kellogg, Oklahoma City	1984	23	373	16.2
Courtney Paris, Oklahoma	2006	30	485	16.2
Deborah Mitchell, Mississippi Coll.	1983	28	447	16.0
Cheryl Miller, USC	1985	30	474	15.8

*School changed name to Missouri State after 2004–05 season

Single Season Records *(Cont.)*

FIELD-GOAL PERCENTAGE

Player and Team	Year	GP	FG	FGA	Pct
Myndee Larsen, Southern Utah	1998	28	249	344	72.4
Chantelle Anderson, Vanderbilt	2001	34	292	404	72.3
Deneka Knowles, SE Louisiana	1996	26	199	276	72.1
Crystal Langhorne, Maryland	2006	32	202	280	72.1
Barbara Farris, Tulane	1998	27	151	210	71.9
Renay Adams, Tennessee Tech	1991	30	185	258	71.7
Regina Days, Georgia Southern	1986	27	234	332	70.5
Kim Wood, UW-Green Bay	1994	27	188	271	69.4
Kelly Lyons, Old Dominion	1990	31	308	444	69.4
Alisha Hill, Howard	1995	28	194	281	69.0

Based on qualifiers for annual championship.

FREE-THROW PERCENTAGE

Player and Team	Year	GP	FT	FTA	Pct
Adrienne Squire, Penn St	2006	29	80	83	96.4
Shanna Zolman, Tennessee	2004	35	88	92	95.7
Ginny Doyle, Richmond	1992	29	96	101	95.0
Jill Marano, La Salle	2003	29	88	93	94.6
Sue Bird, Connecticut	2002	39	98	104	94.2
Paula Corder-King, SE Missouri St	1999	28	111	118	94.1
Kandi Brown, Morehead St	2003	28	104	111	93.7
Linda Cyborski, Delaware	1991	29	74	79	93.7
Kandi Brown, Morehead St	2002	29	74	79	93.7
Kristin Iwanaga, California	2005	29	85	91	93.4

Based on qualifiers for annual championship.

Career Records

POINTS

Player and Team	Yrs	GP	Pts
Jackie Stiles, SW Missouri St*	1997–01	129	3393
Patricia Hoskins, Mississippi Valley St	1985–89	110	3122
Lorri Bauman, Drake	1981–84	120	3115
Chamique Holdsclaw, Tennessee	1995–99	148	3025
Cheryl Miller, USC	1983–86	128	3018
Cindy Blodgett, Maine	1994–98	118	3005
LaToya Thomas, Mississippi St	1999–2003	125	2981
Valorie Whiteside, Appalachian St	1984–88	116	2944
Kelly Mazzante, Penn St	2000–04	133	2919
Joyce Walker, LSU	1981–84	117	2906

SCORING AVERAGE

Player and Team	Yrs	GP	FG	3FG	FT	Pts	Avg
Patricia Hoskins, Mississippi Valley St	1985–89	110	1196	24	706	3122	28.4
Sandra Hodge, New Orleans	1981–84	107	1194	—	472	2860	26.7
Jackie Stiles, SW Missouri St*	1997–01	129	1160	221	852	3393	26.3
Lorri Bauman, Drake	1981–84	120	1104	—	907	3115	26.0
Andrea Congreaves, Mercer	1989–93	108	1107	153	429	2796	25.9
Cindy Blodgett, Maine	1994–98	118	1055	219	676	3005	25.5
Valorie Whiteside, Appalachian St	1984–88	116	1153	0	638	2944	25.4
Joyce Walker, LSU	1981–84	117	1259	—	388	2906	24.8
Tarcha Hollis, Grambling	1989–91	84	891	3	246	2031	24.2
Korie Hlede, Duquesne	1994–98	109	1045	162	379	2631	24.1
Karen Pelphrey, Marshall	1983–86	114	1175	—	396	2746	24.1
Erma Jones, Bethune-Cookman	1982–84	87	961	—	173	2095	24.1

*School changed name to Missouri State after 2004–05 season

NCAA Men's Division II Championship Results

Year	Winner	Score	Runner-up	Third Place	Fourth Place
1957	Wheaton (Ill.)	89–65	Kentucky Wesleyan	Mt. St. Mary's (Md.)	CSU-Los Angeles
1958	South Dakota	75–53	St. Michael's	Evansville	Wheaton (Ill.)
1959	Evansville	83–67	SW Missouri St	North Carolina A&T	CSU-Los Angeles
1960	Evansville	90–69	Chapman	Kentucky Wesleyan	Cornell College
1961	Wittenberg	42–38	SE Missouri St	South Dakota St	Mt. St. Mary's (Md.)
1962	Mt. St. Mary's (Md.)	58–57 (OT)	CSU-Sacramento	Southern Illinois	Nebraska Wesleyan
1963	South Dakota St	44–42	Wittenberg	Oglethorpe	Southern Illinois
1964	Evansville	72–59	Akron	North Carolina A&T	Northern Iowa
1965	Evansville	85–82 (OT)	Southern Illinois	North Dakota	St. Michael's
1966	Kentucky Wesleyan	54–51	Southern Illinois	Akron	North Dakota
1967	Winston-Salem	77–74	SW Missouri St	Kentucky Wesleyan	Illinois St
1968	Kentucky Wesleyan	63–52	Indiana St	Trinity (Tex.)	Ashland
1969	Kentucky Wesleyan	75–71	SW Missouri St	†Vacated	Ashland
1970	Philadelphia Textile	76–65	Tennessee St	UC-Riverside	Buffalo St
1971	Evansville	97–82	Old Dominion	†Vacated	Kentucky Wesleyan
1972	Roanoke	84–72	Akron	Tennessee St	Eastern Mich
1973	Kentucky Wesleyan	78–76 (OT)	Tennessee St	Assumption	Brockport St
1974	Morgan St	67–52	SW Missouri St	Assumption	New Orleans
1975	Old Dominion	76–74	New Orleans	Assumption	Tenn.-Chattanooga
1976	Puget Sound	83–74	Tenn.-Chattanooga	Eastern Illinois	Old Dominion
1977	Tenn.-Chattanooga	71–62	Randolph-Macon	North Alabama	Sacred Heart
1978	Cheyney	47–40	UW-Green Bay	Eastern Illinois	Central Florida
1979	North Alabama	64–50	UW-Green Bay	Cheyney	Bridgeport
1980	Virginia Union	80–74	New York Tech	Florida Southern	North Alabama
1981	Florida Southern	73–68	Mt. St. Mary's (Md.)	Cal Poly-SLO	UW-Green Bay
1982	District of Columbia	73–63	Florida Southern	Kentucky Wesleyan	CSU-Bakersfield
1983	Wright St	92–73	District of Columbia	*CSU-Bakersfield	*Morningside
1984	Central Missouri St	81–77	St. Augustine's	*Kentucky Wesleyan	*N Alabama
1985	Jacksonville St	74–73	South Dakota St	*Kentucky Wesleyan	*Mt. St. Mary's (Md.)
1986	Sacred Heart	93–87	SE Missouri St	*Cheyney	*Florida Southern
1987	Kentucky Wesleyan	92–74	Gannon	*Delta St	*Eastern Montana
1988	Lowell	75–72	Ak.-Anchorage	Florida Southern	Troy St
1989	North Carolina Central	73–46	SE Missouri St	UC-Riverside	Jacksonville St
1990	Kentucky Wesleyan	93–79	CSU-Bakersfield	North Dakota	Morehouse
1991	North Alabama	79–72	Bridgeport (Conn.)	*CSU-Bakersfield	*Virginia Union
1992	Virginia Union	100–75	Bridgeport (Conn.)	*CSU-Bakersfield	*California (Pa.)
1993	CSU-Bakersfield	85–72	Troy St (Ala.)	*New Hampshire Coll	*Wayne St (Mich.)
1994	CSU-Bakersfield	92–86	Southern Indiana	*New Hampshire Coll	*Washburn
1995	Southern Indiana	71–63	UC-Riverside	*Norfolk St	*Indiana (Pa.)
1996	Fort Hays St	70–63	Northern Kentucky	*California (Pa.)	*Virginia Union
1997	CSU-Bakersfield	57–56	Northern Kentucky	*Lynn	*Salem-Teikyo
1998	UC-Davis	83–77	Kentucky Wesleyan	*St. Rose	*Virginia Union
1999	Kentucky Wesleyan	75–60	Metropolitan St	*Truman St	*Florida Southern
2000	Metropolitan St	97–79	Kentucky Wesleyan	*Missouri Southern	*Seattle Pacific
2001	Kentucky Wesleyan	72–63	Washburn	*Western Washington	*Tampa
2002	Metropolitan St	80–72	Kentucky Wesleyan	*Shaw	*Indiana (Pa.)
2003	Northeastern St (Okla.)	75–64	†Vacated	*Bowie St	*Queens (N.Y.)
2004	Kennesaw St	84–59	Southern Indiana	*Humboldt St	*Metropolitan St
2005	Virginia Union	63–58	Bryant	*Lynn	*Tarleton St
2006	Winona St (Minn.)	73–61	Virginia Union	*Seattle Pacific	*Stonehill
2007	Barton	77–75	Winona St (Minn.)	*CSU-San Bernardino	*Central Missouri
2008	Winona St (Minn.)	87–76	Augusta St	*Bentley	*Ak.-Anchorage
2009	Findlay	56–53 (OT)	Cal Poly.-Pomona	*Augusta St	*Central Missouri
2010	Cal Poly	65–53	Indiana Univ. (Pa.)	*Bentley	*St. Cloud St

*Indicates tied for third. †Student-athletes representing American International in 1969, Southwestern Louisiana in 1971, and Kentucky Wesleyan in 2003 were declared ineligible subsequent to the tournament. Under NCAA rules, the teams' and ineligible student-athletes' records were deleted, and the teams' places in the final standings were vacated.

SINGLE-GAME SCORING HIGHS

Pts	Player and Team vs Opponent	Date
113	Bevo Francis, Rio Grande vs Hillsdale	1954
84	Bevo Francis, Rio Grande vs Alliance	1954
82	Bevo Francis, Rio Grande vs Bluffton	1954
80	Paul Crissman, USC vs Pacific Christian	1966
77	William English, Winston-Salem vs Fayetteville St	1968

Single Season Records
SCORING AVERAGE

Player and Team	Year	GP	FG	FT	Pts	Avg
Bevo Francis, Rio Grande	1954	27	444	367	1255	46.5
Earl Glass, Mississippi Industrial	1963	19	322	171	815	42.9
Earl Monroe, Winston-Salem	1967	32	509	311	1329	41.5
John Rinka, Kenyon	1970	23	354	234	942	41.0
Willie Shaw, Lane	1964	18	303	121	727	40.4

REBOUND AVERAGE

Player and Team	Year	GP	Reb	Avg
Tom Hart, Middlebury	1955	22	649	29.5
Tom Hart, Middlebury	1956	21	620	29.5
Frank Stronczek, American Int'l	1966	26	717	27.6
R.C. Owens, College of Idaho	1954	25	677	27.1
Maurice Stokes, St. Francis (Pa.)	1954	26	689	26.5

ASSISTS

Player and Team	Year	GP	Asst
Steve Ray, Bridgeport	1989	32	400
Steve Ray, Bridgeport	1990	33	385
Tony Smith, Pfeiffer	1992	35	349
Jim Ferrer, Bentley	1989	31	309
Rob Paternostro, New Hamp. Coll.	1995	33	309

ASSIST AVERAGE

Player and Team	Year	GP	Asst	Avg
Steve Ray, Bridgeport	1989	32	400	12.5
Steve Ray, Bridgeport	1990	33	385	11.7
Demetri Beekman, Assumption	1993	23	264	11.5
Ernest Jenkins, N.M.-Highlands	1995	27	291	10.8
Brian Gregory, Oakland	1989	28	300	10.7

FIELD-GOAL PERCENTAGE

Player and Team	Year	Pct
Garret Siler, Augusta St	2008	78.9
Todd Linder, Tampa	1987	75.2
Maurice Stafford, North Alabama	1984	75.0
Matthew Cornegay, Tuskegee	1982	74.8
Callistus Eziukwu, Grand Valley St	2005	73.7

FREE-THROW PERCENTAGE

Player and Team	Year	Pct
Paul Cluxton, Northern Kentucky	1997	100.0
Tomas Rimkus, Pace	1997	95.6
C.J. Cowgill, Chaminade	2001	95.0
Kent Andrews, McNeese St	1968	94.4
Billy Newton, Morgan St	1976	94.4

Career Records
POINTS

Player and Team	Yrs	Pts
Travis Grant, Kentucky St	1969–72	4045
Bob Hopkins, Grambling	1953–56	3759
Tony Smith, Pfeiffer	1989–92	3350
Earnest Lee, Clark Atlanta	1984–87	3298
Joe Miller, Alderson-Broaddus	1954–57	3294

CAREER SCORING AVERAGE

Player and Team	Yrs	GP	Pts	Avg
Travis Grant, Kentucky St	1969–72	121	4045	33.4
John Rinka, Kenyon	1967–70	99	3251	32.8
Florindo Vieira, Quinnipiac	1954–57	69	2263	32.8
Willie Shaw, Lane	1961–64	76	2379	31.3
Mike Davis, Virginia Union	1966–69	89	2758	31.0

REBOUND AVERAGE

Player and Team	Yrs	GP	Reb	Avg
Tom Hart, Middlebury	1953, 55–56	63	1738	27.6
Maurice Stokes, St. Francis (Pa.)	1953–55	72	1812	25.2
Frank Stronczek, American Int'l	1965–67	62	1549	25.0
Bill Thieben, Hofstra	1954–56	76	1837	24.2
Hank Brown, Lowell Tech	1965–67	49	1129	23.0

Career Records *(Cont.)*

ASSISTS

Player and Team	Yrs	Asst
Demetri Beekman, Assumption	1990–93	1044
Adam Kaufman, Edinboro	1998–01	936
Rob Paternostro, New Hamp. Coll.	1992–95	919
Luke Cooper, Alaska-Anchorage	2005–08	880
Tony Smith, Pfeiffer	1989–92	828

ASSIST AVERAGE

Player and Team	Yrs	GP	Asst	Avg
Steve Ray, Bridgeport	1989–90	65	785	12.1
Demetri Beekman, Assumption	1990–93	119	1044	8.8
Ernest Jenkins, N.M.-Highlands	1992–95	84	699	8.3
Zack Whiting, Chaminade	2004–07	86	703	8.2
Adam Kaufman, Edinboro	1998–01	116	936	8.1

Note: Minimum 550 Assists.

FIELD-GOAL PERCENTAGE

Player and Team	Yrs	Pct
Garrett Siler, Augusta St	2006–09	74.5
Todd Linder, Tampa	1984–87	70.8
Tom Schurfranz, Bellarmine	1989–92	70.2
Chad Scott, California (Pa.)	1991–94	70.0
Ed Phillips, Alabama A&M	1968–71	68.9

Note: Minimum 400 FGM.

FREE-THROW PERCENTAGE

Player and Team	Yrs	Pct
Paul Cluxton, Northern Kentucky	1994–97	93.5
Jake Linton, St. Martin's	2006–09	92.4
Kent Andrews, McNeese St	1967–69	91.6
Chris Brunson, Souther Ind.	2002–05	90.1
Jon Hagen, Minnesota St–Mankato	1963–65	90.0

Note: Minimum 250 FTM.

NCAA Men's Division III Championship Results

Year	Winner	Score	Runner-up	Third Place	Fourth Place
1975	LeMoyne-Owen	57–54	Glassboro St	Augustana (Ill.)	Brockport St
1976	Scranton	60–57	Wittenberg	Augustana (Ill.)	Plattsburgh St
1977	Wittenberg	79–66	Oneonta St	Scranton	Hamline
1978	North Park	69–57	Widener	Albion	Stony Brook
1979	North Park	66–62	Potsdam St	Franklin & Marshall	Centre
1980	North Park	83–76	Upsala	Wittenberg	Longwood
1981	Potsdam St	67–65 (OT)	Augustana (Ill.)	Ursinus	Otterbein
1982	Wabash	83–62	Potsdam St	Brooklyn	CSU-Stanislaus
1983	Scranton	64–63	Wittenberg	Roanoke	UW–Whitewater
1984	UW–Whitewater	103–86	Clark (Mass.)	DePauw	Upsala
1985	North Park	72–71	Potsdam St	Nebraska Wesleyan	Widener
1986	Potsdam St	76–73	LeMoyne-Owen	Nebraska Wesleyan	Jersey City St
1987	North Park	106–100	Clark (Mass.)	Wittenberg	Stockton St
1988	Ohio Wesleyan	92–70	Scranton	Nebraska Wesleyan	Hartwick
1989	UW–Whitewater	94–86	Trenton St	Southern Maine	Centre
1990	Rochester	43–42	DePauw	Washington (Md.)	Calvin
1991	UW–Platteville	81–74	Franklin & Marshall	Otterbein	Ramapo (N.J.)
1992	Calvin	62–49	Rochester	UW–Platteville	Jersey City St
1993	Ohio Northern	71–68	Augustana	Mass.–Dartmouth	Rowan
1994	Lebanon Valley Coll	66–59 (OT)	NYU	Wittenberg	St Thomas (Minn.)
1995	UW–Platteville	69–55	Manchester	Rowan	Trinity (Conn.)
1996	Rowan	100–93	Hope (Mich.)	Illinois Wesleyan	Franklin & Marshall
1997	Illinois Wesleyan	89–86	Nebraska Wesleyan	Williams	Alvernia
1998	UW–Platteville	69–56	Hope (Mich.)	Williams	Wilkes
1999	UW–Platteville	76–75 (2 OT)	Hampden-Sydney	William Paterson	Connecticut Coll.
2000	Calvin	79–74	UW-Eau Claire	Salem St	Franklin & Marshall
2001	Catholic	76–62	William Paterson	Illinois Wesleyan	Ohio Northern
2002	Otterbein	102–83	Elizabethtown	Carthage	Rochester
2003	Williams	67–65	Gustavus Adolphus	Wooster	Hampden Sydney
2004	UW–Stevens Point	84–82	Williams	John Carroll	Amherst
2005	UW–Stevens Point	73–49	Rochester	Calvin	York
2006	Virginia Wesleyan	59–56	Wittenberg	Illinois Wesleyan	Amherst
2007	Amherst	80–67	Virginia Wesleyan	Washington (Mo.)	Wooster
2008	Washington-St. Louis	90–86	Amherst	Hope	Ursinus
2009	Washington-St. Louis	61–52	Richard Stockton	Guilford	Franklin & Marshall
2010	UW–Stevens Point	78–73	Williams	*Guilford	*Randolph Macon

*Indicates tied for third. In 2010, the NCAA eliminated the consolation game to determine third place.

SINGLE-GAME SCORING HIGHS

Pts	Player and Team vs Opponent	Year
77	Jeff Clement, Grinnell vs Illinois College	1998
69	Sami Wylie, Lincoln (Pa.) vs Ohio St-Marion	2007
69	Steve Diekmann, Grinnell vs Simpson	1995
64	Tim Russell, Albertus Magnus	2005
63	Ryan Hodges, Cal-Lutheran	2005
63	Joe DeRoche, Thomas vs St. Joseph's (Me.)	1988
62	Shannon Lilly, Bishop vs Southwest Assembly of God	1983
62	Nick Pelotte, Plymouth St	2005
62	Kyle Myrick, Lincoln (Pa.) vs. Penn St.-Abington	2006

Three tied at 61.

Single Season Records

SCORING AVERAGE

Player and Team	Year	GP	FG	FT	Pts	Avg
Steve Diekmann, Grinnell	1995	20	223	162	745	37.3
Rickey Sutton, Lyndon St	1976	14	207	93	507	36.2
Shannon Lilly, Bishop	1983	26	345	218	908	34.9
Dana Wilson, Husson	1974	20	288	122	698	34.9
Rickey Sutton, Lyndon St	1977	16	223	112	558	34.9

REBOUND AVERAGE

Player and Team	Year	GP	Reb	Avg
Joe Manley, Bowie St	1976	29	579	20.0
Fred Petty, New Hampshire Coll.	1974	22	436	19.8
Larry Williams, Pratt	1977	24	457	19.0
Larry Parker, Plattsburgh St	1975	23	430	18.7
harles Greer, Thomas	1977	17	318	18.7

ASSISTS

Player and Team	Year	GP	Asst
Robert James, Kean	1989	29	391
Tennyson Whitted, Ramapo	2002	29	319
Ricky Spicer, UW-Whitewater	1989	31	295
Joe Marcotte, New Jersey Tech	1995	30	292
Andre Bolton, Chris. Newport	1996	30	289

ASSIST AVERAGE

Player and Team	Year	GP	Asst	Avg
Robert James, Kean	1989	29	391	13.5
Albert Kirchner, Mt. St. Vincent	1990	24	267	11.1
Tennyson Whitted, Ramapo	2002	29	319	11.0
Ron Torgalski, Hamilton	1989	26	275	10.6
Louis Adams, Rust	1989	22	227	10.3

FIELD-GOAL PERCENTAGE

Player and Team	Year	Pct
Travis Weiss, St. John's (Minn.)	1994	76.6
Brian Schmitting, Ripon	2006	76.3
Pete Metzelaars, Wabash	1982	75.3
Tony Rychlec, Mass. Maritime	1981	74.9
Tony Rychlec, Mass. Maritime	1982	73.1

FREE-THROW PERCENTAGE

Player and Team	Year	Pct
Korey Coon, Illinois Wesleyan	2000	96.3
Ryan Junghans, Hood	2008	95.9
Nick Wilkins, Coe	2003	95.7
Chanse Young, Manchester	1998	95.6
Andy Enfield, Johns Hopkins	1991	95.3

Career Records

POINTS

Player and Team	Yrs	Pts
Andre Foreman, Salisbury St	1989–92	2940
Willie Chandler, Misericordia	2000–03	2898
John Grotberg, Grinnell	2006–09	2848
Lamont Strothers, Chris. Newport	1988–91	2709
Matt Hancock, Colby	1987–90	2678

SCORING AVERAGE

Player and Team	Yrs	GP	Avg
Dwain Govan, Bishop	1974–75	55	32.8
Dave Russell, Shepherd	1974–75	60	30.6
Kyle Myrick, Lincoln (Pa.)	2005–06	57	30.2
Rickey Sutton, Lyndon St	1976–79	80	29.7
John Grotberg, Grinnell	2006–09	96	29.7

REBOUND AVERAGE

Player and Team	Yrs	GP	Reb	Avg
Larry Parker, Plattsburgh St	1975–78	85	1482	17.4
Charles Greer, Thomas	1975–77	58	926	16.0
Willie Parr, LeMoyne-Owen	1974–76	76	1182	15.6
Michael Smith, Hamilton	1989–92	107	1632	15.2
Dave Kufeld, Yeshiva	1977–80	81	1222	15.1

ASSIST AVERAGE

Player and Team	Yrs	Avg
David Arsenault, Grinnell	2006–09	9.4
Phil Dixon, Shenandoah	1993–96	8.6
Tennyson Whitted, Ramapo	2000–03	8.5
Steve Artis, Chris. Newport	1990–93	8.1
David Genovese, Mt. St. Vincent	1992–95	7.5

Hockey

Jonathan Toews led
the Chicago Blackhawks
to that team's first
NHL title in 49 years

Blackhawks Crowned

Two young guns led the way as Chicago defeated the Philadelphia Flyers—this year's playoff Cinderella— to win its first Stanley Cup in nearly five decades

BY CHRIS MANNIX

RUN, CLOCK. RUN. THOSE words echoed through the heads of everyone on the Chicago Blackhawks bench as they stared up at the Wachovia Center scoreboard, willing the clock to tick closer to zero. It was Game 6 of the 2010 Stanley Cup Finals and the favored 'Hawks were clinging to a 3–2 game and series lead against Philadelphia. But the Flyers, an upstart bunch who snuck into the playoffs on the last day of the season with a league-low 88 points, who shocked the world by coming back from a 3–0 series deficit to defeat Boston, and who looked like a team of destiny after wiping the ice with Montreal in five games, just wouldn't go away. Sure enough, with Chicago trying to soak up the seconds with a conservative trap—hockey's version of the prevent defense—Flyers forward Villa Leino zipped a pass from the corner to the front of the net that Scott Hartnell banged in to tie the game with just under four minutes to play.

In previous years, such a demoralizing goal might be a series changer for Chicago. The 'Hawks, after all, had not raised Lord Stanley's Cup since 1961 and were denied at the doorstep each of the last five times they

played for it. This group, however, was different. Young and skilled, they didn't play with history on their shoulders. Not Jonathan Toews, the decorated 22-year old center dubbed 'Captain Serious' by his teammates for his dedication to the game. "He reminds me of a young Steve Yzerman," said Red Wings GM Ken Holland. "How he raises his play in big games, how he gets upset when things don't go well. He's a blue-chipper, a guy who wins face-offs and plays two ways and leans on guys down low."

Not Patrick Kane, either. The 21-year old winger won the Calder Trophy in 2007–08 and led the team in goals (30) in the '09–'10 season. Indeed, it was off of Kane's stick that the 49-year drought ended and the hard work of a franchise record 112-point season finally paid off. A little over four minutes into the overtime period Kane blasted a low shot that slipped through the pads of Michael Leighton and disappeared in the leather goal support behind the goal line. The shot was reviewed—what big moment isn't subject to scrutiny anymore?—but the goal stood. "The pressure on those kids was unbelievable," said veteran Blackhawks winger Andrew Ladd. "The way they handled it, you wouldn't know they were kids. The compete

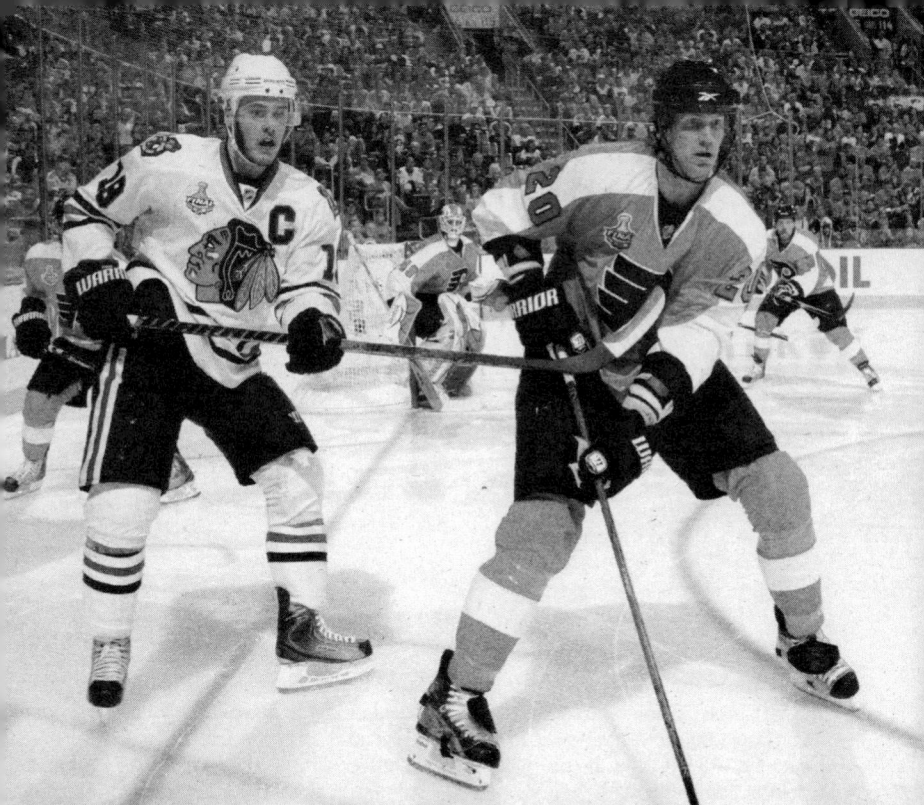

22-year-old Blackhawks captain Jonathan Toews (l.) and veteran Flyers defenseman Chris Pronger battled each other througout the Stanley Cup Final.

level, the maturity level...great, just great."

Kane's heroics were a fitting end to a razor thin series. Four games were decided by one goal. The Blackhawks took Game 1 in a wild shootout that began with a five-goal first period and ended when Tomas Kopecky—he of the career 22 goals in 257 regular season games—potted the game winner midway through the third period. Chicago appeared to put a stranglehold on the series in Game 2 thanks to the brilliance of goaltender Antti Niemi. With the 'Hawks clinging to a 2–1 lead, Niemi turned back 15 Flyers shots in the third period to preserve the win in a game that was watched by 5.89 million viewers, an American audience record. "We asked a lot of our goaltender tonight," said Chicago winger Marian Hossa. "He's the reason we're up 2–0."

Philadelphia refused to cave, however. "When our backs are against the wall," said Hartnell, "we just seem to lay it on the line." In Game 3 Leino knocked in the game-tying

goal in the third period and Claude Giroux redirected a Matt Carle pass by Niemi to give the Flyers their first win of the series. They kept that momentum going in Game 4, building a 4–1 lead before holding on for a 5–3 win.

Game 5 was one Chris Pronger would like to forget. The 35-year old Flyer's defenseman was on the ice for six of Chicago's goals and seated in the penalty box for the seventh. The win was the first blowout of the series and set the stage for the Blackhawks dramatic Game 6 victory. "We're going to enjoy this," said Blackhawks coach Joel Quenneville. "The party in Chicago is going to be all-world."

The Blackhawks victory brought a little levity to a serious season. Concussions,

94.6 percent of the shots thrown at him and setting an American Olympic record with a 1.35 goals against average. Back in Buffalo, Miller set career bests in goals-against average (2.22) and save percentage (92.9), while tying a career high in shutouts (five). He was the game's ultimate closer: Buffalo was 30–0–0 when leading after two periods.

especially those caused by blind-side hits, were a hot topic in the NHL. In October, Florida's David Booth was flattened by what was deemed a legal blow to the head by Philadelphia's Mike Richards.

The Penguins' Matt Cooke brought the issue to the forefront again when he knocked out Boston's Marc Savard with a blind side hit in March. Though the referees deemed the hit legal, Cooke—no stranger to questionable shots—was branded a headhunter. Canadian hockey analyst Don Cherry decried Cooke as 'gutless' and 'backstabbing' while the league vowed to discuss blind-side hits at the general managers meetings. Sure enough, the GM's proposed a rule that would issue a five-minute major and game misconduct for a "'lateral, back-pressure or blind-side hit to an opponent where the head is targeted and/or the principal point of contact." "We believe this is the right thing to do for the game and for the safety of our players," said NHL Commissioner Gary Bettman.

The careers of a handful of stars were launched during the '09–'10 season. Sabres goalie Ryan Miller became a household name at the Winter Olympics in Vancouver, saving

More importantly, Miller's quick glove propelled the Sabres to their sixth division championship.

Since 2006 the Hart Trophy has belonged to either Sidney Crosby or Alexander Ovechkin. But in 2010 a new (old) face emerged. Vancouver's Henrik Sedin, along with his brother and teammate Daniel, was once a heralded prospect but at 29 was considered ancient next to the baby faced phenoms Crosby and Ovechkin. But with Daniel sidelined because of a broken foot—the first time the Sedin's were ever separated for an extended time—Henrik enjoyed the finest season of his career. Noted for his passing, Sedin notched his first career hat trick in November. In the final game of the season, Sedin trailed Ovechkin by one point for the scoring lead. But he picked up four points to finish with 112 for the season, points that earned Sedin the votes necessary to narrowly edge Ovechkin and Crosby for the Hart Trophy.

For his next trick, maybe Sedin will lead the Canucks to a Stanley Cup. Vancouver has never won a title since coming into the league in 1970. But as the Blackhawks once again proved this season, even the longest of droughts will eventually be broken.

2009–10 NHL Final Regular Season Standings

Western Conference

CENTRAL DIVISION

	GP	W	L	OTL	Pts	GF	GA
†Chicago	82	52	22	8	112	271	209
*Detroit	82	44	24	14	102	229	216
*Nashville	82	47	29	6	100	225	225
St. Louis	82	40	32	10	90	225	223
Columbus	82	32	35	15	79	216	259

NORTHWEST DIVISION

	GP	W	L	OTL	Pts	GF	GA
†Vancouver	82	49	28	5	103	272	222
*Colorado	82	43	30	9	95	244	233
Calgary	82	40	32	10	90	204	210
Minnesota	82	38	36	8	84	219	246
Edmonton	82	27	47	8	62	214	284

PACIFIC DIVISION

	GP	W	L	OTL	Pts	GF	GA
†San Jose	82	51	20	11	113	264	215
*Phoenix	82	50	25	7	107	225	202
*Los Angeles	82	46	27	9	101	241	219
Anaheim	82	39	32	11	89	238	251
Dallas	82	37	31	14	88	237	254

OTL=overtime loss; worth 1 pt.

Eastern Conference

NORTHEAST DIVISION

	GP	W	L	OTL	Pts	GF	GA
†Buffalo	82	45	27	10	100	235	207
*Ottawa	82	44	32	6	94	225	238
*Boston	82	39	30	13	91	206	200
*Montreal	82	39	33	10	88	217	223
Toronto	82	30	38	14	74	214	267

ATLANTIC DIVISION

	GP	W	L	OTL	Pts	GF	GA
†New Jersey	82	48	27	7	103	222	191
*Pittsburgh	82	47	28	7	101	257	237
*Philadelphia	82	41	35	6	88	236	225
NY Rangers	82	38	33	11	87	222	218
NY Islanders	82	34	37	11	79	222	264

SOUTHEAST DIVISION

	GP	W	L	OTL	Pts	GF	GA
†Washington	82	54	15	13	121	318	233
Atlanta	82	35	34	13	83	234	256
Carolina	82	35	37	10	80	230	256
Tampa Bay	82	34	36	12	80	217	260
Florida	82	32	37	13	77	208	244

†Division winner. *Playoff team.

2010 Stanley Cup Playoffs

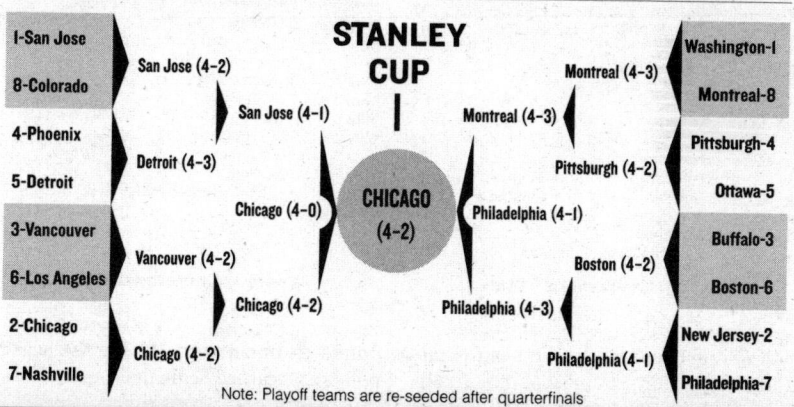

WESTERN CONFERENCE

QUARTERFINALS · SEMIFINALS · CONFERENCE FINAL

| 1-San Jose |
| 8-Colorado |
San Jose (4-2)
San Jose (4-1)
| 4-Phoenix |
| 5-Detroit |
Detroit (4-3)
Chicago (4-0)
| 3-Vancouver |
| 6-Los Angeles |
Vancouver (4-2)
Chicago (4-2)
| 2-Chicago |
| 7-Nashville |
Chicago (4-2)

STANLEY CUP — CHICAGO (4-2)

EASTERN CONFERENCE

CONFERENCE FINAL · SEMIFINALS · QUARTERFINALS

Montreal (4-3)
Montreal (4-3)
| Washington-1 |
| Montreal-8 |
Pittsburgh (4-2)
| Pittsburgh-4 |
| Ottawa-5 |
Philadelphia (4-1)
Boston (4-2)
| Buffalo-3 |
| Boston-6 |
Philadelphia (4-3)
Philadelphia (4-1)
| New Jersey-2 |
| Philadelphia-7 |

Note: Playoff teams are re-seeded after quarterfinals

Stanley Cup Playoff Results

Conference Quarterfinals

EASTERN CONFERENCE

April 15	Montreal	3	at Washington	2*
April 17	Montreal	5	at Washington	6*
April 19	Washington	5	at Montreal	1
April 21	Washington	6	at Montreal	3

*overtime

April 23	Montreal	2	at Washington	1
April 26	Washington	1	at Montreal	4
April 28	Montreal	2	at Washington	1

Montreal won series 4–3.

Conference Quarterfinals *(Cont.)*

EASTERN CONFERENCE *(CONT.)*

April 14	Philadelphia	2	at New Jersey	1			
April 16	Philadelphia	3	at New Jersey	5			
April 18	New Jersey	2	at Philadelphia	3*			
April 20	New Jersey	1	at Philadelphia	4			
April 22	Philadelphia	3	at New Jersey	0			

Philadelphia won series 4–1.

April 14	Ottawa	5	at Pittsburgh	4
April 16	Ottawa	1	at Pittsburgh	2
April 18	Pittsburgh	4	at Ottawa	2
April 20	Pittsburgh	7	at Ottawa	4

April 22	Ottawa	4	at Pittsburgh	3†
April 24	Pittsburgh	4	at Ottawa	3*

Pittsburgh won series 4–2.

April 15	Boston	1	at Buffalo	2
April 17	Boston	5	at Buffalo	3
April 19	Buffalo	1	at Boston	2
April 21	Buffalo	2	at Boston	3**
April 23	Boston	1	at Buffalo	4
April 26	Buffalo	3	at Boston	4

Boston won series 4–2.

WESTERN CONFERENCE

April 14	Colorado	2	at San Jose	1
April 16	Colorado	5	at San Jose	6*
April 18	San Jose	0	at Colorado	1*
April 20	San Jose	2	at Colorado	1*
April 22	Colorado	0	at San Jose	5
April 24	San Jose	5	at Colorado	2

San Jose won series 4–2.

April 14	Detroit	2	at Phoenix	3
April 16	Detroit	7	at Phoenix	4
April 18	Phoenix	4	at Detroit	2
April 20	Phoenix	0	at Detroit	3
April 23	Detroit	4	at Phoenix	1
April 25	Phoenix	5	at Detroit	4
April 27	Detroit	6	at Phoenix	1

Detroit won series 4–3.

April 16	Nashville	4	at Chicago	1
April 18	Nashville	0	at Chicago	2
April 20	Chicago	1	at Nashville	4
April 22	Chicago	3	at Nashville	0
April 24	Nashville	4	at Chicago	5*
April 26	Chicago	5	at Nashville	3

Chicago won series 4–2.

April 15	Los Angeles	2	at Vancouver	3*
April 17	Los Angeles	3	at Vancouver	2*
April 19	Vancouver	3	at Los Angeles	5
April 21	Vancouver	6	at Los Angeles	4
April 23	Los Angeles	2	at Vancouver	7
April 25	Vancouver	4	at Los Angeles	2

Vancouver won series 4–2.

Conference Semifinals

EASTERN CONFERENCE

May 1	Philadelphia	4	at Boston	5*
May 3	Philadelphia	2	at Boston	3
May 5	Boston	4	at Philadelphia	1
May 7	Boston	4	at Philadelphia	5*
May 9	Philadelphia	4	at Boston	0
May 12	Boston	1	at Philadelphia	2
May 13	Philadelphia	4	at Boston	3

Philadelphia won series 4–3.

April 30	Montreal	3	at Pittsburgh	6
May 2	Montreal	3	at Pittsburgh	1
May 4	Pittsburgh	2	at Montreal	0
May 6	Pittsburgh	2	at Montreal	3
May 8	Montreal	1	at Pittsburgh	2
May 10	Pittsburgh	3	at Montreal	4
May 12	Montreal	5	at Pittsburgh	2

Montreal won series 4–3.

WESTERN CONFERENCE

April 29	Detroit	3	at San Jose	4
May 2	Detroit	3	at San Jose	4
May 4	San Jose	4	at Detroit	3*
May 6	San Jose	1	at Detroit	7
May 8	Detroit	1	at San Jose	2

San Jose won series 4–1.

May 1	Vancouver	5	at Chicago	1
May 3	Vancouver	2	at Chicago	4
May 6	Chicago	5	at Vancouver	2
May 7	Chicago	7	at Vancouver	4
May 9	Vancouver	4	at Chicago	1
May 11	Chicago	5	at Vancouver	1

Chicago won series 4–2.

Eastern Conference Finals

May 16	Montreal	0	at Philadelphia	6
May 18	Montreal	0	at Philadelphia	3
May 20	Philadelphia	1	at Montreal	5
May 22	Philadelphia	3	at Montreal	0
May 24	Montreal	2	at Philadelphia	4

Philadelphia won series 4–1.

Western Conference Finals

May 16	Chicago	2	at San Jose	1
May 18	Chicago	4	at San Jose	2
May 21	San Jose	2	at Chicago	3*
May 23	San Jose	2	at Chicago	4

Chicago won series 4–0.

Stanley Cup Finals

May 29	Philadelphia	5	at Chicago	6
May 31	Philadelphia	1	at Chicago	2
June 2	Chicago	3	at Philadelphia	4*
June 4	Chicago	3	at Philadelphia	5

June 6	Philadelphia	4	at Chicago	7
June 9	Chicago	4	at Philadelphia	3*

Chicago won series 4–2.

*Overtime game. **Double overtime game. †Triple overtime game.

Stanley Cup Final Box Scores

Game 1

Philadelphia............3	2	0——5	
Chicago....................2	3	1——6	

FIRST PERIOD

Scoring: 3, Philadelphia, Leino (Briere, Pronger), 6:38, Hartnell (PP-Briere, Pronger), 16:37, Briere (Leino, Hartnell), 19:33; 2, Chicago, Brouwer (Hossa, Sopel), 7:46, Bolland, SH-11:50. Penalties: 3, Chicago, Eager (cross checking); 3:26, Kane (slashing), 9:58; Campbell (high-sticking), 15:51.

SECOND PERIOD

Scoring: 2, Philadelphia, Betts (Asham, Powe) 7:20, Asham (Briere, Hartnell), 18:49; 3, Chicago, Sharp, (Brouwer, Hjalmarsson), 1:11, Versteeg (Kopecky, Keith), 9:31, Brouwer (Hossa, Hjalmarsson), 15:18. Penalties: 1, Chicago, Burish (boarding), 4:49.

THIRD PERIOD

Scoring: 1, Chicago, Kopecky (Versteeg, Bolland), 8:25. Penalties: None.

Shots on goal: PHI 17-9-6—32; CHI 9-15-8—32.

Power-play opportunities: PHI 1-4, CHI 0-0.

Goalies: Phi, Boucher (12 shots, 11 saves), Leighton (20 shots, 15 saves); Chi, Niemi (32 shots, 27 saves).

Referees: McCreary, O'Halloran. Linesmen: Devorski, Racicot.

A: 22,312.

Game 2

Philadelphia............0	0	1——1	
Chicago....................0	2	0——2	

FIRST PERIOD

Scoring: None. Penalties: 3, Philadelphia, Betts (cross checking), 14:48, Richards (elbowing), 17:27, Carcillo (unsportsmanlike conduct), 17:27; 2, Chicago, Versteeg (interference), 7:26, Kopecky (roughing), 17:27.

SECOND PERIOD

Scoring: 2, Chicago, Hossa (Brouwer, Sharp), 17:09, Eager (Byfuglien), 17:37. Penalties: 1, Philadelphia, Richards (hooking), 5:08; 1, Chicago, Brouwer (roughing), 19:24.

THIRD PERIOD

Scoring: 1, Philadelphia, Gagne (PP-Richards, Carter), 5:20. Penalties: 1, Philadelphia, Pronger (major misconduct), 20:00; 2, Chicago, Sharp (tripping), 3:21, Eager (major misconduct), 20:00.

Shots on goal: PHI 3-15-15—33; CHI 9-13-4—26.

Power-play opportunities: PHI 1–3, CHI 0–2.

Goalies: Phi, Leighton (26 shots, 24 saves). Chi, Niemi (33 shots, 32 saves).

Referees: Walkom, Sutherland. Linesmen: Morin, Miller.

A: 22,275.

Game 3

Chicago 0	2	1	0——3
Philadelphia..........1	1	1	1——4

FIRST PERIOD

Scoring: 2, Chicago, Hossa (slashing), 13:54, Byfuglien (roughing), 20:00; 1, Philadelphia, Briere (PP-Hartnell, Coburn), 14:58. Penalties: 1, Philadelphia, Carcillo (charging), 18:05.

SECOND PERIOD

Scoring: 2, Chicago, Keith (Kane, Hossa), 2:49, Sopel (Madden), 17:52; 1, Philadelphia, Hartnell (PP-Pronger, Giroux), 9:55. Penalties: 1, Chicago, Byfuglien (slashing), 9:31; 2, Philadelphia, Pronger (high-sticking), 3:36, Leighton, served by Leino (delay of game), 14:59.

THIRD PERIOD

Scoring: 1, Philadelphia, Leino (Giroux, Carle), 3:10; 1, Chicago, Kane (Toews, Eager), 2:50. Penalties: None.

OVERTIME

Scoring: 1, Philadelphia, Giroux (Carle, Briere), 5:59. Penalties: None.

Shots on goal: CHI 9-12-4-2—27; PHI 9-7-15-1—32.

Power-play opportunities: CHI 0-5, PHI 2-8.

Goalies: Chi, Niemi (32 shots, 29 saves). Phi, Leighton (27 shots, 24 saves).

Referees: O'Halloran, McCreary. Linesmen: Devorski, Racicot.

A: 20,297.

Game 4

Chicago	1	0	2—3
Philadelphia	3	0	2—5

FIRST PERIOD

Scoring: 1, Chicago, Sharp (Keith), 18:32; 3, Philadelphia, Richards PP-4:35, Carle, 14:48, Giroux (Timonen, Hartnell), 19:23. Penalties: 2, Chicago, Ladd (interference), 00:36, Kopecky (high-sticking), 4:30; 1, Philadelphia, Timonen (hooking), 8:16.

SECOND PERIOD

Scoring: None. Penalties: 3, Chicago, Bolland (high-sticking), 1:27, Sharp (slashing), 12:53, Boyton (slashing), 18:22; 1, Philadelphia, Hartnell (cross checking), 18:22.

THIRD PERIOD

Scoring: 2, Chicago, Bolland (PP-Keith, Kane), 12:01, Campbell (Ladd, Keith), 15:50; 2, Philadelphia, Leino (Briere, van Riemsdyk), 6:43; Carter EN-19:35. Penalties: 2, Chicago, Seabrook (cross checking), 8:03, Versteeg (slashing), 19:42; 2, Philadelphia, Hartnell (unsportsmanlike conduct), 10:46, Coburn (holding), 11:49.

Shots on goal: CHI 11–13–10—34; PHI 8–10–13—31. Power-play opportunities: CHI 1–7, PHI 1–6.

Goalies: Chi, Niemi (30 shots, 26 saves). Phi, Leighton (34 shots, 31 saves).

Referees: Walkom, Sutherland. Linesmen: Morin, Miller.

A: 20,304

Game 5

Philadelphia	0	2	2—4
Chicago	3	2	2—7

FIRST PERIOD

Scoring: 3, Chicago, Seabrook (PP-Versteeg, Brouwer), 12:17, Bolland (Sopel, Byfuglien), 15:26, Versteeg (Seabrook, Byfuglien), 18:15. Penalties: 2, Philadelphia, Krajicek (cross checking), 2:50, Hartnell (high-sticking), 11:16; 1, Chicago, Bolland (cross checking), 9:15.

SECOND PERIOD

Scoring: 2, Philadelphia, Hartnell (Leino, Briere), 00:32, Timonen (Briere, Leino), 4:38; 2, Chicago, Kane (Ladd, Sharp), 3:13, Byfuglien (PP-Toews, Keith), 15:45. Penalties: 2, Philadelphia, Hartnell (elbowing), 7:19, Pronger (hooking), 15:18; 1, Chicago, Seabrook (closing hand on puck), 9:51.

THIRD PERIOD

Scoring: 2, Philadelphia, van Riemsdyk (Krajicek, Timonen), 6:36, Gagne (Leino), 17:24; 2, Chicago, Sharp (Kane), 16:08, Byfuglien (EN-Versteeg, Bolland), 17:55. Penalties: 1, Chicago, Versteeg (slashing), 10:38.

Shots on goal: PHI 7–10–10—27; CHI 13–8–7—28. Power-play opportunities: PHI 0–3, CHI 2–3.

Goalies: Phi, Boucher (14 shots, 11 saves); Leighton (13 shots, 10 saves); Chi, Niemi (27 shots, 23 saves).

Referees: McCreary, O'Halloran. Linesmen: Devorski Racicot.

A: 22,305.

Game 6

Chicago	1	2	0	1—4
Philadelphia	1	1	1	0—3

FIRST PERIOD

Scoring: 1, Chicago, Byfuglien (PP-Toews, Kane), 16:49; 1, Philadelphia, Hartnell (PP-Briere, Pronger), 19:33. Penalties: 3, Chicago, Sopel (interference), 13:28, Seabrook (elbowing), 16:59, Sopel (interference), 19:07; 2, Philadelphia, Pronger (holding), 8:42, Pronger (high-sticking), 16:29.

SECOND PERIOD

Scoring: 2, Chicago, Sharp (Bolland, Keith), 9:58, Ladd (Hjalmarsson, Kane), 17:43; 1, Philadelphia, Briere (Leino, Krajicek), 8:00. Penalties: 1, Chicago, Hossa (interference on goalie), 9:29; 3, Philadelphia, Hartnell (high-sticking), 1:56, Coburn (cross checking), 8:09, Briere (cross checking), 18:32.

THIRD PERIOD

Scoring: 1, Philadelphia, Hartnell (Leino, Briere), 16:01. Penalties: None.

OVERTIME

Scoring: 1, Chicago, Kane (Campbell), 4:06. Penalties: None.

Shots on goal: CHI 17–10–12–2—41; PHI 7–6–9–2—24. Power-play opportunities: CHI 1–7, PHI 1–3.

Goalies: Chi, Niemi (24 shots, 21 saves). Phi, Leighton (41 shots, 37 saves).

Referees: Walkom, Sutherland. Linesmen: Morin, Miller.

A: 20,327.

Individual 2010 Playoff Leaders

Scoring

POINTS

Player and Team	GP	G	Ast	Pts	+/-	PM	Player and Team	GP	G	Ast	Pts	+/-	PM
Danny Briere, Phi	23	12	18	30	9	18	Joe Pavelski, SJ	15	9	8	17	6	6
Jonathan Toews, Chi	22	7	22	29	-1	4	Scott Hartnell, Phi	23	8	9	17	4	25
Patrick Kane, Chi	22	10	18	28	-2	6	Duncan Keith, Chi	22	2	15	17	2	10
Mike Richards, Phi	23	7	16	23	-1	18	Dustin Byfuglien, Chi	22	11	5	16	-4	20
Patrick Sharp, Phi	22	11	11	22	10	16	Dave Bolland, Chi	22	8	8	16	6	30
Claude Giroux, Phi	23	10	11	21	7	4	Brian Gionta, Mtl	19	9	6	15	-6	14
Ville Leino, Phi	29	7	14	21	10	6	Mikael Samuelsson, Van	12	8	7	15	7	16
Michael Cammalleri, Mtl	19	13	6	19	-6	6	Henrik Zetterberg, Det	12	7	8	15	11	6
Sidney Crosby, Pit	13	6	13	19	6	6	Marian Hossa, Chi	22	3	12	15	7	25
Johan Franzen, Det	12	6	12	18	8	16	Five tied at 14 points.						
Chris Pronger, Phi	23	4	14	18	5	36							

GOALS

Player and Team	GP	G
Michael Cammalleri, Mtl	19	13
Danny Briere, Phi	23	12
Patrick Sharp, Phi	22	11
Dusitn Byfuglien, Chi	22	11
Patrick Kane, Chi	22	10
Claude Giroux, Phi	23	10
Joe Pavelski, SJ	15	9
Brian Gionta, Mtl	19	9
Simon Gagne, Phi	19	9

SHORT-HANDED GOALS

Player and Team	GP	SH
Dave Bolland, Chi	22	2
Eleven players tied at one goal.		

POWER PLAY GOALS

Player and Team		PP
Simon Gagne,, Phi	19	5
Dustin Byfuglien, Chi	22	5
Jonathan Toews, Chi	22	5
Joe Pavelski, SJ	15	5
Five players tied at four goals.		

ASSISTS

Player and Team	GP	A
Jonathan Toews, Chi	22	22
Danny Briere, Phi	23	18
Patrick Kane, Chi	22	18
Mike Richards, Phi	23	16
Duncan Keith, Chi	22	15

PLUS/MINUS

Player and Team	GP	+/-
Henrik Zetterberg, Det	12	11
Brian Campbell, Chi	19	11
Ville Leino, Phi	19	10
Patrick Sharp, Chi	22	10
Niklas Hjalmarsson, Chi	22	9
Danny Briere, Phi	23	9
Tom Poti, Wsh	6	9
Alexander Edler, Van	12	9
Johan Franzen, Det	12	8
Brent Seabrook, Chi	22	8
Six players tied at 7.		

Goaltending*

GOALS AGAINST AVERAGE

Player and Team	GP	W-L	Avg
Michael Leighton, Phi	14	8-3	2.46
Brian Boucher, Phi	12	6-6	2.47
Jaroslav Halak, Mtl	18	9-9	2.55
Evgeni Nabokov, SJ	15	8-7	2.56
Tuukka Rask, Bos	13	7-6	2.61
Antti Neimi, Chi	22	16-6	2.63
*minimum of 420 minutes			

SAVE PERCENTAGE

Player and Team		W-L	GAA	GA	SV	SV%	SA
Craig Anderson, Col	6	2-4	2.62	16	223	.933	239
Ryan Miller, Buf	6	2-4	2.34	15	189	.926	204
Jaroslav Halak, Mtl	18	9-9	2.55	43	519	.923	562
M. Leighton, Phi	14	8-3	2.46	31	340	.916	371
Jimmy Howard, Det	12	5-7	2.75	33	354	.915	387
Tuukka Rask, Bos	13	7-6	2.61	36	373	.912	409
Pekka Rinne, Nsh	6	2-4	2.68	16	163	.911	179

NHL Awards

Award	Player and Team
Hart Trophy (MVP)	Henrik Sedin, Van
Lindsay Award (NHLPA MOP)	Alexander Ovechkin, Wsh
Calder Trophy (top rookie)	Tyler Myers, Buf
Vezina Trophy (top goaltender)	Ryan Miller, Buf
Norris Trophy (top defenseman)	Duncan Keith, Chi
Lady Byng Trophy (for gentlemanly play)	Martin St. Louis, TB
Adams Award (top coach)	Dave Tippett, Phx
Selke Trophy (top defensive forward)	Pavel Datsyuk, Det
Jennings Trophy (goaltender on club allowing fewest goals)	Martin Brodeur, NJ
Conn Smythe Trophy (playoff MVP)	Jonathan Toews, Chi

Individual 2009-10 Regular Season Leaders

Scoring

POINTS

Player and Team	GP	G	Ast	Pts	+/-	PIM	Player and Team	GP	G	Ast	Pts	+/-	PIM
Henrik Sedin, Van	82	29	83	112	35	48	Daniel Sedin, Van	63	29	56	85	36	28
Sidney Crosby, Pit	81	51	58	109	15	71	Alexander Semin, Wsh	73	40	44	84	36	66
Alex Ovechkin, Wsh	72	50	59	109	45	89	Patrick Marleau, SJ	82	44	39	83	21	22
Nicklas Backstrom, Wsh	82	33	68	101	37	50	Dany Heatley, SJ	82	39	43	82	14	54
Steven Stamkos, TB	82	51	44	95	-2	38	Zach Parise, NJ	81	38	44	82	24	32
Martin St. Louis, TB	82	29	65	94	-8	12	Anze Kopitar, LA	82	34	47	81	6	16
Brad Richards, Dal	80	24	67	91	-12	14	Paul Stastny, Col	81	20	59	79	2	50
Joe Thornton, SJ	79	20	69	89	17	54	Evgeni Malkin, Pit	67	28	49	77	-6	100
Patrick Kane, Chi	82	30	58	88	16	20	Corey Perry, Ana	82	27	49	76	0	111
Marian Gaborik, NYR	76	42	44	86	15	37	Mike Green, Wsh	75	19	57	76	39	54
Ilya Kovalchuk, Atl	76	41	44	85	10	53							

Scoring *(Cont.)*

GOALS

Player and Team	GP	G
Sidney Crosby, Pit	81	51
Steven Stamkos, TB	82	51
Alex Ovechkin, Wsh	72	50
Patrick Marleau, SJ	82	44
Marian Gaborik, NYR	76	42
Ilya Kovalchuk, Atl, NJ	76	41
Alexander Semin, Wsh	73	40
Dany Heatley, SJ	82	39
Zach Parise, NJ	81	38
Alexandre Burrows, Van	82	35
Bobby Ryan, Ana	81	35
Anze Kopitar, LA	82	34

POWER PLAY GOALS

Player and Team	GP	PP
Steven Stamkos, TB	82	24
Dany Heatley, SJ	82	18
Marian Gaborik, NYR	76	14
Anze Kopitar, LA	82	14
Teemu Selanne, Ana	68	14

SHORT-HANDED GOALS

Player and Team	GP	SHG
Marian Hossa, Chi	57	5
Alexandre Burrows, Van	82	5
Patrick Marleau, SJ	82	4
Rene Bourque, Cgy	73	4
Eight tied with three goals.		

ASSISTS

Player and Team	GP	Ast
Henrik Sedin, Van	82	83
Joe Thornton, SJ	79	69
Nicklas Backstrom, Wsh	82	68
Brad Richards, Dal	80	67
Martin St. Louis, TB	82	65
Alex Ovechkin, Wsh	72	59
Paul Stastny, Col	81	59
Sidney Crosby, Pit	81	58
Patrick Kane, Chi	82	58
Mike Green, Wsh	75	57
Daniel Sedin, Van	63	56

GAME-WINNING GOALS

Player and Team	GP	GW
Dany Heatley, SJ	82	9
Patric Hornqvist, Nsh	80	8
Daniel Sedin, Van	63	8
Six tied with seven goals.		

PLUS/MINUS

Player and Team	GP	+/-
Jeff Schultz, Wsh	73	50
Alex Ovechkin, Wsh	72	45
Mike Green, Wsh	75	39
Nicklas Backstrom, Wsh	82	37
Daniel Sedin, Van	63	36
Alexander Semin, Wsh	73	36
Christian Ehrhoff, Van	80	36
Henrik Sedin, Van	82	35
Alexandre Burrows, Van	82	34
Mark Fistric, Dal	67	27
Tom Poti, Wsh	70	26
Patrick Sharp, Chi	82	24
Zach Parise, NJ	81	24

Goaltending
(Minimum 25 games)

GOALS AGAINST AVERAGE

Player and Team	GP	W–L	GAA	GA
Tuukka Rask, Bos	45	22–12	1.97	84
Ryan Miller, Buf	69	41–18	2.22	150
Martin Brodeur, NJ	77	45–25	2.24	168
Antti Niemi, Chi	39	26–7	2.25	82
Jimmy Howard, Det	63	37–15	2.26	141
Ilya Bryzgalov, Phx	69	42–20	2.29	156
Miikka Kiprusoff, Cgy	73	35–28	2.31	163
Henrik Lundqvist, NYR	73	35–27	2.38	167

WINS

Player and Team	GP	GAA	W	L
Martin Brodeur, NJ	77	2.24	45	25
Evgeni Nabokov, SJ	71	2.43	44	16
Ilya Bryzgalov, Phx	69	2.29	42	20
Ryan Miller, Buf	69	2.22	41	18
Roberto Luongo, Van	68	2.57	40	22
Jonathan Quick, LA	72	2.54	39	24
Craig Anderson, Col	71	2.64	38	25

SAVE PERCENTAGE

Player and Team	GP	W–L	GA	SV	SV%
Tuukka Rask, Bos	45	22–12	84	1137	.931
Ryan Miller, Buf	69	41–18	150	1948	.929
Tomas Vokoun, Fla	63	23–28	157	1924	.925
Jaroslav Halak, Mtl	45	26–13	105	1281	.924
Jimmy Howard, Det	63	37–15	141	1708	.924
Evgeni Nabokov, SJ	71	44–16	170	1998	.922
Ty Conklin, StL	26	10–10	60	704	.921
H. Lundqvist, NYR	73	35–27	167	1942	.921

SHUTOUTS

Player and Team	GP	W	L	SO
Martin Brodeur, NJ	77	45	25	9
Ilya Bryzgalov, Phx	69	42	20	8
Craig Anderson, Col	71	38	25	7
Pekka Rinne, Nsh	58	32	16	7
Antti Niemi, Chi	39	26	7	7
Tomas Vokoun, Fla	63	23	28	7

NHL Team-by-Team Statistical Leaders

Anaheim Ducks

SCORING

Player	GP	G	Ast	Pts	+/-	PM
Corey Perry, RW	82	27	49	76	0	111
Ryan Getzlaf, C	66	19	50	69	4	79
Bobby Ryan, RW	81	35	29	64	9	81
Saku Koivu, C	71	19	33	52	14	36
Teemu Selanne, RW	54	27	21	48	3	16
Scott Niedermayer, D	80	10	38	48	-9	38
Lubomir Visnovsky, D	73	15	30	45	-10	20
Jason Blake, LW	82	16	25	41	-10	36
James Wisniewski, D	69	3	27	30	-5	56
Todd Marchant, C	78	9	13	22	-16	32
Dan Sexton, RW	41	9	10	19	-3	16
Matt Beleskey, LW	60	11	7	18	-10	35
Steve Eminger, D	63	4	12	16	1	30
Joffrey Lupul, RW	23	10	4	14	3	18
Aaron Ward, D	77	1	12	13	-15	62
Kyle Chipchura, C	74	6	6	12	-12	72
Sheldon Brookbank, D	66	0	9	9	10	114

SCORING *(CONT.)*

Player	GP	G	Ast	Pts	+/-	PM
Ryan Carter, C	38	4	5	9	0	31
Troy Bodie, RW	44	5	2	7	-8	80
Mike Brown, RW	75	6	1	7	1	106
George Parros, RW	57	4	0	4	4	136
Brett Festerling, D	42	0	3	3	1	15
Kyle Calder, LW	14	0	2	2	-7	8
Brendan Mikkelson, D	28	0	2	2	-5	14
Nick Bonino, C	9	1	1	2	0	6
Nathan Oystrick, D	3	0	0	0	-1	2
Luca Sbisa, D	8	0	0	0	-1	6
MacGregor Sharp, C	8	0	0	0	0	0

GOALTENDING

Player	GP	Mins	W	L	TGA	GAA	SO
Jonas Hiller	59	3338	30	23	152	2.73	2
Curtis McElhinney	20	1024	8	5	51	2.99	0
Joey MacDonald	6	319	1	4	17	3.2	0

Atlanta Thrashers

SCORING

Player	GP	G	Ast	Pts	+/−	PM
Nik Antropov, RW	76	24	43	67	13	44
Maxim Afinogenov, RW	82	24	37	61	-17	46
Rich Peverley, C	82	22	33	55	-14	36
Tobias Enstrom, D	82	6	44	50	-5	30
Niclas Bergfors, RW	81	21	23	44	-10	10
Pavel Kubina, D	76	6	32	38	0	66
Clarke MacArthur, LW	81	16	19	35	-16	49
Bryan Little, RW	79	13	21	34	-6	20
Colby Armstrong, RW	79	15	14	29	6	61
Vyacheslav Kozlov, LW	55	8	18	26	-15	33
Todd White, C	65	7	19	26	-11	24
Ron Hainsey, D	80	5	21	26	-6	39
Evander Kane, LW	66	14	12	26	2	62
Zach Bogosian, D	81	10	13	23	-18	61
Jim Slater, C	61	11	7	18	1	60
Marty Reasoner, C	80	4	13	17	-3	24
Evgeny Artyukhin, RW	54	9	7	16	-4	72
Chris Thorburn, RW	76	4	9	13	6	89
Johnny Oduya, D	67	3	10	13	8	30
Eric Boulton, LW	62	2	6	8	-1	113
Christoph Schubert, D	47	2	5	7	-6	69
Mark Popovic, D	37	2	2	4	0	10
Boris Valabik, D	23	0	2	2	2	36
Tim Stapleton, RW	6	2	0	2	1	2
Arturs Kulda, D	4	0	2	2	2	2
Chris Chelios, D	7	0	0	0	-2	0

GOALTENDING

Player	GP	Mins	W	L	TGA	GAA	SO
Johan Hedberg	47	2632	21	16	115	2.62	3
Ondrej Pavelec	42	2317	14	18	127	3.29	2

Boston Bruins

SCORING

Player	GP	G	Ast	Pts	+/−	PM
Patrice Bergeron, C	73	19	33	52	6	28
David Krejci, C	79	17	35	52	8	26
Zdeno Chara, D	80	7	37	44	19	87
Mark Recchi, RW	81	18	25	43	4	34
Blake Wheeler, RW	82	18	20	38	-4	53
Marco Sturm, LW	76	22	15	37	14	30
Marc Savard, C	41	10	23	33	2	14
Michael Ryder, RW	82	18	15	33	3	35
Dennis Seidenberg, D	79	4	28	32	6	39
Dennis Wideman, D	76	6	24	30	-14	34
Daniel Paille, LW	76	10	10	20	-3	12
Milan Lucic, LW	50	9	11	20	-7	44
Johnny Boychuk, D	51	5	10	15	10	43
Miroslav Satan, RW	38	9	5	14	8	12
Steve Begin, LW	77	5	9	14	-7	53
Matt Hunwick, D	76	6	8	14	-16	32
Shawn Thornton, LW	74	1	9	10	-9	141
Vladimir Sobotka, C	61	4	6	10	-7	30
Andrew Ference, D	51	0	8	8	-7	16
Mark Stuart, D	56	2	5	7	1	80
Trent Whitfield, C	16	0	1	1	-2	7
Adam McQuaid, D	19	1	0	1	-5	21
Brad Marchand, C	20	0	1	1	-3	20
Zach Hamill, C	1	0	1	1	1	0
Guillaume Lefebvre, LW	1	0	0	0	0	0
Drew Larman, C	4	0	0	0	-1	0
Andy Wozniewski, D	2	0	0	0	0	0
Mikko Lehtonen, RW	1	0	0	0	-1	0
Andrew Bodnarchuk, D	5	0	0	0	-2	2

GOALTENDING

Player	GP	Mins	W	L	TGA	GAA	SO
Tuukka Rask	45	2562	22	12	84	1.97	5
Tim Thomas	43	2442	17	18	104	2.56	5

Buffalo Sabres

SCORING

Player	GP	G	Ast	Pts	+/−	PM
Derek Roy, C	80	26	43	69	9	48
Tim Connolly, C	73	17	48	65	10	28
Jason Pominville, RW	82	24	38	62	13	22
Thomas Vanek, LW	71	28	25	53	9	42
Tyler Myers, D	82	11	37	48	13	32
Jochen Hecht, C	79	21	21	42	14	35
Raffi Torres, LW	74	19	17	36	-11	34
Drew Stafford, RW	71	14	20	34	4	35
Tim Kennedy, LW	78	10	16	26	-3	50
Steve Montador, D	78	5	18	23	0	75
Mike Grier, RW	73	10	12	22	-4	14
Paul Gaustad, C	65	12	10	22	-7	82
Chris Butler, D	59	1	20	21	-15	22
Toni Lydman, D	67	4	16	20	10	30
Henrik Tallinder, D	82	4	16	20	13	32
Craig Rivet, D	78	1	14	15	-6	100

SCORING (CONT.)

Player	GP	G	Ast	Pts	+/−	PM
Patrick Kaleta, RW	55	10	5	15	2	89
Adam Mair, C	69	6	8	14	-2	73
Matt Ellis, LW	72	3	10	13	-1	12
Andrej Sekera, D	49	4	7	11	-1	6
Tyler Ennis, LW	10	3	6	9	1	6
Nathan Gerbe, C	10	2	3	5	1	4
Mark Mancari, RW	6	1	1	2	3	4

GOALTENDING

Player	GP	Mins	W	L	TGA	GAA	SO
Ryan Miller	69	4047	41	18	150	2.22	5
Patrick Lalime	16	854	4	8	40	2.81	0
Jhonas Enroth	1	58	0	1	4	4.14	0

Calgary Flames

SCORING

Player	GP	G	Ast	Pts	+/−	PM
Jarome Iginla, RW	82	32	37	69	−2	58
Rene Bourque, LW	73	27	31	58	7	88
Matt Stajan, C	82	19	38	57	−6	32
Niklas Hagman, LW	82	25	19	44	−4	25
Ian White, D	83	13	25	38	8	51
Daymond Langkow, C	72	14	23	37	2	30
Curtis Glencross, LW	67	15	18	33	11	58
Nigel Dawes, LW	66	14	18	32	1	18
Mark Giordano, D	82	11	19	30	17	81
Jay Bouwmeester, D	82	3	26	29	−4	48
Ales Kotalik, RW	71	11	16	27	−17	67
Eric Nystrom, LW	82	11	8	19	0	54
Robyn Regehr, D	81	2	15	17	2	80
David Moss, RW	64	8	9	17	−9	20
Chris Higgins, LW	67	8	9	17	−9	32
Craig Conroy, C	63	3	12	15	−6	25
Jamal Mayers, RW	71	3	11	14	−3	131
Steve Staios, D	58	1	9	10	−27	75
Mikael Backlund, C	23	1	9	10	5	6
Adam Pardy, D	57	2	7	9	−3	48
Cory Sarich, D	57	1	5	6	4	58
Brian McGrattan, RW	34	1	3	4	3	86
Staffan Kronwall, D	11	1	2	3	−1	2
Jason Jaffray, RW	3	0	0	0	−1	0
Brett Sutter, C	10	0	0	0	−1	5

GOALTENDING

Player	GP	Mins	W	L	TGA	GAA	SO
Miikka Kiprusoff	73	4235	35	28	163	2.31	4
Vesa Toskala	32	1605	9	12	93	3.48	1

Carolina Hurricanes

SCORING

Player	GP	G	Ast	Pts	+/−	PM
Eric Staal, C	70	29	41	70	4	68
Jussi Jokinen, LW	81	30	35	65	3	36
Ray Whitney, LW	80	21	37	58	−6	26
Joni Pitkanen, D	71	6	40	46	−11	72
Brandon Sutter, C	72	21	19	40	−1	2
Tuomo Ruutu, RW	54	14	21	35	−4	50
Sergei Samsonov, LW	72	14	15	29	−15	32
Chad Larose, RW	56	11	17	28	−2	24
Tom Kostopoulos, RW	82	8	13	21	4	106
Rod Brind'Amour, C	80	9	10	19	−29	36
Tim Gleason, D	61	5	14	19	0	78
Erik Cole, RW	40	5	16	19	−9	29
Brian Pothier, D	61	5	10	15	4	21
Alexandre Picard, D	54	4	11	15	0	26
Patrick Dwyer, RW	58	7	5	12	−3	6
Brett Carson, D	54	2	10	12	5	12
Bryan Rodney, D	22	1	10	11	−4	8
Jamie McBain, D	14	3	7	10	6	0
Zach Boychuk, C	31	3	6	9	1	2
Jay Harrison, D	38	1	5	6	−8	50
Jiri Tlusty, C	20	1	5	6	0	6
Drayson Bowman, LW	9	2	0	2	−1	4
Jerome Samson, RW	7	0	2	2	−1	10
Steven Goertzen, RW	6	0	0	0	−2	5
Tim Conboy, RW	12	0	0	0	−5	24
Casey Borer, D	2	0	0	0	−1	0
Oskar Osala, LW	1	0	0	0	0	0

GOALTENDING

Player	GP	Mins	W	L	TGA	GAA	SO
Cam Ward	47	2651	18	23	119	2.69	0
Manny Legace	28	1472	10	7	69	2.81	1
Justin Peters	9	488	6	3	23	2.83	0

Chicago Blackhawks

SCORING

Player	GP	G	Ast	Pts	+/−	PM
Duncan Keith, D	82	14	55	69	21	51
Jonathan Toews, C	76	25	43	68	22	47
Patrick Sharp, LW	82	25	41	66	24	28
Marian Hossa, RW	57	24	27	51	24	18
Kris Versteeg, LW	79	20	24	44	8	35
Troy Brouwer, LW	78	22	18	40	9	66
Brian Campbell, D	68	7	31	38	18	18
Andrew Ladd, LW	82	17	21	38	2	67
Dustin Byfuglien, LW	82	17	17	34	−7	94
Brent Seabrook, D	78	4	26	30	20	59
John Madden, C	79	10	13	23	−2	12
Tomas Kopecky, RW	74	10	11	21	0	28
Colin Fraser, C	70	7	12	19	6	44
Kim Johnsson, D	60	7	10	17	10	30
Niklas Hjalmarsson, D	77	2	15	17	9	20
Ben Eager, LW	60	7	9	16	9	120

SCORING *(CONT.)*

Player	GP	G	Ast	Pts	+/−	PM
Dave Bolland, C	39	6	10	16	5	28
Brent Sopel, D	73	1	7	8	3	34
Nick Boynton, D	49	1	7	8	5	71
Jordan Hendry, D	43	2	6	8	5	10
Adam Burish, RW	13	1	3	4	2	14
Bryan Bickell, LW	16	3	1	4	4	5
Jake Dowell, C	3	1	1	2	1	5
Jack Skille, RW	6	1	1	2	−3	0
Radek Smolenak, LW	1	0	0	0	0	5

GOALTENDING

Player	GP	Mins	W	L	TGA	GAA	SO
Cristobal Huet	48	2731	26	14	114	2.50	4
Antti Niemi	39	2190	26	7	82	2.25	7
Corey Crawford	1	59	0	1	3	3.05	0

Colorado Avalanche
SCORING

Player	GP	G	Ast	Pts	+/-	PM
Paul Stastny, C	81	20	59	79	2	50
Chris Stewart, RW	77	28	36	64	4	73
Matt Duchene, C	81	24	31	55	1	16
Milan Hejduk, RW	56	23	21	44	6	10
T.J. Galiardi, LW	70	15	24	39	6	28
Peter Mueller, C	69	13	24	37	-1	16
John-Michael Liles, D	59	6	25	31	-2	30
Kyle Quincey, D	79	6	23	29	9	76
Ryan O'Reilly, C	81	8	18	26	4	18
Darcy Tucker, RW	71	10	14	24	-3	47
Ryan Wilson, D	61	3	18	21	13	36
Brett Clark, D	64	3	17	20	6	28
Kyle Cumiskey, D	61	7	13	20	0	20
Brandon Yip, RW	32	11	8	19	5	22
Cody Mcleod, LW	74	7	11	18	-13	138
Scott Hannan, D	81	2	14	16	2	40
Matt Hendricks, C	56	9	7	16	1	74
David Jones, RW	23	10	6	16	1	2
Marek Svatos, RW	54	7	4	11	-13	35
Adam Foote, D	67	0	9	9	8	64
Stephane Yelle, C	70	4	4	8	-6	32
Chris Durno, LW	41	4	4	8	3	47
Ruslan Salei, D	14	1	5	6	-1	10
Kevin Porter, C	20	2	1	3	-3	0
Ryan Stoa, C	12	2	1	3	-3	0
TJ Hensick, C	7	1	2	3	0	0
Justin Mercier, C	9	1	1	2	2	0
David Koci, LW	43	1	0	1	-2	84

GOALTENDING

Player	GP	Mins	W	L	TGA	GAA	SO
Craig Anderson	71	4235	38	25	186	2.64	7
Peter Budaj	15	728	5	5	32	2.64	1

Dallas Stars
SCORING

Player	GP	G	Ast	Pts	+/-	PM
Brad Richards, C	80	24	67	91	-12	14
Loui Eriksson, LW	82	29	42	71	-4	26
James Neal, LW	78	27	28	55	-5	64
Mike Ribeiro, C	66	19	34	53	-5	38
Brenden Morrow, LW	76	20	26	46	-3	69
Stephane Robidas, D	82	10	31	41	-10	70
Jamie Benn, LW	82	22	19	41	-1	45
Steve Ott, LW	73	22	14	36	-14	153
Mike Modano, C	59	14	16	30	-6	22
Trevor Daley, D	77	6	16	22	3	25
Jere Lehtinen, RW	58	4	13	17	-8	8
Toby Petersen, C	78	9	6	15	3	6
Matt Niskanen, D	74	3	12	15	-15	18
Tom Wandell, C	50	5	10	15	2	14
Karlis Skrastins, D	79	2	11	13	-4	24
Brandon Segal, RW	44	6	6	12	3	38
Fabian Brunnstrom, LW	44	2	9	11	-3	10
Mark Fistric, D	67	1	9	10	27	69
Brian Sutherby, C	46	5	4	9	8	66
Nicklas Grossman, D	71	0	7	7	-3	32
Krystofer Barch, RW	63	0	6	6	0	130
Jeff Woywitka, D	36	0	3	3	-6	11
Warren Peters, C	11	1	0	1	1	2
Maxime Fortunus, D	8	0	0	0	-6	4
Francis Wathier, LW	5	0	0	0		5

GOALTENDING

Player	GP	Mins	W	L	TGA	GAA	SO
Marty Turco	53	3088	22	20	140	2.72	4
Kari Lehtonen	12	663	6	4	31	2.81	0

Columbus Blue Jackets
SCORING

Player	GP	G	Ast	Pts	+/-	PM
Rick Nash, RW	76	33	34	67	-2	58
Antoine Vermette, C	82	27	38	65	2	32
Kristian Huselius, LW	74	23	40	63	-4	36
RJ Umberger, LW	82	23	32	55	-16	40
Jakub Voracek, RW	81	16	34	50	-7	26
Derick Brassard, C	79	9	27	36	-17	48
Anton Stralman, D	73	6	28	34	-17	37
Fedor Tyutin, D	80	6	26	32	-7	49
Kris Russell, D	70	7	15	22	3	32
Chris Clark, RW	74	7	13	20	-12	48
Samuel Pahlsson, C	79	3	13	16	-9	32
Derek Dorsett, RW	51	4	10	14	6	105
Jan Hejda, D	62	3	10	13	-14	36
Mike Commodore, D	57	2	9	11	-9	62
Mathieu Roy, D	31	0	10	10	-2	17
Marc Methot, D	60	2	6	8	-8	51
Rostislav Klesla, D	26	2	6	8	-7	26
Milan Jurcina, D	44	1	6	7	2	24
Andrew Murray, C	46	5	2	7	-6	6
Jared Boll, RW	68	4	3	7	-8	149
Derek MacKenzie, C	18	1	3	4	3	0
Mike Blunden, RW	40	2	2	4	3	59
Grant Clitsome, D	11	1	2	3	0	6
Nikita Filatov, LW	13	2	0	2	0	8
Nathan Paetsch, D	21	1	1	2	-3	12
Tomas Kana, C	6	0	2	2	2	2
Maksim Mayorov, LW	4	0	0	0	-1	0
Alexandre Picard, LW	9	0	0	0	-3	10

GOALTENDING

Player	GP	Mins	W	L	TGA	GAA	SO
Steve Mason	58	3201	20	26	163	3.06	5
Mathieu Garon	35	1771	12	9	83	2.81	2

Detroit Red Wings
SCORING

Player	GP	G	Ast	Pts	+/-	PM
Pavel Datsyuk, C	80	27	43	70	17	18
Henrik Zetterberg, LW	74	23	47	70	12	26
Nicklas Lidstrom, D	82	9	40	49	22	24
Tomas Holmstrom, LW	68	25	20	45	5	60
Todd Bertuzzi, RW	82	18	26	44	-7	80
Brian Rafalski, D	78	8	34	42	23	26
Valtteri Filppula, C	55	11	24	35	-4	24
Dan Cleary, RW	64	15	19	34	-3	29
Darren Helm, C	75	11	13	24	-2	18
Kris Draper, C	81	7	15	22	-2	28
Niklas Kronwall, D	48	7	15	22	5	32
Patrick Eaves, RW	65	12	10	22	0	26
Johan Franzen, RW	27	10	11	21	1	22
Brad Stuart, D	82	4	16	20	-12	22
Drew Miller, LW	80	10	9	19	2	12
Jason Williams, C	44	6	9	15	-7	8
Jonathan Ericsson, D	62	4	9	13	-15	44
Brett Lebda, D	63	1	7	8	-2	24
Kirk Maltby, LW	52	4	2	6	1	32
Derek Meech, D	49	2	4	6	-12	19
Justin Abdelkader, LW	50	3	3	6	-11	35
Doug Janik, D	13	0	2	2	-3	18
Andreas Lilja, D	20	1	1	2	-2	4
Brad May, LW	40	0	1	1	-5	66
Kris Newbury, C	4	1	0	1	1	4

GOALTENDING

Player	GP	Mins	W	L	TGA	GAA	SO
Jimmy Howard	63	3740	37	15	141	2.26	3
Chris Osgood	23	1252	7	9	63	3.02	1

Edmonton Oilers

SCORING

Player	GP	G	Ast	Pts	+/-	PM
Dustin Penner, RW	82	32	31	63	6	38
Sam Gagner, C	68	15	26	41	-8	33
Ryan Whitney, D	81	7	32	39	1	70
Gilbert Brule, C	65	17	20	37	-8	38
Shawn Horcoff, C	77	13	23	36	-29	51
Patrick O'Sullivan, C	73	11	23	34	-35	32
Ryan Potulny, C	64	15	17	32	-21	28
Tom Gilbert, D	82	5	26	31	-10	16
Andrew Cogliano, C	82	10	18	28	-5	31
Robert Nilsson, RW	60	11	16	27	-17	12
Ales Hemsky, RW	22	7	15	22	7	8
Mike Comrie, C	43	13	8	21	-9	30
Ethan Moreau, LW	76	9	9	18	-18	62
Marc Pouliot, C	35	7	7	14	-4	21
Sheldon Souray, D	37	4	9	13	-19	65
Zack Stortini, RW	77	4	9	13	3	155
Ryan Jones, LW	49	8	4	12	0	26
J.-F. Jacques, LW	49	4	7	11	-15	78
Aaron Johnson, D	41	4	6	10	-6	35
Ladislav Smid, D	51	1	8	9	5	39
Fernando Pisani, RW	40	4	4	8	-16	10
Jason Strudwick, D	72	0	6	6	-18	50
Ryan Stone, C	27	0	6	6	2	48
Taylor Chorney, D	42	0	3	3	-21	12
Liam Reddox, LW	9	0	2	2	-2	4
Christopher Minard, LW	5	0	1	1	-3	0
Theo Peckham, D	15	0	1	1	-8	43
Alex Plante, D	4	0	1	1	1	2

GOALTENDING

Player	GP	Mins	W	L	TGA	GAA	SO
Jeff Deslauriers	48	2798	16	28	152	3.26	3
Nikolai Khabibulin	18	1089	7	9	55	3.03	0
Devan Dubnyk	19	1075	4	10	64	3.57	0

Florida Panthers

SCORING

Player	GP	G	Ast	Pts	+/-	PM
Stephen Weiss, C	80	28	32	60	-7	40
Nathan Horton, RW	65	20	37	57	-1	42
Bryan McCabe, D	82	8	35	43	-4	83
Michael Frolik, C	82	21	22	43	-4	43
Steven Reinprecht, C	82	16	22	38	-1	18
Cory Stillman, LW	58	15	22	37	-3	22
Radek Dvorak, RW	76	14	18	32	-7	20
Rostislav Olesz, LW	78	14	15	29	-4	28
Keith Ballard, D	82	8	20	28	-7	88
Gregory Campbell, C	60	2	15	17	-5	53
David Booth, LW	28	8	8	16	-3	23
Shawn Matthias, C	55	7	9	16	-3	10
Dmitry Kulikov, D	68	3	13	16	-5	32
Kamil Kreps, C	76	5	9	14	-7	18
Bryan Allen, D	74	4	9	13	-8	99
Byron Bitz, RW	52	5	6	11	-8	33
Jason Garrison, D	39	2	6	8	5	23
Victor Oreskovich, RW	50	2	4	6	-8	26
Michal Repik, RW	19	3	2	5	1	6
Ville Koistinen, D	17	1	3	4	1	8
Nick Tarnasky, C	31	1	2	3	-5	85
Kenndal McArdle, LW	19	1	2	3	-4	29
Jeff Taffe, LW	21	1	1	2	-1	4
Steve MacIntyre, LW	22	0	1	1	-3	24
Mike Duco, C	10	0	0	0	-3	50
Evgeny Dadonov, RW	4	0	0	0	-1	0
Keaton Ellerby, D	22	0	0	0	-1	2

GOALTENDING

Player	GP	Mins	W	L	TGA	GAA	SO
Tomas Vokoun	63	3695	23	28	157	2.55	7
Scott Clemmensen	23	1215	9	8	59	2.91	1
Alexander Salak	2	67	0	1	6	5.37	0

Los Angeles Kings

SCORING

Player	GP	G	Ast	Pts	+/-	PM
Anze Kopitar, C	82	34	47	81	6	16
Drew Doughty, D	82	16	43	59	20	54
Dustin Brown, RW	82	24	32	56	-6	41
Ryan Smyth, LW	67	22	31	53	8	42
Alexander Frolov, LW	81	19	32	51	-1	26
Jarret Stoll, C	73	16	31	47	13	40
Michal Handzus, C	81	20	22	42	4	38
Wayne Simmonds, RW	78	16	24	40	22	116
Jack Johnson, D	80	8	28	36	-15	48
Justin Williams, RW	49	10	19	29	3	39
Brad Richardson, C	81	11	16	27	1	37
Scott Parse, LW	59	11	13	24	13	22
Randy Jones, D	48	5	16	21	-3	28
Jeff Halpern, C	71	9	10	19	-14	39
Sean O'Donnell, D	78	3	12	15	14	70
Fredrik Modin, LW	44	5	6	11	-8	26
Rob Scuderi, D	73	0	11	11	16	21
Matt Greene, D	75	2	7	9	4	83

SCORING *(CONT.)*

Player	GP	G	Ast	Pts	+/-	PM
Davis Drewiske, D	42	1	7	8	-4	14
Oscar Moller, C	34	4	3	7	-6	4
Peter Harrold, D	39	1	2	3	-2	8
Rich Clune, LW	14	0	2	2	1	26
Corey Elkins, C	3	1	0	1	-2	0
Raitis Ivanans, LW	61	0	0	0	-8	136
Marc-Andre Cliche, C	1	0	0	0	1	0
Trevor Lewis, C	5	0	0	0	-3	0
Alec Martinez, D	4	0	0	0	-2	2
Andrei Loktionov, C	1	0	0	0	0	0
Brayden Schenn, C	1	0	0	0	-1	0

GOALTENDING

Player	GP	Mins	W	L	TGA	GAA	SO
Jonathan Quick	72	4258	39	24	180	2.54	4
Erik Ersberg	11	551	4	3	22	2.40	0
Jonathan Bernier	3	185	3	0	4	1.30	1

Minnesota Wild

SCORING

Player	GP	G	Ast	Pts	+/-	PM
Mikko Koivu, C	80	22	49	71	-2	50
Andrew Brunette, LW	82	25	36	61	-5	12
Martin Havlat, RW	73	18	36	54	-19	34
Marek Zidlicky, D	78	6	37	43	-16	67
Antti Miettinen, RW	79	20	22	42	-2	44
Guill. Latendresse, LW	78	27	13	40	-3	16
Owen Nolan, RW	73	16	17	33	-12	40
Kyle Brodziak, C	82	9	23	32	-3	22
Cam Barker, D	70	5	16	21	5	68
Cal Clutterbuck, RW	74	13	8	21	-8	52
Nick Schultz, D	80	1	19	20	-8	43
Brent Burns, D	47	3	17	20	-15	32
Andrew Ebbett, C	61	9	6	15	-8	8
Greg Zanon, D	81	2	13	15	-10	36
Chuck Kobasew, RW	49	9	6	15	-11	18
Shane Hnidy, D	70	2	12	14	-6	66
Robbie Earl, LW	32	6	0	6	1	6
James Sheppard, C	64	2	4	6	-14	38
Casey Wellman, C	12	1	3	4	-2	0
Derek Boogaard, LW	57	0	4	4	-12	105
Clayton Stoner, D	8	0	2	2	1	12

GOALTENDING

Player	GP	Mins	W	L	TGA	GAA	SO
Niklas Backstrom	60	3489	26	23	158	2.72	2
Josh Harding	25	1300	9	12	66	3.05	1
Wade Dubielewicz	3	101	1	1	5	2.97	0

Nashville Predators

SCORING

Player	GP	G	Ast	Pts	+/-	PM
Steve Sullivan, LW	82	17	34	51	2	35
Patric Hornqvist, RW	80	30	21	51	18	40
Martin Erat, RW	74	21	28	49	-7	50
Jason Arnott, C	63	19	27	46	0	26
JP Dumont, RW	74	17	28	45	8	20
Shea Weber, D	78	16	27	43	0	36
David Legwand, C	82	11	27	38	-5	18
Ryan Suter, D	82	4	33	37	4	48
Joel Ward, RW	71	13	21	34	-5	18
Marcel Goc, C	73	12	18	30	10	14
Dan Hamuis, D	78	5	19	24	4	49
Dustin Boyd, C	78	11	13	24	6	19
Denis Grebeshkov, D	51	7	14	21	-16	32
Cody Franson, D	61	6	15	21	15	16
Jordin Tootoo, RW	51	6	10	16	2	40
Colin Wilson, C	35	8	7	15	-2	7
Jerred Smithson, C	69	9	4	13	-4	54
Francis Bouillon, D	81	3	8	11	5	50
Kevin Klein, D	81	1	10	11	-13	27
Cal O'Reilly, C	31	2	9	11	1	4
Dave Scatchard, C	16	3	2	5	3	17
Michael Santorelli, C	25	2	1	3	-8	8
Nick Spaling, LW	20	0	3	3	3	0
Andreas Thuresson, RW	22	1	2	3	-5	4
Wade Belak, RW	39	0	2	2	0	58
Alexander Sulzer, D	20	0	2	2	4	4
Ben Guite, RW	6	0	0	0	-3	4
Triston Grant, LW	3	0	0	0	-1	9
Teemu Laakso, D	7	0	0	0	-2	2

GOALTENDING

Player	GP	Mins	W	L	TGA	GAA	SO
Pekka Rinne	58	3246	32	16	137	2.53	7
Dan Ellis	31	1715	15	13	77	2.69	1

Montreal Canadiens

SCORING

Player	GP	G	Ast	Pts	+/-	PM
Tomas Plekanec, C	82	25	45	70	5	50
Scott Gomez, C	78	12	47	59	1	60
Michael Cammalleri, LW	65	26	24	50	7	16
Brian Gionta, RW	61	28	18	46	3	26
Andrei Markov, D	45	6	28	34	11	32
Marc Bergeron, D	60	13	21	34	-7	16
Andrei Kostitsyn, LW	59	15	18	33	1	32
Glen Metropolit, C	69	16	13	29	-1	24
Dominic Moore, C	69	10	18	28	-3	43
Benoit Pouliot, LW	53	17	11	28	8	43
Roman Hamrlik, D	75	6	20	26	-2	56
Jaroslav Spacek, D	74	3	18	21	9	50
Travis Moen, LW	81	8	11	19	-2	57
Sergei Kostitsyn, LW	47	7	11	18	4	8
Maxim Lapierre, C	76	7	7	14	-14	61
Max Pacioretty, LW	52	3	11	14	-5	20
Hal Gill, D	68	2	9	11	-10	68
Mathieu Darche, LW	29	5	5	10	2	4
Josh Gorges, D	82	3	7	10	2	39
Paul Mara, D	42	0	8	8	-16	48
Tom Pyatt, C	40	2	3	5	-5	10
Ryan O'Byrne, D	55	1	3	4	-3	74
Georges Laraque, RW	28	1	2	3	-6	28
Ryan White, C	16	0	2	2	-6	16
PK Subban, D	2	0	2	2	1	2

GOALTENDING

Player	GP	Mins	W	L	TGA	GAA	SO
Jaroslav Halak	45	2630	26	13	105	2.40	5
Carey Price	41	2358	13	20	109	2.77	0

New Jersey Devils

SCORING

Player	GP	G	Ast	Pts	+/-	PM
Ilya Kovalchuk, LW	76	41	44	85	10	53
Zach Parise, LW	81	38	44	82	24	32
Travis Zajac, C	82	25	42	67	22	24
J. Langenbrunner, RW	81	19	42	61	6	44
Patrik Elias, LW	58	19	29	48	18	40
Brian Rolston, LW	80	20	17	37	2	22
Andy Greene, D	78	6	31	37	9	14
Dainius Zubrus, LW	51	10	17	27	4	28
David Clarkson, RW	46	11	13	24	3	85
Rob Niedermayer, C	71	10	12	22	3	45
Mike Mottau, D	79	2	16	18	4	41
Dean McAmmond, C	62	8	9	17	-1	40
Bryce Salvador, D	79	4	10	14	8	57
Colin White, D	81	2	10	12	8	46
Martin Skoula, D	52	3	8	11	3	10
Paul Martin, D	22	2	9	11	10	2
Rod Pelley, C	63	2	8	10	-4	40
Vladimir Zharkov, RW	40	0	10	10	2	8
Jay Pandolfo, LW	52	4	5	9	-10	6
Anssi Salmela, D	38	2	6	8	-1	22
Mark Fraser, D	61	3	3	6	3	36
Ilkka Pikkarainen, RW	33	1	3	4	-3	10
Cory Murphy, D	12	2	1	3	-2	2
P. Letourn.-Leblond, LW	27	0	2	2	-4	48
Matt Halischuk, RW	20	1	1	2	-4	2
Tyler Eckford, D	3	0	1	1	0	4
Tim Sestito, C	9	0	1	1	-2	2
Patrick Davis, RW	8	1	0	1	-2	0

GOALTENDING

Player	GP	Mins	W	L	TGA	GAA	SO
Martin Brodeur	77	4499	45	25	168	2.24	9
Yann Danis	12	467	3	2	16	2.06	0

New York Islanders
SCORING

Player	GP	G	Ast	Pts	+/-	PM
John Tavares, C	82	24	30	54	-15	22
Kyle Okposo, RW	80	19	33	52	-22	34
Mark Streit, D	82	11	38	49	0	48
Matt Moulson, LW	82	30	18	48	-1	16
Frans Nielsen, C	76	12	26	38	4	6
Blake Comeau, RW	61	17	18	35	-2	40
Josh Bailey, C	73	16	19	35	5	18
Richard Park, RW	81	9	22	31	-9	28
Trent Hunter, RW	61	11	17	28	3	18
Rob Schremp, C	44	7	18	25	-4	8
Sean Bergenheim, LW	63	10	13	23	1	45
Jon Sim, LW	77	13	9	22	-4	44
Jack Hillen, D	69	3	18	21	-5	44
Doug Weight, C	36	1	16	17	-1	8
Bruno Gervais, D	71	3	14	17	-15	31
Freddy Meyer, D	64	4	11	15	-2	40
Jeff Tambellini, LW	36	7	7	14	-8	14
Tim Jackman, RW	54	4	5	9	-4	98
Andrew MacDonald, D	46	1	6	7	4	20
Brendan Witt, D	42	2	3	5	-18	45
Dylan Reese, D	19	2	2	4	4	14
Dustin Kohn, D	22	0	4	4	-2	4
Radek Martinek, D	16	2	1	3	-1	12
Matt Martin, LW	5	0	2	2	-1	26
Trevor Gillies, LW	14	0	1	1	-2	75
Mark Flood, D	6	0	1	1	-4	0
Jesse Joensuu, LW	11	1	0	1	4	4

GOALTENDING

Player	GP	Mins	W	L	TGA	GAA	SO
Dwayne Roloson	50	2897	23	18	145	3.00	1
Martin Biron	29	1634	9	14	89	3.27	1
Rick DiPietro	8	462	2	5	20	2.60	1

Ottawa Senators
SCORING

Player	GP	G	Ast	Pts	+/-	PM
Daniel Alfredsson, RW	70	20	51	71	8	22
Jason Spezza, C	60	23	34	57	0	20
Mike Fisher, C	79	25	28	53	1	59
Alexei Kovalev, RW	77	18	31	49	-8	54
Matt Cullen, C	81	16	32	48	-7	34
Milan Michalek, LW	66	22	12	34	-12	18
Chris Kelly, C	81	15	17	32	-7	38
Peter Regin, C	75	13	16	29	10	20
Filip Kuba, D	53	3	25	28	-5	28
Jarkko Ruutu, LW	82	12	14	26	-2	121
Nick Foligno, LW	61	9	17	26	6	53
Erik Karlsson, D	60	5	21	26	-5	24
Chris Phillips, D	82	8	16	24	8	45
Chris Neil, RW	68	10	12	22	-1	175
Chris Campoli, D	67	4	14	18	-3	16
Ryan Shannon, RW	66	5	11	16	-12	20
Jonathan Cheechoo, RW	61	5	9	14	-13	20
Anton Volchenkov, D	64	4	10	14	2	38
Andy Sutton, D	72	5	8	13	-10	107
Jesse Winchester, C	52	2	11	13	-1	22
Matt Carkner, D	81	2	9	11	0	190
Shean Donovan, RW	30	2	3	5	-4	40
Brian Lee, D	23	2	1	3	-5	12
Zack Smith, C	15	2	1	3	1	14

GOALTENDING

Player	GP	Mins	W	L	TGA	GAA	SO
Brian Elliott	55	3038	29	18	130	2.57	5
Pascal Leclaire	34	1745	12	14	93	3.20	0
Mike Brodeur	3	180	3	0	3	1.00	1

New York Rangers
SCORING

Player	GP	G	Ast	Pts	+/-	PM
Marian Gaborik, RW	76	42	44	86	15	37
Vinny Prospal, C	75	20	38	58	8	32
Olli Jokinen, C	82	15	35	50	3	75
Brandon Dubinsky, C	69	20	24	44	9	54
Ryan Callahan, RW	77	19	18	37	-12	48
Michael Del Zotto, D	80	9	28	37	-20	32
Chris Drury, C	77	14	18	32	-10	31
Sean Avery, LW	69	11	20	31	0	160
Artem Anisimov, C	82	12	16	28	-2	32
Marc Staal, D	82	8	19	27	11	44
Erik Christensen, C	58	8	18	26	11	26
Dan Girardi, D	82	6	18	24	-2	53
Michal Rozsival, D	82	3	20	23	3	78
Matt Gilroy, D	69	4	11	15	0	23
Wade Redden, D	75	2	12	14	8	27
Enver Lisin, RW	57	6	8	14	-1	18
Brandon Prust, LW	69	5	9	14	9	163
Jody Shelley, LW	57	2	7	9	5	115
PA Parenteau, LW	22	3	5	8	-2	4
Aaron Voros, LW	41	3	4	7	-2	89
Brian Boyle, C	71	4	2	6	-6	47
Anders Eriksson, D	20	0	5	5	2	2
Donald Brashear, LW	36	0	1	1	-9	73
Dane Byers, LW	5	1	0	1	1	31

GOALTENDING

Player	GP	Mins	W	L	TGA	GAA	SO
Henrik Lundqvist	73	4204	35	27	167	2.38	4
Alex Auld	24	1299	9	7	64	2.96	0
Steve Valiquette	6	305	2	3	19	3.74	1
Chad Johnson	5	281	1	2	11	2.35	0

Philadelphia Flyers
SCORING

Player	GP	G	Ast	Pts	+/-	PM
Mike Richards, C	82	31	31	62	-2	79
Jeff Carter, C	74	33	28	61	2	38
Chris Pronger, D	82	10	45	55	22	79
Danny Briere, RW	75	26	27	53	-2	71
Claude Giroux, RW	82	16	31	47	-9	23
Scott Hartnell, LW	81	14	30	44	-6	155
Simon Gagne, LW	58	17	23	40	-1	47
Kimmo Timonen, D	82	6	33	39	-2	50
J. van Riemsdyk, LW	78	15	20	35	-1	30
Matt Carle, D	80	6	29	35	19	16
Arron Asham, RW	72	10	14	24	-2	126
Dan Carcillo, LW	76	12	10	22	5	207
Ian Laperriere, RW	82	3	17	20	-1	162
Braydon Coburn, D	81	5	14	19	-6	54
Blair Betts, C	63	8	10	18	7	14
Darroll Powe, C	63	9	6	15	0	54
Ville Leino, LW	55	6	5	11	-8	10
Oskars Bartulis, D	53	1	8	9	-12	28
Danny Syvret, D	21	2	2	4	1	12
Mika Pyorala, C	36	2	2	4	-3	10
David Laliberte, RW	11	2	1	3	1	6
Lukas Krajicek, D	50	1	2	3	-14	35
Ryan Parent, D	48	1	2	3	-14	20
Ole-Kristian Tollefsen, D	18	0	2	2	1	23
Jon Kalinski, LW	10	0	2	2	-2	0
Andreas Nodl, RW	10	0	1	1	-2	0

GOALTENDING

Player	GP	Mins	W	L	TGA	GAA	SO
Michael Leighton	34	1799	17	9	85	2.83	1
Brian Boucher	33	1742	9	18	80	2.76	1
Ray Emery	29	1684	16	11	74	2.64	3

Phoenix Coyotes

SCORING

Player	GP	G	Ast	Pts	+/-	PM
Wojtek Wolski, LW	80	23	42	65	21	27
Shane Doan, LW	82	18	37	55	3	41
Matthew Lombardi, C	78	19	34	53	8	36
Lee Stempniak, RW	80	28	20	48	0	26
Radim Vrbata, RW	82	24	19	43	6	24
Keith Yandle, D	82	12	29	41	16	45
Ed Jovanovski, D	62	10	24	34	-12	55
Martin Hanzal, C	81	11	22	33	0	104
Scottie Upshall, RW	49	18	14	32	5	50
Vernon Fiddler, C	76	8	22	30	13	46
Robert Lang, C	64	9	20	29	-4	28
Derek Morris, D	76	4	25	29	2	37
Adrian Aucoin, D	82	8	20	28	2	56
Taylor Pyatt, LW	74	12	11	23	13	39
Petr Prucha, RW	79	13	9	22	-2	23
Daniel Winnik, LW	74	4	15	19	1	12
Zbynek Michalek, D	72	3	14	17	5	30
Petteri Nokelainen, C	67	5	8	13	-9	27
James Vandermeer, D	62	4	8	12	3	60
Lauri Korpikoski, LW	71	5	6	11	-10	16
Sami Lepisto, D	66	1	10	11	14	60
Mathieu Schneider, D	25	2	7	9	5	16
Paul Bissonnette, LW	41	3	2	5	-2	117
David Schlemko, D	17	1	4	5	1	8
Mikkel Boedker, RW	14	1	2	3	2	0
Shaun Heshka, D	8	0	2	2	0	4
Joel Perrault, C	2	1	0	1	-1	0

GOALTENDING

Player	GP	Mins	W	L	TGA	GAA	SO
Ilya Bryzgalov	69	4084	42	20	156	2.29	8
Jason LaBarbera	17	928	8	5	33	2.13	0

Pittsburgh Penguins

SCORING

Player	GP	G	Ast	Pts	+/-	PM
Sidney Crosby, C	81	51	58	109	15	71
Evgeni Malkin, C	67	28	49	77	-6	100
Sergei Gonchar, D	62	11	39	50	-4	49
Alexei Ponikarovsky, LW	77	21	29	50	-1	61
Jordan Staal, C	82	21	28	49	19	57
Bill Guerin, RW	78	21	24	45	-9	75
Pascal Dupuis, RW	81	18	20	38	5	16
Alex Goligoski, D	69	8	29	37	7	22
Chris Kunitz, LW	50	13	19	32	3	39
Matt Cooke, LW	79	15	15	30	17	106
Ruslan Fedotenko, LW	80	11	19	30	-17	50
Kris Letang, D	73	3	24	27	1	51
Jordan Leopold, D	81	11	15	26	-2	28
Brooks Orpik, D	73	2	23	25	6	64
Tyler Kennedy, C	64	13	12	25	10	31
Mike Rupp, C	81	13	6	19	5	120
Mark Eaton, D	79	3	13	16	5	26
Jay McKee, D	62	1	9	10	6	54
Craig Adams, RW	82	0	10	10	-5	72
Maxime Talbot, C	45	2	5	7	-9	30
Eric Godard, RW	45	1	2	3	2	76
Chris Conner, RW	8	2	1	3	-1	0
Ben Lovejoy, D	12	0	3	3	8	2
Deryk Engelland, D	9	0	2	2	-2	17
Nick Johnson, RW	6	1	1	2	-2	2
Mark Letestu, C	10	1	0	1	-2	2
Nathan Guenin, D	2	0	0	0	-2	0
Tim Wallace, RW	1	0	0	0	0	0

GOALTENDING

Player	GP	Mins	W	L	TGA	GAA	SO
Marc-Andre Fleury	67	3798	37	21	168	2.65	1
Brent Johnson	23	1108	10	6	51	2.76	0

San Jose Sharks

SCORING

Player	GP	G	Ast	Pts	+/-	PM
Joe Thornton, C	79	20	69	89	17	54
Patrick Marleau, LW	82	44	39	83	21	22
Dany Heatley, RW	82	39	43	82	14	54
Dan Boyle, D	76	15	43	58	6	70
Ryane Clowe, LW	82	19	38	57	0	131
Joe Pavelski, C	67	25	26	51	1	26
Devin Setoguchi, RW	70	20	16	36	0	19
Manny Malhotra, C	71	14	19	33	17	41
Rob Blake, D	70	7	23	30	14	60
Kent Huskins, D	82	3	19	22	6	47
Jason Demers, D	51	4	17	21	5	21
Jed Ortmeyer, RW	76	8	11	19	4	37
Scott Nichol, C	79	4	15	19	0	72
Douglas Murray, D	79	4	13	17	3	66
Marc Vlasic, D	64	3	13	16	21	33
Jamie McGinn, LW	59	10	3	13	-3	38
Torrey Mitchell, C	56	2	9	11	6	27

SCORING *(CONT.)*

Player	GP	G	Ast	Pts	+/-	PM
Logan Couture, C	25	5	4	9	4	6
Niclas Wallin, D	70	0	7	7	-5	49
Frazer McLaren, LW	23	1	5	6	6	54
Brad Staubitz, RW	47	3	3	6	0	110
Benn Ferriero, C	24	2	3	5	4	8
Ryan Vesce, RW	9	3	2	5	-1	0
Derek Joslin, D	24	0	3	3	1	12
Jay Leach, D	35	1	1	2	3	25
Joe Callahan, D	1	0	1	1	1	0
Dwight Helminen, C	4	1	0	1	-1	0
John McCarthy, LW	4	0	0	0	-3	0
Steven Zalewski, C	3	0	0	0	-2	0

GOALTENDING

Player	GP	Mins	W	L	TGA	GAA	SO
Evgeni Nabokov	71	4194	44	16	170	2.43	3
Thomas Greiss	16	782	7	4	35	2.69	0

St. Louis Blues

SCORING

Player	GP	G	Ast	Pts	+/-	PM
Andy McDonald, C	79	24	33	57	-9	18
David Backes, RW	79	17	31	48	-4	106
T.J. Oshie, C	76	18	30	48	-1	36
Alexander Steen, C	68	24	23	47	6	30
David Perron, LW	82	20	27	47	-10	60
Paul Kariya, LW	75	18	25	43	-7	36
Brad Boyes, C	82	14	28	42	1	26
Erik Johnson, D	79	10	29	39	1	79
Keith Tkachuk, LW	67	13	19	32	-2	56
Carlo Colaiacovo, D	67	7	25	32	8	60
Jay McClement, C	82	11	18	29	0	22
Patrik Berglund, C	71	13	13	26	-5	12
Roman Polak, D	78	4	17	21	7	59
Barret Jackman, D	66	2	15	17	3	81
Eric Brewer, D	59	8	7	15	-17	46
Brandon Crombeen, RW	79	7	8	15	-5	168
Mike Weaver, D	77	1	9	10	10	29
Darryl Sydor, D	47	0	8	8	-6	15
Brad Winchester, LW	64	3	5	8	3	108
Matt D'Agostini, RW	47	2	2	4	-15	28
Tyson Strachan, D	8	0	2	2	3	4
Jonas Junland, D	3	0	2	2	-3	0
Lars Eller, C	7	2	0	2	2	4
Alex Pietrangelo, D	9	1	1	2	-9	6
Yan Stastny, C	4	1	0	1	1	0
Derek Armstrong, C	6	0	0	0	-2	2
Cam Janssen, RW	43	0	0	0	-3	190
DJ King, LW	12	0	0	0	-4	33

GOALTENDING

Player	GP	Mins	W	L	TGA	GAA	SO
Chris Mason	61	3512	30	22	148	2.53	2
Ty Conklin	26	1451	10	10	60	2.48	4

Tampa Bay Lightning

SCORING

Player	GP	G	Ast	Pts	+/-	PM
Steven Stamkos, C	82	51	44	95	-2	38
Martin St Louis, RW	82	29	65	94	-8	12
Vincent Lecavalier, C	82	24	46	70	-16	63
Ryan Malone, LW	69	21	26	47	-8	68
Steve Downie, RW	79	22	24	46	14	208
Kurtis Foster, D	71	8	34	42	-5	48
Alex Tanguay, LW	80	10	27	37	-2	32
Victor Hedman, D	74	4	16	20	-3	79
Andrej Meszaros, D	81	6	11	17	-14	50
Teddy Purcell, RW	60	6	9	15	-9	10
Mattias Ohlund, D	67	0	13	13	-8	59
Brandon Bochenski, RW	28	4	9	13	-1	2
Mike Lundin, D	49	3	10	13	-4	18
Nate Thompson, C	71	2	8	10	-17	56
Stephane Veilleux, LW	77	3	6	9	-14	48
Paul Szczechura, C	52	5	2	7	-15	18
Todd Fedoruk, LW	50	3	3	6	-12	54
Matt Walker, D	66	2	3	5	-11	90
Zenon Konopka, C	74	2	3	5	-11	265
James Wright, C	48	2	3	5	-9	18
David Hale, D	39	0	4	4	-2	25
Mark Parrish, RW	16	0	2	2	-5	4
Paul Ranger, D	8	1	1	2	-2	6
Matt Smaby, D	33	0	2	2	-4	27
Ryan Craig, C	3	0	0	0	0	5
Matt Lashoff, D	5	0	0	0	-2	21
Vladimir Mihalik, D	4	0	0	0	-4	2
Scott Jackson, D	1	0	0	0	0	0
Blair Jones, C	14	0	0	0	-5	10

GOALTENDING

Player	GP	Mins	W	L	TGA	GAA	SO
Antero Niittymaki	49	2657	21	18	127	2.87	1
Mike Smith	42	2273	13	18	117	3.09	2

Toronto Maple Leafs

SCORING

Player	GP	G	Ast	Pts	+/-	PM
Phil Kessel, RW	70	30	25	55	-8	21
Tomas Kaberle, D	82	7	42	49	-16	24
Nikolai Kulemin, LW	78	16	20	36	0	16
Mikhail Grabovski, C	59	10	25	35	3	10
Dion Phaneuf, D	81	12	20	32	1	83
Tyler Bozak, C	37	8	19	27	-5	6
Francois Beauchemin, D	82	5	21	26	-13	33
John Mitchell, C	60	6	17	23	-7	31
Luke Schenn, D	79	5	12	17	2	50
Carl Gunnarsson, D	43	3	12	15	8	10
Viktor Stalberg, LW	40	9	5	14	-13	30
Jamie Lundmark, C	36	5	7	12	-7	20
Fredrik Sjostrom, LW	65	3	8	11	-2	12
Jeff Finger, D	39	2	8	10	-11	20
Rickard Wallin, C	60	2	7	9	-7	20
Wayne Primeau, C	59	3	5	8	-1	35

SCORING *(CONT.)*

Player	GP	G	Ast	Pts	+/-	PM
Luca Caputi, LW	23	2	6	8	-1	12
Christian Hanson, C	31	2	5	7	-2	16
Colton Orr, RW	82	4	2	6	-4	239
Garnet Exelby, D	51	1	3	4	-8	73
Mike Komisarek, D	34	0	4	4	-9	40
Jay Rosehill, LW	15	1	1	2	-2	67
Tim Brent, C	1	0	0	0	0	0
Andre Deveaux, C	1	0	0	0	-1	0
Nazem Kadri, C	1	0	0	0	-1	0
Brayden Irwin, C	2	0	0	0	0	2

GOALTENDING

Player	GP	Mins	W	L	TGA	GAA	SO
Jonas Gustavsson	42	2340	16	15	112	2.87	1
Jean-S. Giguere	35	2024	10	15	96	2.85	3

Vancouver Canucks

SCORING

Player	GP	G	Ast	Pts	+/–	PM
Henrik Sedin, C	82	29	83	112	35	48
Daniel Sedin, LW	63	29	56	85	36	28
Ryan Kesler, C	82	25	50	75	1	104
Alex Burrows, LW	82	35	32	67	34	121
Mikael Samuelsson, RW	74	30	23	53	10	64
Mason Raymond, LW	82	25	28	53	0	48
Christian Ehrhoff, D	80	14	30	44	36	42
Alexander Edler, D	76	5	37	42	0	40
Sami Salo, D	68	9	19	28	14	18
Kyle Wellwood, C	75	14	11	25	6	12
Kevin Bieksa, D	55	3	19	22	-5	85
Steve Bernier, RW	59	11	11	22	0	21
Pavol Demitra, RW	28	3	13	16	3	0
Jannik Hansen, LW	47	9	6	15	-5	18
Willie Mitchell, D	48	4	8	12	13	48
Andrew Alberts, D	76	3	9	12	6	87
Tanner Glass, LW	67	4	7	11	5	115

SCORING

Player	GP	G	Ast	Pts	+/–	PM
Michael Grabner, RW	20	5	6	11	2	8
Shane O'Brien, D	65	2	6	8	15	79
Rick Rypien, C	69	4	4	8	-3	126
Ryan Johnson, C	58	1	4	5	-4	12
Aaron Rome, D	49	0	4	4	-2	24
Matt Pettinger, LW	9	1	2	3	3	6
Nolan Baumgartner, D	12	1	1	2	7	2
Brad Lukowich, D	13	1	1	2	5	4
Darcy Hordichuk, LW	56	1	1	2	-7	142
Alexandre Bolduc, C	15	0	.0	0	-3	13
Mario Bliznak, C	2	0	0	0	-2	0
Sergei Shirokov, RW	6	0	0	0	-4	2

GOALTENDING

Player	GP	Mins	W	L	TGA	GAA	SO
Roberto Luongo	68	3899	40	22	167	2.57	4
Andrew Raycroft	21	967	9	5	39	2.42	1
Cory Schneider	2	79	0	1	5	3.80	0

Washington Capitals

SCORING

Player	GP	G	Ast	Pts	+/–	PM
Alex Ovechkin, LW	72	50	59	109	45	89
Nicklas Backstrom, C	82	33	68	101	37	50
Alexander Semin, LW	73	40	44	84	36	66
Mike Green, D	75	19	57	76	39	54
Brooks Laich, C	78	25	34	59	16	34
Mike Knuble, RW	69	29	24	53	23	59
Tomas Fleischmann, C	69	23	28	51	9	28
Brendan Morrison, C	74	12	30	42	23	40
Eric Belanger, C	77	15	26	41	2	32
Eric Fehr, RW	69	21	18	39	18	24
Jason Chimera, LW	78	15	19	34	-1	98
Tom Poti, D	70	4	20	24	26	42
Matt Bradley, RW	77	10	14	24	6	47
Jeff Schultz, D	73	3	20	23	50	32
Joe Corvo, D	52	6	12	18	-10	12
David Steckel, LW	79	5	11	16	4	19
Shaone Morrisonn, D	68	1	11	12	8	68

SCORING

Player	GP	G	Ast	Pts	+/–	PM
Mathieu Perreault, C	21	4	5	9	4	6
Scott Walker, RW	42	5	3	8	-3	32
John Erskine, D	50	1	5	6	16	66
Tyler Sloan, D	40	2	4	6	-1	22
John Carlson, D	22	1	5	6	11	8
Keith Aucoin, RW	9	1	4	5	-2	0
Karl Alzner, D	21	0	5	5	-2	8
Quintin Laing, LW	36	2	2	4	2	21
Alexandre Giroux, LW	9	1	2	3	3	4
Chris Bourque, LW	21	0	3	3	-6	10
Kyle Wilson, C	2	0	2	2	1	0
Jay Beagle, RW	7	1	1	2	-1	2

GOALTENDING

Player	GP	Mins	W	L	TGA	GAA	SO
Jose Theodore	47	2586	30	7	121	2.81	1
Semyon Varlamov	26	1527	15	4	65	2.55	2
Michal Neuvirth	17	872	9	4	40	2.75	0

2010 NHL Draft

First Round

The opening round of the 2010 NHL entry draft was held on June 26 in Los Angeles, California.

	Team	Selection	Position		Team	Selection	Position
1.	Edmonton	Taylor Hall	LW	16.	St. Louis	Vladimir Tarasenko	RW
2.	Boston	Tyler Seguin	C	17.	Colorado	Joey Hishon	C
3.	Florida	Erik Gudbranson	D	18.	Nashville	Austin Watson	LW
4.	Columbus	Ryan Johansen	C	19.	Florida	Nick Bjugstad	C
5.	NY Islanders	Nino Niederreiter	C	20.	Pittsburgh	Beau Bennett	RW
6.	Tampa Bay	Brett Connolly	RW	21.	Detroit	Riley Sheahan	C
7.	Carolina	Jeff Skinner	RW	22.	Montreal	Jarred Tinordi	D
8.	Atlanta	Alexander Burmistov	C	23.	Buffalo	Mark Pysyk	D
9.	Minnesota	Mikael Granlund	C	24.	Chicago	Kevin Hayes	RW
10.	NY Rangers	Dylan McIlrath	D	25.	Florida	Quinton Howden	C
11.	Dallas	Jack Campbell	D	26.	Washington	Evgeny Kuznetsov	C
12.	Anaheim	Cam Fowler	G	27.	Phoenix	Mark Visentin	G
13.	Phoenix	Brandon Gormley	D	28.	San Jose	Charlie Coyle	C
14.	St. Louis	Jaden Schwartz	D	29.	Anaheim	Emerson Etem	RW
15.	Los Angeles	Derek Forbort	C	30.	NY Islanders	Brock Nelson	C

The Stanley Cup

Awarded annually to the team that wins the NHL's best-of-seven final-round playoffs. The Stanley Cup is the oldest trophy competed for by professional athletes in North America. It was donated in 1893 by Frederick Arthur, Lord Stanley of Preston.

Results

1892–93	Montreal A.A.A.
1893–94	Montreal A.A.A.
1894–95	Montreal Victorias
1895–96	Winnipeg Victorias (Feb)
1895–96	Montreal Victorias (Dec)
1896–97	Montreal Victorias
1897–98	Montreal Victorias
1898–99	Montreal Victorias (Feb)
1898–99	Montreal Shamrocks (Mar)
1899–1900	Montreal Shamrocks
1900–01	Winnipeg Victorias
1901–02	Winnipeg Victorias (Jan)
1901–02	Montreal A.A.A. (Mar)
1902–03	Montreal A.A.A. (Feb)
1902–03	Ottawa Silver Seven (Mar)
1903–04	Ottawa Silver Seven
1904–05	Ottawa Silver Seven
1905–06	Ottawa Silver Seven (Feb)
1905–06	Montreal Wanderers (Mar)
1906–07	Kenora Thistles (Jan)
1906–07	Montreal Wanderers (Mar)
1907–08	Montreal Wanderers
1908–09	Ottawa Senators
1909–10	Montreal Wanderers
1910–11	Ottawa Senators
1911–12	Quebec Bulldogs
1912–13	Quebec Bulldogs
1913–14	Toronto Blueshirts
1914–15	Vancouver Millionaires
1915–16	Montreal Canadiens
1916–17	Seattle Metropolitans

NHL WINNERS AND FINALISTS

Season	Champion	Finalist	GP in Final
1917–18	Toronto Arenas	Vancouver Millionaires	5
1918–19	No decision*	No decision*	5
1919–20	Ottawa Senators	Seattle Metropolitans	5
1920–21	Ottawa Senators	Vancouver Millionaires	5
1921–22	Toronto St. Pats	Vancouver Millionaires	5
1922–23	Ottawa Senators	Vancouver Maroons, Edmonton Eskimos	2, 4
1923–24	Montreal Canadiens	Vancouver Maroons, Calgary Tigers	2, 2
1924–25	Victoria Cougars	Montreal Canadiens	4
1925–26	Montreal Maroons	Victoria Cougars	4
1926–27	Ottawa Senators	Boston Bruins	4
1927–28	New York Rangers	Montreal Maroons	5
1928–29	Boston Bruins	New York Rangers	2
1929–30	Montreal Canadiens	Boston Bruins	2
1930–31	Montreal Canadiens	Chicago Black Hawks	5
1931–32	Toronto Maple Leafs	New York Rangers	3
1932–33	New York Rangers	Toronto Maple Leafs	4
1933–34	Chicago Black Hawks	Detroit Red Wings	4
1934–35	Montreal Maroons	Toronto Maple Leafs	3
1935–36	Detroit Red Wings	Toronto Maple Leafs	4
1936–37	Detroit Red Wings	New York Rangers	5
1937–38	Chicago Black Hawks	Toronto Maple Leafs	4
1938–39	Boston Bruins	Toronto Maple Leafs	5
1939–40	New York Rangers	Toronto Maple Leafs	6
1940–41	Boston Bruins	Detroit Red Wings	4
1941–42	Toronto Maple Leafs	Detroit Red Wings	7
1942–43	Detroit Red Wings	Boston Bruins	4
1943–44	Montreal Canadiens	Chicago Black Hawks	4
1944–45	Toronto Maple Leafs	Detroit Red Wings	7
1945–46	Montreal Canadiens	Boston Bruins	5
1946–47	Toronto Maple Leafs	Montreal Canadiens	6
1947–48	Toronto Maple Leafs	Detroit Red Wings	4
1948–49	Toronto Maple Leafs	Detroit Red Wings	4
1949–50	Detroit Red Wings	New York Rangers	7
1950–51	Toronto Maple Leafs	Montreal Canadiens	5
1951–52	Detroit Red Wings	Montreal Canadiens	4
1952–53	Montreal Canadiens	Boston Bruins	5
1953–54	Detroit Red Wings	Montreal Canadiens	7
1954–55	Detroit Red Wings	Montreal Canadiens	7

NHL WINNERS AND FINALISTS

Season	Champion	Finalist	GP in Final
1955–56	Montreal Canadiens	Detroit Red Wings	5
1956–57	Montreal Canadiens	Boston Bruins	5
1957–58	Montreal Canadiens	Boston Bruins	6
1958–59	Montreal Canadiens	Toronto Maple Leafs	5
1959–60	Montreal Canadiens	Toronto Maple Leafs	4
1960–61	Chicago Blackhawks	Detroit Red Wings	6
1961–62	Toronto Maple Leafs	Chicago Blackhawks	6
1962–63	Toronto Maple Leafs	Detroit Red Wings	5
1963–64	Toronto Maple Leafs	Detroit Red Wings	7
1964–65	Montreal Canadiens	Chicago Blackhawks	7
1965–66	Montreal Canadiens	Detroit Red Wings	6
1966–67	Toronto Maple Leafs	Montreal Canadiens	6
1967–68	Montreal Canadiens	St. Louis Blues	4
1968–69	Montreal Canadiens	St. Louis Blues	4
1969–70	Boston Bruins	St. Louis Blues	4
1970–71	Montreal Canadiens	Chicago Blackhawks	7
1971–72	Boston Bruins	New York Rangers	6
1972–73	Montreal Canadiens	Chicago Blackhawks	6
1973–74	Philadelphia Flyers	Boston Bruins	6
1974–75	Philadelphia Flyers	Buffalo Sabres	6
1975–76	Montreal Canadiens	Philadelphia Flyers	4
1976–77	Montreal Canadiens	Boston Bruins	4
1977–78	Montreal Canadiens	Boston Bruins	6
1978–79	Montreal Canadiens	New York Rangers	5
1979–80	New York Islanders	Philadelphia Flyers	6
1980–81	New York Islanders	Minnesota North Stars	5
1981–82	New York Islanders	Vancouver Canucks	4
1982–83	New York Islanders	Edmonton Oilers	4
1983–84	Edmonton Oilers	New York Islanders	5
1984–85	Edmonton Oilers	Philadelphia Flyers	5
1985–86	Montreal Canadiens	Calgary Flames	5
1986–87	Edmonton Oilers	Philadelphia Flyers	7
1987–88	Edmonton Oilers	Boston Bruins	4
1988–89	Calgary Flames	Montreal Canadiens	6
1989–90	Edmonton Oilers	Boston Bruins	5
1990–91	Pittsburgh Penguins	Minnesota North Stars	6
1991–92	Pittsburgh Penguins	Chicago Blackhawks	4
1992–93	Montreal Canadiens	Los Angeles Kings	5
1993–94	New York Rangers	Vancouver Canucks	7
1994–95	New Jersey Devils	Detroit Red Wings	4
1995–96	Colorado Avalanche	Florida Panthers	4
1996–97	Detroit Red Wings	Philadelphia Flyers	4
1997–98	Detroit Red Wings	Washington Capitals	4
1998–99	Dallas Stars	Buffalo Sabres	6
1999–2000	New Jersey Devils	Dallas Stars	6
2000–01	Colorado Avalanche	New Jersey Devils	7
2001–02	Detroit Red Wings	Carolina Hurricanes	5
2002–03	New Jersey Devils	Anaheim Mighty Ducks	7
2003–04	Tampa Bay Lightning	Calgary Flames	7
2004–05	No Stanley Cup due to season lockout		
2005–06	Carolina Hurricanes	Edmonton Oilers	7
2006–07	Anaheim Ducks	Ottawa Senators	5
2007–08	Detroit Red Wings	Pittsburgh Penguins	6
2008–09	Pittsburgh Penguins	Detroit Red Wings	7
2009–10	Chicago Blackhawks	Philadelphia Flyers	6

*In 1919 the Montreal Canadiens traveled to meet Seattle, the PCHL champions. After five games had been played—the teams were tied at two wins and one tie—the series was called off by the local Department of Health because of the influenza epidemic and the death of Canadiens defenseman Joe Hall from influenza.

Conn Smythe Trophy

Awarded to the Most Valuable Player of the Stanley Cup playoffs, as selected by the Professional Hockey Writers Association. The trophy is named after the former coach, general manager, president and owner of the Toronto Maple Leafs.

1965	Jean Beliveau, Mtl
1966	Roger Crozier, Det
1967	Dave Keon, Tor
1968	Glenn Hall, StL
1969	Serge Savard, Mtl
1970	Bobby Orr, Bos
1971	Ken Dryden, Mtl
1972	Bobby Orr, Bos
1973	Yvan Cournoyer, Mtl
1974	Bernie Parent, Phi
1975	Bernie Parent, Phi
1976	Reggie Leach, Phi
1977	Guy Lafleur, Mtl
1978	Larry Robinson, Mtl
1979	Bob Gainey, Mtl
1980	Bryan Trottier, NYI
1981	Butch Goring, NYI
1982	Mike Bossy, NYI
1983	Bill Smith, NYI
1984	Mark Messier, Edm
1985	Wayne Gretzky, Edm
1986	Patrick Roy, Mtl
1987	Ron Hextall, Phi
1988	Wayne Gretzky, Edm
1989	Al MacInnis, Cgy
1990	Bill Ranford, Edm
1991	Mario Lemieux, Pit
1992	Mario Lemieux, Pit
1993	Patrick Roy, Mtl
1994	Brian Leetch, NYR
1995	Claude Lemieux, NJ
1996	Joe Sakic, Col
1997	Mike Vernon, Det
1998	Steve Yzerman, Det
1999	Joe Nieuwendyk, Dal
2000	Scott Stevens, NJ
2001	Patrick Roy, Col
2002	Nicklas Lidstrom, Det
2003	J.-S. Giguere, Ana
2004	Brad Richards, TB
2005	No Award–No Season
2006	Cam Ward, Car
2007	Scott Niedermayer, Ana
2008	Henrik Zetterberg, Det
2009	Evgeni Malkin, Pit
2010	Jonathan Toews, Chi

Alltime Stanley Cup Playoff Leaders

Points

	Playoff Seasons	GP	G	Ast	Pts
Wayne Gretzky, four teams	16	208	122	260	382
Mark Messier, Edm, Van, NYR	18	236	109	186	295
Jari Kurri, four teams	15	200	106	127	233
Glenn Anderson, four teams	15	225	93	121	214
Paul Coffey, six teams	16	194	59	137	196
Brett Hull, four teams	19	202	103	87	190
Doug Gilmour, seven teams	18	182	60	128	188
Joe Sakic, Que, Col	13	172	84	104	188
Steve Yzerman, Det	20	196	70	115	185
Bryan Trottier, NYI, Pit	17	221	71	113	184
Jaromir Jagr, Pit, Wsh, NYR	15	169	77	104	181
Ray Bourque, Bos, Col	21	214	41	139	180
Jean Beliveau, Mtl	17	162	79	97	176
Sergei Fedorov, Det, Wsh	15	183	52	124	176
Denis Savard, Chi, Mtl	16	169	66	109	175
*Nicklas Lidstrom, Det	18	247	50	125	175
Mario Lemieux, Pit	8	107	76	96	172
Peter Forsberg, Que, Col, Phi	13	151	64	107	171
Denis Potvin, NYI	14	185	56	108	164
Mike Bossy, NYI	10	129	85	75	160
Gordie Howe, Det, Hfd	20	157	68	92	160
Bobby Smith, Min, Mtl	13	184	64	96	160
Al MacInnis, Cgy, StL	19	177	39	121	160
Claude Lemieux, six teams	18	234	80	77	157
Adam Oates, six teams	15	163	42	114	156

Goals

	Playoff Seasons	GP	G
Wayne Gretzky, four teams	16	208	122
Mark Messier, Edm, NYR	18	236	109
Jari Kurri, five teams	15	200	106
Brett Hull, Cgy, StL, Dal, Det	19	202	103
Glenn Anderson, four teams	15	225	93
Mike Bossy, NYI	10	129	85
Joe Sakic, Que, Col	13	172	84
Maurice Richard, Mtl	15	133	82
Claude Lemieux, six teams	18	234	80
Jean Beliveau, Mtl	17	162	79
Jaromir Jagr, Pitt, Wsh, NYR	15	169	77
Mario Lemieux, Pitt	8	107	76
Dino Ciccarelli, Min, Wsh, Det	14	141	73
Esa Tikkanen, five teams	13	186	72
Bryan Trottier, NYI, Pit	17	221	71
Steve Yzerman, Det	20	196	70
Gordie Howe, Det, Hfd	20	157	68
Denis Savard, Chi Mtl	16	169	66
Joe Nieuwendyk, Cgy, Dal, NJ, Tor	16	158	66

Assists

	Playoff Seasons	GP	Ast
Wayne Gretzky, four teams	16	208	260
Mark Messier, Edm, NYR	18	236	186
Ray Bourque, Bos, Col	21	214	139
Paul Coffey, six teams	16	194	137
Doug Gilmour, seven teams	18	182	128
Jari Kurri, five teams	15	200	127
*Nicklas Lidstrom, Det	18	247	125
Sergei Fedorov, Det, Wsh	15	183	124
Glenn Anderson, four teams	15	225	121
Al MacInnis, Cgy, StL	19	177	121
Larry Robinson, Mtl, LA	20	227	116
Steve Yzerman, Det	20	196	115
Lawrence Murphy, six teams	20	215	115
Adam Oates, six teams	15	163	114
Bryan Trottier, NYI, Pit	17	221	113
*Chris Chelios, Mtl, Chi, Det	24	266	113
Denis Savard, Det, Mtl	16	169	109
Denis Potvin, NYI	14	185	108
Peter Forsberg, Que, Col, Phi	13	151	107
Joe Sakic, Que, Col	13	172	104

*Active in 2009–10.

Alltime Stanley Cup Playoff Goaltending Leaders

WINS	W	L	Pct
Patrick Roy, Mtl, Col	151	94	.616
*Martin Brodeur, NJ	99	82	.547
Grant Fuhr, five teams	92	50	.648
Billy Smith, LA, NYI	88	36	.710
Ed Belfour, four teams	88	68	.564
Ken Dryden, Mtl	80	32	.714
Mike Vernon, four teams	77	56	.579
*Chris Osgood, NYI, StL, Det	74	49	.602
Jacques Plante, five teams	71	36	.663
Andy Moog, four teams	68	57	.544
Dominik Hasek, Chi, Buf, Det	65	49	.570
Curtis Joseph, four teams	63	66	.488
Tom Barrasso, Buf, Pit, Ott	61	54	.530
Turk Broda, Tor	60	39	.606

*Active in 2009–10.

SHUTOUTS	GP	W	SO
Patrick Roy, Mtl, Col	247	151	23
*Martin Brodeur, NJ	181	99	23
Curtis Joseph, four teams	133	63	16
*Chris Osgood, NYI, StL, Det	129	74	15

GOALS AGAINST AVG	Avg
George Hainsworth, Mtl, Tor	1.93
Turk Broda, Tor	1.98
*Martin Brodeur, NJ	2.01
Dominik Hasek, Chi, Buf, Det	2.02
*Jean-Sebastien Giguere, Ana	2.08
*Chris Osgood, NYI, StL, Det	2.09
Jacques Plante, Mtl, StL, Tor, Bos	2.14

Note: At least 50 games played.
*Active in 2009–10.

Alltime Stanley Cup Team Playoff Record, by Wins

TEAM	W	L	Pct	TEAM	W	L	Pct
Montreal	407	287	.586	Calgary*	94	114	.452
Detroit	305	269	.531	Vancouver	83	106	.439
Boston	257	281	.478	Washington	82	100	.451
Toronto	251	269	.483	San Jose	67	73	.479
Pittsburgh	218	191	.533	Los Angeles	67	109	.381
Chicago	213	232	.479	Carolina§	59	68	.465
Philadelphia	205	186	.524	Anaheim	53	39	.576
NY Rangers	197	212	.482	Ottawa	51	58	.468
Edmonton	152	99	.606	Phoenix††	32	67	.323
Dallas#	148	149	.498	Tampa Bay	26	25	.551
St. Louis	138	169	.450	Florida	13	18	.419
Colorado**	132	117	.530	Minnesota	10	14	.417
NY Islanders	131	102	.562	Nashville	7	16	.304
New Jersey†	122	108	.530	Columbus	0	4	.000
Buffalo	121	128	.486				

*Atlanta Flames 1972–80. †Colorado Rockies 1976–82, Kansas City Scouts 1974–76. #Minnesota North Stars 1967–93. **Quebec Nordiques 1979–95. ††Winnipeg Jets 1979–96. §Hartford Whalers 1979–97.

Stanley Cup Playoff Coaching Records

Coach	Team	Yrs	Series			Games				Cups	Pct
			Series	W	L	Games	W	L	T		
Glen Sather	Edm	10	27	21	6	†126	89	37	0	4	.706
Toe Blake	Mtl	13	23	18	5	119	82	37	0	8	.689
Scott Bowman	Five teams	28	68	49	19	353	223	130	0	9	.632
*Mike Babcock	Ana, Det	6	19	13	6	101	63	38	0	1	.624
Hap Day	Tor	9	14	10	4	80	49	31	0	5	.613
Al Arbour	StL, NYI	16	42	30	12	209	123	86	0	4	.589
Bob Hartley	Col, Atl	5	14	10	4	84	49	35	0	1	.583
*Lindy Ruff	Buf	12	17	10	7	94	54	40	0	0	.574
Fred Shero	Phi, NYR	8	21	15	6	110	63	47	0	2	.573
Mike Keenan	five teams	13	30	18	12	173	96	77	0	1	.555
*Ken Hitchcock	Dal, Phi, CBJ	9	21	13	8	121	66	55	0	1	.545

†Does not include suspended game, May 24, 1988. *Active in 2009–10.
Note: Coaches ranked by winning percentage. Minimum: 65 games.

The 10 Longest Overtime Games

Date	Result	OT	Scorer	Series	Series Winner
3-24-36	Det 1 vs Mtl M 0	116:30	Mud Bruneteau	SF	Det
4-3-33	Tor 1 vs Bos 0	104:46	Ken Doraty	SF	Tor
5-4-00	Phi 2 vs Pit 1	92:01	Keith Primeau	CSF	Phil
4-24-03	Ana 4 vs Dal 3	80:48	Petr Sykora	CSF	Ana
4-24-96	Pit 3 vs Wsh 2	79:15	Petr Nedved	CQF	Pitt
3-23-43	Tor 3 vs Det 2	70:18	Jack McLean	SF	Det
3-28-30	Mtl 2 vs NYR 1	68:52	Gus Rivers	SF	Mtl
4-18-87	NYI 3 vs Wsh 2	68:47	Pat LaFontaine	DSF	NYI
4-27-94	Buf 1 vs NJ 0	65:43	Dave Hannan	CQF	NJ
3-27-51	Mtl 3 vs Det 2	61:09	Maurice Richard	SF	Mtl

Hart Memorial Trophy

Awarded annually "to the player adjudged to be the most valuable to his team." The original trophy was donated by Dr. David A. Hart, father of Cecil Hart, former manager-coach of the Montreal Canadiens. In the 1980s Wayne Gretzky won the award nine times.

Year	Winner	Key Statistics	Runner-Up
1924	Frank Nighbor, Ott	10 goals, 3 assists in 20 games	Sprague Cleghorn, Mtl
1925	Billy Burch, Ham	20 goals, 4 assists in 27 games	Howie Morenz, Mtl
1926	Nels Stewart, Mtl M	42 points in 36 games	Sprague Cleghorn, Mtl
1927	Herb Gardiner, Mtl	12 points in 44 games as defenseman	Bill Cook, NYR
1928	Howie Morenz, Mtl	33 goals, 18 assists	Roy Worters, Pitt
1929	Roy Worters, NYA	1.21 goals against, 13 shutouts	Ace Bailey, Tor
1930	Nels Stewart, Mtl M	39 goals, 16 assists	Lionel Hitchman, Bos
1931	Howie Morenz, Mtl	28 goals, 23 assists	Eddie Shore, Bos
1932	Howie Morenz, Mtl	24 goals, 25 assists	Ching Johnson, NYR
1933	Eddie Shore, Bos	27 assists in 48 games as defenseman	Bill Cook, NYR
1934	Aurel Joliat, Mtl	27 points	Lionel Conacher, Chi
1935	Eddie Shore, Bos	26 assists in 48 games as defenseman	Charlie Conacher, Tor
1936	Eddie Shore, Bos	16 assists in 46 games as defenseman	Hooley Smith, Mtl M
1937	Babe Siebert, Mtl	28 points	Lionel Conacher, Mtl M
1938	Eddie Shore, Bos	17 points in 47 games as defenseman	Paul Thompson, Chi
1939	Toe Blake, Mtl	led NHL in points (47)	Syl Apps, Tor
1940	Ebbie Goodfellow, Det	28 points	Syl Apps, Tor
1941	Bill Cowley, Bos	led NHL in assists (45) and points (62)	Dit Clapper, Bos
1942	Tom Anderson, Bos	41 points	Syl Apps, Tor
1943	Bill Cowley, Bos	57 points in 50 games	Doug Bentley, Chi
1944	Babe Pratt, Tor	led NHL in assists (54) and points (80)	Bill Cowley, Bos
1945	Elmer Lach, Mtl	61 points in 47 games	Maurice Richard, Mtl
1946	Max Bentley, Chi	led NHL in goals (45); 26 assists	Gaye Stewart, Tor
1947	Maurice Richard, Mtl	60 points in 60 games	Milt Schmidt, Bos
1948	Buddy O'Connor, NYR	28 goals, 26 assists	Frank Brimsek, Bos
1949	Sid Abel, Det	6 shutouts	Bill Durnan, Mtl
1950	Charlie Rayner, NYR	61 points in 62 games	Ted Kennedy, Tor
1951	Milt Schmidt, Bos	led NHL in goals (47) and points (86)	Maurice Richard, Mtl
1952	Gordie Howe, Det	led NHL in goals (49) and points (95)	Elmer Lach, Mtl
1953	Gordie Howe, Det	5 shutouts	Al Rollins, Chi
1954	Al Rollins, Chi	52 points	Red Kelly, Det
1955	Ted Kennedy, Tor	led NHL in goals (47) and points (88)	Harry Lumley, Tor
1956	Jean Beliveau, Mtl	led NHL in goals (44) and points (89)	Tod Sloan, Tor
1957	Gordie Howe, Det	74 points in 70 games	Jean Beliveau, Mtl
1959	Andy Bathgate, NYR	45 assists, 73 points	Gordie Howe, Det
1960	Gordie Howe, Det	50 goals, 95 points	Bobby Hull, Chi
1961	Bernie Geoffrion, Mtl	42 wins, 2.37 goals against avg.	Johnny Bower, Tor
1962	Jacques Plante, Mtl	47 assists, 73 points	Doug Harvey, NYR
1963	Gordie Howe, Det	50 assists, 78 points	Stan Mikita, Chi
1964	Jean Beliveau, Mtl	39 goals, 32 assists	Bobby Hull, Chi
1965	Bobby Hull, Chi	led NHL in goals (54) and points (97)	Norm Ullman, Det
1966	Bobby Hull, Chi	led NHL in assists (62) and points (97)	Jean Beliveau, Mtl
1967	Stan Mikita, Chi	40 goals, 47 assists	Ed Giacomin, NYR
1968	Stan Mikita, Chi	led NHL in assists (77) and points (126)	Jean Beliveau, Mtl
1969	Phil Esposito, Bos	led NHL in assists (87) and points (120)	Jean Beliveau, Mtl
1970	Bobby Orr, Bos	102 assists, 139 points	Tony Esposito, Chi
1971	Bobby Orr, Bos	80 assists, 117 points	Phil Esposito, Bos
1972	Bobby Orr, Bos	67 assists, 104 points	Ken Dryden, Mtl
1973	Bobby Clarke, Phi	led NHL in goals (68) and points (145)	Phil Esposito, Bos
1974	Phil Esposito, Bos	89 assists, 116 points	Bernie Parent, Phi
1975	Bobby Clarke, Phi	89 assists, 119 points	Rogatien Vachon, LA
1976	Bobby Clarke, Phi	led NHL in assists (80) and points (136)	Denis Potvin, NYI
1977	Guy Lafleur, Mtl	led NHL in goals (60) and points (132)	Bobby Clarke, Phi
1978	Guy Lafleur, Mtl	led NHL in assists (87) and points (134)	Bryan Trottier, NYI
1979	Bryan Trottier, NYI	51 goals, 86 assists	Guy Lafleur, Mtl
1980	Wayne Gretzky, Edm	led NHL in assists (109) and points (164)	Marcel Dionne, LA
1981	Wayne Gretzky, Edm	NHL-record 92 goals and 212 points	Mike Liut, StL
1982	Wayne Gretzky, Edm	led NHL in goals (71) and points (196)	Bryan Trottier, NYI
1983	Wayne Gretzky, Edm	led NHL in goals (87) and points (205)	Pete Peeters, Bos
1984	Wayne Gretzky, Edm	led NHL in goals (73) and points (208)	Rod Langway, Wsh
1985	Wayne Gretzky, Edm	NHL-record 163 assists and 215 points	Dale Hawerchuk, Win
1986	Wayne Gretzky, Edm	led NHL in assists (121) and points (183)	Mario Lemieux, Pit
1987	Wayne Gretzky, Edm	led NHL in goals (70) and points (168)	Ray Bourque, Bos
1988	Mario Lemieux, Pit		Grant Fuhr, Edm

Hart Memorial Trophy *(Cont.)*

Year	Winner	Key Statistics	Runner-Up
1989	Wayne Gretzky, LA	114 assists, 168 points	Mario Lemieux, Pit
1990	Mark Messier, Edm	84 assists, 129 points	Ray Bourque, Bos
1991	Brett Hull, StL	led NHL in goals (86); 131 points	Wayne Gretzky, LA
1992	Mark Messier, NYR	72 assists, 107 points	Patrick Roy, Mtl
1993	Mario Lemieux, Pitt	69 goals, 91 assists in 60 games	Doug Gilmour, Tor
1994	Sergei Fedorov, Det	56 goals, 64 assists	Dominik Hasek, Buf
1995	Eric Lindros, Phi	29 goals, 41 assists in 46 games	Jaromir Jagr, Pit
1996	Mario Lemieux, Pit	led NHL in goals (69) and points (161)	Mark Messier, NYR
1997	Dominik Hasek, Buf	5 shutouts, 2.27 goals against avg.	Paul Kariya, Ana
1998	Dominik Hasek, Buf	13 shutouts, 2.09 goals against avg.	Jaromir Jagr, Pit
1999	Jaromir Jagr, Pit	44 goals, 127 points	Alexei Yashin, Ott
2000	Chris Pronger, StL	62 points, +52 plus/minus rating	Jaromir Jagr, Pit
2001	Joe Sakic, Col	118 points, +45 plus/minus rating	Mario Lemieux, Pit
2002	Jose Theodore, Mtl	2.11 goals against avg./7 shutouts	Jarome Iginla, Cal
2003	Peter Forsberg, Col	77 assists, +52 plus/minus rating	Markus Naslund, Van
2004	Martin St. Louis, TB	94 points, +35 plus/minus rating	Jarome Iginla, Cal
2005	No Award–No Season.		
2006	Joe Thornton, Bos/SJ	29 goals, 96 assists; 125 points	Jaromir Jagr, NYR
2007	Sidney Crosby, Pit	36 goals, 84 assists; 120 points	Roberto Luongo, Van
2008	Alexander Ovechkin, Wsh	65 goals, 47 assists; 112 points	Evgeni Malkin, Pit
2009	Alexander Ovechkin, Wsh	56 goals, 54 assists; 110 points	Evgeni Malkin, Pit
2010	Henrik Sedin, Van	29 goals, 83 assists; 112 points	Sidney Crosby, Pit

Art Ross Trophy

Awarded annually "to the player who leads the league in scoring points at the end of the regular season." The trophy was presented to the NHL in 1947 by Arthur Howie Ross, former manager-coach of the Boston Bruins. The tie-breakers, in order, are: (1) most goals, (2) fewer games played, (3) first goal of the season. Bobby Orr is the only defenseman in NHL history to win this trophy, and he won it twice (1970 and 1975).

Year	Winner	Pts	Year	Winner	Pts
1919	Newsy Lalonde, Mtl	44	1956	Jean Beliveau, Mtl	88
1920	Joe Malone, Que	30	1957	Gordie Howe, Det	89
1921	Newsy Lalonde, Mtl	48	1958	Dickie Moore, Mtl	84
1922	Punch Broadbent, Ott	41	1959	Dickie Moore, Mtl	96
1923	Babe Dye, Tor	46	1960	Bobby Hull, Chi	81
1924	Cy Denneny, Ott	37	1961	Bernie Geoffrion, Mtl	95
1925	Babe Dye, Tor	23	1962	Bobby Hull, Chi	84
1926	Nels Stewart, Mtl M.	44	1963	Gordie Howe, Det	86
1927	Bill Cook, NYR	42	1964	Stan Mikita, Chi	89
1928	Howie Morenz, Mtl	37	1965	Stan Mikita, Chi	87
1929	Ace Bailey, Tor	51	1966	Bobby Hull, Chi	97
1930	Cooney Weiland, Bos	32	1967	Stan Mikita, Chi	97
1931	Howie Morenz, Mtl	73	1968	Stan Mikita, Chi	87
1932	Harvey Jackson, Tor	51	1969	Phil Esposito, Bos	126
1933	Bill Cook, NYR	53	1970	Bobby Orr, Bos	120
1934	Charlie Conacher, Tor	50	1971	Phil Esposito, Bos	152
1935	Charlie Conacher, Tor	57	1972	Phil Esposito, Bos	133
1936	Sweeney Schriner, NYA	45	1973	Phil Esposito, Bos	130
1937	Sweeney Schriner, NYA	46	1974	Phil Esposito, Bos	145
1938	Gordie Drillon, Tor	52	1975	Bobby Orr, Bos	135
1939	Toe Blake, Mtl	47	1976	Guy Lafleur, Mtl	125
1940	Milt Schmidt, Bos	52	1977	Guy Lafleur, Mtl	136
1941	Bill Cowley, Bos	62	1978	Guy Lafleur, Mtl	132
1942	Bryan Hextall, NYR	56	1979	Bryan Trottier, NYI	134
1943	Doug Bentley, Chi	73	1980	Marcel Dionne, LA	137
1944	Herb Cain, Bos	82	1981	Wayne Gretzky, Edm	164
1945	Elmer Lach, Mtl	80	1982	Wayne Gretzky, Edm	212
1946	Max Bentley, Chi	61	1983	Wayne Gretzky, Edm	196
1947	*Max Bentley, Chi	72	1984	Wayne Gretzky, Edm	205
1948	Elmer Lach, Mtl	61	1985	Wayne Gretzky, Edm	208
1949	Roy Conacher, Chi	68	1986	Wayne Gretzky, Edm	215
1950	Ted Lindsay, Det	78	1987	Wayne Gretzky, Edm	183
1951	Gordie Howe, Det	86	1988	Mario Lemieux, Pit	168
1952	Gordie Howe, Det	86	1989	Mario Lemieux, Pit	199
1953	Gordie Howe, Det	95	1990	Wayne Gretzky, LA	142
1954	Gordie Howe, Det	81	1991	Wayne Gretzky, LA	163
1955	Bernie Geoffrion, Mtl	75	1992	Mario Lemieux, Pit	131

Art Ross Trophy *(Cont.)*

Year	Winner	Pts	Year	Winner	Pts
1993	Mario Lemieux, Pit	160	2002	Jarome Iginla, Cgy	96
1994	Wayne Gretzky, LA	130	2003	Peter Forsberg, Col	106
1995	Jaromir Jagr, Pit	70	2004	Martin St. Louis, TB	94
1996	Mario Lemieux, Pit	161	2005	No award/no season	
1997	Mario Lemieux, Pit	122	2006	Joe Thornton, Bos/SJ	125
1998	Jaromir Jagr, Pit	102	2007	Sidney Crosby, Pit	120
1999	Jaromir Jagr, Pit	127	2008	Alexander Ovechkin, Wsh	112
2000	Jaromir Jagr, Pit	96	2009	Evgeni Malkin, Pit	113
2001	Jaromir Jagr, Pit	121	2010	Henrik Sedin, Van	112

Note: Listing includes scoring leaders prior to inception of Art Ross Trophy in 1947–48.

Lady Byng Memorial Trophy

Awarded annually "to the player adjudged to have exhibited the best type of sportsmanship and gentlemanly conduct combined with a high standard of playing ability." Lady Byng, who first presented the trophy in 1925, was the wife of Canada's Governor-General. She donated a second trophy in 1936 after the first was given permanently to Frank Boucher of the New York Rangers, who won it seven times in eight seasons. Stan Mikita, one of the league's most penalized players during his early years in the NHL, won the trophy twice late in his career (1967 and 1968).

1925 Frank Nighbor, Ott	1954 Red Kelly, Det	1983 Mike Bossy, NYI
1926 Frank Nighbor, Ott	1955 Sid Smith, Tor	1984 Mike Bossy, NYI
1927 Billy Burch, NYA	1956 Earl Reibel, Det	1985 Jari Kurri, Edm
1928 Frank Boucher, NYR	1957 Andy Hebenton, NYR	1986 Mike Bossy, NYI
1929 Frank Boucher, NYR	1958 Camille Henry, NYR	1987 Joe Mullen, Cgy
1930 Frank Boucher, NYR	1959 Alex Delvecchio, Det	1988 Mats Naslund, Mtl
1931 Frank Boucher, NYR	1960 Don McKenney, Bos	1989 Joe Mullen, Cgy
1932 Joe Primeau, Tor	1961 Red Kelly, Tor	1990 Brett Hull, StL
1933 Frank Boucher, NYR	1962 Dave Keon, Tor	1991 Wayne Gretzky, LA
1934 Frank Boucher, NYR	1963 Dave Keon, Tor	1992 Wayne Gretzky, LA
1935 Frank Boucher, NYR	1964 Ken Wharram, Chi	1993 Pierre Turgeon, NYI
1936 Doc Romnes, Chi	1965 Bobby Hull, Chi	1994 Wayne Gretzky, LA
1937 Marty Barry, Det	1966 Alex Delvecchio, Det	1995 Ron Francis, Pit
1938 Gordie Drillon, Tor	1967 Stan Mikita, Chi	1996 Paul Kariya, Ana
1939 Clint Smith, NYR	1968 Stan Mikita, Chi	1997 Paul Kariya, Ana
1940 Bobby Bauer, Bos	1969 Alex Delvecchio, Det	1998 Ron Francis, Pit
1941 Bobby Bauer, Bos	1970 Phil Goyette, StL	1999 Wayne Gretzky, NYR
1942 Syl Apps, Tor	1971 John Bucyk, Bos	2000 Pavol Demitra, StL
1943 Max Bentley, Chi	1972 Jean Ratelle, NYR	2001 Joe Sakic, Col
1944 Clint Smith, Chi	1973 Gilbert Perreault, Buf.	2002 Ron Francis, Car
1945 Billy Mosienko, Chi	1974 John Bucyk, Bos	2003 Alexander Mogilny, Det
1946 Toe Blake, Mtl	1975 Marcel Dionne, Det	2004 Brad Richards, TB
1947 Bobby Bauer, Bos	1976 Jean Ratelle, NYR-Bos	2005 No Award
1948 Buddy O'Connor, NYR	1977 Marcel Dionne, LA	2006 Pavel Datsyuk, Det
1949 Bill Quackenbush, Det	1978 Butch Goring, LA	2007 Pavel Datsyuk, Det
1950 Edgar Laprade, NYR	1979 Bob MacMillan, Atl	2008 Pavel Datsyuk, Det
1951 Red Kelly, Det	1980 Wayne Gretzky, Edm	2009 Pavel Datsyuk, Det
1952 Sid Smith, Tor	1981 Rick Kehoe, Pitt	2010 Martin St. Louis, TB
1953 Red Kelly, Det	1982 Rick Middleton, Bos	

James Norris Memorial Trophy

Awarded annually "to the defense player who demonstrates throughout the season the greatest all-around ability in the position." James Norris was the former owner-president of the Detroit Red Wings. Bobby Orr holds the record for most consecutive times winning the award (eight, 1968–1975).

1954 Red Kelly, Det	1969 Bobby Orr, Bos	1984 Rod Langway, Wsh
1955 Doug Harvey, Mtl	1970 Bobby Orr, Bos	1985 Paul Coffey, Edm
1956 Doug Harvey, Mtl	1971 Bobby Orr, Bos	1986 Paul Coffey, Edm
1957 Doug Harvey, Mtl	1972 Bobby Orr, Bos	1987 Ray Bourque, Bos
1958 Doug Harvey, Mtl	1973 Bobby Orr, Bos	1988 Ray Bourque, Bos
1959 Tom Johnson, Mtl	1974 Bobby Orr, Bos	1989 Chris Chelios, Mtl
1960 Doug Harvey, Mtl	1975 Bobby Orr, Bos	1990 Ray Bourque, Bos
1961 Doug Harvey, Mtl	1976 Denis Potvin, NYI	1991 Ray Bourque, Bos
1962 Doug Harvey, NYR	1977 Larry Robinson, Mtl	1992 Brian Leetch, NYR
1963 Pierre Pilote, Chi	1978 Denis Potvin, NYI	1993 Chris Chelios, Chi
1964 Pierre Pilote, Chi	1979 Denis Potvin, NYI	1994 Ray Bourque, Bos
1965 Pierre Pilote, Chi	1980 Larry Robinson, Mtl	1995 Paul Coffey, Det
1966 Jacques Laperriere, Mtl	1981 Randy Carlyle, Pit	1996 Chris Chelios, Chi
1967 Harry Howell, NYR	1982 Doug Wilson, Chi	1997 Brian Leetch, NYR
1968 Bobby Orr, Bos	1983 Rod Langway, Wsh	1998 Rob Blake, LA

James Norris Memorial Trophy *(Cont.)*

1999 ......Al MacInnis, StL	2003 ......Nicklas Lidstrom, Det	2007 ......Nicklas Lidstrom, Det
2000 ......Chris Pronger, StL	2004 ......Scott Niedermayer, NJ	2008 ......Nicklas Lidstrom, Det
2001 ......Nicklas Lidstrom, Det	2005 ......No Award	2009 ......Zdeno Chara, Bos
2002 ......Nicklas Lidstrom, Det	2006 ......Nicklas Lidstrom, Det	2010 ......Duncan Keith, Chi

Calder Memorial Trophy

Awarded annually "to the player selected as the most proficient in his first year of competition in the National Hockey League." Frank Calder was a former NHL president. Sergei Makarov, who won the award in 1989–90, was the oldest recipient of the trophy, at 31. Players are no longer eligible for the award if they are 26 or older as of September 15th of the season in question.

1933 ......Carl Voss, Det	1960 ......Bill Hay, Chi	1987 ......Luc Robitaille, LA
1934 ......Russ Blinko, Mtl M	1961 ......Dave Keon, Tor	1988 ......Joe Nieuwendyk, Cgy
1935 ......Dave Schriner, NYA	1962 ......Bobby Rousseau, Mtl	1989 ......Brian Leetch, NYR
1936 ......Mike Karakas, Chi	1963 ......Kent Douglas, Tor	1990 ......Sergei Makarov, Cgy
1937 ......Syl Apps, Tor	1964 ......Jacques Laperriere, Mtl	1991 ......Ed Belfour, Chi
1938 ......Cully Dahlstrom, Chi	1965 ......Roger Crozier, Det	1992 ......Pavel Bure, Van
1939 ......Frank Brimsek, Bos	1966 ......Brit Selby, Tor	1993 ......Teemu Selanne, Win
1940 ......Kilby MacDonald, NYR	1967 ......Bobby Orr, Bos	1994 ......Martin Brodeur, NJ
1941 ......Johnny Quilty, Mtl	1968 ......Derek Sanderson, Bos	1995 ......Peter Forsberg, Que
1942 ......Grant Warwick, NYR	1969 ......Danny Grant, Min	1996 ......Daniel Alfredsson, Ott
1943 ......Gaye Stewart, Tor	1970 ......Tony Esposito, Chi	1997 ......Bryan Berard, NYI
1944 ......Gus Bodnar, Tor	1971 ......Gilbert Perreault, Buf	1998 ......Sergei Samsonov, Bos
1945 ......Frank McCool, Tor	1972 ......Ken Dryden, Mtl	1999 ......Chris Drury, Col
1946 ......Edgar Laprade, NYR	1973 ......Steve Vickers, NYR	2000 ......Scott Gomez, NJ
1947 ......Howie Meeker, Tor	1974 ......Denis Potvin, NYI	2001 ......Evgeni Nabokov, SJ
1948 ......Jim McFadden, Det	1975 ......Eric Vail, Atl	2002 ......Dany Heatley, Atl
1949 ......Pentti Lund, NYR	1976 ......Bryan Trottier, NYI	2003 ......Barret Jackman, StL
1950 ......Jack Gelineau, Bos	1977 ......Willi Plett, Atl	2004 ......Andrew Raycroft, Bos
1951 ......Terry Sawchuk, Det	1978 ......Mike Bossy, NYI	2005 ......No Award
1952 ......Bernie Geoffrion, Mtl	1979 ......Bobby Smith, Min	2006.........Alexander Ovechkin, Wsh
1953 ......Gump Worsley, NYR	1980 ......Ray Bourque, Bos	2007.........Evgeni Malkin, Pit
1954 ......Camille Henry, NYR	1981 ......Peter Stastny, Que	2008.........Patrick Kane, Chi
1955 ......Ed Litzenberger, Chi	1982 ......Dale Hawerchuk, Win	2009.........Steve Mason, CBJ
1956 ......Glenn Hall, Det	1983 ......Steve Larmer, Chi	2010.........Tyler Myers, Buf
1957 ......Larry Regan, Bos	1984 ......Tom Barrasso, Buf	
1958 ......Frank Mahovlich, Tor	1985 ......Mario Lemieux, Pit	
1959 ......Ralph Backstrom, Mtl	1986 ......Gary Suter, Cgy	

Vezina Trophy

Awarded annually "to the goalkeeper adjudged to be the best at his position." The trophy is named after Georges Vezina, an outstanding goalie for the Montreal Canadiens who collapsed during a game on November 28, 1925, and died four months later of tuberculosis. The general managers of the NHL teams vote on the award.

1927 ......George Hainsworth, Mtl	1953 ......Terry Sawchuk, Det	1973 ......Ken Dryden, Mtl
1928 ......George Hainsworth, Mtl	1954 ......Harry Lumley, Tor	1974 ......Bernie Parent, Phi
1929 ......George Hainsworth, Mtl	1955 ......Terry Sawchuk, Det	Tony Esposito, Chi
1930 ......Tiny Thompson, Bos	1956 ......Jacques Plante, Mtl	1975 ......Bernie Parent, Phi
1931 ......Roy Worters, NYA	1957 ......Jacques Plante, Mtl	1976 ......Ken Dryden, Mtl
1932 ......Charlie Gardiner, Chi	1958 ......Jacques Plante, Mtl	1977 ......Ken Dryden, Mtl
1933 ......Tiny Thompson, Bos	1959 ......Jacques Plante, Mtl	Michel Larocque, Mtl
1934 ......Charlie Gardiner, Chi	1960 ......Jacques Plante, Mtl	1978 ......Ken Dryden, Mtl
1935 ......Lorne Chabot, Chi	1961 ......Johnny Bower, Tor	Michel Larocque, Mtl
1936 ......Tiny Thompson, Bos	1962 ......Jacques Plante, Mtl	1979 ......Ken Dryden, Mtl
1937 ......Normie Smith, Det	1963 ......Glenn Hall, Chi	Michel Larocque, Mtl
1938 ......Tiny Thompson, Bos	1964 ......Charlie Hodge, Mtl	1980 ......Bob Sauve, Buf
1939 ......Frank Brimsek, Bos	1965 ......Terry Sawchuk, Tor	Don Edwards, Buf
1940 ......Dave Kerr, NYR	Johnny Bower, Tor	1981 ......Richard Sevigny, Mtl
1941 ......Turk Broda, Tor	1966 ......Gump Worsley, Mtl	Michel Larocque, Mtl
1942 ......Frank Brimsek, Bos	Charlie Hodge, Mtl	1982 ......Billy Smith, NYI
1943 ......Johnny Mowers, Det	1967 ......Glenn Hall, Chi	Denis Herron, Mtl
1944 ......Bill Durnan, Mtl	Denis DeJordy, Chi	1983 ......Pete Peeters, Bos
1945 ......Bill Durnan, Mtl	1968 ......Lorne Worsley, Mtl	1984 ......Tom Barrasso, Buf
1946 ......Bill Durnan, Mtl	1969 ......Jacques Plante, StL	1985 ......Pelle Lindbergh, Phi
1947 ......Bill Durnan, Mtl	Glenn Hall, StL	1986 ......John Vanbiesbrouck, NYR
1948 ......Turk Broda, Tor	1970 ......Tony Esposito, Chi	1987 ......Ron Hextall, Phi
1949 ......Bill Durnan, Mtl	1971 ......Ed Giacomin, NYR	1988 ......Grant Fuhr, Edm
1950 ......Bill Durnan, Mtl	Gilles Villemure, NYR	1989 ......Patrick Roy, Mtl
1951 ......Al Rollins, Tor	1972 ......Tony Esposito, Chi	1990 ......Patrick Roy, Mtl
1952 ......Terry Sawchuk, Det	Gary Smith, Chi	1991 ......Ed Belfour, Chi

Vezina Trophy *(Cont.)*

1992 .... Patrick Roy, Mtl	1999 .... Dominik Hasek, Buf	2006 .... Miikka Kiprusoff, Cgy
1993 .... Ed Belfour, Chi	2000 .... Olaf Kolzig, Wash	2007 .... Martin Brodeur, NJ
1994 .... Dominik Hasek, Buf	2001 .... Dominik Hasek, Buf	2008 .... Martin Brodeur, NJ
1995 .... Dominik Hasek, Buf	2002 .... Jose Theodore, Mtl	2009 .... Tim Thomas, Bos
1996 .... Jim Carey, Wsh	2003 .... Martin Brodeur, NJ	2010 .... Ryan Miller, Buf
1997 .... Dominik Hasek, Buf	2004 .... Martin Brodeur, NJ	
1998 .... Dominik Hasek, Buf	2005 .... No Award	

Selke Trophy

Awarded annually "to the forward who best excels in the defensive aspects of the game." The trophy is named after Frank J. Selke, the architect of the Montreal Canadians dynasty that won five consecutive Stanley Cups in the late '50s. The winner is selected by a vote of the Professional Hockey Writers' Association.

1978 .... Bob Gainey, Mtl	1990 .... Rick Meagher, StL	2002 .... Michael Peca, NYI
1979 .... Bob Gainey, Mtl	1991 .... Dirk Graham, Chi	2003 .... Jere Lehtinen, Dal
1980 .... Bob Gainey, Mtl	1992 .... Guy Carbonneau, Mtl	2004 .... Kris Draper, Det
1981 .... Bob Gainey, Mtl	1993 .... Doug Gilmour, Tor	2005 .... No Award
1982 .... Steve Kasper, Bos	1994 .... Sergei Fedorov, Det	2006 .... Rod Brind'Amour, Car
1983 .... Bobby Clarke, Phi	1995 .... Ron Francis, Pit	2007 .... Rod Brind'Amour, Car
1984 .... Doug Jarvis, Wsh	1996 .... Sergei Fedorov, Det	2008 .... Pavel Datsyuk, Det
1985 .... Craig Ramsay, Buf	1997 .... Michael Peca, Buf	2009 .... Pavel Datsyuk, Det
1986 .... Troy Murray, Chi	1998 .... Jere Lehtinen, Dal	2010 .... Pavel Datsyuk, Det
1987 .... Dave Poulin, Phi	1999 .... Jere Lehtinen, Dal	
1988 .... Guy Carbonneau, Mtl	2000 .... Steve Yzerman, Det	
1989 .... Guy Carbonneau, Mtl	2001 .... John Madden, NJ	

Adams Award

Awarded annually "to the NHL coach adjudged to have contributed the most to his team's success." The trophy is named in honor of Jack Adams, longtime coach and general manager of the Detroit Red Wings. The winner is selected by a vote of the National Hockey League Broadcasters' Association.

1974 ..... Fred Shero, Phi	1987 ..... Jacques Demers, Det	2000 ..... Joel Quenneville, StL
1975 ..... Bob Pulford, LA	1988 ..... Jacques Demers, Det	2001 ..... Bill Barber, Phi
1976 ..... Don Cherry, Bos	1989 ..... Pat Burns, Mtl	2002 ..... Bob Francis, Phx
1977 ..... Scott Bowman, Mtl	1990 ..... Bob Murdoch, Win	2003 ..... Jacques Lemaire, Min
1978 ..... Bobby Kromm, Det	1991 ..... Brian Sutter, StL	2004 ..... John Tortorella, TB
1979 ..... Al Arbour, NYI	1992 ..... Pat Quinn, Van	2005 ..... No Award
1980 ..... Pat Quinn, Phi	1993 ..... Pat Burns, Tor	2006 ..... Lindy Ruff, Buf
1981 ..... Red Berenson, StL	1994 ..... Jacques Lemaire, NJ	2007 ..... Alain Vigneault, Van
1982 ..... Tom Watt, Win	1995 ..... Marc Crawford, Que	2008 ..... Bruce Boudreau, Wsh
1983 ..... Orval Tessier, Chi	1996 ..... Scotty Bowman, Det	2009 ..... Claude Julien, Bos
1984 ..... Bryan Murray, Wsh	1997 ..... Ted Nolan, Buf	2010 ..... Dave Tippett, Phx
1985 ..... Mike Keenan, Phi	1998 ..... Pat Burns, Bos	
1986 ..... Glen Sather, Edm	1999 ..... Jacques Martin, Ott	

Career Records

Alltime Point Leaders

Player	Yrs	GP	G	A	Pts	Pts/game
Wayne Gretzky, Edm, LA, StL, NYR	20	1487	894	1963	2857	1.921
Mark Messier, Edm, NYR, Van	25	1756	694	1193	1887	1.074
Gordie Howe, Det, Hfd	26	1767	801	1049	1850	1.047
Ron Francis, Hfd, Pit, Car, Tor	23	1731	549	1249	1798	1.039
Marcel Dionne, Det, LA, NYR	18	1348	731	1040	1771	1.314
Steve Yzerman, Det	22	1514	692	1063	1755	1.159
Mario Lemieux, Pit	17	915	690	1033	1723	1.883
Joe Sakic, Que, Col	20	1378	625	1016	1641	1.191
Jaromir Jagr, Pit, Wsh, NYR	17	1273	646	953	1599	1.256
Phil Esposito, Chi, Bos, NYR	18	1282	717	873	1590	1.240
Ray Bourque, Bos, Col	22	1612	410	1169	1579	.980
Paul Coffey, eight teams	21	1409	396	1135	1531	1.087
*Mark Recchi, seven teams	21	1571	563	922	1485	.945
Stan Mikita, Chi	22	1394	541	926	1467	1.052
Bryan Trottier, NYI, Pit	18	1279	524	901	1425	1.114

*Active in 2009–10.

Alltime Goal-Scoring Leaders

Player	Yrs	GP	G	G/game
Wayne Gretzky, Edm, LA, StL, NYR	20	1487	894	.601
Gordie Howe, Det, Hfd	26	1767	801	.453
Brett Hull, Cgy, StL, Dal, Det	19	1269	741	.584
Marcel Dionne, Det, LA, NYR	18	1348	731	.542
Phil Esposito, Chi, Bos, NYR	18	1282	717	.559
Mike Gartner, Wsh, Min, NYR, Tor, Phx	19	1432	708	.494
Mark Messier, Edm, NYR, Van	25	1756	694	.395
Steve Yzerman, Det.	22	1514	692	.457
Mario Lemieux, Pit	17	915	690	.754
Luc Robitaille, LA, Pit, NYR, Det	19	1431	668	.467
Brendan Shanahan, NJ, StL, Hfd, Det, NYR	21	1524	656	.430

Alltime Assist Leaders

Player	Yrs	GP	A	A/game
Wayne Gretzky, Edm, LA, StL, NYR	20	1487	1963	1.320
Ron Francis, Hfd, Pit, Car	23	1731	1249	.722
Mark Messier, Edm, NYR, Van	25	1756	1193	.679
Ray Bourque, Bos, Col	22	1612	1169	.725
Paul Coffey, eight teams	21	1409	1135	.806
Adam Oates, seven teams	22	1337	1079	.807
Steve Yzerman, Det.	22	1514	1063	.702
Gordie Howe, Det, Hfd	26	1767	1049	.594
Marcel Dionne, Det, LA, NYR	18	1348	1040	.772
Mario Lemieux, Pit	17	915	1033	1.129
Joe Sakic, Que, Col	20	1378	1016	.737

Alltime Penalty Minutes Leaders

Player	Yrs	GP	PIM	Min/game
Dave Williams, Tor, Van, Det, LA, Hfd	14	962	3966	4.12
Dale Hunter, Que, Wsh, Col	19	1407	3565	2.53
Tie Domi, Tor, NYR, Win	16	1020	3515	3.45
Marty McSorley, Pit, Edm, LA, NYR, SJ, Bos	17	961	3381	3.52
Bob Probert, Det, Chi	16	935	3300	3.53
Rob Ray, Buf, Ott	15	900	3207	3.56
Craig Berube, Phi, Tor, Cgy, Wsh, NYI	17	1054	3149	2.99
Tim Hunter, Cgy, Que, Van, SJ	16	815	3146	3.86
Chris Nilan, Mtl, NYR, Bos	13	688	3043	4.42
Rick Tocchet, Phi, Pit, LA, Bos, Wsh, Phx	18	1144	2972	2.60

Goaltending Records

ALLTIME GOALTENDING LEADERS, BY WINS

Goaltender	W	L	T/OTL	Pct
*Martin Brodeur, NJ	602	324	156	.627
Patrick Roy, Mtl, Col	551	315	131	.618
Ed Belfour, five teams	484	320	121	.590
Curtis Joseph, five teams	454	352	96	.557
Terry Sawchuk, five teams	447	330	172	.562
Jacques Plante, five teams	437	246	145	.615
Tony Esposito, Mtl, Chi	423	306	151	.566
Glenn Hall, Det, Chi, StL	407	326	163	.545
Grant Fuhr, six teams	403	295	114	.567
*Chris Osgood, Det, NYI, StL, Det.	396	213	106	.628
Dominik Hasek, Chi, Buf, Ott, Det	389	223	91	.618

*Active in 2009–10.

ACTIVE GOALTENDING LEADERS, BY PERCENTAGE

Goaltender	W	L	T/OTL	Pct
Manny Legace, LA, Det, StL	187	99	44	.633
Chris Osgood, Det, NYI, StL, Det	396	213	106	.628
Martin Brodeur, NJ	602	324	156	.627
Ryan Miller, Buf	187	104	36	.622
Marty Turco, Dal	262	154	66	.612
Evgeni Nabokov, SJ	293	178	80	.604
Henrik Lundqvist, NYR	177	110	44	.601
Miikka Kiprusoff, SJ, Cgy	239	153	57	.596
Cristobal Huet, LA, Mtl, Wsh, Chi	129	90	37	.576
Marc-Andre Fleury, Pit	148	106	34	.573

Note: Minimum 250 games played.

ALLTIME SHUTOUT LEADERS

Goaltender	Team	Yrs	GP	SO
*Martin Brodeur	NJ	17	1076	110
Terry Sawchuk	Det, Bos, Tor, LA, NYR	21	971	103
George Hainsworth	Mtl, Tor	11	465	94
Glenn Hall	Det, Chi, StL	18	906	84
Jacques Plante	Mtl, NYR, StL, Tor, Bos	18	837	82
Tiny Thompson	Bos, Det	12	553	81
Alex Connell	Ott, Det, NYA, Mtl M	12	417	81
Dominik Hasek	Chi, Buf, Ott, Det	16	735	81
Tony Esposito	Mtl, Chi	16	886	76
Ed Belfour	Chi, SJ, Dal, Tor	17	963	76

ALLTIME GOALS-AGAINST AVERAGE LEADERS (PRE-1950)

Goaltender	Team	Yrs	GP	GA	GAA
Alec Connell	Ott, Det, NYA, Mtl M	12	417	830	1.91
George Hainsworth	Mtl, Tor	11	465	937	1.93
Chuck Gardiner	Chi	7	316	664	2.02
Lorne Chabot	NYR, Tor, Mtl, Chi, Mtl M, NYA	11	411	860	2.04
Tiny Thompson	Bos, Det	12	553	1183	2.08

ALLTIME GOALS-AGAINST AVERAGE LEADERS (POST-1950)

Goaltender	Team	Yrs	GP	GA	GAA
Dominik Hasek	Chi, Buf, Det, Ott	16	735	1572	2.20
*Martin Brodeur	NJ	17	1076	2340	2.21
Ken Dryden	Mtl	8	397	870	2.24
Roman Turek	Dal, StL, Cgy	8	328	734	2.31
*Marty Turco	Dal	9	509	1118	2.31
*Henrik Lundqvist	NYR	5	338	771	2.33

*Active in 2009–10. Note: Minimum 250 games played. GAA equals goals against per 60 minutes played.

Alltime Coaching Leaders

Coach	Team	Seasons	W	L	T	OTL	Pct
Scotty Bowman	five teams	1967–87, 91–2002	1244	584	313	0	.654
Toe Blake	Mtl	1955–68	500	255	159	0	.634
Fred Shero	Phi, NYR	1971–81	390	225	119	0	.612
*Joel Quenneville	StL, Col, Chi	1996–	535	327	77	60	.604
Glen Sather	Edm, NYR	1979-89, 93-94, 2003-04	497	314	121	0	.598
*Ken Hitchcock	Dal, Phi, CBJ	1995–	534	350	88	70	.588
Emile Francis	NYR, StL	1965–77, 81–83	388	273	117	0	.574
Billy Reay	Tor, Chi	1957–59, 63–77	542	385	175	0	.571
Pat Burns	Mtl, Tor, Bos, NJ	1988–2001, 2002–05	501	367	151	0	.566
Al Arbour	StL, NYI	1970–94	781	577	248	0	.564
Pat Quinn	Phi, LA, Van, Tor	1978–2006	657	499	154	8	.560

*Active in 2009–10. Note: Minimum 600 regular-season games. Ranked by win percentage. Overtime losses up through 2004 are counted as losses. After 2004, ties were eliminated and overtime losses were awarded one point and so are listed in separate OTL column (and counted like ties).

Single-Season Records

Goals

Player	Season	GP	G	Player	Season	GP	G
Wayne Gretzky, Edm	1981–82	80	92	Wayne Gretzky, Edm	1982–83	80	71
Wayne Gretzky, Edm	1983–84	74	87	Brett Hull, StL	1991–92	73	70
Brett Hull, StL	1990–91	78	86	Mario Lemieux, Pit	1987–88	77	70
Mario Lemieux, Pit	1988–89	76	85	Bernie Nicholls, LA	1988–89	79	70
Alexander Mogilny, Buf	1992–93	77	76	Mario Lemieux, Pit	1992–93	60	69
Phil Esposito, Bos	1970–71	78	76	Mario Lemieux, Pit	1995–96	70	69
Teemu Selanne, Win	1992–93	84	76	Mike Bossy, NYI	1978–79	80	69
Wayne Gretzky, Edm	1984–85	80	73	Phil Esposito, Bos	1973–74	78	68
Brett Hull, StL	1989–90	80	72	Jari Kurri, Edm	1985–86	78	68
Jari Kurri, Edm	1984–85	73	71	Mike Bossy, NYI	1980–81	79	68

Assists

Player	Season	GP	Asst	Player	Season	GP	Asst
Wayne Gretzky, Edm	1985–86	80	163	Bobby Orr, Bos	1970–71	78	102
Wayne Gretzky, Edm	1984–85	80	135	Mario Lemieux, Pit	1987–88	77	98
Wayne Gretzky, Edm	1982–83	80	125	Adam Oates, Bos	1992–93	84	97
Wayne Gretzky, LA	1990–91	78	122	Joe Thornton, SJ	2005-06	81	96
Wayne Gretzky, Edm	1986–87	79	121	Doug Gilmour, Tor	1992–93	83	95
Wayne Gretzky, Edm	1981–82	80	120	Pat LaFontaine, Buf	1992–93	84	95
Wayne Gretzky, Edm	1983–84	74	118	Mario Lemieux, Pit	1985–86	79	93
Mario Lemieux, Pit	1988–89	76	114	Peter Stastny, Que	1981–82	80	93
Wayne Gretzky, LA	1988–89	78	114	Wayne Gretzky, LA	1993–94	81	92
Wayne Gretzky, Edm	1987–88	64	109	Mario Lemieux, Pit	1995–96	70	92
Wayne Gretzky, Edm	1980–81	80	109	Ron Francis, Pit	1995–96	77	92
Wayne Gretzky, LA	1989–90	73	102	Joe Thornton, SJ	2006-07	82	92

Points

Player	Season	G	Asst	Pts	Player	Season	G	Asst	Pts
Wayne Gretzky, Edm	1985–86	52	163	215	Wayne Gretzky, LA	1990–91	41	122	163
Wayne Gretzky, Edm	1981–82	92	120	212	Mario Lemieux, Pit	1995–96	69	92	161
Wayne Gretzky, Edm	1984–85	73	135	208	Mario Lemieux, Pit	1992–93	69	91	160
Wayne Gretzky, Edm	1983–84	87	118	205	Steve Yzerman, Det	1988–89	65	90	155
Mario Lemieux, Pit	1988–89	85	114	199	Phil Esposito, Bos	1970–71	76	76	152
Wayne Gretzky, Edm	1982–83	71	125	196	Bernie Nicholls, LA	1988–89	70	80	150
Wayne Gretzky, Edm	1986–87	62	121	183	Wayne Gretzky, Edm	1987–88	40	109	149
Mario Lemieux, Pit	1987–88	70	98	168	Pat LaFontaine, Buf	1992–93	53	95	148
Wayne Gretzky, LA	1988–89	54	114	168	Mike Bossy, NYI	1981–82	64	83	147
Wayne Gretzky, Edm	1980–81	55	109	164	Phil Esposito, Bos	1973–74	68	77	145

Points per Game

Player	Season	GP	Pts	Avg	Player	Season	GP	Pts	Avg
Wayne Gretzky, Edm	1983–84	74	205	2.77	Mario Lemieux, Pit	1987–88	77	168	2.18
Wayne Gretzky, Edm	1985–86	80	215	2.69	Wayne Gretzky, LA	1988–89	78	168	2.15
Mario Lemieux, Pit	1992–93	60	160	2.67	Wayne Gretzky, LA	1990–91	78	163	2.09
Wayne Gretzky, Edm	1981–82	80	212	2.65	Mario Lemieux, Pit	1989–90	59	123	2.08
Mario Lemieux, Pit	1988–89	76	199	2.62	Wayne Gretzky, Edm	1980–81	80	164	2.05
Wayne Gretzky, Edm	1984–85	80	208	2.60	Mario Lemieux, Pit	1991–92	64	131	2.05
Wayne Gretzky, Edm	1982–83	80	196	2.45	Bill Cowley, Bos	1943–44	36	71	1.97
Wayne Gretzky, Edm	1987–88	64	149	2.33	Phil Esposito, Bos	1970–71	78	152	1.95
Wayne Gretzky, Edm	1986–87	79	183	2.32	Wayne Gretzky, LA	1989–90	73	142	1.95
Mario Lemieux, Pitt	1995–96	70	161	2.30	Steve Yzerman, Det	1988–89	80	155	1.94

Note: Minimum 50 points in one season.

Goals per Game

Player	Season	GP	G	Avg
Joe Malone, Mtl	1917–18	20	44	2.20
Cy Denneny, Ott	1917–18	20	36	1.80
Newsy Lalonde, Mtl	1917–18	14	23	1.64
Joe Malone, Que	1919–20	24	39	1.63
Newsy Lalonde, Mtl	1919–20	23	36	1.57
Reg Noble, Tor	1917–18	20	30	1.50
Babe Dye, Ham-Tor	1920–21	24	35	1.46
Cy Denneny, Ott	1920–21	24	34	1.42
Joe Malone, Ham	1920–21	20	28	1.40
Newsy Lalonde, Mtl	1920–21	24	33	1.38

Note: Minimum 20 goals in one season.

Assists per Game

Player	Season	GP	Asst	Avg
Wayne Gretzky, Edm	1985–86	80	163	2.04
Wayne Gretzky, Edm	1987–88	64	109	1.70
Wayne Gretzky, Edm	1984–85	80	135	1.69
Wayne Gretzky, Edm	1983–84	74	118	1.59
Wayne Gretzky, Edm	1982–83	80	125	1.56
Wayne Gretzky, LA	1990–91	78	122	1.56
Wayne Gretzky, Edm	1986–87	79	121	1.53
Mario Lemieux, Pit	1992–93	60	91	1.52
Wayne Gretzky, Edm	1981–82	80	120	1.50
Mario Lemieux, Pit	1988–89	76	114	1.50

Note: Minimum 35 assists in one season.

Shutout Leaders

Player	Season	SO	Length of Schedule	Player	Season	SO	Length of Schedule
George Hainsworth, Mtl	1928–29	22	44	George Hainsworth, Mtl	1927–28	13	44
Alec Connell, Ott	1925–26	15	36	John Roach, NYR	1928–29	13	44
Alec Connell, Ott	1927–28	15	44	Roy Worters, NYA	1928–29	13	44
Hal Winkler, Bos	1927–28	15	44	Harry Lumley, Tor	1953–54	13	70
Tony Esposito, Chi	1969–70	15	76	Dominik Hasek, Buf	1997–98	13	82
George Hainsworth, Mtl	1926–27	14	44	Tiny Thompson, Bos	1928–29	12	44
Clint Benedict, Mtl M	1926–27	13	44	Chuck Gardiner, Chi	1930–31	12	44
Alec Connell, Ott	1926–27	13	44	Terry Sawchuk, Det	1951–52	12	70

Shutout Leaders *(Cont.)*

	Season	SO	Length of Schedule		Season	SO	Length of Schedule
Terry Sawchuk, Det	1953–54	12	70	John Roach, Det	1932–33	10	48
Terry Sawchuk, Det	1954–55	12	70	Chuck Gardiner, Chi	1933–34	10	48
Glenn Hall, Det	1955–56	12	70	Tiny Thompson, Bos	1935–36	10	48
Bernie Parent, Phi	1973–74	12	78	Frank Brimsek, Bos	1938–39	10	48
Bernie Parent, Phi	1974–75	12	80	Bill Durnan, Mtl	1948–49	10	60
Martin Brodeur, NJ	2006–07	12	82	Gerry McNeil, Mtl	1952–53	10	70
Lorne Chabot, NYR	1927–28	11	44	Harry Lumley, Tor	1952–53	10	70
Harry Holmes, Det	1927–28	11	44	Tony Esposito, Chi	1973–74	10	78
Roy Worters, Pit Pirates	1927–28	11	44	Ken Dryden, Mtl	1976–77	10	80
Lorne Chabot, Tor	1928–29	11	44	Martin Brodeur, NJ	1996–97	10	82
Clint Benedict, Mtl M	1928–29	11	44	Martin Brodeur, NJ	1997–98	10	82
Joe Miller, Pit Pirates	1928–29	11	44	Roman Cechmanek, Phi	2000–01	10	82
Tiny Thompson, Bos	1932–33	11	48	Byron Dafoe, Bos	1998–99	10	82
Terry Sawchuk, Det	1950–51	11	70	Ed Belfour, Tor	2003–04	10	82
Dominik Hasek, Buf	2000–01	11	82	Miikka Kiprusoff, Cgy	2005–06	10	82
Martin Brodeur, NJ	2003–04	11	82	Henrik Lundqvist, NYR	2007–08	10	82
Lorne Chabot, NYR	1926–27	10	44	Steve Mason, CBJ	2008–09	10	82
Clarence Dolson, Det	1928–29	10	44				

Wins

	Season	Record*		Season	Record*
Martin Brodeur, NJ	2006–07	48–23	Martin Brodeur, NJ	1997–98	43–17–8
Roberto Luongo, Van	2006–07	47–22	Martin Brodeur, NJ	1999–00	43–20–8
Bernie Parent, Phi	1973–74	47–13–12	Martin Brodeur, NJ	2005–06	43–23
Evgeni Nabokov, SJ	2007–08	46–21	Ken Dryden, Mtl	1975–76	42–10–6
Miikka Kiprusoff, Cgy	2008–09	45–24	Mike Richter, NYR	1993–94	42–12–6
Martin Brodeur, NJ	2009–10	45–25	Jacques Plante, Mtl	1955–56	42–12–10
Terry Sawchuk, Det	1950–51	44–13–13	Jacques Plante, Mtl	1961–62	42–14–14
Bernie Parent, Phi	1974–75	44–14–9	Roman Turek, StL	1999–00	42–15–9
Terry Sawchuk, Det	1951–52	44–14–12	Martin Brodeur, NJ	2000–01	42–17–11
Evgeni Nabokov, SJ	2009–10	44–16	Miikka Kiprusoff, Cgy	2005–06	42–20
Martin Brodeur, NJ	2007–08	44–27	Ilya Bryzgalov, Phx	2009–10	42–20
Tom Barrasso, Pit	1992–93	43–14–5			
Ed Belfour, Chi	1990–91	43–19–7	*Starting with the 2005–06 season, ties were eliminated.		

Goals Against Average

(PRE-1950)

	Season	GP	GAA
George Hainsworth, Mtl	1928–29	44	0.92
George Hainsworth, Mtl	1927–28	44	1.05
Alec Connell, Ott	1925–26	36	1.12
Tiny Thompson, Bos	1928–29	44	1.15
Roy Worters, NYA	1928–29	38	1.15

(POST-1950)

	Season	GP	GAA
Miika Kiprusoff, Cal	2003–04	38	1.69
Marty Turco, Dal	2002–03	55	1.73
Tony Esposito, Chi	1971–72	48	1.770
Al Rollins, Tor	1950–51	40	1.774
Ron Tugnutt, Ott	1998–99	43	1.79

Single-Game Records

Goals

	Date	G
Joe Malone, Que vs Tor	1-31-20	7
Newsy Lalonde, Mtl vs Tor	1-10-20	6
Joe Malone, Que vs Ott	3-10-20	6
Corb Denneny, Tor vs Ham	1-26-21	6
Cy Denneny, Ott vs Ham	3-7-21	6
Syd Howe, Det vs NYR	2-3-44	6
Red Berenson, StL vs Phi	11-7-68	6
Darryl Sittler, Tor vs Bos	2-7-76	6

Assists

	Date	A
Billy Taylor, Det vs Chi	3-16-47	7
Wayne Gretzky, Edm vs Wsh	2-15-80	7
Wayne Gretzky, Edm vs Chi	12-11-85	7
Wayne Gretzky, Edm vs Que	2-14-86	7

Note: 24 tied with 6.

Points

	Date	G	A	Pts
Darryl Sittler, Tor vs Bos	2-7-76	6	4	10
Maurice Richard, Mtl vs Det	12-28-44	5	3	8
Bert Olmstead, Mtl vs Chi	1-9-54	4	4	8
Tom Bladon, Phi vs Clev	12-11-77	4	4	8
Bryan Trottier, NYI vs NYR	12-23-78	5	3	8
Peter Stastny, Que vs Wsh	2-22-81	4	4	8
Anton Stastny, Que vs Wsh	2-22-81	3	5	8
Wayne Gretzky, Edm vs NJ	11-19-83	3	5	8
Wayne Gretzky, Edm vs Min	1-4-84	4	4	8
Paul Coffey, Edm vs Det	3-14-86	2	6	8
Mario Lemieux, Pit vs StL	10-15-88	2	6	8
Bernie Nicholls, LA vs Tor	12-1-88	2	6	8
Mario Lemieux, Pit vs NJ	12-31-88	5	3	8

Points

Season	Player and Club	Pts	Season	Player and Club	Pts
1917–18	Joe Malone, Mtl	44	1965–66	Bobby Hull, Chi	97
1918–19	Newsy Lalonde, Mtl	30	1966–67	Stan Mikita, Chi	97
1919–20	Joe Malone, Que	48	1967–68	Stan Mikita, Chi	87
1920–21	Newsy Lalonde, Mtl	41	1968–69	Phil Esposito, Bos	126
1921–22	Punch Broadbent, Ott	46	1969–70	Bobby Orr, Bos	120
1922–23	Babe Dye, Tor	37	1970–71	Phil Esposito, Bos	152
1923–24	Cy Denneny, Ott	23	1971–72	Phil Esposito, Bos	133
1924–25	Babe Dye, Tor	44	1972–73	Phil Esposito, Bos	130
1925–26	Nels Stewart, Mtl M	42	1973–74	Phil Esposito, Bos	145
1926–27	Bill Cook, NY	37	1974–75	Bobby Orr, Bos	135
1927–28	Howie Morenz, Mtl	51	1975–76	Guy Lafleur, Mtl	125
1928–29	Ace Bailey, Tor	32	1976–77	Guy Lafleur, Mtl	136
1929–30	Cooney Weiland, Bos	73	1977–78	Guy Lafleur, Mtl	132
1930–31	Howie Morenz, Mtl	51	1978–79	Bryan Trottier, NYI	134
1931–32	Harvey Jackson, Tor	53	1979–80	Marcel Dionne, LA	137
1932–33	Bill Cook, NY	50		Wayne Gretzky, Edm	137
1933–34	Charlie Conacher, Tor	52	1980–81	Wayne Gretzky, Edm	164
1934–35	Charlie Conacher, Tor	57	1981–82	Wayne Gretzky, Edm	212
1935–36	Sweeney Schriner, NYA	45	1982–83	Wayne Gretzky, Edm	196
1936–37	Sweeney Schriner, NYA	46	1983–84	Wayne Gretzky, Edm	205
1937–38	Gord Drillon, Tor	52	1984–85	Wayne Gretzky, Edm	208
1938–39	Hector Blake, Mtl	47	1985–86	Wayne Gretzky, Edm	215
1939–40	Milt Schmidt, Bos	52	1986–87	Wayne Gretzky, Edm	183
1940–41	Bill Cowley, Bos	62	1987–88	Mario Lemieux, Pit	168
1941–42	Bryan Hextall, NY	54	1988–89	Mario Lemieux, Pit	199
1942–43	Doug Bentley, Chi	73	1989–90	Wayne Gretzky, LA	142
1943–44	Herb Cain, Bos	82	1990–91	Wayne Gretzky, LA	163
1944–45	Elmer Lach, Mtl	80	1991–92	Mario Lemieux, Pit	131
1945–46	Max Bentley, Chi	61	1992–93	Mario Lemieux, Pit	160
1946–47	Max Bentley, Chi	72	1993–94	Wayne Gretzky, LA	130
1947–48	Elmer Lach, Mtl	61	1994–95	Jaromir Jagr, Pit	70
1948–49	Roy Conacher, Chi	68	1995–96	Mario Lemieux, Pit	161
1949–50	Ted Lindsay, Det	78	1996–97	Mario Lemieux, Pit	122
1950–51	Gordie Howe, Det	86	1997–98	Jaromir Jagr, Pit	102
1951–52	Gordie Howe, Det	86	1998–99	Jaromir Jagr, Pit	127
1952–53	Gordie Howe, Det	95	1999–00	Jaromir Jagr, Pit	96
1953–54	Gordie Howe, Det	81	2000–01	Jaromir Jagr, Pit	121
1954–55	Bernie Geoffrion, Mtl	75	2001–02	Jarome Iginla, Cgy	96
1955–56	Jean Beliveau, Mtl	88	2002–03	Peter Forsberg, Col	106
1956–57	Gordie Howe, Det	89	2003–04	Martin St. Louis, TB	94
1957–58	Dickie Moore, Mtl	84	2004–05	No season	
1958–59	Dickie Moore, Mtl	96	2005–06	Joe Thornton, Bos/SJ	125
1959–60	Bobby Hull, Chi	81	2006–07	Sidney Crosby, Pit	120
1960–61	Bernie Geoffrion, Mtl	95	2007–08	Alexander Ovechkin, Wsh	112
1961–62	Andy Bathgate, NY	84	2008–09	Evgeni Malkin, Pit	113
	Bobby Hull, Chi	84	2009–10	Henrik Sedin, Van	112
1962–63	Gordie Howe, Det	86			
1963–64	Stan Mikita, Chi	89			
1964–65	Stan Mikita, Chi	87			

Goals

Season	Player and Club	G	Season	Player and Club	G
1917–18	Joe Malone, Mtl	44	1930–31	Charlie Lonacher, Tor	31
1918–19	Odie Cleghorn, Mtl	23	1931–32	Charlie Conacher, Tor	34
1919–20	Joe Malone, Que	39		Bill Cook, NY	34
1920–21	Babe Dye, Ham-Tor	35	1932–33	Bill Cook, NY	28
1921–22	Punch Broadbent, Ott	32	1933–34	Charlie Conacher, Tor	32
1922–23	Babe Dye, Tor	26	1934–35	Charlie Conacher, Tor	36
1923–24	Cy Denneny, Ott	22	1935–36	Charlie Conacher, Tor	23
1924–25	Babe Dye, Tor	38		Bill Thoms, Tor	23
1925–26	Nels Stewart, Mtl	34	1936–37	Larry Aurie, Det	23
1926–27	Bill Cook, NY	33		Nels Stewart, Bos-NYA	23
1927–28	Howie Morenz, Mtl	33	1937–38	Gord Drillon, Tor	26
1928–29	Ace Bailey, Tor	22	1938–39	Roy Conacher, Bos	26
1929–30	Cooney Weiland, Bos	43	1939–40	Bryan Hextall, NY	24

Goals *(Cont.)*

Season	Player and Club	G		Season	Player and Club	G
1940–41	Bryan Hextall, NY	26		1978–79	Mike Bossy, NYI	69
1941–42	Lynn Patrick, NY	32		1979–80	Charlie Simmer, LA	56
1942–43	Doug Bentley, Chi	33			Blaine Stoughton, Hart	56
1943–44	Doug Bentley, Chi	38		1980–81	Mike Bossy, NYI	68
1944–45	Maurice Richard, Mtl	50		1981–82	Wayne Gretzky, Edm	92
1945–46	Gaye Stewart, Tor	37		1982–83	Wayne Gretzky, Edm	71
1946–47	Maurice Richard, Mtl	45		1983–84	Wayne Gretzky, Edm	87
1947–48	Ted Lindsay, Det	33		1984–85	Wayne Gretzky, Edm	73
1948–49	Sid Abel, Det	28		1985–86	Jari Kurri, Edm	68
1949–50	Maurice Richard, Mtl	43		1986–87	Wayne Gretzky, Edm	62
1950–51	Gordie Howe, Det	43		1987–88	Mario Lemieux, Pit	70
1951–52	Gordie Howe, Det	47		1988–89	Mario Lemieux, Pit	85
1952–53	Gordie Howe, Det	49		1989–90	Brett Hull, StL	72
1953–54	Maurice Richard, Mtl	37		1990–91	Brett Hull, StL	86
1954–55	Bernie Geoffrion, Mtl	38		1991–92	Brett Hull, StL	70
	Maurice Richard, Mtl	38		1992–93	Alexander Mogilny, Buf	76
1955–56	Jean Beliveau, Mtl	47			Teemu Selanne, Win	76
1956–57	Gordie Howe, Det	44		1993–94	Pavel Bure, Van	60
1957–58	Dickie Moore, Mtl	36		1994–95	Peter Bondra, Wsh	34
1958–59	Jean Beliveau, Mtl	45		1995–96	Mario Lemieux, Pit	69
1959–60	Bronco Horvath, Bos	39		1996–97	Keith Tkachuk, Phx	52
	Bobby Hull, Chi	39		1997–98	Peter Bondra, Wsh	52
1960–61	Bernie Geoffrion, Mtl	50			Teemu Selanne, Ana	52
1961–62	Bobby Hull, Chi	50		1998–99	Teemu Selanne, Ana	47
1962–63	Gordie Howe, Det	38		1999–00	Pavel Bure, Fla	58
1963–64	Bobby Hull, Chi	43		2000–01	Pavel Bure, Fla	59
1964–65	Norm Ullman, Det	42		2001–02	Jarome Iginla, Cgy	52
1965–66	Bobby Hull, Chi	54		2002–03	Milan Hejduk, Col	50
1966–67	Bobby Hull, Chi	52		2003–04	Jarome Iginla, Cgy	41
1967–68	Bobby Hull, Chi	44			Ilya Kovalchuk, Atl	41
1968–69	Bobby Hull, Chi	58			Rick Nash, CBJ	41
1969–70	Phil Esposito, Bos	43		2004–05	No season	
1970–71	Phil Esposito, Bos	76		2005–06	Jonathan Cheechoo, SJ	56
1971–72	Phil Esposito, Bos	66		2006–07	Vincent Lecavalier, TB	52
1972–73	Phil Esposito, Bos	55		2007–08	Alexander Ovechkin, Wsh	65
1973–74	Phil Esposito, Bos	68		2008–09	Alexander Ovechkin, Wsh	56
1974–75	Phil Esposito, Bos	61		2009–10	Sidney Crosby, Pit	51
1975–76	Guy Lafleur, Mtl	56			Steven Stamkos, TB	51
1976–77	Steve Shutt, Mtl	60				
1977–78	Guy Lafleur, Mtl	60				

Assists

Season	Player and Club	Asst		Season	Player and Club	Asst
1917–18	statistic not kept			1940–41	Bill Cowley, Bos	45
1918–19	Newsy Lalonde, Mtl	9		1941–42	Phil Watson, NY	37
1919–20	Corbett Denneny, Tor	12		1942–43	Bill Cowley, Bos	45
1920–21	Louis Berlinquette, Mtl	9		1943–44	Clint Smith, Chi	49
1921–22	Punch Broadbench, Ott	14		1944–45	Elmer Lach, Mtl	54
1922–23	Babe Dye, Tor	11		1945–46	Elmer Lach, Mtl	34
1923–24	Billy Boucher, Mtl	6		1946–47	Billy Taylor, Det	46
1924–25	Cy Denneny, Ott	15		1947–48	Doug Bentley, Chi	37
1925–26	Frank Nighbor, Ott	13		1948–49	Doug Bentley, Chi	43
1926–27	Dick Irvin, Chi	18		1949–50	Ted Lindsay, Det	55
1927–28	Howie Morenz, Mtl	18		1950–51	Gordie Howe, Det	43
1928–29	Frank Boucher, NY	16			Ted Kennedy, Tor	43
1929–30	Frank Boucher, NY	36		1951–52	Elmer Lach, Mtl	50
1930–31	Joe Primeau, Tor	32		1952–53	Gordie Howe, Det	46
1931–32	Joe Primeau, Tor	37		1953–54	Gordie Howe, Det	48
1932–33	Frank Boucher, NY	28		1954–55	Bert Olmstead, Mtl	48
1933–34	Joe Primeau, Tor	32		1955–56	Bert Olmstead, Mtl	56
1934–35	Art Chapman, NYA	34		1956–57	Ted Lindsay, Det	55
1935–36	Art Chapman, NYA	28		1957–58	Henri Richard, Mtl	52
1936–37	Syl Apps, Tor	29		1958–59	Dickie Moore, Mtl	55
1937–38	Syl Apps, Tor	29		1959–60	Bobby Hull, Chi	42
1938–39	Bill Cowley, Bos	34		1960–61	Jean Beliveau, Mtl	58
1939–40	Milt Schmidt, Bos	30		1961–62	Andy Bathgate, NY	56

Assists *(Cont.)*

Season	Player and Club	Asst	Season	Player and Club	Asst
1962–63	Henri Richard, Mtl	50	1988–89	Wayne Gretzky, LA	114
1963–64	Andy Bathgate, NY-Tor	58		Mario Lemieux, Pit	114
1964–65	Stan Mikita, Chi	59	1989–90	Wayne Gretzky, LA	102
1965–66	Jean Beliveau, Mtl	48	1990–91	Wayne Gretzky, LA	122
	Bobby Rousseau, Mtl	48	1991–92	Wayne Gretzky, LA	90
	Stan Mikita, Chi	48	1992–93	Adam Oates, Bos	97
1966–67	Stan Mikita, Chi	62	1993–94	Wayne Gretzky, LA	92
1967–68	Phil Esposito, Bos	49	1994–95	Ron Francis, Pit	48
1968–69	Phil Esposito, Bos	77	1995–96	Ron Francis, Pit	92
1969–70	Bobby Orr, Bos	87		Mario Lemieux, Pit	92
1970–71	Bobby Orr, Bos	102	1996–97	Mario Lemieux, Pit	72
1971–72	Bobby Orr, Bos	80	1997–98	Wayne Gretzky, NYR	67
1972–73	Phil Esposito, Bos	75		Jaromir Jagr, Pit	67
1973–74	Bobby Orr, Bos	90	1998–99	Jaromir Jagr, Pit	83
1974–75	Bobby Clarke, Phi	89	1999–00	Mark Recchi, Phi	63
	Bobby Orr, Bos	89	2000–01	Jaromir Jagr, Pit	69
1975–76	Bobby Clarke, Phi	89		Adam Oates, Wsh	69
1976–77	Guy Lafleur, Mtl	80	2001–02	Adam Oates, Wsh	64
1977–78	Bryan Trottier, NYI	77	2002–03	Peter Forsberg, Col	77
1978–79	Bryan Trottier, NYI	87	2003–04	Scott Gomez, NJ	56
1979–80	Wayne Gretzky, Edm	86		Martin St. Louis, TB	56
1980–81	Wayne Gretzky, Edm	109	2004–05	No season	
1981–82	Wayne Gretzky, Edm	120	2005–06	Joe Thornton, Bos/SJ	96
1982–83	Wayne Gretzky, Edm	125	2006–07	Joe Thornton, SJ	92
1983–84	Wayne Gretzky, Edm	118	2007–08	Joe Thornton, SJ	67
1984–85	Wayne Gretzky, Edm	135	2008–09	Evgeni Malkin, Pit	78
1985–86	Wayne Gretzky, Edm	163	2009–10	Henrik Sedin, Van	83
1986–87	Wayne Gretzky, Edm	121			
1987–88	Wayne Gretzky, Edm	109			

Goals Against Average

Season	Goaltender and Club	GP	Min	GA	SO	Avg
1917–18	Georges Vezina, Mtl	21	1282	84	1	3.93
1918–19	Clint Benedict, Ott	18	1113	53	2	2.86
1919–20	Clint Benedict, Ott	24	1444	64	5	2.66
1920–21	Clint Benedict, Ott	24	1457	75	2	3.09
1921–22	Clint Benedict, Ott	24	1508	84	2	3.34
1922–23	Clint Benedict, Ott	24	1478	54	4	2.18
1923–24	Georges Vezina, Mtl	24	1459	48	3	1.97
1924–25	Georges Vezina, Mtl	30	1860	56	5	1.81
1925–26	Alec Connell, Ott	36	2251	42	15	1.12
1926–27	Clint Benedict, Mtl M	43	2748	65	13	1.42
1927–28	George Hainsworth, Mtl	44	2730	48	13	1.05
1928–29	George Hainsworth, Mtl	44	2800	43	22	0.92
1929–30	Tiny Thompson, Bos	44	2680	98	3	2.19
1930–31	Roy Worters, NYA	44	2760	74	8	1.61
1931–32	Chuck Gardiner, Chi	48	2989	92	4	1.85
1932–33	Tiny Thompson, Bos	48	3000	88	11	1.76
1933–34	Wilf Cude, Det-Mtl	30	1920	47	5	1.47
1934–35	Lorne Chabot, Chi	48	2940	88	8	1.80
1935–36	Tiny Thompson, Bos	48	2930	82	10	1.68
1936–37	Normie Smith, Det	48	2980	102	6	2.05
1937–38	Tiny Thompson, Bos	48	2970	89	7	1.80
1938–39	Frank Brimsek, Bos	43	2610	68	10	1.56
1939–40	Dave Kerr, NYR	48	3000	77	8	1.54
1940–41	Turk Broda, Tor	48	2970	99	5	2.00
1941–42	Frank Brimsek, Bos	47	2930	115	3	2.35
1942–43	Johnny Mowers, Det	50	3010	124	6	2.47
1943–44	Bill Durnan, Mtl	50	3000	109	2	2.18
1944–45	Bill Durnan, Mtl	50	3000	121	1	2.42
1945–46	Bill Durnan, Mtl	40	2400	104	4	2.60
1946–47	Bill Durnan, Mtl	60	3600	138	4	2.30
1947–48	Turk Broda, Tor	60	3600	143	5	2.38

Goals Against Average *(Cont.)*

Season	Goaltender and Club	GP	Min	GA	SO	Avg
1948–49	Bill Durnan, Mtl	60	3600	126	10	2.10
1949–50	Bill Durnan, Mtl	64	3840	141	8	2.20
1950–51	Al Rollins, Tor	40	2367	70	5	1.77
1951–52	Terry Sawchuk, Det	70	4200	133	12	1.90
1952–53	Terry Sawchuk, Det	63	3780	120	9	1.90
1953–54	Harry Lumley, Tor	69	4140	128	13	1.86
1954–55	Harry Lumley, Tor	69	4140	134	8	1.94
1955–56	Jacques Plante, Mtl	64	3840	119	7	1.86
1956–57	Jacques Plante, Mtl	61	3660	122	9	2.00
1957–58	Jacques Plante, Mtl	57	3386	119	9	2.11
1958–59	Jacques Plante, Mtl	67	4000	144	9	2.16
1959–60	Jacques Plante, Mtl	69	4140	175	3	2.54
1960–61	Charlie Hodge, Mtl	30	1800	74	4	2.47
1961–62	Jacques Plante, Mtl	70	4200	166	4	2.37
1962–63	Don Simmons, Tor	28	1680	69	1	2.46
1963–64	Johnny Bower, Tor	51	3009	106	5	2.11
1964–65	Johnny Bower, Tor	34	2040	81	3	2.38
1965–66	Johnny Bower, Tor	35	1998	75	3	2.25
1966–67	Glenn Hall, Chi	32	1664	66	2	2.38
1967–68	Gump Worsley, Mtl	40	2213	73	6	1.98
1968–69	Jacques Plante, StL	37	2139	70	5	1.96
1969–70	Ernie Wakely, StL	30	1651	58	4	2.11
1970–71	Jacques Plante, Tor	40	2329	73	4	1.88
1971–72	Tony Esposito, Chi	48	2780	82	9	1.77
1972–73	Ken Dryden, Mtl	54	3165	119	6	2.26
1973–74	Bernie Parent, Phi	73	4314	136	12	1.89
1974–75	Bernie Parent, Phi	68	4041	137	12	2.03
1975–76	Ken Dryden, Mtl	62	3580	121	8	2.03
1976–77	Michel Larocque, Mtl	26	1525	53	4	2.09
1977–78	Ken Dryden, Mtl	52	3071	105	5	2.05
1978–79	Ken Dryden, Mtl	47	2814	108	5	2.30
1979–80	Bob Sauve, Buff	32	1880	74	4	2.36
1980–81	Richard Sevigny, Mtl	33	1777	71	2	2.40
1981–82	Denis Herron, Mtl	27	1547	68	3	2.64
1982–83	Pete Peeters, Bos	62	3611	142	8	2.36
1983–84	Pat Riggin, Wsh	41	2299	102	4	2.66
1984–85	Tom Barrasso, Buf	54	3248	144	5	2.66
1985–86	Bob Froese, Phi	51	2728	116	5	2.55
1986–87	Brian Hayward, Mtl	37	2178	102	1	2.81
1987–88	Pete Peeters, Wsh	35	1896	88	2	2.78
1988–89	Patrick Roy, Mtl	48	2744	113	4	2.47
1989–90	Mike Liut, Hfd-Wsh	37	2161	91	4	2.53
	Patrick Roy, Mtl	54	3173	134	3	2.53
1990–91	Ed Belfour, Chi	74	4127	170	4	2.47
1991–92	Patrick Roy, Mtl	67	3935	155	5	2.36
1992–93	Felix Potvin, Tor	48	2781	116	2	2.50
1993–94	Dominik Hasek, Buf	58	3358	109	7	1.95
1994–95	Dominik Hasek, Buf	41	2416	85	5	2.11
1995–96	Ron Hextall, Phi	53	3102	112	4	2.17
	Chris Osgood, Det	50	2932	106	5	2.17
1996–97	Martin Brodeur, NJ	67	3838	120	10	1.88
1997–98	Ed Belfour, Dal	61	3581	112	9	1.88
1998–99	Ron Tugnutt, Ott	43	2508	75	3	1.79
1999–00	Brian Boucher, Phi	35	2038	65	4	1.91
2000–01	Marty Turco, Dal	26	1266	40	3	1.90
2001–02	Patrick Roy, Col	63	3773	122	9	1.94
2002–03	Marty Turco, Dal	55	3202	92	7	1.72
2003–04	Miikka Kiprusoff, Cgy	38	2301	65	4	1.69
2004–05	No season					
2005–06	Miikka Kiprusoff, Cgy	74	4379	151	10	2.07
2006–07	Niklas Backstrom, Min	41	2226	73	5	1.97
2007–08	Chris Osgood, Det	43	2409	84	4	2.09
2008–09	Tim Thomas, Bos	54	3259	114	5	2.10
2009–10	Tuukka Rask, Bos	45	2562	84	5	1.97

Penalty Minutes

Season	Player and Club	GP	PIM	Season	Player and Club	GP	PIM
1918–19	Joe Hall, Mtl	17	135	1964–65	Carl Brewer, Tor	70	177
1919–20	Cully Wilson, Tor	23	79	1965–66	Reggie Fleming, Bos-NYR	69	166
1920–21	Bert Corbeau, Mtl	24	86	1966–67	John Ferguson, Mtl	67	177
1921–22	Sprague Cleghorn, Mtl	24	63	1967–68	Barclay Plager, StL	49	153
1922–23	Billy Boucher, Mtl	24	55	1968–69	Forbes Kennedy, Phi-Tor	77	219
1923–24	Bert Corbeau, Tor	24	55	1969–70	Keith Magnuson, Chi	76	213
1924–25	Billy Boucher, Mtl	30	92	1970–71	Keith Magnuson, Chi	76	291
1925–26	Bert Corbeau, Tor	36	121	1971–72	Brian Watson, Pit	75	212
1926–27	Nels Stewart, Mtl M	44	133	1972–73	Dave Schultz, Phi	76	259
1927–28	Eddie Shore, Bos	44	165	1973–74	Dave Schultz, Phi	73	348
1928–29	Red Dutton, Mtl M	44	139	1974–75	Dave Schultz, Phi	76	472
1929–30	Joe Lamb, Ott	44	119	1975–76	Steve Durbano, Pit-KC	69	370
1930–31	Harvey Rockburn, Det	42	118	1976–77	Dave Williams, Tor	77	338
1931–32	Red Dutton, NYA	47	107	1977–78	Dave Schultz, LA-Pit	74	405
1932–33	Red Horner, Tor	48	144	1978–79	Dave Williams, Tor	77	298
1933–34	Red Horner, Tor	42	126	1979–80	Jimmy Mann, Win	72	287
1934–35	Red Horner, Tor	46	125	1980–81	Dave Williams, Van	77	343
1935–36	Red Horner, Tor	43	167	1981–82	Paul Baxter, Pit	76	409
1936–37	Red Horner, Tor	48	124	1982–83	Randy Holt, Wsh	70	275
1937–38	Red Horner, Tor	47	82	1983–84	Chris Nilan, Mtl	76	338
1938–39	Red Horner, Tor	48	85	1984–85	Chris Nilan, Mtl	77	358
1939–40	Red Horner, Tor	30	87	1985–86	Joey Kocur, Det	59	377
1940–41	Jimmy Orlando, Det	48	99	1986–87	Tim Hunter, Cgy	73	361
1941–42	Pat Egan, Bklyn	48	124	1987–88	Bob Probert, Det	74	398
1942–43	Jimmy Orlando, Det	40	89	1988–89	Tim Hunter, Cgy	75	375
1943–44	Mike McMahon, Mtl	42	98	1989–90	Basil McRae, Min	66	351
1944–45	Pat Egan, Bos	48	86	1990–91	Rob Ray, Buf	66	350
1945–46	Jack Stewart, Det	47	73	1991–92	Mike Peluso, Chi	63	408
1946–47	Gus Mortson, Tor	60	133	1992–93	Marty McSorley, LA	81	399
1947–48	Bill Barilko, Tor	57	147	1993–94	Tie Domi, Win	81	347
1948–49	Bill Ezinicki, Tor	52	145	1994–95	Enrico Ciccone, TB	41	225
1949–50	Bill Ezinicki, Tor	67	144	1995–96	Matthew Barnaby, Buf	73	335
1950–51	Gus Mortson, Tor	60	142	1996–97	Gino Odjick, Van	70	371
1951–52	Gus Kyle, Bos	69	127	1997–98	Donald Brashear, Van	77	372
1952–53	Maurice Richard, Mtl	70	112	1998–99	Rob Ray, Buf	76	261
1953–54	Gus Mortson, Chi	68	132	1999–00	Denny Lambert, Atl	73	219
1954–55	Fern Flaman, Bos	70	150	2000–01	Matthew Barnaby, TB	76	265
1955–56	Lou Fontinato, NYR	70	202	2001–02	Peter Worrell, Fla	79	354
1956–57	Gus Mortson, Chi	70	147	2002–03	Jody Shelley, CBJ	68	249
1957–58	Lou Fontinato, NYR	70	152	2003–04	Sean Avery, LA	76	261
1958–59	Ted Lindsay, Chi	70	184	2004–05	No season		
1959–60	Carl Brewer, Tor	67	150	2005–06	Sean Avery, LA	75	257
1960–61	Pierre Pilote, Chi	70	165	2006–07	Ben Eager, Phi	63	233
1961–62	Lou Fontinato, Mtl	54	167	2007–08	Daniel Carcillo, Phx	57	324
1962–63	Howie Young, Det	64	273	2008–09	Daniel Carcillo, Phi	74	254
1963–64	Vic Hadfield, NYR	69	151	2009–10	Zenon Konopka, TB	74	265

NHL All-Star Game

First played in 1947, this game started before the regular season and was used to match the defending Stanley Cup champions against the league All-Stars from other teams. In 1966 the game was moved to midseason, although there was no game that year. The format changed to a inter-conference showdown in 1969.

Results

Year	Site	Score	MVP	Attendance
1947	Toronto	All-Stars 4, Toronto 3	None named	14,169
1948	Chicago	All-Stars 3, Toronto 1	None named	12,794
1949	Toronto	All-Stars 3, Toronto 1	None named	13,541
1950	Detroit	Detroit 7, All-Stars 1	None named	9,166
1951	Toronto	1st team 2, 2nd team 2	None named	11,469
1952	Detroit	1st team 1, 2nd team 1	None named	10,680
1953	Montreal	All-Stars 3, Montreal 1	None named	14,153
1954	Detroit	All-Stars 2, Detroit 2	None named	10,689
1955	Detroit	Detroit 3, All-Stars 1	None named	10,111
1956	Montreal	All-Stars 1, Montreal 1	None named	13,095
1957	Montreal	All-Stars 5, Montreal 3	None named	13,003
1958	Montreal	Montreal 6, All-Stars 3	None named	13,989
1959	Montreal	Montreal 6, All-Stars 1	None named	13,818
1960	Montreal	All-Stars 2, Montreal 1	None named	13,949
1961	Chicago	All-Stars 3, Chicago 1	None named	14,534
1962	Toronto	Toronto 4, All-Stars 1	Eddie Shack, Tor	14,236
1963	Toronto	All-Stars 3, Toronto 3	Frank Mahovlich, Tor	14,034
1964	Toronto	All-Stars 3, Toronto 2	Jean Beliveau, Mtl	14,232
1965	Montreal	All-Stars 5, Montreal 2	Gordie Howe, Det	13,529
1967	Montreal	Montreal 3, All-Stars 0	Henri Richard, Mtl	14,284
1968	Toronto	Toronto 4, All-Stars 3	Bruce Gamble, Tor	15,753
1969	Montreal	East 3, West 3	Frank Mahovlich, Det	16,260
1970	St. Louis	East 4, West 1	Bobby Hull, Chi	16,587
1971	Boston	West 2, East 1	Bobby Hull, Chi	14,790
1972	Minnesota	East 3, West 2	Bobby Orr, Bos	15,423
1973	NY Rangers	East 5, West 4	Greg Polis, Pit	16,986
1974	Chicago	West 6, East 4	Garry Unger, StL	16,426
1975	Montreal	Wales 7, Campbell 1	Syl Apps Jr, Pit	16,080
1976	Philadelphia	Wales 7, Campbell 5	Pete Mahovlich, Mtl	16,436
1977	Vancouver	Wales 4, Campbell 3	Rick Martin, Buf	15,607
1978	Buffalo	Wales 3, Campbell 2 (OT)	Billy Smith, NYI	16,433
1980	Detroit	Wales 6, Campbell 3	Reg Leach, Phi	21,002
1981	Los Angeles	Campbell 4, Wales 1	Mike Liut, StL	15,761
1982	Washington	Wales 4, Campbell 2	Mike Bossy, NYI	18,130
1983	NY Islanders	Campbell 9, Wales 3	Wayne Gretzky, Edm	15,230
1984	New Jersey	Wales 7, Campbell 6	Don Maloney, NYR	18,939
1985	Calgary	Wales 6, Campbell 4	Mario Lemieux, Pit	16,825
1986	Hartford	Wales 4, Campbell 3 (OT)	Grant Fuhr, Edm	15,100
1988	St. Louis	Wales 6, Campbell 5 (OT)	Mario Lemieux, Pit	17,878
1989	Edmonton	Campbell 9, Wales 5	Wayne Gretzky, LA	17,503
1990	Pittsburgh	Wales 12, Campbell 7	Mario Lemieux, Pit	16,236
1991	Chicago	Campbell 11, Wales 5	Vince Damphousse, Tor	18,472
1992	Philadelphia	Campbell 10, Wales 6	Brett Hull, StL	17,380
1993	Montreal	Wales 16, Campbell 6	Mike Gartner, NYR	17,137
1994	NY Rangers	East 9, West 8	Mike Richter, NYR	18,200
1996	Boston	East 5, West 4	Ray Bourque, Bos	17,565
1997	San Jose	East 11, West 7	Mark Recchi, Mtl	17,422
1998	Vancouver	North America 8, World 7	Teemu Selanne, Ana (World)	18,422
1999	Tampa Bay	North America 8, World 6	Wayne Gretzky, NYR (N. America)	19,758
2000	Toronto	World 9, North America 4	Pavel Bure, Fla (World)	19,300
2001	Denver	North America 14, World 12	Bill Guerin, Bos (North America)	18,646
2002	Los Angeles	World 8, North America 5	Eric Daze, Chi (North America)	18,118
2003	Sunrise, Fla.	West 6, East 5 (shootout)	Dany Heatley, Atl (East)	19,250
2004	St. Paul, Minn.	East 6, West 4	Joe Sakic, Col (West)	19,434
2005	No game played (season lockout)			
2006	No game played (2006 Winter Olympics)			
2007	Dallas	West 12, East 9	Daniel Briere, Buf (East)	18,532

Year	Site	Score	MVP	Attendance
2008	Atlanta	East 8, West 7	Eric Staal, Car (East)	18,644
2009	Montreal	East 12, West 11	Alexei Kovalev, Mtl (East)	21,273
2010	No game played (2010 Winter Olympics)			

Note: The Challenge Cup, a series between the NHL All-Stars and the Soviet Union, was played instead of the All-Star Game in 1979. Eight years later, Rendez-Vous '87, a two-game series matching the Soviet Union and the NHL All-Stars, replaced the All-Star Game. The 1995 NHL All-Star game was cancelled due to a labor dispute. The 1998 NHL All-Star game, billed as a preview to the 1998 Winter Olympics in Nagano, Japan, matched North Amercian–born All-Stars and All-Stars born elsewhere.

Hockey Hall of Fame

Located in Toronto, the Hockey Hall of Fame was officially opened on August 26, 1961. The current chairman is William C. Hay. There are, at present, 306 members of the Hockey Hall of Fame—209 players, 84 "builders," and 14 on-ice officials. (One member, Alan Eagleson, resigned from the Hall March 25, 1998.) To be eligible, player and referee/linesman candidates should have been out of the game for three years, but the Hall's Board of Directors can make exceptions.

Players

Sid Abel (1969)
Jack Adams (1959)
Glenn Anderson (2008)
Charles (Syl) Apps (1961)
George Armstrong (1975)
Irvine (Ace) Bailey (1975)
Donald H. (Dan) Bain (1945)
Hobey Baker (1945)
Bill Barber (1990)
Marty Barry (1965)
Andy Bathgate (1978)
Bobby Bauer (1996)
Jean Beliveau (1972)
Clint Benedict (1965)
Douglas Bentley (1964)
Max Bentley (1966)
Hector (Toe) Blake (1966)
Leo Boivin (1986)
Dickie Boon (1952)
Mike Bossy (1991)
Emile (Butch) Bouchard (1966)
Frank Boucher (1958)
George (Buck) Boucher (1960)
Ray Bourque (2004)
Johnny Bower (1976)
Russell Bowie (1945)
Frank Brimsek (1966)
Harry L. (Punch) Broadbent (1962)
Walter (Turk) Broda (1967)
John Bucyk (1981)
Billy Burch (1974)
Harry Cameron (1962)
Gerry Cheevers (1985)
Dino Ciccarelli (2010)
Francis (King) Clancy (1958)
Aubrey (Dit) Clapper (1947)
Bobby Clarke (1987)
Sprague Cleghorn (1958)
Paul Coffey (2004)
Neil Colville (1967)
Charlie Conacher (1961)
Lionel Conacher (1994)

Roy Conacher (1998)
Alex Connell (1958)
Bill Cook (1952)
Fred (Bun) Cook (1995)
Arthur Coulter (1974)
Yvan Cournoyer (1982)
Bill Cowley (1968)
Samuel (Rusty) Crawford (1962)
Jack Darragh (1962)
Allan M. (Scotty) Davidson (1950)
Clarence (Hap) Day (1961)
Alex Delvecchio (1977)
Cy Denneny (1959)
Marcel Dionne (1992)
Gordie Drillon (1975)
Charles Drinkwater (1950)
Ken Dryden (1983)
Terrance (Dick) Duff (2006)
Woody Dumart (1992)
Thomas Dunderdale (1974)
Bill Durnan (1964)
Mervyn A. (Red) Dutton (1958)
Cecil (Babe) Dye (1970)
Phil Esposito (1984)
Tony Esposito (1988)
Arthur F. Farrell (1965)
Bernie Federko (2002)
Viacheslav Fetisov (2001)
Ferdinand (Fern) Flaman (1990)
Frank Foyston (1958)
Ron Francis (2007)
Frank Frederickson (1958)
Grant Fuhr (2003)
Bill Gadsby (1970)
Bob Gainey (1992)
Chuck Gardiner (1945)
Herb Gardiner (1958)
Jimmy Gardner (1962)
Mike Gartner (2001)
Bernie (Boom Boom) Geoffrion (1972)
Eddie Gerard (1945)

Note: Year of election to the Hall of Fame is in parentheses after the member's name.

Players *(Cont.)*

Ed Giacomin (1987)
Rod Gilbert (1982)
Clark Gillies (2002)
Hamilton (Billy) Gilmour (1962)
Frank (Moose) Goheen (1952)
Ebenezer R. (Ebbie)
 Goodfellow (1963)
Michel Goulet (1998)
Cammi Granato (2010)
Mike Grant (1950)
Wilfred (Shorty) Green (1962)
Jim Gregory (2007)
Wayne Gretzky (1999)
Si Griffis (1950)
George Hainsworth (1961)
Glenn Hall (1975)
Joe Hall (1961)
Doug Harvey (1973)
Dale Hawerchuk (2001)
George Hay (1958)
William (Riley) Hern (1962)
Bryan Hextall (1969)
Harry (Hap) Holmes (1972)
Tom Hooper (1962)
George (Red) Horner (1965)
Miles (Tim) Horton (1977)
Gordie Howe (1972)
Syd Howe (1965)
Harry Howell (1979)
Bobby Hull (1983)
Brett Hull (2009)
John (Bouse) Hutton (1962)
Harry M. Hyland (1962)
James (Dick) Irvin (1958)
Angela James (2010)
Harvey (Busher) Jackson (1971)
Ernest (Moose) Johnson (1952)
Ivan (Ching) Johnson (1958)
Tom Johnson (1970)
Aurel Joliat (1947)
Gordon (Duke) Keats (1958)
Leonard (Red) Kelly (1969)
Ted (Teeder) Kennedy (1966)
Dave Keon (1986)
Valeri Kharlamov (2005)
Jari Kurri (2001)
Elmer Lach (1966)
Guy Lafleur (1988)
Pat LaFontaine (2003)
Edouard (Newsy) Lalonde (1950)
Rod Langway (2002)
Jacques Laperriere (1987)
Guy Lapointe (1993)
Edgar Laprade (1993)
Igor Larionov (2008)
Jean (Jack) Laviolette (1962)
Brian Leetch (2009)
Hugh Lehman (1958)
Jacques Lemaire (1984)
Mario Lemieux (1997)
Percy LeSueur (1961)
Herbert A. Lewis (1989)
Ted Lindsay (1966)

Harry Lumley (1980)
Lanny McDonald (1992)
Frank McGee (1945)
Billy McGimsie (1962)
George McNamara (1958)
Al MacInnis (2007)
Duncan (Mickey) MacKay (1952)
Frank Mahovlich (1981)
Joe Malone (1950)
Sylvio Mantha (1960)
Jack Marshall (1965)
Fred G. (Steamer) Maxwell (1962)
Mark Messier (2007)
Stan Mikita (1983)
Dicky Moore (1974)
Patrick (Paddy) Moran (1958)
Howie Morenz (1945)
Billy Mosienko (1965)
Joe Mullen (2000)
Larry Murphy (2004)
Cam Neely (2005)
Frank Nighbor (1947)
Reg Noble (1962)
Herbert (Buddy) O'Connor (1988)
Harry Oliver (1967)
Bert Olmstead (1985)
Bobby Orr (1979)
Bernie Parent (1984)
Brad Park (1988)
Lester Patrick (1947)
Lynn Patrick (1980)
Gilbert Perreault (1990)
Tommy Phillips (1945)
Pierre Pilote (1975)
Didier (Pit) Pitre (1962)
Jacques Plante (1978)
Denis Potvin (1991)
Walter (Babe) Pratt (1966)
Joe Primeau (1963)
Marcel Pronovost (1978)
Bob Pulford (1991)
Harvey Pulford (1945)
Hubert (Bill) Quackenbush (1976)
Frank Rankin (1961)
Jean Ratelle (1985)
Claude (Chuck) Rayner (1973)
Kenneth Reardon (1966)
Henri Richard (1979)
Maurice (Rocket) Richard (1961)
George Richardson (1950)
Gordon Roberts (1971)
Larry Robinson (1995)
Luc Robitaille (2009)
Art Ross (1945)
Patrick Roy (2006)
Blair Russel (1965)
Ernest Russell (1965)
Jack Ruttan (1962)
Borje Salming (1996)
Denis Savard (2000)
Serge Savard (1986)
Terry Sawchuk (1971)

Note: Year of election to the Hall of Fame is in parentheses after the member's name.

Players *(Cont.)*

Fred Scanlan (1965)
Milt Schmidt (1961)
Dave (Sweeney) Schriner (1962)
Earl Seibert (1963)
Oliver Seibert (1961)
Eddie Shore (1947)
Steve Shutt (1993)
Albert C. (Babe) Siebert (1964)
Harold (Bullet Joe) Simpson (1962)
Daryl Sittler (1989)
Alfred E. Smith (1962)
Billy Smith (1993)
Clint Smith (1991)
Reginald (Hooley) Smith (1972)
Thomas Smith (1973)
Allan Stanley (1981)
Russell (Barney) Stanley (1962)
Peter Stastny (1998)
Scott Stevens (2007)
John (Black Jack) Stewart (1964)
Nels Stewart (1962)
Bruce Stuart (1961)

Hod Stuart (1945)
Frederic (Cyclone) Taylor (O.B.E.) (1947)
Cecil R. (Tiny) Thompson (1959)
Vladislav Tretiak (1989)
Harry J. Trihey (1950)
Bryan Trottier (1997)
Norm Ullman (1982)
Georges Vezina (1945)
Jack Walker (1960)
Marty Walsh (1962)
Harry Watson (1994)
Harry E. Watson (1962)
Ralph (Cooney) Weiland (1971)
Harry Westwick (1962)
Fred Whitcroft (1962)
Gordon (Phat) Wilson (1962)
Lorne (Gump) Worsley (1980)
Roy Worters (1969)
Steve Yzerman (2009)

Builders

Charles Adams (1960)
Weston W. Adams (1972)
Thomas (Frank) Ahearn (1962)
John (Bunny) Ahearne (1977)
Montagu Allan (C.V.O.) (1945)
Keith Allen (1992)
Al Arbour (1996)
Harold Ballard (1977)
David Bauer (1989)
John Bickell (1978)
Scott Bowman (1991)
Herb Brooks (2006)
George V. Brown (1961)
Walter A. Brown (1962)
Frank Buckland (1975)
Walter L. Bush (2000)
Jack Butterfield (1980)
Frank Calder (1947)
Angus D. Campbell (1964)
Clarence Campbell (1966)
Joe Cattarinich (1977)
Ed Chynoweth (2008)
Bob Cole (1996, Media)
Murray Costello (2005)
Joseph (Leo) Dandurand (1963)
Jimmy Devellano (2010)
Francis Dilio (1964)
George S. Dudley (1958)
James A. Dunn (1968)
*Robert Alan Eagleson (1989–98)
Cliff Fletcher (2004)
Emile Francis (1982)
Jack Gibson (1976)
Tommy Gorman (1963)
Frank Griffiths (1993)

William Hanley (1986)
Charles Hay (1974)
James C. Hendy (1968)
Foster Hewitt (1965)
William Hewitt (1947)
Harley Hotchkiss (2006)
Fred J. Hume (1962)
Mike Ilitch (2003)
George (Punch) Imlach (1984)
Tommy Ivan (1974)
William M. Jennings (1975)
Bob Johnson (1992)
Gordon W. Juckes (1979)
John Kilpatrick (1960)
Brian Kilrea (2003)
Seymour Knox III (1993)
Lou Lamoriello (2009)
George Leader (1969)
Robert LeBel (1970)
Thomas F. Lockhart (1965)
Paul Loicq (1961)
Frederic McLaughlin (1963)
John Mariucci (1985)
Frank Mathers (1992)
John (Jake) Milford (1984)
Hartland Molson (1973)
Scotty Morrison (1999)
Msgr. Athol (Pere) Murray (1998)
Roger Neilson (2002)
Francis Nelson (1947)
Bruce A. Norris (1969)
James Norris, Sr. (1958)
James D. Norris (1962)
William M. Northey (1947)
John O'Brien (1962)

*Eagleson resigned from Hall March 25, 1998.
Note: Year of election to the Hall of Fame is in parentheses after the member's name.

Builders *(Cont.)*

Brian O'Neill (1994)
Fred Page (1993)
Craig Patrick (1996)
Frank Patrick (1958)
Allan W. Pickard (1958)
Rudy Pilous (1985)
Norman (Bud) Poile (1990)
Samuel Pollock (1978)
Donat Raymond (1958)
John Robertson (1947)
Claude C. Robinson (1947)
Philip D. Ross (1976)
Gunther Sabetzki (1995)
Glen Sather (1997)
Daryl "Doc" Seaman (2010)
Frank J. Selke (1960)

Harry Sinden (1983)
Frank D. Smith (1962)
Conn Smythe (1958)
Edward M. Snider (1988)
Lord Stanley of Preston (1945)
James T. Sutherland (1947)
Anatoli V. Tarasov (1974)
Bill Torrey (1995)
Lloyd Turner (1958)
William Tutt (1978)
Carl Potter Voss (1974)
Fred C. Waghorn (1961)
Arthur Wirtz (1971)
Bill Wirtz (1976)
John A. Ziegler, Jr. (1987)

Referees/Linesmen

Neil Armstrong (1991)
John Ashley (1981)
William L. Chadwick (1964)
John D'Amico (1993)
Chaucer Elliott (1961)
George Hayes (1988)
Robert W. Hewitson (1963)
Fred J. (Mickey) Ion (1961)

Matt Pavelich (1987)
Mike Rodden (1962)
Ray Scapinello (2008)
J. Cooper Smeaton (1961)
Roy (Red) Storey (1967)
Frank Udvari (1973)
Andy Van Hellemond (1999)

Note: Year of election to the Hall of Fame is in parentheses after the member's name.

Though the hockey team fell just short of gold, they still helped the U.S. set an Olympic record for most medals won at a single Winter Games

BOB MARTIN

Home Cookin'

After a balmy, balky, and tragedy-marred beginning, the 2010 Winter Games in Vancouver turned into a dazzling display of North American dominance

BY MERRELL NODEN

ONE WAG DUBBED THEM THE Glitch Games, and in the months leading up to the Vancouver Winter Olympics, that seemed a fair description. Very little was going right: Polls showed that 70% of the local population thought too much money was being spent, and the freakishly mild weather had organizers in fits. On February 12, the day of the Opening Ceremonies, the temperature hit a balmy 50 degrees. Though desperate organizers raced to import snow by truck and helicopter, several practice sessions had to be cancelled and competitions delayed. And though the Opening Ceremonies themselves started right on time, they were tarnished by a glaring technical failure during the flame-lighting portion, one that left Canada's national hero, Wayne Gretzky, awkwardly smiling on live TV for several excruciating minutes as technicians tried to fix the problem to no avail.

But all those worries were put into grim perspective by the terrible accident that occurred just hours before the Opening Ceremonies. During a practice run at the Whistler Sliding Center Nodar Kumaritashvili, a 21-year-old Georgian luger, lost control and was tossed like a rag doll against a steel pole at 90 mph, dying soon afterwards at a nearby hospital. It was the first death at an Olympics since 1992, when a Swiss skier collided with a snow-grooming tractor. What was tragic became scandalous when it emerged that a number of lugers had complained about the dangers posed by the hyper-fast track in general and by that turn in particular. There was talk of cancelling the luge, but after a few minor alterations to the track, the event went ahead, with many questions still unresolved.

The warm weather and the delays it necessitated were actually good news for Lindsey Vonn, the U.S.'s top woman skier. Vonn had suffered a deep tissue bruise on her right shin in a crash on Feb. 2, and welcomed every extra recovery day she could get. It did not help that this downhill course was especially bumpy, aggravating her injury. Still, Vonn beat her teammate Julia Mancuso to become the first American to win gold in the downhill. She added a bronze in the super-G but then seemed to lose focus, crashing out in several other events. On the men's side, Bode Miller began to make up for his perplexing subpar performance four years earlier in Turin by winning gold in the super-combined, silver in the super-G, and bronze in the closest downhill competition in Olympic history. In the downhill, just .09 seconds separated the third-place Miller from the winner, Didier Defago of Switzerland.

The U.S. team had by far its most successful Winter Games, winning a record 37 medals, nine of them gold. Some went to familiar heroes. Short-track speed skater

Apolo Anton Ohno won three medals to push his career total to nine and pass Bonnie Blair as the alltime winningest U.S. Winter Olympian. Snowboard king Shaun White unveiled a new trick called the "double cork" and won his second straight gold in the halfpipe, while Seth Westcott defended his title in snowboard cross. Shani Davis became the first man to repeat as champion in 1500-meter speed skating.

The U.S. team also won medals in unlikely events. The four-man bobsled team piloted by Steve Holcomb won the U.S.'s first gold in that event since 1948, and Billy Demong and Johnny Spillane went 1-2 in the Nordic combined large hill,

In 2010, Andrew Weibrecht, Lindsey Vonn, Bode Miller, and Julia Mancuso (l. to r.) redeemed a U.S. ski team that had suffered several recent Olympic letdowns, winning a combined eight medals at Vancouver, including two golds.

an event in which the U.S. had never previously medaled. The ice dance pair of Meryl Davis and Charlie White took silver, though the shine was taken off that somewhat by the fact that the U.S. women went without a medal in ladies singles for the first time since 1964.

A pleasant surprise came when Evan Lysacek edged Evgeni Plushenko of Russia

Sidney Crosby (w. flag) scored the overtime goal against the U.S. that gave Canada the Olympic hockey gold medal.

heads the organizing committee for the 2014 host city, Sochi, Russia, "Russia's team performance will be addressed to the proper authorities."

Contrast the grim Russians with the jubilant Canadians. The host nation had never won an Olympic gold medal on home soil, not in Montreal in 1976 or in Calgary (1988). The country invested $117 million in a booster program called Own the Podium, and it seemed to pay off. After a slow start in Vancouver, Canada won 14 golds—a record for any country in a Winter Games—including both ice hockey golds. Canada's most moving medal was the bronze won by Joannie Rochette. Just days after her mother had died from a heart attack, Rochette skated with courage and grace to claim the bronze medal behind the peerless South Korean, Kim Yu-Na.

The last of those Canadian gold medals was surely the sweetest. After a last-minute game-tying comeback by the Americans, Sidney Crosby's overtime goal gave the host nation a 4–3 win over the U.S. in the gold medal men's hockey game. In truth, Canadians could probably have won just this one gold and been satisfied. Instead, they can congratulate themselves on overcoming numerous obstacles and serving as gracious hosts.

in the men's skating despite not performing a quadruple jump in his routine. "Now it's not men's figure skating, now it's dancing," griped Plushenko, who was not the only Russian moaning. His country, traditionally a Winter Games powerhouse, won 15 total medals, only three of which were gold. This did not sit well with the folks back home. Vowed Dmitry Chernyshenko, who

FOR THE RECORD

2010 Winter Olympic Games

BIATHLON

Men
10 KILOMETERS SPRINT
1..........Vincent Jay, France	24:07.8
2..........Emil Hegle Svendsen, Norway	24:20.0
3..........Jakov Fak, Croatia	24:21:8

12.5 KILOMETERS PURSUIT
1..........Bjorn Ferry, Sweden	33:38.4
2..........Christoph Sumann, Austria	33:54.9
3..........Vincent Jay, France	34:06.6

15 KILOMETERS MASS START
1..........Evgeny Ustyugov, Russia	35:35.7
2..........Martin Fourcade, France	35:46.2
3..........Pavol Hurajt, Slovakia	35:52.3

20 KILOMETERS INDIVIDUAL
1..........Emil Hegle Svendsen, Norway	48:22.3
2..........Ole Einar Bjoerndalen, Norway	48:32.0
2..........Sergey Novikov, Belarus	48:32.0

4 X 7.5-KILOMETER RELAY
1..........Norway	1:21:38.1
2..........Austria	1:22:16.7
3..........Russia	1:22:16.9

Women
7.5 KILOMETERS SPRINT
1..........Anastazia Kuzmina, Slovakia	19:55.6
2..........Magdalena Neuner, Germany	19:57.1
3..........Marie Dorin, France	20:06.5

10 KILOMETERS PURSUIT
1..........Magdalena Neuner, Germany	30:16.0
2..........Anastazia Kuzmina, Slovakia	30:28.3
3..........Marie Laure Brunet, France	30:44.3

12.5 KILOMETERS MASS START
1..........Magdalena Neuner, Germany	35:19.6
2..........Olga Zaitseva, Russia	35:25.1
3..........Simone Hauswald, Germany	35:26.9

15 KILOMETERS INDIVIDUAL
1..........Tora Berger, Norway	40:52.8
2..........Elena Khrustaleva, Kazakhstan	41:13.5
3..........Darya Domracheva, Belarus	41:21.0

4 X 6-KILOMETER RELAY
1..........Russia	1:09:36.3
2..........France	1:10:09.1
3..........Germany	1:10:13.4

BOBSLED

Men
TWO
1......A. Lange/ K. Kuske, Germany I	3:26.65
2......T. Florschuetz, R. Adjei, Germany II	3:26.87
3......A. Zubkov/ A. Voevoda, Russia I	3:27.51

FOUR
1......USA I	3:24.46
2......Germany I	3:24.84
3......Canada I	3:24.85

Women
TWO
1......K. Humphries/H. Moyse, Canada I	3:32.28
2......H. Upperton/S. Brown, Canada II	3:33.13
3......E. Pac/E. Meyers, USA II	3:33.40

CURLING

Men
1..........Canada
2..........Norway
3..........Switzerland

Women
1..........Sweden
2..........Canada
3..........China

FIGURE SKATING

Men
	Pts
1......Evan Lysacek, United States	257.67
2......Evgeni Plushenko, Russia	256.36
3......Daisuke Takahashi, Japan	247.23

Women
	Pts
1......Kim Yu-Na, South Korea	228.56
2......Mao Asada, Japan	205.50
3......Joannie Rochette, Canada	202.64

Pairs
	Pts
1......Xue Shen/Hongbo Zhao, China	216.57
2......Qing Pang/Jian Tong, China	213.31
3......Aliona Savchenko/Robin Szolkowy, Germany	210.60

Ice Dancing
	Pts
1......Tessa Virtue/Scott Moir, Canada	221.57
2......Meryl Davis/Charlie White, United States	215.74
3......Oksana Domnina/Maxim Shabalin, Russia	207.64

ICE HOCKEY

Men
1..........Canada
2..........United States
3..........Finland

Women
1..........Canada
2..........United States
3..........Finland

LUGE

Men
SINGLES
1....Felix Loch, Germany	3:13.085
2....David Moeller, Germany	3:13.764
3....Armin Zoeggeler, Italy	3:14.375

DOUBLES
1....Andreas Linger/Wolfgang Linger, Austria	1:22.705
2....Andre Sics/Juris Sics, Latvia	1:22.969
3....Patric Leitner/Alexander Resch, Germany	1:23.040

Women
SINGLES
1....Tatjana Huefner, Germany	2:46.524
2....Nina Reithmayer, Austria	2:47.014
3....Natalie Geisenberger, Germany	2:47.101

SKELETON

Men
1.	Jon Montgomery, Canada	3:29.73
2.	Martins Dukurs, Latvia	3:29.80
3.	Alexander Tretyakov, Russia	3:30.75

Women
1.	Amy Williams, United Kingdom	3:35.64
2.	Kerstin Szymkowiak, Germany	3:36.20
3.	Anja Huber, Germany	3:36.36

SPEED SKATING

Men

500 METERS*
1....Tae-Bum Mo, South Korea	1:09.82
2....Keiichiro Nagashima, Japan	1:09.98
3....Joji Kato, Japan	1:10.01

1,000 METERS
1....Shani Davis, United States	1:08.94
2....Tae-Bum Mo, South Korea	1:09.12
3....Chad Hedrick, United States	1:09.32

1,500 METERS
1....Mark Tuitert, Netherlands	1:45.57
2....Shani Davis, United States	1:46.10
3....Havard Bokko, Norway	1:46.13

5,000 METERS
1....Sven Kramer, Netherlands	6:14.60 OR
2....Lee Seung-Hoon, South Korea	6:16.95
3....Ivan Skobrev, Russia	6:18.05

10,000 METERS
1....Seung-Hoon Lee, South Korea	12:58.55 OR
2....Ivan Skobrev, Russia	13:02.07
3....Bob de Jong, Netherlands	13:06.73

TEAM PURSUIT
1....Canada	3:41.37
2....United States	3:41.58
3....Netherlands	3:39.95 OR

500 METERS SHORT TRACK
1....Charles Hamelin, Canada	40.770
2....Si-Bak Sung, South Korea	40.821
3....Francois-Louis Tremblay, Canada	41.326

1,000 METERS SHORT TRACK
1....Jung-Su Lee, South Korea	1:23.747 OR
2....Ho-Suk Lee, South Korea	1:23.801
3....Apolo Anton Ohno, United States	1:24.128

1,500 METERS SHORT TRACK
1....Jung-Su Lee, South Korea	2:10.949
2....Apolo Anton Ohno, United States	2:11.072
3....J.R. Celski, United States	2:12.460

5,000-METER SHORT TRACK RELAY
1....Canada	6:43.610
2....South Korea	6:43.845
3....United States	6:44.498

Women

500 METERS*
1....Sang-Hwa Lee, South Korea	1:16.09
2....Jenny Wolf, Germany	1:16.14
3....Beixing Wang, China	1:16.63

1,000 METERS
1....Christine Nesbitt, Canada	1:16.56
2....Annette Gerritsen, Netherlands	1:16.58
3....Laurine van Riessen, Netherlands	1:16.72

1,500 METERS
1....Ireen Wust, Netherlands	1:56.89
2....Kristina Groves, Canada	1:57.14
3....Martina Sablikova, Czech Republic	1:57.96

3,000 METERS
1....Martina Sablikova, Czech Republic	4:02.53
2...:Stephanie Beckert, Germany	4:04.62
3....Kristina Groves, Canada	4:04.84

5,000 METERS
1....Martina Sablikova, Czech Republic	6:50.91
2....Stephanie Beckert, Germany	6:51.39
3...Clara Hughes, Canada	6:55.73

TEAM PURSUIT
1....Germany	3:02.82
2....Japan	3:02.84
3....Poland	3:03.73

500 METERS SHORT TRACK
1....Meng Wang, China	42.985
2....Marianne St-Gelais, Canada	43.241
3....Arianna Fontana, Italy	43.804

1,000 METERS SHORT TRACK
1....Meng Wang, China	1:29.213
2....Katherine Reutter, United States	1:29.324
3....Seung-Hi Park, South Korea	1:29.379

1,500 METERS SHORT TRACK
1....Yang Zhou, China	2:16.993
2....Eun-Byul Lee, South Korea	2:17.849
3....Seung-Hi Park, South Korea	2:17.927

3,000-METER SHORT TRACK RELAY
1....China	4:06.610 WR
2....Canada	4:09.137
3....United States	4:14.081

*Combined time.
Note: OR=Olympic Record; WR=World Record; EOR=Equals Olympic Record; EWR=Equals World Record; WB=World Best.

FREESTYLE SKIING

Men

MOGULS

	Pts
1. ...Alexandre Bilodeau, Canada	26.75
2. ...Dale Begg-Smith, Australia	26.58
3. ...Byron Wilson, United States	26.08

AERIALS

	Pts
1. ...Alexei Grishin, Belarus	248.41
2. ...Jeret Peterson, United States	247.21
3. ...Zhongqing Liu, China	242.53

Women

MOGULS

	Pts
1. ...Hannah Kearney, United States	26.63
2. ...Jennifer Heil, Canada	25.69
3. ...Shannon Bahrke, United States	25.43

AERIALS

	Pts
1. ...Lydia Lassila, Australia	214.74
2. ...Nina Li, China	207.23
3. ...Xinxin Guo, China	205.22

ALPINE SKIING

Men

DOWNHILL

1. ...Didier Defago, Switzerland	1:54.31
2. ...Aksel Lund Svindal, Norway	1:54.38
3. ...Bode Miller, United States	1:54.40

SLALOM

1. ...Giuliano Razzoli, Italy	1:39.32
2. ...Ivica Kostelic, Croatia	1:39.48
3. ...Andre Myhrer, Sweden	1:39.76

GIANT SLALOM

1. ...Carlo Janka, Switzerland	2:37.83
2. ...Kjetil Jansrud, Norway	2:38.22
3. ...Aksel Lund Svindal, Norway	2:38.44

SUPER GIANT SLALOM

1. ...Aksel Lund Svindal, Norway	1:30.34
2. ...Bode Miller, United States	1:30.62
3. ...Andrew Weibrecht, United States	1:30.65

SUPER COMBINED

1. ...Bode Miller, United States	2:44.92
2. ...Ivica Kostelic, Croatia	2:44.25
3. ...Silvan Zurbriggen, Switzerland	2:45.32

Women

DOWNHILL

1. ...Lindsey Vonn, United States	1:44.19
2. ...Julia Mancuso, United States	1:44.75
3. ...Elisabeth Goergl, Austria	1:45.65

SLALOM

1. ...Maria Riesch, Germany	1:42.89
2. ...Marlies Schild, Austria	1:43.32
3. ...Sarka Zahrobska, Czech Republic	1:43.90

GIANT SLALOM

1. ...Viktoria Rebensburg, Germany	2:27.11
2. ...Tina Maze, Slovenia	2:27.15
3. ...Elisabeth Goergl, Austria	2:27.25

SUPER GIANT SLALOM

1. ...Andrea Fischbacher, Austria	1:20.14
2. ...Tina Maze, Slovenia	1:20.63
3. ...Lindsey Vonn, United States	1:20.88

SUPER COMBINED

1. ...Maria Riesch, Germany	2:09.14
2. ...Julia Mancuso, United States	2:10.08
3. ...Anja Paerson, Sweden	2:10.19

NORDIC SKIING

Men

INDIVIDUAL SPRINT CLASSIC

1. ...Nikita Kriukov, Russia	3:36.3
2. ...Alexander Panzhinsky, Russia	3:36.3
3. ...Petter Northug, Norway	3:45.5

TEAM SPRINT

1. ...Norway	19:01.0
2. ...Germany	19:02.3
2. ...Russia	19:02.5

15 KILOMETERS FREESTYLE

1. ...Dario Cologna, Switzerland	33:36.3
2. ...Pietro Piller Cottrer, Italy	34:00.9
3. ...Lukas Bauer, Czech Republic	34:12.0

30 KILOMETERS PURSUIT (15K FREE + 15K CLASSIC)

1. ...Marcus Hellner, Sweden	1:15:11.4
2. ...Tobias Angerer, Germany	1:15:13.5
3. ...Johan Olsson, Sweden	1:15:14.2

50 KILOMETERS CLASSIC MASS START

1. ...Petter Northug, Norway	2:05:35.5
2. ...Axel Teichmann, Germany	2:05:35.8
3. ...Johan Olsson, Sweden	2:05:36.5

4 X 10-KILOMETER RELAY MIXED

1. ...Sweden	1:45:05.4
2. ...Norway	1:45:21.3
3. ...Czech Republic	1:45:21.9

NORMAL (90-M) HILL SKI JUMPING

	Pts
1. ...Simon Ammann, Switzerland	276.5
2. ...Adam Malysz, Poland	269.5
3. ...Gregor Schlierenzauer, Austria	268.0

LARGE (120-M) HILL SKI JUMPING

	Pts
1. ...Simon Ammann, Switzerland	283.6
2. ...Adam Malysz, Poland	269.4
3. ...Gregor Schlierenzauer, Austria	262.2

LARGE (120-M) HILL TEAM SKI JUMPING

	Pts
1. ...Austria	1107.9
2. ...Germany	1035.8
3. ...Norway	1030.3

90-METER JUMP/10 KM CC NORDIC COMBINED

1. ...Jason Chappuis Lamy, France	25:47.1
2. ...Johnny Spillane, United States	25:47.5
3. ...Alessandro Pittin, Italy	25:47.9

120-METER JUMP/10 KM CC NORDIC COMBINED

1. ...Bill Demong, United States	25:32.9
2. ...Johnny Spillane, United States	25:36.9
3. ...Bernhard Gruber, Austria	25:41.7

4 X 5-KILOMETER TEAM RELAY

1. ...Austria	49:31.6
2. ...United States	49:36.8
3. ...Germany	49:51.1

NORDIC SKIING *(Cont.)*
Women

INDIVIDUAL SPRINT CLASSIC
1. ...Marit Bjoergen, Norway   3:39.2
2. ...Justyna Kowalczyk, Poland   3:40.3
3. ...Petra Majdic, Slovenia   3:41.0

TEAM SPRINT
1. ...Germany   18:03.7
2. ...Sweden   18:04.3
3. ...Russia   18:07.7

10 KILOMETERS FREESTYLE
1. ...Charlotte Kalla, Sweden   24:58.4
2. ...Kristina Smigun-Vaehi, Estonia   25:05.0
3. ...Marit Bjoergen, Norway   25:14.3

15 KILOMETERS PURSUIT (7.5K FREE + 7.5K CLASSIC)
1. ...Marit Bjoergen, Norway   39:58.1
2. ...Anna Haag, Sweden   40:07.0
3. ...Justyna Kowalczyk, Poland   40:07.4

30 KILOMETERS CLASSIC MASS START
1. ...Justyna Kowalczyk, Poland   1:30:33.7
2. ...Marit Bjoergen, Norway   1:30:34.0
3. ...Aino-Kaisa Saarinen, Finland   1:31:38.7

4 X 5-KILOMETER RELAY MIXED
1. ...Norway   55:19.5
2. ...Germany   55:44.1
3. ...Finland   55:49.9

SKI CROSS

Men
1. ...Michael Schmid, Switzerland
2. ...Andreas Matt, Austria
3. ...Audun Groenvold, Norway

Women
1. ...Ashleigh McIvor, Canada
2. ...Hedda Berntsen, Norway
3. ...Marion Josserand, France

SNOWBOARDING

Men

PARALLEL GIANT SLALOM
1. ...Jasey Jay Anderson, Canada
2. ...Benjamin Karl, Austria
3. ...Mathieu Bozzetto, France

HALF-PIPE   Pts
1. ...Shaun White, United States   48.4
2. ...Peetu Piiroinen, Finland   45.0
3. ...Scott Lago, United States   42.8

SNOWBOARD CROSS
1. ...Seth Wescott, United States
2. ...Mike Robertson, Canada
3. ...Tony Ramoin, France

Women

PARALLEL GIANT SLALOM
1. ...Nicolien Sauerbreij, Netherlands
2. ...Ekaterina Ilyukhina, Russia
3. ...Marion Kreiner, Austria

HALF-PIPE   Pts
1. ...Torah Bright, Australia   45.0
2. ...Hannah Teter, United States   42.4
3. ...Kelly Clark, United States   42.2

SNOWBOARD CROSS
1. ...Maelle Ricker, Canada
2. ...Deborah Anthonioz, France
3. ...Olivia Nobs, Switzerland

FOR THE RECORD • Year by Year

Summer

	Year	Site	Dates	COMPETITORS			Most Medals	US Medals
				Men	Women	Nations		
I	1896	Athens, Greece	Apr 6–15	311	0	13	Greece (10-19-18—47)	11-6-2—19 (2nd)
II	1900	Paris, France	May 20–Oct 28	1319	11	22	France (29-41-32—102)	20-14-19—53 (2nd)
III	1904	St Louis, United States	July 1–Nov 23	681	6	12	United States (80-86-72—238)	—
—	1906	Athens, Greece	Apr 22–May 28	77	7	20	France (15-9-16—40)	12-6-5—23 (4th)
IV	1908	London, Great Britain	Apr 27–Oct 31	1999	36	23	Britain (56-50-39—145)	23-12-12—47 (2nd)
V	1912	Stockholm, Sweden	May 5–July 22	2490	57	28	Sweden (24-24-17—65)	23-19-19—61 (2nd)
VI	1916	Berlin, Germany	Canceled because of war					
VII	1920	Antwerp, Belgium	Apr 20–Sep 12	2543	64	29	United States (41-27-28—96)	—
VIII	1924	Paris, France	May 4–July 27	2956	136	44	United States (45-27-27—99)	—
IX	1928	Amsterdam, Netherlands	May 17–Aug 12	2724	290	46	United States (22-18-16—56)	—
X	1932	Los Angeles, United States	July 30–Aug 14	1281	127	37	United States (41-32-31—104)	—
XI	1936	Berlin, Germany	Aug 1–16	3738	328	49	Germany (33-26-30—89)	24-20-12—56 (2nd)
XII	1940	Tokyo, Japan	Canceled because of war					
XIII	1944	London, Great Britain	Canceled because of war					
XIV	1948	London, Great Britain	July 29–Aug 14	3714	385	59	United States (38-27-19—84)	—
XV	1952	Helsinki, Finland	July 19–Aug 3	4407	518	69	United States (40-19-17—76)	—
XVI	1956	Melbourne, Australia*	Nov 22–Dec 8	2958	384	67	USSR (37-29-32—98)	32-25-17—74 (2nd)
XVII	1960	Rome, Italy	Aug 25–Sep 11	4738	610	83	USSR (43-29-31—103)	34-21-16—71 (2nd)
XVIII	1964	Tokyo, Japan	Oct 10–24	4457	683	93	United States (36-26-28—90)	—
XIX	1968	Mexico City, Mexico	Oct 12–27	4750	781	112	United States (45-28-34—107)	—
XX	1972	Munich, West Germany	Aug 26–Sep 10	5848	1299	122	USSR (50-27-22—99)	33-31-30—94 (2nd)
XXI	1976	Montreal, Canada	July 17–Aug 1	4834	1251	92†	USSR (49-41-35—125)	34-35-25—94 (3rd)
XXII	1980	Moscow, USSR	July 19–Aug 3	4265	1088	81‡	USSR (80-69-46—195)	Did not compete
XXIII	1984	Los Angeles, United States	July 28–Aug 12	5458	1620	141#	United States (83-61-30—174)	—
XXIV	1988	Seoul, South Korea	Sep 17–Oct 2	7105	2476	160	USSR (55-31-46—132)	36-31-27—94 (3rd)
XXV	1992	Barcelona, Spain	July 25–Aug. 9	7555	3008	172	Unified Team (45-38-29—112)	37-34-37—108 (2nd)

Summer *(Cont.)*

	Year	Site	Dates	COMPETITORS Men	Women	Nations	Most Medals	US Medals
XXVI	1996	Atlanta, United States	July 19–Aug 4	6984	3766	197	United States (44-32-25—101)	
XXVII	2000	Sydney, Australia	Sept 15–Oct 1	6862	4254	199	United States (39-25-33—97)	
XXVIII	2004	Athens, Greece	Aug 11–Aug 29	11099 total		202	United States (35-39-29—103)	
XXIX	2008	Beijing, China	Aug 8–Aug 24	11028 total		204	United States (36-38-36—110)	—

*The equestrian events were held in Stockholm, Sweden, June 10–17, 1956.
†This figure includes Cameroon, Egypt, Morocco, and Tunisia, countries that boycotted the 1976 Olympics after some of their athletes had already competed.
‡The U.S. was among 65 countries that did not participate in the 1980 Summer Games in Moscow.
#The USSR, East Germany, and 14 other countries did not participate in the 1984 Summer Games in Los Angeles.

Winter

	Year	Site	Dates	Competitors Men	Women	Nations	Most Medals	US Medals
I	1924	Chamonix, France	Jan 25–Feb 4	281	13	16	Norway (4-7-6—17)	1-2-1—4 (3rd)
II	1928	St. Moritz, Switzerland	Feb 11–19	366	27	25	Norway (6-4-5—15)	2-2-2—6 (2nd)
III	1932	Lake Placid, United States	Feb 4–13	277	30	17	United States (6-4-2—12)	
IV	1936	Garmisch-Partenkirchen, Germany	Feb 6–16	680	76	28	Norway (7-5-3—15)	1-0-3—4 (T-5th)
—	1940	Garmisch-Partenkirchen, Germany	Canceled because of war					
—	1944	Cortina d'Ampezzo, Italy	Canceled because of war					
V	1948	St. Moritz, Switzerland	Jan 30–Feb 8	636	77	28	Norway (4-3-3—10) Sweden (4-3-3—10) Switzerland (3-4-3—10)	3-4-2—9 (4th)
VI	1952	Oslo, Norway	Feb 14–25	624	108	30	Norway (7-3-6—16)	4-6-1—11 (2nd)
VII	1956	Cortina d'Ampezzo, Italy	Jan 26–Feb 5	687	132	32	USSR (7-3-6—16)	2-3-2—7 (T-4th)
VIII	1960	Squaw Valley, United States	Feb 18–28	502	146	30	USSR (7-5-9—21)	3-4-3—10 (2nd)
IX	1964	Innsbruck, Austria	Jan 29–Feb 9	758	175	36	USSR (11-8-6—25)	1-2-3—6 (7th)
X	1968	Grenoble, France	Feb 6–18	1063	230	37	Norway (6-6-2—14)	1-5-1—7 (T-7th)
XI	1972	Sapporo, Japan	Feb 3–13	927	218	35	USSR (8-5-3—16)	3-2-3—8 (6th)
XII	1976	Innsbruck, Austria	Feb 4–15	1013	248	37	USSR (13-6-8—27)	3-3-4—10 (T-3rd)
XIII	1980	Lake Placid, United States	Feb 13–24	1012	271	37	East Germany (9-7-7—23)	6-4-2—12 (3rd)
XIV	1984	Sarajevo, Yugoslavia	Feb 8–19	1127	283	49	USSR (6-10-9—25)	4-4-0—8 (T-5th)
XV	1988	Calgary, Canada	Feb 13–28	1270	364	57	USSR (11-9-9—29)	2-1-3—6 (T-8th)
XVI	1992	Albertville, France	Feb 8–23	1313	488	65	Germany (10-10-6—26)	5-4-2—11 (6th)

Winter *(Cont.)*

	Year	Site	Dates	Competitors			Most Medals	US Medals
				Men	Women	Nations		
XVII	1994	Lillehammer, Norway	Feb 12–27	1302	542	67	Norway (10-11-5—26)	6-5-2—13 (T-5th)
XVIII	1998	Nagano, Japan Sweden	Feb 7–22	2302 total		72	Germany (12-9-8—29)	6-3-4—13 (6th)
XIX	2002	Salt Lake City, United States	Feb 8–24	1513	886	77	Germany (12-16-7—35)	10-13-11—34 (2nd)
XX	2006	Turin, Italy	Feb 10–26	1627	1006	80	Germany (11-12-6—29)	9-9-7—25 (2nd)
XX	2010	Vancouver, Canada	Feb 12–28	2622 total		92	United States (9-15-13—37)	—

Alltime Olympic Medal Winners

Summer

NATIONS

Nation	Gold	Silver	Bronze	Total
United States	934	730	643	2307
USSR (1952–88)	395	319	296	1010
Great Britain	209	259	258	725
Germany	196	222	241	659
(1896–1936, 1992–)				
France	191	208	241	640
Italy	190	158	173	523
Sweden	142	160	173	475
Hungary	159	141	160	460
Australia	134	141	169	444
East Germany (1956–88)	153	129	127	409
China	163	117	106	386
Japan	123	112	125	360
Russia	109	101	112	322
Finland	103	80	113	296
Romania	86	89	117	292
Poland	62	80	119	261
Canada	57	95	106	258
The Netherlands	72	80	96	248
South Korea	68	74	73	215
Bulgaria	51	84	77	212
West Germany (1952–88)	56	67	81	204
Cuba	67	62	60	189
Switzerland	45	69	65	179

INDIVIDUALS — OVERALL

Men

Athlete, Nation	Sport	G	S	B	Tot
Michael Phelps, United States	Swim	14	0	2	16
Nikolai Andrianov, USSR	Gym	7	5	3	15
Boris Shakhlin, USSR	Gym	7	4	2	13
Edoardo Mangiarotti, Italy	Fenc	6	5	2	13
Takashi Ono, Japan	Gym	5	4	4	13
Paavo Nurmi, Finland	Track	9	3	0	12
Sawao Kato, Japan	Gym	8	3	1	12
Alexei Nemov, Russia	Gym	4	2	6	12
Mark Spitz, United States	Swim	9	1	1	11
Matt Biondi, United States	Swim	8	2	1	11
Viktor Chukarin, USSR	Gym	7	3	1	11
Carl Osburn, United States	Shoot	5	4	2	11
Ray Ewry, United States	Track	10	0	0	10
Carl Lewis, United States	Track	9	1	0	10
Aladár Gerevich, Hungary	Fen	7	1	2	10
Akinori Nakayama, Japan	Gym	6	2	2	10
Vitaly Scherbo, UT/Belarus	Gym	6	0	4	10
Aleksandr Dityatin, USSR	Gym	3	6	1	10

Women

Athlete, Nation	Sport	G	S	B	Tot
Larissa Latynina, USSR	Gym	9	5	4	18
Jenny Thompson, United States	Swim	8	3	1	12
Vera Cáslavská, Czech	Gym	7	4	0	11
Agnes Keleti, Hungary	Gym	5	3	2	10
Polina Astaknova, USSR	Gym	5	2	3	10
Dara Torres, United States	Swim	4	1	4	9
Nadia Comaneci, Romania	Gym	5	3	1	9
Lyudmila Touricheva, USSR	Gym	4	3	2	8
Kornelia Ender, E Germany	Swim	4	4	0	8
Dawn Fraser, Australia	Swim	4	4	0	8
Shirley Babashoff, United States	Swim	2	6	0	8
Sofia Muratova, USSR	Gym	2	2	4	8
Inge de Bruijn, Netherlands	Swim	4	2	2	8
Eight tied with seven.					

Summer *(Cont.)*

INDIVIDUALS — GOLD

Men

Micheal Phelps, United States ...14
Ray Ewry, United States 10
Paavo Nurmi, Finland 9
Carl Lewis, United States 9

Mark Spitz, United States 9
Sawao Kato, Japan 8
Matt Biondi, United States 8
Nikolai Andrianov, USSR 7

Boris Shakhlin, USSR 7
Viktor Chukarin, USSR...............7
Aladár Gerevich, Hungary 7

Women

Larissa Latynina, USSR.............9
Jenny Thompson, United States ..8
Vera Cáslavská, Czech 7
Kristin Otto, E Germany 6
Agnes Keleti, Hungary................5
Nadia Comaneci, Romania 5
Polina Astaknova, USSR 5

Krisztina Egerszegi, Hungary 5
Kornelia Ender, E Germany 4
Dawn Fraser, Australia...............4
Lyudmila Tourischeva, USSR.....4
Evelyn Ashford, United States ...4
Janet Evans, United States 4
Fanny Blankers-Koen, Neth 4

Betty Cuthbert, Australia...........4
Pat McCormick, United States ..4
Bärbel Eckert Wöckel, E Ger.....4
Amy Van Dyken, United States ...4
Inge de Bruijn, Netherlands.......4
Yana Klochkova, Ukraine...........4
Dara Torres, United States........4

Winter

NATIONS

Nation	Gold	Silver	Bronze	Total	Nation	Gold	Silver	Bronze	Total
Norway	107	106	90	303	Italy	37	32	37	106
United States	87	95	71	253	France	27	27	38	92
Germany	78	78	53	209	Russia	36	29	26	91
Austria	55	70	76	201	Netherlands	29	31	26	86
USSR (1956–88)	78	57	59	194	South Korea	23	14	8	45
Finland	42	58	56	156	China	9	18	17	44
Canada	52	45	48	145	West Germany (1956–88)	11	15	13	39
Sweden	48	32	48	128	Japan	9	13	15	37
Switzerland	43	37	46	126	Czechoslovakia (1924–92)	2	8	15	25
East Germany (1956–88)	39	36	35	110	United Kingdom	8	3	10	21

INDIVIDUALS — OVERALL

Men

Athlete, Nation	Sport	G	S	B	Tot
Bjørn Dæhlie, Norway	N Ski	8	4	0	12
Sixten Jernberg, Sweden	N Ski	4	3	2	9
Apolo Anton Ohno, U.S.	Shrt Trk	2	2	4	8

Seven tied with 7.

Women

Athlete, Nation	Sport	G	S	B	Tot
Raisa Smetanina, USSR/UT	N Ski	4	5	1	10
Lyubov Egorova, UT/Russia	N Ski	6	3	0	9
Larissa Lazutina, UT/Russia	N Ski	5	3	1	9
Stefania Belmondo, Italy	N Ski	2	3	4	9

Four tied with 8.

INDIVIDUALS — GOLD

Men

Bjørn Dæhlie, Norway :............................8
A. Clas Thunberg, Finland 5
O. Bjoerndalen, Norway............................5
Eric Heiden, United States.......................5

Nine tied with 4.

Women

Lyubov Egorova, UT/Russia.....................6
Lydia Skoblikova, USSR...........................6
Larissa Lazutina, UT/Russia 5
Bonnie Blair, United States 5

Four tied with 4.

BIATHLON
Men

10 KILOMETERS SPRINT

1980	Frank Ullrich, East Germany	32:10.69
1984	Eirik Kvalfoss, Norway	30:53.8
1988	Frank-Peter Rötsch, West Germany	25:08.1
1992	Mark Kirchner, Germany	26:02.3
1994	Sergei Tchepikov, Russia	28:07.0
1998	Ole Einar Bjorndalen, Norway	27:16.2
2002	Ole Einar Bjorndalen, Norway	24:51.3
2006	Sven Fischer, Germany	24:11.6
2010	Vincent Jay, France	24:07.8

12.5 KILOMETERS PURSUIT

2002	Ole Einar Bjorndalen, Norway	24:51.3
2006	Vincent Defrasne, France	35:20.2
2010	Bjorn Ferry, Sweden	33:38.4

15 KILOMETERS MASS START

2006	Michael Greis, Germany	47:20.0
2010	Evgeny Ustyugov, Russia	35:35.7

20 KILOMETERS INDIVIDUAL

1960	Klas Lestander, Sweden	1:33:21.6
1964	Vladimir Melyanin, USSR	1:20:26.8
1968	Magnar Solberg, Norway	1:13:45.9
1972	Magnar Solberg, Norway	1:15:55.5
1976	Nikolay Kruglov, USSR	1:14:12.26

20 KILOMETERS INDIVIDUAL (CONT.)

1980	Anatoliy Alyabiev, USSR	1:08:16.31
1984	Peter Angerer, West Germany	1:11:52.7
1988	Frank-Peter Rötsch, W. Germany	56:33.3
1992	Evgueni Redkine, Unified Team	57:34.4
1994	Sergei Tarasov, Russia	57:25.3
1998	Halvard Hanevold, Norway	56:16.4
2002	Ole Einar Bjordalen, Norway	51:03.3
2006	Michael Greis, Germany	54:23.0
2010	Emil Hegle Svendsen, Norway	48:22.3

4 X 7.5-KILOMETER RELAY

1968	USSR	2:13:02.4
1972	USSR	1:51:44.92
1976	USSR	1:57:55.64
1980	USSR	1:34:03.27
1984	USSR	1:38:51.7
1988	USSR	1:22:30.0
1992	Germany	1:24:43.5
1994	Germany	1:30:22.1
1998	Germany	1:19:43.3
2002	Norway	1:23:42.3
2006	Germany	1:21:51.5
2010	Norway	1:21:38.1

Women

7.5 KILOMETERS SPRINT

1992	Antissa Restzova, Unified Team	24:29.2
1994	Myriam Bedard, Canada	26:08.8
1998	Galina Koukleva, Russia	23:08.0
2002	Kati Wilhemn, Germany	20:41.4
2006	Florence Baverel-Robert, France	22:31.4
2010	Anastazia Kuzmina, Slovakia	19:55.6

10 KILOMETERS PURSUIT

2002	Olga Pyleva, Russia	31:07.7
2006	Kati Wilhemn, Germany	36:43.6
2010	Magdalena Neuner, Germany	30:16.0

12.5 KILOMETERS MASS START

2006	Anna Carin Olofsson, Sweden	40:36.5
2010	Magdalena Neuner, Germany	35:19.6

15 KILOMETERS INDIVIDUAL

1992	Antje Misersky, Germany	51:47.2
1994	Myriam Bedard, Canada	52:06.6
1998	Ekaterina Dofovska, Bulgaria	54:52.0
2002	Andrea Henkel, Germany	47:29.1
2006	Svetlana Ishmouratova, Russia	49:24.1
2010	Tora Berger, Norway	40:52.8

3 X 7.5-KILOMETER RELAY

1992	France	1:15:55.6
1994	Russia	1:47:19.5
1998	Germany	1:40:13.6
2002	Germany	1:27:55.0

4 X 6-KILOMETER RELAY

2006	Russia	1:16:12.5
2010	Russia	1:09:36.3

BOBSLED
Men

FOURS

1924	Switzerland (Eduard Scherrer)	5:45.54
1928	United States (William Fiske) (5-man)	3:20.50
1932	United States (William Fiske)	7:53.68
1936	Switzerland (Pierre Musy)	5:19.85
1948	United States (Francis Tyler)	5:20.10
1952	Germany (Andreas Ostler)	5:07.84
1956	Switzerland (Franz Kapus)	5:10.44
1960	Not held	
1964	Canada (Victor Emery)	4:14.46
1968	Italy (Eugenio Monti) (2 runs)	2:17.39
1972	Switzerland (Jean Wicki)	4:43.07

FOURS (CONT.)

1976	E Germany (Meinhard Nehmer)	3:40.43
1980	E Germany (Meinhard Nehmer)	3:59.92
1984	E Germany (Wolfgang Hoppe)	3:20.22
1988	Switzerland (Ekkehard Fasser)	3:47.51
1992	Austria (Ingo Appelt)	3:53.90
1994	Germany (Harald Czudaj)	3:27.78
1998	Germany (Christoph Langen)	2:39.41
2002	Germany (Andre Lange)	3:10.11
2006	Germany (Andre Lange)	3:40.42
2010	United States (Steven Holcomb)	3:24.46

Note: Driver in parentheses.

BOBSLED *(Cont.)*

Men *(Cont.)*

DOUBLES

1932	United States (Hubert Stevens)	8:14.74
1936	United States (Ivan Brown)	5:29.29
1948	Switzerland (Felix Endrich)	5:29.20
1952	Germany (Andreas Ostler)	5:24.54
1956	Italy (Lamberto Dalla Costa)	5:30.14
1960	Not held	
1964	Great Britain (Anthony Nash)	4:21.90
1968	Italy (Eugenio Monti)	4:41.54
1972	West Germany (Wolfgang Zimmerer)	4:57.07

DOUBLES *(CONT.)*

1976	East Germany (Meinhard Nehmer)	3:44.42
1980	Switzerland (Erich Schärer)	4:09.36
1984	East Germany (Wolfgang Hoppe)	3:25.56
1988	USSR (Janis Kipours)	3:53.48
1992	Switzerland (Gustav Weder)	4:03.26
1994	Switzerland (Gustav Weder)	3:30.81
1998	Canada (Pierre Lueders)	3:37.24
	Italy (Guenther Huber)	3:37.24
2002	Germany (Martin Langen)	3:10:11
2006	Germany (Andre Lange)	3:43.38
2010	Germany (Andre Lange)	3:26.65

Note: Driver in parentheses.

Women

DOUBLES

2002	United States (Jill Bakken)	1:37:76
2006	Germany (Sandra Kiriasis)	3:49.98
2010	Canada (Kaillie Humphries)	3:32.28

Note: Driver in parentheses.

CURLING

Men	Women
1998 .....Switzerland, Canada, Norway	1998 .....Canada, Denmark, Sweden
2002 .....Norway, Canada, Switzerland	2002 .....Britain, Switzerland, Canada
2006 .....Canada, Finland, United States	2006 .....Sweden, Switzerland, Canada
2010 .....Canada, Norway, Switzerland	2010 .....Sweden, Canada, China
Note: In order: gold, silver, and bronze medals.	Note: In order: gold, silver, and bronze medals.

ICE HOCKEY

Men

1920* ....Canada, United States, Czechoslovakia	1976 .....USSR, Czechoslovakia, West Germany
1924 .....Canada, United States, Great Britain	1980 .....United States, USSR, Sweden
1928 .....Canada, Sweden, Switzerland	1984 .....USSR, Czechoslovakia, Sweden
1932 .....Canada, United States, Germany	1988 .....USSR, Finland, Sweden
1936 .....Great Britain, Canada, United States	1992 .....Unified Team, Canada, Czechoslovakia
1948 .....Canada, Czechoslovakia, Switzerland	1994 .....Sweden, Canada, Finland
1952 .....Canada, United States, Sweden	1998 .....Czech Republic, Russia, Finland
1956 .....USSR, United States, Canada	2002 .....Canada, United States, Russia
1960 .....United States, Canada, USSR	2006 .....Sweden, Finland, Czech Republic
1964 .....USSR, Sweden, Czechoslovakia	2010 .....Canada, United States, Finland
1968 .....USSR, Czechoslovakia, Canada	*Competition held at Summer Games in Antwerp.
1972 .....USSR, United States, Czechoslovakia	Note: In order: gold, silver, and bronze medals.

Women

1998 .....United States, Canada, Finland	2006 .....Canada, Sweden, United States
2002 .....Canada, United States, Sweden	2010 .....Canada, United States, Finland
	Note: In order: gold, silver, and bronze medals.

LUGE

Men

SINGLES

1964	Thomas Köhler, East Germany	3:26.77
1968	Manfred Schmid, Austria	2:52.48
1972	Wolfgang Scheidel, West Germany	3:27.58
1976	Detlef Guenther, West Germany	3:27.688
1980	Bernhard Glass, West Germany	2:54.796
1984	Paul Hildgartner, Italy	3:04.258
1988	Jens Müller, West Germany	3:05.548
1992	Georg Hackl, Germany	3:02.363
1994	Georg Hackl, Germany	3:21.571
1998	Georg Hackl, Germany	3:18.44
2002	Armin Zoeggeler, Italy	2:57.941
2006	Armin Zoeggeler, Italy	3:26.088
2010	Felix Loch, Germany	3:13.085

DOUBLES

1964	Austria	1:41.62
1968	East Germany	1:35.85
1972	East Germany	1:28.35
1976	East Germany	1:25.604
1980	East Germany	1:19.331
1984	West Germany	1:23.620
1988	East Germany	1:31.940
1992	Germany	1:32.053
1994	Italy	1:36.720
1998	Germany	1:41.105
2002	Germany	1:26.082
2006	Austria	1:34.497
2010	Austria	1:22.705

Women

SINGLES

1964	Ortrun Enderlein, Germany	3:24.67
1968	Erica Lechner, Italy	2:28.66
1972	Anna-Maria Müller, East Germany	2:59.18
1976	Margit Schumann, East Germany	2:50.621
1980	Vera Zozulya, USSR	2:36.537
1984	Steffi Martin, East Germany	2:46.570
1988	Steffi Walter (Martin), East Germany	3:03.973

SINGLES *(CONT.)*

1992	Doris Neuner, Austria	3:06.696
1994	Gerda Weissensteiner, Italy	3:15.517
1998	Silke Kraushaar, Germany	3:23.779
2002	Sylke Otto, Germany	2:52.464
2006	Sylke Otto, Germany	3:07.979
2010	Tatjana Huefner, Germany	2:46.524

FIGURE SKATING

Men	PTS	Women	PTS
1908* Ulrich Salchow, Sweden		1908* Madge Syers, Great Britain	
1920† Gillis Grafström, Sweden		1920† Magda Julin, Sweden	
1924 Gillis Grafström, Sweden		1924 Herma Szabo-Planck, Austria	
1928 Gillis Grafström, Sweden		1928 Sonja Henie, Norway	
1932 Karl Schäfer, Austria		1932 Sonja Henie, Norway	
1936 Karl Schäfer, Austria		1936 Sonja Henie, Norway	
1948 Dick Button, United States		1948 Barbara Ann Scott, Canada	
1952 Dick Button, United States		1952 Jeanette Altwegg, Great Britain	
1956 Hayes Alan Jenkins, United States		1956 Tenley Albright, United States	
1960 David Jenkins, United States		1960 Carol Heiss, United States	
1964 Manfred Schnelldorfer, W Germany		1964 Sjoukje Dijkstra, Netherlands	
1968 Wolfgang Schwarz, Austria		1968 Peggy Fleming, United States	
1972 Ondrej Nepela, Czechoslovakia		1972 Beatrix Schuba, Austria	
1976 John Curry, Great Britain		1976 Dorothy Hamill, United States	
1980 Robin Cousins, Great Britain		1980 Anett Pötzsch, E Germany	
1984 Scott Hamilton, United States		1984 Katarina Witt, E Germany	
1988 Brian Boitano, United States		1988 Katarina Witt, E Germany	
1992 Victor Petrenko, Unified Team		1992 Kristi Yamaguchi, United States	
1994 Alexei Urmanov, Russia		1994 Oksana Baiul, Ukraine	
1998 Ilia Kulik, Russia		1998 Tara Lipinski, United States	
2002 Alexei Yagudin, Russia		2002 Sarah Hughes, United States	
2006‡ Evgeni Plushenko, Russia	258.33	2006‡ Shizuka Arakawa, Japan	191.34
2010 Evan Lysacek, United States	257.67	2010 Kim Yu-Na, South Korea	228.56

*Competition held at Summer Games in London.
†Competition held at Summer Garnes in Antwerp.
‡In 2004, the ISU adopted a new overall scoring system.

*Competition held at Summer Games in London.
†Competition held at Summer Games in Antwerp.
‡In 2004, the ISU adopted a new overall scoring system.

FIGURE SKATING *(Cont.)*

Mixed

PAIRS

1908* ....Anna Hübler, Heinrich Burger, Germany
1920† ...Ludowika, Walter Jakobsson-Eilers, Finland
1924 .....Helene Engelmann, Alfred Berger, Austria
1928 .....Andree Joly, Pierre Brunet, France
1932 .....Andree Brunet (Joly), Pierre Brunet, France
1936 .....Maxi Herber, Ernst Baier, Germany
1948 .....Micheline Lannoy, Pierre Baugniet, Belgium
1952 .....Ria Falk and Paul Falk, W Germany
1956 .....Elisabeth Schwartz, Kurt Oppelt, Austria
1960 .....Barbara Wagner, Robert Paul, Canada
1964 .....Lyudmila Beloussova, Oleg Protopopov, USSR
1968 .....Lyudmila Beloussova, Oleg Protopopov, USSR
1972 .....Irina Rodnina, Alexei Ulanov, USSR
1976 .....Irina Rodnina, Aleksandr Zaitsev, USSR
1980 .....Irina Rodnina, Aleksandr Zaitsev, USSR
1984 .....Elena Valova, Oleg Vasiliev, USSR
1988 .....Ekaterina Gordeeva, Sergei Grinkov, USSR
1992 .....Natalia Michkouteniok, Artour Dmitriev, Unified Team
1994 .....Ekaterina Gordeeva, Sergei Grinkov, Russia

PAIRS *(CONT.)*	Pts
1998 .....Oksana Kazakova, Artur Dmitriev, Russia	
2002 .....E. Berezhnaya, A. Sikharulidze, Russia	
J. Sales, D. Pelletier, Canada	
2006‡ ...T. Totmianina, M. Marinin, Russia	204.48
2010 .....Xue Shen/Hongbo Zhao, China	216.57

ICE DANCING	Pts
1976 .....L. Pakhomova, A. Gorshkov, USSR	
1980 .....N. Linichuk, G. Karponosov, USSR	
1984 .....Jayne Torvill, Christopher Dean, UK	
1988 .....N. Bestemianova, A. Bukin, USSR	
1992 .....M. Klimova, S. Ponomarenko, Unified Team	
1994 .....Oksana Grishuk, Evgeny Platov, Russia	
1998 .....Pasha Grishuk, Evgeny Platov, Russia	
2002 .....Marina Anissina, Gwendal Peizeralt, France	
2006‡ ...T. Navka, R. Kostomarov, Russia	200.6
2010 .....Tessa Virtue/Scott Moir, Canada	221.5

*Competition held at Summer Games in London.
†Competition held at Summer Games in Antwerp.
‡In 2004, the ISU adopted a new overall point-scoring syste[m]

SKELETON

Men

1928	Jennison Heaton, United States	3:01.8
1948	Nino Bibbia, Italy	5:23.2
2002	Jim Shea Jr., United States	1:41.96
2006	Duff Gibson, Canada	1:55.88
2010	Jon Montgomery, Canada	3:29.73

Women

2002	Tristan Gale, United States	1:45.11
2006	Maya Pedersen, Switzerland	1:59.83
2010	Amy Williams, United Kingdom	3:35.64

SPEED SKATING

Men

500 METERS

1924	Charles Jewtraw, United States	44.0
1928	Clas Thunberg, Finland	43.4 OR
	Bernt Evensen, Norway	43.4 OR
1932	John Shea, United States	43.4 EOR
1936	Ivar Ballangrud, Norway	43.4 EOR
1948	Finn Helgesen, Norway	43.1 OR
1952	Kenneth Henry, United States	43.2
1956	Yevgeny Grishin, USSR	40.2 EWR
1960	Yevgeny Grishin, USSR	40.2 EWR
1964	Terry McDermott, United States	40.1 OR
1968	Erhard Keller, West Germany	40.3
1972	Erhard Keller, West Germany	39.44 OR
1976	Yevgeny Kulikov, USSR	39.17 OR
1980	Eric Heiden, United States	38.03 OR
1984	Sergei Fokichev, USSR	38.19
1988	Uwe-Jens Mey, East Germany	36.45 WR
1992	Uwe-Jens Mey, East Germany	37.14
1994	Aleksandr Golubev, Russia	36.33
1998	Hiroyasu Shimizu, Japan (second run)	35.59 OR
2002	Casey FitzRandolph, United States	1:09.23*
2006	Joey Cheek, United States	1:09.76*
2010	Tae-Bum Mo, South Korea	1:09.82*

*Combined time.

1,000 METERS

1976	Peter Mueller, United States	1:19.32
1980	Eric Heiden, United States	1:15.18 OR
1984	Gaetan Boucher, Canada	1:15.80
1988	Nikolai Gulyaev, USSR	1:13.03 OR
1992	Olaf Zinke, Germany	1:14.85
1994	Dan Jansen, United States	1:12.43 WR
1998	Ids Postma, Netherlands	1:10.64 OR
2002	Gerard van Velde, Netherlands	1:07.18
2006	Shani Davis, United States	1:08.89
2010	Shani Davis, United States	1:08.94

1,500 METERS

1924	Clas Thunberg, Finland	2:20.8
1928	Clas Thunberg, Finland	2:21.1
1932	John Shea, United States	2:57.5
1936	Charles Mathisen, Norway	2:19.2 OR
1948	Sverre Farstad, Norway	2:17.6 OR
1952	Hjalmar Andersen, Norway	2:20.4
1956	Yevgeny Grishin, USSR	2:08.6 WR
	Yuri Mikhailov, USSR	2:08.6 WR
1960	Roald Aas, Norway	2:10.4
	Yevgeny Grishin, USSR	2:10.4
1964	Ants Anston, USSR	2:10.3
1968	Cornelis Verkerk, Netherlands	2:03.4 OR
1972	Ard Schenk, Netherlands	2:02.96 OR
1976	Jan Egil Storholt, Norway	1:59.38 OR

Note: OR=Olympic Record; WR=World Record; EOR=Equals Olympic Record; EWR=Equals World Record; WB=World Best.

SPEED SKATING *(Cont.)*
Men *(Cont.)*

1,500 METERS *(CONT.)*

1980	Eric Heiden, United States	1:55.44 OR
1984	Gaetan Boucher, Canada	1:58.36
1988	Andre Hoffmann, E Germany	1:52.06 WR
1992	Johann Olav Koss, Norway	1:54.81
1994	Johann Olav Koss, Norway	1:51.29 WR
1998	Aadne Sondral, Norway	1:47.87 WR
2002	Derek Parra, United States	1:43.95
2006	Enrico Fabris, Italy	1:45.97
2010	Mark Tuitert, Netherlands	1:45.57

5,000 METERS

1924	Clas Thunberg, Finland	8:39.0
1928	Ivar Ballangrud, Norway	8:50.5
1932	Irving Jaffee, United States	9:40.8
1936	Ivar Ballangrud, Norway	8:19.6 OR
1948	Reidar Liaklev, Norway	8:29.4
1952	Hjalmar Andersen, Norway	8:10.6 OR
1956	Boris Shilkov, USSR	7:48.7 OR
1960	Viktor Kosichkin, USSR	7:51.3
1964	Knut Johannesen, Norway	7:38.4 OR
1968	Fred Anton Maier, Norway	7:22.4 WR
1972	Ard Schenk, Netherlands	7:23.61
1976	Sten Stensen, Norway	7:24.48
1980	Eric Heiden, United States	7:02.29 OR
1984	Sven Tomas Gustafson, Sweden	7:12.28
1988	Tomas Gustafson, Sweden	6:44.63 WR
1992	Geir Karlstad, Norway	6:59.97
1994	Johann Olav Koss, Norway	6:34.96 WR
1998	Gianni Romme, Netherlands	6:22.20 WR
2002	Jo. Uytdehaage, Netherlands	6:41.66
2006	Chad Hedrick, United States	6:14.68
2010	Sven Kramer, Netherlands	6:14.60 OR

10,000 METERS

1924	Julius Skutnabb, Finland	18:04.8
1928	Not held due to thawing of ice	
1932	Irving Jaffee, United States	19:13.6
1936	Ivar Ballangrud, Norway	17:24.3 OR
1948	Ake Seyffarth, Sweden	17:26.3
1952	Hjalmar Andersen, Norway	16:45.8 OR
1956	Sigvard Ericsson, Sweden	16:35.9 OR
1960	Knut Johannesen, Norway	15:46.6 WR
1964	Jonny Nilsson, Sweden	15:50.1
1968	Johnny Höglin, Sweden	15:23.6 OR
1972	Ard Schenk, Netherlands	15:01.35 OR
1976	Piet Kleine, Netherlands	14:50.59 OR
1980	Eric Heiden, United States	14:28.13 WR
1984	Igor Malkov, USSR	14:39.90
1988	Tomas Gustafson, Sweden	13:48.20 WR
1992	Bart Veldkamp, Netherlands	14:12.12
1994	Johann Olav Koss, Norway	13:30.55 WR
1998	Gianni Romme, Netherlands	13:15.33 WR
2002	Jochem Uytdehaage, Netherlands	12:58.92 WR
2006	Bob de Jong, Netherlands	13:01.57
2010	Seung-Hoon Lee, South Korea	12:58.55 OR

TEAM PURSUIT

2006	Italy
2010	Canada

Women

500 METERS

1960	Helga Haase, East Germany	45.9
1964	Lydia Skoblikova, USSR	45.0 OR
1968	Lyudmila Titova, USSR	46.1
1972	Anne Henning, United States	43.33 OR
1976	Sheila Young, United States	42.76 OR
1980	Karin Enke, East Germany	41.78 OR
1984	Christa Rothenburger, E Germany	41.02 OR
1988	Bonnie Blair, United States	39.10 WR
1992	Bonnie Blair, United States	40.33
1994	Bonnie Blair, United States	39.25
1998	Catriona LeMay Doan, Canada (second run)	38.21 OR
2002	Catriona LeMay, Canada	1:14.75*
2006	Svetlana Zhurova, Russia	1:16.57*
2010	Sang-Hwa Lee, South Korea	1:06.09*

1,000 METERS

1960	Klara Guseva, USSR	1:34.1
1964	Lydia Skoblikova, USSR	1:33.2 OR
1968	Carolina Geijssen, Netherlands	1:32.6 OR
1972	Monika Pflug, West Germany	1:31.40 OR
1976	Tatiana Averina, USSR	1:28.43 OR
1980	Natalya Petruseva, USSR	1:24.10 OR
1984	Karin Enke, East Germany	1:21.61 OR

1,000 METERS *(CONT.)*

1988	Christa Rothenburger, East Germany	1:17.65 WR
1992	Bonnie Blair, United States	1:21.90
1994	Bonnie Blair, United States	1:18.74
1998	Marianne Timmer, Netherlands	1:16.51 OR
2002	Chris Witty, United States	1:13.83
2006	Marianne Timmer, Netherlands	1:16.05
2010	Christine Nesbitt, Canada	1:16.56

1,500 METERS

1960	Lydia Skoblikova, USSR	2:25.2 WR
1964	Lydia Skoblikova, USSR	2:22.6 OR
1968	Kaija Mustonen, Finland	2:22.4 OR
1972	Dianne Holum, United States	2:20.85 OR
1976	Galina Stepanskaya, USSR	2:16.58 OR
1980	Anne Borckink, Netherlands	2:10.95 OR
1984	Karin Enke, East Germany	2:03.42 WR
1988	Yvonne van Gennip, Netherlands	2:00.68 OR
1992	Jacqueline Boerner, Germany	2:05.87
1994	Emese Hunyady, Austria	2:02.19
1998	Marianne Timmer, Netherlands	1:57.58 WR
2002	Anni Friesinger, Germany	1:54.02
2006	Cindy Klassen, Canada	1:55.27
2010	Ireen Wust, Netherlands	1:56.89

*Combined time.

Note: OR=Olympic Record; WR=World Record; EOR=Equals Olympic Record; EWR=Equals World Record; WB=World Best.

SPEED SKATING *(Cont.)*
Women *(Cont.)*

3,000 METERS

1960	Lydia Skoblikova, USSR	5:14.3
1964	Lydia Skoblikova, USSR	5:14.9
1968	Johanna Schut, Netherlands	4:56.2 OR
1972	Christina Baas-Kaiser, Netherlands	4:52.14 OR
1976	Tatiana Averina, USSR	4:45.19 OR
1980	Bjorg Eva Jensen, Norway	4:32.13 OR
1984	Andrea Schöne, East Germany	4:24.79 OR
1988	Yvonne van Gennip, Netherlands	4:11.94 WR
1992	Gunda Niemann, Germany	4:19.90
1994	Svetlana Bazhanova, Russia	4:17.43
1998	G. Niemann-Stirnemann, Germany	4:07.29 OR
2002	Claudia Pechstein, Germany	3:57.70

3,000 METERS *(CONT.)*

2006	Ireen Wust, Netherlands	4:02.43
2010	Martina Sablikova, Czech Republic	4:02.53

5,000 METERS

1988	Yvonne van Gennip, Netherlands	7:14.13 WR
1992	Gunda Niemann, Germany	7:31.57
1994	Claudia Pechstein, Germany	7:14.37
1998	Claudia Pechstein, Germany	6:59.61 WR
2002	Claudia Pechstein, Germany	6:46.91 WR
2006	Clara Hughes, Canada	6:59.07
2010	Martina Sablikova, Czech Republic	6:50.91

TEAM PURSUIT

2006	Germany
2010	Germany

SHORT TRACK SPEED SKATING

Men

500 METERS

1994	Chae Ji-Hoon, South Korea	43.54
1998	Takafumi Nishitani, Japan	42.862
2002	Marc Gagnon, Canada	41.802 OR
2006	Apolo Anton Ohno, United States	41.935
2010	Charles Hamelin, Canada	40.770

1,000 METERS

1992	Kim Ki-Hoon, South Korea	1:30.76
1994	Kim Ki-Hoon, South Korea	1:34.57
1998	Kim Dong Sung, South Korea	1:32.375
2002	Steve Bradbury, Australia	1:29.109
2006	Hyun-Soo Ahn, South Korea	1:26.739 OR
2010	Jung-Su Lee, South Korea	1:23.747 OR

1,500 METERS

2002	Apolo Anton Ohno, United States	2:18.541
2006	Hyun-Soo Ahn, South Korea	2:25.341
2010	Jung-Su Lee, South Korea	2:10.949

5,000-METER RELAY

1992	South Korea	7:14.02
1994	Italy	7:11.74
1998	Canada	7:06.075
2002	Canada	6:51.579
2006	South Korea	6:43.376 OR
2010	Canada	6:43.610

Women

500 METERS

1992	Cathy Turner, United States	47.04
1994	Cathy Turner, United States	45.98
1998	Annie Perreault, Canada	46.568
2002	Yang Yang, China	44.187
2006	Meng Wang, China	44.345
2010	Meng Wang, China	42.985

1,000 METERS

1994	Chun Lee Kyung, South Korea	1:36.87
1998	Chun Lee Kyung, South Korea	1:42.776
2002	Yang A. Yang, China	1:36.391
2006	Sun-Yu Jin, South Korea	1:32.859
2010	Meng Wang, China	1:29.213

1,500 METERS

2002	Ko Gi-Hyun, South Korea	2:31.581
2006	Sun-Yu Jin, China	2:23.494
2010	Yang Zhou, China	2:16.993

3,000-METER RELAY

1992	Canada	4:36.62
1994	South Korea	4:26.64
1998	South Korea	4:16.260
2002	South Korea	4:12.793
2006	South Korea	4:17.040
2010	China	4:06.610 WR

ALPINE SKIING

Men

DOWNHILL

1948	Henri Oreiller, France	2:55.0
1952	Zeno Colo, Italy	2:30.8
1956	Anton Sailer, Austria	2:52.2
1960	Jean Vuarnet, France	2:06.0
1964	Egon Zimmermann, Austria	2:18.16
1968	Jean-Claude Killy, France	1:59.85
1972	Bernhard Russi, Switzerland	1:51.43
1976	Franz Klammer, Austria	1:45.73
1980	Leonhard Stock, Austria	1:45.50
1984	Bill Johnson, United States	1:45.59
1988	Pirmin Zurbriggen, Switzerland	1:59.63
1992	Patrick Ortlieb, Austria	1:50.37
1994	Tommy Moe, United States	1:45.75
1998	Jean-Luc Crétier, France	1:50.11
2002	Fritz Strobl, Austria	1:39.13
2006	Antoine Deneriaz, France	1:48.80
2010	Didier Defago, Switzerland	1:54.31

SLALOM*

1948	Edi Reinalter, Switzerland	2:10.3
1952	Othmar Schneider, Austria	2:00.0
1956	Anton Sailer, Austria	3:14.7
1960	Ernst Hinterseer, Austria	2:08.9
1964	Josef Stiegler, Austria	2:11.13
1968	Jean-Claude Killy, France	1:39.73
1972	F. Fernandez Ochoa, Spain	1:49.27
1976	Piero Gros, Italy	2:03.29
1980	Ingemar Stenmark, Sweden	1:44.26
1984	Phil Mahre, United States	1:39.41
1988	Alberto Tomba, Italy	1:39.47
1992	Finn Christian Jagge, Norway	1:44.39
1994	Thomas Stangassinger, Austria	2:02.02
1998	Hans-Petter Buraas, Norway	1:49.31
2002	Jean-Pierre Vidal, France	1:41.06
2006	Benjamin Raich, Austria	1:43.14
2010	Giuliano Razzoli, Italy	1:39.32

*Combined time.

Note: OR=Olympic Record; WR=World Record; EOR=Equals Olympic Record; EWR=Equals World Record; WB=World Best.

ALPINE SKIING (Cont.)
Men (Cont.)

GIANT SLALOM*

1952	Stein Eriksen, Norway	2:25.0
1956	Anton Sailer, Austria	3:00.1
1960	Roger Staub, Switzerland	1:48.3
1964	Francois Bonlieu, France	1:46.71
1968	Jean-Claude Killy, France	3:29.28
1972	Gustav Thöni, Italy	3:09.62
1976	Heini Hemmi, Switzerland	3:26.97
1980	Ingemar Stenmark, Sweden	2:40.74
1984	Max Julen, Switzerland	2:41.18
1988	Alberto Tomba, Italy	2:06.37
1992	Alberto Tomba, Italy	2:06.98
1994	Markus Wasmeier, Germany	2:52.46
1998	Hermann Maier, Austria	2:38.51
2002	Stephan Eberharter, Austria	2:23.28
2006	Benjamin Raich, Austria	2:35.00
2010	Carlo Janka, Switzerland	2:37.83

SUPER COMBINED (SLALOM + DOWNHILL)†

1936	Franz Pfnür, Germany	99.25
1948	Henri Oreiller, France	3.2
1988	Hubert Strolz, Austria	36.55
1992	Josef Polig, Italy	14.58
1994	Lasse Kjus, Norway	3:17.53
1998	Mario Reiter, Austria	3:08.06
2002	Kjetil André Aamodt, Norway	3:17.56
2006	Ted Ligety, United States	3:09.35
2010	Bode Miller, United States	2:44.92

SUPER GIANT SLALOM

1988	Franck Piccard, France	1:39.66
1992	Kjetil André Aamodt, Norway	1:13.04
1994	Markus Wasmeier, Germany	1:32.53
1998	Hermann Maier, Austria	1:34.82
2002	Kjetil André Aamodt, Norway	1:21.58
2006	Kjetil André Aamodt, Norway	1:30.65
2010	Aksel Lund Svindal, Norway	1:30.34

Women

DOWNHILL

1948	Hedy Schlunegger, Switzerland	2:28.3
1952	Trude Jochum-Beiser, Austria	1:47.1
1956	Madeleine Berthod, Switzerland	1:40.7
1960	Heidi Biebl, West Germany	1:37.6
1964	Christl Haas, Austria	1:55.39
1968	Olga Pall, Austria	1:40.87
1972	Marie-Theres Nadig, Switzerland	1:36.68
1976	Rosi Mittermaier, West Germany	1:46.16
1980	Annemarie Moser-Pröll, Austria	1:37.52
1984	Michela Figini, Switzerland	1:13.36
1988	Marina Kiehl, West Germany	1:25.86
1992	Kerrin Lee-Gartner, Canada	1:52.55
1994	Katja Seizinger, Germany	1:35.93
1998	Katja Seizinger, Germany	1:28.89
2002	Carole Montillet, France	1:39.56
2006	Michaela Dorfmeister, Austria	1:56.49
2010	Lindsey Vonn, United States	1:44.19

GIANT SLALOM*

1952	Andrea Mead Lawrence, U.S.	2:06.8
1956	Ossi Reichert, West Germany	1:56.5
1960	Yvonne Rüegg, Switzerland	1:39.9
1964	Marielle Goitschel, France	1:52.24
1968	Nancy Greene, Canada	1:51.97
1972	Marie-Theres Nadig, Switzerland	1:29.90
1976	Kathy Kreiner, Canada	1:29.13
1980	Hanni Wenzel, Liechtenstein (2 runs)	2:41.66
1984	Debbie Armstrong, United States	2:20.98
1988	Vreni Schneider, Switzerland	2:06.49
1992	Pernilla Wiberg, Sweden	2:12.74
1994	Deborah Compagnoni, Italy	2:30.97
1998	Deborah Compagnoni, Italy	2:50.59
2002	Janica Kostelic, Croatia	2:30.01
2006	Julia Mancuso, United States	2:09.19
2010	Viktoria Rebensburg, Germany	2:27.11

SLALOM*

1948	Gretchen Fraser, United States	1:57.2
1952	Andrea Mead Lawrence, United States	2:10.6
1956	Renee Colliard, Switzerland	1:52.3
1960	Anne Heggtveigt, Canada	1:49.6
1964	Christine Goitschel, France	1:29.86
1968	Marielle Goitschel, France	1:25.86
1972	Barbara Cochran, United States	1:31.24
1976	Rosi Mittermaier, West Germany	1:30.54
1980	Hanni Wenzel, Liechtenstein	1:25.09
1984	Paoletta Magoni, Italy	1:36.47
1988	Vreni Schneider, Switzerland	1:36.69
1992	Petra Kronberger, Austria	1:32.68
1994	Vreni Schneider, Switzerland	1:56.01
1998	Hilde Gerg, Germany	1:32.40
2002	Janica Kostelic, Croatia	1:46.10
2006	Anja Paerson, Sweden	1:29.04
2010	Maria Riesch, Germany	1:42.89

SUPER COMBINED (SLALOM + DOWNHILL)†

1988	Anita Wachter, Austria	29.25
1992	Petra Kronberger, Austria	2.55
1994	Pernilla Wiberg, Sweden	3:05.16
1998	Katja Seizinger, Germany	2:40.74
2002	Janica Kostelic, Croatia	2:43.28
2006	Janica Kostelic, Croatia	2:51.08
2010	Maria Riesch, Germany	2:09.14

SUPER GIANT SLALOM

1988	Sigrid Wolf, Austria	1:19.03
1992	Deborah Compagnoni, Italy	1:21.22
1994	Diann Roffe-Steinrotter, U.S.	1:22.15
1998	Picabo Street, United States	1:18.02
2002	Daniela Ceccarelli, Italy	1:13.59
2006	Michaela Dorfmeister, Austria	1:32.47
2010	Andrea Fischbacher, Austria	1:20.14

*Combined time. †Beginning in 1994, Super Combined race scoring based on time.

FREESTYLE SKIING

Men

MOGULS
		Pts
1992	Edgar Grospiron, France	25.81
1994	Jean-Luc Brassard, Canada	27.24
1998	Jonny Moseley, United States	26.93
2002	Janne Lahtela, Finland	27.97
2006	Dale Begg-Smith, Australia	26.77
2010	Alexandre Bilodeau, Canada	26.75

AERIALS
		Pts
1994	Andreas Schoenbaechler, Switz.	234.67
1998	Eric Bergoust, United States	255.64
2002	Ales Valenta, Czech Republic	257.02
2006	Han Xiaopeng, China	250.77
2010	Alexei Grishin, Belarus	248.41

SKI CROSS
2010	Michael Schmid, Switzerland

Women

MOGULS
		Pts
1992	Donna Weinbrecht, United States	23.69
1994	Stine Lise Hattestad, Norway	25.97
1998	Tae Satoya, Japan	25.06
2002	Kari Traa, Norway	25.94
2006	Jennifer Heil, Canada	26.50
2010	Hannah Kearney, United States	26.63

AERIALS
		Pts
1994	Lina Cherjazova, Uzbekistan	166.84
1998	Nikki Stone, United States	193.00
2002	Alisa Camplin, Australia	193.47
2006	Evelyne Leu, Switzerland	202.55
2010	Lydia Lassila, Australia	214.74

SKI CROSS
2010	Ashleigh McIvor, Canada

NORDIC SKIING

Men

10 KILOMETERS CLASSICAL
1992	Vegard Ulvang, Norway	27:36.0
1994	Bjørn Dæhlie, Norway	24:20.1
1998	Bjørn Dæhlie, Norway	27:24.5
1976	Nikolay Bajukov, Unified Team	43:58.47
1980	Thomas Wassberg, Sweden	41:57.63
1984	Gunde Swan, Sweden	41:25.6
1988	Michael Deviatyarov, USSR	41:18.9
2002	Andrus Veerpalu, Estonia	37:07.4
2006	Andrus Veerpalu, Estonia	38:01.3

15 KILOMETERS FREESTYLE
2010	Dario Cologna, Switzerland	33:36.3

15 KILOMETERS PURSUIT FREESTYLE
1992	Bjørn Dæhlie, Norway	1:05:37.9
1994	Bjørn Dæhlie, Norway	1:00:08.8
1998	Thomas Alsgaard, Norway	1:07:01.7

30 KILOMETERS CLASSICAL
1956	Veikko Hakulinen, Finland	1:44:06.0
1960	Sixten Jernberg, Sweden	1:51:03.9
1964	Eero Mantyränta, Finland	1:30:50.7
1968	Franco Nones, Italy	1:35:39.2
1972	Viaceslav Vedenine, USSR	1:36:31.2
1976	Sergei Savelyev, USSR	1:30:29.38
1980	Nikolai Simyatov, USSR	1:27:02.80
1984	Nikolai Simyatov, USSR	1:28:56.3
1988	Alexey Prokororov, USSR	1:24:26.3
1992	Vegard Ulvang, Norway	1:22:27.8
1994	Thomas Alsgaard, Norway	1:12:26.4
1998	Mika Myllylae, Finland	1:33:55.8

30 KILOMETERS PURSUIT
2006	Eugeni Dementiev, Russia	1:17:00.8
2010	Marcus Hellner, Sweden	1:15:11.4

50 KILOMETERS CLASSIC MASS START
2010	Petter Northug, Norway	2:05:35.5

50 KILOMETERS FREESTYLE
1924	Thorleif Haug, Norway	3:44:32.0
1928	Per Erik Hedlund, Sweden	4:52:03.0
1932	Veli Saarinen, Finland	4:28:00.0

50 KILOMETERS FREESTYLE *(CONT.)*
1936	Elis Wiklund, Sweden	3:30:11.0
1948	Nils Karlsson, Sweden	3:47:48.0
1952	Veikko Hakulinen, Finland	3:33:33.0
1956	Sixten Jernberg, Sweden	2:50:27.0
1960	Kalevi Hämäläinen, Finland	2:59:06.3
1964	Sixten Jernberg, Sweden	2:43:52.6
1968	Olle Ellefsaeter, Norway	2:28:45.8
1972	Paal Tyldrum, Norway	2:43:14.75
1976	Ivar Formo, Norway	2:37:30.50
1980	Nikolai Simyatov, USSR	2:27:24.60
1984	Thomas Wassberg, Sweden	2:15:55.8
1988	Gunde Svan, Sweden	2:04:30.9
1992	Bjørn Dæhlie, Norway	2:03:41.5
1994	Vladimir Smirnov, Kazakhstan	2:07:20.3
1998	Bjørn Dæhlie, Norway	2:05:08.2
2002	Mikhail Ivanov, Russia	2:06:20.8
2006	Giorgio di Centa, Italy	2:06:11.8

4 X 10-KILOMETER RELAY MIXED
1936	Finland	2:41:33.0
1948	Sweden	2:32:80.0
1952	Finland	2:20:16.0
1956	USSR	2:15:30.0
1960	Finland	2:18:45.6
1964	Sweden	2:18:34.6
1968	Norway	2:08:33.5
1972	USSR	2:04:47.94
1976	Finland	2:07:59.72
1980	USSR	1:57:03.46
1984	Sweden	1:55:06.3
1988	Sweden	1:43:58.6
1992	Norway	1:39:26.0
1994	Italy	1:41:15.0
1998	Norway	1:40:55.7
2002	Norway	1:32:45.5
2006	Italy	1:43:45.7
2010	Sweden	1:45:05.4

TEAM SPRINT
2006	Sweden	17:02.9
2010	Norway	19:01.0

INDIVIDUAL SPRINT
2006	Bjoern Lind, Sweden	2:26.5
2010	Nikita Kriukov, Russia	3:36.3

* Different scoring system; 1924–1952 distance was 18 km; 1952–present, 15 km.
† Times in the cross-country race were not converted into points. According to the Gundersen Method, used since 1988, starting times in the race are staggered in proportion to points earned in the ski jumping segment of the event.

NORDIC SKIING *(Cont.)*
Men *(Cont.)*

SKI JUMPING, NORMAL (90-M) HILL		Pts
1964	Veikko Kankkonen, Finland	229.90
1968	Jiri Raska, Czechoslovakia	216.5
1972	Yukio Kasaya, Japan	244.2
1976	Hans-Georg Aschenbach, East Germany	252.0
1980	Toni Innauer, Austria	266.3
1984	Jens Weissflog, East Germany	215.2
1988	Matti Nykänen, Finland	229.1
1992	Ernst Vettori, Austria	222.8
1994	Espen Bredesen, Norway	282.0
1998	Jani Soininen, Finland	234.5
2002	Simon Ammann, Switzerland	269.0
2006	Lars Bystoel, Norway	266.5
2010	Simon Ammann, Switzerland	276.5

SKI JUMPING, LARGE (120-M) HIL)		Pts
1924	Jacob Tullin Thams, Norway	18.960
1928	Alf Andersen, Norway	19.208
1932	Birger Ruud, Norway	228.1
1936	Birger Ruud, Norway	232.0
1948	Petter Hugsted, Norway	228.1
1952	Arnfinn Bergmann, Norway	226.0
1956	Antti Hyvärinen, Finland	227.0
1960	Helmut Recknagel, East Germany	227.2
1964	Toralf Engan, Norway	230.70
1968	Vladimir Beloussov, USSR	231.3
1972	Wojciech Fortuna, Poland	219.9
1976	Karl Schnabl, Austria	234.8
1980	Jouko Tormanen, Finland	271.0
1984	Matti Nykänen, Finland	231.2
1988	Matti Nykänen, Finland	224.0
1992	Toni Nieminen, Finland	239.5
1994	Jens Weissflog, Germany	274.5
1998	Kazuyoshi Funaki, Japan	272.3
2002	Simon Amman, Switzerland	281.4
2006	Thomas Morgenstern, Austria	276.9
2010	Simon Ammann, Switzerland	283.6

TEAM SKI JUMPING, LARGE (120-M) HILL		Pts
1988	Finland	634.4
1992	Finland	644.4
1994	Germany	970.1

TEAM SKI JUMPING, LARGE (120-M) HILL *(CONT.)*		Pts
1998	Japan	933.0
2002	Germany	974.1
2006	Austria	984.0
2010	Austria	1107.9

NORDIC COMBINED		Pts
1924	Thorleif Haug, Norway	18.906
1928	Johan Gröttumsbraaten, Norway	17.833
1932	Johan Gröttumsbraaten, Norway	446.0
1936	Oddbjörn Hagen, Norway	430.30
1948	Heikki Hasu, Finland	448.80
1952	Simon Slattvik, Norway	451.621
1956	Sverre Stenersen, Norway	455.0
1960	Georg Thoma, West Germany	457.952
1964	Tormod Knutsen, Norway	469.28
1968	Frantz Keller, West Germany	449.04
1972	Ulrich Wehling, East Germany	413.34
1976	Ulrich Wehling, East Germany	423.39
1980	Ulrich Wehling, East Germany	432.20
1984	Tom Sandberg, Norway	422.595
1988	Hippolyt Kempf, Switzerland	432.230
1992	Fabrice Guy, France	426.47
1994	Fred B. Lundberg, Norway	457.970
1998	Bjarte Engen Vik, Norway	41:21.1†
2002	Samppa Lajunen, Finland	38:18.7†
2006	Georg Hettich, Norway	39:44.6†
2010	Jason Chappuis Lamy, France	25:47.1†

SPRINT NORDIC COMBINED		
2002	Samppa Lajunen, Finland	123.8
2006	Felix Gottwald, Austria	17:35.0†
2010	Bill Demong, United States	25:32.9†

TEAM NORDIC COMBINED RELAY	
1988	West Germany
1992	Japan
1994	Japan
1998	Norway
2002	Finland
2006	Austria
2010	Austria

Women

INDIVIDUAL SPRINT		
2002	Julija Tchepalova, Russia	3:10.6
2006	Chandra Crawford, Canada	2:12.3
2010	Marit Bjoergen, Norway	3:39.2

5 KILOMETERS PURSUIT		
2002	Olga Danilova, Russia	24:52.1

5 KILOMETERS CLASSIC		
1964	Klaudia Boyarskikh, USSR	17:50.5
1968	Toini Gustafsson, Sweden	16:45.2
1972	Galina Kulakova, USSR	17:00.50
1976	Helena Takalo, Finland	15:48.69
1980	Raisa Smetanina, USSR	15:06.92
1984	Marja-Liisa Hamalainen, Finland	17:04.0
1988	Marjo Matikainen, Finland	15:04.0
1992	Marjut Lukkarinen, Finland	14:13.8
1994	Lyubova Egorova, Russia	14:08.8
1998	Larissa Lazhutina, Russia	17:37.9

10 KILOMETERS CLASSIC		
1952	Lydia Widemen, Finland	41:40.0
1956	Lyubov Kosyryeva, USSR	38:11.0

10 KILOMETERS CLASSIC *(CONT.)*		
1960	Maria Gusakova, USSR	39:46.6
1964	Klaudia Boyarskikh, USSR	40:24.3
1968	Toini Gustafsson, Sweden	36:46.5
1972	Galina Kulakova, USSR	34:17.8
1976	Raisa Smetanina, USSR	30:13.41
1980	Barbara Petzold, East Germany	30:31.54
1984	Marja-Lissa Hamalainen, Finland	31:44.2
1988	Vida Ventsene, USSR	30:08.3
2002	Bante Skari, Norway	28:05.6
2006	Kristina Smigun, Estonia	27:51.4

10 KILOMETERS FREESTYLE		
2010	Charlotte Kalla, Sweden	24:58.4

10 KILOMETERS PURSUIT FREESTYLE		
1992	Lyubov Egorova, Unified Team	40:07.7
1994	Lyubov Egorova, Russia	41:38.1
1998	Larissa Lazhutina, Russia	46:06.9

15 KILOMETERS CLASSIC		
1992	Lyubov Egorova, Unified Team	42:20.8
1994	Manuela Di Centa, Italy	39:44.5
1998	Olga Danilova, Russia	46:55.04

†Beginning in 1998, Nordic combined races based on time.

NORDIC SKIING *(Cont.)*
Women *(Cont.)*

15 KILOMETERS FREESTYLE

2002 ....Stefania Belmondo, Italy   39:54.4

15 KILOMETERS PURSUIT FREESTYLE

2006 ....Kristina Smigun, Estonia   42:48.7
2010 ....Marit Bjoergen, Norway   39:58.1

20 KILOMETERS FREESTYLE

1984 ....Marja-Liisa Hamalainen, Finland   1:01:45.0
1988 ....Tamara Tikhonova, USSR   55:53.6

30 KILOMETERS CLASSIC MASS START

2010 ....Justyna Kowalczyk, Poland   1:30:33.7

30 KILOMETERS FREESTYLE

1992 ....Stefania Belmondo, Italy   1:22:30.1
1994 ....Manuela Di Centa, Italy   1:25:41.6
1998 ....Julija Tchepalova, Russia   1:22:01.5
2002 ....Gabriela Paruzzi, Italy   1:30:57.1
2006 ....Katerina Neumannova, Czech Rep. 1:22:25.4

TEAM SPRINT

2006 ....Sweden   16:36.9
2010 ....Germany   18:03.7

4 X 5-KILOMETER RELAY MIXED

1956 ....Finland   1:9:01.0
1960 ....Sweden   1:4:21.4
1964 ....USSR   59:20.0
1968 ....Norway   57:30.0
1972 ....USSR   48:46.15
1976 ....USSR   1:07:49.75
1980 ....E Germany   1:02:11.10
1984 ....Norway   1:06:49.7
1988 ....USSR   59:51.1
1992 ....Unified Team   59:34.8
1994 ....Russia   57:12.5
1998 ....Russia   55:13.5
2002 ....Germany   49:30.6
2006 ....Russia   54:47.7
2010 ....Norway   55:19.5

SNOWBOARDING

Men

GIANT SLALOM

1998 .....Ross Rebagliati, Canada   2:03.96

PARALLEL GIANT SLALOM

2002 .....Philipp Schoch, Switzerland
2006 .....Philipp Schoch, Switzerland
2010 .....Jasey Jay Anderson, Canada

HALF-PIPE   Pts

1998 .....Gian Simmen, Switzerland   85.2
2002 .....Ross Powers, United States   46.1
2006 .....Shaun White, United States   46.8
2010 .....Shaun White, United States   48.4

SNOWBOARD CROSS

2006 .....Seth Wescott, United States
2010 .....Seth Wescott, United States

Women

GIANT SLALOM

1998 .....Karine Ruby, France   2:17.34

PARALLEL GIANT SLALOM

2002 .....Isabella Blanc, France
2006 ....Daniela Meuli, Switzerland
2010 .....Nicolien Sauerbreij, Netherlands

HALF-PIPE   Pts

1998 .....Nicola Thost, Germany   74.6
2002 ....Kelly Clark, United States   47.9
2006 .....Hannah Teter, United States   46.4
2010 .....Torah Bright, Australia   45.0

SNOWBOARD CROSS

2006 .....Tanja Frieden, Switzerland
2010 .....Maelle Ricker, Canada

Tennis

Rafael Nadal won three Grand Slam titles in 2010 and became the world's No. 1 tennis player

FOR THE RECORD • 2010

2010 Grand Slam Champions

Australian Open

Men's Singles

	Winner	Runner-up	Score
Quarterfinals	Roger Federer	Nikolay Davydenko	2–6, 6–3, 6–0, 7–5
	Jo-Wilfried Tsonga	Novak Djokovic	7–6 (10–8), 6–7 (5–7)
	Andy Murray	Rafael Nadal†	6–3, 7–5 (7–2), 3–0
	Marin Cilic	Andy Roddick	7–6 (7–4), 6–3, 3–6, 2–6, 6–
Semifinals	Andy Murray	Marin Cilic	3–6, 6–4, 6–4, 6–2
	Roger Federer	Jo-Wilfried Tsonga	6–2, 6–3, 6–2
Final	Roger Federer	Andy Murray	6–3, 6–4, 7–6 (13–11)

† retired match in third set due to injury

Women's Singles

	Winner	Runner-up	Score
Quarterfinals	Serena Williams	Victoria Azarenka	4–6, 7–6 (7–4), 6–2
	Na Li	Venus Williams	2–6, 7–6 (7–4), 7–5
	Jie Zheng	Maria Kirilenko	6–1, 6–3
	Justine Henin	Nadia Petrova	7–6 (7–3), 7–5
Semifinals	Serena Williams	Na Li	7–6 (7–4), 7–6 (7–1)
	Justine Henin	Jie Zheng	6–1, 6–0
Final	Serena Williams	Justine Henin	6–4, 3–6, 6–2

Doubles

	Winner	Runner-up	Score
Men's Final	Bob Bryan/ Mike Bryan	Daniel Nestor/ Nenad Zimonjic	6–3, 6–7 (5–7), 6–3
Women's Final	Serena Williams/ Venus Williams	Cara Black/ Liezel Huber	6–4, 6–3
Mixed Final	Cara Black/ Leander Paes	Ekaterina Makarova/ Jaroslav Levinsky	7–5, 6–3

French Open

Men's Singles

	Winner	Runner-up	Score
Quarterfinals	Rafael Nadal	Nicolas Almagro	7–6 (7–2), 7–6 (7–3), 6–4
	Jurgen Melzer	Novak Djokovic	3–6, 2–6, 6–2, 7–6 (7–3), 6–4
	Tomas Berdych	Mikhail Youzhny	6–3, 6–1, 6–2
	Robin Soderling	Roger Federer	3–6, 6–3, 7–5, 6–4
Semifinals	Rafael Nadal	Jurgen Melzer	3–6, 7–6 (7–2), 2–6, 6–1, 6–4
	Robin Soderling	Tomas Berdych	6–3, 3–6, 5–7, 6–3, 6–3
Final	Rafael Nadal	Robin Soderling	6–4, 6–2, 6–4

Women's Singles

	Winner	Runner-up	Score
Quarterfinals	Francesca Schiavone	Caroline Wozniacki	7–6 (7–3), 5–7, 7–5
	Elena Dementieva	Nadia Petrova	2–6, 6–2, 6–0
	Jelena Jankovic	Yaroslava Shvedova	7–5, 6–4
	Samantha Stosur	Serena Williams	6–2, 6–7 (2–7), 8–6
Semifinals	Francesca Schiavone	Elena Dementieva‡	7–6 (7–3)
	Samantha Stosur	Jelena Jankovic	6–1, 6–2
Final	Francesca Schiavone	Samantha Stosur	6–4, 7–6 (7–2)

‡-retired in second set due to injury

Doubles

	Winner	Runner-Up	Score
Men's Final	Daniel Nestor/ Nenad Zimonjic	Lukas Dlouhy/ Leander Paes	7–5, 6–2
Women's Final	Serena Williams/ Venus Williams	Kveta Peschke/ Katarina Srebotnik	6–2, 6–3
Mixed Final	Katarina Srebotnik/ Nenad Zimonjic	Yaroslava Shvedova/ Julian Knowle	4–6, 7–6 (7–5), 1–0 (11–9)

Wimbledon

Men's Singles

	Winner	Runner-Up	Score
Quarterfinals	Rafael Nadal ....Robin Soderling		3–6, 6–3, 7–6 (7–4), 6–1
	Andy Murray ....Jo-Wilfried Tsonga		6–7 (5–7), 7–6 (7–5) 6–2, 6–2
	Novak Djokovic ....Yen-Hsun Lu		6–3, 6–2, 6–2
Semifinals	Tomas Berdych.......................Roger Federer		6–4, 3–6, 6–1, 6–4
	Rafael Nadal ....Andy Murray		6–4, 7–6 (8–6), 6–4
Final	Tomas Berdych ....Novak Djokovic		6–3, 7–6 (11–9), 6–3
	Rafael Nadal ....Tomas Berdych		6–3, 7–5, 6–4

Women's Singles

	Winner	Runner-Up	Score
Quarterfinals	Serena Williams......................Na Li		7–5, 6–3
	Petra Kvitova ....Kaia Kanepi		4–6, 7–6 (10–8), 8–6
	Tsvetana Pironkova ....Venus Williams		6–2, 6–3
Semifinals	Vera Zvonareva ....Kim Clijsters		3–6, 6–4, 6–2
	Serena Williams......................Petra Kvitova		7–6 (7–5), 6–2
Final	Vera Zvonareva ....Tsvetana Pironkova		3–6, 6–3, 6–2
	Serena Williams......................Vera Zvonareva		6–3, 6–2

Doubles

	Winner	Runner-Up	Score
Men's Final	Jurgen Melzer/ ....Robert Lindstedt		6–1, 7–5, 7–5
	Philipp Petzchner	Horia Tecau	
Women's Final	Vania King/ ....Elena Vesnina/		7–6 (8–6), 6–2
	Yaroslava Shvedova	Vera Zvonareva	
Mixed Final	Cara Black/ ....Lisa Raymond/		6–4, 7–6 (7–5)
	Leander Paes	Wesley Moodie	

U.S. Open

Men's Singles

	Winner	Runner-Up	Score
Quarterfinals	Rafael Nadal ....Fernando Verdasco		7–5, 6–3, 6–4
	Mikhail Youzhny ....Stanislas Wawrinka		3–6, 7–6 (9–7), 3–6 6–3, 6–3
	Roger Federer.........................Robin Soderling		6–4, 6–4, 7–5
Semifinals	Novak Djokovic ....Gael Monfils		7–6 (7–2), 6–1, 6–2
	Novak Djokovic ....Roger Federer		5–7, 6–1, 5–7, 6–2, 7–5
Final	Rafael Nadal ....Mikhail Youzhny		6–2, 6–3, 6–4
	Rafael Nadal ....Novak Djokovic		6–4, 5–7, 6–4, 6–2

Women's Singles

	Winner	Runner-Up	Score
Quarterfinals	Kim Clijsters ....Samantha Stosur		6–4, 5–7, 6–3
	Venus Williams ....Francesca Schiavone		7–6 (7–5), 6–4
	Caroline Wozniacki ....Dominika Cibulkova		6–2, 7–5
Semifinals	Vera Zvonareva ....Kaia Kanepi		6–3, 7–5
	Kim Clijsters ....Venus Williams		4–6, 7–6 (7–2), 6–4
Final	Vera Zvonareva ....Caroline Wozniacki		6–4, 6–3
	Kim Clijsters ....Vera Zvonareva		6–2, 6–1

Doubles

	Winner	Runner-Up	Score
Men's Final	Bob Bryan/ ....Rohan Bopanna/		7–6 (7–5), 7–6 (7–4)
	Mike Bryan	Aisam-Ul-Haq Qureshi	
Women's Final	Vania King/ ....Liezel Huber/		2–6, 6–4, 7–6 (7–4)
	Yaroslava Shvedova	Nadia Petrova	
Mixed Final	Liezel Huber/ ....Kveta Peschke/		6–4, 6–4
	Bob Bryan	Aisam-Ul-Haq Qureshi	

ATP-Men's Tour (Late 2009 through Summer 2010)

Date	Tournament	Site	Singles Winner	Surface	Total Purse
Oct 5	Japan Open	Tokyo, Japan	Jo-Wilifried Tsonga	Outdoor Hard	$1,226,600
Oct 5	ChinaOpen	Beijing, China	Novak Djokovic	Indoor Hard	$2,100,600
Oct 12	Shanghai Masters	Shanghai, China	Nikolay Davydenko	Indoor Hard	$5,250,000
Oct 19	Stockholm Open	Stockholm, Sweden	Marcos Baghdatis	Indoor Hard	€600,000
Oct 19	Kremlin Cup	Moscow, Russia	Mikhail Youzhny	Indoor Hard	$1,080,500
Oct 26	Austria Trophy	Vienna, Austria	Jurgen Melzer	Indoor Hard	€650,000
Oct 26	Lyon Grand Prix	Lyon, France	Ivan Ljubicic	Indoor Carpet	€766,750
Oct 26	St. Petersburg Open	St. Petersburg, Russia	Sergiy Stakhovsky	Indoor Hard	$750,000
Nov 2	Swiss Indoor	Basel, Switzerland	Novak Djokovic	Indoor Hard	€1,755,000
Nov 2	Valencia Open	Valencia, Spain	Andy Murray	Indoor Hard	€2,019,000
Nov 9	Paris Masters	Paris, France	Jo Wilfried Tsonga	Indoor Hard	€2,270,000
Nov 23	ATP World Tour Finals	London, England	Nikolay Davydenko	Indoor Hard	$5,000,000
Jan 3	Qatar Open	Doha, Qatar	Nikolay Davydenko	Outdoor Hard	$1,110,250
Jan 3	Brisbane International	Brisbane, Australia	Andy Roddick	Outdoor Hard	$372,500
Jan 4	Chennai Open	Chennai, India	Marin Cilic	Outdoor Hard	$398,250
Jan 11	Heineken Open	Auckland, New Zealand	John Isner	Outdoor Hard	$355,500
Jan 11	Medibank International	Sydney, Australia	Marco Badgdatis	Outdoor Hard	$484,750
Jan 18	Australian Open	Melbourne, Australia	Roger Federer	Outdoor Hard	A$11,048,640
Feb 1	SA Open	Johannesburg, S. Africa	Feliciano Lopez	Outdoor Hard	$442,500
Feb 1	Zagreb Indoors	Zagreb, Croatia	Marin Cilic	Indoor Hard	€398,250
Feb 1	Movistar Open	Santiago, Chile	Thomaz Bellucci	Outdoor Clay	$398,250
Feb 8	Brasil Open	Costa de Sauipe, Brazil	Juan Carlos Ferrero	Outdoor Clay	$562,500
Feb 8	SAP Open	San Jose, California	Fernando Verdasco	Indoor Hard	$531,000
Feb 8	ABM/Amro	Rotterdam, Neth.	Robin Soderling	Indoor Hard	€1,150,000
Feb 15	Regions Championships	Memphis, Tennessee	Sam Querrey	Indoor Hard	$1,100,000
Feb 15	Telmex Copa	Buenos Aires, Argentina	Juan Carlos Ferrero	Outdoor Clay	$475,300
Feb 22	Open 13	Marseille, France	Michael Llodra	Indoor Hard	€512,750
Feb 22	Dubai Open	Dubai, U.A.E.	Novak Djokovic	Outdoor Hard	$1,619,500
Feb 22	Mexican Open	Acapulco, Mexico	David Ferrer	Outdoor Clay	$955,000
Feb 22	Delray Beach Int'l	Delray Beach, Fla.	Ernets Gulbis	Outdoor Hard	$442,500
Mar 9	BNP Paribas Open	Indian Wells, Calif.	Ivan Ljubicic	Outdoor Hard	$3,645,000
Mar 23	Sony Ericsson Open	Miami, Fla.	Andy Roddick	Outdoor Hard	$3,645,000
Apr 5	Grand Prix Hassan II	Casablanca, Morocco	Stanislas Wawrinka	Outdoor Clay	€398,250
Apr 5	US Clay Champ'ship	Houston, Texas	Juan Ignacio Chela	Outdoor Clay	$442,500
Apr 11	Monte Carlo Masters	Monte Carlo, Monaco	Rafael Nadal	Outdoor Clay	€2,227,500
Apr 19	Barcelona Open	Barcelona, Spain	Fernando Verdasco	Outdoor Clay	€1,550 ,000
Apr 26	Italia International	Rome, Italy	Rafael Nadal	Outdoor Clay	€2,227,500
May 3	Estoril Open	Estoril, Portugal	Albert Montanes	Outdoor Clay	€398,250
May 3	BMW Open	Munich, Germany	Mikhail Youzhny	Outdoor Clay	€398,250
May 3	Serbia Open	Belgrade, Serbia	Sam Querrey	Outdoor Clay	€373,200
May 9	Madrid Masters	Madrid, Spain	Rafael Nadal	Outdoor Clay	€2,835,000
May 16	Nice Open	Nice, France	Richard Gasquet	Outdoor Clay	€398,250
May 23	French Open	Paris, France	Rafael Nadal	Outdoor Clay	€7,580,800
June 7	Gerry Weber Open	Halle, Germany	Lleyton Hewitt	Outdoor Grass	€663,750
June 7	AEGON Championships	London, England	Sam Querrey	Outdoor Grass	€627,700
June 13	UNICEF Open	's-Hertogenbosch, Netherlands	Sergiy Stakhovsky	Outdoor Grass	€398,250
June 13	AEGON International	Eastbourne, England	Michael Llodra	Outdoor Grass	£405,000
June 21	Wimbledon	Wimbledon, England	Rafael Nadal	Outdoor Grass	£6,196,000
July 5	Hall of Fame Champ's	Newport, R.I.	Mardy Fish	Outdoor Grass	$442,500
July 12	Swedish Open	Bastad, Sweden	Nicolas Almagro	Outdoor Clay	€398,250
July 12	Mercedes Cup	Stuttgart, Germany	Albert Montanes	Outdoor Clay	€398,250
July 19	Atlanta Champ's	Atlanta, Georgia	Mardy Fish	Outdoor Hard	$531,000
July 19	German Open	Hamburg, Germany	Andrey Golubev	Outdoor Clay	€1,000,000
July 25	Allianz Suisse Open	Gstaad, Switzerland	Nicolas Almagro	Outdoor Clay	€450,000
July 26	Farmer's Classic	Los Angeles	Sam Querrey	Outdoor Hard	$619,500
Aug 2	Croatia Open	Umag, Croatia	Juan Carlos Ferrero	Outdoor Clay	€398,250

ATP-Men's Tour (Summer 2010 through September 2010)

Date	Tournament	Site	Singles Winner	Surface	Total Purse
Aug 1	Legg Mason Classic	Washington, D.C.	David Nalbandian	Oudoor Hard	$1,165,500
Aug 9	Rogers Cup	Toronto, Canada	Andy Murray	Outdoor Hard	$2,430,000
Aug 15	Western & Southern	Cincinnati, Ohio	Roger Federer	Outdoor Hard	$2,430000
Aug 22	Pilot Pen Championship	New Haven, Conn.	Sergiy Stakhovsky	Outdoor Hard	$663,750
Sept 14	U.S. Open	New York City	Rafael Nadal	Outdoor Hard	$10,508,000
Sept 20	Moselle Open	Metz, France	Gilles Simon	Indoor Hard	€398,250
Sept 20	Romania Open	Bucharest, Romania	Juan Ignacio Chela	Outdoor Clay	€368,450
Sept 27	Thailand Open	Bangkok, Thailand	Guillermo Garcia Lopez	Outdoor Hard	$551,000
Sept 27	Malaysia Open	Kuala Lumpur, Malaysia	Mikhail Youzhny	Indoor Hard	$850,000

WTA-Women's Tour (Late 2009 through Spring 2010)

Date	Tournament	Site	Winner	Runner-Up	Total Purse
Oct 5	China Open	Bejing, China	Svetlana Kuznetsova	Agnieszka Radwanska	$4,500,000
Oct 12	HP Open	Tokyo, Japan	Samantha Stosur	Francecsa Schiavone	$220,000
Oct 12	Generali Ladies Open	Linz, Austia	Yanina Wickmayer	Petra Kvitova	$220,000
Oct 19	Ladies Kremlin Cup	Moscow, Russia	Francesca Schiavone	Olga Govortsova	$1,000,000
Oct 26	Sony Ericsson Champ's	Doha, Qatar	Serena Williams	Venus Williams	$4,500,000
Nov 2	WTA Tour Championships	Bali, Indonesia	Aravane Rezai	Marion Bartoli	$600,000
Jan 3	Brisbane Int'l	Brisbane, Australia	Kim Clijsters	Justine Henin	$220,000
Jan 4	ASB Classic	Auckland, N.Z.	Yania Wickmayer	Flavia Pennetta	$220,000
Jan 10	Medibank Int'l	Sydney, Australia	Elena Dementieva	Serena Williams	$600,000
Jan 10	Hobart Int'l	Hobart, Australia	Alona Bondarenko	Shahar Peer	$220,000
Jan 18	Australian Open	Melbourne, Australia	Serena Williams	Justine Henin	$9,264,098
Feb 8	GDF Suez Open	Paris, France	Elena Dementieva	Lucie Safarova	$700,000
Feb 8	Pattaya Open	Patttaya, Thailand	Vera Zvonareva	Tamarine Tanasugarn	$220,000
Feb 14	Dubai Championships	Dubai, U.A.E.	Venus Williams	Victoria Azarenka	$2,000,000
Feb 14	Regions Championships	Memphis, Tenn.	Maria Sharpova	Sofia Arvidsson	$220,000
Feb 15	Copa Colsanitas	Bogota, Colombia	Mariana Marino	Angelique Kerber	$220,000
Feb 22	Mexicano Open	Acapulco, Mexico	Venus Williams	Polona Hercog	$220,000
Feb 22	Malaysia Open	Kuala Lumpru, Mal.	Alisa Lkeybanova	Elena Dementieva	$220,000
Mar 1	Monterrey Open	Monterrey, Mexico	A. Pavlyuchenkova	Daniela Hantuchova	$220,000
Mar 10	BNP Paribas Open	Indian Wells, Calif.	Jelena Jankovic	Samantha Stosur	$4,500,000
Mar 23	Sony Ericsson Open	Miami, Florida	Kim Clijsters	Venus Williams	$4,500,000
Apr 5	Andalucia Int'l	Marbella, Spain	Flavia Pennetta	Carla Suarez Navarro	$220,000
Apr 5	MPS Championships	Pontra Vedra Beach, Fla.	Caroline Wozniacki	Olga Govortsova	$220,000
Apr 12	Family Circle Cup	Charleston, S.C.	Samantha Stosur	Vera Zvonareva	$700,000
Apr 12	Barcelona Open	Barcelona, Spain	Fran. Schiavone	Roberts Vinci	$220,000
Apr 26	Morocco Grand Prix	Fez, Morocco	Iveta Benesova	Simona Halep	$220,000
May 2	Italian International	Rome, Italy	Maria M. Sanchez	Jelena Jankovic	$2,000,000
May 3	Estoril Open	Estoril, Portugal	Ana. Sevastova	Arantxa Parra Santonja	$220,000
May 8	Madrid Open	Madrid, Spain	Aravane Rezai	Venus Williams	$4,500,000
May 17	Warsaw Open	Warsaw, Poland	Alexandra Dulgheru	Jie Zheng	$600,000
May 17	Strasbourg Int'l	Strasbourg, France	Maria Sharpova	Kristina Barrois	$220,000
May 23	French Open	Paris, France	Francesca Schiavone	Samantha Stosur	$9,938,926
June 7	AEGON Classic	Birmingham, England	Na Li	Maria Sharpova	$220,000

WTA-Women's Tour (Spring 2010 through September 2010)

Date	Tournament	Site	Winner	Runner-Up	Total Purse
June 13	UNICEF Open	's-Hertogenbosch, Neth.	Justine Henin	Andrea Petkovic	$220,000
June 14	AEGON Int'l	Eastbourne, England	Ekaterina Makarova	Victoria Azarenka	$600,000
June 21	Wimbledon	Wimbledon, England	Serena Williams	Vera Zvonareva	$9,781,631
July 5	Swedish Open	Bastad, Sweden	Aravane Rezai	Gisela Dulko	$220,000
July 5	GDF Suez Grand Prix	Budapest, Hungary	Agnes Szavay	Patty Schnyder	$220,000
July 12	Palermo International	Palermo, Italy	Kaia Kanepi	Flavia Pennetta	$220,000
July 12	Prague Open	Prague, Czech Rep.	Agnes Szavay	Barbora Strycova	$220,000
July 19	Slovenia Open	Portoroz, Slovenia	Anna Chakvetadze	Johanna Larsson	$220,000
July 19	Gastein International	Bad Gastein, Austria	Julia Goerges	Timea Bacsinszky	$220,000
July 26	Bank of the West Classic	Stanford, California	Victoria Azarenka	Maria Sharapova	$700,000
Julu 26	Istanbul Cup	Istanbul, Turkey	A. Pavlyuchenkova	Elena Vesnina	$220,000
Aug 2	Mercury Insurance Open	San Diego, Calif.	Svet. Kuznetsova	Ag. Radawanska	$700,000
Aug 2	Copenhagen Open	Copenhagen, Den.	Caroline Wozniacki	Klara Zakopalova	$220,000
Aug 9	Western & Southern Open	Cincinnati, Ohio	Kim Clijsters	Maria Sharapova	$2,000,000
Aug 16	Rogers Cup	Toronto, Canada	Caroline Wozniacki	Vera Zvonareva	$2,000,000
Aug 22	Pilot Pen Int'l	New Haven, Conn.	Caroline Wozniacki	Nadia Petrova	$600,000
Aug 30	U.S. Open	New York City	Kim Clijsters	Vera Zvonareva	$10,258,000
Sept 13	Guangzhou Open	Guangzhou, China	Jarmilla Groth	Alla Kudryavtseva	$220,000
Sept 13	Bell Challenge	Quebec City, Canada	Tamira Paszek	Beth. Mattek-Sands	$220,000
Sept 20	Hansol Korea Open	Seoul, South Korea	Alisa Kleybanova	Klara Zakopalova	$220,000
Sept 20	Tashkent Open	Tashkent, Uzbekistan	Alla Kudryavtseva	Elena Vesnina	$220,000
Sept 26	Pan Pacific Open	Tokyo, Japan	Caroline Wozniacki	Elena Dementieva	$2,000,000

2009 Final Season Singles Points Leaders

Men

Rank	Player	Country	Points	Events
1.	Roger Federer	SUI	10550	19
2.	Rafael Nadal	ESP	9205	19
3.	Novak Djokovic	SRB	8310	23
4.	Andy Murray	GBR	7030	19
5.	Juan Martin del Potro	ARG	6785	22
6.	Nikolay Davydenko	RUS	4930	26
7.	Andy Roddick	USA	4410	20
8.	Robin Soderlin	SWE	3410	27
9.	Fernando Verdasco	ESP	3300	24
10.	Jo-Wilfried Tsonga	FRA	2875	26

Note: Compiled by the ATP Tour, through the end of the 2009 season.

Women

Rank	Player	Country	Points
1.	Dinara Safina	RUS	7731
2.	Serena Williams	USA	7576
3.	Svetlana Kuznetsova	RUS	5772
4.	Caroline Wozniacki	DEN	5475
5.	Elena Dementieva	RUS	5415
6.	Victoria Azarenka	BLR	4451
7.	Venus Williams	USA	4397
8.	Jelena Jankovic	SRB	3555
9.	Vera Zvonareva	RUS	3550
10.	Agnieszka Radwanska	POL	3340

Note: Compiled by the WTA, through the end of the 2009 season.

FOR THE RECORD • Year by Year

Grand Slam Tournaments

MEN

Australian Open Championships

Year	Winner	Finalist	Score
1905	Rodney Heath	A. H. Curtis	4–6, 6–3, 6–4, 6–4
1906	Tony Wilding	H. A. Parker	6–0, 6–4, 6–4
1907	Horace M. Rice	H. A. Parker	6–3, 6–4, 6–4
1908	Fred Alexander	A. W. Dunlop	3–6, 3–6, 6–0, 6–2, 6–3
1909	Tony Wilding	E. F. Parker	6–1, 7–5, 6–2
1910	Rodney Heath	Horace M. Rice	6–4, 6–3, 6–2
1911	Norman Brookes	Horace M. Rice	6–1, 6–2, 6–3
1912	J. Cecil Parke	A. E. Beamish	3–6, 6–3, 1–6, 6–1, 7–5
1913	E. F. Parker	H. A. Parker	2–6, 6–1, 6–2, 6–3
1914	Pat O'Hara Wood	G. L. Patterson	6–4, 6–3, 5–7, 6–1
1915	Francis G. Lowe	Horace M. Rice	4–6, 6–1, 6–1, 6–4
1916–18	No tournament		
1919	A. R. F. Kingscote	E. O. Pockley	6–4, 6–0, 6–3
1920	Pat O'Hara Wood	Ron Thomas	6–3, 4–6, 6–8, 6–1, 6–3
1921	Rhys H. Gemmell	A. Hedeman	7–5, 6–1, 6–4
1922	Pat O'Hara Wood	Gerald Patterson	6–0, 3–6, 3–6, 6–3, 6–2
1923	Pat O'Hara Wood	C. B. St John	6–1, 6–1, 6–3
1924	James Anderson	R. E. Schlesinger	6–3, 6–4, 3–6, 5–7, 6–3
1925	James Anderson	Gerald Patterson	11–9, 2–6, 6–2, 6–3
1926	John Hawkes	J. Willard	6–1, 6–3, 6–1
1927	Gerald Patterson	John Hawkes	3–6, 6–4, 3–6, 18–16, 6–3
1928	Jean Borotra	R. O. Cummings	6–4, 6–1, 4–6, 5–7, 6–3
1929	John C. Gregory	R. E. Schlesinger	6–2, 6–2, 5–7, 7–5
1930	Gar Moon	Harry C. Hopman	6–3, 6–1, 6–3
1931	Jack Crawford	Harry C. Hopman	6–4, 6–2, 2–6, 6–1
1932	Jack Crawford	Harry C. Hopman	4–6, 6–3, 3–6, 6–3, 6–1
1933	Jack Crawford	Keith Gledhill	2–6, 7–5, 6–3, 6–2
1934	Fred Perry	Jack Crawford	6–3, 7–5, 6–1
1935	Jack Crawford	Fred Perry	2–6, 6–4, 6–4, 6–4
1936	Adrian Quist	Jack Crawford	6–2, 6–3, 4–6, 3–6, 9–7
1937	Vivian B. McGrath	John Bromwich	6–3, 1–6, 6–0, 2–6, 6–1
1938	Don Budge	John Bromwich	6–4, 6–2, 6–1
1939	John Bromwich	Adrian Quist	6–4, 6–1, 6–3
1940	Adrian Quist	Jack Crawford	6–3, 6–1, 6–2
1941–45	No tournament		
1946	John Bromwich	Dinny Pails	5–7, 6–3, 7–5, 3–6, 6–2
1947	Dinny Pails	John Bromwich	4–6, 6–4, 3–6, 7–5, 8–6
1948	Adrian Quist	John Bromwich	6–4, 3–6, 6–3, 2–6, 6–3
1949	Frank Sedgman	Ken McGregor	6–3, 6–3, 6–2
1950	Frank Sedgman	Ken McGregor	6–3, 6–4, 4–6, 6–1
1951	Richard Savitt	Ken McGregor	6–3, 2–6, 6–3, 6–1
1952	Ken McGregor	Frank Sedgman	7–5, 12–10, 2–6, 6–2
1953	Ken Rosewall	Mervyn Rose	6–0, 6–3, 6–4
1954	Mervyn Rose	Rex Hartwig	6–2, 0–6, 6–4, 6–2
1955	Ken Rosewall	Lew Hoad	9–7, 6–4, 6–4
1956	Lew Hoad	Ken Rosewall	6–4, 3–6, 6–4, 7–5
1957	Ashley Cooper	Neale Fraser	6–3, 9–11, 6–4, 6–2
1958	Ashley Cooper	Mal Anderson	7–5, 6–3, 6–4
1959	Alex Olmedo	Neale Fraser	6–1, 6–2, 3–6, 6–3
1960	Rod Laver	Neale Fraser	5–7, 3–6, 6–3, 8–6, 8–6
1961	Roy Emerson	Rod Laver	1–6, 6–3, 7–5, 6–4
1962	Rod Laver	Roy Emerson	8–6, 0–6, 6–4, 6–4
1963	Roy Emerson	Ken Fletcher	6–3, 6–3, 6–1
1964	Roy Emerson	Fred Stolle	6–3, 6–4, 6–2
1965	Roy Emerson	Fred Stolle	7–9, 2–6, 6–4, 7–5, 6–1
1966	Roy Emerson	Arthur Ashe	6–4, 6–8, 6–2, 6–3
1967	Roy Emerson	Arthur Ashe	6–4, 6–1, 6–1
1968	Bill Bowrey	Juan Gisbert	7–5, 2–6, 9–7, 6–4
1969*	Rod Laver	Andres Gimeno	6–3, 6–4, 7–5

MEN *(Cont.)*
Australian Open Championships *(Cont.)*

Year	Winner	Finalist	Score
1970	Arthur Ashe	Dick Crealy	6–4, 9–7, 6–2
1971	Ken Rosewall	Arthur Ashe	6–1, 7–5, 6–3
1972	Ken Rosewall	Mal Anderson	7–6, 6–3, 7–5
1973	John Newcombe	Onny Parun	6–3, 6–7, 7–5, 6–1
1974	Jimmy Connors	Phil Dent	7–6, 6–4, 4–6, 6–3
1975	John Newcombe	Jimmy Connors	7–5, 3–6, 6–4, 7–5
1976	Mark Edmondson	John Newcombe	6–7, 6–3, 7–6, 6–1
1977 (Jan)	Roscoe Tanner	Guillermo Vilas	6–3, 6–3, 6–3
1977 (Dec)	Vitas Gerulaitis	John Lloyd	6–3, 7–6, 5–7, 3–6, 6–2
1978	Guillermo Vilas	John Marks	6–4, 6–4, 3–6, 6–3
1979	Guillermo Vilas	John Sadri	7–6, 6–3, 6–2
1980	Brian Teacher	Kim Warwick	7–5, 7–6, 6–3
1981	Johan Kriek	Steve Denton	6–2, 7–6, 6–7, 6–4
1982	Johan Kriek	Steve Denton	6–3, 6–3, 6–2
1983	Mats Wilander	Ivan Lendl	6–1, 6–4, 6–4
1984	Mats Wilander	Kevin Curren	6–7, 6–4, 7–6, 6–2
1985 (Dec)	Stefan Edberg	Mats Wilander	6–4, 6–3, 6–3
1987 (Jan)	Stefan Edberg	Pat Cash	6–3, 6–4, 3–6, 5–7, 6–3
1988	Mats Wilander	Pat Cash	6–3, 6–7, 3–6, 6–1, 8–6
1989	Ivan Lendl	Miloslav Mecir	6–2, 6–2, 6–2
1990	Ivan Lendl	Stefan Edberg	4–6, 7–6, 5–2, ret.
1991	Boris Becker	Ivan Lendl	1–6, 6–4, 6–4, 6–4
1992	Jim Courier	Stefan Edberg	6–3, 3–6, 6–4, 6–2
1993	Jim Courier	Stefan Edberg	6–2, 6–1, 2–6, 7–5
1994	Pete Sampras	Todd Martin	7–6, 6–4, 6–4
1995	Andre Agassi	Pete Sampras	4–6, 6–1, 7–6, 6–4
1996	Boris Becker	Michael Chang	6–2, 6–4, 2–6, 6–2
1997	Pete Sampras	Carlos Moya	6–2, 6–3, 6–3
1998	Petr Korda	Marcelo Ríos	6–2, 6–2, 6–2
1999	Yevgeny Kafelnikov	Thomas Enqvist	4–6, 6–0, 6–3, 7–6
2000	Andre Agassi	Yevgeny Kafelnikov	3–6, 6–3, 6–2, 6–4
2001	Andre Agassi	Arnaud Clement	6–4, 6–2, 6–2
2002	Thomas Johansson	Marat Safin	3–6, 6–4, 6–4, 7–6 (7-4)
2003	Andre Agassi	Rainer Schuettler	6–2, 6–2, 6–1
2004	Roger Federer	Marat Safin	7–6 (7–3), 6–4, 6–2
2005	Marat Safin	Lleyton Hewitt	1–6, 6–3, 6–4, 6–4
2006	Roger Federer	Marcos Baghdatis	5–7, 7–5, 6–0, 6–2
2007	Roger Federer	Fernando Gonzalez	7–6 (7–2), 6–4, 6–4
2008	Novak Djokovic	Jo-Wilfried Tsonga	4–6, 6–4, 6–3, 7–6 (7–2)
2009	Rafael Nadal	Roger Federer	7–5, 3–6, 7–6 (7–3), 3–6, 6–2
2010	Roger Federer	Andy Murray	6–3, 6–4, 7–6 (13–11)

*Became Open (amateur and professional) in 1969.

MEN *(Cont.)*

French Championships

Year	Winner	Finalist	Score
1925†	Rene Lacoste	Jean Borotra	7–5, 6–1, 6–4
1926	Henri Cochet	Rene Lacoste	6–2, 6–4, 6–3
1927	Rene Lacoste	Bill Tilden	6–4, 4–6, 5–7, 6–3, 11–9
1928	Henri Cochet	Rene Lacoste	5–7, 6–3, 6–1, 6–3
1929	Rene Lacoste	Jean Borotra	6–3, 2–6, 6–0, 2–6, 8–6
1930	Henri Cochet	Bill Tilden	3–6, 8–6, 6–3, 6–1
1931	Jean Borotra	Claude Boussus	2–6, 6–4, 7–5, 6–4
1932	Henri Cochet	Giorgio de Stefani	6–0, 6–4, 4–6, 6–3
1933	Jack Crawford	Henri Cochet	8–6, 6–1, 6–3
1934	Gottfried von Cramm	Jack Crawford	6–4, 7–9, 3–6, 7–5, 6–3
1935	Fred Perry	Gottfried von Cramm	6–3, 3–6, 6–1, 6–3
1936	Gottfried von Cramm	Fred Perry	6–0, 2–6, 6–2, 2–6, 6–0
1937	Henner Henkel	Henry Austin	6–1, 6–4, 6–3
1938	Don Budge	Roderick Menzel	6–3, 6–2, 6–4
1939	Don McNeill	Bobby Riggs	7–5, 6–0, 6–3
1940	No tournament		
1941‡	Bernard Destremau	n/a	n/a
1942‡	Bernard Destremau	n/a	n/a
1943‡	Yvon Petra	n/a	n/a
1944‡	Yvon Petra	n/a	n/a
1945‡	Yvon Petra	Bernard Destremau	7–5, 6–4, 6–2
1946	Marcel Bernard	Jaroslav Drobny	3–6, 2–6, 6–1, 6–4, 6–3
1947	Joseph Asboth	Eric Sturgess	8–6, 7–5, 6–4
1948	Frank Parker	Jaroslav Drobny	6–4, 7–5, 5–7, 8–6
1949	Frank Parker	Budge Patty	6–3, 1–6, 6–1, 6–4
1950	Budge Patty	Jaroslav Drobny	6–1, 6–2, 3–6, 5–7, 7–5
1951	Jaroslav Drobny	Eric Sturgess	6–3, 6–3, 6–3
1952	Jaroslav Drobny	Frank Sedgman	6–2, 6–0, 3–6, 6–4
1953	Ken Rosewall	Vic Seixas	6–3, 6–4, 1–6, 6–2
1954	Tony Trabert	Arthur Larsen	6–4, 7–5, 6–1
1955	Tony Trabert	Sven Davidson	2–6, 6–1, 6–4, 6–2
1956	Lew Hoad	Sven Davidson	6–4, 8–6, 6–3
1957	Sven Davidson	Herbie Flam	6–3, 6–4, 6–4
1958	Mervyn Rose	Luis Ayala	6–3, 6–4, 6–4
1959	Nicola Pietrangeli	Ian Vermaak	3–6, 6–3, 6–4, 6–1
1960	Nicola Pietrangeli	Luis Ayala	3–6, 6–3, 6–4, 4–6, 6–3
1961	Manuel Santana	Nicola Pietrangeli	4–6, 6–1, 3–6, 6–0, 6–2
1962	Rod Laver	Roy Emerson	3–6, 2–6, 6–3, 9–7, 6–2
1963	Roy Emerson	Pierre Darmon	3–6, 6–1, 6–4, 6–4
1964	Manuel Santana	Nicola Pietrangeli	6–3, 6–1, 4–6, 7–5
1965	Fred Stolle	Tony Roche	3–6, 6–0, 6–2, 6–3
1966	Tony Roche	Istvan Gulyas	6–1, 6–4, 7–5
1967	Roy Emerson	Tony Roche	6–1, 6–4, 2–6, 6–2
1968*	Ken Rosewall	Rod Laver	6–3, 6–1, 2–6, 6–2
1969	Rod Laver	Ken Rosewall	6–4, 6–3, 6–4
1970	Jan Kodes	Zeljko Franulovic	6–2, 6–4, 6–0
1971	Jan Kodes	Ilie Nastase	8–6, 6–2, 2–6, 7–5
1972	Andres Gimeno	Patrick Proisy	4–6, 6–3, 6–1, 6–1
1973	Ilie Nastase	Nikki Pilic	6–3, 6–3, 6–0
1974	Bjorn Borg	Manuel Orantes	6–7, 6–0, 6–1, 6–1
1975	Bjorn Borg	Guillermo Vilas	6–2, 6–3, 6–4
1976	Adriano Panatta	Harold Solomon	6–1, 6–4, 4–6, 7–6
1977	Guillermo Vilas	Brian Gottfried	6–0, 6–3, 6–0
1978	Bjorn Borg	Guillermo Vilas	6–1, 6–1, 6–3
1979	Bjorn Borg	Victor Pecci	6–3, 6–1, 6–7, 6–4
1980	Bjorn Borg	Vitas Gerulaitis	6–4, 6–1, 6–2
1981	Bjorn Borg	Ivan Lendl	6–1, 4–6, 6–2, 3–6, 6–1
1982	Mats Wilander	Guillermo Vilas	1–6, 7–6, 6–0, 6–4
1983	Yannick Noah	Mats Wilander	6–2, 7–5, 7–6
1984	Ivan Lendl	John McEnroe	3–6, 2–6, 6–4, 7–5, 7–5
1985	Mats Wilander	Ivan Lendl	3–6, 6–4, 6–2, 6–2
1986	Ivan Lendl	Mikael Pernfors	6–3, 6–2, 6–4
1987	Ivan Lendl	Mats Wilander	7–5, 6–2, 3–6, 7–6

†1925 was the first year that entries were accepted from all countries.
‡From 1941 to 1945 the event was called Tournoi de France and was closed to all foreigners.

MEN *(Cont.)*

French Championships *(Cont.)*

Year	Winner	Finalist	Score
1988	Mats Wilander	Henri Leconte	7–5, 6–2, 6–1
1989	Michael Chang	Stefan Edberg	6–1, 3–6, 4–6, 6–4, 6–2
1990	Andres Gomez	Andre Agassi	6–3, 2–6, 6–4, 6–4
1991	Jim Courier	Andre Agassi	3–6, 6–4, 2–6, 6–1, 6–4
1992	Jim Courier	Petr Korda	7–5, 6–2, 6–1
1993	Sergi Bruguera	Jim Courier	6–4, 2–6, 6–2, 3–6, 6–3
1994	Sergi Bruguera	Alberto Berasategui	6–3, 7–5, 2–6, 6–1
1995	Thomas Muster	Michael Chang	7–5, 6–2, 6–4
1996	Yevgeny Kafelnikov	Michael Stich	7–6, 7–5, 7–6
1997	Gustavo Kuerten	Sergi Bruguera	6–3, 6–4, 6–2
1998	Carlos Moya	Alex Corretja	6–3, 7–5, 6–3
1999	Andre Agassi	Andrei Medvedev	1–6, 2–6, 6–4, 6–3, 6–4
2000	Gustavo Kuerten	Magnus Norman	6–2, 6–3, 2–6, 7–6
2001	Gustavo Kuerten	Alex Corretja	6–7, 7–5, 6–2, 6–0
2002	Albert Costa	Juan Carlos Ferrero	6–1, 6–0, 4–6, 6–3
2003	Juan Carlos Ferrero	Martin Verkerk	6–1, 6–3, 6–2
2004	Gaston Gaudio	Guillermo Coria	0–6, 3–6, 6–4, 6–1, 8–6
2005	Rafael Nadal	Mariano Puerta	6–7, 6–3, 6–1, 7–5
2006	Rafael Nadal	Roger Federer	1–6, 6–1, 6–4, 7–6
2007	Rafael Nadal	Roger Federer	6–3, 4–6, 6–3, 6–4
2008	Rafael Nadal	Roger Federer	6–1, 6–3, 6–0
2009	Roger Federer	Robin Soderling	6–1, 7–6 (7–1), 6–4
2010	Rafael Nadal	Robin Soderling	6–4, 6–2, 6–4

*Became Open (amateur and professional) in 1968, but restricted to only contract professionals in 1972.

MEN *(Cont.)*

Wimbledon Championships

Year	Winner	Finalist	Score
1877	Spencer W. Gore	William C. Marshall	6–1, 6–2, 6–4
1878	P. Frank Hadow	Spencer W. Gore	7–5, 6–1, 9–7
1879	John T. Hartley	V. St Leger Gould	6–2, 6–4, 6–2
1880	John T. Hartley	Herbert F. Lawford	6–0, 6–2, 2–6, 6–3
1881	William Renshaw	John T. Hartley	6–0, 6–2, 6–1
1882	William Renshaw	Ernest Renshaw	6–1, 2–6, 4–6, 6–2, 6–2
1883	William Renshaw	Ernest Renshaw	2–6, 6–3, 6–3, 4–6, 6–3
1884	William Renshaw	Herbert F. Lawford	6–0, 6–4, 9–7
1885	William Renshaw	Herbert F. Lawford	7–5, 6–2, 4–6, 7–5
1886	William Renshaw	Herbert F. Lawford	6–0, 5–7, 6–3, 6–4
1887	Herbert F. Lawford	Ernest Renshaw	1–6, 6–3, 3–6, 6–4, 6–4
1888	Ernest Renshaw	Herbert F. Lawford	6–3, 7–5, 6–0
1889	William Renshaw	Ernest Renshaw	6–4, 6–1, 3–6, 6–0
1890	William J. Hamilton	William Renshaw	6–8, 6–2, 3–6, 6–1, 6–1
1891	Wilfred Baddeley	Joshua Pim	6–4, 1–6, 7–5, 6–0
1892	Wilfred Baddeley	Joshua Pim	4–6, 6–3, 6–3, 6–2
1893	Joshua Pim	Wilfred Baddeley	3–6, 6–1, 6–3, 6–2
1894	Joshua Pim	Wilfred Baddeley	10–8, 6–2, 8–6
1895	Wilfred Baddeley	Wilberforce V. Eaves	4–6, 2–6, 8–6, 6–2, 6–3
1896	Harold S. Mahoney	Wilfred Baddeley	6–2, 6–8, 5–7, 8–6, 6–3
1897	Reggie F. Doherty	Harold S. Mahoney	6–4, 6–4, 6–3
1898	Reggie F. Doherty	H. Laurie Doherty	6–3, 6–3, 2–6, 5–7, 6–1
1899	Reggie F. Doherty	Arthur W. Gore	1–6, 4–6, 6–2, 6–3, 6–3
1900	Reggie F. Doherty	Sidney H. Smith	6–8, 6–3, 6–1, 6–2
1901	Arthur W. Gore	Reggie F. Doherty	4–6, 7–5, 6–4, 6–4
1902	H. Laurie Doherty	Arthur W. Gore	6–4, 6–3, 3–6, 6–0
1903	H. Laurie Doherty	Frank L. Riseley	7–5, 6–3, 6–0
1904	H. Laurie Doherty	Frank L. Riseley	6–1, 7–5, 8–6
1905	H. Laurie Doherty	Norman E. Brookes	8–6, 6–2, 6–4
1906	H. Laurie Doherty	Frank L. Riseley	6–4, 4–6, 6–2, 6–3
1907	Norman E. Brookes	Arthur W. Gore	6–4, 6–2, 6–2
1908	Arthur W. Gore	H. Roper Barrett	6–3, 6–2, 4–6, 3–6, 6–4
1909	Arthur W. Gore	M. J. G. Ritchie	6–8, 1–6, 6–2, 6–2, 6–2
1910	Anthony F. Wilding	Arthur W. Gore	6–4, 7–5, 4–6, 6–2
1911	Anthony F. Wilding	H. Roper Barrett	6–4, 4–6, 2–6, 6–2, ret.
1912	Anthony F. Wilding	Arthur W. Gore	6–4, 6–4, 4–6, 6–4
1913	Anthony F. Wilding	Maurice E. McLoughlin	8–6, 6–3, 10–8
1914	Norman E. Brookes	Anthony F. Wilding	6–4, 6–4, 7–5
1915–18	No tournament		
1919	Gerald L. Patterson	Norman E. Brookes	6–3, 7–5, 6–2
1920	Bill Tilden	Gerald L. Patterson	2–6, 6–3, 6–2, 6–4
1921	Bill Tilden	Brian I. C. Norton	4–6, 2–6, 6–1, 6–0, 7–5
1922	Gerald L. Patterson	Randolph Lycett	6–3, 6–4, 6–2
1923	Bill Johnston	Francis T. Hunter	6–0, 6–3, 6–1
1924	Jean Borotra	Rene Lacoste	6–1, 3–6, 6–1, 3–6, 6–4
1925	Rene Lacoste	Jean Borotra	6–3, 6–3, 4–6, 8–6
1926	Jean Borotra	Howard Kinsey	8–6, 6–1, 6–3
1927	Henri Cochet	Jean Borotra	4–6, 4–6, 6–3, 6–4, 7–5
1928	Rene Lacoste	Henri Cochet	6–1, 4–6, 6–4, 6–2
1929	Henri Cochet	Jean Borotra	6–4, 6–3, 6–4
1930	Bill Tilden	Wilmer Allison	6–3, 9–7, 6–4
1931	Sidney B. Wood Jr	Francis X. Shields	walkover
1932	Ellsworth Vines	Henry Austin	6–4, 6–2, 6–0
1933	Jack Crawford	Ellsworth Vines	4–6, 11–9, 6–2, 2–6, 6–4
1934	Fred Perry	Jack Crawford	6–3, 6–0, 7–5
1935	Fred Perry	Gottfried von Cramm	6–2, 6–4, 6–4
1936	Fred Perry	Gottfried von Cramm	6–1, 6–1, 6–0
1937	Don Budge	Gottfried von Cramm	6–3, 6–4, 6–2
1938	Don Budge	Henry Austin	6–1, 6–0, 6–3
1939	Bobby Riggs	Elwood Cooke	2–6, 8–6, 3–6, 6–3, 6–2
1940–45	No tournament		
1946	Yvon Petra	Geoff E. Brown	6–2, 6–4, 6–7 (7–9), 5–7, 6–4
1947	Jack Kramer	Tom P. Brown	6–1, 6–3, 6–2
1948	Bob Falkenburg	John Bromwich	7–5, 0–6, 6–2, 3–6, 7–5
1949	Ted Schroeder	Jaroslav Drobny	3–6, 6–0, 6–3, 4–6, 6–4

Note: Prior to 1922 the tournament was run on a challenge-round system. The previous year's winner "stood out" of an All Comers event, which produced a challenger to play him for the title.

MEN *(Cont.)*

Wimbledon Championships *(Cont.)*

Year	Winner	Finalist	Score
1950	Budge Patty	Frank Sedgman	6–1, 6–7 (8–10), 6–2, 6–3
1951	Dick Savitt	Ken McGregor	6–4, 6–4, 6–4
1952	Frank Sedgman	Jaroslav Drobny	4–6, 6–3, 6–2, 6–3
1953	Vic Seixas	Kurt Nielsen	9–7, 6–3, 6–4
1954	Jaroslav Drobny	Ken Rosewall	13–11, 4–6, 6–2, 9–7
1955	Tony Trabert	Kurt Nielsen	6–3, 7–5, 6–1
1956	Lew Hoad	Ken Rosewall	6–2, 4–6, 7–5, 6–4
1957	Lew Hoad	Ashley Cooper	6–2, 6–1, 6–2
1958	Ashley Cooper	Neale Fraser	3–6, 6–3, 6–4, 13–11
1959	Alex Olmedo	Rod Laver	6–4, 6–3, 6–4
1960	Neale Fraser	Rod Laver	6–4, 3–6, 9–7, 7–5
1961	Rod Laver	Chuck McKinley	6–3, 6–1, 6–4
1962	Rod Laver	Martin Mulligan	6–2, 6–2, 6–1
1963	Chuck McKinley	Fred Stolle	9–7, 6–1, 6–4
1964	Roy Emerson	Fred Stolle	6–4, 12–10, 4–6, 6–3
1965	Roy Emerson	Fred Stolle	6–2, 6–4, 6–4
1966	Manuel Santana	Dennis Ralston	6–4, 11–9, 6–4
1967	John Newcombe	Wilhelm Bungert	6–3, 6–1, 6–1
1968*	Rod Laver	Tony Roche	6–3, 6–4, 6–2
1969	Rod Laver	John Newcombe	6–4, 5–7, 6–4, 6–4
1970	John Newcombe	Ken Rosewall	5–7, 6–3, 6–2, 3–6, 6–1
1971	John Newcombe	Stan Smith	6–3, 5–7, 2–6, 6–4, 6–4
1972	Stan Smith	Ilie Nastase	4–6, 6–3, 6–3, 4–6, 7–5
1973	Jan Kodes	Alex Metreveli	6–1, 9–8, 6–3
1974	Jimmy Connors	Ken Rosewall	6–1, 6–1, 6–4
1975	Arthur Ashe	Jimmy Connors	6–1, 6–1, 5–7, 6–4
1976	Bjorn Borg	Ilie Nastase	6–4, 6–2, 9–7
1977	Bjorn Borg	Jimmy Connors	3–6, 6–2, 6–1, 5–7, 6–4
1978	Bjorn Borg	Jimmy Connors	6–2, 6–2, 6–3
1979	Bjorn Borg	Roscoe Tanner	6–7, 6–1, 3–6, 6–3, 6–4
1980	Bjorn Borg	John McEnroe	1–6, 7–5, 6–3, 6–7, 8–6
1981	John McEnroe	Bjorn Borg	4–6, 7–6, 7–6, 6–4
1982	Jimmy Connors	John McEnroe	3–6, 6–3, 6–7, 7–6, 6–4
1983	John McEnroe	Chris Lewis	6–2, 6–2, 6–2
1984	John McEnroe	Jimmy Connors	6–1, 6–1, 6–2
1985	Boris Becker	Kevin Curren	6–3, 6–7, 7–6, 6–4
1986	Boris Becker	Ivan Lendl	6–4, 6–3, 7–5
1987	Pat Cash	Ivan Lendl	7–6, 6–2, 7–5
1988	Stefan Edberg	Boris Becker	4–6, 7–6, 6–4, 6–2
1989	Boris Becker	Stefan Edberg	6–0, 7–6, 6–4
1990	Stefan Edberg	Boris Becker	6–2, 6–2, 3–6, 3–6, 6–4
1991	Michael Stich	Boris Becker	6–4, 7–6, 6–4
1992	Andre Agassi	Goran Ivanisevic	6–7, 6–4, 6–4, 1–6, 6–4
1993	Pete Sampras	Jim Courier	7–6, 7–6, 3–6, 6–3
1994	Pete Sampras	Goran Ivanisevic	7–6, 7–6, 6–0
1995	Pete Sampras	Boris Becker	6–7, 6–2, 6–4, 6–2
1996	Richard Krajicek	MaliVai Washington	6–3, 6–4, 6–3
1997	Pete Sampras	Cedric Pioline	6–4, 6–2, 6–4
1998	Pete Sampras	Goran Ivanisevic	6–7, 7–6, 6–4, 3–6, 6–2
1999	Pete Sampras	Andre Agassi	6–3, 6–4, 7–5
2000	Pete Sampras	Patrick Rafter	6–7, 7–6, 6–4, 6–2
2001	Goran Ivanisevic	Patrick Rafter	6–3, 3–6, 6–3, 2–6, 9–7
2002	Lleyton Hewitt	David Nalbandian	6–1, 6–3, 6–2
2003	Roger Federer	Mark Philippoussis	7–6 (7-5), 6–2, 7–6 (7-3)
2004	Roger Federer	Andy Roddick	4–6, 7–5, 7–6 (7-3), 6–4
2005	Roger Federer	Andy Roddick	6–2, 7–6 (7-2), 6–4
2006	Roger Federer	Rafael Nadal	6–0, 7–6, (7-5), 6–7 (2-7), 6–3
2007	Roger Federer	Rafael Nadal	7–6 (9-7), 4–6, 7–6 (7-3), 2–6, 6–2
2008	Rafael Nadal	Roger Federer	6–4, 6–4, 6–7 (5-7), 6–7 (8-10) 9–7
2009	Roger Federer	Andy Roddick	5–7, 7–6 (8-6), 7–6 (7-5), 3–6, 16–14
2010	Rafael Nadal	Tomas Berdych	6–3, 7–5, 6–4

*Became Open (amateur and professional) in 1968, but restricted to only contract professionals in 1972.

MEN (Cont.)
United States Championships

Year	Winner	Finalist	Score
1881	Richard D. Sears	W.E. Glyn	6–0, 6–3, 6–2
1882	Richard D. Sears	C.M. Clark	6–1, 6–4, 6–0
1883	Richard D. Sears	James Dwight	6–2, 6–0, 9–7
1884	Richard D. Sears	H.A. Taylor	6–0, 1–6, 6–0, 6–2
1885	Richard D. Sears	G.M. Brinley	6–3, 4–6, 6–0, 6–3
1886	Richard D. Sears	R.L. Beeckman	4–6, 6–1, 6–3, 6–4
1887	Richard D. Sears	H.W. Slocum Jr	6–1, 6–3, 6–2
1888†	H. W. Slocum Jr	H.A. Taylor	6–4, 6–1, 6–0
1889	H. W. Slocum Jr	Q.A. Shaw	6–3, 6–1, 4–6, 6–2
1890	Oliver S. Campbell	H.W. Slocum Jr	6–2, 4–6, 6–3, 6–1
1891	Oliver S. Campbell	Clarence Hobart	2–6, 7–5, 7–9, 6–1, 6–2
1892	Oliver S. Campbell	Frederick H. Hovey	7–5, 3–6, 6–3, 7–5
1893†	Robert D. Wrenn	Frederick H. Hovey	6–4, 3–6, 6–4, 6–4
1894	Robert D. Wrenn	M.F. Goodbody	6–8, 6–1, 6–4, 6–4
1895	Frederick H. Hovey	Robert D. Wrenn	6–3, 6–2, 6–4
1896	Robert D. Wrenn	Frederick H. Hovey	7–5, 3–6, 6–0, 1–6, 6–1
1897	Robert D. Wrenn	Wilberforce V. Eaves	4–6, 8–6, 6–3, 2–6, 6–2
1898†	Malcolm D. Whitman	Dwight F. Davis	3–6, 6–2, 6–2, 6–1
1899	Malcolm D. Whitman	J. Parmly Paret	6–1, 6–2, 3–6, 7–5
1900	Malcolm D. Whitman	William A. Larned	6–4, 1–6, 6–2, 6–2
1901†	William A. Larned	Beals C. Wright	6–2, 6–8, 6–4, 6–4
1902	William A. Larned	Reggie F. Doherty	4–6, 6–2, 6–4, 8–6
1903	H. Laurie Doherty	William A. Larned	6–0, 6–3, 10–8
1904†	Holcombe Ward	William J. Clothier	10–8, 6–4, 9–7
1905	Beals C. Wright	Holcombe Ward	6–2, 6–1, 11–9
1906	William J. Clothier	Beals C. Wright	6–3, 6–0, 6–4
1907†	William A. Larned	Robert LeRoy	6–2, 6–2, 6–4
1908	William A. Larned	Beals C. Wright	6–1, 6–2, 8–6
1909	William A. Larned	William J. Clothier	6–1, 6–2, 5–7, 1–6, 6–1
1910	William A. Larned	Thomas C. Bundy	6–1, 5–7, 6–0, 6–8, 6–1
1911	William A. Larned	Maurice E. McLoughlin	6–4, 6–4, 6–2
1912‡	Maurice E. McLoughlin	Bill Johnson	3–6, 2–6, 6–2, 6–4, 6–2
1913	Maurice E. McLoughlin	Richard N. Williams	6–4, 5–7, 6–3, 6–1
1914	Richard N. Williams	Maurice E. McLoughlin	6–3, 8–6, 10–8
1915	Bill Johnston	Maurice E. McLoughlin	1–6, 6–0, 7–5, 10–8
1916	Richard N. Williams	Bill Johnston	4–6, 6–4, 0–6, 6–2, 6–4
1917#	R.L. Murray	N. W. Niles	5–7, 8–6, 6–3, 6–3
1918	R.L. Murray	Bill Tilden	6–3, 6–1, 7–5
1919	Bill Johnston	Bill Tilden	6–4, 6–4, 6–3
1920	Bill Tilden	Bill Johnston	6–1, 1–6, 7–5, 5–7, 6–3
1921	Bill Tilden	Wallace F. Johnson	6–1, 6–3, 6–1
1922	Bill Tilden	Bill Johnston	4–6, 3–6, 6–2, 6–3, 6–4
1923	Bill Tilden	Bill Johnston	6–4, 6–1, 6–4
1924	Bill Tilden	Bill Johnston	6–1, 9–7, 6–2
1925	Bill Tilden	Bill Johnston	4–6, 11–9, 6–3, 4–6, 6–3
1926	Rene Lacoste	Jean Borotra	6–4, 6–0, 6–4
1927	Rene Lacoste	Bill Tilden	11–9, 6–3, 11–9
1928	Henri Cochet	Francis T. Hunter	4–6, 6–4, 3–6, 7–5, 6–3
1929	Bill Tilden	Francis T. Hunter	3–6, 6–3, 4–6, 6–2, 6–4
1930	John H. Doeg	Francis X. Shields	10–8, 1–6, 6–4, 16–14
1931	Ellsworth Vines	George M. Lott Jr	7–9, 6–3, 9–7, 7–5
1932	Ellsworth Vines	Henri Cochet	6–4, 6–4, 6–4
1933	Fred Perry	Jack Crawford	6–3, 11–13, 4–6, 6–0, 6–1
1934	Fred Perry	Wilmer L. Allison	6–4, 6–3, 1–6, 8–6
1935	Wilmer L. Allison	Sidney B. Wood Jr	6–2, 6–2, 6–3
1936	Fred Perry	Don Budge	2–6, 6–2, 8–6, 1–6, 10–8
1937	Don Budge	Gottfried von Cramm	6–1, 7–9, 6–1, 3–6, 6–1
1938	Don Budge	Gene Mako	6–3, 6–8, 6–2, 6–1
1939	Bobby Riggs	Welby Van Horn	6–4, 6–2, 6–4
1940	Don McNeill	Bobby Riggs	4–6, 6–8, 6–3, 6–3, 7–5
1941	Bobby Riggs	Francis Kovacs II	5–7, 6–1, 6–3, 6–3
1942	Ted Schroeder	Frank Parker	8–6, 7–5, 3–6, 4–6, 6–2
1943	Joseph R. Hunt	Jack Kramer	6–3, 6–8, 10–8, 6–0
1944	Frank Parker	William F. Talbert	6–4, 3–6, 6–3, 6–3
1945	Frank Parker	William F. Talbert	14–12, 6–1, 6–2
1946	Jack Kramer	Tom P. Brown	9–7, 6–3, 6–0

†No challenge round played. ‡Challenge round abolished. #National Patriotic Tournament.

MEN (Cont.)
United States Championships (Cont.)

Year	Winner	Finalist	Score
1947	Jack Kramer	Frank Parker	4–6, 2–6, 6–1, 6–0, 6–3
1948	Pancho Gonzales	Eric W. Sturgess	6–2, 6–3, 14–12
1949	Pancho Gonzales	Ted Schroeder	16–18, 2–6, 6–1, 6–2, 6–4
1950	Arthur Larsen	Herbie Flam	6–3, 4–6, 5–7, 6–4, 6–3
1951	Frank Sedgman	Vic Seixas	6–4, 6–1, 6–1
1952	Frank Sedgman	Gardnar Mulloy	6–1, 6–2, 6–3
1953	Tony Trabert	Vic Seixas	6–3, 6–2, 6–3
1954	Vic Seixas	Rex Hartwig	3–6, 6–2, 6–4, 6–4
1955	Tony Trabert	Ken Rosewall	9–7, 6–3, 6–3
1956	Ken Rosewall	Lew Hoad	4–6, 6–2, 6–3, 6–3
1957	Mal Anderson	Ashley J. Cooper	10–8, 7–5, 6–4
1958	Ashley J. Cooper	Mal Anderson	6–2, 3–6, 4–6, 10–8, 8–6
1959	Neale Fraser	Alex Olmedo	6–3, 5–7, 6–2, 6–4
1960	Neale Fraser	Rod Laver	6–4, 6–4, 9–7
1961	Roy Emerson	Rod Laver	7–5, 6–3, 6–2
1962	Rod Laver	Roy Emerson	6–2, 6–4, 5–7, 6–4
1963	Rafael Osuna	Frank Froehling III	7–5, 6–4, 6–2
1964	Roy Emerson	Fred Stolle	6–4, 6–2, 6–4
1965	Manuel Santana	Cliff Drysdale	6–2, 7–9, 7–5, 6–1
1966	Fred Stolle	John Newcombe	4–6, 12–10, 6–3, 6–4
1967	John Newcombe	Clark Graebner	6–4, 6–4, 8–6
1968*	Arthur Ashe	Tom Okker	14–12, 5–7, 6–3, 3–6, 6–3
1968**	Arthur Ashe	Bob Lutz	4–6, 6–3, 8–10, 6–0, 6–4
1969	Rod Laver	Tony Roche	7–9, 6–1, 6–3, 6–2
1969**	Stan Smith	Bob Lutz	9–7, 6–3, 6–1
1970	Ken Rosewall	Tony Roche	2–6, 6–4, 7–6, 6–3
1971	Stan Smith	Jan Kodes	3–6, 6–3, 6–2, 7–6
1972	Ilie Nastase	Arthur Ashe	3–6, 6–3, 6–7, 6–4, 6–3
1973	John Newcombe	Jan Kodes	6–4, 1–6, 4–6, 6–2, 6–3
1974	Jimmy Connors	Ken Rosewall	6–1, 6–0, 6–1
1975	Manuel Orantes	Jimmy Connors	6–4, 6–3, 6–3
1976	Jimmy Connors	Bjorn Borg	6–4, 3–6, 7–6, 6–4
1977	Guillermo Vilas	Jimmy Connors	2–6, 6–3, 7–6, 6–0
1978	Jimmy Connors	Bjorn Borg	6–4, 6–2, 6–2
1979	John McEnroe	Vitas Gerulaitis	7–5, 6–3, 6–3
1980	John McEnroe	Bjorn Borg	7–6, 6–1, 6–7, 5–7, 6–4
1981	John McEnroe	Bjorn Borg	4–6, 6–2, 6–4, 6–3
1982	Jimmy Connors	Ivan Lendl	6–3, 6–2, 4–6, 6–4
1983	Jimmy Connors	Ivan Lendl	6–3, 6–7, 7–5, 6–0
1984	John McEnroe	Ivan Lendl	6–3, 6–4, 6–1
1985	Ivan Lendl	John McEnroe	7–6, 6–3, 6–4
1986	Ivan Lendl	Miloslav Mecir	6–4, 6–2, 6–0
1987	Ivan Lendl	Mats Wilander	6–7, 6–0, 7–6, 6–4
1988	Mats Wilander	Ivan Lendl	6–4, 4–6, 6–3, 5–7, 6–4
1989	Boris Becker	Ivan Lendl	7–6, 1–6, 6–3, 7–6
1990	Pete Sampras	Andre Agassi	6–4, 6–3, 6–2
1991	Stefan Edberg	Jim Courier	6–2, 6–4, 6–0
1992	Stefan Edberg	Pete Sampras	3–6, 6–4, 7–6, 6–2
1993	Pete Sampras	Cedric Pioline	6–4, 6–4, 6–3
1994	Andre Agassi	Michael Stich	6–1, 7–6, 7–5
1995	Pete Sampras	Andre Agassi	6–4, 6–3, 4–6, 7–5
1996	Pete Sampras	Michael Chang	6–1, 6–4, 7–6
1997	Patrick Rafter	Greg Rusedski	6–3, 6–2, 4–6, 7–5
1998	Patrick Rafter	Mark Philippoussis	6–3, 3–6, 6–2, 6–0
1999	Andre Agassi	Todd Martin	6–4, 6–7, 6–7, 6–3, 6–2
2000	Marat Safin	Pete Sampras	6–4, 6–3, 6–3
2001	Lleyton Hewitt	Pete Sampras	7–6, 6–1, 6–1
2002	Pete Sampras	Andre Agassi	6–3, 6–4, 5–7, 6–4
2003	Andy Roddick	Juan Carlos Ferrero	6–3, 7–6 (7-2), 6–3
2004	Roger Federer	Lleyton Hewitt	6–0, 7–6 (7-3), 6–0
2005	Roger Federer	Andre Agassi	6–3, 2–6, 7–6 (7-1), 6–1
2006	Roger Federer	Andy Roddick	6–2, 4–6, 7–5, 6–1
2007	Roger Federer	Novak Djokovic	7–6 (7-4), 7–6 (7-2), 6–4
2008	Roger Federer	Andy Murray	6–2, 7–5, 6–2
2009	Juan Martin del Potro	Roger Federer	3–6, 7–6 (7-5), 4–6, 7–6 (7-4), 6–2
2010	Rafael Nadal	Novak Djokovic	6–4, 5–7, 6–4, 6–2

*Became Open (amateur and professional) in 1968. **Amateur event held.

WOMEN
Australian Open Championships

Year	Winner	Finalist	Score
1922	Margaret Molesworth	Esna Boyd	6–3, 10–8
1923	Margaret Molesworth	Esna Boyd	6–1, 7–5
1924	Sylvia Lance	Esna Boyd	6–3, 3–6, 6–4
1925	Daphne Akhurst	Esna Boyd	1–6, 8–6, 6–4
1926	Daphne Akhurst	Esna Boyd	6–1, 6–3
1927	Esna Boyd	Sylvia Harper	5–7, 6–1, 6–2
1928	Daphne Akhurst	Esna Boyd	7–5, 6–2
1929	Daphne Akhurst	Louise Bickerton	6–1, 5–7, 6–2
1930	Daphne Akhurst	Sylvia Harper	10–8, 2–6, 7–5
1931	Coral Buttsworth	Margorie Crawford	1–6, 6–3, 6–4
1932	Coral Buttsworth	Kathrine Le Messurier	9–7, 6–4
1933	Joan Hartigan	Coral Buttsworth	6–4, 6–3
1934	Joan Hartigan	Margaret Molesworth	6–1, 6–4
1935	Dorothy Round	Nancye Wynne Bolton	1–6, 6–1, 6–3
1936	Joan Hartigan	Nancye Wynne Bolton	6–4, 6–4
1937	Nancye Wynne Bolton	Emily Westacott	6–3, 5–7, 6–4
1938	Dorothy Bundy	D. Stevenson	6–3, 6–2
1939	Emily Westacott	Nell Hopman	6–1, 6–2
1940	Nancye Wynne Bolton	Thelma Coyne	5–7, 6–4, 6–0
1941–45	No tournament		
1946	Nancye Wynne Bolton	Joyce Fitch	6–4, 6–4
1947	Nancye Wynne Bolton	Nell Hopman	6–3, 6–2
1948	Nancye Wynne Bolton	Marie Toomey	6–3, 6–1
1949	Doris Hart	Nancye Wynne Bolton	6–3, 6–4
1950	Louise Brough	Doris Hart	6–4, 3–6, 6–4
1951	Nancye Wynne Bolton	Thelma Long	6–1, 7–5
1952	Thelma Long	H. Angwin	6–2, 6–3
1953	Maureen Connolly	Julia Sampson	6–3, 6–2
1954	Thelma Long	J. Staley	6–3, 6–4
1955	Beryl Penrose	Thelma Long	6–4, 6–3
1956	Mary Carter	Thelma Long	3–6, 6–2, 9–7
1957	Shirley Fry	Althea Gibson	6–3, 6–4
1958	Angela Mortimer	Lorraine Coghlan	6–3, 6–4
1959	Mary Carter-Reitano	Renee Schuurman	6–2, 6–3
1960	Margaret Smith	Jan Lehane	7–5, 6–2
1961	Margaret Smith	Jan Lehane	6–1, 6–4
1962	Margaret Smith	Jan Lehane	6–0, 6–2
1963	Margaret Smith	Jan Lehane	6–2, 6–2
1964	Margaret Smith	Lesley Turner	6–3, 6–2
1965	Margaret Smith	Maria Bueno	5–7, 6–4, 5–2, ret.
1966	Margaret Smith	Nancy Richey	Default
1967	Nancy Richey	Lesley Turner	6–1, 6–4
1968	Billie Jean King	Margaret Smith	6–1, 6–2
1969*	Margaret Smith Court	Billie Jean King	6–4, 6–1
1970	Margaret Smith Court	Kerry Melville Reid	6–3, 6–1
1971	Margaret Smith Court	Evonne Goolagong	2–6, 7–6, 7–5
1972	Virginia Wade	Evonne Goolagong	6–4, 6–4
1973	Margaret Smith Court	Evonne Goolagong	6–4, 7–5
1974	Evonne Goolagong	Chris Evert	7–6, 4–6, 6–0
1975	Evonne Goolagong	Martina Navratilova	6–3, 6–2
1976	Evonne Goolagong Cawley	Renata Tomanova	6–2, 6–2
1977 (Jan)	Kerry Melville Reid	Dianne Balestrat	7–5, 6–2
1977 (Dec)	Evonne Goolagong Cawley	Helen Gourlay	6–3, 6–0
1978	Chris O'Neil	Betsy Nagelsen	6–3, 7–6
1979	Barbara Jordan	Sharon Walsh	6–3, 6–3
1980	Hana Mandlikova	Wendy Turnbull	6–0, 7–5
1981	Martina Navratilova	Chris Evert Lloyd	6–7, 6–4, 7–5
1982	Chris Evert Lloyd	Martina Navratilova	6–3, 2–6, 6–3
1983	Martina Navratilova	Kathy Jordan	6–2, 7–6
1984	Chris Evert Lloyd	Helena Sukova	6–7, 6–1, 6–3
1985 (Dec)	Martina Navratilova	Chris Evert Lloyd	6–2, 4–6, 6–2
1987 (Jan)	Hana Mandlikova	Martina Navratilova	7–5, 7–6
1988	Steffi Graf	Chris Evert	6–1, 7–6
1989	Steffi Graf	Helena Sukova	6–4, 6–4
1990	Steffi Graf	Mary Joe Fernandez	6–3, 6–4
1991	Monica Seles	Jana Novotna	5–7, 6–3, 6–1

*Became Open (amateur and professional) in 1969.

WOMEN *(Cont.)*
Australian Championships *(Cont.)*

Year	Winner	Finalist	Score
1992	Monica Seles	Mary Joe Fernandez	6–2, 6–3
1993	Monica Seles	Steffi Graf	4–6, 6–3, 6–2
1994	Steffi Graf	Arantxa Sánchez Vicario	6–0, 6–2
1995	Mary Pierce	Arantxa Sánchez Vicario	6–3, 6–2
1996	Monica Seles	Anke Huber	6–4, 6–1
1997	Martina Hingis	Mary Pierce	6–2, 6–2
1998	Martina Hingis	Conchita Martinez	6–3, 6–3
1999	Martina Hingis	Amelie Mauresmo	6–2, 6–3
2000	Lindsay Davenport	Martina Hingis	6–1, 7–5
2001	Jennifer Capriati	Martina Hingis	6–4, 6–3
2002	Jennifer Capriati	Martina Hingis	4–6, 7–6 (9–7), 6–2
2003	Serena Williams	Venus Williams	7–6 (7-4), 3–6, 6–4
2004	Justine Henin-Hardenne	Kim Clijsters	6–3, 4–6, 6–3
2005	Serena Williams	Lindsay Davenport	2–6, 6–3, 6–0
2006	Amelie Mauresmo	Justine Henin-Hardenne	6–1, 2–0, ret.
2007	Serena Williams	Maria Sharapova	6–1, 6–2
2008	Maria Sharapova	Ana Ivanovic	7–5, 6–3
2009	Serena Williams	Dinara Safina	6–0, 6–3
2010	Serena Williams	Justine Henin	6–4, 3–6, 6–2

French Championships

Year	Winner	Finalist	Score
1925†	Suzanne Lenglen	Kathleen McKane	6–1, 6–2
1926	Suzanne Lenglen	Mary K. Browne	6–1, 6–0
1927	Kea Bouman	Irene Peacock	6–2, 6–4
1928	Helen Wills	Eileen Bennett	6–1, 6–2
1929	Helen Wills	Simone Mathieu	6–3, 6–4
1930	Helen Wills Moody	Helen Jacobs	6–2, 6–1
1931	Cilly Aussem	Betty Nuthall	8–6, 6–1
1932	Helen Wills Moody	Simone Mathieu	7–5, 6–1
1933	Margaret Scriven	Simone Mathieu	6–2, 4–6, 6–4
1934	Margaret Scriven	Helen Jacobs	7–5, 4–6, 6–1
1935	Hilde Sperling	Simone Mathieu	6–2, 6–1
1936	Hilde Sperling	Simone Mathieu	6–3, 6–4
1937	Hilde Sperling	Simone·Mathieu	6–2, 6–4
1938	Simone Mathieu	Nelly Landry	6–0, 6–3
1939	Simone Mathieu	Jadwiga Jedrzejowska	6–3, 8–6
1940–45	No tournament		
1946	Margaret Osborne	Pauline Betz	1–6, 8–6, 7–5
1947	Patricia Todd	Doris Hart	6–3, 3–6, 6–4
1948	Nelly Landry	Shirley Fry	6–2, 0–6, 6–0
1949	Margaret Osborne duPont	Nelly Adamson	7–5, 6–2
1950	Doris Hart	Patricia Todd	6–4, 4–6, 6–2
1951	Shirley Fry	Doris Hart	6–3, 3–6, 6–3
1952	Doris Hart	Shirley Fry	6–4, 6–4
1953	Maureen Connolly	Doris Hart	6–2, 6–4
1954	Maureen Connolly	Ginette Bucaille	6–4, 6–1
1955	Angela Mortimer	Dorothy Knode	2–6, 7–5, 10–8
1956	Althea Gibson	Angela Mortimer	6–0, 12–10
1957	Shirley Bloomer	Dorothy Knode	6–1, 6–3
1958	Zsuzsi Kormoczi	Shirley Bloomer	6–4, 1–6, 6–2
1959	Christine Truman	Zsuzsi Kormoczi	6–4, 7–5
1960	Darlene Hard	Yola Ramirez	6–3, 6–4
1961	Ann Haydon	Yola Ramirez	6–2, 6–1
1962	Margaret Smith	Lesley Turner	6–3, 3–6, 7–5
1963	Lesley Turner	Ann Haydon Jones	2–6, 6–3, 7–5
1964	Margaret Smith	Maria Bueno	5–7, 6–1, 6–2
1965	Lesley Turner	Margaret Smith	6–3, 6–4
1966	Ann Jones	Nancy Richey	6–3, 6–1
1967	Francoise Durr	Lesley Turner	4–6, 6–3, 6–4
1968*	Nancy Richey	Ann Jones	5–7, 6–4, 6–1

†1925 was the first year that entries were accepted from all countries. *Became Open (amateur and professional) in 1968, but restricted to only contract professionals in1972.

WOMEN *(Cont.)*
French Championships *(Cont.)*

Year	Winner	Finalist	Score
1969	Margaret Smith Court	Ann Jones	6–1, 4–6, 6–3
1970	Margaret Smith Court	Helga Niessen	6–2, 6–4
1971	Evonne Goolagong	Helen Gourlay	6–3, 7–5
1972	Billie Jean King	Evonne Goolagong	6–3, 6–3
1973	Margaret Smith Court	Chris Evert	6–7, 7–6, 6–4
1974	Chris Evert	Olga Morozova	6–1, 6–2
1975	Chris Evert	Martina Navratilova	2–6, 6–2, 6–1
1976	Sue Barker	Renata Tomanova	6–2, 0–6, 6–2
1977	Mima Jausovec	Florenza Mihai	6–2, 6–7, 6–1
1978	Virginia Ruzici	Mima Jausovec	6–2, 6–2
1979	Chris Evert Lloyd	Wendy Turnbull	6–2, 6–0
1980	Chris Evert Lloyd	Virginia Ruzici	6–0, 6–3
1981	Hana Mandlikova	Sylvia Hanika	6–2, 6–4
1982	Martina Navratilova	Andrea Jaeger	7–6, 6–1
1983	Chris Evert Lloyd	Mima Jausovec	6–1, 6–2
1984	Martina Navratilova	Chris Evert Lloyd	6–3, 6–1
1985	Chris Evert Lloyd	Martina Navratilova	6–3, 6–7, 7–5
1986	Chris Evert Lloyd	Martina Navratilova	2–6, 6–3, 6–3
1987	Steffi Graf	Martina Navratilova	6–4, 4–6, 8–6
1988	Steffi Graf	Natalia Zvereva	6–0, 6–0
1989	Arantxa Sánchez Vicario	Steffi Graf	7–6, 3–6, 7–5
1990	Monica Seles	Steffi Graf	7–6, 6–4
1991	Monica Seles	Arantxa Sánchez Vicario	6–3, 6–4
1992	Monica Seles	Steffi Graf	6–2, 3–6, 10–8
1993	Steffi Graf	Mary Joe Fernàndez	4–6, 6–2, 6–4
1994	Arantxa Sánchez Vicario	Mary Pierce	6–4, 6–4
1995	Steffi Graf	Arantxa Sánchez Vicario	7–5, 4–6, 6–0
1996	Steffi Graf	Arantxa Sánchez Vicario	6–3, 6–7 (4–7), 10–8
1997	Iva Majoli	Martina Hingis	6–4, 6–2
1998	Arantxa Sánchez Vicario	Monica Seles	7–6 (7–5), 0–6, 6–2
1999	Steffi Graf	Martina Hingis	4–6, 7–5, 6–2
2000	Mary Pierce	Conchita Martinez	6–2, 7–5
2001	Jennifer Capriati	Kim Clijsters	1–6, 6–4, 12–10
2002	Serena Williams	Venus Williams	7–5, 6–3
2003	Justine Henin-Hardenne	Kim Clijsters	6–0, 6–4
2004	Anastasia Myskina	Elena Dementieva	6–1, 6–2
2005	Justine Henin-Hardenne	Mary Pierce	6–1, 6–1
2006	Justine Henin-Hardenne	Svetlana Kuznetsova	6–4, 6–4
2007	Justine Henin	Ana Ivanovic	6–1, 6–2
2008	Ana Ivanovic	Dinara Safina	6–4, 6–3
2009	Svetlana Kuznetsova	Dinara Safina	6–4, 6–2
2010	Francesca Schiavone	Samantha Stosur	6–4, 7–6 (7–2)

Wimbledon Championships

Year	Winner	Finalist	Score
1884	Maud Watson	Lilian Watson	6–8, 6–3, 6–3
1885	Maud Watson	Blanche Bingley	6–1, 7–5
1886	Blanche Bingley	Maud Watson	6–3, 6–3
1887	Charlotte Dod	Blanche Bingley	6–2, 6–0
1888	Charlotte Dod	Blanche Bingley Hillyard	6–3, 6–3
1889	Blanche Bingley Hillyard	n/a	n/a
1890	Lena Rice	n/a	n/a
1891	Charlotte Dod	n/a	n/a
1892	Charlotte Dod	Blanche Bingley Hillyard	6–1, 6–1
1893	Charlotte Dod	Blanche Bingley Hillyard	6–8, 6–1, 6–4
1894	Blanche Bingley Hillyard	n/a	n/a
1895	Charlotte Cooper	n/a	
1896	Charlotte Cooper	Mrs. W. H. Pickering	6–2, 6–3
1897	Blanche Bingley Hillyard	Charlotte Cooper	5–7, 7–5, 6–2
1898	Charlotte Cooper	n/a	n/a
1899	Blanche Bingley Hillyard	Charlotte Cooper	6–2, 6–3
1900	Blanche Bingley Hillyard	Charlotte Cooper	4–6, 6–4, 6–4
1901	Charlotte Cooper Sterry	Blanche Bingley Hillyard	6–2, 6–2
1902	Muriel Robb	Charlotte Cooper Sterry	7–5, 6–1
1903	Dorothea Douglass	n/a	n/a
1904	Dorothea Douglass	Charlotte Cooper Sterry	6–0, 6–3

WOMEN *(Cont.)*
Wimbledon Championships *(Cont.)*

Year	Winner	Finalist	Score
1905	May Sutton	Dorothea Douglass	6–3, 6–4
1906	Dorothea Douglass	May Sutton	6–3, 9–7
1907	May Sutton	Dorothea Douglass Lambert Chambers	6–1, 6–4
1908	Charlotte Cooper Sterry	n/a	n/a
1909	Dora Boothby	n/a	n/a
1910	Dorothea Douglass Lambert Chambers	Dora Boothby	6–2, 6–2
1911	Dorothea Douglass Lambert Chambers	Dora Boothby	6–0, 6–0
1912	Ethel Larcombe	n/a	n/a
1913	Dorothea Douglass Lambert Chambers		
1914	Dorothea Douglass Lambert Chambers	Ethel Larcombe	7–5, 6–4
1915–18	No tournament		
1919	Suzanne Lenglen	Dorothea Douglass Lambert Chambers	10–8, 4–6, 9–7
1920	Suzanne Lenglen	Dorothea Douglass Lambert Chambers	6–3, 6–0
1921	Suzanne Lenglen	Elizabeth Ryan	6–2, 6–0
1922	Suzanne Lenglen	Molla Mallory	6–2, 6–0
1923	Suzanne Lenglen	Kathleen McKane	6–2, 6–2
1924	Kathleen McKane	Helen Wills	4–6, 6–4, 6–2
1925	Suzanne Lenglen	Joan Fry	6–2, 6–0
1926	Kathleen McKane Godfree	Lili de Alvarez	6–2, 4–6, 6–3
1927	Helen Wills	Lili de Alvarez	6–2, 6–4
1928	Helen Wills	Lili de Alvarez	6–2, 6–3
1929	Helen Wills	Helen Jacobs	6–1, 6–2
1930	Helen Wills Moody	Elizabeth Ryan	6–2, 6–2
1931	Cilly Aussem	Hilde Kranwinkel	7–5, 7–5
1932	Helen Wills Moody	Helen Jacobs	6–3, 6–1
1933	Helen Wills Moody	Dorothy Round	6–4, 6–8, 6–3
1934	Dorothy Round	Helen Jacobs	6–2, 5–7, 6–3
1935	Helen Wills Moody	Helen Jacobs	6–3, 3–6, 7–5
1936	Helen Jacobs	Hilde Kranwinkel Sperling	6–2, 4–6, 7–5
1937	Dorothy Round	Jadwiga Jedrzejowska	6–2, 2–6, 7–5
1938	Helen Wills Moody	Helen Jacobs	6–4, 6–0
1939	Alice Marble	Kay Stammers	6–2, 6–0
1940–45	No tournament		
1946	Pauline Betz	Louise Brough	6–2, 6–4
1947	Margaret Osborne	Doris Hart	6–2, 6–4
1948	Louise Brough	Doris Hart	6–3, 8–6
1949	Louise Brough	Margaret Osborne duPont	10–8, 1–6, 10–8
1950	Louise Brough	Margaret Osborne duPont	6–1, 3–6, 6–1
1951	Doris Hart	Shirley Fry	6–1, 6–0
1952	Maureen Connolly	Louise Brough	6–4, 6–3
1953	Maureen Connolly	Doris Hart	8–6, 7–5
1954	Maureen Connolly	Louise Brough	6–2, 7–5
1955	Louise Brough	Beverly Fleitz	7–5, 8–6
1956	Shirley Fry	Angela Buxton	6–3, 6–1
1957	Althea Gibson	Darlene Hard	6–3, 6–2
1958	Althea Gibson	Angela Mortimer	8–6, 6–2
1959	Maria Bueno	Darlene Hard	6–4, 6–3
1960	Maria Bueno	Sandra Reynolds	8–6, 6–0
1961	Angela Mortimer	Christine Truman	4–6, 6–4, 7–5
1962	Karen Hantze Susman	Vera Sukova	6–4, 6–4
1963	Margaret Smith	Billie Jean Moffitt	6–3, 6–4
1964	Maria Bueno	Margaret Smith	6–4, 7–9, 6–3
1965	Margaret Smith	Maria Bueno	6–4, 7–5
1966	Billie Jean King	Maria Bueno	6–3, 3–6, 6–1
1967	Billie Jean King	Ann Haydon Jones	6–3, 6–4
1968*	Billie Jean King	Judy Tegart	9–7, 7–5

Note: Prior to 1922 the tournament was run on a challenge-round system. The previous year's winner "stood out" of an All-Comers event, which produced a challenger to play her for the title.

*Became Open (amateur and professional) in 1968, but restricted to only contract professionals in 1972.

WOMEN (Cont.)
Wimbledon Championships (Cont.)

Year	Winner	Finalist	Score
1969	Ann Haydon Jones	Billie Jean King	3–6, 6–3, 6–2
1970	Margaret Smith Court	Billie Jean King	14–12, 11–9
1971	Evonne Goolagong	Margaret Smith Court	6–4, 6–1
1972	Billie Jean King	Evonne Goolagong	6–3, 6–3
1973	Billie Jean King	Chris Evert	6–0, 7–5
1974	Chris Evert	Olga Morozova	6–0, 6–4
1975	Billie Jean King	Evonne Goolagong Cawley	6–0, 6–1
1976	Chris Evert	Evonne Goolagong Cawley	6–3, 4–6, 8–6
1977	Virginia Wade	Betty Stove	4–6, 6–3, 6–1
1978	Martina Navratilova	Chris Evert	2–6, 6–4, 7–5
1979	Martina Navratilova	Chris Evert Lloyd	6–4, 6–4
1980	Evonne Goolagong Cawley	Chris Evert Lloyd	6–1, 7–6
1981	Chris Evert Lloyd	Hana Mandlikova	6–2, 6–2
1982	Martina Navratilova	Chris Evert Lloyd	6–1, 3–6, 6–2
1983	Martina Navratilova	Andrea Jaeger	6–0, 6–3
1984	Martina Navratilova	Chris Evert Lloyd	7–6, 6–2
1985	Martina Navratilova	Chris Evert Lloyd	4–6, 6–3, 6–2
1986	Martina Navratilova	Hana Mandlikova	7–6, 6–3
1987	Martina Navratilova	Steffi Graf	7–5, 6–3
1988	Steffi Graf	Martina Navratilova	5–7, 6–2, 6–1
1989	Steffi Graf	Martina Navratilova	6–2, 6–7, 6–1
1990	Martina Navratilova	Zina Garrison	6–4, 6–1
1991	Steffi Graf	Gabriela Sabatini	6–4, 3–6, 8–6
1992	Steffi Graf	Monica Seles	6–2, 6–1
1993	Steffi Graf	Jana Novotna	7–6, 1–6, 6–4
1994	Conchita Martinez	Martina Navratilova	6–4, 3–6, 6–3
1995	Steffi Graf	Arantxa Sánchez Vicario	4–6, 6–1, 7–5
1996	Steffi Graf	Arantxa Sánchez Vicario	6–3, 7–5
1997	Martina Hingis	Jana Novotna	2–6, 6–3, 6–3
1998	Jana Novotna	Nathalie Tauziat	6–4, 7–6
1999	Lindsay Davenport	Steffi Graf	6–4, 7–5
2000	Venus Williams	Lindsay Davenport	6–3, 7–6
2001	Venus Williams	Justine Henin	6–1, 3–6, 6–0
2002	Serena Williams	Venus Williams	7–6 (7–4), 6–3
2003	Serena Williams	Venus Williams	4–6, 6–4, 6–2
2004	Maria Sharapova	Serena Williams	6–1, 6–4
2005	Venus Williams	Lindsay Davenport	4–6, 7–6 (7–4), 9–7
2006	Amelie Mauresmo	Justine Henin-Hardenne	2–6, 6–3, 6–4
2007	Venus Williams	Marion Bartoli	6–4, 6–1
2008	Venus Williams	Serena Williams	7–5, 6–4
2009	Serena Williams	Venus Williams	7–6 (7–3), 6–2
2010	Serena Williams	Vera Zvonareva	6–3, 6–2

United States Championships

Year	Winner	Finalist	Score
1887	Ellen Hansell	Laura Knight	6–1, 6–0
1888	Bertha L. Townsend	Ellen Hansell	6–3, 6–5
1889	Bertha L. Townsend	Louise Voorhes	7–5, 6–2
1890	Ellen C. Roosevelt	Bertha L. Townsend	6–2, 6–2
1891	Mabel Cahill	Ellen C. Roosevelt	6–4, 6–1, 4–6, 6–3
1892	Mabel Cahill	Elisabeth Moore	5–7, 6–3, 6–4, 4–6, 6–2
1893	Aline Terry	Alice Schultze	6–1, 6–3
1894	Helen Hellwig	Aline Terry	7–5, 3–6, 6–0, 3–6, 6–3
1895	Juliette Atkinson	Helen Hellwig	6–4, 6–2, 6–1
1896	Elisabeth Moore	Juliette Atkinson	6–4, 4–6, 6–2, 6–2
1897	Juliette Atkinson	Elisabeth Moore	6–3, 6–3, 4–6, 3–6, 6–3
1898	Juliette Atkinson	Marion Jones	6–3, 5–7, 6–4, 2–6, 7–5
1899	Marion Jones	Maud Banks	6–1, 6–1, 7–5
1900	Myrtle McAteer	Edith Parker	6–2, 6–2, 6–0
1901	Elisabeth Moore	Myrtle McAteer	6–4, 3–6, 7–5, 2–6, 6–2
1902*	Marion Jones	Elisabeth Moore	6–1, 1–0, ret.
1903	Elisabeth Moore	Marion Jones	7–5, 8–6
1904	May Sutton	Elisabeth Moore	6–1, 6–2
1905	Elisabeth Moore	Helen Homans	6–4, 5–7, 6–1
1906	Helen Homans	Maud Barger-Wallach	6–4, 6–3

*Five-set final abolished;

WOMEN (Cont.)
United States Championships (Cont.)

Year	Winner	Finalist	Score
1907	Evelyn Sears	Carrie Neely	6–3, 6–2
1908	Maud Barger–Wallach	Evelyn Sears	6–3, 1–6, 6–3
1909	Hazel Hotchkiss	Maud Barger–Wallach	6–0, 6–1
1910	Hazel Hotchkiss	Louise Hammond	6–4, 6–2
1911	Hazel Hotchkiss	Florence Sutton	8–10, 6–1, 9–7
1912†	Mary K. Browne	Eleanora Sears	6–4, 6–2
1913	Mary K. Browne	Dorothy Green	6–2, 7–5
1914	Mary K. Browne	Marie Wagner	6–2, 1–6, 6–1
1915	Molla Bjurstedt	Hazel Hotchkiss Wightman	4–6, 6–2, 6–0
1916	Molla Bjurstedt	Louise Hammond Raymond	6–0, 6–1
1917‡	Molla Bjurstedt	Marion Vanderhoef	4–6, 6–0, 6–2
1918	Molla Bjurstedt	Eleanor Goss	6–4, 6–3
1919	Hazel Hotchkiss Wightman	Marion Zinderstein	6–1, 6–2
1920	Molla Bjurstedt Mallory	Marion Zinderstein	6–3, 6–1
1921	Molla Bjurstedt Mallory	Mary K. Browne	4–6, 6–4, 6–2
1922	Molla Bjurstedt Mallory	Helen Wills	6–3, 6–1
1923	Helen Wills	Molla Bjurstedt Mallory	6–2, 6–1
1924	Helen Wills	Molla Bjurstedt Mallory	6–1, 6–3
1925	Helen Wills	Kathleen McKane	3–6, 6–0, 6–2
1926	Molla Bjurstedt Mallory	Elizabeth Ryan	4–6, 6–4, 9–7
1927	Helen Wills	Betty Nuthall	6–1, 6–4
1928	Helen Wills	Helen Jacobs	6–2, 6–1
1929	Helen Wills	Phoebe Holcroft Watson	6–4, 6–2
1930	Betty Nuthall	Anna McCune Harper	6–1, 6–4
1931	Helen Wills Moody	Eileen Whitingstall	6–4, 6–1
1932	Helen Jacobs	Carolin Babcock	6–2, 6–2
1933	Helen Jacobs	Helen Wills Moody	8–6, 3–6, 3–0, ret.
1934	Helen Jacobs	Sarah Palfrey	6–1, 6–4
1935	Helen Jacobs	Sarah Palfrey Fabyan	6–2, 6–4
1936	Alice Marble	Helen Jacobs	4–6, 6–3, 6–2
1937	Anita Lizane	Jadwiga Jedrzejowska	6–4, 6–2
1938	Alice Marble	Nancye Wynne	6–0, 6–3
1939	Alice Marble	Helen Jacobs	6–0, 8–10, 6–4
1940	Alice Marble	Helen Jacobs	6–2, 6–3
1941	Sarah Palfrey Cooke	Pauline Betz	7–5, 6–2
1942	Pauline Betz	Louise Brough	4–6, 6–1, 6–4
1943	Pauline Betz	Louise Brough	6–3, 5–7, 6–3
1944	Pauline Betz	Margaret Osborne	6–3, 8–6
1945	Sarah Palfrey Cooke	Pauline Betz	3–6, 8–6, 6–4
1946	Pauline Betz	Patricia Canning	11–9, 6–3
1947	Louise Brough	Margaret Osborne	8–6, 4–6, 6–1
1948	Margaret Osborne duPont	Louise Brough	4–6, 6–4, 15–13
1949	Margaret Osborne duPont	Doris Hart	6–4, 6–1
1950	Margaret Osborne duPont	Doris Hart	6–4, 6–3
1951	Maureen Connolly	Shirley Fry	6–3, 1–6, 6–4
1952	Maureen Connolly	Doris Hart	6–3, 7–5
1953	Maureen Connolly	Doris Hart	6–2, 6–4
1954	Doris Hart	Louise Brough	6–8, 6–1, 8–6
1955	Doris Hart	Patricia Ward	6–4, 6–2
1956	Shirley Fry	Althea Gibson	6–3, 6–4
1957	Althea Gibson	Louise Brough	6–3, 6–2
1958	Althea Gibson	Darlene Hard	3–6, 6–1, 6–2
1959	Maria Bueno	Christine Truman	6–1, 6–4
1960	Darlene Hard	Maria Bueno	6–4, 10–12, 6–4
1961	Darlene Hard	Ann Haydon	6–3, 6–4
1962	Margaret Smith	Darlene Hard	9–7, 6–4
1963	Maria Bueno	Margaret Smith	7–5, 6–4
1964	Maria Bueno	Carole Graebner	6–1, 6–0
1965	Margaret Smith	Billie Jean Moffitt	8–6, 7–5
1966	Maria Bueno	Nancy Richey	6–3, 6–1
1967	Billie Jean King	Ann Haydon Jones	11–9, 6–4
1968**	Virginia Wade	Billie Jean King	6–4, 6–4
1968#	Margaret Smith Court	Maria Bueno	6–2, 6–2
1969	Margaret Smith Court	Nancy Richey	6–2, 6–2
1969#	Margaret Smith Court	Virginia Wade	4–6, 6–3, 6–0

†Challenge round abolished. ‡National Patriotic Tournament.
**Became Open (amateur and professional) in 1968. #Amateur event held.

WOMEN (Cont.)

United States Championships (Cont.)

Year	Winner	Finalist	Score
1970	Margaret Smith Court	Rosie Casals	6–2, 2–6; 6–1
1971	Billie Jean King	Rosie Casals	6–4, 7–6
1972	Billie Jean King	Kerry Melville	6–3, 7–5
1973	Margaret Smith Court	Evonne Goolagong	7–6, 5–7, 6–2
1974	Billie Jean King	Evonne Goolagong	3–6, 6–3, 7–5
1975	Chris Evert	Evonne Goolagong Cawley	5–7, 6–4, 6–2
1976	Chris Evert	Evonne Goolagong Cawley	6–3, 6–0
1977	Chris Evert	Wendy Turnbull	7–6, 6–2
1978	Chris Evert	Pam Shriver	7–6, 6–4
1979	Tracy Austin	Chris Evert Lloyd	6–4, 6–3
1980	Chris Evert Lloyd	Hana Mandlikova	5–7, 6–1, 6–1
1981	Tracy Austin	Martina Navratilova	1–6, 7–6, 7–6
1982	Chris Evert Lloyd	Hana Mandlikova	6–3, 6–1
1983	Martina Navratilova	Chris Evert Lloyd	6–1, 6–3
1984	Martina Navratilova	Chris Evert Lloyd	4–6, 6–4, 6–4
1985	Hana Mandlikova	Martina Navratilova	7–6, 1–6, 7–6
1986	Martina Navratilova	Helena Sukova	6–3, 6–2
1987	Martina Navratilova	Steffi Graf	7–6, 6–1
1988	Steffi Graf	Gabriela Sabatini	6–3, 3–6, 6–1
1989	Steffi Graf	Martina Navratilova	3–6, 6–4, 6–2
1990	Gabriela Sabatini	Steffi Graf	6–2, 7–6
1991	Monica Seles	Martina Navratilova	7–6, 6–1
1992	Monica Seles	Arantxa Sánchez Vicario	6–3, 6–2
1993	Steffi Graf	Helena Sukova	6–3, 6–3
1994	Arantxa Sánchez Vicario	Steffi Graf	1–6, 7–6, 6–4
1995	Steffi Graf	Monica Seles	7–6, 0–6, 6–3
1996	Steffi Graf	Monica Seles	7–5, 7–4
1997	Martina Hingis	Venus Williams	6–0, 6–4
1998	Lindsay Davenport	Martina Hingis	6–3, 7–5
1999	Serena Williams	Martina Hingis	6–3, 7–6
2000	Venus Williams	Lindsay Davenport	6–4, 7–5
2001	Venus Williams	Serena Williams	6–2, 6–4
2002	Serena Williams	Venus Williams	6–4, 6–3
2003	Justine Henin-Hardenne	Kim Clijsters	7–5, 6–1
2004	Svetlana Kuznetsova	Elena Dementieva	6–3, 7–5
2005	Kim Clijsters	Mary Pierce	6–3, 6–1
2006	Maria Sharapova	Justine Henin-Hardenne	6–4, 6–4
2007	Justine Henin	Svetlana Kuznetsova	6–1, 6–3
2008	Serena Williams	Jelena Jankovic	6–4, 7–5
2009	Kim Clijsters	Caroline Wozniacki	7–5, 6–3
2010	Kim Clijsters	Vera Zvonareva	6–2, 6–1

Single-Year Grand Slam Winners

Singles

Don Budge, 1938
Maureen Connolly, 1953
Rod Laver, 1962, 1969
Margaret Smith Court, 1970
Steffi Graf, 1988

Doubles

Frank Sedgman and Ken McGregor, 1951
Martina Navratilova and Pam Shriver, 1984
Maria Bueno and two partners, 1960
    Christine Truman (Australian),
    Darlene Hard (French, Wimbledon
    and U.S.)
Martina Hingis and two partners, 1998
    Mirjana Lucic (Australian),
    Jana Novotna (French, Wimbledon
    and U.S.)

Mixed Doubles

Margaret Smith and Ken Fletcher, 1963
Owen Davidson and two partners, 1967
    Lesley Turner (Australian),
    Billie Jean King (French, Wimbledon
    and U.S.)

Alltime Grand Slam Champions

Alltime Grand Slam Champions (Singles, Doubles, and Mixed Doubles)

MEN

Player	Aus. S-D-M	French S-D-M	Wim. S-D-M	U.S. S-D-M	Total
Roy Emerson	6-3-0	2-6-0	2-3-0	2-4-0	28
John Newcombe	2-5-0	0-3-0	3-6-0	2-3-1	25
Frank Sedgman	2-2-2	0-3-2	1-2-2	2-2-2	22
Todd Woodbridge	0-3-1	0-1-1	0-9-1	0-3-3	22
Bill Tilden	†	0-0-1	3-1-0	7-5-4	21
Rod Laver	3-4-0	2-1-1	4-1-2	2-0-0	20
John Bromwich	2-8-1	0-0-0	0-2-2	0-3-1	19
Jean Borotra	1-1-1	1-5-2	2-3-1	0-0-1	18
Fred Stolle	0-3-1	1-2-0	0-2-3	1-3-2	18
Ken Rosewall	4-3-0	2-2-0	0-2-0	2-2-1	18
Neale Fraser	0-3-1	0-3-0	1-2-0	2-3-3	18
Adrian Quist	3-10-0	0-1-0	0-2-0	0-1-0	17
John McEnroe	0-0-0	0-0-1	3-4-0	4-5-0	17
Jack Crawford	4-4-3	1-1-1	1-1-1	0-0-0	17
Mark Woodforde	0-2-2	0-1-1	0-6-1	0-3-1	17

†Did not compete.

WOMEN

Player	Aus. S-D-M	French S-D-M	Wim. S-D-M	U.S. S-D-M	Total
Margaret Smith Court	11-8-2	5-4-4	3-2-5	5-5-8	62
Martina Navratilova	3-8-1	2-7-2	9-7-4	4-9-3	59
Billie Jean King	1-0-1	1-1-2	6-10-4	4-5-4	39
Doris Hart	1-1-2	2-5-3	1-4-5	2-4-5	35
Helen Wills Moody	†	4-2-0	8-3-1	7-4-2	31
Louise Brough	1-1-0	0-3-0	4-5-4	1-8-3	30**
Margaret Osborne duPont	†	2-3-0	1-5-1	3-8-6	29**
*Serena Williams	5-4-0	1-2-0	4-4-1	3-2-1	27
Elizabeth Ryan	†	0-4-0	0-12-7	0-1-2	26
Steffi Graf	4-0-0	6-0-0	7-1-0	5-0-0	23
Pam Shriver	0-7-0	0-4-1	0-5-0	0-5-0	22
Chris Evert	2-0-0	7-2-0	3-1-0	6-0-0	21
Darlene Hard	†	1-3-2	0-4-3	2-6-0	21
Suzanne Lenglen	†	2-2-2#	6-6-3	0-0-0	21
*Venus Williams	0-4-1	0-2-1	5-4-0	2-2-0	21
Nancye Wynne Bolton	6-10-4	0-0-0	0-0-0	0-0-0	20
Maria Bueno	0-1-0	0-1-1	3-5-0	4-4-0	19
Thelma Coyne Long	2-12-4	0-0-1	0-0-0	0-0-0	19

*Active player in 2010. †Did not compete. #Suzanne Lenglen won four singles titles at the French Championships before competition was opened to entries from all nations in 1925. **From 1940–45, with competition in the U.S. Championships thinned due to war, Louise Brough Clapp won four doubles titles (1942–45) and one mixed doubles title (1942); and Margaret Osborne duPont won five doubles titles (1941–45) and three mixed doubles titles (1943–45).

Alltime Grand Slam Singles Champions

MEN

Player	Aus.	French	Wim.	U.S.	Total
*Roger Federer	4	1	6	5	16
Pete Sampras	2	0	7	5	14
Roy Emerson	6	2	2	2	12
Bjorn Borg	0	6	5	0	11
Rod Laver	3	2	4	2	11
Bill Tilden	†	0	3	7	10
*Rafael Nadal	1	5	2	1	9
Jimmy Connors	1	0	2	5	8
Ivan Lendl	2	3	0	3	8
Fred Perry	1	1	3	3	8
Ken Rosewall	4	2	0	2	8
Andre Agassi	4	1	1	2	8
Henri Cochet	†	4	2	1	7
Rene Lacoste	†	3	2	2	7
Bill Larned	†	†	0	7	7
John McEnroe	0	0	3	4	7
John Newcombe	2	0	3	2	7
Willie Renshaw	†	†	7	†	7
Dick Sears	†	†	0	7	7

WOMEN

Player	Aus.	French	Wim.	U.S.	Total
Margaret Smith Court	11	5	3	5	24
Steffi Graf	4	6	7	5	22
Helen Wills Moody	†	4	8	7	19
Chris Evert	2	7	3	6	18
Martina Navratilova	3	2	9	4	18
*Serena Williams	5	1	4	3	13
Billie Jean King	1	1	6	4	12
Maureen Connolly	1	2	3	3	9
Monica Seles	4	3	0	2	9
Suzanne Lenglen	†	2#	6	0	8
Molla Bjurstedt Mallory	†	†	0	8	8
Maria Bueno	0	0	3	4	7
Evonne Goolagong	4	1	2	0	7
Dorothea D.L. Chambers	†	†	7	0	7
Justine Henin	1	4	0	2	7
*Venus Williams	0	0	5	2	7

*Active player in 2010. †Did not compete.

Golf

Phil Mickelson (l.) and Tiger Woods both closed out a disappointing 2009 on an upbeat note at the PGA TOUR Championship

Men's Majors

The Masters
Augusta National GC (par 72; 7,435 yds);
Augusta, Ga., April 8–11, 2010

Player	Score	Earnings ($)
Phil Mickelson	67-71-67-67--272	1,350,000
Lee Westwood	67-69-68-71--275	810,000
Anthony Kim	68-70-73-65--276	510,000
K.J. Choi	67-71-70-69--277	330,000
Tiger Woods	68-70-70-69--277	330,000
Fred Couples	66-75-68-70--279	270,000
Nick Watney	68-76-71-65--280	251,250
Y.E. Yang	67-72-72-70--281	225,000
Hunter Mahan	71-71-68-71--281	225,000
Ricky Barnes	68-70-72-73--283	195,000
Ian Poulter	68-68-74-73--283	195,000
Miguel Angel Jimenez	72-75-72-66--285	165,000
Jerry Kelly	72-74-67-72--285	165,000
Ryan Moore	72-73-73-68--286	131,250
David Toms	69-75-71-71--286	131,250
Trevor Immelman	69-73-72-72--286	131,250
Steve Marino	71-73-69-73--286	131,250
Ernie Els	71-73-75-68--287	94,500
Scott Verplank	73-73-73-68--287	94,500
Adam Scott	69-75-72-71--287	94,500
Angel Cabrera	73-74-69-71--287	94,500
Heath Slocum	72-73-70-72--287	94,500
Tom Watson	67-74-73-73--287	94,500

U.S. Open
Pebble Beach G.C. (par 71; 7,040 yds);
Pebble Beach, Calif., June 17–20, 2010

Player	Score	Earnings ($)
Graeme McDowell	71-68-71-74--284	1,350,000
Gregory Havret	73-71-69-72--285	810,000
Ernie Els	73-68-72-73--286	480,687
Phil Mickelson	75-66-73-73--287	303,119
Tiger Woods	74-72-66-75--287	303,119
Matt Kuchar	74-72-74-68--288	228,255
Davis Love III	75-74-68-71--288	228,255
Brandt Snedeker	75-74-69-71--289	177,534
Martin Kaymer	74-71-72-72--289	177,534
Alex Cejka	70-72-74-73--289	177,534
Dustin Johnson	71-70-66-82--289	177,534
Sean O'Hair	76-71-70-73--290	143,714
Tim Clark	72-72-72-74--290	143,714
Ben Curtis	78-70-75-68--291	127,779
Justin Leonard	72-73-73-73--291	127,779
Peter Hanson	73-76-74-69--292	108,458
a-Scott Langley	75-69-77-71--292	—
Lee Westwood	74-71-76-71--292	108,458
Jim Furyk	72-75-74-71--292	108,458
a-Russel Henley	73-74-72-73--292	—
Charl Schwartzel	74-71-74-73--292	108,458
Sergio Garcia	73-76-73-71--293	83,634
Shaun Micheel	69-77-75-72--293	83,634
Angel Cabrera	75-72-74-72--293	83,634
Padraig Harrington	73-73-74-73--293	83,634
John Mallinger	77-72-70-74--293	83,634

a-Amateur.

British Open
St. Andrews G.C. (par 72; 7,377 yds);
St. Andrews, Scotland, July 15–18, 2010

Player	Score	Earnings ($)
Louis Oosthuizen	65-67-69-71--272	1,305,593
Lee Westwood	67-71-71-70--279	767,996
Paul Casey	69-69-67-75--280	394,238
Rory McIlroy	63-80-69-68--280	394,238
Henrik Stenson	68-74-67-71--280	394,238
Retief Goosen	69-70-72-70--281	268,799
Martin Kaymer	69-71-68-74--282	186,239
Sean O'Hair	67-72-72-71--282	186,239
Robert Rock	68-78-67-69--282	186,239
Nick Watney	67-73-71-71--282	186,239
Luke Donald	73-72-69-69--283	125,439
Jeff Overton	73-69-72-69--283	125,439
Alvaro Quiros	72-70-74-67--283	125,439
Rickie Fowler	79-67-71-67--284	87,840
Sergio Garcia	71-71-70-72--284	87,840
Ignacio Garrido	69-71-73-71--284	87,840
J.B. Holmes	70-72-70-72--284	87,840
Dustin Johnson	69-72-69-74--284	87,840
Robert Karlsson	69-71-72-72--284	87,840
Tom Lehman	71-68-75-70--284	87,840
Charl Schwatzel	71-75-68-70--284	87,840
a-Jin Jeong	68-70-74-72--284	—

a-Amateur.

PGA Championship
Whistling Straits G.C. (par 72; 7,507 yds);
Kohler, Wisc., August 12–15, 2010

Player	Score	Earnings ($)
*Martin Kaymer	72-68-67-70--277	1,350,000
Bubba Watson	68-71-70-68--277	810,000
Zach Johnson	39-70-69-70--278	435,000
Rory McIlroy	71-68-67-72--278	435,000
Jason Dufner	73-66-69-71--279	270,833
Steve Elkington	71-70-67-71--279	270,833
Dustin Johnson	71-68-67-73--279	270,833
WC Liang	72-71-64-73--280	210,000
Camilo Villegas	71-71-70-68--280	210,000
Jason Day	69-72-66-74--281	175,800
Matt Kuchar	67-69-73-72--281	175,800
Paul Casey	72-71-70-69--282	138,050
Simon Dyson	71-71-68-72--282	138,050
Phil Mickelson	73-69-73-67--282	138,050
Bryce Molder	72-67-70-73--282	138,050
Robert Karlsson	71-71-71-70--283	110,050
D.A. Points	70-72-70-71--283	110,050
Stephen Gallacher	71-69-72-72--284	84,733
Charl Schwartzel	73-69-72-70--284	84,733
Stewart Cink	77-68-66-73--284	84,733
Ernie Els	68-74-69-73--284	84,733
Steve Stricker	72-72-68-72--284	84,733
Nick Watney	68-68-66-81--284	84,733

*won in playoff

Late 2009 PGA Tour Events

Tournament	Final Round	Winner	Score/Under Par	Earnings ($)
*Turning Stone Championship	Oct 4	Matt Kuchar	271/-17	1,080,000
*Shriners Hosptials for Children Open	Oct 18	Martin Laird	265/-19	756,000
*Frys.com Open	Oct 25	Troy Matteson	262/-18	900,000
Viking Classic	Nov 1	cancelled because of rain		
*Children's Miracle Network Classic	Nov 15	Stephen Ames	270/-18	846,000

2010 PGA Tour Events

Tournament	Final Round	Winner	Score/Under Par	Earnings ($)
SBS Championship	Jan 10	Geoff Ogilvy	270/-22	1,120,000
Sony Open in Hawaii	Jan 17	Ryan Palmer	265/-15	990,000
†Bob Hope Chrysler Classic	Jan 24	Bill Haas	330/-30	900,000
Farmers Insurance Open	Jan 31	Ben Crane	275/-13	954,000
Northern Trust Open	Feb 7	Steve Stricker	268/-16	1,152,000
**AT&T Pebble Beach National Pro-Am	Feb 14	Dustin Johnson	270/-16	1,116,000
Mayakoba Classic at Riviera Maya	Feb 14	Cameron Beckman	269/-15	648,000
WGC Match Play Championship	Feb 21	Ian Poulter	4 & 2	1,400,000
Phoenix Open	Feb 28	Hunter Mahan	268/-16	1,080,000
Honda Classic	Mar 7	Camilo Villegas	267/13	1,008,000
Puerto Rico Open	Mar 14	Derek Lamely	269/-19	630,000
WGC-CA Championship	Mar 14	Ernie Els	270/-18	1,400,000
Transitions Championship	Mar 21	Jim Furyk	271/-13	972,000
Arnold Palmer Invitational	Mar 29	Ernie Els	277/-11	1,080,000
*Shell Houston Open	Apr 4	Anthony Kim	276/-12	1,044,000
The Masters	Apr 11	Phil Mickelson	272/-16	1,350,000
*Verizon Heritage	Apr 18	Jim Furyk	271/-13	1,026,000
Zurich Classic	Apr 25	Jason Bohn	270/-18	1,152,000
Wells Fargo Championship	May 2	Rory McIlroy	273/-15	1,170,000
The Players Championship	May 9	Tim Clark	272/-16	1,710,000
Valero Texas Open	May 16	Adam Scott	274/-14	1,098,000
Byron Nelson Championship	May 23	Jason Day	270/-10	1,170,000
Crowne Plaza Invitational at Colonial	May 30	Zach Johnson	259/-21	1,116,000
Memorial Tournament	June 6	Justin Rose	270/-18	1,080,000
St. Jude Classic	June 13	Lee Westwood	270/-10	1,008,000
U.S. Open Championship	June 20	Graeme McDowell	284/E	1,350,000
*Travelers Championship	June 27	Bubba Watson	266/-14	1,080,000
AT&T National	July 4	Justin Rose	270/-10	1,116,000
John Deere Classic	July 11	Steve Stricker	258/-26	792,000
Reno-Tahoe Open	July 18	Matt Bettencourt	277/-11	540,000
The Open Championship (British Open)	July 18	Louis Oosthuizen	272/-16	1,305,593
Canadian Open	July 25	Carl Pettersson	266/-14	918,000
Greenbrier Classic	Aug 1	Stuart Appleby	258/-22	1,080,000
Turning Stone Resort Championship	Aug 8	Bill Lunde	271/-17	720,000
WGC-Bridgestone Invitational	Aug 8	Hunter Mahan	268/-12	1,400,000
*PGA Championship	Aug 15	Martin Kaymer	277/-11	1,350,000
*Wyndham Championship	Aug 22	Arjun Atwal	260/-20	918,000
*‡The Barclays	Aug 29	Matt Kuchar	272/-12	1,350,000
‡Deutsche Bank Championship	Sept 5	Charley Hoffman	262/-22	1,350,000
‡BMW Championship	Sept 12	Dustin Johnson	275/-9	1,350,000
‡TOUR Championship	Sept 26	Jim Furyk	272/-8	1,350,000
Viking Classic	Oct 3	Bill Haas	273/-15	648,000

† Five-round tournament. * Won in playoff. **Rain shortened tournament to three rounds. ‡Events part of four-tournament FedEx Cup, the PGA Tour's 30-player playoff.

2010 FedEx Cup Playoff Results

Player	Points	Earnings ($)
1. Jim Furyk	2,980	10,000,000
2. Matt Kuchar	2,728	3,000,000
3. Luke Donald	2,700	2,000,000
4. Charley Hoffman	2,500	1,500,000
5. Dustin Johnson	2,493	1,000,000
6. Paul Casey	2,250	800,000
7. Steve Stricker	2,028	700,000
8. Jason Day	1,660	600,000
9. Ernie Els	1,438	550,000
10. Retief Goosen	1,360	500,000

Kraft Nabisco Championship

Mission Hills CC (par 72; 6,702 yds);
Rancho Mirage, Ca., April 1–4, 2010

Player	Score	Earnings ($)
Yani Tseng	69-71-67-68--275	300,000
Suzann Pettersen	67-73-67-69--276	183,814
Song-Hee Kim	69-68-72-70--279	133,344
Lorena Ochoa	68-70-71-73--282	103,152
Jiyai Shin	72-72-69-71--284	64,408
Cristie Kerr	71-67-74-72--284	64,408
Karrie Webb	69-70-72-73--284	64,408
Karen Stupples	69-69-68-78--284	64,408
Chie Arimura	73-72-68-72--285	44,784
Inbee Park	73-74-70-69--286	35,544
Anna Nordqvist	74-72-69-71--286	35,544
Grace Park	71-74-68-73--286	35,544
Sophie Gustafson	70-73-70-73--286	35,544
Brittany Lang	72-71-69-74--286	35,544
Se Ri Pak	79-71-67-70--286	35,544
Hee Young Park	73-71-70-73--287	26,971
Angela Stanford	78-68-69-72--287	26,971
Catriona Matthew	73-74-67-73--287	26,971
Morgan Pressel	71-72-72-73--288	23,549
Stacy Lewis	71-68-75-74--288	23,549
a-Jennifer Song	71-71-76-71--289	—
Hee Kyung Seo	72-73-76-68--289	21,939
Brittany Lincicome	70-74-72-73--289	21,939
a-Alexis Thompson	74-72-73-71--290	—
Gwladys Nocera	75-70-71-74--290	20,329
Katherine Hull	72-71-72-75--290	20,329

a-Amateur.

U.S. Women's Open

Oakmont C.C. (par 71; 6,613 yds);
Oakmont, Pa., July 8–11, 2010

Player	Score	Earnings ($)
Paula Creamer	72-70-70-69--281	585,000
Na Yeon Choi	75-72-72-66--285	284,468
Suzann Pettersen	73-71-72-69--285	284,468
In Kyung Kim	74-71-73-68--286	152,565
Jiyai Shin	76-71-72-68--287	110,481
Brittany Lang	69-74-75-69--287	110,481
Amy Yang	70-75-71-71--287	110,481
Inbee Park	70-78-73-68--289	87,202
Christina Kim	72-72-72-73--289	87,202
Yani Tseng	73-76-73-68--290	72,131
Sakura Yokomine	71-71-76-72--290	72,131
Alexis Thompson	73-74-70-73--290	72,131
Song-Hee Kim	72-76-78-65--291	63,524
Stacy Lewis	75-70-75-72--292	56,659
Natalie Gulbis	73-73-72-74--292	56,659
Wendy Ward	72-73-70-77--292	56,659
Karrie Webb	74-72-73-74--293	49,365
Cristie Kerr	72-71-75-75--293	49,365
Kristy McPherson	72-78-74-70--293	49,365
Shi Hyun Ahn	72-77-73-72--294	39,285
Azahara Munoz	75-74-71-74--294	39,285
Angela Stanford	73-72-74-75--294	39,285
Jeong Jang	73-72-74-75--294	39,285
Sophie Gustafson	72-72-74-76--294	39,285

LPGA Championship

Bulle Rock GC (par 72; 6,641 yds);
Havre de Grace, Md., June 11–14, 2010

Player	Score	Earnings ($)
Cristie Kerr	68-66-69-66--269	337,500
Song-Hee Kim	72-71-69-69--281	207,790
Ai Miyazato	76-71-70-66--283	133,672
Jiyai Shin	72-70-70-71--283	133,672
In-Kyung Kim	72-70-72-70--284	85,323
Karrie Webb	72-72-69-71--284	85,323
Morgan Pressel	72-76-68-69--285	54,323
Inbee Park	69-70-75-71--285	54,323
Meaghan Francella	73-71-70-71--285	54,323
Jimin Kang	74-67-70-74--285	54,323
Suzann Pettersen	74-72-69-71--286	41,238
Azahara Munoz	72-69-70-75--286	41,328
Mika Miyazato	69-70-72-76--287	37,314
Amy Yang	73-67-76-72--288	31,398
Brittany Lincicome	71-69-75-73--288	31,398
Stacy Lewis	68-74-73-73--288	31,398
Lindsey Wright	69-74-72-73--288	31,398
Sarah Jane Smith	74-71-69-74--288	31,398
Meena Lee	71-76-74-68--289	24,800
Karin Sjodin	74-73-74-68--289	24,800
Michelle Wie	72-74-73-70--289	24,800
Yani Tseng	75-71-70-73--289	24,800
Na On Min	74-67-74-74--289	24,800
Seon Hwa Lee	68-74-73-74--289	24,800

Women's British Open

Royal Birkdale CC (par 72; 6,458 yds);
Merseyside, England, July 29–August 1, 2010

Player	Score	Earnings ($)
Yani Tseng	68-68-68-73--277	408,714
Katherine Hull	68-74-66-70--278	256,209
Na Yeon Choi	74-70-69-68--281	159,825
In-Kyung Kim	70-72-68-71--281	159,825
Amy Yang	69-71-74-68--282	101,670
Cristie Kerr	73-67-72-70--282	101,670
Hee Kyung Seo	73-69-70-70--282	101,670
Morgan Pressel	77-71-65-71--284	81,743
Inbee Park	72-71-77-66--286	61,978
Ai Miyazato	76-70-73-67--286	61,978
Christina Kim	74-68-70-74--286	61,978
Momoko Ueda	72-70-70-74--286	61,978
Brittany Lincicome	69-71-71-75--286	61,978
Maria Hernandez	73-70-73-71--287	43,311
Jiyai Shin	71-71-72-73--287	43,311
Suzann Pettersen	73-68-71-75--287	43,311
Gwladys Nocera	71-75-72-70--288	37,516
Michelle Wie	70-76-71-71--288	37,516
Song-Hee Kim	75-73-71-70--289	33,856
Azahara Munoz	74-71-72-72--289	33,856
Jeong Jang	74-73-74-69--290	28,722
Paula Creamer	74-74-70-72--290	28,722
Juli Inkster	71-70-76-73--290	28,722
Lee-Anne Pace	74-72-71-73--290	28,722
Becky Brewerton	73-73-71-73--290	28,722
Chie Arimura	77-68-70-75--290	28,722

Late 2009 LPGA Tour Events

Tournament	Final Round	Winner	Score/ Under Par	Earnings ($)
Samsung World Championship	Sept 20	Na Yeon Choi	272/-16	250,000
CVS/pharmacy Challenge	Sept 27	Sophie Gustafson	268/-20	165,000
Navistar Classic	Oct 4	Lorena Ochoa	270/-18	195,000
Hana Bank Championship	Nov 1	Na Yeon Choi	206/-10	255,000
Mizuno Classic	Nov 8	Bo Bae Song	201/-15	210,000
Lorena Ochoa Invitational	Nov 15	Michelle Wie	275/-13	220,000
ADT Championship	Nov 23	Jiyai Shin	286/-2	1,000,000

2010 LPGA Tour Events

Tournament	Final Round	Winner	Score/ Under Par	Earnings ($)
Honda LPGA Thailand	Feb 21	Ai Miyazato	267/-21	195,000
HSBC Championship	Feb 28	Ai Miyazato	278/-10	195,000
KIA Classic	Mar 28	Hee Kyung Seo	256/-12	255,000
Kraft Nabisco Championship	Apr 4	Yani Tseng	275/-13	300,000
The Mojo 6	Apr 16	Anna Nordqvist	1-up	350,000
Tres Marias Championship	May 2	Ai Miyazato	273/-19	195,000
Bell Micro Classic	May 16	Se Ri Pak	203/-13	195,000
Sybase Match Play Championship	May 23	Sun Young Yoo	3 & 1	375,000
Brasil Cup	May 30	Meaghan Francella	140/-6	105,000
State Farm Classic	June 13	Cristie Kerr	266/-22	255,000
ShopRite Classic	June 20	Ai Miyazato	197/-16	225,000
McDonald's LPGA Championship	June 27	Cristie Kerr	269/-19	337,500
Wegman's Rochester LPGA	June 28	Jiyai Shin	271/-17	300,000
*Jamie Farr Owens Corning Classic	July 4	Na Yeon Choi	270/-14	150,000
U.S. Women's Open	July 11	Paula Creamer	281/-3	585,000
Evian Masters	July 25	Jiyai Shin	274/-14	487,500
Women's British Open	Aug 1	Yani Tseng	277/-11	408,714
Safeway Classic	Aug 22	Ai Miyazato	205/-11	225,000
Canadian Women's Open	Aug 29	Michelle Wie	276/-12	337,500
NW Arkansas Championship	Sept 12	Yani Tseng	200/-13	300,000

* Won in playoff.

Late 2009 Champions Tour Events

Tournament	Final Round	Winner	Score/ Under Par	Earnings ($)
Senior Players Championship	Oct 10	Jay Haas	267/-13	405,000
Administaff Small Business Classic	Oct 24	John Cook	205/-11	255,000
AT&T Championship	Oct 31	Phil Blackmar	203/-10	255,000
Charles Schwab Cup Championship	Nov 7	John Cook	266/-22	442,000

2010 Champions Tour Events

Tournament	Final Round	Winner	Score/ Under Par	Earnings ($)
Mitsubishi Electric Championship	Jan 22	Tom Watson	194/-22	315,000
ACE Group Classic	Feb 14	Fred Couples	199/-14	240,000
Allianz Championship	Feb 21	Bernhard Langer	199/-17	247,500
Toshiba Senior Classic	Mar 7	Fred Couples	195/-18	255,000
Cap Cana Championship	Mar 28	Fred Couples	195/-21	240,000
**Outback Steakhouse Pro-Am	Apr 18	Bernhard Langer	133/-9	255,000
Legends of Golf	Apr 25	Mark O'Meara/Nick Price	188/-28	230,000 each
Mississippi Gulf Resort Classic	May 2	David Eger	205/-11	240,000
Regions Charity Classic	May 16	Dan Forsman	196/-20	255,000
*Senior PGA Championship	May 30	Tom Lehman	281/-7	360,000
Principal Charity Classic	June 6	Nick Price	199/-14	258,750
Dick's Sporting Goods Open	June 27	Loren Roberts	201/-15	255,000
Montreal Championship	July 4	Larry Mize	199/-17	270,000
*Senior Open Championship (British)	July 25	Bernhard Langer	279/-5	315,600
U.S. Senior Open Championship	Aug 1	Bernhard Langer	272/-8	470,000
3M Championship	Aug 8	David Frost	191/-25	262,500
JELD-WEN Tradition	Aug 22	Fred Funk	276/-12	392,000
Boeing Classic	Aug 29	Bernhard Langer	198/-18	270,000
First Tee Open at Pebble Beach	Sept 5	Ted Schulz	202/-14	315,000
*Songdo Championship	Sept 12	Russ Cochran	204/-12	450,000
SAS Championship	Sept 26	Russ Cochran	202/-14	315,000
Ensure Classic at Rock Barn	Oct 3	Gary Hallberg	198/-11	262,500

* Won in playoff. **Rain shortened tournament to two rounds.

2010 U.S. Amateur Championships Results*

Tournament	Final Round	Winner	Score	Runner-Up
Women's Amateur Public Links	June 26	Emily Tubert	3 & 2	Lisa McCloskey
Men's Amateur Public Links	July 17	Lion Kim	6 & 5	David McDaniel
Girls' Junior Amateur	July 24	Doris Chen	3 & 2	Katelyn Dambaugh
Boys' Junior Amateur	July 24	Jim Liu	4 & 2	Justin Thomas
Women's Amateur	Aug 15	Danielle Kang	3 & 1	Jessica Korda
Men's Amateur	Aug 29	Peter Uihlein	4 & 2	David Chung
Women's Mid-Amateur	Oct 3	Meghan Stasi	2-up	Carol Robertson
Men's Mid-Amateur	Oct 3	Nathan Smith	7 & 5	Tim Hogarth

*Results through 10/04/10.

2010 International Results

Tournament	Final Round	Winner	Score	Runner-Up
Curtis Cup	June 14	United States	12½–7½	Great Britian & Ireland
Ryder Cup	Oct 3	Europe	14½–13½	United States

PGA Tour Final 2009 Money Leaders

Name	Events	Best Finish	Scoring Average*	Money ($)
Tiger Woods	18	1 (6)	68.05	10,508,163
Steve Stricker	23	1 (3)	69.29	6,332,636
Phil Mickelson	19	1 (3)	70.22	5,332,755
Zach Johnson	26	1 (2)	69.58	4,583,213
Kenny Perry	25	1 (2)	69.79	4,445,562
Sean O'Hair	24	1 (1)	69.95	4,316,493
Jim Furyk	24	2 (2)	69.48	3,946,515
Geoff Ogilvy	21	1 (2)	70.32	3,866,270
Lucas Glover	27	1 (1)	69.97	3,692,580
Y.E. Yang	24	1 (2)	70.46	3,489,516

*Adjusted for average score of field in each tournament entered.

LPGA Tour Final 2009 Money Leaders

Name	Events	Best Finish	Scoring Average	Money ($)
Jiyai Shin	25	1 (3)	70.26	1,807,334
Cristie Kerr	25	1 (1)	70.28	1,519,722
Ai Miyazato	22	1 (1)	70.33	1,517,149
Lorena Ochoa	22	1 (3)	70.16	1,489,395
Suzann Pettersen	23	1 (1)	70.49	1,369,717
Na Yeon Choi	26	1 (2)	70.51	1,341,078
Yani Tseng	27	1 (1)	70.44	1,293,755
In-Kyung Kim	25	1 (1)	71.00	1,238,396
Paula Creamer	24	2 (2)	70.62	1,151,864
Angela Stanford	21	1 (1)	70.64	1,081,916

Champions Tour Final 2009 Money Leaders

Name	Events	Best Finish	Scoring Average	Money ($)
Bernhard Langer	21	1 (4)	68.92	2,164,451
Jay Haas	23	1 (2)	69.25	1,963,395
Loren Roberts	22	1 (3)	69.65	1,960,613
John Cook	23	1 (2)	69.71	1,798,664
Fred Funk	22	1 (1)	69.72	1,673,810
Jeff Sluman	25	1 (1)	70.04	1,378,094
Andy Bean	24	2 (2)	69.75	1,313,217
Mark O'Meara	20	1 (1)	69.69	1,278,985
Nick Price	20	1 (1)	69.91	1,254,452
Dan Forsman	23	1 (1)	69.86	1,203,638

Men's Golf

THE MAJOR TOURNAMENTS
The Masters

Year	Winner	Score	Runner-Up
1934	Horton Smith	284	Craig Wood
1935	Gene Sarazen* (144)	282	Craig Wood (149)
	(only 36-hole playoff)		
1936	Horton Smith	285	Harry Cooper
1937	Byron Nelson	283	Ralph Guldahl
1938	Henry Picard	285	Ralph Guldahl
			Harry Cooper
1939	Ralph Guldahl	279	Sam Snead
1940	Jimmy Demaret	280	Lloyd Mangrum
1941	Craig Wood	280	Byron Nelson
1942	Byron Nelson* (69)	280	Ben Hogan (70)
1943–45	No tournament		
1946	Herman Keiser	282	Ben Hogan
1947	Jimmy Demaret	281	Byron Nelson
			Frank Stranahan
1948	Claude Harmon	279	Cary Middlecoff
1949	Sam Snead	282	Johnny Bulla
			Lloyd Mangrum
1950	Jimmy Demaret	283	Jim Ferrier
1951	Ben Hogan	280	Skee Riegel
1952	Sam Snead	286	Jack Burke Jr..
1953	Ben Hogan	274	Ed Oliver Jr.
1954	Sam Snead* (70)	289	Ben Hogan (71)
1955	Cary Middlecoff	279	Ben Hogan
1956	Jack Burke Jr.	289	Ken Venturi
1957	Doug Ford	282	Sam Snead
1958	Arnold Palmer	284	Doug Ford
			Fred Hawkins
1959	Art Wall Jr.	284	Cary Middlecoff
1960	Arnold Palmer	282	Ken Venturi
1961	Gary Player	280	Charles R. Coe
			Arnold Palmer
1962	Arnold Palmer* (68)	280	Gary Player (71)
			D. Finsterwald (77)
1963	Jack Nicklaus	286	Tony Lema
1964	Arnold Palmer	276	Dave Marr
			Jack Nicklaus
1965	Jack Nicklaus	271	Arnold Palmer
			Gary Player
1966	Jack Nicklaus* (70)	288	Tommy Jacobs (72)
			Gay Brewer Jr. (78)
1967	Gay Brewer Jr.	280	Bobby Nichols
1968	Bob Goalby	277	Roberto DeVicenzo
1969	George Archer	281	Billy Casper
			George Knudson
			Tom Weiskopf
1970	Billy Casper* (69)	279	Gene Littler (74)
1971	Charles Coody	279	Johnny Miller
			Jack Nicklaus
1972	Jack Nicklaus	286	Bruce Crampton
			Bobby Mitchell
			Tom Weiskopf
1973	Tommy Aaron	283	J.C. Snead
1974	Gary Player	278	Tom Weiskopf
			Dave Stockton
1975	Jack Nicklaus	276	Johnny Miller
			Tom Weiskopf
1976	Ray Floyd	271	Ben Crenshaw
1977	Tom Watson	276	Jack Nicklaus
1978	Gary Player	277	Hubert Green
			Rod Funseth
			Tom Watson
1979	Fuzzy Zoeller* (4–3)†	280	Ed Sneed (4–4)
			Tom Watson (4–4)
1980	Seve Ballesteros	275	Gibby Gilbert
			Jack Newton
1981	Tom Watson	280	Johnny Miller
			Jack Nicklaus
1982	Craig Stadler* (4)	284	Dan Pohl (5)
1983	Seve Ballesteros	280	Ben Crenshaw
			Tom Kite
1984	Ben Crenshaw	277	Tom Watson
1985	Bernhard Langer	282	Curtis Strange
			Seve Ballesteros
			Ray Floyd
1986	Jack Nicklaus	279	Greg Norman
			Tom Kite
1987	Larry Mize* (4–3)	285	Seve Ballesteros (5)
			Greg Norman (4–4)
1988	Sandy Lyle	281	Mark Calcavecchia
1989	Nick Faldo* (5–3)	283	Scott Hoch (5–4)
1990	Nick Faldo* (4–4)	278	Ray Floyd (4–x)
1991	Ian Woosnam	277	José María
			Olazábal
1992	Fred Couples	275	Ray Floyd
1993	Bernhard Langer	277	Chip Beck
1994	José María Olazábal	279	Tom Lehman
1995	Ben Crenshaw	274	Davis Love III
1996	Nick Faldo	276	Greg Norman
1997	Tiger Woods	270	Tom Kite
1998	Mark O'Meara	279	David Duval
			Fred Couples
1999	José María Olazábal	280	Davis Love III
2000	Vijay Singh	278	Ernie Els
2001	Tiger Woods	272	David Duval
2002	Tiger Woods	276	Retief Goosen
2003	Mike Weir	281	Len Mattiace
2004	Phil Mickelson	279	Ernie Els
2005	Tiger Woods	276	Chris DiMarco
2006	Phil Mickelson	281	Tim Clark
2007	Zach Johnson	289	Tiger Woods
			Retief Goosen
			Rory Sabbatini
2008	Trevor Immelman	280	Tiger Woods
2009	Angel Cabrera	276	Chad Campbell
			Kenny Perry
2010	Phil Mickelson	272	Lee Westwood

*Winner in playoff. Playoff scores are in parentheses. †Playoff cut from 18 holes to sudden death.
Note: Played at Augusta National Golf Club, Augusta, GA.

United States Open Championship

Year	Winner	Score	Runner-Up	Site
1895	Horace Rawlins	†173	Willie Dunn	Newport GC, Newport, RI
1896	James Foulis	†152	Horace Rawlins	Shinnecock Hills GC, Southampton, NY
1897	Joe Lloyd	†162	Willie Anderson	Chicago GC, Wheaton, IL
1898	Fred Herd	328	Alex Smith	Myopia Hunt Club, Hamilton, MA
1899	Willie Smith	315	George Low	Baltimore CC, Baltimore, MD
			Val Fitzjohn	
			W.H. Way	
1900	Harry Vardon	313	John H. Taylor	Chicago GC, Wheaton, IL
1901	Willie Anderson* (85)	331	Alex Smith (86)	Myopia Hunt Club, Hamilton, MA
1902	Laurie Auchterlonie	307	Stewart Gardner	Garden City GC, Garden City, NY
1903	Willie Anderson* (82)	307	David Brown (84)	Baltusrol GC, Springfield, NJ
1904	Willie Anderson	303	Gil Nicholls	Glen View Club, Golf, IL
1905	Willie Anderson	314	Alex Smith	Myopia Hunt Club, Hamilton, MA
1906	Alex Smith	295	Willie Smith	Onwentsia Club, Lake Forest, IL
1907	Alex Ross	302	Gil Nicholls	Philadelphia Cricket Club, Chestnut Hill, PA
1908	Fred McLeod* (77)	322	Willie Smith (83)	Myopia Hunt Club, Hamilton, MA
1909	George Sargent	290	Tom McNamara	Englewood GC, Englewood, NJ
1910	Alex Smith* (71)	298	John McDermott (75)	Philadelphia Cricket Club, Chestnut Hill, PA
			Macdonald Smith (77)	
1911	John McDermott* (80)	307	Mike Brady (82)	Chicago GC, Wheaton, IL
			George Simpson (85)	
1912	John McDermott	294	Tom McNamara	CC of Buffalo, Buffalo, NY
1913	Francis Ouimet* (72)	304	Harry Vardon (77)	The Country Club, Brookline, MA
			Edward Ray (78)	
1914	Walter Hagen	290	Chick Evans	Midlothian CC, Blue Island, IL
1915	Jerry Travers	297	Tom McNamara	Baltusrol GC, Springfield, NJ
1916	Chick Evans	286	Jock Hutchison	Minikahda Club, Minneapolis. MN
1917–18	No tournament			
1919	Walter Hagen* (77)	301	Mike Brady (78)	Brae Burn CC, West Newton, MA
1920	Edward Ray	295	Harry Vardon	Inverness CC, Toledo, OH
			Jack Burke	
			Leo Diegel	
			Jock Hutchison	
1921	Jim Barnes	289	Walter Hagen	Columbia CC, Chevy Chase, MD
			Fred McLeod	
1922	Gene Sarazen	288	John L. Black	Skokie CC, Glencoe, IL
			Bobby Jones	
1923	Bobby Jones* (76)	296	Bobby Cruickshank (78)	Inwood CC, Inwood, NY
1924	Cyril Walker	297	Bobby Jones	Oakland Hills CC, Birmingham, MI
1925	W. MacFarlane* (75–72)	291	Bobby Jones (75–73)	Worcester CC, Worcester, MA
1926	Bobby Jones	293	Joe Turnesa	Scioto CC, Columbus, OH
1927	Tommy Armour* (76)	301	Harry Cooper (79)	Oakmont CC, Oakmont, PA
1928	Johnny Farrell* (143)	294	Bobby Jones (144)	Olympia Fields CC, Matteson, IL
1929	Bobby Jones* (141)	294	Al Espinosa (164)	Winged Foot GC, Mamaroneck, NY
1930	Bobby Jones	287	Macdonald Smith	Interlachen CC, Hopkins, MN
1931	Billy Burke* (149–148)	292	George Von Elm	Inverness Club, Toledo, OH
			(149–149)	
1932	Gene Sarazen	286	Phil Perkins	Fresh Meadows CC, Flushing, NY
			Bobby Cruickshank	
1933	Johnny Goodman	287	Ralph Guldahl	North Shore CC, Glenview, IL
1934	Olin Dutra	293	Gene Sarazen	Merion Cricket Club, Ardmore, PA
1935	Sam Parks Jr.	299	Jimmy Thompson	Oakmont CC, Oakmont, PA
1936	Tony Manero	282	Harry Cooper	Baltusrol GC (Upper Course), Springfield, NJ
1937	Ralph Guldahl	281	Sam Snead	Oakland Hills CC, Birmingham, MI
1938	Ralph Guldahl	284	Dick Metz	Cherry Hills CC, Denver, CO
1939	Byron Nelson* (68–70)	284	Craig Wood (68–73)	Philadelphia CC, Philadelphia, PA
			Denny Shute (76)	
1940	Lawson Little* (70)	287	Gene Sarazen (73)	Canterbury GC, Cleveland, OH
1941	Craig Wood	284	Denny Shute	Colonial Club, Fort Worth, TX
1942–45	No tournament			
1946	Lloyd Mangrum* (72–72)	284	Vic Ghezzi (72–73)	Canterbury GC, Cleveland, OH
			Byron Nelson (72–73)	
1947	Lew Worsham* (69)	282	Sam Snead (70)	St. Louis CC, Clayton, MO
1948	Ben Hogan	276	Jimmy Demaret	Riviera CC, Los Angeles, CA
1949	Cary Middlecoff	286	Sam Snead	Medinah CC, Medinah, IL
			Clayton Heafner	
1950	Ben Hogan* (69)	287	Lloyd Mangrum (73)	Merion GC, Ardmore, PA
			George Fazio (75)	

United States Open Championship *(Cont.)*

Year	Winner	Score	Runner-Up	Site
1951	Ben Hogan	287	Clayton Heafner	Oakland Hills CC, Birmingham, MI
1952	Julius Boros	281	Ed Oliver	Northwood CC, Dallas, TX
1953	Ben Hogan	283	Sam Snead	Oakmont CC, Oakmont, PA
1954	Ed Furgol	284	Gene Littler	Baltusrol GC (Lower Course), Springfield, NJ
1955	Jack Fleck* (69)	287	Ben Hogan (72)	Olympic Club (Lake Course), San Fran., CA
1956	Cary Middlecoff	281	Ben Hogan	Oak Hill CC, Rochester, NY
			Julius Boros	
1957	Dick Mayer* (72)	282	Cary Middlecoff (79)	Inverness Club, Toledo, OH
1958	Tommy Bolt	283	Gary Player	Southern Hills CC, Tulsa, OK
1959	Billy Casper	282	Bob Rosburg	Winged Foot GC, Mamaroneck, NY
1960	Arnold Palmer	280	Jack Nicklaus	Cherry Hills CC, Denver, CO
1961	Gene Littler	281	Bob Goalby	Oakland Hills CC, Birmingham, MI
			Doug Sanders	
1962	Jack Nicklaus* (71)	283	Arnold Palmer (74)	Oakmont CC, Oakmont, PA
1963	Julius Boros* (70)	293	Jacky Cupit (73)	The Country Club, Brookline, MA
			Arnold Palmer (76)	
1964	Ken Venturi	278	Tommy Jacobs	Congressional CC, Bethesda, MD
1965	Gary Player* (71)	282	Kel Nagle (74)	Bellerive CC, St. Louis, MO
1966	Billy Casper* (69)	278	Arnold Palmer (73)	Olympic Club (Lake Course), San Fran., CA
1967	Jack Nicklaus	275	Arnold Palmer	Baltusrol GC (Lower Course), Springfield, NJ
1968	Lee Trevino	275	Jack Nicklaus	Oak Hill CC, Rochester, NY
1969	Orville Moody	281	Deane Beman	Champions GC (Cypress Creek Course),
			Al Geiberger	Houston, TX
			Bob Rosburg	
1970	Tony Jacklin	281	Dave Hill	Hazeltine GC, Chaska, MN
1971	Lee Trevino* (68)	280	Jack Nicklaus (71)	Merion GC (East Course), Ardmore, PA
1972	Jack Nicklaus	290	Bruce Crampton	Pebble Beach GL, Pebble Beach, CA
1973	Johnny Miller	279	John Schlee	Oakmont CC, Oakmont, PA
1974	Hale Irwin	287	Forrest Fezler	Winged Foot GC, Mamaroneck, NY
1975	Lou Graham* (71)	287	John Mahaffey (73)	Medinah CC, Medinah, IL
1976	Jerry Pate	277	Tom Weiskopf	Atlanta Athletic Club, Duluth, GA
			Al Geiberger	
1977	Hubert Green	278	Lou Graham	Southern Hills CC, Tulsa, OK
1978	Andy North	285	Dave Stockton	Cherry Hills CC, Denver, CO
			J.C. Snead	
1979	Hale Irwin	284	Gary Player	Inverness Club, Toledo, OH
			Jerry Pate	
1980	Jack Nicklaus	272	Isao Aoki	Baltusrol GC (Lower Course), Springfield, NJ
1981	David Graham	273	George Burns	Merion GC, Ardmore, PA
			Bill Rogers	
1982	Tom Watson	282	Jack Nicklaus	Pebble Beach GL, Pebble Beach, CA
1983	Larry Nelson	280	Tom Watson	Oakmont CC, Oakmont, PA
1984	Fuzzy Zoeller* (67)	276	Greg Norman (75)	Winged Foot GC, Mamaroneck, NY
1985	Andy North	279	Dave Barr	Oakland Hills CC, Birmingham, MI
			T.C. Chen	
			Denis Watson	
1986	Ray Floyd	279	Lanny Wadkins	Shinnecock Hills GC, Southampton, NY
			Chip Beck	
1987	Scott Simpson	277	Tom Watson	Olympic Club (Lake Course), San Fran., CA
1988	Curtis Strange* (71)	278	Nick Faldo (75)	The Country Club, Brookline, MA
1989	Curtis Strange	278	Chip Beck	Oak Hill CC, Rochester, NY
			Mark McCumber	
			Ian Woosnam	
1990	Hale Irwin* (74) (3)	280	Mike Donald (74) (4)	Medinah CC, Medinah, IL
1991	Payne Stewart* (75)	282	Scott Simpson (77)	Hazeltine GC, Chaska, MN
1992	Tom Kite	285	Jeff Sluman	Pebble Beach GL, Pebble Beach, CA
1993	Lee Janzen	272	Payne Stewart	Baltusrol GC, Springfield, NJ
1994	Ernie Els*	279	Loren Roberts	Oakmont CC, Oakmont, PA
			Colin Montgomerie	
1995	Corey Pavin	280	Greg Norman	Shinnecock Hills GC, Southampton, NY
1996	Steve Jones	278	Davis Love III	Oakland Hills CC, Birmingham, MI
			Tom Lehman	
1997	Ernie Els	276	Colin Montgomerie	Congressional CC, Bethesda, MD
1998	Lee Janzen	280	Payne Stewart	Olympic Club (Lake Course), San Fran., CA
1999	Payne Stewart	279	Phil Mickelson	Pinehurst Resort and CC, Pinehurst, NC
2000	Tiger Woods	272	Miguel Angel Jiménez	Pebble Beach GL, Pebble Beach, CA
			Ernie Els	
2001	Retief Goosen* (70)	276	Mark Brooks (72)	Southern Hills CC, Tulsa, OK

United States Open Championship *(Cont.)*

Year	Winner	Score	Runner-Up	Site
2002	Tiger Woods	277	Phil Mickelson	Bethpage State Park (Black), Farmingdale, NY
2003	Jim Furyk	272	Stephen Leaney	Olympia Fields CC, Olympia Fields, IL
2004	Retief Goosen	276	Phil Mickelson	Shinnecock Hills GC, Southampton, NY
2005	Michael Campbell	280	Tiger Woods	Pinehurst Resort and CC, Pinehurst, NC
2006	Geoff Ogilvy	285	Jim Furyk	Winged Foot GC, Mamaroneck, NY
			Colin Montgomerie	
			Phil Mickelson	
2007	Angel Cabrera	285	Jim Furyk	Oakmont CC, Oakmont, PA
			Tiger Woods	
2008	Tiger Woods* (71) (4)	283	Rocco Mediate	Torrey Pines GC (South), San Diego, CA
2009	Lucas Glover	276	Phil Mickelson	Bethpage State Park (Black), Farmingdale, NY
			David Duval	
			Ricky Barnes	
2010	Graeme McDowell	284	Gregory Havret	Pebble Beach GL, Pebble Beach, CA

*Winner in playoff. Playoff scores are in parentheses. The 1990 and 2008 playoffs went to one hole of sudden death after an 18-hole playoff. In the 1994 playoff, Montgomerie was eliminated after 18 playoff holes, and Els beat Roberts on the 20th.
†Before 1898, 36 holes. From 1898 on, 72 holes.

The Open Championship (British Open)

Year	Winner	Score	Runner-Up	Site
1860†	Willie Park	174	Tom Morris Sr.	Prestwick, Scotland
1861‡	Tom Morris Sr.	163	Willie Park	Prestwick, Scotland
1862	Tom Morris Sr.	163	Willie Park	Prestwick, Scotland
1863	Willie Park	168	Tom Morris Sr.	Prestwick, Scotland
1864	Tom Morris, Sr.	160	Andrew Strath	Prestwick, Scotland
1865	Andrew Strath	162	Willie Park	Prestwick, Scotland
1866	Willie Park	169	David Park	Prestwick, Scotland
1867	Tom Morris Sr.	170	Willie Park	Prestwick, Scotland
1868	Tom Morris Jr.	154	Tom Morris Sr.	Prestwick, Scotland
1869	Tom Morris Jr.	157	Tom Morris Sr.	Prestwick, Scotland
1870	Tom Morris Jr.	149	David Strath	Prestwick, Scotland
			Bob Kirk	
1871	No tournament			
1872	Tom Morris Jr.	166	David Strath	Prestwick, Scotland
1873	Tom Kidd	179	Jamie Anderson	St. Andrews, Scotland
1874	Mungo Park	159	No record	Musselburgh, Scotland
1875	Willie Park	166	Bob Martin	Prestwick, Scotland
1876	Bob Martin#	176	David Strath	St. Andrews, Scotland
1877	Jamie Anderson	160	Bob Pringle	Musselburgh, Scotland
1878	Jamie Anderson	157	Robert Kirk	Prestwick, Scotland
1879	Jamie Anderson	169	Andrew Kirkaldy	St. Andrews, Scotland
			James Allan	
1880	Robert Ferguson	162	No record	Musselburgh, Scotland
1881	Robert Ferguson	170	Jamie Anderson	Prestwick, Scotland
1882	Robert Ferguson	171	Willie Fernie	St. Andrews, Scotland
1883	Willie Fernie*	159	Robert Ferguson	Musselburgh, Scotland
1884	Jack Simpson	160	Douglas Rolland	Prestwick, Scotland
			Willie Fernie	
1885	Bob Martin	171	Archie Simpson	St. Andrews, Scotland
1886	David Brown	157	Willie Campbell	Musselburgh, Scotland
1887	Willie Park Jr.	161	Bob Martin	Prestwick, Scotland
1888	Jack Burns	171	Bernard Sayers	St. Andrews, Scotland
			David Anderson	
1889	Willie Park Jr.* (158)	155	Andrew Kirkaldy (163)	Musselburgh, Scotland
1890	John Ball	164	Willie Fernie	Prestwick, Scotland
1891	Hugh Kirkaldy	166	Andrew Kirkaldy	St. Andrews, Scotland
			Willie Fernie	
1892	Harold Hilton	**305	John Ball	Muirfield, Scotland
			Hugh Kirkaldy	
1893	William Auchterlonie	322	John E. Laidlay	Prestwick, Scotland
1894	John H. Taylor	326	Douglas Rolland	Royal St. George's, England
1895	John H. Taylor	322	Alexander Herd	St. Andrews, Scotland
1896	Harry Vardon* (157)	316	John H. Taylor (161)	Muirfield, Scotland
1897	Harold Hilton	314	James Braid	Royal Liverpool (Hoylake), England
1898	Harry Vardon	307	Willie Park Jr.	Prestwick, Scotland
1899	Harry Vardon	310	Jack White	Royal St. George's, England
1900	John H. Taylor	309	Harry Vardon	St. Andrews, Scotland
1901	James Braid	309	Harry Vardon	Muirfield, Scotland

The Open Championship (British Open) *(Cont.)*

Year	Winner	Score	Runner-Up	Site
1902	Alexander Herd	307	Harry Vardon	Royal Liverpool (Hoylake), England
1903	Harry Vardon	300	Tom Vardon	Prestwick, Scotland
1904	Jack White	296	John H. Taylor	Royal St. George's, England
1905	James Braid	318	John H. Taylor	St. Andrews, Scotland
			Rolland Jones	
1906	James Braid	300	John H. Taylor	Muirfield, Scotland
1907	Arnaud Massy	312	John H. Taylor	Royal Liverpool (Hoylake), England
1908	James Braid	291	Tom Ball	Prestwick, Scotland
1909	John H. Taylor	295	James Braid	Deal, England
			Tom Ball	
1910	James Braid	299	Alexander Herd	St. Andrews, Scotland
1911	Harry Vardon	303	Arnaud Massy	Royal St. George's, England
1912	Ted Ray	295	Harry Vardon	Muirfield, Scotland
1913	John H. Taylor	304	Ted Ray	Royal Liverpool (Hoylake), England
1914	Harry Vardon	306	John H. Taylor	Prestwick, Scotland
1915–19	No tournament			
1920	George Duncan	303	Alexander Herd	Deal, England
1921	Jock Hutchison* (150)	296	Roger Wethered (159)	St. Andrews, Scotland
1922	Walter Hagen	300	George Duncan	Royal St. George's, England
			Jim Barnes	
1923	Arthur G. Havers	295	Walter Hagen	Troon, Scotland
1924	Walter Hagen	301	Ernest Whitcombe	Royal Liverpool (Hoylake), England
1925	Jim Barnes	300	Archie Compston	Prestwick, Scotland
			Ted Ray	
1926	Bobby Jones	291	Al Watrous	Royal Lytham & St. Annes, England
1927	Bobby Jones	285	Aubrey Boomer	St. Andrews, Scotland
1928	Walter Hagen	292	Gene Sarazen	Royal St. George's, England
1929	Walter Hagen	292	Johnny Farrell	Muirfield, Scotland
1930	Bobby Jones	291	Macdonald Smith	Royal Liverpool (Hoylake), England
			Leo Diegel	
1931	Tommy Armour	296	Jose Jurado	Carnoustie, Scotland
1932	Gene Sarazen	283	Macdonald Smith	Prince's, England
1933	Denny Shute* (149)	292	Craig Wood (154)	St. Andrews, Scotland
1934	Henry Cotton	283	Sidney F. Brews	Royal St. George's, England
1935	Alfred Perry	283	Alfred Padgham	Muirfield, Scotland
1936	Alfred Padgham	287	James Adams	Royal Liverpool (Hoylake), England
1937	Henry Cotton	290	Reginald A. Whitcombe	Carnoustie, Scotland
1938	Reginald A. Whitcombe	295	James Adams	Royal St. George's, England
1939	Richard Burton	290	Johnny Bulla	St. Andrews, Scotland
1940–45	No tournament			
1946	Sam Snead	290	Bobby Locke	St. Andrews, Scotland
			Johnny Bulla	
1947	Fred Daly	293	Reginald W. Horne	Royal Liverpool (Hoylake), England
			Frank Stranahan	
1948	Henry Cotton	294	Fred Daly	Muirfield, Scotland
1949	Bobby Locke* (135)	283	Harry Bradshaw (147)	Royal St. George's, England
1950	Bobby Locke	279	Roberto DeVicenzo	Troon, Scotland
1951	Max Faulkner	285	Tony Cerda	Portrush, Ireland
1952	Bobby Locke	287	Peter Thomson	Royal Lytham & St. Annes, England
1953	Ben Hogan	282	Frank Stranahan	Carnoustie, Scotland
			Dai Rees	
			Peter Thomson	
			Tony Cerda	
1954	Peter Thomson	283	Sidney S. Scott	Royal Birkdale, Southport, England
			Dai Rees	
			Bobby Locke	
1955	Peter Thomson	281	John Fallon	St. Andrews, Scotland
1956	Peter Thomson	286	Flory Van Donck	Royal Liverpool (Hoylake), England
1957	Bobby Locke	279	Peter Thomson	St. Andrews, Scotland
1958	Peter Thomson* (139)	278	Dave Thomas (143)	Royal Lytham & St. Annes, England
1959	Gary Player	284	Fred Bullock	Muirfield, Scotland
			Flory Van Donck	
1960	Kel Nagle	278	Arnold Palmer	St. Andrews, Scotland
1961	Arnold Palmer	284	Dai Rees	Royal Birkdale, Southport, England
1962	Arnold Palmer	276	Kel Nagle	Troon, Scotland
1963	Bob Charles* (140)	277	Phil Rodgers (148)	Royal Lytham & St. Annes, England
1964	Tony Lema	279	Jack Nicklaus	St. Andrews, Scotland

The Open Championship (British Open) (Cont.)

Year	Winner	Score	Runner-Up	Site
1965	Peter Thomson	285	Brian Huggett	Royal Birkdale, Southport, England
			Christy O'Connor	
1966	Jack Nicklaus	282	Doug Sanders	Muirfield, Scotland
			Dave Thomas	
1967	Robert DeVicenzo	278	Jack Nicklaus	Royal Liverpool (Hoylake), England
1968	Gary Player	289	Jack Nicklaus	Carnoustie, Scotland
			Bob Charles	
1969	Tony Jacklin	280	Bob Charles	Royal Lytham & St. Annes, England
1970	Jack Nicklaus* (72)	283	Doug Sanders (73)	St. Andrews, Scotland
1971	Lee Trevino	278	Lu Liang Huan	Royal Birkdale, Southport, England
1972	Lee Trevino	278	Jack Nicklaus	Muirfield, Scotland
1973	Tom Weiskopf	276	Johnny Miller	Troon, Scotland
1974	Gary Player	282	Peter Oosterhuis	Royal Lytham & St. Annes, England
1975	Tom Watson* (71)	279	Jack Newton (72)	Carnoustie, Scotland
1976	Johnny Miller	279	Jack Nicklaus	Royal Birkdale, Southport, England
			Seve Ballesteros	
1977	Tom Watson	268	Jack Nicklaus	Turnberry, Scotland
1978	Jack Nicklaus	281	Ben Crenshaw	St. Andrews, Scotland
			Tom Kite	
			Ray Floyd	
			Simon Owen	
1979	Seve Ballesteros	283	Ben Crenshaw	Royal Lytham & St. Annes, England
			Jack Nicklaus	
1980	Tom Watson	271	Lee Trevino	Muirfield, Scotland
1981	Bill Rogers	276	Bernhard Langer	Royal St. George's, England
1982	Tom Watson	284	Nick Price	Troon, Scotland
			Peter Oosterhuis	
1983	Tom Watson	275	Andy Bean	Royal Birkdale, Southport, England
1984	Seve Ballesteros	276	Tom Watson	St. Andrews, Scotland
			Bernhard Langer	
1985	Sandy Lyle	282	Payne Stewart	Royal St. George's, England
1986	Greg Norman	280	Gordon Brand	Turnberry, Scotland
1987	Nick Faldo	279	Paul Azinger	Muirfield, Scotland
			Rodger Davis	
1988	Seve Ballesteros	273	Nick Price	Royal Lytham & St. Annes, England
1989††	Mark Calcavecchia* (4-3-3-3)	275	Wayne Grady (4-4-4-4)	Troon, Scotland
			Greg Norman (3-3-4-x)	
1990	Nick Faldo	270	Payne Stewart	St. Andrews, Scotland
			Mark McNulty	
1991	Ian Baker-Finch	272	Mike Harwood	Royal Birkdale, Southport, England
1992	Nick Faldo	272	John Cook	Muirfield, Scotland
1993	Greg Norman	267	Nick Faldo	Royal St. George's, England
1994	Nick Price	268	Jesper Parnevik	Turnberry, Scotland
1995	John Daly* (4-3-4-4)	282	C. Rocca (5-4-7-3)	St. Andrews, Scotland
1996	Tom Lehman	271	Mark McCumber	Royal Lytham & St. Annes, England
			Ernie Els	
1997	Justin Leonard	272	Jesper Parnevik	Troon, Scotland
			Darren Clarke	
1998	Mark O'Meara* (4-4-5-4)	280	Brian Watts (5-4-5-5)	Royal Birkdale, Southport, England
1999	Paul Lawrie* (5-4-3-3)	290	Jean Van de Velde (6-4-3-5)	Carnoustie, Scotland
			Justin Leonard (5-4-4-5)	
2000	Tiger Woods	269	Thomas Bjorn	St. Andrews, Scotland
			Ernie Els	
2001	David Duval	274	Niclas Fasth	Royal Lytham & St. Annes, England
2002	Ernie Els*	278	Stuart Appleby	Muirfield, Scotland
2003	Ben Curtis	283	Vijay Singh	Royal St. George's, England
2004	Todd Hamilton*	274	Ernie Els	Troon, Scotland
2005	Tiger Woods	274	Colin Montgomerie	St. Andrews, Scotland
2006	Tiger Woods	270	Chris DiMarco	Royal Liverpool (Hoylake), England
2007	Padraig Harrington*	277	Sergio Garcia	Carnoustie, Scotland
2008	Padraig Harrington	283	Ian Poulter	Royal Birkdale, Southport, England
2009	Stewart Cink*	278	Tom Watson	Turnberry, Scotland
2010	Louis Oosthuizen	272	Lee Westwood	St. Andrews, Scotland

*Winner in playoff. †The first event was open only to professional golfers.
‡The second annual open was open to amateurs and pros. #Tied, but refused playoff.
**Championship extended from 36 to 72 holes. ††Playoff cut from 18 holes to 4 holes.

PGA Championship

Year	Winner	Score	Runner-Up	Site
1916	Jim Barnes	1 up	Jock Hutchison	Siwanoy CC, Bronxville, NY
1917–18	No tournament			
1919	Jim Barnes	6 & 5	Fred McLeod	Engineers CC, Roslyn, NY
1920	Jock Hutchison	1 up	J. Douglas Edgar	Flossmoor CC, Flossmoor, IL
1921	Walter Hagen	3 & 2	Jim Barnes	Inwood CC, Far Rockaway, NY
1922	Gene Sarazen	4 & 3	Emmet French	Oakmont CC, Oakmont, PA
1923	Gene Sarazen	1 up / 38 holes	Walter Hagen	Pelham CC, Pelham, NY
1924	Walter Hagen	2 up	Jim Barnes	French Lick CC, French Lick, IN
1925	Walter Hagen	6 & 5	William Mehlhorn	Olympia Fields CC, Olympia Fields, IL
1926	Walter Hagen	5 & 3	Leo Diegel	Salisbury GC, Westbury, NY
1927	Walter Hagen	1 up	Joe Turnesa	Cedar Crest CC, Dallas, TX
1928	Leo Diegel	6 & 5	Al Espinosa	Five Farms CC, Baltimore, MD
1929	Leo Diegel	6 & 4	Johnny Farrell	Hillcrest CC, Los Angeles, CA
1930	Tommy Armour	1 up	Gene Sarazen	Fresh Meadow CC, Flushing, NY
1931	Tom Creavy	2 & 1	Denny Shute	Wannamoisett CC, Rumford, RI
1932	Olin Dutra	4 & 3	Frank Walsh	Keller GC, St. Paul, MN
1933	Gene Sarazen	5 & 4	Willie Goggin	Blue Mound CC, Milwaukee, WI
1934	Paul Runyan	1 up	Craig Wood	Park CC, Williamsville, NY
1935	Johnny Revolta	5 & 4 / 38 holes	Tommy Armour	Twin Hills CC, Oklahoma City, OK
1936	Denny Shute	3 & 2	Jimmy Thomson	Pinehurst CC, Pinehurst, NC
1937	Denny Shute	1 up / 37 holes	Harold McSpaden	Pittsburgh FC, Aspinwall, PA
1938	Paul Runyan	8 & 7	Sam Snead	Shawnee CC, Shawnee-on-Delaware, PA
1939	Henry Picard	1 up / 37 holes	Byron Nelson	Pomonok CC, Flushing, NY
1940	Byron Nelson	1 up	Sam Snead	Hershey CC, Hershey, PA
1941	Vic Ghezzi	1 up / 38 holes	Byron Nelson	Cherry Hills CC, Denver, CO
1942	Sam Snead	2 & 1	Jim Turnesa	Seaview CC, Atlantic City, NJ
1943	No tournament			
1944	Bob Hamilton	1 up	Byron Nelson	Manito G & CC, Spokane, WA
1945	Byron Nelson	4 & 3	Sam Byrd	Morraine CC, Dayton, OH
1946	Ben Hogan	6 & 4	Ed Oliver	Portland GC, Portland, OR
1947	Jim Ferrier	2 & 1	Chick Harbert	Plum Hollow CC, Detroit, MI
1948	Ben Hogan	7 & 6	Mike Turnesa	Norwood Hills CC, St. Louis, MO
1949	Sam Snead	3 & 2	Johnny Palmer	Hermitage CC, Richmond, VA
1950	Chandler Harper	4 & 3	Henry Williams Jr.	Scioto CC, Columbus, OH
1951	Sam Snead	7 & 6	Walter Burkemo	Oakmont CC, Oakmont, PA
1952	Jim Turnesa	1 up	Chick Harbert	Big Spring CC, Louisville, KY
1953	Walter Burkemo	2 & 1	Felice Torza	Birmingham CC, Birmingham, MI
1954	Chick Harbert	4 & 3	Walter Burkemo	Keller GC, St. Paul, MN
1955	Doug Ford	4 & 3	Cary Middlecoff	Meadowbrook CC, Detroit, MI
1956	Jack Burke	3 & 2	Ted Kroll	Blue Hill CC, Boston, MA
1957	Lionel Hebert	2 & 1	Dow Finsterwald	Miami Valley CC, Dayton, OH
1958	Dow Finsterwald	276	Billy Casper	Llanerch CC, Havertown, PA
1959	Bob Rosburg	277	Jerry Barber / Doug Sanders	Minneapolis GC, St. Louis Park, MN
1960	Jay Hebert	281	Jim Ferrier	Firestone CC, Akron, OH
1961	Jerry Barber* (67)	277	Don January (68)	Olympia Fields CC, Olympia Fields, IL
1962	Gary Player	278	Bob Goalby	Aronimink GC, Newton Square, PA
1963	Jack Nicklaus	279	Dave Ragan Jr.	Dallas Athletic Club, Dallas, TX
1964	Bobby Nichols	271	Jack Nicklaus / Arnold Palmer	Columbus CC, Columbus, OH
1965	Dave Marr	280	Billy Casper / Jack Nicklaus	Laurel Valley CC, Ligonier, PA
1966	Al Geiberger	280	Dudley Wysong	Firestone CC, Akron, OH
1967	Don January* (69)	281	Don Massengale (71)	Columbine CC, Littleton, CO
1968	Julius Boros	281	Bob Charles / Arnold Palmer	Pecan Valley CC, San Antonio, TX
1969	Ray Floyd	276	Gary Player	NCR CC, Dayton, OH
1970	Dave Stockton	279	Arnold Palmer / Bob Murphy	Southern Hills CC, Tulsa, OK
1971	Jack Nicklaus	281	Billy Casper	PGA Nat'l GC, Palm Beach Gardens, FL

PGA Championship *(Cont.)*

Year	Winner	Score	Runner-Up	Site
1972	Gary Player	281	Tommy Aaron	Oakland Hills CC, Birmingham, MI
			Jim Jamieson	
1973	Jack Nicklaus	277	Bruce Crampton	Canterbury GC, Cleveland, OH
1974	Lee Trevino	276	Jack Nicklaus	Tanglewood GC, Winston-Salem, NC
1975	Jack Nicklaus	276	Bruce Crampton	Firestone CC, Akron, OH
1976	Dave Stockton	281	Ray Floyd	Congressional CC, Bethesda, MD
			Don January	
1977†	Lanny Wadkins* (4-4-4)	282	Gene Littler (4-4-5)	Pebble Beach GL, Pebble Beach, CA
1978	John Mahaffey* (4–3)	276	Jerry Pate (4–4)	Oakmont CC, Oakmont, PA
			Tom Watson (4–5)	
1979	David Graham* (4-4-2)	272	Ben Crenshaw (4-4-4)	Oakland Hills CC, Birmingham, MI
1980	Jack Nicklaus	274	Andy Bean	Oak Hill CC, Rochester, NY
1981	Larry Nelson	273	Fuzzy Zoeller	Atlanta Athletic Club, Duluth, GA
1982	Raymond Floyd	272	Lanny Wadkins	Southern Hills CC, Tulsa, OK
1983	Hal Sutton	274	Jack Nicklaus	Riviera CC, Pacific Palisades, CA
1984	Lee Trevino	273	Gary Player	Shoal Creek, Birmingham, AL
			Lanny Wadkins	
1985	Hubert Green	278	Lee Trevino	Cherry Hills CC, Denver, CO
1986	Bob Tway	276	Greg Norman	Inverness CC, Toledo, OH
1987	Larry Nelson* (4)	287	Lanny Wadkins (5)	PGA Natl GC, Palm Beach Gardens, FL
1988	Jeff Sluman	272	Paul Azinger	Oak Tree GC, Edmond, OK
1989	Payne Stewart	276	Mike Reid	Kemper Lakes GC, Hawthorn Woods, IL
1990	Wayne Grady	282	Fred Couples	Shoal Creek, Birmingham, AL
1991	John Daly	276	Bruce Lietzke	Crooked Stick GC, Carmel, IN
1992	Nick Price	278	Jim Gallagher Jr.	Bellerive CC, St. Louis, MO
1993	Paul Azinger* (4–4)	272	Greg Norman (4–5)	Inverness CC, Toledo, OH
1994	Nick Price	269	Corey Pavin	Southern Hills CC, Tulsa, OK
1995	Steve Elkington* (3)	267	Colin Montgomerie (4)	Riviera CC, Pacific Palisades, CA
1996	Mark Brooks* (3)	277	Kenny Perry (x)	Valhalla GC, Louisville, KY
1997	Davis Love III	269	Justin Leonard	Winged Foot GC, Mamaroneck, NY
1998	Vijay Singh	271	Steve Stricker	Sahalee CC, Redmond, WA
1999	Tiger Woods	277	Sergio Garcia	Medinah CC, Medinah, IL
2000	Tiger Woods* (3-4-5)	270	Bob May (4-4-x)	Valhalla GC, Louisville, KY
2001	David Toms	265	Phil Mickelson	Atlanta AC, Duluth, GA
2002	Rich Beem	278	Tiger Woods	Hazeltine National GC, Shaska, MN
2003	Shaun Micheel	276	Chad Campbell	Oak Hill CC, Rochester, NY
2004	Vijay Singh*	280	Chris DiMarco	Whistling Straits GC, Kohler, WI
2005	Phil Mickelson	276	Steve Elkington	Baltusrol GC, Springfield, NJ
2006	Tiger Woods	270	Shaun Micheel	Medinah CC, Medinah, IL
2007	Tiger Woods	272	Woody Austin	Southern Hills CC, Tulsa, OK
2008	Padraig Harrington	277	Sergio Garcia	Oakland Hills CC, Birmingham, MI
2009	Y.E. Yang	280	Tiger Woods	Hazeltine National GC, Chaska, MN
2010	Martin Kaymer* (4-2-5)	277	Bubba Watson (3-3-6)	Whistling Straits GC, Kohler, WI

*Winner in playoff. †Playoff changed from 18 holes to sudden death.

THE PGA TOUR
Most Career Wins†

	Wins		Wins		Wins
Sam Snead	82	Billy Casper	51	Lloyd Mangrum	36
Jack Nicklaus	73	Walter Hagen	44	*Vijay Singh	34
*Tiger Woods	71	Cary Middlecoff	40	Horton Smith	32
Ben Hogan	64	Gene Sarazen	39	Harry Cooper	31
Arnold Palmer	62	Tom Watson	39	Jimmy Demaret	31
Byron Nelson	52	*Phil Mickelson	38	Leo Diegel	30

† Through 10/05/10. * Active player.

Alltime Major Championship Winners

	Masters	U.S. Open	British Open	PGA Champ.	U.S. Amateur	British Amateur	Total
Jack Nicklaus	6	4	3	5	2	0	20
*Tiger Woods	4	3	3	4	3	0	17
Bobby Jones	0	4	3	0	5	1	13
Walter Hagen	0	2	4	5	0	0	11
Ben Hogan	2	4	1	2	0	0	9
Gary Player	3	1	3	2	0	0	9
John Ball	0	0	1	0	0	8	9
Arnold Palmer	4	1	2	0	1	0	8
Tom Watson	2	1	5	0	0	0	8
Harold Hilton	0	0	2	0	1	4	7
Gene Sarazen	1	2	1	3	0	0	7
Sam Snead	3	0	1	3	0	0	7
Harry Vardon	0	1	6	0	0	0	7

*Active PGA Tour player.

Alltime Multiple Professional Major Winners

MASTERS

Jack Nicklaus	6
Arnold Palmer	4
*Tiger Woods	4
Jimmy Demaret	3
Nick Faldo	3
*Phil Mickelson	3
Gary Player	3
Sam Snead	3
Seve Ballesteros	2
Ben Crenshaw	2
Ben Hogan	2
*Bernhard Langer	2
Byron Nelson	2
*José María Olazábal	2
Horton Smith	2
Tom Watson	2

U.S. OPEN

Willie Anderson	4
Ben Hogan	4
Bobby Jones	4
Jack Nicklaus	4
Hale Irwin	3
*Tiger Woods	3
Julius Boros	2
Billy Casper	2
*Ernie Els	2
*Retief Goosen	2
Ralph Guldahl	2
Walter Hagen	2
*Lee Janzen	2
John McDermott	2
Cary Middlecoff	2
Andy North	2
Gene Sarazen	2
Alex Smith	2
Payne Stewart	2
Curtis Strange	2
Lee Trevino	2

BRITISH OPEN

Harry Vardon	6
James Braid	5
J.H. Taylor	5
Peter Thomson	5
Tom Watson	5
Walter Hagen	4
Bobby Locke	4
Tom Morris Sr.	4
Tom Morris Jr.	4
Willie Park	4
Jamie Anderson	3
Seve Ballesteros	3
Henry Cotton	3
Nick Faldo	3
Robert Ferguson	3
Bobby Jones	3
Jack Nicklaus	3
Gary Player	3
*Tiger Woods	3
*Padraig Harrington	2
Harold Hilton	2
Bob Martin	2
*Greg Norman	2
Arnold Palmer	2
Willie Park Jr.	2
Lee Trevino	2

PGA CHAMPIONSHIP

Walter Hagen	5
Jack Nicklaus	5
*Tiger Woods	4
Gene Sarazen	3
Sam Snead	3
Jim Barnes	2
Leo Diegel	2
Raymond Floyd	2
Ben Hogan	2
Byron Nelson	2
Larry Nelson	2
Gary Player	2
Paul Runyan	2
Denny Shute	2
Dave Stockton	2
Lee Trevino	2
*Vijay Singh	2

*Active PGA Tour player.

THE PGA TOUR (Cont.)

Season Money Leaders

	Earnings ($)			Earnings ($)			Earnings ($)
1934 ...Paul Runyan	6,767.00		1960 ...Arnold Palmer	75,262.85		1986 ...Greg Norman	653,296.00
1935 ...Johnny Revolta	9,543.00		1961 ...Gary Player	64,540.45		1987 ...Curtis Strange	925,941.00
1936 ...Horton Smith	7,682.00		1962 ...Arnold Palmer	81,448.33		1988 ...Curtis Strange	1,147,644.00
1937 ...Harry Cooper	14,138.69		1963 ...Arnold Palmer	128,230.00		1989 ...Tom Kite	1,395,278.00
1938 ...Sam Snead	19,534.49		1964 ...Jack Nicklaus	113,284.50		1990 ...Greg Norman	1,165,477.00
1939 ...Henry Picard	10,303.00		1965 ...Jack Nicklaus	140,752.14		1991 ...Corey Pavin	979,430.00
1940 ...Ben Hogan	10,655.00		1966 ...Billy Casper	121,944.92		1992 ...Fred Couples	1,344,188.00
1941 ...Ben Hogan	18,358.00		1967 ...Jack Nicklaus	188,998.08		1993 ...Nick Price	1,478,557.00
1942 ...Ben Hogan	13,143.00		1968 ...Billy Casper	205,168.67		1994 ...Nick Price	1,499,927.00
1943 ...No statistics compiled			1969 ...Frank Beard	164,707.11		1995 ...Greg Norman	1,654,959.00
1944 ...Byron Nelson*	37,967.69		1970 ...Lee Trevino	157,037.63		1996 ...Tom Lehman	1,780,159.00
1945 ...Byron Nelson*	63,335.66		1971 ...Jack Nicklaus	244,490.50		1997 ...Tiger Woods	2,066,833.00
1946 ...Ben Hogan	42,556.16		1972 ...Jack Nicklaus	320,542.26		1998 ...David Duval	2,591,031.00
1947 ...Jimmy Demaret	27,936.83		1973 ...Jack Nicklaus	308,362.10		1999 ...Tiger Woods	6,616,585.00
1948 ...Ben Hogan	32,112.00		1974 ...Johnny Miller	353,021.59		2000 ...Tiger Woods	9,188,321.00
1949 ...Sam Snead	31,593.83		1975 ...Jack Nicklaus	298,149.17		2001 ...Tiger Woods	5,687,777.00
1950 ...Sam Snead	35,758.83		1976 ...Jack Nicklaus	266,438.57		2002 ...Tiger Woods	6,912,625.00
1951 ...Lloyd Mangrum	26,088.83		1977 ...Tom Watson	310,653.16		2003 ...Vijay Singh	7,573,907.00
1952 ...Julius Boros	37,032.97		1978 ...Tom Watson	362,428.93		2004 ...Vijay Singh	10,905,166.00
1953 ...Lew Worsham	34,002.00		1979 ...Tom Watson	462,636.00		2005 ...Tiger Woods	10,628,024.00
1954 ...Bob Toski	65,819.81		1980 ...Tom Watson	530,808.33		2006 ...Tiger Woods	9,941,563.00
1955 ...Julius Boros	63,121.55		1981 ...Tom Kite	375,698.84		2007 ...Tiger Woods	10,867,052.00
1956 ...Ted Kroll	72,835.83		1982 ...Craig Stadler	446,462.00		2008 ...Vijay Singh	6,601,094.00
1957 ...Dick Mayer	65,835.00		1983 ...Hal Sutton	426,668.00		2009 ...Tiger Woods	10,508,163.00
1958 ...Arnold Palmer	42,607.50		1984 ...Tom Watson	476,260.00			
1959 ...Art Wall	53,167.60		1985 ...Curtis Strange	542,321.00			

* War bonds. Note: Total money listed from 1968 through 1974. Official money listed from 1975 on.

Year-by-Year Statistical Leaders

SCORING AVERAGE			DRIVING DISTANCE		Yds		DRIVING ACCURACY	
1980 ....Lee Trevino	69.73		1980 ......Dan Pohl		274.3		1980 ....Mike Reid	79.5
1981 ....Tom Kite	69.80		1981 ......Dan Pohl		280.1		1981 ....Calvin Peete	81.9
1982 ....Tom Kite	70.21		1982 ......Bill Calfee		275.3		1982 ....Calvin Peete	84.6
1983 ....Raymond Floyd	70.61		1983 ......John McComish		277.4		1983 ....Calvin Peete	81.3
1984 ....Calvin Peete	70.56		1984 ......Bill Glasson		276.5		1984 ....Calvin Peete	77.5
1985 ....Don Pooley	70.36		1985 ......Andy Bean		278.2		1985 ....Calvin Peete	80.6
1986 ....Scott Hoch	70.08		1986 ......Davis Love III		285.7		1986 ....Calvin Peete	81.7
1987 ....David Frost	70.09		1987 ......John McComish		283.9		1987 ....Calvin Peete	83.0
1988 ....Greg Norman	69.38		1988 ......Steve Thomas		284.6		1988 ....Calvin Peete	82.5
1989 ....Payne Stewart	69.485†		1989 ......Ed Humenik		280.9		1989 ....Calvin Peete	82.6
1990 ....Greg Norman	69.10		1990 ......Tom Purtzer		279.6		1990 ....Calvin Peete	83.7
1991 ....Fred Couples	69.59		1991 ......John Daly		288.9		1991 ....Hale Irwin	78.3
1992 ....Fred Couples	69.38		1992 ......John Daly		283.4		1992 ....Doug Tewell	82.3
1993 ....Greg Norman	68.90		1993 ......John Daly		288.9		1993 ....Doug Tewell	82.5
1994 ....Greg Norman	68.81		1994 ......Davis Love III		283.8		1994 ....David Edwards	81.6
1995 ....Greg Norman	69.06		1995 ......John Daly		289.0		1995 ....Fred Funk	81.3
1996 ....Tom Lehman	69.32		1996 ......John Daly		288.8		1996 ....Fred Funk	78.7
1997 ....Nick Price	68.98		1997 ......John Daly		302.0		1997 ....Allen Doyle	80.8
1998 ....David Duval	69.13		1998 ......John Daly		299.4		1998 ....Bruce Fleisher	81.4
1999 ....Tiger Woods	68.43		1999 ......John Daly		305.6		1999 ....Fred Funk	80.2
2000 ....Tiger Woods	67.79		2000 ......John Daly		301.4		2000 ....Fred Funk	79.7
2001 ....Tiger Woods	68.81		2001 ......John Daly		306.7		2001 ....Joe Durant	81.1
2002 ....Tiger Woods	68.13 ‒		2002 ......John Daly		306.8		2002 ....Fred Funk	81.2
2003 ....Tiger Woods	68.41		2003 ......Hank Kuehne		321.4		2003 ....Fred Funk	77.9
2004 ....Vijay Singh	69.19		2004 ......Hank Kuehne		314.4		2004 ....Fred Funk	77.2
2005 ....Tiger Woods	68.66		2005 ......Scott Hend		318.9		2005 ....Jeff Hart	76.0
2006 ....Tiger Woods	68.11		2006 ......Bubba Watson		319.6		2006 ....Joe Durant	78.4
2007 ....Tiger Woods	67.79		2007 ......Bubba Watson		315.2		2007 ....Jose Coceres	75.5
2008 ....Sergio Garcia	69.12		2008 ......Bubba Watson		315.1		2008 ....Olin Browne	80.4
2009 ....Tiger Woods	68.05		2009 ......Robert Garrigus		312.3		2009 ....Joe Durant	74.8

Note: Scoring average per round, with adjustments made at each round for the field's course scoring average.

Note: Average computed by charting distance of two tee shots on a predetermined par-four or par-five hole (front & back).

Note: Percentage of fairways hit on number of par-four and par-five holes played; par-three holes excluded.

THE PGA TOUR (Cont.)

Year by Year Statistical Leaders (Cont.)

GREENS IN REGULATION

1980	Jack Nicklaus	72.1
1981	Calvin Peete	73.1
1982	Calvin Peete	72.4
1983	Calvin Peete	71.4
1984	Andy Bean	72.1
1985	John Mahaffey	71.9
1986	John Mahaffey	72.0
1987	Gil Morgan	73.3
1988	John Adams	73.9
1989	Bruce Lietzke	72.6
1990	Doug Tewell	70.9
1991	Bruce Lietzke	73.3
1992	Tim Simpson	74.0
1993	Fuzzy Zoeller	73.6
1994	Bill Glasson	73.0
1995	Lenny Clements	72.3
1996	Fred Couples	71.8
	Mark O'Meara	71.8
1997	Tom Lehman	72.7
1998	Hal Sutton	71.3
1999	Tiger Woods	71.4
2000	Tiger Woods	75.2
2001	Tom Lehman	74.5
2002	Tiger Woods	74.0
2003	Joe Durant	72.9
2004	Joe Durant	73.3
2005	Sergio Garcia	71.8
2006	Tiger Woods	74.2
2007	Tiger Woods	71.0
2008	Joe Durant	71.1
2009	John Senden	70.9

Note: Average of greens reached in regulation out of total holes played; hole is considered hit in regulation if any part of the ball rests on the putting surface in two shots less than the hole's par—a par-5 hit in two shots is one green in regulation.

PUTTING

1980	Jerry Pate	28.81
1981	Alan Tapie	28.70
1982	Ben Crenshaw	28.65
1983	Morris Hatalsky	27.96
1984	Gary McCord	28.57
1985	Craig Stadler	28.627†
1986	Greg Norman	1.736
1987	Ben Crenshaw	1.743
1988	Don Pooley	1.729
1989	Steve Jones	1.734
1990	Larry Rinker	1.7467†
1991	Jay Don Blake	1.7326†
1992	Mark O'Meara	1.731
1993	David Frost	1.739
1994	Loren Roberts	1.737
1995	Jim Furyk	1.708
1996	Brad Faxon	1.709
1997	Don Pooley	1.718
1998	Rick Fehr	1.722
1999	Brad Faxon	1.723
2000	Brad Faxon	1.704
2001	David Frost	1.708

PUTTING (Cont.)

2002	Bob Heintz	1.682
2003	John Huston	1.713
2004	Stewart Cink	1.723
2005	Arjun Atwal	1.710
2006	Daniel Chopra	1.712
2007	Tim Clark	1.727
2008	Bob Tway	1.718
2009	Patrick Sheehan	1.358

Note: Average number of putts taken for all holes played; prior to 1986, based on average number of putts per 18 holes.

SAND SAVES

1980	Bob Eastwood	65.4
1981	Tom Watson	60.1
1982	Isao Aoki	60.2
1983	Isao Aoki	62.3
1984	Peter Oosterhuis	64.7
1985	Tom Purtzer	60.8
1986	Paul Azinger	63.8
1987	Paul Azinger	63.2
1988	Greg Powers	63.5
1989	Mike Sullivan	66.0
1990	Paul Azinger	67.2
1991	Ben Crenshaw	64.9
1992	Mitch Adcock	66.9
1993	Ken Green	64.4
1994	Corey Pavin	65.4
1995	Billy Mayfair	68.6
1996	Gary Rusnak	64.0
1997	Bob Estes	70.3
1998	Keith Fergus	71.0
1999	Jeff Sluman	67.3
2000	Fred Couples	67.0
2001	Franklin Langham	68.9
2002	J. Olazabal	64.9
2003	Stuart Appleby	62.1
2004	Dan Forsman	62.3
2005	Pat Perez	63.0
2006	Luke Donald	63.6
2007	Tim Clark	68.1
2008	Dudley Hart	63.7
2009	Luke Donald	64.4

Note: Percentage of up-and-down efforts from greenside sand traps only—fairway bunkers excluded.

EAGLES

1980	Dave Eichelberger	16
1981	Bruce Lietzke	12
1982	Tom Weiskopf	10
	J.C. Snead	10
	Andy Bean	10
1983	Chip Beck	15
1984	Gary Hallberg	15
1985	Larry Rinker	14
1986	Joey Sindelar	16
1987	Phil Blackmar	20
1988	Ken Green	21
1989	Lon Hinkle	14
	Duffy Waldorf	14
1990	Paul Azinger	14

EAGLES (Cont.)

1991	Andy Bean	15
1992	Dan Forsman	18
1993	Davis Love III	15
1994	Davis Love III	18
1995	Kelly Gibson	16
1996	Tom Watson	97.2
1997	Tiger Woods	104.1
1998	Davis Love III	83.3
1999	Vijay Singh	104.8
2000	Tiger Woods	72.0
2001	Phil Mickelson	73.8
2002	John Daly	78.4
2003	Tiger Woods	76.5
2004	Nick Price	90.0
2005	Brenden Pappas	70.6
2006	J.B. Holmes	72.9
2007	Chris Tidland	88.5
2008	Chad Campbell	105.8
2009	Bubba Watson	75.2

Note: Total of eagles scored 1980–1995. Since 1996 winner determined by number of holes played per eagle.

BIRDIES

1980	Andy Bean	388
1981	Vance Heafner	388
1982	Andy Bean	392
1983	Hal Sutton	399
1984	Mark O'Meara	419
1985	Joey Sindelar	411
1986	Joey Sindelar	415
1987	Dan Forsman	409
1988	Dan Forsman	465
1989	Ted Schulz	415
1990	Mike Donald	401
1991	Scott Hoch	446
1992	Jeff Sluman	417
1993	John Huston	426
1994	Brad Bryant	397
1995	Steve Lowery	410
1996	Fred Couples	4.20
1997	Tiger Woods	4.25
1998	David Duval	4.29
1999	Tiger Woods	4.46
2000	Tiger Woods	4.92
2001	Phil Mickelson	4.49
2002	Tiger Woods	4.47
2003	Vijay Singh	4.41
2004	Vijay Singh	4.40
2005	Tiger Woods	4.57
2006	Tiger Woods	4.65
2007	Tiger Woods	4.03
2008	Ryan Palmer	4.16
2009	Tiger Woods	4.15

Note: Total of birdies scored 1980–95. Since 1996, winner determined by average number of birdies per round.

† Number had to be carried to extra decimal place to determine winner.

THE PGA TOUR (Cont.)

Year-by-Year Statistical Leaders (Cont.)

ALL-AROUND			ALL-AROUND (Cont.)			ALL-AROUND (Cont.)	
1987	Dan Pohl	170	1996	Fred Couples	214	2005	Tiger Woods	265
1988	Payne Stewart	170	1997	Bill Glasson	282	2006	Tiger Woods	216
1989	Paul Azinger	250	1998	John Huston	151	2007	Tiger Woods	240
1990	Paul Azinger	162	1999	Tiger Woods	120	2008	Pat Perez	323
1991	Scott Hoch	283	2000	Tiger Woods	113	2009	Tiger Woods	151
1992	Fred Couples	256	2001	Phil Mickelson	174			
1993	Gil Morgan	252	2002	Phil Mickelson	259			
1994	Bob Estes	227	2003	Tiger Woods	206			
1995	Justin Leonard	323	2004	Jeff Ogilvy	268			

Note: Sum of the places of standing from the other statistical categories; the player with the number closest to zero leads.

PGA Player of the Year Award

1948	Ben Hogan	1969	Orville Moody	1990	Wayne Levi
1949	Sam Snead	1970	Billy Casper	1991	Fred Couples
1950	Ben Hogan	1971	Lee Trevino	1992	Fred Couples
1951	Ben Hogan	1972	Jack Nicklaus	1993	Nick Price
1952	Julius Boros	1973	Jack Nicklaus	1994	Nick Price
1953	Ben Hogan	1974	Johnny Miller	1995	Greg Norman
1954	Ed Furgol	1975	Jack Nicklaus	1996	Tom Lehman
1955	Doug Ford	1976	Jack Nicklaus	1997	Tiger Woods
1956	Jack Burke	1977	Tom Watson	1998	David Duval
1957	Dick Mayer	1978	Tom Watson	1999	Tiger Woods
1958	Dow Finsterwald	1979	Tom Watson	2000	Tiger Woods
1959	Art Wall	1980	Tom Watson	2001	Tiger Woods
1960	Arnold Palmer	1981	Bill Rogers	2002	Tiger Woods
1961	Jerry Barber	1982	Tom Watson	2003	Tiger Woods
1962	Arnold Palmer	1983	Hal Sutton	2004	Vijay Singh
1963	Julius Boros	1984	Tom Watson	2005	Tiger Woods
1964	Ken Venturi	1985	Lanny Wadkins	2006	Tiger Woods
1965	Dave Marr	1986	Bob Tway	2007	Tiger Woods
1966	Billy Casper	1987	Paul Azinger	2008	Padraig Harrington
1967	Jack Nicklaus	1988	Curtis Strange	2009	Tiger Woods
1968	Not awarded	1989	Tom Kite		

Vardon Trophy: Scoring Average

Year	Winner	Avg	Year	Winner	Avg	Year	Winner	Avg
1937	Harry Cooper	*500	1964	Arnold Palmer	70.01	1987	Don Pohl	70.25
1938	Sam Snead	520	1965	Billy Casper	70.85	1988	Chip Beck	69.46
1939	Byron Nelson	473	1966	Billy Casper	70.27	1989	Greg Norman	69.49
1940	Ben Hogan	423	1967	Arnold Palmer	70.18	1990	Greg Norman	69.10
1941	Ben Hogan	494	1968	Billy Casper	69.82	1991	Fred Couples	69.59
1942–46	No avg		1969	Dave Hill	70.34	1992	Fred Couples	69.38
1947	Jimmy Demaret	69.90	1970	Lee Trevino	70.64	1993	Nick Price	69.11
1948	Ben Hogan	69.30	1971	Lee Trevino	70.27	1994	Greg Norman	68.81
1949	Sam Snead	69.37	1972	Lee Trevino	70.89	1995	Steve Elkington	69.62
1950	Sam Snead	69.23	1973	Bruce Crampton	70.57	1996	Tom Lehman	69.32
1951	Lloyd Mangrum	70.05	1974	Lee Trevino	70.53	1997	Nick Price	68.98
1952	Jack Burke	70.54	1975	Bruce Crampton	70.51	1998	David Duval	69.13
1953	Lloyd Mangrum	70.22	1976	Don January	70.56	1999	Tiger Woods	68.43
1954	E.J. Harrison	70.41	1977	Tom Watson	70.32	2000	Tiger Woods	67.79
1955	Sam Snead	69.86	1978	Tom Watson	70.16	2001	Tiger Woods	68.81
1956	Cary Middlecoff	70.35	1979	Tom Watson	70.27	2002	Tiger Woods	68.13
1957	Dow Finsterwald	70.30	1980	Lee Trevino	69.73	2003	Tiger Woods	68.41
1958	Bob Rosburg	70.11	1981	Tom Kite	69.80	2004	Vijay Singh	68.84
1959	Art Wall	70.35	1982	Tom Kite	70.21	2005	Tiger Woods	68.66
1960	Billy Casper	69.95	1983	Raymond Floyd	70.61	2006	Jim Furyk	68.86
1961	Arnold Palmer	69.85	1984	Calvin Peete	70.56	2007	Tiger Woods	67.79
1962	Arnold Palmer	70.27	1985	Don Pooley	70.36	2008	Sergio Garcia	69.12
1963	Billy Casper	70.58	1986	Scott Hoch	70.08	2009	Tiger Woods	68.05

*Point system used, 1937–41. NOTE: As of 1988, based on minimum of 60 rounds per year. Adjusted for average score of field in tournaments entered.

THE MAJOR TOURNAMENTS

LPGA Championship

Year	Winner	Score	Runner-Up	Site
1955	Beverly Hanson†(4 & 3)	220	Louise Suggs	Orchard Ridge CC, Ft Wayne, IN
1956	Marlene Hagge*	291	Patty Berg	Forest Lake CC, Detroit, MI
1957	Louise Suggs	285	Wiffi Smith	Churchill Valley CC, Pittsburgh, PA
1958	Mickey Wright	288	Fay Crocker	Churchill Valley CC, Pittsburgh, PA
1959	Betsy Rawls	288	Patty Berg	Sheraton Hotel CC, French Lick, IN
1960	Mickey Wright	292	Louise Suggs	Sheraton Hotel CC, French Lick, IN
1961	Mickey Wright	287	Louise Suggs	Stardust CC, Las Vegas, NV
1962	Judy Kimball	282	Shirley Spork	Stardust CC, Las Vegas, NV
1963	Mickey Wright	294	Mary Lena Faulk	Stardust CC, Las Vegas, NV
			Mary Mills	
			Louise Suggs	
1964	Mary Mills	278	Mickey Wright	Stardust CC, Las Vegas, NV
1965	Sandra Haynie	279	Clifford A. Creed	Stardust CC, Las Vegas, NV
1966	Gloria Ehret	282	Mickey Wright	Stardust CC, Las Vegas, NV
1967	Kathy Whitworth	284	Shirley Englehorn	Pleasant Valley CC, Sutton, MA
1968	Sandra Post*	294	Kathy Whitworth (75)	Pleasant Valley CC, Sutton, MA
1969	Betsy Rawls	293	Susie Berning	Concord GC, Kiameshia Lake, NY
			Carol Mann	
1970	Shirley Englehorn*	285	Kathy Whitworth (78)	Pleasant Valley CC, Sutton, MA
1971	Kathy Whitworth	288	Kathy Ahern	Pleasant Valley CC, Sutton, MA
1972	Kathy Ahern	293	Jane Blalock	Pleasant Valley CC, Sutton, MA
1973	Mary Mills	288	Betty Burfeindt	Pleasant Valley CC, Sutton, MA
1974	Sandra Haynie	288	JoAnne Carner	Pleasant Valley CC, Sutton, MA
1975	Kathy Whitworth	288	Sandra Haynie	Pine Ridge GC, Baltimore, MD
1976	Betty Burfeindt	287	Judy Rankin	Pine Ridge GC, Baltimore, MD
1977	Chako Higuchi	279	Pat Bradley	Bay Tree Golf Plantation, N Myrtle Beach, SC
			Sandra Post	
			Judy Rankin	
1978	Nancy Lopez	275	Amy Alcott	Jack Nicklaus GC, Kings Island, OH
1979	Donna Caponi	279	Jerilyn Britz	Jack Nicklaus GC, Kings Island, OH
1980	Sally Little	285	Jane Blalock	Jack Nicklaus GC, Kings Island, OH
1981	Donna Caponi	280	Jerilyn Britz	Jack Nicklaus GC, Kings Island, OH
			Pat Meyers	
1982	Jan Stephenson	279	JoAnne Carner	Jack Nicklaus GC, Kings Island, OH
1983	Patty Sheehan	279	Sandra Haynie	Jack Nicklaus GC, Kings Island, OH
1984	Patty Sheehan	272	Beth Daniel	Jack Nicklaus GC, Kings Island, OH
			Pat Bradley	
1985	Nancy Lopez	273	Alice Miller	Jack Nicklaus GC, Kings Island, OH
1986	Pat Bradley	277	Patty Sheehan	Jack Nicklaus GC, Kings Island, OH
1987	Jane Geddes	275	Betsy King	Jack Nicklaus GC, Kings Island, OH
1988	Sherri Turner	281	Amy Alcott	Jack Nicklaus GC, Kings Island, OH
1989	Nancy Lopez	274	Ayako Okamoto	Jack Nicklaus GC, Kings Island, OH
1990	Beth Daniel	280	Rosie Jones	Bethesda CC, Bethesda, MD
1991	Meg Mallon	274	Pat Bradley	Bethesda CC, Bethesda, MD
			Ayako Okamoto	
1992	Betsy King	267	Karen Noble	Bethesda CC, Bethesda, MD
1993	Patty Sheehan	275	Lauri Merten	Bethesda CC, Bethesda, MD
1994	Laura Davies	279	Alice Ritzman	DuPont CC, Wilmington, DE
1995	Kelly Robbins	274	Laura Davies	DuPont CC, Wilmington, DE
1996	Laura Davies	213†	Julie Piers	DuPont CC, Wilmington, DE
1997	Chris Johnson*	281	Leta Lindley	DuPont CC, Wilmington, DE
1998	Se Ri Pak	273	Donna Andrews	DuPont CC, Wilmington, DE
1999	Juli Inkster	268	Liselotte Neumann	DuPont CC, Wilmington, DE
2000	Juli Inkster*	281	Stefania Croce	DuPont CC, Wilmington, DE
2001	Karrie Webb	270	Laura Diaz	DuPont CC, Wilmington, DE
2002	Se Ri Pak	279	Beth Daniel	DuPont CC, Wilmington, DE
2003	Annika Sorenstam*	278	Grace Park	DuPont CC, Wilmington, DE
2004	Annika Sorenstam	271	Shi Hyun Ahn	Bulle Rock GC, Havre de Grace, MD
2005	Annika Sorenstam	277	Michelle Wie	Bulle Rock GC, Havre de Grace, MD
2006	Se Ri Pak*	280	Karrie Webb	Bulle Rock GC, Havre de Grace, MD
2007	Suzann Pettersen	274	Karrie Webb	Bulle Rock GC, Havre de Grace, MD
2008	Yani Tseng*	276	Maria Hjorth	Bulle Rock GC, Havre de Grace, MD
2009	Anna Nordqvist	273	Lindsey Wright	Bulle Rock GC, Havre de Grace, MD
2010	Cristie Kerr	269	Song-Hee Kim	Bulle Rock GC, Havre de Grace, MD

*Won playoff. †Won match-play final. #Shortened due to rain.

U.S. Women's Open

Year	Winner	Score	Runner-Up	Site
1946	Patty Berg	5 & 4	Betty Jameson	Spokane CC, Spokane, WA
1947	Betty Jameson	295	Sally Sessions	Starmount Forest CC, Greensboro, NC
			Polly Riley	
1948	Babe Zaharias	300	Betty Hicks	Atlantic City CC, Northfield, NJ
1949	Louise Suggs	291	Babe Zaharias	Prince George's G & CC, Landover, MD
1950	Babe Zaharias	291	Betsy Rawls	Rolling Hills CC, Wichita, KS
1951	Betsy Rawls	293	Louise Suggs	Druid Hills GC, Atlanta, GA
1952	Louise Suggs	284	Marlene Bauer	Bala GC, Philadelphia, PA
			Betty Jameson	
1953	Betsy Rawls* (71)	302	Jackie Pung (77)	CC of Rochester, Rochester, NY
1954	Babe Zaharias	291	Betty Hicks	Salem CC, Peabody, MA
1955	Fay Crocker	299	Mary Lena Faulk	Wichita CC, Wichita, KS
			Louise Suggs	
1956	Kathy Cornelius* (75)	302	Barbara McIntire (82)	Northland CC, Duluth, MN
1957	Betsy Rawls	299	Patty Berg	Winged Foot GC, Mamaroneck, NY
1958	Mickey Wright	290	Louise Suggs	Forest Lake CC, Detroit, MI
1959	Mickey Wright	287	Louise Suggs	Churchill Valley CC, Pittsburgh
1960	Betsy Rawls	292	Joyce Ziske	Worcester CC, Worcester, MA
1961	Mickey Wright	293	Betsy Rawls	Baltusrol GC (Lower Course), Springfield, NJ
1962	Murle Breer	301	Jo Ann Prentice	Dunes GC, Myrtle Beach, SC
			Ruth Jessen	
1963	Mary Mills	289	Sandra Haynie	Kenwood CC, Cincinnati, OH
			Louise Suggs	
1964	Mickey Wright* (70)	290	Ruth Jessen (72)	San Diego CC, Chula Vista, CA
1965	Carol Mann	290	Kathy Cornelius	Atlantic City CC, Northfield, NJ
1966	Sandra Spuzich	297	Carol Mann	Hazeltine Natl GC, Chaska, MN
1967	Catherine LaCoste	294	Susie Berning	Hot Springs GC (Cascades Course),
			Beth Stone	Hot Springs, VA
1968	Susie Berning	289	Mickey Wright	Moslem Springs GC, Fleetwood, PA
1969	Donna Caponi	294	Peggy Wilson	Scenic Hills CC, Pensacola, FL
1970	Donna Caponi	287	Sandra Haynie	Muskogee CC, Muskogee, OK
			Sandra Spuzich	
1971	JoAnne Carner	288	Kathy Whitworth	Kahkwa CC, Erie, PA
1972	Susie Berning	299	Kathy Ahern	Winged Foot GC, Mamaroneck, NY
			Pam Barnett	
			Judy Rankin	
1973	Susie Berning	290	Gloria Ehret	CC of Rochester, Rochester, NY
			Shelley Hamlin	
1974	Sandra Haynie	295	Carol Mann	La Grange CC, La Grange, IL
			Beth Stone	
1975	Sandra Palmer	295	JoAnne Carner	Atlantic City CC, Northfield, NJ
			Sandra Post	
			Nancy Lopez	
1976	JoAnne Carner* (76)	292	Sandra Palmer (78)	Rolling Green CC, Springfield, PA
1977	Hollis Stacy	292	Nancy Lopez	Hazeltine Natl GC, Chaska, MN
1978	Hollis Stacy	289	JoAnne Carner	CC of Indianapolis, Indianapolis, IN
			Sally Little	
1979	Jerilyn Britz	284	Debbie Massey	Brooklawn CC, Fairfield, CT
			Sandra Palmer	
1980	Amy Alcott	280	Hollis Stacy	Richland CC, Nashville, TN
1981	Pat Bradley	279	Beth Daniel	La Grange CC, La Grange, IL
1982	Janet Anderson	283	Beth Daniel	Del Paso CC, Sacramento, CA
			Sandra Haynie	
			Donna White	
			JoAnne Carner	
1983	Jan Stephenson	290	JoAnne Carner	Cedar Ridge CC, Tulsa, OK
			Patty Sheehan	
1984	Hollis Stacy	290	Rosie Jones	Salem CC, Peabody, MA
1985	Kathy Baker	280	Judy Dickinson	Baltusrol GC (Upper Course), Springfield, NJ
1986	Jane Geddes* (71)	287	Sally Little (73)	NCR GC, Dayton, OH
1987	Laura Davies* (71)	285	Ayako Okamoto (73)	Plainfield CC, Plainfield, NJ
			JoAnne Carner (74)	
1988	Liselotte Neumann	277	Patty Sheehan	Baltimore CC, Baltimore, MD
1989	Betsy King	278	Nancy Lopez	Indianwood G & CC, Lake Orion, MI
1990	Betsy King	284	Patty Sheehan	Atlanta Athletic Club, Duluth, GA
1991	Meg Mallon	283	Pat Bradley	Colonial Club, Fort Worth, TX

U.S. Women's Open (Cont.)

Year	Winner	Score	Runner-Up	Site
1992	Patty Sheehan* (72)	280	Juli Inkster	Oakmont CC, Oakmont, PA
1993	Lauri Merten	280	Donna Andrew	Crooked Stick, Carmel, IN
			Helen Alfredsson	
1994	Patty Sheehan	277	Tammie Green	Indianwood G & CC, Lake Orion, MI
1995	Annika Sorenstam	278	Meg Mallon	The Broadmoor GC, Colorado Springs,CO
1996	Annika Sorenstam	272	Kris Tschetter	Pine Needles GC, Southern Pines, NC
1997	Alison Nicholas	274	Nancy Lopez	Pumpkin Ridge CC, North Plains, OR
1998	Se Ri Pak†	290	Jenny Chuasiriporn	Blackwolf Run Golf Resort, Kohler, WI
1999	Juli Inkster	272	Sherri Turner	Old Waverly GC, West Point, MS
2000	Karrie Webb	282	Cristie Kerr/ Meg Mallon	Merit GC, Libertyville, IL
2001	Karrie Webb	273	Se Ri Pak	Pine Needles GC, Southern Pines, NC
2002	Juli Inkster	276	Annika Sorenstam	Prairie Dunes CC, Hutchinson, KS
2003	Hilary Lunke*	283	Kelly Robbins	Pumpkin Ridge GC, North Plains, OR
2004	Meg Mallon	274	Annika Sorenstam	The Orchards GC, South Hadley, MA
2005	Birdie Kim	287	Brittany Lang	Cherry Hills CC, Cherry Hills Village, CO
			Morgan Pressel	
2006	Annika Sorenstam*	284	Pat Hurst	Newport CC, Newport, RI
2007	Cristie Kerr	279	Angela Park	Pine Needles GC, Southern Pines, NC
			Lorena Ochoa	
2008	Inbee Park	283	Helen Alfredsson	Interlachen CC, Edina, MN
2009	Eun-Hee Ji	284	Candie Kung	Saucon Valley CC-Old Course, Bethlehem, PA
2010	Paula Creamer	281	Na Yeon Choi	Oakmont CC, Oakmont, PA

* Winner in playoff. † Winner on second hole of sudden death after 18-hole playoff ended in a tie.

Kraft Nabisco Championship

Year	Winner	Score	Runner-Up
1972	Jane Blalock	213	Carol Mann
			Judy Rankin
1973	Mickey Wright	284	Joyce Kazmierski
1974	Jo Ann Prentice*	289	Jane Blalock
			Sandra Haynie
1975	Sandra Palmer	283	Kathy McMullen
1976	Judy Rankin	285	Betty Burfeindt
1977	Kathy Whitworth	289	JoAnne Carner
			Sally Little
1978	Sandra Post*	283	Penny Pulz
1979	Sandra Post	276	Nancy Lopez
1980	Donna Caponi	275	Amy Alcott
1981	Nancy Lopez	277	Carolyn Hill
1982	Sally Little	278	Hollis Stacy
			Sandra Haynie
1983	Amy Alcott	282	Beth Daniel
			Kathy Whitworth
1984	Juli Inkster*	280	Pat Bradley
1985	Alice Miller	275	Jan Stephenson
1986	Pat Bradley	280	Val Skinner
1987	Betsy King*	283	Patty Sheehan
1988	Amy Alcott	274	Colleen Walker
1989	Juli Inkster	279	Tammie Green
			JoAnne Carner
1990	Betsy King	283	Kathy Postlewait
			Shirley Furlong
1991	Amy Alcott	273	Dottie Mochrie
1992	Dottie Mochrie*	279	Juli Inkster

Year	Winner	Score	Runner-Up
1993	Helen Alfredsson	284	Amy Benz
			Tina Barrett
			Betsy King
1994	Donna Andrews	276	Laura Davies
1995	Nanci Bowen	285	Susie Redman
1996	Patti Sheehan	281	Kelly Robbins
			Meg Mallon
			Annika Sorenstam
1997	Betsy King	276	Kris Tschetter
1998	Pat Hurst	281	Helen Dobson
1999	Dottie Pepper	269	Meg Mallon
2000	Karrie Webb	274	Dottie Pepper
2001	Annika Sorenstam	281	five players
2002	Annika Sorenstam	280	Liselotte Neumann
2003	P. Meunier-Lebouc	281	Annika Sorenstam
2004	Grace Park	277	Aree Song
2005	Annika Sorenstam	273	Rosie Jones
			Lorena Ochoa
2006	Karrie Webb*	279	Catriona Matthew
2007	Morgan Pressel	285	Brittany Lincicome
			Suzann Pettersen
2008	Lorena Ochoa	277	Annika Sorenstam
2009	Brittany Lincicome	279	Kristy McPherson
			Cristie Kerr
2010	Yani Tseng	275	Suzann Pettersen

*Winner in sudden-death playoff. Note: Designated fourth major in 1983; played at Mission Hills CC, Rancho Mirage, CA.

du Maurier Classic

Year	Winner	Score	Runner-Up	Site
1973	Jocelyne Bourassa*	214	Sandra Haynie	Montreal GC, Montreal
			Judy Rankin	
1974	Carole Jo Callison	208	JoAnne Carner	Candiac GC, Montreal
1975	JoAnne Carner*	214	Carol Mann	St. George's CC, Toronto
1976	Donna Caponi*	212	Judy Rankin	Cedar Brae G & CC, Toronto
1977	Judy Rankin	214	Pat Meyers	Lachute G & CC, Montreal
			Sandra Palmer	
1978	JoAnne Carner	278	Hollis Stacy	St. George's CC, Toronto
1979	Amy Alcott	285	Nancy Lopez	Richelieu Valley CC, Montreal
1980	Pat Bradley	277	JoAnne Carner	St. George's CC, Toronto
1981	Jan Stephenson	278	Nancy Lopez	Summerlea CC, Dorion, Quebec
			Pat Bradley	
1982	Sandra Haynie	280	Beth Daniel	St. George's CC, Toronto
1983	Hollis Stacy	277	JoAnne Carner	Beaconsfield GC, Montreal
			Alice Miller	
1984	Juli Inkster	279	Ayako Okamoto	St. George's G & CC, Toronto
1985	Pat Bradley	278	Jane Geddes	Beaconsfield CC, Montreal
1986	Pat Bradley*	276	Ayako Okamoto	Board of Trade CC, Toronto
1987	Jody Rosenthal	272	Ayako Okamoto	Islesmere GC, Laval, Quebec
1988	Sally Little	279	Laura Davies	Vancouver GC, Coquitlam, British Columbia
1989	Tammie Green	279	Pat Bradley	Beaconsfield GC, Montreal
			Betsy King	
1990	Cathy Johnston	276	Patty Sheehan	Westmount G & CC, Kitchener, Ontario
1991	Nancy Scranton	279	Debbie Massey	Vancouver GC, Coquitlam, British Columbia
1992	Sherri Steinhauer	277	Judy Dickinson	St. Charles CC, Winnipeg, Manitoba
1993	Brandie Burton	277	Betsy King	London Hunt and CC, London, Ontario
1994	Martha Nause	279	Michelle McGann	Ottawa Hunt and GC, Ottawa, Ont.
1995	Jenny Lidback	280	Liselotte Neumann	Beaconsfield GC, Pointe-Claire, Quebec
1996	Laura Davies	277	Nancy Lopez	Edmonton CC, Edmonton, Alberta
			Karrie Webb	
1997	Colleen Walker	278	Liselotte Neumann	Glen Abbey GC, Oakville, Ontario
1998	Brandie Burton	270	Annika Sorenstam	Essex G & CC, Windsor, Ontario
1999	Karrie Webb	277	Laura Davies	Priddis Greens G & CC, Calgary, Alberta
2000	Meg Mallon	282	Rosie Jones	Royal Ottawa GC, Aylmer, Quebec

*Winner in sudden-death playoff. Note: Designated third major in 1979. Tournament discontinued in 2001.

Women's British Open

Year	Winner	Score	Runner-Up	Site
2001	Se Ri Pak	277	Mi Hyun Kim	Sunningdale GC, Berkshire, England
2002	Karrie Webb	273	Michelle Ellis	Turnberry GC, Ailsa, Scotland
			Paula Marti	
2003	Annika Sorenstam	278	Se Ri Pak	Royal Lytham & St. Annes, England
2004	Karen Stupples	269	Rachel Teske	Sunningdale GC, Berklshire, England
2005	Jeong Jang	272	Sophie Gustafson	Royal Birkdale CC, Merseyside, England
2006	Sherri Steinhauer	281	Cristie Kerr	Royal Lytham & St. Anne's, England
2007	Lorena Ochoa	287	Jee Young Lee	Old Course, St. Andrew's, Scotland
			Maria Hjorth	
2008	Ji-Yai Shin	270	Yani Tseng	Sunningdale GC, Berkshire, England
2009	Catriona Matthew	285	Karrie Webb	Royal Lytham & St. Annes, England
2010	Yani Tseng	277	Katherine Hull	Royal Birkdale CC, Merseyside, England

Note: Designated fourth major in 2001.

THE LPGA TOUR

Most Career Wins†

	Wins		Wins		Wins
Kathy Whitworth	88	Sandra Haynie	42	*Juli Inkster	31
Mickey Wright	82	Babe Zaharias	41	Amy Alcott	29
Annika Sorenstam	72	Carol Mann	38	Jane Blalock	27
Patty Berg	60	*Karrie Webb	36	*Lorena Ochoa	27
Louise Suggs	58	Patty Sheehan	35	Marlene Hagge	26
Betsy Rawls	55	Betsy King	34	Judy Rankin	26
Nancy Lopez	48	Beth Daniel	33	*Se Ri Pak	25
JoAnne Carner	43	Pat Bradley	31	Donna Caponi	24

†Through 10/05/10. *Active player.

Alltime Major Championship Winners

	LPGA	U.S. Open	Nabisco	Brit. Open	‡du Maurier	#Titleholders	†Western	U.S. Am	Brit. Am	Total
Patty Berg	0	1	0	0	0	7	7	1	0	16
Mickey Wright	4	4	0	0	0	2	3	0	0	13
Louise Suggs	1	2	0	0	0	4	4	1	1	13
Babe Zaharias	0	3	0	0	0	3	4	1	1	12
*Juli Inkster	2	2	2	0	1	0	0	3	0	10
Annika Sorenstam	3	3	3	1	0	0	0	0	0	10
Betsy Rawls	2	4	0	0	0	0	2	0	0	8
JoAnne Carner	0	2	0	0	0	0	0	5	0	7
*Karrie Webb	1	2	2	1	1	0	0	0	0	7
Kathy Whitworth	3	0	0	0	0	2	1	0	0	6
Pat Bradley	1	1	1	0	3	0	0	0	0	6
Patty Sheehan	3	2	1	0	0	0	0	0	0	6
Glenna Vare	0	0	0	0	0	0	0	6	0	6
Betsy King	1	2	3	0	0	0	0	0	0	6

*Active LPGA player.
#Major from 1937–1972. †Major from 1937–1967. ‡Major from 1979–2000.

Alltime Multiple Professional Major Winners

LPGA

Mickey Wright	4
Nancy Lopez	3
Se Ri Pak	3
Patty Sheehan	3
Annika Sorenstam	3
Kathy Whitworth	3
Donna Caponi	2
Sandra Haynie	2
Mary Mills	2
Betsy Rawls	2
Laura Davies	2
*Juli Inkster	2

U.S. OPEN

Betsy Rawls	4
Mickey Wright	4
Susie Maxwell Berning	3
Hollis Stacy	3
Babe Zaharias	3
Annika Sorenstam	3
JoAnne Carner	2
Donna Caponi	2
Betsy King	2
Meg Mallon	2
Patty Sheehan	2
Louise Suggs	2
Karrie Webb	2
*Juli Inkster	2

NABISCO/DINAH SHORE

Amy Alcott	3
Betsy King	3
Annika Sorenstam	3
*Juli Inkster	2
*Karrie Webb	2

TITLEHOLDERS

Patty Berg	7
Louise Suggs	4
Babe Zaharias	3
Dorothy Kirby	2
Marilynn Smith	2
Kathy Whitworth	2
Mickey Wright	2

WESTERN OPEN

Patty Berg	7
Louise Suggs	4
Babe Zaharias	4
Mickey Wright	3
June Beebe	2
Opal Hill	2
Betty Jameson	2
Betsy Rawls	2

DU MAURIER

Pat Bradley	3
Brandie Burton	2
JoAnne Carner	2

*Active player.

THE LPGA TOUR (Cont.)

Season Money Leaders

Year	Player	Earnings ($)	Year	Player	Earnings ($)	Year	Player	Earnings ($)
1950	Babe Zaharias	14,800	1970	Kathy Whitworth	30,235	1990	Beth Daniel	863,578
1951	Babe Zaharias	15,087	1971	Kathy Whitworth	41,181	1991	Pat Bradley	763,118
1952	Betsy Rawls	14,505	1972	Kathy Whitworth	65,063	1992	Dottie Mochrie	693,335
1953	Louise Suggs	19,816	1973	Kathy Whitworth	82,864	1993	Betsy King	595,992
1954	Patty Berg	16,011	1974	JoAnne Carner	87,094	1994	Laura Davies	687,201
1955	Patty Berg	16,492	1975	Sandra Palmer	76,374	1995	Annika Sorenstam	666,533
1956	Marlene Hagge	20,235	1976	Judy Rankin	150,734	1996	Karrie Webb	1,002,000
1957	Patty Berg	16,272	1977	Judy Rankin	122,890	1997	Annika Sorenstam	1,236,789
1958	Beverly Hanson	12,639	1978	Nancy Lopez	189,814	1998	Annika Sorenstam	1,092,748
1959	Betsy Rawls	26,774	1979	Nancy Lopez	197,489	1999	Karrie Webb	1,591,959
1960	Louise Suggs	16,892	1980	Beth Daniel	231,000	2000	Karrie Webb	1,876,853
1961	Mickey Wright	22,236	1981	Beth Daniel	206,998	2001	Annika Sorenstam	2,105,868
1962	Mickey Wright	21,641	1982	JoAnne Carner	310,400	2002	Annika Sorenstam	2,863.904
1963	Mickey Wright	31,269	1983	JoAnne Carner	291,404	2003	Annika Sorenstam	2,029,506
1964	Mickey Wright	29,800	1984	Betsy King	266,771	2004	Annika Sorenstam	2,544,707
1965	Kathy Whitworth	28,658	1985	Nancy Lopez	416,472	2005	Annika Sorenstam	2,588,240
1966	Kathy Whitworth	33,517	1986	Pat Bradley	492,021	2006	Lorena Ochoa	2,592,872
1967	Kathy Whitworth	32,937	1987	Ayako Okamoto	466,034	2007	Lorena Ochoa	4,364,994
1968	Kathy Whitworth	48,379	1988	Sherri Turner	350,851	2008	Lorena Ochoa	2,763,193
1969	Carol Mann	49,152	1989	Betsy King	654,132	2009	Jiyai Shin	1,807,334

LPGA Player of the Year

Year	Player	Year	Player	Year	Player
1966	Kathy Whitworth	1981	JoAnne Carner	1996	Laura Davies
1967	Kathy Whitworth	1982	JoAnne Carner	1997	Annika Sorenstam
1968	Kathy Whitworth	1983	Patty Sheehan	1998	Annika Sorenstam
1969	Kathy Whitworth	1984	Betsy King	1999	Karrie Webb
1970	Sandra Haynie	1985	Nancy Lopez	2000	Karrie Webb
1971	Kathy Whitworth	1986	Pat Bradley	2001	Annika Sorenstam
1972	Kathy Whitworth	1987	Ayako Okamoto	2002	Annika Sorenstam
1973	Kathy Whitworth	1988	Nancy Lopez	2003	Annika Sorenstam
1974	JoAnne Carner	1989	Betsy King	2004	Annika Sorenstam
1975	Sandra Palmer	1990	Beth Daniel	2005	Annika Sorenstam
1976	Judy Rankin	1991	Pat Bradley	2006	Lorena Ochoa
1977	Judy Rankin	1992	Dottie Mochrie	2007	Lorena Ochoa
1978	Nancy Lopez	1993	Betsy King	2008	Lorena Ochoa
1979	Nancy Lopez	1994	Beth Daniel	2009	Lorena Ochoa
1980	Beth Daniel	1995	Annika Sorenstam		

Vare Trophy: Best Scoring Average*

Year	Player	Avg	Year	Player	Avg	Year	Player	Avg
1953	Patty Berg	75.00	1972	Kathy Whitworth	72.38	1991	Pat Bradley	70.76
1954	Babe Zaharias	75.48	1973	Judy Rankin	73.08	1992	Dottie Mochrie	70.80
1955	Patty Berg	74.47	1974	JoAnne Carner	72.87	1993	Nancy Lopez	70.83
1956	Patty Berg	74.57	1975	JoAnne Carner	72.40	1994	Beth Daniel	70.90
1957	Louise Suggs	74.64	1976	Judy Rankin	72.25	1995	Annika Sorenstam	71.00
1958	Beverly Hanson	74.92	1977	Judy Rankin	72.16	1996	Annika Sorenstam	70.47
1959	Betsy Rawls	74.03	1978	Nancy Lopez	71.76	1997	Karrie Webb	70.00
1960	Mickey Wright	73.25	1979	Nancy Lopez	71.20	1998	Annika Sorenstam	69.99
1961	Mickey Wright	73.55	1980	Amy Alcott	71.51	1999	Karrie Webb	69.43
1962	Mickey Wright	73.67	1981	JoAnne Carner	71.75	2000	Karrie Webb	70.05
1963	Mickey Wright	72.81	1982	JoAnne Carner	71.49	2001	Annika Sorenstam	69.42
1964	Mickey Wright	72.46	1983	JoAnne Carner	71.41	2002	Annika Sorenstam	68.70
1965	Kathy Whitworth	72.61	1984	Patty Sheehan	71.40	2003	Se Ri Pak	70.03
1966	Kathy Whitworth	72.60	1985	Nancy Lopez	70.73	2004	Grace Park	69.99
1967	Kathy Whitworth	72.74	1986	Pat Bradley	71.10	2005	Annika Sorenstam	69.33
1968	Carol Mann	72.04	1987	Betsy King	71.14	2006	Lorena Ochoa	69.23
1969	Kathy Whitworth	72.38	1988	Colleen Walker	71.26	2007	Lorena Ochoa	69.69
1970	Kathy Whitworth	72.26	1989	Beth Daniel	70.38	2008	Lorena Ochoa	69.70
1971	Kathy Whitworth	72.88	1990	Beth Daniel	70.54	2009	Lorena Ochoa	70.16

*Must play 70 rounds or more to qualify; Annika Sorenstam compiled an average of 69.02 in 60 rounds in 2003.

CHAMPIONS TOUR

U.S. Senior Open

Year	Winner	Score	Runner-Up	Site
1980	Roberto DeVicenzo	285	William C. Campbell	Winged Foot GC, Mamaroneck, NY
1981	Arnold Palmer* (70)	289	Bob Stone (74)	Oakland Hills CC, Birmingham, MI
			Billy Casper (77)	
1982	Miller Barber	282	Gene Littler, Dan Sikes, Jr.	Portland GC, Portland, OR
1983	Billy Casper* (75) (3)	288	Rod Funseth (75) (4)	Hazeltine GC, Chaska, MN
1984	Miller Barber	286	Arnold Palmer	Oak Hill CC, Rochester, NY
1985	Miller Barber	285	Roberto DeVicenzo	Edgewood Tahoe GC, Stateline, NV
1986	Dale Douglass	279	Gary Player	Scioto CC, Columbus, OH
1987	Gary Player	270	Doug Sanders	Brooklawn CC, Fairfield, CT
1988	Gary Player* (68)	288	Bob Charles (70)	Medinah CC, Medinah, IL
1989	Orville Moody	279	Frank Beard	Laurel Valley GC, Ligonier, PA
1990	Lee Trevino	275	Jack Nicklaus	Ridgewood CC, Paramus, NJ
1991	Jack Nicklaus* (65)	282	Chi Chi Rodriguez (69)	Oakland Hills CC, Birmingham, MI
1992	Larry Laoretti	275	Jim Colbert	Saucon Valley CC, Bethlehem, PA
1993	Jack Nicklaus	278	Tom Weiskopf	Cherry Hills CC, Englewood, CO
1994	Simon Hobday	274	Jim Albus	Pinehurst Resort & CC, Pinehurst, NC
1995	Tom Weiskopf	275	Jack Nicklaus	Congressional CC, Bethesda, MD
1996	Dave Stockton	277	Hale Irwin	Canterbury GC, Beachwood, OH
1997	Graham Marsh	280	Hale Irwin	Olympia Fields CC, Olympia Fields, IL
1998	Hale Irwin	285	Vicente Fernandez	Riviera CC, Pacific Palisades, CA
1999	Dave Eichelberger	281	Ed Dougherty	Des Moines G & CC, Des Moines, IA
2000	Hale Irwin	267	Bruce Fleisher	Saucon Valley CC, Bethlehem, PA
2001	Bruce Fleisher	280	Isao Aoki, Gil Morgan	Salem CC, Peabody, MA
2002	Don Pooley* (19) (5)	274	Tom Watson (18)	Caves Valley GC, Owings Mill, MD
2003	Bruce Lietzke	277	Tom Watson	Inverness GC, Toledo, OH
2004	Peter Jacobsen	272	Hale Irwin	Bellerive CC, St. Louis, MO
2005	Allen Doyle	274	D.A. Weibring	NCR GC, Kettering, OH
			Loren Roberts	
2006	Allen Doyle	272	Tom Watson	Prairie Dunes CC, Hutchinson, KS
2007	Brad Bryant	282	Ben Crenshaw	Whistling Straits GC, Kohler, WI
2008	Eduardo Romero	274	Fred Funk	Broadmoor GC, Colorado Springs, CO
2009	Fred Funk	268	Joey Sindelar	Crooked Stick GC, Carmel, IN
2010	Bernhard Langer	272	Fred Couples	Sahalee CC, Sammamish, WA

*Winner in playoff. Playoff scores are in parentheses. The 1983 playoff went to one hole of sudden death after an 18-hole playoff.

Season Money Leaders

	Earnings ($)		Earnings ($)		Earnings ($)
1980...Don January	44,100	1990...Lee Trevino	1,190,518	2000...Larry Nelson	2,708,005
1981...Miller Barber	83,136	1991...Mike Hill	1,065,657	2001...Allen Doyle	2,553,582
1982...Miller Barber	106,890	1992...Lee Trevino	1,027,002	2002...Hale Irwin	3,028,304
1983...Don January	237,571	1993...Dave Stockton	1,175,944	2003...Tom Watson	1,853,108
1984...Don January	328,597	1994...Dave Stockton	1,402,519	2004...Craig Stadler	2,306,066
1985...Peter Thomson	386,724	1995...Jim Colbert	1,444,386	2005...Dana Quigley	2,170,258
1986...Bruce Crampton	454,299	1996...Jim Colbert	1,627,890	2006...Jay Haas	2,420,227
1987...Chi Chi Rodriguez	509,145	1997...Hale Irwin	2,449,420	2007...Jay Haas	2,581,001
1988...Bob Charles	533,929	1998...Hale Irwin	2,861,945	2008...Bernhard Langer	2,035,073
1989...Bob Charles	725,887	1999...Bruce Fleisher	2,515,705	2009...Bernhard Langer	2,164,451

Most Career Wins†

	Wins		Wins
Hale Irwin	45	*Gary Player	19
Lee Trevino	29	Larry Nelson	19
Gil Morgan	25	Bruce Fleisher	18
Miller Barber	24	Mike Hill	18
Bob Charles	23	Raymond Floyd	14
Don January	23	*Jay Haas	14
Chi Chi Rodriguez	22	*Dave Stockton	14
Jim Colbert	20	*Bernhard Langer	13
Bruce Crampton	20	*Jim Thorpe	13
		*Tom Watson	13

*Active player.
†Through 10/05/10.

Ryder Cup Matches

Year	Results	Site
1927	United States 9½, Great Britain 2½	Worcester CC, Worcester, MA
1929	Great Britain 7, United States 5	Moortown GC, Leeds, England
1931	United States 9, Great Britain 3	Scioto CC, Columbus, OH
1933	Great Britain 6½, United States 5½	Southport and Ainsdale Courses, Southport, England
1935	United States 9, Great Britain 3	Ridgewood CC, Ridgewood, NJ
1937	United States 8, Great Britain 4	Southport and Ainsdale Courses, Southport, England
1939–1945	No tournament	
1947	United States 11, Great Britain 1	Portland GC, Portland, OR
1949	United States 7, Great Britain 5	Ganton GC, Scarborough, England
1951	United States 9½, Great Britain 2½	Pinehurst CC, Pinehurst, NC
1953	United States 6½, Great Britain 5½	Wentworth Club, Surrey, England
1955	United States 8, Great Britain 4	Thunderbird Ranch & CC, Palm Springs, CA
1957	Great Britain 7½, United States 4½	Lindrick GC, Yorkshire, England
1959	United States 8½, Great Britain 3½	Eldorado CC, Palm Desert, CA
1961	United States 14½, Great Britain 9½	Royal Lytham & St. Annes GC, St Anne's-on-the-Sea, England
1963	United States 23, Great Britain 9	East Lake CC, Atlanta
1965	United States 19½, Great Britain 12½	Royal Birkdale GC, Southport, England
1967	United States 23½, Great Britain 8½	Champions GC, Houston
1969	United States 16, Great Britain 16	Royal Birkdale GC, Southport, England
1971	United States 18½, Great Britain 13½	Old Warson CC, St. Louis
1973	United States 19, Great Britain 13	Hon Co of Edinburgh Golfers, Muirfield, Scotland
1975	United States 21, Great Britain 11	Laurel Valley GC, Ligonier, PA
1977	United States 12½, Great Britain 7½	Royal Lytham & St. Annes GC, St. Annes-on-the-Sea, Eng.
1979	United States 17, Europe 11	Greenbrier, White Sulphur Springs, WV
1981	United States 18½, Europe 9½	Walton Heath GC, Surrey, England
1983	United States 14½, Europe 13½	PGA National GC, Palm Beach Gardens, FL
1985	Europe 16½, United States 11½	Belfry GC, Sutton Coldfield, England
1987	Europe 15, United States 13	Muirfield GC, Dublin, OH
1989	Europe 14, United States 14	Belfry GC, Sutton Coldfield, England
1991	United States 14½, Europe 13½	Ocean Course, Kiawah Island, SC
1993	United States 15, Europe 13	Belfry GC, Sutton Coldfield, England
1995	Europe 14½, United States 13½	Oak Hill CC, Rochester, NY
1997	Europe 14½, United States 13½	Valderrama GC, Sotogrande, Spain
1999	United States 14½, Europe 13½	The Country Club, Brookline, MA
2002	Europe 15½, Unites States 12½	Belfry GC, Sutton Coldfield, England
2004	Europe 18½, United States 9½	Oakland Hills CC, Bloomfield Hills, MI
2006	Europe 18½, United States 9½	The K Club, County Kildare, Ireland
2008	United States 16½, Europe 11½	Valhalla GC, Louisville, KY
2010	Europe 14½, United States 13½	Celtic Manor GC, Newport, Wales

Team matches held every odd year between U.S. professionals and those of Great Britain/Europe. Team members selected on basis of finishes in PGA and European tour events. Match in 2001 canceled due to 9/11 terrorist attacks.

Presidents Cup Matches

Year	Results	Site
1994	United States 20, International 12	Robert Trent Jones GC, Lake Manassas, VA
1996	United States 16½, International 15½	Robert Trent Jones GC, Lake Manassas, VA
1998	International 20½ United States 11½	Royal Melbourne GC, Melbourne, Australia
2000	United States 21½, International 10½	Robert Trent Jones GC, Lake Manassas, VA
2003	International 17, United States 17	Fan Court Hotel CC, George, South Africa
2005	United States 18½, International 15½	Robert Trent Jones GC, Lake Manassas, VA
2007	United States 19½, International 14½	Royal Montreal GC, Bizard, Quebec
2009	United States 19½, International 14½	Harding Park GC, San Francisco, CA

A biennial event played in non-Ryder Cup years designed to provide non-European players with international team and match play.

Curtis Cup Matches

Year	Results	Site
1932	United States 5½, British Isles 3½	Wentworth GC, Wentworth, England
1934	United States 6½, British Isles 2½	Chevy Chase Club, Chevy Chase, MD
1936	United States 4½ British Isles 4½	King's Course, Gleneagles, Scotland
1938	United States 5½, British Isles 3½	Essex CC, Manchester, MA
1940–46	No tournament	
1948	United States 6½, British Isles 2½	Birkdale GC, Southport, England
1950	United States 7½, British Isles 1½	CC of Buffalo, Williamsville, NY
1952	British Isles 5, United States 4	Muirfield, Scotland
1954	United States 6, British Isles 3	Merion GC, Ardmore, PA
1956	British Isles 5, United States 4	Prince's GC, Sandwich Bay, England
1958	British Isles 4½, United States 4½	Brae Burn CC, West Newton, Mass.
1960	United States 6½, British Isles 2½	Lindrick GC, Worksop, England
1962	United States 8, British Isles 1	Broadmoor CG, Colorado Springs,CO
1964	United States 10½, British Isles 7½	Royal Porthcawl GC, Porthcawl, South Wales
1966	United States 13, British Isles 5	Va. Hot Springs G & TC, Hot Springs, VA
1968	United States 10½, British Isles 7½	Royal County Down GC, Newcastle, N. Ire.
1970	United States 11½, British Isles 6½	Brae Burn CC, West Newton, MA
1972	United States 10, British Isles 8	Western Gailes, Ayrshire, Scotland
1974	United States 13, British Isles 5	San Francisco GC, San Francisco
1976	United States 11½, British Isles 6½	Royal Lytham & St. Annes GC, England
1978	United States 12, British Isles 6	Apawamis Club, Rye, NY
1980	United States 13, British Isles 5	St. Pierre G & CC, Chepstow, Wales
1982	United States 14½, British Isles 3½	Denver CC, Denver
1984	United States 9½ British Isles 8½	Muirfield, Scotland
1986	British Isles 13, United States 5	Prairie Dunes CC, Hutchinson, KS
1988	British Isles 11, United States 7	Royal St. George's GC, Sandwich, England
1990	United States 14, British Isles 4	Somerset Hills CC, Bernardsville, NJ
1992	Great Britain/Ireland 10, United States 8	Royal Liverpool GC, Hoylake, England
1994	Great Britain/Ireland 9, United States 9	The Honors Course, Ooltewah, TN
1996	Great Britain/Ireland 11½, United States 6½	Killarney Golf & Fishing Club, Killarney, Ireland
1998	United States 10, Great Britain/Ireland 8	The Minikahda Club, Minneapolis
2000	United States 10, Great Britain/Ireland 8	Ganton GC, North Yorkshire, England
2002	United States 11, Great Britain/Ireland 7	Fox Chapel GC, Pittsburgh, PA
2004	United States 10, Great Britain/Ireland 8	Formby GC, Merseyside, England
2006	United States 11½, Great Britain/Ireland 6½	Bandon Dunes GC, Bandon, OR
2008	United States 13, Great Britain/Ireland 7	Old Course, St. Andrews, Scotland
2010	United States 12½, Great Britain/Ireland 7½	Essex County Club, Manchester, Mass.

Women's amateur team competition every other year between the United States and Great Britain/Ireland. U.S. team members selected by USGA.

Solheim Cup Matches

Year	Results	Site
1990	United States 11½, Europe 4½	Lake Nona GC, Orlando, FL
1992	Europe 11½, United States 6½	Dalmahoy Hotel GC, Edinburgh
1994	United States 13, Europe 7	The Greenbriar, White Sulpher Springs, WV
1996	United States 17, Europe 11	Marriot St Pierre Hotel & CC, Chepstow, Wales
1998	United States 16, Europe 12	Muirfield Village GC, Dublin, OH
2000	Europe 14½, United States, 11 ½	Loch Lomond GC, Luss, Scotand
2002	United States 15½, Europe 12 ½	Interlachen CC, Minneapolis, MN
2003	Europe 17½, United States 10 ½	Barseback G&CC, Malmo, Sweden
2005	United States 15½, Europe 12 ½	Crooked Stick GC, Carmel, IN
2007	United States 16, Europe 12	Halmstad GC, Halmstad, Sweden
2009	United States 16, Europe 12	Rich Harvest Farms GC, Sugar Grove, IL

Women's team matches held every other year between U.S. professionals and those of Europe. Team members selected on the basis of finishes in LPGA and European tour events.

Soccer

Thanks to the brilliant play of goalkeeper Iker Casillas (center), Spain won its first-ever World Cup in 2010, defeating the Netherlands 1–0 in the Cup final

SIMON BRUTY

2009 Major League Soccer

2009 Final Standings

EASTERN CONFERENCE

Team	GP	W	L	T	Pts	GF	GA
†Columbus	30	13	7	10	49	41	31
*Chicago	30	11	7	12	45	39	34
*New England	30	11	10	9	42	33	37
D.C. United	30	9	8	13	40	43	44
Toronto FC	30	10	11	9	39	37	46
Kansas City	30	8	13	9	33	33	42
New York	30	5	19	6	21	27	47

WESTERN CONFERENCE

Team	GP	W	L	T	Pts	GF	GA
†Los Angeles	30	12	6	12	48	36	31
*Houston	30	13	8	9	48	39	29
*Seattle	30	12	7	11	47	38	29
*Chivas USA	30	13	11	6	45	34	31
*Real Salt Lake	30	11	12	7	40	43	35
Colorado	30	10	10	10	40	42	38
FC Dallas	30	11	13	6	39	50	47
San Jose	30	7	14	9	30	36	50

Note: Three points for a win. One point for a tie. †Conference champion. *Qualified for playoffs

SCORING LEADERS

Player, Team	GP	G	A	Pts
Jeff Cunningham, DAL	28	17	8	25
Omar Cummings, COL	28	8	12	20
Fredy Montero, SEA	27	12	7	19
Landon Donovan, LA	25	12	6	18
Conor Casey, COL	24	16	1	17
Dwayne De Rosario, TOR	28	11	6	17
Brad Davis, HOU	27	5	12	17
Robbie Findley, RSL	27	12	4	16
Nate Jaqua, SEA	28	9	7	16
Shalrie Joseph, NE	27	8	8	16

ASSISTS LEADERS

Player, Team	GP	A
Omar Cummings, COL	28	12
Brad Davis, HOU	27	12
Dave van den Bergh, DAL	27	11
Freddie Ljungberg, SEA	22	9
Cuauhtemoc Blanco, CHI	21	8
Jeff Cunningham, DAL	28	8
Shalrie Joseph, NE	27	8
Claudio Lopez, KC	29	8

Eight players tied with 7.

GOALS-AGAINST-AVERAGE LEADERS

Player, Team	GAA
Zach Thornton, CHV	0.87
Kasey Keller, SEA	0.92
William Hesmer, CLB	0.95
Matt Reis, NE	0.96
Pat Onstad, HOU	0.97
Donovan Ricketts, LA	1.03
Jon Busch, CHI	1.13
Nick Rimando, RSL	1.14
Matt Pickens, COL	1.16

GOALS LEADERS

Player, Team	GP	G
Jeff Cunningham, DAL	28	17
Conor Casey, COL	24	16
Juan Pablo Angel, NY	25	12
Guillermo Barros Schelotto, CLB	24	12
Landon Donovan, LA	25	12
Robbie Findley, RSL	27	12
Fredy Montero, SEA	27	12
Dwayne De Rosario, TOR	28	11
Ryan Johnson, SJ	30	11
Josh Wolff, KC	27	11

Western Conference Playoffs

1ST ROUND (TWO LEGS)

Los Angeles	2	1—3
Chivas USA	2	0—2

Houston	0	1—1
Seattle	0	0—0

CONF. FINALS

Los Angeles	2
Houston	0

Eastern Conference Playoffs

1ST ROUND (TWO LEGS)

Columbus	0	2—2
Real Salt Lake	1	3—4

New England	2	0—2
Chicago	1	2—3

CONF. FINALS

Chicago	0 (4)
Real Salt Lake	0 (5)

2009 MLS CUP (November 22, 2009 in Seattle, Washington)

Real Salt Lake	0	1 —— 1 (5)
Los Angeles	1	0 —— 1 (4)

FIRST HALF: Scoring: 1, Los Angeles, Magee (Beckham, Donovan), 41st minute.

SECOND HALF: Scoring: 1, Real Salt Lake, Findley, 64th minute.

SHOOTOUT: LA: 4, Beckham (goal), Berhalter (goal), Kirovski (saved), Donovan (high), Magee (goal), Klein (goal), Buddle (saved). RSL: 5, Mathis (goal), Findley (goal), Beckerman (saved), Grabavoy (goal), Williams (saved), Wingert (goal), Russell (goal).

Real Salt Lake: Rimando, Beckerman, Russell, Borchers, Findely, Johnson (Grabavoy 46), Movsisyan (Espinoda 75), Olave, Morales (Mathis 22), Williams, Wingert.

Los Angeles: Ricketts (Saunders 66), Donovan, Berhalter, Magee, Dunivant, Gonzalez (DeLaGarza 89), Birchall (Klein 79), Beckham, Franklin, Buddle, Kirovski.

Attendance: 46,011. Referee: Kevin Stott. Asst. Referees: C.J. Morgante, Robert Fereday.

MLS Cup MVP: Nick Rimando (keeper), Real Salt Lake.

2010 World Cup Results

Group Stage

GROUP A

Country	MP	W	L	T	Pts
*Uruguay	3	2	0	1	7
*Mexico	3	1	1	1	4
South Africa	3	1	1	1	4
France	3	0	2	1	1

GROUP D

Country	MP	W	L	T	Pts
*Germany	3	2	1	0	6
*Ghana	3	1	1	1	4
Australia	3	1	1	1	4
Serbia	3	1	2	0	3

GROUP G

Country	MP	W	L	T	Pts
*Brazil	3	2	0	1	7
*Portugal	3	1	0	2	5
Cote d-Ivoire	3	1	1	1	4
North Korea	3	0	3	0	0

GROUP B

Country	MP	W	L	T	Pts
*Argentina	3	3	0	0	9
*South Korea	3	1	1	1	4
Greece	3	1	2	0	3
Nigeria	3	0	2	1	1

GROUP E

Country	MP	W	L	T	Pts
*Netherlands	3	3	0	0	9
*Japan	3	2	1	0	6
Denmark	3	1	2	0	3
Cameroon	3	0	3	0	0

GROUP H

Country	MP	W	L	T	Pts
*Spain	3	2	1	0	6
*Chile	3	2	1	0	6
Switzerland	3	1	1	1	4
Honduras	3	0	2	1	1

GROUP C

Country	MP	W	L	T	Pts
*United States	3	1	0	2	5
*England	3	1	0	2	5
Slovenia	3	1	1	1	4
Algeria	3	0	2	1	1

GROUP F

Country	MP	W	L	T	Pts
*Paraguay	3	1	0	2	5
*Slovakia	3	1	1	1	4
New Zealand	3	0	0	3	3
Italy	3	0	1	2	2

*Moved on to Round of 16.
Note: in group play, three points are
awarded for a win, one for a tie.

Round of 16

Uruguay	1	1—2
South Korea	0	1—1

Argentina	2	1—3
Mexico	0	1—1

Netherlands	1	1—2
Slovakia	0	0—1

Paraguay	0 0	0—0 (5)
Japan	0 0	0—0 (3)

a.e.t.(penalty kick shootout)

United States	1	0—1
Ghana	1	1—2

Germany	2	2—4
England	1	0—1

Brazil	2	1—3
Chile	0	0—0

Spain	1	0—1
Portugal	0	0—0

Quarterfinals

Uruguay	0 1	0—1 (4)
Ghana	1 0	0—1 (2)

a.e.t. (penalty kick shootout)

Argentina	0	0—0
Germany	1	3—4

Netherlands	0	2—2
Brazil	1	0—1

Paraguay	0	0—0
Spain	1	0—1

Semifinals

Uruguay	1	1—2
Netherlands	1	2—3

Spain	0	1—1
Germany	0	0—0

World Cup Final

Spain	0 0 0 1	1
Netherlands	0 0 0 0	0

2.a.e.t.

Third-Place Consolation Match

Uruguay	1	1—2
Germany	1	2—3

FOR THE RECORD • Year by Year

The World Cup

Results—Men

Year	Champion	Score	Runner-Up	Winning Coach
1930	Uruguay	4–2	Argentina	Alberto Supicci
1934	Italy	2–1	Czechoslovakia	Vittorio Pozzo
1938	Italy	4–2	Hungary	Vittorio Pozzo
1950	Uruguay	2–1	Brazil	Juan Lopez
1954	West Germany	3–2	Hungary	Sepp Herberger
1958	Brazil	5–2	Sweden	Vicente Feola
1962	Brazil	3–1	Czechoslovakia	Aymore Moreira
1966	England	4–2	West Germany	Alf Ramsey
1970	Brazil	4–1	Italy	Mario Zagalo
1974	West Germany	2–1	Netherlands	Helmut Schoen
1978	Argentina	3–1	Netherlands	César Menotti
1982	Italy	3–1	West Germany	Enzo Bearzot
1986	Argentina	3–2	West Germany	Carlos Bilardo
1990	West Germany	1–0	Argentina	Franz Beckenbauer
1994	Brazil	0–0 (3–2)	Italy	Carlos Alberto Parreira
1998	France	3–0	Brazil	Aime Jacquet
2002	Brazil	2–0	Germany	Luis Felipe Scolari
2006	Italy	1–1 (5–3)	France	Marcello Lippi
2010	Spain	1–0 (2ot)	Netherlands	Vicente Del Bosque

Alltime World Cup Participation

Nation	Matches	W	T	L	Goals For	Goals Against	Nation	Matches	W	T	L	Goals For	Goals Against
Brazil	97	67	15	15	210	89	Senegal	5	2	2	1	7	6
*Germany	99	60	19	20	206	119	Ukraine	5	2	1	2	5	7
Italy	80	44	21	15	126	78	East Germany	6	2	2	2	5	6
Argentina	70	37	13	20	123	79	Norway	8	2	3	3	7	9
Spain	56	28	12	16	88	57	Cote d'Ivoire	6	2	1	3	9	9
England	59	26	19	14	77	52	South Africa	9	2	4	3	11	15
France	54	25	11	18	96	70	Republic of Ireland	13	2	8	3	10	10
Netherlands	43	22	10	11	71	42	Algeria	9	2	2	5	6	12
Uruguay	47	18	12	17	76	64	Morocco	13	2	4	7	12	17
†Russia	37	17	6	14	64	44	Saudi Arabia	13	2	2	9	9	32
Yugoslavia	37	17	6	14	60	46	Australia	10	2	3	5	8	16
Sweden	46	16	13	17	74	71	Wales	5	1	3	1	4	4
Poland	31	15	5	11	44	40	Cuba	3	1	1	1	5	12
Hungary	32	15	3	14	87	58	Slovakia	3	1	1	1	4	5
Portugal	23	12	3	8	39	23	Jamaica	3	1	0	2	3	9
Austria	29	12	4	13	43	49	Slovenia	6	1	1	4	5	10
Czech Republic	33	12	5	16	47	48	North Korea	7	1	1	5	6	21
Mexico	49	12	13	24	52	87	Serbia	6	1	0	5	4	13
Belgium	36	10	9	17	46	64	Greece	6	1	0	5	2	15
Switzerland	29	9	6	14	38	51	Iran	9	1	2	6	6	17
Chile	29	9	6	14	34	45	Tunisia	12	1	4	7	8	17
Denmark	16	8	2	6	27	24	Angola	3	0	2	1	1	2
Romania	21	8	5	8	30	32	Israel	3	0	2	1	1	3
Paraguay	27	7	10	10	30	38	Indonesia	1	0	0	1	0	6
United States	29	7	5	17	32	57	Egypt	4	0	2	2	3	6
Croatia	13	6	2	5	15	11	Kuwait	3	0	1	2	2	6
Turkey	10	5	1	4	20	17	Trinidad and Tobago	3	0	1	2	0	4
South Korea	28	5	8	15	28	60	New Zealand	6	0	3	3	4	14
Ghana	9	4	2	3	9	10	Honduras	6	0	3	3	2	6
Japan	14	4	3	7	12	16	United Arab Emirates	3	0	0	3	2	11
Nigeria	14	4	2	8	17	21	Haiti	3	0	0	3	2	14
Peru	15	4	3	8	19	31	Iraq	3	0	0	3	1	4
Cameroon	20	4	7	9	17	34	Togo	3	0	0	3	1	6
Scotland	23	4	7	12	25	41	Canada	3	0	0	3	0	5
Ecuador	7	3	0	4	7	8	China	3	0	0	3	0	9
Northern Ireland	13	3	5	5	13	23	Dem. Rep. of Congo	3	0	0	3	0	14
Costa Rica	10	3	1	6	12	21	Bolivia	6	0	1	5	1	20
Colombia	13	3	2	8	14	22	El Salvador	6	0	0	6	1	22
Bulgaria	26	3	8	15	22	52							

*Includes West Germany 1950–90. †Includes USSR 1930–1990.
Note: Matches decided by penalty kicks are shown as drawn games.

World Cup Final Box Scores

URUGUAY 1930

Uruguay 1   3 — —4
Argentina 2   0 — —2

FIRST HALF: Scoring: 1, Uruguay, Dorado (12); 2, Argentina, Peucelle (20); 3, Argentina, Stabile (37).

SECOND HALF: Scoring: 4, Uruguay, Cea (57); 5, Uruguay, Iriarte (68); 6, Uruguay, Castro (89).

Argentina: Botosso, Della Toree, Paternoster, J. Evaristo, Monti, Suarez, Peucelle, Varallo, Stabile, Ferreira, M. Evaristo.

Uruguay: Ballesteros, Nasazzi, Mascheroni, Andrade, Fernandez, Gestido, Dorado, Scarone, Castro, Cea, Iriarte.

Referee: Langenus (Belgium).

ITALY 1934

Italy 0   1   1 — —2
Czechoslovakia 0   0   0 — —1

SECOND HALF: Scoring: 1, Czech., Puc (70); 2, Italy, Orsi (80).

OVERTIME: Scoring: 3, Italy, Schiavio (95).

Italy: Combi, Monzeglio, Allemandi, Ferraris Monti, Monti, Bertolini, Guaita, Meazza, Schiavio, Ferrari, Orsi.

Czechoslovakia: Planicka, Zenisek, Ctyroky, Kostalek, Cambal, Cambal, Krcil, Junek, Svoboda, Sobotka, Nejedly, Puc.

Referee: Eklind (Sweden).

FRANCE 1938

Italy 3   1 — —4
Hungary 1   1 — —2

FIRST HALF: Scoring: 1, Italy, Colaussi (5); 2, Hungary, Titkos (7); 3, Italy, Piola (16); 4, Italy, Piola (35).

SECOND HALF: Scoring: 5, Hungary, Sarosi (70); 6, Italy, Colaussi (82).

Italy: Olivieri, Foni, Rava, Serantoni, Andreolo, Locatelli, Biavati, Meazza, Piola, Ferrari, Colaussi.

Hungary: Szabo, Polger, Biro, Szalay, Szucs, Lazar, Sas, Vincze, Sarosi, Zsengeller, Titkos.

Referee: Capdeville (France).

BRAZIL 1950

Uruguay 0   2 — —2
Brazil 0   1 — —1

SECOND HALF: Scoring: 1, Brazil, Friaca (47); 2, Uruguay, Schiaffino (66); 3, Uruguay, Ghiggia (79).

Uruguay: Maspoli, Gonzales, Tejera, Gambretta, Varela, Andrade, Ghiggia, Perez, Miguez, Schiffiano, Moran.

Brazil: Barbosa, Augusto, Juvenal, Bauer, Banilo, Bigode, Friaca, Zizinho, Ademir, Jair, Chico.

Referee: Reader (England).

SWITZERLAND 1954

West Germany 2   1 — —3
Hungary 2   0 — —2

FIRST HALF: Scoring: 1, Hungary, Puskas (6); 2, Hungary, Czibor (8); 3, W Germ., Morlock (10); 4, W Germ., Rahn (18).

SECOND HALF: Scoring: 5, W Germany, Rahn (84).

West Germany: Turek, Posipal, Kohlmeyer, Eckel, Liebrich, Mai, Rahn, Morlock, O.Walter, F. Walter, Schaefer.

Hungary: Grosics, Buzansky, Lantos, Bozsik, Lorant, Zakarias, Czibor, Kocsis, Hidegkuti, Puskas, Toth.

Referee: Ling (England).

SWEDEN 1958

Brazil 2   3 — —5
Sweden 1   1 — —2

FIRST HALF: Scoring:1, Sweden, Liedholm (3); 2, Brazil, Vava (9); 3, Brazil, Vava (32).

SECOND HALF: Scoring: 4, Brazil, Pelé (55); 5, Brazil, Zagalo (68); 6, Sweden Simonsson (80); 7, Brazil, Pelé (90).

Brazil: Glymar, D. Santos, N. Santos, Zito, Bellini, Orlando, Garrincha, Didi, Vava, Pelé, Zagalo.

Sweden: Svensson, Bergmark, Axbom, Boerjesson, Gustavsson, Parling, Hamrin, Gren, Simonsson, Liedholm, Skoglund.

Referee: Guigue (France).

CHILE 1962

Brazil 1   2 — —3
Czechoslovakia ... 1   0 — —1

FIRST HALF: Scoring: 1, Czech., Masopust (15); 2, Brazil, Amarildo (17).

SECOND HALF: Scoring: 3, Brazil, Zito (68); 4, Brazil, Vava (77).

Brazil: Glymar, D. Santos, N. Santos, Zito, Mauro, Zozimo, Garrincha, Didi, Vava, Amarildo, Zagalo.

Czechoslovakia: Schroiff, Tichy, Novak, Pluskal, Popluhar, Masopust, Pospichal, Scherer, Kvasnak, Kadraba, Jelinek.

Referee: Latychev (USSR).

ENGLAND 1966

England 1   1   2 — —4
West Germany ..1   1   0 — —2

FIRST HALF: Scoring: 1, W Germany, Haller (12); 2, England, Hurst (18).

SECOND HALF: Scoring: 3, England, Peters (78); 4, W. Germany, Weber (90).

OVERTIME: Scoring: 5, England, Hurst (101); 6, England, Hurst (120).

England: Banks, Cohen, Wilson, Stiles, J. Charlton, Moore, Ball, Hurst, Hunt, R. Charlton, Peters.

West Germany: Tilkowski, Hottges, Schmellinger, Beckenbauer, Schulz, Weber, Held, Haller, Seeler, Overath, Emmerich.

Referee: Dienst (Switzerland).

World Cup Final Box Scores *(Cont.)*

MEXICO 1970

```
Brazil.....................1    3 — —4
Italy .......................1    0 — —1
```

FIRST HALF: Scoring: 1, Brazil, Pelé (18); 2, Italy, Boninsegna (32).

SECOND HALF: Scoring: 3, Brazil, Gerson (65); 4, Brazil, Jairzinho (70); 5, Brazil, Alberto (86).

Brazil: Feliz, Alberto, Brito, Wilson, Piazza, Everaldo, Clodoaldo, Gerson, Jairzinho, Tostao, Pelé, Rivelino.

Italy: Albertosi, Burgnich, Cera, Rosato, Facchetti, Bertini (Juliano), Mazzola, De Sisti, Domenghini, Boninsegna (Rivera), Riva.

Referee: Glockner (E Germany).

WEST GERMANY 1974

```
West Germany......2    0 — —2
Netherlands............1    0 — —1
```

FIRST HALF: Scoring: 1, Netherlands, Neeskens, PK (1); 2, W Germany, Breitner, PK (26); 3, W Germany, Müller (44).

West Germany: Maier, Vogts, Beckenbauer, Schwarzenbeck, Breitner, Hoeness, Bonhof, Overath, Grabowski, Müller, Holzenbein.

Netherlands: Jongbloed, Suurbier, Rijsbergen (de Jong), Haan, Krol, Jansen, Neeskens, van Hanagem, Cruyff, Rensenbrink (van der Kerkhof).

Referee: Taylor (England).

ARGENTINA 1978

```
Argentina ...............1    0    2 — —3
Netherlands...........0    1    0 — —1
```

FIRST HALF: Scoring: 1, Argentina, Kempes (38).

SECOND HALF: Scoring: 2, Netherlands, Nanninga (81).

OVERTIME: Scoring: 3, Arg., Kempes (104); 4, Arg., Bertoni (114).

Argentina: Fillol, Olguin, Galvan, Passarella, Tarantini, Ardiles (Larrosa), Gallego, Kempes, Bertoni, Luque, Ortiz (Houseman).

Netherlands: Jongbloed, Jansen (Suurbier), Krol, Brandts, Poortvliet, Neeskens, Haan, W. van der Kerkhoff, R. van der Kerkhoff, Rep (Nanninga), Rensenbrink.

Referee: Gonella (Italy).

ITALY 1982

```
Italy ......................0    3 — —3
West Germany......0    1 — —1
```

SECOND HALF: Scoring: 1, Italy, Rossi (57); 2, Italy, Tardelli (68); 3, Italy, Altobelli (81); 4, W Germany, Breitner (83).

Italy: Zoff, Bergomi, Scirea, Collovati, Cabrini, Oriali, Gentile, Tardelli, Conti, Rossi, Graziani (Altobelli, Causio).

West Germany: Schumacher, Kaltz, Stielike, K. Foerster, B. Foerster, Dremmler (Hrubesch), Breitner, Briegel, Rummenigge (Müller), Fischcher (Littbarski).

Referee: Coelho (Brazil).

MEXICO 1986

```
Argentina ...............1    2 — —3
West Germany......0    2 — —2
```

FIRST HALF: Scoring: 1, Argentina, Brown (22).

SECOND HALF: Scoring: 2, Arg., Valdano (55); 3, W Germ., Rummenigge (73); 4, W Germ., Voller (81); 5, Arg., Burruchaga (83).

Argentina: Pumpido, Brown, Cuciuffo, Ruggeri, Olarticoecha, Bastista, Giusti, Burruchaga (Trobbiani 90), Enrique, Maradona, Valdona.

West Germany: Schumacher, Jakobs, Forster, Eder, Brehme, Matthaus, Berthold, Magath (Hoeness 62), Briegel, Rummenigge, Allofs (Voller 46).

Referee: Filho (Brazil).

ITALY 1990

```
West Germany .........0    1 — — 1
Argentina ...................0    0 — —0
```

SECOND HALF: Scoring: 1, W Germany, Brehme, PK (84).

West Germany: Illgner, Brehme, Kohler, Augenthaler, Buchwald, Berthold (Reuter), Littbarski, Haessler, Mattaeus, Voeller, Klinsmann.

Argentina: Goychoechea, Lorenzo, Serrizuela, Sensini, Ruggeri (Monzon), Simon, Basualdo, Burruchag (Calderon), Maradona, Troglio, Dezottir.

Referee: Coelho (Brazil).

UNITED STATES 1994

```
Italy ........................0    0    0— —0
Brazil........................0    0    0— —0
```

Scoring: None. Shootout goals: Italy—2: Albertini, Evani; Brazil—3: Romario, Branco, Dunga.

Italy: Pagliuca, Benarrivo, Maldini, Baresi, Mussi (Apolloni 35), Albertini, D. Baggio (Evani 95), Berti, Donadoni, Baggio, Massaro.

Brazil: Taffarel, Jorginho (Cafu 21), Branco, Aldair, Santos, Silva, Dunga, Zinho (Viola 106), Mazinho, Bebeto, Romario.

Referee: Puhl (Hungary).

FRANCE 1998

```
Brazil .........................0    0— —0
France.........................2    1— —3
```

FIRST HALF: Scoring: 1, France, Zidane (27); 2, France, Zidane (45).

SECOND HALF: Scoring: 3, France, Petit (90).

Brazil: Taffarel, Cafu, Aldair, Baiano, Carlos, Sampaio (Edmundo 74), Dunga, Rivaldo, Leonardo, (Denilson 46), Bebeto, Ronaldo.

France: Barthez, Lizarazu, Desailly, Thuram, Leboeuf, Djorkaeff (Vieira 75) Deschamps, Zidane, Petit, Karembeu (Boghossian 57), Guivarc'h (Dugarry 66).

Referee: Belqola (Morocco).

World Cup Final Box Scores (Cont.)

KOREA/JAPAN 2002

Brazil	0		2——2
Germany	0		0——0

SECOND HALF: Scoring: 1, Brazil, Ronaldo (67); 2, Brazil, Ronaldo (79).

Brazil: Marcos, Cafu, Lucio, Roque Junior, Edmilson, Carlos, Silva, Ronaldo (Denilson, 90), Rivaldo, Ronaldinho (Juninho, 85), Kleberson.

Germany: Kahn, Linke, Ramelow, Neuville, Hamann, Klose (Bierhoff, 74), Jeremies (Asamoah, 77), Bode (Ziege, 84), Schneider, Metzelder, Frings.

Referee: Collina (Italy).

GERMANY 2006

Italy	1	0	0 ——1
France	1	0	0 ——1

Italy won on penalty kicks, 5–3.

FIRST HALF: Scoring: 1, France, Zidane (7); 1, Italy, Materazzi (19).

SHOOTOUT GOALS: Italy—Pirlo, Materazzi, De Rossi, Del Piero, Grosso; France—Wiltord, Abidal, Sagnol.

Italy: Buffon, Zambrotta, Cannavaro, Materazzi, Grosso, Camoranesi (Del Piero 86), Pirlo, Gattuso, Perrotta (Iaquinta 61), Totti (De Rossi 61), Toni.

France: Barthez, Sagnol, Thuram, Gallas, Abidal, Ribery (Trezeguet 100), Vieira (Diarra 56), Makelele, Zidane, Malouda, Henry (Wiltord 107).

Referee: Elizondo (Argentina).

SOUTH AFRICA 2010

Spain	0	0	0	1——1
Netherlands	0	0	0	0——0

2ND EXTRA TIME: Scoring: 1, Spain, Iniesta (Fabregas), 116.

Spain: Casillas, Pique, Puyol, Iniesta, Pedro (Navas 60), Xavi, Capdevila, Fabregas (Alonso 87), Ramos, Busquets, Villa (Torres 105).

Netherlands: Stekelenburg, Van der Wiel, Heitinga, Mathijsen, Van Brommel, Robben, Sneijder, Kuyt (Elia 71), De Jong (Van der Vaart 99), Van Bronckhorst (Braafheid 105), Van Persie.

Referee: Howard Webb (England).

Alltime Leaders

GOALS

Player, Nation	Tournaments	Goals
Ronaldo, Brazil	1994, '98, 2002, '06	15
Gerd Müller, West Germany	1970, '74	14
Miroslav Klose, Germany	2002, '06, '10	14
Just Fontaine, France	1958	13
Pelé, Brazil	1958, '62, '66, '70	12
Sandor Kocsis, Hungary	1954	11
Jurgen Klinsmann, Germany	1990, '94, '98	11
Helmut Rahn, West Germany	1954, '58	10
Gary Lineker, England	1986, '90	10
Gabriel Batistuta, Argentina	1998, 2002	10
Teofilo Cubillas, Peru	1970, '78, '82	10
Grzegorz Lato, Poland	1974, '78, '82	10
Ademir, Brazil	1950	9
Eusebio, Portugal	1966	9
Jairzinho, Brazil	1970, '74	9
Paolo Rossi, Italy	1982, '86	9
K.H. Rummenigge, W. Germany	1978, '82, '86	9
Uwe Seeler, West Germany	1958, '62, '66, '70	9
Vava, Brazil	1958, '62	9
Christian Vieri, Italy	1998, 2002	9

LEADING SCORER, CUP BY CUP

Year	Player, Nation	Goals
1930	Guillermo Stabile, Argentina	8
1934	Oldrich Nejedly, Czechoslovakia	5
1938	Leonidas da Silva, Brazil	8
1950	Ademir de Menenzes, Brazil	9
1954	Sandor Kocsis, Hungary	11
1958	Just Fontaine, France	13
1962	Florian Albert, Hungary	4
	Valentin Ivanov, USSR, Garrincha, Brazil,	
	Vava, Brazil, Drazan Jerkovic, Yugoslavia	
	Leonel Sanchez, Chile	9
1966	Eusebio Ferreira, Portugal	9
1970	Gerd Müller, W Germany	10
1974	Gregorz Lato, Poland	7
1978	Mario Kempes, Argentina	6
1982	Paolo Rossi, Italy	6
1986	Gary Lineker, England	6
1990	Salvatore Schillaci, Italy	6
1994	Hristo Stoichkov, Bulgaria	
	Oleg Salenko, Russia	6
1998	Davor Suker, Croatia	6
2002	Ronaldo, Brazil	8
2006	Miroslav Klose, Germany	5
2010	Thomas Mueller, Germany	5
	Diego Forlan, Uruguay	
	Wesley Sneijder, Netherlands	
	David Villa, Spain	

Most Goals, Individual, One Game

Goals	Player, Nation	Score	Date
5	Oleg Salenko, Russia	Russia–Cameroon, 6–1	6-28-94
4	Leonidas, Brazil	Brazil–Poland, 6–5	6-5-38
4	Ernest Willimowski, Poland	Brazil–Poland, 6–5	6-5-38
4	Gustav Wetterstrîm, Sweden	Sweden–Cuba, 8–0	6-12-38
4	Juan Alberto Schiaffino, Uruguay	Uruguay–Bolivia, 8–0	7-2-50
4	Ademir, Brazil	Brazil–Sweden, 7–1	7-9-50
4	Sandor Kocsis, Hungary	Hungary–W Germany, 8–3	6-20-54
4	Just Fontaine, France	France–W Germany, 6–3	6-28-58
4	Eusebio, Portugal	Portugal–N Korea, 5–3	7-23-66
4	Emilio Butragueño, Spain	Spain–Denmark, 5–1	6-18-86

Note: 31 players have scored 32 World Cup hat tricks. Gerd Müller of West Germany is the only man to have two World Cup hat tricks, both in 1970. The last hat tricks were 6-1-02, Miroslav Klose (Ger) vs. Saudi Arabia; 6-21-98, Gabriel Batistuta (Arg) vs. Jamaica; 6-23-90, Tomas Skuhravy (Czech) vs. Costa Rica; and 6-17-90, Michel (Spain) vs. S Korea.

Attendance and Goal Scoring, Year by Year

Year	Site	No. of Games	Goals	Goals/Game	Attendance	Avg Att
1930	Uruguay	18	70	3.89	434,500	24,139
1934	Italy	17	70	4.12	395,000	23,235
1938	France	18	84	4.67	483,000	26,833
1950	Brazil	22	88	4.00	1,337,000	60,773
1954	Switzerland	26	140	5.38	943,000	36,269
1958	Sweden	35	126	3.60	868,000	24,800
1962	Chile	32	89	2.78	776,000	24,250
1966	England	32	89	2.78	1,614,677	50,459
1970	Mexico	32	95	2.97	1,673,975	52,312
1974	W Germany	38	97	2.55	1,774,022	46,685
1978	Argentina	38	102	2.68	1,610,215	42,374
1982	Spain	52	146	2.80	1,856,277	35,698
1986	Mexico	52	132	2.54	2,441,731	46,956
1990	Italy	52	115	2.21	2,514,443	48,354
1994	United States	52	140	2.69	3,567,415	68,604
1998	France	64	171	2.67	2,775,400	43,366
2002	Korea/Japan	64	161	2.52	2,705,216	42,269
2006	Germany	64	147	2.23	3,353,655	52,400
2010	South Africa	64	145	2.27	3,178,856	49,670
Totals		708	2,046	2.89	31,597,166	44,629

Results—Women's World Cup

Year	Champion	Score	Runner-Up	Third Place	Fourth Place
1991	United States	2–1	Norway	Sweden	Germany
1995	Norway	2–0	Germany	United States	China
1999	United States	0–0 (5–4 pk)	China	Brazil	Norway
2003	Germany	2–1	Sweden	United States	Canada
2007	Germany	2–0	Brazil	United States	Norway

Major League Soccer Finals

MLS Cup Results

Year	Champion	Score	Runner-up	Regular Season MVP
1996	D.C. United	3–2 (ot)	Los Angeles	Carlos Valderrama, TB
1997	D.C. United	2–1	Colorado	Preki, Kansas City
1998	Chicago	2–0	D.C. United	Marco Etcheverry, D.C.
1999	D.C. United	2–0	Los Angeles	Jason Kreis, Dallas
2000	Kansas City	1–0	Chicago	Tony Meola, Kansas City
2001	San Jose	2–1 (ot)	Los Angeles	Alex Pineda Chacon, Miami
2002	Los Angeles	1–0 (ot)	New England	Carlos Ruiz, Los Angeles
2003	San Jose	4–2	Chicago	Preki, Kansas City
2004	D.C. United	3–2	Kansas City	Amado Guevara, MetroStars
2005	Los Angeles	1–0 (ot)	New England	Taylor Twellman, NE
2006	Houston	1–1 (ot, 4-3 pks)	New England	Christian Gomez, D.C.
2007	Houston	2–1	New England	Luciano Emilio, D.C.
2008	Columbus	3–1	New York	Guillermo Schelotto, Clb
2009	Real Salt Lake	1–1 (ot, 5–4 pks)	Los Angeles	Landon Donovan, LA

United Soccer League Finals

Year	Champion	Score	Runner-Up	Regular Season MVP
1991	San Francisco	1–3, 2–0 (1–0 on PKs)	Albany	Jean Harbor, Maryland
1992	Colorado	1–0	Tampa Bay	Taifour Diane, Colorado
1993	Colorado	3–1 (OT)	Los Angeles	Taifour Diane, Colorado
1994	Montreal	1–0	Colorado	Paulinho, Los Angeles
1995	Seattle	1–2 (SO), 3–0, 2–1 (SO)	Atlanta	Peter Hattrup, Seattle
1996	Seattle	2–0	Rochester	Wolde Harris, Colorado
1997	Milwaukee	2–1 (SO)	Carolina	Doug Miller, Rochester
1998	Rochester	3–1	Minnesota	Mark Baena, Seattle
1999	Minnesota	2–1	Rochester	John Swallen, Minnesota
2000	Rochester	3–1	Minnesota	Vitalis Takawira, Mil
2001	Rochester	2–0	Vancouver	Paul Conway, Charleston
2002	Milwaukee	2–1 (2 OT)	Richmond	Leighton O'Brien, Seattle
2003	Charleston	3–0	Minnesota	Thiago Martins, Pittsburgh
2004	Montreal	2–0	Seattle	Greg Sutton, Montreal
2005	Seattle	1–1 (4–3 on PKs)	Richmond	Jason Jordan, Vancouver
2006	Vancouver	3–0	Rochester	Joey Gjertsen, Vancouver
2007	Seattle	4–0	Atlanta	Sebastien Le Toux, Seattle
2008	Vancouver	2–1	Puerto Rico	Jonathan Steele, Puerto Rico
2009	Montreal	6–3 (two legs)	Vancouver	Cristian Arietta, Puerto Rico
2010	Puerto Rico	3–1 (two legs)	Carolina	Ryan Pore, Portland

Motor Sports

Dario Franchitti raced his way to a second career Indy 500 title in 2010

Indy Racing League

Indianapolis 500

Results of the 94th running of the Indianapolis 500 and sixth race of the 2010 Indy Racing League season. Held Sunday, May 30, 2010, at the 2.5-mile Indianapolis Motor Speedway in Indianapolis, Indiana. Distance, 500 miles; starters, 33; winning time of race, 3 hours, 5 mins., 37.0131 seconds; average speed, 161.623 mph; margin of victory, 0.1536 seconds (under caution); caution flags, 9 for 44 laps; lead changes, 13 among eight drivers.

TOP 10 FINISHERS

Pos.	Driver (start pos.)	C/E/T	Qual. Speed	Laps	Status
1	Dario Franchitti (3)	D/H/F	226.990	200	running
2	Dan Wheldon (18)	D/H/F	224.464	200	running
3	Marco Andretti (16)	D/H/F	224.575	200	running
4	Alex Lloyd (26)	D/H/F	224.783	200	running
5	Scott Dixon (6)	D/H/F	226.323	200	running
6	Danica Patrick (23)	D/H/F	224.217	200	running
7	Justin Wilson (11)	D/H/F	225.050	200	running
8	Will Power (2)	D/H/F	227.578	200	running
9	Helio Castroneves (1)	D/H/F	227.970	200	running
10	Alex Tagliani (5)	D/H/F	226.390	200	running

2010 Indy Racing League Results

Date	Race	Winner (start pos.)	C/E/T	Qual. Speed
Mar 14	Sao Paulo 300	Will Power (5)	D/H/F	103.727
Mar 29	Grand Prix of St. Petersburg	Will Power (1)	D/H/F	105.190
Apr 11	Grand Prix of Alabama	Helio Castroneves (3)	D/H/F	117.186
Apr 18	Grand Prix of Long Beach	Ryan Hunter-Reay (2)	D/H/F	101.573
May 1	Kansas 300	Scott Dixon (2)	D/H/F	211.298
May 30	Indianapolis 500	Dario Franchitti (3)	D/H/F	226.990
May 31	Milwaukee 225	Scott Dixon (4)	D/H/F	167.089
June 5	Texas 550	Ryan Briscoe (1)	D/H/F	215.273
June 20	Iowa 250	Tony Kanaan (15)	D/H/F	179.109
July 4	Grand Prix of Watkins Glen	Will Power (1)	D/H/F	135.832
July 18	Toronto 200	Will Power (2)	D/H/F	104.505
July 25	Edmonton 95*	Scott Dixon (3)	D/H/F	115.984
Aug 8	Mid-Ohio 200	Dario Franchitti (2)	D/H/F	120.812
Aug 22	Sonoma Grand Prix	Will Power (1)	D/H/F	108.337
Aug 28	Chicago 300	Dario Franchitti (2)	D/H/F	215.593
Sept 4	Kentucky 300	Helio Castroneves (8)	D/H/F	216.857
Sept 18	Japan 300	Helio Castroneves (1)	D/H/F	201.992
Oct 2	Miami 300	Scott Dixon (2)	D/H/F	212.908

Note: Distances are in miles unless followed by * (laps).

2010 Final IRL Standings

Driver	Pts
Dario Franchitti	602
Will Power	597
Scott Dixon	547
Helio Castroneves	531
Ryan Briscoe	482
Tony Kanaan	453
Ryan Hunter-Reay	445
Marco Andretti	392
Dan Wheldon	388
Danica Patrick	367

Daytona 500†

Results of the 52nd Daytona 500, the opening round of the 2010 Sprint Cup series. Held Sunday, February 14, 2010, at the 2.5-mile high-banked Daytona International Speedway. Distance, 500 miles; starters, 43; winning time of race, 3:47:16; average speed, 137.284 mph; margin of victory 0.119 seconds; caution flags, 9 for 40 laps; lead changes,52.

TOP 10 FINISHERS

Pos.	Driver (start pos.)	Car	Laps	Winnings ($)
1	Jamie McMurray (13)	Chevrolet	208	1,508,450
2	Dale Earnhardt Jr. (2)	Chevrolet	208	1,096,990
3	Greg Biffle (23)	Ford	208	793,370
4	Clint Bowyer (9)	Chevrolet	208	648,545
5	David Reutimann (20)	Toyota	208	533,726
6	Martin Truex Jr. (14)	Toyota	208	403,545
7	Kevin Harvick (5)	Chevrolet	208	421,796
8	Matt Kenseth (24)	Ford	208	375,521
9	Carl Edwards (27)	Ford	208	355,143
10	Juan Montoya (8)	Chevrolet	208	362,676

2009 Sprint Chase for the Cup* Final Season Standings

Driver	Pts	Starts	Wins	Top 5	Top 10
Jimmie Johnson	6652	36	7	16	24
Mark Martin	6511	36	5	14	21
Jeff Gordon	6473	36	1	16	25
Kurt Busch	6446	36	2	10	21
Denny Hamlin	6335	36	4	15	20
Tony Stewart	6309	36	4	15	23
Greg Biffle	6292	36	0	10	16
Juan Montoya	6252	36	0	7	18
Ryan Newman	6175	36	0	5	15
Kasey Kahne	6128	36	2	7	14
Carl Edwards	6118	36	0	7	14
Brian Vickers	5929	36	1	4	13

2009 Sprint Cup* Final Season Driver Winnings

Driver	Winnings ($)
Jimmie Johnson	7,339,630
Matt Kenseth	7,085,710
Tony Stewart	6,836,150
Jeff Gordon	6,476,460
Kyle Busch	6,204,750
Kevin Harvick	6,104,740
Kasey Kahne	5,760,140
Carl Edwards	5,607,550
Jeff Burton	5,530,110
Denny Hamlin	5,478,040
Joey Logano	5,375,110
Mark Martin	5,279,000

2010 Sprint Chase for the Cup Late-Season Standings†

Driver	Pts	Starts	Wins	Top 5	Top 10
Jimmie Johnson	5998	32	6	15	19
Denny Hamlin	5992	32	7	13	16
Kevin Harvick	5936	32	3	14	22
Kyle Busch	5826	32	3	10	18
Jeff Gordon	5795	32	0	11	16
Carl Edwards	5785	32	0	7	17
Tony Stewart	5762	32	2	9	16
Jeff Burton	5752	32	0	6	15
Kurt Busch	5721	32	2	9	16
Matt Kenseth	5705	32	0	5	12
Greg Biffle	5682	32	2	7	16
Clint Bowyer	5592	32	1	6	16

*Series name changed from Winston Cup to Nextel Cup after 2003 season, then to Sprint Cup beginning in 2008.
†2010 Sprint Chase for the Cup standings through October 25, 2010 (32 of 36 races).

Late 2009 Sprint Cup Series Results

Date	Track/Distance	Winner (start pos.)	Car	Laps	Winnings ($)
*Oct 17	Charlotte 500	Jimmie Johnson (1)	Chevrolet	334	328,826
*Oct 25	Martinsville 500	Denny Hamlin (17)	Chevrolet	501	189,500
*Nov 1	Talladega 500	Jamie McMurray (22)	Ford	325	229,275
*Nov 8	Texas 500	Kurt Busch (3)	Dodge	334	440,575
*Nov 15	Phoenix 500	Jimmie Johnson (3)	Chevrolet	312	267,001
*Nov 22	Homestead/Miami 400	Denny Hamlin (38)	Toyota	267	347,975

2010 Sprint Cup Series Results†

Date	Track/Distance	Winner (start pos.)	Car	Laps	Winnings ($)
Feb 14	Daytona 500	Jamie McMurray (13)	Chevrolet	152	1,508,450
Feb 21	Fontana 500	Jimmie Johnson (7)	Chevrolet	250	333,103
Feb 28	Las Vegas 427	Jimmie Johnson (20)	Chevrolet	267	405,628
Mar 7	Atlanta 500	Kurt Busch (11)	Dodge	341	176,498
Mar 21	Bristol 500	Jimmie Johnson (4)	Chevrolet	500	199,978
Mar 29	Martinsville 500	Denny Hamlin (19)	Chevrolet	508	179,225
Apr 10	Phoenix 500	Ryan Newman (14)	Chevrolet	378	235,804
Apr 19	Texas 500	Denny Hamlin (29)	Toyota	334	502,075
Apr 25	Talladega 499	Kevin Harvick (4)	Chevrolet	200	344,501
May 1	Richmond 400	Kyle Busch (1)	Toyota	400	264,506
May 8	Darlington 500	Denny Hamlin (8)	Toyota	367	288,525
May 16	Dover 400	Kyle Busch (4)	Toyota	400	327,706
May 22	Showdown	Martin Truex Jr. (20)	Toyota	40	N/A
May 22	All-Star Race	Kurt Busch (1)	Dodge	100	N/A
May 30	Charlotte 600	Kurt Busch (2)	Dodge	400	399,623
June 6	Pocono 500	Denny Hamlin (5)	Toyota	204	212,875
June 13	Michigan 400	Denny Hamlin (7)	Toyota	200	188,350
June 20	Sonoma 350	Jimmie Johnson (2)	Chevrolet	110	326,153
June 27	New Hampshire 301	Jimmie Johnson (10)	Chevrolet	301	264,928
July 3	Daytona 400	Kevin Harvick (1)	Chevrolet	166	344,751
July 10	Chicagoland 400	David Reutimann (7)	Toyota	267	321,531
July 25	Brickyard 400	Jamie McMurray (4)	Chevrolet	160	438,877
Aug 1	Pocono 500	Greg Biffle (12)	Ford	200	205,850
Aug 8	Watkins Glen 220	Juan Montoya (3)	Chevrolet	90	247,306
Aug 15	Michigan 400	Kevin Harvick (8)	Chevrolet	200	211,901
Aug 21	Bristol 500	Kyle Busch (19)	Toyota	500	331,731
Aug 31	California 500	Jimmie Johnson (1)	Chevrolet	250	314,611
*Sept 5	Atlanta 500	Tony Stewart (5)	Chevrolet	325	357,198
*Sept 11	Richmond 400	Denny Hamlin (14)	Toyota	400	219,975
*Sept 19	New Hampshire 300	Clint Bowyer (2)	Chevrolet	300	248,250
*Sept 26	Dover 400	Jimmie Johnson (1)	Chevrolet	400	262,803
*Oct 3	Kansas 400	Greg Biffle (5)	Ford	267	298,525
*Oct 10	Fontana 500	Tony Stewart (22)	Chevrolet	200	262,598
*Oct 16	Charlotte 500	Jamie McMurray (27)	Chevrolet	334	266,129
*Oct 24	Martinsville 500	Denny Hamlin (1)	Toyota	500	189,500

† Through October 25, 2010.
* Part of 10-race Chase for the Cup.

Formula One Grand Prix Racing

2010 Formula One Results†

Grand Prix	Date	Winner	Car	Laps	Time
Bahrain	Mar 14	Fernando Alonso	Ferrari	49	1:39:20.396
Australia	Mar 28	Jenson Button	McLaren-Mercecdes	58	1:33:36.531
Malaysia	Apr 4	Sebastian Vettel	RBR-Renault	56	1:33:48.412
China	Apr 18	Jenson Button	McLaren-Mercecdes	56	1:46:42.163
Spain	May 9	Mark Webber	RBR-Renault	66	1:35:44.101
Monaco	May 16	Mark Webber	RBR-Renault	48	1:50:13.355
Turkey	May 30	Lewis Hamilton	McLaren-Mercedes	58	1:28:47.620
Canada	June 13	Lewis Hamilton	McLaren-Mercedes	70	1:33:53.456
Europe	June 27	Sebastian Vettel	RBR-Renault	57	1:40:29.571
Great Britain	July 11	Mark Webber	RBR-Renault	52	1:24:38.200
Germany	July 25	Fernando Alonso	Ferrari	67	1:27:38.864
Hungary	Aug 1	Mark Webber	RBR-Renault	70	1:41:05.571
Belguim	Aug 29	Lewis Hamilton	McLaren-Mercedes	44	1:29:04.268
Italy	Sept 12	Fernando Alonso	Ferrari	53	1:16:24.572
Singapore	Sept 26	Fernando Alonso	Ferrari	61	1:57:53.579
Japan	Oct 10	Sebastian Vettel	RBR-Renault	53	1:30:27.323

† Through October 10, 2010.

2009 World Championship Final Standings

Drivers compete in Grand Prix races for the title of World Driving Champion. Below are the top 10 drivers from the 2009 season. Points are awarded for places 1–6 as follows: 10-6-4-3-2-1.

Driver	Country	Team	Pts
Jenson Button	Great Britain	Brawn-Mercedes	95
Sebastian Vettel	Germany	RBR-Renault	84
Rubens Barrichello	Brazil	Brawn-Mercedes	77
Mark Webber	Australia	RBR-Renault	69.5
Lewis Hamilton	Great Britain	McLaren-Mercedes	49
Kimi Rakikkonen	Finland	Ferrari	48
Nico Rosberg	Germany	Williams-Toyota	34.5
Jarno Trulli	Italy	Toyota	32.5
Fernando Alonso	Spain	Renault	26
Timo Glock	Germany	Toyota	24

Professional Sports Car Racing

The 24 Hours of Daytona

Held at the Daytona International Speedway on Jan 30–31, 2010, the 24 Hours of Daytona serves as the opening round of the Grand American Road Racing Association's season.

Place	Drivers	Car (Class)	Distance
1	J. Barbosa, T. Borcheller, R. Dalziel, M. Rockenfeller	Porsche Riley	755 laps (111.930 mph)
2	M. Papis, S. Pruett, M. Rojas, J. Wilson	BMW Riley	755
3	R. Hunter-Reay, L. Luhr, S. Tucker, R. Westbrook	BMW Riley	751
4	C. Braun, N. Jonsson, T. Krohn, R. Zonta	Ford Lola	735
5	B. Friselle, O. Negri, J. Pew, M. Wilkins	Ford Riley	725

2010 American Le Mans Series—Prototype Class

Date	Race	Winners	Car
Mar 20	12 Hours of Sebring	A. Wurz, M. Gene, A. Davidson	Peugeot 908 HDI
April 17	Grand Prix of Long Beach	D. Brabham, S. Pagenaud	Honda ARX-01c
May 22	Laguna Seca	D. Brabham, S. Pagenaud	Honda ARX-01c
July 11	Utah Grand Prix	D. Brabham, S. Pagenaud	Honda ARX-01c
July 24	Northeast Grand Prix	G. Pickett, K. Graf	Porsche RS Spyder
Aug 7	Mid Ohio	G. Smith, C. Dyson	Lola B09 86 Mazda
Aug 22	Road America 500	P. Drayson, J. Cocker	Lola B09 60
Aug 29	Grand Prix of Mosport	R. Dumas, K. Graf	Porsche RS Spyder
Oct 2	Petit Le Mans	S. Sarrazin, F. Montagny, P. Lamy	Peugeot 908 HDI

2010 American Le Mans Series—GT Class

Date	Race	Winners	Car
Mar 20	12 Hours of Sebring	J. Melo, G. Bruni, P. Kaffer	BMW E92 M3
April 17	Grand Prix of Long Beach	P. Long, J. Bergmeister	Porsche 911 GT3 RSR
May 22	Laguna Seca	P. Long, J. Bergmeister	Porsche 911 GT3 RSR
July 11	Utah Grand Prix	G. Bruni, J. Melo	Ferrari 430 GT
July 24	Northeast Grand Prix	P. Long, J. Bergmeister	Porsche 911 GT3 RSR
Aug 7	Mid Ohio	O. Beretta, O. Gavin	Chevrolet Corvette ZR1
Aug 22	Road America 500	J. Hand, D. Muller	BMW M3 GT
Aug 29	Grand Prix of Mosport	P. Long, J. Bergmeister	Porsche 911 GT3 RSR
Oct 2	Petit Le Mans	J. Magnussen, O. Gavin, E. Collard	Chevrolet Corvette ZR1

2010 American Le Mans Series—GTC Class

Date	Race	Winners	Car
Mar 20	12 Hours of Sebring	L. Keen, J. Gonzalez, B. Leitzinger	Porsche 911 GT3
April 17	Grand Prix of Long Beach	J. Gonzalez, B. Leitzinger	Porsche 911 GT3
May 22	Laguna Seca	J. Bleekelmolen, S. Bleekemolen, T. Pappas	Porsche 911 GT3
July 11	Utah Grand Prix	J. Bleekelmolen, T. Pappas	Porsche 911 GT3
July 24	Northeast Grand Prix	H. Richard, A. Lally	Porsche 911 GT3
Aug 7	Mid Ohio	J. Bleekelmolen, T. Pappas	Porsche 911 GT3
Aug 22	Road America 500	J. Bleekelmolen, T. Pappas	Porsche 911 GT3
Aug 29	Grand Prix of Mosport	S. Lewis, L. Aschenbach	Porsche 911 GT3
Oct 2	Petit Le Mans	H. Richard, A. Lally, D. Ende	Ferrari F430GT

2010 American Le Mans Series Championship Final Standings

PROTOTYPE CLASS	Pts	GTC CLASS	Pts	GT CLASS	Pts
David Brabham	182	Timothy Pappas	146	Jorg Bergmeister	157
Simon Pagenaud	182	Jeroen Bleekemolen	146	Patrick Long	157
Klaus Graf	162	Shane Lewis	126	Gianmaria Bruni	140
Jonny Cocker	110	Andy Lally	113	Bill Auberlen	125
Chris Dyson	98	Henri Richard	111	Tommy Milner	125
Paul Drayson	94	Bill Sweedler	109	Jamie Melo	115
				Oliver Gavin	110

24 Hours of Le Mans

Held at Le Mans, France, on June 12–13, 2010, the 24 Hours of Le Mans is the most prestigious international event in endurance racing.

Place	Drivers	Car	Laps
1	T. Bernhard, R. Dumas, M. Rockenfeller	Audi R15 TDI	397 (139.95 mph)
2	M. Faessler, A. Lotterer, B. Treluyer	Audi R15 TDI	396
3	D. Capello, T. Kristensen, A. McNish	Audi R15 TDI	394
4	S. Ayari, D. Andre, A. Meyrick	Oreca 01 - AIM	369
5	N. Leventis, D. Watts, J. Kane	Honda ARX-01	367

FOR THE RECORD • Year by Year

Indianapolis 500

First held in 1911, the Indianapolis 500—200 laps of the 2.5-mile Indianapolis Motor Speedway Track (called the Brickyard in honor of its original pavement)—grew to become the most famous auto race in the world. Though the Memorial Day weekend event lost participants and prestige in the mid-1990s due to feuding in the world of U.S. open-wheel racing, it annually attracts crowds of over 100,000.

Year	Winner (start pos.)	Chassis-Engine	Avg Speed	Pole Winner	Speed
1911	Ray Harroun (28)	Marmon-Marmon	74.590	Lewis Strang	First entered
1912	Joe Dawson (7)	National-National	78.720	Gil Anderson	First entered
1913	Jules Goux (7)	Peugeot-Peugeot	75.930	Caleb Bragg	Drew pole
1914	Rene Thomas (15)	Delage-Delage	82.470	Jean Chassagne	Drew pole
1915	Ralph DePalma (2)	Mercedes-Mercedes	89.840	Howard Wilcox	98.90
1916	Dario Resta (4)	Peugeot-Peugeot	84.000	John Aitken	96.69
1917–18	No race				
1919	Howard Wilcox (2)	Peugeot-Peugeot	88.050	Rene Thomas	104.78
1920	Gaston Chevrolet (6)	Frontenac-Frontenac	88.620	Ralph DePalma	99.15
1921	Tommy Milton (20)	Frontenac-Frontenac	89.620	Ralph DePalma	100.75
1922	Jimmy Murphy (1)	Duesenberg-Miller	94.480	Jimmy Murphy	100.50
1923	Tommy Milton (1)	Miller-Miller	90.950	Tommy Milton	108.17
1924	L.L. Corum	Duesenberg-Duesenberg	98.230	Jimmy Murphy	108.037
	Joe Boyer (21)				
1925	Peter DePaolo (2)	Duesenberg-Duesenberg	101.130	Leon Duray	113.196
1926	Frank Lockhart (20)	Miller-Miller	95.904	Earl Cooper	111.735
1927	George Souders (22)	Duesenberg-Duesenberg	97.545	Frank Lockhart	120.100
1928	Louis Meyer (13)	Miller-Miller	99.482	Leon Duray	122.391
1929	Ray Keech (6)	Miller-Miller	97.585	Cliff Woodbury	120.599
1930	Billy Arnold (1)	Summers-Miller	100.448	Billy Arnold	113.268
1931	Louis Schneider (13)	Stevens-Miller	96.629	Russ Snowberger	112.796
1932	Fred Frame (27)	Wetteroth-Miller	104.144	Lou Moore	117.363
1933	Louis Meyer (6)	Miller-Miller	104.162	Bill Cummings	118.524
1934	Bill Cummings (10)	Miller-Miller	104.863	Kelly Petillo	119.329
1935	Kelly Petillo (22)	Wetteroth-Offy	106.240	Rex Mays	120.736
1936	Louis Meyer (28)	Stevens-Miller	109.069	Rex Mays	119.664
1937	Wilbur Shaw (2)	Shaw-Offy	113.580	Bill Cummings	123.343
1938	Floyd Roberts (1)	Wetteroth-Miller	117.200	Floyd Roberts	125.681
1939	Wilbur Shaw (3)	Maserati-Maserati	115.035	Jimmy Snyder	130.138
1940	Wilbur Shaw (2)	Maserati-Maserati	114.277	Rex Mays	127.850
1941	Floyd Davis	Wetteroth-Offy	115.117	Mauri Rose	128.691
	Mauri Rose (17)				
1942–45	No race				
1946	George Robson (15)	Adams-Sparks	114.820	Cliff Bergere	126.471
1947	Mauri Rose (3)	Deidt-Offy	116.338	Ted Horn	126.564
1948	Mauri Rose (3)	Deidt-Offy	119.814	Rex Mays	130.577
1949	Bill Holland (4)	Deidt-Offy	121.327	Duke Nalon	132.939
1950	Johnnie Parsons (5)	Kurtis-Offy	124.002	Walt Faulkner	134.343
1951	Lee Wallard (2)	Kurtis-Offy	126.244	Duke Nalon	136.498
1952	Troy Ruttman (7)	Kuzma-Offy	128.922	Fred Agabashian	138.010
1953	Bill Vukovich (1)	KK500A-Offy	128.740	Bill Vukovich	138.392
1954	Bill Vukovich (19)	KK500A-Offy	130.840	Jack McGrath	141.033
1955	Bob Sweikert (14)	KK500C-Offy	128.209	Jerry Hoyt	140.045
1956	Pat Flaherty (1)	Watson-Offy	128.490	Pat Flaherty	145.596
1957	Sam Hanks (13)	Salih-Offy	135.601	Pat O'Connor	143.948
1958	Jim Bryan (7)	Salih-Offy	133.791	Dick Rathmann	145.974
1959	Rodger Ward (6)	Watson-Offy	135.857	Johnny Thomson	145.908
1960	Jim Rathmann (2)	Watson-Offy	138.767	Eddie Sachs	146.592
1961	A.J. Foyt (7)	Trevis-Offy	139.130	Eddie Sachs	147.481
1962	Rodger Ward (2)	Watson-Offy	140.293	Parnelli Jones	150.370
1963	Parnelli Jones (1)	Watson-Offy	143.137	Parnelli Jones	151.153
1964	A.J. Foyt (5)	Watson-Offy	147.350	Jim Clark	158.828
1965	Jim Clark (2)	Lotus-Ford	150.686	A.J. Foyt	161.233
1966	Graham Hill (15)	Lola-Ford	144.317	Mario Andretti	165.899
1967	A.J. Foyt (4)	Coyote-Ford	151.207	Mario Andretti	168.982
1968	Bobby Unser (3)	Eagle-Offy	152.882	Joe Leonard	171.559
1969	Mario Andretti (2)	Hawk-Ford	156.867	A.J. Foyt	170.568
1970	Al Unser (1)	PJ Colt-Ford	155.749	Al Unser	170.221
1971	Al Unser (5)	PJ Colt-Ford	157.735	Peter Revson	178.696
1972	Mark Donohue (3)	McLaren-Offy	162.962	Bobby Unser	195.940

Year	Winner (start pos.)	Chassis-Engine	Avg speed	Pole Winner	Speed
1973	Gordon Johncock (11)	Eagle-Offy	159.036	Johnny Rutherford	198.413
1974	Johnny Rutherford (25)	McLaren-Offy	158.589	A.J. Foyt	191.632
1975	Bobby Unser (3)	Racers Eagle-Offy	149.213	A.J. Foyt	193.976
1976	Johnny Rutherford (1)	McLaren-Offy	148.725	Johnny Rutherford	188.957
1977	A.J. Foyt (4)	Coyote-Ford	161.331	Tom Sneva	198.884
1978	Al Unser (5)	Lola-Cosworth	161.361	Tom Sneva	202.156
1979	Rick Mears (1)	Penske-Cosworth	158.899	Rick Mears	193.736
1980	Johnny Rutherford (1)	Chaparral-Coswoth	142.862	Johnny Rutherford	192.256
1981	Bobby Unser (1)	Penske-Cosworth	139.084	Bobby Unser	200.546
1982	Gordon Johncock (5)	Wildcat-Cosworth	162.026	Rick Mears	207.004
1983	Tom Sneva (4)	March-Cosworth	162.117	Teo Fabi	207.395
1984	Rick Mears (3)	March-Cosworth	163.612	Tom Sneva	210.029
1985	Danny Sullivan (8)	March-Cosworth	152.982	Pancho Carter	212.583
1986	Bobby Rahal (4)	March-Cosworth	170.722	Rick Mears	216.828
1987	Al Unser (20)	March-Cosworth	162.175	Mario Andretti	215.390
1988	Rick Mears (1)	Penske-Chevrolet	144.809	Rick Mears	219.198
1989	Emerson Fittipaldi (3)	Penske-Chevrolet	167.581	Rick Mears	223.885
1990	Arie Luyendyk (3)	Lola-Chevrolet	185.981*	Emerson Fittipaldi	225.301
1991	Rick Mears (1)	Penske-Chevrolet	176.457	Rick Mears	224.113
1992	Al Unser Jr. (12)	Galmer-Chevrolet	134.477	Roberto Guerrero	232.482
1993	Emerson Fittipaldi (9)	Penske-Chevrolet	157.207	Arie Luyendyk	223.967
1994	Al Unser Jr. (1)	Penske-Mercedes	160.872	Al Unser Jr.	228.011
1995	Jacques Villeneuve (5)	Reynard-Ford	153.616	Scott Brayton	231.616
1996	Buddy Lazier (5)	Reynard-Ford	147.956	Tony Stewart	233.100†
1997	Arie Luyendyk (1)	G Force-Oldsmobile	145.827	Arie Luyendyk	231.468
1998	Eddie Cheever (17)	Dallara-Oldsmobile	145.155	Billy Boat	223.503
1999	Kenny Brack (8)	Dallara-Oldsmobile	153.176	Arie Luyendyk	225.179
2000	Juan Montoya (2)	G Force-Oldsmobile	167.607	Greg Ray	223.471
2001	Helio Castroneves (11)	Dallara-Oldsmobile	153.601	Scott Sharp	226.037
2002	Helio Castroneves (13)	Dallara-Chevrolet	166.499	Bruno Junqueira	231.342
2003	Gil de Ferran (10)	Panoz-Toyota	156.291	Helio Castroneves	231.725
2004	Buddy Rice (1)	G Force-Honda	138.518	Buddy Rice	222.024
2005	Dan Wheldon (16)	Dallara-Honda	157.603	Tony Kanaan	227.566
2006	Sam Hornish Jr.(1)	Dallara-Honda	157.085	Sam Hornish Jr.	228.985
2007	Dario Franchitti (3)	Dallara-Honda	151.744	Helio Castroneves	225.817
2008	Scott Dixon (1)	Dallara-Honda	143.567	Scott Dixon	226.366
2009	Helio Castroneves (1)	Dallara-Honda	150.138	Helio Castroneves	224.864
2010	Dario Franchitti (3)	Dallara-Honda	161.623	Helio Castroneves	227.970

*Track record, winning speed. †Track record, qualifying speed.

Indianapolis 500 Rookie of the Year Award

1952 ....Art Cross	1973 ....Graham McRae	1992 ....Lyn St. James
1953 ....Jimmy Daywalt	1974 ....Pancho Carter	1993 ....Nigel Mansell
1954 ....Larry Crockett	1975 ....Bill Puterbaugh	1994 ....Jacques Villeneuve*
1955 ....Al Herman	1976 ....Vern Schuppan	1995 ....Gil de Ferran*
1956 ....Bob Veith	1977 ....Jerry Sneva	1996 ....Tony Stewart
1957 ....Don Edmunds	1978 ....Rick Mears*	1997 ....Jeff Ward
1958 ....George Amick	............Larry Rice	1998 ....Steve Knapp
1959 ....Bobby Grim	1979 ....Howdy Holmes	1999 ....Robby McGehee
1960 ....Jim Hurtubise	1980 ....Tim Richmond	2000 ....Juan Montoya*
1961 ....Parnelli Jones*	1981 ....Josele Garza	2001 ....Helio Castroneves*
............Bobby Marshman	1982 ....Jim Hickman	2002 ....Alex Barron
1962 ....Jimmy McElreath	1983 ....Teo Fabi	............Tomas Scheckter
1963 ....Jim Clark*	1984 ....Michael Andretti	2003 ....Tora Tagaki
1964 ....Johnny White	............Roberto Guerrero	2004 ....Kosuke Matsuura
1965 ....Mario Andretti*	1985 ....Arie Luyendyk*	2005 ....Danica Patrick
1966 ....Jackie Stewart	1986 ....Randy Lanier	2006 ....Marco Andretti
1967 ....Denis Hulme	1987 ....Fabrizio Barbazza	2007 ....Phil Giebler
1968 ....Billy Vukovich	1988 ....Billy Vukovich III	2008 ....Ryan Hunter-Reay
1969 ....Mark Donohue*	1989 ....Bernard Jourdain	2009 ....Alex Tagliani
1970 ....Donnie Allison	............Scott Pruett	2010 ....Simona De Silvestro
1971 ....Denny Zimmerman	1990 ....Eddie Cheever*	
1972 ....Mike Hiss	1991 ....Jeff Andretti	

*Future winner of Indy 500.

Champ Car World Series Champions

From 1909 to 1955, this championship was awarded by the American Automobile Association (AAA), and from 1956 to 1979 by the United States Auto Club (USAC). During the 1979 season, Championship Auto Racing Teams (CART) split from the USAC and conducted the championship. Known as PPG CART World Series until 1998. Series name changed to Champ Car World Series for 2005 racing season. On Februray 22, 2008, the Champ Car World Series merged with the Indy Racing League.

1909 ....George Robertson	1942–45 ....No racing	1978 ....Tom Sneva
1910 ....Ray Harroun	1946 ....Ted Horn	1979 .............A.J. Foyt (USAC)
1911 ....Ralph Mulford	1947 ....Ted Horn	1979 ....Rick Mears (CART)
1912 ....Ralph DePalma	1948 ....Ted Horn	1980 ....Johnny Rutherford
1913 ....Earl Cooper	1949 ....Johnnie Parsons	1981 ....Rick Mears
1914 ....Ralph DePalma	1950 ....Henry Banks	1982 ....Rick Mears
1915 ....Earl Cooper	1951 ....Tony Bettenhausen	1983 ....Al Unser
1916 ....Dario Resta	1952 ....Chuck Stevenson	1984 ....Mario Andretti
1917 ....Earl Cooper	1953 ....Sam Hanks	1985 ....Al Unser
1918 ....Ralph Mulford	1954 ....Jimmy Bryan	1986 ....Bobby Rahal
1919 ....Howard Wilcox	1955 ....Bob Sweikert	1987 ....Bobby Rahal
1920 ....Tommy Milton	1956 ....Jimmy Bryan	1988 ....Danny Sullivan
1921 ....Tommy Milton	1957 ....Jimmy Bryan	1989 ....Emerson Fittipaldi
1922 ....Jimmy Murphy	1958 ....Tony Bettenhausen	1990 ....Al Unser Jr.
1923 ....Eddie Hearne	1959 ....Rodger Ward	1991 ....Michael Andretti
1924 ....Jimmy Murphy	1960 .............A.J. Foyt	1992 ....Bobby Rahal
1925 ....Peter DePaolo	1961 .............A.J. Foyt	1993 ....Nigel Mansell
1926 ....Harry Hartz	1962 ....Rodger Ward	1994 ....Al Unser Jr.
1927 ....Peter DePaolo	1963 .............A.J. Foyt	1995 ....Jacques Villeneuve
1928 ....Louis Meyer	1964 .............A.J. Foyt	1996 ....Jimmy Vasser
1929 ....Louis Meyer	1965 ....Mario Andretti	1997 ....Alex Zanardi
1930 ....Billy Arnold	1966 ....Mario Andretti	1998 ....Alex Zanardi
1931 ....Louis Schneider	1967 .............A.J. Foyt	1999 ....Juan Montoya
1932 ....Bob Carey	1968 ....Bobby Unser	2000 ....Gil de Ferran
1933 ....Louis Meyer	1969 ....Mario Andretti	2001 ....Gil de Ferran
1934 ....Bill Cummings	1970 ....Al Unser	2002 ....Cristiano da Matta
1935 ....Kelly Petillo	1971 ....Joe Leonard	2003 ....Paul Tracy
1936 ....Mauri Rose	1972 ....Joe Leonard	2004 ....Sebastian Bourdais
1937 ....Wilbur Shaw	1973 ....Roger McCluskey	2005 ....Sebastian Bourdais
1938 ....Floyd Roberts	1974 ....Bobby Unser	2006 ....Sebastian Bourdais
1939 ....Wilbur Shaw	1975 .............A.J. Foyt	2007 ....Sebastian Bourdais
1940 ....Rex Mays	1976 ....Gordon Johncock	
1941 ....Rex Mays	1977 ....Tom Sneva	

Alltime Champ Car* Leaders

WINS		POLE POSITIONS	
A.J. Foyt	67	Mario Andretti	67
Mario Andretti	52	A.J. Foyt	53
Michael Andretti	42	Bobby Unser	49
Al Unser	39	Rick Mears	40
Bobby Unser	35	Michael Andretti	32
Al Unser Jr	31	†Sebastian Bourdais	28
†Paul Tracy	31	Al Unser	27
Rick Mears	29	†Paul Tracy	25
†Sebastian Bourdais	29	Johnny Rutherford	23
Johnny Rutherford	27	Gordon Johncock	20
Rodger Ward	26	Rex Mays	19
Gordon Johncock	25	Danny Sullivan	19
Bobby Rahal	24	Bobby Rahal	18
Ralph DePalma	24	Emerson Fittipaldi	17
Tommy Milton	23	Gil de Ferran	16
Tony Bettenhausen	22	Tony Bettenhausen	14
Emerson Fittipaldi	22	Juan Montoya	14
Earl Cooper	20	Don Branson	14
Jimmy Bryan	19	Tom Sneva	14
Jimmy Murphy	19	Parnelli Jones	12
Danny Sullivan	17		
Ralph Mulford	17		

*Series known as CART prior to 2003 season

Stock Car Racing's Major Events

In 1985, Winston began offering a $1 million bonus to any driver to win three of the top four NASCAR events in the same season. A fifth event, the Brickyard 400 (in Indianapolis) was added in 1994. As of 1998 the Winston million was awarded to any driver who won three of the five events. The other four races are the richest (Daytona 500), the fastest (Talladega 500), the longest (Charlotte 600) and the oldest (Southern 500 at Darlington). Only five drivers, Lee Roy Yarbrough (1969), David Pearson (1976), Bill Elliott (1985), Dale Jarrett (1996) and Jeff Gordon (1997, '98) have scored the three-track hat trick.

Daytona 500

Year	Winner (start pos.)	Chassis-Engine	Avg speed	Pole Winner	Qual. speed
1959	Lee Petty	Oldsmobile	135.520	Cotton Owens	143.198
1960	Junior Johnson	Chevrolet	124.740	Fireball Roberts	151.556
1961	Marvin Panch	Pontiac	149.601	Fireball Roberts	155.709
1962	Fireball Roberts	Pontiac	152.529	Fireball Roberts	156.995
1963	Tiny Lund	Ford	151.566	Johnny Rutherford	165.183
1964	Richard Petty	Plymouth	154.345	Paul Goldsmith	174.910
1965	Fred Lorenzen	Ford	141.539	Darel Dieringer	171.151
1966	Richard Petty	Plymouth	160.627	Richard Petty	175.165
1967	Mario Andretti	Ford	149.926	Curtis Turner	180.831
1968	Cale Yarborough	Mercury	143.251	Cale Yarborough	189.222
1969	Lee Roy Yarbrough	Ford	157.950	David Pearson	190.029
1970	Pete Hamilton	Plymouth	149.601	Cale Yarborough	194.015
1971	Richard Petty	Plymouth	144.462	A.J. Foyt	182.744
1972	A.J. Foyt	Mercury	161.550	Bobby Isaac	186.632
1973	Richard Petty	Dodge	157.205	Buddy Baker	185.662
1974	Richard Petty	Dodge	140.894	David Pearson	185.017
1975	Benny Parsons	Chevrolet	153.649	Donnie Allison	185.827
1976	David Pearson	Mercury	152.181	A.J. Foyt	185.943
1977	Cale Yarborough	Chevrolet	153.218	Donnie Allison	188.048
1978	Bobby Allison	Ford	159.730	Cale Yarborough	187.536
1979	Richard Petty	Oldsmobile	143.977	Buddy Baker	196.049
1980	Buddy Baker	Oldsmobile	177.602*	A.J. Foyt	195.020
1981	Richard Petty	Buick	169.651	Bobby Allison	194.624
1982	Bobby Allison	Buick	153.991	Benny Parsons	196.317
1983	Cale Yarborough	Pontiac	155.979	Ricky Rudd	198.864
1984	Cale Yarborough	Chevrolet	150.994	Cale Yarborough	201.848
1985	Bill Elliott	Ford	172.265	Bill Elliott	205.114
1986	Geoff Bodine	Chevrolet	148.124	Bill Elliott	205.039
1987	Bill Elliott	Ford	176.263	Bill Elliott	210.364†
1988	Bobby Allison	Buick	137.531	Ken Schrader	193.823
1989	Darrell Waltrip	Chevrolet	148.466	Ken Schrader	196.996
1990	Derrike Cope	Chevrolet	165.761	Ken Schrader	196.515
1991	Ernie Irvan	Chevrolet	148.148	Davey Allison	195.955
1992	Davey Allison	Ford	160.256	Sterling Marlin	192.213
1993	Dale Jarrett	Chevrolet	154.972	Kyle Petty	189.426
1994	Sterling Marlin	Chevrolet	156.931	Loy Allen Jr	190.158
1995	Sterling Marlin	Chevrolet	141.710	Dale Jarrett	193.498
1996	Dale Jarrett	Ford	154.308	Dale Earnhardt	189.510
1997	Jeff Gordon	Chevrolet	148.295	Mike Skinner	189.813
1998	Dale Earnhardt	Chevrolet	172.712	Bobby Labonte	192.415
1999	Jeff Gordon	Chevrolet	161.551	Jeff Gordon	195.067
2000	Dale Jarrett	Ford	155.669	Dale Jarrett	191.091
2001	Michael Waltrip	Chevrolet	161.783	Bill Elliott	183.570
2002	Ward Burton	Dodge	142.971	Jimmie Johnson	185.831
2003	Michael Waltrip	Chevrolet	133.870	Jeff Green	186.606
2004	Dale Earnhardt Jr.	Chevrolet	156.345	Greg Biffle	188.387
2005	Jeff Gordon	Chevrolet	135.173	Dale Jarrett	188.312
2006	Jimmie Johnson	Chevrolet	142.667	Jeff Burton	188.887
2007	Kevin Harvick	Chevrolet	149.335	David Gilliland	186.320
2008	Ryan Newman	Dodge	152.672	Jimmie Johnson	187.075
2009	Matt Kenseth	Ford	132.816	Martin Truex Jr.	188.001
2010	Jamie McMurray	Chevrolet	137.284	Mark Martin	191.188

Note: The Daytona 500, held annually in February, now opens the NASCAR season with 200 laps around the 2.5-mile high-banked Daytona International Speedway. Starting in 1988, cars racing at Daytona have used restrictor plates that lower power and acceleration.

*Track record, winning speed. †Track record, qualifying speed.

Brickyard 400

Year	Winner	Car	Avg Speed	Pole Winner	Qual. Speed
1994	Jeff Gordon	Chevrolet	131.977	Rick Mast	172.414
1995	Dale Earnhardt	Chevrolet	155.206	Jeff Gordon	172.536
1996	Dale Jarrett	Ford	139.508	Jeff Gordon	176.419
1997	Ricky Rudd	Ford	130.814	Ernie Irvan	177.736
1998	Jeff Gordon	Chevrolet	126.772	Ernie Irvan	179.394
1999	Dale Jarrett	Ford	148.194	Jeff Gordon	179.612
2000	Bobby Labonte	Pontiac	155.912*	Ricky Rudd	181.068
2001	Jeff Gordon	Chevrolet	130.790	Jimmy Spencer	179.666
2002	Bill Elliott	Dodge	125.033	Tony Stewart	182.960
2003	Kevin Harvick	Chevrolet	134.554	Kevin Harvick	184.343
2004	Jeff Gordon	Chevrolet	115.037	Casey Mears	186.293†
2005	Tony Stewart	Chevrolet	148.782	Elliott Sadler	184.117
2006	Jimmie Johnson	Chevrolet	137.182	Jeff Burton	182.778
2007	Tony Stewart	Chevrolet	117.379	Reed Sorenson	184.207
2008	Jimmie Johnson	Chevrolet	115.117	Jimmie Johnson	181.763
2009	Jimmie Johnson	Chevrolet	145.882	Mark Martin	182.054
2010	Jamie McMurray	Chevrolet	137.284	Mark Martin	191.188

Note: Held at the 2.5-mile Indianapolis Motor Speedway.
*Track record, winning speed. †Track record, qualifying speed

Talladega 500

Year	Winner	Car	Avg Speed	Pole Winner	Qual Speed
1970	Pete Hamilton	Plymouth	152.321	Bobby Isaac	199.658
1971	Donnie Allison	Mercury	147.419	Donnie Allison	185.869
1972	David Pearson	Mercury	134.400	Bobby Isaac	192.428
1973	David Pearson	Mercury	131.956	Buddy Baker	193.435
1974	David Pearson	Mercury	130.220	David Pearson	186.086
1975	Buddy Baker	Ford	144.94	Buddy Baker	189.947
1976	Buddy Baker	Ford	169.887	Dave Marcis	189.197
1977	Darrell Waltrip	Chevrolet	164.887	A.J. Foyt	192.424
1978	Cale Yarborough	Oldsmobile	155.699	Cale Yarborough	191.904
1979	Bobby Allison	Ford	154.770	Darrell Waltrip	195.644
1980	Buddy Baker	Oldsmobile	170.481	David Pearson	197.704
1981	Bobby Allison	Buick	149.376	Bobby Allison	195.864
1982	Darrell Waltrip	Buick	156.697	Benny Parsons	200.176
1983	Richard Petty	Pontiac	135.936	Cale Yarborough	202.650
1984	Cale Yarborough	Chevrolet	172.988	Cale Yarborough	202.692
1985	Bill Elliott	Ford	186.288	Bill Elliott	209.398
1986	Bobby Allison	Buick	157.698	Bill Elliott	212.229
1987	Davey Allison	Ford	154.228	Bill Elliott	221.809†
1988	Phil Parsons	Oldsmobile	156.547	Davey Allison	198.969
1989	Davey Allison	Ford	155.869	Mark Martin	193.061
1990	Dale Earnhardt	Chevrolet	159.571	Bill Elliott	199.388
1991	Harry Gant	Oldsmobile	165.620	Ernie Irvan	195.186
1992	Davey Allison	Ford	167.609	Ernie Irvan	192.831
1993	Ernie Irvan	Chevrolet	155.412	Dale Earnhardt	192.355
1994	Dale Earnhardt	Chevrolet	157.478	Ernie Irvan	193.298
1995	Mark Martin	Ford	178.902	Terry Labonte	196.532
1996	Sterling Marlin	Chevrolet	149.999	Ernie Irvan	192.855
1997	Mark Martin	Ford	188.354*	John Andretti	193.627
1998	Dale Jarrett	Ford	159.318	Ken Schrader	196.153
1999	Dale Earnhardt	Chevrolet	166.632	Joe Nemechek	198.331
2000	Dale Earnhardt	Chevrolet	165.681	Joe Nemechek	190.279
2001	Dale Earnhardt Jr.	Chevrolet	164.185	Stacy Compton	185.240
2002	Dale Earnhardt Jr.	Chevrolet	183.665	qualifying cancelled	—
2003	Michael Waltrip	Chevrolet	156.045	Elliott Sadler	189.943
2004	Jeff Gordon	Chevrolet	129.396	Ricky Rudd	191.180
2005	Dale Jarrett	Ford	143.818	Elliott Sadler	189.260
2006	Brian Vickers	Chevrolet	157.602	David Gilliland	191.712
2007	Jeff Gordon	Chevrolet	143.438	Michael Waltrip	189.070
2008	Kyle Busch	Toyota	157.409	Joe Nemechek	187.396
2009	Brad Keselowski	Chevrolet	147.565	Juan Pablo Montoya	188.171
2010	Kevin Harvick	Chevrolet	150.590	qualifying cancelled	—

*Track record, winning speed. †Track record, qualifying speed.

Charlotte 600

Year	Winner	Car	Avg Speed	Pole Winner
1960	Joe Lee Johnson	Chevrolet	107.752	Joe Lee Johnson
1961	David Pearson	Pontiac	111.634	Richard Petty
1962	Nelson Stacy	Ford	125.552	Fireball Roberts
1963	Fred Lorenzen	Ford	132.418	Junior Johnson
1964	Jim Paschal	Plymouth	125.772	Junior Johnson
1965	Fred Lorenzen	Ford	121.772	Fred Lorenzon
1966	Marvin Panch	Plymouth	135.042	Paul Goldsmith
1967	Jim Paschal	Plymouth	135.832	Cale Yarborough
1968	Buddy Baker	Dodge	104.207	Donnie Allison
1969	Lee Roy Yarbrough	Mercury	134.631	Donnie Allison
1970	Donnie Allison	Ford	129.680	Bobby Isaac
1971	Bobby Allison	Mercury	140.442	Charlie Glotzbach
1972	Buddy Baker	Dodge	142.255	Bobby Allison
1973	Buddy Baker	Dodge	134.890	Buddy Baker
1974	David Pearson	Mercury	135.720	David Pearson
1975	Richard Petty	Dodge	145.327	David Pearson
1976	David Pearson	Mercury	137.352	David Pearson
1977	Richard Petty	Dodge	137.636	David Pearson
1978	Darrell Waltrip	Chevrolet	138.355	David Pearson
1979	Darrell Waltrip	Chevrolet	136.674	Neil Bonnet
1980	Benny Parsons	Chevrolet	119.265	Cale Yarborough
1981	Bobby Allison	Buick	129.326	Neil Bonnett
1982	Neil Bonnett	Ford	130.508	David Pearson
1983	Neil Bonnett	Chevrolet	140.406	Buddy Baker
1984	Bobby Allison	Buick	129.233	Harry Gant
1985	Darrell Waltrip	Chevrolet	141.807	Bill Elliott
1986	Dale Earnhardt	Chevrolet	140.406	Geoff Bodine
1987	Kyle Petty	Ford	131.483	Bill Elliott
1988	Darrell Waltrip	Chevrolet	124.460	Davey Allison
1989	Darrell Waltrip	Chevrolet	144.077	Alan Kulwicki
1990	Rusty Wallace	Pontiac	137.650	Ken Schrader
1991	Davey Allison	Ford	138.951	Mark Martin
1992	Dale Earnhardt	Chevrolet	132.980	Bill Elliott
1993	Dale Earnhardt	Chevrolet	145.504	Ken Schrader
1994	Jeff Gordon	Chevrolet	139.445	Jeff Gordon
1995	Bobby Labonte	Chevrolet	151.952*	Jeff Gordon
1996	Dale Jarrett	Ford	147.581	Jeff Gordon
1997	Jeff Gordon	Chevrolet	136.745	Jeff Gordon
1998	Jeff Gordon	Chevrolet	136.424	Jeff Gordon
1999	Jeff Burton	Ford	151.367	Bobby Labonte
2000	Matt Kenseth	Ford	142.640	Dale Earnhardt Jr
2001	Jeff Burton	Ford	138.107	Ryan Newman
2002	Mark Martin	Ford	137.729	Jimmie Johnson
2003	Jimmie Johnson	Chevrolet	126.198	Ryan Newman
2004	Jimmie Johnson	Chevrolet	142.763	Jimmie Johnson
2005	Jimmie Johnson	Chevrolet	114.698	Ryan Newman
2006	Kasey Kahne	Dodge	128.840	Scott Riggs
2007	Casey Mears	Chevrolet	130.222	Ryan Newman
2008	Kasey Kahne	Dodge	135.772	Kyle Busch
2009	David Reutimann	Toyota	120.899	Ryan Newman
2010	Kurt Busch	Dodge	144.966	Ryan Newman

Note: Held at the 1.5 mile high-banked Lowe's Motor Speedway in Charlotte on Memorial Day weekend.
*Track record, winning speed.

Darlington 500

Note: Formerly the Winston 500, held at the 2.66-mile Talladega Superspeedway. Starting in 1988, cars racing at Talladega have used restrictor plates that lower power and acceleration.

Year	Winner	Car	Avg Speed	Pole Winner
1950	Johnny Mantz	Plymouth	76.260	Wally Campbell
1951	Herb Thomas	Hudson	76.900	Marshall Teague
1952	Fonty Flock	Oldsmobile	74.510	Dick Rathman
1953	Buck Baker	Oldsmobile	92.780	Fonty Flock
1954	Herb Thomas	Hudson	94.930	Buck Baker
1955	Herb Thomas	Chevrolet	92.281	Tim Flock
1956	Curtis Turner	Ford	95.067	Buck Baker
1957	Speedy Thompson	Chevrolet	100.100	Paul Goldsmith
1958	Fireball Roberts	Chevrolet	102.590	Fireball Roberts
1959	Jim Reed	Chevrolet	111.836	Fireball Roberts
1960	Buck Baker	Pontiac	105.901	Cotton Owens
1961	Nelson Stacy	Ford	117.880	Fireball Roberts
1962	Larry Frank	Ford	117.965	Fireball Roberts
1963	Fireball Roberts	Ford	129.784	Fireball Roberts
1964	Buck Baker	Dodge	117.757	Richard Petty
1965	Ned Jarrett	Ford	115.924	Junior Johnson
1966	Darel Dieringer	Mercury	114.830	Lee Yarborough
1967	Richard Petty	Plymouth	131.933	David Pearson
1968	Cale Yarborough	Mercury	126.132	Charlie Glotzbach
1969	Lee Roy Yarbrough	Ford	105.612	Cale Yarborough
1970	Buddy Baker	Dodge	128.817	David Pearson
1971	Bobby Allison	Mercury	131.398	Bobby Allison
1972	Bobby Allison	Chevrolet	128.124	David Pearson
1973	Cale Yarborough	Chevrolet	134.033	David Pearson
1974	Cale Yarborough	Chevrolet	111.075	Richard Petty
1975	Bobby Allison	Matador	116.825	David Pearson
1976	David Pearson	Mercury	120.534	David Pearson
1977	David Pearson	Mercury	106.797	Darrell Waltrip
1978	Cale Yarborough	Oldsmobile	116.828	David Pearson
1979	David Pearson	Chevrolet	126.259	Bobby Allison
1980	Terry Labonte	Chevrolet	115.210	Darrell Waltrip
1981	Neil Bonnett	Ford	126.410	Harry Gant
1982	Cale Yarborough	Buick	126.703	David Pearson
1983	Bobby Allison	Buick	123.343	Neil Bonnett
1984	Harry Gant	Chevrolet	128.270	Harry Gant
1985	Bill Elliott	Ford	121.254	Bill Elliott
1986	Tim Richmond	Chevrolet	121.068	Tim Richmond
1987	Dale Earnhardt	Chevrolet	115.520	Davey Allison
1988	Bill Elliott	Ford	128.297	Bill Elliott
1989	Dale Earnhardt	Chevrolet	135.462	Alan Kulwicki
1990	Dale Earnhardt	Chevrolet	123.141	Dale Earnhardt
1991	Harry Gant	Oldsmobile	133.508	Davey Allison
1992	Darrell Waltrip	Chevrolet	129.114	Sterling Marlin
1993	Mark Martin	Ford	137.932	Ken Schrader
1994	Bill Elliott	Ford	127.915	Geoff Bodine
1995	Jeff Gordon	Chevrolet	121.231	John Andretti
1996	Jeff Gordon	Chevrolet	135.757	Dale Jarrett
1997	Jeff Gordon	Chevrolet	121.149	Bobby Labonte
1998	Jeff Gordon	Chevrolet	139.031*	Dale Jarrett
1999	Jeff Burton	Ford	100.816	Kenny Irwin
2000	Bobby Labonte	Pontiac	108.275	Jeremy Mayfield
2001	Ward Burton	Dodge	122.773	Kurt Busch
2002	Jeff Gordon	Chevrolet	118.617	Sterling Marlin
2003	Terry Labonte	Chevrolet	120.744	Ryan Newman
2004	Jimmie Johnson	Chevrolet	125.044	Kurt Busch
2005	Greg Biffle	Ford	135.127	Kasey Kahne
2006	Greg Biffle	Ford	123.031	Kasey Kahne
2007	Jeff Gordon	Chevrolet	124.372	Clint Bowyer
2008	Kyle Busch	Toyota	140.350	Greg Biffle
2009	Mark Martin	Chevrolet	119.687	Matt Kenseth
2010	Denny Hamlin	Toyota	126.605	Jamie McMurray

Through 2004, results listed were for the Southern 500, traditionally the second race of the year at the 1.366-mile Darlington (S.C.) Raceway. Starting in 2005, Darlington only hosted one race a year, in May.

*Track record, winning speed.

Sprint Cup* NASCAR Champions

Year	Driver	Car	Wins	Poles	Winnings ($)
1949	Red Byron	Oldsmobile	2	1	5,800
1950	Bill Rexford	Oldsmobile	1	0	6,175
1951	Herb Thomas	Hudson	7	4	18,200
1952	Tim Flock	Hudson	8	4	20,210
1953	Herb Thomas	Hudson	11	10	27,300
1954	Lee Petty	Dodge	7	3	26,706
1955	Tim Flock	Chrysler	18	19	33,750
1956	Buck Baker	Chrysler	14	12	29,790
1957	Buck Baker	Chevrolet	10	5	24,712
1958	Lee Petty	Oldsmobile	7	4	20,600
1959	Lee Petty	Plymouth	10	2	45,570
1960	Rex White	Chevrolet	6	3	45,260
1961	Ned Jarrett	Chevrolet	1	4	27,285
1962	Joe Weatherly	Pontiac	9	6	56,110
1963	Joe Weatherly	Mercury	3	6	58,110
1964	Richard Petty	Plymouth	9	8	98,810
1965	Ned Jarrett	Ford	13	9	77,966
1966	David Pearson	Dodge	14	7	59,205
1967	Richard Petty	Plymouth	27	18	130,275
1968	David Pearson	Ford	16	12	118,824
1969	David Pearson	Ford	11	14	183,700
1970	Bobby Isaac	Dodge	11	13	121,470
1971	Richard Petty	Plymouth	21	9	309,225
1972	Richard Petty	Plymouth	8	3	227,015
1973	Benny Parsons	Chevrolet	1	0	114,345
1974	Richard Petty	Dodge	10	7	299,175
1975	Richard Petty	Dodge	13	3	378,865
1976	Cale Yarborough	Chevrolet	9	2	387,173
1977	Cale Yarborough	Chevrolet	9	3	477,499
1978	Cale Yarborough	Oldsmobile	10	8	530,751
1979	Richard Petty	Chevrolet	5	1	531,292
1980	Dale Earnhardt	Chevrolet	5	0	588,926
1981	Darrell Waltrip	Buick	12	11	693,342
1982	Darrell Waltrip	Buick	12	7	873,118
1983	Bobby Allison	Buick	6	0	828,355
1984	Terry Labonte	Chevrolet	2	2	713,010
1985	Darrell Waltrip	Chevrolet	3	4	1,318,735
1986	Dale Earnhardt	Chevrolet	5	1	1,783,880
1987	Dale Earnhardt	Chevrolet	11	1	2,099,243
1988	Bill Elliott	Ford	6	6	1,574,639
1989	Rusty Wallace	Pontiac	6	4	2,247,950
1990	Dale Earnhardt	Chevrolet	9	4	3,083,056
1991	Dale Earnhardt	Chevrolet	4	0	2,396,685
1992	Alan Kulwicki	Ford	2	6	2,322,561
1993	Dale Earnhardt	Chevrolet	6	2	3,353,789
1994	Dale Earnhardt	Chevrolet	4	2	3,400,733
1995	Jeff Gordon	Chevrolet	7	9	4,347,343
1996	Terry Labonte	Chevrolet	2	4	4,030,648
1997	Jeff Gordon	Chevrolet	10	1	4,201,227
1998	Jeff Gordon	Chevrolet	13	7	6,175,867
1999	Dale Jarrett	Ford	4	0	3,608,829
2000	Bobby Labonte	Pontiac	4	2	4,041,750
2001	Jeff Gordon	Chevrolet	6	8	6,649,076
2002	Tony Stewart	Pontiac	3	4	4,695,150
2003	Matt Kenseth	Ford	1	2	4,038,120
2004	Kurt Busch	Ford	3	1	4,200,330
2005	Tony Stewart	Chevrolet	5	3	6,987,530
2006	Jimmie Johnson	Chevrolet	5	1	8,909,140
2007	Jimmie Johnson	Chevrolet	10	4	7,646,420
2008	Jimmie Johnson	Chevrolet	7	6	7,354,860
2009	Jimmie Johnson	Chevrolet	7	4	7,339,630

*Series name changed from Winston Cup after 2003 season, then to Sprint Cup beginning in 2008.

Alltime NASCAR Leaders

	WINS		WINS	POLE POSITIONS		POLE POSITIONS	
Richard Petty	200	Lee Petty	54	Richard Petty	126	*Mark Martin	49
David Pearson	105	*Jimmie Johnson	53	David Pearson	113	Junior Johnson	47
Bobby Allison	84	Ned Jarrett	50	Cale Yarborough	70	*Ryan Newman	46
Darrell Waltrip	84	Junior Johnson	50	*Jeff Gordon	69	Buck Baker	44
Cale Yarborough	83	Herb Thomas	48	Darrell Waltrip	59	Buddy Baker	40
*Jeff Gordon	82	Buck Baker	46	Bobby Allison	57	Tim Flock	39
Dale Earnhardt	76	David Pearson	45	Bill Elliott	54	Herb Thomas	39
Rusty Wallace	55	Bill Elliott	44	Bobby Isaac	51	Geoff Bodine	37

*Active drivers. Note: NASCAR wins leaders and pole position leaders through Oct 11, 2010.

Formula One Grand Prix Racing

World Driving Champions

Year	Winner	Car	Year	Winner	Car
1950	Guiseppe Farina, Italy	Alfa Romeo	1977	Niki Lauda, Austria	Ferrari
1951	Juan-Manuel Fangio, Argentina	Alfa Romeo	1978	Mario Andretti, U.S.	Lotus-Ford
1952	Alberto Ascari, Italy	Ferrari	1979	Jody Scheckter, S Africa	Ferrari
1953	Alberto Ascari, Italy	Ferrari	1980	Alan Jones, Australia	Williams-Ford
1954	Juan-Manuel Fangio, Argentina	Maserati-Mercedes	1981	Nelson Piquet, Brazil	Brabham-Ford
1955	Juan-Manuel Fangio, Argentina	Mercedes	1982	Keke Rosberg, Finland	Williams-Ford
			1983	Nelson Piquet, Brazil	Brabham-BMW
1956	Juan-Manuel Fangio, Argentina	Ferrari	1984	Niki Lauda, Austria	McLaren-Porsche
			1985	Alain Prost, France	McLaren-Porsche
1957	Juan-Manuel Fangio, Argentina	Maserati	1986	Alain Prost, France	McLaren-Porsche
			1987	Nelson Piquet, Brazil	Williams-Honda
1958	Mike Hawthorn, Grt Britain	Ferrari	1988	Ayrton Senna, Brazil	McLaren-Honda
1959	Jack Brabham, Australia	Cooper-Climax	1989	Alain Prost, France	McLaren-Honda
1960	Jack Brabham, Australia	Cooper-Climax	1990	Ayrton Senna, Brazil	McLaren-Honda
1961	Phil Hill, U.S.	Ferrari	1991	Ayrton Senna, Brazil	McLaren-Honda
1962	Graham Hill, Grt Britain	BRM	1992	Nigel Mansell, Grt. Britain	Williams-Renault
1963	Jim Clark, Scotland	Lotus-Climax	1993	Alain Prost, France	Williams-Renault
1964	John Surtees, Grt Britain	Ferrari	1994	Michael Schumacher, Ger	Benetton-Ford
1965	Jim Clark, Scotland	Lotus-Climax	1995	Michael Schumacher, Ger	Benetton-Renault
1966	Jack Brabham, Australia	Brabham-Repco	1996	Damon Hill, Grt Britain	Williams-Renault
1967	Denny Hulme, New Zealand	Brabham-Repco	1997	Jacques Villeneuve, Can	Williams-Renault
			1998	Mika Hakkinen, Finland	McLaren-Mercedes
1968	Graham Hill, Grt Britain	Lotus-Ford	1999	Mika Hakkinen, Finland	McLaren-Mercedes
1969	Jackie Stewart, Scotland	Matra-Ford	2000	Michael Schumacher, Ger	Ferrari
1970	Jochen Rindt, Austria*	Lotus-Ford	2001	Michael Schumacher, Ger	Ferrari
1971	Jackie Stewart, Scotland	Tyrell-Ford	2002	Michael Schumacher, Ger	Ferrari
1972	Emerson Fittipaldi, Brazil	Lotus-Ford	2003	Michael Schumacher, Ger	Ferrari
1973	Jackie Stewart, Scotland	Tyrell-Ford	2004	Michael Schumacher, Ger	Ferrari
1974	Emerson Fittipaldi, Brazil	McLaren-Ford	2005	Fernando Alonso, Spain	Renault
1975	Niki Lauda, Austria	Ferrari	2006	Fernando Alonso, Spain	Renault
1976	James Hunt, Grt Britain	McLaren-Ford	2007	Kimi Raikkonen, Finland	Ferrari
			2008	Lewis Hamilton, Great Britain	McLaren-Mercedes
			2009	Jenson Button, Great Britain	Brawn-Mercedes

*The championship was awarded posthumously, after Rindt was killed during practice for the Italian Grand Prix.

Alltime F/I Grand Prix Winners

Driver	Wins	Driver	Wins
*Michael Schumacher, Germany	91	*Fernando Alonso, Spain	26
Alain Prost, France	51	Jim Clark, Great Britain	25
Ayrton Senna, Brazil	41	Niki Lauda, Austria	25
Nigel Mansell, Great Britain	31	Juan Manuel Fangio, Argentina	24
Jackie Stewart, Great Britain	27	Nelson Piquet, Brazil	23

Alltime F/I Grand Prix Pole Winners

Driver	Poles	Driver	Poles
*Michael Schumacher, Germany	68	Mika Hakkinen, Finland	26
Ayrton Senna, Brazil	65	Niki Lauda, Austria	24
Alain Prost, France	33	Nelson Piquet, Brazil	24
Jim Clark, Great Britain	33	Damon Hill, Great Britain	20
Nigel Mansell, Great Britain	31	*Fernando Alonso, Spain	20
Juan Manuel Fangio, Argentina	29	*Lewis Hamilton, Great Britain	19

*Active driver in 2010. Note: Grand Prix winners through Oct 10, 2010.

The 24 Hours of Daytona

Year	Winner	Car	Avg Speed	Distance
1962	Dan Gurney	Lotus 19-Class SP11	104.101 mph	3 hrs (312.42 mi)
1963	Pedro Rodriguez	Ferrari-Class 12	102.074 mph	3 hrs (308.61 mi)
1964	Pedro Rodriguez/Phil Hill	Ferrari 250 LM	98.230 mph	2,000 km
1965	Ken Miles/Lloyd Ruby	Ford	99.944 mph	2,000 km
1966	Ken Miles/Lloyd Ruby	Ford Mark II	108.020 mph	24 hrs (2,570.63 mi)
1967	Lorenzo Bandini/Chris Amon	Ferrari 330 P4	105.688 mph	24 hrs (2,537.46 mi)
1968	Vic Elford/Jochen Neerpasch	Porsche 907	106.697 mph	24 hrs (2,565.69 mi)
1969	Mark Donohue/Chuck Parsons	Chevy Lola	99.268 mph	24 hrs (2,383.75 mi)
1970	Pedro Rodriguez/Leo Kinnunen	Porsche 917	114.866 mph	24 hrs (2,758.44 mi)
1971	Pedro Rodriguez/Jackie Oliver	Porsche 917K	109.203 mph	24 hrs (2,621.28 mi)
1972*	Mario Andretti/Jacky Ickx	Ferrari 312/P	122.573 mph	6 hrs (738.24 mi)
1973	Peter Gregg/Hurley Haywood	Porsche Carrera	106.225 mph	24 hrs (2,552.7 mi)
1974	(No race)			
1975	Peter Gregg/Hurley Haywood	Porsche Carrera	108.531 mph	24 hrs (2,606.04 mi)
1976†	Peter Gregg/Brian Redman/ John Fitzpatrick	BMW CSL	104.040 mph	24 hrs (2,092.8 mi)
1977	John Graves/Hurley Haywood/ Dave Helmick	Porsche Carrera	108.801 mph	24 hrs (2,615 mi)
1978	Rolf Stommelen/ Antoine Hezemans/Peter Gregg	Porsche Turbo	108.743 mph	24 hrs (2,611.2 mi)
1979	Ted Field/Danny Ongais/ Hurley Haywood	Porsche Turbo	109.249 mph	24 hrs (2,626.56 mi)
1980	Volkert Meri/Rolf Stommelen/ Reinhold Joest	Porsche Turbo	114.303 mph	24 hrs
1981	Bob Garretson/Bobby Rahal/ Brian Redman	Porsche Turbo	113.153 mph	24 hrs
1982	John Paul Jr/John Paul Sr/ Rolf Stommelen	Porsche Turbo	114.794 mph	24 hrs
1983	Preston Henn/Bob Wollek/ Claude Ballot-Lena/A.J. Foyt	Porsche Turbo	98.781 mph	24 hrs
1984	Sarel van der Merwe/ Graham Duxbury/Tony Martin	Porsche March	103.119 mph	24 hrs (2,476.8 mi)
1985	A.J. Foyt/Bob Wollek/ Al Unser/Thierry Boutsen	Porsche 962	104.162 mph	24 hrs (2,502.68 mi)
1986	Al Holbert/Derek Bell/Al Unser Jr.	Porsche 962	105.484 mph	24 hrs (2,534.72 mi)
1987	Chip Robinson/Derek Bell/ Al Holbert/Al Unser Jr.	Porsche 962	111.599 mph	24 hrs (2,680.68 mi)
1988	Martin Brundle/John Nielsen/ Raul Boesel	Jaguar XJR-9	107.943 mph	24 hrs (2,591.68 mi)
1989	John Andretti/Derek Bell/ Bob Wollek	Porsche 962	92.009 mph	24 hrs (2,210.76 mi)
1990	Davy Jones/ Jan Lammers/ Andy Wallace	Jaguar XJR-12	112.857 mph	24 hrs (2,709.16 mi)
1991	Hurley Haywood/ John Winter/ Frank Jelinski/ Henri Pescarolo/ Bob Wollek	Porsche 962C	106.633 mph	24 hrs (2,559.64 mi)
1992	Massahiro Hasemi/ Kazuoyshi Hoshino/ Toshio Suzuki/ Anders Olofsson	Nissan R91CP	112.987 mph	24 hrs (2,712.72 mi)
1993	P.J. Jones/Mark Dismore/ Rocky Moran	Toyota Eagle MK III	103.537 mph	24 hrs (2,484.88 mi)
1994	Paul Gentilozzi/ Scott Pruett/ Butch Leitzinger/ Steve Millen	Nissan 300 ZX	104.80 mph	24 hrs (2,693.67 mi)
1995	Jurgen Lassig/ Christophe Buochut/ Giovanni Lavaggi/ Marco Werner	Porsche Spyder K8	102.28 mph	690 laps (2,456.4 mi)
1996	Wayne Taylor/ Scott Sharp/ Jim Pace	Oldsmobile Mark III	103.32 mph	697 laps (2,481.32 mi)
1997	Elliot Forbes-Robinson/ John Schneider/Rob Dyson/ John Paul Jr/Butch Leitzinger/James Weaver/Andy Wallace	Ford R & S MK III	102.292 mph	690 laps (2,456.4 mi)
1998	Arie Luyendyk/Didier Theys/ Mauro Baldi	Ferrari 333 SP	105.565 mph	711 laps (2,531.16 mi)
1999	Elliott Forbes-Robinson/ Butch Leitzinger/ Andy Wallace	Ford R & S MK III	104.9 mph	708 laps (2,520.48 mi)
2000	Olivier Beretta/Karl Wendlinger/ Dominique Dupuy	Dodge Viper	107.207 mph	723 laps (2,573.88 mi)
2001	Ron Fellows/Chris Kneifel/ Franck Freon/Johnny O'Connell	Corvette	97.293 mph	656 laps (2,335.360 mi)

The 24 Hours of Daytona (Cont.)

Year	Winner	Car	Speed	Distance
2002	Didier Theys/Fredy Lienhard/Max Papis/Mauro Baldi	Dallara-Judd (SRP)	106.143 mph	716 laps (2,548.96 mi)
2003	Kevin Buckler/Michael Schrom Timo Bernhard/Jorg Bergmeister	Porsche GT3 RS	114.068 mph‡	694 laps (2,470.64 mi)
2004	Forest Barber/Terry Borcheller Andy Pilgrim/Christian Fittipaldi	Pontiac Doran	117.651 mph	526 laps (1,872.56 mi)
2005	Wayne Taylor, Max Angelelli, Emmanuel Collard	Pontiac Riley	119.397 mph	710 laps (2,527.60 mi)
2006	Scott Dixon/Dan Wheldon Casey Mears	Lexus Riley	108.826 mph	734 laps (2,613.04 mi)
2007	Scott Pruett/Salvador Duran Juan Pablo Montoya	Lexus Riley	99.020 mph	668 laps (2,378.08 mi)
2008	Scott Pruett/Memo Rojas Juan Pablo Montoya Dario Franchitti	Lexus Riley	103.057 mph	695 laps (2,474.20 mi)
2009	Darren Law/David Donohue Buddy Rice/Antonio Garcia	Porsche Riley	108.994 mph	735 laps (2,616.60 mi.)
2010	Terry Borcheller0Joao Barbosa Ryan Dalziel/Mike Rockenfeller	Porsche Riley	111.930 mph	755 laps (2,687.77 mi.)

*Race shortened due to fuel crisis. †Course lengthened from 3.81 miles to 3.84 miles. ‡Top speed.

World SportsCar Champions*

Year	Winner	Car	Year	Winner	Car
1978	Peter Gregg	Porsche 935	1989	Geoff Brabham	Nissan GTP
1979	Peter Gregg	Porsche 935	1990	Geoff Brabham	Nissan GTP
1980	John Fitzpatrick	Porsche 935	1991	Geoff Brabham	Nissan NPT
1981	Brian Redman	Chevy Lola	1992	Juan Fangio II	Toyota EGL MKIII
1982	John Paul Jr	Chevy Lola	1993	Juan Fangio II	Toyota EGL MKIII
1983	Al Holbert	Chevy March	1994	Wayne Taylor	Mazda Kudzu
1984	Randy Lanier	Chevy March	1995	Fermin Velez	Ferrari 333 SP
1985	Al Holbert	Porsche 962	1996	Wayne Taylor	Mazda Kudzu
1986	Al Holbert	Porsche 962	1997	Butch Leitzinger	Ford R&S MKIII
1987	Chip Robinson	Porsche 962	1998	Butch Leitzinger	Ford R&S MKIII
1988	Geoff Brabham	Nissan GTP			

Year	Prototype	GTS	GT
1999	Elliott Forbes-Robinson	Olivier Beretta	Cort Wagner
2000	Allan McNish	Olivier Beretta	Sascha Maassen
2001	Emanuele Pirro	Terry Borcheller	Jörg Müller
2002	Tom Kristensen	Ron Fellows	Lucas Luhr
2003	Frank Biela/Marco Werner	Ron Fellows/John O'Connell	Sascha Maassen/L. Luhr
2004	Frank Biela/Emanuele Pirro	Oliver Gavin/Olivier Beretta	Patrick Long/Jorg Bergmeister
2005	Frank Biela/Emanuele Pirro	Oliver Gavin/Olivier Beretta	Patrick Long/Jorg Bergmeister
2006	R. Capello/A. McNish	Oliver Gavin/Olivier Beretta	Johannes van Overbeek
2007	R. Capello/A. McNish	Oliver Gavin/Olivier Beretta	Mika Salo/Jaime Melo
2008	Lucas Luhr/Marco Werner	Jan Magnussen/J. O'Connell	Jorg Bergmeister/Wolf Henzler
2009	David Brabham/Scott Sharp	Oliver Gavin/Olivier Beretta	Jorg Bergmeister/Patrick Long
2010	D. Brabham/Simon Pagenaud	Tim. Pappas/Jer. Bleekemolen	Jorg Bergmeister/Patrick Long

*1978–93 champions raced in the GT series, which in 1994 was replaced by the World SportsCar series. Beginning in 1999, racing was reclassified according to the American Le Mans Series. The Series is comprised of two different types of race cars divided into two categories and five separate classes. The Prototype category features open-cockpit prototype as well as Grand Touring Prototype (GTP) class cars. The Grand Touring category features the Grand Touring S (GTS) class cars, formerly known as GT2, and Grand Touring (GT) cars, formerly known as GT3. Both classes feature purpose-built race cars with an emphasis on spectator car identification.

Alltime SportsCar Leaders

PROTOTYPE WINS

*Rinaldo Capello	34
*Allan McNish	27
Marco Werner	25
Frank Biela	22
J.J. Lehto	19
*Emanuele Pirro	19
James Weaver	16

GTS AND GT WINS

Al Holbert	49
*Olivier Beretta	41
Peter Gregg	41
*Johnny O'Connell	38
*Oliver Gavin	33
*Jorg Bergmeister	33
Hurley Haywood	31

* Active driver in 2010.

Year	Winning Drivers	Car
1923	André Lagache/René Léonard	Chenard & Walker
1924	John Duff/Francis Clement	Bentley
1925	Gérard de Courcelles/André Rossignol	La Lorraine
1926	Robert Bloch/André Rossignol	La Lorraine
1927	J. Dudley Benjafield/Sammy Davis	Bentley
1928	Woolf Barnato/Bernard Rubin	Bentley
1929	Woolf Barnato/Sir Henry Birkin	Bentley Speed 6
1930	Woolf Barnato/Glen Kidston	Bentley Speed 6
1931	Earl Howe/Sir Henry Birkin	Alfa Romeo 8C-2300 sc
1932	Raymond Sommer/Luigi Chinetti	Alfa Romeo 8C-2300 sc
1933	Raymond Sommer/Tazio Nuvolari	Alfa Romeo 8C-2300 sc
1934	Luigi Chinetti/Philippe Etancelin	Alfa Romeo 8C-2300 sc
1935	John Hindmarsh/Louis Fontés	Lagonda M45R
1936	RACE CANCELLED	
1937	Jean-Pierre Wimille/Robert Benoist	Bugatti 57G sc
1938	Eugene Chaboud/Jean Tremoulet	Delahaye 135M
1939	Jean-Pierre Wimille/Pierre Veyron	Bugatti 57G sc
1940–48	RACES CANCELLED	
1949	Luigi Chinetti/Lord Selsdon	Ferrari 166MM
1950	Louis Rosier/Jean-Louis Rosier	Talbot-Lago
1951	Peter Walker/Peter Whitehead	Jaguar C
1952	Hermann Lang/Fritz Reiss	Mercedes-Benz 300 SL
1953	Tony Rolt/Duncan Hamilton	Jaguar C
1954	Froilan Gonzales/Maurice Trintignant	Ferrari 375
1955	Mike Hawthorn/Ivor Bueb	Jaguar D
1956	Ron Flockhart/Ninian Sanderson	Jaguar D
1957	Ron Flockhart/Ivor Bueb	Jaguar D
1958	Olivier Gendebien/Phil Hill	Ferrari 250 TR58
1959	Carroll Shelby/Roy Salvadori	Aston Martin DBR1
1960	Olivier Gendebien/Paul Frère	Ferrari 250 TR59/60
1961	Olivier Gendebien/Phil Hill	Ferrari 250 TR61
1962	Olivier Gendebien/Phil Hill	Ferrari 250P
1963	Lodovico Scarfiotti/Lorenzo Bandini	Ferrari 250P
1964	Jean Guichel/Nino Vaccarella	Ferrari 275P
1965	Jochen Rindt/Masten Gregory	Ferrari 250LM
1966	Chris Amon/Bruce McLaren	Ford Mk2
1967	Dan Gurney/A.J. Foyt	Ford Mk4
1968	Pedro Rodriguez/Lucien Bianchi	Ford GT40
1969	Jacky Ickx/Jackie Oliver	Ford GT40
1970	Hans Herrmann/Richard Attwood	Porsche 917
1971	Helmut Marko/Gijs van Lennep	Porsche 917
1972	Henri Pescarolo/Graham Hill	Matra-Simca MS670
1973	Henri Pescarolo/Gérard Larrousse	Matra-Simca MS670B
1974	Henri Pescarolo/Gérard Larrousse	Matra-Simca MS670B
1975	Jacky Ickx/Derek Bell	Mirage-Ford MB
1976	Jacky Ickx/Gijs van Lennep	Porsche 936
1977	Jacky Ickx/Jurgen Barth/Hurley Haywood	Porsche 936
1978	Jean-Pierre Jaussaud/Didier Pironi	Renault-Alpine A442
1979	Klaus Ludwig/Bill Whittington/Don Whittington	Porsche 935
1980	Jean-Pierre Jaussaud/Jean Rondeau	Rondeau-Ford M379B
1981	Jacky Ickx/Derek Bell	Porsche 936-81
1982	Jacky Ickx/Derek Bell	Porsche 956
1983	Vern Schuppan/Hurley Haywood/Al Holbert	Porsche 956-83
1984	Klaus Ludwig/Henri Pescarolo	Porsche 956B
1985	Klaus Ludwig/Paolo Barilla/John Winter	Porsche 956B
1986	Derek Bell/Hans-Joachim Stuck/Al Holbert	Porsche 962C
1987	Derek Bell/Hans-Joachim Stuck/Al Holbert	Porsche 962C
1988	Jan Lammers/Johnny Dumfries/Andy Wallace	Jaguar XJR9LM
1989	Jochen Mass/Manuel Reuter/Stanley Dickens	Sauber-Mercedes C9-88
1990	John Nielsen/Price Cobb/Martin Brundle	TWR Jaguar XJR-12
1991	Volker Weidler/Johnny Herbert/Bertrand Gachof	Mazda 787B
1992	Derek Warwick/Yannick Dalmas/Mark Blundell	Peugeot 905B
1993	Geoff Brabham/Christophe Bouchut/Eric Helary	Peugeot 905
1994	Yannick Dalmas/Hurley Haywood/Mauro Baldi	Porsche 962
1995	Yannick Dalmas/J.J. Lehto/Masanori Sekiya	McLaren BMW
1996	Manuel Reuter/Davy Jones/Alexander Wurz	TWR Porsche
1997	Michele Alboreto/Stefan Johansson/Tom Kristensen	TWR Porsche
1998	Allan McNish/Laurent Aiello/Stephane Ortelli	Porsche GT One
1999	Yannick Dalmas/Joachim Winkelhock/Pierluigi Martini	BMW V12 LMR
2000	Frank Biela/Tom Kristensen/Emanuele Pirro	Audi R8
2001	Frank Biela/Tom Kristensen/Emanuele Pirro	Audi R8
2002	Frank Biela/Tom Kristensen/Emanuele Pirro	Audi R8
2003	Rinaldo Capello/Tom Kristensen/Guy Smith	Bentley EXP Speed 8
2004	Rinaldo Capello/Seiji Ará/Tom Kristensen	Audi R8
2005	J.J. Lehto/Marco Werner/Tom Kristensen	Audi R8
2006	Frank Biela/Emanuele Pirro/Marco Werner	Audi R10
2007	Frank Biela/Emanuele Pirro/Marco Werner	Audi R10
2008	Rinaldo Capello/Tom Kristensen/Allan McNish	Audi R10
2009	Marc Gene/Alexander Wurz/David Brabham	Peugeot 908
2010	Timo Bernhard/Romain Dumas/Mike Rockenfeller	Audi R15

Horse Racing

Jockey Calvin Borel won for the second straight year at the Kentucky Derby, this year on the mount Super Saver

THOROUGHBRED RACING

The Triple Crown

136th Kentucky Derby

May 1, 2010. Grade I, 3-year-olds; 11th race, Churchill Downs, Louisville. All 126 lbs. Distance: 1¼ miles. Purse: $2,000,000 guaranteed. Track: Sloppy (sealed). Off: 6:32 p.m. Winner: Super Saver (By Maria's Mom, out of Supercharger by A.P. Indy) ; Times: 0:22.63, 0:46.16, 1:10.58, 1:37.65, 2:04.45. Won: Driving. Breeder: Winstar Farms LLC. Scratched: I Want Revenge.

Horse	Finish-PP	Margin	Jockey/Trainer
Super Saver	1–4	2½	Calvin Borel/Todd Pletcher
Ice Box	2–2	neck	Jose Lezcano/Nick Zito
Paddy O'Prado	3–10	2	Kent Desormeaux/Dale Romans
Make Music for Me	4–9	1¼	Joel Rosario/Alexis Barba
Noble's Promise	5–3	1	Willie Martinez/Kenneth McPeek
Lookin At Lucky	6–1	½	Garrett Gomez/Bob Baffert
Dublin	7–17	1¼	Terry Thompson/D. Wayne Lukas
Stately Victor	8–6	2	Alan Garcia/Michael Maker
Mission Impazible	9–14	1¼	Rajiv Maragh/Todd Pletcher
Devil May Care	10–11	6¾	John Velazquez/Todd Pletcher
American Lion	11–7	neck	David Flores/Eoin Harty
Jackson Bend	12–13	6½	Mike Smith/Nick Zito
Discreetly Mine	13–15	3¼	Javier Castellano/Todd Pletcher
Dean's Kitten	14–8	14½	Robby Albarado/Michael Maker
Conveyance	15–12	10½	Martin Garcia/Bob Baffert
Homeboykris	16–19	½	Ramon Dominguez/Richard Dutrow Jr.
Sidney's Candy	17–20	6¼	Joe Talamo/John Sadler
Line of David	18–5	neck	Rafael Bejarano/John Sadler
Awesome Act	19–16	9½	Julien Leparoux/Jeremy Noseda
Backtalk	20–18	—	M Mena/Thomas Amoss

135th Preakness Stakes

May 15, 2010. Grade I, 3-year-olds; 12th race, Pimlico Race Course, Baltimore. All 126 lbs. Distance: 1³⁄₁₆ miles; Stakes value: $1,100,000. Track: Fast. Off: 6:19 p.m. Winner: Looking at Lucky (By Smart Strike out of Private Feeling by Belong to Me); Times: 0:22.91 0:46.47, 1:11.22, 1:36.26, 1:55.47. Won: Driving. Breeder: Gulf Coast Farms LLC

Horse	Finish-PP	Margin	Jockey/Trainer
Lookin at Lucky	1–7	1¾	Martin Garcia/Bob Baffert
First Dude	2–11	head	Ramon Dominguez/Dale Romans
Jackson Bend	3–6	1	Mike Smith/Nick Zito
Yawanna Twist	4–5	4	Edgar Prado/Richard Dutrow Jr.
Dublin	5–12	4¾	Garrett Gomez/D. Wayne Lukas
Paddy O'Prado	6–10	nose	Kent Desormeaux/Dale Romans
Caracortado	7–9	1	Paul Atkinson/Michael Machowsky
Super Saver	8–8	¾	Calvin Borel/Todd Pletcher
Schoolyard Dreams	9–2	2½	Eibar Coa/Derek Ryan
Aikenite	10–1	3½	Javier Castellano/Todd Pletcher
Pleasant Prince	11–3	3½	Julien Leparoux/Wesley Ward
Northern Giant	12–4	–	Terry Thompson/D. Wayne Lukas

142nd Belmont Stakes

June 5, 2010. Grade I, 3-year-olds; 11th race, Belmont Park, Elmont, NY. All 126 lbs. Distance: 1½ miles. Stakes value: $1,000,000. Track: Fast. Off: 6:35 p.m. Winner: Drosselmeyer (By Distorted Humor out of Golden Ballet by Moscow Ballet); Times: 0:24.15, 49.19, 1:14.94, 1:40.25, 2:04.97, 2:31.57. Won: Driving. Breeder: Aaron U. and Marie D. Jones

Horse	Finish-PP	Margin	Jockey/Trainer
Drosselmeyer	1–7	1¾	Mike Smith/William Mott
Fly Down	2–5	neck	John Velazquez/Nick Zito
First Dude	3–11	1½	Ramon Dominguez/Dale Romans
Game On Dude	4–8	½	Martin Garcia/Bob Baffert
Uptowncharlybrown	5*–3	3¾	Rajiv Maragh/Kiaran McLaughlin
Stay Put	6–10	1¼	Jamie Theriot/Steve Margolis
Interactif	7–12	2½	Javier Castellano/Todd Pletcher
Stately Victor	8–9	¾	Alan Garcia/Michael Maker
Ice Box	9–6	4½	Jose Lezcano/Nick Zito
Make Music for Me	10–4	11¼	Joel Rosario/Alexis Barba
Dave in Dixie	11–1	19½	Calvin Borel/John Sadler
Spangled Star	12–2	—	Garrett Gomez/Richard Dutrow Jr.

*disqualified after race for losing lead pad on backstretch and placed 12th

Major Stakes Races

Late 2009

Date	Race	Track	Distance	Winner	Trainer/Jockey	Purse ($)
Oct 3	Hirsch Turf Classic Invt'l	Belmont	1½ miles	Interpretation	R. Barbara/ R. Albarado	600,000
Oct 3	Flower Bowl Invitational	Belmont	1¼ miles	Pure Clan	R. Holthus/ J. Leparoux	600,000
Oct 3	Indiana Derby	Hoosier	1¹⁄₁₆ miles	Misremembered	B. Baffert/ V. Espinoza	512,600
Oct 3	Fitz Dixon Cotillion	Philadelphia	1¹⁄₁₆ miles	Careless Jewel	J. Carroll/ R. Landry	750,000
Oct 3	Beldame Stakes	Belmont	1⅛ miles	Music Note	S. b. Suroor/ R. Maragh	588,000
Oct 3	Hawthorne Gold Cup	Hawthorne	1¼ miles	Awesome Gem	C. Dollase/ D. Romero	500,000
Oct 4	Prix de L'Arc De Triomphe	Longchamp	1½ miles	Sea The Stars	J. Oxx/ M. Kinane	4,000,000
Oct 10	First Lady Stakes	Keeneland	1 mile	Diamondarella	A. Penna Jr./ R. Maragh	400,000
Oct 10	Shadwell Turf Mile	Keeneland	1 mile	Court Vision	R. Dutrow/ R. Albarado	600,000
Oct 10	Champagne Stakes	Belmont	1 mile	Homeboykris	R. Dutrow/ E. Prado	400,000
Oct 10	Frizette Stakes	Belmont	1 mile	Devil May Care	T. Pletcher/ J. Velazquez	400,000
Oct 17	Queen Elizabeth II Challenge Cup	Keeneland	1⅛ miles	Hot Cha Cha	P. Sims/ J. Graham	500,000
Oct 17	Nearctice Stakes	Woodbine	6 furlongs	Field Commission	D. Vella/ J. Leparoux	527,254
Oct 17	E.P. Taylor Stakes	Woodbine	1¼ miles	Lahaleeb	M. Channon/ W. Buick	964,355
Oct 17	Pattison Canadian International	Woodbine	1½ miles	Champs Elysees	R. Frankel/ G. Gomez	1,927,555
Oct 17	Juddmonte Spinster Stakes	Keeneland	1⅛ miles	Mushka	W. Mott/ K. Desormeaux	500,000
Oct 18	West Virginia Classic Sprint	Charles Town	7 furlongs	My Sister Margaret	W. Mogge/ S. Spieth	450,000
Oct 18	West Virginia Classic Stakes	Charles Town	1⅛ miles	Russell Road	J. Caesy/ T. Dunkelberger	450,000
Nov 6	Breeders Cup Juvenile Fillies	Santa Anita	1¹⁄₁₆ miles	She Be Wild	W. Catalano/ J. Leparoux	1,818,000
Nov 6	Breeders Cup Juvenile Fillies Turf	Santa Anita	1 mile	Tapitsfly	D.Romans/ R. Albaradao	909,000
Nov 6	Breeders Cup F & M Turf	Santa Anita	1¼ miles	Midday	H. Cecil/ T. Queally	1,818,000
Nov 6	Breeders Cup Ladies' Classic	Santa Anita	1⅛ miles	Life is Sweet	J. Shirreffs/ G. Gomez	1,818,000
Nov 6	Breeders Cup F & M Sprint	Santa Anita	7 furlongs	Informed Decision	J. Sheppard/ J. Leparoux	909,000
Nov 6	Breeders Cup Marathon	Santa Anita	1½ miles	Man of Iron	A. O'Brien/ J. Murtagh	454,500
Nov 7	Breeders Cup Classic	Santa Anita	1¼ miles	Zenyatta	J. Shirreffs/ M. Smith	4,545,000
Nov 7	Breeders Cup Turf	Santa Anita	1½ miles	Conduit	M. Stoute/ R. Moore	2,727,000
Nov 7	Breeders Cup Turf Sprint	Santa Anita	6½ furlongs	California Flag	B. Koriner/ J. Talamo	909,000
Nov 7	Breeders Cup Mile	Santa Anita	1 mile	Goldikova	F. Head/ O. Peslier	1,818,000
Nov 7	Breeders Cup Dirt Mile	Santa Anita	1 mile	Furthest Land	M. Maker/ J. Leparoux	909,000
Nov 7	Breeders Cup Juvenile	Santa Anita	1¹⁄₁₆ miles	Vale of York	S. b. Suroor/ A. Ajtebi	1,818,000
Nov 7	Breeders Cup Juvenile Turf	Santa Anita	1 miles	Pounced	J. Gosden/ L. Dettori	909,000
Nov 7	Breeders Cup Sprint	Santa Anita	6 furlongs	Dancing in Silks	C. Gaines/ J. Rosario	1,818,000
Nov 27	Clark Handicap	Churchill Downs	1⅛ miles	Blame	A. Stall/ J. Theriot	460,600
Dec 19	Cashcall Futurity	Hollywood Park	1¹⁄₁₆ miles	Lookin at Lucky	B. Baffert/ G. Gomez	750,000

2010

Date	Race	Track	Distance	Winner	Trainer/Jockey	Purse ($)
Feb 6	Donn Handicap	Gulfstream	1⅛ miles	Quality Road	T. Pletcher/ J. Velazquez	500,000
Mar 6	Santa Anita Handicap	Santa Anita	1¼ miles	Misremembered	B. Baffert/ M. Garcia	750,000
Mar 20	Florida Derby	Gulfstream	1⅛ miles	Ice Box	N. Zito/ R. LaPenta	750,000
Mar 27	Dubai World Cup	Nad al Sheba	1¼ miles	Gloria de Campeao	P. Bary/ T. Pereira	10,000,000
Mar 27	Louisiana Derby	La. Fair Grounds	1¹⁄₁₆ miles	Mission Impazible	T. Pletcher/ R. Maragh	750,000
Mar 28	Sunland Derby	Sunland	1⅛ miles	Endorsement Alexandra	S. Ritter/ R. Albarado	800,000
Apr 3	Wood Memorial Stakes	Aqueduct	1⅛ miles	Eskenderaya	T. Pletcher/ J. Velazquez	750,000
Apr 3	Santa Anita Derby	Santa Anita	1⅛ miles	Sidney's Candy	J. Sadler/ J. Talamo	750,000
Apr 3	Illinois Derby	Hawthorne	1⅛ miles	American Lion	E. Harty/ D. Flores	500,000
Apr 3	Oaklawn Handicap	Oaklawn	1⅛ miles	Duke of Mischief	D. Fawkes/ E. Coa	500,000
Apr 10	Blue Grass Stakes	Keeneland	1⅛ miles	Stately Victor	M. Maker/ A. Garcia	750,000
Apr 10	Arkansas Derby	Oaklawn	1⅛ miles	Line of David	J. Sadler/ J. Court	1,000,000
Apr 17	Charles Town Classic	Charles Town	1⅛ miles	Researcher	J. Runco/ L. Perez	1,000,000
May 1	Kentucky Derby	Churchill Downs	1¼ miles	Super Saver	T. Pletcher/ C. Borel	2,185,200
May 1	Woodford Reserve Turf Classic	Churchill Downs	1⅛ miles	General Quarters	T. McCarthy/ R. Bejarano	553,100
May 15	Preakness Stakes	Pimlico	1³⁄₁₆ miles	Lookin at Lucky	B. Baffert/ M. Garcia	1,000,000
May 30	Metropolitan Handicap	Belmont	1 mile	Quality Road	T. Pletcher/ J. Velazquez	500,000
May 25	Lone Star Handicap	Lone Star	1¹⁄₁₆ miles	It's a Bird	M. Wolfson/ J. Leparoux	400,000
June 5	Belmont Stakes	Belmont	1½ miles	Drosselmeyer	W. Mott/ M. Smith	1,000,000
June 5	Just a Game Stakes	Belmont	1 mile	Proviso	W. Mott/ M. Smith	400,000
June 5	Manhattan Handicap Turf	Belmont	1¼ miles	Winchester	C. Clement/ C. Velasquez	400,000
June 12	Stephen Foster Handicap	Churchill Downs	1⅛ miles	Blame	A. Stall/ G. Gomez	671,700
July 10	Gold Cup Handicap	Hollywood	1¼ miles	Awesome Gem	C. Dollase/ D. Flores	500,000
July 10	Man O'War Stakes Turf	Belmont	1⅜ miles	Gio Ponti	C. Clement/ R. Dominguez	600,000
July 17	Virginia Derby	Colonial Downs	1¼ miles	Paddy O'Prado	D. Romans/ K. Desormeaux	600,000
July 17	Delaware Handicap	Delaware	1¼ miles	Life At Ten Temper	T. Pletcher/ J. Velazquez	750,000
July 24	Lady's Secret Stakes	Monmouth	1⅛ miles	Rachel Alexandra	S. Asmussen/ C. Borel	412,000
July 25	Prince of Wales Stakes	Fort Erie	1³⁄₁₆ miles	Golden Moka	B. Lynch/ A. Stephen	482,600
July 31	Diana Stakes Turf	Saratoga	1⅛ miles	Proviso	W. Mott/ M. Smith	500,000
July 31	Jim Dandy Stakes	Saratoga	1⅛ miles	A Little Warm	A. Dutrow/ J. Velazquez	500,000
Aug 1	Haskell Invitational	Monmouth	1⅛ miles	Lookin at Lucky	B. Baffert/ M. Garcia	1,010,000
Aug 7	Whitney Handicap	Saratoga	1⅛ miles	Blame	A. Stall Jr./ G. Gomez	750,000
Aug 7	West Virginia Derby	Mountaineer	1⅛ miles	Concord Point	B. Baffert/ M. Garcia	750,000

2010 (through September 30) *(Cont.)*

Date	Race	Track	Distance	Winner	Trainer/Jockey	Purse ($)
Aug 14	Sword Dancer Invitational	Saratoga	1½ miles	Telling	S. Hobby/ G. Gomez	500,000
Aug 15	Breeder's Stakes Turf	Woodbine	1½ miles	Miami Deco	B. Lynch/ R. Anthony	483,172
Aug 21	Alabama Stakes	Saratoga	1¼ miles	Blind Luck	J. Hollendorfer/ J. Rosario	500,000
Aug 21	Arlington Million Stakes Turf	Arlington	1¼ miles	Debussy	J. Gosden/ W. Buick	1,000,000
Aug 21	Beverly D. Stakes	Arlington	1³⁄₁₆ miles	Eclair De Lune	R. McAnally/ J. Alvarado	750,000
Aug 21	Secretariat Stakes	Arlington	1¼ miles	Paddy O'Prado	D. Romans/ K. Desormeaux	400,000
Aug 28	Travers Stakes	Saratoga	1¼ miles	Afleet Express	J. Jerkens/ J. Castellano	1,000,000
Aug 28	Pacific Classic	Del Mar	1¼ miles	Richard's Kid	B. Baffert/ M. Smith	1,000,000
Sept 4	Woodward Stakes	Saratoga	1⅛ miles	Quality Road	T. Pletcher/ J. Velazquez	750,000
Sept 11	Presque Isle Master	Presque Isle	6½ furlongs	Informed Decision	J. Sheppard/ J. Leparoux	400,400
Sept 19	Woodbine Mile	Woodbine	1 mile	Court Vision	R. Dutrow/ R. Albarado	972,704
Sept 19	Northern Dancer Stakes Turf	Woodbine	1½ miles	Redwood	B. Hills/ M. Hills	748,144
Sept 25	Super Derby XXXI	Louisiana Downs	1⅛ miles	Apart	A. Stall/ J. Campbell	500,000
Sept 25	Pennsylvania Derby	Philadelphia	1⅛ miles	Morning Line	N. Zito/ J. Velazquez	1,000,000

FOR THE RECORD • Year by Year

THOROUGHBRED RACING

Kentucky Derby

Run at Churchill Downs, Louisville, KY, on the first Saturday in May.

Year	Winner (Margin)	Jockey	Second	Third	Time
1875	Aristides (1)	Oliver Lewis	Volcano	Verdigris	2:37¾
1876	Vagrant (2)	Bobby Swim	Creedmoor	Harry Hill	2:38¼
1877	Baden-Baden (2)	William Walker	Leonard	King William	2:38
1878	Day Star (2)	Jimmie Carter	Himyar	Leveler	2:37¼
1879	Lord Murphy (1)	Charlie Shauer	Falsetto	Strathmore	2:37
1880	Fonso (1)	George Lewis	Kimball	Bancroft	2:37½
1881	Hindoo (4)	Jimmy McLaughin	Lelex	Alfambra	2:40
1882	Apollo (½)	Babe Hurd	Runnymede	Bengal	2:40¼
1883	Leonatus (3)	Billy Donohue	Drake Carter	Lord Raglan	2:43
1884	Buchanan (2)	Isaac Murphy	Loftin	Audrain	2:40¼
1885	Joe Cotton (Neck)	Erskine Henderson	Bersan	Ten Booker	2:37¼
1886	Ben Ali (½)	Paul Duffy	Blue Wing	Free Knight	2:36½
1887	Montrose (2)	Isaac Lewis	Jim Gore	Jacobin	2:39¼
1888	MacBeth II (1)	George Covington	Gallifet	White	2:38¼
1889	Spokane (Nose)	Thomas Kiley	Proctor Knott	Once Again	2:34½
1890	Riley (2)	Isaac Murphy	Bill Letcher	Robespierre	2:45
1891	Kingman (1)	Isaac Murphy	Balgowan	High Tariff	2:52¼
1892	Azra (Nose)	Alonzo Clayton	Huron	Phil Dwyer	2:41½
1893	Lookout (5)	Eddie Kunze	Plutus	Boundless	2:39¼
1894	Chant (2)	Frank Goodale	Pearl Song	Sigurd	2:41
1895	Halma (3)	Soup Perkins	Basso	Laureate	2:37½
1896	Ben Brush (Nose)	Willie Simms	Ben Eder	Semper Ego	2:07¼
1897	Typhoon II (Head)	Buttons Garner	Ornament	Dr. Catlett	2:12½
1898	Plaudit (Neck)	Willie Simms	Lieber Karl	Isabey	2:09
1899	Manuel (2)	Fred Taral	Corsini	Mazo	2:12
1900	Lieut. Gibson (4)	Jimmy Boland	Florizar	Thrive	2:06¼
1901	His Eminence (2)	Jimmy Winkfield	Sannazarro	Driscoll	2:07¾
1902	Alan-a-Dale (Nose)	Jimmy Winkfield	Inventor	The Rival	2:08¾
1903	Judge Himes (¾)	Hal Booker	Early	Bourbon	2:09
1904	Elwood (½)	Frankie Prior	Ed Tierney	Brancas	2:08½
1905	Agile (3)	Jack Martin	Ram's Horn	Layson	2:10¾
1906	Sir Huon (2)	Roscoe Troxler	Lady Navarre	James Reddick	2:08⅕
1907	Pink Star (2)	Andy Minder	Zal	Ovelando	2:12⅗
1908	Stone Street (1)	Arthur Pickens	Sir Cleges	Dunvegan	2:15⅕
1909	Wintergreen (4)	Vincent Powers	Miami	Dr. Barkley	2:08⅕
1910	Donau (½)	Fred Herbert	Joe Morris	Fighting Bob	2:06⅖
1911	Meridian (¾)	George Archibald	Governor Gray	Colston	2:05
1912	Worth (Neck)	Carroll H. Schilling	Duval	Flamma	2:09⅖
1913	Donerail (½)	Roscoe Goose	Ten Point	Gowell	2:04⅘
1914	Old Rosebud (8)	John McCabe	Hodge	Bronzewing	2:03⅖
1915	Regret (2)	Joe Notter	Pebbles	Sharpshooter	2:05⅖
1916	George Smith (Neck)	Johnny Loftus	Star Hawk	Franklin	2:04
1917	Omar Khayyam (2)	Charles Borel	Ticket	Midway	2:04⅗
1918	Exterminator (1)	William Knapp	Escoba	Viva America	2:10⅘
1919	Sir Barton (5)	Johnny Loftus	Billy Kelly	Under Fire	2:09⅘
1920	Paul Jones (Head)	Ted Rice	Upset	On Watch	2:09
1921	Behave Yourself (Head)	Charles Thompson	Black Servant	Prudery	2:04⅕
1922	Morvich (½)	Albert Johnson	Bet Mosie	John Finn	2:04⅗
1923	Zev (1½)	Earl Sande	Martingale	Vigil	2:05⅖
1924	Black Gold (½)	John Mooney	Chilhowee	Beau Butler	2:05⅕
1925	Flying Ebony (1½)	Earl Sande	Captain Hal	Son of John	2:07⅗
1926	Bubbling Over (5)	Albert Johnson	Bagenbaggage	Rock Man	2:03⅗
1927	Whiskery (Head)	Linus McAtee	Osmond	Jock	2:06
1928	Reigh Count (3)	Chick Lang	Misstep	Toro	2:10⅖
1929	Clyde Van Dusen (2)	Linus McAtee	Naishapur	Panchio	2:10⅘
1930	Gallant Fox (2)	Earl Sande	Gallant Knight	Ned O.	2:07⅗
1931	Twenty Grand (4)	Charles Kurtsinger	Sweep All	Mate	2:01⅘
1932	Burgoo King (5)	Eugene James	Economic	Stepenfetchit	2:05⅕
1933	Brokers Tip (Nose)	Don Meade	Head Play	Charley O.	2:06⅘

Kentucky Derby *(Cont.)*

Year	Winner (Margin)	Jockey	Second	Third	Time
1934	Cavalcade (2½)	Mack Garner	Discovery	Agrarian	2:04
1935	Omaha (1½)	Willie Saunders	Roman Soldier	Whiskolo	2:05
1936	Bold Venture (Head)	Ira Hanford	Brevity	Indian Broom	2:03⅗
1937	War Admiral (1¾)	Charles Kurtsinger	Pompoon	Reaping Reward	2:03⅕
1938	Lawrin (1)	Eddie Arcaro	Dauber	Can't Wait	2:04⅘
1939	Johnstown (8)	James Stout	Challedon	Heather Broom	2:03⅗
1940	Gallahadion (1½)	Carroll Bierman	Bimelech	Dit	2:05
1941	Whirlaway (8)	Eddie Arcaro	Staretor	Market Wise	2:01⅖
1942	Shut Out (2½)	Wayne Wright	Alsab	Valdina Orphan	2:04⅖
1943	Count Fleet (3)	John Longden	Blue Swords	Slide Rule	2:04
1944	Pensive (4½)	Conn McCreary	Broadcloth	Stir Up	2:04⅕
1945	Hoop Jr. (6)	Eddie Arcaro	Pot o' Luck	Darby Dieppe	2:07
1946	Assault (8)	Warren Mehrtens	Spy Song	Hampden	2:06⅗
1947	Jet Pilot (Head)	Eric Guerin	Phalanx	Faultless	2:06⅘
1948	Citation (3½)	Eddie Arcaro	Coaltown	My Request	2:05⅖
1949	Ponder (3)	Steve Brooks	Capot	Palestinian	2:04⅕
1950	Middleground (1¼)	William Boland	Hill Prince	Mr. Trouble	2:01⅗
1951	Count Turf (4)	Conn McCreary	Royal Mustang	Ruhe	2:02⅗
1952	Hill Gail (2)	Eddie Arcaro	Sub Fleet	Blue Man	2:01⅗
1953	Dark Star (Head)	Hank Moreno	Native Dancer	Invigorator	2:02
1954	Determine (1½)	Ray York	Hasty Road	Hasseyampa	2:03
1955	Swaps (1½)	Bill Shoemaker	Nashua	Summer Tan	2:01⅘
1956	Needles (¾)	Dave Erb	Fabius	Come On Red	2:03⅖
1957	Iron Liege (Nose)	Bill Hartack	Gallant Man	Round Table	2:02⅕
1958	Tim Tam (½)	Ismael Valenzuela	Lincoln Road	Noureddin	2:05
1959	Tomy Lee (Nose)	Bill Shoemaker	Sword Dancer	First Landing	2:02⅕
1960	Venetian Way (3½)	Bill Hartack	Bally Ache	Victoria Park	2:02⅖
1961	Carry Back (¾)	John Sellers	Crozier	Bass Clef	2:04
1962	Decidedly (2¼)	Bill Hartack	Roman Line	Ridan	2:00⅖
1963	Chateaugay (1¼)	Braulio Baeza	Never Bend	Candy Spots	2:01⅘
1964	Northern Dancer (Neck)	Bill Hartack	Hill Rise	The Scoundrel	2:00
1965	Lucky Debonair (Neck)	Bill Shoemaker	Dapper Dan	Tom Rolfe	2:01⅕
1966	Kauai King (½)	Don Brumfield	Advocator	Blue Skyer	2:02
1967	Proud Clarion (1)	Bobby Ussery	Barbs Delight	Damascus	2:00⅗
1968	Forward Pass (Disq.)	Ismael Valenzuela	Francie's Hat	T.V. Commercial	2:02⅕
1969	Majestic Prince (Neck)	Bill Hartack	Arts and Letters	Dike	2:01⅘
1970	Dust Commander (5)	Mike Manganello	My Dad George	High Echelon	2:03⅖
1971	Canonero II (3¾)	Gustavo Avila	Jim French	Bold Reason	2:03⅕
1972	Riva Ridge (3¼)	Ron Turcotte	No Le Hace	Hold Your Peace	2:01⅘
1973	Secretariat (2½)	Ron Turcotte	Sham	Our Native	1:59⅖
1974	Cannonade (2¼)	Angel Cordero Jr.	Hudson County	Agitate	2:04
1975	Foolish Pleasure (1¾)	Jacinto Vasquez	Avatar	Diabolo	2:02
1976	Bold Forbes (1)	Angel Cordero Jr.	Honest Pleasure	Elocutionist	2:01⅗
1977	Seattle Slew (1¾)	Jean Cruguet	Run Dusty Run	Sanhedrin	2:02⅕
1978	Affirmed (1½)	Steve Cauthen	Alydar	Believe It	2:01⅕
1979	Spectacular Bid (2¾)	Ronald J. Franklin	General Assembly	Golden Act	2:02⅖
1980	Genuine Risk (1)	Jacinto Vasquez	Rumbo	Jaklin Klugman	2:02
1981	Pleasant Colony (¾)	Jorge Velasquez	Woodchopper	Partez	2:02
1982	Gato Del Sol (2½)	Eddie Delahoussaye	Laser Light	Reinvested	2:02⅕
1983	Sunny's Halo (2)	Eddie Delahoussaye	Desert Wine	Caveat	2:02⅕
1984	Swale (3¼)	Laffit Pincay Jr.	Coax Me Chad	At the Threshold	2:02⅖
1985	Spend A Buck (5)	Angel Cordero Jr.	Stephan's Odyssey	Chief's Crown	2:00⅕
1986	Ferdinand (2¼)	Bill Shoemaker	Bold Arrangement	Broad Brush	2:02⅘
1987	Alysheba (¾)	Chris McCarron	Bet Twice	Avies Copy	2:03⅖
1988	Winning Colors (Neck)	Gary Stevens	Forty Niner	Risen Star	2:02⅕
1989	Sunday Silence (2½)	Pat Valenzuela	Easy Goer	Awe Inspiring	2:05
1990	Unbridled (3½)	Craig Perret	Summer Squall	Pleasant Tap	2:02
1991	Strike the Gold (1¾)	Chris Antley	Best Pal	Mane Minister	2:03
1992	Lil E. Tee (1)	Pat Day	Casual Lies	Dance Floor	2:03
1993	Sea Hero (2½)	Jerry Bailey	Prairie Bayou	Wild Gale	2:02⅖
1994	Go for Gin (2½)	Chris McCarron	Strodes Creek	Blumin Affair	2:03⅗
1995	Thunder Gulch (2¼)	Gary Stevens	Tejano Run	Timber Country	2:01⅕
1996	Grindstone (Nose)	Jerry Bailey	Cavonnier	Prince of Thieves	2:01
1997	Silver Charm (Head)	Gary Stevens	Captain Bodgit	Free House	2:02⅖
1998	Real Quiet (½)	Kent Desormeaux	Victory Gallop	Indian Charlie	2:02⅒
1999	Charismatic (Neck)	Chris Antley	Menifee	Cat Thief	2:03⅕

Kentucky Derby *(Cont.)*

Year	Winner (Margin)	Jockey	Second	Third	Time
2000	Fusaichi Pegasus (1½)	Kent Desormeaux	Aptitude	Impeachment	2:01.12
2001	Monarchos (4¾)	Jorge Chavez	Invisible Ink	Congaree	1:59.97
2002	War Emblem (4)	Victor Espinoza	Proud Citizen	Perfect Drift	2:01.13
2003	Funny Cide (1¾)	Jose Santos	Empire Maker	Peace Rules	2:01.19
2004	Smarty Jones (2¾)	Stewart Elliott	Lion Heart	Imperialism	2:04.06
2005	Giacomo (½)	Mike Smith	Closing Argument	Afleet Alex	2:02.75
2006	Barbaro (1½)	Edgar Prado	Bluegrass Cat	Steppenwolfer	2:01.36
2007	Street Sense (2¼)	Calvin Borel	Hard Spun	Curlin	2:02.17
2008	Big Brown (4¾)	Kent Desormeaux	Eight Belles	Denis of Cork	2:01.82
2009	Mine That Bird (6¾)	Calvin Borel	Pioneerof the Nile	Musket Man	2:02.66
2010	Super Saver (2½)	Calvin Borel	Ice Box	Paddy O'Prado	2:04.45

Note: Distance: 1½ miles (1875–95), 1¼ miles (1896–present).

Preakness

Run at Pimlico Race Course, Baltimore, Md., two weeks after the Kentucky Derby.

Year	Winner (Margin)	Jockey	Second	Third	Time
1873	Survivor (10)	G. Barbee	John Boulger	Artist	2:43
1874	Culpepper (¾)	W. Donohue	King Amadeus	Scratch	2:56½
1875	Tom Ochiltree (2)	L. Hughes	Viator	Bay Final	2:43½
1876	Shirley (4)	G. Barbee	Rappahannock	Algerine	2:44¾
1877	Cloverbrook (4)	C. Holloway	Bombast	Lucifer	2:45½
1878	Duke of Magenta (6)	C. Holloway	Bayard	Albert	2:41¾
1879	Harold (3)	L. Hughes	Jericho	Rochester	2:40½
1880	Grenada (¾)	L. Hughes	Oden	Emily F.	2:40½
1881	Saunterer (½)	T. Costello	Compensation	Baltic	2:40½
1882	Vanguard (Neck)	T. Costello	Heck	Col Watson	2:44½
1883*	Jacobus (4)	G. Barbee	Parnell		2:42½
1884*	Knight of Ellerslie (2)	S. Fisher	Welcher		2:39½
1885	Tecumseh (2)	Jim McLaughlin	Wickham	John C.	2:49
1886	The Bard (3)	S. Fisher	Eurus	Elkwood	2:45
1887	Dunboyne (1)	W. Donohue	Mahoney	Raymond	2:39½
1888	Refund (3)	F. Littlefield	Judge Murray	Glendale	2:49
1889*	Buddhist (8)	W. Anderson	Japhet		2:17½
1890	Montague (3)	W. Martin	Philosophy	Barrister	2:36¾
1894	Assignee (3)	Fred Taral	Potentate	Ed Kearney	1:49¼
1895	Belmar (1)	Fred Taral	April Fool	Sue Kittie	1:50½
1896	Margrave (1)	H. Griffin	Hamilton II	Intermission	1:51
1897	Paul Kauvar (1½)	C. Thorpe	Elkins	On Deck	1:51¼
1898	Sly Fox (2)	C. W. Simms	The Huguenot	Nuto	1:49⅗
1899	Half Time (1)	R. Clawson	Filigrane	Lackland	1:47
1900	Hindus (Head)	H. Spencer	Sarmation	Ten Candles	1:48⅖
1901	The Parader (2)	F. Landry	Sadie S.	Dr. Barlow	1:47⅕
1902	Old England (Nose)	L. Jackson	Major Daingerfield	Namtor	1:45⅘
1903	Flocarline (½)	W. Gannon	Mackey Dwyer	Rightful	1:44⅘
1904	Bryn Mawr (1)	E. Hildebrand	Wotan	Dolly Spanker	1:44⅕
1905	Cairngorm (Head)	W. Davis	Kiamesha	Coy Maid	1:45⅘
1906	Whimsical (4)	Walter Miller	Content	Larabie	1:45
1907	Don Enrique (1)	G. Mountain	Ethon	Zambesi	1:45⅖
1908	Royal Tourist (4)	E. Dugan	Live Wire	Robert Cooper	1:46⅖
1909	Effendi (1)	Willie Doyle	Fashion Plate	Hilltop	1:39⅘
1910	Layminster (½)	R. Estep	Dalhousie	Sager	1:40⅗
1911	Watervale (1)	E. Dugan	Zeus	The Nigger	1:51
1912	Colonel Holloway (5)	C. Turner	Bwana Tumbo	Tipsand	1:56⅗
1913	Buskin (Neck)	J. Butwell	Kleburne	Barnegat	1:53⅖
1914	Holiday (¾)	A. Schuttinger	Brave Cunarder	Defendum	1:53⅘
1915	Rhine Maiden (1½)	Douglas Hoffman	Half Rock	Runes	1:58
1916	Damrosch (1½)	Linus McAtee	Greenwood	Achievement	1:54⅘
1917	Kalitan (2)	E. Haynes	Al M. Dick	Kentucky Boy	1:54⅖
1918*	War Cloud (¾)	Johnny Loftus	Sunny Slope	Lanius	1:53⅗
1918*	Jack Hare, Jr (2)	C. Peak	The Porter	Kate Bright	1:53⅖
1919	Sir Barton (4)	Johnny Loftus	Eternal	Sweep On	1:53
1920	Man o' War (1½)	Clarence Kummer	Upset	Wildair	1:51⅗

Preakness (*Cont.*)

Year	Winner (Margin)	Jockey	Second	Third	Time
1921	Broomspun (¾)	F. Coltiletti	Polly Ann	Jeg	1:54⅕
1922	Pillory (Head)	L. Morris	Hea	June Grass	1:51⅗
1923	Vigil (1¼)	B. Marinelli	General Thatcher	Rialto	1:53⅗
1924	Nellie Morse (1½)	J. Merimee	Transmute	Mad Play	1:57⅕
1925	Coventry (4)	Clarence Kummer	Backbone	Almadel	1:59
1926	Display (Head)	J. Maiben	Blondin	Mars	1:59⅘
1927	Bostonian (½)	A. Abel	Sir Harry	Whiskery	2:01⅗
1928	Victorian (Nose)	Sonny Workman	Toro	Solace	2:00⅕
1929	Dr. Freeland (1)	Louis Schaefer	Minotaur	African	2:01⅗
1930	Gallant Fox (¾)	Earl Sande	Crack Brigade	Snowflake	2:00⅗
1931	Mate (1½)	G. Ellis	Twenty Grand	Ladder	1:59
1932	Burgoo King (Head)	E. James	Tick On	Boatswain	1:59⅘
1933	Head Play (4)	Charles Kurtsinger	Ladysman	Utopian	2:02
1934	High Quest (Nose)	R. Jones	Cavalcade	Discovery	1:58⅕
1935	Omaha (6)	Willie Saunders	Firethorn	Psychic Bid	1:58⅖
1936	Bold Venture (Nose)	George Woolf	Granville	Jean Bart	1:59
1937	War Admiral (Head)	Charles Kurtsinger	Pompoon	Flying Scot	1:58⅖
1938	Dauber (7)	M. Peters	Cravat	Menow	1:59⅘
1939	Challedon (1¼)	George Seabo	Gilded Knight	Volitant	1:59⅘
1940	Bimelech (3)	F. A. Smith	Mioland	Gallahadion	1:58⅗
1941	Whirlaway (5½)	Eddie Arcaro	King Cole	Our Boots	1:58⅘
1942	Alsab (1)	B. James	Requested Sun Again	(dead heat for second)	1:57
1943	Count Fleet (8)	Johnny Longden	Blue Swords	Vincentive	1:57⅖
1944	Pensive (¾)	Conn McCreary	Platter	Stir Up	1:59⅕
1945	Polynesian (2½)	W. D. Wright	Hoop Jr.	Darby Dieppe	1:58⅘
1946	Assault (Neck)	Warren Mehrtens	Lord Boswell	Hampden	2:01⅖
1947	Faultless (1¼)	Doug Dodson	On Trust	Phalanx	1:59
1948	Citation (5½)	Eddie Arcaro	Vulcan's Forge	Boyard	2:02⅖
1949	Capot (Head)	Ted Atkinson	Palestinian	Noble Impulse	1:56
1950	Hill Prince (5)	Eddie Arcaro	Middleground	Dooley	1:59⅕
1951	Bold (7)	Eddie Arcaro	Counterpoint	Alerted	1:56⅖
1952	Blue Man (3½)	Conn McCreary	Jampol	One Count	1:57⅖
1953	Native Dancer (Neck)	Eric Guerin	Jamie K.	Royal Bay Gem	1:57⅘
1954	Hasty Road (Neck)	Johnny Adams	Correlation	Hasseyampa	1:57⅖
1955	Nashua (1)	Eddie Arcaro	Saratoga	Traffic Judge	1:54⅗
1956	Fabius (¾)	Bill Hartack	Needles	No Regrets	1:58⅖
1957	Bold Ruler (2)	Eddie Arcaro	Iron Liege	Inside Tract	1:56⅕
1958	Tim Tam (1½)	I. Valenzuela	Lincoln Road	Gone Fishin'	1:57⅕
1959	Royal Orbit (4)	William Harmatz	Sword Dancer	Dunce	1:57
1960	Bally Ache (4)	Bobby Ussery	Victoria Park	Celtic Ash	1:57⅗
1961	Carry Back (¾)	Johnny Sellers	Globemaster	Crozier	1:57⅗
1962	Greek Money (Nose)	John Rotz	Ridan	Roman Line	1:56⅕
1963	Candy Spots (3½)	Bill Shoemaker	Chateaugay	Never Bend	1:56⅕
1964	Northern Dancer (2¼)	Bill Hartack	The Scoundrel	Hill Rise	1:56⅘
1965	Tom Rolfe (Neck)	Ron Turcotte	Dapper Dan	Hail to All	1:56⅕
1966	Kauai King (1¾)	Don Brumfield	Stupendous	Amberoid	1:55⅖
1967	Damascus (2¼)	Bill Shoemaker	In Reality	Proud Clarion	1:55⅕
1968	Forward Pass (6)	I. Valenzuela	Out of the Way	Nodouble	1:56⅘
1969	Majestic Prince (Head)	Bill Hartack	Arts and Letters	Jay Ray	1:55⅗
1970	Personality (Neck)	Eddie Belmonte	My Dad George	Silent Screen	1:56⅕
1971	Canonero II (1½)	Gustavo Avila	Eastern Fleet	Jim French	1:54
1972	Bee Bee Bee (1¼)	Eldon Nelson	No Le Hace	Key to the Mint	1:55⅗
1973	Secretariat (2½)	Ron Turcotte	Sham	Our Native	1:54⅖
1974	Little Current (7)	Miguel Rivera	Neapolitan Way	Cannonade	1:54⅗
1975	Master Derby (1)	Darrel McHargue	Foolish Pleasure	Diabolo	1:56⅖
1976	Elocutionist (3)	John Lively	Play the Red	Bold Forbes	1:55
1977	Seattle Slew (1½)	Jean Cruguet	Iron Constitution	Run Dusty Run	1:54⅖
1978	Affirmed (Neck)	Steve Cauthen	Alydar	Believe It	1:54⅖
1979	Spectacular Bid (5½)	Ron Franklin	Golden Act	Screen King	1:54⅕
1980	Codex (4¾)	Angel Cordero Jr.	Genuine Risk	Colonel Moran	1:54⅕
1981	Pleasant Colony (1)	Jorge Velasquez	Bold Ego	Paristo	1:54⅗
1982	Aloma's Ruler (½)	Jack Kaenel	Linkage	Cut Away	1:55⅖
1983	Deputed Testamony (2¾)	Donald Miller Jr.	Desert Wine	High Honors	1:55⅖
1984	Gate Dancer (1½)	Angel Cordero Jr.	Play On	Fight Over	1:53⅗
1985	Tank's Prospect (Head)	Pat Day	Chief's Crown	Eternal Prince	1:53⅖
1986	Snow Chief (4)	Alex Solis	Ferdinand	Broad Brush	1:54⅘
1987	Alysheba (½)	Chris McCarron	Bet Twice	Cryptoclearance	1:55⅘

Preakness (*Cont.*)

Year	Winner (Margin)	Jockey	Second	Third	Time
1988	Risen Star (1¼)	E. Delahoussaye	Brian's Time	Winning Colors	1:56⅕
1989	Sunday Silence (Nose)	Pat Valenzuela	Easy Goer	Rock Point	1:53⅘
1990	Summer Squall (2¼)	Pat Day	Unbridled	Mister Frisky	1:53⅗
1991	Hansel (Head)	Jerry Bailey	Corporate Report	Mane Minister	1:54
1992	Pine Bluff (¾)	Chris McCarron	Alydeed	Casual Lies	1:55⅗
1993	Prairie Bayou (½)	Mike Smith	Cherokee Run	El Bakan	1:56⅗
1994	Tabasco Cat (¾)	Pat Day	Go For Gin	Concern	1:56⅖
1995	Timber Country (½)	Pat Day	Oliver's Twist	Thunder Gulch	1:54⅖
1996	Louis Quatorze (3¼)	Pat Day	Skip Away	Editor's Note	1:53⅖
1997	Silver Charm (Head)	Gary Stevens	Free House	Captain Bodgit	1:54⅖
1998	Real Quiet (2¼)	Kent Desormeaux	Victory Gallop	Classic Cat	1:54⅗
1999	Charismatic (1½)	Chris Antley	Menifee	Badge	1:55⅕
2000	Red Bullet (3¾)	Jerry Bailey	Fusaichi Pegasus	Impeachment	1:56.04
2001	Point Given (2¼)	Gary Stevens	A P Valentine	Congaree	1:55.51
2002	War Emblem (¾)	Victor Espinoza	Magic Weisner	Proud Citizen	1:56.36
2003	Funny Cide (9¾)	Jose Santos	Midway Road	Scrimshaw	1:55.61
2004	Smarty Jones (11½)	Stewart Elliott	Rock Hard Ten	Eddington	1:55.59
2005	Afleet Alex (7)	Jeremy Rose	Scrappy T	Giacomo	1:55.04
2006	Bernardini (5¼)	Javier Castellano	Sweetnorthernsaint	Hemingway's Key	1:54.65
2007	Curlin (Head)	Robby Albarado	Street Sense	Hard Spun	1:53.46
2008	Big Brown (5¼)	Kent Desormeaux	Macho Again	Icabad Crane	1:54.80
2009	Rachel Alexandra (1)	Calvin Borel	Mine That Bird	Musket Man	1:55.08
2010	Lookin at Lucky (1¾)	Martin Garcia	First Dude	Jackson Bend	1:55.47

*Preakness was a two-horse race in 1883, '84 and '89. It was not run 1891–1893; and in 1918, it was run in two divisions.
Note: Distance: 1½ miles (1873–88), 1¼ miles (1889), 1½ miles (1890), 1⅟₁₆ miles (1894–1900), 1 mile and 70 yards (1901–1907), 1⅟₁₆ miles (1908), 1 mile (1909–10), 1⅛ miles (1911–24), 1³⁄₁₆ miles (1925–present).

Belmont

Run at Belmont Park, Elmont, NY, three weeks after the Preakness Stakes. Held previously at two locations in the Bronx (NY): Jerome Park (1867–1889) and Morris Park (1890–1904).

Year	Winner (Margin)	Jockey	Second	Third	Time
1867	Ruthless (Head)	J. Gilpatrick	De Courcy	Rivoli	3:05
1868	General Duke (2)	R. Swim	Northumberland	Fannie Ludlow	3:02
1869	Fenian (Unknown)	C. Miller	Glenelg	Invercauld	3:04¼
1870	Kingfisher (½)	E. Brown	Foster	Midday	2:59½
1871	Harry Bassett (3)	W. Miller	Stockwood	By-the-Sea	2:56
1872	Joe Daniels (¾)	James Rowe	Meteor	Shylock	2:58¼
1873	Springbok (4)	James Rowe	Count d'Orsay	Strachino	3:01¾
1874	Saxon (Neck)	G. Barbee	Grinstead	Aaron Pennington	2:39½
1875	Calvin (2)	R. Swim	Aristides	Milner	2:40¼
1876	Algerine (Head)	W. Donahue	Fiddlestick	Barricade	2:40½
1877	Cloverbrook (1)	C. Holloway	Loiterer	Baden-Baden	2:46
1878	Duke of Magenta (2)	L. Hughes	Bramble	Sparta	2:43½
1879	Spendthrift (5)	S. Evans	Monitor	Jericho	2:42¾
1880	Grenada (½)	L. Hughes	Ferncliffe	Turenne	2:47
1881	Saunterer (Neck)	T. Costello	Eole	Baltic	2:47
1882	Forester (5)	James McLaughlin	Babcock	Wyoming	2:43
1883	George Kinney (2)	James McLaughlin	Trombone	Renegade	2:42½
1884	Panique (½)	James McLaughlin	Knight of Ellerslie	Himalaya	2:42
1885	Tyrant (3½)	Paul Duffy	St. Augustine	Tecumseh	2:43
1886	Inspector B (1)	James McLaughlin	The Bard	Linden	2:41
1887*	Hanover (28-32)	James McLaughlin	Oneko		2:43½
1888*	Sir Dixon (12)	James McLaughlin	Prince Royal		2:40¼
1889	Eric (Head)	W. Hayward	Diable	Zephyrus	2:47
1890	Burlington (1)	S. Barnes	Devotee	Padishah	2:07¾
1891	Foxford (Neck)	E. Garrison	Montana	Laurestan	2:08¾
1892*	Patron (Unknown)	W. Hayward	Shellbark		2:17
1893	Comanche (Head)	Willie Simms	Dr. Rice	Rainbow	1:53¼
1894	Henry of Navarre (2-4)	Willie Simms	Prig	Assignee	1:56½
1895	Belmar (Head)	Fred Taral	Counter Tenor	Nanki Pooh	2:11½
1896	Hastings (Neck)	H. Griffin	Handspring	Hamilton II	2:24½
1897	Scottish Chieftain (1)	J. Scherrer	On Deck	Octagon	2:23¼
1898	Bowling Brook (8)	P. Littlefield	Previous	Hamburg	2:32
1899	Jean Bereaud (Head)	R. R. Clawson	Half Time	Glengar	2:23

Belmont (*Cont.*)

Year	Winner (Margin)	Jockey	Second	Third	Time
1900	Ildrim (Head)	N. Turner	Petrucio	Missionary	2:21½
1901	Commando (½)	H. Spencer	The Parader	All Green	2:21
1902	Masterman (2)	John Bullmann	Ranald	King Hanover	2:22½
1903	Africander (2)	John Bullmann	Whorler	Red Knight	2:23⅕
1904	Delhi (3½)	George Odom	Graziallo	Rapid Water	2:06⅗
1905	Tanya (1/2)	E. Hildebrand	Blandy	Hot Shot	2:08
1906	Burgomaster (4)	L. Lyne	The Quail	Accountant	2:20
1907	Peter Pan (1)	G. Mountain	Superman	Frank Gill	Unknown
1908	Colin (Head)	Joe Notter	Fair Play	King James	Unknown
1909	Joe Madden (8)	E. Dugan	Wise Mason	Donald MacDonald	2:21⅗
1910*	Sweep (6)	J. Butwell	Duke of Ormonde		2:22
1913	Prince Eugene (½)	Roscoe Troxler	Rock View	Flying Fairy	2:18
1914	Luke McLuke (8)	M. Buxton	Gainer	Charlestonian	2:20
1915	The Finn (4)	G. Byrne	Half Rock	Pebbles	2:18⅗
1916	Friar Rock (3)	E. Haynes	Spur	Churchill	2:22
1917	Hourless (10)	J. Butwell	Skeptic	Wonderful	2:17⅘
1918	Johren (2)	Frank Robinson	War Cloud	Cum Sah	2:20⅖
1919	Sir Barton (5)	Johnny Loftus	Sweep On	Natural Bridge	2:17⅖
1920*	Man o' War (20)	Clarence Kummer	Donnacona		2:14⅕
1921	Grey Lag (3)	Earl Sande	Sporting Blood	Leonardo II	2:16⅘
1922	Pillory (2)	C. H. Miller	Snob II	Hea	2:18⅘
1923	Zev (1½)	Earl Sande	Chickvale	Rialto	2:19
1924	Mad Play (2)	Earl Sande	Mr. Mutt	Modest	2:18⅘
1925	American Flag (8)	Albert Johnson	Dangerous	Swope	2:16⅘
1926	Crusader (1)	Albert Johnson	Espino	Haste	2:32⅕
1927	Chance Shot (1½)	Earl Sande	Bois de Rose	Flambino	2:32⅖
1928	Vito (3)	Clarence Kummer	Genie	Diavolo	2:33⅕
1929	Blue Larkspur (¾)	Mack Garner	African	Jack High	2:32⅘
1930	Gallant Fox (3)	Earl Sande	Whichone	Questionnaire	2:31⅗
1931	Twenty Grand (10)	Charles Kurtsinger	Sun Meadow	Jamestown	2:29⅗
1932	Faireno (1½)	T. Malley	Osculator	Flag Pole	2:32⅘
1933	Hurryoff (1½)	Mack Garner	Nimbus	Union	2:32⅗
1934	Peace Chance (6)	W. D. Wright	High Quest	Good Goods	2:29⅕
1935	Omaha (1½)	Willie Saunders	Firethorn	Rosemont	2:30⅗
1936	Granville (Nose)	James Stout	Mr. Bones	Hollyrood	2:30
1937	War Admiral (3)	Charles Kurtsinger	Sceneshifter	Vamoose	2:28⅗
1938	Pasteurized (Neck)	James Stout	Dauber	Cravat	2:29⅖
1939	Johnstown (5)	James Stout	Belay	Gilded Knight	2:29⅗
1940	Bimelech (¾)	F. A. Smith	Your Chance	Andy K	2:29⅗
1941	Whirlaway (2½)	Eddie Arcaro	Robert Morris	Yankee Chance	2:31
1942	Shut Out (2)	Eddie Arcaro	Alsab	Lochinvar	2:29⅕
1943	Count Fleet (25)	Johnny Longden	Fairy Manhurst	Deseronto	2:28⅕
1944	Bounding Home (½)	G. L. Smith	Pensive	Bull Dandy	2:32⅕
1945	Pavot (5)	Eddie Arcaro	Wildlife	Jeep	2:30⅕
1946	Assault (3)	Warren Mehrtens	Natchez	Cable	2:30⅘
1947	Phalanx (5)	R. Donoso	Tide Rips	Tailspin	2:29⅖
1948	Citation (8)	Eddie Arcaro	Better Self	Escadru	2:28⅕
1949	Capot (½)	Ted Atkinson	Ponder	Palestinian	2:30⅕
1950	Middleground (1)	William Boland	Lights Up	Mr. Trouble	2:28⅗
1951	Counterpoint (4)	D. Gorman	Battlefield	Battle Morn	2:29
1952	One Count (2½)	Eddie Arcaro	Blue Man	Armageddon	2:30⅕
1953	Native Dancer (Neck)	Eric Guerin	Jamie K.	Royal Bay Gem	2:38⅗
1954	High Gun (Neck)	Eric Guerin	Fisherman	Limelight	2:30⅘
1955	Nashua (9)	Eddie Arcaro	Blazing Count	Portersville	2:29
1956	Needles (Neck)	David Erb	Career Boy	Fabius	2:29⅘
1957	Gallant Man (8)	Bill Shoemaker	Inside Tract	Bold Ruler	2:26⅗
1958	Cavan (6)	Pete Anderson	Tim Tam	Flamingo	2:30⅕
1959	Sword Dancer (¾)	Bill Shoemaker	Bagdad	Royal Orbit	2:28⅖
1960	Celtic Ash (5½)	Bill Hartack	Venetian Way	Disperse	2:29⅗
1961	Sherluck (2¼)	Braulio Baeza	Globemaster	Guadalcanal	2:29⅕
1962	Jaipur (Nose)	Bill Shoemaker	Admiral's Voyage	Crimson Satan	2:28⅘
1963	Chateaugay (2½)	Braulio Baeza	Candy Spots	Choker	2:30⅕
1964	Quadrangle (2)	Manuel Ycaza	Roman Brother	Northern Dancer	2:28⅖
1965	Hail to All (Neck)	John Sellers	Tom Rolfe	First Family	2:28⅖
1966	Amberold (2½)	William Boland	Buffle	Advocator	2:29⅗
1967	Damascus (2½)	Bill Shoemaker	Cool Reception	Gentleman James	2:28⅘

Belmont *(Cont.)*

Year	Winner (Margin)	Jockey	Second	Third	Time
1968	Stage Door Johnny (1¼)	Hellodoro Gustines	Forward Pass	Call Me Prince	2:27⅕
1969	Arts and Letters (5½)	Braulio Baeza	Majestic Prince	Dike	2:28⅘
1970	High Echelon (¾)	John L. Rotz	Needles N Pins	Naskra	2:34
1971	Pass Catcher (¾)	Walter Blum	Jim French	Bold Reason	2:30⅖
1972	Riva Ridge (7)	Ron Turcotte	Ruritania	Cloudy Dawn	2:28
1973	Secretariat (31)	Ron Turcotte	Twice a Prince	My Gallant	2:24
1974	Little Current (7)	Miguel A. Rivera	Jolly Johu	Cannonade	2:29⅕
1975	Avatar (Neck)	Bill Shoemaker	Foolish Pleasure	Master Derby	2:28⅕
1976	Bold Forbes (Neck)	Angel Cordero Jr.	McKenzie Bridge	Great Contractor	2:29
1977	Seattle Slew (4)	Jean Cruguet	Run Dusty Run	Sanhedrin	2:29⅗
1978	Affirmed (Head)	Steve Cauthen	Alydar	Darby Creek Road	2:26⅘
1979	Coastal (3¼)	Ruben Hernandez	Golden Act	Spectacular Bid	2:28⅗
1980	Temperence Hill (2)	Eddie Maple	Genuine Risk	Rockhill Native	2:29⅘
1981	Summing (Neck)	George Martens	Highland Blade	Pleasant Colony	2:29
1982	Conquistador Cielo (14½)	Laffit Pincay, Jr.	Gato Del Sol	Illuminate	2:28⅕
1983	Caveat (3½)	Laffit Pincay Jr.	Slew o'Gold	Barberstown	2:27⅘
1984	Swale (4)	Laffit Pincay Jr.	Pine Circle	Morning Bob	2:27⅕
1985	Creme Fraiche (½)	Eddie Maple	Stephan's Odyssey	Chief's Crown	2:27
1986	Danzig Connection (1¼)	Chris McCarron	Johns Treasure	Ferdinand	2:29⅘
1987	Bet Twice (14)	Craig Perret	Cryptoclearance	Gulch	2:28⅕
1988	Risen Star (14¾)	Eddie Delahoussaye	Kingpost	Brian's Time	2:26⅖
1989	Easy Goer (8)	Pat Day	Sunday Silence	Le Voyageur	2:26
1990	Go and Go (8¼)	Michael Kinane	Thirty Six Red	Baron de Vaux	2:27⅕
1991	Hansel (Head)	Jerry Bailey	Strike the Gold	Mane Minister	2:28
1992	A.P. Indy (¾)	Eddie Delahoussaye	My Memoirs	Pine Bluff	2:26
1993	Colonial Affair (2¼)	Julie Krone	Kissin Kris	Wild Gale	2:29⅘
1994	Tabasco Cat (2)	Pat Day	Go For Gin	Strodes Creek	2:26⅘
1995	Thunder Gulch (2)	Gary Stevens	Star Standard	Citadeed	2:32
1996	Editor's Note (1)	Rene Douglas	Skip Away	My Flag	2:28⅘
1997	Touch Gold (¾)	Chris McCarron	Silver Charm	Free House	2:28⅘
1998	Victory Gallop (Nose)	Gary Stevens	Real Quiet	Thomas Jo	2:28⅘
1999	Lemon Drop Kid (Head)	Jose Santos	Vision and Verse	Charismatic	2:27⅘
2000	Commendable (1½)	Pat Day	Aptitude	Unshaded	2:31.19
2001	Point Given (12¼)	Gary Stevens	A P Valentine	Monarchos	2:26.56
2002	Sarava (½)	Edgar Prado	Medaglia d'Oro	Sunday Break	2:29.71
2003	Empire Maker (¾)	Jerry Bailey	Ten Most Wanted	Funny Cide	2:28.26
2004	Birdstone (1)	Edgar Prado	Smarty Jones	Royal Assault	2:27.59
2005	Afleet Alex(4¾)	Jeremy Rose	Andromeda's Hero	Nolan's Cat	2:28.75
2006	Jazil (1¼)	Fernando Jara	Bluegrass Cat	Sunriver	2:27.86
2007	Rags to Riches (Head)	John Velazquez	Curlin	Tiago	2:28.74
2008	Da' Tara (5¼)	Alan Garcia	Denis of Cork	Ready's Echo	2:29.65
2009	Summer Bird (2¾)	Kent Desormeaux	Dunkirk	Mine That Bird	2:27.54
2010	Drosselmeyer (1¾)	Mike Smith	Fly Down	First Dude	2:31.57

*Belmont was a two-horse race in 1887, '88, '92, 1910 and '20; and was not held in 1911–1912.
Note: Distance: 1 mile 5 furlongs (1867–89), 1¼ miles (1890–1905), 1⅜ miles (1906–25), 1½ miles (1926–present).

Triple Crown Winners

Year	Horse	Jockey	Owner	Trainer
1919	Sir Barton	John Loftus	J. K. L. Ross	H. G. Bedwell
1930	Gallant Fox	Earle Sande	Belair Stud	James Fitzsimmons
1935	Omaha	William Saunders	Belair Stud	James Fitzsimmons
1937	War Admiral	Charles Kurtsinger	Samuel D. Riddle	George Conway
1941	Whirlaway	Eddie Arcaro	Calumet Farm	Ben Jones
1943	Count Fleet	John Longden	Mrs J. D. Hertz	Don Cameron
1946	Assault	Warren Mehrtens	King Ranch	Max Hirsch
1948	Citation	Eddie Arcaro	Calumet Farm	Jimmy Jones
1973	Secretariat	Ron Turcotte	Meadow Stable	Lucien Laurin
1977	Seattle Slew	Jean Cruguet	Karen L. Taylor	William H. Turner Jr.
1978	Affirmed	Steve Cauthen	Harbor View Farm	Laz Barrera

Boxing

Floyd Mayweather Jr. (r.) kept his unbeaten streak alive when he scored a unanimous decision over "Sugar" Shane Mosley in one of 2010's biggest bouts

FOR THE RECORD • 2009—2010

Current World Champions

Division	Weight Limit	WBA Champion	WBC Champion	IBF Champion
Heavyweight	None	David Haye	Vitali Klitschko	Wladimir Klitschko
Cruiserweight	200	Guillermo Jones	Krzysztof Wlodarczyk	Steve Cunningham
Light Heavyweight	175	Beibut Shumenov	Jean Pascal	Tavoris Cloud
Super Middleweight	168	Andre Ward*	Mikkel Kessler	Lucian Bute
Middleweight	160	Felix Sturm	Kelly Pavlik	Sebastian Sylvester
Super Welterweight	154	Miguel Cotto	Vacant	Cory Spinks
Welterweight	147	Vyacheslav Senchenko	Andre Berto	Dejan Zavec
Super Lightweight	140	Amir Khan	Devon Alexander	Juan Urango
Lightweight	135	Juan Manuel Marquez*	Humberto Soto	Vacant
Super Featherweight	130	Takashi Uchiyama	Vitaly Tajbert	Robert Guerrero
Featherweight	126	Yuriorkis Gamboa*	Elio Rojas*	Cristobal Cruz
Super Bantamweight	122	P. Kratingdaenggym	Toshiaki Nishioka	Cellestino Caballero
Bantamweight	118	Anselmo Moreno	Fernando Montiel	Yohnny Perez
Super Flyweight	115	Vic Darchinyan*	Vic Darchinyan*	Simphiwe Nongqayi
Flyweight	112	Daiki Kameda	Pongsaklek Wonjongkam	Vacant
Light Flyweight	108	Giovanni Segura	Omar Nino	Brian Viloria
Strawweight	105	Roman Gonzalez	Oley. Sithsamerchai	Nkosinathi Joyi

Note: WBA=World Boxing Association; WBC=World Boxing Council; IBF=International Boxing Federation. Champions as of October 1, 2010. *Denotes unified, mulit-title or super champion.

Title and Major Boxing Matches of Late 2009 and 2010

Abbreviations: WBC=World Boxing Council; WBA= World Boxing Association; IBF=International Boxing Federation; KO=knockout; TKO=technical knockout; UD=unanimous decision; SD=split decision; DQ=disqualification; MD=majority decision; TD=technical decision. Bouts from Oct. 1, 2009 to Oct. 1, 2010.

	Date	Winner	Loser	Result	Title/Org.	Site
HEAVYWEIGHT	Dec 12	Vitali Klitschko	Kevin Johnson	UD	WBC	Berne, Switzerland
	Mar 20	Wladimir Klitschko	Eddie Chambers	KO 12	IBF	Dusseldorf, Germany
	Apr 3	David Haye	John Ruiz	TKO 9	WBA	Manchester, England
	May 29	Vitali Klitschko	Alberto Sosnowski	KO 10	WBC	Gelsenkirchen, Germany
	Sept 11	Wladimir Klitschko	Samuel Peter	TKO 10	IBF	Frankfurt, Germany
CRUISERWEIGHT	Nov 21	Zsolt Erdei	Giacobbe Fragomeni	MD	WBC	Kiel, Germany
	May 15	Krzysztof Wlodarczyk	Giacobbe Fragomeni	TKO 8	WBC	Lodz, Poland
	June 5	Steve Cunningham	Troy Ross	TKO 4	IBF	Neubrandenburg, Germany
	July 3	Steve Herelius	Firat Arslan	TKO 11	WBA	Stuttgart, Germany
	Sept 25	Krzysztof Wlodarczyk	Jason Robinson	UD	WBC	Warsaw, Poland
LIGHT HEAVYWEIGHT	Nov 7	Chad Dawson	Glen Johnson	UD	WBC	Hartford, Connecticut
	Dec 11	Jean Pascal	Adrian Diaconu	UD	WBC	Montreal
	Jan 29	Beibut Shumenov	Gabriel Campillo	SD	WBA	Las Vegas, Nevada
	July 23	Beibut Shumenov	Viacheslav Uzelkov	UD	WBA	Lemoore, California
	Aug 7	Tavoris Cloud	Glen Johnson	UD	IBF	St. Louis, Missouri
	Aug 14	Jean Pascal	Chad Dawson	TD 11	WBC	Montreal, Canada
SUPER MIDDLEWEIGHT	Oct 17	Carl Froch	Andre Dirrell	SD	WBC	Nottingham, England
	Nov 28	Lucian Bute	Librado Andrade	KO 4	IBF	Quebec City, Canada
	Apr 17	Lucian Bute	Edison Miranda	TKO 3	IBF	Montreal, Canada
	Apr 24	Mikkel Kessler	Carl Froch	UD	WBC	Herning, Denmark
	June 19	Andre Ward	Allan Green	UD	WBA	Oakland, California
MIDDLEWEIGHT	Dec 19	Sebastian Zbik	Emanuele Della Rossa	SD	WBC	Schwerin, Germany
	Dec 19	Kelly Pavlik	Miguel Espino	TKO 5	WBC	Youngstown, Ohio
	Jan 30	Sebastian Sylvester	Billy Lyell	TKO 10	IBF	Neubrandenburg, Germany
	Apr 17	Sebastian Zbik	Domenico Spada	UD	WBC	Magdeburg, Germany
	Apr 17	Sergio Martinez	Kelly Pavlik	UD	WBC	Atlantic City, New Jersey
	June 5	Sebastian Sylvester	Roman Karmazin	S.Draw	IBF	Neubrandenburg, Germany
	July 31	Sebastian Zbik	Jorge Heiland	UD	WBC	Hamburg, Germany
	Aug 14	Gennady Golovkin	Milton Nunez	KO 1	WBA	Panama City, Panama
	Sept 4	Felix Sturm	Giovanni Lorenzo	UD	WBA	Cologne, Germany

	Date	Winner	Loser	Result	Title/Org.	Site
JR. MIDDLEWT. (SUPER WELTERT.)	Dec 29	Nobuhiro Ishida	Oney Valdez	UD	WBA	Osaka, Japan
	June 5	Miguel Cotto	Yuir Foreman	TKO 9	WBA	Bronx, New York
	July 31	Dimitri Sartison	Khoren Gevor	UD	WBA	Hamburg, Germany
	Aug 7	Cornelius Bundgrage	Cory Spinks	TKO 5	IBF	St. Louis, Missouri
WELTERWEIGHT	Oct 3	Vyacheslav Senchenko	Motoki Sasaki	UD	WBA	Donetsk, Ukraine
	Dec 11	Dejan Zavec	Isaac Hlathshwayo	TKO 3	IBF	Johannesburg, S. Africa
	Apr 9	Dejan Zavec	Rodolfo Martinez	TKO 12	IBF	Ljubljana, Slovenia
	Apr 10	Andre Berto	Carlos Quintana	TKO 9	WBC	Sunrise, Florida
	May 1	Floyd Mayweather Jr.	Shane Mosley	UD	No Title	Las Vegas, Nevada
	May 28	Souleymane M'Baye	Antonin Decarie	UD	WBA	Levallois-Perret, France
	Aug 30	Vyacheslav Senchenko	Charlie Jose Navarro	UD	WBA	Donetsk, Ukraine
	Sept 4	Dejan Zavec	Rafal Jackiewicz	MD	IBF	Ljubljana, Slovenia
SUPER LIGHTWEIGHT (JUNIOR WELTERWEIGHT)	Mar 6	Devon Alexander	Juan Urango	TKO 8	WBC/IBF	Uncasville, Connecticut
	Mar 27	Marcos Maidana	Victor Manuel Cayo	KO 6	WBA	Las Vegas, Nevada
	May 15	Amir Khan	Paulie Malignaggi	TKO 11	WBA	New York, New York
	Aug 7	Devon Alexander	Andriy Kotelnik	UD	WBC/IBF	St. Louis, Missouri
	Aug 28	Marcos Maidana	DeMarcus Corley	UD	WBA	Buenos Aires, Argentina
LIGHTWEIGHT	Oct 31	Antonio DeMarco	Jose Alfaro	TKO 10	WBC	Las Vegas, Nevada
	Dec 19	Edwin Valero	Hector Velazquez	TKO 6	WBC	La Guaira, Venezuela
	Feb 6	Edwin Valero	Antonio DeMarco	TKO 10	WBC	Monterrey, Mexico
	Mar 13	Humberto Soto	David Diaz	UD	WBC	Arlington, Texas
	Mar 27	Joan Guzman	Ali Funeka	SD	IBF	Las Vegas, Nevada
	May 15	Humberto Soto	Ricardo Dominguez	UD	WBC	Los Mochis, Mexico
	May 29	Miguel Acosta	Paulus Moses	KO 6	WBA	Windhoek, Namibia
	July 31	Juan Manuel Marquez	Juan Diaz	UD	WBA	Las Vegas, Nevada
	Aug 14	Miguel Vazquez	Kim Ji-Hoon	UD	IBF	Laredo, Texas
	Sept 18	Humberto Soto	Fidel Monterrosa	UD	WBC	Culiacan, Mexico
SUPER FEATHERWEIGHT (JUNIOR LIGHTWEIGHT)	Nov 21	Vitaly Tajbert	Humberto Gutierrez	UD	WBC	Kiel, Germany
	Jan 11	Takashi Uchiyama	Juan Carlos Salgado	TKO 12	WBA	Tokyo, Japan
	May 8	Jorge Solis	Mario Santiago	UD	WBA	Aguascalientes, Mexico
	May 17	Takashi Uchiyama	Angel Granados	TKO 6	WBA	Saitama, Japan
	May 22	Vitaly Tajbert	Hector Velazquez	TKO 9	WBC	Rostock, Germany
	Sept 1	Mzonke Fana	Cassius Baloyi	UD	IBF	Brakpan, South Africa
	Sept 4	Jorge Solis	Francisco Cordero	TKO 6	WBA	Guadalajara, Mexico
	Sept 20	Takashi Uchiyama	Roy Mukhlis	TKO 5	WBA	Saitama, Japan
FEATHERWEIGHT	Dec 19	Cristobal Cruz	Richard Castillo	T. Draw	IBF	Tuxtla Gutierrez, Mexico
	Jan 23	Yuriorkis Gamboa	Rogers Mtagwa	TKO 2	WBA	New York, New York
	Feb 20	Elio Rojas	Guty Espadas Jr.	UD	WBC	Merida, Mexico
	Mar 27	Yuiorkis Gamboa	Jonathan Barros	UD	WBA	Hamburg, Germany
	May 15	Orlando Salido	Cristobal Cruz	UD	IBF	Ciudad Obregon, Mexico
	Sept 11	Yuriorkis Gamboa	Orlando Salido	UD	WBA/IBF	Las Vegas, Nevada
SUPER BANTAMWEIGHT (JUNIOR FEATHERWEIGHT)	Jan 11	P. Kratingdaenggym	Satoshi Hosono	MD	WBA	Tokyo, Japan
	Feb 6	Jorge Solis	Likar Ramos	KO 7	WBA	Merida, Mexico
	Mar 27	Steve Molitor	Takalani Ndlovu	UD	IBF	Rama, Canada
	Apr 30	Celestino Caballero	Jeffrey Mathebula	SD	WBA/IBF	Panama City, Panama
	Apr 30	Toshiaki Nishioka	Balwe Bangoyan	TKO 5	WBC	Tokyo, Japan
	May 20	P. Kratingdaenggym	Shoji Kimura	TKO 4	WBA	Maha Sarakham, Thailand
	Sept 11	Steve Molitor	Jason Booth	MD	IBF	Houghton-le-Spring, England
BANTAMWEIGHT	Dec 18	Hozumi Hasegawa	Alvaro Perez	TKO 4	WBC	Kobe, Japan
	Dec 19	Nehomar Cermeno	Alejandro Valdez	KO 11	WBA	Ciudad Obregon, Mexico
	Mar 27	Anselmo Moreno	Nehomar Cermeno	SD	WBA	La Guaira, Venezuela
	Apr 30	Fernando Montiel	Hozumi Hasegawa	TKO 4	WBC	Tokyo, Japan
	May 22	Yhonny Perez	Abner Mares	M.Draw	IBF	Los Angeles, California
	July 17	Fernando Montiel	Rafael Concepcion	KO 3	WBC	Tuxtla Gutierrez, Mexico
	Aug 14	Anselmo Moreno	Nehomar Cermeno	SD	WBA	Panama City, Panama

	Date	Winner	Loser	Result	Title/Org.	Site
SUPER FLYWEIGHT (JUNIOR BANTAMWEIGHT)	Oct 24	Tomas Rojas	Evans Mbamba	UD	WBC	Boca del Rio, Mexico
	Dec 12	Vic Darchinyan	Tomas Rojas	KO 2	WBA/WBC	Rancho Mirage, California
	Mar 6	Vic Darchinyan	Rodrigo Guerrero	UD	WBA/WBC	Rancho Mirage, California
	Apr 9	Simphiwe Nongqayi	Malik Bouziane	Draw	IBF	Massy, France
	May 8	Hugo Cazares	Nobuo Nashiro	UD	WBA	Osaka, Japan
	July 3	Hugo Cazares	Everardo Morales	TKO 7	WBA	Tlalnepantla, Mexico
	July 10	Noniot Donaire	Herman Marquez	TKO 8	WBA	San Juan, Puerto Rico
	July 31	Jual Alberto Rosas	Simphiwe Nongqayi	TKO 6	IBF	Tepic, Mexico
	Sept 20	Tomas Rojas	Kohei Kono	UD	WBC	Saitama, Japan
FLYWEIGHT	Oct 6	Denkaosaen Kaovichit	Daiki Kameda	MD	WBA	Osaka, Japan
	Nov 20	Moruti Mthalane	Julio Cesar Miranda	KO 4	IBF	Johannesburg, South Africa
	Nov 29	Koki Kameda	Daisuke Natio	UD	WBC	Saitama, Japan
	Feb 7	Daiki Kameda	Denk. Kaovichit	UD	WBA	Kobe, Japan
	Mar 27	P. Wongjongkam	Koki Kameda	MD	WBC	Tokyo, Japan
	Apr 22	Luis Concepcion	Eric Ortiz	TKO 4	WBA	Panama City, Panama
	Sept 1	Moruti Mthalane	Zolani Tete	TKO 5	IBF	Brakpan, South Africa
	Sept 25	Takefumi Sakata	Daiki Kameda	UD	WBA	Tokyo, Japan
LIGHT FLYWEIGHT (JUNIOR FLYWEIGHT)	Nov 21	Rodel Mayol	Edgar Sosa	TKO 2	WBC	Tuxtla Gutierrez, Mexico
	Dec 18	Juan Carlos Reveco	Ronald Barrera	KO 3	WBA	Junin, Argentina
	Jan 23	Brian Viloria	Carlos Tamara	TKO 12	IBF	Manila, Philippines
	Feb 20	Giovanni Segura	Walter Tello	TKO 3	WBA	Acapulco, Mexico
	Feb 27	Rodel Mayol	Omar Nino Romero	T. Draw	WBC	Guadalajara, Mexico
	May 29	Luis Lazarte	Carlos Tamara	SD	IBF	Mar del Plata, Argentina
	June 19	Omar Nino Romero	Rodel Mayol	UD	WBC	San Juan del Rio, Mexico
	July 17	Juan Carlos Reveco	Armando Torres	TKO 5	WBA	Las Heras, Argentina
	Aug 28	Giovanni Segura	Ivan Calderon	KO 8	WBA	Guaynabo, Puerto Rico
	Sept 4	Omar Nino Romero	Ronald Barrera	TKO 6	WBC	Guadalajara, Mexico
	Sept 4	Luis Lazarte	Nerys Espinoza	UD	IBF	Mar del Plata, Argentina
STRAWWEIGHT (MINI FLYWT.) (MINIMUM WT.)	Nov 27	O. Sithsamerchai	Juan Palacios	MD	WBC	Rangsit, Thailand
	Jan 30	Roman Gonzalez	Ivan Meneses	TKO 4	WBA	Puebla, Mexico
	Mar 26	Nkosinathi Joyi	Raul Garcia	UD	IBF	East London, South Africa
	Mar 27	O. Sithsamerchai	Yasutaka Kuroki	UD	WBC	Tokyo, Japan
	Sept 3	O. Sithsamerchai	P. Popramook	M.Draw	WBC	Chiang Mai, Thailand

World Champions

Sanctioning bodies: the National Boxing Association (NBA), the New York State Athletic Commission (NY), the World Boxing Association (WBA), the World Boxing Council (WBC), and the International Boxing Federation (IBF).

Heavyweights (Weight: Unlimited)

Champion	Reign	Champion	Reign	Champion	Reign	Champion	Reign
John L. Sullivan*	1885–92	Muhammad Ali*	1964–70†	Trevor Berbick WBC	1986	Hasim Rahman* WBC,	
James J. Corbett*	1892–97	Ernie Terrell WBA	1965–67	Mike Tyson WBC	1986–87	IBF	2001–05
Bob Fitzsimmons*	1897–99	Joe Frazier* NY	1968–70	James Smith WBA	1986–87	Chris Byrd IBF	2002–06
James J. Jeffries*	1899–05†	Jimmy Ellis WBA	1968–70	Tony Tucker IBF	1987	Roy Jones Jr. WBA	2003–05
Marvin Hart*	1905–06	Joe Frazier*	1970–73	Mike Tyson*	1987–90	Lennox Lewis* WBC	2001–04
Tommy Burns*	1906–08	George Foreman*	1973–74	Buster Douglas*	1990	John Ruiz, WBA	2003–05
Jack Johnson*	1908–15	Muhammad Ali*	1974–78	Evander Holyfield*	1990–92	Vitali Klitschko WBC	2004–05
Jess Willard*	1915–19	Leon Spinks*	1978	Lennox Lewis WBC	1993–95	Hasim Rahman WBC	2005–06
Jack Dempsey*	1919–26	Ken Norton WBC	1978	Riddick Bowe*	1992–93	Nikolay Valuev WBA	2005–07
Gene Tunney*	1926–28†	Larry Holmes WBC	1978–80	Evander Holyfield*	1993–94	Oleg Maskaev WBC	2006–08
Max Schmeling*	1930–32	Muhammad Ali*	1978–79†	Michael Moorer*	1994	Wladimir Klitschko.	
Jack Sharkey*	1932–33	John Tate WBA	1979–80	George Foreman*	1994–95	IBF	2006–
Primo Carnera*	1933–34	Mike Weaver WBA	1980–82	Oliver McCall WBC	1995	Ruslan Chagaev WBA	2007–08
Max Baer*	1934–35	Larry Holmes*	1980–85	Frank Bruno WBC	1995–96	Samuel Peter WBC	2008
James J. Braddock*	1935–37	Michael Dokes WBA	1982–83	Bruce Seldon WBA	1995–96	Nikolai Valuev WBA	2008–09
Joe Louis*	1937–49†	Gerrie Coetzee WBA	1983–84	Mike Tyson WBA	1996	Vitali Klitschko WBC	2008–
Ezzard Charles*	1949–51	Tim Witherspoon		Michael Moorer IBF	1996–97	David Haye WBA	2009–
Jersey Joe Walcott*	1951–52	WBC	1984	Shannon Briggs*	1997–98		
Rocky Marciano*	1952–56†	Pinklon Thomas WBC	1984–86	Lennox Lewis* WBC	1997–01		
Floyd Patterson*	1956–59	Greg Page WBA	1984–85	E. Holyfield WBA, IBF	1996–99		
Ingemar Johansson*	1959–60	Michael Spinks*	1985–87	Lennox Lewis	1999–01		
Floyd Patterson*	1960–62	Tim Witherspoon		E. Holyfield WBA	2000–01		
Sonny Liston*	1962–64	WBA	1986	John Ruiz WBA	2001–03		

Cruiserweights (Weight Limit: 200 pounds)

Champion	Reign	Champion	Reign	Champion	Reign	Champion	Reign
Marvin Camel* WBC	1980	Evander Holyfield*	1988†	Imamu Mayfield IBF	1997–98	David Haye WBC	2007–08
Carlos De Leon* WBC	1980–82	Toufik Belbouli WBA	1989	Fabrice Tiozzo WBA	1997–00	David Haye WBA	2007–08†
Ossie Ocasio WBA	1982–84	Robert Daniels WBA	1989–91	J.C. Gomez* WBC	1998–02†	Guillermo Jones	
S.T. Gordon* WBC	1982–83	Carlos De Leon* WBC	1989–90	Arthur Williams IBF	1998–99	WBA	2009–
Carlos De Leon* WBC	1983–85	Glenn McCrory IBF	1989–90	Vassiliy Girov* IBF	1999–03	Giacobbe Fragomeni	
Marvin Camel IBF	1983–84	Jeff Lampkin IBF	1990	James Toney* IBF	2003	WBC	2008–09
Lee Roy Murphy IBF	1984–86	M. Duran* WBC	1990–91	Virgil Hill WBA	2000–02	Zsolt Erdei WBC	2009–10
Piet Crous WBA	1984–85	Bobby Czyz WBA	1991–92†	Wayne Braithwaite		Tomasz Adamek IBF	2008–09†
Alfonso Ratliff*		Anaclet Wamba* WBC	1991–95†	WBC	2002–05	Kryzysztof Wlodarczyk	
WBC	1985	James Pritchard IBF	1991	J.M. Mormeck WBA	2002–05	WBC	2010–
Dwight Braxton WBA	1985–86	James Warring IBF	1991–92	J.M. Mormeck WBC	2005–06	Steve Cunningham	
Bernard Benton* WBC	1985–86	Alfred Cole IBF	1992–96	Melvin Davis IBF	2004–05	IBF	2010–
Carlos De Leon* WBC	1986–88	Orlin Norris WBA	1993–95	O'Neil Bell IBF	2005–06		
Evander Holyfield*		Nate Miller WBA	1995–97	O'Neil Bell WBC/WBA	2006–07		
WBA	1986–87	M. Dominguez*		Steve Cunningham			
Ricky Parkey IBF	1986–87	WBC	1996–98	IBF	2006–08		
Evander Holyfield*		A. Washington IBF	1996–97	J.M. Mormeck			
WBA, IBF	1987–88	Uriah Grant IBF	1997	WBC/WBA	2007		

*Lineal champion.   †Champion relinquished title to retire or switch weight classes, or had title stripped by boxing organization.

Light Heavyweights (Weight Limit: 175 pounds)

Champion	Reign	Champion	Reign	Champion	Reign	Champion	Reign
Jack Root*	1903	Jose Torres*	1965–66	Bobby Czyz IBF	1986–87	Silvio Branco WBA	2003–04
George Gardner*	1903	Dick Tiger*	1966–68	Leslie Stewart WBA	1987	Antonio Tarver	
Bob Fitzsimmons*	1903–05	Bob Foster*	1968–74†	Virgil Hill* WBA	1987–91	WBC, IBF	2003
Jack O'Brien*	1905–12†	Vicente Rondon WBA	1971–72	Pr Charles Williams		Roy Jones Jr. WBC	2003
Jack Dillon*	1914–16	John Conteh WBC	1974–77	IBF	1987–93	Glencoffe Johnson	
Battling Levinsky*	1916–20	Victor Galindez* WBA	1974–78	Thomas Hearns WBC	1987†	IBF	2004–05
Georges Carpentier*	1920–22	Miguel A. Cuello WBC	1977–78	Donny Lalonde WBC	1987–88	Fabrice Tiozzo WBA	2004–5
Battling Siki*	1922–23	Mate Parlov WBC	1978	Sugar Ray Leonard		Antonio Tarver* WBC	2004–05
Mike McTigue*	1923–25	Mike Rossman*		WBC	1988	Silvio Branco WBA	2005–07
Paul Berlenbach*	1925–26	WBA	1978–79	Dennis Andries WBC	1989	Clinton Woods IBF	2005–08
Jack Delaney*	1926–27†	Victor Galindez*		Jeff Harding WBC	1989–90	Tomasz Adamek WBC	2005–07
Jimmy Slattery NBA	1927	WBA	1979	Dennis Andries WBC	1990–91	Stipe Drews WBA	2007
Tommy Loughran*	1927–29†	Marvin Johnson*		Thomas Hearns* WBA	1991–92	Chad Dawson WBC	2007–08
Maxie Rosenbloom*	1930–34	WBC	1978–79	Jeff Harding WBC	1991–94		2008–09†
George Nichols NBA	1932	M.S. Muhammad*		Iran Barkley* WBA	1992	Danny Green WBA	2007–08
Bob Godwin NBA	1933	WBC	1979–81	Virgil Hill* WBA	1992–97	Hugo Garay WBA	2008–09
Bob Olin*	1934–35	Marvin Johnson		Henry Maske IBF	1993–96	Antonio Tarver IBF	2008
John Henry Lewis*	1935–38†	WBA	1979–80	Mike McCallum WBC	1994–95	Adrian Diaconu WBC	2008–09
Melio Bettina	1939	E.M. Muhammad*		Fabrice Tiozzo WBC	1995–96	Gabriel Campillo WBA	2009–10
Billy Conn*	1939–40†	WBA	1980–81	D. Michalczewski*		Jean Pascal WBC	2009–
Anton Christoforidis	1941	Michael Spinks* WBA	1981–83	IBF	1997†	Tavoris Cloud IBF	2009–
Gus Lesnevich*	1941–48	Dwight Qawi WBC	1981–83	Roy Jones Jr.		Beibut Shumenov	
Freddie Mills*	1948–50	Michael Spinks*	1983–85†	WBC, WBA	1997–03	WBA	2010–
Joey Maxim*	1950–52	J. B. Williamson WBC	1985–86	William Guthrie IBF	1997–98		
Archie Moore*	1952–62†	Slobodan Kacar IBF	1985–86	Reggie Johnson IBF	1998–99		
Harold Johnson NBA	1961	Marvin Johnson*		Roy Jones Jr.*	1999–03		
Harold Johnson*	1962–63	WBA	1986–87	Bruno Girard WBA	2001–03		
Willie Pastrano*	1963–65	Dennis Andries WBC	1986–87	Mehdi Sahnoune			
				WBA	2003		

Super Middleweights (Weight Limit: 168 pounds)

Champion	Reign	Champion	Reign	Champion	Reign	Champion	Reign
Murray Sutherland*		Nigel Benn WBC	1992–96	Markus Beyer WBC	1999–00	Mikkel Kessler WBC	2006–07
IBF	1984	James Toney IBF	1992–94	Bruno Girard* WBA	2000–01†	Robert Stieglitz IBF	2007
Chong-Pal Park* IBF	1984–87	Michael Nunn* WBA	1992–94	Glenn Catley WBC	2000–01	Alejandro Berrio IBF	2007
Chong-Pal Park* WBA	1987–88	Steve Little* WBA	1994	Eric Lucas WBC	2000–03	Joe Calzaghe, WBC	2007–08
G. Rocchigiani IBF	1988–89	Frank Liles* WBA	1994–99	Byron Mitchell WBA	2000–03	Lucian Bute, IBF	2007–
F. Obelmejias* WBA	1988–89	Roy Jones Jr. IBF	1994–96	Sven Ottke WBA	2003†	Joe Calzaghe, WBA	2007–08
Sugar Ray Leonard		Thulane Malinga WBC	1996	Anthony Mundine WBA	2003	Carl Froch WBC	2008–10
WBC	1988–90†	V. Nardiello WBC	1996	Markus Beyer WBC	2003–04	Mikkel Kessler WBA	2008–09
In-Chul Baek* WBA	1989–90	Robin Reid WBC	1996–97	Sven Ottke, IBF	2003–05	Andre Ward WBA	2009–
Lindell Holmes IBF	1990–91	Charles Brewer IBF	1997–98	Cristian Sanavia WBC	2004	Mikkel Kessler WBC	2010–
Chris Tiozzo* WBA	1990–91	Thulane Malinga		Manny Siaca, WBA	2004		
Mauro Galvano WBC	1990–92	WBC	1997–98	Mikel Kessler WBA	2004–07		
Victor Cordova* WBA	1991	Richie Woodhall WBC	1998–99	Markus Beyer WBC	2004–06		
Darrin Van Horn IBF	1991–92	Sven Ottke IBF	1998–03	Jeff Lacy IBF	2005		
Iran Barkley IBF	1992	Byron Mitchell* WBA	1999–00	Joe Calzaghe IBF	2006–07		

*Lineal champion. †Champion relinquished title to retire or switch weight classes, or had title stripped by boxing organization.

Middleweights (Weight Limit: 160 pounds)

Champion	Reign	Champion	Reign	Champion	Reign	Champion	Reign
Jack Dempsey*	1884–91	Rocky Graziano*	1947–48	Rodrigo Valdez WBC	1974–76	Bernard Hopkins*	
Bob Fitzsimmons*	1891–97†	Tony Zale*	1948	Rodrigo Valdez*	1977–78	IBF	1994–
Kid McCoy*	1897–98	Marcel Cerdan*	1948–49	Hugo Corro*	1978–79	Keith Holmes WBC	1996–98
Tommy Ryan*	1898–07†	Jake La Motta*	1949–51	Vito Antuofermo*	1979–80	William Joppy WBA	1996–97
Stanley Ketchel*	1908	Sugar Ray Robinson*	1951	Alan Minter*	1980	J.C. Green WBA	1997
Billy Papke*	1908	Randy Turpin*	1951	Marvin Hagler*	1980–87	William Joppy WBA	1998–01
Stanley Ketchel*	1908–10†	Sugar Ray Robinson*	1951–52†	Sugar Ray Leonard*	1987†	Hassine Cherifi WBC	1998–99
Frank Klaus*	1913	Bobo Olson*	1953–55	Frank Tate IBF	1987–88	Keith Holmes WBC	1999–00
George Chip*	1913–14	Sugar Ray Robinson*	1955–57	Sumbu Kalambay		Felix Trinidad WBA	2001
Al McCoy*	1914–17	Gene Fullmer*	1957	WBA	1987–89	William Joppy WBA	2001–03
Mike O'Dowd*	1917–20	Sugar Ray Robinson*	1957	Thomas Hearns*		Bernard Hopkins*	
Johnny Wilson*	1920–23	Carmen Basilio*	1957–58	WBC	1987–89	WBC/IBF	2001–05
Harry Greb*	1923–26	Sugar Ray Robinson*	1958–60	Iran Barkley* WBC	1988–89	Bernard Hopkins WBA	2003–05
Tiger Flowers*	1926	Gene Fullmer NBA	1959–62	Michael Nunn IBF	1988–91	Jermain Taylor IBF	2005
Mickey Walker*	1926–31†	Paul Pender*	1960–61	Roberto Duran* WBC	1989–90†	Jermain Taylor WBA	2005–06
Gorilla Jones*	1931–32	Terry Downes*	1961–62	Michael Nunn* IBF	1991	Jermain Taylor WBA	2005–06
Marcel Thil*	1932–37	Paul Pender*	1962–63†	Mike McCallum WBA	1989–91	Jermain Taylor WBC	2005–07
Fred Apostoli*	1937–39	Dick Tiger WBA	1962–63	Julian Jackson WBC	1990–93	Arthur Abraham IBF	2005–09†
Al Hostak NBA	1938	Dick Tiger*	1963	James Toney* IBF	1991–93†	Felix Sturm WBA	2006
Solly Krieger NBA	1938–39	Joey Giardello*	1963–65	Reggie Johnson WBA	1992–94	Javier Castillejo WBA	2006–07
Al Hostak NBA	1939–40	Dick Tiger*	1965–66	Roy Jones Jr.* IBF	1993–95†	Felix Sturm WBA	2007–
Ceferino Garcia*	1939–40	Emile Griffith*	1966–67	G. McClellan WBC	1993–95†	Kelly Pavlik WBC	2007–
Ken Overlin*	1940–41	Nino Benvenuti*	1967	Jorge Castro WBA	1994–95	Sebastian Sylvester	
Tony Zale NBA	1940–41	Emile Griffith*	1967–68	Shinji Takehara WBA	1995–96	IBF	2009–
Billy Soose*	1941	Nino Benvenuti*	1968–70	Jullian Jackson WBC	1995		
Tony Zale*	1941–47	Carlos Monzon*	1970–77†	Quincy Taylor WBC	1995–96		

Junior Middleweights (Weight Limit: 154 pounds)

Champion	Reign	Champion	Reign	Champion	Reign	Champion	Reign
Emile Griffith (EBU)	1962–63	Davey Moore WBA	1982–83	Simon Brown* WBC	1993–94	Ronald Wright	
Dennis Moyer*	1962–63	Thomas Hearns*		Terry Norris* WBC	1994	WBA/WBC	2004–05
Ralph Dupas*	1963	WBC	1982–84	Luis Santana* WBC	1995–95	Verno Phillips IBF	2004–05
Sandro Mazzinghi*	1963–65	Roberto Duran WBA	1983–84	Vincent Pettway IBF	1994–95	Ricardo Mayora	
Nino Benvenuti*	1965–66	Mark Medal IBF	1984	Paul Vaden IBF	1995	WBC	2005–06
Ki-Soo Kim*	1966–68	Thomas Hearns*	1984–86†	Carl Daniels WBA	1995	Alex T. Garcia WBA	2005–06
Sandro Mazzinghi*	1968	Mike McCallum*		Terry Norris* WBC	1995–97	Roman Karmazin	
Freddie Little*	1969–70	WBA	1984–87†	Terry Norris* IBF	1995–96†	IBF	2005–06
Carmelo Bossi*	1970–71	Carlos Santos IBF	1984–86	L. Boudouani WBA	1996–99	Jose A. Rivera WBA	2006–07
Koichi Wajima*	1971–74	Buster Drayton IBF	1986–87	Raul Marquez IBF	1997	Oscar De La Hoya	
Oscar Albarado*	1974–75	Duane Thomas		Keith Mullings* WBC	1997–99	WBC	2006–07
Koichi Wajima*	1975	WBC	1986–87	Yori Boy Campas IBF	1997–98	Cory Spinks IBF	2006–08
Miguel de Oliveira WBC	1975–76	Matthew Hilton IBF	1987–88	Fernando Vargas IBF	1998–00		2009–
Jae-Do Yuh*	1975–76	Lupe Aquino WBC	1987	F. Javier Castillejo*		Travis Simms WBA	2007
Elisha Obed WBC	1975–76	Gianfranco Rosi		WBC	1999–01	Floyd Mayweather Jr.	
Koichi Wajima*	1976	WBC	1987–88	David Reid WBA	1999–00	WBC	2007
Jose Duran*	1976	Julian Jackson WBC	1987–90	Felix Trinidad WBA	2000–01	Joachim Alcine WBA	2007–08
Eckhard Dagge WBC	1976–77	Donald Curry WBC	1988–89	Felix Trinidad		Vernon Forrest WBC	2007–08
Miguel Angel		Robert Hines IBF	1988–89	WBA, IBF	2001†	Sergio Mora WBC	2008
Castellini*	1976–77	Darrin Van Horn IBF	1989	Oscar De La Hoya*		Verno Phillips IBF	2008†
Eddie Gazo*	1977–78	Rene Jacquot WBC	1989	WBC	2001–03	Daniel Santos WBA	2008–09
Rocky Mattioli WBC	1977–79	John Mugabi* WBC	1989–90	Fernando Vargas		Vernon Forrest	
Masashi Kudo*	1978–79	Gianfranco Rosi IBF	1989–94	WBA	2001–02	WBC	2008–09
Maurice Hope WBC	1979–81	Terry Norris* WBC	1990–93	Ronald Wright IBF†	2001–04	Sergio Gabriel Martinez	
Ayub Kalule*	1979–81	Gilbert Dele WBA	1991	Oscar De La Hoya*		WBC	2009–10†
Wilfred Benitez WBC	1981–82	Vinny Pazienza		WBC/WBA	2002–03	Yuri Foreman WBA	2009–10
Sugar Ray Leonard*	1981–82†	WBA	1991–92	Shane Mosley* WBC	2003–04	Miguel Cotto WBA	2010–
Tadashi Mihara WBA	1981–82	Julio C. Vasquez WBA	1992–95	Alejandro Garcia WBA	2003–05		

*Lineal champion. †Champion relinquished title to retire or switch weight classes, or had title stripped by boxing organization.

Welterweights (Weight Limit: 147 pounds)

Champion	Reign
Paddy Duffy*	1888–90†
Mysterious Billy Smith*	1892–94
Tommy Ryan*	1894–98†
Mysterious Billy Smith*	1898–1900
Rube Ferns*	1900
Matty Matthews*	1900–01
Rube Ferns*	1901
Joe Walcott*	1901–04
The Dixie Kid*	1904–05†
Honey Mellody*	1906–07
Mike Sullivan*	1907–08†
Jimmy Gardner*	1908†
Jimmy Clabby*	1910–1†
Waldemar Holberg*	1914
Tom McCormick*	1914
Matt Wells*	1914–15
Mike Glover*	1915
Jack Britton*	1915
Ted "Kid" Lewis*	1915–16
Jack Britton*	1916–17
Ted "Kid" Lewis*	1917–19
Jack Britton*	1919–22
Mickey Walker*	1922–26
Pete Latzo*	1926–27
Joe Dundee*	1927–29
Jackie Fields*	1929–30
Young Jack Thompson*	1930
Tommy Freeman*	1930–31
Young Jack Thompson*	1931
Lou Brouillard*	1931–32
Jackie Fields*	1932–33
Young Corbett III*	1933
Jimmy McLarnin*	1933–34
Barney Ross*	1934
Jimmy McLarnin*	1934–35
Barney Ross*	1935–38
Henry Armstrong*	1938–40
Fritzie Zivic*	1940–41
Red Cochrane*	1941–46
Marty Servo*	1946
Sugar Ray Robinson*	1946–51†
Johnny Bratton*	1951
Kid Gavilan*	1951–54
Johnny Saxton*	1954–55
Tony DeMarco*	1955
Carmen Basilio*	1955–56
Johnny Saxton*	1956
Carmen Basilio*	1956–57†
Virgil Akins*	1958
Don Jordan*	1958–60
Kid Paret*	1960–61
Emile Griffith*	1961
Kid Paret*	1961–62
Emile Griffith*	1962–63
Luis Rodriguez*	1963
Emile Griffith*	1963–66†
Curtis Cokes*	1966–69
Jose Napoles*	1969–70
Billy Backus*	1970–71
Jose Napoles*	1971–75
Hedgemon Lewis NY	1972–73
Angel Espada WBA	1975–76
John H. Stracey*	1975–76
Carlos Palomino*	1976–79
Pipino Cuevas WBA	1976–80
Wilfredo Benitez*	1979
Sugar Ray Leonard*	1979–80
Roberto Duran*	1980
Thomas Hearns WBA	1980–81
Sugar Ray Leonard*	1980–82†
Donald Curry* WBA	1983–85
Milton McCrory WBC	1983–85
Donald Curry*	1985–86
Lloyd Honeyghan*	1986–87
Jorge Vaca* WBC	1987–88
Lloyd Honeyghan* WBC	1988–89
Mark Breland WBA	1987
Marlon Starling WBA	1987–88
Tomas Molinares WBA	1988–89
Simon Brown IBF	1988–91
Mark Breland WBA	1989–90
Marlon Starling* WBC	1989–90
Aaron Davis WBA	1990–91
Maurice Blocker* WBC	1990–91
Meldrick Taylor WBA	1991–92
Simon Brown* WBC	1991
Buddy McGirt* WBC	1991–93
Felix Trinidad IBF	1993–00
Pernell Whitaker* WBC	1993–97
Crisanto Espana WBA	1992–94
Ike Quartey WBA	1994–97†
Oscar De La Hoya* WBC	1997–99
James Page WBA	1998–01
Felix Trinidad* IBF, WBC	1999–00†
Shane Mosley* WBC	2000–02
Andrew Lewis WBA	2001–02
Vernon Forrest IBF	2001
Vernon Forrest* WBC	2001–03
Ricardo Mayorga WBA	2002
Ricardo Mayorga* WBC	2003–05
Michele Piccirillo IBF	2002–03
Jose Rivera WBA	2003
Cory Spinks IBF, WBC, WBA	2003–05
Zab Judah WBA/WBC/IBF	2005–06
Luis Collazo WBA	2006
Ricky Hatton WBA	2006
Carlos Baldomir WBC	2006
F. Mayweather, Jr. IBF	2006
Miguel Cotto WBA	2006–08
F. Mayweather Jr. WBC	2006–08
Kermit Cintron IBF	2006–08
A. Margarito IBF	2008
Joshua Clottey IBF	2008–09†
Ant. Margarito WBA	2008–09
Andre Berto WBC	2008–
Shane Mosley WBA	2009
Isaac Hlatshwayo IBF	2009
Vyacheslav Senchenko WBA	2009–
Dejan Zavec IBF	2009–

Super Lightweights (Weight Limit: 140 pounds)

Champion	Reign
Pinkey Mitchell*	1922–25
Red Herring	1925
Mushy Callahan*	1926–30
Jack (Kid) Berg*	1930–31
Tony Canzoneri*	1931–32
Johnny Jadick*	1932–33
Sammy Fuller*	1932–33
Battling Shaw*	1933
Tony Canzoneri*	1933
Barney Ross*	1933–35†
Tippy Larkin*	1946
Carlos Ortiz*	1959–60
Duilio Loi*	1960–62
Eddie Perkins*	1962
Duilio Loi*	1962–63†
Roberto Cruz WBA	1963
Eddie Perkins*	1963–65
Carlos Hernandez*	1965–66
Sandro Lopopolo*	1966–67
Paul Fujii*	1967–68
Nicolino Loche*	1968–72
Pedro Adigue WBC	1968–70
Bruno Arcari WBC	1970–74
Alfonso Frazer*	1972
Antonio Cervantes*	1972–76
Perico Fernandez WBC	1974–75
S. Muangsurin WBC	1975–76
Wilfred Benitez*	1976–79†
M. Velasquez WBC	1976
S. Muangsurin WBC	1976–78
A. Cervantes WBA	1977–80
Sang-Hyun Kim WBC	1978–80
Saoul Mamby WBC	1980–82
Aaron Pryor* WBA	1980–83
Leroy Haley WBC	1982–83
Aaron Pryor* IBF	1983–85†
Bruce Curry WBC	1983–84
Johnny Bumphus WBA	1984
Bill Costello WBC	1984–85
Gene Hatcher WBA	1984–85
Ubaldo Sacco WBA	1985–86
Lonnie Smith* WBC	1985–86
Patrizio Oliva WBA	1986–87
Gary Hinton IBF	1986
Rene Arredondo* WBC	1986
Tsuyoshi Hamada WBC	1986–87
Joe Louis Manley IBF	1986–87
Terry Marsh IBF	1987
Juan Coggi WBA	1987–90
Rene Arredondo WBC	1987
R. Mayweather* WBC	1987–89
James McGirt IBF	1988
Meldrick Taylor IBF	1988–90
Julio César Chávez* WBC	1989–94
Julio César Chávez* IBF	1990–91
Loreto Garza WBA	1990–91
Juan Coggi WBA	1991
Edwin Rosario WBA	1991–92
Rafael Pineda IBF	1991–92
Akinobu Hiranaka WBA	1992
Pernell Whitaker IBF	1992–93†
Charles Murray IBF	1993–94
Jake Rodriguez IBF	1994–95
Juan Coggi WBA	1993–94
Frankie Randall* WBC	1994
Frankie Randall WBA	1994–96
Juan Coggi WBA	1996
Julio César Chávez* WBC	1994–96
Kostya Tszyu IBF	1995–97
Frankie Randall WBA	1996–97
Oscar De La Hoya* WBC	1996–97†
Khalid Rahilou WBA	1997–98
Vincent Phillips* IBF	1997–99
Sharmba Mitchell WBA	1998–01
Kostya Tszyu WBC	1998–
Terronn Millett* IBF	1999–00
Zab Judah* IBF	2000–01
Kostya Tszyu*† WBA/C	2001–03
Kostya Tszyu* IBF	2003–05
Vivian Harris WBA	2003–05
Arturo Gatti WBA	2004–05
F. Mayweather Jr. WBC	2005–06
Carlos Maussa WBA	2005–06
Ricky Hatton IBF	2005–06
Souleymane M'baye WBA	2006–07
Juan Urango IBF	2006–07
Junior Witter WBC	2006–08
Gavin Rees WBA	2007–08
Ricky Hatton IBF	2007
Lovemore N'Dou IBF	2007
Paul Malignaggi IBF	2007–09†

*Lineal champion. †Champion relinquished title to retire or switch weight classes, or had title stripped by boxing organization.

Super Lightweights (Cont.)

Champion	Reign	Champion	Reign	Champion	Reign	Champion	Reign
Timothy Bradley WBC	2008–09	Andreas Kotelnik WBA	2008–09	Devon Alexander WBC	2009–	Amir Khan WBA	2009–
						Juan Urango IBF	2009–

Lightweights (Weight Limit: 135 pounds)

Champion	Reign	Champion	Reign	Champion	Reign	Champion	Reign
Jack McAuliffe*	1886–94†	Joe Brown*	1956–62	Julio César Chávez*		Steve Johnston*	
Kid Lavigne*	1896–99	Carlos Ortiz*	1962–65	WBA	1987–88	WBC	1999–00
Frank Erne*	1899–1902	Ismael Laguna*	1965	Jose Luis Ramirez		Julien Lorcy WBA	1999
Joe Gans*	1902–04	Carlos Ortiz*	1965–68	WBC	1987–88	Stefano Zoff WBA	1999
Jimmy Britt*	1904–05	Carlos Teo Cruz*	1968–69	Julio César Chávez*	1988–89†	Paul Spadafora IBF	1999–03
Battling Nelson*	1905–06	Mando Ramos*	1969–70	Vinny Pazienza IBF	1987–88	Gilbert Serrano WBA	1999–00
Joe Gans*	1906–08	Ismael Laguna*	1970	Greg Haugen IBF	1988–89	T. Hatakeyama WBA	2000–01
Battling Nelson*	1908–10	Ken Buchanan*	1970–72	P. Whitaker*		Jose Luis Castillo*	
Ad Wolgast*	1910–12	Roberto Duran*	1972–79†	WBC, IBF	1989–90	WBC	2000–02
Willie Ritchie*	1912–14	Chango Carmona		Edwin Rosario WBA	1989–90	Julien Lorcy WBA	2001
Freddie Welsh*	1915–17	WBC	1972	Juan Nazario WBA	1990	Raul Balbi WBA	2001
Benny Leonard*	1917–25†	Rodolfo Gonzalez		P. Whitaker*		F. Mayweather* WBC	2002–03
Jimmy Goodrich*	1925	WBC	1972–74	WBA, WBC	1990–92†	Javier Jauregui IBF	2003–04
Rocky Kansas*	1925–26	Ishimatsu Suzuki		Pernell Whitaker*		Leonard Dorin WBA	2002–03
Sammy Mandell*	1926–30	WBC	1974–76	IBF	1991–92†	Julio Diaz IBF	2004–05
Al Singer*	1930	Estaban DeJesus		Julio César Chávez		Lakva Sim WBA	2004
Tony Canzoneri*	1930–33	WBC	1976–78	IBF	1990–91	Juan Diaz WBA	2004–08
Barney Ross*	1933–35†	Jim Watt WBC*	1979–81	Edwin Rosario WBA	1991–92	Jose Luis Castillo	
Tony Canzoneri*	1935–36	Ernesto Espana		Julio César Chávez		WBC	2004–05
Lou Ambers*	1936–38	WBA	1979–80	WBC	1990–92	Diego Corrales WBC	2005–06
Henry Armstrong*	1938–39	Sean O'Grady WBA	1981	Miguel Gonzalez		Jesus Chavez IBF	2005–07
Lou Ambers*	1939–40	Claude Noel WBA	1981	WBC	1992–95	Joel Casamayor	
Sammy Angott NBA	1940–41	Alexis Arguello*		Joey Gamache		WBC	2006–08
Lew Jenkins*	1940–41	WBC	1981–82†	WBA	1992–93	Julio Diaz IBF	2007
Sammy Angott*	1941–42†	Arturo Frias WBA	1981–82	Dingaan Thobela		Juan Diaz	2007–08
Beau Jack* NY	1942–43	Ray Mancini* WBA	1982–84	WBA	1993	David Diaz WBC	2008
Bob Montgomery*		Alexis Arguello	1982–83	Fred Pendleton* IBF	1993–94	Yusuke Kobori WBA	2008–
NY	1943	Edwin Rosario WBC	1983–84	Orzubek Nazarov		Nate Campbell IBF	2008–09†
Sammy Angott NBA	1943–44	Choo Choo Brown		WBA	1993–98	Manny Pacquiao	
Beau Jack* NY	1943–44	IBF	1984	Rafael Ruelas* IBF	1994–95	WBC	2008–09†
Bob Montgomery*		Jose Luis Ramirez		Oscar De La Hoya*		Juan Manual Marquez	
NY	1944–47	WBC	1984–85	IBF	1995†	WBA	2009–
Juan Zurita NBA	1944–45	Harry Arroyo IBF	1984–85	Phillip Holiday IBF	1995–97	Edwin Valero WBC	2009–10†
Ike Williams*	1947–51	Jimmy Paul IBF	1985–86	Jean B. Mendy*		Humberto Soto WBC	2010–
James Carter*	1951–52	Hector Camacho		WBC	1996–97		
Lauro Salas*	1952	WBC	1985–86	Steve Johnston*			
James Carter*	1952–54	Greg Haugen IBF	1986–87	WBC	1997–98		
Paddy DeMarco*	1954	Edwin Rosario* WBA	1986–87	Shane Mosley IBF	1997–99†		
James Carter*	1954–55			Jean B. Mendy WBA	1998–99		
Wallace Smith*	1955–56			Cesar Bazan* WBC	1998–99		

*Lineal champion. †Champion relinquished title to retire or switch weight classes, or had title stripped by boxing organization.

Super Featherweights (Weight Limit: 130 pounds)

Champion	Reign	Champion	Reign	Champion	Reign
Johnny Dundee*	1921–23	Roger Mayweather*	1983–84	Jong Kwon Baek WBA	1999–00
Jack Bernstein*	1923	Hector Camacho WBC	1983–84	Joel Casamayor WBA	2000–02
Johnny Dundee*	1923–24	Rocky Lockridge*	1984–85	Steve Forbes IBF	2000–02†
Steve (Kid) Sullivan*	1924–25	Hwan-Kil Yuh IBF	1984–85	Acelino Freitas* WBA	2002–04
Mike Ballerino*	1925	Julio César Chávez WBC	1984–87	Y. Nantchachai WBA	2002–05
Tod Morgan*	1925–29	Lester Ellis IBF	1985	S. Singmanassak WBC	2002–03
Benny Bass*	1929–31	Wilfredo Gomez*	1985–86	Jesus Chavez WBC	2003–04
Kid Chocolate*	1931–33	Barry Michael IBF	1985–87	Carlos Hernandez IBF	2003–04
Frankie Klick*	1933–34†	Alfredo Layne* WBA	1986	Erik Morales WBC/IBF	2004–05
Sandy Saddler*	1949–50†	Brian Mitchell* WBA	1986–91†	Erik Morales IBF	2004–05
Harold Gomes*	1959–60	Rocky Lockridge IBF	1987–88	Marco A. Barrera WBC	2005–07
Gabriel (Flash) Elorde*	1960–67	Azumah Nelson* WBC	1988–94	Vicente Mosquera WBA	2005–06
Yoshiaki Numata*	1967	Tony Lopez IBF	1988–89	Robbie Peden IBF	2005
Hiroshi Kobayashi*	1967–71	Juan Molina IBF	1989–90	Marco A. Barrera, IBF	2005–06
Rene Barrientos WBC	1969–70	Tony Lopez IBF	1990–91	Cassius Baloyi IBF	2006
Yoshiaki Numata WBC	1970–71	Joey Gamache WBA	1991	Edwin Valero WBA	2006–08
Alfredo Marcano*	1971–72	Brian Mitchell IBF	1991	Gairy St. Clair IBF	2006
R. Arredondo WBC	1971–74	Genaro Hernandez WBA	1991–95	Malcolm Klassen IBF	2006–07
Ben Villaflor*	1972–73	James Leija* WBC	1994	Mzonke Fana IBF	2007–08
Kuniaki Shibata*	1973	Juan Molina IBF	1991–95	Juan Manuel Marquez WBC	2007–08
Ben Villaflor*	1973–76	Gabriel Ruelas* WBC	1994–95	Manny Pacquiao WBC	2008
Kuniaki Shibata WBC	1974–75	Eddie Hopson IBF	1995	Jorge Llnares WBA	2008–09
Alfredo Escalera WBC	1975–78	Tracy Patterson IBF	1995	Cassius Baloyi IBF	2008–09
Samuel Serrano*	1976–80	Azumah Nelson* WBC	1995–97	Humberto Soto WBC	2008–10†
Alexis Arguello WBC	1978–80	Choi Yong-Soo WBA	1995–98	Malcom Klassen IBF	2009
Yasutsune Uehara*	1980–81	Arturo Gatti IBF	1995–98†	Juan Carlos Salgado IBF	2009
Rafael Limon WBC	1980–81	Genaro Hernandez* WBC	1997–98	Juan Carlos Salgado WBA	2009–10
C. Boza-Edwards WBC	1981	Roberto Garcia IBF	1998–99	Robert Guerrero IBF	2009–
Samuel Serrano*	1981–83	Floyd Mayweather Jr.* WBC	1998–01†	Takashi Uchiyama WBA	2010–
R. Navarrete WBC	1981–82	T. Hatakeyama WBA	1998–99	Vitaly Tajbert WBC	2010–
Rafael Limon WBC	1982	Lakva Sim WBA	1999		
Bobby Chacon WBC	1982–83	Diego Corrales IBF	1999–01		

Featherweights (Weight Limit: 126 pounds)

Champion	Reign	Champion	Reign	Champion	Reign
Torpedo Billy Murphy*	1890	Joey Archibald*	1941	Poison Kotey WBC	1975–76
Young Griffo*	1890–92†	Richie Lamos NBA	1941	Danny Lopez* WBC	1976–80
George Dixon*	1892–97	Chalky Wright*	1941–42	Rafael Ortega WBA	1977
Solly Smith*	1897–98	Jackie Wilson NBA	1941–43	Cecilio Lastra WBA	1977–78
Dave Sullivan*	1898	Willie Pep*	1942–48	Eusebio Pedroza* WBA	1978–85
George Dixon*	1898–1900	Jackie Callura NBA	1943	S. Sanchez* WBC	1980–82†
Terry McGovern*	1900–01	Phil Terranova NBA	1943–44	Juan LaPorte WBC	1982–84
Young Corbett II*	1901–03†	Sal Bartolo NBA	1944–46	Wilfredo Gomez WBC	1984
Abe Attell*	1903–04	Sandy Saddler*	1948–49	Min-Keun Oh IBF	1984–85
Tommy Sullivan*	1904–05†	Willie Pep*	1949–50	Azumah Nelson WBC	1984–88
Abe Attell*	1906–12	Sandy Saddler*	1950–57†	Barry McGuigan* WBA	1985–86
Johnny Kilbane*	1912–23	Kid Bassey*	1957–59	Ki Young Chung IBF	1985–86
Eugene Criqui*	1923	Davey Moore*	1959–63	Steve Cruz* WBA	1986–87
Johnny Dundee*	1923–24†	Sugar Ramos*	1963–64	Antonio Rivera IBF	1986–88
"Kid" Kaplan*	1925–26†	Vicente Saldivar*	1964–67†	A. Esparragoza* WBA	1987–91
Tony Canzoneri*	1927–28	Paul Rojas WBA	1968	Calvin Grove IBF	1988
Andre Routis*	1928–29	Jose Legra WBC	1968–69	Jorge Paez IBF	1988–91
Battling Battalino*	1929–32†	Shozo Saijyo WBA	1968–71	Jeff Fenech WBC	1988–90†
Tommy Paul NBA	1932–33	J. Famechon* WBC	1969–70	Marcos Villasana WBC	1990–91
Kid Chocolate NY	1932–33†	Vicente Saldivar* WBC	1970	Paul Hodkinson WBC	1991–93
Freddie Miller NBA	1933–36	Kuniaki Shibata* WBC	1970–72	Troy Dorsey IBF	1991
Mike Beloise NY	1936–37	Antonio Gomez WBA	1971–72	Manuel Medina IBF	1991–93
Petey Sarron NBA	1936–37	C. Sanchez* WBC	1972	Yung Kyun Park* WBA	1991–93
Maurice Holtzer*	1937–38	Ernesto Marcel WBA	1972–74	Gregorio Vargas WBC	1993
Henry Armstrong*	1937–38†	Jose Legra* WBC	1972–73	Tom Johnson IBF	1993–97†
Joey Archibald* NY	1938–39	Eder Jofre* WBC	1973–74†	Eloy Rojas* WBA	1993–96
Leo Rodak NBA	1938–39	Ruben Olivares WBA	1974	Kevin Kelley WBC	1993–95
Joey Archibald	1939–40	Bobby Chacon WBC	1974–75	A. Gonzalez WBC	1995
Petey Scalzo NBA	1940–41	Alexis Arguello* WBA	1974–76†	Manuel Medina WBC	1995–96
Harry Jeffra*	1940–41	Ruben Olivares WBA	1975	Luisito Espinosa WBC	1995–99

*Lineal champion. †Champion relinquished title to retire or switch weight classes, or had title stripped by boxing organization.

Featherweights (Cont.)

Champion	Reign
Wilfredo Vazquez* WBA	1996–98
Hector Lizarraga IBF	1997–98
Naseem Hamed* WBA	1998†
Naseem Hamed*	1998–01
Freddy Norwood WBA	1998
Manuel Medina IBF	1998–99
Antonio Cermeno WBA	1998–99
Cesar Soto WBC	1999
Freddy Norwood WBA	1999–00
Naseem Hamed* WBC	1999†
Paul Ingle IBF	1999–00
Guty Espadas WBC	2000–01
Erik Morales WBC	2000–02
Derrick Gainer WBA	2000–03
Mbulelo Botile IBF	2001
Frankie Toledo IBF	2001
Manuel Medina IBF	2001–02

Champion	Reign
Marco A. Barrera*WBA/WBC	2001–03
Johnny Tapia IBF	2002
Marco A. Barrera* WBC	2002†
Erik Morales WBC	2002–03
Juan Marquez IBF	2003–06
Chris John WBA	2003–09
In Jin Chi WBC	2004–06
Valdemir Pereira, IBF	2006
Eric Aiken IBF	2006
T. Koshimoto, WBC	2006
Rudolfo Lopez WBC	2006
Robert Guerrero IBF	2006
Orlando Salido IBF	2006
In Jin Chi WBC	2006–07
Robert Guerrero IBF	2007–08†
Jorge Linares WBC	2007–08
Oscar Larios WBC	2008–09

Champion	Reign
Cristobal Cruz IBF	2008–
Takahiro Aoh WBC	2009
Elio Rojas WBC	2009–
Yuriorkis Gamboa WBA	2009–

Super Bantamweights (Weight Limit: 122 pounds)

Champion	Reign
Jack (Kid) Wolfe*	1922–23
Carl Duane*	1923–24
Rigoberto Riasco* WBC	1976
R. Kobayashi* WBC	1976
Dong-Kyun Yum* WBC	1976–77
Wilfredo Gomez* WBC	1977–83†
Soo-Hwan Hong WBA	1977–78
Ricardo Cardona WBA	1978–80
Leo Randolph WBA	1980
Sergio Palma WBA	1980–82
Leonardo Cruz WBA	1982–84
Jaime Garza* WBC	1983
Bobby Berna IBF	1983–84
Loris Stecca WBA	1984
Seung-Il Suh IBF	1984–85
Victor Callejas WBA	1984–86
Juan Meza* WBC	1984–85
Ji-Won Kim IBF	1985–86
Lupe Pintor* WBC	1985–86
S. Payakaroon* WBC	1986–87
Seung-Hoon Lee IBF	1987–88
Louie Espinoza WBA	1987
Jeff Fenech* WBC	1987†
Julio Gervacio WBA	1987–88
Daniel Zaragoza* WBC	1988–90

Champion	Reign
Jose Sanabria IBF	1988–89
B. Pinango WBA	1988
J.J. Estrada WBA	1988–89
Fabrice Benichou IBF	1989–90
Jesus Salud WBA	1989–90
Welcome Ncita IBF	1990–92
Paul Banke* WBC	1990
Luis Mendoza WBA	1990–91
Raul Perez WBA	1992
Pedro Decima* WBC	1990–91
K. Hatanaka* WBC	1991
Daniel Zaragoza* WBC	1991–92
Thiery Jacob* WBC	1992
Tracy Patterson* WBC	1992–94
Kennedy McKinney IBF	1993–94
Wilfredo Vasquez WBA	1992–95
Vuyani Bungu IBF	1994–99†
H. Acero* Sanchez WBC	1994–95
Antonio Cermeno WBA	1995–98†
Daniel Zaragoza* WBC	1995–97
Erik Morales* WBC	1997–00†
Enrique Sanchez WBA	1998
Nestor Garza WBA	1998–00
Benedict Ledwaba IBF	1999–01
Clarence Adams WBA	2000–01†

Champion	Reign
Willie Jorrin WBC	2000–02
Manny Pacquiao IBF	2001–04
Yober Ortega WBA	2001–02
Y. Sithyodthong WBA	2002
Osamu Sato WBA	2002
Salim Medjkoune WBA	2002–03
Mahyar Monshipour WBA	2003–06
Oscar Larios WBC	2002–05
Israel Vazquez IBF	2004–05
S. Sithchatchawal WBA	2006
Israel Vazquez WBC	2005–07
C. Caballero WBA	2006–09
IBF	2008–
Michael Hunter IBF	2006
Steve Molitor IBF	2006–08
Rafael Marquez WBC	2007
Israel Vazquez WBC	2007–08
Toshiaki Nishioka WBC	2008–
Poon. Kratingdaenggym WBA	2009–

Bantamweights (Weight Limit: 118 pounds)

Champion	Reign
Spider Kelly	1887
Hughey Boyle	1887–88
Spider Kelly	1889
Chappie Moran	1889–90
George Dixon	1890–91
Pedlar Palmer	1895–99
Terry McGovern*	1899–00†
Harry Harris	1901
Harry Forbes*	1901–03
Frankie Neil*	1903–04
Joe Bowker*	1904–05†
Jimmy Walsh*	1905–06†
Owen Moran	1907–08
Monte Attell	1909–10
Frankie Conley	1910–11
Johnny Coulon*	1910–14

Champion	Reign
Kid Williams*	1914–17
Kewpie Ertle	1915
Pete Herman*	1917–20
Joe Lynch*	1920–21
Pete Herman*	1921
Johnny Buff*	1921–22
Joe Lynch*	1922–24
Abe Goldstein*	1924
Cannonball Martin*	1924–25
Phil Rosenberg*	1925–27†
Bud Taylor NBA	1927–28
Bushy Graham NY	1928–29
Panama Al Brown*	1929–35
Sixto Escobar NBA	1934–35
Baltazar Sangchilli*	1935–36
Lou Salica NBA	1935

Champion	Reign
Sixto Escobar NBA	1935–36
Tony Marino*	1936
Sixto Escobar*	1936–37
Harry Jeffra*	1937–38
Sixto Escobar*	1938–39†
Georgie Pace NBA	1939–40
Lou Salica*	1940–42
Manuel Ortiz*	1942–47
Harold Dade*	1947
Manuel Ortiz*	1947–50
Vic Toweel*	1950–52
Jimmy Carruthers*	1952–54†
Robert Cohen*	1954–56
Paul Macias NBA	1955–57
Mario D'Agata*	1956–57
Alphonse Halimi*	1957–59

Champion	Reign
Joe Becerra*	1959–60†
Eder Jofre*	1961–65
Fighting Harada*	1965–68
Lionel Rose*	1968–69
Ruben Olivares*	1969–70
Chucho Castillo*	1970–71
Ruben Olivares*	1971–72
Rafael Herrera*	1972
Enrique Pinder*	1972–73
Romeo Anaya*	1973
Arnold Taylor*	1973–74
Rafael Herrera WBC	1973–74
Soo-Hwan Hong*	1974–75
Rodolfo Martinez WBC	1974–76
Alfonso Zamora*	1975–77

*Lineal champion. †Champion relinquished title to retire or switch weight classes, or had title stripped by boxing organization.

Bantamweights ((Cont.)

Champion	Reign
Carlos Zarate* WBC	1976–79
Jorge Lujan	1977–80
Lupe Pintor* WBC	1979–83†
Julian Solis	1980
Jeff Chandler*	1980–84
Albert Davila WBC	1983–85
Richard Sandoval*	1984–86
Satoshi Shingaki IBF	1984–85
Jeff Fenech IBF	1985
Daniel Zaragoza WBC	1985
Miguel Lora WBC	1985–88
Gaby Canizales*	1986
Bernardo Pinango*	1986–87†
W. Vasquez WBA	1987–88
Kevin Seabrooks* IBF	1987–88
Kaokor Galaxy WBA	1988

Champion	Reign
Moon Sung-Kil WBA	1988–89
Kaokor Galaxy WBA	1989
Raul Perez WBC	1988–91
O. Canizales* IBF	1988–95†
Luisito Espinosa WBA	1989–91
Israel Contreras WBA	1991–92
Eddie Cook WBA	1992–93
Greg Richardson WBC	1991
J. Tatsuyoshi, WBC	1991–92
Victor Rabanales WBC	1992–93
Jung-Il Byun WBC	1993
Jorge Julio WBA	1993
Yasuei Yakushiji WBC	1993–95
Junior Jones WBA	1994

Champion	Reign
John M. Johnson WBA	1994
D. Chuvatana WBA	1994–95
V. Sahaprom* WBA	1995–96
W. McCullough WBC	1995–96
Harold Mestre IBF	1995
Mbulelo Botile IBF	1995–97
Nana Konadu* WBA	1996–98
S. Singmanassak	1996–97
Tim Austin IBF	1997–03
J.Tatsuyoshi IBF	1997–98
Johnny Tapia* WBA	1998–99
V. Sahaprom* WBC	1998–05
Paulie Ayala* WBA	1999–01†
Eidy Moya WBA	2001–02

Champion	Reign
Johnny Bredahl WBA	2002–05
Rafael Marquez IBF	2003–07
W. Sidorenko WBA	2005–08
H. Hasegawa WBC	2005–10
Luis Perez IBF	2007
Joseph Agbeko IBF	2007–09
Anselmo Moreno WBA	2008–
Yohnny Perez IBF	2009–
Fernando Montiel WBC	2010–

Super Flyweights (Weight Limit: 115 pounds)

Champion	Reign
Rafael Orono* WBC	1980–81
Chul-Ho Kim* WBC	1981–82
Gustavo Ballas WBA	1981
Rafael Pedroza WBA	1981–82
Jiro Watanabe WBA	1982–84
Rafael Orono* WBC	1982–83
Payao Poontarat* WBC	1983–84
Joo-Do Chun IBF	1983–85
Jiro Watanabe*	1984–86
Kaosai Galaxy WBA	1984
Ellyas Pical IBF	1985–86
Cesar Polanco IBF	1986
Gilberto Roman* WBC	1986–87
Ellyas Pical IBF	1986
Santos Laciar* WBC	1987
Tae-Il Chang IBF	1987

Champion	Reign
Sugar Rojas* WBC	1987–88
Ellyas Pical IBF	1987–89
Giberto Roman* WBC	1988–89
Juan Polo Perez IBF	1989–90
Nana Konadu* WBC	1989–90
Sung-Kil Moon* WBC	1990–93
Robert Quiroga IBF	1990–93
Julio Borboa IBF	1993–94
Katsuya Onizuka WBA	1993–94
Lee Hyung-Chul WBA	1994–95
Jose Luis Bueno* WBC	1993–94
H. Kawashima* WBC	1994–97
Harold Grey IBF	1994–95

Champion	Reign
Alimi Goitia WBA	1995–96
Yokthai Sith-Oar WBA	1996–97
Carlos Salazar IBF	1995–96
Harold Grey IBF	1996
Danny Romero IBF	1996–97
Gerry Penalosa* WBC	1997–98
Johnny Tapia IBF	1997–99†
Satoshi Iida WBA	1997–98
In-Joo Cho* WBC	1998–00
Jesus Rojas WBA	1998–99
Mark Johnson IBF	1999–00
Hideki Todaka WBA	1999–00
Felix Machado IBF	2000–03
M. Tokuyama* WBC	2000–04
Leo Gamez WBA	2000–01
Celes Kobayashi	

Champion	Reign
WBA	2001–02
Alexander Munoz WBA	2002–05
Luis Alberto Perez IBF	2003–06
Katsushige Kawashima WBC	2004–05
M. Tokuyama WBC	2005–06
Jose M. Castillo WBA	2005–06
Nobuo Nashiro WBA	2006–08
Cristian Mijares WBC	2006–08
Dmitri Kirilov IBF	2007–08
Vic Darchinyan WBC, WBA	2008–
IBF	2006–09†
Simphiwe Nongqayi IBF	2009–

Flyweights (Weight Limit: 112 pounds)

Champion	Reign
Sid Smith*	1913
Bill Ladbury*	1913–14
Percy Jones*	1914†
Joe Symonds*	1914–16
Jimmy Wilde*	1916–23
Pancho Villa*	1923–25†
Fidel La Barba*	1925–27†
Frenchy Belanger* NBA	1927–28
Izzy Schwartz NY	1927–29
Frankie Genaro* NBA	1928–29
Spider Pladner* NBA	1929
Frankie Genaro* NBA	1929–31
Midget Wolgast NY	1930–35
Young Perez* NBA	1931–32
Jackie Brown* NBA	1932–35
Benny Lynch*	1935–38†
Small Montana NY	1935–37
Peter Kane*	1938–43
Little Dado NY	1938–40

Champion	Reign
Jackie Paterson*	1943–48
Rinty Monaghan*	1948–50†
Terry Allen*	1950
Dado Marino*	1950–52
Yoshio Shirai*	1952–54
Pascual Perez*	1954–60
Pone Kingpetch*	1960–62
Masahiko Harada*	1962–63
Pone Kingpetch*	1963
Hiroyuki Ebihara*	1963–64
Pone Kingpetch*	1964–65
Salvatore Burrini*	1965–66
H. Accavallo WBA	1966–68
Walter McGowan*	1966
Chartchai Chionoi*	1966–69
Efren Torres*	1969–70
Hiroyuki Ebihara WBA	1969
B. Villacampo WBA	1969–70
Chartchai Chionoi*	1970
B. Chartvanchai WBA	1970
Masao Ohba WBA	1970–73

Champion	Reign
Erbito Salavarria*	1970–73†
B. Gonzalez WBA	1972
V. Borkorsor WBC	1972–73†
Venice Borkorsor*	1973†
Chartchai Chionoi WBA	1973–74
B. Gonzalez* WBA	1973–74
Shoji Oguma* WBC	1974–75
S. Hanagata WBA	1974–75
Miguel Canto* WBC	1975–79
Erbito Salavarria WBA	1975–76
Alfonso Lopez WBA	1976
G. Espadas WBA	1976–78
B. Gonzalez WBA	1978–79
Chan-Hee Park* WBC	1979–80
Luis Ibarra WBA	1979–80
Tae-Shik Kim WBA	1980
Shoji Oguma* WBC	1980–81
Peter Mathebula WBA	1980–81
Santos Laciar WBA	1981
Antonio Avelar* WBC	1981–82

Champion	Reign
Luis Ibarra WBA	1981
Juan Herrera WBA	1981–82
P. Cardona* WBC	1982
Santos Laciar WBA	1982–85
Freddie Castillo* WBC	1982
E. Mercedes* WBA	1982–83
Charlie Magri* WBC	1983
Frank Cedeno* WBC	1983–84
Soon-Chun Kwon IBF	1983–85
Koji Kobayashi* WBC	1984
Gabriel Bernal* WBC	1984
Sot Chitalada* WBC	1984–88
Hilario Zapate WBA	1985–87
Chong-Kwan Chung IBF	1985–86
Bi-Won Chung IBF	1986
Hi-Sup Shin IBF	1986–87
Dodie Penalosa IBF	1987
Fidel Bassa WBA	1987–89

*Lineal champion. †Champion relinquished title to retire or switch weight classes, or had title stripped by boxing organization.

Flyweights *(Cont.)*

Champion	Reign
Choi-Chang Ho IBF	1987–88
Rolando Bohol IBF	1988
Yong-Kang Kim*	
WBC	1988–89
Duke McKenzie IBF	1988–89
Sot Chitalada* WBC	1989–91
Dave McAuley IBF	1989–92
Jesus Rojas WBA	1989–90
Yul-Woo Lee WBA	1990
L. Tamakuma WBA	1990–91
M. Kittikasem* WBC	1991–92
Yuri Arbachakov*	
WBC	1992–97

Champion	Reign
Yong Kang Kim	
WBA	1991–92
Rodolfo Blanco IBF	1992–93
P. Sithbangprachan IBF	1992–93
David Griman WBA	1992–94
S.S. Ploenchit WBA	1994–96
Francisco Tejedor IBF	1995
Danny Romero IBF	1995–96
Mark Johnson IBF	1996–99†
Jose Bonilla WBA	1996–98
Chatchai Sasakul*	
WBC	1997–98
Hugo Soto WBA	1998–99

Champion	Reign
Manny Pacquiao* WBC	1998–99
Leo Gamez WBA	1999
Irene Pacheco IBF	1999–05
S. Pisnurachan WBA	1999–00
M. Sinsurat* WBC	1999–00
Malcolm Tunacao* WBC	2000–01
Eric Morel WBA	2000–03
P. Wonjongkam*	
WBC	2001–07
Lorenzo Parra WBA	2003–07
Vic Darchinyan IBF	2005–07
Takefumi Sakata	
WBA	2007–08

Champion	Reign
Daisuke Naito WBC	2007–09
Nonito Donaire IBF	2007–09†
Denkaosan Kaovichit	
WBA	2008–10
Koki Kameda WBC	2009–10
Daiki Kameda WBA	2010–
Pongsaklek Wonjongkam	
WBC	2010–

Light Flyweights (Weight Limit: 108 pounds)

Champion	Reign
Franco Udella WBC	1975
Jaime Rios WBA	1975–76
Luis Estaba* WBC	1975–78
Juan Guzman WBA	1976
Yoko Gushiken WBA	1976–81
Freddy Castillo* WBC	1978
Sor Vorasingh* WBC	1978
Sung-Jun Kim* WBC	1978–80
Shigeo Nakajima* WBC	1980
Hilario Zapata* WBC	1980–82
Pedro Flores WBA	1981
Hwan-Jin Kim WBA	1981
Katsuo Tokashiki WBA	1981–83
Amado Urzua* WBC	1982
Tadashi Tomori* WBC	1982
Hilario Zapata* WBC	1982–83
Jung-Koo Chang* WBC	1983–88†
Lupe Madera WBA	1983–84
Dodie Penalosa IBF	1983–86
Francisco Quiroz WBA	1984–85
Joey Olivo WBA	1985
Myung-Woo Yuh* WBA	1985–91
Jum-Hwan Choi IBF	1986–88

Champion	Reign
Tacy Macalos IBF	1988–89
German Torres WBC	1988–89
Yul-Woo Lee WBC	1989
M. Kittikasem IBF	1989–90
H. Gonzalez WBC	1989–90
Michael Carbajal IBF	1990–94
R. Pascua WBC	1990
M. C. Castro WBC	1991
H. Gonzalez WBC	1991–93
Hirokia Ioka* WBA	1991–92
Myung-Woo Yuh* WBA	1993†
Michael Carbajal* WBC	1993–94
Leo Gamez WBA	1993–95
H. Gonzalez* WBC, IBF	1994–95
Choi Hi-Yong	1995–96
S. Sor Jaturong WBC, IBF	1995–96
Carlos Murillo WBA	1996
Keiji Yamaguchi WBA	1996
Michael Carbajal IBF	1996–97
Saman Jaturong* WBC	1995–99
Phichitchor Siriwat WBA	1996–00
Mauricio Pastrana IBF	1997–98†
Will Grigsby IBF	1998–99

Champion	Reign
Ricardo Lopez IBF	1999–02
Yo-Sam Choi* WBC	1999–02
Beibis Mendoza WBA	2000–01
Rosendo Alvarez WBA	2001–05
Jorge Arce* WBC	2002–05
Jose Burgos IBF	2003–05
Brian Viloria WBC	2005–06
R. Vasquez WBA	2005–06
Will Grigsby IBF	2005–06
Koki Kameda WBA	2006–07
Omar Nino Rivero WBC	2006–07
Ulises Solis IBF	2006–09
Juan Carlos Reveco WBA	2007
Edgar Sosa WBC	2007–09
Brahim Asloum WBA	2007–09†
Giovanni Segura WBA	2009–
Brian Viloria IBF	2009–
Rodel Mayol WBC	2009–10
Omar Nino Romero WBC	2010–

Strawweights (Weight Limit: 105 pounds)

Champion	Reign
Kyung-Yun Lee* IBF	1987
Hiroki Ioka* WBC	1987–88
Leo Gamez WBA	1988–89
S. Sithnaruepol IBF	1988–89
N. Kiatwanchai* WBC	1988–89
Bong-Jun Kim WBA	1989–91
Nico Thomas IBF	1989
Eric Chavez IBF	1989–90
Jum-Hwan Choi* WBC	1989–90
Hideyuki Ohashi* WBC	1990
F. Lookmingkwan IBF	1990–92
Ricardo Lopez* WBC	1990–98†
Hi-Yong Choi WBA	1991–92
Manny Melchor IBF	1992
Hideyuki Ohashi WBA	1992–93
R.S. Voraphin IBF	1992–96
Chana Porpaoin WBA	1993–95

Champion	Reign
Rosendo Alvarez WBA	1995–98
R. Sor Vorapin IBF	1996–97
Zolani Petelo* IBF	1997–00†
W. Chor Charoen WBC	1998–00
R. Lopez* WBA, WBC	1998–99†
Songkram Popaoin WBA	1999
Noel Arambulet WBA	1999–00
Jose Aguirre* WBC	2000–04
Joma Gamboa WBA	2000
Keitaro Hoshino WBA	2000–01
Chana Porpaoin WBA	2001
Roberto Leyva IBF	2001–02
Yutaka Niida WBA	2001†
Miguel Barrera IBF	2002–03
Edgar Cardenas IBF	2003
Noel Arambulet WBA	2002–04
Daniel Reyes IBF	2003–05

Champion	Reign
Eagle Junlaphan WBC	2004
Isaac Bustos WBC	2004–05
Yutaka Niida WBA	2004–08
K. Takayama WBC	2005
Eagle Junlaphan WBC	2005–07
M. Rachman IBF	2005–07
Florante Condes IBF	2007–08
O. Sithsamerchai WBC	2007–
Roman Gonzalez WBA	2008–
Raul Garcia IBF	2008–10
Nkosinathi Joyi IBF	2010–

*Lineal champion.   †Champion relinquished title to retire or switch weight classes, or had title stripped by boxing organization.

Lineal Heavyweight Champions

Champion	Reign	Age*	Career	W-L-D (KO)	SD
John L. Sullivan	1885–92	26	1878–92	38-1-3 (33)	0
James J. Corbett	1892–97	26	1884–03	11-4-2 (7)	1
Bob Fitzsimmons	1897–99	33	1880–16	74-8-3 (67)	0
James J. Jeffries†	1899–05	24	1896–10	18-1-2 (15)	7
Marvin Hart	1905–06	28	1899–10	28-7-4 (19)	0
Tommy Burns	1906–08	24	1900–20	46-5-8 (37)	11
Jack Johnson	1908–15	30	1894–28	77-13-14 (48)	9
Jess Willard	1915–19	33	1911–23	23-6-1 (20)	1
Jack Dempsey	1919–26	24	1914–27	60-6-8 (50)	5
Gene Tunney†	1926–28	29	1915–28	61-1-1 (45)	2
Max Schmeling	1930–32	24	1924–48	56-10-4 (39)	1
Jack Sharkey	1932–33	29	1924–36	38-13-3 (14)	0
Primo Carnera	1933–34	26	1928–37	88-14-0 (69)	2
Max Baer	1934–35	25	1929–41	72-12-0 (53)	0
James J. Braddock	1935–37	29	1926–38	51-26-7 (26)	0
Joe Louis†	1937–49	23	1934–51	68-3-0 (54)	25
Ezzard Charles	1949–51	27	1940–59	96-25-1 (59)	8
Jersey Joe Walcott	1951–52	37	1930–53	53-18-1 (33)	1
Rocky Marciano†	1952–56	29	1947–56	49-0-0 (43)	6
Floyd Patterson	1956–59	21	1952–72	55-8-1 (40)	4
Ingemar Johansson	1959–60	26	1952–63	26-2-0 (17)	0
Floyd Patterson	1960–62	25	1952–72	55-8-1 (40)	2
Sonny Liston	1962–64	30	1953–70	50-4-0 (39)	1
Muhammad Ali	1964–71	22	1960–81	56-5-0 (37)	9
Joe Frazier	1971–73	27	1965–81	32-4-1 (27)	2
George Foreman	1973–74	24	1969–97	76-5-0 (68)	2
Muhammad Ali	1974–78	32	1960–81	56-5-0 (37)	10
Leon Spinks	1978	24	1977–95	26-17-3 (14)	0
Muhammad Ali†	1978–79	36	1960–81	56-5-0 (37)	0
Larry Holmes	1980–85	29	1973–2002	69-6-0 (44)	20
Michael Spinks	1985–88	29	1977–88	32-1-0 (21)	3
Mike Tyson	1988–90	21	1985–2005	49-4-0 (43)	2
Buster Douglas	1990	29	1981–99	38-6-1 (25)	0
Evander Holyfield	1990–92	28	1984–	38-5-2 (26)	3
Riddick Bowe	1992–93	25	1989–96	40-1-0 (32)	2
Evander Holyfield	1993–94	31	1984–	38-5-2 (26)	0
Michael Moorer	1994	26	1988–97	39-2-0 (31)	0
George Foreman	1994–97	45	1969–97	76-5-0 (68)	3
Shannon Briggs	1997–98	25	1992–00	32-3-1 (25)	0
Lennox Lewis	1998–01	32	1989–2004	40-2-1 (31)	5
Hasim Rahman	2001	28	1994–	35-4-0 (29)	0
Lennox Lewis†	2001–04	36	1989–2004	41-2-1 (32)	2
Chris Byrd	2002–06	35	1993–	38-2-1 (20)	3
John Ruiz	2001–03	31	1992–	38-5-1 (28)	2
Roy Jones, Jr.	2003	34	1989–	49-3-0 (38)	0
John Ruiz	2003–05	33	1992–	41-6-1 (28)	2
Vitali Klitschko†	2004–05	34	1996–2005; 2007–	34-2-0 (33)	1
Hasim Rahman	2005-06	33	1994–	41-5-2 (33)	1
Oleg Maskaev	2006–08	37	1993–	32-5-0 (26)	0
Wladimir Klitschko	2006–	33	1996–	55-3-0 (49)	0
Nikolay Valuev	2005–07	32	1993–	44-0-0 (32)	1
Ruslan Chagaev	2007–08	28	2001	24-0-1 (17)	1
Samuel Peter	2008	28	2004–	30-2-0 (23)	0
Vitali Klitschko^	2008–	38	1996–2005; 2007–	40-2-0 (38)	0
Nikolay Valuev	2008–09	36	1993–	50-1-0 (34)	0
David Haye	2009–	30	2002–	24-1-0 (22)	0

*Age when boxer won world championship.
† Boxer retired or relinquished world title.
^ Boxer returned from retirement.

NCAA
Sports

The NCAA men's Division I
championship trophy simply moved a
few miles down Commonwealth Ave.
between 2009 and 2010, from
Boston University to Boston College

FOR THE RECORD • 2009—2010

NCAA Team Champions

Fall 2009

			Champion	Runner-Up
Cross-Country	MEN	Division I:	Oklahoma St	Oregon
		Division II:	Adams St	Western St
		Division III:	North Central (Ill.)	Williams
	WOMEN	Division I:	Villanova	Florida St
		Division II:	Adams St	Grand Valley St
		Division III:	UW-Eau Claire	St. Lawrence
Field Hockey	WOMEN	Division I:	North Carolina	Maryland
		Division II	Bloomsburg	UMass-Lowell
		Division III:	Messiah	Salisbury
Football	MEN	FCS (I-AA):	Villanova	Montana
		Division II:	NW Missouri St	Grand Valley St
		Division III:	UW-Whitewater	Mount Union
Soccer	MEN	Division I:	Virginia	Akron
		Division II:	Fort Lewis	Lees-McRae
		Division III:	Messiah	Calvin
	WOMEN	Division I:	North Carolina	Stanford
		Division II:	Grand Valley St	CSU-Dominguez Hills
		Division III:	Messiah	Washington-St. Louis
Volleyball	WOMEN	Division I:	Penn St	Texas
		Division II:	Concordia-St. Paul	West Texas A&M
		Division III:	Washington-St. Louis	Juniata
Water Polo	MEN		USC	UCLA

Winter 2009–10

			Champion	Runner-Up
Bowling	WOMEN		Fairleigh Dickinson	Nebraska
Basketball	MEN	Division I:	Duke	Butler
		Division II:	Cal. Poly-Pomona	Indiana (Pa.)
		Division III:	UW-Stevens Point	Williams
	WOMEN	Division I:	Connecticut	Stanford
		Division II:	Emporia St	Gannon
		Division III:	Washington-St. Louis	Hope
Fencing			Penn St	St. John's
Gymnastics	MEN		Michigan	Stanford
	WOMEN		UCLA	Oklahoma
Ice Hockey	MEN	Division I:	Boston College	Wisconsin
		Division III:	Norwich	St. Norbert
	WOMEN	Division I:	Minn.-Duluth	Cornell
		Division III:	Amherst	Norwich
Rifle			TCU	Alaska-Fairbanks
Skiing			Denver	Colorado
Swimming and Diving	MEN	Division I:	Texas	California
		Division II:	Drury	Incarnate Word
		Division III:	Kenyon	Denison
	WOMEN	Division I:	California	Georgia
		Division II:	Drury	Wayne St
		Division III:	Emory	Denison

Winter 2009-2010 (Cont.)

			Champion	Runner-Up
Wrestling	MEN	Division I:	Iowa	Cornell
		Division II:	Neb.-Omaha	Augustana
		Division III:	Augsburg (Minn.)	UW-La Crosse
Indoor Track and Field	MEN	Division I:	Florida	Florida
		Division II:	Adams St	St. Augustine's (N.C.)
		Division III:	North Central (Ill.)	UW-Stevens Point
	WOMEN	Division I:	Oregon	Texas A&M
		Division II:	Lincoln (Mo.)	Ashland/ Grand Valley St
		Division III:	Wartburg	Oshkosh

Spring 2010

			Champion	Runner-Up
Baseball		Division I:	South Carolina	UCLA
		Division II:	Southern Indiana	UC-San Diego
		Division III:	Illinois-Wesleyan	SUNY-Cortland
Golf	MEN	Division I:	Augusta St	Oklahoma St
		Division II:	Florida Southern	Central Missouri
		Division III:	Methodist	Guilford
	WOMEN	Division I:	Purdue	USC
		Division II:	Nova Southeastern	Rollins
		Division III	Methodist	Gustavus Adolphus
Lacrosse	MEN	Division I:	Duke	Notre Dame
		Division II:	LIU-C.W. Post	Le Moyne
		Division III:	Tufts	Salisbury
	WOMEN	Division I:	Maryland	Northwestern
		Division II	Adelphi	West Chester
		Division III:	Salisbury	Hamilton
Rowing	WOMEN	Division I:	Virginia	California
		Division II	Western Washington	Seattle Pacific
		Division III:	Williams	Bates
Softball		Division I:	UCLA	Arizona
		Division II:	Hawaii Pacific	Valdosta St
		Division III:	East Texas Baptist	Linfield
Tennis	MEN	Division I:	USC	Tennessee
		Division II:	Barry	Valdosta St
		Division III:	Middlebury	Amherst
	WOMEN	Division I:	Stanford	Florida
		Division II:	Armstrong Atlantic St	BYU-Hawaii
		Division III:	Williams	Emory
Outdoor Track and Field	MEN	Division I:	Texas A&M	Florida
		Division II:	St. Augustine's (N.C.)	Abilene Christian
		Division III:	North Central (Ill.)	Salisbury
	WOMEN	Division I:	Texas A&M	Oregon
		Division II:	Angelo St	Lincoln (Mo.)
		Division III:	Illinois Wesleyan	UW-Oshkosh
Volleyball	MEN		Stanford	Penn St
Water Polo	MEN		USC	UCLA
	WOMEN		USC	Stanford

NCAA Division I Individual Champions

Fall 2009 – Cross Country

	Champion	Runner-Up
MEN	Samuel Chelanga, Liberty	David McNeill, Northern Arizona
WOMEN	Angela Bizzarri, Illinois	Kendra Schaaf, Villanova

Winter 2009-10

Gymnastics

MEN

	Champion	Runner-Up
All-around	Chris Cameron, Michigan	Steven Legendre, Oklahoma
Vault	Eddie Penev, Stanford	Geoff Reins, Iowa
Parallel bars	Ryan Lieberman, Stanford	Mel Anton Santander, Michigan
Horizontal bar	Ryan McCarthy, Michigan	Ian Mackowske, Michigan
Floor exercise	Steven Legendre, Oklahoma	Eddie Penev, Stanford
Pommel horse	Alex Naddour, Oklahoma	Glen Ishino, California
Rings	Brandon Wynn, Ohio St	Tyler Williamson, Illinois

WOMEN

	Champion	Runner-Up
All-around	Susan Jackson, LSU	Kristina Baskett, Utah
Balance beam	Susan Jackson, LSU	Courtney McCool, Georgia/ Carly Janiga, Stanford
Uneven bars	Carly Janiga, Stanford	Summer Hubbard, LSU
Floor exercise	Brittani McCullough, UCLA	Ashleigh Clare-Kearney, LSU
Vault	Vanessa Zamarripa, UCLA	Susan Jackson, LSU

Skiing

MEN

	Champion	Runner-Up
Slalom	Andreas Adde, Ak.-Anchorage	Torjus Krogdahl, Utah
Giant slalom	Leif Haugen, Denver	Ace Tarberry, Dartmouth
10-kilometer classic	Matt Gelso, Colorado	Franz Bernstein, Vermont
20-kilometer free	Franz Bernstein, Vermont	Martin Kaas, Vermont

WOMEN

	Champion	Runner-Up
Slalom	Malin Hemmingsson, New Mexico	Lindsay Cone, Denver
Giant slalom	Eva Huckova, Utah	Lindsay Cone, Denver
5-kilometer classic	Antje Maempel, Denver	Rosie Brennan, Dartmouth
15-kilometer free	Antje Maempel, Denver	Alexa Turzian, Colorado

Wrestling

	Champion	Runner-Up
125 lb	Matt McDonough, Iowa	Andrew Long, Iowa St
133 lb	Jayson Ness, Minnesota	Dan Dennis, Iowa
141 lb	Kyle Dake, Cornell	Montel Marion, Iowa
149 lb	Brent Metcalf, Iowa	Lance Palmer, Ohio St
157 lb	J.P. O'Connor, Harvard	Chase Pami, Cal Poly
165 lb	Andrew Howe, Wisconsin	Dan Vallimont, Penn St
174 lb	Jay Borschel, Iowa	Mack Lewnes, Cornell
184 lb	Max Askren, Missouri	Kirk Smith, Boise St
197 lb	Jake Varner, Iowa St	Craig Brester, Nebraska
285 lb	David Zabriskie, Iowa St	Jared Rosholt, Oklahoma St

Swimming and Diving — Men

	Champion	Time	Runner-Up	Time
50-yd freestyle	Josh Schneider, Cincinnati	18.93	Nathan Adrian, California	19.02
100-yd freestyle	Nathan Adrian, California	41.50	James Feigen, Texas	41.91
200-yd freestyle	Conor Dwyer, Florida	1:32.31	Shaune Fraser, Florida	1:32.53
500-yd freestyle	Conor Dwyer, Florida	4:13.64	Jean Besson, Arizona	4:13.65
1650-yd freestyle	Chad La Tourette, Stanford	14:42.87	Martin Grodzki, Georgia	14:48.15
100-yd backstroke	Eugene Godsoe, Stanford	45.11	Jake Tapp, Arizona	46.16
200-yd backstroke	Cory Chitwood, Arizona	1:39.29	Tyler Clary, Michigan	1:39.89
100-yd breaststroke	Damir Dugonjic, California	51.65	Scott Spann, Texas	52.22
200-yd breaststroke	Clark Burckle, Arizona	1:53.19	Scott Spann, Texas	1:53.21
100-yd butterfly	Thomas Shields, California	44.91	Mathias Gydesen, California	45.83
200-yd butterfly	Shaune Fraser, Florida	1:41.45	Thomas Shields, California	1:41.52
200-yd IM	Austin Surhoff, Texas	1:42.95	Shaune Fraser, Florida	1:42.99
400-yd IM	Tyler Clary, Michigan	3:38.89	Gal Nevo, Georgia Tech	3:40.68
200-yd free relay	California	1:15.71	Auburn	1:16.01
400-yd free relay	California	2:48.78	Texas	2:49.90
800-yd free relay	Texas	6:12.77	Florida	6:14.72
200-yd medley relay	California	1:23.08	Auburn	1:24.13
400-yd medley relay	California	3:02.83	Auburn	3:05.24
1-meter diving	David Boudia, Purdue	468.65	Terry Horner, Florida St	432.45
3-meter diving	David Boudia, Purdue	494.90	Nick McCrory, Duke	459.15
Platform	Nick McCrory, Duke	534.00	Riley McCormick, Arizona St	469.50

Winter 2009-10 (Cont.)
Swimming and Diving — Women

	Champion	Time/Pts	Runner-Up	Time/Pts
50-yd freestyle	Liv Jensen, California	22.04	Elizabeth Webb, Stanford	22.07
100-yd freestyle	Julia Wilkinson, Texas A&M	47.61	Morgan Scroggy, Georgia	47.72
200-yd freestyle	Allison Schmitt, Georgia	1:42.84	Morgan Scroggy, Georgia	1:42.94
500-yd freestyle	Allison Schmitt, Georgia	4:34.14	Lauren Boyle, California	4:37.18
1650-yd freestyle	Wendy Trott, Georgia	15:48.87	Ali Aemisegger, Princeton	15:57.02
100-yd backstroke	Gemma Spofforth, Florida	50.92	Kateryna Fesenko, Indiana	51.15
200-yd backstroke	Kateryna Fesenko, Indiana	1:49.92	Gemma Spofforth, Florida	1:50.24
100-yd breaststroke	Annie Chandler, Arizona	58.06-*	Ashley Danner, George Mason	59.29
200-yd breaststroke	Alia Atkinson, Texas A&M	2:07.38	Elizabeth Smith, Stanford	2:07.50
100-yd butterfly	Elaine Breeden, Stanford	51.43	Lyndsey DePaul, USC	51.72
200-yd butterfly	Elaine Breeden, Stanford	1:52.39	Katinka Hosszu, USC	1:52.52
200-yd IM	Julia Smit, Stanford	1:53.56	Julia Wilkinson, Texas A&M	1:54.45
400-yd IM	Julia Smit, Stanford	4:00.90	Teresa Crippen, Florida	4:02.91
200-yd free relay	Florida	1:27.79	Stanford	1:28.38
400-yd free relay	Stanford	3:12.32	California	3:12.67
800-yd free relay	Georgia	6:55.61	California	7:00.00
200-yd medley relay	Arizona	1:36.61	Tennessee	1:36.90
400-yd medley relay	Arizona	3:29.76	Stanford	3:30.45
1-meter diving	Anas. Pozdniakova, Houston	356.20	Kelci Bryant, Minnesota	352.65
3-meter diving	Kelci Bryant, Minnesota	415.50	Anas. Pozdniakova, Houston	406.45
Platform	Chen Ni, IUPUI	325.50	Carrie Dragland, Alabama	323.05

Indoor Track and Field — Men

	Champion	Time/Mark	Runner-Up	Time/Mark
60-meter dash	Jeff Demps, Florida	6.57	Gerald Phiri, Texas A&M	6.60
60-meter hurdles	Ronnie Ash, Oklahoma	7.56	Booker Nunley, South Carolina	7.58
200-meter dash	Curtis Mitchell, Texas A&M	20.38	Brandon Byram, Florida St	20.46
400-meter dash	Torrin Lawrence, Georgia	45.23	Kirani James, Alabama	45.63
800-meter run	Robby Andrews, Virginia	1:48.39	Andrew Wheating, Oregon	1:48.40
4x400-meter relay	Texas A&M	3:04.40	Baylor	3:05.01
Mile run	Lee Emanuel, New Mexico	3:59.26	Mac Fleet, Oregon	4:01.63
3,000-meter run	Dorian Ulrey, Arkansas	8:10.52	David McNeill, Northern Arizona	8:10.96
5,000-meter run	David McNeill, Northern Arizona	13:36.41	Sam Chelanga, Liberty	13:37.01
Distance medley	Oregon	9:36.87	Arkansas	9:37.53
High jump	Derek Drouin, Indiana	2.28m	Ricky Roberston, Mississippi	2.25m
Pole Vault	Scott Roth, Washington	5.60m	Jason Colwick, Rice	5.50m
Long jump	Alain Bailey, Arkansas	8.17m	Christian Taylor, Florida	7.93m
Triple jump	Christian Taylor, Florida	17.18m	Zedric Thomas, LSU	16.30m
Shot put	Ryan Whiting, Arizona St	21.52m	Kemal Mesic, Florida	19.26m
35-pound wt throw	Walter Henning, LSU	23.56m	Steffen Nerdal, Memphis	23.22m
Heptathlon	Ashton Eaton, Oregon	6.499 pts-a	Mateo Sossah, North Carolina	5,886 pts

Indoor Track and Field — Women

	Champion	Time/Mark	Runner-Up	Time/Mark
60-meter dash	Blessing Okagbare, UTEP	7.18	Gabby Mayo, Texas A&M	7.18
60-meter hurdles	Queen Harrison, Virginia Tech	7.95	Kristi Castlin, Virginia Tech	8.01
200-meter dash	Shaniqua Ferguson, Auburn	23.09	Nivea Smith, Auburn	23.12
400-meter dash	Francena McCorory, Hampton	50.54-a	Keshia Baker, Oregon	51.63
800-meter run	Phoebe Wright, Tennessee	2:02.55	Lacey Cramer, LSU	2:03.89
4x400-meter relay	Oregon	3:32.97	LSU	3:33.79
Mile run	Charlotte Browning, Florida	4:35.36	Katie Follett, Washington	4:36.39
3,000-meter run	Angela Bizzarri, Illinois	8:57.40	Lisa Koll, Iowa St	8.57.52
5,000-meter run	Lisa Koll, Iowa St	15:39.65	Marie Louise Asselin, W. Virginia	15:50.53
Distance medley	Tennessee	10:58.37	Oregon	10:58.96
High jump	Elizabeth Patterson, Arizona	1.93m	Amber Kaufman, Hawaii	1.90m
Pole vault	Kylie Hutson, Indiana St	4.50m	Melissa Gergel, Oregon	4.45m
Long jump	Blessing Okagbare, UTEP	6.87m	Mindy McClurkin, BYU	6.69m
Triple jump	Kimberly Williams, Florida St	13.95m	Patricia Mamona, Clemson	13.85m
Shot Put	Miriam Kevkhishvili, Florida	18.59m	Ashley Muffet, Kentucky	17.31m
20-pound wt throw	D'Ana McCarty, Louisville	22.76m	Victoria Flowers, Connecticut	21.44m
Pentathlon	Brianne Theisen, Oregon	4,396 pts	Kiani Profit, Maryland	4,242 pts

Rifle

	Champion	Pts	Runner-Up	Pts
Smallbore	Sarah Scherer, TCU	685.0	Patrik Sartz, Ak.-Anchorage	682.7
Air rifle	Jonathan Hall, Columbus St (Ga.)	699.9	Ashley Jackson, Kentucky	697.4

a-American record. *-NCAA record.

Spring 2010

Golf

	Champion	Score	Runners-Up	Score
MEN	Scott Langley, Purdue	206	Alex Ching, San Diego	208
			Peter Uihlein, Oklahoma St	
WOMEN	Caroline Hedwall, Oklahoma St	276	Jennifer Johnson, Arizona St	280

Outdoor Track and Field

MEN

	Champion	Mark	Runner-Up	Mark
100-meter dash	Jeff Demps, Florida	9.96	Rondel Sorrillo, Kentucky	10.09
200-meter dash	Rondel Sorrillo, Kentucky	20.36	Curtis Mitchell, Texas A&M	20.45
400-meter dash	Kirani James, Alabama	45.05	Donald Sanford, Arizona St	45.21
4x100-meter relay	Florida	39.04	Florida St	39.07
800-meter run	Andrew Wheating, Oregon	1:45.69	Robby Andrews, Virginia	1:46.83
1,500-meter run	Andrew Wheating, Oregon	3:47.94	A.J. Acosta, Oregon	3:48.01
4x400-meter relay	Texas A&M	3:00.89	Mississippi St	3:01.66
5,000-meter run	David McNeil, Northern Arizona	13:44.81	Sam Chelanga, Liberty	13:45.35
10,000-meter run	Sam Chelanga, Liberty	28:37.40	John Kosgei, Oklahoma St	28:55.93
110-meter hurdles	Andrew Riley, Illinois	13.45	Barrett Nugent, LSU	13.49
400-meter hurdles	Johnny Dutch, South Carolina	48.75	Jeshua Anderson, Washington St	49.31
3,000-meter steeple	Matt Hughes, Louisville	8:34.18	Donn Cabral, Princeton	8:38.90
High jump	Derek Drouin, Indiana	2.26m	Manjula Kumara, USC	2.23m
Pole vault	Jordan Scott, Kansas	5.40m	Josh Dominguez, LSU	5.40m
Long jump	Marquise Goodwin, Texas	8.15m	Stanley Gbagbeke, Mid. Tenn. St	7.96m
Triple jump	Christian Taylor, Florida	17.09m	Tyron Stewart, Texas A&M	16.38m
Shot put	Ryan Whiting, Arizona St	21.97m	Mason Finley, Kansas	20.68m
Discus throw	Ryan Whiting, Arizona St	59.06m	Mason Finley, Kansas	58.35m
Hammer throw	Walter Henning, LSU	72.79m	Alexander Ziegler, Virginia Tech	72.43m
Javelin throw	Craig Kinsley, Brown	76.29m	Pontus Thomee, Boise St	73.60m
Decathlon	Ashton Eaton, Oregon	8,457 pts	Michael Morrison, California	7,801 pts

WOMEN

	Champion	Mark	Runner-Up	Mark
100-meter dash	Blessing Okagbare, UTEP	10.98	Porscha Lucas, Texas A&M	11.12
200-meter dash	Porscha Lucas, Texas A&M	22.83	Jeneba Tarmoh, Texas A&M	22.92
400-meter dash	Francena McCorory, Hampton	50.69	Jessica Beard, Texas A&M	51.02
4x100-meter relay	Texas A&M	42.82	LSU	43.72
800-meter run	Phoebe Wright, Tennessee	2:01.40	Molly Beckwith, Indiana	2:02.14
1,500-meter run	Charlotte Browning, Florida	4:15.84	Gabriele Anderson, Minnesota	4:16.25
4x400-meter relay	Oregon	3:28.54	Texas A&M	3:28.57
5,000-meter run	Lisa Koll, Iowa St	15:23.80	Marie Louise Asselin, W. Virginia	15:53.93
10,000-meter run	Lisa Koll, Iowa St	32:49.35	Betsy Saina, Iowa St	33:13.13
100-meter hurdles	Queen Harrison, Virginia Tech	12.67	Ti'erra Brown, Miami (Fla.)	12.84
400-meter hurdles	Queen Harrison, Virginia Tech	54.55	Ti'erra Brown, Miami (Fla.)	55.22
3,000-meter steeple	Bridget Franck, Penn St	9:38.86	Emma Coburn, Colorado	9:51.86
High jump	Amber Kaufman, Hawaii-Manoa	1.86m	Elizabeth Patterson, Arizona	1.83m
Pole vault	Kylie Hutson, Indiana St	4.45m	Tina Sutej, Arkansas	4.40m
Long jump	Blessing Okagbare, UTEP	6.79m	Arantxa King, Stanford	6.57m
Triple jump	Patricia Mamona, Clemson	14.01m	Sarah Nambawa, Mid. Tenn. St	13.82m
Shot put	Mariam Kevkhishvili, Florida	18.11m	Karen Shump, Oklahoma	17.14m
Discus throw	Jeneva McCall, Southern Illinois	54.98m	Brittany Borman, Oklahoma	54.33m
Hammer throw	Nikola Lomnicka, Georgia	65.57m	Dorotea Habazin, Virginia Tech	64.05m
Javelin throw	Evelien Dekkers, Florida	58.99m	Brittany Borman, Oklahoma	53.00m
Heptathlon	Brianne Theisen, Oregon	6,094 pts	Kiani Profit, Maryland	5,682 pts

Tennis

		Champion	Score	Runner-Up
MEN	Singles	Bradley Klahn, Stanford	6–1, 6–2	Austen Childs, Louisville
	Doubles	D. Courtney/M. Shabaz, Virginia	6–7 (4), 6–2, 6–3	D. Sandgren/J.P. Smith, Tennessee
WOMEN	Singles	Chelsey Gullickson, Georgia	6–3, 7–6 (7)	Jana Juricova, California
	Doubles	H. Barte/L. Burdette, Stanford	7–5, 4–6, 6–0	N. Pluskota/C. Whoriskey, Tennessee

CHAMPIONSHIP RESULTS

Baseball

DIVISION I

Year	Champion	Coach	Score	Runner-Up	Most Outstanding Player
1947	California*	Clint Evans	8–7	Yale	No award
1948	USC	Sam Barry	9–2	Yale	No award
1949	Texas*	Bibb Falk	10–3	Wake Forest	Charles Teague, Wake Forest, 2B
1950	Texas	Bibb Falk	3–0	Washington St	Ray VanCleef, Rutgers, CF
1951	Oklahoma*	Jack Baer	3–2	Tennnessee	Sidney Hatfield, Tennessee, P-1B
1952	Holy Cross	Jack Barry	8–4	Missouri	James O'Neill, Holy Cross, P
1953	Michigan	Ray Fisher	7–5	Texas	J.L. Smith, Texas, P
1954	Missouri	John (Hi) Simmons	4–1	Rollins	Tom Yewcic, Michigan St, C
1955	Wake Forest	Taylor Sanford	7–6	Western Michigan	Tom Borland, Oklahoma St, P
1956	Minnesota	Dick Siebert	12–1	Arizona	Jerry Thomas, Minnesota, P
1957	California*	George Wolfman	1–0	Penn St	Cal Emery, Penn St, P-1B
1958	USC	Rod Dedeaux	8–7†	Missouri	Bill Thom, USC, P
1959	Oklahoma St	Toby Greene	5–3	Arizona	Jim Dobson, Oklahoma St, 3B
1960	Minnesota	Dick Siebert	2–1‡	USC	John Erickson, Minnesota, 2B
1961	USC*	Rod Dedeaux	1–0	Oklahoma St	Littleton Fowler, Oklahoma St, P
1962	Michigan	Don Lund	5–4	Santa Clara	Bob Garibaldi, Santa Clara, P
1963	USC	Rod Dedeaux	5–2	Arizona	Bud Hollowell, USC, C
1964	Minnesota	Dick Siebert	5–1	Missouri	Joe Ferris, Maine, P
1965	Arizona St	Bobby Winkles	2–1#	Ohio St	Sal Bando, Arizona St, 3B
1966	Ohio St	Marty Karow	8–2	Oklahoma St	Steve Arlin, Ohio St, P
1967	Arizona St	Bobby Winkles	11–2	Houston	Ron Davini, Arizona St, C
1968	USC*	Rod Dedeaux	4–3	Southern Illinois	Bill Seinsoth, USC, 1B
1969	Arizona St	Bobby Winkles	10–1	Tulsa	John Dolinsek, Arizona St, LF
1970	USC	Rod Dedeaux	2–1	Florida St	Gene Ammann, Florida St, P
1971	USC	Rod Dedeaux	7–2	Southern Illinois	Jerry Tabb, Tulsa, 1B
1972	USC	Rod Dedeaux	1–0	Arizona St	Russ McQueen, USC, P
1973	USC*	Rod Dedeaux	4–3	Arizona St	Dave Winfield, Minnesota, P-OF
1974	USC	Rod Dedeaux	7–3	Miami (Fla.)	George Milke, USC, P
1975	Texas	Cliff Gustafson	5–1	S Carolina	Mickey Reichenbach, Texas, 1B
1976	Arizona	Jerry Kindall	7–1	Eastern Michigan	Steve Powers, Arizona, P-DH
1977	Arizona St	Jim Brock	2–1	S Carolina	Bob Horner, Arizona St, 3B
1978	USC*	Rod Dedeaux	10–3	Arizona St	Rod Boxberger, USC, P
1979	CSU–Fullerton	Augie Garrido	2–1	Arkansas	Tony Hudson, CSU–Fullerton, P
1980	Arizona	Jerry Kindall	5–3	Hawaii	Terry Francona, Arizona, LF
1981	Arizona St	Jim Brock	7–4	Oklahoma St	Stan Holmes, Arizona St, LF
1982	Miami (Fla.)*	Ron Fraser	9–3	Wichita St	Dan Smith, Miami (Fla.), P
1983	Texas*	Cliff Gustafson	4–3	Alabama	Calvin Schiraldi, Texas, P
1984	CSU–Fullerton	Augie Garrido	3–1	Texas	John Fishel, CSU–Fullerton, LF
1985	Miami (Fla.)	Ron Fraser	10–6	Texas	Greg Ellena, Miami (Fla.), DH
1986	Arizona	Jerry Kindall	10–2	Florida St	Mike Senne, Arizona, LF
1987	Stanford	Mark Marquess	9–5	Oklahoma St	Paul Carey, Stanford, RF
1988	Stanford	Mark Marquess	9–4	Arizona St	Lee Plemel, Stanford, P
1989	Wichita St	Gene Stephenson	5–3	Texas	Greg Brummett, Wichita St, P
1990	Georgia	Steve Webber	2–1	Oklahoma St	Mike Rebhan, Georgia, P
1991	LSU	Skip Bertman	6–3	Wichita St	Gary Hymel, LSU, C
1992	Pepperdine	Andy Lopez	3–2	CSU–Fullerton	Phil Nevin, CSU–Fullerton, 3B
1993	LSU	Skip Bertman	8–0	Wichita St	Todd Walker, LSU, 2B
1994	Oklahoma	Larry Cochell	13–5	Georgia Tech	Chip Glass, Oklahoma, CF
1995	CSU–Fullerton*	Augie Garrido	11–5	USC	Mark Kotsay, CSU–Fullerton, CF-P
1996	LSU*	Skip Bertman	9–8	Miami (Fla.)	Pat Burrell, Miami (Fla.), 3B
1997	LSU*	Skip Bertman	13–6	Alabama	Brandon Larson, LSU, SS
1998	USC	Mike Gillespie	21–14	Arizona St	Wes Rachels, USC, 2B
1999	Miami (Fla.)	Jim Morris	6–5	Florida St	Marshall McDougall, FSU 3B/2B
2000	LSU*	Skip Bertman	6–5	Stanford	Trey Hodges, LSU, P
2001	Miami (Fla.)*	Jim Morris	12–1	Stanford	Charlton Jimerson, Miami (Fla.), OF
2002	Texas	Augie Garrido	12–6	South Carolina	Huston Street, Texas, P
2003	Rice	Wayne Graham	14–2^	Stanford	John Hudgins, Stanford, P
2004	CSU–Fullerton	George Horton	3–2^	Texas	Jason Windsor, CSU–Fullerton

*Undefeated teams in College World Series play.
†12 innings.   ‡10 innings.   #15 innings.   ^Score of decisive game of best-of-three series.

DIVISION I (CONT.)

Year	Champion	Coach	Score	Runner-Up	Most Outstanding Player
2005 ....Texas		Augie Garrido	6–2^	Florida	David Maroul, Texas
2006 ....Oregon St		Pat Casey	3–2^	North Carolina	Jonah Nickerson, Oregon St, P
2007 ....Oregon St		Pat Casey	9–3^	North Carolina	Jorge Reyes, Oregon St, P.
2008 ....Fresno St		Mike Batesole	6–1^	Georgia	Tommy Mendonca. Fresno St, 3B
2009 ....LSU		Paul Mainieri	11–4^	Texas	Jared Mitchell, LSU, OF
2010 ....South Carolina		Ray Tanner	2–1^†	UCLA	Jackie Bradley Jr., South Carolina, OF

*Undefeated teams in College World Series play.
†11 innings.   ^Score of decisive game of best-of-three series.

DIVISION II

Year	Champion
1968 ...Chapman*
1969 ...Illinois St*
1970 ...CSU–Northridge
1971 ...Florida Southern
1972 ...Florida Southern
1973 ...UC–Irvine*
1974 ...UC–Irvine
1975 ...Florida Southern
1976 ...Cal Poly–Pomona
1977 ...UC–Riverside
1978 ...Florida Southern
1979 ...Valdosta St
1980 ...Cal Poly–Pomona*
1981 ...Florida Southern*
1982 ...UC–Riverside*

Year	Champion
1983 ...Cal Poly–Pomona*
1984 ...CSU–Northridge
1985 ...Florida Southern*
1986 ...Troy St
1987 ...Troy St*
1988 ...Florida Southern*
1989 ...Cal Poly–SLO
1990 ...Jacksonville St
1991 ...Jacksonville St
1992 ...Tampa*
1993 ...Tampa
1994 ...Central Missouri St
1995 ...Florida Southern*
1996 ...Kennesaw St*

Year	Champion
1997 ...CSU–Chico*
1998 ...Tampa*
1999 ...CSU–Chico
2000 ...SE Oklahoma St
2001 ...St. Mary's (Tex.)
2002 ...Columbus St
2003 ...Central Missouri St
2004 ...Kennesaw St
2005 ...Florida Southern
2006 ...Tampa
2007 ...Tampa
2008 ...Mount Olive
2009 ...Lynn
2010 ...Southern Indiana

DIVISION III

Year	Champion
1976 ....CSU–Stanislaus
1977 ....CSU–Stanislaus
1978 ....Glassboro St
1979 ....Glassboro St
1980 ....Ithaca
1981 ....Marietta
1982 ....Eastern Connecticut St
1983 ....Marietta
1984 ....Ramapo
1985 ....UW-Oshkosh
1986 ....Marietta

Year	Champion
1987 ....Montclair St
1988 ....Ithaca
1989 ....N. Carolina Wesleyan
1990 ....Eastern Connecticut St
1991 ....Southern Maine
1992 ....William Paterson
1993 ....Montclair St
1994 ....UW-Oshkosh
1995 ....La Verne
1996 ....William Paterson
1997 ....Southern Maine
1998 ....Eastern Connecticut St

Year	Champion
1999 ....N.Carolina Wesleyan
2000 ....Montclair St
2001 ....St. Thomas (Minn.)
2002 ....Eastern Connecticut St.
2003 ....Chapman
2004 ....UW-Stevens Pt
2005 ....Wisconsin
2006 ....Marietta
2007 ....Kean
2008 ....Trinity (Conn.)
2009 ....St. Thomas (Minn.)
2010 ....Illinois Wesleyan

*Undefeated teams in final series.

Ice Hockey

Men

DIVISION I

Year	Champion	Coach	Score	Runner-Up	Most Outstanding Player
1948 ....Michigan	Vic Heyliger	8–4	Dartmouth	Joe Riley, Dartmouth, F
1949 ....Boston College	John Kelley	4–3	Dartmouth	Dick Desmond, Dartmouth, G
1950 ....Colorado College	Cheddy Thompson	13–4	Boston University	Ralph Bevins, Boston University, G
1951 ....Michigan	Vic Heyliger	7–1	Brown	Ed Whiston, Brown, G
1952 ....Michigan	Vic Heyliger	4–1	Colorado College	Kenneth Kinsley, Colorado Coll, G
1953 ....Michigan	Vic Heyliger	7–3	Minnesota	John Matchefts, Michigan, F
1954 ....Rensselaer	Ned Harkness	5–4 (OT)	Minnesota	Abbie Moore, Rensselaer, F
1955 ....Michigan	Vic Heyliger	5–3	Colorado College	Philip Hilton, Colorado College, D
1956 ....Michigan	Vic Heyliger	7–5	Michigan Tech	Lorne Howes, Michigan, F
1957 ....Colorado College	Thomas Bedecki	13–6	Michigan	Bob McCusker, Colorado Coll, F
1958 ....Denver	Murray Armstrong	6–2	North Dakota	Murray Massier, Denver, F
1959 ....North Dakota	Bob May	4–3 (OT)	Michigan St	Reg Morelli, North Dakota, F
1960 ....Denver	Murray Armstrong	5–3	Michigan Tech	Bob Marquis, Boston University, F
1961 ....Denver	Murray Armstrong	12–2	St. Lawrence	Barry Urbanski, Boston Univ, G
1962 ....Michigan Tech	John MacInnes	7–1	Clarkson	Louis Angotti, Michigan Tech, F
1963 ....North Dakota	Barney Thorndycraft	6–5	Denver	Al McLean, North Dakota, F
1964 ....Michigan	Allen Renfrew	6–3	Denver	Bob Gray, Michigan, G
1965 ....Michigan Tech	John MacInnes	8–2	Boston College	Gary Milroy, Michigan Tech, F
1966 ....Michigan St	Amo Bessone	6–1	Clarkson	Gaye Cooley, Michigan St, G
1967 ....Cornell	Ned Harkness	4–1	Boston University	Walt Stanowski, Cornell, D

Men *(Cont.)*

DIVISION I *(CONT.)*

Year	Champion	Coach	Score	Runner-Up	Most Outstanding Player
1968	Denver	Murray Armstrong	4–0	North Dakota	Gerry Powers, Denver, G
1969	Denver	Murray Armstrong	4–3	Cornell	Keith Magnuson, Denver, D
1970	Cornell	Ned Harkness	6–4	Clarkson	Daniel Lodboa, Cornell, D
1971	Boston University	Jack Kelley	4–2	Minnesota	Dan Brady, Boston University, G
1972	Boston University	Jack Kelley	4–0	Cornell	Tim Regan, Boston University, G
1973	Wisconsin	Bob Johnson	4–2	Vacated	Dean Talafous, Wisconsin, F
1974	Minnesota	Herb Brooks	4–2	Michigan Tech	Brad Shelstad, Minnesota, G
1975	Michigan Tech	John MacInnes	6–1	Minnesota	Jim Warden, Michigan Tech, G
1976	Minnesota	Herb Brooks	6–4	Michigan Tech	Tom Vanelli, Minnesota, F
1977	Wisconsin	Bob Johnson	6–5 (OT)	Michigan	Julian Baretta, Wisconsin, G
1978	Boston University	Jack Parker	5–3	Boston College	Jack O'Callahan, Boston Univ, D
1979	Minnesota	Herb Brooks	4–3	North Dakota	Steve Janaszak, Minnesota, G
1980	North Dakota	John Gasparini	5–2	Northern Michigan	Doug Smail, North Dakota, F
1981	Wisconsin	Bob Johnson	6–3	Minnesota	Marc Behrend, Wisconsin, G
1982	North Dakota	John Gasparini	5–2	Wisconsin	Phil Sykes, North Dakota, F
1983	Wisconsin	Jeff Sauer	6–2	Harvard	Marc Behrend, Wisconsin, G
1984	Bowling Green	Jerry York	5–4 (OT)	Minn.–Duluth	Gary Kruzich, Bowling Green, G
1985	Rensselaer	Mike Addesa	2–1	Providence	Chris Terreri, Providence, G
1986	Michigan St	Ron Mason	6–5	Harvard	Mike Donnelly, Michigan St, F
1987	North Dakota	John Gasparini	5–3	Michigan St	Tony Hrkac, North Dakota, F
1988	Lake Superior St	Frank Anzalone	4–3 (OT)	St. Lawrence	Bruce Hoffort, Lake Superior St, G
1989	Harvard	Bill Cleary	4–3 (OT)	Minnesota	Ted Donato, Harvard, F
1990	Wisconsin	Jeff Sauer	7–3	Colgate	Chris Tancill, Wisconsin, F
1991	Northern Michigan	Rick Comley	8–7 (3OT)	Boston University	Scott Beattie, Northern Michigan, F
1992	Lake Superior St	Jeff Jackson	4–2	Wisconsin	Paul Constantin, Lake Superior St, F
1993	Maine	Shawn Walsh	5–4	Lake Superior St	Jim Montgomery, Maine, F
1994	Lake Superior St	Jeff Jackson	9–1	Boston University	Sean Tallaire, Lake Superior St, F
1995	Boston University	Jack Parker	6–2	Maine	Chris O'Sullivan, Boston Univ, F
1996	Michigan	Red Berenson	3–2 (OT)	Colorado College	Brendan Morrison, Michigan, F
1997	North Dakota	Dean Blais	6–4	Boston University	Matt Henderson, North Dakota, F
1998	Michigan	Red Berenson	3–2 (OT)	Boston College	Marty Turco, Michigan, G
1999	Maine	Shawn Walsh	3–2 (OT)	New Hampshire	Alfie Michaud, Maine, G
2000	North Dakota	Dean Blais	4–2	Boston College	Lee Goren, North Dakota, F
2001	Boston College	Jerry York	3–2 (OT)	North Dakota	Chuck Kobasew, Boston Coll, F
2002	Minnesota	Don Lucia	4–3 (OT)	Maine	Grant Potulny, Minnesota, F
2003	Minnesota	Don Lucia	5–1	New Hampshire	Thomas Vanek, Minnesota, F
2004	Denver	George Gwozdecky	1–0	Maine	Adam Berkhoel, Denver, G
2005	Denver	George Gwozdecky	4–1	North Dakota	Peter Mannino, Denver
2006	Wisconsin	Mike Eaves	2–1	Boston College	Robbie Earl, Wisconsin, F
2007	Michigan St	Rick Comley	3–1	Boston College	Justin Abdelkader, Michigan St, F
2008	Boston College	Jerry York	4–1	Notre Dame	Nathan Gerbe, Boston Coll, F
2009	Boston University	Jack Parker	4–3 (OT)	Miami (Ohio)	Colby Cohen, Boston University, D
2010	Boston College	Jerry York	5–0	Wisconsin	Ben Smith, Boston College, F

DIVISION II *(Discontinued)*

Year	Champion	Coach	Score	Runner-Up
1978	Merrimack	Thom Lawler	12–2	Lake Forest
1979	Lowell	Bill Riley Jr	6–4	Mankato St
1980	Mankato St	Don Brose	5–2	Elmira
1981	Lowell	Bill Riley Jr	5–4	Plattsburgh St
1982	Lowell	Bill Riley Jr	6–1	Plattsburgh St
1983	RIT	Brian Mason	4–2	Bemidji St
1984	Bemidji St	R.H. (Bob) Peters	14–4*	Merrimack
1993	Bemidji St	R.H. (Bob) Peters	15–6*	Mercyhurst
1994	Bemidji St	R.H. (Bob) Peters	7–6*	Ala.–Huntsville
1995	Bemidji St	R.H. (Bob) Peters	11–6*	Mercyhurst
1996	Ala.–Huntsville	Doug Ross	10–1*	Bemidji St
1997	Bemidji St	R.H. (Bob) Peters	7–4*	Ala.–Huntsville
1998	Ala.–Huntsville	Doug Ross	11–4*	Bemidji St
1999	St. Michael's (Vt.)	Lou DiMasi	12–9*	New Hamp. Coll

*Two-game, total-goal series.

Men (Cont.)
DIVISION III

Year	Champion	Coach	Score	Runner-Up
1984	Babson	Bob Riley	8–0	Union (N.Y.)
1985	RIT	Bruce Delventhal	5–1	Bemidji St
1986	Bemidji St	R.H. (Bob) Peters	8–5	Vacated
1987	Vacated			Oswego St
1988	UW-River Falls	Rick Kozuback	7–1, 3–5, 3–0	Elmira
1989	UW-Stevens Point	Mark Mazzoleni	3–3, 3–2	RIT
1990	UW-Stevens Point	Mark Mazzoleni	10–1, 3–6, 1–0	Plattsburgh St
1991	UW-Stevens Point	Mark Mazzoleni	6–2	Mankato St
1992	Plattsburgh St	Bob Emery	7–3	UW-Stevens Point
1993	UW-Stevens Point	Joe Baldarotta	4–3	UW-River Falls
1994	UW-River Falls	Dean Talafous	6–4	UW-Superior
1995	Middlebury	Bill Beaney	1–0	Fredonia St
1996	Middlebury	Bill Beaney	3–2	RIT
1997	Middlebury	Bill Beaney	3–2	UW-Superior
1998	Middlebury	Bill Beaney	2–1	UW-Stevens Point
1999	Middlebury	Bill Beaney	5–0	UW-Superior
2000	Norwich	Michael McShane	2–1	St. Thomas (Minn.)
2001	Plattsburgh	Bob Emery	6–2	RIT
2002	UW-Superior	Dan Stauber	3–2	Norwich
2003	Norwich	Michael McShane	2–1	Oswego St
2004	Middlebury	Bill Beaney	1–0	St. Norbert
2005	Middlebury	Bill Beaney	5–0	St. Thomas (Minn.)
2006	Middlebury	Bill Beaney	3–0	St. Norbert
2007	Oswego	Ed Gosek	4–3	Middlebury
2008	St. Norbert	Tim Coghlin	2–0	Plattsburgh St
2009	Neumann	Dominick Dawes	4–1	Gustavus Adolphus
2010	Norwich	Michael McShane	2–1	St. Norbert

Women – DIVISION I

Year	Champion	Coach	Score	Runner-Up
2001	Minn.-Duluth	Shannon Miller	4–2	St. Lawrence
2002	Minn.-Duluth	Shannon Miller	3–2	Brown
2003	Minn.-Duluth	Shannon Miller	4–3 (2 OT)	Harvard
2004	Minnesota	Laura Holldorson	6–2	Harvard
2005	Minnesota	Laura Holldorson	4–3	Harvard
2006	Wisconsin	Mark Johnson	3–0	Minnesota
2007	Wisconsin	Mark Johnson	4–1	Minnesota
2008	Minn.-Duluth	Shannon Miller	4–0	Wisconsin
2009	Wisconsin	Mark Johnson	5–0	Mercyhurst
2010	Minn.-Duluth	Shannon Miller	3–2 (3 OT)	Cornell

Soccer

Men – DIVISION I

Year	Champion	Coach	Score	Runner-Up
1959	St. Louis	Bob Guelker	5–2	Bridgeport
1960	St. Louis	Bob Guelker	3–2	Maryland
1961	West Chester	Mel Lorback	2–0	St. Louis
1962	St. Louis	Bob Guelker	4–3	Maryland
1963	St. Louis	Bob Guelker	3–0	Navy
1964	Navy	F.H. Warner	1–0	Michigan St
1965	St. Louis	Bob Guelker	1–0	Michigan St
1966	San Francisco	Steve Negoesco	5–2	LIU–Brooklyn
1967	Michigan St	Gene Kenney	0–0	Game called due to
	St. Louis	Harry Keough		inclement weather
1968	Maryland	Doyle Royal	2–2 (2 OT)	
	Michigan St	Gene Kenney		
1969	St. Louis	Harry Keough	4–0	San Francisco
1970	St. Louis	Harry Keough	1–0	UCLA
1971	Vacated		3–2	St. Louis
1972	St. Louis	Harry Keough	4–2	UCLA
1973	St. Louis	Harry Keough	2–1 (OT)	UCLA
1974	Howard	Lincoln Phillips	2–1 (4 OT)	St. Louis
1975	San Francisco	Steve Negoesco	4–0	SIU–Edwardsville
1976	San Francisco	Steve Negoesco	1–0	Indiana
1977	Hartwick	Jim Lennox	2–1	San Francisco
1978	Vacated		2–0	Indiana

Men - DIVISION I *(CONT.)*

Year	Champion	Coach	Score	Runner-Up
1979	SIU–Edwardsville	Bob Guelker	3–2	Clemson
1980	San Francisco	Steve Negoesco	4–3 (OT)	Indiana
1981	Connecticut	Joe Morrone	2–1 (OT)	Alabama A&M
1982	Indiana	Jerry Yeagley	2–1 (8 OT)	Duke
1983	Indiana	Jerry Yeagley	1–0 (2 OT)	Columbia
1984	Clemson	I.M. Ibrahim	2–1	Indiana
1985	UCLA	Sigi Schmid	1–0 (8 OT)	American
1986	Duke	John Rennie	1–0	Akron
1987	Clemson	I.M. Ibrahim	2–0	San Diego St
1988	Indiana	Jerry Yeagley	1–0	Howard
1989	Santa Clara	Steve Sampson	1–1 (2 OT)	
	Virginia	Bruce Arena		
1990	UCLA	Sigi Schmid	1–0 (OT)	Rutgers
1991	Virginia	Bruce Arena	0–0*	Santa Clara
1992	Virginia	Bruce Arena	2–0	San Diego
1993	Virginia	Bruce Arena	2–0	South Carolina
1994	Virginia	Bruce Arena	1–0	Indiana
1995	Wisconsin	Jim Launder	2–0	Duke
1996	St. John's (N.Y.)	Dave Masur	4–1	Florida International
1997	UCLA	Sigi Schmid	2–1	Virginia
1998	Indiana	Jerry Yeagley	3–1	Stanford
1999	Indiana	Jerry Yeagley	1–0	Santa Clara
2000	Connecticut	Ray Reid	2–0	Creighton
2001	N.Carolina	Elmar Bolowich	2–0	Indiana
2002	UCLA	Tom Fitzgerald	1–0	Stanford
2003	Indiana	Jerry Yeagley	2–1	St. John's (N.Y.)
2004	Indiana	Jerry Yeagley	1–1 (2 OT 3-2)	UC–Santa Barbara
2005	Maryland	Sasho Cirovski	1–0	New Mexico
2006	UC-Santa Barbara	Tim Vom Steeg	2–1	UCLA
2007	Wake Forest	Tony da Luz	2–0	Ohio St
2008	Maryland	Sasha Cirovski	1–0	North Carolina
2009	Virginia	George Gelnovatch	0–0 (3–2 PKs)	Akron

*Under a rule passed in 1991, the NCAA determined that when a score is tied after regulation and overtime, and the championship is determined by penalty klcks, the official score will be 0–0.

Men - DIVISION II

Year	Champion	Year	Champion	Year	Champion
1972	SIU–Edwardsville	1985	Seattle Pacific	1998	Southern Conn St
1973	Missouri–St. Louis	1986	Seattle Pacific	1999	Southern Conn St
1974	Adelphi	1987	Southern Conn St	2000	CSU–Dominguez Hills
1975	Baltimore	1988	Florida Tech	2001	Tampa
1976	Loyola (Md.)	1989	New Hampshire College	2002	Sonoma St
1977	Alabama A&M	1990	Southern Conn St	2003	Lynn
1978	Seattle Pacific	1991	Florida Tech	2004	Seattle
1979	Alabama A&M	1992	Southern Conn St	2005	Fort Lewis
1980	Lock Haven	1993	Seattle Pacific	2006	Dowling (N.Y.)
1981	Tampa	1994	Tampa	2007	Franklin Pierce
1982	Florida International	1995	Southern Conn St	2008	Cal St.-Dominguez Hills
1983	Seattle Pacific	1996	Grand Canyon	2009	Fort Lewis
1984	Florida International	1997	CSU-Bakersfield		

Men - DIVISION III

Year	Champion	Year	Champion	Year	Champion
1974	Brockport St	1987	NC–Greensboro	2000	Messiah
1975	Babson	1988	UC–San Diego	2001	Richard Stockton
1976	Brandeis	1989	Elizabethtown	2002	Messiah
1977	Lock Haven	1990	Glassboro St	2003	Trinity (Tex.)
1978	Lock Haven	1991	UC–San Diego	2004	Messiah
1979	Babson	1992	Kean	2005	Messiah
1980	Babson	1993	UC–San Diego	2006	Messiah
1981	Glassboro St	1994	Bethany (W.V.)	2007	Middlebury
1982	NC–Greensboro	1995	Williams	2008	Messiah
1983	NC–Greensboro	1996	College of New Jersey*	2009	Messiah
1984	Wheaton (Ill.)	1997	Wheaton (Ill.)		
1985	NC–Greensboro	1998	Ohio Wesleyan		
1986	NC–Greensboro	1999	St. Lawrence		

*Formerly Trenton St

Women - DIVISION I

Year	Champion	Coach	Score	Runner-Up
1982	North Carolina	Anson Dorrance	2–0	Central Florida
1983	North Carolina	Anson Dorrance	4–0	George Mason
1984	North Carolina	Anson Dorrance	2–0	Connecticut
1985	George Mason	Hank Leung	2–0	North Carolina
1986	North Carolina	Anson Dorrance	2–0	Colorado College
1987	North Carolina	Anson Dorrance	1–0	Massachusetts
1988	North Carolina	Anson Dorrance	4–1	North Carolina St
1989	North Carolina	Anson Dorrance	2–0	Colorado College
1990	North Carolina	Anson Dorrance	6–0	Connecticut
1991	North Carolina	Anson Dorrance	3–1	Wisconsin
1992	North Carolina	Anson Dorrance	9–1	Duke
1993	North Carolina	Anson Dorrance	6–0	George Mason
1994	North Carolina	Anson Dorrance	5–0	Notre Dame
1995	Notre Dame	Chris Petrucelli	1–0	Portland
1996	North Carolina	Anson Dorrance	1–0	Notre Dame
1997	North Carolina	Anson Dorrance	2–0	Connecticut
1998	Florida	Becky Burleigh	1–0	North Carolina
1999	North Carolina	Anson Dorrance	2–0	Notre Dame
2000	North Carolina	Anson Dorrance	2–1	UCLA
2001	Santa Clara	Jerry Smith	1–0	North Carolina
2002	Portland	Clive Charles	2–1	Santa Clara
2003	North Carolina	Anson Dorrance	6–0	Connecticut
2004	Norte Dame	Randy Waldrum	1–1 (OT 4–3)	UCLA
2005	Portland	Garrett Smith	4–0	UCLA
2006	North Carolina	Anson Dorrance	2–1	Notre Dame
2007	USC	Ali Khosroshahin	2–0	Florida St
2008	North Carolina	Anson Dorrance	2–1	Notre Dame
2009	North Carolina	Anson Dorrance	1–0	Stanford

Women - DIVISION II

Year	Champion
1988	CSU–Hayward
1989	Barry
1990	Sonoma St
1991	CSU–Dominguez Hills
1992	Barry
1993	Barry
1994	Franklin Pierce
1995	Franklin Pierce
1996	Franklin Pierce
1997	Franklin Pierce
1998	Lynn
1999	Franklin Pierce
2000	UC–San Diego
2001	UC–San Diego
2002	Christian Brothers
2003	Kennesaw St
2004	Metro St
2005	Nebraska-Omaha
2006	Metro St
2007	Tampa
2008	Seattle Pacific
2009	Grand Valley St

Women - DIVISION III

Year	Champion
1986	Rochester
1987	Rochester
1988	William Smith
1989	UC–San Diego
1990	Ithaca
1991	Ithaca
1992	Cortland St
1993	Trenton St
1994	Trenton St
1995	UC–San Diego
1996	UC–San Diego
1997	UC–San Diego
1998	Macalester
1999	UC–San Diego
2000	College of New Jersey*
2001	Ohio Wesleyan
2002	Ohio Wesleyan
2003	Oneonta St
2004	Wheaton College
2005	Messiah
2006	Wheaton (Ill.)
2007	Wheaton (Ill.)
2008	Messiah
2009	Messiah

*formerly Trenton St

Track & Field

Jamaican sprinter Usain Bolt's undefeated streak came to a halt in 2010, when American Tyson Gay sped past him in the 100m at Stockholm, Sweden

2009 IAAF World Championships

Berlin, Germany, August 15–23, 2009

Men

100 METERS
1. ....Usain Bolt, Jamaica   9.59WR
2. ....Tyson Gay, United States   9.71
3. ....Asafa Powell, Jamaica   9.84

200 METERS
1. ....Usain Bolt, Jamaica   19.19WR
2. ....Alonso Edward, Panama   19.81
3. ....Wallace Spearmon, United States   19.85

400 METERS
1. ....LaShawn Merritt, United States   44.06
2. ....Jeremy Wariner, United States   44.60
3. ....Renny Quow, Trinidad & Tobago   45.02

800 METERS
1. ....Mbulaeni Mulaudzi, South Africa   1:45.29
2. ....Alfred Kirwa Yego, Kenya   1:45.35
3. ....Yusuf Saad Kamel, Bahrain   1:45.35

1,500 METERS
1. ....Yusuf Saad Kamel, Bahrain   3:35.93
2. ....Deresse Mekonnen, Ethiopia   3:36.01
3. ....Bernard Lagat, United States   3:36.20

3,000-METER STEEPLECHASE
1. ....Ezekiel Kemboi, Kenya   8:00.43
2. ....Richard Mateelong, Kenya   8:00.89
3. ....Bouabdellah Tahri, France   8:01.18

5,000 METERS
1. ....Kenenisa Bekele, Ethiopia   13:17.09
2. ....Bernard Lagat, United States   13:17.33
3. ....James Kwalia C'Kurui, Bahrain   13:17.78

10,000 METERS
1. ....Kenenisa Bekele, Ethiopia   26:46.31
2. ....Zersenay Tadese, Eritrea   26:50.12
3. ....Moses Ndiema Masai, Kenya   26:57.39

110-METER HURDLES
1. ....Ryan Brathwaite, Barbados   13.14
2. ....Terrence Trammell, United States   13.15
3. ....David Payne, United States   13.15

400-METER HURDLES
1. ....Kerron Clement, United States   47.91
2. ....Javier Culson, Puerto Rico   48.09
3. ....Bershawn Jackson, United States   48.23

4 x 100-METER RELAY
1. ....Jamaica   37.31
    (Mullings, Frater, Bolt, Powell)
2. ....Trinidad & Tobago   37.62
    (Brown, Burns, Callander, Thompson)
3. ....United Kingdom   38.02
    (Williamson, Edgar, Devonish, Alkines-Aryeetey)

4 x 400-METER RELAY
1. ....United States   2:57.86
    (Taylor, Wariner, Clement, Merritt)
2. ....United Kingdom   3:00.53
    (Williams, Bingham, Tobin, Rooney)
3. ....Australia   3:00.90
    (Steffensen, Offereins, Thomas, Wroe)

20-KILOMETER RACE WALK
1. ....Valeriy Borchin, Russia   1:18:41
2. ....Hao Wang, China   1:19:06
3. ....Eder Sanchez, Mexico   1:19:22

50-KILOMETER RACE WALK
1. ....Sergey Kirdyapkin, Russia   3:38:35
2. ....Trond Nymark, Norway   3:41:16
3. ....Jesus Angel Garcia, Spain   3:41:37

MARATHON
1. ....Able Kirui, Kenya   2:06:54
2. ....Emmanuel Mutai, Kenya   2:07:48
3. ....Tsegay Kebede, Ethiopia   2:08:35

POLE VAULT
1. ....Steven Hooker, Australia   5.90m
2. ....Romain Mesnil, France   5.85m
3. ....Renaud Lavillenie, France   5.80m

LONG JUMP
1. ....Dwight Phillips, United States   8.54m
2. ....Godfrey Mokoena, South Africa   8.47m
3. ....Mitchell Watt, Australia   8.37m

TRIPLE JUMP
1. ....Phillips Idowu, United Kingdom   17.73m
2. ....Nelson Evora, Portugal   17.55m
3. ....Alexis Copello, Cuba   17.36m

HIGH JUMP
1. ....Yaroslav Rybakov, Russia   §2.32m
2. ....Kyriakos Ioannau, Cyprus   §2.32m
*3. ....Raul Spank, Germany   §2.32m
*3. ....Sylwester Bednarek, Poland   §2.32m

SHOT PUT
1. ....Christian Cantwell, United States   22.03m
2. ....Tomasz Majewski, Poland   21.91m
3. ....Ralf Bartels, Germany   21.37m

DISCUS THROW
1. ....Robert Harting, Germany   69.43m
2. ....Piotr Malachowski, Poland   69.15m
3. ....Gerd Kanter, Estonia   66.88m

HAMMER THROW
1. ....Primoz Kozmus, Slovenia   80.84m
2. ....Szymon Ziolkowski, Poland   79.30m
3. ....Aleksey Zagornyi, Russia   78.09m

JAVELIN THROW
1. ....Andreas Thorkildsen, Norway   89.59m
2. ....Guillermo Martinez, Cuba   86.41m
3. ....Yukifumi Murakami, Japan   82.97m

DECATHLON
1. ....Trey Hardee, United States   8790pts
2. ....Leonel Suarez, Cuba   8640pts
3. ....Aleksandr Pogorelov, Russia   8528pts

Women

100 METERS
1. ....Shelly-Ann Fraser, Jamaica   10.73
2. ....Kerron Stewart, Jamaica   10.75
3. ....Carmelita Jeter, United States   10.90

200 METERS
1. ....Allyson Felix, United States   22.02
2. ....Veronica Campbell-Brown, Jamaica   22.35
3. ....Debbie Ferguson-McKenzie, Bahamas   22.41

400 METERS
1. ....Sanya Richards, United States   49.00
2. ....Shericka Williams, Jamaica   49.32
3. ....Antonina Krivoshapka, Russia   49.71

800 METERS
1. ....Caster Semenya, South Africa   1:55.45
2. ....Janeth Busienei, Kenya   1:57.90
3. ....Jennifer Meadows, U.K.   1:57.93

1,500 METERS
1. ....Maryam Yusuf Jamal, Bahrain   4:03.74
2. ....Lisa Dobriskey, United Kingdom   4:03.75
3. ....Shannon Rowbury, United States   4:04.18

3,000-METER STEEPLECHASE
1. ....Marta Dominguez, Spain   9:07.32
2. ....Yuliya Zarudneva, Russia   9:08.39
3. ....Milcah Chemos Cheyma, Kenya   9:08.57

5,000 METERS
1. ....Vivian Cheruiyot, Kenya   14:57.97
2. ....Sylvia Jebiwott Kibet, Kenya   14:58.33
3. ....Meseret Defar, Ethiopia   14:58.41

10,000 METERS
1. ....Linet Masai, Kenya   30:51.24
2. ....Meselech Melkamu, Ethiopia   30:51.34
3. ....Wude Ayalew, Ethiopia   30:51.95

100-METER HURDLES
1. ....Brigitte Foster-Hylton, Jamaica   12.51
2. ....Priscilla Lopes-Schilep, Canada   12.54
3. ....Delloreen Ennis-London, Jamaica   12.55

400-METER HURDLES
1. ....Melaine Walker, Jamaica   52.42
2. ....Lashinda Demus, United States   52.96
3. ....Josanne Lucas, Trin. & Tob.   53.20

4 x 100-METER RELAY
1. ....Jamaica   42.06
    (Facey, Fraser, Bailey, Stewart)
2. ....Bahamas   42.29
    (Ferguson, Sturrup, Amertil, Ferguson-Mckenzie)
3. ....Germany   42.87
    (Wagner, Mollinger, Tschirch, Sailer)

WR–World record. *Athletes tied after clearing same height same number of times. §Place decided by which athlete cleared height first.

Berlin, Germany, August 15–23, 2009
Women (*Cont.*)

4 x 400-METER RELAY
1. ....United States   3:17.83
(Dunn, Felix, Demus, Richards)
2. ....Jamaica   3:21.15
(Whyte, Williams-Mills, Lloyd, Williams)
3. ....Russia   3:21.64
(Kapachinskaya, Firova, Litvinova, Krivoshapka)

20-KILOMETER RACE WALK
1. ....Olga Kaniskina, Russia   1:28:09
2. ....Olive Loughnane, Ireland   1:28:58
3. ....Hong Liu, China   1:29:10

MARATHON
1. ....Xue Bai, China   2:25:15
2. ....Yoshimi Ozaki, Japan   2:25:25
3. ....Aselefech Mergia, Ethiopia 2:25:32

HIGH JUMP
1. ....Blanka Vlasic, Croatia   2.04m
2. ....Anna Chicherova, Russia   §2.02m
3. ....Ariane Friedrich, Germany §2.02m

POLE VAULT
1. ....Anna Rogowska, Poland   4.75m
*2. ....Monika Pyrek, Poland   4.65m
*2. ....Chelsea Johnson, United States 4.65m

LONG JUMP
1. ....Brittney Reese, United States 7.10m
2. ....Tatyana Lebedeva, Russia   6.97m
3. ....Karin May Melis, Turkey   6.80m

TRIPLE JUMP
1. ....Yargeris Savigne, Cuba   14.95m
2. ....Mabel Gay, Cuba   14.61m
3. ....Anna Pyatykh, Russia   14.58m

SHOT PUT
1. ....Valerie Vili, New Zealand   20.44m
2. ....Nadine Kleinert, Germany   20.20m
3. ....Lijiao Gong, China   19.89m

DISCUS THROW
1. ....Dani Samuels, Australia   65.44m
2. ....Yarelis Barrios, Cuba   65.31m
3. ....Nicoleta Grasu, Romania   65.20m

HAMMER THROW
1. ....Anita Wlodarczyk, Poland   77.96mWR
2. ....Betty Heidler, Germany   77.12m
3. ....Martina Hrasnova, Slovakia 74.79m

JAVELIN THROW
1. ....Steffi Nerius, Germany   67.30m
2. ....Barbora Spotakova, Czech Rep. 66.42m
3. ....Maria Abakumova, Russia   66.06m

HEPTATHLON
1. ....Jessica Ennis, United Kingdom 6731pts
2. ....Jennifer Oeser, Germany   6493pts
3. ....Kamila Chudzik, Poland   6471pts

WR–World record. *Athletes tied after clearing same height same number of times. § Final place decided by which athlete cleared height first.

World and American Outdoor Records

As of October 1, 2010. World outdoor records are recognized by the International Amateur Athletics Federation (IAAF). American records recognized by U.S.A. Track & Field.

Men

Event	Mark	Record Holder	Date	Site
100 meters	9.58	Usain Bolt, Jamaica (W)	8-16-09	Berlin
	9.69	Tyson Gay (A)	9-20-09	Shanghai
200 meters	19.19	Usain Bolt, Jamaica (W)	8-20-09	Berlin
	19.32	Michael Johnson (A)	8-01-96	Atlanta
400 meters	43.18	Michael Johnson, U.S. (W,A)	8-26-99	Seville, Spain
800 meters	1:41.01	David Lekuta Rudisha, Kenya (W)	8-29-10	Rieti, Italy
	1:42.60	Johnny Gray (A)	8-28-85	Koblenz, Germany
1,000 meters	2:11.96	Noah Ngeny, Kenya (W)	9-05-99	Rieti, Italy
	2:13.90	Rick Wohlhuter (A)	7-20-74	Oslo
1,500 meters	3:26.00	Hicham El Guerrouj, Morocco (W)	7-14-98	Rome
	3:29.30	Bernard Lagat (A)	8-28-05	Rieti, Italy
Mile	3:43.13	Hicham El Guerrouj, Morocco (W)	7-07-99	Rome
	3:46.91	Alan Webb (A)	7-21-07	Brasschaat, Belguim
2,000 meters	4:44.79	Hicham El Guerrouj, Morocco (W)	9-07-99	Berlin
	4:52.44	Jim Spivey (A)	9-15-87	Lausanne, Switzerland
3,000 meters	7:20.67	Daniel Komen, Kenya (W)	9-01-96	Rieti, Italy
	7:30.84	Bob Kennedy (A)	8-08-98	Fontvielle, Monaco
3,000-m Steeplechase	7:53.63	Saif Saaeed Shaheen, Qatar (W)	9-03-04	Brussels
	8:08.82	Daniel Lincoln (A)	7-14-06	Rome
5,000 meters	12:37.35	Kenenisa Bekele, Ethiopia (W)	5-31-04	Hengelo, Netherlands
	12:56.27	Dathan Ritzenhein (A)	8-28-09	Zurich
10,000 meters	26:17.53	Kenenisa Bekele, Ehtiopia (W)	8-26-05	Brussels
	27:13.98	Meb Keflezighi (A)	5-04-01	Stanford, Calif.
Marathon	2:03:59	Haile Gebrselassie, Ethiopia (W)	9-28-08	Berlin
	2:05:38	Khalid Khannouchi (A)	4-14-02	London
110-meter hurdles	12.87	Dayron Robles, Cuba (W)	6-12-08	Ostrava, Czech Republic
	12.90	Dominique Arnold (A)	7-11-06	Lausanne, Switzerland
400-meter hurdles	46.78	Kevin Young, United States (W,A)	8-6-92	Barcelona
20-kilometer walk	1:17.16	Vladimir Kanaykin, Russia (W)	9-29-07	Saransk, Russia
	1:23:40	Tim Seaman (A)	3-07-99	Chula Vista, Calif.
50-kilometer walk	3:34:14	Denis Nizhegorodov, Russia (W)	5-11-08	Cheboksary, Russia
4 x 100-meter relay	37.10	Jamaica (Nesta Carter, (W)	8-22-08	Beijing
		Michael Prater, Usain Bolt, Asafa Powell)		

Men (*Cont.*)

Event	Mark	Record Holder	Date	Site
4 x 100-meter relay	37.40	Mike Marsh, Leroy Burrell, (A) Dennis Mitchell, Carl Lewis	8-08-92	Barcelona
	37.40	Jon Drummond, Andrew Canson, (A) Dennis Mitchell, Leroy Burrell	8-21-93	Stuttgart, Germany
4 x 200-meter relay	1:18.68	U.S. (Mike Marsh, Leroy Burrell, (W,A) Floyd Heard, Carl Lewis)	4-17-94	Walnut, Calif.
4 x 400-meter relay	2:54.29	United States (Andrew Valmon, (W,A) Quincy Watts, Harry Reynolds, Michael Johnson)	7-22-93	Stuttgart, Germany
4 x 800-meter relay	7:02.43	Kenya (Wilfred Bungei, (W) William Yiampoy, Joseph Mutua, Ismael Kombich)	8-25-06	Brussels
	7:02.82	Jebreh Harris, Khadevis Robinson, (A) Sam Burley, David Krummenacker	8-25-06	Brussels
4 x 1,500-meter relay	14:36.28	Kenya (W) (Willaim Biwoot Tanui, Gideon Gathimba, Geoffrey Kipkoech Rono, Augustine Kiprono Choge)	9-04-09	Brussels
	14:46.30	Dan Aldridge, Andy Clifford, (A) Todd Harbour, Tom Dults	6-24-79	Bourges, France
High jump	2.45m	Javier Sotomayor, Cuba (W)	7-27-93	Salamanca, Spain
	2.40m	Charles Austin (A)	8-07-91	Zurich
Pole vault	6.14m	Sergei Bubka, Ukraine (W)	7-31-94	Sestriere, Italy
	6.04m	Brad Walker (A)	6-08-08	Eugene, Oregon
Long jump	8.95m	Mike Powell, United States (W,A)	8-30-91	Tokyo
Triple jump	18.29m	Jonathan Edwards, U.K. (W)	8-07-95	Göteborg, Sweden
	18.09m	Kenny Harrison (A)	7-27-96	Atlanta
Shot put	23.12m	Randy Barnes, United States (W,A)	5-20-90	Westwood, Calif.
Discus throw	74.08m	Jürgen Schult, East Germany (W)	6-06-86	Neubrandenburg, Germ.
	72.34m	Ben Plucknett (A)	7-07-81	Stockholm
Hammer throw	86.74m	Yuriy Sedykh, USSR (W)	8-30-86	Stuttgart, Germany
	82.52m	Lance Deal (A)	9-17-96	Milan
Javelin throw	98.48m	Jan Zelezny, Czech Republic (W)	5-25-96	Jena, Germany
	91.29m	Breaux Greer (A)	6-21-07	Indianapolis
Decathlon	9026 pts	Roman Sebrle, Czech Rep. (W)	5-27-01	Goetzis, Austria
	8891pts	Dan O'Brien (A)	9-04-92	Talence, France

Note: The decathlon consists of 10 events: the 100 meters, long jump, shot put, high jump and 400 meters on the first day; the 110-meter hurdles, discus, pole vault, javelin and 1,500 meters on the second.

Women

Event	Mark	Record Holder	Date	Site
100 meters	10.49	Florence Griffith Joyner, U.S. (W,A)	7-16-88	Indianapolis
200 meters	21.34	Florence Griffith Joyner, U.S. (W,A)	9-29-88	Seoul
400 meters	47.60	Marita Koch, E Germany (W)	10-6-85	Canberra, Australia
	48.70	Sanya Richards (A)	9-17-06	Athens
800 meters	1:53.28	Jarmila Kratochvilová, Czech. (W)	7-26-83	Munich
	1:56.40	Jearl Miles-Clark (A)	8-11-99	Zurich
1,000 meters	2:28.98	Svetlana Masterkova, Russia (W)	8-23-96	Brussels
	2:31.80	Regina Jacobs (A)	7-02-99	Brunswick, Maine
1,500 meters	3:50.46	Yunxia Qu, China (W)	9-11-93	Beijing
	3:57.12	Mary Slaney (A)	7-26-83	Stockholm
Mile	4:12.56	Svetlana Masterkova, Russia (W)	8-14-96	Zurich
	4:16.71	Mary Slaney (A)	8-21-85	Zurich
2,000 meters	5:25.36	Sonia O'Sullivan, Ireland (W)	7-08-94	Edinburgh
	5:32.70	Mary Slaney (A)	8-03-84	Eugene, Oregon
3,000 meters	8:06.11	Junxia Wang, China (W)	9-13-93	Beijing
	8:25.83	Mary Slaney (A)	9-07-85	Rome
3,000-m Steeplechase	8:58.81	Gulnara Samitova-Galkina, Russia (W)	8-17-08	Beijing
	9:12.50	Jenny Barringer (A)	8-17-09	Berlin
5,000 meters	14:11.15	Tirunesh Dibaba, Ethiopia (W)	6-06-08	Oslo
	14:44.80	Shalane Flanagan (A)	5-14-07	Walnut Creek, Calif.
10,000 meters	29:31.78	Junxia Wang, China (W)	9-08-93	Beijing
	30:22.22	Shalane Flanagan (A)	8-15-08	Beijing
Marathon	2:15:25	Paula Radcliffe, Great Britain (W)	4-13-03	London
	2:19:36	Deena Kastor (A)	4-23-06	London

Women *(Cont.)*

Event	Record	Name	Date	Location
100-meter hurdles	12.21	Yordanka Donkova, Bulgaria (W)	8-20-88	Stara Zagora, Bulgaria
	12.33	Gail Devers (A)	7-23-00	Sacramento, Calif,.
400-meter hurdles	52.34	Yuliya Pechenkina, Russia (W)	8-08-03	Tula, Russia
	52.61	Kim Batten (A)	8-11-95	Gothenburg, Sweden
20-kilometer walk	1:25:41	Olimpiada Ivanova, Russia (W)	8-07-05	Helsinki
	1:33:28.15	Teresa Vaill (A)	6-25-05	Carson, Calif.
4 x 100-meter relay	41.37	East Germany (Silke Gladisch, (W) Sabine Reiger, Ingrid Auerswald, Marlies Göhr)	10-6-85	Canberra, Australia
	42.36	Khrystal Carter, Porscha Lucas, (A) Dominique Duncan, Gabby Mayo	6-12-09	Fayetteville, Ark.
4 x 200-meter relay	1:27.46	United States (LaTasha Jenkins, (W,A) LaTasha Colander-Richardson, Nanceen Perry, Marion Jones)	4-29-00	Philadelphia
4 x 400-meter relay	3:15.17	USSR (Tatyana Ledovskaya, (W) Olga Nazarova, Maria Pinigina, Olga Bryzgina)	10-01-88	Seoul
	3:15.51	Denean Howard, Diane Dixon (A) Valerie Brisco, Florence Griffith-Joyner	10-01-88	Seoul
4 x 800-meter relay	7:50.17	USSR (Nadezhda Olizarenko, (W) Lyubov Gurina, Lyudmila Borisova, Irina Podyalovskaya)	8-05-84	Moscow
	8:17.91	Chanelle Price, Phoebe Wright (A) Rolanda Bell, Sarah Bowman	4-24-09	Philadelphia
High jump	2.09m	Stefka Kostadinova, Bulgaria (W)	8-30-87	Rome
	2.03m	Louise Ritter (A)	7-08-88	Austin, Texas
	2.03m	Louise Ritter (A)	9-30-88	Seoul
Pole vault	5.06m	Yelena Isinbayeva, Russia (W)	8-28-09	Zurich
	4.92m	Jenn Stuczynski (A)	7-06-08	Eugene, Ore.
Long jump	7.52m	Galina Chistyakova, USSR (W)	6-11-88	Leningrad
	7.49m	Jackie Joyner-Kersee (A)	7-31-94	Sestriere, Italy
Triple jump	15.50m	Inessa Kravets, Ukraine (W)	8-10-95	Gothenburg, Sweden
	14.45m	Tiombe Hurd (A)	7-11-04	Sacramento, Calif..
Shot put	22.63m	Natalya Lisovskaya, USSR (W)	6-07-87	Moscow
	20.18m	Ramona Pagel (A)	6-25-88	San Diego, Calif.
Discus throw	76.80m	Gabriele Reinsch, East Germany (W)	7-09-88	Neubrandenburg, Germ.
	67.67m	Suzy Powell-Roos (A)	4-14-07	Wailuku, Haw.
Hammer throw	78.30m	Anita Wlodarczyk, Poland (W)	6-06-10	Bydgoszcz, Poland
	73.87m	Erin Gilreath (A)	6-25-05	Carson, Calif.
Javelin throw	72.28m	Barbora Spotakova, Czech Rep. (W)	9-13-08	Stuttgart
	64.19m	Kim Kreiner (A)	5-16-07	Fortaleza, Brazil
Heptathlon	7291 pts	Jackie Joyner-Kersee, U.S. (W,A)	9-24-88	Seoul

Note: The heptathlon consists of 7 events: the 100-meter hurdles, high jump, shot put and 200 meters on the first day; the long jump, javelin and 800 meters on the second.

World and American Indoor Records

As of October 1, 2010. American indoor records are recognized by USA Track and Field. World Indoor records are recognized by the International Amateur Athletics Federation (IAAF). (A) represents an American record, (W) represents a World record.

Men

Event	Mark	Record Holder	Date	Site
50 meters	5.56	Donovan Bailey, Canada (W)	2-09-96	Reno, Nev.
	5.56	Maurice Greene (A)	2-12-99	Los Angeles
55 meters*	6.00	Lee McRae (A)	3-14-86	Oklahoma City
60 meters	6.39	Maurice Greene (W, A)	2-03-98	Madrid
	6.39	Maurice Greene (W, A)	3-03-01	Atlanta
200 meters	19.92	Frankie Fredericks, Namibia (W)	2-18-96	Liévin, France
	20.10	Wallace Spearmon(A)	3-11-05	Fayetteville, Ark.
400 meters	44.57	Kerron Clement (W, A)	3-12-05	Fayetteville, Ark.
800 meters	1:42.67	Wilson Kipketer, Denmark (W)	3-09-97	Paris
	1:45.00	Johnny Gray (A)	3-08-92	Sindelfingen, Germany
1,000 meters	2:14.96	Wilson Kipketer, Denmark (W)	2-20-00	Birmingham, England
	2:17.86	David Krummenacker (A)	1-27-02	Boston
1,500 meters	3:31.18	Hicham El Guerrouj, Morocco (W)	2-02-97	Stuttgart, Germany
	3:33.34	Bernard Lagat (A)	2-11-05	Fayetteville, Ark.
Mile	3:48.45	Hicham El Guerrouj, Morocco (W)	2-12-97	Ghent, Belgium
	3:49.89	Bernard Lagat (A)	2-11-05	Fayetteville, Ark.
3,000 meters	7:24.90	Daniel Komen, Kenya (W)	2-06-98	Budapest, Hungary
	7:32.43	Bernard Lagat (A)	2-17-07	Birmingham, England
5,000 meters	12:49.60	Kenenisa Bekele, Ethiopia (W)	2-20-04	Birmingham, England
	13:18.22	Galen Rupp (A)	2-13-09	Fayetteville, Ark.
50-meter hurdles	6.25	Mark McKoy, Canada (W)	3-05-86	Kobe, Japan
	6.35	Greg Foster (A)	1-31-87	Ottawa
	6.35	Greg Foster (A)	1-27-85	Rosemont, Illinois
55-meter hurdles*	6.89	Renaldo Nehemiah (A)	1-20-79	New York City
60-meter hurdles	7.30	Colin Jackson, Great Britain (W)	3-6-94	Sindelfingen, Germany
	7.36	Greg Foster (A)	1-16-87	Los Angeles
	7.36	Allen Johnson (A)	3-06-04	Budapest, Hungary
5,000-meter walk	18:07.08	Mikhail Shchennikov, Russia (W)	2-14-95	Moscow
	19:15.88	Tim Seaman (A)	2-14-95	Indianapolis
4 x 200-meter relay	1:22.11	United Kingdom (Linford Christie, (W) Darren Braithwaite, Ade Mafe, John Regis)	3-03-91	Glasgow
	1:22.71	National Team (A) (Thomas Jefferson, Raymond Pierre, Antonio McKay, Kevin Little)	3-03-91	Glasgow
4 x 400-meter relay	3:01.96	United States (W, A) (Kerron Clement, Wallace Spearmon, Darold Williamson, Jeremy Wariner)	2-11-06	Fayetteville, Ark.
4 x 800-meter relay	7:13.94	United States (W, A) (Joey Woody, Karl Paranya, Rich Kenah, David Krummenacker)	2-06-00	Boston
High jump	2.43m	Javier Sotomayor, Cuba (W)	3-4-89	Budapest, Hungary
	2.40m	Hollis Conway (A)	3-10-91	Seville
Pole vault	6.15m	Sergei Bubka, Ukraine (W)	2-21-93	Donetsk, Ukraine
	6.02m	Jeff Hartwig (A)	3-10-02	Sindelfingen, Germany
Long jump	8.79m	Carl Lewis (W, A)	1-27-84	New York City
Triple jump	17.90m	Teddy Tamgho, France (W)	3-14-10	Doha, Qatar
	17.76m	Mike Conley (A)	2-27-87	New York City
Shot put	22.66m	Randy Barnes (W, A)	1-20-89	Los Angeles
Weight throw*	25.86m	Lance Deal (A)	3-04-95	Atlanta
Pentathlon*	4478 pts	Steve Fritz, (A)	1-14-95	Lawrence, Kan.
Heptathlon	6499 pts	Ashton Eaton (W, A)	3-12-10	Fayetteville, Ark.

*No recognized world record.

Women

Event	Mark	Record Holder	Date	Site
50 meters	5.96	Irina Privolova, Russia (W)	2-09-95	Madrid
	6.02	Gail Devers (A)	2-22-99	Liévin, France
55 meters*	6.56	Gwen Torrence (A)	3-14-87	Oklahoma City, Okla.
60 meters	6.92	Irina Privalova, Russia (W)	2-11-93	Madrid
	6.95	Gail Devers (A)	3-12-93	Toronto
	6.95	Marion Jones (A)	3-07-98	Maebashi, Japan
200 meters	21.87	Merlene Ottey, Jamaica (W)	2-13-93	Liévin, France
	22.33	Gwen Torrence (A)	3-02-66	Atlanta
400 meters	49.59	Jarmila Kratochvilová, Czecho. (W)	3-07-82	Milan
	50.64	Diane Dixon (A)	3-10-91	Seville
800 meters	1:55.82	Jolanda Batageli, Slovenia (W)	3-03-02	Vienna
	1:58.71	Nicole Teter (A)	3-02-02	New York City
1,000 meters	2:30.94	Maria Mutola, Mozambique (W)	2-25-99	Stockholm
	2:34.19	Jennifer Toomey (A)	2-20-04	Birmingham, England
1,500 meters	3:58.28	Yelena Soboleva, Russia (W)	2-18-06	Moscow
	3:59.98	Regina Jacobs, United States (A)	2-01-03	Boston
Mile	4:17.14	Doina Melinte, Romania (W)	2-09-90	East Rutherford, N.J.
	4:20.50	Mary Slaney (A)	2-19-82	San Diego
3,000 meters	8:23.72	Meseret Defar, Ethiopia (W)	2-03-07	Stuttgart
	8:33.25	Shalane Flanagan (A)	1-27-07	Boston
5,000 meters	14:24.37	Meseret Defar, Ethiopia (W)	2-18-09	Stockholm
	14:47.62	Shalane Flanagan (A)	2-07-09	Boston
50-meter hurdles	6.58	Cornelia Oschkenat, E Germany (W)	2-20-88	Berlin
	6.67	Jackie Joyner-Kersee (A)	2-10-95	Reno, Nev.
55-meter hurdles*	7.37	Jackie Joyner-Kersee (A)	2-03-89	New York City
60-meter hurdles	7.68	Susanna Kallur, Sweden (W)	2-20-08	Berlin
	7.74	Gail Devers (A)	3-01-03	Boston
3,000-meter walk	11:40.33	Claudia Stef, Romania	1-30-99	Bucharest, Romania
	12:20.79	Debbi Lawrence (A)	3-12-93	Toronto
4 x 200-meter relay	1:32.41	Russia (Y, Kondratyeva, (W) I. Khabarova, Y.Pechonkina, Y. Gushchina)	1-29-05	Glasgow
	1:33.24	Flirtisha Harris, Chryste Gaines, (A) Terri Dendy, Michele Collins	2-12-94	Glasgow
4 x 400-meter relay	3:23.37	Russia (Y. Gushchina, (W) O. Kotlyarova, O. Zaytseva, O. Krasnomovets)	1-28-06	Glasgow
	3:27.59	Michelle Collins, Monique Hennagan (A) Zundra Feagin-Alexander, Shanelle Porter	3-07-99	Maebashi, Japan
4 x 800-meter relay	8:12.41	Russia, (T. Andrianova, E. Kofanova (W) O. Sukhachova-Spasovkhodskaya, Y. Zinurova)	2-28-10	Moscow, Russia
	8:28.41	Univ. of Wisconsin (Sarah Renk, (A) Kim Sherman, Sue Gentes, Amy Wickus)	3-14-92	Indianapolis
High jump	2.08m	Kajsa Bergqvist, Sweden (W)	2-4-06	Arnstadt, Germany
	2.01m	Tisha Waller (A)	2-28-98	Atlanta
Pole vault	5.00m	Yelena Isinbaeva, Russia (W)	2-15-09	Donetsk, Ukraine
	4.83m	Jenn Stuczynski (A)	3-01-09	Boston
Long jump	7.37m	Heike Drechsler, East Germany (W)	2-13-88	Vienna
	7.13m	Jackie Joyner-Kersee (A)	3-5-94	Atlanta
Triple jump	15.36m	Tatyana Lebedeva, Russia (W)	3-6-04	Budapest, Hungary
	14.23m	Sheila Hudson-Strudwick (A)	3-4-95	Atlanta
Shot put	22.50m	Helena Fibingerová, Czecho. (W)	2-19-77	Jablonec, Czecho.
	19.83m	Ramona Pagel (A)	2-20-87	Inglewood, Calif.
Weight throw*	25.56m	Brittany Riley (A)	3-10-07	Fayetteville, Ark.
Pentathlon	4991 pts	Irina Belova, Russia (W)	2-15-92	Berlin
	4753 pts	DeDee Nathan (A)	3-4/5-99	Maebashi, Japan

*No recognized world record.

Men

100 METERS

1983	Carl Lewis, United States	10.07
1987*	Carl Lewis, United States	9.93 WR
1991	Carl Lewis, United States	9.86 WR
1993	Linford Christie, Great Britain	9.87
1995	Donovan Bailey, Canada	9.97
1997	Maurice Greene, United States	9.86
1999	Maurice Greene, United States	9.80
2001	Maurice Greene, United States	9.82
2003	Kim Collins, St. Kitts & Nevis	10.07
2005	Justin Gatlin, United States	9.88
2007	Tyson Gay, United States	9.85
2009	Usain Bolt, Jamaica	9.58WR

200 METERS

1983	Calvin Smith, United States	20.14
1987	Calvin Smith, United States	20.16
1991	Michael Johnson, United States	20.01
1993	Frank Fredericks, Namibia	19.85
1995	Michael Johnson, United States	19.79
1997	Ato Boldon, Trinidad and Tobago	20.04
1999	Maurice Greene, United States	19.90
2001	Konstadínos Kedéris, Greece	20.04
2003	John Capel, United States	20.30
2005	Justin Gatlin, United States	20.04
2007	Tyson Gay, United States	19.76
2009	Usain Bolt, Jamaica	19.19WR

400 METERS

1983	Bert Cameron, Jamaica	45.05
1987	Thomas Schoenlebe, E Germany	44.33
1991	Antonio Pettigrew, United States	44.57
1993	Michael Johnson, United States	43.65
1995	Michael Johnson, United States	43.39
1997	Michael Johnson, United States	44.12
1999	Michael Johnson, United States	43.18 WR
2001	Avard Moncur, Bahamas	44.64
2003	Jerome Young, United States	44.50
2005	Jeremy Wariner, United States	43.93
2007	Jeremy Wariner, United States	43.45
2009	LaShawn Merritt, United States	44.06

800 METERS

1983	Willi Wulbeck, W Germany	1:43.65
1987	Billy Konchellah, Kenya	1:43.06
1991	Billy Konchellah, Kenya	1:43.99
1993	Paul Ruto, Kenya	1:44.71
1995	Wilson Kipketer, Denmark	1:45.08
1997	Wilson Kipketer, Denmark	1:43.38
1999	Wilson Kipketer, Denmark	1:43.30
2001	André Bucher, Switzerland	1:43.70
2003	Djabir Saïd-Guerni, Algeria	1:44.81
2005	Rashid Ramzi, Brunei	1:44.24
2007	Alfred Kirwa Yego	1:47.09
2009	Mbulaeni Mulaudzi, South Africa	1:45.29

1,500 METERS

1983	Steve Cram, Great Britain	3:41.59
1987	Abdi Bile, Somalia	3:36.80
1991	Noureddine Morceli, Algeria	3:32.84
1993	Noureddine Morceli, Algeria	3:34.24
1995	Noureddine Morceli, Algeria	3:33.73
1997	Hicham El Guerrouj, Morocco	3:35.83
1999	Hicham El Guerrouj, Morocco	3:27.65
2001	Hicham El Guerrouj, Morocco	3:30.68
2003	Hicham El Guerrouj, Morocco	3:31.77
2005	Rashid Ramzi, Brunei	3:37.88
2007	Bernard Lagat, United States	3:34.77
2009	Yusuf Kamel, Bahrain	3:35.93

3,000-METER STEEPLECHASE

1983	Patriz Ilg, W Germany	8:15.06
1987	Francesco Panetta, Italy	8:08.57
1991	Moses Kiptanui, Kenya	8:12.59
1993	Moses Kiptanui, Kenya	8:06.36
1995	Moses Kiptanui, Kenya	8:04.16
1997	Wilson Boit Kipketer, Kenya	8:05.84
1999	Christopher Koskei, Kenya	8:11.76
2001	Reuben Kosgei, Kenya	8:15.16
2003	Saif Saaeed Shaheen, Qatar	8:04.39
2005	Saif Saaeed Shaheen, Qatar	8:13.31
2007	Brimin Kipruto, Kenya	8:13.82
2009	Ezekiel Kemboi, Kenya	8:00.43

5,000 METERS

1983	Eamonn Coghlan, Ireland	13:28.53
1987	Said Aouita, Morocco	13:26.44
1991	Yobes Ondieki, Kenya	13:14.45
1993	Ismael Kirui, Kenya	13:02.75
1995	Ismael Kirui, Kenya	13:16.77
1997	Daniel Komen, Kenya	13:07.38
1999	Salah Hissou, Morocco	12:58.13
2001	Richard Limo, Kenya	13:00.77
2003	Eliud Kipchoge, Kenya	12:52.79
2005	Benjamin Limo, Kenya	13:32.55
2007	Bernard Lagat, United States	13:45.87
2009	Kenenisa Bekele, Ethiopia	13:17.09

10,000 METERS

1983	Alberto Cova, Italy	28:01.04
1987	Paul Kipkoech, Kenya	27:38.63
1991	Moses Tanui, Kenya	27:38.74
1993	Haile Gebrselassie, Ethiopia	27:46.02
1995	Haile Gebrselassie, Ethiopia	27:12.95
1997	Haile Gebrselassie, Ethiopia	27:24.58
1999	Haile Gebrselassie, Ethiopia	27:57.27
2001	Charles Kamathi, Kenya	27:53.25
2003	Kenenisa Bekele, Ethiopia	26:49.57
2005	Kenenisa Bekele, Ethiopia	27:08.33
2007	Kenenisa Bekele, Ethiopia	27:05.90
2009	Kenenisa Bekele, Ethiopia	26:46.31

MARATHON

1983	Rob de Castella, Australia	2:10:03
1987	Douglas Wakiihuri, Kenya	2:11:48
1991	Hiromi Taniguchi, Japan	2:14:57
1993	Mark Plaatjes, United States	2:13:57
1995	Martín Fiz, Spain	2:11:41
1997	Abel Anton, Spain	2:13:16
1999	Abel Anton, Spain	2:13:36
2001	Gezahegne Abera, Ethiopia	2:12:42
2003	Jaouad Gharib, Morocco	2:08:31
2005	Jaouad Gharib, Morocco	2:10:10
2007	Luke Kibet, Kenya	2:15:59
2009	Abel Kirui, Kenya	2:06:54

110-METER HURDLES

1983	Greg Foster, United States	13.42
1987	Greg Foster, United States	13.21
1991	Greg Foster, United States	13.06
1993	Colin Jackson, Great Britain	12.91 WR
1995	Allen Johnson, United States	13.00
1997	Allen Johnson, United States	12.93
1999	Colin Jackson, Great Britain	13.04
2001	Allen Johnson, United States	13.04
2003	Allen Johnson, United States	13.12
2005	Ladji Doucoure, France	13.07
2007	Liu Xiang, China	12.95
2009	Ryan Brathwaite, Barbados	13.14

WR=World record. *Ben Johnson, Canada, disqualified.

Men (Cont.)

400-METER HURDLES

1983	Edwin Moses, United States	47.50
1987	Edwin Moses, United States	47.46
1991	Samuel Matete, Zambia	47.64
1993	Kevin Young, United States	47.18
1995	Derrick Adkins, United States	47.98
1997	Stéphane Diagana, France	47.70
1999	Fabrizio Mori, Italy	47.72
2001	Felix Sánchez, Dominican Rep.	47.49
2003	Felix Sánchez, Dominican Rep.	47.25
2005	Bershawn Jackson, United States	47.30
2007	Kerron Clement, United States	47.61
2009	Kerron Clement, United States	47.91

20-KILOMETER WALK

1983	Ernesto Canto, Mexico	1:20:49
1987	Maurizio Damilano, Italy	1:20:45
1991	Maurizio Damilano, Italy	1:19:37
1993	Valentin Massana, Spain	1:22:31
1995	Michele Didoni, Italy	1:19:59
1997	Daniel Garcia, Mexico	1:21:43
1999	Ilya Markov, Russia	1:23:34
2001	Roman Rasskazov, Russia	1:20:31
2003	Jefferson Pérez, Ecuador	1:17.21 WR
2005	Jefferson Pérez, Ecuador	1:18:35
2007	Jefferson Pérez, Ecuador	1:22:20
2009	Valeriy Borchin, Russia	1:18.41

50-KILOMETER WALK

1983	Ronald Weigel, East Germany	3:43:08
1987	Hartwig Gauder, East Germany	3:40:53
1991	Aleksandr Potashov, USSR	3:53:09
1993	Jesus Angel Garcia, Spain	3:41:41
1995	Valentin Kononen, Finland	3:43:42
1997	Robert Korzeniowski, Poland	3:44:46
1999	German Skurygin, Russia	3:44:23
2001	Robert Korzeniowski, Poland	3:42:08
2003	R. Korzeniowski, Poland	3:36:03 WR
2005	S. Kirdyapkin, Russia	3:38:08
2007	Nathan Deakes, Australia	3:43:53
2009	Sergey Kirdyapkin, Russia	3:38.35

4 X 100-METER RELAY

1983	United States (Emmit King, Willie Gault, Calvin Smith, Carl Lewis)	37.86
1987	United States (Lee McRae, Lee McNeil, Harvey Glance, Carl Lewis)	37.90
1991	United States (A. Cason L. Burrell, D. Mitchell, C. Lewis)	37.50 WR
1993	United States (J. Drummond, A. Cason, D. Mitchell, L. Burrell)	37.48
1995	Canada (Robert Esmie, Glenroy Gilbert, Bruny Surin, Donovan Bailey)	38.31
1997	Canada (Robert Esmie, Glenroy Gilbert, Bruny Surin, Donovan Bailey)	37.86
1999	United States (Jon Drummond, Tim Montgomery, Brian Lewis, Maurice Greene)	37.59
2001	United States (Mickey Grimes, Bernard Williams, Dennis Mitchell, Tim Montgomery)	37.96
2003	United States (J. Capel, B. Williams D.Patton, J. Johnson)	38.06
2005	Trinidad and Tobago (L. Doucoure, R. Pognon, E. De Lepine, Dovy Lueyi)	38.08
2007	United States (D. Patton, W. Spearmon, T. Gay, L. Dixon)	37.78
2009	Jamaica (Steve Mullings, Michael Frater, Usain Bolt, Asafa Powell)	37.31

4 X 400-METER RELAY

1983	USSR (S. Lovachev, A. Troschilo, N. Chernyetski, V. Markin)	3:00.79
1987	United States (Danny Everett Rod Haley, Antonio McKay, Butch Reynolds)	2:57.29
1991	Great Britain (Roger Black Derek Redmond, John Regis, Kriss Akabusi)	2:57.53
1993	United States (Andrew Valmon, Quincy Watts, Butch Reynolds, Michael Johnson)	2:54.29 WR
1995	United States (Marlon Ramsey, Derek Mills, Butch Reynolds, Michael Johnson)	2:57.32
1997	United States (J. Young, A. Pettigrew, C. Jones, T. Washington)	2:56.47
1999	United States (Jerome Davis, Antonio Pettigrew, Angelo Taylor, Michael Johnson)	2:56.45
2001	United States (L. Byrd, A. Pettigrew, D. Brew, A. Taylor)	2:57.54
2003	United States (C. Harrison, T. Washington, D. Brew, J. Young)	2:58.88
2005	United States (D. Brew, R. Andrew, D. Williamson, B. Wariner)	2:56.91
2007	United States (LaShawn Merritt, Angelo Taylor, Darold Williamson, Jeremy Wariner)	2:55.56
2009	United States (Angelo Taylor, Jeremy Wariner, Kerron Clement, LaShawn Merritt)	2:57.86

HIGH JUMP

1983	Gennadi Avdeyenko, USSR	2.32m
1987	Patrik Sjoberg, Sweden	2.38m
1991	Charles Austin, United States	2.38m
1993	Javier Sotomayor, Cuba	2.40mWR
1995	Troy Kemp, Bahamas	2.37m
1997	Javier Sotomayor, Cuba	2.37m
1999	Vyacheslav Voronin, Russia	2.37m
2001	Martin Buss, Germany	2.36m
2003	Jacques Freitag, South Africa	2.35m
2005	Yuriy Krymarenko, Ukraine	2.32m
2007	Donald Thoma, Bahamas	2.35m
2009	Yaroslav Rybakov, Russia	2.32m

POLE VAULT

1983	Sergei Bubka, USSR	5.70m
1987	Sergei Bubka, USSR	5.85m
1991	Sergei Bubka, USSR	5.95m
1993	Sergei Bubka, Ukraine	6.00m
1995	Sergei Bubka, Ukraine	5.92m
1997	Sergei Bubka, Ukraine	6.01m
1999	Maksim Tarasov, Russia	6.02m
2001	Dmitri Markov, Australia	6.05mWR
2003	Guiseppe Gibilisco, Italy	5.90m
2005	Rens Blom, Netherlands	5.80m
2007	Brad Walker, United States	5.86m
2009	Steven Hooker, Australia	5.90m

LONG JUMP

1983	Carl Lewis, United States	8.55m
1987	Carl Lewis, United States	8.67m
1991	Mike Powell, United States	8.95mWR
1993	Mike Powell, United States	8.59m
1995	Iván Pedroso, Cuba	8.71m
1997	Iván Pedroso, Cuba	8.51m
1999	Iván Pedroso, Cuba	8.62m
2001	Iván Pedroso, Cuba	8.43m
2003	Dwight Phillips, United States	8.29m

Men *(Cont.)*

LONG JUMP *(Cont.)*

2005	Dwight Phillips, United States	8.60m
2007	Irving Saladino, Panama	8.57m
2009	Dwight Phillips, United States	8.54m

TRIPLE JUMP

1983	Zdzislaw Hoffmann, Poland	17.42m
1987	Hristo Markov, Bulgaria	17.92m
1991	Kenny Harrison, United States	17.78m
1993	Mike Conley, United States	17.86m
1995	Jonathan Edwards, G.B.	18.29m WR
1997	Yoelvis Quesada, Cuba	17.85m
1999	Charles Friedek, Germany	17.59m
2001	Jonathan Edwards, G. Britain	17.92m
2003	Christian Olsson, Sweden	17.72m
2005	Walter Davis, United States	17.57m
2007	Nelson Evora, Portugal	17.74m
2009	Phillips Idowu, United Kingdom	17.73m

SHOT PUT

1983	Edward Sarul, Poland	21.39m
1987	Werner Günthör, Switz.	22.23mWR
1991	Werner Günthör, Switz.	21.67m
1993	Werner Günthör, Switz.	21.97m
1995	John Godina, United States	21.47m
1997	John Godina, United States	21.44m
1999	C.J. Hunter, United States	21.79m
2001	John Godina, United States	21.87m
2003	Andrei Mikahnevic, Bulgaria	21.69m
2005	Adam Nelson, United States	21.73m
2007	Reese Hoffa, United States	22.04m
2009	Christian Cantwell, United States	22.03m

DISCUS THROW

1983	Imrich Bugar, Czechoslovakia	67.72m
1987	Juergen Schult, E Germany	68.74m
1991	Lars Riedel, Germany	66.20m
1993	Lars Riedel, Germany	67.72m
1995	Lars Riedel, Germany	68.76m
1997	Lars Riedel, Germany	68.54m
1999	Anthony Washington, U.S.	69.08m
2001	Lars Riedel, Germany	69.72m
2003	Virgilijus Alekna, Lithuania	69.69m
2005	Virgilijus Alekna, Lithuania	70.17mWR
2007	Gerd Kanter, Estonia	68.94m
2009	Robert Harting, Germany	69.43m

HAMMER THROW

1983	Sergei Litvinov, USSR	82.68m
1987	Sergei Litvinov, USSR	83.06m
1991	Yuriy Sedykh, USSR	81.70m
1993	Andrey Abduvaliyev, Tajikistan	81.64m
1995	Andrey Abduvaliyev, Tajikistan	81.56m
1997	Heinz Weis, Germany	81.78m
1999	Karsten Kobs, Germany	80.24m
2001	Szymon Ziolkowski, Poland	83.38m
2003	Ivan Tikhon, Belarus	83.05m
2005	Ivan Tikhon, Belarus	83.89mWR
2007	Ivan Tsikhan, Belarus	83.63m
2009	Primoz Kozmus, Slovenia	80.84

JAVELIN

1983	Detlef Michel, East Germany	89.48m
1987	Seppo Räty, Finland	83.54m
1991	Kimmo Kinnunen, Finland	90.82m
1993	Jan Zelezny, Czech Rep.	85.98m
1995	Jan Zelezny, Czech Rep.	89.58m
1997	Marius Corbett, South Africa	88.40m
1999	Aki Parviainen, Finland	89.52m
2001	Jan Zelezny, Czech Rep.	92.80mWR
2003	Sergey Makarov, Russia	85.44m
2005	Andrus Varnik, Estonia	87.17m
2007	Tero Pitkämäki, Finland	90.33m
2009	Andreas Thorkildsen, Norway	89.59m

DECATHLON

1983	Daley Thompson, Great Britain	8666 pts
1987	Torsten Voss, East Germany	8680 pts
1991	Dan O'Brien, United States	8812 pts
1993	Dan O'Brien, United States	8817 pts
1995	Dan O'Brien, United States	8695 pts
1997	Tomás Dvorák, Czech Rep.	8837 pts
1999	Tomás Dvorák, Czech Rep.	8744 pts
2001	Tomás Dvorák, Czech Rep.	8902 ptsWR
2003	Tom Pappas, United States	8750 pts
2005	Bryan Clay, United States	8732 pts
2007	Roman Sebrle, Czech Rep.	8676 pts
2009	Trey Hardee, United States	8790 pts

Women

100 METERS

1983	Marlies Gohr, East Germany	10.97
1987	Silke Gladisch, East Germany	10.90
1991	Katrin Krabbe, Germany	10.99
1993	Gail Devers, United States	10.82
1995	Gwen Torrence, United States	10.85
1997	Marion Jones, United States	10.83
1999	Marion Jones, United States	10.70
2001	Zhanna Pintusevich-Block, Ukraine	10.82
2003	Kelli White, United States	10.85
2005	Lauryn Williams, United States	10.93
2007	Veronica Campbell, Jamaica	11.01
2009	Shelly-Ann Fraser, Jamaica	10.73

200 METERS

1983	Marita Koch, East Germany	22.13
1987	Silke Gladisch, East Germany	21.74
1991	Katrin Krabbe, Germany	22.09
1993	Merlene Ottey, Jamaica	21.98
1995	Merlene Ottey, Jamaica	22.12
1997	Zhanna Pintusevich, Ukraine	22.32

200 METERS *(Cont.)*

1999	Inger Miller, United States	21.77
2001	Marion Jones, United States	22.39
2003	Kelli White, United States	22.05
2005	Allyson Felix, United States	22.16
2007	Allyson Felix, United States	21.81
2009	Allyson Felix, United States	22.02

400 METERS

1983	Jarmila Kratochvilova, Czech.	47.99
1987	Olga Bryzgina, USSR	49.38
1991	Marie-José Pérec, France	49.13
1993	Jearl Miles, United States	49.82
1995	Marie-José Pérec, France	49.28
1997	Cathy Freeman, Australia	49.77
1999	Cathy Freeman, Australia	49.67
2001	Amy Mbacke Thiam, Senegal	49.86
2003	Ana Guevara, Mexico	48.89
2005	Darling Williams, Bahamas	49.55
2007	Christine Ohuruogu, Great Britain	49.61
2009	Sanya Richards, United States	49.00

WR=World record. EWR=Equals world record.

Women (Cont.)

800 METERS

1983	Jarmila Kratochvilova, Czech.	1:54.68
1987	Sigrun Wodars, East Germany	1:55.26
1991	Lilia Nurutdinova, USSR	1:57.50
1993	Maria Mutola, Mozambique	1:55.43
1995	Ana Quirot, Cuba	1:56.11
1997	Ana Quirot, Cuba	1:57.14
1999	Ludmila Formanová, Czech Rep.	1:56.68
2001	Maria Mutola, Mozambique	1:57.17
2003	Maria Mutola, Mozambique	1:59.89
2005	Zulia Calatayud, Cuba	1:58.82
2007	Janeth Jepkosgei, Kenya	1:56.04
2009	Caster Semenya, South Africa	1:55.45

1,500 METERS

1983	Mary Slaney, United States	4:00.90
1987	Tatyana Samolenko, USSR	3:58.56
1991	Hassiba Boulmerka, Algeria	4:02.21
1993	Dong Liu, China	4:00.50
1995	Hassiba Boulmerka, Algeria	4:02.42
1997	Carla Sacramento, Portugal	4:04.24
1999	Svetlana Masterkova, Russia	3:59.53
2001	Gabriela Szabo, Romania	4:00.57
2003	Tatyana Tomashova, Russia	3:58.52
2005	Tatyana Tomashova, Russia	4:00.35
2007	Maryam Yusuf Jamal, Bahrain	3:58.75
2009	Maryam Yusuf Jamal, Bahrain	4:03.74

3,000 METERS

1983	Mary Slaney, United States	8:34.62
1987	Tatyana Samolenko, USSR	8:38.73
1991	Tatyana Dorovskikh, USSR	8:35.82
1993	Qu Yunxia, China	8:28.71

3,000 METER STEEPLECHASE

2005	Docus Inzikuru, Uganda	9:18.24
2007	Yekaterina Volkova, Russia	9:06.57
2009	Marta Dominguez, Spain	9:07.32

5,000 METERS

1995	Sonia O'Sullivan, Ireland	14:46.47
1997	Gabriela Szabo, Romania	14:57.68
1999	Gabriela Szabo, Romania	14:41.82
2001	Olga Yegorova, Russia	15:03.39
2003	Tirunesh Dibaba, Ethiopia	14:51.72
2005	Tirunesh Dibaba, Ethiopia	14:38.59
2007	Meseret Defar, Ethiopia	14:57.91
2009	Vivian Cheruiyot, Kenua	14:57.97

10,000 METERS

1987	Ingrid Kristiansen, Norway	31:05.85
1991	Liz McColgan, Great Britain	31:14.31
1993	Wang Junxia, China	30:49:30
1995	Fernanda Ribeiro, Portugal	31:04.99
1997	Sally Barsosio, Kenya	31:32.92
1999	Gete Wami, Ethiopia	30:24.56
2001	Derartu Tulu, Ethiopia	31:48.81
2003	Berhane Adere, Ethiopia	30:04.18
2005	Tirunesh Dibaba, Ethiopia	30:24.02
2007	Tirunesh Dibaba, Ethiopia	31:55.41
2009	Linet Masai, Kenya	30:51.24

MARATHON

1983	Grete Waitz, Norway	2:28:09
1987	Rosa Mota, Portugal	2:25:17
1991	Wanda Panfil, Poland	2:29:53
1993	Junko Asari, Japan	2:30:03
1995	Manuela Machado, Portugal	2:25:39*
1997	Hiromi Suzuki, Japan	2:29:48
1999	Jong Song-Ok, North Korea	2:26:59
2001	Lidia Simon, Romania	2:26.01

*400 meters short. WR=World Record.

MARATHON (Cont.)

2003	Catherine Ndereba, Kenya	2:23:55
2005	Paula Radcliffe, Great Britain	2:20:57
2007	Catherine Ndereba, Kenya	2:30:37
2009	Xue Bai, China	2:25.15

100-METER HURDLES

1983	Bettine Jahn, East Germany	12.35
1987	Ginka Zagorcheva, Bulgaria	12.34
1991	Lyudmila Narozhilenko, USSR	12.59
1993	Gail Devers, United States	12.46
1995	Gail Devers, United States	12.68
1997	Ludmila Engquist, Sweden	12.50
1999	Gail Devers, United States	12.37
2001	Anjanette Kirkland, United States	12.42
2003	Perdita Felicien, Canada	12.53
2005	Michelle Perry, United States	12:66.
2007	Michelle Perry, United States	12:46
2009	Brigitte Foster-Hylton, Jamaica	12.51

400-METER HURDLES

1983	Yekaterina Fesenko, USSR	54.14
1987	Sabine Busch, East Germany	53.62
1991	Tatyana Ledovskaya, USSR	53.11
1993	Sally Gunnell, Great Britain	52.74WR
1995	Kim Batten, United States	52.61
1997	Nezha Bidouane, Morocco	52.97
1999	Daimi Pernia, Cuba	52.89
2001	Nezha Bidouane, Morocco	53.34
2003	Jana Pittman, Australia	53.22
2005	Yuliya Pechonkina, Russia	52.90
2007	Jana Rawlinson, Australia	53.31
2009	Melaine Walker, Jamaica	52.42

20-KILOMETER WALK

1999	Hongyu Liu, China	1:30:50
2001	Olimpiada Ivanova, Russia	1:27:48
2003	Yelena Nikolayeva, Russia	1:26:52
2005	Olimpiada Ivanova, Russia	1:25:41
2007	Olga Kaniskina, Russia	1:30:09
2009	Olga Kaniskina, Russia	1:28.09

4 X 100-METER RELAY

1983	E Germany (S. Gladisch, M. Koch, I. Auerswald, M. Gohr)	41.76
1987	United States (A. Brown, D. Williams, F. Griffith, P. Marshall)	41.58
1991	Jamaica (Dalia Duhaney, Juliet Cuthbert, Beverley McDonald, Merlene Ottey)	41.94
1993	Russia (Olga Bogoslovskaya, Galina Malchugina, Natalya Voronova, Irina Privalova)	41.49
1995	United States (Celena Mondie-Milner, Carlette Guidry, Chryste Gaines, Gwen Torrence)	42.12
1997	United States (C. Gaines, M. Jones, I. Miller, G.Devers)	41.47
1999	Bahamas (S. Fynes, C. Sturrup, P. Davis-Thompson, D. Ferguson)	41.92
2001	United States (Kelli White, Chryste Gaines, Inger Miller, Marion Jones)	41.71
2003	France (P. Girard, M. Hurtis S. Félix, C. Arron)	41.78
2005	Jamaica, (A. Daigie, M. Lee, M. Billiams	41.78
2007	United States (Lauryn Williams, Allyson Felix, Mikele Barber, Torri Edwards)	41.98
2009	Jamaica (Simone Facey, S. Fraser, Aleen Bailey, Kerron Stewart)	42.06

Women (Cont.)

4 X 400-METER RELAY

Year	Team	Time
1983	East Germany (Kerstin Walther, Sabine Busch, Marita Koch, Dagmar Rubsam)	3:19.73
1987	East Germany (Dagmar Neubauer, Kirsten Emmelmann, Petra Müller, Sabine Busch)	3:18.63
1991	USSR (Tatyana Ledovskaya, Lyudmila Dzhigalova, Olga Nazarova, Olga Bryzgina)	3:18.43
1993	United States (Gwen Torrence, Maicel Malone, Natasha Kaiser-Brown, Jearl Miles)	3:16.71
1995	United States (Kim Graham, Rochelle Stevens, Camara Jones, Jearl Miles)	3:22.39
1997	Germany (A. Feller, U. Rohlander, A. Rucker, G. Breuer)	3:20.92
1999	Russia (Tatyana Chebykina, Svetlana Goncharenko, Olga Kotylarova, Natalya Nazarova)	3:21.98
2001	Jamaica (Sandie Richards, Catherine Scott, Debbie Ann Parris, Lorraine Fenton)	3:20.65
2003	United States (M. Barber, D. Washington, J. Miles-Clark, S. Richards)	3:22.63
2005	Russia (Y. Pechonkina, O. Krasnomovets, N. Antyukh, S. Pospelova)	3:20.95
2007	United States (D. Trotter, A. Felix, M. Wineberg, S.Richards)	3:18.55
2009	United States (Debbie Dunn, A. Felix, Lashinda Demus, Sanya Richards)	3:17.83

HIGH JUMP

1983	Tamara Bykova, USSR	2.01m
1987	Stefka Kostadinova, Bulgaria	2.09mWR
1991	Heike Henkel, Germany	2.05m
1993	Ioamnet Quintero, Cuba	1.99m
1995	Stefka Kostadinova, Bulgaria	2.01m
1997	Hanne Haugland, Norway	1.99m
1999	Inga Babakova, Ukraine	1.99m
2001	Hestrie Cloete, South Africa	2.00m
2003	Hestrie Cloete, South Africa	2.06m
2005	Kajsa Bergvist, Sweden	2.02m
2007	Blanka Vlasic, Croatia	2.05m
2009	Blanka Vlasic, Croatia	2.04m

POLE VAULT

1999	Stacy Dragila, United States	4.06mEWR
2001	Stacy Dragila, United States	4.75m
2003	Svetlana Feofanova, Russia	4.75m
2005	Yelena Isinbayeva, Russia	5.01mWR
2007	Yelena Isinbayeva, Russia	4.80m
2009	Anna Rogowska, Poland	4.75m

LONG JUMP

1983	Heike Daute, E Germany	7.27m
1987	Jackie Joyner-Kersee, U.S.	7.36mWR
1991	Jackie Joyner-Kersee, United States	7.32m
1993	Heike Drechsler, Germany	7.11m
1995	Fiona May, Italy	6.98m
1997	Lyudmila Galkina, Russia	7.05m
1999	Niurka Montalvo, Spain	7.06m
2001	Fiona May, Italy	6.87m
2003	Eunice Barber, France	6.99m
2005	Tianna Madison, United States	6.89m
2007	Tatyana Lebedeva, Russia	7.03m
2009	Brittney Reese, United States	7.10m

TRIPLE JUMP

1993	Ana Biryukova, Russia	15.09m
1995	Inessa Kravets, Ukraine	15.50mWR

TRIPLE JUMP (Cont.)

1997	S. Kasparkova, Czech Rep.	15.20m
1999	Paraskevi Tsiamíta, Greece	14.88m
2001	Tatyana Lebedeva, Russia	15.25m
2003	Tatyana Lebedeva, Russia	15.18m
2005	Trecia Smith, Jamaica	15.11m
2007	Yargeris Savigne, Cuba	15.28m
2009	Yargeris Savigne, Cuba	14.95m

SHOT PUT

1983	Helena Fibingerova, Czech.	21.05m
1987	Natalya Lisovskaya, USSR	21.24mWR
1991	Zhihong Huang, China	20.83m
1993	Zhihong Huang, China	20.57m
1995	Astrid Kumbernuss, Germany	21.22m
1997	Astrid Kumbernuss, Germany	20.71m
1999	Astrid Kumbernuss, Germany	19.85m
2001	Yanina Korolchik, Belarus	20.61m
2003	Svetlana Krivelyova, Russia	20.63m
2005	Nadezhda Ostapchuk, Russia	20.51m
2007	Valerie Vili, New Zealand	20.54m
2009	Valerie Vili, New Zealand	20.44m

HAMMER THROW

1999	Mihaela Melinte, Romania	75.20mWR
2001	Yipsi Moreno, Cuba	70.65m
2003	Yipsi Moreno, Cuba	70.30m
2005	Olga Kuzenkova, Russia	75.10m
2007	Betty Heidler, Germany	74.76m
2009	Anita Wlodarczyk, Poland	77.96mWR

JAVELIN

1983	Tiina Lillak, Finland	70.82m
1987	Fatima Whitbread, United Kingdom	76.64m
1991	Xu Demei, China	68.78m
1993	Trine Solberg-Hattestad, Norway	69.18m
1995	Natalya Shikolenko, Belarus	67.56m
1997	Trine Hattestad, Norway	68.78m
1999	Mirela Manjani-Tzelili, Greece	67.09m
2001	Osleidys Menendez, Cuba	69.53m
2003	Mirela Manjani, Greece	66.52m
2005	Osleidys Menendez, Cuba	71.70m
2007	Barbora Spotakova, Czech Rep.	67.07m
2009	Steffi Nerius, Germany	67.30m

DISCUS THROW

1983	Martina Opitz, E Germany	68.94m
1987	Martina Hellmann, East Germ.	71.62mWR
1991	Tsvetanka Khristova, Bulgaria	71.02m
1993	Olga Burova, Russia	67.40m
1995	Ellina Zvereva, Belarus	68.64m
1997	Beatrice Faumuina, New Zeal.	66.82m
1999	Franka Dietzsch, Germany	68.14m
2001	Ellina Zvereva,, Belarus	67.10m
2003	Irina Yatchenko, Belarus	67.32m
2005	Franka Dietzsch, Germany	66.56m
2007	Franka Dietzsch, Germany	66.61m
2009	Dani Samuels, Australia	65.44m

HEPTATHLON

1983	Ramona Neubert, E. Germany	6714 pts
1987	Jackie Joyner-Kersee, U.S.	7128 pts
1991	Sabine Braun, Germany	6672 pts
1993	Jackie Joyner-Kersee, U.S.	6831 pts
1995	Ghada Shouaa, Syria	6651 pts
1997	Sabine Braun, Germany	6739 pts
1999	Eunice Barber, France	6861 pts
2001	Yelena Prokhorova, Russia	6694 pts
2003	Carolina Kluft, Sweden	7001 pts
2005	Carolina Kluft, Sweden	6887 pts
2007	Carolina Kluft, Sweden	7032 pts
2009	Jessica Ennis, United Kingdom	6731 pts

WR=World Record. EWR=Equals world record.

Swimming

HEINZ KLUETMEIER

World and American Records

Men

Freestyle	Time	Record Holder	Date	Site
50 meters	20.91	Cesar Cielo Filho, Brazil (W)	12-18-09	Sao Paulo
	21.40	Cullen Jones (A)	8-01-09	Rome
100 meters	46.91	Cesar Cielo Filho, Brazil (W)	7-30-09	Rome
	47.33	David Walters (A)	7-30-09	Rome
200 meters	1:42.00	Paul Biedermann, Germany (W)	7-28-09	Rome
	1:42.96	Michael Phelps (A)	8-12-08	Beijing
400 meters	3:40.07	Paul Biedermann, Germany (W)	7-26-09	Rome
	3:42.78	Larsen Jensen (A)	8-10-08	Beijing
800 meters	7:32.12	Lin Zhang, China (W)	7-29-09	Rome
	7:45.63	Larsen Jensen (A)	7-27-05	Montreal
1,500 meters	14:34.56	Grant Hackett, Australia (W)	7-29-01	Fukuoka, Japan
	14:45.29	Larsen Jensen (A)	8-21-04	Athens

Backstroke	Time	Record Holder	Date	Site
50 meters	24.04	Liam Tancock, United Kingdom (W)	8-02-09	Rome
	24.33	Randall Bal (A)	12-05-08	Eindhoven, Neth.
100 meters	51.94	Aaron Peirsol (W,A)	7-08-09	Indianapolis
200 meters	1:51.92	Aaron Peirsol (W,A)	7-31-09	Rome

Breaststroke	Time	Record Holder	Date	Site
50 meters	26.67	Cameron Van Der Burgh, South Africa (W)	7-29-09	Rome
	26.86	Mark Gangloff (A)	7-29-09	Rome
100 meters	58.58	Brenton Rickard, Australia (W)	7-27-09	Rome
	58.96	Eric Shanteau (A)	7-26-09	Rome
200 meters	2:07.31	Christian Sprenger, Australia (W)	7-30-09	Rome
	2:07.42	Eric Shanteau (A)	7-11-09	Indianapolis

Butterfly	Time	Record Holder	Date	Site
50 meters	22.43	Rafael Munoz, Spain (W)	4-05-09	Malaga, Spain
	22.91	Bryan Lundqvist (A)	7-18-09	Knoxville, Tenn.
100 meters	49.82	Michael Phelps (W,A)	8-01-09	Rome
200 meters	1:51.51	Michael Phelps (W,A)	7-29-09	Rome

Individual Medley	Time	Record Holder	Date	Site
200 meters	1:54.10	Ryan Lochte (W,A)	7-30-09	Rome
400 meters	4:03.84	Michael Phelps (W,A)	8-10-08	Beijing

Relays	Time	Record Holder	Date	Site
4 x100-meter medley	3:27.28	United States (W,A)	8-02-09	Rome
		(Aaron Peirsol, Eric Shanteau, Michael Phelps, and David Walters)		
4 x100-meter freestyle	3:08.24	United States (W,A)	8-11-08	Beijing
		(Michael Phelps, Garrett Weber-Gale, Cullen Jones and Jason Lezak)		
4 x 200-meter freestyle	6:58.55	United States (W,A)	7-31-09	Rome
		(Michael Phelps, Ricky Berens, David Walters and Ryan Lochte)		

Note: Records through Oct 1, 2010.

Women

Freestyle

	Time	Record Holder	Date	Site
50 meters	23.73	Britta Steffen, Germany (W)	8-02-09	Rome
	24.07	Dara Torres (A)	8-17-08	Beijing
100 meters	52.07	Britta Steffen, Germany (W)	7-31-09	Rome
	53.02	Amanda Weir (A)	7-30-09	Rome
200 meters	1:52.98	Federica Pellegrini, Italy (W)	7-29-09	Rome
	1:54.96	Allison Schmitt (A)	7-29-09	Rome
400 meters	3:59.15	Federica Pellegrini, Italy (W)	7-26-09	Rome
	4:02.20	Katie Hoff (A)	2-16-08	Columbia, Mo.
800 meters	8:14.10	Rebecca Adlington, Great Britain (W)	8-16-08	Beijing
	8:16.22	Janet Evans (A)	8-20-89	Tokyo
1,500 meters	15:42.54	Kate Ziegler (W,A)	6-17-07	Mission Viejo, Calif.

Backstroke

	Time	Record Holder	Date	Site
50 meters	27.06	Jing Zhao, China (W)	7-30-09	Rome
	27.80	Hayley McGregory (A)	6-07-08	Austin, Tex.
100 meters	58.12	Gemma Spofforth, United Kingdom (W)	7-28-09	Rome
	58.94*	Natalie Coughlin (A)	8-17-08	Beijing
200 meters	2:04.81	Kirsty Coventry, Zimbabwe (W)	8-01-09	Rome
	2:06.09	Margaret Hoelzer (A)	7-5-08	Omaha, Neb.

Breaststroke

	Time	Record Holder	Date	Site
50 meters	29.80	Jessica Hardy (W,A)	8-07-09	Federal Way, Wash.
100 meters	1:04.45	Jessica Hardy (W,A)	8-07-09	Federal Way, Wash.
200 meters	2:20.12	Annamay Pierse, Canada (W)	7-30-09	Rome
	2:20.22	Rebecca Soni (A)	8-15-08	Beijing

Butterfly

	Time	Record Holder	Date	Site
50 meters	25.07	Therese Alshammar, Sweden (W)	7-31-09	Rome
	25.50	Dara Torres (A)	7-11-09	Indianapolis
100 meters	56.06	Sarah Sjostrom, Sweden (W)	7-27-09	Rome
	56.94	Dana Vollmer (A)	7-27-09	Rome
200 meters	2:01.81	Liu Zige, China (W)	10-21-09	Jinan, China
	2:04.14	Mary DeScenza (A)	7-30-09	Rome

Individual Medley

	Time	Record Holder	Date	Site
200 meters	2:06.15	Ariana Kukors (W,A)	7-27-09	Rome
400 meters	4:29.45	Stephanie Rice, Australia (W)	8-10-08	Beijing
	4:31.12	Katie Hoff (A)	6-29-08	Omaha, Neb.

Relays

	Time	Record Holder	Date	Site
4 x100-meter medley	3:52.19	China (W)	8-01-09	Rome
		(Jing Zhao, Huijia Chen, Liuyang Jiao and Zhesi Li)		
	3:53.30	United States (A)	8-17-08	Beijing
		(Natalie Coughlin, Rebecca Soni, Christine Magnuson and Dara Torres)		
4 x100-meter freestyle	3:31.72	Netherlands (W)	7-26-09	Rome
		(Inge Dekker, Ranomi Kromowidjojo, Femke Heemskerk and Marleen Veldhuis)		
	3:34.33	United States (A)	8-10-08	Beijing
		(Natalie Coughlin, Lacey Nymeyer, Kara Lynn Joyce and Dara Torres)		
4 x 200-meter freestyle	7:42.08	China (W)	7-30-09	Rome
		(Yu Yang, Qian Wei Zhu, Jing Liu, Jiaying Pang)		
	7:42.56	United States (A)	7-30-09	Rome
		(Dana Vollmer, Lacey Nymeyer, Ariana Kukors and Allison Schmitt)		

Note: Records through Oct 1, 2010. *relay lead-off split.

World Championships History

Men

50-METER FREESTYLE

1986	Tom Jager, United States	22.49‡
1991	Tom Jager, United States	22.16‡
1994	Alexander Popov, Russia	22.17
1998	Bill Pilczuk, United States	22.29
2001	Anthony Ervin, United States	22.09
2003	Alexander Popov, Russia	21.92‡
2005	Roland Schoeman, Russia	21.69
2007	Benjamin Wildman-Tobriner, U.S.	21.88
2009	Cesar Cielo Filho, Brazil	21.08‡

100-METER FREESTYLE

1973	Jim Montgomery, United States	51.70
1975	Andy Coan, United States	51.25
1978	David McCagg, United States	50.24
1982	Jorg Woithe, E. Germany	50.18
1986	Matt Biondi, United States	48.94
1991	Matt Biondi, United States	49.18
1994	Alexander Popov, Russia	49.12
1998	Alexander Popov, Russia	48.93‡
2001	Anthony Ervin, United States	48.33‡
2003	Alexander Popov, Russia	48.42
2005	Filippo Magnini, Italy	48:12
2007	Filippo Magnini, Italy	48.43
2009	Cesar Cielo Filho, Brazil	46.91*

200-METER FREESTYLE

1973	Jim Montgomery, United States	1:53.02
1975	Tim Shaw, United States	1:52.04‡
1978	Billy Forrester, United States	1:51.02‡
1982	Michael Gross, W Germany	1:49.84
1986	Michael Gross, W Germany	1:47.92
1991	Giorgio Lamberti, Italy	1:47.27‡
1994	Antti Kasvio, Finland	1:47.32
1998	Michael Klim, Australia	1:47.41
2001	Ian Thorpe, Australia	1:44.06*
2003	Ian Thorpe, Australia	1:45.14
2005	Michael Phelps, United States	1:45.20
2007	Michael Phelps, United States	1:43.86*
2009	Paul Biedermann, Germany	1:42.00*

400-METER FREESTYLE

1973	Rick DeMont, United States	3:58.18‡
1975	Tim Shaw, United States	3:54.88‡
1978	Vladimir Salnikov, U.S.S.R.	3:51.94‡
1982	Vladimir Salnikov, U.S.S.R.	3:51.30‡
1986	Rainer Henkel, W Germany	3:50.05
1991	Joerg Hoffman, Germany	3:48.04‡
1994	Kieran Perkins, Australia	3:43.80*
1998	Ian Thorpe, Australia	3:46.29
2001	Ian Thorpe, Australia	3:40.17*
2003	Ian Thorpe, Australia	3:42.58
2005	Grant Hackett, Australia	3:42.91
2007	Tae Hwan Park, Korea	3:44.30
2009	Paul Biedermann, Germany	3:40.07*

800-METER FREESTYLE

2001	Ian Thorpe, Australia	7:39.16*
2003	Grant Hackett, Australia	7:43.82
2005	Grant Hackett, Australia	7:38.65*
2007	Przemyslav Stanczyk, Poland	7:47.91†
2009	Lin Zhag, China	7:32.12*

1,500-METER FREESTYLE

1973	Stephen Holland, Australia	15:31.85
1975	Tim Shaw, United States	15:28.92‡
1978	Vladimir Salnikov, U.S.S.R.	15:03.99‡
1982	Vladimir Salnikov, U.S.S.R.	15:01.77‡
1986	Rainer Henkel, W Germany	15:05.31
1991	Joerg Hoffman, Germany	14:50.36*
1994	Kieran Perkins, Australia	14:50.52
1998	Grant Hackett, Australia	14:51.70
2001	Grant Hackett, Australia	14:34.56*
2003	Grant Hackett, Australia	14:43.14
2005	Grant Hackett, Australia	14:42.58
2007	Mateusz Sawrymowicz, Poland	14:45.94
2009	Oussama Mellouli, Tunisia	14:37.28

50-METER BACKSTROKE

2001	Randall Bal, United States	25.34
2003	Thomas Rupprath, Germany	24.80*
2005	Aristeidis Grigoriadis, Greece	24.95
2007	Gerhard Zandberg, South Africa	24.98
2009	Liam Tancock, United Kingdom	24.04*

100-METER BACKSTROKE

1973	Roland Matthes, E. Germany	57.47
1973	Roland Matthes, E. Germany	58.15
1978	Bob Jackson, United States	56.36‡
1982	Dirk Richter, E. Germany	55.95
1986	Igor Polianski, U.S.S.R.	55.58‡
1991	Jeff Rouse, United States	55.23‡
1994	Martin Lopez Zubero, Spain	55.17‡
1998	Lenny Krayzelburg, United States	55.00‡
2001	Matt Welsh, Australia	54.31‡
2003	Aaron Peirsol, United States	53.61‡
2005	Aaron Peirsol, United States	53:62
2007	Aaron Peirsol, United States	52.98*
2009	Junya Koga, Japan	52.26‡

200-METER BACKSTROKE

1973	Roland Matthes, E. Germany	2:01.87‡
1975	Zoltan Varraszto, Hungary	2:05.05
1978	Jesse Vassallo, United States	2:02.16
1982	Rick Carey, United States	2:00.82‡
1986	Igor Polianski, U.S.S.R.	1:58.78‡
1991	Martin Zubero, Spain	1:59.52
1994	Vladimir Selkov, Russia	1:57.42‡
1998	Lenny Krayzelburg, United States	1:58.84
2001	Aaron Peirsol, United States	1:57.13‡
2003	Aaron Peirsol, United States	1:55.92
2005	Aaron Peirsol, United States	1:54.66*
2007	Ryan Lochte, United States	1:54.32*
2009	Aaron Peirsol, United States	1:51.92*

Men (*Cont.*)

50-METER BREASTSTROKE

2001	Oleg Lisogor, Ukraine	27.52
2003	James Gibson, United Kingdom	27.56
2005	Mark Warnecke, Germany	27.63
2007	Oleg Lisogor, Ukraine	27.66
2009	Cameron Van Der Burgh, S. Africa	26.67*

100-METER BREASTSTROKE

1973	Roland Matthes, E. Germany	2:01.87‡
1973	John Hencken, United States	1:04.02‡
1975	David Wilkie, Great Britain	1:04.26‡
1978	Walter Kusch, W Germany	1:03.56‡
1982	Steve Lundquist, United States	1:02.75‡
1986	Victor Davis, Canada	1:02.71
1991	Norbert Rozsa, Hungary	1:01.45*
1994	Norbert Rozsa, Hungary	1:01.24‡
1998	Frederik Deburghgraeve, Belgium	1:01.34
2001	Roman Sloudnov, Russia	1:00.16
2003	Kosuke Kitajima, Japan	59.78*
2005	Brendan Hansen, United States	59:13*
2007	Brendan Hansen, United States	59.80
2009	Brenton Rickard, Australia	58.58*

200-METER BREASTSTROKE

1973	David Wilkie, Great Britain	2:19.28‡
1975	David Wilkie, Great Britain	2:18.23‡
1978	Nick Nevid, United States	2:18.37
1982	Victor Davis, Canada	2:14.77*
1986	Jozsef Szabo, Hungary	2:14.27‡
1991	Mike Barrowman, United States	2:11.23*
1994	Norbert Rozsa, Hungary	2:12.81
1998	Kurt Grote, United States	2:13.40
2001	Brendan Hansen, United States	2:10.69‡
2003	Kosuke Kitajima, Japan	2:09.42*
2005	Brendan Hansen, United States	2:08.74*
2007	Kosuke Kitajima, Japan	2:09.80
2009	Daniel Gyurta, Hungary	2:07.64

50-METER BUTTERFLY

2001	Geoff Huegill, Australia	23.50
2003	Matt Welsh, Australia	23.43*
2005	Roland Schoeman, South Africa	22.96*
2007	Roland Schoeman, South Africa	23.18
2009	Milorad Cavic, Serbia	22.67‡

100-METER BUTTERFLY

1973	Bruce Robertson, Canada	55.69
1975	Greg Jagenburg, United States	55.63
1978	Joe Bottom, United States	54.30
1982	Matt Gribble, United States	53.88‡
1986	Pablo Morales, United States	53.54‡
1991	Anthony Nesty, Suriname	53.29‡
1994	Rafal Szukala, Poland	53.51
1998	Michael Klim, Australia	52.25‡
2001	Lars Frolander, Sweden	52.10‡
2003	Ian Crocker, United States	50.98*

100-METER BUTTERFLY (*Cont.*)

2005	Ian Crocker, United States	50:40*
2007	Michael Phelps, United States	50.77
2009	Michael Phelps, United States	49.82*

200-METER BUTTERFLY

1973	Robin Backhaus, United States	2:03.32
1975	Bill Forrester, United States	2:01.95‡
1978	Mike Bruner, United States	1:59.38‡
1982	Michael Gross, E. Germany	1:58.85‡
1986	Michael Gross, E. Germany	1:56.53‡
1991	Melvin Stewart, United States	1:55.69*
1994	Denis Pankratov, Russia	1:56.54
1998	Denys Sylantyev, Ukraine	1:56.61
2001	Michael Phelps, United States	1:54.58*
2003	Michael Phelps, United States	1:54.35
2005	Pawel Korzeniowski, Poland	1:55.02
2007	Michael Phelps, United States	1:52.09*
2009	Michael Phelps, United States	1:51.51*

200-METER INDIVIDUAL MEDLEY

1973	Gunnar Larsson, Sweden	2:08.36
1975	Andras Hargitay, Hungary	2:07.72
1978	Graham Smith, Canada	2:03.65*
1982	Aleksandr Sidorenko, U.S.S.R.	2:03.30‡
1986	Tamás Darnyi, Hungary	2:01.57‡
1991	Tamás Darnyi, Hungary	1:59.36*
1994	Jani Sievin, Finland	1:58.16*
1998	Marcel Wouda, Netherlands	2:01.18
2001	Massimiliano Rosolino, Italy	1:59.71
2003	Michael Phelps, United States	1:56.04*
2005	Ryan Lochte, United States	1:58.06
2007	Michael Phelps, United States	1:54.98*
2009	Ryan Lochte, United States	1:54.10*

400-METER INDIVIDUAL MEDLEY

1975	Andras Hargitay, Hungary	4:32.57
1978	Jesse Vassallo, United States	4:20.05*
1982	Ricardo Prado, Brazil	4:19.78*
1986	Tamás Darnyi, Hungary	4:18.98‡
1991	Tamás Darnyi, Hungary	4:12.36*
1994	Tom Dolan, United States	4:12.30*
1998	Tom Dolan, United States	4:14.95
2001	Alessio Boggiatto, Italy	4:13.15
2003	Michael Phelps, United States	4:09.09*
2005	Laszlo Cseh, Hungary	4:09.63
2007	Michael Phelps, United States	4:06.22*
2009	Ryan Lochte, United States	4:07.01

* World Record; ‡ Meet Record.

Men *(Cont.)*

4 x 100-METER MEDLEY RELAY

Year	Team	Time
1973	United States (Mike Stamm, John Hencken, Joe Bottom, Jim Montgomery)	3:49.49
1975	United States (John Murphy, Rick Colella, Greg Jagenburg, Andy Coan)	3:49.00
1978	United States (Robert Jackson, Nick Nevid, Joe Bottom, David McCagg)	3:44.63
1982	United States (Rick Carey, Steve Lundquist, Matt Gribble, Rowdy Gaines)	3:40.84*
1986	United States (Dan Veatch, David Lundberg, Pablo Morales, Matt Biondi)	3:41.25
1991	United States (Jeff Rouse, Eric Wunderlich, Mark Henderson, Matt Biondi)	3:39.66‡
1994	United States (Jeff Rouse, Eric Wunderlich, Mark Henderson, Gary Hall Jr.)	3:37.74‡
1998	Australia (Matt Welsh, Phil Rogers, Robin Backhaus, Rick Klatt, Jim Montgomery)	3:37.98
2001	Australia (Matt Welsh, Ian Thorpe, Geoff Huegill, Regan Harrison)	3:35.35
2003	United States (Aaron Peirsol, Brendan Hansen, Ian Crocker, Jason Lezak)	3:31.54*
2005	United States (Aaron Peirsol, Brendan Hansen, Ian Crocker, Jason Lezak)	3:31.85
2007	Australia (Matt Welsh, Brenton Rickard, Andrew Lauterstein, Eamon Sullivan)	3:34.93
2009	United States (Aaron Peirsol, Eric Shanteau, Michael Phelps, David Walters)	3:27.28*

4 x 100-METER FREESTYLE RELAY

Year	Team	Time
1973	United States (Mel Nash, Joe Bottom, Jim Montgomery, John Murphy)	3:27.18
1975	United States (Bruce Furniss, Jim Montgomery, Andy Coan, John Murphy)	3:24.85
1978	United States (Jack Babashoff, Rowdy Gaines, Jim Montgomery, David McCagg)	3:19.74
1982	United States (Chris Cavanaugh, Robin Leamy, David McCagg, Rowdy Gaines)	3:19.26*
1986	United States (Tom Jager, Mike Heath, Paul Wallace, Matt Biondi)	3:19.89
1991	United States (Tom Jager, Brent Lang, Doug Gjertsen, Matt Biondi)	3:17.15‡
1994	United States (Jon Olsen, Josh Davis, Ugur Taner, Gary Hall Jr.)	3:16.90‡
1998	United States (Bryan Jones, Jon Olsen, Bradley Schumacher, Gary Hall Jr.)	3:16.69‡
2001	Australia (Michael Klim, Ian Thorpe, Todd Pearson, Ashley Callus)	3:14.10‡
2003	Russia (Andrei Kapralov, Ivan Usov, Denis Pimankov, Alexander Popov)	3:14.06‡
2005	United States (Michael Phelps, Neil Walker, Nate Dusing, Jason Lezak)	3:13.77
2007	United States (Michael Phelps, Neil Walker, Cullen Jones, Jason Lezak)	3:12.72
2009	United States (Michael Phelps, Ryan Lochte, Mattew Grevers, Nathan Adrian)	3:09.21‡

4 x 200-METER FREESTYLE RELAY

Year	Team	Time
1973	United States (Kurt Krumpholz, Robin Backhaus, Rick Klatt, Jim Montgomery)	7:33.22*
1975	W Germany (Klaus Steinbach, Werner Lampe, Hans Joachim Geisler, Peter Nocke)	7:39.44
1978	United States (Bruce Furniss, Billy Forrester, Bobby Hackett, Rowdy Gaines)	7:20.82
1982	United States (Rich Saeger, Jeff Float, Kyle Miller, Rowdy Gaines)	7:21.09
1986	E. Germany (Lars Hinneburg, Thomas Flemming, Dirk Richter, Sven Lodziewski)	7:15.91‡
1991	Germany (Peter Sitt, Steffan Zesner, Stefan Pfeiffer, Michael Gross)	7:13.50‡
1994	Sweden (Christer Waller, Tommy Werner, Lars Frolander, Anders Holmertz)	7:17.34
1998	Australia (Daniel Kowalski, Grant Hackett, Ian Thorpe, Anthony Rogis)	7:12.48‡
2001	Australia (Michael Klim, Ian Thorpe, William Kirby, Grant Hackett)	7:04.66*
2003	Australia (Grant Hackett, Craig Stevens, Nicholas Springer, Ian Thorpe)	7:08.58
2005	United States (Michael Phelps, Ryan Lochte, Peter Vanderkaay, Klete Keller)	7:06.58
2007	United States (Michael Phelps, Ryan Lochte, Peter Vanderkaay, Klete Keller)	7:03.24*
2009	United States (Michael Phelps, Ricky Berens, David Walters, Ryan Lochte)	6:58.55*

Note: Records through Oct 1, 2010. * World record; ‡Meet record

Women

50-METER FREESTYLE

1986....Tamara Costache, Romania	25.28*
1991....Zhuang Yong, China	25.47
1994....Le Jingyi, China	24.51*
1998....Amy Van Dyken, United States	25.15
2001....Inge de Bruijn, Netherlands	24.47
2003....Inge de Bruijn, Netherlands	24.47
2005....Lisbeth Lenton, Australia	24.59
2007....Lisbeth Lenton, Australia	24.53
2009....Britta Steffen, Germany	23.73*

100-METER FREESTYLE

1973....Kornelia Ender, E. Germany	57.54
1975....Kornelia Ender, E. Germany	56.50
1978....Barbara Krause, E. Germany	55.68‡
1982....Birgit Meineke, E. Germany	55.79
1986....Kristin Otto, E. Germany	55.05‡
1991....Nicole Haislett, United States	55.17
1994....Le Jingyi, China	54.01*
1998....Jenny Thompson, United States	54.95
2001....Inge de Bruijn, Netherlands	54.18
2003....Hanna-Maria Seppälä, Finland	54.37
2005....Britta Steffen, Germany	53.30*
2007....Lisbeth Lenton, Australia	53.40
2009....Britta Steffen, Germany	52.07*

200-METER FREESTYLE

1973.....Keena Rothhammer, United States	2:04.99
1975....Shirley Babashoff, United States	2:02.50
1978....Cynthia Woodhead, United States	1:58.53*
1982.....Annemarie Verstappen, Netherlands	1:59.53‡
1986....Heike Friedrich, E. Germany	1:58.26‡
1991....Hayley Lewis, Australia	2:00.48
1994....Franziska Van Almsick, Germany	1:56.78*
1998....Claudia Poll, Costa Rica	1:58.90
2001....Giaan Rooney, Australia	1:58.57
2003....Alena Popchanka, Bulgaria	1:58.32
2005....Solenne Figues, France	1:58.60
2007....Laure Manaudou, France	1:55.52*
2009....Federica Pellegrini, Italy	1:52.98*

400-METER FREESTYLE

1973.....Heather Greenwood, United States	4:20.28
1975....Shirley Babashoff, United States	4:22.70
1978....Tracey Wickham, Australia	4:06.28*
1982....Carmela Schmidt, E. Germany	4:08.98
1986....Heike Friedrich, E. Germany	4:07.45
1991....Janet Evans, United States	4:08.63
1994....Yang Aihua, China	4:09.64
1998....Chen Yan, China	4:06.72
2001....Yana Klochkova, Ukraine	4:07.30
2003....Hannah Stockbauer, Germany	4:06.75
2005....Laure Manaudou, France	4:02.13*
2007....Laure Manaudou, France	4:02.61
2009....Federia Pellegrini, Italy	3:59.15*

800-METER FREESTYLE

1973....Novella Calligaris, Italy	8:52.97
1975 Jenny Turrall, Australia	8:44.75‡
1978....Tracey Wickham, Australia	8:24.94‡
1982....Kim Linehan, United States	8:27.48
1986....Astrid Strauss, E. Germany	8:28.24
1991....Janet Evans, United States	8:24.05‡
1994....Janet Evans, United States	8:29.85
1998....Brooke Bennett, United States	8.28.71
2001....Hannah Stockbauer, Germany	8:24.66
2003....Hannah Stockbauer, Germany	8:23.66‡
2005....Kate Ziegler, United States	8:25.31
2007....Kate Ziegler, United States	8:18.62
2009....Lotte Friis, Denmark	8:15.92‡

1,500-METER FREESTYLE

2001....Hannah Stockbauer, Germany	16:01.02
2003....Hannah Stockbauer, Germany	16:00.108
2005....Kate Ziegler, United States	16:00.41
2007....Kate Ziegler, United States	15:53.05
2009....Alessia Filippi, Italy	15:44.93‡

* World record; ‡Meet record.

Women *(Cont.)*

50-METER BACKSTROKE

2001	Haley Cope, United States	28.51
2003	Nina Zhivanevskaya, Spain	28.48
2005	Giaan Rooney, Australia	28.63
2007	Leila Vaziri, United States	28.16e
2009	Jiing Zhao, China	27.06*

50-METER BREASTSTROKE

2001	Xuejuan Luo, China	30.84
2003	Xuejuan Luo, China	30.67
2005	Jade Edmistone, Australia	30.45*
2007	Jessica Hardy, United States	30.63
2009	Yuliya Efimova, Russia	30.09*

100-METER BACKSTROKE

1973	Ulrike Richter, E. Germany	1:05.42
1975	Ulrike Richter, E. Germany	1:03.30‡
1978	Linda Jezek, United States	1:02.55‡
1982	Kristin Otto, E. Germany	1:01.30‡
1986	Betsy Mitchell, United States	1:01.74
1991	Krisztina Egerszegi, Hungary	1:01.78
1994	He Cihong, China	1:00.57
1998	Lea Maurer, United States	1:01.16
2001	Natalie Coughlin, United States	1:00.37
2003	Antje Buschschulte, Germany	1:00.50
2005	Kirsty Coventry, Zimbabwe	1:00.24
2007	Natalie Coughlin, United States	59.44*
2009	Gemma Spofforth, United Kingdom	58.12*

100-METER BREASTSTROKE

1973	Renate Vogel, E. Germany	1:13.74
1975	Hannalore Anke, E. Germany	1:12.72
1978	Julia Bogdanova, U.S.S.R.	1:10.31*
1982	Ute Geweniger, E. Germany	1:09.14‡
1986	Sylvia Gerasch, E. Germany	1:08.11*
1991	Linley Frame, Australia	1:08.81
1994	Samantha Riley, Australia	1:07.96*
1998	Kristy Kowal, United States	1:08.42
2001	Xuejuan Luo, China	1:07.18‡
2003	Xuejuan Luo, China	1:06.80
2005	Leisel Jones, Australia	1:05.09*
2007	Leisel Jones, Australia	1:05.72
2009	Rebecca Soni, United States	1:04.93

200-METER BACKSTROKE

1973	Melissa Belote, United States	2:20.52
1975	Birgit Treiber, E. Germany	2:15.46*
1978	Linda Jezek, United States	2:11.93*
1982	Cornelia Sirch, E. Germany	2:09.91*
1986	Cornelia Sirch, E. Germany	2:11.37
1991	Krisztina Egerszegi, Hungary	2:09.15‡
1994	He Cihong, China	2:07.40
1998	Roxanna Maracineanu, France	2:11.26
2001	Diana Mocanu, Romania	2:09.94
2003	Katy Sexton, Great Britain	2:08.74
2005	Kirsty Coventry, Zimbabwe	2:08.52
2007	Margaret Hoelzer, United States	2:07.16
2009	Kirsty Coventry, Zimbabwe	2:04.81*

200-METER BREASTSTROKE

1973	Renate Vogel, E. Germany	2:40.01
1975	Hannalore Anke, E. Germany	2:37.25‡
1978	Lina Kachushite, U.S.S.R.	2:31.42*
1982	Svetlana Varganova, U.S.S.R.	2:28.82‡
1986	Silke Hoerner, E. Germany	2:27.40*
1991	Elena Volkova, U.S.S.R.	2:29.53
1994	Samantha Riley, Australia	2:26.87‡
1998	Agnes Kovacs, Hungary	2:25.45‡
2001	Agnes Kovacs, Hungary	2:24.90
2003	Amanda Beard, United States	2:22.99*
2005	Leisel Jones, Australia	2:20.54*
2007	Leisel Jones, Australia	2:21.84
2009	Nadja Higl, Serbia	2:21.62

Note: Records through Oct 1, 2010. * World record; ‡Meet record

Women *(Cont.)*

50-METER BUTTERFLY

2001	Inge De Bruijn, Netherlands	25.90
2003	Inge De Bruijn, Netherlands	25.84
2005	Danni Miatke, Australia	26.11
2007	Therese Alshammar, Sweden	25.91
2009	Marieke Guehrer, Australia	25.48

100-METER BUTTERFLY

1973	Kornelia Ender, E. Germany	1:02.53
1975	Kornelia Ender, E. Germany	1:01.24*
1978	Joan Pennington, United States	1:00.20‡
1982	Mary T. Meagher, United States	59.41‡
1986	Kornelia Gressler, E. Germany	59.51
1991	Qian Hong, China	59.68
1994	Liu Limin, China	58.98‡
1998	Jenny Thompson, United States	58.46‡
2001	Petria Thomas, Australia	58:27
2003	Jenny Thompson, United States	57.96‡
2005	Jessicah Schipper, Australia	57.23‡
2007	Lisbeth Lenton, Australia	57.15
2009	Sarah Sjostrom, Sweden	56.06*

200-METER BUTTERFLY

1973	Rosemarie Kother, E. Germany	2:13.76‡
1975	Rosemarie Kother, E. Germany	2:15.92
1978	Tracy Caulkins, United States	2:09.87*
1982	Ines Geissler, E. Germany	2:08.66‡
1986	Mary T. Meagher, United States	2:08.41‡
1991	Summer Sanders, United States	2:09.24
1994	Liu Limin, China	2:07.25‡
1998	Susie O'Neill, Australia	2:07.93‡
2001	Petria Thomas, Australia	2:06.73‡
2003	Otylia Jedrzejczak, Poland	2:07.56
2005	Otylia Jedrzejczak, Poland	2:05.61*
2007	Jessicah Schipper, Australia	2:06.39
2009	Jessicah Schipper, Australia	2:03.41*

200-METER INDIVIDUAL MEDLEY

1973	Andrea Huebner, E. Germany	2:20.51
1975	Kathy Heddy, United States	2:19.80
1978	Tracy Caulkins, United States	2:14.07*
1982	Petra Schneider, E. Germany	2:11.79
1986	Kristin Otto, E. Germany	2:15.56
1991	Li Lin, China	2:13.40
1994	Lu Bin, China	2:12.34‡
1998	Wu Yanyan, China	2:10.88
2001	Martha Bowen, United States	2:11.93
2003	Yana Klochkova, Ukraine	2:10.75‡
2005	Katie Hoff, United States	2:10.41‡
2007	Katie Hoff, United States	2:10.13
2009	Ariana Kukors, United States	2:06.15*

400-METER INDIVIDUAL MEDLEY

1973	Gudrun Wegner, E. Germany	4:57.71
1975	Ulrike Tauber, E. Germany	4:52.76‡
1978	Tracy Caulkins, United States	4:40.83*
1982	Petra Schneider, E. Germany	4:36.10*
1986	Kathleen Nord, E. Germany	4:43.75
1991	Lin Li, China	4:41.45
1994	Dai Guohong, China	4:39.14
1998	Chen Yan, China	4:36.66
2001	Yana Klochkova, Ukraine	4:36.98
2003	Yana Klochkova, Ukraine	4:36.74
2005	Katie Hoff, United States	4:36.07‡
2007	Katie Hoff, United States	4:32.89*
2009	Katinka Hosszu, Hungary	4:30.31‡

---

* World record; ‡ Meet record.

Women *(Cont.)*

4 x 100-METER MEDLEY RELAY

1973 ....E. Germany (Ulrike Richter, 4:16.84
Renate Vogel, Rosemarie Kother, Kornelia Ender)
1975 ....E. Germany (Ulrike Richter, 4:14.74
Hannelore Anke, Rosemarie Kother,
Kornelia Ender)
1978 ....United States (Linda Jezek, 4:08.21‡
Tracy Caulkins, Joan Pennington,
Cynthia Woodhead)
1982 ....E. Germany (K. Otto, U. Gewinger, 4:05.8*
I. Geissler, B. Meineke)
1986 ....E. Germany (K. Zimmermann, S. Gerasch, 4:04.82
K. Gressler, K. Otto)
1991 ....United States (Janie Wagstaff, 4:06.51
Tracey McFarlane, Crissy
Ahmann-Leighton, Nicole Haislett)
1994 ....China (He Cihong, Dai Guohong, 4:01.67*
Liu Limin, Lu Bin)
1998 ....United States (K. Kowal, L. Maurer, 4:01.93
J.Thompson, A. Van Dyken)
2001 ....Australia (Dyana Calub, Sarah 4:07.30
Ryan, Petria Thomas, Leisel Jones)
2003 ....China (Shu Xhan, Xuejuan Luo, 3:59.89‡
Yafei Zhou, Yu Yang)
2005 ....Australia (S. Edington, L. Jones, 3:56.30*
J. Schipper, L. Lenton)
2007 ....Australia (E. Seebohm, L. Jones, 3:55.74*
J. Schipper, L. Lenton)
2009 ....China (Jing Zhao, Huijia Chen, 3:52.19*
Liuyang Jiao, Zhesi Li)

4 x 100-METER FREESTYLE RELAY

1973 ....E. Germany (K. Ender, A. Eife, 3:52.45
A. Huebner, S. Eichner)
1975 ....E. Germany (K. Ender, B. Krause, 3:49.37
C. Hempel, U. Bruckner)
1978 ....United States (T. Caulkins, 3:43.43*
S. Elkins, J. Pennington, C. Woodhead)
1982 ....E. Germany (B. Meineke, S. Link, 3:43.97
K. Otto, C. Metschuk)
1986 ....E. Germany (K. Otto, M. Stellmach, 3:40.57*
S. Schulze, H. Friedrich)
1991 ....United States (N. Haislett, 3:43.26
J.Cooper, W. Hedgepeth, J. Thompson)
1994 ....China (Le Jingyi, Ying Shan, 3:37.91*
Le Ying, Lu Bin)
1998 .....United States (C. Fox, L. Farella, 3:42.11
M. Valerio, B.J. Bedford)
2001 ....Germany (P. Dallman, 3:39.58
A. Buschschulte, K. Meissner, S. Volkner)
2003 ....United States (N. Coughlin, 3:38.09
L. Benko, R. Jeffrey, J. Thompson)
2005 ....Germany (P. Dallman, 3:35.22*
D. Goetz, B. Steffen, A. Liebs)
2007 ....Netherlands (I. Dekker, 3:35.48
R. Kromowidjojo, F. Heemskerk, M. Veldhuis)
2009 Netherlands (I. Dekker, 3:31.72*
R. Kromowidjojo, F. Heemskerk, M. Veldhuis)

4 x 200-METER FREESTYLE RELAY

1986 ....E. Germany (Manuela 7:59.33*
Stellmach, Astrid Strauss,
Nadja Bergknecht, Heike Friedrich)
1991 ....Germany (Kerstin Kielgass, Manuela 8:02.56
Stellmach, Dagmar Hase, Stephanie
Ortwig)
1994 China (Le Ying, Yang Alhua, 7:57.96
Zhou Guabin, Lu Bin)
1998 ....Germany (Silvia Szalai, Antje 8:02.56
Buschschulte, Janina Goetz,
Franziska Van Almsick)
2001 ....Great Britain (Nicola Jackson, Janine 7:58.69
Belton, Karen Legg, Karen Pickering)
2003 ....United States (L. Benko, R. Komisarz 7:55.70‡
R. Jeffrey, D. Munz)
2005 ....Germany (Petra Dallman, Daniela 7:50.82*
Samulski, Britta Steffen, Annika Liebs)
2007 ....United States (Natalie Coughlin, 7:50.09*
Dana Vollmer, Lacey Nymeyer, Katie Hoff)
2009 ....China (Yu Yang, Qian Wei Zhu, 7:42.08*
Jing Liu, Jiaying Pang)

JOE KLAMAR/AFP/GETTY IMAGES

Lindsey Vonn dominated the FIS World Cup Tour again in 2010, topping the overall season standings for a third straight year

Miscellaneous Sports

Miscellaneous Sport Champions

Archery	2010 U.S. Outdoor Championships **MEN** **WOMEN**	**Winner (Recurve)** Taylor Worth Khatuna Lorig	**Winner (Compound)** Rodger Willett Jr. Erika Anschutz
Bowling	2009–10 PBA Tour **TOUR LEADERS**	**Money Winner ($)** Walter Ray Williams Jr. ($152,670)	**Highest Average (pts.)** Walter Ray Williams Jr. (222.98)
	2009–10 PBA Senior Tour **TOUR LEADERS**	**Money Winner ($)** Wayne Webb ($41,900)	**Highest Average (pts.)** Walter Ray Williams Jr. (225.49)
Curling	2010 World Championships **MEN** **WOMEN**	**Country** Canada Germany	**Skip** Kevin Koe Andrea Schopp
	2010 U.S. Club National Championships **MEN** **WOMEN**	**Club** Bemidji, Minnesota Madison, Wisconsin	**Skip** Pete Fenson Erika Brown
Cycling	**2010 ROAD RACE WORLD CHAMPIONSHIP** **2010 TOUR DE FRANCE**	**Winner** Thor Hushovd Alberto Contador, Spain	**Time** 6:21:49 98:58:48
Sled Dog Racing	**2010 IDITAROD**	**Winner** Lance Mackey	**Time** 8 days, 23:59:9
Figure Skating	2010 ISU World Championships **MEN** **WOMEN** **PAIRS** **ICE DANCING**	**Winner** Daisuke Takahashi Mao Asada Qing Pang/ Jian Tong Tessa Virtue/ Scott Moir	**Country** Japan Japan China Canada
	2010 U.S. Figure Skating Nat'l Championships **MEN** **WOMEN** **PAIRS** **ICE DANCING**	**Winner** Jeremy Abbott Rachael Flatt Caydee Denney/ Jeremy Barrett Meryl Davis/ Charlie White	**Club** Detroit SC Broadmoor SC Southwest Florida FSC/ Southwest Florida FSC Arctic FSC/ Detroit SC
Handball	2010 U.S.One-Wall Nat'l Championships **MEN** **WOMEN** 2010 U.S.Three-Wall Nat'l Championships **MEN** **WOMEN**	**Winner** Tyree Bastidas Sandy Ng **Winner** David Chapman Tracy Davis	**Runner-up** Willie Polanco Theresa McCourt **Runner-up** Tyree Bastidas Megan Mehilos
Lacrosse	League **AMERICAN LACROSSE LEAGUE** **NATIONAL LACROSSE LEAGUE** **MAJOR LEAGUE LACROSSE**	**Winner (Score)** GMH-Philadelphia (9–7) Washington Stealth (15–11) Chesapeake Bayhawks (13–9)	**Runner-up** Dewalt Toronto Rock Long Island Lizards
Little League Baseball	**WORLD SERIES CHAMPION**	**Winner** Tokyo, Japan	**Runner-up** **Score** Waipahu, Hawaii 4–1
Motor Boat Racing	American Power Boat Association **GOLD CUP CHAMPION (UNLIMITED)**	**Winning Boat** U-96 Spirit of Qatar	**Winning Driver** Dave Villwock
Polo	2010 U.S. Open **U.S. POLO ASSOCIATION**	**Winner** Crab Orchard (13–8)	**Runner-up** Audi

Miscellaneous Sport Champions

Rodeo

2009 PRCA World Champions	Winner(s)	
ALL-AROUND	Trevor Brazile	
SADDLE BRONC RIDING	Jesse Kruse	
BAREBACK RIDING	Bobby Mote	
BULL RIDING	J.W. Harris	
STEER WRESTLING	Lee Graves	
STEER ROPING	Rocky Patterson	
CALF TIE-DOWN ROPING	Trevor Brazile	
TEAM ROPING (Header, Heeler)	Nick Sartain, Kollin VonAhn	

Rowing

2010 Intercollegiate Rowing Association	Winner	Runner-Up
MEN (VARSITY EIGHTS)	California	Washington

Rugby

2010 Rugby Union	Winner	Runner-Up
MEN'S CLUB (DIV. I)	Las Vegas	Belmont Shore
MEN'S COLLEGIATE (DIV. I)	California	BYU

2010 American National Rugby League	Winner	Runner-Up
U.S. CHAMPION	Jacksonville Axemen	New Haven Warriors

Skiing

FIS World Champion	Men's Winner (Season)	Women's Winner (Season)
OVERALL	Carlo Janka (SUI)	Lindsey Vonn (USA)
DOWNHILL	Didier Cuche (SUI)	Lindsey Vonn (USA)
SLALOM	Rienfried Herbst (AUT)	Maria Riesch (GER)
GIANT SLALOM	Ted Ligety (USA)	Kathrin Hoelzl (GER)
SUPER G	Erik Guay (CAN)	Lindsey Vonn (USA)
COMBINED	Benjamin Raich (AUT)	Lindsey Vonn (USA)

Softball

2010 U.S. ASA Championship	Major Fast Pitch Winner	Major Slow Pitch Winner
MEN	Rivershark Twins	Windy City
WOMEN	None (tournament cancelled)	

Speed Skating

2010 ISU All-Around World Champion	Winner	
MEN	Sven Kramer (NET)	
WOMEN	Martina Sablikova (CZE)	

Squash

U.S. Championship	Hard Ball Winner	Soft Ball (S.L. Green) Winner
MEN	Eric Pearson	Julian Illingworth
WOMEN	N/A	Natalie Grainger

Triathlon

2010 Ironman World Championship	Winner	Time
MEN	Chris McCormack (AUS)	8:10:37
WOMEN	Mirinda Carfrae (AUS)	8:58:36

2010 U.S. Elite Triathlon Championship	Winner	Time
MEN	Brendon Sexton (AUS)	1:53:48
WOMEN	Laura Bennett (USA)	2:04:13

Volleyball

2010 U.S. Adult Championship (Open Div.)	Winner	Runner-Up
MEN	2ndcity/Premier	OCVC/Smack
WOMEN	USA Blue	The Exterminators

Wrestling

2010 U.S. Championship	Freestyle	Greco-Roman
121 LBS.	Obe Blanc	Spenser Mango
132 LBS.	Shawn Bunch	Nathan Piasecki
145.5 LBS.	Jared Frayer	Glenn Garrison
163 LBS.	Andrew Howe*	Jake Fisher
185 LBS.	Jake Herbert	Cheney Haight*
211.5 LBS.	J.D. Bergman	Justin Ruiz
264.5 LBS.	Les Sigman	Dremiel Byers
TEAM	New York AC (Div. I)	U.S. Army (Div. I)
	Gator WC (Div. II)	Sunkist Kids (Div. II)

*Most Outstanding Wrestler

Bowling

2009–10 PBA TOUR RESULTS

Date	Event	Winner	Earnings ($)	Runner-Up
Aug 2–6	Motor City Open	Walter Ray Williams Jr.	25,000	Chris Barnes
Aug 6–9	Viper Championship	Norm Duke	25,000	Ryan Ciminelli
Aug 8–13	Cheetah Championship	Rhino Page	25,000	Ryan Ciminelli
Aug 13–16	Chameleon Championship	Bill O'Neill	25,200	Ronnie Russell
Aug 22–23	Scorpion Championship	Mike DeVaney	25,000	Jason Belmonte
Aug 22–30	Shark Championship	Jack Jurek	25,000	Michael Fagan
Aug 30–Dec 13	PBA World Championship	Tom Smallwood	50,000	Wes Malott
Dec 7–13	Pepsi Open	Mike Scroggins	25,070	Wayne Garber
Jan 12–17	Earl Anthony Medford Classic	Anthoy LaCaze	25,000	Michael Machuga
Jan 19–24	PBA Tournament of Champions	Kelly Kulick	40,000	Walter Ray Williams Jr.
Jan 26–31	Dick Weber Open	Michael Fagan	25,000	Walter Ray Williams Jr.
Feb 9–14	USBC Masters	Walter Ray Williams Jr.	50,000	Chris Barnes
Feb 15–21	Mixed Doubles Championship	Brian Voss	25,000	Jason Belmonte
Feb 21–28	67th U.S. Open	Bill O'Neill	60,000	Mike Scroggins
Mar 1–7	Don Johnson Eliminator	Mike Scroggins	25,000	Brian Kretzer
Mar 17–21	Match Play Championship	Brian Kretzer	25,000	Patrick Allen
Feb. 18–22	GEICO Plastic Ball Championship	Brian Ziesig	25,000	Jason Belmonte
Mar 29– Apr 4	Marathon Open	Pete Weber	25,200	Mike Scroggins
April 22–25	Japan Cup	Tommy Jones	40,000	Dino Castillo

2010 SENIOR PBA TOUR RESULTS

Date	Event	Winner	Earnings ($)	Runner-Up
Apr 17–20	Dayton Classic	Steve Ferraro	8,000	Wayne Webb
Apr 24–27	Columbus Open	Wayne Webb	8,050	Mark Williams
May 2–5	Miller High Life Classic	Walter Ray Williams Jr.	8,000	Keith Sharp
May 30–June 2	Northern California Classic	Don Sylvia	8,050	J.P. Muller
June 6–11	Senior U.S. Open	Mark Williams	15,200	Ron Mohr
June 13–18	USBC Senior Masters	Wayne Webb	16,000	Walter Ray Williams Jr.
Aug 9–12	Lake County Indiana Open	Michael Henry	8,000	Timothy Kauble
Aug 14–17	Senior Pepsi Open	Tom Baker	8,050	Dale Csuhta
Aug 21–24	Jackson Open	Wayne Webb	8,000	Ray Johnson

TOUR LEADERS - PBA: 2009–10

MONEY LEADERS	Events	Earnings ($)	AVERAGE	Events	Average
Walter Ray Williams Jr.	19	152,670	Walter Ray Williams Jr.	19	222.92
Bill O'Neill	19	147,275	Wes Malott	18	221.33
Mike Scroggins	19	130,705	Chris Barnes	19	220.73
Chris Barnes	19	116,510	Mike Fagan	19	220.49
Tommy Jones	19	110,910	Mike Scroggins	19	220.27

TOUR LEADERS - SENIOR PBA: 2009–10

MONEY LEADERS	Events	Earnings ($)	AVERAGE	Events	Average
Wayne Webb	7	41,900	Walter Ray Williams Jr.	6	225.49
Mark Williams	8	26,653	Ron Mohr	6	223.15
Walter Ray Williams Jr.	6	24,550	Tom Baker	9	221.28
Tom Baker	9	20,450	Mark Williams	8	220.06
Steve Ferraro	8	15,300	Wayne Webb	7	219.48

PBA Career Statistics

CAREER EARNINGS		CAREER TITLES	
*Walter Ray Williams Jr.	$4,094,622	*Walter Ray Williams Jr.	47
*Pete Weber	$3,201,603	Earl Anthony	43
*Norm Duke	$2,805,671	*Pete Weber	35
*Parker Bohn III	$2,671,754	Mark Roth	34
*Brian Voss	$2,426,102	*Norm Duke	33
*Chris Barnes	$1,690,579	*Parker Bohn III	32
Mark Roth	$1,619,136	Dick Weber	30
*Jason Couch	$1,572,178	Mike Aulby	29
Tom Baker	$1,450,000	Don Johnson	26
Earl Anthony	$1,441,061	*Brian Voss	25

Note: Career leaders through Sept. 1, 2010. *Active in 2009–10 season.

Cycling

Tour de France Winners

Year	Winner	Time
1903	Maurice Garin, France	94 hrs, 33 min
1904	Henry Cornet, France	96 hrs, 5 min, 56 sec
1905	Louis Trousselier, France	110 hrs, 26 min, 58 sec
1906	Rene Pottier, France	Not available
1907	Lucien Petit-Breton, France	158 hrs, 54 min, 5 sec
1908	Lucien Petit-Breton, France	Not available
1909	Francois Faber, Luxembourg	157 hrs, 1 min, 22 sec
1910	Octave Lapize, France	162 hrs, 41 min, 30 sec
1911	Gustave Garrigou, France	195 hrs, 37 min
1912	Odile Defraye, Belgium	190 hrs, 30 min, 28 sec
1913	Philippe Thys, Belgium	197 hrs, 54 min
1914	Philippe Thys, Belgium	200 hrs, 28 min, 48 sec
1915–18	NO RACE	
1919	Firmin Lambot, Belgium	231 hrs, 7 min, 15 sec
1920	Philippe Thys, Belgium	228 hrs, 36 min, 13 sec
1921	Leon Scieur, Belgium	221 hrs, 50 min, 26 sec
1922	Firmin Lambot, Belgium	222 hrs, 8 min, 6 sec
1923	Henri Pelissier, France	222 hrs, 15 min, 30 sec
1924	Ottavio Bottechia, Italy	226 hrs, 18 min, 21 sec
1925	Ottavio Bottechia, Italy	219 hrs, 10 min, 18 sec
1926	Lucien Buysse, Belgium	238 hrs, 44 min, 25 sec
1927	Nicolas Frantz, Luxembourg	198 hrs, 16 min, 42 sec
1928	Nicolas Frantz, Luxembourg	192 hrs, 48 min, 58 sec
1929	Maurice Dewaele, Belgium	186 hrs, 39 min, 16 sec
1930	Andre Leducq, France	172 hrs, 12 min, 16 sec
1931	Antonin Magne, France	177 hrs, 10 min, 3 sec
1932	Andre Leducq, France	154 hrs, 12 min, 49 sec
1933	Georges Speicher, France	147 hrs, 51 min, 37 sec
1934	Antonin Magne, France	147 hrs, 13 min, 58 sec
1935	Romain Maes, Belgium	141 hrs, 32 min
1936	Sylvere Maes, Belgium	142 hrs, 47 min, 32 sec
1937	Roger Lapebie, France	138 hrs, 58 min, 31 sec
1938	Gino Bartali, Italy	148 hrs, 29 min, 12 sec
1939	Sylvere Maes, Belgium	132 hrs, 3 min, 17 sec
1940–46	NO RACE	
1947	Jean Robic, France	148 hrs, 11 min, 25 sec
1948	Gino Bartali, Italy	147 hrs, 10 min, 36 sec
1949	Fausto Coppi, Italy	149 hrs, 40 min, 49 sec
1950	Ferdi Kubler, Switzerland	145 hrs, 36 min, 56 sec
1951	Hugo Koblet, Switzerland	142 hrs, 20 min, 14 sec
1952	Fausto Coppi, Italy	151 hrs, 57 min, 20 sec
1953	Louison Bobet, France	129 hrs, 23 min, 25 sec
1954	Louison Bobet, France	140 hrs, 6 min, 5 sec
1955	Louison Bobet, France	130 hrs, 29 min, 26 sec
1956	Roger Walkowiak, France	124 hrs, 1 min, 16 sec
1957	Jacques Anquetil, France	129 hrs, 46 min, 11 sec
1958	Charly Gaul, Luxembourg	116 hrs, 59 min, 5 sec
1959	Federico Bahamontes, Spain	123 hrs, 46 min, 45 sec
1960	Gastone Nencini, Italy	112 hrs, 8 min, 42 sec
1961	Jacques Anquetil, France	122 hrs, 1 min, 33 sec

Year	Winner	Time
1962	Jacques Anquetil, France	114 hrs, 31 min, 54 sec
1963	Jacques Anquetil, France	113 hrs, 30 min, 5 sec
1964	Jacques Anquetil, France	127 hrs, 9 min, 44 sec
1965	Felice Gimondi, Italy	116 hrs, 42 min, 6 sec
1966	Lucien Aimar, France	117 hrs, 34 min, 21 sec
1967	Roger Pingeon, France	136 hrs, 53 min, 50 sec
1968	Jan Janssen, Netherlands	133 hrs, 49 min, 32 sec
1969	Eddy Merckx, Belgium	116 hrs, 16 min, 2 sec
1970	Eddy Merckx, Belgium	119 hrs, 31 min, 49 sec
1971	Eddy Merckx, Belgium	96 hrs, 45 min, 14 sec
1972	Eddy Merckx, Belgium	108 hrs, 17 min, 18 sec
1973	Luis Ocana, Spain	122 hrs, 25 min, 34 sec
1974	Eddy Merckx, Belgium	116 hrs, 16 min, 58 sec
1975	Bernard Thevenet, France	114 hrs, 35 min, 31 sec
1976	Lucien Van Impe, Belgium	116 hrs, 22 min, 23 sec
1977	Bernard Thevenet, France	115 hrs, 38 min, 30 sec
1978	Bernard Hinault, France	108 hrs, 18 min
1979	Bernard Hinault, France	103 hrs, 6 min, 50 sec
1980	Joop Zoetemelk, Netherlands	109 hrs, 19 min, 14 sec
1981	Bernard Hinault, France	96 hrs, 19 min, 38 sec
1982	Bernard Hinault, France	92 hrs, 8 min, 46 sec
1983	Laurent Fignon, France	105 hrs, 7 min, 52 sec
1984	Laurent Fignon, France	112 hrs, 3 min, 40 sec
1985	Bernard Hinault, France	113 hrs, 24 min, 23 sec
1986	Greg LeMond, United States	110 hrs, 35 min, 19 sec
1987	Stephen Roche, Ireland	115 hrs, 27 min, 42 sec
1988	Pedro Delgado, Spain	84 hrs, 27 min, 53 sec
1989	Greg LeMond, United States	87 hrs, 38 min, 35 sec
1990	Greg LeMond, United States	90 hrs, 43 min, 20 sec
1991	Miguel Induráin, Spain	101 hrs, 1 min, 20 sec
1992	Miguel Induráin, Spain	100 hrs, 49 min, 30 sec
1993	Miguel Induráin, Spain	95 hrs, 57 min, 9 sec
1994	Miguel Induráin, Spain	103 hrs, 38 min, 38 sec
1995	Miguel Induráin, Spain	92 hrs, 44 min, 59 sec
1996	Bjarne Riis, Denmark	95 hrs, 57 min, 16 sec
1997	Jan Ullrich, Germany	100 hrs, 30 min, 35 sec
1998	Marco Pantani, Italy	92 hrs, 49 min, 46 sec
1999	Lance Armstrong, United States	91 hrs, 32 min, 16 sec
2000	Lance Armstrong, United States	92 hrs, 33 min, 8 sec
2001	Lance Armstrong, United States	86 hrs, 17 min, 28 sec
2002	Lance Armstrong, United States	82 hrs, 5 min, 12 sec
2003	Lance Armstrong, United States	83 hrs, 41 min, 12 sec
2004	Lance Armstrong, United States	83 hrs, 36 min, 2 sec
2005	Lance Armstrong, United States	82 hrs, 34 min, 5 sec
2006	Oscar Pereiro, Spain†	82 hrs, 48 min, 30 sec
2007	Alberto Contador, Spain	91 hrs, 26 sec
2008	Carlos Sastre, Spain	87 hrs, 52 min, 52 sec
2009	Alberto Contador, Spain	85 hrs, 48 min, 35 sec
2010	Alberto Contador, Spain	91 hrs, 58 min, 48 sec

†Floyd Landis, the initial winner, was officially stripped of his title on Sept. 20, 2007 by the ICU after a hearing affirmed that he had tested positive for using banned substances during Stage 17 of the 2006 Tour.

WORLD CHAMPIONS
Women

Year	Champion
1906	Madge Sayers-Cave, Great Britain
1907	Madge Sayers-Cave, Great Britain
1908	Lily Kronberger, Hungary
1909	Lily Kronberger, Hungary
1910	Lily Kronberger, Hungary
1911	Lily Kronberger, Hungary
1912	Opika von Meray Horvath, Hungary
1913	Opika von Meray Horvath, Hungary
1914	Opika von Meray Horvath, Hungary
1915–21	NO COMPETITION
1922	Herma Plank-Szabo, Austria
1923	Herma Plank-Szabo, Austria
1924	Herma Plank-Szabo, Austria
1925	Herma Jaross-Szabo, Austria
1926	Herma Jaross-Szabo, Austria
1927	Sonja Henie, Norway
1928	Sonja Henie, Norway
1929	Sonja Henie, Norway
1930	Sonja Henie, Norway
1931	Sonja Henie, Norway
1932	Sonja Henie, Norway
1933	Sonja Henie, Norway
1934	Sonja Henie, Norway
1935	Sonja Henie, Norway
1936	Sonja Henie, Norway
1937	Cecilia Colledge, Great Britain
1938	Megan Taylor, Great Britain
1939	Megan Taylor, Great Britain
1940–46	NO COMPETITION
1947	Barbara Ann Scott, Canada
1948	Barbara Ann Scott, Canada
1949	Alena Vrzanova, Czechoslovakia
1950	Alena Vrzanova, Czechoslovakia
1951	Jeannette Altwegg, Great Britain
1952	Jacqueline duBief, France
1953	Tenley Albright, United States
1954	Gundi Busch, W. Germany
1955	Tenley Albright, United States
1956	Carol Heiss, United States
1957	Carol Heiss, United States
1958	Carol Heiss, United States
1959	Carol Heiss, United States
1960	Carol Heiss, United States
1961	NO COMPETITION
1962	Sjoukje Dijkstra, Netherlands
1963	Sjoukje Dijkstra, Netherlands
1964	Sjoukje Dijkstra, Netherlands
1965	Petra Burka, Canada
1966	Peggy Fleming, United States
1967	Peggy Fleming, United States
1968	Peggy Fleming, United States
1969	Gabriele Seyfert, E. Germany
1970	Gabriele Seyfert, E. Germany
1971	Beatrix Schuba, Austria
1972	Beatrix Schuba, Austria
1973	Karen Magnussen, Canada
1974	Christine Errath, E. Germany
1975	Dianne DeLeeuw, Netherlands
1976	Dorothy Hamill, United States
1977	Linda Fratianne, United States
1978	Annett Poetzsch, E. Germany
1979	Linda Fratianne, United States
1980	Annett Poetzsch, E. Germany
1981	Denise Biellmann, Switzerland
1982	Elaine Zayak, United States
1983	Rosalynn Sumners, United States
1984	Katarina Witt, E. Germany
1985	Katarina Witt, E. Germany
1986	Debi Thomas, United States
1987	Katarina Witt, E. Germany
1988	Katarina Witt, E. Germany
1989	Midori Ito, Japan
1990	Jill Trenary, United States
1991	Kristi Yamaguchi, United States
1992	Kristi Yamaguchi, United States
1993	Oksana Baiul, Ukraine
1994	Yuka Sato, Japan
1995	Chen Lu, China
1996	Michelle Kwan, United States
1997	Tara Lipinski, United States
1998	Michelle Kwan, United States
1999	Maria Butyrskaya, Russia
2000	Michelle Kwan, United States
2001	Michelle Kwan, United States
2002	Irina Slutskaya, Russia
2003	Michelle Kwan, United States
2004	Shizuka Arakawa, Japan
2005	Irina Slutskaya, Russia
2006	Kimmie Meissner, United States
2007	Miki Ando, Japan
2008	Mao Asada, Japan
2009	Yu-Na Kim, South Korea
2010	Mao Asada, Japan

Men

Year	Champion
1896	Gilbert Fuchs, Germany
1897	Gustav Hugel, Austria
1898	Henning Grenander, Sweden
1899	Gustav Hugel, Austria
1900	Gustav Hugel, Austria
1901	Ulrich Salchow, Sweden
1902	Ulrich Salchow, Sweden
1903	Ulrich Salchow, Sweden
1904	Ulrich Salchow, Sweden
1905	Ulrich Salchow, Sweden
1906	Gilbert Fuchs, Germany
1907	Ulrich Salchow, Sweden
1908	Ulrich Salchow, Sweden
1909	Ulrich Salchow, Sweden
1910	Ulrich Salchow, Sweden
1911	Ulrich Salchow, Sweden
1912	Fritz Kachler, Austria
1913	Fritz Kachler, Austria
1914	Gosta Sandhal, Sweden
1915–21	NO COMPETITION
1922	Gillis Grafstrom, Sweden
1923	Fritz Kachler, Austria
1924	Gillis Grafstrom, Sweden
1925	Willy Bockl, Austria
1926	Willy Bockl, Austria
1927	Willy Bockl, Austria
1928	Willy Bockl, Austria
1929	Gillis Grafstrom, Sweden
1930	Karl Schafer, Austria
1931	Karl Schafer, Austria
1932	Karl Schafer, Austria
1933	Karl Schafer, Austria
1934	Karl Schafer, Austria
1935	Karl Schafer, Austria
1936	Karl Schafer, Austria
1937	Felix Kaspar, Austria
1938	Felix Kaspar, Austria
1939	Graham Sharp, Great Britain
1940–46	NO COMPETITION
1947	Hans Gerschwiler, Switzerland
1948	Dick Button, United States
1949	Dick Button, United States
1950	Dick Button, United States
1951	Dick Button, United States
1952	Dick Button, United States
1953	Hayes Alan Jenkins, United States
1954	Hayes Alan Jenkins, United States
1955	Hayes Alan Jenkins, United States
1956	Hayes Alan Jenkins, United States
1957	David W. Jenkins, United States
1958	David W. Jenkins, United States
1959	David W. Jenkins, United States
1960	Alan Giletti, France
1961	No competition
1962	Donald Jackson, Canada
1963	Donald McPherson, Canada
1964	Manfred Schneldorfer, W. Germany
1965	Alain Calmat, France
1966	Emmerich Danzer, Austria
1967	Emmerich Danzer, Austria
1968	Emmerich Danzer, Austria
1969	Tim Wood, United States
1970	Tim Wood, United States
1971	Andrej Nepela, Czechoslovakia
1972	Andrej Nepela, Czechoslovakia
1973	Andrej Nepela, Czechoslovakia
1974	Jan Hoffmann, E. Germany
1975	Sergei Volkov, USSR
1976	John Curry, Great Britain
1977	Vladimir Kovalev, USSR
1978	Charles Tickner, United States
1979	Vladimir Kovalev, USSR
1980	Jan Hoffmann, E. Germany
1981	Scott Hamilton, United States
1982	Scott Hamilton, United States
1983	Scott Hamilton, United States
1984	Scott Hamilton, United States
1985	Aleksandr Fadeev, USSR

WORLD CHAMPIONS (Cont.)

Men (Cont.)

1986.....Brian Boitano, United States	1995.....Elvis Stojko, Canada
1987.....Brian Orser, Canada	1996.....Todd Eldredge, United States
1988.....Brian Boitano, United States	1997.....Elvis Stojko, Canada
1989.....Kurt Browning, Canada	1998.....Alexei Yagudin, Russia
1990.....Kurt Browning, Canada	1999.....Alexei Yagudin, Russia
1991.....Kurt Browning, Canada	2000.....Alexei Yagudin, Russia
1992.....Viktor Petrenko, CIS	2001.....Evgeni Plushenko, Russia
1993.....Kurt Browning, Canada	2002.....Alexei Yagudin, Russia
1994.....Elvis Stojko, Canada	2003.....Evgeni Plushenko, Russia

2004.....Evgeni Plushenko, Russia
2005.....Stephane Lambiel, Switzerland
2006.....Stephane Lambiel, Switzerland
2007.....Brian Joubert, France
2008.....Jeffrey Buttle, Canada
2009.....Evan Lysacek, United States
2010.....Daisuke Takahaski, Japan

Pairs

1908.....Anna Hubler, Heinrich Burger, Germany
1909.....Phyllis Johnson, James H. Johnson, Great Britain
1910.....Anna Hubler, Heinrich Burger, Germany
1911.....Ludowika Eilers, Walter Jakobsson, Germany/Finland
1912.....Phyllis Johnson, James H. Johnson, Great Britain
1913.....Helene Engelmann, Karl Majstrik, Germany
1914.....Ludowika Jakobsson-Eilers, Walter Jakobsson-Eilers, Finland
1915–21   NO COMPETITION
1922.....Helene Engelmann, Alfred Berger, Germany
1923.....Ludowika Jakobsson-Eilers, Walter Jakobsson-Eilers, Finland
1924.....Helene Engelmann, Alfred Berger, Germany
1925.....Herma Jaross-Szabo, Ludwig Wrede, Austria
1926.....Andree Joly, Pierre Brunet, France
1927.....Herma Jaross-Szabo, Ludwig Wrede, Austria
1928.....Andree Joly, Pierre Brunet, France
1929.....Lilly Scholz, Otto Kaiser, Austria
1930.....Andree Brunet-Joly, Pierre Brunet-Joly, France
1931.....Emilie Rotter, Laszlo Szollas, Hungary
1932.....Andree Brunet-Joly, Pierre Brunet-Joly, France
1933.....Emilie Rotter, Laszlo Szollas, Hungary
1934.....Emilie Rotter, Laszlo Szollas, Hungary
1935.....Emilie Rotter, Laszlo Szollas, Hungary
1936.....Maxi Herber, Ernst Bajer, Germany
1937.....Maxi Herber, Ernst Bajer, Germany
1938.....Maxi Herber, Ernst Bajer, Germany
1939.....Maxi Herber, Ernst Bajer, Germany
1940–46   NO COMPETITION
1947.....Micheline Lannoy, Pierre Baugniet, Belgium
1948.....Micheline Lannoy, Pierre Baugniet, Belgium
1949.....Andrea Kekessy, Ede Kiraly, Hungary
1950.....Karol Kennedy, Peter Kennedy, United States
1951.....Ria Baran, Paul Falk, W. Germany
1952.....Ria Baran Falk, Paul Falk, W. Germany
1953.....Jennifer Nicks, John Nicks, Great Britain
1954.....Frances Dafoe, Norris Bowden, Canada
1955.....Frances Dafoe, Norris Bowden, Canada
1956.....Sissy Schwarz, Kurt Oppelt, Austria
1957.....Barbara Wagner, Robert Paul, Canada
1958.....Barbara Wagner, Robert Paul, Canada
1959.....Barbara Wagner, Robert Paul, Canada
1960.....Barbara Wagner, Robert Paul, Canada
1961.....NO COMPETITION
1962.....Maria Jelinek, Otto Jelinek, Canada
1963.....Marika Kilius, Hans-Jurgen Baumler, W Germany
1964.....Marika Kilius, Hans-Jurgen Baumler, W Germany

1965.....Ljudmila Protopopov, Oleg Protopopov, USSR
1966.....Ljudmila Protopopov, Oleg Protopopov, USSR
1967.....Ljudmila Protopopov, Oleg Protopopov, USSR
1968.....Ljudmila Protopopov, Oleg Protopopov, USSR
1969.....Irina Rodnina, Aleksey Ulanov, USSR
1970.....Irina Rodnina, Aleksey Ulanov, USSR
1971.....Irina Rodnina, Aleksey Ulanov, USSR
1972.....Irina Rodnina, Aleksey Ulanov, USSR
1973.....Irina Rodnina, Aleksandr Zaytsev, USSR
1974.....Irina Rodnina, Aleksandr Zaytsev, USSR
1975.....Irina Rodnina, Aleksandr Zaytsev, USSR
1976.....Irina Rodnina, Aleksandr Zaytsev, USSR
1977.....Irina Rodnina, Aleksandr Zaytsev, USSR
1978.....Irina Rodnina, Aleksandr Zaytsev, USSR
1979.....Tai Babilonia, Randy Gardner, United States.
1980.....Maria Cherkasova, Sergei Shakhrai, USSR
1981.....Irina Vorobieva, Igor Lisovsky, USSR
1982.....Sabine Baess, Tassilio Thierbach, E. Germany
1983.....Elena Valova, Oleg Vasiliev, USSR
1984.....Barbara Underhill, Paul Martini, Canada
1985.....Elena Valova, Oleg Vasiliev, USSR
1986.....Ekaterina Gordeeva, Sergei Grinkov, USSR
1987.....Ekaterina Gordeeva, Sergei Grinkov, USSR
1988.....Elena Valova, Oleg Vasiliev, USSR
1989.....Ekaterina Gordeeva, Sergei Grinkov, USSR
1990.....Ekaterina Gordeeva, Sergei Grinkov, USSR
1991.....Natalia Mishkutienok, Artur Dmitriev, USSR
1992.....Natalia Mishkutienok, Artur Dmitriev, CIS
1993.....Isabelle Brasseur, Lloyd Eisler, Canada
1994.....Evgenia Shishkova, Vadim Naumov, Russia
1995.....Radka Kovarikova, Rene Novotny, Czech Republic
1996.....Marina Eltsova, Andrey Buskhov, Russia
1997.....Mandy Wötzel, Ingo Steuer, Germany
1998.....Jenni Meno, Todd Sand, United States
1999.....Elena Berezhnaya, Anton Sikharulidze, Russia
2000.....Maria Petrova, Aleksei Tikhonov, Russia
2001.....Jamie Salé, David Pelletier, Canada
2002.....Xue Shen, Hongbo Zhao, China
2003.....Xue Shen, Hongbo Zhao, China
2004.....Tatiana Totmianina, Maxim Marinin, Russia
2005.....Tatiana Totmianina, Maxim Marinin, Russia
2006.....Qing Pang, Jian Tong, China
2007.....Shen Xue, Zhao Hongbo, China
2008.....Aliona Savchenko, Robin Szolkowy, Germany
2009.....Aliona Savchenko, Robin Szolkowy, Germany
2010.....Qin Pang, Jian Tong, China

WORLD CHAMPIONS (Cont.)

Dance

1950 ....Lois Waring, Michael McGean, United States	1981 ....Jayne Torvill, Christopher Dean, Great Britain
1951 ....Jean Westwood, Lawrence Demmy, Great Britain	1982 ....Jayne Torvill, Christopher Dean, Great Britain
1952 ....Jean Westwood, Lawrence Demmy, Great Britain	1983 ....Jayne Torvill, Christopher Dean, Great Britain
1953 ....Jean Westwood, Lawrence Demmy, Great Britain	1984 ....Jayne Torvill, Christopher Dean, Great Britain
1954 ....Jean Westwood, Lawrence Demmy, Great Britain	1985 ....Natalia Bestemianova, Andrei Bukin, USSR
1955 ....Jean Westwood, Lawrence Demmy, Great Britain	1986 ....Natalia Bestemianova, Andrei Bukin, USSR
1956 ....Pamela Wieght, Paul Thomas, Great Britain	1987 ....Natalia Bestemianova, Andrei Bukin, USSR
1957 ....June Markham, Courtney Jones, Great Britain	1988 ....Natalia Bestemianova, Andrei Bukin, USSR
1958 ....June Markham, Courtney Jones, Doreen D. Denny, Courtney Jones, Great Britain	1989 ....Marina Klimova, Sergei Ponomarenko, USSR
1960 ....Doreen D. Denny, Courtney Jones, Great Britain	1990 ....Marina Klimova, Sergei Ponomarenko, USSR
1961 ....NO COMPETITION	1991 ....Isabelle Duchesnay, Paul Duchesnay, France
1962 ....Eva Romanova, Pavel Roman, Czechoslovakia	1992 ....Marina Klimova, Sergei Ponomarenko, CIS
1963 ....Eva Romanova, Pavel Roman, Czechoslovakia	1993 ....Renee Roca, Gorsha Sur, United States
1964 ....Eva Romanova, Pavel Roman, Czechoslovakia	1994 ....Oksana Grishuk, Evgeny Platov, Russia
1965 ....Eva Romanova, Pavel Roman, Czechoslovakia	1995 ....Oksana Grishuk, Evgeny Platov, Russia
1966 ....Diane Towler, Bernard Ford, Great Britain	1996 ....Oksana Grishuk, Evgeny Platov, Russia
1967 ....Diane Towler, Bernard Ford, Great Britain	1997 ....Oksana Grishuk, Evgeny Platov, Russia
1968 ....Diane Towler, Bernard Ford, Great Britain	1998 ....Anjelika Krylova, Oleg Ovsyannikov, Russia
1969 ....Diane Towler, Bernard Ford, Great Britain	1999 ....Anjelika Krylova, Oleg Ovsyannikov, Russia
1970 ....Ljudmila Pakhomova, Aleksandr Gorshkov, USSR	2000 ....Marina Anissina, Gwendal Peizerat, France
1971 ....Ljudmila Pakhomova, Aleksandr Gorshkov USSR	2001 ....Barbara Fusar Poli, Maurizio Margaglio, Italy
1972 ....Ljudmila Pakhomova, Aleksandr Gorshkov USSR	2002 ....Irina Lobacheva, Ilia Averbukh, Russia
1973 ....Ljudmila Pakhomova, Aleksandr Gorshkov USSR	2003 ....Shae-Lynn Bourne, Victor Kraatz, Canada
1974 ....Ljudmila Pakhomova, Aleksandr Gorshkov USSR	2004 ....Tatiana Navka, Roman Kostomarov, Russia
1975 ....Irina Moiseeva, Andreij Minenkov, USSR	2005 ....Tatiana Navka, Roman Kostomarov, Russia
1976 ....Ljudmila Pakhomova, Aleksandr Gorshkov, USSR	2006 ....Albena Denkova, Maxim Staviski, Bulgaria
1977 ....Irina Moiseeva, Andreij Minenkov, USSR	2007 ....Albena Denkova ,Maxim Staviski, Bulgaria
1978 ....Natalia Linichuk, Gennadi Karponosov, USSR	2008 ....Isabelle Delobel, Olivier Schoenfelder, France
1979 ....Natalia Linichuk, Gennadi Karponosov, USSR	2009 ....Oksana Domnina, Maxim Shabalin, Russia
1980 ....Krisztina Regoeczy, Andras Sallai, Hungary	2010 ....Tessa Virtue, Scott Moir, Canada

CHAMPIONS OF THE UNITED STATES

Women

The championships held in 1914, 1918, 1920 and 1921 under the auspices of the International Skating Union of America were open to Canadians, although the competitions were considered to be United States championships. Beginning in 1922, the championships have been held under the auspices of the United States Figure Skating Association.

1914 ....Theresa Weld, SC of Boston	1932 ....Maribel Y. Vinson, SC of Boston	1947 ....Gretchen Van Zandt Merrill, SC of Boston
1915–17 NO COMPETITION	1933 ....Maribel Y. Vinson, SC of Boston	1948 ....Gretchen Van Zandt Merrill, SC of Boston
1918 ....Rosemary S. Beresford, New York SC	1934 ....Suzanne Davis, SC of Boston	1949 ....Yvonne Claire Sherman, SC of New York
1919 NO COMPETITION	1935 ....Maribel Y. Vinson, SC of Boston	1950 ....Yvonne Claire Sherman, SC of New York
1920 ....Theresa Weld, SC of Boston	1936 ....Maribel Y. Vinson, SC of Boston	1951 ....Sonya Klopfer, Junior SC of New York
1921 ....Theresa Weld Blanchard, SC of Boston	1937 ....Maribel Y. Vinson, SC of Boston	1952 ....Tenley E. Albright, SC of Boston
1922 ....Theresa Weld Blanchard, SC of Boston	1938 ....Joan Tozzer, SC of Boston	1953 ....Tenley E. Albright, SC of Boston
1923 ....Theresa Weld Blanchard, SC of Boston	1939 ....Joan Tozzer, SC of Boston	1954 ....Tenley E. Albright, SC of Boston
1924 ....Theresa Weld Blanchard, SC of Boston	1940 ....Joan Tozzer, SC of Boston	1955 ....Tenley E. Albright, SC of Boston
1925 ....Beatrix Loughran, New York SC	1941 ....Jane Vaughn, Philadelphia SC & HS	1956 ....Tenley E. Albright, SC of Boston
1926 ....Beatrix Loughran, New York SC	1942 ....Jane Vaughn Sullivan, Philadelphia SC & HS	1957 ....Carol E. Heiss, SC of New York
1927 ....Beatrix Loughran, New York SC	1943 ....Gretchen Van Zandt Merrill, SC of Boston	1958 ....Carol E. Heiss, SC of New York
1928 ....Maribel Y. Vinson, SC of Boston	1944 ....Gretchen Van Zandt Merrill, SC of Boston	1959 ....Carol E. Heiss, SC of New York
1929 ....Maribel Y. Vinson, SC of Boston	1945 ....Gretchen Van Zandt Merrill, SC of Boston	1960 ....Carol E. Heiss, SC of New York
1930 ....Maribel Y. Vinson, SC of Boston	1946 ....Gretchen Van Zandt Merrill, SC of Boston	1961 ....Laurence R. Owen, SC of Boston
1931 ....Maribel Y. Vinson, SC of Boston		

CHAMPIONS OF THE UNITED STATES (Cont.)
Women (Cont.)

1962 ....Barbara Roles Pursley, Arctic Blades FSC
1963 ....Lorraine G. Hanlon, SC of Boston
1964 ....Peggy Fleming, Arctic Blades FSC
1965 ....Peggy Fleming, Arctic Blades FSC
1966 ....Peggy Fleming, City of Colorado Springs
1967 ....Peggy Fleming, Broadmoor SC
1968 ....Peggy Fleming, Broadmoor SC
1969 ....Janet Lynn, Wagon Wheel FSC
1970 ....Janet Lynn, Wagon Wheel FSC
1971 ....Janet Lynn, Wagon Wheel FSC
1972 ....Janet Lynn, Wagon Wheel FSC
1973 ....Janet Lynn, Wagon Wheel FSC
1974 ....Dorothy Hamill, SC of New York
1975 ....Dorothy Hamill, SC of New York

1976 ....Dorothy Hamill, SC of New York
1977 ....Linda Fratianne, Los Angeles FSC
1978 ....Linda Fratianne, Los Angeles FSC
1979 ....Linda Fratianne, Los Angeles FSC
1980 ....Linda Fratianne, Los Angeles FSC
1981 ....Elaine Zayak, SC of New York
1982 ....Rosalynn Sumners, Seattle SC
1983 ....Rosalynn Sumners, Seattle SC
1984 ....Rosalynn Sumners, Seattle SC
1985 ....Tiffany Chin, San Diego FSC
1986 ....Debi Thomas, Los Angeles FSC
1987 ....Jill Trenary, Broadmoor SC
1988 ....Debi Thomas, Los Angeles FSC
1989 ....Jill Trenary, Broadmoor SC
1990 ....Jill Trenary, Broadmoor SC
1991 ....Tonya Harding, Carousel FSC
1992 ....Kristi Yamaguchi, St Moritz ISC
1993 ....Nancy Kerrigan, Colonial FSC
1994 ....Tonya Harding, Portland FSC

1995 ....Nicole Bobek, Los Angeles FSC
1996 ....Michelle Kwan, Los Angeles FSC
1997 ....Tara Lipinski, Detroit SC
1998 ....Michelle Kwan, Los Angeles FSC
1999 ....Michelle Kwan, Los Angeles FSC
2000 ....Michelle Kwan, Los Angeles FSC
2001 ....Michelle Kwan, Los Angeles FSC
2002 ....Michelle Kwan, Los Angeles FSC
2003 ....Michelle Kwan, Los Angeles FSC
2004 ....Michelle Kwan, Los Angeles FSC
2005 ....Michelle Kwan, Los Angeles FSC
2006 ....Sasha Cohen, Orange County FSC
2007 ....Kimmie Meissner, Univ. of Delaware FSC
2008 ....Mirai Nagasu, Pasadena FSC
2009 ....Alissa Czisny, Detroit SC
2010 ....Rachael Flatt, Broadmoor SC

Men

1914   Norman M. Scott, WC of Montreal
1915–17   NO COMPETITION
1918 ....Nathaniel W. Niles, SC of Boston
1919   NO COMPETITION
1920 ....Sherwin C. Badger, SC of Boston
1921 ....Sherwin C. Badger, SC of Boston
1922 ....Sherwin C. Badger, SC of Boston
1923 ....Sherwin C. Badger, SC of Boston
1924 ....Sherwin C. Badger, SC of Boston
1925 ....Nathaniel W. Niles, SC of Boston
1926   Chris I. Christenson, Twin City FSC
1927 ....Nathaniel W. Niles, SC of Boston
1928 ....Roger F. Turner, SC of Boston
1929 ....Roger F. Turner, SC of Boston
1930 ....Roger F. Turner, SC of Boston
1931 ....Roger F. Turner, SC of Boston
1932 ....Roger F. Turner, SC of Boston
1933 ....Roger F. Turner, SC of Boston
1934 ....Roger F. Turner, SC of Boston
1935 ....Robin H. Lee, SC of New York
1936 ....Robin H. Lee, SC of New York
1937 ....Robin H. Lee, SC of New York
1938 ....Robin H. Lee, Chicago FSC
1939 ....Robin H. Lee, St Paul FSC
1940 ....Eugene Turner, Los Angeles FSC
1941 ....Eugene Turner, Los Angeles FSC
1942 ....Robert Specht, Chicago FSC
1943   Arthur R. Vaughn Jr., Phila. SC & HS
1944–45   NO COMPETITION
1946   Dick Button, Philadelphia SC & HS
1947 ....Dick Button, Philadelphia SC & HS
1948 ....Dick Button, Philadelphia SC & HS
1949 ....Dick Button, Philadelphia SC & HS

1950 ....Dick Button, SC of Boston
1951 ....Dick Button, SC of Boston
1952 ....Dick Button, SC of Boston
1953 ....Hayes Alan Jenkins, Cleveland SC
1954 ....Hayes Alan Jenkins, Broadmoor SC
1955 ....Hayes Alan Jenkins, Broadmoor SC
1956 ....Hayes Alan Jenkins, Broadmoor SC
1957 ....David Jenkins, Broadmoor SC
1958 ....David Jenkins, Broadmoor SC
1959 ....David Jenkins, Broadmoor SC
1960 ....David Jenkins, Broadmoor SC
1961 ....Bradley R. Lord, SC of Boston
1962 ....Monty Hoyt, Broadmoor SC
1963 ....Thomas Litz, Hershey FSC
1964 ....Scott Ethan Allen, SC of New York
1965 ....Gary C. Visconti, Detroit SC
1966 ....Scott Ethan Allen, SC of New York
1967 ....Gary C. Visconti, Detroit SC
1968 ....Tim Wood, Detroit SC
1969 ....Tim Wood, Detroit SC
1970 ....Tim Wood, City of Colorado Springs
1971 ....John Misha Petkevich, Great Falls FSC
1972 ....Kenneth Shelley, Arctic Blades FSC
1973 ....Gordon McKellen Jr., SC of Lake Placid
1974 ....Gordon McKellen Jr., SC of Lake Placid
1975 ....Gordon McKellen Jr., SC of Lake Placid
1976 ....Terry Kubicka, Arctic Blades FSC
1977 ....Charles Tickner, Denver FSC
1978 ....Charles Tickner, Denver FSC

1979 ....Charles Tickner, Denver FSC
1980 ....Charles Tickner, Denver FSC
1981 ....Scott Hamilton, Philadelphia SC & HS
1982 ....Scott Hamilton, Philadelphia SC & HS
1983 ....Scott Hamilton, Philadelphia SC & HS
1984 ....Scott Hamilton, Philadelphia SC & HS
1985 ....Brian Boitano, Peninsula FSC
1986 ....Brian Boitano, Peninsula FSC
1987 ....Brian Boitano, Peninsula FSC
1988 ....Brian Boitano, Peninsula FSC
1989 ....Christopher Bowman, Los Angeles FSC
1990 ....Todd Eldredge, Los Angeles FSC
1991 ....Todd Eldredge, Los Angeles FSC
1992 ....Christopher Bowman, Los Angeles FSC
1993 ....Scott Davis, Broadmoor SC
1994 ....Scott Davis, Broadmoor SC
1995 ....Todd Eldredge, Detroit SC
1996 ....Rudy Galindo, St Moritz ISC
1997 ....Todd Eldredge, Detroit SC
1998 ....Todd Eldredge, Detroit SC
1999 ....Michael Weiss, Washington FSC
2000 ....Michael Weiss, Washington FSC
2001 ....Timothy Goebel, Winterhurst FSC
2002 ....Todd Eldredge, Los Angeles FSC
2003 ....Michael Weiss, Washington FSC
2004 ....Johnny Weir, SC of New York
2005 ....Johnny Weir, SC of New York
2006 ....Johnny Weir, SC of New York
2007 ....Evan Lysacek, DuPage FSC
2008 ....Evan Lysacek, DuPage FSC
2009 ....Jeremy Abbott, Broadmoor SC
2010 ....Jeremy Abbott, Detroit SC

CHAMPIONS OF THE UNITED STATES (Cont.)
Pairs

1914	Jeanne Chevalier, Norman M. Scott, WC of Montreal
1915–17	NO COMPETITION
1918	Theresa Weld, Nathaniel W. Niles, SC of Boston
1919	No competition
1920	Theresa Weld, Nathaniel W. Niles, SC of Boston
1921	Theresa Weld Blanchard, Nathaniel W. Niles, SC of Boston
1922	Theresa Weld Blanchard, Nathaniel W. Niles, SC of Boston
1923	Theresa Weld Blanchard, Nathaniel W. Niles, SC of Boston
1924	Theresa Weld Blanchard, Nathaniel W. Niles, SC of Boston
1925	Theresa Weld Blanchard, Nathaniel W. Niles, SC of Boston
1926	Theresa Weld Blanchard, Nathaniel W. Niles, SC of Boston
1927	Theresa Weld Blanchard, Nathaniel W. Niles, SC of Boston
1928	Maribel Y. Vinson, Thornton L. Coolidge, SC of Boston
1929	Maribel Y. Vinson, Thornton L. Coolidge, SC of Boston
1930	Beatrix Loughran, Sherwin C. Badger, SC of New York
1931	Beatrix Loughran, Sherwin C. Badger, SC of New York
1932	Beatrix Loughran, Sherwin C. Badger, SC of New York
1933	Maribel Y. Vinson, George E. B. Hill, SC of SC of Boston
1936	Maribel Y. Vinson, George E. B. Hill, SC of Boston
1937	Maribel Y. Vinson, George E. B. Hill, SC of Boston
1938	Joan Tozzer, M. Bernard Fox, SC of Boston
1939	Joan Tozzer, M. Bernard Fox, SC of Boston
1940	Joan Tozzer, M. Bernard Fox, SC of Boston
1941	Donna Atwood, Eugene Turner, Mercury FSC/Los Angeles FSC
1942	Doris Schubach, Walter Noffke, Springfield Ice Birds
1943	Doris Schubach, Walter Noffke, Springfield Ice Birds
1944	Doris Schubach, Walter Noffke, Springfield Ice Birds
1945	Donna Jeanne Pospisil, Jean-Pierre Brunet, SC of New York
1946	Donna Jeanne Pospisil, Jean-Pierre Brunet, SC of New York
1947	Yvonne Claire Sherman, Robert J. Swenning, SC of New York
1948	Karol Kennedy, Peter Kennedy, Seattle SC
1949	Karol Kennedy, Peter Kennedy, Seattle SC
1950	Karol Kennedy, Peter Kennedy, Broadmoor SC
1951	Karol Kennedy, Peter Kennedy, Broadmoor SC
1952	Karol Kennedy, Peter Kennedy, Broadmoor SC

1953	Carole Ann Ormaca, Robin Greiner, SC of Fresno
1954	Carole Ann Ormaca, Robin Greiner, SC of Fresno
1955	Carole Ann Ormaca, Robin Greiner, St Moritz ISC
1956	Carole Ann Ormaca, Robin Greiner, St Moritz ISC
1957	Nancy Rouillard Ludington, Ronald Ludington, Commonwealth FSC/SC of Boston
1958	Nancy Rouillard Ludington, Ronald Ludington, Commonwealth FSC/SC of Boston
1959	Nancy Rouillard Ludington, Ronald Ludington, Commonwealth FSC
1960	Nancy Rouillard Ludington, Ronald Ludington, Commonwealth FSC
1961	Maribel Y. Owen, Dudley S. Richards, SC of Boston
1962	Dorothyann Nelson, Pieter Kollen, Village of Lake Placid
1963	Judianne Fotheringill, Jerry J. Fotheringill, Broadmoor SC
1964	Judianne Fotheringill, Jerry J. Fotheringill, Broadmoor SC
1965	Vivian Joseph, Ronald Joseph, Chicago FSC
1966	Cynthia Kauffman, Ronald Kauffman, Seattle SC
1967	Cynthia Kauffman, Ronald Kauffman, Seattle SC
1968	Cynthia Kauffman, Ronald Kauffman, Seattle SC
1969	Cynthia Kauffman, Ronald Kauffman, Seattle SC
1970	Jo Jo Starbuck, Kenneth Shelley, Arctic Blades FSC
1971	Jo Jo Starbuck, Kenneth Shelley, Arctic Blades FSC
1972	Jo Jo Starbuck, Kenneth Shelley, Arctic Blades FSC
1973	Melissa Militano, Mark Militano, SC of New York
1974	Melissa Militano, Johnny Johns, SC of New York/Detroit SC
1975	Melissa Militano, Johnny Johns, SC of New York/Detroit SC
1976	Tai Babilonia, Randy Gardner, LA FSC
1977	Tai Babilonia, Randy Gardner, LA FSC
1978	Tai Babilonia, Randy Gardner, Los Angeles FSC/Santa Monica FSC
1979	Tai Babilonia, Randy Gardner, Los Angeles FSC/Santa Monica FSC
1980	Tai Babilonia, Randy Gardner, Los Angeles FSC/Santa Monica FSC
1981	Caitlin Carruthers, Peter Carruthers, SC of Wilmington

1982	Caitlin Carruthers, Peter Carruthers, SC of Wilmington
1983	Caitlin Carruthers, Peter Carruthers, SC of Wilmington
1984	Caitlin Carruthers, Peter Carruthers, SC of Wilmington
1985	Jill Watson, Peter Oppegard, LA FSC
1986	Gillian Wachsman, Todd Waggoner, SC of Wilmington
1987	Jill Watson, Peter Oppegard, LA FSC
1988	Jill Watson, Peter Oppegard, LA FSC
1989	Kristi Yamaguchi, Rudy Galindo, St Mortiz ISC
1990	Kristi Yamaguchi, Rudy Galindo, St Mortiz ISC
1991	Natasha Kuchiki, Todd Sand, LA FSC
1992	Calla Urbanski, Rocky Marval, U of Delaware FSC/SC of New York
1993	Calla Urbanski, Rocky Marval, U of Delaware FSC/SC of New York
1994	Jenni Meno, Todd Sand, Winterhurst FSC/Los Angeles FSC
1995	Jenni Meno, Todd Sand, Winterhurst FSC/Los Angeles FSC
1996	Jenni Meno, Todd Sand, Winterhurst FSC/Los Angeles FSC
1997	Kyoko Ina, Jason Dungjen, SC of New York
1998	Kyoko Ina, Jason Dungjen, SC of New York
1999	Danielle Hartsell, Steve Hartsell, Detroit SC
2000	Kyoko Ina, John Zimmerman, SC of New York/Birmingham FSC
2001	Kyoko Ina, John Zimmerman, SC of New York/Birmingham FSC
2002	Kyoko Ina, John Zimmerman, SC of New York/Birmingham FSC
2003	Tiffany Scott, Philip Dulebohn, Colonial FSC/Univ of Delaware FSC
2004	Rena Inoue, John Baldwin, All Year FSC
2005	Kathryn Orscher, Garrett Lucash, Charter Oak FSC
2006	Rena Inoue, John Baldwin, All Year FSC
2007	Brooke Castile, Benjamin Okolski, Arctic FSC
2008	Keauna McLaughlin, Los Angeles FSC/Rockne Brubaker, Broadmoor SC
2009	Keauna McLaughlin, Los Angeles FSC/Rockne Brubaker, Broadmoor SC
2010	Caydee Denney, SW Florida FSC/Jeremy Barrett, SW Florida FSC

CHAMPIONS OF THE UNITED STATES *(Cont.)*

Dance

1914 Waltz: Theresa Weld, Nathaniel W. Niles, SC of Boston

1915–19 NO COMPETITION

1920 Waltz: Theresa Weld, Nathaniel W. Niles, SC of Boston
Fourteenstep: Gertrude Cheever Porter, Irving Brokaw, New York SC

1921 Waltz and Fourteenstep: Theresa Weld Blanchard, Nathaniel W. Niles, SC of Boston

1922 Waltz: Beatrix Loughran, Edward M. Howland, New York SC/ SC of Boston
Fourteenstep: Theresa Weld Blanchard, Nathaniel W. Niles, SC of Boston

1923 Waltz: Mr. & Mrs. Henry W. Howe, New York SC
Fourteenstep: Sydney Goode, James B. Greene, New York SC

1924 Waltz: Rosaline Dunn, Frederick Gabel, New York SC
Fourteenstep: Sydney Goode, James B. Greene, New York SC

1925 Waltz and Fourteenstep: Virginia Slattery, Ferrier T. Martin, New York SC

1926 Waltz: Rosaline Dunn, Joseph K. Savage, New York SC
Fourteenstep: Sydney Goode, James B. Greene, New York SC

1927 Waltz and Fourteenstep: Rosaline Dunn, Joseph K. Savage, New York SC

1928 Waltz: Rosaline Dunn, Joseph K. Savage, New York SC
Fourteenstep: Ada Bauman Kelly, George T. Braakman, New York SC

1929 Waltz and Original Dance combined: Edith C. Secord, Joseph K. Savage, SC of New York

1930 Waltz: Edith C. Secord, Joseph K. Savage, SC of New York
Original: Clara Rotch Frothingham, George E. B. Hill, SC of Boston

1931 Waltz: Edith C. Secord, Ferrier T. Martin, SC of New York
Original: Theresa Weld Blanchard, Nathaniel W. Niles, SC of Boston

1932 Waltz: Edith C. Secord, Joseph K. Savage, SC of New York
Original: Clara Rotch Frothingham, George E. B. Hill, SC of Boston

1933 Waltz: Ilse Twaroschk, Frederick F. Fleishmann, Brooklyn FSC
Original: Suzanne Davis, Frederick Goodridge, SC of Boston

1934 Waltz: Nettie C. Prantel, Roy Hunt, SC of New York
Original: Suzanne Davis, Frederick Goodridge, SC of Boston

1935 Waltz: Nettie C. Prantel, Roy Hunt, SC of New York

1936 Marjorie Parker, Joseph K. Savage, SC of New York

1937 Nettie C. Prantel, Harold Hartshorne, SC of New York

1938 Nettie C. Prantel, Harold Hartshorne, SC of New York

1939 Sandy Macdonald, Harold Hartshorne,SC of New York

1940 Sandy Macdonald, Harold Hartshorne, SC of New York

1941 Sandy Macdonald, Harold Hartshorne, SCNY

1942 Edith B. Whetstone, Alfred N. Richards, Jr, Philadelphia SC & HS

1943 Marcella May, James Lochead Jr., Skate & Ski Club

1944 Marcella May, James Lochead Jr., Skate & Ski Club

1945 Kathe Mehl Williams, Robert J. Swenning,SC of New York

1946 Anne Davies, Carleton C. Hoffner Jr., Washington FSC

1947 Lois Waring, Walter H. Bainbridge Jr., Baltimore FSC/Washigton FSC

1948 Lois Waring, Walter H. Bainbridge Jr.,Baltimore FSC/Washington FSC

1949 Lois Waring, Walter H. Bainbridge Jr.,Baltimore FSC/Washington FSC

1950 Lois Waring, Michael McGean, Baltimore FSC

1951 Carmel Bodel, Edward L. Bodel, St. Moritz ISC

1952 Lois Waring, Michael McGean, Baltimore FSC

1953 Carol Ann Peters, Daniel C. Ryan, Washington FSC

1954 Carmel Bodel, Edward L. Bodel, St Moritz ISC

1955 Carmel Bodel, Edward L. Bodel, St Moritz ISC

1956 Joan Zamboni, Roland Junso, Arctic Blades FSC

1957 Sharon McKenzie, Bert Wright, Los Angeles FSC

1958 Andree Anderson, Donald Jacoby, Buffalo SC

1959 Andree Anderson Jacoby, Donald Jacoby, Buffalo SC

1960 Margie Ackles, Charles W. Phillips Jr., Los Angeles FSC/Arctic Blades FSC

1961 Diane C. Sherbloom, Larry Pierce, Los Angeles FSC/ WC of Indianapolis

1962 Yvonne N. Littlefield, Peter F. Betts, Arctic Blades FSC/ Paramount, CA

1963 Sally Schantz, Stanley Urban, SC of Boston/Buffalo SC

1964 Darlene Streich, Charles D. Fetter Jr., WC of Indianapolis

1965 Kristin Fortune, Dennis Sveum, Los Angeles FSC

1966 Kristin Fortune, Dennis Sveum, Los Angeles FSC

1967 Lorna Dyer, John Carrell, Broadmoor SC

1968 Judy Schwomeyer, James Sladky, WC of Indianapolis/Genesee FSC

1969 Judy Schwomeyer, James Sladky, WC of Indianapolis/Genesee FSC

1970 Judy Schwomeyer, James Sladky, WC of Indianapolis/Genesee FSC

1971 Judy Schwomeyer, James Sladky, WC of Indianapolis/Genesee FSC

1972 Judy Schwomeyer, James Sladky, WC of Indianapolis/Genesee FSC

1973 Mary Karen Campbell, Johnny Johns, Lansing SC/Detroit SC

1974 Colleen O'Connor, Jim Millns, Broadmoor SC/ City of Colorado Springs

1975 Colleen O'Connor, Jim Millns, Broadmoor SC

1976 Colleen O'Connor, Jim Millns, Broadmoor SC

1977 Judy Genovesi, Kent Weigle, SC of Hartford/Charter Oak FSC

1978 Stacey Smith, John Summers, SC of Wilmington

1979 Stacey Smith, John Summers, SC of Wilmington

1980 Stacey Smith, John Summers, SC of Wilmington

1981 Judy Blumberg, Michael Seibert, Broadmoor SC/ISC of Indianapolis

1982 Judy Blumberg, Michael Seibert, Broadmoor SC/ISC of Indianapolis

1983 Judy Blumberg, Michael Seibert, Pittsburgh FSC

1984 Judy Blumberg, Michael Seibert, Pittsburgh FSC

1985 Judy Blumberg, Michael Seibert, Pittsburgh FSC

1986 Renee Roca, Donald Adair, Genesee FSC/Academy FSC

1987 Suzanne Semanick, Scott Gregory, U of Delaware SC

1988 Suzanne Semanick, Scott Gregory, U of Delaware SC

1989 Susan Wynne, Joseph Druar, Broadmoor SC/Seattle SC

1990 Susan Wynne, Joseph Druar, Broadmoor SC/Seattle SC

1991 Elizabeth Punsalan, Jerod Swallow, Broadmoor SC

1992 April Sargent, Russ Witherby, Ogdensburg FSC/ U of Delaware FSC

1993 Renee Roca, Gorsha Sur, Broadmoor SC

1994 Elizabeth Punsalan, Jerod Swallow, Broadmoor SC/Detroit SC

1995 Renee Roca, Gorsha Sur, Broadmoor SC

1996 Elizabeth Punsalan, Jerod Swallow, Detroit SC

1997 Elizabeth Punsalan, Jerod Swallow, Detroit SC

CHAMPIONS OF THE UNITED STATES *(CONT.)*
Dance *(Cont.)*

1998	Elizabeth Punsalan, Jerod Swallow, Detroit SC	2003	Naomi Lang, Peter Tchernyshev, American Academy FSC	2008	Tanith Belbin, Ben Agosto, Arctic FSC
1999	Naomi Lang, Peter Tchernyshev, Detroit SC	2004	Tanith Belbin, Ben Agosto, Detroit SC	2009	Meryl Davis, Arctic FSC/ Charlie White, Detroit SC
2000	Naomi Lang, Peter Tchernyshev, Detroit SC	2005	Tanith Belbin, Ben Agosto, Detroit SC	2010	Meryl Davis, Arctic FSC/ Charlie White, Detroit SC
2001	Naomi Lang, Peter Tchernyshev, Detroit SC	2006	Tanith Belbin, Ben Agosto, Arctic FSC		
2002	Naomi Lang, Peter Tchernyshev, American Academy FSC	2007	Tanith Belbin, Ben Agosto, Arctic FSC		

Gymnastics

WORLD CHAMPIONS — Men

All-Around

Year	Champion, Nation
1903	Joseph Martinez, France
1905	Marcel Lalue, France
1907	Joseph Czada, Czechoslovakia
1909	Marcos Torres, France
1911	Ferdinand Steiner, Czechoslovakia
1913	Marcos Torres, France
1922	Peter Sumi, Yugoslavia
	F. Pechacek, Czechoslovakia
1926	Peter Sumi, Yugoslavia
1930	Josip Primozic, Yugoslavia
1934	Eugene Mack, Switzerland
1938	Jan Gajdos, Czechoslovakia
1950	Walter Lehmann, Switzerland
1954	Valentin Mouratov, USSR
	Victor Chukarin, USSR
1958	Boris Shaklin, USSR
1962	Yuri Titov, USSR
1966	Mikhail Voronin, USSR
1970	Eizo Kenmotsu, Japan
1974	Shigeru Kasamatsu, Japan
1978	Nikolai Andrianov, USSR
1979	Alexander Ditiatin, USSR
1981	Yuri Korolev, USSR
1983	Dimitri Bilozertchev, USSR
1985	Yuri Korolev, USSR
1987	Dimitri Bilozertchev, USSR
1989	Igor Korobchinsky, USSR
1991	Grigori Misutin, CIS
1993	Vitaly Scherbo, Belarus
1994	Ivan Ivankov, Belarus
1995	Li Xiaoshuang, China
1997	Ivan Ivankov, Belarus
1999	Nicolae Krukov, Russia
2001	Feng Jing, China
2003	Paul Hamm, United States
2005	Hiroyuki Tomita, Japan
2007	Yang Wei, China
2009	Kohei Uchimura, Japan

Pommel Horse

Year	Champion, Nation
1930	Josip Primozic, Yugoslavia
1934	Eugene Mack, Switzerland
1938	Michael Reusch, Switzerland
1950	Josef Stalder, Switzerland
1954	Grant Chaguinjan, USSR
1958	Boris Shaklin, USSR
1962	Miroslav Cerar, Yugoslavia
1966	Miroslav Cerar, Yugoslavia
1970	Miroslav Cerar, Yugoslavia
1974	Zoltan Magyar, Hungary
1978	Zoltan Magyar, Hungary
1979	Zoltan Magyar, Hungary
1981	Michael Mikolai, East Germany
1983	Dmitri Bilozertchev, USSR
1985	Valentin Moguilny, USSR
1987	Zsolt Borkai, Hungary
	Dmitri Bilozertchev, USSR
1989	Valentin Moguilny, USSR
1991	Valeri Belenki, USSR
1992	Pae Gil Su, North Korea
	Vitaly Scherbo, CIS
	Li Jing, China
1993	Pae Gil Su, North Korea
1994	Marius Urzica, Romania
1995	Li Donghua, Switzerland
1996	Pae Gil Su, North Korea
1997	Valeri Belenki, Germany
1999	Alexei Nemov, Russia
2001	Marius Urzica, Romania
2003	Teng Haibin, China
	Takehiro Kashima, Japan
2005	Qin Xiao, China
2007	Qin Xiao, China
2009	Hongtao Zhang, China

Floor Exercise

Year	Champion, Nation
1930	Josip Primozic, Yugoslavia
1934	Georges Miesz, Switzerland
1938	Jan Gajdos, Czechoslovakia
1950	Josef Stalder, Switzerland
1954	Valentin Mouratov, USSR
	Masao Takemoto, Japan
1958	Masao Takemoto, Japan
1962	Nobuyuki Aihara, Japan
	Yukio Endo, Japan
1966	Akinori Nakayama, Japan
1970	Akinori Nakayama, Japan
1974	Shigeru Kasamatsu, Japan
1978	Kurt Thomas, United States
1979	Kurt Thomas, United States
	Roland Brucker, East Germ.
1981	Yuri Korolev, USSR,
	Li Yuejui, China
1983	Tong Fei, China
1985	Tong Fei, China
1987	Lou Yun, China
1989	Igor Korobchinsky, USSR
1991	Igor Korobchinsky, USSR
1993	Grigori Misutin, Ukraine
1994	Vitaly Scherbo, Belarus
1995	Vitaly Scherbo, Belarus
1996	Vitaly Scherbo, Belarus
1997	Alexei Nemov, Russia
1999	Alexei Nemov, Russia
2001	Marian Dragulescu, Romania
2003	Paul Hamm, United States
	Jordan Jovtchev, Bulgaria
2005	Diego Hypolito, Brazil
2007	Zou Kai, China
2009	Marian Dragulescu, Romania

WORLD CHAMPIONS — Men

Rings

Year	Champion, Nation
1930	Emanuel Loffler, Czechoslovakia
1934	Alois Hudec, Czechoslovakia
1938	Alois Hudec, Czechoslovakia
1950	Walter Lehmann, Switzerland
1954	Albert Azarian, USSR
1958	Albert Azarian, USSR
1962	Yuri Titov, USSR
1966	Mikhail Voronin, USSR
1970	Akinori Nakayama, Japan
1974	N. Andrianov, USSR D. Grecu, Rom.
1978	Nikolai Andrianov, USSR
1979	Alexander Ditiatin, USSR
1981	Alexander Ditiatin, USSR
1983	Dimitri Bilozertchev, USSR
1985	Li Ning, China, Yuri Korolev, USSR
1987	Yuri Korolev, USSR
1989	Andreas Aguilar, West Germ.
1991	Grigory Misutin, USSR
1992	Vitaly Scherbo, CIS
1993	Yuri Chechi, Italy
1994	Yuri Chechi, Italy
1995	Yuri Chechi, Italy
1996	Yuri Chechi, Italy
1997	Yuri Chechi, Italy
1999	Zhen Dong, China
2001	Jordan Jovtchev, Bulgaria
2003	Jordan Jovtchev, Bulgaria
	Dimosthenis Tampakos, Greece
2005	Yuri Van Gelder, Netherlands
2007	Diego Hypolito, Brazil
2009	Mingyong Yan, China

Parallel Bars

Year	Champion, Nation
1930	Josip Primozic, Yugoslavia
1934	Eugene Mack, Switzerland
1938	Michael Reusch, Switzerland
1950	Hans Eugster, Switzerland
1954	Victor Chukarin, USSR
1958	Boris Shaklin, USSR
1962	Miroslav Cerar, Yugoslavia
1966	Sergei Diamidov, USSR
1970	Akinori Nakayama, Japan
1974	Eizo Kenmotsu, Japan
1978	Eizo Kenmotsu, Japan
1979	Bart Conner, United States
1981	Koji Gushiken, Japan
	Alexandr Ditiatin, USSR
1983	Vladimir Artemov, USSR
	Lou Yun, China
1985	Sylvio Kroll, East Germany
	Valentin Moguilny, USSR
1987	Vladimir Artemov, USSR
1989	Li Jing, China
	Vladimir Artemov, USSR
1991	Li Jing, China
1992	Li Jin, China, Alexei Voropaev, CIS
1993	Vitaly Scherbo, Belarus
1994	Huang Liping, China
1995	Vitaly Scherbo, Belarus
1996	Rustam Sharipov, Ukraine
1997	Zhang Jinjing, China

Parallel Bar (Cont.)

Year	Champion, Nation
1999	Joo-Hyung Lee, South Korea
2001	Sean Townsend, U.S.
2003	Li Xiao-Peng, China
2005	Mitja Petkovsek, Slovenia
2007	Mitja Petkovsek, Slovenia
2009	Guanyin Yang, China

High Bar

Year	Champion, Nation
1930	Istvan Pelle, Hungary
1934	Ernst Winter, Germany
1938	Michael Reusch, Switzerland
1950	Paavo Aaltonen, Finland
1954	Valentin Mouratov, USSR
1958	Boris Shaklin, USSR
1962	Takashi Ono, Japan
1966	Akinori Nakayama, Japan
1970	Eizo Kenmotsu, Japan
1974	Eberhard Gienger, W Germany
1978	Shigeru Kasamatsu, Japan
1979	Kurt Thomas, United States
1981	Alexander Takchev, USSR
1983	Dimitri Bilozertchev, USSR
1985	Tong Fei, China
1987	Dimitri Bilozertchev, USSR
1989	Li Chunyang, China
1991	Li Chunyang, China
	R. Buechner, Germ
1992	Grigori Misutin, CIS
1993	Sergei Kharkov, Russia
1994	Vitaly Scherbo, Belarus
1995	Andreas Wecker, Germany
1996	Jesús Carballo, Spain
1997	Jani Tanskanen, Finland
1999	Jesus Carballo, Spain
2001	Vlasios Maras, Greece
2003	Takehiro Kashima, Japan
2005	Vlasios Maras, Greece
2007	Fabian Hambuechen, Germ.
2009	Kai Zou, China

Vault

Year	Champion, Nation
1934	Eugene Mack, Switzerland
1938	Eugene Mack, Switzerland
1950	Ernst Gebendinger, Switzerland
1954	Leo Sotornik, Czechoslovakia
1958	Yuri Titov, USSR
1962	Premysel Krbec, Czechoslovakia
1966	Haruhiro Yamashita, Japan
1970	Mitsuo Tsukahara, Japan
1974	Shigeru Kasamatsu, Japan
1978	Junichi Shimizu, Japan
1979	Alexander Ditiatin, USSR
1981	Ralf-Peter Hemmann, East Germany
1983	Arthur Akopian, USSR
1985	Yuri Korolev, USSR
1987	Lou Yun, China
	Sylvio Kroll, East Germany

Vault (Cont.)

Year	Champion, Nation
1989	Joreg Behrend, East Germany
1991	Yoo Ok Youl, South Korea
1992	Yoo Ok Youl, South Korea
1993	Vitaly Scherbo, Belarus
1994	Vitaly Scherbo, Belarus
1995	G. Misutin, Ukraine A. Nemov, Russia
1996	Alexei Nemov, Russia
1997	Sergei Fedorchenko, Kazakhstan
1999	Li Xiao-Peng, China
2001	Marian Dragulescu, Romania
2003	Li Xiao-Peng, China
2005	Eichi Sekiguchi, Japan
2007	Leszek Blanik, Poland
2009	Marian Dragulescu, Romania

WORLD CHAMPIONS — Women

All-Around

Year	Champion, Nation
1934	Vlasta Dekanova, Czechoslovakia
1938	Vlasta Dekanova, Czechoslovakia
1950	Helena Rakoczy, Poland
1954	Galina Roudiko, USSR
1958	Larissa Latynina, USSR
1962	Larissa Latynina, USSR
1966	Vera Caslavska, Czechoslovakia
1970	Ludmilla Tourischeva, USSR
1974	Ludmilla Tourischeva, USSR
1978	Elena Mukhina, USSR
1979	Nelli Kim, USSR
1981	Olga Bicherova, USSR
1983	Natalia Yurchenko, USSR
1985	Elena Shoushounova, USSR
	Oksana Omeliantchik, USSR
1987	Aurelia Dobre, Romania
1989	Svetlana Bouguinskaia, USSR
1991	Kim Zmeskal, United States
1993	Shannon Miller, United States
1994	Shannon Miller, United States
1995	Lilia Podkopayeva, Ukraine
1997	Svetlana Khorkina, Russia
1999	Maria Olaru, Romania
2001	Svetlana Khorkina, Russia
2003	Svetlana Khorkina, Russia
2005	Chellsie Memmel, United States
2007	Shawn Johnson, United States
2009	Bridget Sloan, United States

Floor Exercise

Year	Champion, Nation
1950	Helena Rakoczy, Poland
1954	Tamara Manina, USSR
1958	Eva Bosakava, Czechoslovakia
1962	Larissa Latynina, USSR
1966	Natalia Kuchinskaya, USSR
1970	Ludmilla Tourischeva, USSR
1974	Ludmilla Tourischeva, USSR
1978	Nelli Kim, USSR
	Elena Mukhina, USSR
1979	Emilia Eberle, Romania
1981	Natalia Ilenko, USSR
1983	Ecaterina Szabo, Romania
1985	Oksana Omeliantchik, USSR
1987	Elena Shoushounova, USSR
	Daniela Silivas, Romania
1989	Svetlana Bouguinskaia, USSR
	Daniela Silivas, Romania
1991	Cristina Bontas, Romania
	Oksana Tchusovitina, USSR
1992	Kim Zmeskal, United States
1993	Shannon Miller, United States
1994	Dina Kochetkova, Russia
1995	Gina Gogean, Romania
1996	Gina Gogean, Romania
1997	Gina Gogean, Romania
1999	Andreea Raducan, Romania
2001	Andreea Raducan, Romania
2003	Daiane Dos Santos, Brazil
2005	Nastia Liukin, United States
2007	Shawn Johnson, United States
2009	Elizabeth Tweddle, United Kingdom

Uneven Bars

Year	Champion, Nation
1950	Gertchen Kolar, Austria
	Anna Pettersson, Sweden
1954	Agnes Keleti, Hungary
1958	Larissa Latynina, USSR
1962	Irina Pervuschina, USSR
1966	Natalia Kuchinskaya, USSR
1970	Karin Janz, East Germany
1974	Annelore Zinke, East Germany
1978	Marcia Frederick, United States
1979	Ma Yanhong, China
	Maxi Gnauck, East Germany
1981	Maxi Gnauck, East Germany
1983	Maxi Gnauck, East Germany
1985	Gabriele Fahnrich, East Germany
1987	Daniela Silivas, Romania
	Doerte Thuemmler, East Germany
1989	Fan Di, China
	Daniela Silivas, Romania
1991	Gwang Suk Kim, North Korea
1992	Lavinia Milosivici, Romania
1993	Shannon Miller, United States
1994	Luo Li, China
1995	Svetlana Khorkina, Russia
1996	Svetlana Khorkina, Russia
1997	Svetlana Khorkina, Russia
1999	Svetlana Khorkina, Russia
2001	Svetlana Khorkina, Russia
2003	Chellsie Memmel, U.S.
	Hollie Vise, United States
2005	Nastia Liukin, United States
2007	Ksenia Semenov, Russia
2009	Kexin He, China

Balance Beam

Year	Champion, Nation
1950	Helena Rakoczy, Poland
1954	Keiko Tanaka, Japan
1958	Larissa Latynina, USSR
1962	Eva Bosakova, Czech.
1966	Natalia Kuchinskaya, USSR
1970	Erika Zuchold, East Germany
1974	Ludmilla Tourischeva, USSR
1978	Nadia Comaneci, Romania
1979	Vera Cerna, Czechoslovakia
1981	Maxi Gnauck, East Germany
1983	Olga Mostepanova, USSR
1985	Daniela Silivas, Romania
1987	Aurelia Dobre, Romania
1989	Daniela Silivas, Romania
1991	Svetlana Boguinskaia, USSR
1992	Kim Zmeskal, United States
1993	Lavinia Milosivici, Romania
1994	Shannon Miller, United States
1995	Mo Huilan, China
1996	Dina Kochetkova, Russia
1997	Gina Gogean, Romania
1999	E. Zamolodchikova, Russia
2001	Andreea Raducan, Romania
2003	Fan Ye, China
2005	Nan Zhang, China
2007	Nastia Liukin, United States
2009	Linlin Deng, China

Vault

Year	Champion, Nation
1950	Helena Rakoczy, Poland
1954	T. Manina, USSR
	Anna Pettersson, Sweden
1958	Larissa Latynina, USSR
1962	Vera Caslavska, Czech.
1966	Vera Caslavska, Czech.
1970	Erika Zuchold, East Germany
1974	Olga Korbut, USSR
1978	Nelli Kim, USSR
1979	Dumitrita Turner, Romania
1981	Maxi Gnauck, East Germany
1983	Boriana Stoyanova, Bulgaria
1985	Elena Shoushounova, USSR
1987	Elena Shoushounova, USSR
1989	Olesia Durnik, USSR
1991	Lavinia Milosovici, Romania
1992	Henrietta Onodi, Hungary
1993	Elena Piskun, Belarus
1994	Gina Gogean, Romania
1995	L. Podkopayeva, Ukraine
	Simona Amanar, Rom.
1996	Gina Gogean, Romania
1997	Simona Amanar, Romania
1999	Jie Ling, China
2001	Svetlana Khorkina, Russia
2003	Oksana Chusovitina, Uzbekistan
2005	Fei Cheng, China
2007	Fei Cheng, China
2009	Kayla Williams, United States

CHAMPIONS OF THE UNITED STATES — Men

All-Around

Year	Champion
1963	Art Shurlock
1964	Rusty Mitchell
1965	Rusty Mitchell
1966	Rusty Mitchell
1967	Katsuzoki Kanzaki
1968	Yoshi Hayasaki
1969	Steve Hug
1970	Makoto Sakamoto, Mas Watanabe
1971	Yoshi Takei
1972	Yoshi Takei
1973	Marshall Avener
1974	John Crosby
1975	Tom Beach, Bart Conner
1976	Kurt Thomas
1977	Kurt Thomas
1978	Kurt Thomas
1979	Bart Conner
1980	Peter Vidmar
1981	Jim Hartung
1982	Peter Vidmar
1983	Mitch Gaylord
1984	Mitch Gaylord
1985	Brian Babcock
1986	Tim Daggett
1987	Scott Johnson
1988	Dan Hayden
1989	Tim Ryan
1990	John Roethlisberger
1991	Chris Waller
1992	John Roethlisberger
1993	John Roethlisberger
1994	Scott Keswick
1995	John Roethlisberger
1996	Blaine Wilson
1997	Blaine Wilson
1998	Blaine Wilson
1999	Blaine Wilson
2000	Blaine Wilson
2001	Sean Townsend
2002	Paul Hamm
2003	Paul Hamm
2004	Paul Hamm
2005	Todd Thornton
2006	Alexander Artemev
2007	David Durante
2008	David Sender
2009	Jonathan Horton
2010	Jonathan Horton

Floor Exercise

Year	Champion
1963	Tom Seward
1964	Rusty Mitchell
1965	Rusty Mitchell
1966	Dan Millman
1967	Katsuzoki Kanzaki, Ron Aure
1968	Katsuzoki Kanzaki
1969	Steve Hug, Dave Thor
1970	Makoto Sakamoto
1971	John Crosby
1972	Yoshi Takei
1973	John Crosby

Floor Exercise (Cont.)

Year	Champion
1974	John Crosby
1975	Peter Korman
1977	Ron Galimore
1978	Kurt Thomas
1979	Ron Galimore
1980	Ron Galimore
1981	Jim Hartung
1982	Jim Hartung
1983	Mitch Gaylord
1984	Peter Vidmar
1985	Mark Oates
1986	Robert Sundstrom
1987	John Sweeney
1988	Mark Oates, Charles Lakes
1989	Mike Racanelli
1990	Bob Stelter
1991	Mike Racanelli
1992	Gregg Curtis
1993	Kerry Huston
1994	Jeremy Killen
1995	Daniel Stover
1996	Jay Thornton
1997	Jason Gatson
1998	Jason Gatson
1999	Jason Gatson
2000	Blaine Wilson
2001	Sean Townsend
2002	Morgan Hamm
2003	Morgan Hamm
2004	Paul Hamm
2005	Guillermo Alvarez
2006	Jonathan Horton
2007	Paul Hamm
2008	Morgan Hamm
2009	Steven Legendre
2010	Joshua Dixon

Pommel Horse

Year	Champion
1963	Larry Spiegel
1964	Sam Bailie
1965	Jack Ryan
1966	Jack Ryan
1967	Paul Mayer/Dave Doty
1968	Katsuoki Kanzaki
1969	Dave Thor
1970	Mas Watanabe
1971	Leonard Caling
1972	Sadao Hamada
1973	Marshall Avener
1974	Marshall Avener
1975	Bart Conner
1977	Gene Whelan
1978	Jim Hartung
1979	Bart Conner
1980	Jim Hartung
1981	Jim Hartung
1982	Jim Hartung
1983	Bart Conner
1984	Tim Daggett
1985	Phil Cahoy
1986	Phil Cahoy

Pommel Horse (Cont.)

Year	Champion
1987	Tim Daggett
1988	Kevin Davis
1989	Kevin Davis
1990	Patrick Kirksey
1991	Chris Waller
1992	Chris Waller
1993	Chris Waller
1994	Mihai Begiu
1995	Mark Sohn
1996	Josh Stein
1997	John Roethlisberger
1998	John Roethlisberger
1999	John Roethlisberger
2000	John Roethlisberger
2001	Brett McClure
2002	Paul Hamm
2003	Paul Hamm
2004	Brett McClure
2005	Yewki Tomita
2006	Alexander Artemev
2007	Alexander Artemev
2008	Yewki Tomita
2009	Luke Stannard
2010	Daniel Ribiero

Rings

Year	Champion
1963	Art Shurlock
1964	Glen Gailis
1965	Glen Gailis
1966	Glen Gailis
1967	Fred Dennis, Don Hatch
1968	Yoshi Hayasaki
1969	Fred Dennis, Bob Emery
1970	Makoto Sakamoto
1971	Yoshi Takei
1972	Yoshi Takei
1973	Jim Ivicek
1974	Tom Weeder
1975	Tom Beach
1977	Kurt Thomas
1978	Mike Silverstein
1979	Bart Conner
1980	Jim Hartung
1981	Jim Hartung
1982	Jim Hartung, Peter Vidmar
1983	Mitch Gaylord
1984	Jim Hartung
1985	Dan Hayden
1986	Dan Hayden
1987	Scott Johnson
1988	Dan Hayden
1989	Scott Keswick
1990	Scott Keswick
1991	Scott Keswick
1992	Tim Ryan
1993	John Roethlisberger
1994	Scott Keswick
1995	Paul O'Neill
1996	Kip Simons
1997	Blaine Wilson
1998	Jeff Johnson

Rings (Cont.)

Year	Champion
1999	Blaine Wilson
2000	Blaine Wilson
2001	Sean Townsend
2002	Blaine Wilson
2003	Blaine Wilson
2004	Raj Bhavsar
2005	Sean Golden
2006	Kevin Tan
2007	Kevin Tan
2008	Kevin Tan
2009	Jonathan Horton
2010	Brandon Wynn

Vault

Year	Champion
1963	Art Shurlock
1964	Gary Hery
1965	Brent Williams
1966	Dan Millman
1967	Jack Kenan, Sid Jensen
1968	Rich Scorza
1969	Dave Butzman
1970	Makoto Sakamoto
1971	Gary Morava
1972	Mike Kelley
1973	Gary Morava
1974	John Crosby
1975	Tom Beach
1977	Ron Galimore
1978	Jim Hartung
1979	Ron Galimore
1980	Ron Galimore
1981	Ron Galimore
1982	Jim Hartung/Jim Mikus
1983	Chris Reigel
1984	Chris Reigel
1985	Scott Johnson, Mark Oates
1986	Scott Wilbanks
1987	John Sweeney
1988	John Sweeney/Bill Paul
1989	Bill Roth
1990	Lance Ringnald
1991	Scott Keswick
1992	Trent Dimas
1993	Bill Roth
1994	Keith Wiley
1995	David St. Pierre
1996	Blaine Wilson
1997	Blaine Wilson
1998	Brent Klaus
1999	Guard Young
2000	Blaine Wilson
2001	Jason Furr
2002	Paul Hamm
2003	Raj Bhavsar
2004	David Sender
2005	Sean Golden
2006	David Sender
2007	Sean Golden
2008	David Sender
2009	Jake Dalton
2010	Steven Legendre

CHAMPIONS OF THE UNITED STATES - Men *(Cont.)*

Parallel Bars

Year	Champion
1963	Tom Seward
1964	Rusty Mitchell
1965	Glen Gailis
1966	Ray Hadley
1967	Katsuzoki Kanzaki
	Tom Goldsborough
1968	Yoshi Hayasaki
1969	Steve Hug
1970	Makoto Sakamoto
1971	Brent Simmons
1972	Yoshi Takei
1973	Marshall Avener
1974	Jim Ivicek
1975	Bart Conner
1977	Kurt Thomas
1978	Bart Conner
1979	Bart Conner
1980	Phil Cahoy/Larry Gerard
1981	Bart Conner
1982	Peter Vidmar
1983	Mitch Gaylord
1984	Peter Vidmar, Mitch Gaylord, Tim Daggett
1985	Tim Daggett
1986	Tim Daggett
1987	Scott Johnson
1988	D. Hayden/K. Davis
1989	Conrad Voorsanger
1990	Trent Dimas

Parallel Bars *(Cont.)*

Year	Champion
1991	Scott Keswick
1992	Jair Lynch
1993	Chainey Umphrey
1994	Steve McCain
1995	John Roethlisberger
1996	Jair Lynch
1997	Blaine Wilson
1998	Blaine Wilson
1999	Jason Gatson
2000	Trent Wells
2001	Sean Townsend
2002	Sean Townsend
2003	Jason Gatson
2004	Alexander Artemev
2005	D.J. Bucher
2006	Alexander Artemev
2007	David Durante
2008	Justin Spring
2009	Tim McNeill
2010	Danell Leyva

High Bars

Year	Champion
1963	Art Shurlock
1964	Glen Gailis
1965	Rusty Mitchell
1966	Katsuzoki Kanzaki
1967	Katsuzoki Kanzaki
	Jerry Fontana
1968	Yoshi Hayasaki
1969	Rich Grisby
1970	Makoto Sakamoto
1971	Yoshi Takei
1972	Tom Lindner
1973	John Crosby
1974	Brent Simmons
1975	Tom Beach
1977	Kurt Thomas
1978	Kurt Thomas
1979	Yoichi Tomita
1980	Jim Hartung
1981	Bart Conner
1982	Mitch Gaylord
1983	Mario McCutcheon
1983	Mario McCutcheon
1984	Peter Vidmar
	Tim Daggett
	Mitch Gaylord
1985	Dan Hayden
1986	D. Hayden/D. Moriel
1987	David Moriel

High Bars *(Cont.)*

Year	Champion
1988	Dan Hayden
1989	Tim Ryan
1990	Trent Dimas
	Lance Ringnald
1991	Lance Ringnald
1992	Jair Lynch
1993	Steve McCain
1994	Scott Keswick
1995	John Roethlisberger
1996	Bill Roth
1997	Douglas Stibel
1998	Jason Gatson
1999	Jamie Natalie
2000	Trent Wells
	Jamie Natalie
2001	Daniel Diaz-Luong
2002	Blaine Wilson
2003	Paul Hamm
2004	Paul Hamm
2005	D.J. Bucher
2006	Chris Brooks
2007	Justin Spring
2008	Joseph Hagerty
2009	Jonathan Horton
2010	Chris Brooks

CHAMPIONS OF THE UNITED STATES — Women

All-Around

Year	Champion
1963	Donna Schanezer
1965	Gail Daley
1966	Donna Schanezer
1968	Linda Scott
1969	Joyce Tanac Schroeder
1970	Cathy Rigby
1971	Joan Moore Gnat
	Linda Metheny Mulvihill
1972	Joan Moore Gnat
	Cathy Rigby
1973	Joan Moore Gnat
1974	Joan Moore Gnat
1975	Tammy Manville
1976	Denise Cheshire
1977	Donna Turnbow
1978	Kathy Johnson
1979	Leslie Pyfer
1980	Julianne McNamara
1981	Tracee Talavera
1982	Tracee Talavera
1983	Dianne Durham
1984	Mary Lou Retton
1985	Sabrina Mar
1986	Jennifer Sey
1987	Kristie Phillips
1988	Phoebe Mills
1989	Brandy Johnson
1990	Kim Zmeskal
1991	Kim Zmeskal

All-Around *(Cont.)*

Year	Champion
1992	Kim Zmeskal
1993	Shannon Miller
1994	Dominique Dawes
1995	Dominique Moceanu
1996	Shannon Miller
1997	V. Adler/ K. Powell
1998	Kristen Maloney
1999	Kristen Maloney
2000	Elise Ray
2001	Tasha Schwikert
2002	Tasha Schwikert
2003	Courtney Kupets
2004	Courtney Kupets/Carly Patterson
2005	Nastia Liukin
2006	Nastia Liukin
2007	Shawn Johnson
2008	Shawn Johnson
2009	Bridget Sloan
2010	Rebecca Bross

Vault

Year	Champion
1963	Donna Schanezer
1965	Gail Daley
1966	Donna Schanezer
1968	Terry Spencer
1969	Joyce Tanac Schroeder
	Cleo Carver
1970	Cathy Rigby

Vault *(Cont.)*

Year	Champion
1971	Joan Moore Gnat/Adele Gleaves
1972	Cindy Eastwood
1973	Roxanne Pierce Mancha
1974	Dianne Dunbar
1975	Kolleen Casey
1976	Debbie Wilcox
1977	Lisa Cawthron
1978	Rhonda Schwandt/Sharon Shapiro
1979	Christa Canary
1980	J. McNamara/B. Kline
1981	Kim Neal
1982	Yumi Mordre
1983	Dianne Durham
1984	Mary Lou Retton
1985	Yolanda Mavity
1986	Joyce Wilborn
1987	Rhonda Faehn
1988	Rhonda Faehn
1989	Brandy Johnson
1990	Brandy Johnson
1991	Kerri Strug
1992	Kerri Strug
1993	Dominique Dawes
1994	Dominique Dawes
1995	Shannon Miller
1996	Dominique Dawes
1997	Vanessa Atler
1998	Dominique Moceanu
1999	Vanessa Atler
2000	Kristen Maloney

CHAMPIONS OF THE UNITED STATES— Women *(Cont.)*

Vault *(Cont.)*

Year	Champion
2001	Mohini Bhardwaj
2002	Elizabeth Tricase
2003	Annia Hatch
2004	Liz Tricase
2005	Alicia Sacramone
2006	Alicia Sacramone
2007	Alicia Sacramone
2008	Alicia Sacramone
2009	Kayla Williams
2010	Alicia Sacramone

Uneven Bars

Year	Champion
1963	Donna Schanezer
1965	Irene Haworth
1966	Donna Schanezer
1968	Linda Scott
1969	Joyce Tanac Schroeder
	Lisa Nelson
1970	Roxanne Pierce Mancha
1971	Joan Moore Gnat
1972	Cathy Rigby
1973	Roxanne Pierce Mancha
1974	Diane Dunbar
1975	Leslie Wolfsberger
1976	Leslie Wolfsberger
1977	Donna Turnbow
1978	Marcia Frederick
1979	Marcia Frederick
1980	Marcia Frederick
1981	Julianne McNamara
1982	Marie Roethlisberger
1983	Julianne McNamara
1984	Julianne McNamara
1985	Sabrina Mar
1986	Marie Roethlisberger
1987	Melissa Marlowe
1988	Chelle Stack
1989	Chelle Stack
1990	Sandy Woolsey
1991	Elisabeth Crandall
1992	Dominique Dawes
1993	Shannon Miller
1994	Dominique Dawes
1995	Dominique Dawes
1996	Dominique Dawes
1997	Kristy Powell
1998	Elise Ray
1999	Jamie Dantzscher
	Jennie Thompson
2000	Elise Ray
2001	Katie Heenan
2002	Tasha Schwikert
2003	Katie Heenan
2004	Courtney Kupets
2005	Nastia Liukin
2006	Nastia Liukin
2007	Nastia Liukin
2008	Nastia Liukin
2009	Bridget Sloan
2010	Rebecca Bross

Balance Beam

Year	Champion
1963	Leissa Krol
1965	Gail Daley
1966	Irene Haworth
	Linda Scott
1968	Linda Scott
1969	Lonna Woodward
1970	Joyce Tanac Schroeder
1971	Linda Metheny Mulvihill
1972	Kim Chace
1973	Nancy Thies Marshall
1974	Joan Moore Gnat
1975	Kyle Gayner
1976	Carrie Englert
1977	Donna Turnbow
1978	Christa Canary
1979	Heidi Anderson
1980	Kelly Garrison-Steves
1981	Tracee Talavera
1982	Julianne McNamara
1983	Dianne Durham
1984	Pam Bileck
	Tracee Talavera
1986	Angie Denkins
1987	Kristie Phillips
1985	Kelly Garrison-Steves
1988	Kelly Garrison-Steves
1989	Brandy Johnson
1990	Betty Okino
1991	Shannon Miller
1992	Kerri Strug
	Kim Zmeskal
1993	Dominique Dawes
1994	Dominique Dawes
1995	Doni Thompson
	Monica Flammer
1996	Dominique Dawes
1997	Kendall Beck
1998	Dominique Moceanu
1999	Vanessa Atler
2000	Alyssa Beckerman
	Amy Chow
2001	Tasha Schwikert
2002	Tasha Schwikert
2003	Hollie Vise
2004	Courtney Kupets
2005	Nastia Liukin
2006	Nastia Liukin
2007	Shawn Johnson
2008	Nastia Liukin
2009	Ivana Hong
2010	Rebecca Bross

Floor Exercise

Year	Champion
1963	Donna Schanezer
1965	Gail Daley
1966	Donna Schanezer
1968	Linda Scott
1970	Cathy Rigby
1971	Joan Moore Gnat
	Linda Metheny Mulvihill
1972	Joan Moore Gnat
1973	Joan Moore Gnat
1974	Joan Moore Gnat
1975	Kathy Howard
1976	Carrie Englert
1977	Kathy Johnson
1978	Kathy Johnson
1979	Heidi Anderson
1980	Beth Kline
1981	Michelle Goodwin
1982	Amy Koopman
1983	Dianne Durham
1984	Mary Lou Retton
1985	Sabrina Mar
1986	Yolanda Mavity
1987	Kristie Phillips
1988	Phoebe Mills
1989	Brandy Johnson
1990	Brandy Johnson
1991	Kim Zmeskal
	Dominique Dawes
1992	Kim Zmeskal
1993	Shannon Miller
1994	Dominique Dawes
1995	Dominique Dawes
1996	Dominique Dawes
1997	Lindsay Wing
1998	Vanessa Atler
1999	Elise Ray
2000	Kristen Maloney
2001	Tabitha Yim
2002	Tasha Schwikert
2003	Ashley Postell
2004	Carly Patterson
2005	Alicia Sacramone
2006	Alicia Sacramone
	Randi Stageberg
2007	Shawn Johnson
2008	Shawn Johnson
2009	Bridget Sloan
2010	Mattie Larson

Skiing

2009–10 World Cup Alpine Final Season Standings

Men

	Pts
OVERALL Carlo Janka, Switzerland	1197
DOWNHILL Didier Cuche, Switzerland	528
SLALOM Reifried Herbst, Austria	534
GIANT SLALOM Ted Ligety, United States	412
SUPER G Erik Guay, Canada	331
COMBINED Benjamin Raich, Austria	246

Women

	Pts
OVERALL Lindsey Vonn, United States	1671
DOWNHILL Lindsey Vonn, United States	725
SLALOM Maria Riesch, Germany	493
GIANT SLALOM Kathrin Hoelzl, Germany	471
SUPER G Lindsey Vonn, United States	620
COMBINED Lindsey Vonn, United States	160

World Cup Season Title Holders

Men – OVERALL

1967	Jean-Claude Killy, France
1968	Jean-Claude Killy, France
1969	Karl Schranz, Austria
1970	Karl Schranz, Austria
1971	Gustavo Thoeni, Italy
1972	Gustavo Thoeni, Italy
1973	Gustavo Thoeni, Italy
1974	Piero Gros, Italy
1975	Gustavo Thoeni, Italy
1976	Ingemar Stenmark, Sweden
1977	Ingemar Stenmark, Sweden
1978	Ingemar Stenmark, Sweden
1979	Peter Lüscher, Switzerland
1980	Andreas Wenzel, Liechtenstein
1981	Phil Mahre, United States
1982	Phil Mahre, United States
1983	Phil Mahre, United States
1984	Pirmin Zurbriggen, Switzerland
1985	Marc Girardelli, Luxembourg
1986	Marc Girardelli, Luxembourg
1987	Pirmin Zurbriggen, Switzerland
1988	Pirmin Zurbriggen, Switzerland
1989	Marc Girardelli, Luxembourg
1990	Pirmin Zurbriggen, Switzerland
1991	Marc Girardelli, Luxembourg
1992	Paul Accola, Switzerland
1993	Marc Girardelli, Luxembourg
1994	Kjetil André Aamodt, Norway
1995	Alberto Tomba, Italy
1996	Lasse Kjus, Norway
1997	Luc Alphand, France
1998	Hermann Maier, Austria
1999	Lasse Kjus, Norway
2000	Hermann Maier, Austria
2001	Hermann Maier, Austria
2002	Stephan Eberharter, Austria
2003	Stephan Eberharter, Austria
2004	Hermann Maier, Austria
2005	Bode Miller, United States
2006	Benjamin Raich, Austria
2007	Aksel Lund Svindal, Norway
2008	Bode Miller, United States
2009	Aksel Lund Svindal, Norway
2010	Carlo Janka, Switzerland

Women – OVERALL

1967	Nancy Greene, Canada
1968	Nancy Greene, Canada
1969	Gertrud Gabl, Austria
1970	Michèle Jacot, France
1971	Annemarie Pröll, Austria
1972	Annemarie Pröll, Austria
1973	Annemarie Pröll, Austria
1974	Annemarie Moser-Proell, Austria
1975	Annemarie Moser-Proell, Austria
1976	Rosi Mitermaier, W Germany
1977	Lise-Marie Morerod, Switzerland
1978	Hanni Wenzel, Liechtenstein
1979	Annemarie Moser-Proell, Austria
1980	Hanni Wenzel, Liechtenstein
1981	Marie-Thérèse Nadig, Switzerland
1982	Erika Hess, Switzerland
1983	Tamara McKinney, United States
1984	Erika Hess, Switzerland
1985	Michela Figini, Switzerland
1986	Maria Walliser, Switzerland
1987	Maria Walliser, Switzerland
1988	Michela Figini, Switzerland
1989	Vreni Schneider, Switzerland
1990	Petra Kronberger, Austria
1991	Petra Kronberger, Austria
1992	Petra Kronberger, Austria
1993	Anita Wachter, Austria
1994	Vreni Schneider, Switzerland
1995	Vreni Schneider, Switzerland
1996	Katja Seizinger, Germany
1997	Pernilla Wiberg, Sweden
1998	Katja Seizinger, Germany
1999	Alexandra Meissnitzer, Austria
2000	Renate Goetschl, Austria
2001	Janica Kostelic, Croatia
2002	Michaela Dorfmeister, Austria
2003	Janica Kostelic, Croatia
2004	Anja Paerson, Sweden
2005	Anja Paerson, Sweden
2006	Janica Kostelic, Croatia
2007	Nicole Hosp, Austria
2008	Lindsey Vonn, United States
2009	Lindsey Vonn, United States
2010	Lindsey Vonn, United States

United States National Champions

1983
FREESTYLE
- 105.5 ......Rich Salamone
- 114.5 ......Joe Gonzales
- 125.5 ......Joe Corso
- 136.5 ......Rich Dellagatta*
- 149.5 ......Bill Hugent
- 163 ....Lee Kemp
- 180.5 ......Chris Campbell
- 198 ....Pete Bush
- 220 ....Greg Gibson
- Hvy ....Bruce Baumgartner
- Team.......Sunkist Kids

GRECO-ROMAN
- 105.5 ......T.J. Jones
- 114.5 ......Mark Fuller
- 125.5 ......Rob Hermann
- 136.5 ......Dan Mello
- 149.5 ......Jim Martinez
- 163 ....James Andre
- 180.5 ......Steve Goss
- 198 ....Steve Fraser*
- 220 ....Dennis Koslowski
- Hvy ....No champion
- Team.......Minn. Wrestling Club

1984
FREESTYLE
- 105.5 ......Rich Salamone
- 114.5 ......Charlie Heard
- 125.5 ......Joe Corso
- 136.5 ......Rich Dellagatta*
- 149.5 ......Andre Metzger
- 163 ....Dave Schultz*
- 180.5 ......Mark Schultz
- 198 ....Steve Fraser
- 220 ....Harold Smith
- Hvy ....Bruce Baumgartner
- Team.......Sunkist Kids

GRECO-ROMAN
- 105.5 ......T.J. Jones
- 114.5 ......Mark Fuller
- 136.5 ......Dan Mello
- 149.5 ......Jim Martinez*
- 163 ....John Matthews
- 180.5 ......Tom Press
- 198 ....Mike Houck
- 220 ....No champion
- Hvy ....No champion
- Team.......Adirondack 3-Style, Wash.

1985
FREESTYLE
- 105.5 ......Tim Vanni
- 114.5 ......Jim Martin
- 125.5 ......Charlie Heard
- 136.5 ......Darryl Burley
- 149.5 ......Bill Nugent*
- 163 ....Kenny Monday
- 180.5 ......Mike Sheets
- 198 ....Mark Schultz
- 220 ....Greg Gibson
- 286 ....Bruce Baumgartner
- Team.......Sunkist Kids

1985 *(Cont.)*
GRECO-ROMAN
- 105.5 ......T.J. Jones
- 114.5 ......Mark Fuller
- 125.5 ......Eric Seward*
- 136.5 ......Buddy Lee
- 149.5 ......Jim Martinez
- 163 ....David Butler
- 180.5 ......Chris Catallo
- 198 ....Mike Houck
- 220 ....Greg Gibson
- 286 ....Dennis Koslowski
- Team.......U.S. Marine Corps

1986
FREESTYLE
- 105.5 ......Rich Salamone
- 114.5 ......Joe Gonzales
- 125.5 ......Kevin Darkus
- 136.5 ......John Smith
- 149.5 ......Andre Metzger*
- 163 ....Dave Schultz
- 180.5 ......Mark Schultz
- 198 ....Jim Scherr
- 220 ....Dan Severn
- 286 ....Bruce Baumgartner
- Team.......Sunkist Kids (Div. I)
- ....Hawkeye Wrestling
- ....Club (Div. II)

GRECO-ROMAN
- 105.5 ......Eric Wetzel
- 114.5 ......Shawn Sheldon
- 125.5 ......Anthony Amado
- 136.5 ......Frank Famiano
- 149.5 ......Jim Martinez
- 163 ....David Butler*
- 180.5 ......Darryl Gholar
- 198 ....Derrick Waldroup
- 220 ....Dennis Koslowski
- 286 ....Duane Koslowski
- Team .......U.S. Marine Corps (Div. I)
- .............U.S. Navy (Div. II)

1987
FREESTYLE
- 105.5 ......Takashi Irie
- 114.5 ......Mitsuru Sato
- 125.5 ......Barry Davis
- 136.5 ......Takumi Adachi
- 149.5 ......Andre Metzger
- 163 ....Dave Schultz*
- 180.5 ......Mark Schultz
- 198 ....Jim Scherr
- 220 ....Bill Scherr
- 286 ....Bruce Baumgartner
- Team.......Sunkist Kids (Div. I)
- ....Team Foxcatcher (Div. II)

1987 *(Cont.)*
GRECO-ROMAN
- 105.5 ......Eric Wetzel
- 114.5 ......Shawn Sheldon
- 125.5 ......Eric Seward
- 136.5 ......Frank Famiano
- 149.5 ......Jim Martinez
- 163 ....David Butler
- 180.5 ......Chris Catallo
- 198 ....Derrick Waldroup*
- 220 ....Dennis Koslowski
- 286 ....Duane Koslowski
- Team .......U.S. Marine Corp (Div. I)
- .............U.S. Army (Div. II)

1988
FREESTYLE
- 105.5 ......Tim Vanni
- 114.5 ......Joe Gonzales
- 125.5 ......Kevin Darkus
- 136.5 ......John Smith*
- 149.5 ......Nate Carr
- 163 ....Kenny Monday
- 180.5 ......Dave Schultz
- 198 ....Melvin Douglas III
- 220 ....Bill Scherr
- 286 ....Bruce Baumgartner
- Team.......Sunkist Kids (Div. I)
- ....Team Foxcatcher (Div. II)

GRECO-ROMAN
- 105.5 ......T.J. Jones
- 114.5 ......Shawn Sheldon
- 125.5 ......Gogi Parseghian*
- 136.5 ......Dalen Wasmund
- 149.5 ......Craig Pollard
- 163 ....Tony Thomas
- 180.5 ......Darryl Gholar
- 198 ....Mike Carolan
- 220 ....Dennis Koslowski
- 286 ....Duane Koslowski
- Team.......U.S. Marine Corps (Div. I)
- ....Sunkist Kids (Div. II)

1989
FREESTYLE
- 105.5 ......Tim Vanni
- 114.5 ......Zeke Jones
- 125.5 ......Brad Penrith
- 136.5 ......John Smith
- 149.5 ......Nate Carr
- 163 ....Rob Koll
- 180.5 ......Rico Chiapparelli
- 198 ....Jim Scherr*
- 220 ....Bill Scherr
- 286 ....Bruce Baumgartner
- Team.......Sunkist Kids (Div. I)
- ....Team Foxcatcher (Div. II)

*Outstanding wrestler.

United States National Champions

1989*(Cont.)*
GRECO-ROMAN
105.5 ....Lew Dorrance
114.5 ....Mark Fuller
125.5 ....Gogi Parseghian
136.5 ....Isaac Anderson
149.5 ....Andy Seras*
163 ....David Butler
180.5 ....John Morgan
198 ....Michial Foy
220 ....Steve Lawson
286 ....Craig Pittman
Team........USMC (Div. I)
              Jets USA (Div. II)

1990
FREESTYLE
105.5 ....Rob Eiter
114.5 ....Zeke Jones
125.5 ....Joe Melchiore
136.5 ....John Smith
149.5 ....Nate Carr
163 ....Rob Koll
180.5 ....Royce Alger
198 ....Chris Campbell*
220 ....Bill Scherr
286 ....Bruce Baumgartner
Team........Sunkist Kids (Div. I)
              Team Foxcatcher (Div. II)

GRECO-ROMAN
105.5 ....Lew Dorrance
114.5 ....Sam Henson
125.5 ....Mark Pustelnik
136.5 ....Isaac Anderson
149.5 ....Andy Seras
163 ....David Butler
180.5 ....Derrick Waldroup
198 ....Randy Couture*
220 ....Chris Tironi
286 ....Matt Ghaffari
Team........Jets USA (Div. I)
              California Jets (Div. II)

1991
FREESTYLE
105.5 ....Tim Vanni
114.5 ....Zeke Jones
125.5 ....Brad Penrith
136.5 ....John Smith*
149.5 ....Townsend Saunders
163 ....Kenny Monday
180.5 ....Kevin Jackson
198 ....Chris Campbell
220 ....Mark Coleman
286 ....Bruce Baumgartner
Team........Sunkist Kids (Div. I)
              Jets USA (Div. II)

1991*(Cont.)*
GRECO-ROMAN
105.5 ....Eric Wetzel
114.5 ....Shawn Sheldon
125.5 ....Frank Famiano
136.5 ....Buddy Lee
149.5 ....Andy Seras
163 ....Gordy Morgan
180.5 ....John Morgan*
198 ....Michial Foy
220 ....Dennis Koslowski
286 ....Craig Pittman
Team........Jets USA (Div. I)
              Sunkist Kids (Div. II)

1992
FREESTYLE
105.5 ....Rob Eiter
114.5 ....Jack Griffin
125.5 ....Kendall Cross*
136.5 ....John Fisher
149.5 ....Matt Demaray
163 ....Greg Elinsky
180.5 ....Royce Alger
198 ....Dan Chaid
220 ....Bill Scherr
286 ....Bruce Baumgartner
Team........Sunkist Kids (Div. I)
              Team Foxcatcher (Div. II)

GRECO-ROMAN
105.5 ....Eric Wetzel
114.5 ....Mark Fuller
125.5 ....Dennis Hall
136.5 ....Buddy Lee*
149.5 ....Rodney Smith
163 ....Travis West
180.5 ....John Morgan
198 ....Michial Foy
220 ....Dennis Koslowski
286 ....Matt Ghaffari
Team........N.Y. Athletic Club (Div. I)
              Sunkist Kids (Div. II)

1993
FREESTYLE
105.5 ....Rob Eiter
114.5 ....Zeke Jones
125.5 ....Brad Penrith
136.5 ....Tom Brands
149.5 ....Matt Demaray
163 ....Dave Schultz*
180.5 ....Kevin Jackson
198 ....Melvin Douglas
220 ....Kirk Trost
286 ....Bruce Baumgartner
Team........Sunkist Kids (Div. I)
              Team Foxcatcher (Div. II)

1993*(Cont.)*
GRECO-ROMAN
105.5 ....Eric Wetzel
114.5 ....Shawn Sheldon
125.5 ....Dennis Hall*
136.5 ....Shon Lewis
149.5 ....Andy Seras
163 ....Gordy Morgan
180.5 ....Dan Henderson
198 ....Randy Couture
220 ....James Johnson
286 ....Matt Ghaffari
Team........N.Y. Athletic Club (Div. I)
              Sunkist Kids (Div. II)

1994
FREESTYLE
105.5 ....Tim Vanni
114.5 ....Zeke Jones
125.5 ....Terry Brands
136.5 ....Tom Brands
149.5 ....Matt Demaray
163 ....Dave Schultz
180.5 ....Royce Alger
198 ....Melvin Douglas
220 ....Mark Kerr
286 ....Bruce Baumgartner*
Team........Sunkist Kids (Div. I)
              Team Foxcatcher (Div. II)

GRECO-ROMAN
105.5 ....Isaac Ramaswamy
114.5 ....Shawn Sheldon
125.5 ....Dennis Hall
136.5 ....Shon Lewis
149.5 ....Andy Seras*
163 ....Gordy Morgan
180.5 ....Dan Henderson
198 ....Derrick Waldroup
220 ....James Johnson
286 ....Matt Ghaffari
Team........Armed Forces (Div. I)
              N.Y. Athletic Club (Div. II)

1995
FREESTYLE
105.5 ....Tim Vanni
114.5 ....Zeke Jones
125.5 ....Terry Brands
136.5 ....Tom Brands
149.5 ....Matt Demaray
163 ....Dave Schultz
180.5 ....Royce Alger
198 ....Melvin Douglas
220 ....Mark Kerr
286 ....Bruce Baumgartner*
Team........Sunkist Kids (Div. I)
              Team Foxcatcher (Div. II)

*Outstanding wrestler.

United States National Champions *(Cont.)*

1995 *(Cont.)*
GRECO-ROMAN

105.5	Isaac Ramaswamy
114.5	Shawn Sheldon
125.5	Dennis Hall
136.5	Shon Lewis
149.5	Andy Seras*
163	Gordy Morgan
180.5	Dan Henderson
198	Derrick Waldroup
220	James Johnson
286	Matt Ghaffari
Team	Armed Forces (Div. I)
	N.Y. Athletic Club (Div. II)

1996
FREESTYLE

105.5	Rob Eiter
114.5	Lou Rosselli
125.5	Kendall Cross*
136.5	Tom Brands
149.5	Matt Demaray
163	Dave Schultz
180.5	Kevin Jackson
198	Melvin Douglas
220	Kurt Angle
286	Bruce Baumgartner
Team	Sunkist Kids (Div. I)
	Team Foxcatcher (Div. II)

GRECO-ROMAN

105.5	Isaac Ramaswamy
114.5	Shawn Sheldon
125.5	Dennis Hall*
136.5	Van Fronhofer
149.5	Heath Sims
163	Matt Lindland
180.5	Marty Morgan
198	Michial Foy
220	James Johnson
286	Rulon Gardner
Team	Armed Forces (Div. I)
	Sunkist Kids (Div. II)

1997
FREESTYLE

110	Kanamti Soloman
119	Zeke Jones
127.75	Terry Brands
138.75	Carl Kolat
152	Lincoln McIlravy*
167.5	Dan St. John
187.25	Les Gutches
213.75	Melvin Douglas
275.5	Tom Erikson
Team	Sunkist Kids (Div. I)
	N.Y. Athletic Club (Div. II)

GRECO-ROMAN

110	Mark Yanagihara
119	Broderick Lee
127.75	Dennis Hall
138.75	Kevin Bracken
152	Chris Saba
167.5	Miguel Spencer
187.25	Dan Henderson
213.75	Randy Couture*
275.5	Rulon Gardner
Team	Armed Forces (Div. I)
	N.Y. Athletic Club (Div. II)

1998
FREESTYLE

119	Sam Henson
127.75	Tony Purler
138.75	Shawn Charles
152	Lincoln McIlravy
167.5	Steve Marianetti
187.25	Les Gutches*
213.75	Melvin Douglas
286	Tolly Thompson
Team	Sunkist Kids (Div. I)
	N.Y. Athletic Club (Div. II)

GRECO-ROMAN

119	Shawn Sheldon
127.75	Dennis Hall
138.75	Shon Lewis
152	Chris Saba
167.5	Matt Lindland
187.25	Dan Niebuhr*
213.75	Jason Klohs
286	Matt Ghaffari
Team	Armed Forces (Div. I)
	Sunkist Kids (Div. II)

1999
FREESTYLE

119	Lou Rosselli
127.75	Terry Brands
138.75	Cary Kolat
152	Lincoln McIlravy
167.5	Joe Williams
187.25	Les Gutches
213.75	Dominic Black
286	Stephen Neal*
Team	Sunkist Kids (Div. I)
	N.Y. Athletic Club (Div. II)

GRECO-ROMAN

119	Steven Mays
127.75	Dennis Hall
138.75	Glen Nieradka
152	David Zuniga
167.5	Matt Lindland
187.25	Quincey Clark
213.75	Randy Couture
286	Dremiel Byers*
Team	Minnesota Storm (Div. I)
	Sunkist Kids (Div. II)

2000
FREESTYLE

119	Sammie Henson
127.75	Keyy Boumans
138.75	Cary Kolat
152	Lincoln McIlravy
167.5	Brandon Slay*
187.25	Les Gutches
213.75	Melvin Douglas
286	Kerry McCoy
Team	Sunkist Kids (Div. I)
	N.Y. Athletic Club (Div. II)

2000 *(Cont.)*
GRECO-ROMAN

119	Brandon Paulson
127.75	Dennis Hall
138.75	Kevin Bracken
152	Heath Sims
167.5	Matt Lindland
187.25	Quincey Clark*
213.75	Jason Gleasman
286	Rulon Gardner
Team	Armed Forces (Div. I)
	Sunkist Kids (Div. II)

2001
FREESTYLE

119	Eric Akin
127.75	Eric Guerrero
138.75	Bill Zadick
152	Ramico Blackmon
167.5	Joe Williams
187.25	Cael Sanderson*
213.75	Dominic Black
286	Kerry McCoy
Team	Sunkist Kids (Div. I)
	New York A.C. (Div. II)

GRECO-ROMAN

119	Jeff Cervone
127.75	Dennis Hall
138.75	Kevin Bracken
152	Marcel Cooper
167.5	Keith Sieracki
187.25	Matt Lindland*
213.75	Garrett Lowney
286	Rulon Gardner
Team	U.S. Army (Div. I)
	Sunkist Kids (Div. II)

2002
FREESTYLE

121	Teague Moore
132	Eric Guerrero
145.5	Bill Zadick
163	Joe Williams*
185	Cael Sanderson
211.5	Tim Hartung
264.5	Kerry McCoy
Team	Sunkist Kids (Div. I)
	New York A.C. (Div. II)

GRECO-ROMAN

121	Brandon Paulson
132	Glenn Nieradka*
145.5	Kevin Bracken
163	Keith Sieracki
185	Ethan Bosch
211.75	Garrett Lowney
264.5	Dremiel Byers
Team	U.S. Army (Div. I)
	New York A.C. (Div. II)

---

*Outstanding wrestler.

Wrestling (Cont.)

United States National Champions

2003

FREESTYLE

121	Stephen Abas
132	Eric Guerrero*
145.5	Chris Bono
163	Joe Williams
185	Cael Sanderson
211.5	Daniel Cormier
264.5	Kerry McCoy
Team	Sunkist Kids (Div. I)
	Gator WC (Div. II)

GRECO-ROMAN

121	Brandon Paulson
132	James Gruenwald*
145.5	Kevin Bracken
163	Keith Sieracki
185	Brad Vering
211.5	Garrett Lowney
264.5	Dremiel Byers
Team	U.S. Army (Div. I)
	Air Force (Div. II)

2004

FREESTYLE

121	Stephen Abbas
132	Eric Guerrero
145.5	Jamill Kelly
163	Joe Williams
185	Lee Fullhart*
211.5	Daniel Cormier
264.5	Kerry McCoy
Team	Sunkist Kids (Div. I)
	Gator WC (Div. II)

GRECO-ROMAN

121	Brandon Paulson
132	James Gruenwald
145.5	Faruk Sahin
163	Darryl Christian
185	Brad Vering
211.5	Justin Ruiz
264.5	Dremiel Byers*
Team	New York A.C. (Div. I)
	Air Force (Div. II)

2005

FREESTYLE

121	Sam Henson
132	Michael Lightner*
145.5	Chris Bono
163	Joe Williams
185	Mo Lawal
211.5	Daniel Cormier
264.5	Tolly Thompson
Team	Sunkist Kids (Div. I)
	Gator WC (Div. II)

GRECO-ROMAN

121	Sam Hazewinkel
132	Joseph Warren
145.5	Harry Lester
163	Darryl Christian
185	Brad Vering
211.5	Justin Ruiz
264.5	Dremiel Byers*
Team	New York A.C. (Div.I)
	Air Force (Div. II)

2006

FREESTYLE

121	Henry Cejudo
132	Zach Roberson
145.5	Chris Bono
163	Donny Pritzlaff*
185	Mo Lawal
211.5	Daniel Cormier
264.5	Tolly Thompson
Team	Sunkist Kids (Div. I)
	Gator WC (Div. II)

GRECO-ROMAN

121	Lindsey Durlacher
132	Joseph Warren
145.5	Marcel Cooper
163	T.C. Dantzler
185	Jacob Clark*
211.5	Justin Ruiz
264.5	Dremiel Byers
Team	U.S. Army (Div. I)
	New York A.C. (Div. II)

2007

FREESTYLE

121	Henry Cejudo
132	Nate Gallick*
145.5	Chris Bono
163	Joe Heskett
185	Joe Williams
211.5	Daniel Cormier
264.5	Tommy Rowlands
Team	Sunkist Kids (Div. I)
	Gator WC (Div. II)

GRECO-ROMAN

121	Sam Hazewinkel*
132	Joseph Warren
145.5	Glenn Garrison
163	T.C. Dantzler
185	Brad Vering
211.5	Justin Ruiz
264.5	Russ Davie
Team	U.S. Army (Div. I)
	New York A.C. (Div. II)

2008

FREESTYLE

121	Matt Azevedo*
132	Shawn Bunch
145.5	Doug Schwab
163	Ben Askren
185	Mo Lawal
211.5	Daniel Cormier
264.5	Tommy Rowlands
Team	Sunkist Kids (Div. I)
	New York A.C. (Div. II)

GRECO-ROMAN

121	Spencer Mango*
132	Jim Gruenwald
145.5	Mark Rial
163	T.C. Dantzler
185	Brad Ahearn
211.5	Justin Ruiz
264.5	Dremiel Byers
Team	U.S. Army (Div. I)
	New York A.C. (Div. II)

2009

FREESTYLE

121	Nick Simmons
132	Mike Zadick
145.5	Trent Paulson
163	Travis Paulson
185	Jake Herbert*
211.5	Jake Varner
264.5	Steve Mocco
Team	Sunkist Kids (Div. I)
	Gator WC (Div. II)

GRECO-ROMAN

121	Jermaine Hodge
132	Joe Betterman
145.5	Faruk Sahin
163	Harry Lester*
185	T.C. Dantzler
211.5	Brad Ahearn
264.5	Dremiel Byers
Team	U.S. Army (Div. I)
	Sunkist Kids (Div. II)

2010

FREESTYLE

121	Obe Blanc
132	Shawn Bunch
145.5	Jared Frayer
163	Andrew Howe*
185	Jake Herbert
211.5	J.D. Bergman
264.5	Les Sigman
Team	New York AC (Div. I)
	Gator WC (Div. II)

GRECO-ROMAN

121	Spenser Mango
132	Nathan Piasecki
145.5	Glenn Garrison
163	Jake Fisher
185	Cheney Haight*
211.5	Justin Ruiz
264.5	Brandon Rupp
Team	U.S. Army (Div. I)
	Sunkist Kids (Div. II)

*Outstanding wrestler.

Awards

DOUBLE ISSUE

SPORTSMAN of the YEAR

Sports Illustrated

SI.COM

Yankees Shortstop
DEREK JETER

161 Street-
Yankee Stadium
Station

Ⓑ Ⓓ ④

161 St & River Av NE

**SPORTS ILLUSTRATED'S
2009 Sportsman of the Year
Derek Jeter**

FOR THE RECORD · Year by Year

Athlete Awards

Sports Illustrated Sportsman of the Year

1954	Roger Bannister, Track and Field	1977	Steve Cauthen, Horse Racing
1955	Johnny Podres, Baseball	1978	Jack Nicklaus, Golf
1956	Bobby Morrow, Track and Field	1979	Terry Bradshaw, Pro Football
1957	Stan Musial, Baseball		Willie Stargell, Baseball
1958	Rafer Johnson, Track and Field	1980	U.S. Olympic Hockey Team
1959	Ingemar Johansson, Boxing	1981	Sugar Ray Leonard, Boxing
1960	Arnold Palmer, Golf	1982	Wayne Gretzky, Hockey
1961	Jerry Lucas, Basketball	1983	Mary Decker, Track and Field
1962	Terry Baker, Football	1984	Mary Lou Retton, Gymnastics
1963	Pete Rozelle, Pro Football		Edwin Moses, Track and Field
1964	Ken Venturi, Golf	1985	Kareem Abdul-Jabbar, Pro Basketball
1965	Sandy Koufax, Baseball	1986	Joe Paterno, Football
1966	Jim Ryun, Track and Field	1987	Athletes Who Care:
1967	Carl Yastrzemski, Baseball		Bob Bourne, Hockey
1968	Bill Russell, Pro Basketball		Kip Keino, Track and Field
1969	Tom Seaver, Baseball		Judi Brown King, Track and Field
1970	Bobby Orr, Hockey		Dale Murphy, Baseball
1971	Lee Trevino, Golf		Chip Rives, Football
1972	B.J. King, Tennis/ J. Wooden, Bask		Patty Sheehan, Golf
1973	Jackie Stewart, Auto Racing		Rory Sparrow, Pro Basketball
1974	Muhammad Ali, Boxing		Reggie Williams, Pro Football
1975	Pete Rose, Baseball	1988	Orel Hershiser, Baseball
1976	Chris Evert, Tennis	1989	Greg LeMond, Cycling
		1990	Joe Montana, Pro Football
		1991	Michael Jordan, Pro Basketball
		1992	Arthur Ashe, Tennis
		1993	Don Shula, Pro Football
		1994	Bonnie Blair, Speed Skating
			Johann Olav Koss, Speed Skating
		1995	Cal Ripken Jr, Baseball
		1996	Tiger Woods, Golf
		1997	Dean Smith, College Basketball
		1998	Mark McGwire, Sammy Sosa, Baseball
		1999	U.S. Women's Soccer Team
		2000	Tiger Woods, Golf
		2001	C. Schilling/ R. Johnson, Baseball
		2002	Lance Armstrong, Cycling
		2003	Tim Duncan/David Robinson, Basketball
		2004	Boston Red Sox, Baseball
		2005	Tom Brady, Pro Football
		2006	Dwyane Wade, Pro Basketball
		2007	Brett Favre, Pro Football
		2008	Michael Phelps, Swimming
		2009	Derek Jeter, Baseball

Associated Press Athletes of the Year

	MEN	WOMEN		MEN	WOMEN
1931	Pepper Martin, Baseball	Helene Madison, Swimming	1958	Herb Elliott, Track and Field	Althea Gibson, Tennis
1932	Gene Sarazen, Golf	Babe Didrikson, Track and Field	1959	Ingemar Johansson, Boxing	Maria Bueno, Tennis
1933	Carl Hubbell, Baseball	Helen Jacobs, Tennis	1960	Rafer Johnson, Track and Field	Wilma Rudolph, Track and Field
1934	Dizzy Dean, Baseball	Virginia Van Wie, Golf	1961	Roger Maris, Baseball	Wilma Rudolph, Track and Field
1935	Joe Louis, Boxing	Helen Wills Moody, Tennis	1962	Maury Wills, Baseball	Dawn Fraser, Swimming
1936	Jesse Owens, Track and Field	Helen Stephens, Track and Field	1963	Sandy Koufax, Baseball	Mickey Wright, Golf
1937	Don Budge, Tennis	Katherine Rawls, Swimming	1964	Don Schollander, Swimming	Mickey Wright, Golf
1938	Don Budge, Tennis	Patty Berg, Golf	1965	Sandy Koufax, Baseball	Kathy Whitworth, Golf
1939	Nile Kinnick, Football	Alice Marble, Tennis	1966	Frank Robinson, Baseball	Kathy Whitworth, Golf
1940	Tom Harmon, Football	Alice Marble, Tennis	1967	Carl Yastrzemski, Baseball	Billie Jean King, Tennis
1941	Joe DiMaggio, Baseball	Betty Hicks Newell, Golf	1968	Denny McLain, Baseball	Peggy Fleming, Skating
1942	Frank Sinkwich, Football	Gloria Callen, Swimming	1969	Tom Seaver, Baseball	Debbie Meyer, Swimming
1943	Gunder Haegg, Track and Field	Patty Berg, Golf	1970	George Blanda, Pro Football	Chi Cheng, Track and Field
1944	Byron Nelson, Golf	Ann Curtis, Swimming	1971	Lee Trevino, Golf	Evonne Goolagong, Tennis
1945	Bryon Nelson, Golf	Babe Didrikson Zaharias, Golf	1972	Mark Spitz, Swimming	Olga Korbut, Gymnastics
1946	Glenn Davis, Football	Babe Didrikson Zaharias, Golf	1973	O.J. Simpson, Pro Football	Billie Jean King, Tennis
1947	Johnny Lujack, Football	Babe Didrikson Zaharias, Golf	1974	Muhammad Ali, Boxing	Chris Evert, Tennis
1948	Lou Boudreau, Baseball	Fanny Blankers-Koen, Track and Field	1975	Fred Lynn, Baseball	Chris Evert, Tennis
1949	Leon Hart, Football	Marlene Bauer, Golf	1976	Bruce Jenner, Track and Field	Nadia Comaneci, Gymnastics
1950	Jim Konstanty, Baseball	Babe Didrikson Zaharias, Golf	1977	Steve Cauthen, Horse Racing	Chris Evert, Tennis
1951	Dick Kazmaier, Football	Maureen Connolly, Tennis	1978	Ron Guidry, Baseball	Nancy Lopez, Golf
1952	Bob Mathias, Track and Field	Maureen Connolly, Tennis	1979	Willie Stargell, Baseball	Tracy Austin, Tennis
1953	Ben Hogan, Golf	Maureen Connolly, Tennis	1980	U.S. Olympic Hockey Team	Chris Evert Lloyd, Tennis
1954	Willie Mays, Baseball	Babe Didrikson Zaharias, Golf	1981	John McEnroe, Tennis	Tracy Austin, Tennis
1955	Hopalong Cassidy, Football	Patty Berg, Golf	1982	Wayne Gretzky, Hockey	Mary Decker, Track and Field
1956	Mickey Mantle, Baseball	Pat McCormick, Diving	1983	Carl Lewis, Track and Field	Martina Navratilova, Tennis
1957	Ted Williams, Baseball	Althea Gibson, Tennis	1984	Carl Lewis, Track and Field	Mary Lou Retton, Gymnastics
			1985	Dwight Gooden, Baseball	Nancy Lopez, Golf
			1986	Larry Bird, Pro Basketball	Martina Navratilova, Tennis
			1987	Ben Johnson, Track and Field	Jackie Joyner-Kersee, Track and Field

Associated Press Athletes of the Year (Cont.)

	MEN	WOMEN		MEN	WOMEN
1988	Orel Hershiser, Baseball	Florence Griffith Joyner, Track and Field	1997	Tiger Woods, Golf	Martina Hingis, Tennis
1989	Joe Montana, Pro Football	Steffi Graf, Tennis	1998	Mark McGwire, Baseball	Se Ri Pak, Golf
1990	Joe Montana, Pro Football	Beth Daniel, Golf	1999	Tiger Woods, Golf	U.S. Women's Soccer Team
1991	Michael Jordan, Pro Basketball	Monica Seles, Tennis	2000	Tiger Woods, Golf	Marion Jones, Track and Field
1992	Michael Jordan, Pro Basketball	Monica Seles, Tennis	2001	Barry Bonds, Baseball	Jennifer Capriati, Tennis
1993	Michael Jordan, Pro Basketball	Sheryl Swoopes, Basketball	2002	Lance Armstrong, Cycling	Serena Williams, Tennis
1994	George Foreman, Boxing	Bonnie Blair, Speed Skating	2003	Lance Armstrong, Cycling	Annika Sorenstam, Golf
1995	Cal Ripken Jr, Baseball	Rebecca Lobo, Basketball	2004	Lance Armstrong, Cycling	Annika Sorenstam, Golf
1996	Michael Johnson, Track and Field	Amy Van Dyken, Swimming	2005	Lance Armstrong, Cycling	Annika Sorenstam, Golf
			2006	Tiger Woods, Golf	Lorena Ochoa, Golf
			2007	Tom Brady, Pro Football	Lorena Ochoa, Golf
			2008	Michael Phelps, Swimming	Candace Parker, Basketball
			2009	Jimmie Johnson, Auto Racing	Serena Williams, Tennis

James E. Sullivan Award

Presented annually by the AAU to the athlete who "by his or her performance, example and influence as an amateur, has done the most during the year to advance the cause of sportsmanship."

1930	Bobby Jones, Golf
1931	Barney Berlinger, Track and Field
1932	Jim Bausch, Track and Field
1933	Glenn Cunningham, Track and Field
1934	Bill Bonthron, Track and Field
1935	Lawson Little, Golf
1936	Glenn Morris, Track and Field
1937	Don Budge, Tennis
1938	Don Lash, Track and Field
1939	Joe Burk, Rowing
1940	Greg Rice, Track and Field
1941	Leslie MacMitchell, Track and Field
1942	Cornelius Warmerdam, Track
1943	Gilbert Dodds, Track and Field
1944	Ann Curtis, Swimming
1945	Doc Blanchard, Football
1946	Arnold Tucker, Football
1947	John B. Kelly Jr, Rowing
1948	Bob Mathias, Track and Field
1949	Dick Button, Skating
1950	Fred Wilt, Track and Field
1951	Bob Richards, Track and Field
1952	Horace Ashenfelter, Track and Field
1953	Sammy Lee, Diving
1954	Mal Whitfield, Track and Field
1955	Harrison Dillard, Track and Field
1956	Pat McCormick, Diving

1957	Bobby Morrow, Track and Field
1958	Glenn Davis, Track and Field
1959	Parry O'Brien, Track and Field
1960	Rafer Johnson, Track and Field
1961	Wilma Rudolph, Track and Field
1962	Jim Beatty, Track and Field
1963	John Pennel, Track and Field
1964	Don Schollander, Swimming
1965	Bill Bradley, Basketball
1966	Jim Ryun, Track and Field
1967	Randy Matson, Track and Field
1968	Debbie Meyer, Swimming
1969	Bill Toomey, Track and Field
1970	John Kinsella, Swimming
1971	Mark Spitz, Swimming
1972	Frank Shorter, Track and Field
1973	Bill Walton, Basketball
1974	Rich Wohlhuter, Track and Field
1975	Tim Shaw, Swimming
1976	Bruce Jenner, Track and Field
1977	John Naber, Swimming
1978	Tracy Caulkins, Swimming
1979	Kurt Thomas, Gymnastics
1980	Eric Heiden, Speed Skating
1981	Carl Lewis, Track and Field
1982	Mary Decker, Track and Field
1983	Edwin Moses, Track and Field

1984	Greg Louganis, Diving
1985	Joan B.-Samuelson, T & F
1986	Jackie Joyner-Kersee, T & F
1987	Jim Abbott, Baseball
1988	Florence Griffith Joyner, Track
1989	Janet Evans, Swimming
1990	John Smith, Wrestling
1991	Mike Powell, Track and Field
1992	Bonnie Blair, Speed Skating
1993	Charlie Ward, Football, Basketball
1994	Dan Jansen, Speed Skating
1995	Bruce Baumgartner, Wrestling
1996	Michael Johnson, Track and Field
1997	Peyton Manning, Football
1998	Chamique Holdsclaw, Basketball
1999	Kelly and Coco Miller, Basketball
2000	Rulon Gardner, Wrestling
2001	Michelle Kwan, Figure Skating
2002	Sarah Hughes, Figure Skating
2003	Michael Phelps, Swimming
2004	Paul Hamm, Gymnastics
2005	J. J. Redick, College Basketball
2006	Jessica Long, Paralympic Swimmer
2007	Tim Tebow, College Football
2008	Shawn Johnson, Gymnastics
2009	Amy Palmiero-Winters, Ultra Marathon

The Sporting News Sportsman of the Year

1968	Denny McLain, Baseball
1969	Tom Seaver, Baseball
1970	John Wooden, Basketball
1971	Lee Trevino, Golf
1972	Charles O. Finley, Baseball
1973	O.J. Simpson, Pro Football
1974	Lou Brock, Baseball
1975	Archie Griffin, Football
1976	Larry O'Brien, Pro Basketball
1977	Steve Cauthen, Horse Racing
1978	Ron Guidry, Baseball
1979	Willie Stargell, Baseball
1980	George Brett, Baseball
1981	Wayne Gretzky, Hockey
1982	Whitey Herzog, Baseball

1983	Bowie Kuhn, Baseball
1984	Peter Ueberroth, LA Olympics
1985	Pete Rose, Baseball
1986	Larry Bird, Pro Basketball
1987	No award
1988	Jackie Joyner-Kersee, T & F
1989	Joe Montana, Pro Football
1990	Nolan Ryan, Baseball
1991	Michael Jordan, Pro Basketball
1992	Mike Krzyzewski, Basketball
1993	Pat Gillick/Cito Gaston, Baseball
1994	Emmitt Smith, Pro Football
1995	Cal Ripken Jr, Baseball
1996	Joe Torre, Baseball
1997	Michael Jordan, Basketball

1998	Mark McGwire, Baseball
1999	New York Yankees, Baseball
2000	Kurt Warner/Marshall Faulk, Pro Football
2001	Curt Schilling, Baseball
2002	Tyrone Willingham, Football
2003	Jack McKeon, Baseball
	Dick Vermeil, Pro Football
2004	Tom Brady, Pro Football
2005	Matt Leinart, College Football
2006	LaDainian Tomlinson, Pro Football
2007	Tom Brady, Pro Football
2008	Eli Manning, Pro Football
2009	Mariano Rivera, Baseball*

*named Pro Athlete of the Year

United Press International Male and Female Athlete of the Year

	MEN	WOMEN
1974	Muhammad Ali, Boxing	Irena Szewinska, Track and Field
1975	Joao Oliveira, Track and Field	Nadia Comaneci, Gymnastics
1976	Alberto Juantorena, Track and Field	Nadia Comaneci, Gymnastics
1977	Alberto Juantorena, Track and Field	Rosie Ackermann, Track and Field
1978	Henry Rono, Track and Field	Tracy Caulkins, Swimming
1979	Sebastian Coe, Track and Field	Marita Koch, Track and Field
1980	Eric Heiden, Speed Skating	Hanni Wenzel, Alpine Skiing
1981	Sebastian Coe, Track and Field	Chris Evert Lloyd, Tennis
1982	Daley Thompson, Track and Field	Marita Koch, Track and Field
1983	Carl Lewis, Track and Field	Jarmila Kratochvilova, Track and Field
1984	Carl Lewis, Track and Field	Martina Navratilova, Tennis
1985	Steve Cram, Track and Field	Mary Decker Slaney, Track and Field
1986	Diego Maradona, Soccer	Heike Drechsler, Track and Field
1987	Ben Johnson, Track and Field	Steffi Graf, Tennis
1988	Matt Biondi, Swimming	Florence Griffith Joyner, Track and Field
1989	Boris Becker, Tennis	Steffi Graf, Tennis
1990	Stefan Edberg, Tennis	Merlene Ottey, Track and Field
1991	Michael Jordan, Pro Basketball	Monica Seles, Tennis
1992	Mario Lemieux, Hockey	Monica Seles, Tennis
1993	Michael Jordan, Pro Basketball	Steffi Graf, Tennis
1994	Nick Price, Golf	Bonnie Blair, Speed Skating
1995	Cal Ripken Jr, Baseball	Steffi Graf, Tennis

Note: Award not given since 1995.

Dial Award

Presented by the Dial Corporation to the male and female national high school athlete/scholar of the year.

	BOYS	GIRLS
		No award
1979	Herschel Walker, Football	Carol Lewis, Track and Field
1980	Bill Fralic, Football	Cheryl Miller, Basketball
1981	Kevin Willhite, Football	Elaine Zayak, Skating
1982	Mike Smith, Basketball	Melanie Buddemeyer, Swimming
1983	Chris Spielman, Football	Nora Lewis, Basketball
1984	Hart Lee Dykes, Football	Gea Johnson, Track and Field
1985	Jeff George, Football	Mya Johnson, Track and Field
1986	Scott Schaffner, Football	Kristi Overton, Water Skiing
1987	Todd Marinovich, Football	Courtney Cox, Basketball
1988	Carlton Gray, Football	Lisa Leslie, Basketball
1989	Robert Smith, Football	Vicki Goetze, Golf
1990	Derrick Brooks, Football	Katie Smith, Basketball, Volleyball, Track
1991	Jeff Buckey, Football, Track and Field	Amanda White, Track and Field, Swimming
1992	Jacque Vaughn, Basketball	Kristin Folkl, Basketball
1993	Tiger Woods, Golf	Shannon Miller, Gymnastics
1994	Taymon Domzalski, Basketball	Shea Ralph, Basketball
1995	Brent Abernathy, Baseball	Grace Park, Golf
1996	Grant Irons, Football	Michelle Kwan, Figure Skating
1997	Ronald Curry, Football	

Note: Award not given since 1997.

Obituaries

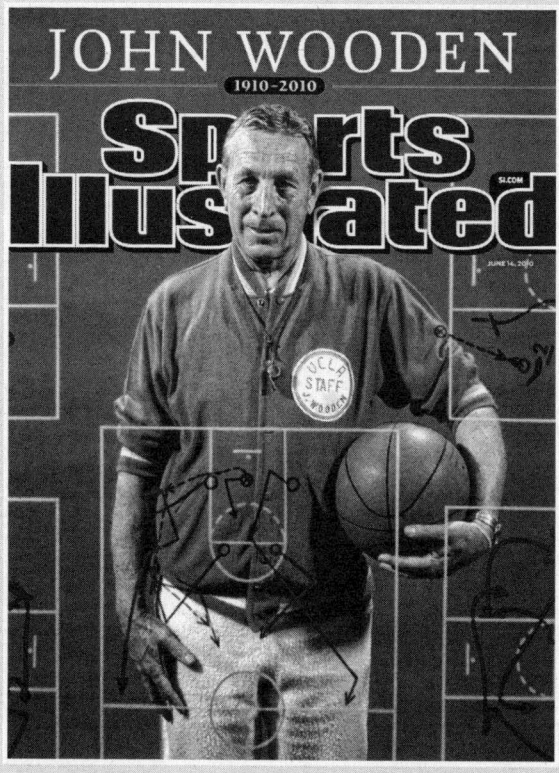

John Wooden
1910–2010

George Blanda, 83, football player. *Hall of Fame kicker and quarterback.*

A seemingly ageless Hall of Fame quarterback and kicker, Blanda's 26-year career was best remembered for a remarkable run of late-game theatrics with the Oakland Raiders. Blanda retired a month shy of his 49th birthday before the 1976 season, playing longer than anyone else in pro football history.

He scored 2,002 points in his career, a pro football record at the time of his retirement, kicking 335 field goals and 943 extra points, running for nine touchdowns and throwing for 236 more. But it was a five-game stretch for Oakland in 1970 that is the lasting imprint from his career. As a 43-year-old, Blanda led the Raiders to four wins and one tie with late touchdown passes or field goals. Later that season, he became the oldest quarterback to play in a championship game. His performance that season earned him the *Associated Press* Male Athlete of the Year award.

Blanda joined the Houston Oilers of the new American Football League in 1960 and led the Oilers to the first two AFL titles, beating the Chargers for the championship in the 1960 and '61 seasons.

In Alameda, Calif., after a brief illness, on September 27, 2010.

David "Satch" Davidson, 75, umpire. *Worked numerous All-Star and World Series games.*

Davidson's major league umpiring career was full of big games—his first month in the majors, he worked no-hitters that Jim Maloney and Don Wilson pitched on back-to-back days at old Crosley Field in Cincinnati. He was on the field for five no-hitters overall, plus a pair of World Series, three NL Championship series and the 1976 All-Star Game. But most memorably, he was the home plate umpire when Hank Aaron hit his historic 715th home run, breaking Babe Ruth's record, and when Carlton Fisk launched his famous, barely-fair shot over the Green Monster in Game 6 of the 1975 World Series.

In Houston, Tex., of complications from Alzheimer's disease, on August 21, 2010.

Bobby Thomson, 86, baseball player. *San Francisco Giant who hit the famous "Shot Heard 'Round the World." in 1951.*

In a decisive Game 3 of the 1951 National League pennant playoff, Thomson hit what is perhaps the game's most famous home run, the game-winning "Shot Heard 'Round the World," Thomson's "shot" was a three-run homer in the bottom of the ninth inning off Brooklyn Dodgers pitcher Ralph Branca and it lifted the New York Giants to the World Series. The drive into the left-field stands at the Polo Grounds and broadcaster Russ Hodges' ecstatic call of "The Giants win the pennant!" remain one of the signature moments in baseball history.

A three-time All-Star as an infielder and outfielder, Thomson hit .270 with 264 career home runs and 1,026 RBIs from 1946–60 with several teams. Yet his drive into the left-field stands vaulted "The Flying Scot" to a place of almost mythic status. There have been plenty of historic home runs over the years—Bill Mazeroski, Kirk Gibson, Carlton Fisk and Joe Carter, to name a few—but Thomson's shot remains the giant among them.

Thomson's home run decided one of baseball's most memorable pennant races, and later led to one of its most-debated questions: Did he know Branca was going to throw the high-and-inside fastball that Thomson hit out of the park? More than a half-century later, it was revealed the Giants during the season had used a buzzer-and-telescope system to steal the signals from opposing catchers. Still, Thomson steadfastly claimed he did not know what pitch was coming when he connected. Branca was never quite so sure.

In Savannah, Ga., of complications from cancer, on August 16, 2010.

Jack Tatum, 61, football player. *Former Oakland Raider linebacker.*

A Pro Bowl safety for the Oakland Raiders, Tatum is best known for his crushing hit that paralyzed Darryl Stingley in an NFL preseason game in 1978. Nicknamed "the Assassin," the hard-hitting Tatum was drafted in the first round by the Raiders in 1971. In nine seasons with the Raiders, Tatum started 106 of 120 games with 30 interceptions and helped Oakland win the 1976 Super Bowl.

Tatum was also a central figure in the famed "Immaculate Reception" play, in which the Raiders lost a 1972 playoff game on a last-ditch, deflected TD pass by the Pittsburgh Steelers. With 22 seconds left, Tatum jarred loose a pass to Frenchy Fuqua from Steelers QB Terry Bradshaw, the ball bounced off Fuqua's foot and ricocheted into the arms of Steelers running back Franco Harris, who never broke stride as he ran 42 yards for the winning touchdown.

In Oakland, Calif., of heart attack, on July 27, 2010.

Ralph Houk, 90, baseball manager. *World Series-winning manager of the 1961–'63 New York Yankees.*

Before reaching the big leagues with the Yankees in 1947 as a player, Houk served in the Army in World War II and rose to the rank of major — a moniker that stuck even when he returned to baseball. Houk spent parts of eight seasons as a backup catcher for New York, appearing in just 91 games. But it was as manager of the powerhouse New York Yankees teams of the early 1960s that he is best remembered, guiding them to two World Series championships in the 1961 and '62 seasons.

Houk also skippered the Detroit Tigers from 1974–78 and the Boston Red Sox from 1981–84 in a managerial career that spanned three decades. In all, Houk managed 3,157 games and won 1,619 with a winning percentage of .514.

In Winter Haven, Fla. of natural causes, on July 21, 2010.

George Steinbrenner, 80, baseball owner. *Longtime owner of the New York Yankees.*

In 37-plus seasons as owner, Steinbrenner led the Yankees to seven World Series championships, 11 American League pennants and 16 AL East titles. New York was 11 years removed from its last championship when Steinbrenner headed a group that bought the team from CBS Inc. on Jan. 3, 1973, for about $10 million.

He revolutionized the franchise—and sports—by starting his own television network and ballpark food company. *Forbes* now values the Yankees at $1.6 billion, trailing only Manchester United ($1.8 billion) and the Dallas Cowboys ($1.65 billion).

He ruled with obsessive dedication to detail, overseeing everything from trades to the airblowers that kept his ballparks spotless. He admittedly was overbearing, screaming at all from commissioners to managers to secretaries. His reign was interrupted for suspensions, including a 15-month ban in 1974 after his guilty plea to conspiring to make illegal contributions to President Richard Nixon's re-election campaign. He was pardoned 15 years later by President Ronald Reagan.

The son of a shipping magnate, Steinbrenner lived up to his billing as "the Boss," a nickname he earned and clearly enjoyed as he ruled with an iron fist. Steinbrenner was known for feuds, clashing with former Yankees catcher and, later, manager Yogi Berra and firing manager Billy Martin five times while repeatedly fighting with him. But as his health declined, Steinbrenner let sons Hal and Hank run more of the family business.

Till the end, Steinbrenner demanded championships. He barbed Joe Torre during the 2007 AL playoffs, then let the popular manager leave after another loss in the opening round. The team responded last year by winning another title in 2009.

In Tampa, Fla., of heart attack, on July 13, 2010.

Bob Sheppard, 99, baseball announcer. *Longtime stadium voice of the New York Yankees.*

The revered Yankees public address announcer for nearly 60 years, Sheppard's elegant introductions earned him the nickname "The Voice of God." Sheppard started with the Yankees in 1951 and he last worked at Yankee Stadium late in the 2007 season, when he became ill with a bronchial infection.

The Yankees' lineup for Sheppard's first game on April 17, 1951, included Joe DiMaggio, Mickey Mantle, Johnny Mize, Yogi Berra, and Phil Rizzuto. And the opponents that day, the Boston Red Sox, were led by Ted Williams. He announced 62 World Series games and a pair of All-Star Games, and introduced more than 70 Hall of Famers across his career.

In Baldwin, N.Y., of natural causes, on July 11, 2010.

Johnny Sellers, 72, jockey. *Hall of fame jockey.*

A Los Angeles native who grew up in Oklahoma, Sellers won 328 races including riding Carry Back to victory in the 1961 Kentucky Derby and Preakness Stakes, earning him the cover of an August 1961 issue of *Sports Illustrated.* He completed his personal Triple Crown by winning the 1965 Belmont Stakes with Hail to All. He finished his riding career in 1977 with 2,787 victories.

He was inducted into the National Museum of Racing Hall of Fame in 2007.

In Fayetteville, Arkansas, of natural causes, on July 2, 2010.

Don Coryell, 85, football coach. *Longtime San Diego Chargers coach and football offense innovator.*

One of the founding fathers of the modern passing game, Coryell started his career as the head football coach at San Diego State, posting a record of 104-19-2 from 1961–72. He left the Aztecs for the NFL, coaching the St. Louis Cardinals to two division titles in 1974 and '75. But his most memorable years came after Coryell returned to San Diego to coach the Chargers.

From 1978-86, "Air Coryell," as the Chargers' offense was known, set records and—thanks to QB Dan Fouts—led the NFL in passing almost every season. Coryell guided the Chargers to the AFC championship game after the 1980 and '81 seasons, but he never reached the Super Bowl. The lack of a Super Bowl on his resume may have hurt Coryell last winter in voting for the Pro Football Hall of Fame. He was a finalist for the first time, but was not selected for induction.

However, the big stars of the Air Coryell years — Fouts, tight end Kellen Winslow and wide receiver Charlie Joiner — all ended up in the Hall of Fame.

In La Mesa, Calif., of complications from pneumonia, on July 1, 2010.

Manute Bol, 47, basketball player. *Second-tallest player in NBA history and African philanthropist.*

The 7-foot, 6-inch Bol played 10 seasons in the NBA, finishing with career averages of 2.6 points, 4.2 rebounds and 3.3 blocks per game. He led the league in blocks in 1985–86 with Washington (5.0 per game) and in 1988–89 with Golden State (4.3 a game). A former Dinka tribesman from Sudan, Bol remained heavily involved in his home country and after retiring from the NBA, founded the humanitarian group Sudan Sunrise to help build schools and foster political reconciliation there.

In Charlottesville, Virginia, of complications from kidney disease and Stevens-Johnson syndrome, a rare skin disease, on June 19, 2010

Les Richter, 79, football player and racing executive. *College Football Hall of Famer and stock car racing pioneer.*

An eight-time Pro Bowl selection for the Los Angeles Rams, Richter went on to become a top NASCAR executive after retiring from the NFL. He was an All-America linebacker and class valedictorian at the University of California and was drafted by the Dallas Texans in 1952, but did not agree to contract terms and subsequently played for the Rams from 1954–62.

His second career started as president of Riverside International Raceway in 1961. He later joined NASCAR and became an adviser to then-chairman Bill France Jr. in 1963. Richter was named NASCAR's executive vice president of competition in 1986, and senior vice president of operations in 1992.

In Riverside, Calif., of a brain aneurysm, on June 12, 2010.

John Wooden, 99, basketball coach. *Hall of Fame college basketball coach and winner of 10 NCAA national titles.*

With his signature rolled-up game program in hand, Wooden led the UCLA Bruins to 10 NCAA championships and 620 victories over his 27 year tenure as head coach, including 88 straight wins during one historic stretch. He coached many of the game's greatest players such as Bill Walton and Lew Alcindor—later known as Kareem Abdul-Jabbar. From the time of his first title following the 1963–64 season through the 10th in 1974–75, Wooden's Bruins were 330–19, including four 30–0 seasons.

As a coach, he was a groundbreaking trendsetter who demanded his players be in great physical condition so they could play an up-tempo style not well-known on the West Coast at the time. But the Wizard of Westwood's legacy extended well beyond that. He was the master of the simple one- or two-sentence homily, instructive little messages best presented in his famous book "Pyramid of Success," which remains must-read material, not only for fellow coaches but for anyone in a leadership position in American business.

He taught the team game and had only three hard-and-fast rules—no profanity, tardiness, or criticizing fellow teammates. Layered beneath that seeming simplicity, though, were a slew of life lessons—primers on everything from how to put on your socks correctly to how to maintain poise.

In Los Angeles, Calif. of natural causes, on June 4, 2010.

Skip Away, 17, thoroughbred. *Award-winning racehorse.*

Skip Away, the third-richest North American racehorse in history, was a three-time Eclipse Award winner, including Horse of the Year in 1998. He was named the champion 3-year-old male in 1996 and champion older horse in 1997-98. During his racing career, he won 18 of 38 starts, including the Breeders' Cup Classic and Woodbine Million, earning a total of $9.6 million. That was second only to Cigar all-time when he retired, but both horses have since been passed by Curlin.

Near Midway, Ky. of a heart attack, on May 14, 2010.

Erica Blasberg, 25, golfer. *LPGA Tour professional.*

A six-time college tournament winner and two-time All-America golfer at the University of Arizona, Blasberg played on the victorious U.S. Curtis Cup team in 2004. She was in her sixth season on the LPGA tour. Her best year as a professional was 2008, when she earned a career-best tie for eighth at the SBS Open in Hawaii and more than $113,000 in winnings.

In Henderson, Nevada, of suicide by asphyxiation, on May 9, 2010.

Robin Roberts, 83, baseball player. *Hall of Fame pitcher.*

The right-handed pitcher Roberts was the most productive pitcher in the National League in the first half of the 1950s and was a prominent member of the 1950 Phillies NL pennant-winning squad dubbed the "Whiz Kids." During his career, Roberts won 286 games and put together six consecutive 20-win seasons. He had 45 career shutouts, 2,357 strikeouts and a lifetime ERA of 3.41. He pitched 305 complete games, but also holds the dubious distinction of giving up more home runs than any other Major League pitcher.

Roberts started five All-Star games and was named to the team seven times. His best years came before the Cy Young Award, but Roberts twice was chosen pitcher of the year by *The Sporting News.* He also was the publication's player of the year in 1952.

The Phillies retired his jersey, No. 36, in 1962 and he remains the Phillies career leader in games pitched, complete games and innings pitched. Long after his career ended, Roberts followed the Phillies closely and was still popular in Philadelphia. A statue of him now sits outside the first base gate at Citizens Bank Park in Philadelphia.

He was elected to the Baseball Hall of Fame in 1976.

In Temple Terrace, Fla. of natural causes, on May 6, 2010.

Ernie Harwell, 92, sports broadcaster. *Longtime broadcast voice of the Detroit Tigers.*

A Hall of Fame announcer, Harwell spent 42 of his 55 years in broadcasting with the Tigers. He was their play-by-play radio voice from 1960–91 and 1993–2002, joining Mel Allen, Jack Buck, Harry Caray and others as some of the game's most famous voices.

By his own count, Harwell called more than 8,300 major league games, starting with the Brooklyn Dodgers in 1948 and continuing with the Giants and Baltimore Orioles before joining the Tigers. He missed two games outside of the '92 season: one for his brother's funeral in 1968, the other when he was inducted into the National Sportscasters and Sportswriters Association Hall of Fame in 1989.

The Georgia native's easygoing manner and love of baseball endeared him to generations of Tigers fans, enhancing the club's finest moments and making its struggles more bearable. Even casual fans could tick off Harwell catchphrases: "Loooooong gone!" for a home run and "Two for the price of one!" for a double play.

The Baseball Hall of Fame honored Harwell in 1981 with the Ford C. Frick Award, given annually to a broadcaster for major contributions to baseball.

In Novi, Mich., of complications from cancer, on May 4, 2010.

Owen Thomas, 21, football player. *Penn college football player diagnosed with chronic traumatic encephalopathy (CTE).*

Thomas, a 6-foot-2, 240-pound defensive end, had been voted one of Quakers' captains for the 2010–11 season. He was a second-team All-Ivy player in 2009, starting all 10 Penn games, recording 29 tackles and finishing second in the league with six sacks.

After Thomas's suicide, a subsequent autopsy revealed chronic traumatic encephalopathy, which he may have developed from a series of subconcussive collisions. Thomas was the youngest and first amateur football player to be found with clear evidence of CTE.

In Philadelphia, Pa., of suicide by hanging, on April 26, 2010.

Juan Antonio Samaranch, 89, sports administrator. *Longtime International Olympic Committee president.*

Samaranch, a courtly former diplomat who served as Spanish ambassador in Moscow, led the IOC from 1980 to 2001. He was considered one of the defining presidents for building the IOC into a powerful global organization and firmly establishing the Olympics as a world force. A reserved but shrewd dealmaker, Samaranch's 21-year term was perhaps the most eventful in IOC history, spanning political boycotts, the end of amateurism and the advent of professionalism, the explosion of commercialization, a boom in growth and popularity of the games, the scourge of doping, and the Salt Lake crisis.

In Barelona, Spain, of heart failure, on April 21, 2010.

Vicki Manolo Draves, 85, diver. *1948 Olympic gold medal-winning diver.*

An Asian-American diver who overcame ethnic prejudice early in her career, Draves became the first woman to win springboard and platform gold medals in the same Olympics, in 1948. Vicki Manalo was the daughter of a Filipino father and an English mother, at a time in which mixed marriages were generally frowned on. In 1941, when she was 17, she was refused entry to the Fairmont Hotel Swimming and Diving Club in San Francisco because of her Filipino surname.

She was elected to the International Swimming Hall of Fame in Fort Lauderdale, Fla., in 1969.

In Palm Springs, of pancreatic cancer, on April 11, 2010.

Merlin Olsen, 69, football player, *Hall of Fame defensive left tackle, sports broadcaster, and actor.*

Considered one of the greatest tackles in NFL history, Olsen was also a longtime color commentator for NBC's pro football and Rose Bowl telecasts and acted on television, most prominently in "Little House on the Prairie" and in his own series, "Father Murphy."

Olsen was voted to the Pro Bowl every one of his 15 years except for his final season. He was known for being a member of the Los Angeles Rams' famed "Fearsome Foursome" defenses of the mid-1960s. He was an All-NFL selection six times, and was chosen by the Maxwell Club of Philadelphia as the NFL's most valuable player in 1974. He was voted into the College Football Hall of Fame in 1980 and the Pro Football Hall of Fame in 1982. He was also named, along with Fearsome Foursome partner Deacon Jones, to the 75th anniversary All-NFL team in 1994.

In Duarte, Calif., of mesothelioma, on March 11, 2010.

Willie Davis, 69, baseball player. *Two-time All-Star and three-time Gold Glove winner for the 1960s Los Angeles Dodgers. SI writes:*

A speedy center fielder, Davis collected two World Series rings, three Gold Gloves and was a two-time All-Star during his 14 seasons with the Los Angeles Dodgers. Davis' teammates included Sandy Koufax, Don Drysdale, and Maury Wills. He won his World Series rings in 1963 and 1965.

During the 1965 World Series, Davis stole three bases in one inning, including one where he had to crawl into second base after stumbling and falling. In Game 2 of the 1966 World Series against the Baltimore Orioles, the last game of Koufax's pitching career, Davis memorably committed a Fall Classic-record three errors in one inning when he lost one fly ball in the sun, dropped the next one, then overthrew third base.

In Burbank, Calif., of natural causes, on March 9, 2010.

Dick Francis, 89, jockey. *British champion steeplechase jockey and best-selling novelist.*

A successful steeplechase jockey, winning over 350 races, Francis retired from racing in 1957 and took up writing, first as a racing correspondent for Britain's *Sunday Express* newspaper. He began writing the first of his 42 mystery novels in 1962.

In the Cayman Islands, of natural causes, on February 14, 2010.

Chris Henry, 26, football player. *Cincinnati Bengals wide receiver.*

Throughout his career, Henry's temper and poor decisions got him in trouble. Drafted by Cincinnati in the third round, Henry become a vital part of the offense as a rookie, helping the Bengals reach the playoffs in 2005 with his ability to run past defenders to grab long passes. But after multiple arrests, NFL Commissioner Roger Goodell suspended Henry for half a season in 2007.

After his fifth arrest, which prompted the Bengals to release him, Henry seemed determined to stay out of trouble and later returned to the team. After only 19 catches and two touchdowns in 12 games in the 2008 season, he set out to remake himself into a topflight receiver and began spending more time with his fiancee and three children.

Upon his death, an autopsy revealed that Henry suffered from a chronic brain injury that may have influenced his mental state and behavior. A microscopic tissue analysis of Henry's brain showed that he had chronic traumatic encephalopathy, a disorder caused by multiple head impacts that many retired professional football players also suffer from at a higher rate than normal.

In Charlotte, N.C., of injuries sustained from falling out of a moving pickup truck, on December 17, 2009.

Mike Penner, 52, sportswriter. *Former Los Angeles Times transgender sportswriter.*

In 25 years with the newspaper, Penner worked at various times as a sports reporter, columnist and the newspaper's Los Angeles Angels beat writer. On April 26, 2007, he wrote a story for the *Times* headlined "Old Mike, New Christine," in which he revealed he was taking a few weeks vacation and when he returned to his job as a sports writer it would be as a woman named Christine Daniels. The announcement sent shock waves through the sports world. After his vacation, Penner did indeed return as Christine Daniels, not only continuing to report on sports for the *Times* but also authoring a blog called "Woman in Transition," detailing her experiences.

However, Daniels eventually dropped the "Woman in Transition" blog and returned to writing under the name Mike Penner.

In Los Angeles, Calif., of injuries sustained from suicide, on November 27, 2009.

Abe Pollin, 85, basketball owner. *Longtime owner of the NBA's Washington franchise.*

Pollin was the NBA's patriarch, an old-school owner who won a championship in 1978 and later had the mettle to stand up to Michael Jordan. He introduced luxury boxes and the large replay screen to big-time professional sports. He used to have 3-point shooting contests with Hall of Fame Bullets center Wes Unseld.

In the changing world of professional sports, Pollin stood out for decades as an owner who tried to run his teams like a family business. He bemoaned the runaway salaries of free agency and said it would have been difficult for him to keep the Wizards if it weren't for the NBA's salary cap.

In Bethesda, Md., of complications from progressive supranuclear palsy, a rare brain disorder, on November 24, 2009.

Bill Chadwick, 94, referee. *Hall of Fame hockey referee.*

Bill "The Big Whistle" Chadwick, was the first U.S.-born official in NHL history and was later a popular broadcaster for the New York Rangers. For 16 seasons, from 1939 to 1955, Chadwick was one of the best officials the NHL, despite being blind in one eye. He invented and perfected the system of hand signals to signify penalties, and the system is now used throughout the world. In 1964, Chadwick was inducted into the Hockey Hall of Fame, only the fifth official, and the first American-born official, to be so honored. In 1974, he was inducted into the U.S. Hockey Hall of Fame.

In Cutchogue, N.Y., on October 24, 2009.

2011 MAJOR EVENTS

JANUARY

Major College BCS Bowl Games	Jan 1–7
NFL Wild-Card Playoffs	Jan 8–9
BCS Championship Game	Jan 10
NFL Divisional Playoffs	Jan 15–16
Australian Open	Jan 17–30
U.S. Figure Skating Championships	Jan 22–30
NFL Conference Championships	Jan 23
Millrose Games	Jan 28
NFL Pro Bowl	Jan 30

FEBRUARY

Super Bowl XLV	Feb 6
NBA All-Star Game	Feb 20
Daytona 500	Feb 20
MLB Spring Training begins (voluntary)	Feb 13

MARCH

MLB Spring Training begins (mandatory)	Mar 1
March Madness Begins	March 17
NCAA Women's Hockey Frozen Four	March 18 & 20
World Figure Skating Championships	March 21–27
Major League Soccer season begins	March 19
Kraft Nabisco Championship	Mar 31–April 3

APRIL

Major League Baseball Opening Day	April 1
NCAA Men's Basketball Final Four	April 2 & 4
NCAA Women's Basketball Final Four	April 3 & 5
NCAA Men's Hockey Frozen Four	April 7 & 9
The Masters	April 7–10
NHL Playoffs begin	April 13
NFL Draft	*April 14–16**
NBA Playoffs begin	*April 15**
Boston Marathon	April 18

MAY

WNBA Season Begins	*May 1**
Kentucky Derby	May 7
The Players Championship (Golf)	May 12–15
NBA Draft Lottery	May 17
Preakness Stakes	May 21
NASCAR All-Star Race	May 21
NHL Stanley Cup Final begins	*May 28**
Indianapolis 500	May 29

JUNE

French Open	May 22–June 5
NBA Finals Begin	*June 2**
Belmont Stakes	June 11
MLB Entry Draft	June 6–8
U.S. Men's Open (Golf)	June 16–19
College World Series	June 18–29
NBA Draft	June 23
LPGA Championship	June 23–26
US Outdoor Track & Field Championships	June 23–26
NHL Entry Draft	June 24–25

JULY

Wimbledon	June 20–July 3
Tour de France	July 2–24
U.S. Women's Open (Golf)	July 7–10
MLB All-Star Game	July 12
Men's British Open	July 14–17
FINA World Swimming Championships	July 23–31
Women's British Open	July 28–31
Brickyard 400	July 31

AUGUST

NFL Hall of Fame Induction	Aug 6
PGA Championship	Aug 11–14
PGA Tour FedEx Playoffs Begin	*Aug 18**
Little League World Series	Aug 19–28

SEPTEMBER

U.S. Open (Tennis)	Aug 22–Sept 4
World Track & Field Championships	Aug 27–Sept 4
College Football Season Begins	*Sept 1**
NFL Season Begins	*Sept 8**
Women's World Cup (Soccer)	Sept 10–30
NASCAR Chase for the Cup Begins	*Sept 11**
WNBA Finals Begin	*Sept 11**
PGA TOUR Championship	Sept 22–25
Solheim Cup (Women's Golf)	Sept 23–25

OCTOBER

MLB Divisional Series Begin	*Oct 1**
NHL Season Begins	*Oct 6**
MLB League Championship Series Begin	*Oct 6**
World Gymnastics Championships	Oct 8–16
World Series Begins	Oct 19
Rugby World Cup	Sept 9–Oct 23
NBA Regular Season Begins	*Oct 25**
Women's World Tour Championships (Tennis)	Oct 25–30

NOVEMBER

Breeders' Cup	Nov 4–5
New York Marathon	Nov 6
NASCAR Chase for the Cup Ends	*Nov 14**
Presidents Cup (Men's Golf)	Nov 17–20
MLS Cup	Nov 20
Men's World Tour Championships (Tennis)	*Nov 20–27**

DECEMBER

Davis Cup Final (Tennis)	Dec 2–4
Heisman Trophy Presentation	Dec 10
Major College Bowl Games Begin	*Dec 17**

* Approximate date.